American Politics Today

Seventh Essentials Edition

VOTE HERE

City of Milwaukee

WARNING
$100 to $500 fine or imprisonment for removing or tampering with this sign
4057

Seventh Essentials Edition

American Politics Today

William T. Bianco
Indiana University, Bloomington

David T. Canon
University of Wisconsin, Madison

W. W. NORTON & COMPANY
Independent Publishers Since 1923

W. W. Norton & Company has been independent since its founding in 1923, when William Warder Norton and Mary D. Herter Norton first published lectures delivered at the People's Institute, the adult education division of New York City's Cooper Union. The firm soon expanded its program beyond the Institute, publishing books by celebrated academics from America and abroad. By midcentury, the two major pillars of Norton's publishing program—trade books and college texts—were firmly established. In the 1950s, the Norton family transferred control of the company to its employees, and today—with a staff of five hundred and hundreds of trade, college, and professional titles published each year—W. W. Norton & Company stands as the largest and oldest publishing house owned wholly by its employees.

Editor: Laura Wilk
Project Editor: Thea Goodrich
Editorial Assistant: Catherine Lillie
Managing Editor, College: Marian Johnson
Managing Editor, College Digital Media: Kim Yi
Production Manager: Eric Pier-Hocking
Media Editor: Spencer Richardson-Jones
Associate Media Editor: Michael Jaoui
Media Project Editor: Marcus Van Harpen
Assistant Media Editor: Lena Nowak-Laird
Marketing Manager, Political Science: Ashley Sherwood
Design Director: Jillian Burr
Text Designer: Open, NY
Photo Editor: Catherine Abelman
Photo Researcher: Lynn Gadson
Director of College Permissions: Megan Schindel
Permissions Consultant: Elizabeth Trammell
Composition: KnowledgeWorks Global Ltd.
Manufacturing: Transcontinental Interglobe, Inc.

Permission to use copyrighted material is included on p. A49.

The Library of Congress has cataloged another edition as follows:

Names: Bianco, William T., 1960– author. | Canon, David T., author.
Title: American politics today / William T. Bianco, David T. Canon.
Description: Seventh edition. | New York : W.W. Norton & Company, 2021. |
    Includes bibliographical references and index.
Identifiers: LCCN 2020051030 | ISBN **9780393427660** (paperback)
Subjects: LCSH: United States—Politics and government—Textbooks.
Classification: LCC JK275 .B54 2021 | DDC 320.473—dc23
LC record available at https://lccn.loc.gov/2020051030

ISBN: **978-0-393-42768-4** (pbk.)

W. W. Norton & Company, Inc., 500 Fifth Avenue, New York, N.Y. 10110
    www.wwnorton.com
W. W. Norton & Company Ltd., 15 Carlisle Street, London W1D 3BS

1 2 3 4 5 6 7 8 9 0

For our families,
Regina, Anna, and Catherine,
Sarah, Neal, Katherine, and Sophia,
who encouraged, empathized, and
helped, with patience,
grace, and love.

About the Authors

William T. Bianco

is professor of political science at Indiana University, Bloomington, where he is also Director of the Indiana Political Analysis Workshop (IPAW). His research focuses on congressional institutions, representation, and science policy. He received his undergraduate degree from SUNY Stony Brook and his MA and PhD from the University of Rochester. He is the author of *Trust: Representatives and Constituents*; *American Politics: Strategy and Choice*; and numerous articles on American politics. His research and graduate students have received funding from the National Science Foundation and the National Council for Eurasian and East European Research. He has also served as a consultant to congressional candidates and party campaign committees, as well as to the U.S. Department of Energy, the U.S. Department of Health and Human Services, and other state and local government agencies. He was also a Fulbright Senior Scholar in Moscow, Russia, during 2011–2012.

David T. Canon

is professor of political science at the University of Wisconsin, Madison. His teaching and research interests focus on American political institutions, especially Congress, and racial representation. He is the author of *Actors, Athletes, and Astronauts: Political Amateurs in the U.S. Congress*; *Race, Redistricting, and Representation: The Unintended Consequences of Black Majority Districts* (winner of the Richard F. Fenno Prize); *The Dysfunctional Congress?* (with Kenneth Mayer); and various articles and book chapters. He is the editor of the *Election Law Journal* and previously served as the Congress editor of *Legislative Studies Quarterly*. He is an AP® consultant and has taught in the University of Wisconsin Summer AP® Institute for U.S. Government & Politics since 1997. Professor Canon is the recipient of a University of Wisconsin Chancellor's Distinguished Teaching Award.

Contents in Brief

Contents

3. Federalism   66

4. Civil Liberties   98

5. Civil Rights   136

8. Elections   246

9. Interest Groups   286

Part III: Institutions

10. Congress 312

11. The Presidency 352

12. The Bureaucracy   384

Part IV: Policy

14. Economic and Social Policy   446

Preface

This book is based on three simple premises: politics is conflictual, political process matters, and politics is everywhere. It reflects our belief that politics is explainable, that political outcomes can be understood in terms of decisions made by individuals—and that the average college undergraduate can make sense of the political world in these terms. It focuses on contemporary American politics, the events and outcomes that our students have lived through and know something about. The result, we believe, is a book that provides an accessible but rigorous account of the American political system.

American Politics Today is also the product of our dissatisfaction. Thirty years ago, we were assistant professors together at the same university, assigned to teach the introductory class in alternate semesters. Though our graduate training was quite different, we found that we shared a deep disappointment with available texts. Their wholesale focus on grand normative concepts such as civic responsibility or their use of advanced analytic themes left students with little idea of how American politics really works, how events in Washington, D.C., affect their everyday lives, and how to piece together all the facts about American politics into a coherent explanation of why things happen as they do. These texts did not engender excitement, fascination, or even passing interest. What they did was put students to sleep.

As with previous editions, the overarching goal of the Seventh Edition is to describe what happens in American politics, but also to explain behavior and outcomes. In part we wish to counter the widespread belief among students that politics is too complicated, too chaotic, or too secretive to make sense of. More than that, we want to empower our students, to demonstrate that everyday American politics is relevant to their lives. This emphasis is also a response to the typical complaint about American government textbooks—that they are full of facts but devoid of useful information, and that after students finish reading, they are no better able to answer "why" questions than they were before they cracked the book.

In this edition, we maintain our focus on conflict and compromise in American politics—identifying what Americans agree and disagree about and assessing how conflict shapes American politics, from campaign platforms to policy outcomes. Though this emphasis seems especially timely given recent elections and the social movements and dynamic global events, including the coronavirus pandemic, that preceded them, our aim is to go beyond these events to identify a fundamental constant in American politics: the reality that much of politics is driven by disagreements over the scope and form of government policy, and that compromise is an essential component of virtually all significant changes in government policy. Indeed, it is impossible to imagine politics without conflict. Conflict was embedded in the American political system by the Founders, who set up a system of checks and balances to make sure that no single group could dominate. The Constitution's division of power guarantees that enacting and implementing laws will involve conflict and compromise. Furthermore, the Constitution itself was constructed as one long series of compromises. Accordingly, despite the general dislike people have for conflict, our students must recognize that conflict and compromise lie at the heart of politics.

Throughout the text, we emphasize common sense, showing students that politics inside the Beltway is often strikingly similar to the students' own everyday interactions. For example, what sustains policy compromises made by members of Congress?

The fact that the members typically have long careers, that they interact frequently with each other, and that they only deal with colleagues who have kept their word in the past. These strategies are not unique to the political world. Rather, they embody rules of thumb that most people follow (or are at least aware of) in their everyday interactions. In short, we try to help students understand American politics by emphasizing how it is not all that different from the world they know.

This focus on common sense is coupled with many references to the political science literature. We believe that contemporary research has something to say about prediction and explanation of events that students care about—and that these insights can be taught without turning students into game theorists or statisticians. Our text presents the essential insights of contemporary research, motivated by real-world political phenomena and explained using text or simple diagrams. This approach gives students a set of tools for understanding politics, provides an introduction to the political science literature, and matches up well with students' commonsense intuitions about everyday life. Moreover, by showing that academic scholarship is not a blind alley or irrelevant, this approach helps bridge the gap between an instructor's teaching and his or her research.

The Seventh Edition builds on these strengths. We've continued to streamline and improve the presentation of text and graphics and enhanced our "How It Works" sections. We've also focused on building students' media literacy skills, starting with a new section in Chapter 1 that includes an infographic titled "Media Checklist for Assessing Reporting on Politics." This theme is carried throughout the "What Do the Facts Say?" sections, where we apply the five-step framework from the checklist to help evaluate news articles, tweets, and quotations. Additionally, new chapter openers use contemporary stories and examples and offer quotations from people on both sides of an issue (from the debate over federal funds for COVID-19 relief to the impeachment of President Trump) to highlight the conflict and compromise theme. We refer to these openers throughout the chapters to illustrate and extend our discussion. The "Take a Stand" sections explicitly argue both sides of policy questions. We have also worked to place the Trump presidency in context, acknowledging the differences between Trump and other presidents, but also explaining how Trump's successes and failures, both in public opinion and in policy terms, can be explained using the same logic we have applied to previous presidents.

The text continues to be ruthlessly contemporary, but also places recent events in context. Although we do not ignore American history, our stress is on contemporary politics—on the debates, actions, and outcomes that most college students are aware of. Focusing on recent events emphasizes the utility of the concepts and insights that we develop in the text. It also goes a long way toward establishing the relevance of the intro class. The new edition focuses on strengthening students' media literacy skills by introducing best practices for evaluating sources of political information. A new easy-to-follow five-step framework introduced in Chapter 1 and applied throughout the text gives students a tool to deploy as they encounter media in their American government class and beyond. We have also devoted considerable space to describing the 2018 and 2020 campaigns, working to show how recent contests at the presidential and congressional levels fit into a broader theory of how candidates campaign and how voters decide.

Finally, our book offers an individual-level perspective on America's government. The essential message is that politics—elections, legislative proceedings, regulatory choices, and everything else we see—is a product of the decisions made by real flesh-and-blood people. This approach grounds our discussion of politics in the real world. Many texts focus on abstractions such as "the eternal debate," "the great questions," or "the pulse of democracy." We believe that these constructs don't explain where the debate, the questions, or even democracy come from. Nor do they help students understand what's going on in Washington, D.C., and elsewhere, as it's not obvious that the participants themselves care much about these sorts of abstractions—quite the opposite, in fact.

We replace these constructs with a focus on real people and actual choices. The primary goal is to make sense of American politics by understanding why politicians, bureaucrats, judges, and citizens act as they do. That is, we are grounding our description of American politics at the most fundamental level—an individual facing a decision. How, for example, does a voter choose among candidates? Stated that way, it is reasonably easy to talk about where the choice came from, how the individual might evaluate different options, and why one choice might look better than the others. Voters' decisions may be understood by examining the different feasible strategies they employ (issue voting, retrospective evaluations, stereotyping, and so on) and by asking why some voters use one strategy while others use a different one.

By focusing on individuals and choices, we can place students in the shoes of the decision makers, and in so doing, give them insight into why people act as they do. We can discuss, for example, why a House member might favor enacting wasteful pork-barrel spending, even though a proposal full of such projects will make his constituents economically worse off—and why constituents might reward such behavior, even if they suspect the truth. By taking this approach, we are not trying to let legislators off the hook. Rather, we believe that any real understanding of the political process must begin with a sense of the decisions the participants make and why they make them. Focusing on individuals also segues naturally into a discussion of consequences, allowing us to move from examining decisions to describing and evaluating outcomes. In this way, we can show students how large-scale outcomes in politics, such as inefficient programs, don't happen by accident or because of malfeasance. Rather, they are the predictable results of choices made by individuals (here, politicians and voters).

The policy chapters in the Full and Essentials Editions also represent a distinctive feature of this book. The discussion of policy at the end of an intro class often fits awkwardly with the material covered earlier. It is supposed to be a culmination of the semester-long discussion of institutions, politicians, and political behavior, but instead it often becomes an afterthought that gets discarded when time runs out in the last few weeks of class. Our policy chapters explicitly draw on previous chapters' discussions of the actors that shape policy: the president, Congress, the courts, interest groups, and parties. By doing so, these chapters show how all the pieces of the puzzle fit together.

Finally, this book reflects our experience as practicing scholars and teachers, as well as interactions with more than 20,000 students in introductory classes at several universities. Rather than thinking of the intro class as a service obligation, we believe it offers a unique opportunity for faculty to develop a broader sense of American politics and American political science, while at the same time giving students the tools they need to behave as knowledgeable citizens or enthusiastic political science majors. We hope that it works for you as well as it does for us.

Features of the Text and Media Package

The book's "three key ideas"
are fully integrated throughout the text.

- **Politics Is Conflictual** and conflict and compromise are a normal, healthy part of politics. The questions debated in elections and the policy options considered by people in government are generally marked by disagreement at all levels. Making policy typically involves important issues on which people disagree, sometimes strongly; so compromise, bargaining, and tough choices about trade-offs are often necessary.
- **Political Process Matters** because it is the mechanism we have established to resolve conflicts and achieve compromise. Governmental actions result from conscious choices made by voters, elected officials, and bureaucrats. The media often cover political issues in the same way they do sporting events, and though this makes for entertaining news, it also leads citizens to overlook the institutions, rules, and procedures that have a decisive influence on American life. Politics really is not just a game.
- **Politics Is Everywhere** in that the results of the political process affect all aspects of Americans' everyday lives. Politics governs what people can and cannot do, their quality of life, and how they think about events, other people, and situations.

New chapter openers and conclusions
present two sides of a controversy that has dominated media headlines—and about which people have passionate, emotion-driven opinions from both points of view—framed by quotes from politicians, pundits, and everyday people who hold these views. These include the impeachment of President Trump (The Constitution and the Founding), the use of excessive force by the police (Civil Rights), and the CARES legislation (Interest Groups). The "Unpacking the Conflict" sections at the end of each chapter show how the nuts and bolts of the chapter topic can be applied to help students understand both sides of these debates.

New coverage of 2020 elections and Trump presidency
provides more than 20 pages and numerous graphics analyzing the 2018 and 2020 elections and the Trump presidency, including coverage of current issues, such as the failure to pass "Trumpcare," executive actions around immigration, the governmental response to COVID-19, tax reform, impeachment, the escalation of the trade war with China, and President Trump's use of social media.

Organization around chapter goals
stresses learning objectives and mastery of core material.

- **Chapter Goals** appear at the beginning of the chapter and then recur at the start of the relevant sections throughout the chapter to create a more active reading experience that emphasizes important learning objectives.

- **Extensive end-of-chapter review sections organized around the Chapter Goals** include section summaries, practice quiz questions, key terms, and suggested reading lists. Students have everything they need to master the material in each section of the chapter.

Special features for critical thinking

reinforce the three key ideas while introducing other important ways to think about American politics.

- **The "Media Checklist for Assessing Reporting on Politics" infographic,** new to this edition in Chapter 1, provides a five-step framework for best practices for assessing media sources ranging from tweets to news articles.
- **"How It Works: In Theory/How It Works: In Practice" graphics,** many new to this edition, highlight key political processes and structures and build graphical literacy. New discussions include the 2020 Democratic primary (Political Parties) and gerrymandering decisions in the court system (The Courts).
- **"What Do the Facts Say?" features** develop quantitative reasoning skills by teaching students to read and interpret data on important political issues and current events. New to this edition are five features focused on honing students' media literacy skills by breaking down various media sources, including tweets, articles, and quotations, using the framework introduced in the new "Media Checklist for Assessing Reporting on Politics."
- **"Why Should I Care?" sections** draw explicit connections between the chapter material and students' lives. These have also been added to the "Nuts & Bolts" features mentioned below to provide students with a big-picture perspective.
- **"Did You Know?" features and pull quotes** give students tidbits of information that may induce questions and even inspire students to get involved.
- **"Take a Stand" features** address contemporary issues in a pro/con format and invite students to consider how they would argue their own position on the topic. Each feature concludes with critical-thinking questions.
- **"Nuts & Bolts" features provide students with concise explanations of key concepts,** like the difference between civil liberties and civil rights, different kinds of gerrymanders, and brief summaries of campaign finance rules. These features provide an easy way for quick study and review.

Tools for a dynamic classroom

- **InQuizitive, Norton's adaptive learning tool,** accompanies the Seventh Edition of *American Politics Today* and reinforces reading comprehension with a focus on the foundations of government and major political science concepts. Guiding feedback helps students understand why their answers were right or wrong and steers them back to the text. Norton recently conducted a within-subjects efficacy study in American government, and among the students who did not earn a perfect score on the pre-test, we saw an average InQuizitive Effect of 17 percentage points. To try it out, go to https://digital.wwnorton.com/amerpoltoday7.
- **The NEW "Evaluating Sources" InQuizitive module,** like the current "How to Read Charts and Graphs" tutorial, walks students step by step through identifying and understanding what a source is, how it is used in an argument, and whether it is a valid source or not (such as fake news). Paired with the new Media Checklist and Weekly News Quizzes, this module will help students be better prepared than ever to understand and evaluate the news.

- **NEW Weekly News Quizzes** prompt students to engage with the major stories of the day and see their connection to American government. Using a variety of media (print, video, and podcast), each quiz takes a major news story from the previous week and pairs it with assessment for students and a suggested class activity for instructors to use.
- **Features for your Learning Management System (LMS)** allow you to easily bring Norton's high-quality digital content into your existing LMS. The content is fully editable and adaptable to your course needs. The Norton Coursepack for *American Politics Today*, Seventh Edition, contains the following activities and quizzes:
  - **"How to Read Charts and Graphs" tutorial** that provides students with extra practice and guidance interpreting common representations of data that they will encounter in this textbook and in the world,
  - **Simulations** tied to each chapter that allow students to inhabit the role of various political actors to help them better understand political decision making,
  - **"How It Works: In Theory/How It Works: In Practice" animated graphics**, with assessment, that guide students through understanding political processes and institutions,
  - **"What Do the Facts Say?" activities** that give students more practice with quantitative skills and more familiarity with how political scientists know what they know, and
  - **"Take a Stand" exercises** that present students with multiple sides of contemporary debates and ask them to consider and refine their own views based on what they've learned.
- **The test bank** contains more than 1,800 questions tagged to chapter learning objectives and keyed to Bloom's taxonomy.
- **An Interactive Instructor's Guide (IIG)** includes chapter outlines, class activities, and discussion questions, and suggestions for additional resources to engage students.
- **Instructor PowerPoints** contain fully customizable lecture slides with clicker questions and "How It Works: In Theory" and "How It Works: In Practice" animated PowerPoint slides for optimal classroom presentation.

Acknowledgments

This edition of *American Politics Today* is again dedicated to our families. Our wives, Regina and Sarah, have continued to accommodate our deadlines and schedules and have again served as our most accurate critics and sources of insight and inspiration. Our children have again been forced to contend with politics and textbook writing as a perennial topic of conversation in their visits home, and have responded with critiques and ideas of their own, which appear throughout the text. In light of important recent and ongoing discussions, we wanted to note that consistent with our strong commitment to diversity and our belief that all should be treated with respect, we are capitalizing the names of all racial, religious, and ethnic groups.

Our colleagues at Indiana University and the University of Wisconsin (and before that, Duke University for both of us) provided many opportunities to talk about American politics and teaching this course.

Bill thanks his colleagues at Indiana University and elsewhere, including Christine Barbour, John Brehm, Laura Bucci, Ted Carmines, Chris DeSante, Mike Ensley, Bernard Fraga, Matthew Hayes, Yanna Krupnikov, Lin Ostrom, Regina Smyth, Steven Webster, Will Winecoff, and Jerry Wright, for sharp insights and encouragement at crucial moments. He is also grateful to many teaching assistants who have helped him organize and teach the intro class at three universities. Finally, he thanks the students at the Higher School of Economics in Moscow, Russia, where he taught the introductory class as a Fulbright Scholar in 2012.

David gives special thanks to Ken Mayer, whose daily "reality checks" and consistently thoughtful professional and personal advice are greatly appreciated. Barry Burden, Kathy Cramer, Ben Marquez, Ryan Owens, Ellie Powell, Howard Schweber, Alex Tahk, Dave Weimer, Susan Yackee, and all the great people at Wisconsin have provided a wonderful community within which to teach and research American politics. John Coleman, who has moved on to become a dean at the University of Minnesota, also deserves special thanks as a former member of the intro American team and good friend and colleague. David would also like to thank the students at the University of Debrecen in Hungary, where he taught American politics as a Fulbright Scholar in 2003–2004, and the Eberhard Karls University of Tübingen, Germany, where he taught as a Fulbright Scholar in 2011–2012. The Hungarian students' unique perspective on democracy, civil liberties, and the role of government required David to think about American politics in a different way. The German students' views on the role of political parties, campaigns, and the social welfare state also provided a strong contrast to the views of his American students.

Both of us are grateful to the political science faculty at Duke University, who, in addition to giving us our first academic jobs, worked to construct a hospitable and invigorating place to research and to teach. In particular, Rom Coles, Ruth Grant, John Aldrich, Tom Spragens, Taylor Cole, and David Barber were model teachers, colleagues, and scholars. We both learned to teach by watching them, and we are better instructors and scholars for it.

We are indebted to the outstanding people at W. W. Norton who have been our full partners through all seven editions. Our editor Laura Wilk is a graceful, insightful taskmaster, and her new perspective has improved the text immensely. Steve Dunn was responsible for getting the process started and providing good counsel from beginning to end. Roby Harrington has been a source of constant encouragement and feedback. Thea Goodrich has been a superb project editor, bringing to the project her talent for clarity of words and visuals. Cat Abelman put together an excellent photo program. Elizabeth Trammell cleared permissions for the figures and tables. Eric Pier-Hocking handled production with efficiency and good humor. Catherine Lillie helped keep the various pieces moving on schedule. Jillian Burr and Open design studio created a beautiful design for the book's interior and cover. Spencer Richardson-Jones and Michael Jaoui's clear vision for the ever-more-complex and rich digital media package has been a major help, as have Marcus Van Harpen's tremendous efforts developing the interactive ebook. We also would like to thank Peter Lesser, Aaron Javsicas, Ann Shin, and Sam Held for their outstanding work on earlier editions. The entire crew at Norton has been incredibly professional and supportive in ways we never expected when we started writing this book. Signing with them 20 years ago was an eyes-shut home run.

We are also indebted to the many reviewers who have commented on the text.

First Edition Reviewers

Dave Adler, *Idaho State University*

Rick Almeida, *Francis Marion University*

Jim Bailey, *Arkansas State University-Mountain Home*

Todd Belt, *University of Hawaii at Hilo*

Scott Buchanan, *Columbus State University*

Randy Burnside, *Southern Illinois University, Carbondale*

Carolyn Cocca, *SUNY College at Old Westbury*

Tom Dolan, *Columbus State University*

Dave Dulio, *Oakland University*

Matt Eshbaugh-Soha, *University of North Texas*

Kevin Esterling, *University of California, Riverside*

Peter Francia, *East Carolina University*

Scott Frisch, *California State University, Channel Islands*

Sarah Fulton, *Texas A&M University*

Keith Gaddie, *University of Oklahoma*

Joe Giammo, *University of Arkansas at Little Rock*

Kate Greene, *University of Southern Mississippi*

Steven Greene, *North Carolina State University*

Phil Habel, *Southern Illinois University, Carbondale*

Charles Hartwig, *Arkansas State University, Jonesboro*

Ted Jelen, *University of Nevada, Las Vegas*

Jennifer Jensen, *Binghamton University, SUNY*

Terri Johnson, *University of Wisconsin-Green Bay*

Luke Keele, *Ohio State University*

Linda Keith, *The University of Texas at Dallas*

Chris Kelley, *Miami University*

Jason Kirksey, *Oklahoma State University*

Jeffrey Kraus, *Wagner College*

Chris Kukk, *Western Connecticut State University*

Mel Kulbicki, *York College*

Joel Lieske, *Cleveland State University*

Steve Light, *University of North Dakota*

Baodong (Paul) Liu, *University of Utah*

Ken Long, *University of Saint Joseph, Connecticut*

Michael Lynch, *University of Kansas*

Cherie Maestas, *Florida State University*

Tom Marshall, *The University of Texas at Arlington*

Scott McClurg, *Southern Illinois University, Carbondale*

Jonathan Morris, *East Carolina University*

Jason Mycoff, *University of Delaware*

Sean Nicholson-Crotty, *University of Missouri, Columbia*

Timothy Nokken, *Texas Tech University*

Sandra O'Brien, *Florida Gulf Coast University*

John Orman, *Fairfield University*

L. Marvin Overby, *University of Missouri, Columbia*

Catherine Paden, *Simmons College*

Dan Ponder, *Drury University*

Paul Posner, *George Mason University*

David Redlawsk, *University of Iowa*

Russell Renka, *Southeast Missouri State University*

Travis Ridout, *Washington State University*

Andy Rudalevige, *Dickinson College*

Denise Scheberle, *University of Wisconsin-Green Bay*

Tom Schmeling, *Rhode Island College*

Pat Sellers, *Davidson College*

Dan Smith, *Northwest Missouri State University*

Dale Story, *The University of Texas at Arlington*

John Vile, *Middle Tennessee State University*

Mike Wagner, *University of Nebraska*

Dave Wigg, *St. Louis Community College*

Maggie Zetts, *Purdue University*

Second Edition Reviewers

Danny Adkison, *Oklahoma State University*
Hunter Bacot, *Elon College*
Tim Barnett, *Jacksonville State University*
Robert Bruhl, *University of Illinois at Chicago*
Daniel Butler, *Yale University*
Jennifer Byrne, *James Madison University*
Jason Casellas, *The University of Texas at Austin*
Jeffrey Christiansen, *Seminole State College*
Richard Conley, *University of Florida*
Michael Crespin, *University of Georgia*
Brian DiSarro, *California State University, Sacramento*
Ryan Emenaker, *College of the Redwoods*
John Evans, *California State University, Northridge*
John Fliter, *Kansas State University*
Jimmy Gleason, *Purdue University*
Dana Glencross, *Oklahoma City Community College*
Jeannie Grussendorf, *Georgia State University*
Phil Habel, *Southern Illinois University, Carbondale*
Lori Han, *Chapman University*
Katy Harriger, *Wake Forest University*
Richard Himelfarb, *Hofstra University*
Doug Imig, *University of Memphis*
Daniel Klinghard, *College of the Holy Cross*
Eddie Meaders, *University of North Texas*

Kristy Michaud, *California State University, Northridge*
Kris Miler, *University of Illinois at Urbana-Champaign*
Melinda Mueller, *Eastern Illinois University*
Michael Mundt, *Oakton Community College*
Emily Neff-Sharum, *The University of North Carolina at Pembroke*
David Nice, *Washington State University*
Tim Nokken, *Texas Tech University*
Stephen Nuño, *Northern Arizona University*
Richard Powell, *University of Maine, Orono*
Travis Ridout, *Washington State University*
Sara Rinfret, *University of Wisconsin-Green Bay*
Martin Saiz, *California State University, Northridge*
Gabriel Ramon Sanchez, *University of New Mexico*
Charles Shipan, *University of Michigan*
Dan Smith, *Northwest Missouri State University*
Rachel Sondheimer, *United States Military Academy*
Chris Soper, *Pepperdine University*
Walt Stone, *University of California, Davis*
Greg Streich, *University of Central Missouri*
Charles Walcott, *Virginia Tech*
Rick Waterman, *University of Kentucky*
Edward Weber, *Washington State University*
Jack Wright, *Ohio State University*

Third Edition Reviewers

Steve Anthony, *Georgia State University*
Marcos Arandia, *North Lake College*
Richard Barberio, *SUNY Oneonta*
Jody Baumgartner, *East Carolina University*
Brian Berry, *The University of Texas at Dallas*
David Birch, *Lone Star College-Tomball*
Eileen Burgin, *University of Vermont*
Randolph Burnside, *Southern Illinois University, Carbondale*
Kim Casey, *Northwest Missouri State University*
Christopher Chapp, *University of Wisconsin-Whitewater*
Daniel Coffey, *University of Akron*
William Corbett, *The University of Texas at El Paso*
Jonathan Day, *Western Illinois University*
Rebecca Deen, *The University of Texas at Arlington*
Brian DiSarro, *California State University, Sacramento*
Nelson Dometrius, *Texas Tech University*

Stan Dupree, *College of the Desert*
David Edwards, *The University of Texas at Austin*
Ryan Emenaker, *College of the Redwoods*
John Evans, *University of Wisconsin-Eau Claire*
Brandon Franke, *Blinn College, Bryan*
Rodd Freitag, *University of Wisconsin-Eau Claire*
Donna Godwin, *Trinity Valley Community College*
Craig Goodman, *Texas Tech University*
Amy Gossett, *Lincoln University*
Tobin Grant, *Southern Illinois University*
Stephanie Hallock, *Harford Community College*
Alexander Hogan, *Lone Star College-CyFair*
Marvin King, *University of Mississippi*
Timothy LaPira, *James Madison University*
Mary Linder, *Grayson University*
Christine Lipsmeyer, *Texas A&M University*
Michael Lyons, *Utah State University*
Jill Marshall, *The University of Texas at Arlington*

Thomas Masterson, *Butte College*
Daniel Matisoff, *Georgia Institute of Technology*
Jason McDaniel, *San Francisco State University*
Mark McKenzie, *Texas Tech University*
Leonard McNeil, *Contra Costa College*
Melissa Merry, *University of Louisville*
Ann Mezzell, *Lincoln University*
Eric Miller, *Blinn College, Bryan*
Jonathan Morris, *East Carolina University*
Leah Murray, *Weber State University*
Farzeen Nasri, *Ventura College*
Brian Newman, *Pepperdine University*
David Nice, *Washington State University*
Stephen Nichols, *California State University San Marcos*

Tim Nokken, *Texas Tech University*
Barbara Norrander, *University of Arizona*
Andrew Reeves, *Boston University*
Michelle Rodriguez, *San Diego Mesa College*
Dan Smith, *Northwest Missouri State University*
Christopher Soper, *Pepperdine University*
Jim Startin, *The University of Texas at San Antonio*
Jeffrey Stonecash, *Syracuse University*
Linda Trautman, *Ohio University*
Kevin Unter, *University of Louisiana Monroe*
Michelle Wade, *Northwest Missouri State University*
Michael Wagner, *University of Nebraska-Lincoln*
Adam Warber, *Clemson University*
Wayne Wolf, *South Suburban College*

Fourth Edition Reviewers

Rickert Althaus, *Southeast Missouri State University*
Eric K. Austin, *Montana State University*
Evelyn Ballard, *Houston Community College Southeast*
Jim Battista, *University at Buffalo, SUNY*
Kenneth C. Blanchard Jr., *Northern State University*
Heidi Brockmann, *United States Military Academy*
Adriana Buliga-Stoian, *Mount Mercy University*
Abbe Allen DeBolt, *Sandhills Community College*
John C. Evans, *University of Wisconsin-Eau Claire*
Babette Faehmel, *Schenectady County Community College*
Daniel Fuerstman, *State College of Florida*
Stephanie Hallock, *Harford Community College*
John Hitt, *North Lake College*
Debra Jenke, *Angelina College*
Ronald A. Kuykendall, *Trident Technical College*
Paul Lewis, *Arizona State University*
Mary Linder, *Grayson College*
Michael Lyons, *Utah State University*

Wendy Martinek, *Binghamton University, SUNY*
Melissa Merry, *University of Louisville*
Javan "J. D." Mesnard, *Mesa Community College*
Monique Mironesco, *University of Hawai'i-West O'ahu*
Tim Nokken, *Texas Tech University*
David Parker, *Montana State University*
Sylvia Peregrino, *El Paso Community College*
Blayne Primozich, *El Paso Community College*
Bryan Rasmussen, *Collin College*
Suzanne M. Robbins, *George Mason University*
Susan Roomberg, *The University of Texas at San Antonio*
Michael Shamgochian, *Worcester State University*
Geoffrey Shine, *Wharton County Junior College*
Rachel Milstein Sondheimer, *United States Military Academy*
Gregory Streich, *University of Central Missouri*
Jeremy Teigen, *Ramapo College*
Dave Wells, *Arizona State University*

Fifth Edition Reviewers

Leslie Baker, *Mississippi State University*
Evelyn Ballard, *Houston Community College*
Jim Battista, *University at Buffalo, SUNY*
Nathaniel A. Birkhead, *Kansas State University*
William Blake, *Indiana University, Purdue University Indianapolis*

Kenneth C. Blanchard Jr., *Northern State University*
Michael P. Bobic, *Glenville State College*
Ben Christ, *Harrisburg Area Community College*
Rosalyn Crain, *Houston Community College, Northwest College*
Brian Cravens, *Blinn College-Schulenburg*

Stephanie R. Davis, *University of South Carolina*

Christi Dayley, *Weatherford College*

Justin B. Dyer, *University of Missouri*

Jonathan P. Euchner, *Missouri Western State University*

John W. Eyster, *University of Wisconsin-Whitewater*

Eddie Feng, *Weatherford College*

John P. Flanagan, *Weatherford College*

Peter L. Francia, *East Carolina University*

Daniel Fuerstman, *State College of Florida*

Willie Hamilton, *Mt. Jacinto College*

David Huseman, *Butler County Community College*

Debra Jenke, *Angelina College*

Catherine Johnson, *Weatherford College*

Joshua Kaplan, *University of Notre Dame*

Tim LaPira, *James Madison University*

Alan Lehmann, *Blinn College*

Morris Levy, *University of Southern California*

Michael S. Lynch, *University of Georgia*

Rob Mellen Jr., *Mississippi State University*

Timothy Nokken, *Texas Tech University*

Anthony O'Kegan, *Los Angeles Valley College*

Hyung Lae Park, *El Paso Community College*

Donna Rhea, *Houston Community College*

Joseph Romance, *Fort Hays State University*

Sam Scinta, *Viterbo University*

Michael Shamgochian, *Worcester State University*

Lenore VanderZee, *SUNY Canton*

Abram J. Trosky, *United States Coast Guard Academy*

Ronald W. Vardy, *Wharton County Community College; University of Houston*

Gordan Vurusic, *Grand Rapids Community College*

Jeremy Walling, *Southeast Missouri State University*

Sixth Edition Reviewers

Brent Andersen, *University of Maine at Presque Isle*

Nick Anspach, *York College of Pennsylvania*

Nick Beatty, *Missouri State University*

Todd Belt, *University of Hawaii*

Mark Brewer, *University of Maine*

Mark Checchia, *Old Dominion University*

Tom Copeland, *Biola University*

Todd Curry, *The University of Texas at El Paso*

Erin Engels, *Indiana University School of Liberal Arts at IUPUI*

Greg Granger, *Northwestern State University of Louisiana*

Jeanette Harvie, *California State University, Los Angeles*

Susan Haynes, *Lipscomb University*

Carol Jasieniecki, *Santiago Canyon College*

Alana Jeydel, *American River College*

Travis Johnston, *University of Massachusetts Boston*

Jesse Kapenga, *The University of Texas at El Paso*

Cassandra Khatri, *Lone Star College—University Park*

David Kimball, *University of Missouri—St. Louis*

Keith Knutson, *Viterbo University*

Julie Lane, *University of North Carolina Wilmington*

Tim LaPira, *James Madison University*

Beth Leech, *Rutgers University*

Eric Loepp, *University of Wisconsin—Whitewater*

Darrell Lovell, *Lone Star College—University Park*

Drew McMurray, *Wabash Valley College*

Melissa Merry, *University of Louisville*

Akira Ruddle Miyamoto, *University of Hawaii*

James Newman, *Southeastern Missouri State University*

Timothy Nokken, *Texas Tech University*

Stephen Northam, *University of North Georgia*

Hyung Park, *El Paso Community College*

Yuhua Qiao, *Missouri State University*

Jason Sides, *Southeastern Missouri State University*

Anand Edward Sokhey, *University of Colorado Boulder*

Herschel Thomas, *The University of Texas at Arlington*

Paul Weizer, *Fitchburg State University*

Maryann Zihala, *Ozarks Technical Community College*

Seventh Edition Reviewers

Audrey Ambrosino, *Middlesex Community College*

Brent Andersen, *University of Maine, Presque Isle*

Sean Anderson, *California State University Stanislaus*

John Aughenbaugh, *Virginia Commonwealth University*

Manuel Avalos, *University of Southern Maine*

Bruce Brady, *Norfolk Public Schools*

Cynthia Breneman, *Erie Community College, City Campus*

Kizmet Chandler, *Nitro High School*

Anne Comiskey, *St. Mary's Dominican High School*
Mark Drake, *West Bend West High School*
Denise Dupas, *Del Norte High School*
Erin Engels, *Indiana University-Purdue University Indianapolis*
John C. Evans, *Century College*
Frank Franz, *James Madison High School*
Annika Hagley, *Roger Williams University*
Rick Henderson, *Texas State University*
Josh Herring, *Jones County High School*
Mark Jendrysik, *University of North Dakota*
Jerrod Kelly, *North Carolina Wesleyan College*
Daniel Kirsch, *California State University, Sacramento*
Ronald Kuykendall, *Trident Technical College*
Denise Lutz, *East Meadow High School*
Thomas Marshall, *University of Texas at Arlington*
Laura Matthews, *Rochester High School*
Markie McBrayer, *University of Idaho*
Dylan McLean, *University of West Georgia*

Peter Meinberg, *Hartford Union High School*
Wendel Morden, *Shadow Hills High School*
Anthony Nownes, *University of Tennessee*
Anthony Peek, *Baton Rouge Magnet High School*
Joseph Pelletier, *Bangor High School*
Curt Portzel, *Pepperdine University*
Christina Rice, *Thomas M. Wootton High School*
Heather M. Rice, *Slippery Rock University of Pennsylvania*
Suzanne Robbins, *University of Florida*
Michael Romano, *Shenandoah University*
Marc Schwarz, *Pflugerville Independent School District*
Jeffrey Sher, *McKinney North High School*
Rebecca Small, *Fairfax County Public Schools*
Christine Soderquist, *Kenowa Hills High School*
Bob Turner, *Skidmore College*
Greg Wall, *Amador High School*
Paul Weizer, *Fitchburg State University*
Dave Wells, *Arizona State University*
Adam Wemmer, *Pacifica High School*

We would like to thank Cory Colby for his thoughtful and considered suggestions for improving the text, as well as his work on the Interactive Instructor's Guide. His innovative teaching strategies make this a valuable resource for instructors. We would also like to thank Eric Loepp for his thought leadership on online teaching, and his efforts authoring and enhancing the PowerPoints that accompany the text. It is a humbling experience to have so many smart people involved in the process of writing and revising this book. Their reviews are often critical, but always insightful, and you the reader are the beneficiaries of their efforts. In many cases, the improvements in this edition are the direct result of their suggestions. They have our profound thanks.

William T. Bianco
David T. Canon
November 2020

American Politics Today

Seventh Essentials Edition

99

In a democracy, oftentimes other people win.

—C. J. Cregg, *The West Wing*

1

Understanding American Politics

How does politics work and why does politics matter?

» "America is indebted as a democratic nation to the free press for truths it has uncovered, for truth it has disseminated, and for falsehoods it has repudiated. The press uncovered the government's lies about the war in Vietnam; it exposed Watergate; it opened our eyes to the sexual abuse of children by priests; and, most recently, it shed a light on the sexual assault by numerous men in power.... The work of a free press is essential."[1]
Senator Mitt Romney (R-UT)

« "Fake news, fake news. They're scum, many of them are scum. You have some good reporters but not many, I'll be honest with you. And that's one of the things we battle.... But they're total —just terrible dishonest people—and they couldn't figure out—'What do we say bad about this conversation?'"[2]
President Donald Trump

Fake news extends beyond print media. Political pundits on cable news channels have also been responsible for the spread of false information. Using his personal Twitter account, President Trump quoted one such pundit, further disseminating the false claim that the Obama administration had spied on his presidential campaign.

One of Donald Trump's favorite responses to unfavorable media coverage of his presidency is to label the accounts as "FAKE NEWS!" From stories detailing Russian involvement in the 2016 election to accounts of the federal government's response to the COVID-19 pandemic, Trump argued that mainstream media outlets (aided by leaks from "deep state" career bureaucrats) were deliberately slanting coverage to build public opposition and ensure Trump's defeat in 2020. The media outlets argued in turn that they were simply reporting facts as facts.

"The Obama people did something that's never been done...They spied on a rival presidential campaign. Would it be OK if Trump did it next? I am losing faith that our system is on the level. I'm beginning to think it is rotten & corrupt. Scary stuff Obama did." @TuckerCarlson DOJ

CHAPTER GOALS

Describe the basic functions of government. pages 4–9

Define *politics* **and identify three key ideas that help explain politics.** pages 9–15

Identify major sources of conflict in American politics. pages 16–21

Explain how the American values of democracy, liberty, and equality work to resolve political conflict. pages 21–24

Understand how to interpret, evaluate, and use political information. pages 24–27

While Trump's defeat in the 2020 elections means that he will likely fade from public view, his protracted conflict with the media illustrates one of the key ideas in this book—that conflict in American politics reflects real disagreements about government policy. While some of Trump's policy goals (such as his support for tax cuts) reflected conventional Republican ideas, others, such as his imposition of punitive tariffs, skepticism about American engagement abroad, proposals for immigration restrictions, and his support for reopening American society in the case of COVID-19, were unpopular even among Republican lawmakers and voters. It's not surprising that Trump wanted more positive coverage as a way of building public support. It's also not surprising that reporters and editors were unwilling to comply, as their goal is to inform a broad audience, and not all of them are Trump supporters. And from the perspective of sustaining a functioning democracy, skeptical and even negative news coverage of political leaders is essential.

Trump's complaints also illustrate a deeper issue in contemporary American politics: while there are many information sources, it is often hard to determine which are reliable. Americans' propensity to share information through social media means that outlandishly false stories can get widespread attention. In 2019 and 2020, stories circulated that House Speaker Nancy Pelosi had diverted Social Security funds to pay for impeachment hearings, that Representative Alexandria Ocasio-Cortez had proposed a ban on motorcycles, that President Trump's grandfather had been a member of the Ku Klux Klan, and that fireworks were being distributed in American cities to increase tensions and create a rationale for law enforcement to crack down on protests against the murder of George Floyd, who died in police custody in Minneapolis.[3] None of these stories are true—but in a world where the public is bombarded with political information, it is easy to see why some truly fake news gets taken seriously. If Americans can't even agree on which news is "fake," how can we know what to trust? In a complex world, how do Americans understand, evaluate, and act on the political information that they encounter? In part, we will explore these questions throughout the book because the answers can tell us a lot about important political outcomes, including how people vote, what kinds of candidates win elections, and why some policies get enacted in Congress while others are defeated. At the same time, we hope to give you some ideas about how to find the information you need to make up your own mind about political debates.

DESCRIBE THE BASIC FUNCTIONS OF GOVERNMENT

Making sense of American government and politics

The premise of this book is simple: *American politics makes sense*. What happens in elections, in Washington, D.C., and everywhere else has a logical and often simple explanation. By the end of this book, we hope you get really good at analyzing the politics you see everywhere—in the news and in your own life.

This claim may seem unrealistic or even naive. On the surface, American politics often makes no sense. Polls show strong support for extreme, unconstitutional, or downright silly proposals. Candidates put more time into insulting their opponents than into making credible campaign promises. Members of Congress seem more interested in beating their political opponents than in getting something done, and the Democratic and Republican caucuses agree on virtually nothing. As we've just described, information from historically trusted national sources is labeled "fake news." The last year has also revealed the limits of government power, showing its inability to prevent a nationwide pandemic or stop the racially biased exercise of police force.

You are also living through an unusual period in American politics. President Trump broke many well-established political norms, most notably threatening to initiate Justice Department probes of prominent Democrats (including his predecessor, former president Barack Obama; his 2016 opponent, former senator Hillary Clinton; and his 2020 opponent and eventual winner of the general election, former vice president Joe Biden), and asked several foreign governments to investigate members of Biden's family—this is the event that triggered impeachment proceedings against him. Trump's agenda on trade, immigration, international alliances, and other issues conflicted with the long-held consensus in both political parties. He refused to place his extensive business holdings in a blind trust or to make his tax returns public, both things that all modern presidents have done.

Whether you approve or disapprove of Trump's behavior in office or his impeachment by the House, it is important to remember two things. First, Trump's presidency has shown that some things we believed about how American politics works were in fact wrong. Four years ago, few political scientists would have believed that presidential candidates could win election (or remain in office) if they were found to have paid hush money to someone with whom they had had an affair, if they were accused of sexual assault by multiple individuals, if they offhandedly used Twitter to criticize and insult political opponents and members of their own party, or if they used a combination of threats, bluffs, and bluster to manage domestic and foreign policy. Trump's presidency revealed new things about how politicians win and hold political support and how presidents can use their official and unofficial powers to shape policy outcomes.

However, for all of Trump's successes, much of what we understood about American politics still holds. It is true that Trump unexpectedly won the 2016 presidential election, gaining support from groups and areas of the country that had been reliably Democratic for nearly a generation. But Trump received a minority of the popular vote in 2016, his party suffered severe losses in the 2018 midterms, and he lost the 2020 election. And many of his policy priorities were stymied by defeats in Congress or the courts. One of our central goals in this book is to explain where Trump came from, why he succeeded in some areas but not others, and what we know about how American politics works in light of these events.

Conflicts within the government—say, over immigration policy—often reflect real divisions among American citizens about what government should do about certain issues. Groups on all sides of controversial issues pressure the government to enact their preferred policies.

The second thing to keep in mind is that the polarization, distrust, anger, and worries about the survival of democracy that seem to be core features of contemporary American politics are actually nothing new. Many people, we believe, are hostile toward American politics because they don't understand the political process, feel helpless to influence election outcomes or policy making, and believe that it is impossible to work within the system to change things (even deeply flawed practices such as racially biased policing). A surprisingly high percentage of Americans dislike both political parties and their candidates and see the conflict between Republicans and Democrats as more evidence that American politics does not work well. Here again, while these beliefs might be somewhat stronger than they were a generation ago, Americans have been skeptical of politicians and political parties since the Founding.

To be clear, it is *not* our goal to turn you into a political junkie or policy wonk (or a Democrat, a Republican, or anything else). You don't need to like politics to make sense of it, but we hope that after finishing this book you will have a basic understanding of how the political process works and why it matters.

One of our goals is to help you take an active role in the political process, if you want to. A functioning democracy allows citizens to defer complicated policy decisions to their elected leaders, but a democracy works better when citizens organize to make demands of government, monitor what politicians do, and hold them accountable at the voting booth. This book will help you be an effective participant by providing the analytical skills you need to make sense of politics, even when it initially appears to make no sense at all.

We are not going to spend time talking about how American politics should be. Rather, our focus will be on explaining American politics as it is. Here are some other questions we will examine:

- Why don't people vote? Why *do* people vote? How do they decide whom to vote for?
- Why do so many people mistrust politicians and the political system?
- Why can't Congress get things done?
- Why is the Supreme Court so political?
- Can presidents do whatever they want? Why can't they do more?
- How much power do bureaucrats have?
- Is the media biased?

We will answer these questions and many others by applying three key ideas about the nature of politics: politics is conflictual, political process matters, and politics is everywhere. But first, we begin with an even more basic question: Why do we have a government?

Why do we have a government?

government
The system for implementing decisions made through the political process.

As we prepare to address this question, let's agree on a definition: **government** is the system for implementing decisions made through the political process. All countries have some form of government, which in general serves two broad purposes: to provide order and to promote the general welfare.

To Provide Order At a basic level, the answer to the question "Why do we have a government?" seems obvious: without government there would be chaos. As the seventeenth-century British philosopher Thomas Hobbes said, life in the "state of nature" (that is, without government) would be "solitary, poor, nasty, brutish, and short."[4] Without government there would be no laws—people could do whatever they wanted. Even if people tried to develop informal rules, there would be no way to guarantee enforcement of those rules. Accordingly, some of the most important roles of government are policing and providing national security.

The Founders of the United States noted this crucial role in the Constitution's preamble: two of the central goals of government are to "provide for the common defense" and to "insure domestic Tranquility." The former refers to military protection against foreign invasion and the defense of our nation's common security interests. The latter refers to policing and law enforcement within the nation, which today includes the National Guard, the Federal Bureau of Investigation (FBI), the Department of Homeland Security, state and local police, and the courts. So at a minimal level, government is necessary to provide security.

However, there's more to it than that. The Founders cited the desire to "establish Justice . . . and secure the Blessings of Liberty to ourselves and our Posterity." But do we need government to do these things? It may be obvious that the police power of the nation is required to prevent anarchy, but can't people have justice and liberty without government? In a perfect world, maybe, but the Founders had a more realistic view of human nature. As James Madison, one of the founding fathers (and the fourth president of the United States), said, "But what is government itself, but the greatest of all reflections on human nature? If men were angels, no government would be necessary. If angels were to govern men, neither external nor internal controls on government would be necessary."[5] Furthermore, Madison continued, people have a variety of interests that have "divided mankind into parties, inflamed them with mutual animosity, and rendered them much more disposed to vex and oppress each other than to co-operate for their common good."[6] That is, without government, we would quickly be headed toward Hobbes's nasty and brutish state of nature because of differences in opinion about what society should look like. Having a government means that people cannot act unilaterally against each other, but it also creates a new problem: people will try to use the government and its powers to impose their views on the rest of society.

Madison's view of human nature might sound pessimistic, but it was also realistic. He assumed that people were self-interested: we want what is best for ourselves and for our families, and to satisfy those interests we tend to form groups with like-minded people. Madison saw these groups, which he called **factions**, as being opposed to the public good, and his greatest fear was of tyranny by a faction imposing its will on the rest of the nation. For example, if one group took power and established an official state religion, that faction would be tyrannizing people who practiced a different religion. This type of oppression is precisely why many of the early American colonists fled Europe in the first place.

As we will discuss in Chapters 2 and 3, America's government seeks to control the effects of factions by dividing government power in three main ways. First, the **separation of powers** divides the government into three branches—judicial, executive, and legislative—and assigns distinct duties to each branch. Second, the system of **checks and balances** gives each branch some power over the other two. (For example, the president can veto legislation passed by Congress; Congress can impeach the president; and the Supreme Court has the power to interpret laws written by Congress to determine whether they are constitutional.) Third, **federalism** divides power yet again by allotting different responsibilities to local, state, and national government. With power divided in this fashion, Madison reasoned, no single faction could dominate the government.

To Promote the General Welfare The preamble to the Constitution also states that the federal government exists to "promote the general Welfare." This means tackling the hard problems that Americans cannot solve on their own, such as taking care of the poor, the

factions
Groups of like-minded people who try to influence the government. American government is set up to avoid domination by any one of these groups.

separation of powers
The division of government power across the judicial, executive, and legislative branches.

checks and balances
A system in which each branch of government has some power over the others.

federalism
The division of power across the local, state, and national levels of government.

Two important government functions described in the Constitution are to "provide for the common defense" and "insure domestic Tranquility." The military and local police are two of the most commonly used forces the government maintains to fulfill those roles.

sick, and the aged and dealing with global issues like climate change, pandemics, terrorist threats, and poverty in other countries. However, government intervention is not inevitable—people can decide that these problems aren't worth solving. But if people *do* want to address these large problems, government action is necessary because **public goods** such as environmental protection or national defense are not efficiently provided by the free market, either because of **collective action problems** or for other reasons.

It is easy for two people or even a small group to tackle a common problem without the help of government, but 1,000 people (to say nothing of the more than 334 million in the United States today) would have a very difficult time. They would suffer from the **free rider problem**—that is, because it is in everyone's own interest to let someone else do the work, the danger is that no one will contribute, even though everyone wants the outcome that collective contributions would create. A government representing more than 334 million people can provide public goods that all those people acting on their own would be unable to provide, so people elect leaders and pay taxes to provide those public goods.

Collective action problems are common in modern society. Education provides a great example. You benefit personally from your primary, secondary, and college education in terms of the knowledge and experience you gain, and from the higher salary and better job you will earn because of your college degree. However, society also benefits from your education. Your employer will benefit from your knowledge and skills, as will people you interact with. If education were provided solely by the free market, those who could afford schooling would be educated, but the rest would not, leaving a large segment of society with little or no education and therefore unemployable. So public education, like many important services, benefits all levels of society and must be provided by the government for the general welfare.

Now that we understand *why* we have a government, the next question is, *What* does the government do to "insure domestic Tranquility" and "promote the general Welfare"? Many visible components of the government promote these goals, from the police and armed services to the Internal Revenue Service, Federal Reserve, Postal Service, Social Security Administration, National Aeronautics and Space Administration, Department of Education, and Food and Drug Administration. In fact, it is hard to find an aspect of everyday life that does not involve the government in some way, either as a provider of public goods, as a protector of civil liberties, as an enforcer of laws and property rights, or as a regulator of individual or corporate behavior. What makes politics both interesting and important is that in most of these cases, Americans disagree on what kinds of public goods the government should provide, or whether government should be involved at all.

Forms of government

While all governments must provide order and promote the general welfare, different types of governments accomplish this in various ways. Greek political philosopher Aristotle, writing in the fourth century BC, developed a classification scheme for governments that is still surprisingly useful. Aristotle distinguished three pure types of government based on the number of rulers versus the number of people ruled: monarchy (rule by one), aristocracy (rule by the few), and polity (rule by the many, such as the general population—this is the most general description of a democracy).

There are many ways to implement democracy. In its purest form, a democracy is a system in which citizens make policy choices directly, such as through referenda. However, all current democracies, including America's national government, are organized as republics, in which elected representatives make policy decisions on behalf of citizens. Republics throughout the world are organized very differently. For example, they allocate power differently among the executive, legislative, and judicial branches. Presidential systems such as the one we have in the United States tend to follow a separation of power among the three branches, while parliamentary systems such as the one in the United Kingdom elect the chief executive from the legislature, resulting in much closer coordination between those two branches. An additional distinction is the relationship among different levels of government. In a federal system (such as the United States), power is shared among the local, state, and national levels of government. In a unitary system (such as France or Japan), all power is held at the national level, and local governments must comply with orders from the central government. A confederation (like Switzerland) is a less common form of government in which states retain their sovereignty and autonomy but form a loose association at the national level.

What is politics?

We define **politics** as the process that determines what government does—whether and how it provides different public and private goods. You may consider politics the same thing as government, but we see government as the institutions that carry out the decisions that are a result of the political process. Many aspects of our discussion of politics will probably sound familiar because your life involves politics on a regular basis. This may sound a little abstract, but it should become clear in light of the three key ideas of this book (see the How It Works graphic in this chapter).

First, *politics is conflictual*. The questions debated in election campaigns and in Washington and the options considered by policy makers generally involve disagreement at all levels. The federal government does not spend much time resolving questions that everyone agrees on the answers to. Rather, making government policy involves issues on which people disagree, sometimes strongly, which makes compromise difficult—and this is a normal, healthy part of politics. Although compromise may be difficult to achieve, it is often necessary to produce outcomes that can be enacted and implemented.

Second, *political process matters*. Governmental actions don't happen by accident—they result from conscious choices made by elected officials and bureaucrats. Politics puts certain individuals into positions of power and makes the rules that structure their choices. The media often cover political campaigns the way they would report on a boxing match or the Super Bowl, focusing on the competition, rivalries, and

DID YOU KNOW?

63%

of the world's population lives in countries considered to be free or partly free. Most countries considered not free are in Asia or Africa.
Source: Freedom House

DEFINE *POLITICS* AND IDENTIFY THREE KEY IDEAS THAT HELP EXPLAIN POLITICS

politics
The process that determines what government does.

entertaining stories, which can lead people to overlook the institutions, rules, and procedures that have a decisive influence on politics. Indeed, the political process is in part a mechanism for resolving conflict. The most obvious example of the political process at work is elections, which democracies use to resolve a fundamental conflict: deciding who should lead the country and make policy choices.

Third, *politics is everywhere*. Decisions about what government should do or who should be in charge are integral to society, and they influence the everyday lives of all Americans. Politics helps determine what people can and cannot do, their quality of life, and how they think about events, people, and situations. Moreover, people's political thought and behavior are driven by the same types of calculations and decision-making rules that shape beliefs and actions in other parts of life. For example, deciding which presidential candidate to vote for is not so different from deciding which college to attend. For candidates, you might consider issue positions, character, and leadership ability, while for college you would weigh how schools fit your academic goals, how much tuition you can afford, and where different schools are located. In both cases you are consciously making a decision that will satisfy the criteria most important to you, given known budgetary and academic constraints.

Politics is conflictual

Political scientists have long recognized the central role of conflict in politics. In fact, one prominent theory in the mid-twentieth century saw conflict between interest groups as explaining most outcomes in American politics. The political scientist E. E. Schattschneider argued that the scope of political conflict—that is, how many people are involved in the fight—determines who wins in politics.[7] Others have argued that some conflict is helpful for group decision making: if nobody challenges a widely shared but flawed view, people may convince themselves that the obvious flaws are not a problem.[8] Bureaucratic politics, congressional politics, elections, and even Supreme Court decision making have all been studied through the lens of political conflict.[9]

Conflict is inherent in American politics. Here, supporters and opponents of same-sex marriage argue in front of the Supreme Court building in Washington on the day the Court heard arguments in *Obergefell v. Hodges*, the 2015 case that legalized same-sex marriage throughout the nation.

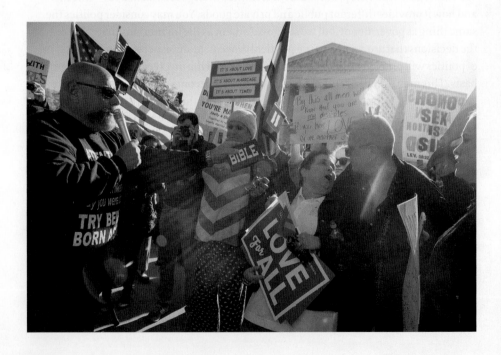

Three Key Ideas for Understanding Politics

Politics Is Conflictual

Conflict and compromise are natural parts of politics.
Political conflict over issues like the national debt, abortion, and health care **reflects disagreements among the American people** and often requires compromises within government.

Political Process Matters

How political conflicts are resolved is important.
Elections determine who represents citizens in government. **Rules and procedures determine who has power** in Congress and other branches of government.

Politics Is Everywhere

What happens in government affects our lives in countless ways.
Policies related to jobs and the economy, food safety and nutrition, student loans, and many other areas shape **our everyday lives**. We see political information in the news and encounter political situations in many areas of our lives.

? Critical Thinking

1. **One implication of the idea that politics is conflictual is that politicians** may not want to negotiate compromises on important policy questions. Why do you think politicians sometimes refuse to compromise rather than work together to get things done?

2. **Think back to the discussion** of fake news at the beginning of this chapter. In what ways do disagreements over what constitutes "fake" news illustrate the three key ideas described here?

Despite the consensus that conflict in politics is inevitable, most people do not like conflict, either in their personal lives or in politics. You probably have heard people say that the three topics one should not discuss in polite company are money, religion, and politics. Indeed, political scientists have found strong evidence that people avoid discussing politics in order to maintain social harmony.[10]

Many people apply their disdain for conflict to politicians as well. "Why is there so much partisan bickering?" our students frequently ask. "Why can't they just get along?" This dislike of conflict, and of politics more generally, produces a desire for what political scientists John R. Hibbing and Elizabeth Theiss-Morse call "stealth democracy"—that is, nondemocratic practices such as running government like a business or taking action without political debate. In essence, this idea reflects the hope that everything would be better if we could just take the politics out of politics. Hibbing and Theiss-Morse argue that, to combat this belief, we need to do a better job of educating people about conflict and policy differences and that the failure to do so "is encouraging students to conclude that real democracy is unnecessary and stealth democracy will do just fine."[11] Conflict cannot be avoided in politics; ignoring fundamental disagreements will not make conflict go away.

The argument over abortion is a good example. Abortion rights have been a perennial topic of debate since a 1973 Supreme Court decision held that state laws banning abortion were unconstitutional. Surveys about abortion rights show that public opinion spans a wide range of policy options, with little agreement about which policy is best. (In Chapter 6, we will examine the political implications of this kind of broad disagreement.) Such conflicts reflect intense differences of opinion that are rooted in self-interest, ideology, and personal beliefs. Moreover, in such situations, no matter what Congress does, many people will be unhappy with the result. You might expect that politicians will ultimately find a compromise that satisfies everyone, but this is not always true. In many cases (abortion rights are a good example), no single policy choice satisfies even a slight majority of elected officials or citizens.

The idea that conflict is nearly always a part of politics should be no surprise. Situations in which everyone (or almost everyone) agrees about what government should be doing are easy to resolve: either a popular new policy is enacted or an unpopular issue is avoided, and the debate moves off the political agenda. Although issues where there is consensus resolve quickly and disappear, conflictual issues remain on the agenda as the winners try to extend their gains and the losers work to roll back policies. Thus, one reason that abortion rights is a perennial issue in campaigns and congressional debates is that there is no national consensus on when to allow abortions, no indication that the issue is becoming less important to citizens or elected officials, and no sign of a compromise policy that would attract widespread support.

An important consequence of the inevitable conflicts in American politics is that compromise and bargaining are essential to getting things done. Politicians who bargain with opponents are not necessarily abandoning their principles; striking a deal may be the only way to make some of the policy changes they want. Moreover, agreement sometimes exists even in the midst of controversy. For example, surveys that measure attitudes about abortion find widespread support for measures such as prohibiting government funding for abortions, requiring parental notification when a minor has an abortion, or requiring doctors who perform the procedure to present their patients with information on alternatives such as adoption, while only 15–25 percent (depending on the survey) think that abortion should always be illegal.[12]

Another consequence of conflict is that it is almost impossible to get exactly what you want from the political process. Even when a significant percentage of the population is united behind common goals—such as supporters of Donald Trump after the 2016 election, who demanded the repeal of Obamacare—these individuals almost always find

One consequence of political conflict is that one party's policy victories last only until the other party wins control of government. Here, President Trump signs a law repealing most of Dodd-Frank, an Obama-era measure that imposed new regulations on the banking industry in the wake of the 2008 financial crisis.

As long as the reason of man continues fallible, and he is at liberty to exercise it, different opinions will be formed.

—James Madison, founding father

that translating these demands into policy change requires them to accept something short of their ideal. Even with Democratic gains in the 2020 election, supporters of initiatives such as free college tuition or Medicare for All are likely to find that they must accept more modest changes or risk winning nothing at all. The need for compromise does not mean that change is impossible, but rather means that what is achievable often falls short of individuals' demands.

Political process matters

The political process is often described like a sporting event. Election coverage often emphasizes the "horse race" (who's ahead in the latest poll), and accounts of negotiations between the president and Congress often make the process sound like a poker game. This emphasis overlooks an important point: politics is the process that determines what government does, none of which is inevitable. Public policy—everything from defending the nation to spending on Medicare—is up for grabs. Changes in federal policy can have profound consequences for large swaths of the population. Politics is not just a game.

Elections are an excellent example. Elections allow voters to give fellow citizens the power to enact laws, write budgets, and appoint senior bureaucrats and federal judges. It matters who gets elected. In the first two years after the 2016 election produced unified Republican control of the presidency and Congress, many Obama-era environmental and employment regulations were repealed, conservatives were appointed to the Supreme Court and other federal courts, corporate tax rates were cut, and the United States withdrew from the Paris Agreement on climate change. Even after Democrats gained majority control of the House in 2018, Senate Republicans continued to confirm conservative federal judges, and the Trump administration continued to revise federal regulations. Clearly, political process matters: if the 2016 election had gone the other way, outcomes in all these important areas would have been significantly different.

Yet politics is more than elections. As you will see, many unelected members of the federal bureaucracy have influence over what government does by virtue of their roles in developing and implementing government policies. The same is true for federal judges, who review government actions to see if they are consistent with the Constitution and other federal laws. These individuals' decisions are part of the political process, even though they are not elected to their positions.

Ordinary citizens are also part of politics. They can vote; donate time or money to interest groups, party organizations, or individual candidates; or demand action from these groups or individuals by writing letters, sending e-mails, or participating in

The political process mattered in the 2020 election, from determining who the candidates were to affecting which states received the most attention from campaigns. Both Joe Biden and Donald Trump spent a lot of time campaigning in Florida in a bid to win the state's Electoral College votes.

public protest. Such actions can influence government policy, either by determining who holds the power to directly change policy or by signaling to policy makers which options have public support.

Another important element of politics is the web of rules and procedures that determines who has the power to make choices about government policy. These rules range from the requirement that the president must be born a U.S. citizen, to the rules that structure debates and voting in the House and the Senate, to the procedures for approving new federal regulations. Seemingly innocuous rules can have an enormous impact on what can or does happen, which means that choices about these rules are actually choices about outcomes. The ability to determine political rules empowers the people who make those choices.

Politics is everywhere

Even though most Americans have little interest in politics, most of us encounter it every day. When you read the newspaper, watch television, go online, or listen to the radio, you'll almost surely encounter a political story. When you are walking down the street, you may see billboards, bumper stickers, or T-shirts advertising a candidate, a political party, an interest group, or an issue position. Someone may ask you to sign a petition. You may walk past a homeless person and wonder whether a winning candidate followed through on her promise to help. You may glance at a headline about a Black Lives Matter protest and wonder why the protection of civil rights is such an enduring problem in America.

Many people have an interest in putting politics in front of us on a daily basis. Interest groups, political parties, and candidates work to raise public awareness of the political process and to shape what people know and want. Moreover, the news media offer extensive coverage of elections, governing, and how government policies affect ordinary Americans. Through efforts like these, politics really is everywhere.

Politics is also a fundamental part of how Americans think about themselves. Virtually all of us can name our party identification (Democrat, Republican, or Independent)[13] and can place our views on a continuum between liberal and conservative.[14]

Politics is everywhere in another important way, too: actions by the federal government touch virtually every aspect of your life. Figure 1.1 shows a time line

FIGURE 1.1

Government in a Student's Daily Life

On a typical day, the government plays a critical role in a student's daily life through federal programs, regulation, and spending. In addition to what is listed here, in what other aspects of your life does government play a part?

7:30	Wake up in dorm funded by federal program.
8:00	Eat cereal regulated by Food and Drug Administration.
8:15	Get dressed in clothing subject to import tariffs and regulations.
8:30	Read weather reports that use data from the National Weather Service.
9:00	Check e-mail using Internet developed with federal funding.
10:00	Drive to school in car whose design is shaped by federal regulations.
10:30	Drive past post office, military recruitment office, and environmental cleanup site.
11:00	Attend lecture by professor whose research receives federal funding.
4:00	Ride home from school on federally subsidized mass transit.
7:30	Pay bursar bill using federally funded student loan.
8:00	Call friend on cellular network regulated by the Federal Communications Commission.
10:00	Watch TV program on station that has federal license.

for a typical college student on a typical day. As you can see, from the moment this student wakes up until the end of the day, his or her actions are influenced by federal programs, spending, and regulations. Moreover, this chart omits actions by state and local governments, which are very active in areas such as education policy and law enforcement. As you will see in later chapters, it's not surprising that the federal government touches your everyday life in many ways. The federal government is extraordinarily large regardless of whether you measure it in terms of spending (more than $4.4 trillion a year), number of employees (over 2 million, not including contract workers and Postal Service employees), or regulations (over 180,000 pages in the *Code of Federal Regulations*).[15]

Moreover, the idea that politics is everywhere has a deeper meaning: people's political behavior is similar to their behavior in the rest of their lives. For example, collective action problems occur when you live with roommates and need to keep common areas neat and clean. Everyone has an interest in a clean area, but each person is inclined to let someone else do the work. The same principles help us understand campus protests over tuition hikes, alcohol bans, or changes in graduation requirements in terms of which kinds of issues and circumstances foster cooperation. In each case, individual free riders acting in their own self-interest may undermine the outcome that most people prefer.

Similarly, convincing like-minded individuals to contribute to a political group's lobbying efforts is no easy task. Each would-be contributor of time or money also has the opportunity to be a free rider who refuses to participate yet reaps the benefits of others' participation. Because of these difficulties, some groups of people with common goals remain unorganized. College students are a good example: many want more student aid and lower interest rates on government-subsidized student loans, but they fail to organize politically toward those ends.

This similarity between behavior in political situations and in the rest of life is no surprise; everything that happens in politics is the result of individuals' choices. And the connections between politics and everyday life mean you already know more about politics than you realize.

The idea that "politics is everywhere" means that government actions touch virtually all aspects of our lives, from regulating the business of Internet service providers to maintain net neutrality to mandating equal funding for men's and women's sports in high schools and colleges. Moreover, everyday life often helps us make sense of politics and politicians; for example, U.S. senator Ted Cruz joked that "The Democrats are the party of Lisa Simpson and Republicans are happily the party of Homer, Bart, Maggie and Marge," riffing on the perceived elitism of Lisa in comparison to the rest of her down-to-earth and highly relatable (and amusing) family members.

Just because you do not take an interest in politics does not mean that politics will not take an interest in you.

—**Pericles,** ancient Greek lawmaker

When you are trying to make sense of a political situation, think first of the three key ideas that we have just discussed. Focusing on conflict helps you understand what is at stake. Focusing on rules helps explain the strategies that participants use to achieve their goals. And the idea that politics is everywhere is there to remind you that conflicts over government policy are not things that happen only to other people—for better or worse, the outcome of political conflicts can touch virtually all aspects of our lives.

"Why Should I Care?"

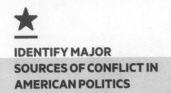
Sources of conflict in American politics

Where does political conflict come from? The reality is that conflict must be addressed in order to find compromise and enact policy. Sometimes, however, disagreements resist resolution because of inherent differences among people and their opinions about government and politics.

Economic interests

People's economic interests today vary widely, and they constitute a source of conflict in politics. In contrast, relative economic equality was a defining characteristic of our nation's early history—at least among White men—since small landowners, businessmen, craftsmen, and their families constituted a large majority of the nation's population. Compared with our European counterparts, the United States has, historically, been relatively free from class-based politics. Over time, our nation has become more stratified by class, to the point that the United States now has one of the highest levels of income inequality among developed nations. Nonetheless, a broad commitment to the **free market** (an economic system based on competition among businesses without government interference) and to *economic individualism* (the autonomy of individuals to manage their own financial decisions without government interference) remains central to our national identity.

Despite this basic consensus on economic principles and a history relatively free of class-based politics, there are important differences among American citizens, interest groups, and political parties in terms of their economic interests and favored economic policies. Democratic politicians and activists tend to favor more **redistributive tax policies** (that is, tax policies that attempt to create greater social equality, such as taxing the rich at higher rates than the middle class or the poor, as in the wealth tax proposed by a 2020 Democratic presidential candidate, Senator Elizabeth Warren) and social spending on programs for the poor. Democrats are also more inclined to regulate industry to protect the environment and ensure worker and product safety, but they tend to favor fewer restrictions on the personal behavior of individuals. Republicans favor lower taxes and less spending on social policies. They are also more supportive than Democrats of the free market and less inclined to interfere with business interests, although many Republicans favor regulation of individual behaviors, such as abortion, same-sex marriage, and marijuana consumption.

Cultural values

Another source of conflict in American politics is differing cultural values. For example, political analysts often focus attention on the **culture wars** in the United States between "red-state" Americans, who tend to have strong religious beliefs, and "blue-state" Americans, who tend to be more secular. (The color coding of the states comes from the election-night maps on television that show the states carried by Republican candidates in red and those won by Democrats in blue—but see the What Do the Facts Say? feature for a more nuanced take on this.)

free market
An economic system based on competition among businesses without government interference.

redistributive tax policies
Policies, generally favored by Democratic politicians, that use taxation to attempt to create social equality (for example, higher taxation of the rich to provide programs for the poor).

culture wars
Political conflict in the United States between "red-state" Americans, who tend to have strong religious beliefs, and "blue-state" Americans, who tend to be more secular.

Purple America: The 2020 Presidential Election

The media create maps of the country on election night with red states indicating where Republicans win and blue states where Democrats win, like the top map here. But what do we see if we look beyond the state level to the county level? And what if we look not just at who won and who lost, but which party was stronger relative to the other? This is what the bottom map, created by Robert Vanderbei at Princeton University, shows. The simple view of two Americas—Republican versus Democrat, red versus blue—starts to look a lot more purple.

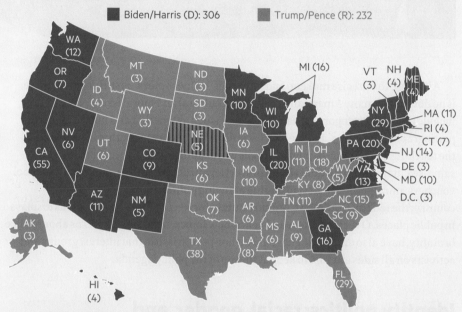

Biden/Harris (D): 306   Trump/Pence (R): 232

Note: 2020 Electoral map represents the authors' estimates as of 11/13/20. Two states split their electoral votes: in Maine, Trump received 1 vote and Biden 3; in Nebraska, Trump received 4 votes and Biden 1.

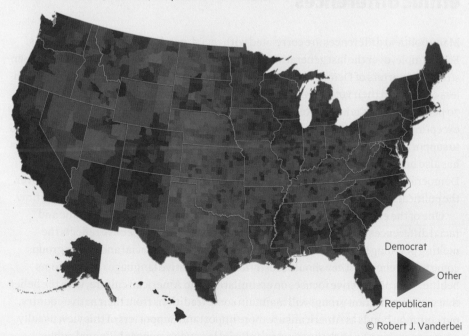

Democrat

Other

Republican

© Robert J. Vanderbei

Source: Provided by Robert J. Vanderbei, Princeton University, "2020 Presidential Election, Purple America," https://vanderbei.princeton.edu/JAVA/election2020/ (accessed 11/12/20).

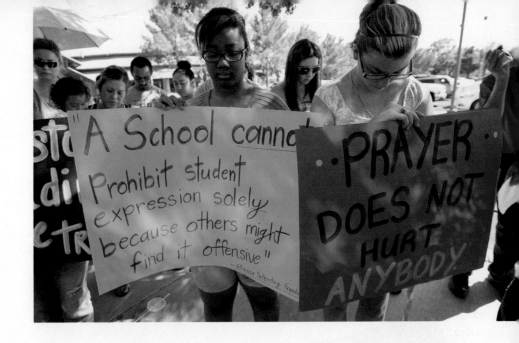

Differing cultural values are a significant source of conflict among groups of voters in the United States. Pictured here are students in Odessa, Texas, protesting a school district policy that changed the names of the "invocation" and "benediction" to "opening" and "closing" at their graduation ceremony.

Civil and voting rights contributed to the realignment of the South in the second half of the twentieth century, as more Whites began supporting the Republican Party, and the Democratic Party came to be seen as the champion of minority rights. Here, Blacks and Whites in Alabama wait in line together to vote at a city hall after the enactment of the 1965 Voting Rights Act.

Although the precise makeup and impact of "values voters" is still debated, there is no doubt that many Americans disagree on cultural and moral issues. These include the broad category of "family values" (such as whether and how to regulate pornography, gambling, and media obscenity and violence); whether to supplement the teaching of evolution in public schools with intelligent design and creationism; same-sex marriage; abortion; school prayer; legalization of drugs; gun control; school vouchers; immigration policy, including allowing political refugees to enter the country; the federal Common Core curriculum for K–12 schools; and religious displays in public places. Over the last several years, new topics, including concerns about police brutality, have also emerged. These are all hot-button issues that interest groups and activists on all sides attempt to keep at the top of the policy agenda.

Identity politics: racial, gender, and ethnic differences

Many political differences are correlated with racial, gender, and ethnic differences. For example, over the last generation about 90 percent of African Americans have been strong supporters of Democratic candidates. Other racial and ethnic groups have been less cohesive in their voting, with their support for a particular party ranging from 55 to 70 percent. Whites tend to vote Republican; Latinos tend to vote Democratic, with the exception of Cuban Americans, who tend to vote Republican; and Asian Americans tend to support Democrats with about 70 percent of the vote. A gender gap in national politics has also been evident in recent elections, with women being more likely to vote for Democrats and men for Republicans. Because these tendencies are not fixed, however, the political implications of racial, gender, and ethnic differences can change over time.

One of the enduring debates in American politics concerns whether ethnic and racial differences *should* be tied to political interests. One perspective reflects the melting pot image of America, which holds that as different racial and ethnic groups come to this country, they should mostly leave their native languages and customs behind. This perspective focuses on assimilation into American culture, with the belief that while immigrant groups will maintain some traditions from their native country, our common bonds as Americans are more important. Supporters of this view usually advocate making English the country's official language, oppose bilingual public education, and, if they favor immigration at all, prefer that it be restricted to well-off people from English-speaking countries.

However, there are varied alternatives to the melting pot view. These range from racial separatists such as the Nation of Islam, whose members see White-dominated society as oppressive and discriminatory, to multiculturalists, who argue that there is strength in diversity and embrace a "tossed salad" version of assimilation (that is, each ingredient remains distinct but contributes to the overall quality of the salad).[16] In general, people holding this viewpoint favor less restrictive immigration laws and oppose policies that encourage immigrants to assimilate. Given that immigrant groups also differ from the population in terms of education levels, occupation, family size, and other factors, it should not be surprising that members of these groups have their own ideas about what government should and should not do.

This debate over culture is one reason why recent discussions about immigration law have been so conflictual—the two sides start from very different premises about the value of diversity. But regardless of how this debate is resolved, our multiracial makeup is clear, as Figure 1.2 shows. In fact, trends in population growth suggest that by 2060 or so, Whites will no longer constitute a majority of the U.S. population. The extent to which this diversity continues to be a source of political conflict depends on the broader role of race in our society. As long as there are racial differences in employment, education, health, housing, and crime, and as long as racial discrimination is present in our society, race will continue to be a source of political conflict, as the Black Lives Matter protests in 2020 illustrate.

Many of the same observations apply to gender and politics. The women's movement is usually viewed as beginning in 1848 at the first Women's Rights Convention in Seneca Falls, New York. The fight for women's suffrage and legal rights dominated the movement through the late nineteenth and early twentieth centuries, with women gaining the right to vote in 1920 after passage of the Nineteenth Amendment to the Constitution. Beginning in the 1960s and 1970s, feminism and the women's liberation movement highlighted a broad range of issues: workplace issues such as maternity leave, equal pay, and sexual harassment; reproductive rights and abortion; domestic violence; and sexual violence.

The Racial Composition of the United States

FIGURE 1.2

Only about 60 percent of Americans describe themselves as White. Moreover, the proportion of Hispanics and Latinos in the population is about 18 percent and rising, although this category contains many distinct subgroups. What changes would you expect in American politics and federal policy if the actual population in 2060 matches the projections?

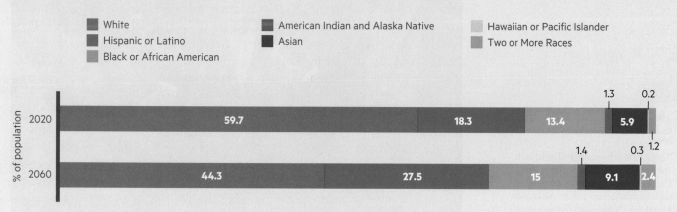

Source: Census data aggregated by author. Raw data available at www.census.gov/programs-surveys/popproj/data/tables.html (accessed 12/2/19).

While progress has occurred on many fronts, including electing women to political office, gender remains an important source of political disagreement and identity politics. While the Congress elected in 2020 has more than 100 female House members and more than 20 female senators, these percentages are far lower than in the general population, and many other nations have a higher percentage of women in elected office. Gender politics became even more central during President Trump's presidency, starting with the January 2017 Women's March, which drew between 3.3 and 4.6 million people in more than 500 U.S. cities, and continuing with the #MeToo movement that has drawn attention to sexual assault (see Chapter 5 for additional details on contemporary civil rights politics).

Ideology

ideology
A cohesive set of ideas and beliefs used to organize and evaluate the political world.

conservative
The side of the ideological spectrum defined by support for lower taxes, a free market, and a more limited government; generally associated with Republicans.

liberal
The side of the ideological spectrum defined by support for stronger government programs and more market regulation; generally associated with Democrats.

libertarians
Those who prefer very limited government and therefore tend to be conservative on issues such as social welfare policy, environmental policy, and government funding for education but liberal on issues involving personal liberty such as free speech, abortion, and the legalization of drugs.

Another source of differences in interests is **ideology**: a cohesive set of ideas and beliefs that allows an individual to organize and evaluate the political world. Ideology may seem most obviously related to political interests through political parties, since Republicans tend to be **conservative** and Democrats tend to be **liberal**. While this is true in a relative sense (most Republicans are more conservative than most Democrats), few Americans consider their own views ideologically extreme.[17]

Ideology shapes beliefs about more specific policies. Conservatives promote traditional social practices and favor lower taxes, a free market, and a more limited government, whereas liberals support social tolerance, stronger government programs, and more market regulation. However, the picture gets cloudy if we look more closely. **Libertarians**, for example, prefer very limited government—they believe government should provide for the national defense and should have only a few other narrowly defined responsibilities. Because they are at the extreme end of the ideological continuum on this issue, libertarians are generally conservative in areas such as social welfare policy, environmental policy, and government funding for education and generally liberal on issues involving personal liberty such as free speech, abortion, and the legalization of drugs. For libertarians, the consistent ideological theme is limiting the role of government in our lives.

Though he is formally affiliated with the Republican party, Senator Rand Paul of Kentucky is often associated with libertarianism and is well known for taking a libertarian conservative stance on economic issues, in particular.

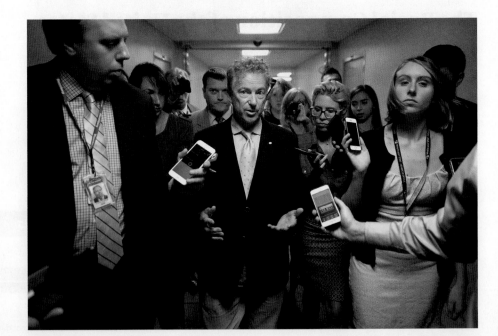

Personal ideologies are not always consistent. Someone can be both a fiscal conservative (favoring balanced budgets) and a social liberal (favoring the pro-choice position on abortion and marital rights for gay men and lesbians), or a liberal on foreign policy issues (supporting humanitarian aid and opposing military intervention overseas) and a conservative on moral issues (being pro-life on abortion and opposing stem-cell research). Ideology is a significant source of conflict in politics, and it does not always operate in a straightforward manner. In Chapter 6, we explore whether America is becoming more ideological and polarized, deepening our conflicts and making compromise more difficult.

Even so, there are clear areas of agreement in American politics, even on issues that once divided us. For example, while there is still considerable disagreement over same-sex marriage, public opinion has clearly shifted toward accepting these unions. Along the same lines, two generations ago Americans were divided on the legality of mixed-race marriage, while today very few people would object. Thus, even though conflict is a constant in American politics, it is wrong to say that we are divided into two groups, red and blue, that oppose each other on all issues of significance.

The first step in understanding any political conflict is to determine who wants what. Who is involved? What do they, or their side, want? In modern American politics, citizens' demands are often connected to their economic interests, values, race, gender, ethnicity, and ideology. As a result, the group affiliations of individuals often tell us a lot about what they want from candidates and the government, and why they want it.

"Why Should I Care?"

EXPLAIN HOW THE AMERICAN VALUES OF DEMOCRACY, LIBERTY, AND EQUALITY WORK TO RESOLVE POLITICAL CONFLICT

Resolving conflict: democracy and American political values

When we say that rules shape how conflicts are worked out in American politics, most of the time we are referring to formal (written-down) constraints that describe how the actions taken by each participant shape the ultimate outcome. For example, most American House and Senate elections are decided using plurality rule (whichever candidate gets the most votes wins), while a few states require winners to receive an absolute majority (50 percent + 1) of votes cast. However, some of the most important rules are not written down—these **norms** constitute America's political culture, or a collective idea of how a government and society should operate, including democracy, equality, and liberty, and more specific ideas about everyday political interactions.[18]

Democracy

The idea of democracy means that policy disagreements are ultimately resolved through decisions made by citizens, such as their votes in elections. In the simplest terms, "**democracy**" means government by the people. As put into practice, this typically means representative democracy rather than direct democracy—that is, the people elect representatives who decide policies and pass laws rather than determining those things directly. There are some examples of direct democracy in the United States, such as the New England town meeting and the referendum process, through

norms
Unwritten rules and informal agreements among citizens and elected officials about how government and society should operate.

democracy
Government by the people. In most contexts, this means representative democracy in which the people elect leaders to enact policies. Democracies must have fair elections with at least two options.

which people in a state directly determine policy.[19] But for the most part, Americans elect politicians to represent us, from school board and city council members at the local level, to state legislators and governors at the state level, to U.S. House members, senators, and the president at the national level.

Democracy is not the only way to resolve conflict, nor do all societies have as strong a belief in democracy as in America. One mechanism used by authoritarian governments is to suppress conflict though violence and limitations on freedom. Some governments, such as those of China and Russia, control political outcomes while allowing relatively free markets. The Iranian government is a theocracy, in which religious leaders have a veto over the government's policy choices. And some countries, such as the oil sheikdoms in the Middle East, like the United Arab Emirates, have a monarchy, in which rulers are determined by heredity. While nondemocratic systems vary widely in terms of their structure and their popularity, the common thread is that some individual or group is in charge of the country and the policy-making process and cannot be removed except by revolution.

In contrast, democracies select rulers and resolve conflict through voting and elections. When the second president of the United States, John Adams, turned over power to his bitter rival, Thomas Jefferson, after losing a hotly contested election in 1800, his departure demonstrated that democratic government by the people had real meaning—electoral winners get to exercise power, while losers go home to strategize about how to increase their popularity and win the next election. Democracy depends on the consent of the governed: if the views of the people change, then the government must eventually be responsive to those views or the people will choose new leaders. It also means that citizens must accept election results as authoritative—you have to obey the laws passed by a new Congress, even if you voted for the other party's candidates.

Liberty

liberty
Political freedom, such as the freedom of speech, press, assembly, and religion. These and other legal and due process rights protecting individuals from government control are outlined in the Bill of Rights of the U.S. Constitution.

To the Founders, **liberty** was a central principle for their new government: they believed that people must have the freedom to express their political views, with the understanding that conflict may arise between different views expressed by different people. The Bill of Rights of the Constitution (discussed in Chapter 4) outlines the nature of those liberties: the freedom of speech, press, assembly, and religion, as well as many legal and due process rights protecting individuals from government control.

Liberty also means that within broad limits, people are free to determine what they want from government and to organize themselves to demand their preferred policies from elected officials. Thus, in the case of immigration policy, it is acceptable to hold the view that America should have open borders, and it is also acceptable to demand (and lobby Congress to enact) a complete ban on immigration—or to hold any view in between these extremes.

A system in which individuals are free to form their own views about what government should do virtually guarantees conflict over government policy. James Madison recognized this essential trade-off between liberty and conflict. He argued that suppressing conflict by limiting freedom was "worse than the disease" (worse than conflict). To put it another way, any political system that prioritizes liberty will have conflict.

Another consequence of valuing liberty (and the inevitable conflict over policy that results) is the need for compromise in the policy-making process. In most policy areas, Americans and their elected officials hold a wide range of views, with no consensus on what government should do. Getting something done requires fashioning an agreement that gives no one what he or she really wants, but is nevertheless better than nothing. Standing on principle and refusing to compromise may sound like a noble strategy, but it often results in getting none of what you want, as other individuals or groups work to change policy without your involvement.

Equality

Another principle of democracy is **equality**. Even though the Declaration of Independence boldly declared that "all men are created equal," this did not mean that all people were entitled to the same income or even the same social status (and the Founders obviously ignored slavery as well). Instead, the most widely embraced notion of equality in the United States today is the equality of opportunity—that is, everyone should have the same chance to realize his or her potential. Political equality also means that people are treated the same in the political system. Everyone has one vote in an election, and everyone is equal in the eyes of the law—that is, we are all subject to the same rules that limit how we can lobby, contribute, work for a candidate, or express our opinions. In practice, political equality has not always existed in America. In our early history, only White men could vote and in many states those men needed to be property owners in order to vote. Slowly, political equality expanded as property requirements were dropped; Black men (in 1870), women (in 1920)—though restrictions for people of color persisted into the 1960s—and 18- to 20-year-olds (in 1971) got the right to vote. (For more on the expansion of the right to vote, see Chapter 5.) Today, although wealthy people clearly can have their voices heard more easily than poor people can (through campaign contributions or independent expenditures on political ads), the notion of political equality is central to our democracy.

Like democracy, political equality also contributes to resolving conflict. First, if people know that they will be treated equally by the political system, they are more likely to respect the system. Indeed, one of the triggers for revolutions around the world is reaction against rigged elections or policies that benefit only the supporters of winning candidates. Political equality also gives us cues about how to get involved in politics. Most fundamentally, it suggests that the way to change policy is to elect candidates who share your views, rather than appealing to a friend or relative who works in the government or offering a bribe to a bureaucrat.

While America's political culture has many other aspects, the concepts of democracy, liberty, and equality are central to understanding how American politics

equality
In the context of American politics, "equality" means equality before the law, political equality (one person, one vote), and equality of opportunity (the equal chance for everyone to realize his or her potential), but not material equality (equal income or wealth).

In democracies like the United States, voting is one of the most visible ways citizens use the political process to express their opinions and resolve conflict.

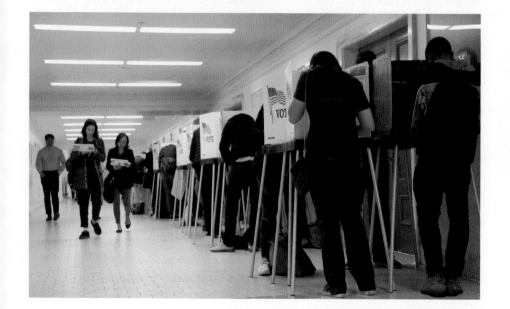

works. Agreement on these principles helps lessen conflicts and limit their scope. For example, when Democratic senators lost the battle to prevent Trump's Supreme Court nominee Amy Coney Barrett from being appointed, they didn't have to worry that Trump would remove them from office or throw them in jail for opposing Barrett. (Indeed, this equality norm is one reason why Trump's threats to investigate prominent Democrats were so controversial.) Moreover, Democrats had a clear path to preventing Trump from appointing more justices like Barrett: regain control of the Senate or win the presidency. Americans and their elected officials have been willing to grant one another political equality and to take political defeats in stride because there is agreement on the basic boundaries of political debate. Again, this consensus does not imply there is no conflict—quite the contrary. However, conflict is easier to resolve if it is over a narrower range of options.

Not surprisingly, many aspects of America's political culture will come up throughout this book. You also might want to look out for them when you are watching the news or reading about national politics. When Democrats in Congress talk about the need to provide health insurance for all Americans, they are emphasizing equality—and when Trump and his Republican allies argue that minimizing government involvement and allowing people more choice (even if it means some people cannot afford insurance) will lead to a better system, they are emphasizing liberty. Moreover, as this example suggests, part of the conflict in American politics is over which aspect of political culture should carry the day. The fact that issues such as health care have been central in recent elections is a reminder of the importance of elections in a democracy and our belief that elections are one venue where conflicts are debated and resolved.

"Why Should I Care?"

To truly understand American politics, you must understand America's core values: democracy, liberty, and equality. These values set broad limits on how political conflicts will be resolved. Democracy implies that the people are the ultimate authority over political outcomes. Liberty implies that people are able to express whatever demands they want and to choose among a wide range of strategies in trying to shape the outcomes of political decisions. And equality means that everyone has an equal share of decision-making power. Despite conflicts over their interpretations, most Americans believe in these core values, and reminding ourselves of this can help us work toward resolving political conflicts.

UNDERSTAND HOW TO INTERPRET, EVALUATE, AND USE POLITICAL INFORMATION

How to be a critical consumer of politics

One of the biggest problems in understanding American politics today is deciding whom you should believe. If you want to justify a particular policy solution or point of view on any political issue, you can find a source that will help you do just that. Would free college tuition for all create a well-informed American citizenry? There are people who think so—and who have spent a great deal of time making this argument on free and paid media. Alternatively, would making college free do nothing except increase enrollments? There are plenty of easily accessible arguments for this position as well.

In one sense, the mountain of available information is an amazing asset. If you want to learn about politics, there are many more sources available now compared to generations ago, from mainstream media to a large number of political observers who put together websites, podcasts, Twitter feeds, or other social media sites. The problem is, if two sources disagree, who should you believe? If a source makes an extraordinary claim ("Space aliens control Congress!"), when should you take it seriously—at least seriously enough to research the claim? What rules should you follow to become well informed without being misled?

The Media Checklist for Assessing Reporting on Politics on p. 27 provides some general guidelines for learning about politics. We will be referring to these rules throughout the text, to help you understand how to put them into practice.

Consider the Author While it is true that the rise of the Internet and social media allows virtually anyone to report on politics, authors are not created alike. Some reporters have covered American politics for several decades and have a track record for cultivating sources, uncovering information, or analyzing and interpreting events. Other reporters essentially come out of nowhere, offering insights on a brand-new blog or website. Other things being equal, who should you believe—someone who has produced reliable reporting in the past or someone whose abilities can't be evaluated? Think about it this way: Whom do you want to fix your car—someone who's been fixing cars for 30 years and has thousands of satisfied customers (including your best friend, once a mechanic herself) or the newbie who just opened a shop last week? The answer is easy: unless the newbie has some identifiable edge, go with the track record.

Look for Verifiable Evidence Another important criterion for evaluating political reports is to see if they provide evidence to back up their claims. Anyone can say that free tuition will create a well-informed citizenry. However, this argument is more credible if it comes with supporting data, such as a study showing that college graduates are better informed than people who never attended. As engineer David Akin once put it, "Analysis without numbers is only an opinion." It's also important for the article to include enough information about the source so that it can be found without too much searching. That way, readers can examine the source themselves to verify that evidence was reported fairly. Of course, many reports on American politics rely on anonymous sources—in these cases, the author's reputation looms especially large in the decision of whether to take the story seriously.

Think about the Size of the Claim Evidence should also match the claims being made by a reporter. If someone claims that space aliens control Congress, we need more than his or her word to believe the report. In fact, in an era when everyone has access to Photoshop, pictures would not be enough. We'd probably want a news conference with a space alien and congressional leaders in which the full plot is revealed in detail. As the astronomer Carl Sagan often said, "Extraordinary claims require extraordinary evidence." The problem, of course, is that in many cases available evidence is fragmentary, contradictory, or even nonexistent. For example, one persistent rumor over the last few years was that the Russian government has some sort of embarrassing information about President Trump and that it was controlling his actions by threatening to release it. However, there is no hard evidence to back up these claims or many other possible explanations for Trump's allegedly pro-Russia actions. Which is to say, some of the time, it makes sense to disregard a potentially explosive story because those reporting it cannot prove what they claim to be true.

> **The further a society drifts from the truth, the more it will hate those who speak it.**
>
> —**George Orwell,** novelist

Read Multiple Reports A story about a political event or outcome is more credible if it is consistent with other reports. For example, on June 16, 2017, Trump tweeted about a Rasmussen Reports poll that showed his approval rate at 50 percent. However, the Rasmussen poll was an outlier; all the other polls taken at the same time showed Trump's approval rating to be significantly lower. In fact, FiveThirtyEight's aggregated estimate that same day was 38.7 percent. Moreover, past Rasmussen polls had also showed higher approval ratings for Trump. We'll talk more about polling and how to interpret poll results in Chapter 6. For now, these numbers illustrate the dangers of relying on a single information source.

Some sources are also better than others. For example, even though pollsters cannot measure public opinion with perfect certainty, they know some techniques are better than others. Accordingly, most public opinion scholars criticize the polling techniques used by Rasmussen Reports, on the grounds that they produce less accurate (and more pro-Republican) findings than the techniques used by other pollsters. Of course, pollsters don't know which techniques are the best in all circumstances—but they can still distinguish better from worse.

Beware of Simple Explanations In general, you should be skeptical about simple explanations for political outcomes. For example, one explanation for Hillary Clinton's defeat in 2016 (or the failure of the presidential campaigns of Senators Elizabeth Warren, Amy Klobuchar, and Kirsten Gillibrand during the 2020 Democratic nomination process) was that Americans were not ready to elect a female president. However, this account ignores the fact that throughout America women are routinely elected as mayors, governors, and members of Congress—and, after Kamala Harris's win in the 2020 election, as vice president. This is not to say that attitudes about gender did not play a role in Clinton's defeat (or that of the others), but rather to note that this outcome was the result of many factors working together. Complex outcomes are rarely explained by a single factor.

Finally, you might ask, If I'm supposed to be skeptical, why should I believe anything in this book? The answer is that throughout this book we've strived to follow all the rules presented here. Our aim is to describe how American politics works, rather than to make an argument about how it *should* work. We are social scientists, not cheerleaders. Rather than shaping your preferences, our goal is to give you the tools to understand, evaluate, and interpret political information and to help you be an informed, effective participant in the political process. As we always tell our students, "My goal is not to tell you *what* to think, but to help you learn *how* to think about politics." We emphasize facts and data (often from multiple sources, with citations and references) because the first step in understanding why things happen is to learn the details of actual events. And while we believe that American politics makes sense and that you can learn to make sense of it, we avoid simple explanations, as these generally do not provide much insight into political behavior or policy outcomes.

"Why Should I Care?"

Which reports about American politics should we take seriously? Those whose authors have reputations for insight and reliability, those that present appropriate evidence given their claims, those that are consistent with what other reporters are saying, and those that reflect the complexity of America's society and its government.

Media Checklist for Assessing Reporting on Politics

① Says who?

✓ **Evaluate the author's reputation**
The Internet and social media allow virtually anyone to report on politics, but authors are not created alike. Trust reporters who have experience covering American politics.

② Fact or "fake news"?

✓ **Verify the information**
Good reporting is the result of good sources, and you should always be able to identify and find the source without too much searching. Take a look at the source yourself—whether it is data, polling results, or even a journal article —to verify that evidence was reported fairly.

③ What's the impact?

✓ **Assess the extent of the claim**
As the astronomer Carl Sagan once put it, "Extraordinary claims require extraordinary evidence." Evidence should also match the claims being made by reporters. We need more than their word to believe what they are saying.

④ Who agrees?

✓ **Corroborate the report**
A story about a political event or outcome is more credible if it is consistent with other reports. Make sure you verify that other credible sources of news and reporters are saying the same thing.

⑤ Tell me more!

1+1=3

✓ **Assess if the explanation is too simple**
Be skeptical about simple explanations for political outcomes. Complex outcomes are rarely explained by a single factor.

Unpacking the Conflict

As we consider the three key ideas about politics that we've discussed in this chapter—politics is conflictual, political process matters, and politics is everywhere—let's return to the problem of defining "fake news" discussed at the beginning of the chapter. If Americans can't even agree on which news is "fake," how can we know what to trust?

Understanding that politics is conflictual reveals important details about the fight between Trump and the mainstream media. Because media coverage shapes public support, Trump wanted stories that said good things about his performance in office. But the job of a reporter is not to support the president—it's to provide a combination of facts and analysis that captures the situation. Virtually all presidents have felt at times that they were being treated unfairly by the media. But those feelings reflect the different goals held by presidents and the people who report on their performance. It's all about conflict, not fake news.

Understanding that process matters also provides insight into fake news. One reason why presidents complain about press coverage (although rarely in as blunt terms as Trump) is that there is very little they can do to stop the media from publishing critical stories. This is because of the First Amendment to our Constitution, which guarantees a free press. Trump can fume in private and publish critical tweets, but he has only marginal influence over what is written about him.

Finally, the media's coverage of Trump illustrates the fact that politics is everywhere. Trump's actions got attention because they affect our lives directly and indirectly. You might prefer that all the stories about Trump were replaced by additional coverage of your hobbies, favorite sports team, or other interests. But even if you ignore politics, politics does not ignore you. Decisions made in Washington have a profound impact on your life, whether you want them to or not.

As you read this book, we hope you will learn important "nuts and bolts" of the American political process as well as some political history that will help you gauge the likely accuracy of what you learn from news reports and help you determine if there might be more to the story than the narratives that are being presented. In general, your reading in this book will focus on contemporary questions, debates, and examples—the kinds of stories that constitute a lot of political news coverage—to illustrate broader points about our nation's political system.

Although you will no doubt disagree with—or even be angry about—some aspects of American politics and some media coverage, our goal is to provide you with the tools to understand *why* government operates as it does. We are not arguing that the federal government is perfect, that one party's agenda (or leadership) is better than the other's, or that imperfect responses to policy problems are inevitable. Rather, we believe that any attempt to explain these outcomes, or to devise ways to prevent similar problems, requires an understanding of why they happened in the first place. After reading this book, you will have a better sense of how American politics really works, and why it matters.

"What's Your Take?"

Is the media the "watchdog" that protects democracy, or is it an out-of-control, self-serving, biased group of partisans?

And if Americans can't even agree on which news is "fake," how can we know what to trust?

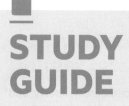

STUDY GUIDE

Making sense of American government and politics

Describe the basic functions of government.
(Pages 4–9)

Summary

Forms of government can be characterized by the number of people who hold power (many versus few) and the number of levels over which power is distributed (national versus state versus local). Government exists primarily to provide order, although it must do so while avoiding oppression by the rulers. Government also needs to provide public goods because they will be underprovided by the free market.

Key terms

government (p. 6)

factions (p. 7)

separation of powers
(p. 7)

checks and balances (p. 7)

federalism (p. 7)

public goods (p. 8)

collective action problems
(p. 8)

free rider problem (p. 8)

Practice Quiz Questions

1. What did Aristotle call a government ruled by the many?

a   monarchy

b   aristocracy

c   polity

d   unitary system

e   democracy

2. Which term describes giving each branch of government power over the other two?

a   separation of powers

b   checks and balances

c   federalism

d   plutocracy

e   unitary system

3. Which term describes the inability to get individuals to cooperate to achieve a common goal?

a   positive externality

b   the Samaritan's dilemma

c   collective action problem

d   principal-agent problem

e   public goods

What is politics?

Define *politics* and identify three key ideas that help explain politics. (Pages 9–15)

Summary

Conflict in politics cannot be avoided: the American people disagree on nearly every issue on which politicians make policy decisions. Compromise and bargaining are essential to enacting policy, but this means that it is almost impossible to get exactly what you want from the political process. Policy outcomes are also influenced by the policy process itself—different procedures of making policy can lead to different outcomes. Whether it is on the news or influencing most aspects of your life, politics is all around us.

Key term

politics (p. 9)

Practice Quiz Questions

4. What is the main reason why politicians have a hard time resolving the issue of abortion?

a   Politicians don't listen to the people.

b   The parties are divided on what abortion policy should look like.

c   Politicians don't know what their constituents' views are.

d   The country is closely divided on what abortion policy should look like.

e   Abortion is a relatively new issue.

5. Which concept describes the idea that actions by the government touch most aspects of your life?

a   Politics is understandable.

b   Politics is conflictual.

c   Political process matters.

d   Politics is everywhere.

e   People have different interests.

6. Rules, such as those regulating debate in the Senate or limiting who can vote in elections, serve as evidence that _____ .

a   politics is understandable

b   politics is conflictual

c   political process matters

d   politics is everywhere

e   people have different interests

Sources of conflict in American politics

Identify major sources of conflict in American politics. (Pages 16–21)

Summary

Although Americans generally agree on a free market system, there is considerable conflict over how much the government should support tax policies that redistribute wealth. Conflict also arises on cultural grounds, pitting religious "red-state" Americans against the more secular "blue-state" Americans. There is also disagreement on the extent to which racial, gender, and ethnic diversity should be celebrated or minimized.

Key terms

free market (p. 16)

redistributive tax policies (p. 16)

culture wars (p. 16)

ideology (p. 20)

conservative (p. 20)

liberal (p. 20)

libertarians (p. 20)

Practice Quiz Questions

7. Democrats tend to favor _____ tax policies and are _____ inclined to regulate industry.

a redistributive; more

b conservative; more

c redistributive; less

d conservative; less

e regressive; less

8. Which issue is commonly associated with the culture wars?

a the national debt

b environmental regulation

c affirmative action

d the tax code

e same-sex marriage

9. An individual who opposes government social welfare policy and supports the legalization of drugs is most likely a _____ .

a libertarian

b socialist

c Democrat

d Republican

e centrist

Resolving conflict: democracy and American political values

Explain how the American values of democracy, liberty, and equality work to resolve political conflict. (Pages 21–24)

Summary

Democracy, liberty, and equality are American political values that are essential for understanding how conflict is resolved. Representative democracies resolve conflict through elections rather than through violence. Although liberty ensures that people will have the freedom to express differing views, democracy is the best system for resolving those conflicts. Political equality ensures that everyone is treated the same before the law and that all votes are equal, and the equality of opportunity means that every person has an equal chance to realize his or her potential.

Key terms

norms (p. 21)

democracy (p. 21)

liberty (p. 22)

equality (p. 23)

Practice Quiz Questions

10. Which type of equality is *not* typically agreed upon in American politics?

a equality of opportunity

b equality before the law

c political equality

d one person, one vote

e material equality (such as equal income)

11. What did James Madison argue was "worse than the disease"?

a giving too much power to state legislatures

b allowing people to have too much freedom, which would lead to chaos

c giving up liberty to get rid of conflict

d allowing politicians to exercise their judgment rather than listen to the people

e taking cod liver oil to treat various ailments

How to be a critical consumer of politics

Understand how to interpret, evaluate, and use political information. (Pages 24–27)

Summary

One of the biggest problems in understanding American politics today is deciding whom you should believe. In one sense, the mountain of available information is an amazing asset. If you want to learn about politics, there are many more sources and much more content available now compared to generations ago. But if sources disagree, whom should you believe? One answer is to focus on sources that provide evidence to back up their claims. It also helps to gather information from multiple sources, especially if the sources have different ideological or other biases. You should also be skeptical about simple explanations for political outcomes. Complex outcomes are rarely explained by a single factor.

Practice Quiz Question

12. Which of the following would be the best source of information regarding a Congress member's position on a particular bill?

a   a podcast produced by a person on the Congress member's staff

b   an article in a national newspaper written by a staff reporter covering Washington, D.C.

c   a blog post written by an organization that will be affected by the bill

d   an interview with the Congress member on a cable news segment

e   a campaign advertisement paid for by a political opponent

Suggested Reading

Bartels, Larry M. *Unequal Democracy: The Political Economy of the New Gilded Age,* 2nd ed. Princeton, NJ: Princeton University Press, 2016.

Dahl, Robert. *A Preface to Democratic Theory*, expanded ed. Chicago: University of Chicago Press, 2013.

Dalton, Russell J. *Citizen Politics: Public Opinion and Political Parties in Advanced Industrial Democracies*, 6th ed. Los Angeles: CQ Press, 2014.

Fiorina, Morris P., with Samuel J. Abrams and Jeremy C. Pope. *Culture War? The Myth of a Polarized America*, 3rd ed. New York: Pearson, Longman, 2010.

Gelman, Andrew, David Park, Boris Shor, Joseph Bafumi, and Jeronimo Cortina. *Red State, Blue State, Rich State, Poor State: Why Americans Vote the Way They Do*. Princeton, NJ: Princeton University Press, 2008.

Lupia, Arthur. *Uninformed: Why People Know So Little about Politics and What We Can Do about It*. New York: Oxford University Press, 2016.

Norris, Pippa. *Democratic Deficit: Critical Citizens Revisited*. New York: Cambridge University Press, 2011.

Putnam, Robert D. *Bowling Alone: The Collapse and Revival of American Community*. New York: Simon and Schuster, 2000.

Schattschneider, E. E. *The Semisovereign People: A Realist's View of Democracy in America*. New York: Holt, Rinehart, and Winston, 1960.

2
The Constitution and the Founding

What are the rules of the political game?

>> **"The call to the Ukrainian President was PERFECT. Read the Transcript! There was NOTHING said that was in any way wrong. Republicans, don't be led into the fools [sic] trap of saying it was not perfect, but is not impeachable. No, it is much stronger than that. NOTHING WAS DONE WRONG!"[1]**
President Donald Trump

<< **"Everybody has read your words on the call. The Ukrainian President asks for military aid to fend off the Russian attack, you say 'I want you to do us a favor though,' and then you spend the rest of the call asking for bogus investigations to smear your political opponents."[2]**
Speaker of the House Nancy Pelosi (D-CA)

In 2019, Donald Trump became the third president in U.S. history to be impeached by the House of Representatives, led by Speaker Pelosi. After several months of House investigations and a brief Senate trial, the president was acquitted almost along party lines. Speaking from the East Room of the White House after the conclusion of the trial, President Trump holds up a copy of the *Washington Post* announcing his acquittal.

In August 2019, a "whistleblower" filed a complaint alleging that President Trump had asked the president of Ukraine, Volodymyr Zelensky, to investigate Joe Biden, who at that point appeared to be Trump's chief rival in the 2020 campaign. The House started investigating the matter in early September and later that month it began an impeachment inquiry. Three different House committees heard testimony from more than a dozen witnesses over the next two months, first in private interviews and then in public hearings. In December, the House impeached the president, passing two articles of impeachment on nearly straight party votes. Article I alleged that Trump had abused his power by threatening to withhold $391 million in military and security assistance and a White House meeting until Ukraine agreed to two demands: (1) announce that it had opened investigations into the Bidens and (2) state that it, rather than Russia, had interfered in the 2016 presidential election. Article II alleged that Trump had obstructed Congress by directing executive branch officials not to testify before Congress and to withhold documents and records concerning the impeachment inquiry.

Although substantial evidence was presented in the impeachment trial to support the allegations, the Senate voted to acquit the president, again on a party-line vote, with the exception of a vote from Republican Mitt Romney of Utah to convict on Article I.

Why was the president acquitted if the evidence was clear? The answer lies in the sparseness of the Constitution's language concerning impeachment and the Senate's interpretation of these words: "The President, Vice President and all civil Officers of the United States, shall be removed from Office on Impeachment for, and Conviction of, Treason, Bribery, or other High Crimes and Misdemeanors" (Article II, Section 4). Treason and bribery are pretty clear, but what is a "high crime and misdemeanor"? When the words of the Constitution are unclear, scholars first look to two sources to figure out the framers' intent: James Madison's notes to the Constitutional Convention and the *Federalist Papers* (which we will talk about in more detail later in the chapter). Madison's notes reveal that initially the framers planned to limit impeachment to treason and bribery, but George Mason objected that the narrowness of those terms would excuse some impeachable behavior and "will not reach many great and dangerous offenses." So the framers added "high crimes and misdemeanors. At the time, misdemeanor meant "misconduct or misbehavior," so the term would have applied to a general abuse of power.

The president's expert on constitutional law in the impeachment trial, Alan Dershowitz, argued that an impeachable offense had to be a crime or "criminal-like behavior." But most constitutional scholars agree with Alexander Hamilton, who argued that impeachment is for "offenses which proceed from the misconduct of public men, or, in other words, from the abuse or violation of public trust. They are of a nature which may with peculiar propriety be denominated POLITICAL, as they relate chiefly to injuries done immediately to the society itself."[3] However, because impeachment is inherently a political process, not a legal process, impeachment means whatever a given House and Senate say that it means. So, when a majority of the Senate decided that President Trump's behavior did not warrant removal from office, many senators explicitly said that the voters should be able to decide, given that an election was coming up in less than a year. Well, the voters *did* decide and elected Joe Biden by extremely thin margins in a handful of states. President Trump claimed the election was stolen and for the first time in U.S. history, a peaceful transition of power was in doubt.

What would have happened if President Trump refused to leave office? Was American democracy in danger? Does the American political system as laid out in the Constitution work to keep conflicts between politicians and branches of government in check, or does it allow space for these conflicts to spiral out of control?

DESCRIBE THE HISTORICAL CIRCUMSTANCES THAT LED TO THE CONSTITUTIONAL CONVENTION OF 1787

The historical context of the Constitution

The Constitution was created through conflict and compromise, and understanding its historical context can help clarify *why* the framers made the specific choices they did. The first event that led many American colonists to question the fairness of British rule and shaped their ideas about self-governance was the Stamp Act of 1765, which imposed a tax on many publications and legal documents in the colonies. The British Parliament enacted the tax to help pay for the French and Indian War (1754–1763), claiming the tax was fair because the American colonists had benefited from the protection of British troops during the war. However, many colonists saw this as unfair "taxation without representation," because they had no say in the legislation's passage (because they had no representation in the British Parliament). A series of escalating events, including the Tea Act (1773) and the Boston Tea Party later that year, in which colonists dumped tea from the British East India Company into the harbor rather than pay the new tax on tea, moved the colonies closer to the inevitable break with Great Britain. Attempts at a political solution failed, so the Continental Congress declared independence from Britain on July 4, 1776.[4]

The Articles of Confederation: the first attempt at government

Throughout the Revolutionary (1775–1783) and early post-Revolutionary era (1783–1787), the future of the American colonies was very much in doubt. While many Americans were eager to sever ties with the oppressive British government and establish a new nation that rejected the trappings of royalty, there was still a large contingent of Tories (supporters of the British monarchy) and probably an even larger group of Americans who wished the conflict would just go away. This context of uncertainty and conflict made the Founders' task of creating a lasting republic extremely difficult.

The first attempt to structure an American government, the **Articles of Confederation**, swung too far in the direction of decentralized and **limited government**. The Articles were written in the summer of 1776 during the Second Continental Congress, which had also authorized and approved the Declaration of Independence. They were submitted to all 13 states in 1777 for approval, but they did not take effect until the last state ratified them in 1781. However, in the absence of any alternative, the Articles of Confederation served as the basis for organizing the government during the Revolutionary War (see Figure 2.1).

In their zeal to reject **monarchy**, the authors of the Articles did not even include provisions for a president or any other executive leader. Instead, they assigned all national power to a Congress in which each state had a single vote. Members of Congress were elected by state legislatures rather than directly by the people. There was no judicial branch. All legal matters were left to the states, with the exception of disputes among the states, which would be resolved by special panels of judges

Articles of Confederation
Sent to the states for ratification in 1777, these were the first attempt at a new American government. It was later decided that the Articles restricted national government too much, and they were replaced by the Constitution.

limited government
A political system in which the powers of the government are restricted to prevent tyranny by protecting property and individual rights.

monarchy
A form of government in which power is held by a single person, or monarch, who comes to power through inheritance rather than election.

FIGURE 2.1

Constitutional Time Line

The sequence of important events leading to independence and the writing and ratification of the Constitution.

January
First publication of Thomas Paine's *Common Sense*

October 19
Cornwallis surrenders the British army at Yorktown

November 15
Articles of Confederation adopted by Congress, sent to the states for ratification

July
Congress adopts the Declaration of Independence

February 6
Treaty of Alliance with France

March 1
Articles of Confederation are ratified by the requisite number of states

September
First Continental Congress

May
Second Continental Congress

| 1774 | 1775 | 1776 | 1777 | 1778 | 1779 | 1780 | 1781 |

1775–1783 Revolutionary War

Source: Compiled by the authors.

appointed on an as-needed basis by Congress. In their eagerness to limit the power of government, the authors of the Articles gave each state veto power over any changes to the Articles and required approval from 9 of the 13 states on any legislation.

More important, the states maintained autonomy and did not sacrifice any significant power to the national government; thus, government power was decentralized in the states, rather than centralized in the national government. For example, the national government and the states could both make treaties and coin money. Congress also lacked any real authority over the states. For example, Congress could suggest the amount of money each state owed to support the Revolutionary army but could not enforce payment. After the Revolutionary War ended with the Treaty of Paris in September 1783, the same weaknesses continued to plague Congress. For example, even though the new government owed millions of dollars to foreign governments and domestic creditors, it had no way to make the states pay their share. And if a foreign government negotiated a trade agreement with Congress, any state government could veto or amend the agreement, which meant that the foreign government might have to negotiate separate agreements with Congress and each state legislature. Even trade among states was complicated and inefficient.

In the face of such issues, a small group of leaders decided that something had to be done. A group from Virginia urged state legislatures to send delegates to a convention on interstate commerce in Annapolis, Maryland, in September 1786. Only five states sent delegates. However, Alexander Hamilton and James Madison salvaged the effort by getting those delegates to agree to convene again in Philadelphia the following May. They also proposed that the next convention examine the defects of the current government and "devise such further provisions as shall appear to them necessary to render the Constitution of the Federal Government adequate to the exigencies of the Union."[5]

The issues that motivated the Annapolis Convention gained new urgency as subsequent events unfolded. Economic chaos and depression in the years after the war had caused many farmers to lose their land because they could not pay their debts or

October 27 • • • • • • • •
Federalist Papers
begin appearing
in New York
newspapers

September 14 • • • • • • • • •
Annapolis
delegates
decide that
Articles need
to be fixed

September 17 • • • •
Constitution
signed

June 21
Constitution
ratified when
New Hampshire
is the ninth
state to ratify

March 4
Constitution
takes effect

September 3
Treaty of Paris signed,
ending the Revolutionary War

August 1786– • • • • • • •
January 1787
Shays's Rebellion

May 25 • • • • • •
Constitutional
Convention
begins in
Philadelphia

| 1783 | 1784 | 1785 | 1786 | 1787 | 1788 | 1789 |

31–1789 Articles of Confederation period

state taxes. Frustration mounted throughout the latter half of 1786, and early in 1787 a former captain in the Revolutionary army, Daniel Shays, led a force of 1,500 men in an attempt to take over the Massachusetts state government arsenal in Springfield. Their goal was to force the state courts to stop prosecuting debtors and taking their land, but the rebels were repelled by a state militia. Similar protests on a smaller scale happened in Pennsylvania and Virginia. Some state legislatures gave in to the debtors' demands, causing national leaders to fear that **Shays's Rebellion** had exposed fundamental discontent with the new government. The very future of the fledgling nation was at risk.

The rebellion exposed the central flaws of the government under the Articles of Confederation. If its leaders could not build a political system that addressed the problems of state sovereignty, redundant or conflicting responsibilities (such as coining money, foreign policy and trade, and taxing power), and the resulting political and economic chaos, then the United States would not be able to unite. Something clearly needed to be done.

Shays's Rebellion
An uprising of about 1,500 men in Massachusetts in 1786 and 1787 to protest oppressive laws and gain payment of war debts. The unrest prompted calls for a new constitution.

Political theories of the framers

Although the leaders who gathered in Philadelphia in the summer of 1787 to write the Constitution were chastened by the failure of the Articles of Confederation (see Nuts & Bolts 2.1), they still supported many of the principles that motivated the Revolution. There was broad consensus on (1) rejection of monarchy, (2) popular control of government through a republican democracy, and (3) limitations on government power that would protect individual rights and personal property (that is, protect against tyranny).

First among these principles was rejection of monarchy in favor of a form of government based on self-rule. **Republicanism** as understood by the framers is a government in which elected leaders represent the views of the people. Thomas Paine,

republicanism
As understood by James Madison and the framers, the belief that a form of government in which the interests of the people are represented through elected leaders is the best form of government. Our form of government is known as a republican democracy.

an influential political writer of the Revolutionary era, wrote a pamphlet titled *Common Sense* in 1776 that was a widely read indictment of monarchy and an endorsement of the principles that fueled the Revolution and underpinned the framers' thinking.[6] Paine wrote that monarchy was the "most bare-faced falsity ever imposed on mankind" and that the common interests of the community should be served by elected representatives.

The Founders' views of republicanism, together with liberal principles of liberty and individual rights, shaped their vision of the proper form of government. Thomas Jefferson's inspirational words in the Declaration of Independence express these core principles:

> *We hold these truths to be self-evident, that all men are created equal, that they are endowed by their Creator with certain unalienable Rights, that among these are Life, Liberty, and the pursuit of Happiness. That to secure these rights, Governments are instituted among Men, deriving their just powers from the consent of the governed. That whenever any Form of Government becomes destructive of these ends, it is the Right of the People to alter or to abolish it, and to institute new Government.*

Comparing the Articles of Confederation and the Constitution

Issue	Articles of Confederation	Constitution
Legislature	Unicameral Congress	Bicameral Congress divided into the House of Representatives and the Senate
Members of Congress	Between two and seven per state (the number was determined by each state)	Two senators per state; representatives apportioned according to population of each state
Voting in Congress	One vote per state	One vote per representative or senator
Selection of members	Appointed by state legislatures	Representatives elected by popular vote; senators appointed by state legislatures
Chief executive	None (there was an Executive Council within Congress, but it had limited executive power)	President
National judiciary	No general federal courts	Supreme Court; Congress authorized to establish national judiciary
Amendments to the document	When approved by all states	When approved by two-thirds of each house of Congress and three-fourths of the states
Power to coin money	Federal government and the states	Federal government only
Taxes	Apportioned by Congress, collected by the states	Apportioned and collected by Congress
Ratification	Unanimous consent required	Consent of nine states required

Source: Compiled by the authors.

"Why Should I Care?" The Constitution, which to this day outlines the rules for American government, provides for a strong federal government. This resolved many of the challenges that handicapped the early republic under the Articles of Confederation.

Three crucial ideas are packed into this passage: equality, self-rule, and natural rights. Equality was not given much attention in the Constitution (later in this chapter we discuss how the problem of slavery was handled), but the notion that a government gains its legitimacy from the "consent of the governed" (the idea of **popular sovereignty**) and that its central purpose is to uphold the "unalienable" or **natural rights** of the people was central to the framers. The "right of the people to alter or abolish" a government that did not protect these rights served both to justify the revolt against the British and to remind the framers of their continuing obligation to ensure that those rights were maintained. The leaders who met in Philadelphia thought the Articles of Confederation had become "destructive to those ends" and therefore needed to be altered.

The most comprehensive statement of the framers' political philosophy and democratic theory was a series of essays written by James Madison, Alexander Hamilton, and John Jay titled the *Federalist Papers*. These essays explained and justified the framework of government created by the Constitution. They also revealed the framers' view of human nature and its implications for democracy. The framers' view of human nature as basically being driven by self-interest led to Madison's assessment that "[i]n framing a government which is to be administered by men over men, the great difficulty lies in this: you must first enable the government to control the governed; and in the next place oblige it to control itself." This analysis (from *Federalist 51*) is often considered the clearest articulation of the need for republican government and a system of separated powers.

In *Federalist 10*, Madison described the central problem for government as the need to control factions. He argued that governments cannot control the causes of factions because differences of opinion—based on the fallibility of reason; differences in wealth, property, and native abilities; and attachments to different leaders—are part of human nature. The only way to eliminate factions would be to either curtail liberty or try to make everyone the same. The first remedy Madison called "worse than the disease" of factions themselves, and the second he found "as impracticable as the first would be unwise." Because people are driven by self-interest, which sometimes conflicts with the common good, government must, however, try to control the effects of factions. This was the task facing the framers at the Constitutional Convention.

popular sovereignty
The idea that government gains its legitimacy through regular elections in which the people living under that government participate to elect their leaders.

natural rights
Also known as "unalienable rights," these rights are defined in the Declaration of Independence as "Life, Liberty, and the pursuit of Happiness." The Founders believed that upholding these rights should be the government's central purpose.

The economic context of the American Founding had an important impact on the framing of the Constitution. Most Americans worked on small farms or as artisans or business owners, which meant that economic power was broadly distributed. This woodcut shows New York City around the time the Constitution was written, viewed from upper Manhattan.

Economic interests

Political ideas were central to the framers' thinking at the Constitutional Convention, but economic context and interests were equally important.

First, while there were certainly class differences among Americans in the late eighteenth century, they were insignificant compared with those in Europe. America did not have the history of feudalism that had created tremendous inequality in Europe between landowners and propertyless serfs who worked the land. In contrast, most Americans owned small farms or worked as middle-class artisans and craftsmen. Thus, while political equality did not figure prominently in the Constitution, citizens' relative economic equality did indeed influence the context of debates at the Constitutional Convention.

Second, despite Americans' general economic equality, there were significant regional differences. The South was largely agricultural, with cotton and tobacco plantations that depended on the labor of enslaved people. The region favored free trade because of its export-based economy (bolstered by westward expansion) and the trading of enslaved people. The middle Atlantic and northern states, however, had smaller farms and a broad economic base of manufacturing, fishing, and trade. These states favored government-managed trade and commercial development.

Despite these differences, the diverse population favored a stronger national government and reform of the Articles of Confederation (see Nuts & Bolts 2.1). Creditors wanted a government that could pay off its debts to them, southern farmers wanted free trade that could be efficiently promoted only by a central government, and manufacturers and traders wanted a single national currency and uniform interstate commerce regulations. However, there was a deep division between those who supported empowering the national government and those who still favored strong state governments and a weak national government. These two groups became known as the **Federalists** and the **Antifederalists**. The stage was set for a productive but contentious convention.

Federalists
Those at the Constitutional Convention who favored a strong national government and a system of separated powers.

Antifederalists
Those at the Constitutional Convention who favored strong state governments and feared that a strong national government would be a threat to individual rights.

"Why Should I Care?"

The historical context and political ideas that shaped the thinking of the framers still resonate today. While we are centuries removed from the oppressive rule of the British monarchy, most Americans still support the ideas of representative democracy and limited government that replaced it. The division between the Federalists and Antifederalists on how to best create a representative government that protected our freedom is evident today in ongoing debates about the proper role of the government in our everyday lives.

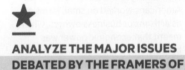

★

ANALYZE THE MAJOR ISSUES DEBATED BY THE FRAMERS OF THE CONSTITUTION

The politics of compromise at the Constitutional Convention

Although the delegates to the Constitutional Convention generally agreed that the Articles of Confederation needed to be changed, there were many tensions over the issues that required political compromise (see Nuts & Bolts 2.2). Among them were the following:

- majority rule versus minority rights
- small states versus large states
- legislative power versus executive power (and how to elect the executive)
- national power versus state and local power
- slave states versus nonslave states

Major Compromises at the Constitutional Convention

Conflict	Position of the Large States	Position of the Small States	Compromise
Apportionment in Congress	By population	State equality	Great Compromise created the Senate and House
Method of election to Congress	By the people	By the states	House elected by the people; Senate elected by the state legislatures*
Electing the executive (president)	By Congress	By the states	By the Electoral College
Who decides federal–state conflicts?	Some federal authority	State courts	State courts to decide†
	Position of the Slave States	**Position of the Nonslave States**	**Compromise**
Control over commerce	By the states	By Congress	By Congress, but with 20-year exemption for the importation of enslaved people
Counting enslaved people toward apportionment	Counted 1:1 like citizens	Not counted	Three-Fifths Compromise
	Position of the Federalists	**Position of the Antifederalists**	**Compromise**
Protection for individual rights‡	Secured by state constitutions; national Bill of Rights not needed	National Bill of Rights needed	Bill of Rights passed by the 1st Congress; ratified by all states as of December 1791

*This was changed by the Seventeenth Amendment in 1913, which allowed for the direct election by the people of two senators from each state.
†This was changed by the Judiciary Act of 1789, which provided for appeals from state to federal courts.
‡This issue was raised but not resolved until after the convention.
Source: Compiled by the authors.

"Why Should I Care?" As we noted in Chapter 1, politics is conflictual. People will always have different goals and objectives. Adhering to one's principles is admirable, but unless one is willing to compromise, no one will get anything he or she wants in politics—or in life. The success of the Constitution is a result of compromises outlined above.

These complex and competing interests meant that the delegates had to focus on pragmatic, achievable solutions rather than on proposals that represented particular groups' ideals but could not gain majority support. The most important initial decision they made was to give up on the original plan to revise the Articles of Confederation; instead, they decided to start from scratch with a new blueprint for government.

Majority rule versus minority rights

A central problem for any representative democracy is protecting minority rights within a system ruled by the majority. The framers thought of this issue not in terms of racial and ethnic minorities (as we might today), but in terms of regional and economic minorities. How could the framers be sure that small landowners and poorer people would not impose onerous taxes on the wealthier minority? How could they guarantee

DID YOU KNOW?

The average age of the delegates to the Constitutional Convention was

42

Four of the delegates were in their 20s, and 14 were in their 30s.
Source: teachingamericanhistory.org

that dominant agricultural interests would not impose punitive tariffs on manufacturing while allowing the free export of farmed commodities? The answers to these questions can be found in Madison's writings on the problem of factions in *Federalist 10*.

Madison defined a "faction" as a group motivated by selfish interests against the common good. If these interests prevailed, he felt, it could produce the very kind of tyranny that the Americans had fought to escape during the Revolutionary War. Madison's solution to this problem provided justification for the American form of government. To control majority tyranny, he argued, factions must be set against one another to counter one another's ambitions and prevent the tyranny of any single majority faction. This would be accomplished through the "double protection" of the separation of powers within the national government in the form of checks and balances, and by further dividing power across the levels of state and local governments through the system of federalism (which we will discuss in detail in the next chapter). Popular majorities were also controlled, as we discuss below, by the indirect election of the president through the Electoral College and senators by state legislatures.

Madison also argued that additional protection against majority tyranny would come from the "size principle." That is, the new nation would be a large and diverse republic in which majority interests would be less likely to organize and therefore less able to dominate. This insight provides the basis for modern **pluralism**, a political theory that makes the same argument about the crosscutting interests of groups today.

The precise contours of Madison's solution still had to be hammered out at the Constitutional Convention, but the general principle pleased both the Antifederalists and the Federalists. State governments would maintain some autonomy, but the national government would become stronger than it had been under the Articles. The issue was how to strike an appropriate balance: none of the framers favored a pure populist majoritarian democracy, and few wanted to protect minority rights to the extent that the Articles had.

Small states versus large states

The question of the appropriate balance came to a head in a debate between small- and large-population states over representation in the national legislature. Under the Articles, every state had a single vote, but this did not seem fair to large states. They pushed for representation based on population. This proposal, along with other proposals to strengthen the national government, constituted the **Virginia Plan**. The small states countered with the **New Jersey Plan**, which proposed maintaining equal representation for every state. Rhode Island, the smallest state, was so concerned about small-state power that it boycotted the convention. Tensions were running high; this issue appeared to have all the elements of a deal breaker, and there seemed to be no way to break the impasse.

Just as it appeared that the convention might grind to a halt before it really got started, Connecticut proposed what became known as the **Great Compromise**, or Connecticut Compromise. The plan suggested establishing a Congress with two houses: a Senate would have two senators from each state, and in the House of Representatives each state's number of representatives would be based on its population. Interestingly, Connecticut's population was ranked seventh of the 13 states (see Figure 2.2). It seemed to be in a perfect position to offer a compromise because it did not have strong vested interests in the plans offered by either the small states or the large states. But the situation was actually much more complicated. First, Rhode Island did not attend the convention, so there was no true median state (with only 12 states at the convention, no one stood alone at the center). Second, given that each state had one

James Madison argued that it is beneficial to put the interests of one group in competition with the interests of other groups, so that no one group can dominate government. He hoped to achieve this through the separation of powers across different branches of the national government and across the national, state, and local levels.

pluralism
The idea that having a variety of parties and interests within a government will strengthen the system, ensuring that no group possesses total control.

Virginia Plan
A plan proposed by the larger states during the Constitutional Convention that based representation in the national legislature on population. The plan also included a variety of other proposals to strengthen the national government.

New Jersey Plan
A plan that was suggested in response to the Virginia Plan; smaller states at the Constitutional Convention proposed that each state should receive equal representation in the national legislature, regardless of size.

FIGURE
2.2

Connecticut's Pivotal Place at the Constitutional Convention

Though there were many disagreements over the details of America's new constitution, one of the most intense focused on how states would be represented in Congress, either allocating representatives equally or based on population. After other plans were considered and rejected, the Connecticut Compromise won out. Why do you think Connecticut was well positioned to find a compromise? How do these graphs help us understand why the Virginia and New Jersey Plans were in conflict and ultimately rejected?

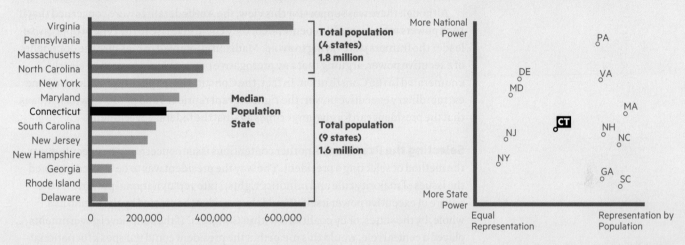

Source: Keith L. Dougherty and Jac C. Heckelman, "A Pivotal Voter from a Pivotal State: Roger Sherman at the Constitutional Convention," *American Political Science Review* 100:2 (May 2006): 298.

vote at the convention, the smallest states could have easily outvoted the biggest ones and insisted on equal representation for each state.

Two of the smaller states, Georgia and South Carolina, focused on their future growth, so they supported representation based on population, the Virginia Plan. But when other smaller states balked at their loss of power, the Connecticut Compromise was able to win the support of North Carolina (and Massachusetts's delegates were divided), so the compromise passed 5-4-1.

Legislative power versus executive power

An equally difficult challenge was how to divide power at the national level. Here the central issues revolved around the executive: the president. How much power should the president have relative to the legislative branch? (The courts also figured here, but they were less central to the discussions.) And how would the president be elected?

Limiting Presidential Power The delegates knew what they did not want: the king of England and his colonial governors were viewed as tramplers of liberty. Many delegates rejected outright the idea of a single executive because they believed it was impossible to have an executive who would not be oppressive. The delegates finally agreed on the single executive because the president would have the most

Great Compromise
A compromise between the large and small states, proposed by Connecticut, in which Congress would have two houses: a Senate with two legislators per state and a House of Representatives in which each state's representation would be based on population (also known as the Connecticut Compromise).

"energy, dispatch, and responsibility for the office" (as explained in *Federalist 70*), but they constrained the president's power through the system of checks and balances. One significant power they granted to the executive was the veto. It could be overridden by Congress, but only with the support of two-thirds of both chambers. This requirement gave the president a significant role in the legislative process. The arguments for a strong executive relied heavily on the work of the English philosopher John Locke. Locke recognized the general superiority of a government of laws created by legislatures, but he also saw the need for an executive with more flexible leadership powers, or what he called "prerogative powers." Legislatures are unable, Locke wrote, "to foresee, and so by laws to provide for all accidents and necessities."[7] They also are, by virtue of their size and unwieldiness, too slow to alter and adapt the law in times of crisis, when the executive could step in to pursue policies in the public's interest.

Although there was support for this view, the Antifederalists were concerned that if such powers were viewed as open-ended, they could give rise to the type of oppressive leader the framers were trying to avoid. Madison attempted to reassure the opponents of executive power, arguing that any prerogative powers would have to be clearly enumerated in the Constitution. In fact, the Constitution explicitly provides only one extraordinary executive power: the right to grant reprieves and pardons, which means that the president can forgive any crimes against the federal government.

Selecting the President Another contentious issue concerning the executive was the method of selecting a president. The way the president was to be elected involved the issues of majority rule and minority rights, state versus national power, and the nature of executive power itself. Would the president be elected by the nation as a whole, by the states, or by coalitions within Congress? If the state-level governments played a central role, would this mean that the president could not speak for national interests? If Congress elected the president, could the executive still provide a check on the legislative branch?

Most Americans do not realize (1) that our presidential system is unique and (2) that we came close to having a parliamentary system, which is the form of government that exists in most other established democracies. In a **parliamentary system**, the executive branch depends on the support of the legislative branch. The Virginia Plan proposed that Congress elect the president, just as Parliament elects the British prime minister. However, facing lingering concerns that the president would be too beholden to Congress, a committee of framers subsequently made the following recommendations: (1) that the president would be selected by an Electoral College, representation in which would be based on the number of representatives and senators each state has in Congress, and (2) that members of each state's legislature would determine the method for choosing their state's electors.[8] The delegates ultimately approved this recommendation.

However, the solution did not work out the way the framers intended. First, if the Electoral College was supposed to provide an independent check on the voters, it never played this role because of the quick emergence of political parties (which the framers did not anticipate). Electors soon became agents of the parties (as they remain today) rather than independent actors who would use their own judgment to pick the most qualified candidate for president. Second, the emergence of parties created a serious technical error in the Constitution: the provision that gave each elector two votes and elected the candidate with the most votes as president and the second-place finisher as vice president. With electors acting as agents of the parties, they ended up casting one vote each for the presidential and vice-presidential candidate of their own party. This created a tie in the 1800 presidential election when Thomas Jefferson and Aaron Burr each received 73 electoral votes. The problem was fixed by the Twelfth Amendment, which required that electors cast separate votes for president and vice president.

parliamentary system
A system of government in which legislative and executive power are closely joined. The legislature (parliament) selects the chief executive (prime minister), who forms the cabinet from members of the parliament.

Jefferson: You hear this guy? Man openly campaigns against me, talking 'bout "I look forward to our partnership!"
Madison: It is crazy that the guy who comes in second gets to be vice president.
Jefferson: OOOH! Y'know what, we can change that! Y'know why?
Madison: Why?
Jefferson: 'Cause I'm the president!

—*Hamilton,* the musical

National power versus state and local power

Tensions over the balance of power cut across virtually every debate at the convention: presidential versus legislative power, whether the national government could supersede state laws, apportionment in the legislature, slavery, regulation of commerce and taxation, and the amendment process. The overall compromise that addressed these tensions was the system of federalism, which divided power among autonomous levels of government that controlled different areas of policy.

Federalism is such an important topic that we devote the entire next chapter to it, but two brief points about it are important here. First, the Tenth Amendment, which was added as part of the Bill of Rights shortly after ratification, was a concession to the Antifederalists, who were concerned that the national government would gain too much power in the new political system. The Tenth Amendment says: "The powers not delegated to the United States by the Constitution, nor prohibited by it to the States, are reserved to the States respectively, or to the people." This definition of **reserved powers** was viewed as setting outer limits on the reach of national power.

Second, the **national supremacy clause** of the Constitution (Article VI) says that any national law is the supreme law of the land and takes precedence over any state law that conflicts with it. This is especially important in areas where the national and state governments have overlapping responsibilities for policy. (The relationship between the national government and the states is discussed in Chapter 3.)

Slave states versus nonslave states

Slavery was another nearly insurmountable issue for the delegates. Southern states would not agree to any provisions limiting slavery; indeed, about 25 of the 55 delegates to the Constitutional Convention owned enslaved people.[9] Although the nonslave

reserved powers
As defined in the Tenth Amendment, powers that are not given to the national government by the Constitution, or not prohibited to the states, are reserved by the states or the people.

national supremacy clause
The part of Article VI, Section 2, of the Constitution stating that the Constitution and the laws and treaties of the United States are the "supreme Law of the Land," meaning national laws take precedence over state laws if the two conflict.

This advertisement from a slave-trading company appeared in a Richmond, Virginia, newspaper shortly after the Constitution was signed. Slavery is often referred to as the "original sin" of our nation and proved to be very problematic at the Constitutional Convention: Would there be limits on the importation of enslaved people? How would enslaved people who had escaped to freedom be dealt with by nonslave states? And how would enslaved people be counted for the purposes of congressional representation?

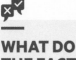

The Three-Fifths Compromise

The Three-Fifths Compromise is often described as the "original sin" of the Constitution, but less recognized is the impact that it had on the Electoral College. The figure shows the number of each state's House members in the 1790s based on the Three-Fifths Compromise, and then how many representatives they would have had if only the free population had been counted or if the total population, including enslaved people, had been counted.

Think about it

- **How many additional seats in the House did southern states get** as a result of the Three-Fifths Compromise, relative to the number of seats they would have had if enslaved people had not been counted at all?

- **How many additional seats in the House would southern states have gotten** if enslaved people had been counted as full members of the population?

- **How did the Three-Fifths Compromise** have an impact on the Electoral College? (Remember: each state's number of electors is equal in number to its combined total of representatives in the House and senators.)

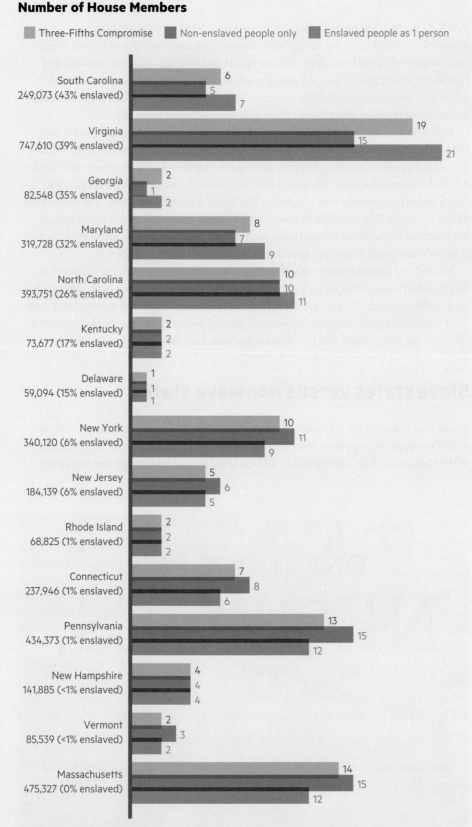

Number of House Members

Three-Fifths Compromise · Non-enslaved people only · Enslaved people as 1 person

South Carolina
249,073 (43% enslaved): 6, 5, 7

Virginia
747,610 (39% enslaved): 19, 15, 21

Georgia
82,548 (35% enslaved): 2, 1, 2

Maryland
319,728 (32% enslaved): 8, 7, 9

North Carolina
393,751 (26% enslaved): 10, 10, 11

Kentucky
73,677 (17% enslaved): 2, 2, 2

Delaware
59,094 (15% enslaved): 1, 1, 1

New York
340,120 (6% enslaved): 10, 11, 9

New Jersey
184,139 (6% enslaved): 5, 6, 5

Rhode Island
68,825 (1% enslaved): 2, 2, 2

Connecticut
237,946 (1% enslaved): 7, 8, 6

Pennsylvania
434,373 (1% enslaved): 13, 15, 12

New Hampshire
141,885 (<1% enslaved): 4, 4, 4

Vermont
85,539 (<1% enslaved): 2, 3, 2

Massachusetts
475,327 (0% enslaved): 14, 15, 12

Note: These numbers reflect total populations according to the 1790 census.

Source: U.S. Census Bureau, "Return of the Whole Number of Persons within the Several Districts of the United States," www2.census.gov/library/publications/decennial/1790/number_of_persons/1790a-02.pdf (accessed 10/2/20); calculations are by the authors.

states opposed the practice, they were not willing to scuttle the entire Constitution by taking a principled stand. Even after these basic positions had been recognized, many unresolved issues remained. Could the importation of enslaved people be restricted in the future? How would northern states deal with enslaved people who had escaped to freedom? Most important in terms of the politics of the issue, how would the enslaved population be counted for the purpose of slave states' representation in Congress?

The states had been through this debate once before, when they addressed the issue of taxation under the Articles of Confederation. At that point, slave states had argued that enslaved people should not be counted because they did not receive the same benefits as citizens and were not the same burden to the government. Nonslave states had countered that enslaved people should be counted in the same way as citizens when determining a state's fair share of the tax burden. They had reached a compromise by agreeing that each enslaved person would count as three-fifths of a person for purposes of taxation. Now the arguments over the issue of representation were even more contentious at the Constitutional Convention. Here the positions were reversed, with slave states arguing that enslaved people should be counted like everyone else for the purposes of determining the number of House representatives for each state. Ultimately, both sides managed to agree on the **Three-Fifths Compromise** (see the What Do the Facts Say? feature).

The other two issues involved the importation of enslaved people and how to deal with enslaved people who had escaped to freedom. In terms of the latter issue, northern states either would be obligated to return freedom seekers to their southern owners or would not. Because there was no middle ground, the opposing sides looked for other issues on which to trade votes. The nonslave states wanted more national government control over commerce and trade than under the Articles, a change that the slave states opposed. So a vote trade developed as a way to compromise the competing regional interests of slavery and regulation of commerce. Northern states agreed to return freedom seekers (the Fugitive Slave Clause), and southern states agreed to allow Congress to pass laws regulating commerce and taxing imports with a simple majority vote (rather than the supermajority required under the Articles).

The importation of enslaved people was included as part of this solution. Northern states wanted to allow future Congresses to ban the importation of enslaved people; southern states wanted to allow the importation of enslaved people to continue indefinitely, arguing that slavery was essential to produce their labor-intensive crops. After much negotiation, the final language prevented a constitutional amendment from banning the slave trade until 1808.[10]

From a modern perspective, it is difficult to understand how the framers could have taken such a purely political approach to the moral issue of slavery. Many of the delegates believed slavery was immoral, yet they were willing to negotiate in order to gain the southern states' support of the Constitution. Some southern delegates were apologetic about slavery, even as they argued for protecting their own interests. Numerous constitutional scholars view the convention's treatment of slavery as its central failure. In fairness to the delegates, the issue of slavery could not be settled, since the goal was to create a document that all states would support. However, the delegates' inability to resolve this issue meant that it would simmer below the surface for the next 70 years, finally boiling over into the bloodiest of all American wars: the Civil War.

The convention ended on a relatively harmonious note with Benjamin Franklin moving for adoption. His motion was worded ambiguously to allow those who still had reservations to sign the Constitution anyway: "Done in Convention by the unanimous consent of the States present the 17th of September . . . In Witness whereof we have hereunto subscribed our names." His clever wording meant that the signers were only bearing witness to the approval by the states and therefore could still, in good faith, oppose substantial parts of the document. Franklin's motion passed with 10 ayes, no nays, and one delegation divided. All but three of the remaining delegates signed.

Three-Fifths Compromise
The states' decision during the Constitutional Convention to count each enslaved person as three-fifths of a person in a state's population for the purposes of determining the number of House members and the distribution of taxes.

DID YOU KNOW?

At only about

8,700

words, the U.S. Constitution is much shorter than the average state constitution (39,604 words).
Source: PARCA, Tableau Public

Union and Confederate troops clash in close combat in the Battle of Cold Harbor, Virginia, in June 1864. The inability of the framers to resolve the issue of slavery allowed tensions over the issue to grow throughout the early nineteenth century, culminating in the Civil War.

"Why Should I Care?"

Politicians today have a very difficult time compromising on issues like gun control, abortion rights, and even the proper levels of taxation and spending. At the Constitutional Convention, the framers had to struggle with fundamental issues such as executive power and state versus national power as well as incredibly divisive issues like slavery. The framers were facing uncertainty about the very survival of their new nation and the nearly impossible task of creating a new framework that would allow our nation to not only survive but also flourish. Yet the framers were able to arrive at workable compromises on all of these issues. Without compromise, our nation would not exist. When you hear a politician today say, "I am going to stick to my principles; I am not going to compromise," reflect on the fact that governing is not possible without compromise. "Compromise" is not a dirty word; it is an essential feature of politics.

CONTRAST THE ARGUMENTS OF THE FEDERALISTS WITH THOSE OF THE ANTIFEDERALISTS

Ratification

Article VII of the Constitution, which described the process for ratifying the document, was also designed to maximize its chance of success. Only nine states were needed to ratify, unlike under the unanimity rule that had applied to changing the Articles of Confederation. Equally important, ratification votes would be taken in state conventions set up specifically for that purpose, bypassing the state legislatures, which would be more likely to resist some of the Constitution's state–federal power-sharing arrangements.

The near-unanimous approval at the Constitutional Convention's end masked the very strong opposition that remained. Subsequently, the ratifying conventions in each state subjected the Constitution to intense scrutiny, as attendees examined every sentence for possible objections. A national debate raged over the next nine months.

The Antifederalists' concerns

The Antifederalists were most worried about the role of the president, the transfer of power from the states to the national government, and the lack of specific guarantees of civil liberties. In short, they feared that a strong, centralized national government would become tyrannical and they favored a small, decentralized republic. This concern was summarized in Brutus 1, an Anitifederalist paper believed to have been written by Robert Yates, a New York judge and delegate to the Constitutional Convention: the Constitution would create a federal government that would "possess absolute and uncontrollable power."[11] State power and the ability to regulate commerce were also central concerns. States such as New York would lose substantial revenue if they could no longer charge tariffs on goods that came into their ports. Other states were concerned that they would pay a disproportionate share of national taxes.

The Antifederalists' foremost objection was to the lack of protections for civil liberties in the new political system. During the last week of the convention, Elbridge Gerry and George Mason offered a resolution "to prepare a Bill of Rights." However, the resolution was unanimously defeated by the state delegations. Some believed that the national government posed no threat to liberties such as freedom of the press because it did not have the power to restrict them in the first place. Others thought that because it would be impossible to enumerate all rights, it was better to list none at all. Federalists such as Roger Sherman argued that state constitutions, most of which protected freedom of speech, freedom of the press, right to a trial by jury, and other civil liberties, would be sufficient to protect liberty. However, many Antifederalists still wanted assurances that the *national* government would not trample their rights.

A lady asked Dr. [Benjamin] Franklin, "Well, Doctor, what have we got—a republic or a monarchy?"
"A republic," replied the Doctor, "if you can keep it."

—**James McHenry,** *The Records of the Federal Convention of 1787*

Alexander Hamilton authored a majority of the *Federalist Papers* and was a strong advocate for ratification of the Constitution.

The Federalists' strategies

The Antifederalists had many strong arguments and there was no denying that the Constitution was really a "leap in the dark"—many of the ideas of the document had never been tested, so the experiment in government had high risks and no guarantee for success. To try to reassure opponents of the Constitution, the Federalists counterattacked on several fronts. First, as we mentioned earlier, they published a series of articles that came to be known as the *Federalist Papers*. Although originally published in New York newspapers, these articles were widely read throughout the nation. The *Federalist Papers* were one-sided arguments aimed at changing public opinion. The authors downplayed potentially unpopular aspects of the new system, such as the power of the president, while emphasizing points they knew would appeal to the opposition. Despite the authors' biased arguments, the *Federalist Papers* are considered the best comprehensive discussion of the political theory underlying the Constitution, such as the framers' views of self-interested human nature and the dangers of factions, and their interpretations of many of the document's key provisions, such as the meaning of impeachment, as noted in the chapter opener.

Second, the Federalists agreed that the new Congress's first order of business would be to add a **Bill of Rights** to the Constitution to protect individual rights and liberties. This promise was essential for securing the support of New York, Massachusetts, and Virginia. The crucial ninth state, New Hampshire, ratified the Constitution on June 21, 1788, but New York and Virginia were still dragging their heels, and their support was viewed as necessary for the legitimacy of the United States, even if it technically was not needed. By the end of the summer, both Virginia and New York finally voted for ratification. Rhode Island and North Carolina refused to ratify until Congress made good on its promise of a Bill of Rights (our civil liberties, which are guaranteed in the Bill of Rights, will be examined in Chapter 4). The 1st Congress submitted 12 amendments to the states, and 10 were ratified by all the states as of December 15, 1791.

Bill of Rights
The first 10 amendments to the Constitution; they protect individual rights and liberties.

> ## "Why Should I Care?"
>
> The ratifying conventions in each state subjected the Constitution to intense scrutiny, as attendees examined every sentence for possible objections. A national debate raged over the next nine months, framed by the arguments of the Federalists and the Antifederalists. As we explained in Chapter 1, all politics is conflictual, but ultimately compromise is necessary in order to move forward. The resulting compromise between these two groups was the addition of the Bill of Rights, securing the civil liberties we hold as central American values to this day.

OUTLINE THE MAJOR PROVISIONS OF THE CONSTITUTION

The Constitution: a framework for government

The Constitution certainly has its flaws (some of which have been corrected through amendments), but the document's longevity is testimony to the framers' foresight in crafting a flexible framework for government. Perhaps its most important feature is the system of separation of powers and checks and balances that prevents majority tyranny while maintaining sufficient flexibility for decisive leadership during times of crisis.

The system of checks and balances means that each branch of national government has certain exclusive powers, some shared powers, and the ability to check the other two branches (see How It Works: Checks and Balances).

Exclusive powers

The framers viewed Congress as the "first branch" of government and granted it significant exclusive powers. Congress was given the specific **enumerated powers** to raise revenue for the federal government through taxes and borrowing, regulate interstate and foreign commerce, coin money, establish post offices and roads, grant patents and copyrights, create the system of federal courts, declare war, "raise and support armies," make rules for the military, and create and maintain a navy. Most important is the so-called **power of the purse**—control over taxation and spending. During the first years of the Trump presidency the "emoluments clause," which gives Congress the sole power to consent to any government official's receipt of anything of value from a foreign state, has received new attention. Lawsuits filed in federal court contend that the Trump family's ownership of hotels that are frequented by foreign officials in business with the federal government constitutes a violation of the emoluments clause. Two of these cases, in the Second and Fourth Circuit Courts of Appeals, have been permitted to proceed. A third case, which was brought by 215 Democratic members of Congress, was thrown out by the D.C. Court of Appeals early in 2020, and the Supreme Court declined to hear the case in October.[12]

Congress's exclusive powers take on additional significance through the **necessary and proper clause**, also known as the elastic clause. It gives Congress the flexibility to "make all Laws which shall be necessary and proper for carrying into Execution the foregoing Powers, and all other Powers vested by this Constitution in the Government

The Constitution is the guide which I never will abandon.

—President George Washington

enumerated powers
Powers explicitly granted to Congress, the president, or the Supreme Court in the first three articles of the Constitution. Examples include Congress's power to "raise and support Armies" and the president's power as commander in chief.

power of the purse
The constitutional power of Congress to raise and spend money. Congress can use this as a negative or checking power over the other branches by freezing or cutting their funding.

necessary and proper clause
The part of Article I, Section 8, of the Constitution that grants Congress the power to pass all laws related to its expressed powers; also known as the elastic clause.

Congress alone has "the power of the purse" to fund government programs. Although Congress appropriated $11 billion to fund the construction of 500 miles of new barriers at the southern U.S. border, President Trump reallocated several billion dollars in Pentagon funds as well to the border wall project, drawing sharp bipartisan criticism from lawmakers who say that this move infringed upon the appropriations power granted solely to Congress by the Constitution.

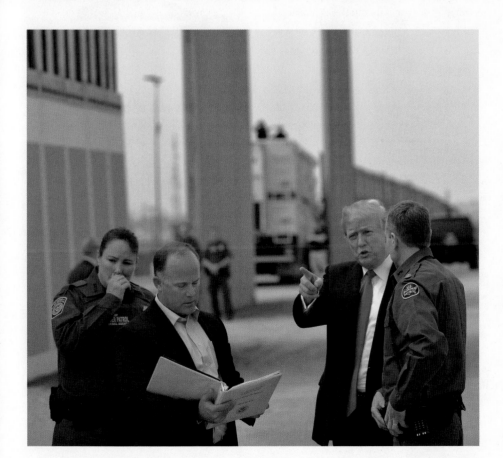

Checks and Balances

The Constitution stipulates that if one branch tries to assert too much power, the other branches have certain key powers that allow them to fight back and restore the balance. (In addition to the powers noted in the diagram, Congress can impeach the president and remove him or her from office.)

The president nominates judges.

The president can veto congressional legislation.

The Senate confirms the president's judicial nominations. Congress can impeach and remove judges from office.

Executive

Legislative

Judicial

The Senate approves presidential nominations, and Congress can override the president's veto and pass laws.

The Court interprets the laws passed by Congress.

The Court interprets actions by the executive branch.

Checks and Balances in the War on Terror

Shortly after the attacks of September 11, 2001, President George W. Bush, acting on his power as commander in chief, authorized the Guantánamo Bay detention center in Cuba to be used as a place to detain, interrogate, and try prisoners related to the War on Terror. President Obama tried to close the facility, but President Trump has advocated keeping it open. At the same time, Trump called for a broad ban restricting travel to the U.S. from several Muslim countries. The controversies and policies surrounding these efforts in the War on Terror show how checks and balances work in practice.

He said...

First prisoners are taken to Guantánamo on January 11, 2002. President George W. Bush asserts that Guantánamo is outside legal U.S. jurisdiction and that prisoners held there do not have protections guaranteed to prisoners of war under the Geneva Convention.

But then...

The Supreme Court disagrees in *Hamdan v. Rumsfeld* on June 29, 2006, ruling that the detainees were entitled to basic legal rights and that the Geneva Convention did apply.

Shut it down?

The detention center is increasingly controversial. Two days after taking office in 2009, President Obama **signs an order to close the center** by the end of the year and to suspend all Guantánamo military commission hearings for 120 days.

Nope.

A week later, a military court judge **overturns the order** to suspend hearings at Guantánamo.

Another plan.

President Obama **wants to move Guantánamo prisoners** to a federal prison in Illinois.

Plan blocked.

A few months later, **Congress votes to block funds** needed for the transfer or release of prisoners held at the facility.

Sigh.

By the end of Obama's presidency, **41 prisoners remained**. President Trump vows to keep the facility open.

New strategy.

In 2017, President Trump tries a new approach by **issuing a ban on travel** from several mostly Muslim countries.

Is this okay?

Several district courts **strike down the ban as religious profiling**, but the Supreme Court reinstates a more limited version of the ban, citing the president's powers over national security and immigration policy.

❓

Critical Thinking

1. **Why do you think it has been so difficult for presidents** to have their way in fighting terrorism, with regard to the travel ban and Guantánamo? Is it because of the issue of terrorism and national security? Or is it because of our system of checks and balances? Why?

2. **Do you think our system of checks and balances creates** too much gridlock, or is it an essential check on potential tyranny?

of the United States, or in any Department or Officer thereof." In other words, Congress could pass laws related to any of its exclusive powers. For example, although the Constitution did not explicitly mention Congress's right to compel people to serve in the military, its power to enact a draft was clearly given by the necessary and proper clause, in conjunction with its power to "raise and support Armies."

In contrast to Congress's numerous and specific exclusive powers, the Constitution grants very limited exclusive powers to the president. The president is the commander in chief of the armed forces, has the power to receive ambassadors and foreign ministers, and may issue pardons. For example, President Trump pulled out of the Paris Agreement on climate change, the Trans-Pacific Partnership, the Iran nuclear agreement, and the Intermediate-Range Nuclear Forces (INF) Treaty. He pulled U.S. troops out of northern Syria, engaged in a lengthy trade war with China, moved the U.S. embassy in Israel to Jerusalem, and threatened war with North Korea and then attempted to get it to stop its nuclear weapons program.

President Trump also created a stir in 2017 when he explored the possibility of preemptively granting pardons to everyone, including himself, targeted by the Justice Department's Russia investigation.[13] Another controversy exploded when he pardoned three army officers accused of war crimes and granted clemency to a navy SEAL. His supporters saw these acts as sticking up for the nation's warriors, but many military leaders saw them as undermining military justice and the Law of Armed Conflict.[14] The president's most important powers are contained in the executive powers clause, which says, "The executive power shall be vested in a President of the United States of America," and in the directive to ensure "that the laws are faithfully executed."

The courts did not receive as much attention in the Constitution as either Congress or the president. The most important positive powers that the framers gave the Supreme Court were lifetime tenure for justices with good behavior and relative independence from the other two branches. The critical negative power of judicial review, the ability to strike down the laws and actions of other branches, will be discussed later in this chapter.

Shared powers

Along with dividing the exclusive powers among the branches of government, the Constitution's system of checks and balances designates some shared powers. These are areas where no branch has exclusive control. For example, the president has the power to negotiate treaties and make appointments to the federal courts and other government offices, but these executive actions are to be undertaken with the "advice and consent" of the Senate, which means they were intended to be shared powers. In the twentieth century, these particular powers became executive centered, with the Senate providing almost no advice to the president and routinely giving its consent. However, the Senate still can assert its shared power, as shown by the Senate's blocking of several of President George W. Bush's and President Barack Obama's lower-court nominees and Obama's nomination of Merrick Garland to the Supreme Court in 2016.

The war powers, which include decisions about when and how to use military force, were also intended to be shared. After serious disagreements, the ultimate compromise that the framers reached shows checks and balances at work, with the president serving as commander in chief of the armed forces, while Congress has the power to declare war and to appropriate the funds to conduct a war. Since very early in the nation's history, the president has taken a lead role in the war powers. Presidents have authorized the use of American troops on hundreds of occasions, but Congress has declared war only five times. Of these, Congress debated the merits of entering only one war, the War of 1812. The other "declarations" recognized a state of war that already existed. If a president is intent on going to war, Congress must go along or get out of the way.

However, since the Vietnam War, Congress has tried to redress the imbalance in the war powers in a variety of ways. In 1970, Congress passed a resolution that prevented any funds from supporting ground troops in Laos or Cambodia (nations that bordered Vietnam). Congress passed the War Powers Resolution in 1973 to further limit the president's war powers (this will be discussed in more detail in Chapter 15. In 2013, Congress was strongly opposed to a military strike against Syria in response to its use of chemical weapons against its own people. A showdown with President Obama, who favored a strike, was averted when Syria agreed to allow weapons inspectors to destroy its chemical weapons stockpile. These examples show that although the president continues to dominate the war powers, Congress can assert its power when it has the will—just as it can by advising the president in treaty negotiations or by withholding approval of the president's nominees for appointed positions. Congress can also express its displeasure when the president acts unilaterally against its will, as it did when the House voted 354–60 to condemn Trump's withdrawal of American forces from northern Syria.[15]

Negative or checking powers

The last part of the system of checks and balances is the negative power that the branches have over one another. These powers are especially important because they ensure that no single branch dominates the national government.

Congressional Checks Congress has two important negative checks on the other branches: impeachment and the power of the purse. The **impeachment** power allows Congress to remove the president, vice president, or other "officers of the United States" (including federal judges) for abuses of power—specifically, "Treason, Bribery, or other high Crimes or Misdemeanors."

Through the power of the purse, Congress can punish executive agencies by freezing or cutting their funding or by holding hearings on, investigations of, or audits of their operations to make sure money is being spent properly. Congress can also freeze judges' salaries to show displeasure with court decisions, and it has the power to limit the issues that federal courts can consider. Even today, the system of checks and balances is not fixed in stone but evolves according to the changing political climate.

impeachment
A negative or checking power over the other branches that allows Congress to remove the president, the vice president, or other "officers of the United States" (including federal judges) for abuses of power.

The president and the Senate share the appointment power to many federal offices: the president makes the nominations, and the Senate provides its "advice and consent." The nomination of Brett Kavanaugh was extremely contentious and prompted several days of Senate hearings regarding past allegations of sexual misconduct. Ultimately, Kavanaugh was confirmed by a vote of 50–48 in the Senate.

In addition to these two formal constitutional checks, Congress may limit presidential power through its legislative powers of lawmaking and oversight. When Congress is controlled by a different party than the president, such checking is common; for example, in the last six years of Obama's presidency, Republicans in Congress tried to stop much of his agenda. But even under unified government, as in the first two years of Trump's presidency, Congress can check presidential power. Republicans passed stronger sanctions against Russia, investigated Russian interference in our elections, failed to provide full funding for the wall at the U.S.-Mexico border, and failed to "repeal and replace" the Affordable Care Act (Obamacare), all in the face of Trump's opposition.

Presidential Checks The framers placed important checks on congressional power as well, and the president's most important check on Congress is the veto. Again there was very little agreement on this topic. The Antifederalists argued that it was "a political error of the greatest magnitude, to allow the executive power a negative, or in fact any kind of control over the proceedings of the legislature." But the Federalists worried that Congress would slowly strip away presidential powers and leave the president too weak. Ultimately, the Federalist view won the day. However, the veto has developed into a major policy-making tool for the president, which is probably broader than the check against "depredations" envisioned by the framers. The Constitution also gives the president a formal check on the courts through the power to appoint judges.

judicial review
The Supreme Court's power to strike down a law or an executive branch action that it finds unconstitutional.

Judicial Review The Constitution did not provide the Supreme Court with any formal checks on the other two branches. Instead, the Court itself (in the landmark decision of *Marbury v. Madison* in 1803) established the practice of **judicial review**— the ability of the Supreme Court to strike down a law or an executive branch action as unconstitutional. For example, early in Trump's first year, federal courts struck down the initial versions of his travel ban because they were viewed as discriminatory against Muslims. Although judicial review is not explicitly mentioned in the Constitution, supporters of the practice justify it by pointing to the supremacy clause, which states that the "Constitution, and the Laws of the United States which shall be made in Pursuance thereof . . . shall be the supreme Law of the Land."

As Chief Justice John Marshall argued in *Marbury v. Madison*, to enforce the Constitution as the supreme law of the land, the Court must determine which laws are "in pursuance thereof." Critics of judicial review argue that the Constitution is supreme because it gains its legitimacy from the people and that therefore elected officials—Congress and the president—should be the primary interpreters of the Constitution rather than the courts. This dispute may never be fully resolved, but Marshall's bold assertion of judicial review made the Supreme Court an equal partner in the system of separate powers and checks and balances.

"Why Should I Care?"

If you remember anything from your elementary civics class, it is probably some foggy notion of the system of checks and balances and separation of powers. But why is this system so important? This institutional framework provides the basis for our government and explains the nature of political conflict and outcomes. When the government shuts down because of a dispute over spending or the Senate blocks the president's court nominees, this is because the president and Congress have different roles but can check each other's powers. Understanding checks and balances and separation of powers helps us be realistic about what government can do and shows us that all parts of the government are critical, but none are dominant, in making policy and enforcing laws.

Is the Constitution a "living" document?

★

EXPLORE HOW THE MEANING OF THE CONSTITUTION HAS EVOLVED

How has the Constitution remained relevant after more than 230 years? Why does this framework of government still work? How can the framers' values still be meaningful to us? There are several reasons that the Constitution continues to be a "living" document that evolves with the changing values and norms of the nation (see the Take a Stand feature).

Changing the Constitution

The most obvious way that the Constitution keeps up with the times is by allowing for changes to its language. The framers broadly supported the idea behind Article V, which lays out the formal process for amending the Constitution: the people must control their own political system, which includes the ability to change it through a regular, nonviolent process.

Proposal and Ratification Although there was strong consensus on including in the Constitution a set of provisions for amending it, there was no agreement on how this should be done. The Virginia Plan envisioned a relatively easy process of changing the Constitution "whensoever it shall seem necessary" by means of ratification by the people, whereas the New Jersey Plan proposed a central role for state governments. Madison suggested the plan that was eventually adopted, which accommodated both those who wanted a stronger national government and those who favored the states.

NUTS & BOLTS 2.3

Amending the Constitution

This flowchart shows how amendments to the Constitution can be proposed and ratified and the frequency with which each method has been used. Interestingly, the president is not a part of the formal process of amending the Constitution.

Source: Compiled by the authors.

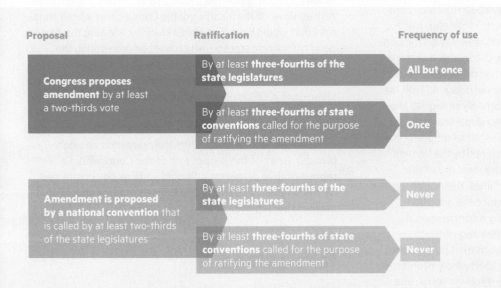

Proposal	Ratification	Frequency of use
Congress proposes amendment by at least a two-thirds vote	By at least **three-fourths of the state legislatures**	All but once
	By at least **three-fourths of state conventions** called for the purpose of ratifying the amendment	Once
Amendment is proposed by a national convention that is called by at least two-thirds of the state legislatures	By at least **three-fourths of the state legislatures**	Never
	By at least **three-fourths of state conventions** called for the purpose of ratifying the amendment	Never

"Why Should I Care?"

The amendment process reflects the idea that the people must control their own political system, which includes the ability to change it through a regular, nonviolent process. Would the country have survived the Civil War if not for the ability to amend the Constitution? Would the Senate be as representative as it is now? How does this process serve as a safeguard for the future?

A Living Constitution?

Should the Constitution be viewed as a flexible framework or a document that has fixed meaning? The public is fairly split on this issue, with 55 percent saying that constitutional interpretation should be based on "what it means in current time" (the living Constitution approach) and 41 percent saying that it should be based on "what it originally meant" (originalism). However, there is a deep partisan divide on this issue, with 78 percent of Democrats taking the living Constitution approach and 77 percent of Republicans supporting originalism.[a]

The meaning of the Constitution doesn't change.

Justice Clarence Thomas is perhaps the strongest advocate of the originalist view. He wrote: "Let me put it this way; there are really only two ways to interpret the Constitution—try to discern as best we can what the framers intended or make it up."[b] Former chief justice William Rehnquist, although generally adhering to the originalist view, took a more nuanced approach. He favorably cited a 1920 Supreme Court opinion by Oliver Wendell Holmes: "When we are dealing with words that also are a constituent act, like the Constitution of the United States, we must realize that they have called into life a being the development of which could not have been foreseen completely by the most gifted of its begetters."[c] John Marshall in *McCulloch v. Maryland* also endorsed this view, saying the Constitution was "intended to endure for ages to come, and consequently to be adapted to the various crises of human affairs." Rehnquist said that "scarcely anyone would disagree" with the idea that the Constitution was written broadly enough to allow principles such as the prohibition against illegal searches and seizures to apply to technologies, such as the telephone or the Internet, that could not have been envisioned by the framers.[d]

However, according to this view, the *meaning* of the Constitution cannot change with the times. Rehnquist wrote that "mere change in public opinion since the adoption of the Constitution, unaccompanied by a constitutional amendment, should not change the meaning of the Constitution. A merely temporary majoritarian groundswell should not abrogate some individual liberty truly protected by the Constitution."[e] Therefore, recent rulings restricting the death penalty (which is clearly endorsed by the Constitution), expanding gay rights, or allowing children to testify remotely against their sexual abusers rather than having to confront them directly in court (as guaranteed by the Sixth Amendment) would all be inconsistent with the originalist view. This view would also hold that anything other than relying on the meaning of the words of the Constitution allows justices to "legislate from the bench," which is undemocratic given that the judges are not elected.

There is a vigorous debate among justices of the Supreme Court as to whether the Constitution is a living document or should be interpreted more strictly according to the original intent of the framers.

The meaning of the Constitution changes with the times.
Proponents of a living Constitution argue for a more flexible view. Justice Thurgood Marshall advocated a living Constitution, noting that the framers "could not have imagined, nor would they have accepted, that the document they were drafting would one day be construed by a Supreme Court to which had been appointed a woman and the descendent of an African slave."[f] If the meaning of the Constitution is fixed, then the Court would have to uphold a state law allowing the death penalty for horse stealing, which was common during the Founding era. Executing horse thieves, or, more realistically, children and the mentally impaired (which was allowed in many states until 2005), is unacceptable in a modern society, even if it would be allowed by a strict reading of the Constitution.

The answer to the question about how justices should interpret the Constitution ultimately depends on one's broader views of the proper role of the Court within a representative democracy. Should justices be constrained by the original meaning of the Constitution, or should that meaning evolve over time?

take a stand

1. If you were on the Supreme Court, would you adopt an originalist or a living Constitution approach? Justify your position.

2. Based on the originalist view, should a state be allowed to execute whomever it wants to, including minors (or horse thieves)? Based on the living Constitution approach, should limits be placed on justices to prevent them from "legislating from the bench"?

Article V describes the two steps necessary to change the Constitution: proposal and ratification. Congress may *propose* an amendment that has the approval of two-thirds of the members in both houses, or an amendment may be proposed by a national convention that has been called by two-thirds of the states' legislatures. In either case, the amendment must be *ratified* by three-fourths of the states' legislatures or state conventions (see Nuts & Bolts 2.3). A national convention has never been used to propose an amendment, and every amendment except for the Twenty-First, which repealed Prohibition, has been ratified by state legislatures rather than state conventions.

A Range of Amendments Amendments have ranged from fairly narrow, technical corrections of errors in the original document (Eleventh and Twelfth Amendments) to important topics such as abolishing slavery (Thirteenth), mandating equal protection of the laws for all citizens (Fourteenth), providing for the popular election of senators (Seventeenth), giving Black men and then women the right to vote (Fifteenth and Nineteenth), and allowing a national income tax (Sixteenth). Potential constitutional amendments have addressed many other issues, with more than 10,000 proposed; of those, 33 were sent to the states and 27 have made it through the amending process (the first 10 came at once in the Bill of Rights). Table 2.1 shows several amendments that were introduced but not ratified.

> "
>
> The people made the Constitution, and the people can unmake it. It is the creature of their will, and lives only by their will.
>
> —**John Marshall,** chief justice, 1801–1835

Flexibility and interpretation

The Constitution also remains relevant because it allows for some flexibility in how it is interpreted. Furthermore, some parts of the Constitution are simply ignored today because they have no meaning in a modern context. For example, Article I, Section 4, says that "Congress shall assemble at least once in every Year," but the modern Congress is in session throughout the year (with various recesses). Nobody pays attention to this passage anymore because it simply does not matter.

Recent Amendments Introduced in Congress That Did Not Pass

TABLE 2.1

Many proposed constitutional amendments have almost no chance of passing. Indeed, most of those listed here did not even make it to the floor of the House or Senate for a vote. Why do you think a member of Congress would propose an amendment that he or she knew would fail?

116th Congress (2019–2020)	Limit the pardon power of the president. Provide equal rights for men and women. Extend the right to vote to citizens 16 and 17 years of age. Limit the number of terms a representative or senator may serve.
115th Congress (2017–2018)	Require that the federal budget be balanced. Abolish the Electoral College to provide for the direct election of the president and vice president. Protect the voting rights of the citizens of the United States. Amend the First Amendment to allow limitations on federal campaign contributions and expenditures.
114th Congress (2015–2016)	Require that the rights extended by the Constitution be granted only to natural persons (not corporations). Repeal the Sixteenth Amendment (income tax).

Source: Compiled by the authors from www.congress.gov (accessed 12/6/19).

Ambiguity The Constitution's inherent ambiguity is a characteristic that has kept the document relevant. Key passages were written in very general language, which has allowed the Constitution to evolve along with changing norms, values, and political contexts. This ambiguity was a political necessity: not only were the framers aware that the document would need to survive for generations, but in many instances the language that they chose was simply the only wording that all the framers could agree on. For instance, the necessary and proper clause gives Congress the power to enact laws that are related to its enumerated powers, or those that are explicitly granted. But what does "necessary and proper" mean? Congress, for the most part, gets to answer that question.

Implied Powers Furthermore, there have been significant changes in the way that the Constitution structures the policy-making process, even though the pertinent text of the Constitution has not changed.[16] This point is best understood by examining the concept of **implied powers**—that is, powers that are not explicitly stated in the Constitution but that can be inferred from an enumerated power. The Supreme Court often defines the boundaries of implied powers, but Congress, the president, and the public can also play key roles.

To take a recent example of Congress's interpretation of implied powers, the president's appointment powers have evolved as the Senate has become much more aggressive in providing "advice and consent" on presidential nominations to the federal courts. As we explore in Chapter 13, in the past 20 years the Senate has blocked court appointments at a significantly higher rate than it did in the first half of the twentieth century. The relevant language in the Constitution is the same, yet the Senate's understanding of its role in this important process has changed. The president's power to remove appointees also recently came into play in May 2017 when President Trump fired FBI Director James Comey, who was investigating the Trump campaign's connections to Russia. This situation raised the constitutional question of when (or whether) the president's removal of one of his or her appointees constitutes an obstruction of justice. Presidential use of executive powers to go around Congress when it declines to act on issues the president deems important also demonstrates the ambiguous nature of constitutional powers. For example, Obama's action on EPA rules concerning carbon emissions and immigration policy and Trump's use of executive orders to impose a travel ban on specific countries to limit the threat of terrorism were viewed as either appropriate and necessary executive action or "constitutional overreach."

Changing Social Norms Public opinion and social norms also influence the prevailing interpretation of the Constitution, as is evident in the evolving meanings of capital punishment (the death penalty) and freedom of speech. When the Constitution was written, capital punishment was broadly accepted, even for horse thieves. Therefore, the prohibition in the Eighth Amendment against "cruel and unusual punishments" certainly did not mean to the framers that the death penalty was unconstitutional. However, in 1972 the Supreme Court struck down capital punishment as unconstitutional because it was being applied arbitrarily.[17] Subsequently, after procedural changes were made, the Court once again upheld the practice. However, the Court has since decided that capital punishment for minors and mentally impaired people constitutes cruel and unusual punishment—decisions that reflect modern sensibilities but not the framers' thinking.[18] Similarly, the text of the First Amendment protections for freedom of speech has never changed, but the Supreme Court has been willing to uphold significant limitations on free speech, especially in wartime. When external threats are less severe, the Court has been more tolerant of controversial speech.

implied powers
Powers supported by the Constitution that are not expressly stated in it.

The Eighth Amendment's ban on "cruel and unusual punishments" is generally viewed as excluding capital punishment, but the execution of juveniles and the mentally impaired has been found unconstitutional. This picture shows the lethal injection chamber at the Arizona State Prison in Florence.

The line between a new interpretation of the Constitution and constitutional change is difficult to define. Clearly, not every new direction taken by the Supreme Court or new interpretation of the constitutional roles of the president or Congress is comparable to a constitutional amendment. In one respect, a constitutional amendment is much more permanent than a new interpretation by the Court. For example, the Court could not unilaterally decide that 18- to 20-year-olds, women, and African Americans no longer have the right to vote. Constitutional amendments expanded the right to vote to include these groups, and only further amendments could either expand or restrict the right to vote. However, gradual changes in constitutional interpretation are probably just as important as the amending process in explaining the Constitution's ability to keep pace with the times.

Amending the Constitution is difficult and can be controversial. Some amendments that are widely accepted today, like the Nineteenth Amendment giving women the right to vote, were intensely debated prior to their ratification.

One of the most remarkable things about the Constitution is its longevity. While there are intense debates about whether a "living Constitution" is a good thing, there is no doubt that its ability to change with the times, whether because of its amending process, multiple interpreters, or ambiguity, has helped make it the oldest constitution in the world. People may joke that the Constitution isn't relevant anymore, but it shapes the boundaries for all of today's policy debates and institutional struggles.

"Why Should I Care?"

Unpacking the Conflict

As we discussed at the beginning of this chapter, the presidency of Donald Trump raises many questions about the strength and resilience of our Constitution. Considering all that we know about how the Constitution works, was American democracy in danger? Is our system of checks and balances working?

While this presidency raised other new, important constitutional questions such as "Can the president pardon himself?" and "How does the emoluments clause apply to the complex real estate holdings of the Trump family?" a look at the facts indicates that the Constitution is working just as the Founders intended. The Trump presidency illustrates many of the themes of this chapter: the conflictual nature of politics established by the Constitution (there has been plenty of conflict!) and the fact that multiple interpreters and ambiguous language provide the flexibility for our political system to respond to challenging times. Most significantly, elections served their function of imposing accountability, and there was a peaceful transition of power.

To protect against majority tyranny, the separation of powers and the system of checks and balances in our political system divide power by giving each branch of government the power to check the others (and the additional check of divided power across levels of government). Therefore, when the presidency starts to drift out of the mainstream of American politics, Congress, the courts, and state governments can reel it back in. We've seen throughout the chapter how our constitutional system has allowed the courts and Congress to effectively check the more extreme aspects of Trump's agenda that have alarmed pundits on the left, from Trump's proposed immigration and environmental policies, to the failure to "repeal and replace" Obamacare, to the early versions of his travel bans, to his relationship with Russia. This self-corrective feature of our constitutional system means that no branch of government will attain disproportionate power for very long, and it has kept the political system stable.

Even more fundamentally, the Constitution promotes long-term stability by providing the basis for resolving conflict through elections and representative government rather than by taking up arms. Losers of one round of elections know that they have an opportunity to compete in the next election and that their voices can be heard in another part of the government. Indeed, after heavy losses in 2016, Democrats were especially energized for the competitive 2018 midterms and taking back the presidency two years later.

Congress, the president, and the Supreme Court all must interpret the Constitution in the normal course of fulfilling their institutional roles, which also helps preserve an institutional balance of power. Having multiple interpreters of the Constitution is built into our system. The Trump presidency also compelled the general public to become more interested in the Constitution.[19] If Americans are more informed about the Constitution, they can become even more significant interpreters of the Constitution.

Finally, the general and ambiguous language of the Constitution means that both supporters and opponents of the president can find evidence for their views. It is impossible to know exactly how the emoluments clause should apply to foreign officials staying in a Trump-owned property or whether the president can pardon himself, because these constitutional questions have never come up before. Therefore, answers to these questions, and the broader health of our American democracy, will continue to be determined by the outcome of the political process and democratic elections as established by the Constitution. While there is no guarantee that our nation will be around for another 230 years, these past four years have demonstrated the Constitution's resilience and strength once again.

A leading constitutional scholar, Walter Murphy, addressed the relevance of the Constitution this way: "The ideals it enshrines, the processes it prescribes, and the actions it legitimizes must either help to change its citizenry or at a minimum reflect their current values. If a constitution does not articulate, at least in general terms, the ideals that form or will re-form its people and express the political character they have . . . , it will soon be replaced or atrophy."[20] The Constitution's ability to change with the times and reflect its citizens' values has enabled it to remain relevant and important today. Its flexibility and general language mean that there will never be definitive answers to the conflict over its meaning, but they ensure that these debates will be enduring and meaningful.

> They keep talking about drafting a constitution for Iraq. Why don't we just give them ours? It was written by a lot of really smart guys. It's worked for over 200 years, and hell, we're not using it anymore.

—**Jay Leno,** late-night television host

"What's Your Take?"

Did Trump's actions as president threaten democracy?

Or did our system of government as laid out in the Constitution work to keep conflicts over Trump's policies in check?

STUDY GUIDE

3. **At the American Founding, what is the best way to describe the economic inequality among classes and the economic diversity among regions?**

a high inequality / high diversity

b high inequality / low diversity

c low inequality / high diversity

d low inequality / low diversity

e none of the above

The historical context of the Constitution

Describe the historical circumstances that led to the Constitutional Convention of 1787. (Pages 34–40)

Summary

The U.S. Constitution was shaped by historical events preceding its creation, particularly the period of British rule over the colonies, the Revolutionary War, and the states' experience under the Articles of Confederation. Under British rule, the colonies were relatively independent of one another, and the framers sought to create a strong nation while still maintaining the autonomy of the states in the system. The framers based the Constitution on three key principles: the rejection of a monarchy, popular control of the government, and a limited government that protected against tyranny.

Key terms

Articles of Confederation (p. 35)

limited government (p. 35)

monarchy (p. 35)

Shays's Rebellion (p. 37)

republicanism (p. 37)

popular sovereignty (p. 39)

natural rights (p. 39)

Federalists (p. 40)

Antifederalists (p. 40)

Practice Quiz Questions

1. **How were members of Congress selected under the Articles of Confederation?**

a by the state governor

b by the state legislature

c by the state supreme court

d by popular election

e by random lot

2. **What power did the president have under the Articles of Confederation?**

a power to raise an army

b power to veto congressional legislation

c power to negotiate foreign agreements

d power to nominate federal judges

e There was no president under the Articles of Confederation.

The politics of compromise at the Constitutional Convention

Analyze the major issues debated by the framers of the Constitution. (Pages 40–48)

Summary

Although the framers of the Constitution agreed that the Articles of Confederation needed to be changed, there was little consensus otherwise. The Federalists and Antifederalists clashed on several issues, though the most important were (1) balancing majority rule with minority rights, (2) allocating power between large and small states, (3) allocating power between the legislature and executive, (4) allocating power between the national government and the states, and (5) determining how to handle slavery.

Key terms

pluralism (p. 42)

Virginia Plan (p. 42)

New Jersey Plan (p. 42)

Great Compromise (p. 43)

parliamentary system (p. 44)

reserved powers (p. 45)

national supremacy clause (p. 45)

Three-Fifths Compromise (p. 47)

Practice Quiz Questions

4. **Madison argued that the best way to prevent the tyranny of factions was to _____ .**

a outlaw political parties

b establish a strong national government

c have various groups compete against one another in the government

d establish strong local governments

e try to ensure that all people were equal

5. **The Great Compromise provided solutions to which issue?**

a balancing majority rule with minority rights

b allocating power between big and small states

c allocating power between the legislature and executive

d allocating power between national and state governments

e determining how to handle slavery

6. **How are executives chosen in most other established democracies?**

a   by popular election

b   by electoral college

c   through selection by the judiciary

d   through selection by the legislature

e   by the United Nations

7. **The outcome of the Three-Fifths Compromise was that each enslaved person counted for three-fifths of a person for the purposes of _____ and _____.**

a   voting; taxation

b   congressional representation; taxation

c   voting; congressional representation

d   taxation; congressional appropriations

e   congressional representation; agricultural subsidies

Ratification

Contrast the arguments of the Federalists with those of the Antifederalists. (Pages 48–50)

Summary

After the Constitution was written and approved at the Constitutional Convention, it still needed to be ratified by nine states. The Constitution was primarily criticized by the Antifederalists, which gave way to a lengthy public debate over the merits of the proposed framework. Ultimately, to win over the necessary support in the states, the framers had to include the Bill of Rights, which was tailored to protect the rights of states and individuals from the national government.

Key term

Bill of Rights (p. 50)

Practice Quiz Questions

8. **What group was concerned about the Constitution's provisions for the strength of the president and the lack of specific guarantees of civil liberties?**

a   Tories

b   Unionists

c   Federalists

d   Antifederalists

e   Free Soilers

9. **A series of arguments originally published in New York newspapers supported the Constitution and outlined the political theory behind it. What are these assembled works called?**

a   *Pickwick Papers*

b   *Federalist Papers*

c   *Antifederalist Papers*

d   *Common Sense*

e   *The Second Treatise of Government*

The Constitution: a framework for government

Outline the major provisions of the Constitution. (Pages 50–56)

Summary

The defining feature of the Constitution is its separation of powers while still maintaining flexibility for leadership in times of crisis. The system of checks and balances gives each branch of the federal government some explicit powers, some shared powers, and some ability to limit the power of the other two branches of government.

Key terms

enumerated powers (p. 51)

power of the purse (p. 51)

necessary and proper clause (p. 51)

impeachment (p. 55)

judicial review (p. 56)

Practice Quiz Questions

10. **The "necessary and proper" clause gives flexibility to which part of government?**

a   the president

b   the Supreme Court

c   the bureaucracy

d   the Congress

e   interest groups

11. **Which branch has the fewest explicit powers?**

a   the president

b   the Supreme Court

c   the bureaucracy

d   the Congress

e   the people

12. Which of the following negative powers does the president enjoy?

a   the power to veto legislation

b   the power to freeze judicial salaries

c   the power to review the constitutionality of a law

d   the power to impeach federal justices

e   the power to dissolve Congress and call new elections

Is the Constitution a "living" document?

Explore how the meaning of the Constitution has evolved. (Pages 57–61)

Summary

The Constitution is more than 230 years old, yet it still provides a blueprint for modern governance. It has maintained its relevance because of its ambiguity in several key passages, its ability to be amended rather than entirely rewritten, and the designation of multiple interpreters of the Constitution.

Key term

implied powers (p. 60)

Practice Quiz Questions

13. Which route for *proposing* a constitutional amendment has been used for all successful amendments to date?

a   approval by two-thirds of the members of Congress

b   approval by a national convention

c   approval by two-thirds of the state legislatures

d   approval by the Supreme Court

e   approval by the president

14. After an amendment is successfully proposed, what step must occur in order for it to become part of the Constitution?

a   signature by the president

b   approval by a popular vote

c   ratification by three-fourths of the states

d   nullification by all 50 state legislatures

e   a national referendum vote

15. Which part of government often defines the boundaries of implied powers?

a   the president

b   the Supreme Court

c   the bureaucracy

d   the Congress

e   the people

Suggested Reading

Allen, Danielle. *Our Declaration: A Reading of the Declaration of Independence in Defense of Equality.* New York: W. W. Norton, 2014.

Amar, Akhil Reed. *The Constitution Today: Timeless Lessons for the Issues of Our Era.* New York: Basic Books, 2016.

Currie, David P. *The Constitution of the United States: A Primer for the People,* 2nd ed. Chicago: University of Chicago Press, 2000.

Dahl, Robert A. *How Democratic Is the American Constitution?* New Haven, CT: Yale University Press, 2001.

Davis, Sue. *Corwin and Peltason's Understanding the Constitution,* 17th ed. Boston: Wadsworth, 2008.

Hamilton, Alexander, James Madison, and John Jay. *The Federalist Papers.* 1788. Reprint, 2nd ed., edited by Roy P. Fairfield. Baltimore, MD: Johns Hopkins University Press, 1981.

Ketcham, Ralph. *The Anti-Federalist Papers and the Constitutional Convention Debates.* New York: Signet Classics, 2003.

Rossiter, Clinton. *1787: The Grand Convention.* New York: Macmillan, 1966.

Strauss, David. *The Living Constitution.* New York: Oxford University Press, 2010.

Sunstein, Cass R. *Designing Democracy: What Constitutions Do.* New York: Oxford University Press, 2001.

West, Thomas G. *The Political Theory of the American Founding: Natural Rights, Public Policy, and the Moral Conditions of Freedom.* New York: Cambridge University Press, 2017.

Wood, Gordon S. *The Creation of the American Republic.* New York: W. W. Norton, 1969.

3

Federalism

States or the federal government: who's got the power?

 "While the White House clings to the past, automakers and American families embrace cleaner cars. The evidence is irrefutable: today's clean car standards are achievable, science-based, and a boon for hardworking American families and public health. It's time to remove your blinders, President Trump, and acknowledge that the only person standing in the way of progress is you. You have no basis and no authority to pull this waiver. We're ready to fight for a future that you seem unable to comprehend; we'll see you in court if you stand in our way."
Xavier Becerra, California attorney general

"We embrace federalism and the role of the states, but federalism does not mean that one state can dictate standards for the nation."
Andrew Wheeler, administrator of the Environmental Protection Agency

How strictly should the government regulate automobile fuel emissions? While individual Americans disagree about this question, the states and the federal government also disagree about the states' role in determining fuel economy standards. EPA Administrator Andrew Wheeler sees California's aggressive regulation as overstepping its bounds.

Since passage of the Clean Air Act of 1970, the state of California has required auto manufacturers to meet higher fuel economy standards for cars and light trucks sold in the state than are required by federal law. This policy was one way that the state met the Clean Air Act's mandates to reduce auto pollution. More recently, California had agreed with auto manufacturers to increase fuel economy standards and tighten emissions limits as a way of fighting climate change. Because California is such a large market, auto companies often implement the changes needed to satisfy California's requirements to all the cars they produce, meaning that California's policies influence the design of cars sold throughout America.

In September 2019, however, the Trump administration revoked California's authority to set its own fuel economy and pollution standards. President Trump argued that revocation would reduce car prices and increase safety. As the quote from California's Attorney General shows, California's response was to fight the administration's move in federal court, a case that is likely to be dropped given the Biden presidency.[1]

CHAPTER GOALS

Define *federalism* and explain its significance. pages 68–72

Explain what the Constitution says about federalism. pages 72–74

Trace the major shifts in state and federal government power over time. pages 74–80

Describe the major trends and debates in federalism today. pages 81–93

This conflict over fuel economy standards reflects a fundamental feature of America's government: federalism. In areas such as education, law enforcement, and environmental policy, the federal government has only limited power to affect policy at the state and local level. Because of federalism, your experiences with government, including the services you receive, the laws you are supposed to obey, and the regulations that constrain your actions, differ depending on where you live.

As we discussed in Chapter 2, one of the reasons we have a federal system is the desire to limit the power of the national government. Federalism also enables state and local governments to take account of citizens' demands or local conditions—information that might not be available to decision makers in Washington. By giving power to state and local governments, federalism can increase citizen satisfaction and governmental efficiency.

However, as the fight over emissions standards suggests, federalism is more than a way to increase responsiveness and efficiency. In many policy areas, federalism sets up conflicts between different levels of government over who gets to make policy choices. In the case of fuel economy standards, while California's policies are designed in part to address local pollution issues, it is also true that a substantial majority of California's citizens would like the federal government to do more to fight climate change. Because auto companies often implement California standards throughout their production line, the state can impose these standards on people elsewhere, whether they like it or not—a concept with which EPA administrator Andrew Wheeler strongly disagrees.[2]

The conflict triggered by fuel economy standards is a great example of the tensions created by a federal system. Joe Biden's victory in the 2020 election means that the conflict is moot—but the potential for disagreement between federal and state governments remains. When local and federal officials disagree about fuel economy and global warming, who wins? What are the responsibilities of the states and what is the domain of the national government? What happens when levels of government disagree? How have the answers to these questions changed over the course of American history—and how does federalism work today?

DEFINE *FEDERALISM* **AND EXPLAIN ITS SIGNIFICANCE**

federalism
The division of power across the local, state, and national governments.

sovereign power
The supreme power of an independent state to regulate its internal affairs without foreign interference.

What is federalism and why does it matter?

Federalism is a form of government that divides sovereign power across at least two political units. Dividing **sovereign power** means that each unit of government (in the United States, national, state, and local governments) has some degree of authority and autonomy. As discussed in Chapter 2, this division of power across levels of government is central to the system of separated powers in the United States. Dividing power across levels of government seems simple, but as we will see later in this chapter, the political battles over *how* that power is divided have been intense. (One important note on terminology: while the national government in Washington, D.C., is referred to as the federal government, it is only one part of the federal system that combines national, state, and local governments.)

In practical terms, federalism is about intergovernmental relations: How do the different levels of government interact, and how is power divided? But even that

The relationship between the national government and states and territories involves cooperation as well as competition. During the COVID-19 pandemic, the Federal Emergency Management Agency (FEMA) partnered with local officials to provide emergency support, including the construction of a temporary hospital in New York City.

may seem a little abstract. Why does federalism matter? On a broad range of issues, the level of government that dictates policy can make a real difference, simply because preferences vary across these levels. Sometimes these disagreements reflect different beliefs about what citizens want from government. But more commonly, conflicts result from differences of opinion about what government should be doing. In the case of fuel economy standards, for example, the national government, represented by President Trump and the Environmental Protection Agency, wants to roll back many current environmental regulations, believing that they provide little benefit and cost too much. While some state and local politicians (as well as their supporters) hold similar feelings, others, such as California's attorney general and many of his constituents, disagree. This divergence between the policies desired by politicians at different levels of government means that decisions about federalism (which level of government does what) affect how environmental laws are ultimately interpreted and enforced. (See the What Do the Facts Say? feature.)

The fact that many policies are administered by multiple levels of government provides multiple access points for citizens and groups who want to influence the details of these policies. Finally, conflicts over federalism create a key role for the federal courts, as their power to interpret the Constitution makes them the ultimate arbiter of conflicts between federal and state governments. As we will see, at various points in American history (including recent years), changes in the composition of the Supreme Court have had important consequences for the balance of power between different levels of government.

Levels of government and their degrees of autonomy

A distinguishing feature of federalism is that each level of government has some degree of autonomy from the other levels—that is, each level can carry out some policies without interference from the others. In the United States, this means that the national and state governments have distinct powers and responsibilities (see Nuts & Bolts 3.1). The national government, for example, has **exclusive powers** for national defense and

exclusive powers
Policy-making responsibilities that are exercised only by the national government.

police powers
The power to enforce laws and provide for public safety.

concurrent powers
Responsibilities for particular policy areas, such as transportation, that are shared by federal, state, and local governments.

foreign policy. State and local governments have primary responsibility for conducting elections and promoting public safety, or **police powers**. In other areas, such as transportation, the different levels of government have **concurrent powers**—they share responsibilities. The national government also has additional responsibilities through implied powers that are inferred from the powers explicitly granted in the Constitution (see the later discussion in this chapter). Local governments—cities, towns, school districts, and counties—are not autonomous units of government. State governments create them and control the types of activities they can engage in by specifying in the state charter what local governments can do and cannot do.

NUTS & BOLTS 3.1

National and State Responsibilities

National Government Powers	State Government Powers	Concurrent Powers
Print money	Issue licenses	Collect taxes
Regulate interstate commerce and international trade	Regulate intrastate (within the state) businesses	Build roads
Make treaties and conduct foreign policy	Conduct elections	Borrow money
Declare war	Establish local governments	Establish courts
Provide an army and navy	Ratify amendments to the Constitution	Make and enforce laws
Establish post offices	Promote public health and safety	Charter banks and corporations
Make laws necessary and proper to carry out these powers	May exert powers the Constitution does not delegate to the national government or does not prohibit the states from using	Spend money for the general welfare; take private property for public purposes, with just compensation

Powers Denied to the National Government	Powers Denied to State Governments
May not violate the Bill of Rights	May not enter into treaties with other countries
May not impose export taxes among states	May not print money
May not use money from the Treasury without an appropriation from Congress	May not tax imports or exports
May not change state boundaries	May not interfere with contracts
	May not suspend a person's rights without due process

Source: Compiled by the authors.

"Why Should I Care?" These provisions of the Constitution define the scope of policy conflict between the state and federal governments—which powers are given exclusively to one level, which are shared, and, most important, which are left unallocated. Modern fights over federalism start with these provisions and how they should be interpreted.

Will New Regulations Save "a Million Lives"?

One of the most important rules when reading a news story about a controversial issue is to look for sources and documentation. We all want media coverage that gives "just the facts"—but a good article also tells readers where the facts came from, so that they can be checked and verified. This is particularly true when a story relies on quotes from participants in a political conflict, as their comments may be designed to persuade rather than inform.

Let's look at an example from Breitbart News' coverage of the Trump administration's fight with the state of California over fuel economy standards. A March 2019 story on the Breitbart site featured an interview with EPA Administrator Andrew Wheeler, who was quoted as follows:

BREITBART

"We were hoping to work something out with California, but it just didn't take place. We are moving forward with our own regulation; it's going to reduce the price of a new car by about $2,300. Right now, people are holding on to their cars longer," the EPA chief said. "The average lifespan for a car is about 12 years; it used to be about eight years. The older cars are less safe, less environmentally friendly, so by getting the older cars off, by reducing the price of a car, hopefully more people will buy newer cars, safer cars that will also save lives. I believe the number is that a million lives will be saved by this proposal as opposed to the Obama proposal, and we get there by reducing the cost of a new car. And we're still reducing pollutants at the same time."

Source: Sean Moran, "Exclusive—EPA's Andrew Wheeler: Green New Deal Activists Don't Want American 'Energy Domination.'" Breitbart, March 2, 2019, www.breitbart.com/politics/2019/03/02/exclusive-epa-administrator-andrew-wheeler-green-new-deal-activists-dont-want-american-energy-domination/ (accessed 11/18/19).

Wheeler's quote gives two of the central arguments for taking away California's waiver: that it will reduce the price of a new car by $2,300, and that it will save a million lives. But he doesn't provide any documentation for these numbers, and the article doesn't question the claims.

A Google search on "EPA $2,300" finds several stories with well-documented critiques of Wheeler's claims.[a] It turns out that the $2,300 figure refers to increased costs over the lifetime of owning a car, which is 12 years—so the actual increase is only about $200 per year, which does not take into account decreased fuel costs from California's higher mileage standards. There is also no formal study or report to justify the claim about saving a million lives—in fact, some internal e-mails sent by EPA analysts to the Office of Management and Budget argued that revoking California's waiver would actually increase deaths from auto accidents.

The point is not that you should think every story on Breitbart is fake or that a source such as Vox can always be trusted. Rather, when trying to make sense of American politics, you should look for stories that give you a way to assess the reliability of the information they provide, whether it is the story's account of political issues and events or information contained in a quote. A lack of sources or documentation is a red flag.

Think about it

- **What are some credible sources** of news you go to for "just the facts"? What do you do when you can't validate the information in a second source?
- **What are the dangers** of spreading misleading or incorrect information? How might these errors lead people make uninformed decisions?

A comparative perspective

unitary government
A system in which the national, centralized government holds ultimate authority. It is the most common form of government in the world.

confederal government
A form of government in which states hold power over a limited national government.

It is useful to compare U.S. federalism with forms of government in other countries. In some countries, power is centralized within the national government. This system is known as a **unitary government**. Unitary governments are the most common in the modern world (about 80 percent); examples include the United Kingdom, Israel, Italy, France, Japan, and Sweden. In these countries, the states or subunit governments are not autonomous; they cannot carry out policies if the national government opposes them. At the opposite end of the spectrum is a **confederal government**, in which the states have most of the power. This was the first type of government in the United States under the Articles of Confederation, but there are very few modern examples. One was the Commonwealth of Independent States, which formed from former Soviet Republics after the dissolution of the Soviet Union in 1991, but exists today only as a forum for discussion and coordination between Russia, Belarus, and a few central Asian republics.

"Why Should I Care?"

Federalism explains why laws and regulations may differ from state to state; it allows for differences of opinion across regions. For example, how do your state's opinions on fuel efficiency differ from California's? How does federalism allow your state to respond differently to address issues of climate change? This is federalism in action.

EXPLAIN WHAT THE CONSTITUTION SAYS ABOUT FEDERALISM

Balancing national and state power in the Constitution

Although the Founders wanted a national government that was stronger than it had been under the Articles of Confederation, they also wanted to preserve states' autonomy. These goals are reflected in different parts of the Constitution, which provides ample support for advocates of both strong state governments and a strong national government. The nation-centered position has its roots in the document's preamble, which begins: "We the People of the United States." The Articles of Confederation, by contrast, began: "We the undersigned delegates of the States." The Constitution's phrasing emphasizes the nation as a whole over the separate states—although as we will see, it also allocates significant powers to the states.

A strong national government

DID YOU KNOW?

Under the Articles of Confederation, all

13

states had their own militia and navy.

Many features of the Constitution reflect the Founders' desire for a strong national government.

In terms of national security, Congress was granted the power to raise and support armies, declare war, and "suppress Insurrections and repel Invasion," while the president, as commander in chief of the armed forces, would oversee the conduct of war. Congress's power to regulate interstate commerce promoted economic efficiency and centralized an important economic power at the national level. The Constitution outlines restrictions on state power that contribute to the centralization of national military and economic power: states were *prohibited* from entering into "any Treaty, Alliance, or Confederation" or keeping troops or "Ships of War" during peacetime. They also could not coin money or impose duties on imports or exports (see Article I, Section 10).

The necessary and proper clause (Article I, Section 8) was another broad grant of power to the national government: it gave Congress the power "[t]o make all Laws which shall be necessary and proper for carrying into Execution the foregoing Powers." Similarly, the national supremacy clause (Article VI) says that the Constitution and all laws and treaties that are made under the Constitution shall be the "supreme Law of the Land" and that "the Judges in every State shall be bound thereby, any Thing in the Constitution or Laws of any State to the Contrary notwithstanding." This is perhaps the clearest statement of the nation-centered focus of the Constitution. If any state law or state constitution conflicts with national law or the Constitution, the national perspective wins. Thus, in the case of same-sex marriages, once the Supreme Court ruled that all laws prohibiting same-sex marriage were unconstitutional, elected officials at all levels knew that if they enacted new prohibitions, the laws would be immediately invalidated by the courts.

State powers and limits on national power

Despite the Founders' nation-centered bias, many parts of the Constitution also address state powers and set limits on national power. Article II gives the states the power to choose electors for the Electoral College, and Article V grants the states a central role in the process of amending the Constitution. Three-fourths of the states must ratify any constitutional amendment (through either conventions or the state legislatures, as specified by Congress), but the states can also bypass Congress in proposing amendments if two-thirds of the states call for a convention. This route to amending the Constitution has never been used.

Article I of the Constitution enumerates many powers for Congress, but the list of state powers is much shorter. One could interpret this as more evidence for the nation-centered perspective, but at the time of the Founding the expectation was that most power would be exercised at the state level. Therefore, the federal powers that were exceptions to this rule had to be clearly specified, while state governments

Jim Obergefell, the plaintiff in the *Obergefell v. Hodges* Supreme Court case that legalized same-sex marriage nationwide, is backed by supporters of the ruling on the steps of the Texas capitol during a rally on June 29, 2015, in Austin. This ruling shows the power of the supremacy clause, as it struck down laws in 14 states.

received authority over all other matters. The Tenth Amendment supports this view, saying: "The powers not delegated to the United States by the Constitution, nor prohibited by it to the states, are reserved to the states respectively, or to the people."

Clauses that favor both perspectives

Article IV of the Constitution includes provisions that favor both the state-centered and the nation-centered perspectives. For example, its **full faith and credit clause** specifies that states must respect one another's laws, granting citizens the "Full Faith and Credit" of their home state's laws if they go to another state. At the same time, though, the article's **privileges and immunities clause** says that citizens of each state are "entitled to all Privileges and Immunities" of citizens in the other states, which means that states must treat visitors from other states the same as their own residents.

There are many examples of the full faith and credit clause and privileges and immunities clause at work today. If you have a Michigan driver's license and are traveling to Texas, you do not need to stop at every state line to get a new license; each state will honor your Michigan license. Similarly, a legal marriage in one state (even a same-sex marriage) must be honored by another state. But not all state licenses are subject to full faith and credit: if you have an open or concealed-carry gun permit in one state, that does not automatically give you the right to carry a firearm in another state. Similarly, states do not have to permit nonresidents to vote in state elections, and public colleges and universities may charge out-of-state residents higher tuition than in-state residents. Therefore, the privileges and immunities clause cuts both ways on the question of the balance of power: it allows the states to determine and uphold their own laws autonomously, but it also emphasizes that national citizenship is more important than state citizenship.

full faith and credit clause
The part of Article IV of the Constitution requiring that each state's laws be honored by the other states. For example, a legal marriage in one state must be recognized across state lines.

privileges and immunities clause
The part of Article IV of the Constitution requiring that states must treat nonstate residents within their borders as they would treat their own residents. This was meant to promote commerce and travel between states.

"Why Should I Care?"

Why is it important to understand the Constitution's role in federalism? The Constitution sets the boundaries for the battles over state and federal power. For example, no state can decide to print its own currency, and the U.S. government cannot take over the public schools. But within those broad boundaries, the balance between national and state power at any given point in history is a political decision, the product of choices made by elected leaders and the courts. The struggle over fuel economy standards is a perfect example: the Trump administration wanted to weaken standards and California's government wanted to increase them.

★
TRACE THE MAJOR SHIFTS IN STATE AND FEDERAL GOVERNMENT POWER OVER TIME

The evolving concept of federalism

The nature of federalism has changed as the size and functions of the national and state governments have evolved. In the first century of our nation's history, the national government played a relatively limited role and the boundaries between the levels of government were distinct. As the national government took on more power in the twentieth century, intergovernmental relations became more cooperative and the boundaries less distinct. Even within this more cooperative framework, federalism remains a source of conflict within our political system, both because the levels of government share lawmaking authority and because they may disagree over the details of government policy.

The early years

As the United States gained its footing, clashes between the advocates of state-centered and nation-centered federalism evolved into a partisan struggle. The Federalists—the party of George Washington, John Adams, and Alexander Hamilton—controlled the new government for its first 12 years and favored strong national power. One of their strongest allies was Chief Justice John Marshall, who wrote several landmark Supreme Court decisions that enhanced the power of the national government. The Federalists' opponents, the Democratic-Republicans (led by Thomas Jefferson and James Madison), favored state power, or, as it came to be known, **dual federalism**. Dual federalism, as we will discuss, was the guiding principle of Marshall's successor as chief justice, Roger Taney. Table 3.1 highlights several important decisions resolved during Marshall's and Taney's tenures on the Court.

Establishing National Supremacy The first confrontation came when the Federalists established a national bank in 1791, followed by a second national bank in 1816. At that time, the state of Maryland, which was controlled by the Democratic-Republicans, tried to tax the National Bank's Baltimore branch out of existence. However, the bank refused to pay the tax, creating a conflict that sent the case to the Supreme Court.

In the landmark decision *McCulloch v. Maryland* (1819), Marshall's Court held that even though the word "bank" does not appear in the Constitution, Congress's power to create one is implied through its relevant enumerated powers—such as the power to coin money, levy taxes, and borrow money. The Court also ruled that Maryland did not have the right to tax the bank because of the Constitution's national supremacy clause.

dual federalism
The form of federalism favored by Chief Justice Roger Taney, in which national and state governments are seen as distinct entities providing separate services. This model limits the power of the national government.

Early Landmark Supreme Court Decisions on Federalism

TABLE 3.1

Case	Holding and Significance for States' Rights	Direction of the Decision
Chisholm v. Georgia (1793)	Held that citizens of one state could sue another state; led to the Eleventh Amendment, which prohibited such lawsuits.	Less state power
McCulloch v. Maryland (1819)	Upheld the national government's right to create a bank and reaffirmed the idea of "national supremacy."	Less state power
Gibbons v. Ogden (1824)	Held that Congress, rather than the states, has broad power to regulate interstate commerce.	Less state power
Barron v. Baltimore (1833)	Endorsed a notion of "dual federalism" in which the rights of a U.S. citizen under the Bill of Rights did not apply to that same person under state law.	More state power
Dred Scott v. Sandford (1857)	Sided with southern states' view that enslaved people were property and ruled that the Missouri Compromise violated the Fifth Amendment, because making slavery illegal in some states deprived owners of enslaved people of property. Contributed to the start of the Civil War.	More state power

Source: Compiled by the authors.

In the early 1800s, the Supreme Court confirmed the national government's right to regulate commerce between the states. The state of New York granted a monopoly to a ferry company serving ports in New York and New Jersey, but this was found to interfere with interstate commerce and was therefore subject to federal intervention.

A few years later, Marshall's Court held in *Gibbons v. Ogden* (1824) that Congress has broad power to regulate interstate commerce. The ruling struck down a New York law that had granted a monopoly to a private company that was operating steamboats on the Hudson River between New York and New Jersey. By granting this monopoly, New York was interfering with interstate commerce, a power reserved to Congress by the Constitution. Even in the modern era, this ruling underlies many of the federal government's regulations on businesses, which are based on the expectation that virtually any commercial activity will involve buying and selling across state lines.

The emergence of states' rights and dual federalism

Under Marshall's successor, Chief Justice Roger Taney, Court decisions involving federalism shifted to reflect a new concept: dual federalism. According to the system of dual federalism, the national and state governments are considered distinct, with little overlap in their activities or the services they provide. In this view, the national government's activities are confined to powers strictly enumerated in the Constitution.

Dual federalism was expressed most consequentially in the *Dred Scott v. Sandford* decision of 1857. Dred Scott was an enslaved man who had lived for many years with his owner in the free state of Illinois and the free Wisconsin Territory but was living in Missouri, a slave state, when his master died. Scott petitioned for his freedom under the Missouri Compromise, which had made slavery illegal in any free state. The Court did not grant Scott his freedom. Its majority decision held that enslaved people were not citizens but private property; therefore, the Missouri Compromise's ban on slavery in certain territories violated the Fifth Amendment because it deprived citizens (owners of enslaved people) of their property without the due process of law. Put another way, the *Dred Scott* decision said that state law, not federal, determined the legal status of enslaved people.

Contrasting Marshall's decisions in favor of national power with Taney's decisions in favor of state power highlights the policy consequences of judicial decisions.

The Taney Court's decision that the Missouri Compromise was unconstitutional is consistent with a dual federalism interpretation of the Constitution—but it also sustained the legality of slavery in southern states and halted attempts by representatives from the North to limit the spread of slavery into the western territories. There is little doubt that Taney favored this outcome on policy grounds. In this sense, debates about dual federalism during this time were really about the legality of slavery, its expansion into new states, and the rights of formerly enslaved people in free states.

states' rights
The idea that states are entitled to a certain amount of self-government, free of federal government intervention. This became a central issue in the period leading up to the Civil War.

Arguments about dual federalism are sometimes framed using the concept of **states' rights**: the idea that states retain some powers under the Constitution (specifically those reserved by the Tenth Amendment) and can ignore federal policies that encroach on these powers. The key question is, where does federal authority end and state authority begin? As this chapter demonstrates, the lines are not always easy to define and are still being debated today. Some people argue that southern states fought the Civil War to preserve the concept of states' rights, but this argument tells only a fraction of the whole story. Southern secessionists were not interested in states' rights per se; what they wanted was to continue slavery without federal intervention. States' rights was a convenient rationale for their proslavery position.

After the Civil War, constitutional amendments banned slavery (Thirteenth Amendment), prohibited states from denying citizens due process or the equal protection of the laws (Fourteenth Amendment), and gave newly freed men the right to vote (Fifteenth Amendment). Congress also passed the 1875 Civil Rights Act (although it was later overturned by the Supreme Court). The Fourteenth Amendment was the most important in terms of federalism because it was the constitutional basis for many of the civil rights laws passed by the federal government during Reconstruction. The Civil War fundamentally changed the way Americans thought about the relationship between the national government and the states: before the war people said "the United States *are* ... ," but after the war they said "the United States *is* ..."

The Supreme Court and Limited National Government The assertion of power by Congress during Reconstruction was short-lived, as the Supreme Court soon stepped in again to limit the power of the national government. In 1873, the Court reinforced the notion of dual federalism, ruling that the Fourteenth Amendment did not change the balance of power between the national and state governments. Specifically, the Court ruled that the Fourteenth Amendment right to due process and equal treatment under the law applied to individuals' rights only as citizens of the

After the Supreme Court struck down the 1875 Civil Rights Act, southern states were free to impose Jim Crow laws. These state and local laws led to complete racial segregation, even for public drinking fountains.

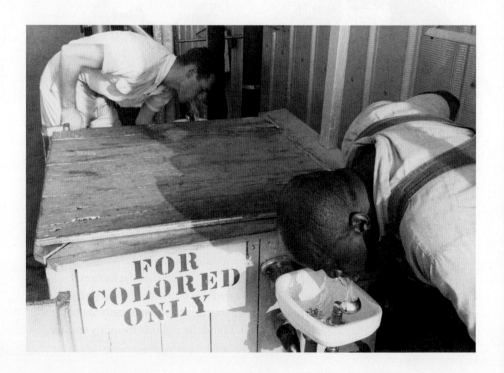

United States, not to their state citizenship.[3] By extension, freedom of speech, freedom of the press, and the other liberties protected in the Bill of Rights applied only to laws passed by Congress, not to state laws. Here again, these decisions can be read as an articulation of a theoretical interpretation of the Constitution, but they are also part of a broader, more concrete debate over how much the government should regulate interactions between individuals and corporations.

In 1883, the Court overturned the 1875 Civil Rights Act, which had guaranteed equal treatment in public accommodations. The Court argued that the Fourteenth Amendment did not give Congress the power to regulate private conduct, such as whether a White restaurant owner had to serve a Black customer; it affected only the conduct of state governments, not individuals in these states.[4] This narrow view of the Fourteenth Amendment left the national government powerless to prevent southern states from implementing state and local laws that led to complete segregation of Blacks and Whites in the South (called Jim Crow laws) and the denial of many basic rights to Blacks after northern troops left the South at the end of Reconstruction.

The Supreme Court also limited the reach of the national government by curtailing Congress's authority to regulate the economy through its commerce clause powers. In several cases in the late nineteenth and early twentieth centuries, the Supreme Court endorsed a view of laissez-faire—French for "leave alone"—capitalism aimed at protecting business from regulation by the national government. To this end, the Court defined clear boundaries between *inter*state and *intra*state commerce, ruling that Congress could not regulate any economic activity that occurred *within* a state (intrastate). On similar grounds, the Court also struck down attempts by Congress to regulate child labor.[5]

Cooperative federalism

In the early years of the twentieth century and through the 1930s, a new era of American federalism emerged in which the national government became much more involved in activities that were formerly reserved for the states, such as transportation,

Franklin Delano Roosevelt's New Deal shifted more power than ever to the national government. Through major new programs to address the Great Depression, such as the Works Progress Administration construction projects pictured here, the federal government expanded its reach into areas that had been primarily the responsibility of state and local governments.

civil rights, agriculture, social welfare, and management–labor relations. Starting in 1937 with the landmark ruling *National Labor Relations Board v. Jones and Laughlin Steel Corporation*, the Supreme Court gave Congress far more latitude to shape economic and social policy for the nation.[6]

Shifting National–State Relations The type of federalism that emerged in this era is called **cooperative federalism**, or "marble cake" federalism, as opposed to the "layer cake" model of dual federalism.[7] As the image of a marble cake suggests, the boundaries of state and national responsibilities are not as well defined under cooperative federalism as under dual federalism. With the increasing industrialization and urbanization of the late 1930s and 1940s, along with the Great Depression, more complex problems arose that could not be solved at one level of government. Cooperative federalism adopted a more practical focus on intergovernmental relations and the efficient delivery of services. State and local governments maintained some influence as the implementers of national programs, but the national government played an enhanced role as the initiator, director, and funder of key policies.

"Cooperative federalism" accurately describes this important shift in national–state relations in the first half of the twentieth century, but it only partially captures the complexity of modern federalism. The marble cake metaphor falls short in one important way: the lines of authority and patterns of cooperation are not as messy as implied by the swirly flow of chocolate through white cake. Instead, the 1960s metaphor of **picket fence federalism** is a better description of cooperative federalism in action. As the How It Works: Versions of Federalism graphic shows, each picket of the fence represents a different policy area and the horizontal boards that hold the pickets together represent the different levels of government. This is a much more orderly image than the marble cake, and it has important implications about how policy is made across levels of government.

The most important point to be drawn from this analogy is that activity in the cooperative federal system occurs *within* pickets of the fence—that is, within policy areas. Policy makers within a given policy area will have more in common with others in that area (even if they are at different levels of government) than they do with people who work in different areas (even if they are at the same level of government). For example, someone working in a state's Department of Natural Resources will have more contact with people working in local park programs and the national Department of the Interior than with people who also work at the state level but who focus on, say, law enforcement. Overall, this version of federalism provides good opportunities for coordination and the sharing of expertise within policy areas.

cooperative federalism
A form of federalism in which national and state governments work together to provide services efficiently. This form emerged in the late 1930s, representing a profound shift toward less concrete boundaries of responsibility in national–state relations.

picket fence federalism
A more refined and realistic form of cooperative federalism in which policy makers within a particular policy area work together across the levels of government.

"Why Should I Care?"

Why is it important to understand the history of federalism? You might think that the Civil War ended the debates over nation-centered versus state-centered federalism (in favor of the national government), but disputes today over immigration, health care, welfare, and education policy all revolve around the balance of power between the levels of government. State legislatures that talk about ignoring federal criticisms of their policy choices are invoking the same arguments used by advocates of states' rights in the 1830s and 1840s concerning tariffs and slavery.

Federalism today

Federalism today is a complex mix of all the types of federalism that our nation's political system has experienced in the past. Our current system is predominantly characterized by cooperative federalism, but it has retained strong elements of national supremacy, dual federalism, and states' rights (see Nuts & Bolts 3.2). Debates over the appropriate role of the federal and state governments continue to occur in areas such as government surveillance of individuals (especially after September 11) and funding of social-welfare programs like public school education and health care. (For more details on these programs, see Chapter 14.) And the courts continue to play a key role in deciding the constitutionality of new laws and regulations.

Cooperative federalism lives on: fiscal federalism

Cooperative federalism refers to situations in which federal and state governments share responsibility for delivering a policy. Most examples of cooperative federalism involve some element of **fiscal federalism**, a system whereby the federal government provides some of the funds needed to sustain the state programs that deliver services to citizens. For example, the federal government pays a large share of state Medicaid costs and a portion of the funding for local school districts. At one level, fiscal federalism is a way for the federal government to help states deal with responsibilities that outstrip their financial resources. However, fiscal federalism also gives the federal government a way to influence the kinds of policies implemented at the state level.

An extreme version of fiscal federalism is **coercive federalism**, which is the use of federal regulations, mandates, or conditions to force or entice the states to change their policies to match national goals or policies established by Congress. A related concept, **federal preemption**, occurs when the federal government passes a law that overrides state law or makes it impossible for a state to enact its own statute. The Clean Air and Clean Water Acts, the Americans with Disabilities Act (ADA) (which promotes making public buildings and commercial facilities more accessible to those with disabilities), and the Motor Voter Act (which requires states to provide voter registration services at motor vehicle departments) are all laws that forced states to change their policies. The laws most objectionable to the states are **unfunded mandates**, which require states to do certain things but carry no federal money to pay for them. Republican criticism of unfunded mandates in the 1990s led to passage of the Unfunded Mandate Reform Act of 1995, which made it more difficult for Congress to impose these mandates on the states.

Types of Federal Aid to States The method used to transfer resources from the federal government to states and localities often determines the effectiveness of fiscal federalism. Today, most federal aid comes in two forms. **Categorical grants** are for specific purposes—they have strings attached. Funds that help states run their Medicaid programs, for example, are delivered as categorical grants. **Block grants** are financial aid to states for use within a specific policy area, but within that area the states have discretion on how to spend the money. An example of a block grant is TANF (Temporary Assistance for Needy Families), which is federal money given to states to

fiscal federalism
A form of federalism in which federal funds are allocated to the lower levels of government through transfer payments or grants.

coercive federalism
A form of federalism in which the federal government pressures the states to change their policies by using regulations, mandates, or conditions (often involving threats to withdraw federal funding).

federal preemption
Imposition of national priorities on the states through national legislation that is based on the Constitution's supremacy clause.

unfunded mandates
Federal laws that require the states to do certain things but do not provide state governments with funding to implement these policies.

categorical grants
Federal aid to state or local governments that is provided for a specific purpose, such as a mass-transit program within the transportation budget or a school lunch program within the education budget.

block grants
Federal aid provided to a state government to be spent within a certain policy area, but the state can decide how to spend the money within that area.

Versions of Federalism

Version 1:
Layer Cake Federalism

1789–1937
No interactions between the levels of government.

Version 2:
Marble Cake Federalism

1937–today
Interactions between the levels of government are common.

Version 3:
Picket Fence Federalism

1960s–today
Horizontal boards represent different levels of government, and the pickets are policy areas within which coordination happens across those levels.

National
State
Local

Agriculture
Environment
Highways
Housing
Education
Medical Care
Tax Policy

Version 4:
Coercive Federalism

1970s–today
National government uses regulations, mandates, and conditions to pressure states to fall into line with national policy goals.

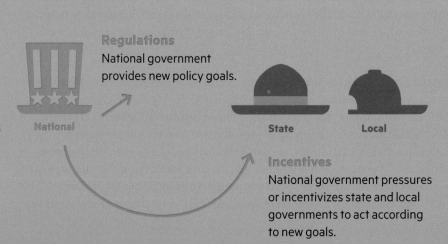

Regulations
National government provides new policy goals.

National

State   Local

Incentives
National government pressures or incentivizes state and local governments to act according to new goals.

Federalism and Environmental Policy

This is who carries out environmental policy in...

The National Government:
Environmental Protection Agency (EPA), Department of the Interior, Department of Energy

The State Government:
State Department of Natural Resources, State Park Service, State Environmental Protection Agencies

The Local Government:
City park system, city and county oversight boards for land use policy and zoning

Environmental policy shows contemporary federalism in action. As you can see on the right, all levels of government combine to effect environmental policy (exemplifying picket fence federalism). Also, the national government provides both rules and incentives for state and local governments to change their environmental policies (exemplifying coercive federalism).

Congress passed new acts.

Over the last several decades, Congress has passed the **Coastal Zone Management Act**, the **Clean Water Act**, the **Endangered Species Act**, and the **Clean Air Act**.

What does that mean?

This legislation has provided states and localities with **federal regulations and mandates**.

Stricter rules...

During the Obama administration, **the EPA set tougher limits on ozone and water pollution** and proposed stricter limits on carbon emissions.

But also incentives.

Other federal programs **provided grants and tax incentives** to encourage use of renewable energy technologies.

Change happens.

Beginning in 2017, the Trump administration **repealed many of the new EPA regulations** but left the tax credits and grant programs largely intact.

The states fight back.

Fifteen states **sued the federal government**, claiming that the regulatory rollbacks violated the Clean Air Act. Litigation is currently underway and will likely end up in the Supreme Court.

?

Critical Thinking

1. **Which do you think is a more effective tool** to change environmental policy—the "stick" of regulation or the "carrot" of incentives? Why?

2. **Should the government provide tax credits and other incentives** for things like renewable energy, or leave such things up to the free market?

In short:

The national government **imposes new rules** on **state and local governments** and **provides incentives** to follow these new rules and goals. However, the content of these rules, as well as whether they stay in place over time, **depends on who is elected to federal office and decisions made by federal courts**.

The Evolution of Federalism

Type of Federalism	Period	Characteristics
Dual federalism (layer cake)	1789–1937	The national and state governments were viewed as very distinct with little overlap in their activities or the services they provided. Within this period, federalism could have been state centered or nation centered, but relations between levels of government were limited.
Cooperative federalism (marble cake)	1937–present	This indicates greater cooperation and collaboration between the levels of government.
Fiscal federalism	1937–present	This system of transfer payments or grants from the national government to lower-level governments involves varying degrees of national control over how the money is spent: categorical grants give the national government a great deal of control whereas block grants involve less national control.
Picket fence federalism	1960–present	This version of cooperative federalism emphasizes that policy makers within a given policy area have more in common with others in their area at different levels of government than with people at the same level of government who work on different issues.
Coercive federalism	1970s–present	This involves federal preemptions of state and local authority and unfunded mandates on state and local governments to force the states to change their policies to match national goals or policies established by Congress.

Source: Compiled by the authors.

"Why Should I Care?"

Over the 240 years of American history, shifts in citizen demands and the expansion of the federal government have changed the nature of policy conflicts between state and federal governments. Even so, the fact that many policy responsibilities are shared or left undetermined, coupled with the fact that politics is conflictual, means that the federal government and the states will always be arguing over who gets to do what.

help fund their welfare programs. However, in contrast to Medicaid, federal welfare funds are given without restrictions about how the states determine benefits or the eligibility of welfare recipients. As a result, both of these factors vary across states. Since the 1970s, grants to the states as a proportion of the size of the national economy (gross domestic product, or GDP) have been relatively constant, whereas the rate of state and local spending has continued to inch up.

Advocates of cooperative federalism often promote block grants as the best way for the levels of government to work together to solve problems: the national government identifies problem areas and then provides money to the states to help solve them. The problem is that state governments may disagree with the president or Congress on how these programs should be implemented, which creates a temptation for the federal government to move to categorical grants as a way to shape state policy.

Expanding national power

Despite the overall shift toward cooperative federalism, strong overtones of national government supremacy remain. Three important characteristics of American politics in the past 60 years have reinforced the role of the national government: (1) reliance on the national government in times of crisis and war; (2) the "rights revolution" of the 1950s and 1960s, as well as the Great Society programs of the 1960s; and (3) the rise of coercive federalism.

Crisis and War Even in the 1800s, during the period of dual federalism and strong state power, the national government's decisive actions were needed during the Civil War to hold the nation together. More recently, during the COVID-19 pandemic that spread across the country, most people looked to the federal government to deliver emergency supplies, aid in emergency medical operations, and allocate funds for affected communities. Policy responses to the other major crises that occurred during the twentieth century (the Great Depression's New Deal policies and the massive mobilization for World War II), as well as the response to the banking meltdown of 2008–2009, also dramatically shifted the balance of power toward Washington.

The "Rights Revolution" and Great Society Programs During the mid-twentieth century, the "rights revolution" initiated by the Supreme Court, as well as President Lyndon Johnson's Great Society programs, contributed to more national control over state policies. Landmark Court decisions thrust the national government into policy areas that had typically been reserved to the states. In the school desegregation and busing cases of the 1950s and 1960s, for example, the Court upheld the national goal of promoting racial equality and fighting discrimination over the earlier norm of local control of school districts.[8] The rights revolution also applied to police powers, another area of traditional state control, including protection against self-incrimination and preventing illegally obtained evidence from being used in a criminal trial.[9]

> **Bureaucrats sometimes do not have the correct information, while citizens and users of resources do.**
>
> —**Elinor Ostrom,** Nobel Laureate

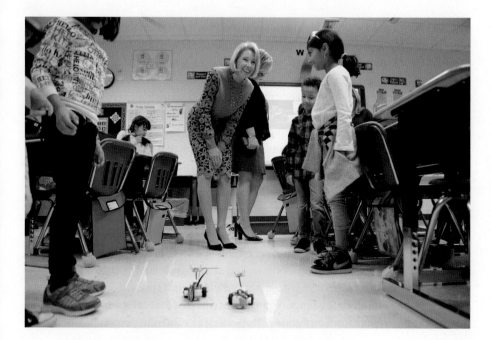

In response to the Bush and Obama administrations' perceived overreach into education policy, Secretary of Education Betsy DeVos led the Trump administration's efforts to roll back the federal government's power over education.

These Court actions were paralleled by a burst of legislation that tackled civil rights, education, the environment, medical care for the poor, and housing. These so-called Great Society policies made the national government much more active in policy areas previously controlled by state and local governments. For example, under the 1965 Voting Rights Act federal marshals were sent to the South to ensure that African Americans were allowed to vote.

In the 1960s, the national government also expanded its reach through a large increase in categorical grants, although most of these funds came with strings attached. For example, the 1964 Civil Rights Act required nondiscrimination as a condition for receiving any kind of federal grants.

More Unfunded Mandates Despite the legislation enacted by Congress designed to curb unfunded mandates, the practice has continued. President George W. Bush imposed significant mandates related to education testing, sales tax collection, emergency management, infrastructure, and election administration. President Barack Obama's administration required state governments to adopt policies preventing discrimination against the disabled and mandated reforms to local school lunch menus. More recently, the Trump administration's crackdown on undocumented immigrants has an unfunded mandate: if local police arrest someone suspected of being undocumented, they are expected to keep these suspects in custody until federal authorities can arrange for a transfer, even though the federal government does not reimburse them for the cost of the detention.

The fact that members of Congress enact unfunded mandates makes sense given the themes of this textbook. First, politics is about conflict, and when there is disagreement between the federal and state government over what policies should look like, we should expect each side to do whatever it can to advance its own priorities. Second, the rules matter. The fact that the Constitution prioritizes federal law over state law, coupled with increased federal aid to state and local governments, gives the federal government considerable leverage to get its way when conflicts arise. In the case of suspected undocumented immigrants, the Trump administration threatened to withhold various forms of federal aid to communities that refuse to hold suspects for transfer, although it never actually did so, and it is questionable whether aid cutoffs would survive a court challenge.

State governments, including Washington D.C., have taken up the mantle of meeting the United States' commitments to the climate goals set by the Paris Agreement. Muriel Bowser, mayor of Washington, D.C., reaffirmed her administration's commitment to fighting climate change.

The States Fight Back Most Americans support some of the national policies that have been imposed on the states: racial equality, clean air and water, a fair legal process, safer highways, and equal access to the voting booth. At the same time, there has always been considerable opposition in some states to federal mandates, whether unfunded or otherwise. For example, about 20 states have refused to accept federal funds to expand Medicaid as outlined in the Affordable Care Act (the ACA, or "Obamacare"). While the law initially did not give states the flexibility to opt out of the expansion, the Supreme Court found that mandating that the states expand their Medicaid programs to receive these funds was unconstitutional.

States appear to be reversing their traditional role of resisting change and protecting the status quo. In recent years, states have followed California's lead on environmental policy, refusing to accept national pollution standards that are too lenient or the lack of national action on issues such as global warming. Many policies to address climate change—including the development of renewable energy sources, carbon emissions limits, and carbon cap and trade programs—have been advocated or enacted at the state level, and some governors have announced that their states will comply with the Paris Agreement on climate change regardless of what the federal government does. States have been out in front on fighting electronic waste, mercury emissions, and air pollution more generally.[10] Similarly, during the COVID-19 pandemic, many states implemented mandatory mask regulations despite the absence of federal action. To take another example, Kansas and Montana passed laws holding that federal gun laws do not apply to guns manufactured in their states (and making it a felony to try to enforce those laws).[11] Many such state laws will not stand up in federal court; the Montana gun law has already been struck down. But the laws are clearly a reflection of state frustration with assertions of federal power, and with the policy goals that underlie these assertions. Simply put, local elected officials and their constituents often disagree with federal directives. From this perspective, federalism provides a way for state and local officials to shape public policy in ways that favor their own policy goals.

States have one important advantage over the national government when it comes to experimenting with new policies: their numbers. There are 50 states potentially trying a mix of different policies—another reason that advocates of state-centered federalism see the states as the proper repository of government power. In this view, such a mix of policies produces **competitive federalism**—competition among states to provide the best policies to attract businesses, create jobs, and maintain a healthy social fabric.[12] For example, one of the arguments in favor of repealing Obamacare and giving the program's funds to states as a block grant was that state governments might develop better, more efficient ways to deliver health care without having to meet federal requirements.

Fighting for states' rights: the role of the modern Supreme Court

Just as the Supreme Court played a central role in defining dual federalism in the nineteenth and early twentieth centuries and in introducing a more nation-centered cooperative federalism in the late 1930s, today's Court is once again reshaping federalism. But this time, the move is decidedly in the direction of state power (see Table 3.2).

The Tenth Amendment The Tenth Amendment ensures that all powers not delegated to the national government are reserved to the states or to the people. Until recent years, this amendment had been overshadowed by federal supremacy—state laws contradicting the Constitution or federal laws and regulations were generally found to be unconstitutional.

For example, state laws enforcing racial segregation were deemed unconstitutional because they conflicted with the equal protection clause of the Fourteenth Amendment. Similarly, a state law concerning public education, traditionally a state power, is void if it conflicts with the Constitution or with a national law that is based on an enumerated power. For example, a state could not compel an 18-year-old to attend school if the student had been drafted to serve in the army. Under the Tenth Amendment, the constitutionally enumerated national power to "raise and support armies" would override the reserved state power to support public education.

But times change. With the appointment of three conservative justices between 1986 and 1991 who favored a stronger role for the states, the Court started to limit the national government's reach. One common thread in these decisions was to require that Congress provide an unambiguous statement of its intent for a particular law to overrule state authority.

The Fourteenth Amendment The Supreme Court has also empowered states by limiting the applicability of the Constitution's Fourteenth Amendment to state laws. The Fourteenth Amendment was intended to give the national government control

Crucial to understanding federalism in modern day America is the concept of mobility, or "the ability to vote with your feet." If you don't support the death penalty and citizens packing a pistol—don't come to Texas. If you don't like medicinal marijuana and gay marriage, don't move to California.

—**Rick Perry,** former Texas governor

competitive federalism
A form of federalism in which states compete to attract businesses and jobs through the policies they adopt.

The immense size and power of the Government of the United States ought not obscure its fundamental character. It remains a Government of enumerated powers.

—**Sandra Day O'Connor,** former Supreme Court justice

TABLE
3.2

Recent Important Supreme Court Decisions on Federalism

Case	Holding and Significance for States' Rights	Direction of the Decision
Gregory v. Ashcroft (1991)	The Missouri constitution's requirement that state judges retire by age 70 did not violate the Age Discrimination in Employment Act.	More state power
United States v. Lopez (1995)	Carrying a gun in a school did not fall within "interstate commerce"; thus, Congress could not prohibit the possession of guns on school property.	More state power
Seminole Tribe v. Florida (1996)	The Court used the Eleventh Amendment to strengthen states' sovereign immunity, ruling that Congress could not compel a state to negotiate with Native American tribes about gaming and casinos.	More state power
City of Boerne v. Flores (1997)	The Court struck down the Religious Freedom Restoration Act as an overly broad attempt to curtail the state-sponsored harassment of religion, saying that national legislation aimed at remedying states' discrimination must be "congruent and proportional" to the harm.	More state power
United States v. Morrison (2000)	The Court struck down part of the Violence Against Women Act, saying that Congress did not have the power under the commerce clause to provide a national remedy for gender-based crimes.	More state power
Alabama v. Garrett (2001)	The Court struck down the portion of the ADA that applied to the states, saying that state governments are not required to make special accommodations for the disabled.	More state power
Nevada Department of Human Resources v. Hibbs (2003)	The Court upheld Congress's power to apply the 1993 Family Leave Act to state employees as "appropriate legislation" under Section 5 of the Fourteenth Amendment.	Less state power
United States v. Bond (2011)	The Court upheld an individual's right to challenge the constitutionality of a federal law under the Tenth Amendment.	More state power
National Federation of Independent Business v. Sebelius (2012)	The Court upheld most provisions of the ACA but struck down the expansion of Medicaid as an unconstitutional use of coercive federalism (states could voluntarily take the additional funding to cover the expansion, but they would not lose existing funds if they opted out).	Mixed
United States v. Windsor (2013)	The Court held that Section 3 of DOMA was unconstitutional because it denied federal benefits to same-sex couples who were legally married under state law.	More state power
Shelby County v. Holder (2013)	The Court struck down Section 4 of the Voting Rights Act on the grounds that it violated the "equal sovereignty" of the states.	More state power

Source: Compiled by the authors.

remedial legislation
National laws that address discriminatory state laws. Authority for such legislation comes from Section 5 of the Fourteenth Amendment.

over the potentially discriminatory laws of southern states after the Civil War. Section 1 guarantees that no state shall make or enforce any law depriving any person of "life, liberty, or property, without due process of law" or denying any person the "equal protection of the laws." Section 5 empowers Congress "to enforce" those guarantees by "appropriate legislation." Throughout most of the twentieth century, the Court interpreted Section 5 to give Congress broad discretion to pass legislation to remedy bad state laws. For example, discriminatory application of literacy tests prevented millions of African Americans from voting in the South before Congress passed the Voting Rights Act in 1965.

As part of the federalism revolution of the 1990s, the Court started to chip away at Congress's Fourteenth Amendment powers. An important case in 1997 established a new standard to justify **remedial legislation**—national legislation that fixes discriminatory state law—under Section 5 of the Fourteenth amendment, saying: "There must be a congruence and proportionality between the injury to be prevented or remedied and the means adopted to that end."[13] In one application of the new standard for remedial legislation, the Court ruled that the Age Discrimination in Employment Act of 1967 could not be applied to state employees because it was not "appropriate legislation."[14]

The Commerce Clause Another category of cases that have been decided in favor of more state power concerns the commerce clause of the Constitution. A significant recent Court case that limited Congress's commerce powers involved the Gun-Free School Zones Act of 1990, which made it a federal offense to have a gun within 1,000 feet of a school. Congress assumed that it had the power to pass this legislation, given the Court's previously expansive interpretation of the commerce clause, even though it concerned a traditional area of state power. Although it was a stretch to claim that carrying a gun in or around a school was related to interstate commerce, Congress could have demonstrated the point by showing that (1) most guns are made in one state and sold in another (thus commercially crossing state lines); (2) crime affects the economy and commerce; and (3) the quality of education, which is also crucial to the economy, is harmed if students and teachers are worrying about guns in their schools. However, members of Congress did not present this evidence.

Alfonso Lopez, a high school senior, was arrested for carrying a concealed handgun with five bullets in it, in violation of the Gun-Free School Zones Act. Lopez moved to dismiss the charges, arguing that the law was unconstitutional because carrying a gun in a school could not be regulated as "interstate commerce." The Court agreed in *United States v. Lopez*.[15] If Congress wanted to encroach on the states' turf in the future, the Court indicated, Congress would have to demonstrate that the law in question was a legitimate exercise of the commerce clause powers.

As a result, the next time Congress passed legislation that affected law enforcement at the state level, it documented the impact on interstate commerce. The Violence Against Women Act was passed in 1994 after testimony and evidence showing the links between violence against women and commerce. Nevertheless, the Supreme Court subsequently ruled that Congress did not have the power under the commerce clause to make a national law that gave victims of gender-motivated violence the right to sue their attackers in federal court (however, the Court struck down only that part of the law; the program funding remained unaffected).[16]

The impact of these cases goes well beyond setting limits on the federal government's ability to regulate commerce. Not only has the Court set new limits on Congress's ability to address national problems, but it has also clearly stated that the

[A] state may, if its citizens choose, serve as a laboratory; and try novel social and economic experiments without risk to the rest of the country.

—**Louis Brandeis,**
former Supreme Court justice

The *Lopez* decision struck down the 1990 Gun-Free School Zones Act, ruling that Congress did not have the power to forbid people to carry guns near schools. After the shooting of 34 people at Marjory Stoneman Douglas High School in Parkland, Florida, on February 14, 2018, students led renewed calls nationwide for strengthening gun control laws.

Court alone will determine which rights warrant protection by Congress. However, the Court does not consistently rule against Congress; it often rules against the states because of broader constitutional principles or general public consensus behind a specific issue. For example, the Court has struck down state laws limiting gay rights as a violation of the equal protection clause of the Fourteenth Amendment.[17] And although the Court rejected the commerce clause as the constitutional justification for national health care reform, it did uphold the ACA based on Congress's taxing power.[18]

It's also important to keep in mind that the national government still has the upper hand in the balance of power and can readily blunt the impact of any Court decision: Congress can pass new laws to clarify its legislative intent and can overturn any cases that involve statutory interpretation. Congress can also use its financial power to impose its will on the states, although this power is not unlimited. For example, in a 2012 case dealing with Obamacare's requirement that states expand Medicaid coverage in order to receive federal subsidies for the program, the Court ruled that the threat embodied in this requirement was a "gun to the head,"[19] meaning states did not have a real choice: without the subsidies, no state could afford to provide Medicaid coverage on its own, even without the expansion in coverage. This was the first time the Court limited Congress's coercive budgetary power over the states, and the boundaries of the new limits will have to be decided in future cases.

Assessing federalism today

There is much to recommend federalism as a cornerstone of our political system. However, there are disadvantages as well, such as inefficiency in the policy process and inequality in policy outcomes. How does federalism in the United States fare from a twenty-first-century perspective?

Policy Preferences Issues concerning federalism have seemed to break down along traditional liberal and conservative lines. Liberals generally favor strong national power to fight discrimination, and they push for progressive national policies on issues such as protecting the environment, providing national health care, and supporting the poor. Conservatives, in contrast, tend to favor limiting intrusion from the national government and allowing the states to decide their own mix of social welfare and regulatory policies.

However, in recent years the tables have turned, and in many cases liberals today are arguing for states' rights while conservatives are advocating the virtues of uniform national laws. On a broad range of new issues, such as gay rights, aid in dying, and the recreational use of marijuana (see the Take a Stand feature), some state governments have enacted socially liberal legislation in recent years. As a result, liberals who might have favored a strong national government as a way of implementing their policy goals have found themselves arguing for states' rights, and conservatives have ended up arguing for the virtues of centralizing power.

Advantages of a Strong Role for the States The advantages of a strong role for the states can be summarized in four main points: (1) states can be laboratories of democracy, (2) state and local government is closer to the people, (3) states provide more access to the political system, and (4) states provide an important check on national power.

DID YOU KNOW?

Owing to a state program that is similar to Obamacare, only

2.8%

of people in Massachusetts don't have health insurance. In Texas, 17.7 percent of people do not have health insurance—the highest percentage in the nation.

Source: Census.gov

TAKE A STAND

Recreational Marijuana and Federalism

Should the federal government be able to tell a state that it cannot allow the recreational use of marijuana? While the use and possession of marijuana is illegal under federal law, 11 states (Alaska, California, Colorado, Illinois, Maine, Massachusetts, Michigan, Nevada, Oregon, Vermont, and Washington) have legalized nonmedical use. In most of these states, commercial activity (growing and sales) has also been legalized. Over 30 states have legalized marijuana use for medical purposes. And in most other states, possession of small amounts of marijuana is no longer treated as a crime. In the coming years, several other states are likely to move toward partial or complete legalization.

The federal government should be "hands off." Up until recently, the federal government responded to these changes in state law by adopting a "hands off" policy. The so-called Cole Memo (named after Deputy Associate Attorney General James Cole, who served during the Obama administration) stated that the federal government would not prosecute marijuana cases unless there had been a violation of both state and federal law. This policy reflected an attitude within the Obama Justice Department that prosecution of marijuana cases was not a high priority. Moreover, some Justice Department staff members (and perhaps President Obama) probably favored federal legalization. However, this step would have required congressional approval, which would have been unlikely during Obama's administration given the Republican majority in the House (and, after January 2015, in the Senate). Thus, deferring to state law helped move parts of the country toward decriminalization without requiring additional legislative action and allowed public support for legalization to build. Opponents of marijuana legalization in Congress may eventually be forced to reconsider their position based on the tides of public opinion.

The federal government should be "hands on." The situation changed after the election of Donald Trump. Throughout 2017, Trump's first Attorney General Jeff Sessions argued that the federal government needed to be more aggressive in its enforcement of marijuana laws as a means of reducing drug abuse, fighting criminal organizations, and decreasing violent crime. In January 2018, Sessions formally

 Federal drug enforcement agents raid a medical marijuana club.

rescinded the Cole Memo, although his new guidelines did not order U.S. attorneys to give marijuana prosecutions a higher priority, distinguish between medical or recreational use, or provide additional resources for anti-marijuana efforts. Sessions did not order states to change their laws or compel local law-enforcement agencies to enforce federal law.

Sessions's successor as attorney general, William Barr, has the option of proposing new federal legislation to increase the penalties for possession or sale of marijuana or providing local governments with funds or other assistance to enforce anti-marijuana laws. However, many Republican legislators, particularly from states that have relaxed marijuana laws, might oppose higher penalties. Similarly, law-enforcement agencies in communities that have decriminalized marijuana would likely decline federal help in prosecuting activities that they no longer consider a crime. On the other hand, insofar as Barr's responsibility is to enforce the laws as written, these steps are reasonable options for increased federal involvement in deterring marijuana production, sale, and consumption.

take a stand

1. As a matter of policy, should marijuana be legalized in all cases or just some cases—ranging from complete legalization to legalization only for medical use when prescribed by a doctor? If some possession is legal, what should policies be for growth and sale?

2. Do you tend to support a state-centered or a nation-centered perspective on federalism? Now revisit your answers to question 1. Are your positions more consistent with your views on federalism or with your policy concerns?

The first point refers to the role that states can play as the source of policy diversity and innovation. If many states are trying to solve problems creatively, they can complement the efforts of the national government. Likewise, successful policies first adopted at the state level often percolate up to the national level. Welfare reform, health care, and environmental policy are key examples of that.

Second, government that is closer to the people can encourage participation in the political process and may be more responsive to local needs. Local politicians know better what their constituents want than further-removed national politicians do. On the one hand, if voters want higher taxes to pay for more public benefits, such as public parks and better schools, they can enact these changes at the state and local levels. On the other hand, if they prefer lower taxes and fewer services, local politicians can be responsive to those desires. In addition, local government provides a broad range of opportunities for direct involvement in politics, from working on local political campaigns to attending city council meetings, which may increase the input that citizens have in the establishment of new policies.

Third, our federalist system provides more access points for interested parties (stakeholders) to influence government policy. For example, the court system allows citizens to pursue complaints under either state or federal law. If a group, such as anti-abortion activists, loses at the federal level, it can try to enact similar legislation at the state level. Likewise, cooperative federalism can draw on the strengths of different levels of government to solve problems.

Finally, federalism provides a check on national tyranny. Competitive federalism ensures that Americans have a broad range of social policies, levels of taxation and regulation, and public services to choose from (see Figure 3.1). When people "vote with their feet" by deciding where to live, they encourage healthy competition among states that would be impossible under a unitary government.

FIGURE 3.1

State Spending per Person

Spending per person varies dramatically by state. What are some of the advantages and disadvantages of living in a low-spending state or in a high-spending state? What type of state would you rather live in? Why?

Source: State and Local Government Finance Data Query System, http://slfdqs.taxpolicycenter.org (accessed 2/13/20).

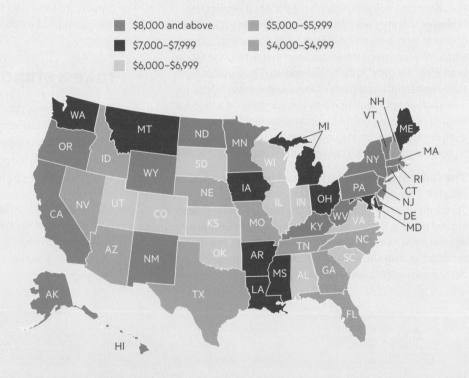

Disadvantages of Too Much State Power A balanced assessment of federalism must acknowledge that there are problems with a system that gives too much power to the states. The disadvantages include unequal distribution of resources, unequal protection for civil rights, competition that produces a "race to the bottom," and the problem of coordinating local responses to truly national issues.

One problem of giving too much responsibility to the states is the huge variation in the distribution of resources. Without federal funding, poor states simply cannot provide an adequate level of benefits because they have the greatest needs but the lowest incomes—a situation that leads to significant disparities in important areas such as public education. The resource problem becomes more acute in dealing with national-level problems that affect different areas differently. For example, many communities across the United States are faced with deteriorating public infrastructure, including highways, bridges, and mass transit. Paying for these repairs can outstrip the resources of state and local governments.

Another problem, unequal civil rights protection, is evident in various federalism cases that have passed before the Supreme Court. These clearly show that states are not uniformly willing to protect the civil liberties and civil rights of their citizens. This was critically important during the 1950s and 1960s when the national government forced southern states to end segregation and passed laws outlawing discrimination in housing, employment, transportation, and voting. The Supreme Court recently stepped in to provide equal rights to marry, but states still vary a great deal in terms of antidiscrimination laws based on sexual orientation. Without national laws, there will continue to be large differences in the levels of protection against discrimination based on age, disability, and sexual orientation. More generally, insofar as we give power to states, we create a situation whereby individuals' rights, as well as the benefits they are entitled to, depend on which state they happen to live in.

Competitive federalism can also create a "race to the bottom" as states attempt to lure businesses by keeping taxes and social spending low. This can place an unfair burden on states that take a more generous position toward the poor or provide services (low college tuition, for example) that others do not.

Finally, state and local governments might be unable to coordinate their response to truly national problems such as climate change. To return to the issues raised at the beginning of the chapter, if holding global temperature increases to a tolerable level requires fuel economy standards such as those established by California, it does little good if only some states adopt these changes while others refuse. Action at the national level is the only way to ensure universal compliance.

Thus, overall, there is no clear "winner" in determining the appropriate balance of national and state power in our nation today. The advantages and disadvantages of our federal system ensure that federalism will always remain a central source of conflict in the policy-making process as the various levels of government fight it out.

Government that is closer to the people can encourage participation in the political process and may be more responsive to local needs. These protesters in Kentucky, for example, are letting the governor know their feelings on a teacher pension overhaul.

Why is it important to understand federalism today? More than at any time in U.S. history, the question of which branch of government has power over a particular policy is up for grabs. This change gives elected officials new opportunities to influence policy—rather than changing the policy itself, they can influence decisions about which level of government implements the policy.

"Why Should I Care?"

Unpacking the Conflict

Considering all that we've discussed in this chapter, let's apply what we know about how federalism works to the example of competing federal and state-level automobile standards from the beginning of the chapter. When local and federal officials disagree about fuel economy standards and global warming, who wins? How can we explain this conflict, or conflicts between federal and state authorities over other policies?

As we have seen, one issue is that even after 230 years, the boundaries between federal authority and state authority are not always clear, particularly given the rise of cooperative federalism and the use of unfunded mandates. In other areas, such as laws governing the legality of marijuana, federal authority and state authority are genuinely overlapping. Thus, at least some of the time, the question of whether the federal government can tell states what to do (or whether states have the right to ignore federal directives) has no clear answer. In these situations, politicians' (or citizens') judgments about federalism probably reflect their ideas about which level of government is more likely to give them an outcome they want.

In other policy areas, the lines of authority between federal and state governments are relatively clear, but federalism can be justified as a way to deliver policies more effectively or efficiently. Like many other regulatory initiatives over the last generation, the Clean Air Act was designed with the idea that some states and communities would implement policies that deviated from federal standards—and that allowing such flexibility would ensure consideration of local needs or conditions. However, nothing in the Constitution mandates that the federal government allow local discretion. You can disagree on policy grounds with the Trump administration's revocation of California's fuel economy waiver, but the decision itself is entirely consistent with how the courts have interpreted the federal government's regulatory powers.

The fight over fuel economy standards also highlights the idea that Americans are citizens of several levels of government simultaneously. Martha Derthick, a leading scholar of American federalism, says that the basic question of federalism involves choices about how many communities we will be.[20] If you asked most people in our nation about their primary geopolitical community, they would probably not say, "I am a Montanan" or "I am an Arizonan." Most people would likely say, "I am an American." Yet we have strong attachments to our local communities and state identities. We are members of multiple communities and subject to several different sets of overlapping laws, a fact that has had an indelible impact on our political system and the policy choices that affect our everyday life.

"What's Your Take?"

Should the federal government be able to force states to comply with national auto fuel efficiency standards?

Or should state and local officials be able to conduct their business without federal interference?

STUDY GUIDE

What is federalism and why does it matter?

Define *federalism* and explain its significance.
(Pages 68–72)

Summary

A federal system simultaneously allocates power to both the state and federal governments, whereas a confederal system gives power only to the states, and a unitary government gives power only to the federal government.

Key terms

federalism (p. 68)   **concurrent powers** (p. 70)

sovereign power (p. 68)   **unitary government** (p. 72)

exclusive powers (p. 69)   **confederal government** (p. 72)

police powers (p. 70)

Practice Quiz Questions

1. **What system of government did the Articles of Confederation establish?**

a   unitary

b   federal

c   confederal

d   monarchy

e   dictatorship

2. **Which is an example of a concurrent power?**

a   printing money

b   building roads

c   conducting elections

d   declaring war

e   establishing post offices

Balancing national and state power in the Constitution

Explain what the Constitution says about federalism.
(Pages 72–74)

Summary

Although the state governments have considerable power in our system, the Founders disproportionately favored the federal government in the Constitution, so that the federal government's interests superseded those of the states in the event of a conflict.

Key terms

full faith and credit   **privileges and immunities**
  clause (p. 74)   **clause** (p. 74)

Practice Quiz Questions

3. **States' rights are protected in which constitutional provisions?**

a   the Ninth Amendment

b   the Tenth Amendment

c   Article I of the Constitution

d   Article III of the Constitution

e   the First Amendment

4. **Which of the following would be best explained by the Tenth Amendment?**

a   Congress increasing the minimum wage to $10 an hour

b   the California state legislature declaring it was going to create its own navy

c   state and local control over education policy

d   the Supreme Court's recent decisions in same-sex marriage cases

e   the Environmental Protection Agency passing a new regulation on carbon emissions that applies to all 50 states

The evolving concept of federalism

Trace the major shifts in state and federal government power over time. (Pages 74–80)

Summary

The relationship between the state and federal governments has changed dramatically over time. Whereas the federal and state governments traditionally operated with little interaction under the era of dual federalism, the trend over the past 80 years has been one of increasing federal interaction with state governments to address particular policy areas.

Key terms

dual federalism (p. 75)   **cooperative federalism** (p. 80)

states' rights (p. 78)   **picket fence federalism** (p. 80)

Practice Quiz Questions

5. Which analogy best describes the federalism arrangement today?

a   layer cake federalism

b   marble cake federalism

c   picket fence federalism

d   gumbo federalism

e   dual federalism

6. Which case bolstered the federal government's power over the states?

a   *Barron v. Baltimore*

b   *McCulloch v. Maryland*

c   *Dred Scott v. Sandford*

d   *Mapp v. Ohio*

e   *Shelby County v. Holder*

7. When did the federal government begin cooperating with the states on policy goals?

a   1890s

b   1930s

c   1950s

d   1970s

e   1990s

Federalism today

Describe the major trends and debates in federalism today. (Pages 81–93)

Summary

Today's federal structure offers a complex mix of all previous components of federalism: some elements of national supremacy combine with states' rights for a varied federal landscape. Although the federal and state governments still exercise cooperative federalism to achieve joint policy goals, the federal government has also utilized coercive federalism to impose federal priorities on the states without offering compensation. However, in several recent cases the Supreme Court has ruled in favor of the states, limiting federal power.

Key terms

fiscal federalism (p. 81)

coercive federalism (p. 81)

federal preemption (p. 81)

unfunded mandates (p. 81)

categorical grants (p. 81)

block grants (p. 81)

competitive federalism (p. 87)

remedial legislation (p. 88)

Practice Quiz Questions

8. Which form of grants is given to the states by the federal government with explicit conditions on how funds are to be allocated?

a   block grant

b   categorical grant

c   general revenue sharing

d   federal mandates

e   tax refund

9. Recent moves in Congress to increase state power over public policy generally increase usage of _____ .

a   block grants

b   categorical grants

c   federal taxes

d   federal mandates

e   state taxes

10. The imposition of national priorities on the states through congressional legislation and imposition of the national supremacy clause is called _____ .

a   cooperative federalism

b   dual federalism

c   competitive federalism

d   federal preemption

e   remedial legislation

11. A state would usually challenge the constitutionality of a federal law under which of the following amendments?

a   Eighth Amendment

b   Tenth Amendment

c   Thirteenth Amendment

d   Fourteenth Amendment

e   First Amendment

12. The Court has recently overturned a number of congressional laws rooted in the _____ .

a   national supremacy clause

b   reserve clause

c   establishment clause

d   commerce clause

e   free exercise clause

Suggested Reading

Banks, Christopher P., and John C. Blakeman. *The U.S. Supreme Court and New Federalism: From the Rehnquist to the Roberts Court*. Lanhan, MD: Rowman & Littlefield, 2012.

Bednar, Jenna. *The Robust Federation: Principles of Design*. New York: Cambridge University Press, 2009.

Chomsky, Aviva. *Undocumented: How Immigration Became Illegal*. New York: Beacon Press, 2014.

Conlan, Timothy. *From New Federalism to Devolution: Twenty-Five Years of Intergovernmental Reform*. Washington, DC: Brookings Institution, 1998.

Derthick, Martha. *Keeping the Compound Republic: Essays on American Federalism*. Washington, DC: Brookings Institution, 2001.

Elkins, Stanley, and Eric McKitrick. *The Age of Federalism: The Early American Republic, 1788–1800*. New York: Oxford University Press, 1993.

LaCroix, Alison L. *The Ideological Origins of American Federalism*. Cambridge, MA: Harvard University Press, 2010.

Manna, Paul. *School's In: Federalism and the National Education Agenda*. Washington, DC: Georgetown University Press, 2006.

Ostrom, Elinor. *Governing the Commons: The Evolution of Institutions for Collective Action*, 2nd ed. New York: Cambridge University Press, 2015.

Peterson, Paul E. *The Price of Federalism*. Washington, DC: Brookings Institution, 1995.

Posner, Paul L. *The Politics of Unfunded Mandates: Whither Federalism?* Washington, DC: Georgetown University Press, 1998.

Scheberle, Denise. *Federalism and Environmental Policy: Trust and the Politics of Implementation*, 2nd ed. Washington, DC: Georgetown University Press, 2004.

4

Civil Liberties

It's a free country ... right?

 "Under the guise of 'speech codes' and 'safe spaces' and 'trigger warnings,' these universities have tried to restrict free thought, impose total conformity, and shut down the voices of great young Americans.... All of that changes starting right now."[1]
President Donald Trump

"If I were president of a university and I had some hate speech person coming, I wouldn't let them come. I just wouldn't."[2]
John Kasich, former Ohio governor

Should controversial figures like Milo Yiannopoulos be allowed to speak on public college campuses in the face of popular opposition to their views? In February 2017, Berkeley students organized protests in response to a planned appearance by Yiannopoulos. Although the speech was eventually canceled, that didn't stop protests from getting violent. Students and supporters of Yiannopoulos clashed on campus.

The constitutional protection for speech is clear and strong: "Congress shall make no law ... abridging the freedom of speech." However, recent protests against controversial speakers booked to speak on college campuses are calling into question the scope of those protections. Must college campuses allow talks by right-wing provocateur Milo Yiannopoulos, who has said child sexual abuse "really is not that big of a deal," or White nationalist Richard Spencer, who has called for a White ethno-state?[3] Must they embrace conservative speakers like political commentator Ann Coulter and economist Charles Murray? All of these speakers met strong and sometimes violent protests at campuses around the country.[4] A CNN headline described the situation as "War on Campus."[5] A speech by Richard Spencer at the University of Florida caused Governor Rick Scott to declare a state of emergency, and the university had to spend nearly $600,000 to provide security for the event. Despite these efforts, three men shouting "Heil Hitler" fired a shot at students demonstrating against Spencer's speech (but nobody was hurt).[6]

Many are calling for limits on the kind of hate speech that some claim speakers like Yiannopoulos and Spencer promote and for the creation of "safe spaces" on campus where students would be protected from hurtful speech within a broader effort to promote social justice. Others see such efforts as "political correctness" run amok and are concerned that free speech is under attack as conservative speakers are prevented from talking. When announcing his executive order on free speech on campus President Trump said, "We will not stand idly by and allow public institutions to violate their students' constitutional rights. If a college or university doesn't allow you to speak, we will not give them money."[7]

The controversy over free speech on campus does not divide neatly along partisan or ideological lines. While strongly disagreeing with the conservative speakers' views, recently President Obama has expressed support for the free speech side, saying college students shouldn't be "coddled and protected from different points of view.... Feel free to disagree with somebody, but don't try to shut them up."[8] The left-leaning American Civil Liberties Union has also defended free speech on campus, arguing, "Speech that deeply offends our morality or is hostile to our way of life warrants the same constitutional protection as other speech because the right of free speech is indivisible: when we grant the government the power to suppress controversial ideas, we are all subject to censorship by the state."[9]

Some have argued that the controversy is overblown, pointing to evidence that there is more support for the First Amendment on college campuses than in the public at large[10] and that the number of disinvited conservative speakers is down from a high of 24 in 2016 to 5 in 2019.[11] However, others argue that the swastikas and nooses, historically symbols of hate and aggression, that have recently been portrayed on campuses, are not free speech and that the real question is where to draw the line.

Defining the boundaries of our liberties and freedoms, like freedom of speech, is messy and complicated. Can controversial speech on college campuses be limited? When we say America is a free country, what does this really mean? Are there limits to those freedoms? If so, how should political actors draw the lines between protected behavior and actions that may be regulated?

DEFINE *CIVIL LIBERTIES* AND EXPLAIN HOW THE BILL OF RIGHTS CAME TO APPLY TO THE STATES

civil liberties
Constitutionally established guarantees and freedoms that protect citizens, opinions, and property against arbitrary government interference.

Defining civil liberties

The terms "civil rights" and "civil liberties" are often used interchangeably, but there are some important differences (see Nuts & Bolts 4.1). To oversimplify a bit, **civil liberties** are about freedom and civil rights are about equality. (For more on this distinction, see Chapter 5.)

Civil liberties are deeply rooted in our key idea that politics is conflictual and that it involves trade-offs. When the Supreme Court rules on civil liberties cases, it must balance an individual's freedom with the government's interests and the public good. For example, in the war on terrorism the government must balance civil liberties with national security. Many Americans have been concerned that government surveillance invades people's privacy and that the treatment of suspected terrorists violates due process rights.[12] At the same time, most Americans would probably agree that in some instances these measures might be warranted. For example, if a nuclear device were set to detonate in Manhattan in three hours, few would insist on protecting the civil liberties of someone who knew where the bomb was hidden. Once we recognize that our freedoms are not absolute, it becomes a question of how they are balanced against other interests, such as national security, public safety, and public health.

Along with balancing competing interests, court rulings must also draw the lines to define the limits of permissible conduct by the government or by an individual in the context of a specific civil liberty. For example, despite the First Amendment's protection of freedom of speech, it is obvious that some speech absolutely cannot be permitted. The classic example is falsely yelling "fire!" in a crowded theater. Therefore, the courts must interpret the law to draw the line between protected speech and impermissible speech. The same challenge applies to other civil liberties such as the establishment of religion, freedom of the press, freedom from illegal searches, or other due process rights (see How It Works: The First Amendment).

Distinguishing Civil Liberties from Civil Rights

Civil Liberties	Civil Rights
Basic freedoms and liberties	Protection from discrimination
Rooted in the Bill of Rights and the "due process" protection of the Fourteenth Amendment	Rooted in laws and the "equal protection" clause of the Fourteenth Amendment
Primarily restrict what the government can do to you ("*Congress* shall make no law . . . abridging the freedom of speech")	Protect you from discrimination both by the government and by individuals

Source: Compiled by the authors.

"Why Should I Care?" One easy way to remember the difference between the two is that civil liberties are about freedom and civil rights concern equality. Also, civil liberties *limit* the actions government can take against you, while civil rights *expand* the actions that you can take as a citizen while also protecting you from discrimination from the government and other citizens.

Courts define the boundaries of civil liberties, but the other branches of government and the public often get involved as well. The earliest debates during the American Founding illustrate the broad public involvement concerning the basic questions of how our civil liberties would be defined: Should government be limited by an explicit statement of individual liberties? Would these limitations apply to the state governments or just the national government? How should these freedoms evolve as our society changes? As we will see in this section, interpretations of these constitutional protections have changed over time.

Origins of the Bill of Rights

Originally, the Constitution provided very limited protection of civil liberties: it guaranteed habeas corpus rights (a protection against illegal incarceration) and prohibited bills of attainder (legislation punishing someone for a crime without the benefit of a trial) and ex post facto laws (laws that retroactively change the legal consequences of some behavior). Delegates to the Constitutional Convention made a few attempts to include a broader statement of civil liberties, including one proposed by George Mason and Elbridge Gerry five days before the convention adjourned. But their motion to appoint a committee to draft a bill of rights was rejected. Charles Pinckney and Gerry also tried to add a provision protecting the freedom of the press, but that too was rejected.[13]

Mason and Gerry opposed ratification of the Constitution partly because it did not include a bill of rights, and many Antifederalists echoed this view, including in the

The First Amendment

Freedom of Expression

Freedom of Religion

The First Amendment states:
"Congress shall make no law respecting an establishment of religion, or prohibiting the free exercise thereof; or abridging the freedom of speech, or of the press; or the right of the people peaceably to assemble, and to petition the government for a redress of grievances."

Freedom of Assembly

Freedom to Petition the Government

Freedom of the Press

Freedom of Speech

@user
!!!!!!
Less-protected forms of speech

Political speech and symbolic speech

Establishment
The government cannot establish an official state religion or favor one religion over others.

Free Exercise
The government cannot prevent people from practicing their religion.

Balancing Interests and Drawing Lines: Government and Religion

While the different branches of the First Amendment on the opposite page are an accurate representation of the various aspects of our religious and expressive freedoms, in practice, the implementation of these civil liberties is more complicated.

Free Exercise:

When they refused...

When Masterpiece Cakeshop **refused to make a wedding cake** for a same-sex couple...

They said...

The baker didn't have to bake the cake... for now (postponing a decision on the broader question).

Here's why.

In cases like these, **courts must balance religious freedom against other state interests**, such as freedom from discrimination.

Establishment Clause:

Banned.

Since 1962 the Supreme Court has **banned school prayer as a violation of the establishment clause**.

What about...?

But does the separation of church and state also apply to town board members who **start their meetings with a prayer**? In 2014, the Court decided by a 5–4 vote that it did not.

It's tough.

The establishment clause often asks courts to **draw lines between what type of religious conduct is allowed** and what would be considered an "excessive entanglement" between church and state.

❓ Critical Thinking

1. **Balancing interests can be tricky**. Consider these two scenarios in which competing interests are in play: Company policy restricts employees from wearing political T-shirts or buttons at work. A pharmacist denies birth control pills to a customer for religious reasons. Which (if either) do you think should be allowed? Why did you select the one(s) you did?

2. **Drawing lines for a given civil liberty** can also be difficult. What if a high school football coach knelt in a private prayer on the field after a game? Should that be allowed? Or, consider a different scenario: Should Congress be able to start its sessions with a prayer? Reference the First Amendment and its interpretations in your answer.

In some cases, the free exercise and establishment clauses are in tension with one another. For example, while the establishment clause prohibits school-sponsored prayer, the free exercise clause guarantees that any student can pray at any time in school on his or her own, **as long as he or she is not bothering others**.

influential Brutus essays, which were written to encourage New Yorkers to reject the Constitution (see especially Brutus 1). Some states ratified the Constitution but urged Congress to draft specific protections for individuals' and states' rights from federal action. (They believed that protection of civil liberties from state actions should reside in state constitutions.) In other states, the Antifederalists who lost the ratification battle continued making their case to the public and Congress.

Madison and other supporters of the Constitution agreed that the 1st Congress would take up the issue, despite their reservations that a Bill of Rights could lead the people into falsely believing that it was an exhaustive list of all their rights. State conventions submitted 124 amendments for consideration. That list was whittled down to 17 by the House and then to 12 by the Senate. This even dozen was approved by the House and sent to the states, which in 1791 ratified the 10 amendments that became the Bill of Rights (see Nuts & Bolts 4.2).[14]

NUTS & BOLTS 4.2

The Bill of Rights: A Statement of Our Civil Liberties

First Amendment	Freedom of religion, speech, press, and assembly; the separation of church and state; and the right to petition the government.
Second Amendment	Right to bear arms.
Third Amendment	Protection against the forced quartering of troops in one's home.
Fourth Amendment	Protection from unreasonable searches and seizures; "probable cause" is required for search warrants, which must specifically describe the "place to be searched, and the persons or things to be seized."
Fifth Amendment	Protection from forced self-incrimination or double jeopardy (being tried twice for the same crime); no person can be deprived of life, liberty, or property without due process of law; private property cannot be taken for public use without just compensation; and no person can be tried for a serious crime without the indictment of a grand jury.
Sixth Amendment	Right of the accused to a speedy and public trial by an impartial jury, to an attorney, to confront witnesses, to a compulsory process for obtaining witnesses in his or her favor, and to counsel in all felony cases.
Seventh Amendment	Right to a trial by jury in civil cases involving common law.
Eighth Amendment	Protection from excessive bail, excessive fines, and cruel and unusual punishment.
Ninth Amendment	The enumeration of specific rights in the Constitution shall not be construed to deny other rights retained by the people. This has been interpreted to include a general right to privacy and other fundamental rights.
Tenth Amendment	Powers not delegated by the Constitution to the national government, nor prohibited by it to the states, are reserved to the states or to the people.

Source: Compiled by the authors.

"Why Should I Care?"

Many of the rights and liberties Americans think of as core American values weren't originally outlined in the Constitution. These first 10 amendments, outlined in the Bill of Rights, affect your daily life: you can practice the religion you choose, you can express your opinions on government actions, and you can choose to carry a gun. Additionally, if you are accused of a crime, the Bill of Rights guarantees your right to a trial by jury and various due process rights.

Despite the document's profound significance, one point limited its reach: it applied only to the laws and actions of the national government and not to those of the states. This decision proved consequential because the national government was quite weak for the first half of our nation's history. Because states exercised at least as much power over people's lives as the national government did, it would have been more important for the Bill of Rights to limit the states than to limit the federal government. The Supreme Court used the Bill of Rights only once before 1866 to invalidate a federal action—in the infamous *Dred Scott* case that contributed to the Civil War (see Chapter 3).

Selective incorporation and the Fourteenth Amendment

The significance of the Bill of Rights increased somewhat with ratification of the Fourteenth Amendment in 1868. It was one of the three **Civil War amendments** that attempted to guarantee the newly freed, formerly enslaved people equal rights as citizens of the United States. (The other two Civil War amendments were the Thirteenth, which abolished slavery, and the Fifteenth, which gave formerly enslaved men the right to vote.) Northern politicians were concerned that southerners would deny basic rights to the formerly enslaved people, so the sweeping language of the Fourteenth Amendment was adopted. Section 1 of the Fourteenth Amendment says:

All persons born or naturalized in the United States, and subject to the jurisdiction thereof, are citizens of the United States and of the State wherein they reside. No State shall make or enforce any law which shall abridge the privileges or immunities of citizens of the United States; nor shall any State deprive any person of life, liberty, or property, without due process of law; nor deny to any person within its jurisdiction the equal protection of the laws.

This language sought to ensure that states would not deny newly freed people the full protection of the law.[15] The **due process clause**, which forbids any state from denying "life, liberty, or property, without due process of law," led to an especially important expansion of civil liberties because the Supreme Court had previously interpreted a similar clause in the Fifth Amendment to apply only to the federal government.

Despite the amendment's clear statement that "no State shall make or enforce any law," in the Supreme Court's first opportunity to interpret the Fourteenth Amendment in 1873 it continued to rule in favor of protecting states from national government actions only, embracing the "dual citizenship" idea set forth in *Barron v. Baltimore*.[16] Over the next 50 years, a few justices tried mightily to interpret the Fourteenth Amendment to protect civil liberties against state government action, culminating in the 1925 case *Gitlow v. New York*.[17] Here the Court said for the first time that the Fourteenth Amendment incorporated one of the amendments in the Bill of Rights and applied it to the states. The case involved Benjamin Gitlow, a radical socialist convicted under New York's Criminal Anarchy Act of 1902 for advocating the overthrow of the government. The Court upheld his conviction, arguing that his writings were the "language of direct incitement," but it also warned state governments that there were limits on such suppression of speech.

Over the ensuing decades, most civil liberties covered in the Bill of Rights were applied to the states on a right-by-right, case-by-case basis through the Fourteenth Amendment. However, this process of **selective incorporation** was not smooth and incremental. Rather, it progressed in surges with flurries of activity in the 1930s and the 1960s (see Table 4.1). As a result, the Bill of Rights has evolved from a narrow range of protections for people from national government actions during the early nineteenth century to a robust set of protections for freedom and liberty that limit national, state, and local government actions today.

Civil War amendments
The Thirteenth, Fourteenth, and Fifteenth Amendments to the Constitution, which abolished slavery and granted civil liberties and voting rights to newly freed people after the Civil War.

due process clause
Part of the Fourteenth Amendment that forbids states from denying "life, liberty, or property" to any person without due process of law. (A nearly identical clause in the Fifth Amendment applies only to the national government.)

selective incorporation
The process through which most of the civil liberties granted in the Bill of Rights were applied to the states on a case-by-case basis through the Fourteenth Amendment.

TABLE 4.1

Selective Incorporation

The process of applying most of the Bill of Rights to the states progressed in two stages. The first, coming in the 1920s and 1930s, applied the First Amendment to the states; the second came a few decades later and involved criminal defendants' rights.

Amendment	Issue	Case
First Amendment	Freedom of speech	*Gitlow v. New York* (1925)
	Freedom of the press	*Near v. Minnesota* (1931)
	Freedom of assembly	*De Jonge v. Oregon* (1937)
	Right to petition the government	*Hague v. CIO* (1939)
	Free exercise of religion	*Hamilton v. Regents of the University of California* (1934); *Cantwell v. Connecticut* (1940)
	Separation of church and state	*Everson v. Board of Education of Ewing Township* (1947)
Second Amendment	Right to bear arms	*McDonald v. Chicago* (2010)
Fourth Amendment	Protection from unreasonable search and seizure	*Wolf v. Colorado* (1949); *Mapp v. Ohio* (1961)*
Fifth Amendment	Protection from forced self-incrimination	*Malloy v. Hogan* (1964)
	Protection from double jeopardy	*Benton v. Maryland* (1969)
Sixth Amendment	Right to a public trial	*In re Oliver* 333 U.S. 257 (1948)
	Right to a fair trial and an attorney in death-penalty cases	*Powell v. Alabama* (1932)
	Right to an attorney in all felony cases	*Gideon v. Wainwright* (1963)
	Right to an attorney in cases involving jail time	*Argersinger v. Hamlin* (1972)
	Right to a jury trial in a criminal case	*Duncan v. Louisiana* (1968)
	Right to cross-examine a witness	*Pointer v. Texas* (1965)
	Right to compel the testimony of witnesses who are vital for the defendant's case	*Washington v. Texas* (1967)
	Right to a unanimous jury verdict	*Ramos v. Louisiana* (2020)
Eighth Amendment	Protection from cruel and unusual punishment	*Robinson v. California* (1962)†
	Protection from excessive bail	*Schilb v. Kuebel* (1971)‡
	Protection from excessive fines	*Timbs v. Indiana* (2019)
Ninth Amendment	Right to privacy and other nonenumerated, fundamental rights	*Griswold v. Connecticut* (1965)§

Not Incorporated

Third Amendment	Prohibition against the quartering of troops in private homes	
Fifth Amendment	Right to indictment by a grand jury	
Seventh Amendment	Right to a jury trial in a civil case	

* *Wolf v. Colorado* applied the Fourth Amendment to the states (which meant that states could not engage in unreasonable searches and seizures); *Mapp v. Ohio* applied the exclusionary rule to the states (which excludes the use in a trial of illegally obtained evidence).

† Some sources list *Louisiana ex rel. Francis v. Resweber* (1947) as the first case that incorporated the Eighth Amendment. While the decision mentioned the Fifth and Eighth Amendments in the context of the due process clause of the Fourteenth Amendment, this argument was not included in the majority opinion that upheld as constitutional the bizarre double electrocution of prisoner Willie Francis (the electric chair malfunctioned on the first attempt but was successful on the second attempt; see Henry J. Abraham and Barbara A. Perry, *Freedom and the Court: Civil Rights and Civil Liberties in the United States*, 8th ed. [Lawrence: University Press of Kansas, 2003], pp. 71–72).

‡ Justice Blackmun "assumed" in this case that "the Eighth Amendment's proscription of excessive bail [applies] to the states through the Fourteenth Amendment," but later decisions did not seem to share this view. However, Justices Stevens and O'Connor agreed with Blackmun's view in *Browning-Ferris v. Kelco Disposal* (1989). Some sources argue that the excessive bail clause of the Eighth Amendment is unincorporated.

§ Justice Goldberg argued for explicit incorporation of the Ninth Amendment in a concurring opinion joined by Justices Warren and Brennan. The opinion of the Court referred more generally to a privacy right rooted in five amendments, including the Ninth, but did not explicitly argue for incorporation.

Source: Compiled by the authors.

Today the Bill of Rights is one of the most revered and important parts of the Constitution. But it didn't start out that way. Initially, the Bill of Rights applied to only the national government, not the states. But through the Fourteenth Amendment and the process of selective incorporation, the Supreme Court has gradually applied most of the Bill of Rights to the states. While all levels of government must respect our civil liberties today, there are many unresolved areas in terms of balancing interests and drawing lines. The next time you feel strongly about an issue concerning civil liberties, take some time to consider the other side—these questions are often not as black-and-white as they seem. Should speakers who hold extreme, even racist, views be allowed to speak on campus? How do we balance our freedom of speech or freedom from illegal searches with the need for national security?

"Why Should I Care?"

Freedom of religion

The First Amendment has two parts that deal with religion: the **establishment clause**, which has been interpreted to mean that Congress cannot sponsor or endorse any particular religion, and the **free exercise clause**, which has been interpreted to mean that Congress cannot interfere in the practice of religion unless there are important secular reasons for doing so. Essentially, the former says that Congress should not *help* religion and the latter that it should not *hurt* religion. The establishment clause is primarily concerned with drawing lines. For example, does a prayer at a public high school football game or a Nativity scene on government property constitute state sponsorship of religion? The free exercise clause has more to do with balancing interests, such as balancing public safety concerns against snake handling in religious services and the use of Amish buggies on public highways.

The combination of the establishment and free exercise clauses results in a general policy of noninterference and government neutrality toward religion. As Thomas Jefferson said in 1802, the First Amendment provides a "wall of eternal separation between church and state." This language continues to be cited in Court cases in which religion and politics intersect.[18] Since both areas carry great moral weight and emotional charge, the boundaries of religious expression remain difficult to draw.

The establishment clause and separation of church and state

Determining the boundaries between church and state—the central issue of the establishment clause—is very difficult. We know that the Founders did not want an official state religion and did not want the government to favor one religion over another, but beyond that it's hard to say. Jefferson's "wall of eternal separation" has been cited in Court decisions that prohibit state aid for religious activities, but lately the Court has been displaying a more "accommodationist" perspective that sometimes allows religious activity in public institutions.

Public Prayer The issue of prohibition of prayer in public schools exploded onto the political scene in 1962 when the Court ruled in *Engel v. Vitale* that a prayer written by the New York State Board of Regents and read every day in the state's public schools

DESCRIBE THE FIRST AMENDMENT LIBERTIES RELATED TO FREEDOM OF RELIGION

establishment clause
Part of the First Amendment that states, "Congress shall make no law respecting an establishment of religion," which has been interpreted to mean that Congress cannot sponsor or favor any religion.

free exercise clause
Part of the First Amendment that states that Congress cannot prohibit or interfere with the practice of religion unless there are important secular reasons for doing so.

The number, the industry, and the morality of the Priesthood, & the devotion of the people have been manifestly increased by the total separation of the Church from the State.

—President James Madison

How can conflicts be resolved between civil liberties and other legitimate interests, such as public safety and public health? Sometimes freedom is forced to give way. Courts have upheld bans on the religious practice of snake handling (though several churches have been undeterred by these bans) and laws requiring the Amish to display reflective triangles when driving slow-moving buggies on public roads, despite religious objections to doing so.

Lemon test
The Supreme Court uses this test, established in *Lemon v. Kurtzman*, to determine whether a practice violates the First Amendment's establishment clause.

violated the establishment clause and the separation of church and state.[19] Banning the prayer caused a public outcry protesting the perceived attack on religion.

Over the next 50 years, Congress repeatedly tried, unsuccessfully, to amend the Constitution to allow school prayer. Meanwhile, the Court continued to take a hard line on school-sponsored prayer. In 1985, the Court struck down the practice of observing a one-minute moment of silence for "meditation or voluntary prayer" in the Alabama public schools, showing that it isn't the *words* of the prayer that are the problem, but the idea of prayer itself.[20] More recently, the Court said that benedictions or prayers at public school graduations and a school policy that allowed an elected student representative to lead a prayer at a high school football game also violated the establishment clause. The former established a strong "coercion test" that prohibited prayers that may appear to be voluntary (students are not required to attend their high school graduation) but in effect are compulsory.[21] Yet the Court has upheld the practice of opening every session of Congress with a prayer, has let stand without comment a lower-court ruling that allowed a prayer that was planned and led by students (rather than recited as school policy) at a high school graduation, and in 2014 upheld prayers by voluntary chaplains for town board meetings in Greece, New York.[22] The latter case was especially significant because the legislative prayers were offered at town meetings that included residents, unlike the previously approved prayers that were intended for the elected leaders only.[23]

Aid to Religious Organizations and Religious Symbols The Court has had an even more difficult time determining principles to govern government aid to religious organizations, either directly, through tax dollars, or indirectly, through the use of public space for religious symbols. One early attempt was known as the **Lemon test**, after one of the parties in a 1971 case involving government support for religious schools (*Lemon v. Kurtzman*). Here the justices ruled that a practice violated the establishment clause if it (1) did not have a "secular legislative purpose," (2) either advanced or inhibited religion, or (3) fostered "an excessive government entanglement with religion."[24] The third part of the test was later found open to interpretation by lower courts and therefore led to conflicting rulings.

The Court started to move away from the Lemon test in a 1984 case involving a city-owned crèche that was displayed in a park owned by a nonprofit corporation. The Court allowed the Nativity display, saying: "The Constitution does not require complete separation of church and state; it affirmatively mandates accommodation, not merely tolerance, of all religions, and forbids hostility toward any.[25] This "endorsement test" simply says that government action is unconstitutional if a "reasonable observer" would think that the action either endorses or disapproves of religion. Later rulings upheld similar religious displays, especially if they conformed to what observers have labeled the "three plastic animals rule"—if the baby Jesus is surrounded by Rudolph the red-nosed reindeer and other secular symbols, the overall display is considered sufficiently nonreligious to pass constitutional muster.[26]

More recently, in a 2019 case the Court upheld the American Legion's right to display a 40-foot cross at a World War I memorial on state property in Bladensburg, Maryland, saying that Lemon should not apply in cases that "involve the use, for ceremonial, celebratory, or commemorative purposes, of words or symbols with religious associations." Instead, the Court ruled, "The cross is undoubtedly a Christian symbol, but that fact should not blind us to everything else that the Bladensburg Cross has come to represent.... [D]estroying or defacing the Cross that has stood undisturbed for nearly a century would not be neutral and would not further the ideals of respect and tolerance embodied in the First Amendment."[27] Three justices wanted to completely overturn Lemon; Justice Gorsuch called it a "dog's breakfast"—a confusing mess. But it still has application to direct government support for religious schools.

In cases involving funding for religious schools, the Court has applied the accommodationist perspective by looking more favorably on providing tax dollars to students' families to subsidize tuition costs at religious schools than on funding parochial schools directly. In 2011, the Court expanded taxpayer support for religious education when it upheld an Arizona law that provides state tax credits for contributions to organizations that provide tuition for religious schools.[28] The Court has also ruled that it is acceptable to use federal funds to buy computers and other educational equipment to be used in public and private schools for "secular, neutral, and nonideological programs"[29] and tax dollars for a sign language interpreter for a deaf student who attended a parochial school.[30]

In a landmark 2020 decision, *Espinoza v. Montana Department of Revenue*, the Supreme Court ruled 5–4 that under the free exercise clause, a state could not prevent the use of state-based, publicly-funded scholarship funds meant for private school tuition from being applied toward religious school tuition. The case was brought by Montana parents who qualified for these income-based scholarships, and whose children attended a Christian school. They were informed that the scholarship funds could not be applied toward the religious school tuition because of a Montana state rule barring the use of "any direct or indirect appropriations or payment" to any religious organizations or schools affiliated with religious organizations. The case went to the Montana Supreme Court, which in 2018 found the entire scholarship program unconstitutional, as it unfairly benefited religious schools. As a result, the public scholarship program was terminated, so the parents appealed to the U.S. Supreme Court. In the majority opinion, Chief Justice Roberts wrote that the program violated the free exercise clause, as it "bars religious schools from public benefits solely because of the religious character of the schools" and "also bars parents who wish to send their children to a religious school from those same benefits, again solely because of the religious character of the school."[31]

The free exercise clause

While the freedom of belief is absolute, freedom of religious conduct cannot be unrestricted. That is, you can believe whatever you want without government interference, but if you *act* on those beliefs, the government may regulate your behavior.

Can a cross be displayed on federal land? This 40-foot cross in Bladensburg, Maryland, is on state property, but serves as a World War I memorial. The Court allowed it to remain in place, stating that though the cross is a Christian symbol, removing the Bladensburg Cross would be a disservice to all that it has come to represent.

And while the government has restricted religious conduct in dozens of cases, the freedom of religion has been among the most consistently protected civil liberties.

Hundreds of cases have come before the Court in the area of the free exercise of religion. Here are some examples of the questions they addressed:[32] May Amish parents be forced to send their children to schools beyond the eighth grade? (No, as established in *Wisconsin v. Yoder* in 1972.) Is animal sacrifice as part of a religious ceremony protected by the First Amendment? (Generally yes.) May Mormons have multiple wives? (No.) Does the First Amendment protect distribution of religious leaflets on public streets? And religious meetings in public parks? (Yes, for both, but the latter is subject to "time, manner, and place" restrictions.) May people be forced to work on Friday night and Saturday if those are their days of worship? (No.) May religious dress be regulated? (Generally not, but in some contexts, such as the military, yes.) Keep in mind that this list is not exhaustive.

One particular case, brought by plaintiffs who had been fired for using peyote as part of a religious ceremony and then denied unemployment benefits because they had broken the law, had broad implications that defined the general basis for government restrictions of religious expression. The Court ultimately ruled that the state of Oregon had not violated the free exercise clause in denying the plaintiffs unemployment benefits. More significantly, with this ruling the Court announced a new interpretation of the free exercise clause: the government does not need a "compelling interest" in regulating a particular behavior to justify a law that limits a religious practice; it only needs a demonstration that the law in question was a "neutral law of general applicability."[33] In other words, after this decision it would be easier for the government to limit the exercise of religion because the Court would no longer require a "compelling" reason for the restrictions.

Congress responded by passing the Religious Freedom Restoration Act (RFRA) in 1993, reinstating the need to demonstrate a "compelling state interest" before limiting religious freedoms. After several cases and congressional actions, the Court made it clear that it would have the final word in deciding when a compelling interest is required in order to limit religious practice.[34] The Court relied on this standard in the controversial 2014 case involving the family-owned Hobby Lobby stores, ruling that

Wisconsin v. Yoder
A 1972 case in which the Supreme Court held that compelling Amish students to attend school past the eighth grade violates the free exercise clause. The ruling opened the door to homeschooling, which is a common practice today.

Cake shop owner Jack Phillips did not want to bake a wedding cake for Charlie Craig and David Mullins because it would have violated his religious beliefs. In a narrow ruling that did not settle the broader free exercise question, the Court sided with the baker because he had not been treated fairly by the commission that heard his case.

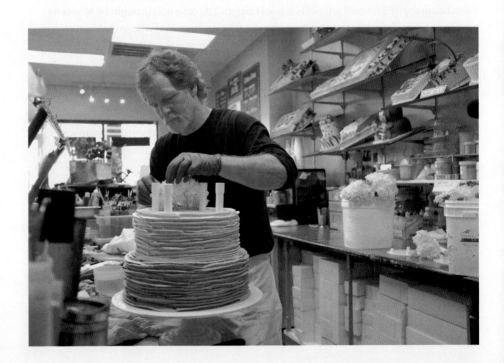

a "closely held" private corporation could not be forced to provide contraception to women under the Affordable Care Act if there was a "less restrictive" means available to have the insurance provide it.[35] This was the first time that a corporation was given First Amendment protections based on the religious beliefs of the owners of the corporation. In 2020, the Court extended the opt-out options to private employers on religious or moral grounds. The Court also expanded religious freedom when it approved, for the first time in 2017, direct government payments to a church in support of a secular purpose (in this case, funds for a playground in a church-run day-care center). The Court ruled that churches should have equal access to state grants made available to fund secular programs.[36]

In a highly anticipated case, the Court was faced with a difficult question concerning the civil rights of a same-sex couple and the religious beliefs of a cake shop owner. The baker had refused to bake a cake for the couple, saying that doing so would violate his religious beliefs. The Court avoided ruling on this central question because the Colorado Civil Rights Commission, which initially heard the case, did not treat religion in a neutral manner and did not give the baker a fair hearing. While concluding that the baker did not have to bake the cake because of the commission's biased behavior, the Court affirmed that the free exercise clause will not provide a basis for such refusals of service when there is not the expression of hostility to religion and that LGBTQ people have the right to "equal access to goods and services under a neutral and generally applicable public accommodations law."[37]

Being familiar with these freedoms and the controversies around them is important because they concern the most deeply personal freedoms debated today. Would you, or do you, send your children to religious schools? Should the government pay for it? If you attend a public college or university, should it be allowed to organize a prayer before a football or basketball game? Should business owners be able to deny equal access to a service (baking a wedding cake) or a public program (health insurance) because of their religious beliefs?

"Why Should I Care?"

DESCRIBE THE MAJOR FIRST AMENDMENT LIBERTIES RELATED TO FREEDOM OF SPEECH

Freedom of speech, assembly, and the press

As noted earlier, defining the scope of our civil liberties depends on balancing interests and drawing lines. This is especially true of the First Amendment's freedom of speech, which can best be envisioned on a continuum from most to least protected types of speech based on the Supreme Court cases that have tested their limits.

Generally protected expression

Any time you attend a religious service or a political rally, post a tweet, write a blog post or letter to the editor, or express a political idea, you are protected by the First Amendment. However, the nature of this protection is continually evolving due to political forces and shifting constitutional interpretations. Only recently have the courts developed a complex continuum ranging from strongly protected political speech to less protected speech.

Standards for Protection The basis for the continuum of protected speech is rooted in the content of the speech. Typically, the Court does not allow content-based regulation of speech (unless it falls into one of the categories of exceptions we discuss later). For example, in 1972 the Court struck down a local ordinance that banned picketing outside schools except for labor picketing.[38] This ordinance was deemed to be content-based regulation because it favored one form of speech (from labor unions) over others. Such regulation is subject to the **strict scrutiny** standard of judicial review, which means the regulation must be narrowly tailored (that is, the least restrictive means) to serve a compelling state interest. In most cases, this means that the speech will be protected and the regulation struck down. If a regulation is "content neutral" and does not favor any given viewpoint, then it is subject to the less demanding **intermediate scrutiny** standard. This means that the government must demonstrate only a substantial interest, the interest must be unrelated to the content of the speech, and there must be alternative opportunities for communication.[39]

Political Speech Freedom of speech got off to a rocky start when Congress passed the Alien and Sedition Acts in 1798. The controversial Sedition Act made it a crime to "write, print, utter or publish . . . any false, scandalous and malicious writing or writings against the government of the United States." Supporters of the acts claimed they were necessary to strengthen the national government in response to the French Revolution, but in reality they were an attempt by the governing Federalist Party to neutralize the opposition—the Democratic-Republican Party. The outcry against the laws helped propel Thomas Jefferson to the presidency in 1800. Jefferson pardoned those who had been convicted under the law (mostly newspaper editors), Congress repealed one of the acts in 1802, and the others were allowed to expire before the Supreme Court had a chance to rule them unconstitutional.

In the twentieth century, World War I prompted the harshest crackdowns on free speech since the Sedition Act of 1798. The most important case from this period involved the general secretary of the Socialist Party, Charles Schenck, who opposed U.S. involvement in the war. He had printed a leaflet urging young men to resist the draft. Schenck was arrested, and he appealed all the way to the Supreme Court, arguing that the First Amendment permitted him to protest the war and urge others to resist the draft. But the Court sustained his conviction, noting that free speech is not an absolute right:

The most stringent protection of free speech would not protect a man in falsely shouting fire in a theatre and causing a panic. . . . The question in every case is whether the words used are used in such circumstances and are of such a nature as to create a clear and present danger that they will bring about the substantive evils that Congress has a right to prevent.[40]

This **clear and present danger test** meant that the government could suppress any speech it deemed dangerous—in this instance, preventing the government from fighting the war. However, critics of the decision argue that Schenck's actions were not dangerous for the country and should have been allowed.[41]

Over the next several decades, the Court struggled to draw the line between dangerous speech and words that were simply unpopular. Then, in 1969, the Court established in *Brandenburg v. Ohio* a strong protection for free speech, superseding the clear and present danger test, that still holds today. This case involved Clarence Brandenburg, a Ku Klux Klan leader in Ohio who made a threatening speech at a cross-burning rally that was subsequently shown on television. Twelve hooded figures were shown, many with weapons. The speech said that "revengence [*sic*]" might be taken if "our president, our Congress, our Supreme Court continues to suppress the white,

Caucasian race." It continued, "We are marching on Congress July the Fourth, four hundred thousand strong." The Klan leader was convicted under an Ohio law banning "sabotage, violence, or unlawful methods of terrorism as a means of accomplishing industrial or political reform," but the Court unanimously reversed his conviction, arguing that threatening speech could not be suppressed just because it sounded dangerous. Specifically, the **direct incitement test** holds that speech is protected "except where such advocacy is directed to inciting or producing imminent lawless action and is likely to incite or produce such action."[42] Under this new standard, *Schenck* and many other previous sedition convictions and limitations on speech during World War I and the Red Scare would have been overturned.

Perhaps the strongest example of protecting unpopular speech comes from the case of the Westboro Baptist Church (WBC). Since 2005, members of the WBC have protested at hundreds of funerals of members of the armed services who were killed in Iraq and Afghanistan. However, these are not typical antiwar protests. Instead, the protesters claim that the troops' deaths were God's punishment for "the homosexual lifestyle of soul-damning, nation-destroying filth." The church and its members have drawn strong reactions and counterprotests for their confrontational approach at the military funerals, including their use of signs that say "God Hates Fags," "Thank God for Dead Soldiers," "God Killed Your Sons," and "God Hates America." Critics, including many veterans groups and attorneys general from 48 states, argue that the protests should not be considered protected speech under the First Amendment. The Veterans of Foreign Wars issued a statement saying, "In a time of profound grief and emotional vulnerability, these personal attacks are an affront of the most egregious kind." However, in 2011 the Supreme Court ruled 8–1 that the WBC's protests were protected speech.[43]

Symbolic Speech The use of signs, symbols, or other unspoken acts or methods to communicate in a political manner—**symbolic speech**—enjoys many of the same protections as regular speech. For example, during the Vietnam War the Court protected the right of a protester to wear an American flag patch sewn on the seat of his pants,[44] a high school student's right to wear an armband to protest the war (*Tinker v. Des Moines School District*, 1969),[45] and an individual's right to tape a peace symbol on the flag and fly it upside down outside an apartment window.[46]

A 1989 case provided the strongest protection for symbolic speech yet, overturning a flag desecration law in Texas on the grounds that symbolic political speech is protected by the First Amendment.[47] In response to this unpopular decision, Congress passed the Flag Protection Act of 1989, which the Court also struck down as an unconstitutional infringement on political expression.[48] Congress then attempted six times to pass a constitutional amendment to overturn the Court decision, but each time the measure failed in the Senate. President Trump reignited this debate shortly after he was elected, tweeting, "Nobody should be allowed to burn the American flag—if they do, there must be consequences—perhaps loss of citizenship or year in jail!" However, Republican leaders in Congress have not been interested in revisiting this fight.[49]

Money as Speech Spending money in political campaigns may also be protected by the First Amendment, since it provides the means for more conventional types of political speech. Here the question is whether the government can control campaign contributions and spending for a broader public purpose such as lessening the potential for corruption, or whether such laws violate the First Amendment rights of candidates or their supporters. You probably have heard the old saying "Money talks," which implies that money is speech. Given the importance of advertising in modern campaigns, limitations on raising and spending money could limit the ability

direct incitement test
Established in *Brandenburg v. Ohio*, this test protects threatening speech under the First Amendment unless that speech aims to and is likely to cause imminent "lawless action."

Restriction of free thought and free speech is the most dangerous of all subversions. It is the one un-American act that could most easily defeat us.

—**William O. Douglas,** former Supreme Court justice

symbolic speech
Nonverbal expression, such as the use of signs or symbols. It benefits from many of the same constitutional protections as verbal speech because of its expressive value.

Tinker v. Des Moines School District
In 1969, the Supreme Court ruled that students may wear armbands to protest the Vietnam War. The Court noted that the students "were not disruptive and did not impinge upon the rights of others" and therefore their conduct was protected by the First and Fourteenth Amendments.

DID YOU KNOW?

73%
of college-educated Black Americans and 45 percent of college-educated White Americans view the Confederate battle flag primarily as a symbol of racism.
Source: YouGov

The American flag is a popular target for protesters: it has been spat upon, shredded, turned into underwear, and burned. Here, protesters burn a U.S. flag as they march through downtown Washington, D.C., following the Ferguson, Missouri, grand jury's decision not to indict Officer Darren Wilson for the shooting death of Michael Brown.

hate speech
Expression that is offensive or abusive, particularly in terms of race, gender, or sexual orientation. It is currently protected under the First Amendment.

of candidates and groups to reach voters with their message. The Court has walked a tightrope on this one, balancing the public interest in honest and ethical elections and the First Amendment rights of candidates and their advocates. The Court has upheld individual candidates' right to spend their own money in federal elections, but presidential candidates give up that right if they accept federal campaign funds (taxpayers' money) in a presidential election. Also, candidates in federal elections are subject to limits on the types and size of contributions they can receive, and they must report all contributions and spending to the Federal Election Commission.[50]

The Bipartisan Campaign Reform Act, which went into effect for the 2004 elections, included a "Millionaires' Amendment" that lifted restrictions on campaign contributions for candidates whose opponent spent more than $350,000 of his or her own money in the election. This attempt to level the campaign finance playing field was struck down by the Supreme Court in 2008 as a violation of wealthy candidates' First Amendment rights.[51] In 2010, the Court also extended First Amendment rights to corporations and labor unions that want to spend money on campaign ads.[52] In 2014, the Court struck down aggregate limits placed on individual contributions.[53] However, the Court upheld a ban on unlimited "soft money" contributions because they have the most potential for corruption.[54]

Hate Speech Free speech has been a hot topic on many college campuses in the context of **hate speech**. Do people have a right to say things that are offensive or abusive, especially in terms of race, gender, and sexual orientation? By the mid-1990s, more than 350 public colleges and universities said no by regulating some forms of hate speech.[55] Many of these speech codes were struck down in federal court, but in the last few years the issue has resurfaced on many college campuses. In addition to the controversial speakers discussed in the chapter opener, a variety of "campus climate" issues consumed dozens of schools. At Yale University in 2015, controversy erupted over the response of a residential college faculty administrator, Erika Christakis, to an e-mail students received cautioning them not to wear Halloween costumes that could be racially or culturally insensitive. Christakis wrote that universities no longer allowed students to be "a little bit inappropriate or provocative or, yes, offensive."[56]

A historic mural illustrating a member of the Ku Klux Klan provoked controversy at Indiana University in 2017, with many students calling for the removal of the offensive imagery.

She resigned a few weeks later, saying, "[T]he current climate at Yale is not, in my view, conducive to the civil dialogue and open inquiry required to solve our urgent societal problems."[57] The president of the University of Missouri also resigned in 2015 after students, including the football team, said that he was racially insensitive and not open to their demands for a more inclusive and supportive environment on campus. In 2017, Indiana University students petitioned to remove part of a mural that depicts the history of the state using imagery of a burning cross and white-hooded Klansmen. University leaders compromised by leaving the artwork but saying that classes would no longer be held in the lecture hall with the mural.[58]

Another significant issue combines the topics of symbolic speech and hate speech. For example, can a person who burned a cross on a Black family's lawn be convicted under a city ordinance that prohibits conduct "arous[ing] anger, alarm, or resentment in others on the basis of race, color, creed, religion, or gender"? Or is the ordinance an unconstitutional limit on First Amendment rights? In this case, the Court said the cross burner could be punished for arson, terrorism, trespassing, or other violations of the law, but he could not be convicted under that particular city ordinance because it was overly broad and vague.[59] However, the Court has since upheld more carefully worded bans of cross burning.[60]

Speech on the Internet Internet hate speech has become increasingly controversial in recent years. Cyberbullying precipitated several suicides, and then in 2013 Facebook cracked down on offensive content that glorified violence against women, such as pages with headlines like "Violently Raping Your Friend Just for Laughs."[61] Facebook's "community standards" have a more restrictive definition of hate speech than is allowed by the direct incitement test. While Facebook makes a distinction between humor and serious speech, it "do[es] not permit individuals or groups to attack others based on their race, ethnicity, national origin, religion, sex, gender, sexual orientation, disability or medical condition."[62] This led law professor Jeff Rosen to conclude that "today, lawyers at Google, YouTube, Facebook, and Twitter have more power over who can speak and who can be heard than any president, judge, or monarch."[63] This may sound like hyperbole, but he is right: corporations are not restricted by the First Amendment (which, after all, says "*Congress* shall make no law . . ."). So if Facebook and other social media want to restrict hate speech, they can. Although free speech advocates are concerned about restrictions on Internet hate speech, civil rights groups such as the Anti-Defamation League, the Leadership Conference on Civil and Human Rights, and the National Organization for Women all support the move. Another controversial area of speech on the Internet is political ads. Late in 2019, Twitter announced that it was banning all political ads for the 2020 elections, while Google restricted "micro-targeting" based on ideology, party, or voting history. Facebook, on the other hand, still allows political ads, but with warnings if they are deemed untrue.[64]

While social media companies have great latitude in what they permit online, the government has limited power to regulate access to social media. In 2017, the Court struck down a North Carolina law that prohibited sex offenders from accessing or using social media sites, saying that these sites are the "principal sources for knowing current events, checking ads for employment, speaking and listening in the modern public square, and otherwise exploring the vast realms of human thought and knowledge." Therefore, limiting access to social media would prevent the "legitimate exercise of First Amendment rights."[65]

Freedom of Assembly The Supreme Court has consistently protected the right to assemble peaceably.[66] Perhaps the most famous assembly case involved a neo-Nazi group that wanted to march in Skokie, a suburb of Chicago whose population of 70,000 was nearly 60 percent Jewish. (And of those, many were Holocaust survivors.) The village passed ordinances that banned the group from marching, arguing that

The August 2017 "Unite the Right" rally in Charlottesville, Virginia—initially organized in opposition to the removal of a statue of Confederate general Robert E. Lee from a public park—raised issues of symbolic speech and freedom of assembly. Can the use of symbols that some deem offensive, such as the Confederate battle flag, be regulated by the government? Should groups promoting hate speech be permitted to peaceably assemble in public areas?

residents would be so upset by the Nazi marchers that they might become violent. But the lower courts did not accept this argument, ruling that if "the audience is so offended by the ideas being expressed that it becomes disorderly and attempts to silence the speaker, it is the duty of the police to attempt to protect the speaker, not to silence his speech."[67] Otherwise, the right to assemble would be restricted by a "heckler's veto."

While broad protection is provided for peaceable assemblies, governments may regulate the time, manner, and place of expression as long as these regulations do not favor certain groups or messages over others. For example, the Court ruled that anti-abortion protesters were not allowed to picket a doctor's home in Brookfield, Wisconsin, on the grounds that the ordinance banning all residential picketing was content neutral; there was a government interest in preserving the "sanctity of the home, the one retreat to which men and women can repair to escape from the tribulations of their daily pursuits."[68] "Time, manner, and place" restrictions also may be invoked for practical reasons. For instance, if the Ku Klux Klan planned to hold a march around a football stadium on the day of a game, the city council could deny it a permit and suggest that it choose another day that would be more convenient. When White supremacist Richard Spencer requested to speak at the University of Florida just a month after the tragic events in Charlottesville, the school initially turned him down, saying that it would not have time to provide adequate security for the event. However, it approved the talk for a date a month later.[69]

The legal standard for "time, manner, and place" regulations is that they must be "reasonable." This standard came into play in a 2014 case in which the Court ruled that a Massachusetts state law creating a 35-foot buffer zone around entrances to abortion clinics violated the First Amendment. While the buffer zone was content neutral, it was unreasonable because it was more restrictive than necessary to allow access to the clinics.[70] While the "reasonableness" standard is vague, it allows the courts to balance the right to assemble against other practical considerations.

Freedom of the Press The task of balancing interests is central to many First Amendment cases involving the freedom of the press. The general issue here is **prior restraint**, the government's right to prevent the media from publishing

prior restraint
A limit on freedom of the press that allows the government to prohibit the media from publishing certain materials.

Through her work as an intelligence analyst for the U.S. military, Chelsea Manning downloaded thousands of classified videos, diplomatic cables, reports, and other information that she then gave to the website WikiLeaks in 2010. Though she was released from prison in 2017, Manning has since spent additional time in jail for refusing to testify in additional WikiLeaks-related investigations.

The freedom of the press is one of the greatest bulwarks of liberty, and can never be restrained but by despotic governments.

—**George Mason,** politician and father of the Bill of Rights

fighting words

Forms of expression that "by their very utterance" can incite violence. These can be regulated by the government but are often difficult to define.

slander

Spoken false statements that damage a person's reputation. They can be regulated by the government but are often difficult to distinguish from permissible speech.

libel

Written false statements that damage a person's reputation. They can be regulated by the government but are often difficult to distinguish from permissible speech.

(or, later, broadcasting) something of social or political significance. Prior restraint has never been clearly defined by the Supreme Court, but several landmark cases have set a very high bar for applying it. One suit, brought in 1971 and known as the Pentagon Papers case (**New York Times Co. v. United States**), involved disclosure of parts of a top-secret report on internal planning for the Vietnam War. Ultimately, the Court decided that the government could not prevent publication of the Pentagon Papers, but at least five justices supported the view that under some circumstances the government could use prior restraint—though they could not agree on the standard.[71]

The debate over restraining the media heated up in 2010 with the sensational leaking of more than 91,000 reports concerning the war in Afghanistan by WikiLeaks. Some members of Congress labeled the leaks "treason" and called for prosecution. However, supporters of an unrestrained press point to the Pentagon Papers case as precedent for the role of journalists in holding the government accountable. They argue that the conduct of war and programs such as warrantless wiretapping of U.S. citizens may violate international or domestic law and that the public has the right to know about them.

The forms of expression discussed in this section—speech, assembly, and press—all have strong protection from the First Amendment. The strongest protections are for content-based expression. However, there are exceptions, such as speech that directly incites an imminent danger. If the regulation is content neutral and does not favor one viewpoint over another, then it is easier to uphold. But even then, the government must have a substantial reason for limiting expression.

Less protected speech and publications

Some forms of speech do not warrant the same level of protection as political speech because they do not contribute to public debate or express ideas that have important social value. Governments may more easily regulate four categories of such speech: fighting words, slander and libel, commercial speech, and obscenity. The first two categories may be prevented by the state if certain conditions are met, and the second two receive some protection, but not as much as political speech.

Fighting Words Governments may regulate **fighting words**, "which by their very utterance inflict injury or tend to incite an immediate breach of the peace."[72] Such laws must be narrowly written; it is not acceptable to ban all foul language, and the prohibited speech must target a single person rather than a group. Moreover, the question of whether certain words provoke a backlash depends on the reaction of the targeted person. Inflammatory words directed at a pacifist would not be fighting words because he or she would turn the other cheek, whereas the same words yelled at a hothead *would* be fighting words because that individual would likely respond with violence. The Court has further clarified the test, based on "what persons of common intelligence would understand to be words likely to cause an average addressee to fight."[73]

Slander and Libel A more extensive line of cases prohibiting speech concerns **slander**, spoken false statements that damage someone's reputation (defamation), and **libel**, written statements that do the same thing. However, it is difficult to draw the line between permissible speech and slander or libel. The current legal standard distinguishes between speech about a public figure, such as a politician or celebrity, and speech about a regular person. It is much more difficult for public figures to prove libel because they must demonstrate that the defamatory statement was made with "actual malice" and "with knowledge that it was false or with reckless disregard of whether it was false or not."[74]

One of the most famous libel cases occurred when Reverend Jerry Falwell, a well-known televangelist and political activist, sued *Hustler* magazine for libel and emotional distress after the magazine published a parody of a liquor advertisement depicting him in a "drunken incestuous rendezvous with his mother in an outhouse" (this quote is from the Supreme Court case).[75] The Court ruled against Falwell, saying that public figures and public officials have to put up with such things, comparing the parody to outrageous political cartoons, which have always been protected by the First Amendment.

Commercial Speech Commercial speech, which mostly refers to advertising, has evolved from having almost no protection under the First Amendment to enjoying quite strong protection. The Court became much more sympathetic to commercial speech in the 1970s when it struck down a law against advertising prescription drug prices and a law prohibiting placing newspaper racks on city streets to distribute commercial publications such as real estate guides.[76] The key decision in 1980 established a test that is still central today: the government may regulate commercial speech if it concerns an illegal activity, if the advertisement is misleading, or if regulating speech directly advances a substantial government interest and the regulation is not excessive. In practice, this test means that commercial speech can be regulated but that the government has to have a very good reason to do it.[77]

Commercial speech is protected even when it could be considered offensive. In 2017, the Court sided with the Slants, an Asian-American rock band, in overturning a provision of U.S. patent and trademark law that prohibited the registration of trademarks that "disparage" or "bring … into contempt or disrepute" any "persons, living or dead." The Slants, whose application to trademark their band name had been denied, argued that their goal was to reclaim the racial slur against Asian Americans, in the same way that the LGBTQ community over time redefined the use of "queer." The Court agreed, saying, "A law that can be directed against speech found offensive to some portion of the public can be turned against minority and dissenting views to the detriment of all." This ruling also means that the Washington Redskins football team will be able to keep its nickname, despite the fact that many find it offensive.[78]

Obscenity One area in which the press has never experienced complete freedom involves the publication of pornography and material considered obscene. The difficulty arises in deciding where to draw the line. Nearly everyone would agree that child pornography should not be published[79] and that pornography should not be available to minors. However, beyond these points there is little consensus. For example, some people are offended by nude paintings in art museums, while others enjoy watching hard-core X-rated movies.

Defining obscenity has proven difficult for the courts. In an often-quoted moment of frustration, Justice Potter Stewart wrote that he could not define obscenity, but "I know it when I see it."[80] The Supreme Court took a stab at it in 1973 in a case that gave rise to the **Miller test**, which is still applied today.[81] The test has three standards that must all be met in order for material to be banned as obscene: (1) it appeals to prurient interests, (2) it is "patently offensive," and (3) the work as a whole lacks serious literary, artistic, political, or scientific value. The Court also clarified that *local* community standards are to apply rather than a single national standard.

Commercial speech may be protected even if some consider its content offensive. The rock band the Slants won the right to trademark their band name even though it refers to a racial slur against the Asian-American community.

commercial speech
Public expression with the aim of making a profit. It has received greater protection under the First Amendment in recent years but remains less protected than political speech.

Miller test
Established in *Miller v. California*, this three-part test is used by the Supreme Court to determine whether speech meets the criteria for obscenity. If so, it can be restricted by the government.

Even if you are not a journalist, do not engage in political protest, or do not contribute to political campaigns, the freedom of speech, the press, and assembly still shapes the world around you. The "marketplace of ideas" ensures that policies are debated and a range of voices can be heard. Our political leaders are held accountable by the free exchange of ideas and a strong independent media that can criticize their actions. Also, other areas of your everyday life that you may not consider to be "speech," such as video games, are protected by the First Amendment. Having an understanding of the law is especially important when the freedom of the press and free speech are regularly challenged in the political world.

EXPLORE WHY THE SECOND AMENDMENT'S MEANING ON GUN RIGHTS IS OFTEN DEBATED

DID YOU KNOW?

39,420

people were killed by guns in the United States in 2019. About 61 percent of these deaths were from suicides.

Source: www.gunviolencearchive.org

The right to bear arms

Between 1791 and 2007, the Court issued only four rulings directly pertaining to the Second Amendment and the right to bear arms. The federal courts had always interpreted the Second Amendment's awkward phrasing—"A well regulated Militia, being necessary to the security of a free State, the right of the people to keep and bear Arms, shall not be infringed"—as a right to bear arms within the context of serving in a militia, rather than an individual right to own a gun.

Interest groups such as the National Rifle Association have long asserted that the Second Amendment guarantees an individual the right to bear arms.[82] Critics of this view emphasize the first clause of the amendment and point to the frequent mentions of state militias in congressional debates at the time the Bill of Rights was adopted.[83] They argue that the Second Amendment was adopted to reassure Antifederalist advocates of states' rights that state militias, not a national standing army, would provide national security. In this view, the national armed forces and the National Guard have made the Second Amendment obsolete.

Before the Court's recent entry into this debate, Congress and state and local lawmakers had largely defined gun ownership and carrying rights, creating significant variation among the states. (Wyoming and Montana have virtually no restrictions on gun ownership, for example, whereas California and Connecticut have many.) However, following an assassination attempt on President Ronald Reagan in 1981 a push for stronger gun control laws intensified. In 1993, Congress passed the Brady bill, which mandates a background check and a five-day waiting period for any handgun purchase.

But not all gun tragedies lead to more gun control. There were 417 mass shootings in 2019 and 464 in 2020 (as of September), defined as incidents in which at least four people were killed or injured, not counting the shooter.[84] By the FBI's definition of an "active shooter" there were 277 incidents from 2000 to 2018, including those in Orlando, Florida; San Bernardino, California; Charleston, South Carolina; and Parkland, Florida.[85] In the deadliest mass shooting by a single gunman, 58 people were killed and 546 injured in October 2017 at a country music festival in Las Vegas. While 45 states have passed new gun safety laws since 2013, including "smart gun" laws, laws concerning mental health and gun ownership, laws restricting ownership of assault weapons, and stronger background checks, 30 states now make it relatively easy to get a permit to carry a concealed weapon and 42 states do not require a permit. Many states have also expanded the places in which guns may be carried, included college campuses, and have passed "stand your ground" laws which allow gun owners to shoot first if they feel threatened.[86]

McDonald v. Chicago

The Supreme Court ruled in 2010 that the Second Amendment's right to keep and bear arms for self-defense in one's home is applicable to the states through the Fourteenth Amendment.

In 2008, a landmark Supreme Court ruling recognized for the first time an individual right to bear arms for self-defense and hunting.[87] The decision struck down the District of Columbia's ban on handguns, while noting that state and local governments could enforce ownership restrictions, such as preventing felons or the mentally impaired from buying guns. The Court did not apply the Second Amendment to the states in this decision, but it did so two years later in striking down a gun control ordinance in Chicago in *McDonald v. Chicago* (2010) and reaffirming the ownership restrictions noted in the Washington, D.C., case.[88]

There is strong public support for gun ownership in the United States, where there are about 393 million privately owned guns. This accounts for 46 percent of the world's total and is more than twice as high a rate of gun ownership as in the second most heavily armed nation: there are 120.5 guns per 100 people in the United States compared to 52.8 in Yemen. The contrast to our closest allies is even more extreme: there are 34.7 guns per 100 people in Canada, 19.6 in Germany, 4.9 in the United Kingdom, and 0.3 in Japan.[89] The fact that so many Americans support gun ownership, combined with the Supreme Court's endorsement of an individual right to bear arms, means that stronger gun control at the national level is highly unlikely (especially given the unsuccessful pushes after the shootings at Sandy Hook Elementary School in 2012 and in Orlando, Florida, in 2016; Las Vegas in 2017; and Parkland, Florida, in 2018).

However, the president and Congress have taken some limited steps in recent years. Early in 2016, President Obama issued an executive order requiring most gun sales to be through federally licensed dealers who would conduct background checks. The order also required the Social Security Administration to release information about mentally ill recipients of Social Security benefits, which would be considered as part of the background checks. This provision essentially prohibited people with mental illnesses from buying guns.[90] The second part of the order was overturned by Congress early in 2017. After a mass shooting at a Parkland, Florida, high school that killed 17 students in 2018, high school students organized the March for Our Lives, which had 1.2 to 2 million participants in more than 800 cities around the world. In Florida, gun control laws were strengthened by raising the age to buy a gun to 18, banning bump stocks that allow bullets to be fired more rapidly, and introducing a three-day waiting period before buying a long rifle. Congress passed legislation strengthening the National Instant Criminal Background Check System and providing $1 billion to fund initiatives intended to enhance school safety, such as the addition of metal detectors. President Trump also signed an executive order banning bump stocks. However, the ban could be challenged in court because bump stocks appear to be legal under current law. Thus, congressional action would be required for a national ban. In addition to this limited legislative and executive action, extensive litigation will be necessary to define the acceptable boundaries of gun control and to identify which state and local restrictions will be allowed to stand.

DESCRIBE THE PROTECTIONS PROVIDED FOR PEOPLE ACCUSED OF A CRIME

due process rights
The idea that laws and legal proceedings must be fair. The Constitution guarantees that the government cannot take away a person's "life, liberty, or property, without due process of law." Other specific due process rights are found in the Fourth, Fifth, Sixth, and Eighth Amendments, such as protection from self-incrimination and freedom from illegal searches.

Law, order, and the rights of criminal defendants

Every advanced democracy protects the rights of people who have been accused of a crime. In the United States, the **due process rights** of the Fourth, Fifth, Sixth, and Eighth Amendments include the right to a fair trial, the right to consult a lawyer, freedom from self-incrimination, the right to know what crime you are accused of, the right to confront the accuser in court, and freedom from unreasonable police searches. Difficulties in applying these abstract principles to concrete situations indicate how hard it is to define due process, especially in a way that protects civil liberties without jeopardizing order.

The difference between abstract principles of due process and their specific application also raises difficult political questions. Most people endorse the principle of "due process of law" and general ideas such as requiring that police legally obtain any evidence used in court. However, when the Court applies these principles to protect the rights of criminal defendants, there is a public outcry that too many suspects are going free on "legal technicalities" (such as having to inform a suspect of his or her right to talk to an attorney before being questioned by the police).

The Fourth Amendment: unreasonable searches and seizures

The Fourth Amendment says: "The right of the people to be secure in their persons, houses, papers, and effects, against unreasonable searches and seizures, shall not be violated." Over the years, the Court has provided strong protections against searches within a person's physical space, typically defined as his or her home. With the introduction of new technology—telephones and wiretapping, then more sophisticated listening and searching devices—the Court has had to confront a broad array of complicated questions. It has attempted to achieve a balance between security and privacy by requiring court approval for search warrants, while carving out limited exceptions to this general rule (see the Take a Stand feature).

Searches and Warrants Under most circumstances, a law-enforcement official seeking a search warrant must provide the court with "personal knowledge" of a "probable cause" of specific criminal activity and outline the evidence that is the target of the search. Broad "fishing expeditions" for evidence are not allowed.

Police searches inherently involve a clash between public safety and the private freedom from government intrusions. These issues came to the fore with passage of the USA PATRIOT Act of 2001 after the terrorist attacks of September 11. Several of the most controversial parts of the act strengthen police surveillance powers; make it

Drug-Sniffing Dogs: An Illegal Search?

In 2013, the Supreme Court was presented with the case of Joelis Jardines, whom police suspected of growing marijuana inside his Miami home based on an anonymous tip. Police went to the home with a trained drug-detection dog. On the front porch, the dog gave a positive signal indicating the presence of drugs. The police returned with a search warrant, found a marijuana-growing operation, and arrested Jardines. However, the Florida Supreme Court threw out the evidence, arguing it was an illegal search. The case then made its way to the U.S. Supreme Court, which was faced with this question: Should drug-sniffing dogs be allowed outside a home without a warrant? More broadly, in the context of rapidly changing technology, what is the public's "reasonable expectation" for privacy?

A drug-sniffing dog is no more invasive than the surveillance technologies we encounter every day. The Court has ruled that police do not need a search warrant to have drug-sniffing dogs search luggage at an airport or a car that has been stopped for a traffic violation unrelated to drugs. Lower courts have also ruled that sniffs are not considered searches in a hotel hallway, at a school locker, outside a passenger train's sleeper compartments, or outside an apartment door. Is a sniff outside someone's home any more invasive?

It might not seem that way, especially when you consider the reach of new surveillance methods that are on the horizon. Other technologies that are becoming more common or will be used soon include RFIDs (radio frequency identifications), which are the size of a grain of rice and transmit information wirelessly through radio waves; facial recognition software and iris scanners; "smart dust devices"—tiny wireless micromechanical sensors—that can detect light and movement; and drones, which have primarily been used for military purposes but also have vast potential for tracking suspects in any situation.

Warrantless surveillance of somebody's home crosses a line. Lower courts have been split on whether drug-sniffing dogs may be used outside a home without a warrant, due, in part, to a Supreme Court precedent giving homes stronger Fourth Amendment protection than cars, lockers, or other areas. For example, in 2001 the Court ruled that police needed a warrant to use a thermal-imaging device outside a home when trying to detect marijuana that was believed to be growing under heat lamps inside.

The U.S. Supreme Court ultimately agreed in the Jardines case, saying that there is a general expectation that anyone may come onto a front porch as long as the uninvited person simply knocks and then leaves if there is no answer. The majority opinion wryly noted: "Complying with the terms of that traditional invitation does not require fine-grained legal knowledge; it is generally managed without incident by the Nation's Girl Scouts and trick-or-treaters." But, they continued, "introducing a trained police dog to explore the area around the home in hopes of discovering incriminating evidence is something else. There is no customary invitation to do *that*."[a]

 A U.S. Customs and Border Patrol agent in Florida uses a drug-sniffing dog to inspect incoming mail at a sorting facility.

New and future technologies continue to complicate the question of just what is "reasonable." Justice Alito raised this question in oral arguments in a Supreme Court case involving a GPS tracking device. He said, "Technology is changing people's expectations of privacy. . . . Maybe 10 years from now 90 percent of the population will be using social networking sites and they will have on average 500 friends and they will have allowed their friends to monitor their location 24 hours a day, 365 days a year, through the use of their cell phones. Then—what would the expectation of privacy be then?"[b]

take a stand

1. If you had to decide the case of the drug-sniffing dog, how would you have ruled? Do you think that homes should have stronger privacy expectations than cars or school lockers? Even when it concerns illegal drugs?

2. How would you answer Justice Alito's question about the expectation of privacy in an era of rapidly changing technology? When should law-enforcement officials have to get a warrant to monitor our behavior?

Can the police search your home without a warrant? After Dollree Mapp was arrested for possession of pornographic material, the case made its way to the Supreme Court and the search was ruled unconstitutional. This case established the exclusionary rule for evidence that is obtained without a warrant.

easier to conduct "sneak and peek" searches (the police enter a home with a warrant, look for evidence, and do not tell the suspect of their search until months later); broaden Internet surveillance; increase the government's access to library, banking, and medical records; and permit roving wiretaps for suspected terrorists.

Most police searches without warrants occur because suspects consent to being searched; officers are not required to tell a suspect that he or she may say no or request a warrant. Other cases in which the Court allows a warrantless search include conducting a search that happens at the time of a legal arrest and "is confined to the immediate vicinity of the arrest"; collecting evidence that was not included in the search warrant but is out in plain view; searching the passenger area and passengers of a car if the driver has been stopped for a traffic offense; and searching school lockers with probable cause.[91] The Supreme Court recently upheld strip searches after an arrest and before the suspect is put in jail even when there is no suspicion of illegal substances. Dissenting justices argued that "the humiliation of a visual strip-search" after being "arrested for driving with a noisy muffler, failing to use a turn signal and riding a bicycle without an audible bell" should not be allowed under the Fourth Amendment.[92]

In 2013, the Court ruled that a DNA swab of an arrested suspect is simply for identification and therefore is no more intrusive than a photograph or fingerprint. The late Justice Scalia, a strong defender of privacy rights, argued in his dissent that DNA evidence could be used to identify the arrestee as a suspect in an unrelated crime and therefore the standard of individualized suspicion should hold before the swab can be taken.[93]

The Court has generally made it easier for law-enforcement officials to conduct searches without warrants, but two important decisions in the other direction were a 2014 case that required a warrant to search cell phones of people who are arrested[94] and a 2012 case that required a warrant to place a GPS tracking device on a vehicle. In the latter case, the FBI suspected Antoine Jones of selling cocaine, so agents placed a tracking device on his vehicle without a warrant, monitored his movements for four weeks, and then used the evidence to convict him. Jones was sentenced to life in prison. While the Court required a warrant in this specific case, the basis for the majority's decision was fairly narrow: the placement of the device was a "physical trespass," and the lengthy monitoring of his movement constituted an illegal search.[95] The Court provided additional protection for privacy in 2018 when it ruled that a search warrant is required to access cell phone location records. While the ruling made exceptions for emergencies such as "bomb threats, active shootings, and child abductions," the four dissenting justices feared that law-enforcement officials were losing an important tool in fighting crime.[96]

If the police illegally obtain evidence, the need to balance security and privacy becomes concrete. Either the evidence is excluded from a criminal trial to protect privacy rights or it is allowed in order to support conviction of the suspect.

The Exclusionary Rule In 1961, the Fourth Amendment was incorporated (applied to the states through the Fourteenth Amendment) in a case that established the **exclusionary rule** for all courts.[97] Previously, the rule, which states that illegally obtained evidence cannot be used in a criminal trial, had applied only at the national level. The landmark case involved police breaking into Dollree Mapp's residence without a warrant to look for a suspect thought to be hiding there. The officers did not find the suspect, but they did find illegal pornographic material. Although the woman was convicted of possessing it, the Court ultimately threw out the conviction.

Subsequent Courts started weakening the exclusionary rule. For example, the Court established a "good faith exception" to the exclusionary rule, allowing evidence to be used as long as the officer believed that he or she had conducted a legal search. In this

exclusionary rule
The principle that illegally or unconstitutionally acquired evidence cannot be used in a criminal trial.

specific case, the officer had a warrant with the wrong address.[98] The bottom line is that the exclusionary rule remains in effect, but lately it has become easier for prosecutors to use evidence obtained under questionable circumstances.

Drug Testing Another area of Fourth Amendment law concerns drug testing. The clause granting people the right "to be secure in their persons" certainly seems to cover drug testing. However, the courts have long recognized the right of private companies to test their employees for illegal drugs, and testing for performance-enhancing drugs is increasingly common in professional sports.

What about drug testing by the state? The Court has upheld random drug testing for high school athletes and mandatory drug testing for any junior high or high school students involved in extracurricular activities.[99] In the case of athletes, proponents of the policy asserted that safety concerns should preclude a 260-pound lineman or a pitcher with a 90-mile-per-hour fastball from using drugs. However, the same arguments could not be made for members of the choir, band, debate club, social dance club, or the chess club, so this decision to include all extracurricular activities was a particularly strong endorsement of schools' antidrug policies.

The Court has upheld drug testing of public employees, with one exception. It struck down a Georgia law that would have required all candidates for state office to pass a drug test within 30 days of announcing a run for office, because candidates are not public employees.[100] Rather than appealing to the courts, former senator Ernest Hollings of South Carolina had a different approach to avoid drug testing. When his opponent challenged him to take a drug test, the senator shot back, "I'll take a drug test if you take an IQ test."[101]

The Post–September 11 Politics of Domestic Surveillance The debate over the trade-off between civil liberties and security intensified in 2005, when a White House–approved domestic surveillance program was revealed. Since the September 11, 2001, attacks, the National Security Agency (NSA) had been monitoring the phone calls of many U.S. citizens who have had contact with suspected terrorists overseas. These calls were intercepted without the approval of the Foreign Intelligence Surveillance Court (FISC), which Congress created in 1978 for approving the interception of calls. A few months later in 2005, another NSA program aimed at creating a database of every phone call made within the borders of the United States was revealed. Phone companies AT&T, Verizon, and BellSouth reportedly had turned over records of millions of customers' phone calls to the government.[102] In 2013, classified information revealed by Edward Snowden showed that the NSA had been monitoring the phone calls of German chancellor Angela Merkel and other leaders of allied countries, in addition to collecting e-mail traffic in the United States that contained the e-mail address or phone number of a foreign target. In April 2017, the NSA announced that it would no longer collect information on communications that simply mentioned someone rather than being sent to or from that person (so-called "about searches"). It also would discontinue "backdoor" searches in which conversations and Internet data from Americans get swooped up in the course of monitoring foreign targets. However, early in 2018, when Congress reauthorized the foreign surveillance for an additional six years, it opened the door to allowing "about" collection and "backdoor" searches to start up again.[103] Critics warn that phone surveillance may be just the tip of the domestic surveillance iceberg because the government might be monitoring travel, credit card, and banking records more widely than we think.[104]

As you can imagine, the debate over domestic surveillance has generated intense disagreement. The idea that government is everywhere may seem threatening if you are concerned about protecting your civil liberties, or it may seem reassuring if you are more concerned about national security. Either way, this issue will remain significant in your daily life for the foreseeable future.

The Fifth Amendment

The familiar phrase "I plead the Fifth" has been part of our criminal justice system since the Bill of Rights was ratified, ensuring that a suspect cannot be compelled to provide court testimony that would cause him or her to be prosecuted for a crime. However, what about outside a court of law? If a police officer coerces a confession out of a suspect, is that self-incrimination?

Coercive police interrogations were allowed until a landmark case in 1966. Ernesto Miranda had been convicted in an Arizona court of kidnapping and rape, on the basis of a confession extracted after two hours of questioning in which he was not read his rights. The Court overturned the conviction, saying that police interrogation "is inherently intimidating" and in these circumstances "no statement obtained from the defendant can truly be the product of his free choice."[105] To ensure that a confession is truly a free choice, the Court established **Miranda rights**. If police do not read a suspect these rights, nothing the suspect says can be used in court.

Miranda rights
The list of civil liberties described in the Fifth Amendment that must be read to a suspect before anything the suspect says can be used in a trial.

Over time, the Court has carved out exceptions to the Miranda rights requirement because the public has viewed the practice as "coddling criminals" and letting too many people go free on legal technicalities. However, in 2000 the Court rejected Congress's attempt to overturn *Miranda* by designating all voluntary confessions as legally admissible evidence. The Court ruled that it, not Congress, has the power to determine constitutional protections for criminal defendants. The justices also affirmed their intent to protect the *Miranda* rule, saying: "*Miranda* has become embedded in routine police practice to the point where the warnings have become part of our national culture."[106]

Another Fifth Amendment right for defendants is protection against being tried more than once for a particular crime. This **double jeopardy** prohibition was extended to the states in 1969.[107] However, prosecutors can exploit two loopholes in this civil liberty: (1) a suspect may be tried in federal court and state court for the same crime,[108] and (2) if a suspect is found innocent of one set of *criminal* charges brought by the state,

double jeopardy
Being tried twice for the same crime. This is prevented by the Fifth Amendment.

This is a typical example of the Miranda warning card that police officers carry with them and read to every suspect after an arrest.

DEFENDANT		LOCATION
SPECIFIC WARNING REGARDING INTERROGATIONS		

1. You have the right to remain silent.

2. Anything you say can and will be used against you in a court of law.

3. You have the right to talk to a lawyer and have him present with you while you are being questioned.

4. If you cannot afford to hire a lawyer one will be appointed to represent you before any questioning, if you wish one.

SIGNATURE OF DEFENDANT	DATE
WITNESS	TIME
☐ REFUSED SIGNATURE SAN FRANCISCO POLICE DEPARTMENT	PR.9.1.4

he or she may still be found guilty of the same or similar offenses based on *civil* charges brought by a private individual.

The final part of the Fifth Amendment is at the heart of a legal debate over property rights and eminent domain. The clause says, "nor shall private property be taken for public use, without just compensation." For most of American history, this civil liberty has been noncontroversial. When the government needs private property for a public use such as a highway or a park, it may enforce "physical takings" by making a property owner sell at a fair market value in a practice known as eminent domain. But lately a controversial interpretation of the "takings" clause has attempted to expand just compensation for "regulatory takings" as well. For example, if the Endangered Species Act protects an animal whose habitat is on your land, you would not be able to develop that property and thus its market value would probably drop. Therefore, the argument goes, because of this law the government has "taken" some of your land's value by protecting the species, so the government should compensate you.

The issue became especially controversial around a case involving a development project in New London, Connecticut. A working-class neighborhood was sold to a private developer to build a waterfront hotel, office space, and higher-end housing, but a homeowner sued the city to stop the development. The Court supported the local government, saying that "promoting economic development is a traditional and long accepted function of government," so a "plausible public use" is satisfied.[109] In reaction to this decision, 42 states passed legislation or constitutional amendments restricting the use of eminent domain for economic development.[110] This is an evolving area of the law, with several recent cases restoring property rights and an important 2017 case providing another setback for property owners.[111] However, in 2019 the Court ruled that property owners who believe their property has been unfairly taken by local governments can sue for compensation directly in federal court without having to first bring the case in state court. This ruling overturned a 1985 precedent and was seen as a major victory for property owners.[112]

The Sixth Amendment: the right to legal counsel and a jury trial

The right to an attorney is one of the civil liberties key to criminal law, because the legal system is too complicated for a layperson to navigate. However, at one time, poor people accused of a state felony had to defend themselves in court if they could not afford a lawyer (except in death-penalty cases, for which the state would provide a lawyer).[113] This changed in 1963 with *Gideon v. Wainwright*, when the Court overturned the conviction of a man who had been accused of breaking into a pool hall to steal beer, wine, and money. Unable to afford an attorney, Clarence Gideon defended himself—quite well, in fact—but the (false) testimony of the actual guilty party brought Gideon a conviction. Ultimately, the Court overturned it, saying: "In our adversary system of criminal justice, any person hauled into court who is too poor to hire a lawyer cannot be assured a fair trial unless counsel is provided for him."[114]

The right to an attorney has been strengthened over time, through both legislation and subsequent Court rulings. One year after *Gideon*, Congress passed the Criminal Justice Act, which provided better legal representation for criminal defendants in federal court; soon 23 states had taken similar action. The Court has defined a general right to *effective* counsel (although the bar is set low in defining "effective") and recently mandated that defense attorneys must conduct any reasonable investigation into possible lines of defense when presenting evidence that could help the defendant.[115]

Gideon v. Wainwright
The 1963 Supreme Court case that guaranteed the right to an attorney for the poor or indigent for felony offenses.

The fight against terrorism has raised controversial questions about due process rights. After the United States killed Anwar al-Awlaki—an Al Qaeda leader living in Yemen, and a U.S. citizen—critics argued that his due process rights, such as the right to a fair trial, had been violated.

The Sixth Amendment also protects the right to a speedy and public trial by an impartial jury in criminal cases. The Court affirmed the right to a speedy trial in 1967,[116] and today under the Federal Speedy Trial Act a trial must begin within 70 days of the defendant's arrest or first appearance in court. In addition, a defendant may not waive the right to a speedy trial.[117] The most important disputes over the "impartial jury" issue concern jury selection and peremptory challenges, in which lawyers may eliminate certain people from the jury pool without providing any reason. Race and gender may not be the basis for a peremptory challenge.[118]

The Eighth Amendment: cruel and unusual punishment

The Founders would be surprised by the intense debates over whether the Eighth Amendment prohibition against "cruel and unusual punishments" applies to the death penalty. Clearly, the death penalty was accepted in their time (even stealing a horse was a capital offense!), and the language of the Constitution reflects that. Both the Fifth and Fourteenth Amendments say that a person may not be deprived of "life, liberty, or property, without due process of law," which implies that someone *could* be deprived of life as long as the state followed due process. In the United States, 28 states still allow capital punishment. However, eight states have abolished the death penalty since 2007 (and four more states have moratoriums on the death penalty imposed by their governors, although Nebraska reinstated the death penalty by state referendum in 2016), and dozens of other countries have done the same in recent years. There were only 22 executions in the United States in 2019, which is the third-lowest number since 1991 and well below the peak of 98 in 1999.[119] A botched execution in Oklahoma in 2014, in which Clayton Lockett writhed and gasped for nearly 30 minutes when one of the lines filled with the lethal drugs failed, led to renewed calls for abolishing the death penalty.[120]

After being silent on this issue for nearly two centuries, the Supreme Court ruled in 1972 that the death penalty was unconstitutional because the process of applying it was inconsistent. Thereafter, Congress and 35 states rushed to make their laws compliant with the Court decision. The typical fix was to make explicit which crimes were punishable by death and to make capital sentencing a two-step process: first, the determination of guilt or innocence, and second, a sentencing phase after a guilty finding. Four years later, the Court allowed states to bring back the death penalty.[121]

While never again challenging the death penalty, the Court has been chipping away at its edges for two decades. The Court has struck down state laws mandating the death penalty in murder cases and another law requiring it for rape. It has also prohibited the execution of insane prisoners and abolished the death penalty for the "mentally retarded," for juveniles, and for child rapists.[122]

Privacy rights

EXPLAIN WHY THE RIGHTS ASSOCIATED WITH PRIVACY ARE OFTEN CONTROVERSIAL

You may be surprised to learn that the word "privacy" does not actually appear in the Constitution. **Privacy rights** were developed in a 1965 case that questioned the constitutionality of an 1879 Connecticut law against using birth control. Estelle Griswold, the director of Planned Parenthood in Connecticut, was arrested after opening a clinic that dispensed contraceptives. She was fined $100 and appealed her conviction all the way to the Supreme Court, which overturned it.

In a fractured decision, the Court agreed that the law was outdated, but the justices agreed on little else. Even those who based their opinions on an implied constitutional right to privacy cited various constitutional roots: the First Amendment right of association, the Third's protection against the quartering of troops, the Fourth's prohibition against unreasonable searches and seizures, the Fifth's protection against self-incrimination, and the Ninth's statement "The enumeration in the Constitution, of certain rights, shall not be construed to deny or disparage others retained by the people."[123] *Griswold* was significant for establishing the constitutional basis for a right to privacy, but the dissenters worried where this right would lead. Justice Black warned that privacy "is a broad, abstract and ambiguous concept" that could be shrunken or expanded in subsequent decisions as judges determine what is constitutional on the basis of their own appraisal of what laws are unwise or unnecessary.[124]

privacy rights
Liberties protected by several amendments in the Bill of Rights that shield certain personal aspects of citizens' lives from governmental interference, such as the Fourth Amendment's protection against unreasonable searches and seizures.

Abortion rights

Eight years after *Griswold,* the landmark ruling in ***Roe v. Wade*** struck down laws in 46 states that limited abortion. Twelve of those states allowed abortions for pregnancies due to rape or incest, to protect the life of the mother, and in cases of severe fetal abnormalities. The much-criticized trimester analysis in the *Roe* ruling said that in the first trimester, states could not limit abortions; in the second trimester, states could regulate abortions in the interests of the health of the mother; and in the third trimester, states could forbid all abortions except those necessary to protect the health or life of the mother.[125]

Subsequent decisions have upheld *Roe* but endorsed various state restrictions on abortion, such as requiring parental consent, a waiting period, or counseling sessions aimed at convincing the woman not to have an abortion (see the What Do the Facts Say? feature for more on restrictions currently in effect). Most significant, the trimester analysis of *Roe* has been replaced by a focus on fetal viability. When the fetus would be viable (generally at 22 or 23 weeks), states can ban abortions "except where it is necessary, in

Roe v. Wade
This 1973 Supreme Court case extended the right of privacy to a woman's decision to have an abortion while recognizing legitimate state interests in potential life and maternal health. The Court noted that the "relative weight of each of these interests varies over the course of pregnancy, and the law must account for this variability."

appropriate medical judgment, for the preservation of the life or health of the mother."[126] Laws passed in 2013 by Arkansas and North Dakota limiting abortions as soon as a fetal heartbeat can be detected (as early as 6 weeks) were struck down by federal courts, but laws in 19 states now ban abortions at 20 weeks, in apparent contradiction with *Roe v. Wade*.

Since *Roe*, most political action concerning abortion has taken place in the courts, but that could all change if the Supreme Court overturns this decision. Overturning *Roe* would shift the politics of abortion back to state legislatures and make it an even more highly contested political issue. One effort to force a challenge to *Roe* was a "personhood amendment" to the Mississippi constitution that defined life as beginning at conception. However, the amendment was soundly defeated in a statewide vote in 2011.[127] The pace of state restrictions on abortions accelerated from 2011 to 2013, with more than 200 limitations on abortion services. In 2013, 22 states enacted 70 new restrictions, including a requirement that abortion doctors have admitting privileges at local hospitals—which would close up one-third of abortion clinics in affected states.[128] In 2016, the Supreme Court struck down the latter as an "undue burden" on the right to an abortion.[129] In June 2020, the Supreme Court also struck down a Louisiana law that would have limited the number of abortion providers in the state to just one. In his deciding vote, Chief Justice Roberts cited precedent in his decision, pointing to the fact that the Court struck down a similar law in Texas in its 2016 decision. When Justice Ruth Bader Ginsburg died shortly before the 2020 elections and was replaced by Amy Coney Barrett, abortion opponents believed they might have the fifth vote needed to overturn *Roe v. Wade*.

Gay rights

Gay rights have typically been seen more as a civil right (that is, freedom from discrimination) than a civil liberty, so these issues will be discussed in the next chapter. However, a recent Court ruling established very broad privacy rights for sexual behavior. The case involved two Houston men who were prosecuted for same-sex sodomy after police entered one of the men's apartments—upon receiving a false tip about an armed man in an apartment complex—and found the two having sex. Under Texas law, sodomy was illegal for homosexuals but not for heterosexuals. In a landmark ruling, the Court said that the liberty guaranteed by the Fourteenth Amendment's due process clause allows homosexuals to have sexual relations. "Freedom presumes an autonomy of self that includes freedom of thought, belief, expression, and certain intimate conduct."[130]

Five members of the majority signed on to the broad "due process" reasoning of the decision, while Justice O'Connor wrote a concurring opinion in which she agreed that the Texas law was unconstitutional but on narrower grounds. With the broader due process logic, 13 state laws that banned sodomy were struck down.

While privacy rights may not be as firmly grounded in the Constitution as the freedom of speech or religion, this evolving area of the law has provided important protections for millions of Americans. These civil liberties also remain among the most controversial political issues in our nation, contributing to our observation that politics is conflictual.

Tyron Garner and John Geddes Lawrence after the Supreme Court decision in *Lawrence v. Texas* in 2003 established broad privacy rights for sexual behavior (including homosexual behavior).

"Why Should I Care?"

Privacy might not seem important. You may think you'll never be accused of a crime or have your privacy invaded or questioned by the government. Indeed, many people think, "I have nothing to hide, so it is fine if the NSA monitors e-mail and Internet traffic to keep tabs on suspected terrorists." What if your e-mail revealed that you had a serious medical or mental health condition? What if the NSA paid special attention to you because of tweets you posted criticizing a government policy? Knowing your rights and how those rights apply to everyone—both criminals and innocent people—will help you make informed decisions about which policies to support.

Parental Consent Laws for Abortions for Minors

- ■ No parental notification or consent laws
- ■ One or both parents must consent
- ■ One or both parents must be informed
- ■ Both parental consent and notification required
- ■ Parental consent or notification laws blocked

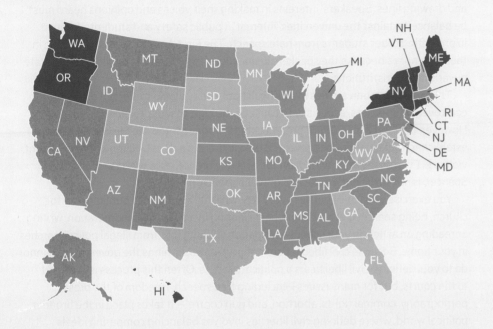

Pre-Abortion Mandatory Waiting Period Laws

- ■ No mandatory waiting period
- ■ Waiting period of less than 24 hours
- ■ Waiting period of 24 hours or more
- ■ Waiting period law blocked

Abortion Rights Today

The Court's 1973 decision in *Roe v. Wade* made abortion legal throughout the United States. How do abortion rights look today? What do the numbers say?

Source: Guttmacher Institute, "An Overview of Abortion Laws," January 6, 2020, www.guttmacher.org/state-policy/explore/overview-abortion-laws (accessed 1/31/20).

Think about it

- **Which states have the most** restrictive policies concerning access to abortions?
- **How do you think waiting periods** and parental notification affect the number of abortions in a state? What about the number of abortions nationwide?

Unpacking the Conflict

Considering all that we've discussed in this chapter, let's apply what we know about how civil liberties work to the example of free speech on college campuses introduced at the beginning of this chapter. Can controversial speech on college campuses be limited? How can we explain this conflict?

The issue of free speech on campus raises difficult questions of balancing interests and drawing lines. Speakers' interests in making their voices and opinions heard must be balanced against the universities' interest in public safety and students' interest in protecting other students from hate speech. The First Amendment is applicable in these instances because the speakers in question are lecturing at public—that is, state government—institutions.

This puts many universities in a difficult spot—they would rather not allow these controversial speakers, especially because of the high cost of providing security. However, the First Amendment protects political speech, and the Supreme Court has established that it cannot be prevented unless there is a direct incitement to imminent violence. Even association with previous acts of violence, as in the case of Richard Spencer, is not sufficient grounds to prevent speech.

You exercise your civil liberties every day, whether speaking in public, going to church, being searched at an airport, participating in a political demonstration, writing or reading an article in your school newspaper, or being free from illegal police searches in your home. Because civil liberties are defined as those things the government cannot do to you, defining civil liberties is a political process. Often this process is confined to the courts, but for many issues—including free speech, freedom of the press, pornography, criminal rights, abortion, and gun control—it takes place in the broader political world, where defining civil liberties involves balancing competing ideals and interests and drawing lines by interpreting and applying the law. For example, debates over how to balance national security and civil liberties—whether newspapers should publish stories about classified government programs that may threaten civil liberties, or whether government surveillance powers should be strengthened to fight terrorism—will rage for years.

Other cases, such as the protests at military funerals or the protection of the due process rights of suspected criminals and terrorists, illustrate how difficult and politically unpopular it can be to protect our freedoms and liberty. Nearly everyone would agree that the behavior of the members of Westboro Baptist Church is completely outrageous. But protecting the freedom of speech is easy if you agree with what is being spoken. It becomes much more difficult if the freedom protects the rights of Nazis to march in Skokie, defends a person accused of a heinous crime, or gives a White supremacist like Richard Spencer a platform.

"What's Your Take?"

Should speakers with controversial, sometimes hateful opinions be allowed to speak on college campuses?

Or do universities' and students' interests outweigh their right to free speech?

STUDY GUIDE

Defining civil liberties

Define *civil liberties* and explain how the Bill of Rights came to apply to the states. (Pages 100–107)

Summary

The Bill of Rights—the first 10 amendments to the Constitution—lists individual protections from the federal government. For the majority of the nineteenth century, these individual freedoms were guaranteed from only the *federal* government and did not extend to protections from *state* governments. With the ratification of the Fourteenth Amendment and the process of selective incorporation, federal freedoms have been gradually extended to the state level.

Key terms

civil liberties (p. 100)　　due process clause (p. 105)

Civil War amendments　　selective incorporation (p. 105)
(p. 105)

Practice Quiz Questions

1. **The Bill of Rights originally protected individuals from which level of government?**

a　all levels of American government

b　state governments

c　local governments

d　federal government

e　the bureaucracy

2. **Which amendment has been used as the basis for selective incorporation?**

a　the Eighth Amendment

b　the Fourteenth Amendment

c　the Tenth Amendment

d　the Nineteenth Amendment

e　the Fifth Amendment

Freedom of religion

Describe the First Amendment liberties related to freedom of religion. (Pages 107–111)

Summary

Religious freedoms are defined by two clauses in the First Amendment: the establishment clause and the free exercise clause. Together, they do not allow the government to do anything to benefit any particular religion, nor do they allow the government to hinder religious practice without adequate justification. As is often the case, the Court has struggled to define exactly what constitutes "excessive government entanglement" in religion.

Key terms

establishment clause (p. 107)　　Lemon test (p. 108)

free exercise clause (p. 107)　　*Wisconsin v. Yoder* (p. 110)

Practice Quiz Questions

3. **The establishment clause is invoked under which of the following circumstances?**

a　allowing "conscientious objectors" to avoid the military draft

b　outlawing polygamy

c　prohibiting prayer in public schools

d　allowing the Amish to keep children home from school after the eighth grade

e　banning the handling of snakes in church services

4. **Which test does the Supreme Court use to establish whether there has been "excessive government entanglement with religion"?**

a　Lemon test

b　Kreutz test

c　Miller test

d　Meyer test

e　Brandenburg test

Freedom of speech, assembly, and the press

Describe the major First Amendment liberties related to freedom of speech. (Pages 111–120)

Summary

The Court's attempt to balance individual freedoms and public good is reflected in the scope of protections guaranteed by the First Amendment. The Court generally prioritizes protecting individual rights to political speech, hate speech, symbolic speech, the freedom to assemble, and the freedom of the press except under extreme circumstances (such as speech that directly incites violence). By contrast, the Court regularly places a lower priority on, and affords less protection to, fighting words, slander, libel, and commercial speech.

Key terms

strict scrutiny (p. 112)

intermediate scrutiny (p. 112)

clear and present danger test (p. 112)

direct incitement test (p. 113)

symbolic speech (p. 113)

Tinker v. Des Moines School District (p. 113)

hate speech (p. 114)

prior restraint (p. 117)

New York Times Co. v. United States (p. 118)

fighting words (p. 118)

slander (p. 118)

libel (p. 118)

commercial speech (p. 119)

Miller test (p. 119)

Practice Quiz Questions

5. Which test does the Court use to determine if speech is considered dangerous and should not be legally protected?

a   Lemon test

b   clear and present danger test

c   Miller test

d   direct incitement test

e   balancing test

6. Flag burning is an example of _____ that is currently _____ under the First Amendment.

a   symbolic speech; protected

b   symbolic speech; not protected

c   hate speech; protected

d   hate speech; not protected

e   offensive slander; not protected

7. Prior restraint involves limits on what form of expression?

a   freedom of assembly

b   freedom of association

c   freedom of speech

d   freedom of the press

e   freedom of religion

The right to bear arms

Explore why the Second Amendment's meaning on gun rights is often debated. (Pages 120–122)

Summary

The Supreme Court has done little to define exactly what freedoms are established in the Second Amendment, largely preferring to allow the national, state, and local governments to make their own laws. The majority of public sentiment appears in favor of continued gun ownership, and limitations on Second Amendment rights appear unlikely.

Key term

McDonald v. Chicago (p. 121)

Practice Quiz Question

8. What is the best summary of the current position of the Supreme Court on the Second Amendment?

a   The Court has upheld most gun control laws, both at the state and national level, arguing that there is no individual right to own guns.

b   The Court has upheld most gun control laws at the state level but struck down federal gun control laws, arguing that the Second Amendment applies only to Congress.

c   The Court has struck down some state and national limitations on gun ownership, arguing that the Second Amendment protects an individual right to bear arms.

d   The Court has struck down *all* state and national limitations on gun ownership, arguing that the Second Amendment protects an individual right to bear arms.

e   The Court has refused to take a general position on the individual right to bear arms.

Law, order, and the rights of criminal defendants

Describe the protections provided for people accused of a crime. (Pages 122–129)

Summary

The Fourth, Fifth, Sixth, and Eighth Amendments provide protections for individuals accused of a crime, known as due process rights. Interpreting these general due process rights in specific cases is difficult, however, because specific standards of fairness and justice are very hard to define.

Key terms

due process rights (p. 122)

exclusionary rule (p. 124)

Miranda rights (p. 126)

double jeopardy (p. 126)

Gideon v. Wainwright (p. 127)

Practice Quiz Questions

9. Protections from unreasonable searches and seizures are guaranteed by which constitutional amendment?

a   the Third Amendment

b   the Fourth Amendment

c   the Fifth Amendment

d   the Seventh Amendment

e   the Eighth Amendment

10. The Miranda rights are protections that primarily fall under which constitutional amendment?

a   the Third Amendment

b   the Fourth Amendment

c   the Fifth Amendment

d   the Seventh Amendment

e   the Eighth Amendment

11. In 1972, the Supreme Court banned the death penalty for what reason?

a   It deprived individuals of their rights to "life, liberty, or property."

b   It was cruel and unusual.

c   It was being inconsistently applied and violated the due process of law.

d   It was racially biased.

e   It was inconsistent with international law.

Privacy rights

Explain why the rights associated with privacy are often controversial. (Pages 129–131)

Summary

The term "privacy rights" is not found in the Constitution—rather, it was established in a 1965 Supreme Court case—but it may be implied in several amendments in the Bill of Rights. The right to privacy is controversial because of the lack of explicit language in the Constitution and the lack of consensus on exactly what the right to privacy means. It has remained a hot-button issue because recognition of the right to privacy is an important facet of the contemporary debate on abortion.

Key terms

privacy rights (p. 129)   *Roe v. Wade* (p. 129)

Practice Quiz Questions

12. Which of the following freedoms guaranteed in the Bill of Rights is thought to imply a right to privacy?

a   right to bear arms

b   freedom from unreasonable search and seizure

c   right to secure legal counsel

d   right to request a jury trial

e   freedom of speech

13. In what case did the Supreme Court first establish the right to privacy?

a   *Roe v. Wade*

b   *Lawrence v. Texas*

c   *Griswold v. Connecticut*

d   *Gonzales v. Oregon*

e   *Lemon v. Kurtzman*

Suggested Reading

Abraham, Henry J., and Barbara A. Perry. *Freedom and the Court: Civil Rights and Liberties in the United States*, 8th ed. Lawrence: University Press of Kansas, 2003.

Abrams, Floyd. *The Soul of the First Amendment*. New Haven, CT: Yale University Press, 2017.

Amar, Akhil Reed. *The Bill of Rights*. New Haven, CT: Yale University Press, 1998.

Chemerinsky, Erwin, and Howard Gillman. *Free Speech on Campus*. New Haven, CT: Yale University Press, 2017.

Lewis, Anthony. *Gideon's Trumpet*. New York: Random House, 1964.

Posner, Richard A. *Not a Suicide Pact: The Constitution in a Time of National Emergency*. New York: Oxford University Press, 2006.

Pritchett, C. Herman. *Constitutional Civil Liberties*. Englewood Cliffs, NJ: Prentice Hall, 1984.

Schweber, Howard. *Speech, Conduct, and the First Amendment*. New York: Peter Lang, 2003.

Walker, Samuel. *Presidents and Civil Liberties from Wilson to Obama: A Story of Poor Custodians*. New York: Cambridge University Press, 2014.

5

Civil Rights

You can't discriminate against me...right?

» **"No one should live in fear of being stopped whenever he leaves his home to go about the activities of daily life."**
Shira A. Scheindlin, former federal judge

« **"Well, I think profiling is something that we're going to have to start thinking about as a country. And other countries do it. . . . And they do it successfully. And I hate the concept of profiling. But we have to start using common sense, and we have to use our heads."**
President Donald Trump

» **"I don't even talk about whether or not racial profiling is legal. I just don't think racial profiling is a particularly good law enforcement tool."**
Eric Holder, former attorney general

Opponents of policing tactics such as "stop-and-frisk" and the use of excessive force have argued that these practices encourage illegal racial profiling. This issue was brought to the fore in 2020 when the killing of an unarmed Black man, George Floyd, by the police set off mass protests across the country against police brutality and racial injustice.

Our civil rights protect us from discrimination by the government and our fellow Americans. This issue came to the fore in 2020 when the killing of an unarmed Black man, George Floyd, by the police set off mass protests across the country against police brutality and racial injustice. Most everyone would agree that selective enforcement of laws depending on the color of one's skin constitutes discrimination—and is unacceptable. However, opinions on discrimination become less clear-cut in the realm of law enforcement, particularly when it comes to strategies that involve racial profiling. Not surprisingly, racial profiling is illegal as a general tool for screening suspects. As Shira Scheindlin, the federal judge who struck down New York City's controversial "stop-and-frisk" policy has made clear, Americans should not be singled out for scrutiny by law-enforcement officers just because of the color of their skin.[1] Under this policy, police officers stopped people based on the "reasonable suspicion" that they were engaged in criminal activity. At its peak in 2011, more than 685,000 New Yorkers were stopped by police; 88 percent were entirely innocent, just over half were between 14 and 24 years old, and 87 percent were African American or Latino. In 2019, 13,459 people were questioned and frisked by police in New York.[2] Stop and frisk became an issue in the 2020 Democratic presidential primary campaign when Mike Bloomberg, the former mayor of New York who expanded the policy, reversed his position and admitted it was a mistake.

However, President Donald Trump and others have called for a "commonsense" approach to profiling when it comes to both matters of local and national security, which would include more intense scrutiny of people who fit a certain profile imagined to be more likely to commit crimes.[3] People who take this position argue that it may be necessary to sacrifice some of our civil rights to more effectively keep neighborhoods safe from crime or secure our borders against terrorism. Many, including former attorney general Eric Holder, disagree with this perspective on purely practical grounds and say that racial profiling is simply not an effective tool of law enforcement.[4]

You probably have experience with questions of profiling and discrimination in your own life, beyond the realm of law enforcement. In fact, civil rights are one of the best examples of the idea that politics is everywhere: policies concerning discrimination in the workplace and in housing and against women, minorities, the LGBTQ community, and disabled people affect millions of Americans every day. Consider the following scenarios:

- Scenario 1: You are driving home one night with a few of your friends after a party. It is late at night, but you have not had anything to drink and you are following all traffic laws. Your heart sinks as you see the flashing lights of a squad car signaling you to pull over. As the police officer approaches your car, you wonder if you have been pulled over because you and your friends are African Americans driving in an all-White neighborhood. Have your civil rights been violated? Change the scene to a car full of White teenagers with all the other facts the same. Can an officer pull them over just because he or she thinks that teenagers are more likely than older people to be engaging in criminal activity?
- Scenario 2: You are a 21-year-old Asian-American woman applying for your first job out of college. After being turned down for a job at an engineering firm, you suspect that you didn't get the job because you are a woman and because management thought that you would not fit in with the "good ol' boy" atmosphere of the firm. Have your civil rights been violated?
- Scenario 3: You and your gay partner are told that "your kind" are not welcome in the apartment complex that you want to live in. Should you call a lawyer?
- Scenario 4: You are a White male graduating from high school. You have just received a letter of rejection from the college that was first on your list. You are very disappointed, but then you get angry when a friend tells you that one of your classmates got into the same school even though he had virtually the same grades as you and his SAT scores were a bit lower. Your friend says that it is probably because of the school's affirmative action policy—the classmate who was accepted is Latino. Are you a victim of "reverse discrimination"? Have your civil rights been violated?

All of these scenarios would seem to be civil rights violations. However, some are, some are not, and some depend on additional considerations (we will return to these examples in the chapter's conclusion). Is it ever acceptable to treat people differently based on the color of their skin, their ethnic status, their gender, or their sexual orientation, in a situation of racial profiling or otherwise? More broadly, when is discrimination legal, and when isn't it? How are civil rights in the United States defined today?

DESCRIBE THE HISTORICAL STRUGGLES GROUPS HAVE FACED IN WINNING CIVIL RIGHTS

The context of civil rights

In general, **civil rights** are rights that guarantee individuals freedom from discrimination. The terms "civil rights" and "civil liberties" are often used interchangeably, but there are important differences. Civil liberties are the freedoms guaranteed in the Bill of Rights, such as freedom of speech, religious expression, and the press, as well as the "due process" protection of the Fourteenth Amendment. In contrast, civil rights protect all persons from discrimination and are rooted in laws and the equal protection clause of the Fourteenth Amendment. Moreover, civil liberties primarily limit what the government can do to you ("*Congress* shall make no law ... abridging the freedom of speech," for example), whereas civil rights protect you from discrimination both by the government and by individuals. As noted in the previous chapter, to oversimplify, civil liberties are about freedom and civil rights are about equality.

Neither civil liberties nor civil rights figured prominently at the Constitutional Convention. Equality is not even mentioned in the Constitution or the Bill of Rights. However, equality was very much on the Founders' minds, as is evident in this ringing passage from the Declaration of Independence: "We hold these truths to be self-evident, that all men are created equal, that they are endowed by their Creator with certain unalienable Rights, that among these are Life, Liberty, and the pursuit of Happiness." Despite the broad language, this was a limited conception of equality, because women had no political or economic rights at that time. Similarly, equality did not apply to enslaved people or to Native Americans. Even propertyless White men did not have full political rights until several decades after the Constitution was ratified. Indeed, equality and civil rights in the United States have been a continually evolving work in progress.

African Americans

From the early nineteenth century and the movement for the abolition of slavery until the mid-twentieth century and the civil rights movement, the central focus of civil rights was on African Americans. Other groups received attention more gradually. For example, starting in the mid-nineteenth century women began their fight for equal rights and over the next century the civil rights movement expanded to include groups such as Native Americans, Latinos, and Asian Americans. Most recently, attention has turned to the elderly, disabled people, and the LGBTQ community (lesbian, gay, bisexual, transgender, and queer/questioning people). The most divisive civil rights issue with the greatest long-term impact, however, has been slavery and its legacy.

civil rights
Rights that guarantee individuals freedom from discrimination. These rights are generally grounded in the equal protection clause of the Fourteenth Amendment and more specifically laid out in laws passed by Congress, such as the 1964 Civil Rights Act.

Slavery was part of the American economy from the 1600s until it was abolished by the Thirteenth Amendment in 1865. The system of slavery in the South created a highly unequal society in which African Americans were denied virtually all rights. Abolitionists worked to undermine and abolish slavery. Harriet Tubman was instrumental in the success of the Underground Railroad, which brought countless enslaved people to freedom.

Slavery and Its Impact Slavery was part of the American economy from nearly the beginning of the nation's history. Dutch traders brought 20 enslaved people to Jamestown, Virginia, in 1619, a year before the Puritans landed at Plymouth Rock. It is impossible to overstate the importance of enslaved people to the southern economy. The 1860 census shows that there were 2.3 million enslaved people in the Deep South (including Georgia, Alabama, South Carolina, Mississippi, and Louisiana), constituting 47 percent of its population, and nearly 4 million enslaved people in the South overall. The economic benefits for owners of enslaved people were clear. By 1860, the per capita income for Whites in the South was $3,978; in the North it was $2,040. The South had only 30 percent of the nation's free population, but it had 60 percent of the wealthiest men.[5]

Abolitionists worked to rid the nation of slavery as its importance to the South grew, setting the nation on a collision course that would not be resolved until the Civil War. Despite the work of some early abolitionists, the Founders largely ducked the issue (see Chapter 2), and subsequent legislatures and courts did not come any closer to resolving the impasse between the North and South over slavery. The Missouri Compromise of 1820, which limited the expansion of slavery and kept the overall balance between slave states and free states, eased tensions for a while, but the issue persisted. By the 1830s, the abolitionist movement gained considerable strength. Owners of enslaved people became increasingly frustrated with the success of the Underground Railroad, which helped some enslaved people escape to freedom in the North. In 1850, the debate over admitting California as a free state or a slave state (or making it half-free and half-slave) threatened to split the nation once again. As part of the Compromise of 1850, southern states agreed to admit California as a free state, but only if Congress passed the Fugitive Slave Act, which required northern states to treat people who had escaped from slavery as property and return them to their owners. The Compromise also established Utah and New Mexico as territories that could decide for themselves if they would permit slavery. This idea of "popular sovereignty" concerning slavery in new states was fully embraced in the Kansas-Nebraska Act of 1854, thus overturning that central part of the Missouri Compromise.[6]

All possibility of further compromise ended with the misguided *Dred Scott v. Sandford* decision of 1857, in which the Supreme Court ruled that at the time of the drafting of the Constitution enslaved people were "considered as a subordinate and inferior class of beings who had been subjugated by the dominant race." Therefore, enslaved people were property rather than citizens and, as such, had no legal rights. The Court also used its power of judicial review for only the second time, ruling that it was unconstitutional for Congress to limit the property rights of owners of enslaved people in the territories. In 1860, believing that slavery was in jeopardy after Abraham Lincoln won the presidency, the southern states seceded from the Union and formed the Confederacy.

When the Civil War ended, national unity was restored and slavery ended, but the price was very high. About 528,000 Americans died in the war, with an astonishingly high casualty rate (25 percent).[7] After the war, Republicans moved quickly to ensure that the changes accomplished by the war could not be easily undone: they promptly adopted the Civil War amendments to the Constitution. The Thirteenth Amendment banned slavery, the Fourteenth guaranteed that states could not deny newly freed people the equal protection of the laws and provided citizenship to anyone born in the United States, and the Fifteenth Amendment gave African-American men the right to vote. These amendments were ratified within five years, although southern states resisted giving freed people and their descendants "equal protection of the laws" over the next 100 years.

A house divided against itself cannot stand. I believe this government cannot endure permanently half-slave and half-free.

—President Abraham Lincoln

Slow Progress after Reconstruction During Reconstruction (1866–1877), Blacks in the South gained political power through institutions such as the Freedmen's Bureau and the Union League. With the protection of the occupying northern army, Blacks were able to vote and even hold public office. However, when federal troops withdrew and the Republican Party abandoned the South, Blacks were almost completely disenfranchised through the imposition of residency requirements, poll taxes, literacy tests, the grandfather clause, physical intimidation, and other forms of disqualification. Later the practice known as the "white primary" allowed only Whites to vote in Democratic primary elections and, given that the Republican Party did not exist in most southern states, Blacks were effectively disenfranchised. Although most of these provisions were claimed to be race neutral, their impact fell disproportionately on Black voters and virtually eliminated Black voting. Despite the constitutional guarantees of the Fourteenth and Fifteenth Amendments, Blacks had little access to the political system in the South and they had little success in winning office at any level in the rest of the nation.[8]

The social and economic position of Blacks in the South followed a path similar to their political fortunes. When Reconstruction ended in 1877, the southern states enacted "black codes," or **Jim Crow laws**, that led to complete segregation of the races. Jim Crow laws forbade interracial marriage and mandated the separation of the races for neighborhoods, hotels, apartments, hospitals, schools, restrooms, drinking fountains, restaurants, elevators, and even cemetery plots. In cases where it would have been inconvenient to completely separate the races, as in public transportation, Blacks had to sit in the back of the bus or in separate cars on the train and give up their seats to Whites if asked. The Supreme Court validated these practices in *Plessy v. Ferguson* (1896) by establishing the **"separate but equal" doctrine**, officially permitting segregation as long as Blacks had equal facilities.

Initially after Reconstruction, the rest of the nation mostly ignored the status of Blacks, because 90 percent of all African Americans lived in the South. The subjugation of Blacks in the South went well beyond the separations of the races. A racist criminal justice system ignored widespread lynchings, church burnings, and general intimidation. The Equal Justice Initiative has documented 4,084 "racial terror lynchings" in 12 southern states between the end of Reconstruction in 1877 and 1950.[9] But as Blacks' northward migration gradually transformed the nation's demographic profile and its racial politics, America's "race problem" was no longer a southern problem. Although conditions for Blacks were generally better outside the South, they still faced discrimination and lived largely segregated lives throughout the nation. In World Wars I and II, Black soldiers fought and died for their country in segregated units. Professional sports teams were segregated, and Black musicians and artists could not perform in many of the nation's leading theaters. Moreover, Blacks largely were hired for the lowest-paying menial jobs.

Real progress began in the 1940s. The Supreme Court struck down the white primary in 1944, Jackie Robinson broke the color line in Major League Baseball in 1947, and President Harry Truman issued an executive order integrating the U.S. armed services in 1948. Then came the landmark decision *Brown v. Board of Education* (1954), which rejected the "separate but equal" doctrine and declared that race-based school segregation violates the Fourteenth Amendment's equal protection clause, followed by *Brown v. Board of Education II* (1955), which ordered that public schools be desegregated "with all deliberate speed." These events set the stage for the growing success of the civil rights movement, discussed later in this chapter.

Jim Crow laws
State and local laws that mandated racial segregation in all public facilities in the South, many border states, and some northern communities between 1876 and 1964.

"separate but equal" doctrine
The idea that racial segregation was acceptable as long as the separate facilities were of equal quality; supported by *Plessy v. Ferguson* and struck down by *Brown v. Board of Education*.

Brown v. Board of Education
(1954) declared that race-based school segregation violates the Fourteenth Amendment's equal protection clause.

Native Americans

The legacy of slavery and racial segregation has been the dominant focus of U.S. civil rights policies, but many other groups have also fought for equal rights. Understanding the history of these struggles is also necessary to understand today's civil rights policies.

Native Americans were the first group to come in contact with the European immigrants. Although initial relations were good, the settlers' appetite for more land and their insensitivity to Native-American culture fostered continual conflict. Native Americans were systematically pushed from their land and placed on reservations. The most infamous example was the removal of 60,000 members of the "Five Civilized Tribes" from the southeastern United States under the Indian Removal Act of 1830. Thousands of Native Americans died on the Trail of Tears on their way to reservations in Oklahoma.[10]

Native Americans had no political rights; the U.S. government considered them "savages" to be eliminated. The American Indian Wars involved about 1,500 different campaigns authorized by the American government between 1622 and the late nineteenth century.[11] By the end of the nineteenth century, the Native-American population had shrunk to 250,000 from at least eight times that many before the Europeans arrived (estimates range from a low of 2.1 million to a high of 18 million).[12] While thousands were killed by the military campaigns, most deaths were caused by European diseases for which the Native Americans did not have immunity, with smallpox being the most deadly.

Native Americans did not gain the right to vote until 1924, just after women and well after Black men. Although the U.S. government signed treaties with Native-American tribes that recognized them as sovereign nations (not as foreign nations but as "domestic dependent nations"),[13] in practice the government ignored most of the agreements. Only recently has the government started to uphold its obligations, although compliance remains spotty. Native Americans have struggled to maintain their cultural history and autonomy in the face of widespread poverty and unemployment and a sustained and concerted effort to force assimilation. The most notorious of these practices was the removal of children from their families to attend Native-American boarding schools that forced assimilation. Founded shortly after the Civil War, these schools continued to operate into the late twentieth century, with a peak attendance of 60,000 Native-American children in 1973. Although Christian

The Carlisle Indian Industrial School in Carlisle, Pennsylvania, was open from 1879 to 1918. The school's Native-American students were forced to cut their hair and change their names.

Native Americans' struggles to maintain the security of their cultural lands were at the forefront of controversy over the construction of the Dakota Access Pipeline. In 2016 and 2017, the Standing Rock Sioux tribe led protests against the oil pipeline and its proposed route, which threatened their ancestral lands and clean water supply.

missionaries originally ran the schools, the Bureau of Indian Affairs took over the operation of many in the twentieth century. This dark chapter in American history has been referred to by its critics as "cultural genocide."[14]

Latinos and Latinas

Latinos also have struggled for political and economic equality. The early history of Latinos in the United States is rooted in the Mexican-American War (1846–1848) and the conquest by the United States of the territory that today makes up most of the southwestern states. Although Latinos had long experienced prejudice and discrimination, one of their first major political successes was Cesar Chavez's effort to organize farmworkers in the 1960s and 1970s. He established the United Farm Workers Union and forced growers to bargain with 50,000 mostly Mexican-American fieldworkers in California and Florida. While many Mexican Americans have roots that go back centuries, most Latinos have been in the United States for less than two generations and have become a political force only recently, although they are now the nation's largest minority.

Latinos' relative lack of political clout when compared with that of African Americans derives from two factors. First, Latinos vote at a much lower rate than African Americans, in part because of language barriers. In addition, about one-third of Latinos cannot vote in national elections because they are not U.S. citizens. Second, unlike African Americans, Latinos are a relatively diverse group politically, composed of people from many Latin American nations. Most Latino voters are loyal to the Democratic Party, but a majority of Cuban Americans are Republicans. Although this diversity means that Latino voters do not speak with one voice, it brings opportunity for increased political clout in the future, because both parties are eager to attract them as new voters. In 2016, Donald Trump surprised many experts by winning a higher percentage of the Latino vote (29 percent) than Mitt Romney did in 2012 (27 percent). Trump defied expectations again in 2020, as this percentage increased to 32 percent despite his immigration policies.

Asian Americans

Asian Americans have experienced discrimination since their arrival in the United States in the nineteenth century. The first wave of Chinese immigrants came with the 1848 California gold rush and staked out their claims along with Americans. But by

1850, when the easy-to-find gold was gone, Americans tried to drive out the Chinese through violence and the Foreign Miners Tax. Subsequently, Chinese immigrants worked on building the intercontinental railroad between 1865 and 1869. However, because they were given the more dangerous jobs, many lost their lives. After the railroad was completed, Chinese workers returned to the West Coast, where they experienced increasing discrimination and violence. When Congress passed the Chinese Exclusion Act of 1882, Chinese already in the United States were prevented from becoming U.S. citizens—although the Supreme Court later granted their American-born children automatic citizenship under the Fourteenth Amendment.[15] The Chinese Exclusion Act also barred virtually all immigration from China—the first time in U.S. history that a specific ethnic group was singled out in this way. Later, during World War II, more than 110,000 Japanese Americans were singled out and placed in internment camps for fear that they were enemy supporters. Although the internment was upheld by the Supreme Court at the time, a 1980 congressional commission determined that it was a "grave injustice" motivated by "racial prejudice, war hysteria and the failure of political leadership." Eight years later, President Ronald Reagan signed into law the Civil Liberties Act, which paid more than $1.6 billion in reparations to the survivors of the camps and their heirs.[16] In 2018, the Court explicitly overturned the 1944 decision that approved the internment, saying, "The forcible relocation of U.S. citizens to concentration camps, solely and explicitly on the basis of race, is objectively unlawful and outside the scope of presidential authority."[17] In recent decades, a much broader range of Asians have immigrated to the United States, including Koreans, Filipinos, Hmong, Vietnamese, and Asian Indians; their diversity in culture means that they display equally diverse political views and voting patterns.

Women and civil rights

On the eve of the United States' declaration of independence in 1776, John Adams's wife, Abigail, advised him not to "put such unlimited power in the hands of the husbands. Remember, all men would be tyrants if they could. . . . If particular care and attention is not paid to the ladies, we . . . will not hold ourselves bound by any laws in which we have no voice or representation."[18] John Adams did not listen to his wife. The Constitution did not give women the right to vote, and they were not guaranteed that civil right until the Nineteenth Amendment was ratified in 1920. Until the early twentieth century, women in most parts of the country could not hold office, serve on juries, bring lawsuits in their own name, own property, or serve as legal guardians for their children. A woman's identity was so closely tied to her husband's that if she married a noncitizen she automatically gave up her citizenship. The rationale for these policies was called **protectionism**: women were considered too frail to compete in the business world and were seen as needing to be protected by men.

While protectionist sentiment waned by the mid-twentieth century, as recently as 1961 a Court upheld a Florida law that automatically exempted women but not men from compulsory jury duty. Later in this chapter, we describe how the Supreme Court has moved away from this discriminatory position and rejected protectionist thinking.

The LGBTQ community

The most recent group to engage in the struggle for civil rights is the LGBTQ community. For most of American history, gay men and lesbians lived secret lives and faced abuse and discrimination if they came out. The critical moment that spurred

protectionism
The idea under which some people have tried to rationalize discriminatory policies by claiming that some groups, like women or African Americans, should be denied certain rights for their own safety or well-being.

the gay rights movement occurred in 1969, during a police raid on the Stonewall Inn in New York City. (Police often raided gay bars to harass patrons and selectively enforce liquor laws.)[19] Rather than submitting to the arrests, the customers fought back, throwing stones and beer bottles, breaking windows, and starting small fires. Several hundred people gathered, and the fighting raged for three nights. The Stonewall rebellion galvanized the gay community by demonstrating the power of collective action.

Since Stonewall, the gay rights movement has made progress through political mobilization and protest, legislative action, and legal action. Public support for gay rights has increased dramatically in recent years. Seventy-five percent believe that same-sex couples should be able to adopt children (compared to only 14 percent in 1977), 89 percent think that businesses should not be able to discriminate against gays and lesbians, and 63 percent believe that same-sex couples should be entitled to the same benefits as heterosexual couples (whereas only 32 percent think they should not).[20] In May 2012, President Obama endorsed same-sex marriage for the first time (and was the first president to take that position), completing his gradual shift on the issue. In 2015, the Supreme Court ruled that same-sex marriage is legal in all 50 states.[21] In the 2016 presidential campaign Donald Trump said, "I will do everything in my power to protect our LGBTQ citizens from the violence and oppression of a hateful foreign ideology. Believe me." But his record on LGBTQ issues has been criticized by civil rights supporters.[22] In 2019, the Trump administration banned transgender people from joining the military and prohibited anyone currently in the military from transitioning genders. This policy was challenged in federal court, and the Supreme Court in 2019 let the ban stand. However, the Court's June 2020 landmark civil rights decision protecting gay and transgender people from discrimination in the workplace complicates the ban. While it remains in effect, a federal court planned to hear the case later in the year.

"Why Should I Care?"

Why does this history matter for politics today? First, the effects of slavery and Jim Crow laws are still quite evident: legal racial segregation ended 50 years ago, but its legacy—especially evident in the difference that exists in the relative quality of education available to most Whites and Blacks—remains. Second, knowing about this history helps us understand where the inequalities (that we discuss in the next section) in our society come from. Finally, active discrimination based on race, gender, and sexual orientation is still evident in our society. Given the importance of race in the everyday lives of millions of Americans and in gaining an understanding of American politics, a grasp of the history that got us to where we are today is an important starting point.

★

ANALYZE INEQUALITY AMONG RACIAL, ETHNIC, AND SOCIAL GROUPS TODAY

The racial divide today

The racial divide today begins with the unequal treatment of racial minorities, women, gays, and lesbians and is rooted in the gulf that remains between minorities and Whites, in terms of their objective condition as well as their political views. Although substantial progress has been made in bridging that gulf, political, social, and economic inequalities remain.

Differences in voting access

The United States has a long history of discriminating against racial and ethnic minorities in the election process. Although African Americans voted at a rate that was quite similar to that of Whites in presidential elections from 2008 to 2020, their turnout in midterm elections has been somewhat lower than that of Whites, and other racial and ethnic minorities have generally lower turnouts (see Figure 5.1). Much of the difference in voter turnout can be accounted for by education and income, but there still are practices and institutions that specifically depress minority-voter turnout. And many of these deterrents are intentional. The National Association for the Advancement

FIGURE 5.1

Turnout in Presidential Elections by Race

Turnout among African Americans has risen steadily over the last 20 years (with a dip in 2016), while turnout of other groups has remained relatively flat. What do you think accounts for these trends? What could state governments do to increase voter turnout?

Source: United States Elections Project, "Voter Turnout Demographics," www. electproject.org/home/voter-turnout/ demographics (accessed 5/14/20).

of Colored People (NAACP), the U.S. Commission on Civil Rights, and the Brennan Center for Justice have all documented such practices in elections going back to 2000, including moving and reducing the number of polling places in areas with predominantly minority voters, changing from district-based to at-large elections, using voter challenges to target minority voters, redistricting to dilute minority voting power, withholding information about registration and voting procedures from Blacks, and "causing or taking advantage of Election Day irregularities."[23]

In recent years many states have restricted access to voting by requiring an ID to vote (which has a disproportionate impact on minorities because they are less likely to have a photo ID), requiring proof of citizenship to vote, cutting back on early voting days and times, and making it more difficult for people to register to vote.[24] In addition, as we will discuss later, in 2013 the Supreme Court struck down an important provision of the Voting Rights Act (VRA) of 1965, making it easier for the nine states that had been covered by this provision of the law to implement discriminatory practices. However, legal challenges in many states pushed back against these changes in voting laws. Those supporting voting rights won at least partial victories in eight states against voter ID laws and restrictions on early voting that had a racial impact. Other states also restored the right to vote for those with past criminal convictions.[25] Also, partly in response to the COVID-19 pandemic, which required restrictions on social gatherings and interactions, many states passed laws to make voting easier, such as automatically registering voters and imposing fewer restrictions on early voting and voting by mail.

Socioeconomic indicators

The racial divide is also evident in social and economic terms. Nearly twice as many Black families are below the poverty line as White families: 18.8 percent compared with 9.1 percent in 2019. The poverty rate of 15.7 percent for Latino families in 2019 was similar to that of Black families. (Poverty thresholds are determined by the amount of money an individual or family earns each year. This figure varies by state, by the composition of the household, and by year, to account for inflation in the cost of living expenses. For 2020, an individual living on an income of less than $12,760, or a family of four living on less than $26,200, would be considered as living in poverty and eligible for certain programs as a result.[26])

While White median household income (that is, income from wages, salaries, interest, and disability and unemployment payments) was $72,204 in 2019, Black median household income was $45,438 (62.9 percent of White family income) and Latino median household income was $56,113 (77.7 percent of White family income).[27] Moreover, the gap in overall wealth is much more dramatic. The average White household has more than six times the assets of the typical non-White family. In 2019, the median household net worth (that is, the sum of all assets, including houses, cars, and stock) was $189,000 for Whites, $24,000 for African Americans, and $36,000 for Latinos.[28] Poverty is not distributed equally throughout the United States but rather is concentrated in areas where the minority population is the highest (see Figure 5.2).

Other indicators show similar patterns. For example, the rate of Black adult male unemployment has been about twice as high as that of White adult male unemployment

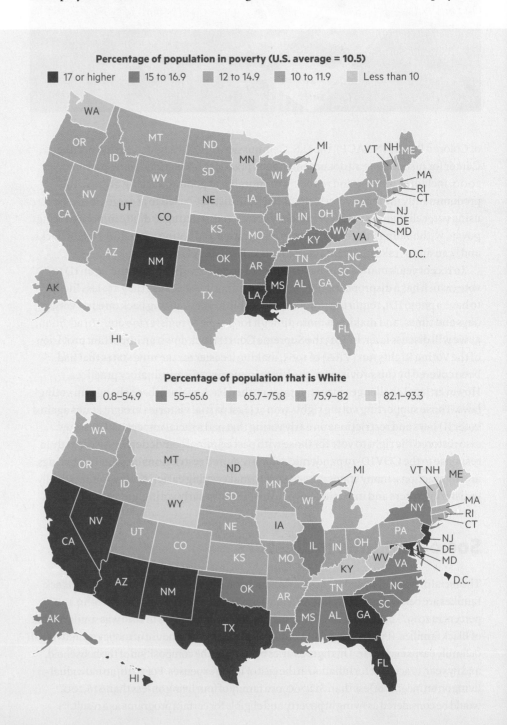

FIGURE 5.2

Poverty and Race, 2020

Carefully examine these maps. What is the relationship between poverty and the minority population? How do you think these patterns might affect the politics of civil rights policies aimed at reducing discrimination in the workplace or housing?

Sources: Poverty data from U.S. Census Bureau, 2019 American Community Survey, www.census.gov/acs; race data from U.S. Census Bureau, Quickfacts, www.census.gov/quickfacts/fact/map (both accessed 9/23/20).

Percentage of population in poverty (U.S. average = 10.5)

17 or higher | 15 to 16.9 | 12 to 14.9 | 10 to 11.9 | Less than 10

Percentage of population that is White

0.8–54.9 | 55–65.6 | 65.7–75.8 | 75.9–82 | 82.1–93.3

for the past 45 years. On every measure of health—life expectancy, infectious diseases, infant mortality, cancer rates, heart disease, and strokes—the gaps between Whites and Blacks are large and, in some cases, increasing.[29] Current research suggests that racial disparities in health outcomes may be caused in part by government policies and business-related decisions. Broadly labeled "environmental racism," these practices mean that minority groups are much more likely to live in areas affected by pollution, toxic waste, and hazardous chemical sites.[30] One of the most extreme examples of this came to light in late 2015 and early 2016 in Flint, Michigan. In 2014, to save money, the city switched its public water supply from Lake Huron to the Flint River. The poor, majority-Black residents of Flint soon reported discolored, foul-looking water, but city and state officials ignored their complaints. Researchers demonstrated that levels of lead in the water far exceeded safe levels. Many residents had elevated levels of lead in their blood, among other serious health issues. President Obama declared the city a disaster area and aid was provided in early 2016, but permanent damage had already been done.[31] More than a dozen officials were charged with felonies for their role in the crisis; none were convicted of the most serious charges, but several plead "no contest" to lesser charges. More than 80 lawsuits have been filed in the case, the most significant a $722 million class-action lawsuit filed in 2017 against the Environmental Protection Agency. Early in 2020, the Supreme Court allowed that case to move forward.[32]

Criminal justice and hate crimes

The greatest disparity between racial minorities and Whites may be in the criminal justice system. Recently, tensions have been high between minority communities and the police in the wake of dozens of cases of police shooting unarmed Black men. In 2019, police killed 1,004 people in the United States; of those, 235 were African Americans (see the What Do the Facts Say? feature).[33] Most of these involved tragic circumstances in which police were acting appropriately given existing protocols. But several highly publicized cases reveal negligent and, in some cases, criminal behavior by police officers. In 2013, following the acquittal of a neighborhood watch member, George Zimmerman, for shooting an unarmed 17-year-old African American, Trayvon Martin, the group Black Lives Matter was formed.[34] The next year in Ferguson, Missouri, thousands of protesters gathered to call attention to the killing of an unarmed man, Michael Brown, by a police officer. The officer was acquitted, but an investigation by the Department of Justice found patterns of discriminatory behavior by the Ferguson Police Department. From 2015 to 2020, other high-profile cases of officers killing unarmed African Americans occurred in Cleveland, Baltimore, Chicago, Staten Island, Baton Rouge, Minneapolis–St. Paul, and Sacramento. One 2015 case in North Charleston, South Carolina, led to a murder charge for the officer. Following a daytime traffic stop for a broken taillight, Officer Michael Slager shot Walter Scott in the back eight times from a distance of 15 to 20 feet as Scott was running away, and lied about what happened to cover up his crime. A bystander's video showed the murder and led to Slager's arrest. State first-degree murder charges were dismissed, however, as part of a plea deal. Slager ultimately plead guilty to a federal civil rights charge of using excessive force and was sentenced to 20 years in prison.[35] Overall, convictions in these cases are rare. One study found that of the roughly 14,000 police shootings from 2005 to 2019, there were 98 officers arrested for murder or manslaughter and just over one-third were convicted of a crime, but only three for murder.[36] There has also been intensive research on the topic of racial bias in police shootings, with more than 50 studies since 2015. Some of the studies have found that African Americans are more than twice as likely to be killed by police as Whites are, while other studies have found no significant differences.[37]

Racial Inequality in Law Enforcement

In 2020, national protests set off by the killing of an unarmed Black man, George Floyd, in Minneapolis, Minnesota, raised the issue of racial inequality in law enforcement and underscored similar killings in Ferguson, Missouri, Baltimore, Maryland, and Staten Island, New York. These graphs show both the total number and the relative number (expressed as a percentage), by race, of people killed by police. Do racial inequalities exist in law enforcement? What do the facts say?

Think about it

- **For all victims (total and unarmed),** what racial category had the highest percentage of deaths? What racial category had the highest percentage of victims unarmed and not attacking? What do you think accounts for this difference?

- **Is there a greater racial disparity** in the second chart (which shows all people killed by police) or the third chart (which shows unarmed people)?

- **What, if anything, surprises you** about these numbers? Why?

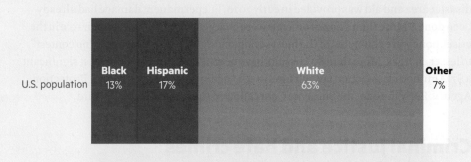

U.S. population — Black 13% | Hispanic 17% | White 63% | Other 7%

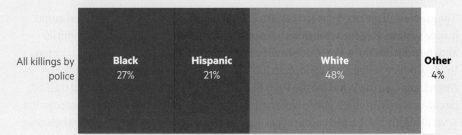

All killings by police — Black 27% | Hispanic 21% | White 48% | Other 4%

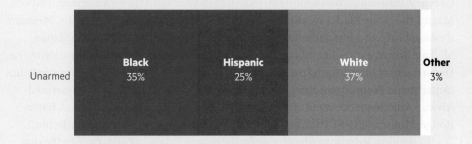

Unarmed — Black 35% | Hispanic 25% | White 37% | Other 3%

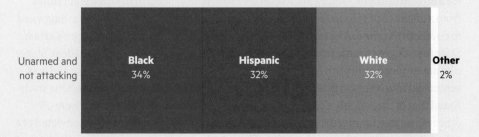

Unarmed and not attacking — Black 34% | Hispanic 32% | White 32% | Other 2%

Source: "2017 Police Violence Report," Mapping Police Violence, https://policeviolencereport.org (accessed 9/23/20).

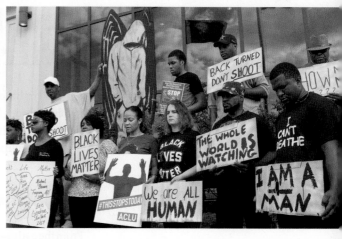

Racial profiling subjects many innocent Blacks to intrusive searches. In addition, Blacks are not only more likely than Whites to be convicted for the same crimes but also more likely to serve longer sentences.[38] And African Americans and other minorities are subjected to hate crimes much more frequently than Whites.[39] According to FBI statistics, in 2018 nearly half of race-related hate crimes in the United States were "anti-Black" (48 percent), while only 19 percent were "anti-White" (57 percent of all hate crimes are race based). This means that the rate of anti-Black hate crimes is nearly four times what would be expected based on the percentage of African Americans in the United States, while the rate of anti-White hate crimes is less than one-third as high as would be expected. One of the most extreme hate crimes in recent years happened in 2015 when Dylann Roof, a 21-year-old White supremacist, shot and killed nine people at a Bible study in the historic Emanuel African Methodist Episcopal Church in Charleston, South Carolina. Roof later confessed that he was trying to ignite a race war.

This backdrop of racial inequality, discrimination, and violence drives civil rights activists to push their agenda in the three branches of government: legislative, executive, and judicial. In some instances, activists work in several arenas simultaneously; in others, they seek redress in one arena after exhausting alternatives in the others. The civil rights movement, which was crucial in the early policy successes, also continues to mobilize from the grass roots.

There have been dozens of high-profile cases in recent years of police shooting unarmed Black men. Walter Scott was killed by North Charleston, South Carolina, police officer Michael Slager following a traffic stop for a broken brake light, inspiring protests throughout the city.

Mourners outside the Emanuel AME Church in Charleston, South Carolina, pray at the memorial for the nine people shot and killed by White supremacist Dylann Roof during a prayer service.

Key players in the conflict over civil rights

Our civil rights policies are produced by several key players. First, the public becomes involved through social movements to put pressure on the political system to change. But Congress, the president, and the courts all also exert their own influence on policies that define civil rights.

Social movements

From the early women's rights movement and abolitionists of the nineteenth century to the gay rights and civil rights movements of the mid-twentieth century, activists have pressured the political system to change civil rights policies. Through collective action, these social movements have made sure that protecting equal rights remained on the policy agenda.

Women started to push for the right to vote at a convention in 1848 in Seneca Falls, New York. Subsequently, a constitutional amendment to give women the right to vote was regularly introduced in Congress between 1878 and 1913 but never was passed, despite the efforts of women such as Sojourner Truth, Ida B. Wells, Susan B. Anthony, and Elizabeth Cady Stanton. After a parallel movement at the state level had some success, the Nineteenth Amendment, giving women the right to vote, was finally passed in 1919 and ratified in 1920 (see Figure 5.3).

The civil rights movement of the 1950s and 1960s, aimed at ending segregation and guaranteeing equal political and social rights for Blacks, is the most famous example of a successful social movement (see Figure 5.4). Although the *Brown v. Board of Education* decision, which struck down segregation in public schools, gave the movement a boost, most southern Blacks saw little change in their daily lives after the ruling. As White school boards and local governments resisted integration, Black leaders became convinced that the only way to change the laws was to get the public, both Black and White, to demand change.

The spark came in 1955 in Montgomery, Alabama, when Rosa Parks refused to give up her seat on a bus to a White person, as she was required to do by law. When she was

FIGURE 5.3   **Women's Rights Time Line**

First women's rights convention held in Seneca Falls, New York.	Territory of Wyoming gives women the right to vote.	Congress requires equal pay for equal work for federal employees (but not for private sector workers).	The Nineteenth Amendment gives women the right to vote (however, this largely only benefits White women, as women of color still face significant barriers to voting, including voter suppression and intimidation at the polls).	Equal Pay Act requires equal pay for equal work.	Title VII of the Civil Rights Act bars employment discrimination based on race, sex, and other grounds.
1848	**1869**	**1872**	**1920**	**1963**	**1964**

Source: Compiled by the authors.

arrested, local civil rights leaders organized a boycott of the bus company. Whites in Montgomery tried to stop the boycott. The police arrested and fined Blacks who arranged a car pool system to get to work: people waiting for a ride were arrested for loitering, and car pool drivers were arrested for lacking appropriate insurance or having too many people in their car. Martin Luther King Jr., the group's elected leader, was subjected to harassment and violence—his house was firebombed, and he was arrested several times. Finally, a federal district court ruled that the segregation policy was unconstitutional and the Supreme Court upheld the ruling.

Nonviolent Protest In 1960, four Black students in Greensboro, North Carolina, went to a segregated lunch counter at a local Woolworth's and asked to be served. They waited for an hour without being served and had to leave when the store closed. When 20 students returned the next day, national wire services picked up the story. Within two weeks, the sit-ins spread to 11 cities. In some cases, the students encountered violence; in others, they were simply arrested. However, they continued to respond with passive resistance, and new waves of protesters replaced those who had been arrested. The Student Nonviolent Coordinating Committee (SNCC) was created to coordinate the protests. The Greensboro Woolworth's was integrated on July 26, 1961, but the protests continued in other cities. By August 1961, the sit-ins had 70,000 participants and there had been 3,000 arrests.[40] The sit-ins marked an important shift in the tactics of the civil rights movement away from the court-based approach, exemplified by the fight against the "separate but equal" doctrine (as we will discuss next), and toward the nonviolent civil disobedience that had been successful in Montgomery.

The next significant events occurred in Birmingham, Alabama, which experienced 18 unsolved bombings of Black churches and homes in a six-year period. During a peaceful protest in 1963, Martin Luther King Jr. and many others were arrested. While in solitary confinement, King wrote his "Letter from Birmingham Jail," an eloquent statement of the principles of nonviolent civil disobedience. Responding to White religious leaders who said that King's actions were "unwise and untimely" and that "when rights are consistently denied, a cause should be pressed in the courts and in negotiations among local leaders, and not in the streets," King wrote a justification for civil disobedience, asserting that everyone had an obligation to follow just laws but an equal obligation to break unjust laws.

As part of the Montgomery Bus Boycott, many African Americans organized car pools or walked to work.

Griswold v. Connecticut legalizes the use of contraceptives by married couples.	Federal affirmative action policies are extended to women by an executive order.	Title IX of the Education Amendments of 1972 requires equal access to programs for men and women in higher education.	Roe v. Wade establishes a constitutional right to abortion.	Thirty-five states ratify the Equal Rights Amendment, passed by Congress in 1971–1972, falling three states short of the number needed to add the amendment to the Constitution. (As of 2020, three additional states ratified the amendment; however, because their approval occurred after the deadline, they don't legally count toward the three-fourths of the states required.)	Lilly Ledbetter Fair Pay Act makes it easier to sue for gender-based pay discrimination.	The social media campaign #MeToo calls attention to sexual violence against women.
1965	1967	1972	1973	1982	2009	2017

FIGURE
5.4

African-American Civil Rights Time Line

Government Action

May 17
U.S. Supreme Court rules segregated schools are unconstitutional in the *Brown v. Board of Education* decision.

September 9
The Federal Civil Rights Act prohibits discrimination.

September 23
President Eisenhower sends troops to escort Black students into a White high school in Little Rock, Arkansas.

1954   1957

Social Movement

December 1
Rosa Parks is arrested for refusing to move to the back of a bus in Montgomery, Alabama.

February 1
Black college students, refused service at a lunch counter in Greensboro, North Carolina, launch a sit-in.

May 4
Freedom Riders test a Supreme Court decision that integrated interstate bus travel, sparking violence.

1955   1960   1961

Source: Adapted from "Civil Rights Movement Timeline," History.com, www.history.com/topics/civil-rights-movement-timeline (accessed 5/13/20).

Public Opinion and Legislative Action Following King's release from jail, the situation escalated. The protest leaders decided to use children in the next round of demonstrations. After more than 1,000 children were arrested and the jails were overflowing, the police turned fire hoses and police dogs on children trying to continue their march. Media coverage turned public opinion in favor of the marchers as the country expressed outrage over the violence in Birmingham. Similar protests occurred in over 100 southern cities.

Mass protest became the preferred tool of many other social movements for civil rights and other causes. Vietnam War protesters marched on Washington by the hundreds of thousands in the late 1960s and early 1970s. Likewise, the women's rights, gay rights, and environmental movements have staged many mass demonstrations in Washington and other major cities. The largest single day of protest in the United States was the Women's March on January 21, 2017, which drew an estimated 4.2 million people in 654 American cities and another 300,000 in 261 cities around the world to protest the election of Donald Trump and call attention to issues concerning women's rights, health care, and immigration reform.[41]

The tools of social movements have evolved in recent years to combine the power of social media and mass protest. #BlackLivesMatter started in 2013 on social

July 2
President Johnson signs the Civil Rights Act.

August 6
The Federal Voting Rights Act prohibits denying anyone the vote on the basis of color or race.

April 11
Fair Housing Act protects against discrimination in housing.

1964   **1965**   **1968**

April 16
Martin Luther King Jr. writes his "Letter from Birmingham Jail," defending nonviolent civil disobedience against unjust laws.

February 21
Malcolm X is shot and killed in New York.

March 7
Six hundred voting rights marchers are attacked by police with clubs and whips on the Edmund Pettus Bridge outside Selma, Alabama. On March 21, about 3,200 marchers head out again on a four-day march to Montgomery in support of voting rights.

August 28
Martin Luther King Jr. delivers his "I Have a Dream" speech at the March on Washington.

September 15
Four girls are killed when a Baptist church in Birmingham, Alabama, is bombed.

June 21
Three civil rights workers are murdered outside Philadelphia, Mississippi.

April 4
Martin Luther King Jr. is slain in Memphis, Tennessee.

1963   **1964**   **1965**   **1968**

media but has since expanded to organize mass protests against police killings in many cities across the country. Black Lives Matter is a large, decentralized movement that is not organized under a traditional hierarchy or national leadership. Black Lives Matter activists have thus used a broad range of tactics to raise awareness and put pressure on police departments to change their policies, including marches, "die-ins" (protests in which participants block traffic by lying in the street), and social media campaigns. Many police departments have responded to the organization's concerns about excessive police violence and a lack of accountability by adopting new policies, such as requiring police officers to wear body cameras and complete bias-reduction training programs.[42] The cause received a boost in 2017 when many NFL players kneeled during the playing of the national anthem before games to call attention to racially biased policing and police violence. President Trump pressured NFL owners to force the players to stand, saying that their actions disrespected the flag and the military personnel who serve the country. However, some players continued their protest throughout the season.[43] Protesters intensified their call for changes to police practices during the summer of 2020 after police killed George Floyd in Minneapolis and Breonna Taylor in Louisville and shot Jacob Blake in Kenosha.

After King's and others' nonviolent protests produced significant successes, mass protests became the preferred tool of many social movements, such as the Women's March on Washington (left) and Black Lives Matter (right).

The legacy of the civil rights movement has been not only to help change unjust laws but also to provide a new tool for political action across a broad range of policy areas. By putting pressure on political leaders through direct, nonviolent protest, millions of Americans have had their voices heard.

The courts

The Supreme Court has played an important role in defining civil rights, including those pushed for by the social movements just discussed. In the mid-twentieth century, the justices moved away from the "separate but equal" doctrine, required the desegregation of public schools, and upheld landmark civil rights legislation passed by Congress. More recently, they have expanded civil rights for women and the LGBTQ community, but they also have endorsed a "color-blind" position that some see as a movement away from protecting civil rights.

Challenging "Separate but Equal" in Education In the 1930s, the NAACP, which was established to fight for equal rights for Black people, started a concerted effort to nibble away at the "separate but equal" doctrine. Rather than tackling segregation head-on, the NAACP first challenged an aspect of segregation that would be familiar to the Supreme Court justices: the ways in which states kept Blacks out of all-White law schools.

After several victories, the signals increasingly indicated that the Supreme Court was ready to strike down the "separate but equal" doctrine. As background, in addition to the law school cases, in 1948 the Court had ruled that "restrictive covenants"—clauses in real estate contracts that prevented a property owner from selling to an African American—could not be enforced by state or local courts because the Fourteenth Amendment prohibited the states from denying Blacks the "equal protection of the laws."[44] This application of the Fourteenth Amendment was expanded in the landmark ruling *Brown v. Board of Education*.

The *Brown* case arrived on the Court's docket in 1951, was postponed for argument until after the 1952 elections, and was re-argued in December 1953. The postponement was intentional, because the Court knew that a firestorm would ensue. In its unanimous decision the Court ruled: "In the field of public education, the doctrine of separate but equal has no place. Separate educational facilities are inherently unequal, depriving the plaintiffs of the equal protection of the laws."[45] The case was significant not only because it required all public schools to desegregate but also because it used the equal protection clause of the Fourteenth Amendment in a way that had potentially far-reaching consequences. Also, even though the decision did not rule segregation unconstitutional in all contexts, *Brown* provided an important boost to the civil rights movement.

The Push to Desegregate Schools In 1955, *Brown v. Board of Education II* addressed the implementation of desegregation and required the states to "desegregate with all deliberate speed."[46] The odd choice of words, "all deliberate speed," was read as a signal by southerners that they could take their time with desegregation. The phrase does seem to be contradictory: being deliberate does not usually involve being speedy. Southern states engaged in "massive resistance" to the desegregation order. In some cases, they even closed public schools rather than integrate them—and then reopened the schools as "private," segregated schools for which the White students received government vouchers. However, Maryland, Kentucky, Tennessee, Missouri, and the District of Columbia desegregated their schools within two years.

Eight years after *Brown I*, little had changed in the Deep South: fewer than 1 percent of Black children attended school with White children.[47] Through the 1960s, the courts had to battle against the continued resistance to integration. In 1971, the Court shifted its focus from **de jure** segregation (segregation mandated by law) to **de facto** segregation (segregation that existed because of segregated housing patterns) and approved school busing as a tool to integrate schools.[48] This approach was extremely controversial. The Court almost immediately limited the application of busing by ruling in a Detroit case that busing could not go beyond the boundaries of a city's school district: students did not have to be bused from suburbs to cities— unless it could be shown that the school district's lines were drawn in an intentionally discriminatory way.[49] This rule encouraged "White flight" from the cities to the suburbs in response to court-ordered busing.

In a significant recent decision, in 2007 the Court invalidated voluntary desegregation plans implemented by public school districts in Seattle and Louisville. Both districts set goals for racial diversity and denied school assignment requests if they tipped the racial balance above or below certain thresholds. In these cases, the discrimination was against White students who wanted to be in schools with few minority students, rather than Black students who wanted to be in integrated schools.[50]

DID YOU KNOW?

75%

of African-American students and 79 percent of Latino students attend schools that are majority minority.
Source: U.S. News & World Report

de jure
Relating to actions or circumstances that occur "by law," such as the legally enforced segregation of schools in the American South before the 1960s.

de facto
Relating to actions or circumstances that occur outside the law or "by fact," such as the segregation of schools that resulted from housing patterns and other factors rather than from laws.

Busing students from one school district to another has been controversial since the 1960s. In Boston in the 1970s, many Black students who were bused into White districts needed police protection against protests.

A 15-year-old civil rights demonstrator, defying an anti-parade ordinance, is attacked by a police dog in Birmingham, Alabama, on May 3, 1963. The next day, during a meeting at the White House, President Kennedy discussed this photo, which had appeared on the front page of the *New York Times*. Reaction against this police brutality helped spur Congress and the president to enact civil rights legislation.

Expanding Civil Rights for African Americans Other significant rulings in the 1960s struck down state laws that forbid interracial marriages (16 states had such laws), upheld all significant parts of the Civil Rights Act, and expanded the scope of the Voting Rights Act (VRA; these important laws will be discussed in the next section). In central cases, the justices ruled that Congress had the power to eliminate segregation in public places, such as restaurants and hotels, under the commerce clause of the Constitution.

One important area of cases was in employment law. In 1971, the Court ruled that employment tests, such as written exams or general aptitude tests, that are not related to job performance and that discriminate against Blacks violate the 1964 Civil Rights Act.[51] This means that if the employment practice has a bad *effect* on a racial group, it doesn't matter whether or not the discrimination is *intended*. The Supreme Court and Congress have gone back and forth in defining this concept, but it is still important in workplace discrimination suits. (See also Nuts & Bolts 5.1.)

The Color-Blind Court and Judicial Activism Recently, the Supreme Court has been gradually imposing a "color-blind jurisprudence" over numerous issues—that is, the Court has reasoned that race should not be considered in determining the outcome of certain kinds of cases. One significant area was the 1992 racial redistricting in which 15 new U.S. House districts were drawn to help elect African Americans and 10 districts were drawn to help elect Latino members. The resulting dramatic change in the number of minorities in Congress (an increase greater than 50 percent) was rooted in the 1982 amendments to the VRA. Instead of mandating a fair *process*, this law and subsequent interpretation by the Supreme Court mandated that minorities have an "equal opportunity" to "elect representatives of their choice" when their numbers and configuration permit. As a result, the legislative redistricting process now had to avoid discriminatory *results* rather than being concerned only with discriminatory *intent*.

However, in several decisions, starting with the 1993 case *Shaw v. Reno*, the Supreme Court's adherence to a color-blind jurisprudence has thrown the constitutionality of Black-majority districts into doubt. The Court has ruled that Black-majority districts are legal as

Race-Related Discrimination as Defined by the Equal Employment Opportunity Commission

Race/Color Discrimination

Race discrimination involves treating someone (an applicant or employee) unfavorably because he/she is of a certain race or because of personal characteristics associated with race (such as hair texture, skin color, or certain facial features). Color discrimination involves treating someone unfavorably because of skin color complexion.... Discrimination can occur when the victim and the person who inflicted the discrimination are the same race or color.

Race/Color Discrimination and Work Situations

The law forbids discrimination when it comes to any aspect of employment, including hiring, firing, pay, job assignments, promotions, layoff, training, fringe benefits, and any other term or condition of employment.

Race/Color Discrimination and Harassment

It is unlawful to harass a person because of that person's race or color. Harassment can include, for example, racial slurs, offensive or derogatory remarks about a person's race or color, or the display of racially offensive symbols. Although the law doesn't prohibit simple teasing, offhand comments, or isolated incidents that are not very serious, harassment is illegal when it is so frequent or severe that it creates a hostile or offensive work environment or when it results in an adverse employment decision (such as the victim being fired or demoted). The harasser can be the victim's supervisor, a supervisor in another area, a coworker, or someone who is not an employee of the employer, such as a client or customer.

Race/Color Discrimination and Employment Policies/Practices

An employment policy or practice that applies to everyone, regardless of race or color, can be illegal if it has a negative impact on the employment of people of a particular race or color and is not job-related and necessary to the operation of the business.

Source: U.S. Equal Employment Opportunity Commission, "Race/Color Discrimination," www.eeoc.gov (accessed 3/20/20).

"Why Should I Care?"

As a job applicant, it is essential to know your rights. These guidelines forbid discrimination when it comes to any aspect of employment, including hiring, firing, pay, job assignments, promotions, layoff, training, fringe benefits, and any other term or condition of employment. They also prohibit retaliation against people who complain of discrimination. Everyone is protected from race and color discrimination: Whites, Blacks, Asians, Latinos, persons of more than one race, and all other persons, whatever their race, color, or ethnicity.

long as they are "done right."[52] But it has consistently held that if race is the predominant factor in drawing district lines, the districts are unconstitutional because they violate the equal protection clause of the Fourteenth Amendment for the White plaintiffs in these cases. Based on this reasoning, Black-majority districts in North Carolina, Georgia, Louisiana, Virginia, Texas, and Florida have been found to be unconstitutional. In 2001, the Court upheld the re-drawn 12th District in North Carolina, which no longer was a Black majority, arguing that when race and partisanship are so intertwined—as they are when 90 percent of African Americans vote for a Democratic candidate—plaintiffs cannot assume that African Americans were placed together for racial reasons. This ruling opens the door for a greater consideration of race than had been allowed in the previous cases.[53]

In 2017, the Court struck down districting plans in North Carolina and Virginia for packing African Americans into districts, thus diluting their ability to have an equal opportunity to elect candidates of their choice.[54] However, racial redistricting remains an unsettled area of the law. According to election law expert Richard Hasen, the Supreme Court's decision in 2019 to no longer decide cases concerning partisan gerrymandering will "force courts to make logically impossible determinations about whether racial reasons or partisan motives predominate when a party gerrymanders for political advantage." That is, a state could redraw districts on racial grounds (which would not be OK), but claim it was for partisan reasons (which now *is* OK, at least in federal court), and there would be no way for the courts to sort this out.[55]

The Court also struck down an important part of the 1965 VRA in a 2013 ruling. This case concerned the "coverage formula" that determines which states have to get approval from the Justice Department before implementing changes in an election law or practice (such as redistricting or closing a polling place). This "preclearance" provision of the law was viewed as one of the best ways to stop discriminatory voting practices because it could prevent them before they were implemented, rather than forcing voters to wait until they went into effect to challenge them. The Court ruled that the coverage formula was an unconstitutional burden on the covered states and was a violation of the Tenth Amendment.[56]

The racial redistricting and voting rights cases illustrate that the Supreme Court is increasingly activist in issues involving civil rights: it is generally unwilling to defer to the other branches of government and will assert its view of discrimination and equal protection regardless of what the other branches think (see Chapter 13 for a broader discussion of judicial activism). In some periods, like the 1950s and 1960s, judicial activism has served to further civil rights. More recently, it has served to limit them.

Women's Rights The Supreme Court has also been central in shaping women's civil rights. Until relatively recently, the Court did not apply the Constitution to protect women's rights, despite the Fourteenth Amendment's language that states may not deny any *person* the equal protection of the laws. Apparently, women were not regarded as people when it came to political and economic rights in the nineteenth and early twentieth centuries. These protectionist notions were finally rejected in three cases between 1971 and 1976, when the Court made it much more difficult for states to treat men and women differently.

The first case involved an Idaho state law that gave a man priority over a woman when they were otherwise equally entitled to execute a person's estate. This law was justified on the "reasonable" grounds that it reduced the state courts' workload by having an automatic rule that would limit challenges. But the Court ruled that the law was arbitrary, did not meet the "reasonableness" test, and therefore violated the woman's equal protection rights under the Fourteenth Amendment.[57] The second case involved a female air force officer who wanted to count her husband as a dependent for purposes of health and housing benefits. Under the law at the time, a military man could automatically count his wife as a dependent, but a woman could claim her husband only if she brought in more than half the family income. The Court struck down this practice, saying that protectionist laws, "in practical effect, put women not on a pedestal, but in a cage."[58]

rational basis test
The use of evidence to suggest that differences in the behavior of two groups can rationalize unequal treatment of these groups.

These two cases relied on the **rational basis test** for discrimination between men and women (which evolved from the reasonableness test). It wasn't until 1976 that the Court established the intermediate scrutiny test (see Chapter 4) in a case involving the drinking age. In the early 1970s, some states had a lower drinking age for women than for men on the "reasonable (or rational) basis" that 18- to 20-year-old women are more mature than men of that age (and thus less likely to abuse alcohol). The new intermediate scrutiny standard meant that the government's policy must be "substantially related" to an "important government objective" to justify the unequal treatment of men and women, so the law was struck down.[59]

Before this case, only two standards served to apply the Fourteenth Amendment to different categories of people: the rational basis test and the strict scrutiny test. The strict scrutiny test gives racial minorities the strongest protection as the "suspect classification" under the Fourteenth Amendment and stipulates that there must be a "compelling state interest" to discriminate among people if race is involved. The other standard, the rational basis test, says that it is acceptable for states to discriminate against a group of people as long as there is a "rational basis" for the state law. Today, for example, states can pass drinking laws that allow only those who are 21 and older to drink on the grounds that traffic fatalities will be lower with that drinking age rather than under a law that allows 18-year-olds to drink (see How It Works: Civil Rights). The intermediate scrutiny standard gives women stronger protections than the rational basis test, but this standard is not as strong as strict scrutiny.

The more aggressive application of the Fourteenth Amendment for women helped in providing them the equal protection of the laws, as shown in a Court decision that struck down the male-only admission policy at the Virginia Military Institute (VMI). The ruling stated that VMI violated the Fourteenth Amendment's equal protection clause because it failed to show an "exceedingly persuasive justification" for its sex-biased admissions policy.[60]

An important gender-equality case in 2017 concerned the law for determining the citizenship of children born overseas to an unmarried couple when one parent is a citizen and the other is not. Federal law requires a single father to have resided in the United States for five years prior to his child's birth in order for that child to have U.S. citizenship, while a child born overseas to a single American mother would be granted U.S. citizenship if the mother had lived continuously in the United States for just one year prior to the child's birth. The Court ruled that this gender-based distinction was unconstitutional. As with earlier cases involving the drinking age and alimony, the remedy in this case was to make things worse for women in the short term—that is, rather than reducing the residency requirement for men from five years to one, the Court increased it for women to match the longer period for men. However, supporters of women's rights applauded the decision for what it means for gender equality in the long term.

Two other areas where the Court has helped advance women's rights are affirmative action and protection against sexual harassment. In 1987, the Court approved affirmative action in a case involving a woman who was promoted over a man despite the fact that he scored slightly higher than she did on a test. The Court ruled that the promotion was acceptable to make up for past discrimination.[61] The Court made it easier to sue employers for sexual harassment in 1993, saying that a woman did not have to reach the point of a nervous breakdown before claiming that she was harassed; it was enough to demonstrate a pattern of "repeated and unwanted" behavior that created a "hostile workplace environment."[62] Later rulings stated that if a single act is flagrant, the conduct does not have to be repeated to create a hostile environment.

The issues of sexual harassment exploded on the national scene in October 2017, when Ashley Judd, Angelina Jolie, Gwyneth Paltrow, and Rose McGowan alleged that Hollywood mogul Harvey Weinstein sexually assaulted them. Ten days later, actress Alyssa Milano encouraged other women to share their stories with the hashtag #MeToo, building on the movement started by activist Tarana Burke to raise awareness of sexual assault. Within 24 hours the messages had been retweeted 500,000 times and shared in 12 million posts on Facebook. In 2020, Weinstein was convicted in New York court and sentenced to 23 years in prison; he faces additional charges in California court.[63] Allegations of sexual harassment or assault have ended the careers of Fox News anchor Bill O'Reilly, Senator Al Franken, comedian Bill Cosby, Representative John Conyers, Alabama Senate nominee Roy Moore, morning show anchors Matt Lauer and Charlie Rose, Olympic gymnast doctor Lawrence G. Nassar, public radio star Garrison Keillor, celebrity chef Mario Batali, conductor James Levine, actor Kevin Spacey, and

Civil Rights

Cases Involving "Suspect Classification"
(race, ethnicity, creed, or national origin)

Strict Scrutiny Test

1. Is unequal treatment justified by a **"compelling state interest"**?

yes   **no**

↓

discrimination is illegal

↓

2. Is unequal treatment the **"least restrictive"** option?

yes   **no**

↓

discrimination is illegal

Very few cases meet this standard.

Cases Involving Sex or Gender Equality

Intermediate Scrutiny Test

1. Is the discriminatory policy **"substantially related"** to an **"important government objective"**?

yes   **no**

↓

discrimination is illegal

2. Is the discrimination **not substantially broader** than it needs to be to protect the important government interest?

yes   **no**

↓

discrimination is illegal

Some discrimination based on gender is permitted, but this test is harder to pass than the rational basis test applied to gender cases in the past.

Cases Involving Age, Economic Status, or Other Criteria

Rational Basis Test

1. Is the law **rationally related to furthering** a legitimate government interest?

yes   **no**

↓

discrimination is illegal

2. Does the policy avoid **"arbitrary, capricious, or deliberate"** discrimination?

yes   **no**

↓

discrimination is illegal

This is the easiest hurdle for a law or policy to pass.

discrimination is legal

Evaluating Discrimination Cases

Strict Scrutiny Test

Case 1:

The University of Michigan Law School's "holistic" race-conscious admissions policy is designed to promote diversity.

Case 2:

The University of Michigan's more rigid race-conscious undergraduate admissions policy was designed to promote diversity.

The Court asked...

1. Is unequal treatment justified by a "compelling state interest"?
2. Is unequal treatment the "least restrictive" option?

The Court said...

In Case 1, discrimination is OK. In *Grutter v. Bollinger* (2003), the Court ruled that the state's interest in **racial diversity in higher education was compelling**, and that this specific admissions policy was narrowly tailored. This was affirmed in *Fisher v. Univ. of Texas* (2016).

In Case 2, discrimination is not OK. In *Gratz v. Bollinger* (2003), the Court **struck down Michigan's undergraduate admissions policy** for not being narrowly tailored.

Intermediate Scrutiny Test

Case 1:

A California state law says that men— but not women— can be guilty of statutory rape.

Case 2:

The Virginia Military Institute maintained a male-only admissions policy.

The Court asked...

1. Is the discriminatory policy "substantially related" to an "important government objective"?
2. Is the discrimination not substantially broader than it needs to be to protect the important government interest?

The Court said...

In Case 1, discrimination is OK. In *Michael M. v. Superior Court* (1981), the Court found that the state had a **strong interest in preventing illegitimate pregnancy** and in punishing only the participant who, by nature, suffers few of the consequences of his conduct.

In Case 2, discrimination is not OK. In *United States v. Virginia* (1996), the Court **struck down the Virginia Military Institute's policy** as a violation of the equal protection clause of the Fourteenth Amendment.

Rational Basis Test

Case 1:

States have a 21-year-old drinking age that applies equally to men and women.

Case 2:

An Oklahoma law allowed 18- to 20-year-old women— but not men—to buy 3.2% ABV ("nonintoxicating") beer.

The Court asked...

1. Is the law rationally related to furthering a legitimate government interest?
2. Does the policy avoid "arbitrary, capricious, or deliberate" discrimination?

The Court said...

In Case 1, discrimination is OK. Various state supreme courts have upheld these laws on the rational basis that **the laws may prevent drunk driving among those younger than 21**.

In Case 2, discrimination is not OK. In *Craig v. Boren* (1976), the Court **struck down this law**, rejecting the rational basis that Oklahoma had claimed and instead applying intermediate scrutiny.

❓ Critical Thinking

1. **Is it easier for the government to discriminate against** someone based on age or race? Why?

2. **What is the standard used by the Court if the state wants** to make distinctions between people based on race? Under what circumstances and in what scenarios is discrimination based on race legal?

many more. *Time* magazine named "The Silence Breakers" their "person of the year" for 2017 for their courage in bringing attention to this problem.[64]

While the court of public opinion and the actual courts have played a central role in bringing justice to the victims of sexual assault and harassment, the Supreme Court has been less sympathetic to plaintiffs in cases involving pay discrimination. Lilly Ledbetter sued Goodyear Tire & Rubber Company because she had received lower pay than men doing the same work over a 20-year period, which she claimed was gender discrimination. The Court rejected her claim, saying that she did not meet the time limit required by law, as the discrimination must have occurred within 180 days of the claim.[65] (This overturned the long-standing policy of the EEOC—the Equal Employment Opportunity Commission—which held that each new paycheck restarted the 180-day clock as a new act of discrimination.) Dissenters pointed out that pay discrimination usually occurs in increments over long periods, so it would be impossible to recognize unequal pay within 180 days of an initial paycheck. Congress overturned the Court's decision and restored the old standard in January 2009 by passing the Lilly Ledbetter Fair Pay Act. But as Figure 5.5 shows, significant pay disparities between men and women remain throughout much of the United States. Early in 2016, President Obama issued an executive order requiring companies with more than 100 employees to report to the federal government what they pay employees by race, gender, and ethnicity. He said, "Women are not getting the fair shot that we believe every single American deserves."[66] However, in 2017, President Trump overturned this order.[67]

Gay Rights The Supreme Court has a similarly mixed record on gay rights. The Court's decisions in early cases were not supportive of gay rights. One of the first cases concerned Georgia's law banning sodomy. The Supreme Court ruled in

DID YOU KNOW?

Women working full-time earn

$0.81

compared to every dollar earned by men.

Source: payscale.com

FIGURE 5.5

Lifetime Wage Gap for Women as Compared to Men

There is a substantial difference between women's and men's earnings in the United States. What could account for this variation? How much do you think it has to do with levels of discrimination, and how much with differences in the nature of the jobs that men and women hold?

Source: National Women's Law Center, "Lifetime Wage Gap Losses for Women: 2019 State Rankings," based on U.S. Census 2019 American Community Survey Data, March 2019, https:// nwlc-ciw49tixgw5lbab.stackpathdns.com/ wp-content/uploads/2019/03/Women-Lifetime-Losses-State-by-State-2019.pdf (accessed 3/22/20).

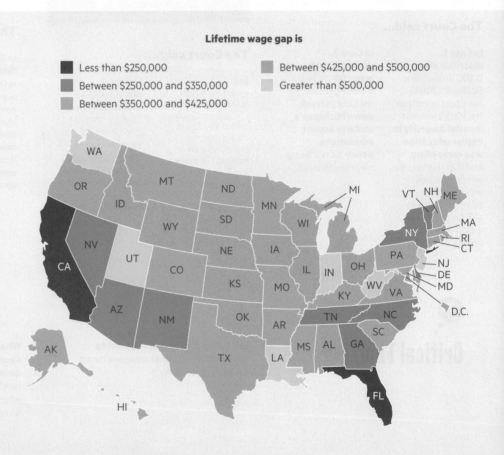

Lifetime wage gap is

- Less than $250,000
- Between $250,000 and $350,000
- Between $350,000 and $425,000
- Between $425,000 and $500,000
- Greater than $500,000

Bowers v. Hardwick (1986) that "homosexual behavior" was not protected by the Constitution and that state laws banning it could be justified under the most lenient "rational basis" test.[68]

After cases in which it sidestepped the issue, the Court first endorsed civil rights for gays in 1996. Here the Court struck down an amendment to the Colorado state constitution that prevented them from suing for discrimination in employment or housing. The Court said that the amendment violated gays' equal protection rights because it "withdrew from homosexuals, but no others, specific legal protection from the injuries caused by discrimination."[69] An important ruling came in 2003 in a case involving two Houston men. As we discussed in Chapter 4, the Supreme Court ruled in a historic decision that the due process clause of the Fourteenth Amendment guarantees freedom of not only thought, belief, and expression but also certain intimate conduct (including same-sex relations).[70]

The Supreme Court issued two important rulings on same-sex marriage in 2013. The first case was a narrow ruling that reinstated same-sex marriage in California but did not affect any other state. The second case was a more far-reaching decision that struck down the Defense of Marriage Act (DOMA) as a violation of the Fifth Amendment's due process clause. The majority opinion said that the federal government cannot deny benefits to same-sex couples who are legally married under state law. The gradual movement toward endorsing same-sex marriage culminated in 2015 in the landmark ruling *Obergefell v. Hodges*, which legalized same-sex marriage in all 50 states.[71] The 5–4 ruling said that the fundamental right to marry is guaranteed by both the due process clause and the equal protection clause of the Fourteenth Amendment.

In 2020, there was another landmark ruling in protection of the rights of gay and transgender people. In a 6–3 ruling on *Bostock v. Clayton County*, the Court said that the language of the Civil Rights Act of 1964 applies to discrimination based on sexual orientation and gender identity. As such, it protects gay and transgender individuals from discrimination in the workforce.[72] The plaintiff, Gerald Bostock, had been fired from his job for expressing interest in forming a gay softball league at work. The Supreme Court consolidated the case with two other similar cases of workplace discrimination: *Altitude Express Inc. v. Zarda* and *R.G. & G.R. Harris Funeral Homes Inc. v. Equal Employment Opportunity Commission*.[73]

Writing for the majority, Justice Neil Gorsuch said, "An employer who fires an individual merely for being gay or transgender defies the law." Prior to this decision, it had been legal in almost half the states to fire an employee for being gay, bisexual, or transgender.

This summary of cases demonstrates that the courts can be both a strong advocate of and an impediment to civil rights. In general, however, the courts have a limited *independent* impact on policy. Indeed, the Supreme Court must rely on the other branches of government to carry out its policy decisions.

The Constitution promises liberty to all within its reach ... [and] extend[s] to certain personal choices central to individual dignity and autonomy, including intimate choices that define personal identity and beliefs.

—Supreme Court's majority opinion in *Obergefell v. Hodges*

Congress

Congress has provided the basis for protection of civil rights through laws enacted starting in the 1960s. Applying to racial and ethnic minorities and women, these laws attempted to ensure a "level playing field" of equal opportunity.

Key Early Legislation The bedrock of equal protection that exists today stems from the 1964 Civil Rights Act, the 1965 VRA, and the 1968 Fair Housing Act. President Lyndon Johnson, a former segregationist, helped push through the

Civil Rights Act when he became president. The act barred discrimination in employment based on race, sex, religion, or national origin; banned segregation in public places; and established the EEOC as the enforcement agency for the legislation.

The VRA eliminated direct obstacles to minority voting in the South, such as discriminatory literacy tests and other voter registration tests, and provided the means to enforce the law: federal marshals were charged with overseeing elections in the South. The VRA, often cited as one of the most significant pieces of civil rights legislation,[74] precipitated an explosion in Black political participation in the South. The most dramatic gains came in Mississippi, where Black registration increased from 6.7 percent before the VRA to 59.8 percent in 1967.

The Fair Housing Act of 1968 barred discrimination in the rental or sale of a home based on race, sex, religion, or national origin. Important amendments to the law enacted in 1988 added disability and familial status (having children under age 18), provided new administrative enforcement mechanisms, and expanded Justice Department jurisdiction to bring suit on behalf of victims in federal district courts.[75]

There have been many other important amendments to civil rights laws since the 1960s. The 1975 amendments to the VRA extended coverage of many of the law's provisions to language minorities, guaranteeing that registration and voting materials are made available to voters in their native language in certain districts with large numbers of citizens who are not proficient in English. The 1982 VRA amendments extended important provisions of the law for 25 years and made it easier to bring a lawsuit under the act. The 1991 Civil Rights Act overruled or altered parts of 12 Supreme Court decisions that had eroded the initial intent of the 1964 civil rights legislation. It also expanded earlier legislation and increased the costs to employers for intentional, illegal discrimination. In 2006, Congress voted to extend the VRA for another 25 years.

Protections for Women Women have also received extensive protection through legislation. In 1966, the National Organization for Women (NOW) was formed to push for enforcement of Title VII of the Civil Rights Act, which barred discrimination based on gender. NOW's members convinced President Johnson to sign an executive order that eliminated sex discrimination in federal agencies and among federal contractors, but it was difficult to enforce. Finally, in 1970, the EEOC started enforcing the law. Before long, one-third of civil rights cases involved sex discrimination, and those numbers remain high.

In 1972, Congress passed Title IX of the Education Amendments, which prohibits sex discrimination in institutions that receive federal funds. The law has had the greatest impact in women's sports. In the 1960s and 1970s, opportunities for women to play sports in college or high school were limited because of few scholarships and small budgets for women's sports. Although it took nearly 30 years to reach parity between men and women, most universities are now in compliance with Title IX. Nonetheless, many men's sports, such as baseball, tennis, wrestling, and gymnastics, were cut at universities that had to bring the number of student athletes into rough parity, and critics argued that such cuts were unfair, especially as the interest in women's sports was not as high as for men's sports. Defenders of the law argue that the gap in interest in women's and men's sports will not change until there is equal opportunity. There is some evidence to support that claim, as interest is increasing in professional women's soccer with the NWSL (National Women's Soccer League) and professional women's basketball with the WNBA (Women's National Basketball Association), as well as in well-established women's professional sports such as golf and tennis.

No person in the United States shall, on the basis of sex, be excluded from participation in, be denied the benefits of, or be subjected to discrimination under any educational program or activity receiving Federal financial assistance.

—Full text of Title IX

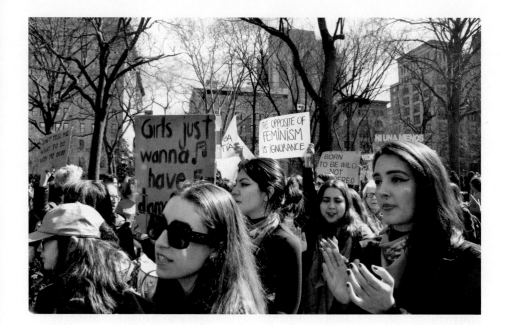

At the fourth annual Washington, D.C., Women's March in 2020, demonstrators gathered to show their support for women's rights.

Another significant legislative effort was the failed Equal Rights Amendment. It was approved by Congress in 1972 with simple wording: "Equality of rights under the law shall not be denied or abridged by the United States or any state on the account of sex." Many states passed it within months, but the process lost momentum and after seven years (the deadline set by Congress for ratification by the states) the amendment fell 3 states short of the required 38 states. The amendment received a three-year extension from Congress, but it still was not passed by the additional three states. Three more states have ratified the ERA since 2017, most recently Virginia in 2020, bringing the total to 38. Then, a few weeks after the Virginia vote, the House passed a bill nullifying the 1982 deadline for the ERA. With abortion rights being weakened by state laws and the possibility that the Supreme Court will overturn *Roe v. Wade*, supporters of abortion rights would like to provide constitutional protection.[76] However, five other states rescinded their ratifications back in the late 1970s and the Senate is unlikely to take up the bill. Therefore, the only way to adopt the ERA would be to start the entire process over again.

In 1994, Congress passed the Violence against Women Act, which allowed women who were the victims of physical abuse and violence to sue in federal court and provided funding for investigating and prosecuting violent crimes against women, for helping the victims of such crimes, and for prevention programs. In 2000, part of this law was overturned by the Supreme Court, which ruled that Congress had exceeded its powers under the commerce clause.[77] Nonetheless, the funding provisions of the act were reauthorized and expanded by Congress in 2000, 2005, and 2013.

Protections for Disabled People and for Gay Rights Other important civil rights legislation included the 1990 Americans with Disabilities Act, which provided federal protections for disabled Americans in terms of workplace discrimination and access to public facilities. This law produced curb cuts in sidewalks, access for wheelchairs on public buses and trains, special seating in sports stadiums, and many other changes that provide disabled people an opportunity to participate more fully in society.[78]

Congress's track record in protecting gay rights has not been as strong. In fact, most of the steps taken by Congress have been to restrict gay rights. In 1996, Congress reacted to the possibility that some liberal states would allow same-sex marriage by passing DOMA. This act defined marriage as only between a man and woman and barred couples in same-sex marriages from receiving federal insurance or Social Security spousal benefits and from filing joint federal tax returns. However, as we noted earlier, this law was struck down by the Supreme Court in 2013, and the entire law was overturned in 2015.

In a possible change of course, in 2009 Congress passed the Matthew Shepard and James Byrd Jr. Hate Crimes Prevention Act. This legislation expanded the hate-crime laws based on race, color, religion, or national origin to include attacks based on sexual orientation, gender identity, or intellectual or physical disability. The law also lifted a requirement that a victim had to be attacked while engaged in a federally protected activity, such as attending school, for it to be a federal hate crime. In signing the bill, President Obama said, "After more than a decade of opposition and delay, we've passed inclusive hate-crimes legislation to help protect our citizens from violence based on what they look like, who they love, how they pray or who they are."[79] The law commemorates the murders of James Byrd Jr., a Black man who in 1998 was dragged behind a pickup truck by White supremacists for three miles until his head and right arm were severed, and Matthew Shepard, a gay teenager who in 1998 was beaten by two men, tied to a fence, and left to die. Also, the Employment Non-Discrimination Act, which would prohibit discrimination in employment based on sexual orientation, has been proposed in nearly every Congress since 1994. A version of the bill passed the House in 2007 but died in the Senate.

The president

The mid-century civil rights movement benefited greatly from presidential action. President Truman integrated the armed services in 1948, and President Eisenhower used the National Guard to enforce a court order to integrate a school in Arkansas in 1957. Executive orders by President Kennedy in 1961 and President Johnson in 1965 established affirmative action, and in 1969 Richard Nixon expanded the "goals and numerical ranges" for hiring minorities in the federal government.

The most significant action by a president in the area of civil rights for gay men and lesbians was President Bill Clinton's effort to end the ban on homosexuals in the military. Under his policy of "don't ask, don't tell," the military would stop actively searching for and discharging homosexuals from the military ranks, and recruits would not need to reveal their sexual orientation. But if the military did find out (without conducting an investigation) that a person was gay, he or she still could be disciplined or discharged. Subsequently, President Obama promised to repeal "don't ask, don't tell," and under his administration Congress passed the Don't Ask, Don't Tell Repeal Act of 2010. The repeal went into effect on September 20, 2011. Minutes afterward, navy lieutenant Gary Ross and his longtime partner were married in Vermont and Ross became the first openly gay married person in the military.[80] President Obama extended the policy to include transgender service members, but President Trump reversed that policy, tweeting that "the United States Government will not accept or allow transgender individuals to serve in any capacity in the U.S. Military." However, an injunction against the ban was ordered by a federal judge, who said that lawsuits against the ban have a strong chance of prevailing and that the ban "does not appear to be supported by any facts."[81] In March 2018, Trump issued a new executive order with essentially the same ban (but with a version of "don't ask, don't tell"), and the Supreme Court allowed the ban to go into effect in 2019 (without ruling

You do not take a person who, for years, has been hobbled by chains and liberate him, bring him up to the starting line of a race and then say "you are free to compete with all the others," and still just believe that you have been completely fair.

—President Lyndon Johnson on affirmative action

In a landmark civil rights decision in 2020, the Supreme Court ruled that employers cannot discriminate against employees because of their sexual orientation or gender identity. This has renewed questions about President Trump's reversal of the Obama-era policy of allowing transgender people to serve in the military, which is currently being challenged in court.

on the constitutionality of the ban) while four lawsuits in federal court challenging the policy play out.[82]

Recent presidential candidates have generally made civil rights policy a low priority, which means that it is less likely that significant and dramatic change will come from unilateral action by the president. Instead, attention to civil rights concerns in the executive branch in the past few decades has primarily been in two areas: racial diversity in presidential appointments and use of the bully pulpit to promote racial concerns and interests.

President Bill Clinton was active in both areas. His cabinet, subcabinet, and judicial appointments achieved the greatest gender and racial balance in history. Clinton also used the bully pulpit to advocate a civil rights agenda. Most significant was his effort to promote a "national conversation on race," which helped focus national attention on many of the problems faced by minorities. President George W. Bush did not achieve the same level of diversity in his appointments as Clinton did, but his administration was more diverse than those of other Republican presidents. Bush also made serious overtures to minorities, especially Latinos, in his effort to expand the Republican Party base. In terms of Barack Obama's presidency, the historical significance of his successful campaign as a minority candidate is clear. And like his predecessors, Obama nominated a diverse cabinet—with 14 men, 7 women, and 7 racial minorities. Eric Holder was the first African American to serve as attorney general, and Sonia Sotomayor is the first Latina on the Supreme Court. Obama also nominated Elena Kagan to the Supreme Court, putting three women on the Court for the first time.

Donald Trump was elected with racially divisive positions, such as building a wall between the United States and Mexico and deporting 12 million undocumented residents. In his election-night victory speech, he emphasized the importance of representing all Americans and uniting the country. As president, Trump has tended to express polarizing opinions on civil rights issues, rather than unifying themes. He failed to condemn the attacks by White supremacists on counterprotesters in Charlottesville, Virginia, instead blaming "both sides" for the violence and saying that some of the White supremacists were "very fine people." He also said that any NFL player who knelt during the national anthem in protest of racial bias in policing was a "son of a bitch," attempted to ban immigration to the United States from several dominantly Muslim countries, said the immigrants from Africa were from "shithole countries," told four House members who are women of color to go back to the "crime infested places from which they came" (three of the four were born in the United States), and banned transgender service members from the military.

"Why Should I Care?"

Why is it important for us to know about who the key players are in civil rights? At various times in our history, different branches of government took the lead in promoting civil rights: Congress in the 1960s with the Civil Rights Act and the VRA, Presidents Clinton and Obama with promoting diversity in presidential appointments, and the Supreme Court in endorsing same-sex marriage. But in recent years, both the Supreme Court and President Trump have moved some civil rights policies in the other direction. If we want to see policies on these kind of issues change, knowing who is involved, and what impact these policies can have, is critical.

★

EXAMINE AFFIRMATIVE ACTION AND OTHER ONGOING CIVIL RIGHTS ISSUES

Civil rights issues today

Today, there is vigorous debate over the likely direction of the civil rights movement in the twenty-first century. These debates play out over a broad range of issues, several of which are outlined in this section.

Affirmative action or reverse discrimination

Even though the Civil Rights Act of 1964 ensured that all Americans would enjoy equality of opportunity, Blacks continued to lag behind Whites in socioeconomic status. In 1965, President Johnson required all federal agencies and government contractors to submit written proposals to provide an equal opportunity for employment of Blacks, women, Asian Americans, and Native Americans within various job categories and to outline programs to achieve those goals. The policy was expanded under President Richard Nixon, and throughout the 1970s and 1980s affirmative action programs grew in the private sector, higher education, and government contracting. Through such programs, employers and universities gave special opportunities to minorities and women.

Affirmative action takes many forms. The most passive type involves recruiting women and minorities for employment or college admission by placing ads in newspapers and magazines, visiting schools with diverse student populations, or sending out targeted mailings. A more active form involves including race or gender as a "plus factor" in admissions or hiring decisions. That is, in a pool of qualified candidates a minority applicant may receive an advantage over White applicants. (Women generally do not receive special consideration in admissions decisions, but gender may be a "plus factor" in some employment decisions.) The strongest form of affirmative action is the use of quotas—strict numerical targets to hire or admit a specific number of applicants from underrepresented groups.

Affirmative action has been a controversial policy. Polls indicate that minorities are much more supportive of the practice than Whites are. Many Whites view it as "preferential treatment" and "reverse discrimination." Two-thirds of Whites support passive affirmative action in general terms to "increase the number of Black and minority students on college campuses," but when asked specifically about race-based admissions or merit-based admissions, only 22 percent said that college admissions should "take race/ethnicity into account" while 76 percent said that admissions should be based "solely on merit" (the comparable numbers for Black respondents were 44 percent and 50 percent).[83]

The Supreme Court has helped define the boundaries of this policy debate. The earliest cases concerning affirmative action in employment upheld preferential treatment and rigid quotas when the policies were necessary to make up for past discrimination.[84] In each instance, there had been a previous pattern of discrimination and exclusion.

The Court moved in a more color-blind direction in an important reverse-discrimination employment case in 2009. In that case, 17 White firefighters and 1 Latino firefighter sued the city of New Haven, Connecticut, for throwing out the results of a test that would have been used to promote them. The city tried to ignore the test results because no African-American firefighters would have qualified for promotion and the city feared a "disparate impact" lawsuit. However, the Court ruled that the exam did appear to be "job related and consistent with business necessity" (as required by Section VII of the Civil Rights Act) and that unless the city could provide a "strong basis in evidence" that it would have been sued, it had to consider the results of the exam.[85]

The landmark decision for affirmative action in higher education was *Regents of the University of California v. Bakke* (1978).[86] Allan Bakke, a White student, sued when he was denied admission to medical school at the University of California, Davis, in successive years. Bakke's test scores and GPA were significantly higher than those of some minority students who were admitted under the school's affirmative action program. The Supreme Court agreed with Bakke that rigid racial quotas were unconstitutional but allowed race to be used in admissions decisions as a "plus factor" to promote diversity in the student body.

In two 2003 cases from the University of Michigan, the Court's rulings were consistent with *Bakke*, saying that the law school's "holistic approach," which considered race as one of the factors in the admission decision, was acceptable. However, the more rigid approach for undergraduate admissions at Michigan, which automatically gave minority students 20 of the 100 points needed to guarantee admission, was unacceptable.[87] Though these two decisions affirmed *Bakke*, it was the first time that a majority of the Court clearly stated that "student body diversity is a compelling state interest that can justify the use of race in university admissions."[88]

Demonstrators protested against an allegedly discriminatory affirmative action policy at Harvard University that disadvantages Asian-American students.

In 2006, voters in Michigan passed Proposal 2, an initiative to make it illegal for state bodies to consider race in admissions and hiring decisions; this policy was upheld by the Supreme Court in 2014.[89] In 2019, voters in Washington State narrowly voted down an affirmative action referendum, 50.6–49.4 percent. This means that states will be able to decide on an individual basis whether to consider affirmative action in higher education, because the policy is neither prohibited nor required by the Constitution.

In 2008, a White student, Abigail Fisher, claimed she was a victim of reverse discrimination and sued the University of Texas at Austin. Texas had achieved a racially diverse student body by extending offers of admission to the top 10 percent of every graduating high school class (in recent years, this policy was changed to the top 7 percent). This approach worked because most high schools in Texas were still segregated. In June 2016, the Court upheld Texas's affirmative action policy by a 4–3 vote.[90] Despite this ruling, documents leaked in August 2017 revealed that the Justice Department was going to "investigate, and potentially sue, colleges and universities over admissions decisions that are perceived as discriminating against White applicants."[91] For more on affirmative action in college admissions, see the Take a Stand feature.

Multicultural issues and immigration policy

Issues involving the multicultural, multiracial nature of American society will become more important as Whites cease to be the majority of the population by mid-century. At their cores, these issues are rooted in the fact that the United States is a nation of immigrants. Will that history continue, and if so, what shape will it take? Is our country a "melting pot," focused on the assimilation of new groups, or is it more like a "tossed salad," in which each immigrant group maintains its cultural identity but creates a new, better collective whole? Groups who favor one or the other of these conceptions of American society often clash over issues such as whether English should be our official language (31 states have such laws) and whether bilingual education should be offered in public schools. But the biggest area for debate on this topic in recent years concerns immigration reform and border security.

Following the September 11 terrorist attacks, some people saw immigration as a threat that must be curtailed. The government asserted that it would not engage in racial profiling of Arab Americans—for example, subjecting them to stricter screening at airports—but many commentators argued that such profiling would be justified, and there was at least anecdotal evidence of increased discrimination against people of Middle Eastern descent. After the terrorist attacks in Paris and San Bernardino, California, in 2016, the debate in the presidential campaign shifted to a strongly anti-immigrant tone. During the campaign, Donald Trump proposed preventing all Muslims from entering the United States until the government could make sure they did not pose a terrorist threat. As president, he issued an executive order narrowly targeting Muslim countries that was struck down by a federal court. A second version was also struck down, but in 2018 the Supreme Court upheld the third version of the travel ban. The Court deferred to the president's ability to define national security, saying that his executive power was not undermined by his political comments about the possible intent of the travel ban.[92]

Over the past two decades, immigration has been central in many political debates. This intensified in 2010, when Arizona enacted an anti-immigration law that requires local law-enforcement officials to check the immigration status of a person in a "lawful stop, detention, or arrest" if there is a "reasonable suspicion" that the person is an

Affirmative Action in College Admissions

Since 1978, the Supreme Court has endorsed the idea of race as a "plus factor" in college admissions while rejecting the idea of strict quotas or point systems. This approach was affirmed in a 2003 case involving the University of Michigan's law school, but many Court-watchers believed that affirmative action would be struck down in the 2016 case *Fisher v. University of Texas, Austin*.[a] Instead, swing vote Justice Kennedy sided with the liberal justices, and the Court upheld the practice.

UT Austin's college admissions process has two parts. First, anyone in the top 10 percent of a Texas public high school is guaranteed admission to UT (in recent years this has been closer to the top 7 percent). Because most high schools in Texas are somewhat segregated by race, the 10 percent plan automatically creates diversity for the entering class. Seventy-five percent of in-state students are admitted via the 10 percent plan. Second, the remaining 25 percent of in-state students are admitted by a "holistic" program that evaluates their entire record and includes race as a "plus factor." It was this second part that Abigail Fisher challenged after being denied admission to UT. The legal question that the Court had to decide was whether the university's affirmative action program violated the equal protection clause of the Fourteenth Amendment and civil rights laws barring discrimination on the basis of race, or whether the program could be justified as serving a "compelling state interest" under the strict scrutiny standard.

Diversity deserves consideration. Advocates of affirmative action argue that a diverse student body promotes viewpoint diversity that is essential to learning. Having racial diversity in the student body is likely to produce more viewpoint diversity

in classroom discussions than would occur with a mostly White student body. The majority opinion in the Texas case also argued that a more diverse student body leads to "the destruction of stereotypes," promotes "cross-racial understanding," and prepares students "for an increasingly diverse work force and society." Furthermore, proponents argue, the courts are not the proper place to decide these issues. Instead, as with the complex and highly charged topic of racial redistricting, the political branches of government are where these decisions should be made. The Court endorsed this position of judicial restraint in a 2014 case involving a ban on affirmative action in Michigan.[b]

The Court argued that the Texas approach was "narrowly tailored" to serve the compelling state interest of viewpoint diversity because the 10 percent plan, by itself, did not produce the desired level of diversity and would create perverse incentives. Justice Kennedy wrote, "Percentage plans encourage parents to keep their children in low-performing segregated schools, and discourage students from taking challenging classes that might lower their grade point averages."

Affirmative action is just another kind of discrimination. Opponents reply that supporters of affirmative action have not provided convincing evidence that racial diversity in colleges has any beneficial effects. They also argue that "viewpoint diversity" arguments assume that members of all racial minorities think alike, drawing a comparison to racial profiling in law enforcement. It is just as offensive, they say, that an admissions committee thinks that one Black student has the same views as another Black student as it is that a police officer may pull over a Black teenage male just because he fits a certain criminal profile.

Opponents also argue that affirmative action amounts to "reverse discrimination" and that any racial classification is harmful. Justice Alito's scathing dissent in the Texas case said, "U.T. has never provided any coherent explanation for its asserted need to discriminate on the basis of race, and . . . U.T.'s position relies on a series of unsupported and noxious racial assumptions." Alito also argued that concepts such as viewpoint diversity and "cross-cultural understanding" are "slippery" and difficult to analyze systematically.

The Texas case will not be the end of the debate concerning affirmative action in higher education. A federal appeals court ruled that Harvard University's affirmative action program did not discriminate against Asian Americans, but that decision is being appealed to the Supreme Court. If you had to rule on the Texas case, how would you have decided? Take a stand.

take a stand

1. To what extent should race be used as a "plus factor" to promote racial diversity and viewpoint diversity, if at all? Is the "top 10 percent" plan a better approach?
2. Think of your own experiences in high school and college. Has racial diversity contributed to viewpoint diversity?

Students protest outside the Supreme Court in support of diversity at the University of Texas.

When President Trump announced his original travel ban preventing individuals from select Muslim-majority countries from entering the United States, people flooded airports across the country in protest.

undocumented immigrant. The law also requires immigrants to always carry papers and bans people without proper documents from seeking work in public places. Many civil rights violations occurred when local law-enforcement officials started enforcing this law. Opponents of the law argue that it requires illegal racial profiling and that the federal government has the sole responsibility for deciding immigration law. In 2012, the Supreme Court struck down three of the four main provisions of the law, citing the supremacy clause of the Constitution. This decision meant that Congress, not the states, determines immigration law when the two laws conflict. The Court upheld the controversial "show me your papers" part of the law, saying that the state was simply enforcing the federal law. However, the Court indicated that the law must be applied in a race-neutral way and could be struck down if there was clear evidence of racial profiling.[93] Several months later, a federal district court judge cleared the way for implementation of the "show me your papers" law, saying that the Supreme Court wanted to see actual evidence of discrimination rather than speculation that the law could have a discriminatory effect.[94]

The immigration system is widely viewed as broken and in need of reform, but neither President Bush nor President Obama was able to get Congress to approve his proposal to provide a "path to citizenship" for undocumented immigrants. In 2019, a Pew poll showed strong support for reform, with 67 percent of those surveyed saying that the government should "establish a way for most immigrants in the country illegally to remain here legally." A nearly identical percentage supported "increasing security along the U.S.-Mexico border."[95] In 2015, President Obama used executive orders to implement part of his immigration policy (concerning the deportation of young adults who were brought to the United States illegally by their parents and the deportation of the parents of children who are citizens). The Supreme Court deadlocked 4–4 in a June 2016 case, upholding the lower court's ruling that struck down the executive order. More than 4 million immigrants had to await the results of the election. President Trump revoked Obama's executive order and, while Congress deadlocked on the issue, the courts allowed the program to continue for those already enrolled. President Trump also instituted a "zero tolerance" policy that led to the separation of thousands of children and parents at the border. The policy violated a federal court order and was reversed, though about 2,500 children remained in detention centers in late 2019.[96]

The debates over affirmative action, English as the country's official language, and immigration reform clearly illustrate the conflictual nature of civil rights policy. However, history has shown that when public opinion strongly supports a given application of civil rights—for example, the integration of African Americans in the South in the 1960s and, more recently, allowing gays to openly serve in the military and recognizing same-sex marriage—public policy soon reflects those views. Although it is impossible to say when there will be comprehensive immigration reform that includes a path to citizenship, it is likely to eventually happen given the trends in public opinion. However, the Trump administration's efforts to move immigration policy in the opposite direction mean that comprehensive immigration reform is probably off the table until at least 2021.

Unpacking the Conflict

Considering all that we've discussed in this chapter, let's apply what we know about how civil rights work to the examples of profiling introduced at the beginning of this chapter. Is it ever acceptable to treat people differently based on the color of their skin, their ethnic status, their gender, or their sexual orientation, in a situation of racial profiling or otherwise?

Enforcing civil rights means providing equal protection of the law to individuals and groups that are discriminated against, which may include noncitizens and illegal immigrants. But figuring out exactly when an individual's civil rights have been violated can be tricky. When does a routine traffic stop by a police officer turn into racial profiling?

To help figure that out, we now can answer the questions about possible civil rights violations that introduced this chapter:

- Scenario 1: On the one hand, the African-American teenagers who were pulled over by the police may or may not have had their civil rights violated, depending on the laws in their state. In Massachusetts, for example, it is prohibited to consider the "race, gender, national or ethnic origin of members of the public in deciding to detain a person or stop a motor vehicle" except in "suspect specific incidents."[97] On the other hand, in the scenario in which the police pulled over White teenagers, the traffic stop would have been acceptable as long as there had been "probable cause" to justify the stop.
- Scenario 2: The Asian-American woman who did not get the job could certainly talk to a lawyer about filing a "disparate impact" discrimination suit. Under the 1991 Civil Rights Act, the employer would have the burden of proof to show that she was not a victim of the "good ol' boy" network.
- Scenario 3: The gay couple who could not rent the apartment because of their sexual orientation might have a basis for a civil rights lawsuit based on the Fourteenth Amendment. But this would depend on where they live, given that there is no federal protection against discrimination against gay men and lesbians (and the Supreme Court has not applied the Fourteenth Amendment in this context).

- Scenario 4: Court decisions concerning affirmative action in Michigan and Texas show that the White student who was not admitted to the university of his choice would have to take his lumps, as long as the affirmative action program considered race as a general "plus factor" rather than assigning more or fewer points for it (and the practice was allowed by his state).

This review of civil rights in the United States has highlighted only some of the most important issues, but a significant agenda remains. The civil rights movement will continue to use the multiple avenues of the legislative, executive, and judicial branches to secure equal rights for all Americans. Although this process may take many years, history demonstrates that when public opinion becomes more supportive of diversity and stronger civil rights, our political institutions support the views of the people.

"What's Your Take?"

Should distinctions between people based on race, ethnic status, gender, or sexual orientation be uniformly prohibited?

Or are they OK under some circumstances?

STUDY GUIDE

The context of civil rights

Describe the historical struggles groups have faced in winning civil rights. (Pages 138–146)

Summary

Civil rights are protections from discrimination both by the government and by individuals and are rooted in laws and the equal protection clause of the Fourteenth Amendment. The concept of equality has evolved over time, with protections now for the LGBTQ community, women, African Americans, Native Americans, Asian Americans, and Latinos. Despite our attempts to live in a color-blind society, awareness of race still influences many people's opinions and behavior.

Key terms

civil rights (p. 139)
Jim Crow laws (p. 141)
"separate but equal" doctrine (p. 141)

Brown v. Board of Education (p. 141)
protectionism (p. 144)

Practice Quiz Questions

1. **The distinction between civil rights and civil liberties is that civil rights _____ while civil liberties _____ .**

a protect against discrimination; are guaranteed in the Bill of Rights

b are guaranteed in the Bill of Rights; protect against discrimination

c are guaranteed in the Bill of Rights; limit what the government can do to you

d limit what the government can do to you; protect against discrimination

e limit what the government can do to you; are guaranteed in the Bill of Rights

2. **The Missouri Compromise _____ .**

a ruled that enslaved people are not protected by the Constitution

b established that three-fifths of the enslaved population could count in a state's population

c limited the expansion of slavery while maintaining the balance of slave states

d gave enslaved people the right to vote

e ended slavery in the South

3. ***Plessy v. Ferguson* established _____ .**

a the legitimacy of poll taxes

b the "separate but equal" doctrine

c that Jim Crow laws were illegal

d the process of desegregation in the South

e the legality of slavery

4. **The principle of _____ was used in many court cases to deny women equal rights.**

a matriarchy

b "separate but equal"

c sectionalism

d misandry

e protectionism

The racial divide today

Analyze inequality among racial, ethnic, and social groups today. (Pages 146–151)

Summary

Beyond the unequal treatment of racial minorities, women, and LGBTQ individuals, inequalities in political, social, and economic conditions also persist. Whites are able to participate in politics at a higher rate, enjoy a better standard of living, and avoid prejudice in the criminal justice system.

Practice Quiz Questions

5. ***Most* of the differences in voter turnout among Whites relative to racial minorities can be accounted for by _____ .**

a contemporary Jim Crow laws

b voter purge lists

c voter ID laws

d poll taxes

e education and income

6. **The gaps between Whites and Blacks on health measures are _____ and in many cases _____ .**

a large; decreasing

b large; increasing

c small; decreasing

d small; increasing

e small; staying the same

Key players in the conflict over civil rights

Explain the approaches used to bring about change in civil rights policies. (Pages 152–170)

Summary

Depending on the political context, each branch of government has played a role in the expansion of civil rights. Moreover, federalism has played a role in this process. Although the state governments often lagged behind the federal government in African Americans' civil rights, they have been on the forefront in protecting the rights of gays and lesbians.

Key terms

de jure (p. 157)   rational basis test (p. 160)
de facto (p. 157)

Practice Quiz Questions

7. **Early in the nation's history, civil rights activism was focused on _____ .**

a   women

b   gays and lesbians

c   African Americans

d   Latinos

e   Native Americans

8. **Early in the civil rights movement (before the 1960s), which governmental body provided most of the successes?**

a   state governments

b   Congress

c   the presidency

d   the bureaucracy

e   the Supreme Court

9. **The difference between de facto segregation and de jure segregation is that de facto segregation _____ , while de jure segregation _____ .**

a   is the result of circumstances; is mandated by law

b   is mandated by law; is the result of circumstances

c   applies to racial minorities; applies to women

d   applies to women; applies to racial minorities

e   applies to all groups; applies to racial minorities

10. **Minorities receive the strongest protection as the "suspect classification" when which test is applied?**

a   rational basis

b   strict scrutiny

c   intermediate scrutiny

d   privileged interest

e   disparate impact

11. **The VRA _____ .**

a   established "majority-minority" districts

b   established compulsory voter registration for African Americans

c   eliminated direct obstacles to minority voting in the South

d   barred discrimination in the rental or sale of a home

e   reduced participation by African Americans in the South

12. **Relative to the protection of individuals with disabilities, Congress's track record in protecting gay rights is _____ .**

a   stronger

b   about the same

c   weaker

d   nonexistent

e   more focused on job discrimination

Civil rights issues today

Examine affirmative action and other ongoing civil rights issues. (Pages 170–175)

Summary

The public is divided on the appropriateness of civil rights policies, with some groups preferring a "color-blind" approach and some groups preferring a "color-conscious" approach. Furthermore, the debates over issues such as affirmative action, immigration reform, and establishing English as the official language in many states indicate the level of conflict over civil rights policy. Nonetheless, when public opinion does strongly support the application of civil rights in a particular arena, policy makers generally respond to these views.

Practice Quiz Question

13. **What did the case Regents of the University of California v. Bakke establish?**

a   that race could play no role in the college admissions process

b   that gender could play no role in the college admissions process

c   that strict racial quotas in the admissions process were legal

d   that race could be used as a "plus factor" in the admissions process

e   that gender could be used as a "plus factor" in the admissions process

Suggested Reading

For various websites devoted to civil rights, see www.justice.gov/crt, https://blacklivesmatter.com, www.womensmarch.com, https://metoomvmt.org/, and http://nationalfairhousing.org.

Berman, Ari. *Give Us the Ballot: The Modern Struggle for Voting Rights in America*. New York: Farrar, Straus and Giroux, 2015.

Canon, David T. *Race, Redistricting, and Representation: The Unintended Consequences of Black-Majority Districts*. Chicago: University of Chicago Press, 1999.

Dawson, Michael C. *Behind the Mule: Race and Class in African-American Politics*. Princeton, NJ: Princeton University Press, 1994.

Hochschild, Jennifer L., Vesla M. Weaver, and Traci R. Burch. *Creating a New Racial Order: How Immigration, Multiracialism, Genomics, and the Young Can Remake Race in America*. Princeton, NJ: Princeton University Press, 2012.

Katznelson, Ira. *When Affirmative Action Was White: An Untold History of Racial Inequality in Twentieth-Century America*. New York: W. W. Norton, 2005.

Kennedy, Randall. *For Discrimination: Race, Affirmative Action, and the Law*. New York: Vintage Books, 2015.

Kousser, J. Morgan. *Colorblind Injustice: Minority Voting Rights and the Undoing of the Second Reconstruction*. Chapel Hill: University of North Carolina Press, 1999.

Tate, Katherine. *Black Lawmaking in the U.S. Congress from Carter to Obama*. Ann Arbor: University of Michigan Press, 2014.

Thernstrom, Stephan, and Abigail Thernstrom. *America in Black and White: One Nation, Indivisible—Race in Modern America*. New York: Simon and Schuster, 1997.

6

Public Opinion and the Media

What do the people want? How should we measure opinion?

 "Leadership does not mean putting the ear to the ground to follow public opinion, but to have the vision of what is necessary and the courage to make it possible."[1]
Representative Shirley Chisholm

 "You have to remember one thing about the will of the people: it wasn't that long ago that we were swept away by the Macarena."[2]
Jon Stewart, comedian

Significant percentages of Americans hold politically consequential beliefs that are factually untrue. For example, even after Barack Obama had been president for eight years and released copies of his birth certificate showing he was born in Hawaii, large numbers of Republicans believed that he was not a U.S. citizen and therefore not eligible to be president. Can we trust public opinion?

One of the foundations of democracy is the belief that public opinion matters: while in office, elected officials act in accordance with their constituents' demands or else face the possibility of being defeated in the next election. Every election season, candidates, political parties, journalists, and political scientists take thousands of polls in an attempt to determine who is likely to vote, who they are planning to vote for, and what sorts of arguments, slogans, and platforms might change their minds.

According to political scientist V. O. Key, basing policy and election strategy on public opinion makes sense because "[i]n the large, the electorate behaves about as rationally and responsibly as we should expect, given the clarity and the alternatives presented to it and the character of the information available to it."[3] The expectation is that citizens' evaluations of what government is, their ideas of what they would like done differently, and their thoughts about what they like and don't like more broadly all have some basis in reality. The only way to assess whether government follows the wishes of the people is to have some idea of what people really want—to actually develop surveys, measure public opinion, and compare it to the policy choices made in Washington.

CHAPTER GOALS

Define *public opinion* **and explain why it matters in American politics.** pages 182–184

Explain how people form political attitudes and opinions. pages 184–191

Describe basic survey methods and potential issues affecting accuracy. pages 191–198

Present findings on what Americans think about government and why it matters. pages 198–206

Describe the major types of news sources and the role they play in American politics. pages 206–212

However, a look at the results of some mass surveys might lead you to comedian and political commentator Jon Stewart's concern that public opinion is fickle and only loosely connected to reality. Even as Republicans doubted President Obama's citizenship,[4] a significant percentage of Democrats believed that the government had advance knowledge of attacks on September 11, 2001. (Needless to say, both claims are false.[5]) And while most Americans would agree with the late Representative Shirley Chisholm that politicians should not blindly respond to public opinion, the persistence of blatantly false beliefs about Obama's citizenship and the September 11 attacks raises questions about whether public opinion is based in reality at all.

Before we blame Americans for believing in conspiracy theories—or take pollsters to task for mismeasuring public opinion—we need to determine how opinions are formed and how they are expressed. What does it mean when someone reveals an opinion, such as support for a conspiracy theory, a desire for change in some policy, or support for a president? Answering this question requires an understanding of how opinions are formed and what goes into them. We also need to determine whether opinions are real, in the sense that they are considered judgments that shape behavior, and what problems arise when we ask people what they think about politics. Do Americans really hold the bizarre beliefs that are sometimes expressed in polling results? Can we take polls seriously, if they produce results like these? Where does public opinion come from? Can politicians trust public opinion as a guide to what Americans want—and can we use opinions to measure the quality of American democracy?

Are Americans poorly informed about political topics? During the height of America's confrontation with Iran in January 2020, only 28 percent of survey respondents could correctly locate Iran on an unlabeled map of the Middle East.[6]

DEFINE *PUBLIC OPINION* AND EXPLAIN WHY IT MATTERS IN AMERICAN POLITICS

public opinion
Citizens' views on politics and government actions.

What is public opinion?

Public opinion describes what the population thinks about politics and government—what government should be doing, evaluations of what government *is* doing, and judgments about elected officials and others who participate in the political process—as well as the wider set of beliefs that shape these opinions.

Public opinion matters for three reasons. First, citizens' political actions—including voting, contributing to campaigns, writing letters to senators, and undertaking other kinds of activism—are driven by their opinions.[7] Therefore, if we want to either understand an individual's behavior or analyze broader political outcomes, such as who wins an election or the fate of a legislative proposal, we need good data on public opinion.

Second, examining public opinion helps explain the behavior of candidates, political parties, and other political actors. Politicians look to public opinion to determine what citizens want them to do and how happy citizens are with their behavior in office.

Third, because public opinion is a key to understanding what motivates citizens and political officials, it can shed light on the reasons for specific policy outcomes. For example, changes in the policy mood—the public's demand for new domestic policies— are linked to changes in government spending.[8] When people want government to do more, spending increases more rapidly; when people want less from government, spending goes down (or increases more slowly).

Different kinds of opinion

Modern theories of public opinion distinguish between two types of opinions: opinions that are preformed and opinions that are formed on the spot as needed. The first type includes broad expressions such as how a person thinks about politics, what he or she wants from government, or principles that apply across a range of issues. These kinds of beliefs typically form early in life and remain stable over time. Some of these beliefs are obviously political, such as party identification, ideology (liberal or conservative), and judgments about society's responsibility to those in need. Liberal or conservative ideology is a good example of a stable opinion: the best way to predict an American's ideology at age 40 is to assume it will match his or her ideology at age 20. The same is true for party identification.

One important thing to understand about public opinion is that although ideology and party identification are largely consistent over time, these particular kinds of opinions are exceptions to the rule.[9] The average person does not maintain a set of fully formed opinions on all political topics. Instead, most Americans' political judgments are **latent opinions**: they are constructed only as needed, such as when answering a survey question or deciding on Election Day how to vote. For example, when most people are asked about the oppression of the Rohingya people in Myanmar, they probably do not have a specific response in mind simply because they have not thought much about the question. Their opinions become concrete only when they are asked about those opinions.

People who follow politics closely have more preformed opinions than the average American, whose interest in politics is relatively low. But very few people are so well informed that they have ready opinions on a wide range of political and policy questions.

> Whoever can change public opinion can change the government.

—President Abraham Lincoln

latent opinion
An opinion formed on the spot, when it is needed (as distinct from a deeply held opinion that is stable over time).

A person's ideological perspective is relatively stable over time. People who subscribe to a conservative ideology generally support small government and decreased spending.

Moreover, even when people do form opinions in advance, they may not remember every factor that influenced their opinions. Thus, an individual may identify as a liberal or a conservative, or as a supporter of a particular party, but may be unable to explain the reasons behind these ideological leanings.[10]

Opinions also vary in intensity. For example, one individual might strongly favor policies that allow handgun ownership and open carry in public, while another might oppose both policies but with less intensity. Intensity matters because it shapes whether and how people act on their opinions. The strongly pro-gun individual would be more likely to consider a candidate's gun rights policy when deciding how to vote, while the individual who opposes gun ownership (but less intensely) would likely base his or her vote on other issues. Variation in intensity is one reason why government policies sometimes reflect minority opinions. In the case of gun rights, members of Congress are well aware of polls showing that a majority of people support restrictions on gun ownership. However, polls also show that most supporters of restrictions do not feel strongly about this issue, while people who oppose restrictions are more likely to be intense in their opposition. Thus, when responding to public opinion about gun control, members of Congress reflect the intense minority opinion, not the weaker opinions held by the majority.

In a democracy, elected officials stay in office by keeping their constituents happy. As a result, knowing what public opinion looks like—what citizens believe, what they want government to do—helps us understand the choices elected officials make. New policy initiatives such as stricter gun control laws are unlikely to be enacted in the absence of strong, sustained public support. Conversely, even controversial proposals such as Obamacare can be enacted over strong opposition, as long as there are enough enthusiastic supporters. Public opinion both motivates and constrains elected officials.

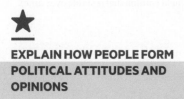

EXPLAIN HOW PEOPLE FORM POLITICAL ATTITUDES AND OPINIONS

Where do opinions come from?

There are numerous sources of public opinion. Some arise from early life experiences, such as exposure to the beliefs of parents, relatives, or teachers; others result from later life events or from informal conversations with friends. Politicians and other political actors also play a critical role in the opinion-formation process.

Socialization: families, communities, and networks

political socialization
The process by which an individual's political opinions are shaped by other people and the surrounding culture.

Theories of **political socialization** show that children develop a liberal or conservative ideology; a level of trust in others; their own class, racial, and ethnic identity; and other political opinions based on what they learn from their parents.[11] Opinions formed through socialization are not necessarily permanent; in fact, people often respond to events by modifying their opinions, even those developed early in life.

Beyond the influence of parents and family, research finds broader aspects of socialization that shape political opinions. Consider the following examples: People are socialized by their communities—by the people they interact with while growing up, such as neighbors, teachers, clergy, and others.[12] Support for democracy as a system of government and for American political institutions is higher for individuals who take a civics class in high school.[13] Growing up in a homogeneous community, where many people share the same cultural, ethnic, or political beliefs, increases adults' sense of civic duty—their belief that voting or other forms of political participation are important social obligations.[14] Volunteering in community organizations as a child shapes political beliefs and participation in later life.[15] Engaging in political activity as a teenager, such as volunteering in a presidential campaign, generates higher levels of political interest as an adult; it also strengthens the belief that people should care about politics and participate in political activities.[16]

Individuals' opinions are also shaped by their network: the people they interact with on a regular basis. For many people, these interactions are an important source of information about political events as well as how these events should be interpreted. Put another way, you might not think that meeting for coffee with a friend would affect your opinions about climate change, but suppose you met on an unusually warm day and your friend mentioned how much hotter this year had been compared to last year. While such conversations are unlikely to have a permanent impact, they might well influence your thinking in the short run—for example, if a week after having coffee, you have to decide how to vote in an election where climate change is an issue.

Events

Although socialization often influences individuals' fairly stable core beliefs, this does not mean that these beliefs or opinions are fixed. All kinds of events—from everyday interactions to traumatic, life-changing disasters—can capture people's attention and cause them to revise their understanding of politics and the role of government.

Some events that shape beliefs are specific, individual experiences. For example, individuals' support for same-sex marriage is strongly influenced by the number of people they know who are gay or lesbian.[17] Major national or world events may also shape beliefs. For example, support for restrictions on gun ownership—such as background checks, bans on certain weapons, or confiscation of weapons from individuals with mental health issues—typically increases after a mass shooting event (although it generally returns to prior levels after a few weeks or months). And political scientists Bethany Albertson and Shana Kushner Gadarian show that feelings of anxiety generated by events (such as the COVID-19 pandemic) can also influence opinion formation by de-emphasizing considerations like partisanship and emphasizing others, such as the opinions of political elites.

Group identity

In the United States, opinions on many issues are correlated with the state or region where a person grew up or lives.[18] People who live in the same region might have common beliefs because they experienced the same historical events at similar points in their lives or learned political viewpoints from one another. Political scientist Katherine Cramer has shown that rural resentment in contemporary American politics stems from the belief that elected officials at the state and national levels do not share the values held by rural residents and will thus shortchange rural communities in the policy process.

Individuals may rely on others who "look like" them as a source of opinions. Some political scientists, for example, argue that group identities shape partisanship: when people decide between being a Republican or a Democrat, they think about which demographic groups are associated with each party and pick the party that has more members from the groups they feel they identify with.[19]

It is important to examine group variations in public opinion because candidates and political consultants often formulate their campaign strategies in terms of groups. For example, analyses of the three previous presidential elections show that the electoral strategies of Democratic candidates are shaped by the goal of attracting support from young Americans, African Americans, Latinos, and women.[20] In contrast, Republican presidential candidates targeted regular churchgoers, as well as older voters and people living in rural areas. Table 6.1 includes data on the variation in opinions across different groups of Americans. There are sharp differences among groups on some questions. For example, people of different education levels respond very differently to both questions about abortion and free speech. However, education has little to do with opinions about affirmative action.

TABLE 6.1

The Importance of Groups

The General Social Survey (GSS) has been conducted since 1972 to assess the opinions of Americans on certain key issues. Those who take the surveys are asked to indicate if they agree or disagree with statements such as those shown in the table. The percentages indicate those who agree with the statements. Group differences based on such factors as gender, age, race, and family income have been shown to affect the answers given by the respondents.

Source: 2018 data from General Social Survey 1972–2018, Cumulative Datafile, Survey Documentation and Analysis (SDA) at UC Berkeley, http://sda.berkeley.edu (accessed 12/30/19).

		"Favor preferences in hiring Blacks" (percentage who strongly support or support)	"Abortions OK if woman wants one for any reason" (percentage who agree)	"OK to allow anti-American Muslim cleric to speak" (percentage who agree)
Gender	Male	15.8%	50.3%	49.2%
	Female	15.6	49.6	37.7
Age	18–30	17.5	56.6	41.1
	31–40	17.8	53.5	44.6
	41–55	15.9	48.5	46.5
	56–89	13.8	43.2	40.3
Education	Less than high school	24.8	30.1	19.4
	High school	15.6	46.3	38.2
	Bachelor's degree	13.2	61.1	59.8
	Advanced degree	16.8	67.5	63.3
Race	White	10.7	51.4	48.8
	African-American	34.9	47.0	34.9
	Latino	16.6	44.9	26.6
	Other	25.5	56.6	36.2
Family Income	Low	18.7	43.0	32.6
	Lower middle	17.7	49.7	40.4
	Higher middle	14.0	47.0	44.9
	High	12.1	59.2	57.2

Politicians and other political actors

Opinions and changes in opinion are also subject to influence by politicians and other political actors (such as political parties and party leaders; interest groups; and leaders of religious, civic, and other large organizations). In part, this link exists because Americans look to these individuals for information because of their presumed expertise. For example, if you do not know what to think about gun control, you might seek out someone who appears to know more about the issues than you do. Insofar as the person's opinions seem reasonable, you might adopt them as your own.[21] Of course, most people take account of an expert's opinions only when they generally agree with the expert—perhaps because they hold matching conservative or liberal views or because they have some other basis for thinking their preferences match the expert's. For example, Donald Trump's claims about a "deep state" of individuals in the federal bureaucracy who were working to thwart his policy agenda probably reinforced his supporters' high levels of distrust of government.

Politicians on both sides of the debate tried to influence public opinion about health care reform. While Democrats sought to convince Americans that maintaining Obamacare was necessary, opponents played up the possible disadvantages, with references to costs and bureaucratic incompetence.

Politicians and other political actors also actively work to shape public opinion. Some political scientists argue that politicians describe proposals through arguments and images designed to tap the public's strong opinions, with the goal of winning support for these proposals.[22] That said, precisely because politicians are working to build support for their preferred policies, it is relatively difficult for them to influence what people think. For example, although President Trump and his allies in Congress expended much time and effort in summer 2020 to convince Americans that lockdowns, masks, and social distancing were not needed to combat COVID-19, only Trump's strongest supporters accepted this view. If anything, perhaps because of the dire news about caseloads and deaths in much of the country, public opinion moved against Trump, and increased support for his Democratic opponent in the election, Joe Biden.

Considerations: the process of forming opinions

When people form opinions on the spot, they are based on *considerations*: pieces of relevant information from sources like the ones we've just discussed—such as ideology, party identification, the influence of family and community members, personal and national events, group identification, or opinions and actions of politicians—that come to mind when the opinion is requested.[23] The process of forming an opinion usually is not thorough or systematic;[24] rather, people use only considerations that come to mind immediately.[25] Highly informed people who follow politics use this process, as do those with low levels of political interest and knowledge.[26]

In some cases, opinions are formed from very little information. For example, suppose you were asked right before the 2020 presidential election whether you approved of President Trump's performance in office. There are many considerations you might have used, from your evaluations of Trump's response to COVID-19 or the Black Lives Matter protests, news coverage of Trump's tariff war with China or a profile of one of his staffers, how Trump's tax reform affected your personal well-being (or that of your parents)—or even what Trump had tweeted that day. Your opinions might have reflected things that have no connection to Trump, such as whether you just received a pay raise, whether you recently watched a video of politicians arguing with each other, or even whether you were just having a bad day. However, if you are like many Americans, your opinion would have centered on Trump's party affiliation: if you are a Republican, you approved, and if you're a Democrat, you disapproved. In fact, in modern American politics, party affiliation is used to form a wide range of political judgments. For example, when Barack Obama (a Democrat) was president, Republicans were much more likely than Democrats to say that economic conditions were poor. This pattern reversed when Donald Trump (a Republican) took office in 2017. There is also evidence that people use partisanship to form broader judgments about people from the other party: if, for example, you are a Republican, you may dislike Democrats simply because they are Democrats, not because of the policy positions you believe they hold.[27]

Basing decisions about presidential approval on party affiliation may seem simplistic, but in an era when the parties disagree on most things, a Republican voter is likely to agree with most decisions made by a Republican president and disagree with most decisions made by a Democrat. In that sense, considerations are a useful shortcut for people who need to make judgments about a president but don't want to spend too much time gathering or evaluating information. In other situations, considerations may lead to inaccurate judgments; this can happen, for example, when individuals decide what they think about the state of the economy based on the party affiliation of the president. But even here, if the goal is to vote for the candidate who is most likely to share your interests, using partisanship to evaluate the economy and then voting based on this evaluation is an easy way to increase the chances that you vote for the right candidate.

That said, as we discussed earlier, partisanship is not the only consideration people use to form political opinions. A generation ago, when differences between the parties were not as strong, evaluations of presidential performance were often shaped by perceptions of economic conditions, which in turn were based on some combination of personal financial well-being and judgments about the state of the economy. The impact of a candidate's personal characteristics has varied over time as well. For example, one of the author's parents reported that in her first presidential election (1952), she could not vote for the Democrat, Adlai Stevenson, because Stevenson was divorced. In the modern era, when the divorce rate is

FIGURE
6.1

First-Term Presidential Approval Ratings

Compared to President Bush's approval ratings, which moved up and down over time, both President Obama's and President Trump's approval ratings were relatively stable. What factors account for the differences in these plots?

Source: FiveThirtyEight, "How Popular Is Donald Trump?," https://projects. fivethirtyeight.com/trump-approval-ratings (accessed 11/2/20).

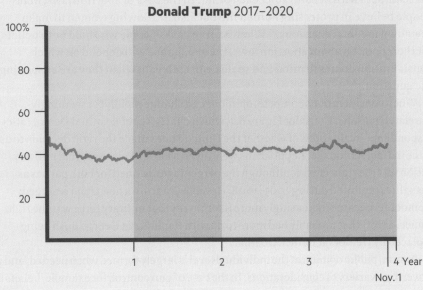

around 50 percent and many politicians are on their second or third marriage, absent unusual circumstances, divorce is unlikely to be a factor many voters think about when forming opinions about candidates. Even in the debate over Trump's performance in office, in which partisanship played an important role, some citizens may have focused on economic conditions, Trump's golf game, or even his preference for well-done steak. So, if we look at individuals, opinions can be hard to predict or understand, because we don't know which considerations will come to mind when we ask them what they think.

Individual Considerations and Mass Public Opinion While public opinion may be difficult to predict on a person-to-person basis, at the aggregate level (where opinions are averaged across the population of a community, state, or nation) opinions are easier to predict.

As an example of how considerations work on an aggregate level, consider Figure 6.1. One important difference is that approval for Bush moved up and down during his first term, while there was no identifiable trend for Obama, and Trump's popularity remained relatively stable until the COVID-19 pandemic reached America in spring 2020, causing his approval to decline. In part, this difference reflects the increasing importance of partisanship in modern American politics. The two sharp upticks in Bush's popularity occurred in November 2001 (after the September 11 attacks) and after the initial successes in the Iraq War in March 2003.

Similarly, Trump's popularity until the pandemic showed no increases in reaction to favorable economic conditions or declines after his impeachment in late 2019. The best explanation is that in the current era, approval ratings are driven by partisanship—for the most part, Americans base their evaluations on whether they share the president's party identification, with other factors, such as evaluations of the man's character or the details of his foreign and domestic policy, playing a much smaller role. There is no guarantee that the predominance of party identification in presidential approval will continue into the future, but until it changes, presidential approval will only modestly reflect other factors such as economic conditions, international crises, or even the president's background or personal characteristics.

How Considerations Interact Opinions are often influenced by considerations that compete with or contradict each other. In the case of abortion laws, many people believe in protecting human life but also in allowing women to make their own medical decisions.[28] When a survey asks people who hold both beliefs for their opinion about abortion laws, their response will depend on which consideration comes to mind and seems most relevant when they are answering the question.

When considerations compete, opinions can change rapidly for seemingly unrelated reasons. Consider Figure 6.2, which charts Republican and Democratic respondents' evaluations of whether the United States made the right decision to use force in Iraq. As you see, Republicans were always more likely to say that military action was the right choice, although the percentage declined for both parties as casualties mounted during 2003–2008. However, in 2009 a new trend emerged: Democrats became increasingly more likely to say that military force was the right choice, a shift that probably had more to do with Republican George Bush being replaced by Democrat Barack Obama.

In sum, public opinion at the individual level is largely formed when needed, and is driven by a variety of considerations. In the case of gun control, for example, beliefs are

FIGURE 6.2

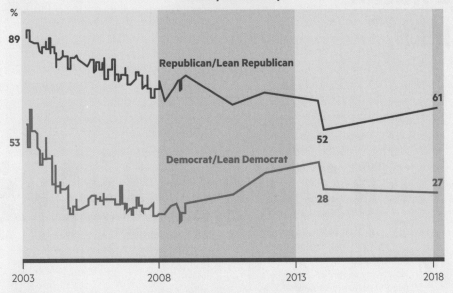

Percentage that says the United States made the *right decision* in using military force in Iraq

%

89

Republican/Lean Republican

61

53

52

Democrat/Lean Democrat

28

27

2003   2008   2013   2018

Evaluations of Military Force in Iraq

The graph shows how Democratic and Republican evaluations of the war in Iraq changed over the last 15 years. What factors might have shaped the observed partisan differences? Why do you think beliefs have largely stayed the same in recent years?

Source: Pew Research Center, "The Iraq War Continues to Divide the U.S. Public, 15 Years after It Began," March 19, 2018, www.people-press.org (accessed 12/30/19).

likely to depend on individuals' backgrounds—whether they own a gun, hunt, or know someone who does; their political beliefs, including their tolerance for government regulation of individual behavior and even their partisanship; and horrific events involving guns. Thus, although public opinion may shift somewhat in response to events such as a mass shooting or domestic terror attack, such events are only one factor that shapes opinion. As a result, even if an event is momentous, the shift in opinion may be quite small and transitory.

mass survey
A way to measure public opinion by interviewing a relatively small sample of a large population.

population
The group of people whom a researcher or pollster wants to study, such as evangelicals, senior citizens, or Americans.

How people form opinions matters because understanding what people say about politics on the news, or in the classroom, or around the dinner table depends on where they are coming from. Perhaps an important event has shaped their opinion, maybe their parents or connection to a social or generational group has influenced them, or maybe a combination of all of these and more has affected them. Knowing what's behind someone's opinions and arguments on an issue can help you decide how you feel about that issue and whether or not the other person's argument carries weight.

"Why Should I Care?"

DESCRIBE BASIC SURVEY METHODS AND POTENTIAL ISSUES AFFECTING ACCURACY

Measuring public opinion

For the most part, information about public opinion comes from **mass surveys**—in-person or phone interviews with a relatively small number of individuals. A mass survey seeks to measure the attitudes of a large **population** or group of people, such as the residents of a specific congressional district, evangelicals, senior citizens, or even the nation's entire adult population (see How It Works: Measuring What a Nation of 330 Million Thinks: A Checklist).

Measuring What a Nation of 330 Million Thinks: A Checklist

✔ **A Random Sample:**
Were the people who participated in the survey selected randomly, such that any member of the population had an equal chance of being selected?

✔ **Sample Size:**
How many people do researchers need to survey to know what 330 million Americans think? Major national surveys usually use a sample of 1,000–2,000 respondents.

± 3%

✔ **Sampling Error:**
For a group of any size (even 330 million), 95 percent of the time a survey of 1,000 randomly selected respondents will measure the average opinion in a population within 3 percentage points. Reputable surveys will usually give the sampling error (sometimes also called "margin of error").

✔ **Question Wording:**
Did the way the question was worded influence the results? Scientific surveys try to phrase questions in a neutral way, but even in reputable polls, differences in question wording can influence answers.

✔ **Reliable Respondents:** Respondents often give socially acceptable answers rather than truthful ones—or invent opinions on the spot. Is there a reason to think people may not have answered a survey honestly and thoughtfully?

Surveying the 2020 Elections: Two Approaches

To illustrate how these requirements for good survey design play out in real life, we examine how two well-known polling organizations, the Pew Research Center and Rasmussen Reports, designed polls to measure presidential preference during the 2020 campaign.

Rasmussen Reports

Use land-lines... mostly.

A partially random sample: Contact people who have **land-line phones** and use a **nonrandom online panel** to sample groups that tend not to have land-lines.

Respondent selection: Survey the **first person who answers the phone**.

Make robo-calls.

Computer-controlled: Use an automated script to survey respondents; do the survey in a **short time period (hours)**.

One-shot: **Don't call back** people who you miss on the first try.

Adjust the results.

Weighting the responses: If there are more Democrats (or Republicans) in your sample than you expect, **adjust your results** to account for the difference.

Pew Research Center

Include cell phones.

A random sample: Generate a **sample of all Americans**, including people who have only cell phones.

Respondent selection: When you call, **talk only to the person who is in your sample**.

Use a person to call.

Live interviewer: Use a live interviewer who can **help respondents who are unsure what a question means**.

Multiple tries: Implement the survey over several days, and **call people back if you missed them**.

Don't adjust results.

Surprises are interesting: If the partisan divide in your sample is not what you expect, **treat it as a finding**—people may be changing their party ID.

Outcome

Rasmussen data are incomplete (at best)...

A random sample: Rasmussen misses many people who use only cell phones (many of whom are younger and are Democrats).

Sample size: Rasmussen is also **biased toward people who are likely to answer the phone**. These people tend to be older and include a higher proportion of men than in the population.

and assume nothing has changed.

Sampling error: Adjusting for partisanship **assumes that no changes in party ID have occurred** since the last election.

Reliable respondents: Rasmussen tactic **lowers response rate**. Rasmussen tactic makes poll results sensitive to short-term events.

Pew is more reliable.

Pew's results were generally regarded as more reliable than Rasmussen's—and generally **made more accurate predictions about results**. Furthermore, Rasmussen kept its data largely private, while Pew released its questionnaire and data. This made Pew's survey verifiable and provided an opportunity for further analysis.

❓ Critical Thinking

1. **When evaluating these two polling organizations,** how would you respond to someone who said he still preferred Rasmussen's polls because they correctly predicted the outcome of a Senate race in his state in 2018?

2. **Which kinds of respondents are likely to be put off by polls** that the computer scripts? How might this affect the findings of the survey?

sample

Within a population, the group of people surveyed in order to gauge the whole population's opinion. Researchers use samples because it would be impossible to interview the entire population.

sampling error

The predicted difference between the average opinion expressed by survey respondents and the average opinion in the population, sometimes called the *margin of error*. Increasing the number of respondents lowers the sampling error.

For large groups such as these, it would be impossible to survey everyone. So surveys typically involve **samples** of between a few hundred and several thousand individuals.

Mass surveys

One of the principal attractions of mass surveys is that they can in theory provide very accurate estimates of public opinion for a large population by using relatively small samples (see Nuts & Bolts 6.1). For example, while polls taken very early in a presidential campaign (such as a year in advance of the general election) are poor predictors of the ultimate outcome, polls taken after the campaign has gotten started, when both parties' nominees are known, provide very good predictions of who will win the election and how many votes that candidate will receive.[29] Large-scale surveys such as the American National Election Study (ANES), conducted every election year (typically both before and after the general election),

NUTS & BOLTS 6.1

Sampling Error in Mass Surveys

The **sampling error** in a survey (the predicted difference between the average opinion expressed by survey respondents and the average opinion in the population, sometimes called the *margin of error*) using a random sample depends on the sample size. Sampling error is large for small samples of around 200 or fewer but decreases rapidly as sample size increases.

The graph shows how the sampling error for a random sample decreases as sample size increases. For example, in surveys with 1,000 respondents the sampling error is about 3 percent, meaning that 95 percent of the time the results of a 1,000-person survey will fall within the range of

3 percentage points above or below the actual percentage of the population who hold a particular opinion. If the sample size was increased to 5,000 people, the sampling error would decline to 1.4 percent. Mass surveys typically interview around 1,000 people. As the figure shows, this is the point where adding interviewees provides relatively little improvement in accuracy.

Sampling errors need to be taken into account when interpreting what a poll says about public opinion. For example, suppose a poll of 1,300 Americans found that 66 percent gave an unfavorable rating of Donald Trump's performance in office and 33 percent rated him favorably. Because the difference between the percentages (33 points) exceeds the sampling error (about 2.5 points), it is reasonable to conclude that, at the time the poll was conducted, more Americans saw Trump unfavorably than favorably.

In contrast, suppose the poll found a narrow 51–49 percent split slightly favoring approval. Because the difference in support is smaller than the sampling error, it would be a mistake to conclude that the majority of Americans had a favorable opinion of Trump. Even though more people in the sample expressed this opinion, there is a good chance that the opposite was true in the overall population.

You don't need to calculate sampling errors to make sense of political polls—just keep two things in mind. First, large samples (1,000 or more) are much more likely to provide accurate information about population opinions than small ones (fewer than 500). Second, be cautious when you read about small differences in survey responses, as these patterns are unlikely to hold true in the entire population.

"Why Should I Care?" Not all data are equal! Statistical errors that occur when researchers don't select a sample that represents the entire population can significantly affect the accuracy of the conclusions they draw from that survey. When looking at survey data, you need to think critically about the size of the sample, as well as the small differences in results.

use various types of questions to measure citizens' opinions. In presidential election years, participants in the ANES are first asked whether they voted for president. If they say yes, they are asked which candidate they voted for: a major-party candidate (for example, Joe Biden or Donald Trump in 2020), an Independent candidate, or some other candidate.

Another kind of survey question uses an *issue scale*. For example, respondents might be asked about the government's role in protecting morality or their own liberal or conservative ideology. Two opposing statements are given for each topic, and respondents are asked to pick the statement, or one of the choices between the two extremes, that comes closest to their views.

A typical survey like the General Social Survey or the ANES will ask several hundred questions related to issues and candidates, along with additional questions about the respondents' age, education, and marital status. Some surveys conducted by media sources, candidates, or political parties are shorter, focusing on voter evaluations of specific candidates and the reasons for these evaluations. In the main, the length of a survey reflects the fact that people have limited attention spans, so there is a trade-off between learning more about each respondent's opinions and getting him or her to agree to be surveyed in the first place.

Problems in measuring public opinion

Polling is an imperfect science. Many pollsters failed to predict Trump's victory in 2016. In 2020, most underpredicted support for Trump in states such as Florida and overestimated support for Democratic congressional candidates. While the COVID-19 pandemic increased the difficulty of collecting and interpreting survey data, the fact is that measuring public opinion is hard to do. The problems begin with gathering an appropriate, representative sample of subjects. These difficulties are compounded by issues pertaining to the wording of the questions and further complicated by the very nature of public opinion itself. Consequently, survey results must be read carefully, taking into account who is being surveyed, when they are being surveyed, what opinions are being asked about, and what mechanism is used to ask survey questions.

Issues with Survey Methods Building a random sample of respondents is not easy. One strategy is to choose households at random from census data and send interviewers out for face-to-face meetings. Another is to contact people by telephone using random digit dialing, which allows surveyors to find people who have unlisted phone numbers or who use only a cell phone. While each technique in theory produces a random sample, in practice they both may deviate from this ideal. Face-to-face interviews of people in their homes during work hours won't include adults who work during the day and are not home, and is very expensive. Even with phone surveys, many people refuse to participate. Pollsters must adjust their survey results to account for these and other potential biases. Sometimes these adjustments successfully predict results, and sometimes they don't.

To keep costs down, many organizations use Internet polling, in which volunteer respondents log on to a website to participate in a survey, or robo-polls, in which an automated system phones people and interviews them. While these techniques are less expensive, there are often doubts about the quality of the samples they produce.

The wording of questions can also influence survey results. Table 6.2 shows different questions asked to measure opinions about President Trump's executive order banning travel to the United States from seven predominantly Muslim countries. As you can see, support depends on how the question is asked: whether Trump's name is mentioned, the specific countries, and the rationale for the ban. These issues shouldn't make you suspicious that pollsters are trying to skew their findings—rather, they show just how hard it is to accurately measure opinions. (See Take a Stand for more on public opinion on immigration.)

TABLE
6.2

The Impact of Question Wording on Opinions

How questions are worded can affect survey results. These surveys (all taken in January to February 2017) ask about President Trump's 2017 executive order banning citizens from certain countries from traveling to the United States, but differ in how they describe the details of the ban as well as the supposed goal. In light of how the responses to survey questions are shaped by the precise wording of these questions, what sort of question would you ask if your goal was to show that Americans favored the travel ban? What if you wanted to show high levels of opposition?

% Support or Favor	Question	Pollster
57	Do you favor or oppose a temporary ban on refugees from Syria, Iraq, Iran, Libya, Somalia, Sudan and Yemen **until the federal government improves its ability to screen out potential terrorists from coming here**?	Rasmussen
55	Do you approve or disapprove of [President Trump's] executive order prohibiting citizens from seven predominantly Muslim countries **from being able to enter the United States for 90 days and halting processing of refugees for 120 days**?	Politico
46	Do you support or oppose **suspending all travel by citizens of Iraq, Syria, Iran, Libya, Somalia, Sudan and Yemen to the U.S. for 90 days**?	Quinnipiac
42	**Thinking now about some of the specific actions Donald Trump has taken since he has been in office,** would you say you approve or disapprove of ordering a temporary ban on entry into U.S. for most people from seven predominantly Muslim countries?	Gallup

Sources: Rasmussen Reports, "Most Support Temporary Ban on Newcomers from Terrorist Havens," January 30, 2017, www.rasmussenreports.com/public_content/politics/current_events/immigration/january_2017/most_support_temporary_ban_on_newcomers_from_terrorist_havens; Jake Sherman, "Poll: Democrats Want Leaders to Block Trump," Politico, February 7, 2017, www.politico.com/story/2017/02/trump-democrats-poll-234778; Quinnipiac Poll, "American Voters Oppose Trump Immigration Ban, Quinnipiac University National Poll Finds," February 7, 2017, https://poll.qu.edu/national/release-detail?ReleaseID=2427; Frank Newport, "About Half of Americans Say Trump Moving Too Fast," Gallup, February 7, 2017, https://news.gallup.com/poll/203264/half-americans-say-trump-moving-fast.aspx (all accessed (1/2/2020).

As always, keep in mind that the poll does not, and cannot, predict the outcome of the election in November.

—Disclaimer on CNN preelection poll

Unreliable Respondents People are sometimes reluctant to reveal their opinions. Rather than speaking truthfully, they often give socially acceptable answers or the ones that they think the interviewers want to hear. In the case of voter turnout in elections, in most surveys up to one-third of respondents who say they voted when surveyed actually did not vote at all. Political scientists refer to this behavior as the social desirability bias, meaning that people are less willing to admit actions or express opinions that they believe their neighbors or society at large will disapprove of, such as racial prejudice.[30] Pollsters use various techniques to address this problem, such as framing a question in terms of the entire country rather than the respondent's own beliefs.

The Accuracy of Public Opinion Because poll results play such an important role in media coverage and public discussions about politics, questions are often raised about the assumptions and corrections that pollsters use to account for the inevitable ambiguities related to poll results. During the 2020 presidential campaign, many Republican politicians and observers argued that polls showing a significant lead for Democrat Joe Biden over Republican Donald Trump were the product of inaccurate polling questions and assumptions about turnout. Some even argued that pollsters were deliberately skewing their findings so as to bolster support for Biden. Of course, Biden won the election, although it appears that pollsters did misestimate turnout of some groups. However, this outcome does not imply that pollsters altered their surveys to

Should Politicians Follow the Polls?

Elected officials in America work hard to cast votes and take other actions that their constituents will like. At first glance, this behavior seems easy. All a politician needs to do is take a poll, measure public opinion in his or her state or district, and comply with the demands expressed in the survey responses. The problem is, poll results need interpretation. As we saw for President Trump's travel ban in Table 6.2, small differences in question wording can produce very different responses, or public opinion can remain vague, despite the polls. As a result, even if representatives want to follow constituent opinion, they may decide that they don't really know enough about these opinions to decide what they should do.

Imagine that a survey on immigration was conducted in your congressional district, asking voters if they favored allowing illegal immigrants to stay in the country or if people here illegally should be deported as soon as possible. Suppose that the poll results indicate strong support for one of the two options and that you yourself have no strong feelings about illegal immigrants. The decision you face is: Should you demand that Congress enact immigration reform consistent with the poll results, or should you quietly ask that immigration reform be kept off the agenda?

Follow the poll. Elected officials often have strong incentives to do what constituents demand—in this case, to push for immigration reform measures that are consistent with the demands expressed in the poll. By this logic, if most constituents want immigrants to gain legal status, then you'd ask for a reform proposal that made legal status possible. Conversely, if the poll indicated that most constituents favored deportation, you would push for legislation that funded a program to achieve this goal. Doing so would allow you to claim some credit for the specifics of the bill, as well as for your vote, which in theory would please most of your constituents and increase your chances of reelection.

Stay quiet. As we discuss throughout the chapter, poll results are highly sensitive to question wording, timing, and other factors, making it hard to interpret even seemingly clear findings. Suppose, for example, the poll indicates support for allowing illegal immigrants to gain legal status. However, the survey did not ask about any of the details of legalization: whether legal status would require learning English, holding a stable job, paying back taxes, or other conditions. Even though none of these conditions were in the question, most of your constituents probably had some of them in mind when they thought about how they wanted to answer the question. In other words, your constituents' support of immigration reform depends on what the reforms look like. Even if you want to act in accordance with their demands, the survey may not tell you much about what exactly they want.

The situation is no easier if your poll indicates support for deportation. Would government officials search for illegals to deport or just deport people they happen to find? What would happen to children whose parents entered the country illegally but who were born in the United States and are therefore citizens? For some respondents, the solution is a nationwide house-to-house search, with children deported with their parents. But others would reject a deportation process that did either of these things. So here again, the poll results, one-sided as they are, don't provide you with foolproof guidance about how to vote.

Americans in both parties agree on the need for immigration reform but differ as to what they think the new immigration policies should be.

take a stand

1. Suppose you are a politician who feels that changes in immigration policy are needed but is faced with the quandary described above. Would you do nothing, so as to avoid alienating your constituency, or would you force a policy change and accept the political consequence—possible removal from office?

2. What poll questions would you use to get a clearer picture of public opinion on immigration?

hurt Trump's chances. The same models that yielded polling errors in 2020 have proved reliable in many other elections; that's why pollsters used them. Their mistake highlights the difficulty of accurately surveying the American people and shows why we should be reluctant to overinterpret survey results.

Claims about Obamacare reform are a good example. A 2015 poll asked people whether health care spending by the federal government was higher or lower than estimates made at the time the program was enacted in 2010. Forty-two percent said spending was higher, 40 percent did not know—and only 5 percent of respondents gave the correct answer, that spending was less than expected.[31] Other surveys were highly correlated with party identification, with Republicans much more likely to say the program cost more than expected and Democrats less likely. How can we explain these findings?

We can offer three explanations: (1) Many respondents likely had not thought about the questions beforehand. When they were asked for an opinion as part of a survey, there was no time to do research or think things through. (2) Respondents may also use partisan considerations: Obama supporters (Democrats) said they didn't know, while Obama opponents (Republicans) said costs were higher than expected. If so, the responses say more about partisanship and attitudes toward President Obama than about the cost of Obamacare. And because opinions are subject to influence by politicians and others, survey respondents might have evaluated Obamacare negatively because they formed their opinions after hearing certain public figures repeatedly describe the program in highly negative terms. (3) Many supposed facts are "contested truths," meaning that it is reasonable for individuals to hold a range of views.[32]

Such problems do not arise in all areas of public opinion. Respondents' ability to express specific opinions, as well as the accuracy of their opinions, rises if the survey questions relate to their everyday life.[33] Thus, the average American would be more likely to have an accurate sense of the state of the economy or his or her own personal economic condition than of the situation in Syria. Everyday life gives us information about the economy; in contrast, we learn about Syria only if we take the time to gather information.

DID YOU KNOW?

90%

of people contacted by phone to participate in a political survey either don't answer or refuse to participate.

Source: Pew Research Center

"Why Should I Care?"

New technologies have made surveys cheaper and easier, allowing groups to poll more often and ask a much wider range of questions. However, polls are not infallible. Believing in survey results without some skepticism can lead to fundamental misunderstandings of public opinion, as exemplified by claims that pollsters failed to predict support for Trump and other Republicans in 2020.

★

PRESENT FINDINGS ON WHAT AMERICANS THINK ABOUT GOVERNMENT AND WHY IT MATTERS

What Americans think about politics

American public opinion encompasses what people think of the federal government and their ideological beliefs. These opinions drive overall support for government action and serve as the basis for opinions on more specific policy questions. To understand what America's national government does and why, we have to determine what Americans ask of it.

Ideological polarization

We begin by examining liberal and conservative ideology and party identification to see if historical data show evidence of **ideological polarization**: sharp difference in Americans' overall ideas of the size and scope of government. The What Do the Facts Say? feature shows two kinds of survey data that can help us evaluate levels of polarization: responses to a question measuring ideology (liberal, moderate, or conservative) and a question that taps a respondent's party identification (Republican, Independent, or Democrat). The ideological data show no evidence of increased polarization; in the case of partisanship, a substantial percentage of Americans in 2019 described themselves as Independents. (For more details on partisanship, see Chapter 7.)

Looking more closely at opinion polarization, the third part of the What Do the Facts Say? feature divides the electorate into nine groups based on answers to questions that tap important principles, from foreign policy to domestic issues, civil liberties, and morality. Principles such as these are a kind of consideration—they form the basis for opinions that people express in surveys or act on when they vote or engage in other political behavior. The figure shows, first, that only about one-fifth of the electorate (Solid Liberals and Country-First Conservatives) hold consistent ideological beliefs—meaning that they generally give one kind of answer (conservative or liberal) when asked questions that tap their underlying principles. Moreover, most people fall into one of the intermediate groups, meaning that they express a mix of liberal and conservative issue positions. It's also important to remember that typologies like these are designed to identify differences and disagreements—there are many other issues on which there is consensus among the American public.[34]

While these data confirm that Americans disagree on important policy questions, they argue against the conception of a polarized America, with a large group of secular liberals opposing another large group of religious conservatives, and few people in the middle. Public opinion is much more complex. Most people could be labeled as liberals or as conservatives, secular or religious, depending on which issues they are asked about. Thus, even though people say they are liberals (or conservatives), this response does not mean that they hold liberal (or conservative) preferences on all issues. In addition, self-professed moderates may hold relatively extreme preferences on certain policy questions. Thus, understanding what Americans think and what they want from government often requires data on specific policy questions rather than broad judgments about the liberal or conservative nature of American public opinion. (Whether elected officials themselves are more polarized than their constituents is a different story, which we will discuss in Chapter 10.)

Given this data, why do political scientists talk so much about high levels of polarization in contemporary America? For the most part, these comments refer to the fact that in contemporary American politics, most of the policy conflicts divide Americans along party lines. These disagreements are magnified by a phenomenon known as negative partisanship, which we discuss in Chapter 7. So the difference between America now and a generation ago is not that we disagree more but that most of our disagreements have Democrats on one side and Republicans on the other. As we have already discussed, presidential approval and beliefs about the state of the economy are highly correlated with partisanship. In Chapter 8, we will show how partisanship drives voter decisions. Data presented throughout this book show partisan and ideological differences on many other political questions. In addition, the opinion data presented in other chapters show sharp partisan and ideological differences on questions about specific public policies. Finally, these partisan differences translate into higher levels of distrust by partisans from one party toward politicians and citizens from the other.[35]

ideological polarization
Sharp differences in Americans' overall ideas of the size and scope of government

WHAT DO THE FACTS SAY?

Are the American People Polarized?

Many commentators describe politics in America as highly conflictual, with most Americans holding either liberal or conservative points of view and identifying with one of the two major parties. Is polarization as strong as these commentators think?

Sources: Data from General Social Survey 1972–2018, Cumulative Datafile, Survey Documentation and Analysis (SDA) at UC Berkeley, https://sda.berkeley.edu/sdaweb/ analysis/;jsessionid=E9829C77CA98B-226C5A8AEAFD3031D92?dataset=gss18; Gallup, "Party Affiliation," June 4, 2020, https://news.gallup.com/poll/15370/party-affiliation.aspx; Pew Research Center, "Political Typology Reveals Deep Fissures on the Right and Left," October 26, 2017, www.people-press.org/2017/10/24/political-typology-reveals-deep-fissures-on-the-right-and-left/ (all accessed 6/30/20).

Think about it

- **According to the top figure,** how have levels of polarization changed since the 1990s?
- **What does the political typology** reveal about divisions within each political party?

Liberal or Conservative Ideology in America

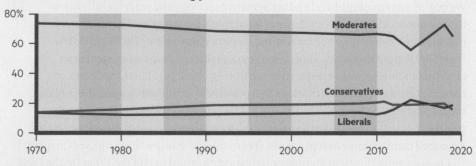

Party Identification in America

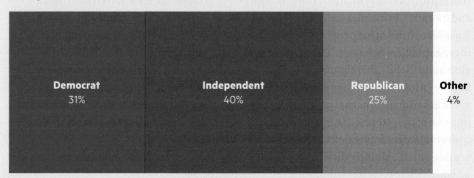

| Democrat 31% | Independent 40% | Republican 25% | Other 4% |

Political Typology in the General Public

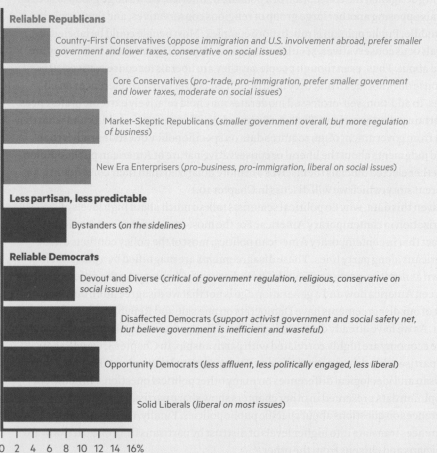

Reliable Republicans

Country-First Conservatives (*oppose immigration and U.S. involvement abroad, prefer smaller government and lower taxes, conservative on social issues*)

Core Conservatives (*pro-trade, pro-immigration, prefer smaller government and lower taxes, moderate on social issues*)

Market-Skeptic Republicans (*smaller government overall, but more regulation of business*)

New Era Enterprisers (*pro-business, pro-immigration, liberal on social issues*)

Less partisan, less predictable

Bystanders (*on the sidelines*)

Reliable Democrats

Devout and Diverse (*critical of government regulation, religious, conservative on social issues*)

Disaffected Democrats (*support activist government and social safety net, but believe government is inefficient and wasteful*)

Opportunity Democrats (*less affluent, less politically engaged, less liberal*)

Solid Liberals (*liberal on most issues*)

0 2 4 6 8 10 12 14 16%

Evaluations of government and officeholders

Another set of politically significant opinions addresses how people view the government: how well or poorly they think it is doing, whether they trust it, and their evaluations of individual politicians. These opinions matter for several reasons. Citizens' judgments about the government's overall performance may shape their evaluations of specific policies, especially if they do not know much about the policies.[36] Evaluations of specific policies may be shaped by how much a citizen trusts the government; greater trust brings more positive evaluations.[37] Trust in government and overall evaluations of it might influence a citizen's willingness to vote for incumbent congressional representatives or a president seeking reelection.[38]

The top graph in Figure 6.3 reveals that the average American is fairly disenchanted with the government. As of 2019, a majority believes that government is not run for the benefit of all the people and that government programs are usually wasteful and inefficient. These beliefs have not changed much over the last generation, nor in light of COVID-19.

This impression of a disenchanted and disapproving public is reinforced by the second graph, which generally shows declining levels of trust in government since the 1960s. Many scholars have argued that low levels of trust make it harder for elected officials to enact new policies, especially those involving large expenditures.[39] Some scholars even argue that low levels of trust raise questions about the future of democracy in America.[40] How can we say that American democracy is a good or popular form of government when so many people are unhappy with the performance of elected officials and bureaucrats and so few people trust the government? Finally, trust in government also has a partisan cast—people are more likely to express trust in the government when someone from their party is serving as president.

One important insight is that although Americans don't like the government in general, they tend to be more satisfied with their own representatives in Washington (see Chapter 10). For example, a survey question asking about "the government" may cause respondents to picture a roomful of bureaucrats pushing paperwork, whereas a question asking about "your representative" may lead respondents to think of someone working on their behalf. Also, as we discuss in Chapter 10, members of Congress work hard to convince their constituents that they are doing everything possible to satisfy constituents' demands. Sometimes members blame the institution of Congress and the government bureaucracy for shortcomings, portraying themselves as standing between their constituents and an inefficient government.

Policy preferences

In a diverse country of more than 330 million, people care about a wide range of policies. One useful measure of Americans' policy preferences is the **policy mood**, which captures the public's collective demands for government action on domestic policies.[41] Policy mood measures are constructed from surveys that address a wide range of policy questions.[42]

Fluctuations in the policy mood in America have led to changes in defense spending, environmental policy, and civil rights, among others—and have influenced elections.[43] Figure 6.4 shows that when the policy mood leans in an activist direction (Americans want government to do more, corresponding to lower values on the

policy mood
The level of public support for expanding the government's role in society; whether the public wants government action on a specific issue.

FIGURE 6.3

What Do Americans Think about Government?

A significant percentage of Americans have always been distrustful and disparaging of the federal government—and the percentage of people holding such views has increased markedly in the last generation. Does the perception that government is wasteful and inefficient make it easier or harder to enact new policies? How might the decline in trust explain the rise of the Tea Party organization and candidates like Donald Trump and Bernie Sanders?

Sources: Pew Research Center, "In a Politically Polarized Era, Sharp Divides in Both Partisan Coalitions," December 17, 2019, www.people-press.org/2019/12/17/in-a-politically-polarized-era-sharp-divides-in-both-partisan-coalitions/ (accessed 4/7/20); Pew Research Center, "Public Trust in Government: 1958–2019," April 11, 2019, www.people-press.org (accessed 5/3/20).

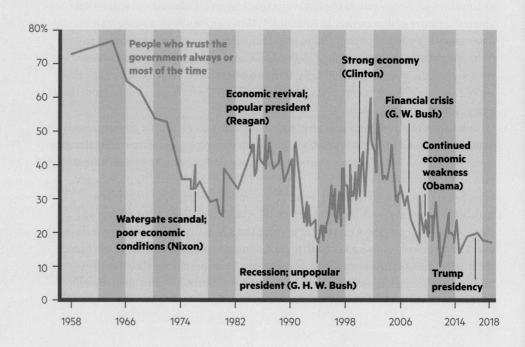

vertical axis), such as in the early 1960s, conditions are ripe for an expansion of the federal government involving more spending and new programs. But when the policy mood leans in the opposite direction (Americans want a smaller, less-active government, corresponding to higher values on the vertical axis), elected officials generally enact smaller increases in government spending and fewer new programs—or, as in recent elections, candidates who support a more active government are more likely to be defeated. At present, support for an activist government is at its highest since Barack Obama's administration. Given these opinions, we should expect

Policy Mood

Surveys assess the public's policy mood by asking questions about specific policy issues such as levels of taxation and government spending and the role of government. The level of conservatism (for example, support for smaller, less-active government) was at a high in 1952 and 1980. Could you have used the policy mood prior to the election to predict the outcomes of the 2020 elections?

FIGURE 6.4

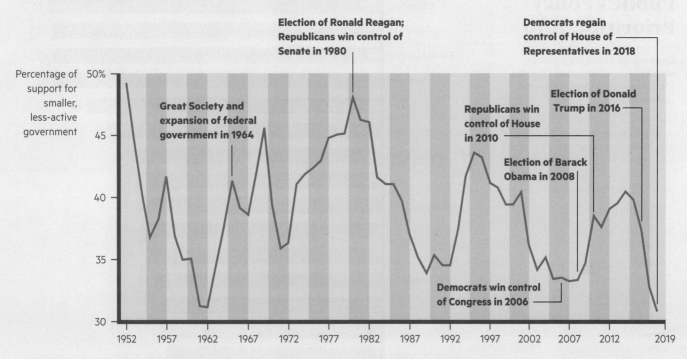

Source: Policy mood data available at http://stimson.web.unc.edu/data (accessed 1/15/20).

expansion in the size and scope of the government, at least until the public policy mood moves in a less activist direction.

Regarding more specific policy preferences, everything we have said in this chapter reinforces the idea that public opinion is often a moving target. While some beliefs and preferences are stable over time, opinions about specific policies can change from year to year, month to month, or even day to day. One of the best ways to take a snapshot of these beliefs is to ask citizens what they see as the top policy priorities facing the nation. Figure 6.5 shows responses to a 2019 survey, which of course does not reflect opinions in the wake of the COVID-19 pandemic or the Black Lives Matter protests of 2020.

The top priorities—the economy, education, and health care—have not changed very much over the last several decades. It is no exaggeration to say that Americans are always worried about the economy. Even when other pressing issues, such as terrorism, surpass the economy as the most important problem to Americans, the economy is typically listed second or third. In general, as the state of the economy declines, more and more people rate the economy as their greatest concern. Moreover, the percentage of people who mention their personal economic concerns—for example, unemployment or worries about retirement—also increases.

One important change in recent years is that concerns about terrorism and international conflict are no longer at the top of the list. In the wake of the September 11 attacks and the U.S. invasion of Iraq in 2003, many Americans saw protecting the

FIGURE 6.5

The American Public's Policy Priorities, 2019

Given this data on policy priorities, what issues would you have expected to be prominent in the 2020 election campaign?

Source: Pew Research Center, "Public's Policy Priorities for 2019," January 24, 2019, www.people-press.org (accessed 5/3/20).

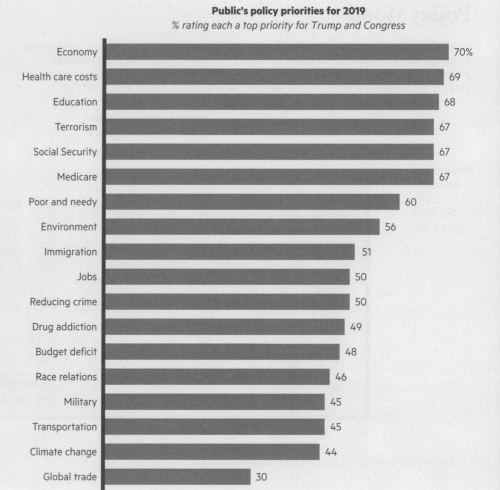

Public's policy priorities for 2019
% rating each a top priority for Trump and Congress

Issue	%
Economy	70%
Health care costs	69
Education	68
Terrorism	67
Social Security	67
Medicare	67
Poor and needy	60
Environment	56
Immigration	51
Jobs	50
Reducing crime	50
Drug addiction	49
Budget deficit	48
Race relations	46
Military	45
Transportation	45
Climate change	44
Global trade	30

country against attack as the top priority. Now, even though U.S. forces are still engaged in fighting groups such as Al Qaeda, the Taliban, and ISIS, Americans see fighting terrorism as less of a priority than domestic policy issues.

These policy priorities frame contemporary political debates and divide the political parties. Think about what Republicans and Democrats in Washington argue about: how best to fight terrorism and secure the United States from attack, how to increase economic growth and reduce the unemployment rate, and what the government's role should be in providing health care and making sure that Americans have secure

Politicians read public-opinion polls closely to gauge whether their behavior will anger or please constituents. Few politicians always follow survey results—but virtually none would agree with Calvin's father that polls should be ignored entirely.

retirements. In fact, there are sharp partisan disagreements on many of these issues; 67 percent of Democrats see climate change as an important problem, while only 21 percent of Republicans give the same response when asked about their public policy priorities.[44] Similar differences exist for economic inequality, racism, and illegal immigration. However, in other areas, such as concerns over jobs and social security, responses do not vary much by party.

The list of policy priorities in Figure 6.5 also explains government inaction on some issues. For example, gun control doesn't even appear on the list. Thus, the fact that Congress has not legislated on this issue in recent years is actually consistent with public opinion. For better or worse, the average American has other priorities for government action.[45]

Does public opinion matter?

We can say with confidence that public opinion remains highly relevant in American politics today. One key piece of evidence is the amount of time and effort politicians, journalists, and political scientists spend trying to find out what Americans think. Of course, it is easy to find examples like gun control in which policy has stayed the same despite a majority supporting change. In other cases, such as the enactment of Obamacare, new policies have been passed even though a majority preferred the status quo at the time of enactment. But these examples do not mean that public opinion is irrelevant. It is not always possible to please a majority of citizens. Politicians' willingness to do so depends on whether the majority is organized into interest groups, how much they care about the issue (and the intensity of the opposition), and, most important, the details of their personal preferences and the views held by their constituents.

More broadly, public opinion exerts a conspicuous influence in widespread areas of government. We mention this broad influence repeatedly throughout this book. In Chapter 10, we describe how legislators endeavor to determine what their constituents want and how their constituents will respond to different actions. In Chapter 8, we see how voters use retrospective evaluations to form opinions about whom to vote for and how candidates incorporate the public's views into campaign platforms that will attract widespread support. And in Chapter 7, we discuss how voters use candidates' party affiliations like brand names to determine how candidates will behave if elected. Scholars have found that congressional actions on a wide range of issues, from votes on defense policy to the confirmation of Supreme Court nominees, are shaped by constituent opinion.[46] Moreover, careful analysis of the connection between opinions and actions shows that this linkage does not exist because politicians are able to shape public opinion in line with what they want to do; rather, politicians behave in line with their constituents' opinions because to do otherwise would place the politicians in jeopardy of losing the next election.[47]

Recent events also speak to the influence of public opinion. Think about the failure of elected officials over the last few years to repeal Obamacare, enact immigration reform, or pass new limits on the ownership of handguns and assault rifles. In all of these cases, a significant portion of Americans wanted policy change, but a substantial percentage were opposed and even the supporters disagreed on what kinds of changes were best. Congressional inaction on these measures does not reflect a willful ignorance of public opinion. Rather, it reflects the lack of a public consensus about what government should do. Inaction on these issues is exactly what we should expect if public opinion is real and relevant to what happens in politics.

★

DESCRIBE THE MAJOR TYPES OF NEWS SOURCES AND THE ROLE THEY PLAY IN AMERICAN POLITICS

mass media
Sources that provide information to the average citizen, such as newspapers, television networks, radio stations, podcasts, and websites.

linking institution
An actor or group of actors in American politics that informs citizens about government actions or helps them exercise control over policy.

DID YOU KNOW?

67%

of American adults report they get at least some of their news from social media.
Source: Pew Research Center

The news media

Closely related to our discussion of public opinion is the role of the news media, for it is generally through the media that Americans receive political information. This section describes the **mass media**, the many sources of political information available to Americans, and how people use (or don't use) this information. Finally, we consider how the media may influence public opinion and politics. The media are the first example in this book of a **linking institution**—an actor or group of actors in American politics that informs citizens about government actions or helps them exercise control over policy. The development of the Internet over the last generation has dramatically increased the number of media sources and the range of information available to the average American. This changing media landscape means that it is less important than it was in the past to describe each media source and what kinds of information it can (and cannot) provide. In contemporary America, there are so many sources and so much information that Americans can become experts on virtually any aspect of politics or public policy—if they are willing to search for information and assess the value of what they find.

Media sources in the twenty-first century

Over the last two decades, the Internet has become a major and often dominant source for information about American politics. Virtually all U.S. newspapers, television networks, radio stations, and cable stations offer free or (increasingly) paid access to most or all of their content via websites and mobile apps as well as providing some Web-only information.

Many Internet-only sites offer a combination of rumor, inside information, and deep analysis of American politics. Some, such as Politico, Vox, and FiveThirtyEight, have paid staff and report on a wide range of topics. Others have a narrower focus: the Monkey Cage (now affiliated with the *Washington Post*) and the Mischiefs of Faction use political science research to explain contemporary American politics.[48] And many websites, some run by ordinary citizens, provide their own insights and information about American politics. Finally, Facebook, Twitter, and other social media sites provide users with links to coverage written by others; people also use these sites to report and comment on political events themselves.

These changes have dramatically increased the amount of information about politics that is available to the average American. Imagine yourself in the late 1940s. Suppose you wanted to learn about President Truman's State of the Union address.

The White House ✔ @WhiteHouse · May 8
"We will be instituting the highest level of economic sanction. Any nation that helps Iran in its quest for nuclear weapons could also be strongly sanctioned by the United States. America will not be held hostage to nuclear blackmail."

◯ 1.1K ⟳ 3.7K ♡ 13K

The White House ✔ @WhiteHouse · May 8
"Therefore, I am announcing today that the United States will withdraw from the Iran nuclear deal."

President Trump is terminating United States participation in the JCPOA, as it failed to protect America's national security interests.

◯ 998 ⟳ 2.6K ♡ 11K

The White House ✔ @WhiteHouse · May 8
Watch LIVE as President Trump delivers remarks on the Joint Comprehensive Plan of Action: 45.wh.gov/RtVRmD

President Trump delivers remarks on the Joint Comprehensive Plan of Action

◯ 157 ⟳ 390 ♡ 1.2K

Information and coverage of important events become instantaneously available through Internet sources like Twitter feeds and blogs. For instance, President Trump relied on Twitter to communicate his foreign policy and economic policy priorities.

If you couldn't go to Washington to hear it in person, where could you have gotten information about the speech? If you lived in a big city, the speech would probably be covered in the next day's newspaper. If you lived in a small town, your local paper might or might not run the story. If it didn't, you would need a subscription to either a big-city paper (which would arrive a week after the fact) or a weekly or monthly news magazine, or you would need to have access to a radio that could pick up a station broadcasting the speech.

Now consider the modern era, in which major political events saturate the media and a virtually unlimited amount of information is available on the Internet. Suppose you want to know about the president's State of the Union message. You can tune in to one of the four major television networks, numerous cable news channels, public television stations, or radio stations. Most television stations will feature pundits' commentaries on the speech and will interview prominent politicians and commentators. Jimmy Fallon and other late-night hosts will probably make jokes about it on television, and John Oliver will skewer the speech on his Sunday show. Tomorrow it will be front-page news and larger papers will publish the full text of the speech online. Countless websites will offer analyses. And you will be able to watch a video of the speech on YouTube and many other sites. Some of your friends (perhaps even you) might offer commentary on

DID YOU KNOW?

Newspaper circulation per capita has declined

66%

since 1970.
Source: Pew Research Center

social media. The point is, there are many places to get information; you would have to work to avoid them.

The Internet creates new opportunities for interaction between citizens, reporters, and government officials. Many reporters host live chat sessions, allowing people to ask follow-up questions about published stories, or interact with their audience through a variety of social media sites. People who know something about political events (or think they do) now have a variety of ways, from blogs to Twitter, to contribute to the commentary on political news stories and put information before a wide audience. While there is much more information available today than there was a generation ago, media sources are constantly in flux. Websites and Web pages come and go. Individuals who post detailed analyses of one political event may be too busy to comment on another. Even well-established media sources can quickly change. For example, in recent years companies that once owned newspapers in Chicago, Philadelphia, and Minneapolis have gone bankrupt, whereas several major U.S. cities, including Seattle, Birmingham, and New Orleans, have a hometown daily newspaper that appears only in digital form. Other newspapers have cut foreign bureaus, reduced their staff, and thinned the amount of news in every edition. (One exception is the *Washington Post*, which expanded its newsroom by over a third under the ownership of Jeff Bezos, the founder of Amazon.) At the same time, the major television networks as well as cable television sources have seen declines in viewership.

The increase in sources has also led to a blurring of fact and opinion in some news coverage. Most mainstream media distinguish between news coverage, where the goal is to present facts and analysis without an ideological agenda, and opinion pieces, which have a clear point of view.[49] In print media, the latter stories are usually reserved for a special op-ed (opinions and editorials) section. Newer media sources, especially solo Web-only operations, may not follow these conventions, meaning that casual readers might assume they are reading a factual account when in fact they are not. See the What Do the Facts Say? feature for an example of this.

Regulating the media

Federal regulation of the news media was driven by the fact that many media sources are profit-seeking businesses—as well as concerns over the media's potential to shape public opinion. For example, the **Federal Communications Commission (FCC)** regulates **broadcast media**, such as radio stations, as well as broadcast and cable television.

Limits on Ownership and Content Until very recently, a central concern of the FCC was that one company or organization might buy enough stations to dominate the airwaves in an area and become a monopoly, offering only one set of programs or point of view. For many years, FCC regulations limited the number of radio and television stations a company could own in a community and the total nationwide audience that a company's television stations could reach.

The FCC also created the **equal time provision**, which states that if a radio or television station gives air time to a candidate outside its news coverage—such as during an entertainment show—it has to give an equivalent amount of time to other candidates running for the same office. In addition, it established a fairness doctrine, whereby broadcasters had to present opposing points of view as part of their coverage of important events; usually this was done by broadcasting editorials during news programs that presented both sides of an issue.

Federal Communications Commission (FCC)
A government agency created in 1934 to regulate American radio stations and later expanded to regulate television, wireless communications technologies, and other broadcast media.

broadcast media
Communications technologies, such as television and radio, that transmit information over airwaves.

equal time provision
An FCC regulation requiring broadcast media to provide equal air time on any non-news programming to all candidates running for an office.

Is Chicago's Murder Rate a "National Crisis"?

Numerous articles published in the last few years raised alarms about a sharp increase in homicides in some large U.S. metropolitan areas, most notably Chicago. A story from the *New York Post* (an opinion piece written by Gianno Caldwell and published in November 2019) treats Chicago as an exemplar of how Democratic city administrations are indifferent to the suffering of their citizens. The writer summarized the situation as a "national crisis."

When people make a claim about a real-world phenomenon like crime, the first thing to check is if they have their facts straight. Crime rates are relatively easy to analyze because the police and medical examiners in most areas release annual statistics to the public. In fact, the *Chicago Tribune* has a Web page that allows you to view trends in Chicago's murder rates over several years (the *Tribune* also provides information on sources so you can check its findings—its data include all cases that Chicago's medical examiner classified as homicides).[b] These *Tribune* data tell a different story: rather than being out of control, murder rates in Chicago have been declining for several years following a spike in 2016.

> In my reporting for Fox News, the people I have spoken with feel so under siege by the gun violence that this tiny drop doesn't even register to them, and any talk from a politician who mentions the reduction in murders is a smack in their face because going on their front porch could be a death sentence.
>
> —**Gianno Caldwell,** *New York Post*[a]

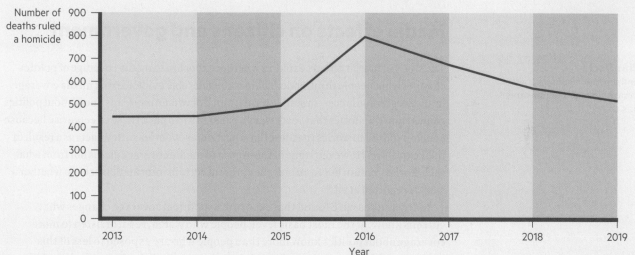

Chicago Murder Rate, 2013–2019

Source: "Tracking Chicago Homicide Victims," *Chicago Tribune*, www.chicagotribune.com/news/breaking/ct-chicago-homicides-data-tracker-htmlstory.html (accessed 1/29/20).

Additional analysis by *The Economist* places murders in Chicago in a broader context.[c] Homicide rates in any city can vary sharply from year to year simply because homicide is a fairly rare crime. Several cities in *The Economist*'s analysis had the same pattern as in Chicago of sharp increases followed by declines.

The *Post*'s article fails one of the key criteria we discussed in Chapter 1: the claims it makes about Chicago's murder rates are very different from those developed by other researchers. Because the story is so anomalous, we should be very skeptical about its conclusions. Remember to always corroborate the report.

Think about it

- **What additional information** might help put Chicago's murder rate as cited in this *New York Post* article in context? Can you think of any comparative data points that might help make better sense of the numbers?

- **What are the dangers** of spreading misleading or incorrect information about public safety? How might these errors lead people to make uninformed decisions?

Deregulation The FCC's limits on ownership and content as well as the fairness doctrine have been eliminated because of the development of new communications technologies. The logic is that with so many sources of information, if one broadcaster ignores a candidate, an issue, or a viewpoint, citizens can still find what they want from another source. Pressure for deregulation also came from the owners of media companies, who wanted to buy more television, radio, and cable stations, as well as from book and magazine publishers, Internet service providers, and newspapers.[50]

These regulatory changes have shaped the current media landscape in two ways. First, they have allowed for concentration: many media companies own multiple media sources in a town or community. For example, iHeartMedia owns over 850 AM and FM radio stations, including multiple stations in more than 30 cities. Similarly, Facebook, which is a major source of news for many Americans, also owns Instagram. Second, the changes have allowed for cross-ownership, in which one company owns several different kinds of media outlets, often in the same community. For example, Nexstar owns various Chicago media outlets, including the WGN radio station, the WGN television station, and the *Chicago Tribune* daily newspaper. These trends have given rise to **media conglomerates**, companies that control a wide range of news sources.[51] Nuts & Bolts 6.2 shows the diverse holdings of one such company, the Walt Disney Company. You may think of Disney in terms of theme parks, cruises, and Avengers or Star Wars movies and TV shows, but the company owns a wide range of media companies, including the ABC broadcast network, Hulu, ESPN, and the political information site FiveThirtyEight.

Media effects on citizens and government

The study of **media effects** explores whether exposure to media coverage of politics changes what people think or do. There is considerable evidence that media coverage influences its audience—in simple terms, much of what Americans know about politics comes from the stories they read, watch, or listen to. In part, these effects arise because people exposed to stories that describe a particular event learn new facts as a result of their exposure. However, some of the impact of media coverage stems not from what such stories contain but from how they present certain information or even whether a story is reported at all.[52]

Many studies have found that exposure to political coverage changes what citizens know: at the most basic level, people who watch, read, or listen to more coverage about politics know more than people who are exposed to less of this coverage.[53] What people learn from the media can shape the demands they place on politicians.[54] However, at least part of the media's effect on people's knowledge level arises because of underlying interest: people who are interested in politics know more in the first place and, because of their interest, watch more media coverage of events as they happen. Moreover, because people can pick and choose which coverage to watch, read, or listen to, what they learn from the media tends to reinforce their preexisting beliefs. That is, a conservative might listen to Sean Hannity, while a liberal might watch MSNBC. Both people may learn something from the coverage, but the most likely result is that they will only grow more certain in the opinion that they already have.[55]

Given this evidence of media effects, one of the central questions is whether reporters and editors have a discernable bias: That is, do their decisions about which events to report on and how they report on them reflect a conscious effort to shape

media conglomerates
Companies that control a large number of media sources across several types of media outlets.

media effects
The influence of media coverage on average citizens' opinions and actions.

Holdings of the Walt Disney Company

The Walt Disney Company is an example of a media conglomerate, a company that controls a variety of media outlets throughout the world. It owns cable television networks, television and radio stations, cable channels, movie-production companies, subscription programming sites, and websites; this table provides just a few examples of its many holdings. This structure allows the company to rebroadcast or reprint stories in different outlets and thus operate more efficiently, but opponents are concerned that conglomerates might expand to control most—or even all—of the sources that are available to the average citizen, making it impossible to access alternate points of view.

Broadcast Stations	Film Companies
ABC broadcast network (owns 8 stations, over 200 affiliates)	20th Century Studios
KRDC-AM (Los Angeles)	Lucasfilm
Radio Disney (available through Internet platforms)	Marvel Studios
	Pixar
	20th Century Fox Television
	Walt Disney Studios

Cable Channels	Other Media
A&E	Vice Media
ESPN	FiveThirtyEight
Freeform	Hulu
FX	Disney+
Lifetime	
National Geographic	
Four Disney-branded channels	

Source: Compiled by the authors.

"Why Should I Care?" Think about where you get your news. If all your top sources for political information were owned by the same company, how might that affect the diversity of stories you see or the perspectives you hear? While conglomerates might help make the process of reporting and distributing the news more efficient, it's important to understand how the owners might influence what you ultimately read.

public opinion in a liberal, conservative, or other direction? Surveys of the American electorate have found a **hostile media effect**: regardless of respondents' partisan leanings, they believe that the media favor candidates and ideas from the other party.[56] It is easy to find examples of suspicious decisions by reporters and their editors that suggest some sort of overt bias in coverage, and many journalists and commentators admit that they take an ideological or partisan perspective.

It is also no surprise that politicians complain that media coverage is biased against them: the stakes for them are very high. For example, during the final weeks of the 2020 election, Donald Trump's campaign wanted more coverage of claims that Joe Biden was a corrupt politician whose son and other family members had

hostile media effect
The tendency of people to see neutral media coverage of an event as biased against their point of view.

used connections to enrich themselves, and less attention paid to the COVID-19 pandemic and the weak American economy. The Biden campaign in turn complained that the media were focusing too much on rumors about Biden's health or conflicts within the Democratic party, and not enough on Trump's missteps. Thus, while both campaigns complained about bias, the simple explanation for their complaints is that they wanted to win the election and therefore wanted media coverage that exposed their opponent's flaws rather than their candidate's flaws.

In fact, while it is easy to find media coverage of politics that is incomplete or sloppily reported, cases in which reporters made predictions that later turned out to be false, or stories that candidates wish had not been reported, it is hard to find cases of systematic bias in media coverage. Moreover, while some academic studies have found evidence of press coverage favoring one type of candidate or issue position over another, an equally large body of work has produced important critiques of these studies. For one thing, a finding that most reporters are liberal (or Democrats) and few are conservative (Republicans) does not imply that political coverage must necessarily favor liberal positions or Democratic candidates. Reporters may prioritize being as objective as possible, fear that favoring one side will cause their audience to decline, or be subject to review by editors who are on guard against bias. Similarly, the fact that a reporter criticizes a politician or party is not evidence of his or her lack of objectivity. Critiques do not in themselves suggest that a reporter is being unfair—the question is, what would a fair analysis look like? Many analyses of President Trump's time in office (before COVID-19) acknowledged the strong American economy but gave little credit to Trump for this outcome. Were these reporters biased against Trump, or had they read the literature on political control of the economy, which shows that presidential actions have little impact on economic conditions, particularly in the short run? Untangling these effects is difficult, and if media bias were as pronounced as some critics claim, it would likely be easier to measure.

Filtering and Framing Compared with overt bias, filtering and framing may produce subtler but stronger impacts on public opinion. **Filtering** (also called *agenda-setting*) refers to the ways in which journalists' and editors' decisions about which stories to report influence which stories people think about. **Framing** refers to how the description or presentation of a story, including the details, explanations, and context, changes the ways people react to and interpret the information. Space limitations mean that some filtering is inevitable as reporters and editors decide which of many potential news stories to cover. Similar decisions about what to report and how to present the information lead to framing effects. Even if everyone in the political media adhered to the highest standards of accuracy, these influences would still exist.

filtering
The influence on public opinion that results from journalists' and editors' decisions about which of many potential news stories to report.

framing
The influence on public opinion caused by the way a story is presented or covered, including the details, explanations, and context offered in the report.

"Why Should I Care?"

It's important to have a clear and accurate understanding of today's media sources. If you're looking for someone to blame for Americans' lack of knowledge about politics, the mass media is not a good candidate. While most sources fall short in one way or another, there is a wealth of information available, most of it for free. But most people never search for political information and ignore much of what they encounter. Journalists can do the most effective reporting possible—providing in-depth, balanced coverage of critical events—but unless people take time to read or view that coverage, they will remain uninformed.

Unpacking the Conflict

Considering all that we've discussed in this chapter, let's apply what we know about how public opinion works to the examples from the beginning of the chapter. Do Americans really hold the bizarre beliefs that are sometimes expressed in polling results? Can we take polls seriously, if they produce results like these? Where does public opinion come from? Can politicians trust public opinion as a guide to what Americans want—and can we use opinions to measure the quality of American democracy?

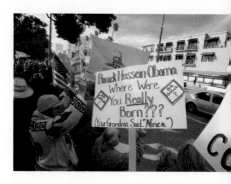

Given how people form opinions, it's easy to see what Jon Stewart was talking about: at least some of the time, public opinion will be incomplete at best and wildly inaccurate at worst. But that's not surprising. For most people, politics is not the most important thing in their lives, and they don't spend much time worrying about it, learning the details, or forming judgments until they need to. This logic also explains why people are sometimes unable to answer seemingly easy questions, as in the survey mentioned alongside the image at the beginning of this chapter in which respondents were asked to find Iran on a map of the Middle East. Most of the time, there's no reason to know where Iran is. Even if the United States and Iran came close to armed conflict, as they did in early 2020, it is unclear whether knowledge of geography would help average citizens decide how they felt about the matter.

When we ask how "good" opinions are, or whether the electorate acts "rationally and responsibly," as V. O. Key argued, the most important thing to remember is that there is no absolute standard of accuracy. One of the fundamental tenets of a democracy is that people are free to hold whatever opinions they want, and to base these opinions on whatever factors they want to consider. If someone says she approves of Trump's performance in office, and we determine that her judgment is based on Trump's being a Republican, this opinion is as legitimate as that of someone whose evaluation is based on a detailed study of multiple factors. Moreover, making sense of politics requires people to make some pretty sophisticated judgments, and it would be no surprise to find that they make mistakes some of the time, particularly given the shortcuts they use to form their opinions. Nevertheless, the model of opinion formation described in this chapter provides observers of American politics with a guide for interpreting public opinion, including how opinions will change given events.

These findings also explain why the proliferation of media sources and the rise of social media has not produced a better-informed public. Even now, the fact that much more information is available has not changed our consumption habits. The value of gathering additional information is simply not worth the trouble, especially given the need to reconcile different sources. In addition, people today have a better sense of which sources they should trust and which they shouldn't. Taken as a group, the media are no less trustworthy than they were a generation ago—but the average American has a much better idea of why they should be suspicious of some media coverage.

Should we take polls seriously? Yes, but not too much. Given all the potential problems with mass surveys, we should be suspicious about surprising results such as the support for conspiracy theories cited at the beginning of this chapter. Respondents may not have taken the question seriously, they may have focused on subtle details of the question—or their reply may have been driven by considerations that have nothing to do with the question at hand. Republican suspicions about Barack Obama's citizenship probably reflected the fact that several of their party's leaders, as well as prominent spokespeople including Donald Trump, had repeatedly voiced their suspicions during the campaign. And Democratic concerns about the government's foreknowledge of the

September 11 attacks were colored by the identity of the president at the time, Republican George W. Bush. More generally, we should take poll results seriously to the extent that they are based on multiple surveys, with differently worded questions; are conducted by reputable pollsters; and are conducted at a time when respondents are aware of the issues they are being asked about. One poll on its own doesn't tell us very much.

In sum, while you can't take every poll result you see at face value, public opinion is real, and it matters. Americans have ideas about what they want government to do, and they use these ideas to guide their political choices. Polls showing deep disagreement between Americans on some issues describe the policy landscape on which elections will be contested and the subsequent debates in Washington. While very few Americans are policy experts, their views on policy are the ultimate driver of our government's policy choices.

"What's Your Take?"

Is public opinion important enough that politicians should follow it? Or is public opinion too unreliable and unpredictable to trust?

And if public opinion cannot be trusted, whose wishes should government follow, if not the people's?

STUDY GUIDE

What is public opinion?

Define *public opinion* and explain why it matters in American politics. (Pages 182–184)

Summary

What the population thinks about politics and government matters for three reasons: people's political actions are driven by their opinions; there is a strong linkage between people's opinions and political actors' behavior; and public opinion helps us understand how specific policy outcomes are achieved.

Key terms

public opinion (p. 182)   latent opinion (p. 183)

Practice Quiz Questions

1. **What does it mean that most political judgments are latent opinions?**

a   Most Americans have preformed opinions.

b   Most Americans have well-thought-out reasons for preferring a policy.

c   Most Americans do not have any meaningful political attitudes.

d   Most Americans form their opinions only as needed.

e   Most opinions are not accurate.

2. **Which of the following is *not* true regarding considerations?**

a   Well-informed and poorly informed people use them in forming opinions.

b   Opinions on morally complex issues do not involve considerations.

c   Political events can become considerations.

d   They may be contradictory.

e   Party identification is often used in considerations.

Where do opinions come from?

Explain how people form political attitudes and opinions. (Pages 184–191)

Summary

Political opinions are influenced by a wide range of factors. The belief systems of our parents and relatives influence our opinions early on, and our social groups influence our perspectives later in life. Personal events such as attending college or moving to a new city may influence how we think about politics, as do national events such as the attacks on September 11. Even political debates by political elites and party leaders shape our political attitudes.

Key term

political socialization (p. 184)

Practice Quiz Questions

3. **Theories of political socialization say that people's opinions are influenced first by _____ .**

a   what they learned from their parents

b   the way political parties change over time

c   their genetic and biological factors

d   their personality traits

e   politicians

4. **The idea that individuals will rely on others who "look like" them for opinions relates to _____ .**

a   party identification

b   political socialization

c   group identity

d   political events

e   generational effects

5. **Which phrase best completes the following statement regarding the sources of public opinion? "Politicians and other political actors work to _____ public opinion."**

a   respond to

b   ignore

c   disregard

d   stabilize

e   shape

Measuring public opinion

Describe basic survey methods and potential issues affecting accuracy. (Pages 191–198)

Summary

Most information about public opinion comes from mass surveys involving hundreds or thousands of respondents. The accuracy of surveys is influenced by several factors, including the size of the sample and whether the people in the sample are randomly selected. Using a randomly selected sample, researchers can draw conclusions about public opinion across the American population.

Key terms

mass survey (p. 191)
population (p. 191)
sample (p. 194)
sampling error (p. 194)

Practice Quiz Question

6. Why is it important to get a large random survey sample?

a   to keep costs down

b   to provide deep insights into why people hold their opinions

c   to help candidates fine-tune their campaign messages

d   to be able to generalize about the broad population

e   to prevent question wording from biasing survey results

What Americans think about politics

Present findings on what Americans think about government and why it matters. (Pages 198–206)

Summary

As a whole, the American electorate is ideologically moderate, with relatively little ideological polarization. Paradoxically, while trust in the government has declined steadily since the 1960s, people are still generally rather happy with their own representatives in Washington, D.C., and low trust in government does not preclude Americans from approving of specific government programs and activities. Government policy and congressional outcomes are responsive to changes in public mood, and most policy decisions (and arguments) reflect the priorities of a majority of Americans.

Key terms

ideological polarization (p. 199)
policy mood (p. 201)

Practice Quiz Questions

7. Americans generally _____ of the government; Americans generally _____ of their own representatives.

a   approve; approve

b   approve; disapprove

c   disapprove; approve

d   disapprove; disapprove

e   have no opinion; have no opinion

8. What is policy mood?

a   public support for Congress

b   presidential approval rating

c   trust in government

d   public demand for government action on domestic policies

e   public demand for government action on international policies

9. Which policy area is always near the top of Americans' concerns?

a   economic conditions

b   health care

c   same-sex marriage

d   immigration

e   the environment

The news media

Describe the major types of news sources and the role they play in American politics. (Pages 206–212)

Summary

While the term "media" traditionally referred only to print sources, technological advances allowed political information to be spread through radio, television, and the Internet. The creation of the Internet and the proliferation of media sources more generally have drastically increased the amount of information about politics that is available to the average American. Much of what Americans know about politics comes not only from the stories that they are exposed to in the news but also from the way these stories are presented (if the stories are reported at all). Potential media bias, filtering, and framing all may influence the type and scope of information that reporters choose to disseminate.

Key terms

mass media (p. 206)
linking institution (p. 206)
Federal Communications
    Commission (FCC) (p. 208)
broadcast media (p. 208)
equal time provision (p. 208)
media conglomerates (p. 210)
media effects (p. 210)
hostile media effect (p. 211)
filtering (p. 212)
framing (p. 212)

Practice Quiz Questions

10. Which is the result of the decreased barriers to publication on the Internet?

a Few opportunities exist for citizens to interact with reporters or government officials.

b People with no official connection to politics can contribute to the commentary and reach a wide audience.

c The accuracy of political information has improved.

d Few average citizens report on events as they happen.

e Like-minded political supporters have difficulty organizing and staying informed on issues.

11. The deregulation of the media has resulted in _____.

a increasing enforcement of the equal time provision

b increasing enforcement of the fairness doctrine

c increasing use of the Internet

d increasing scrutiny of media concentration

e increasing frequency of cross-ownership

12. What is one problem with research on media bias?

a Few scholars are interested in studying media bias.

b It is difficult to measure bias.

c No journalist will admit that bias exists.

d There's little chance that media sources are biased.

e There are not enough media sources to create a sample.

13. Space limitations mean that some _____ is inevitable.

a filtering

b slant

c priming

d framing

e soft news

Suggested Reading

Achen, Christopher H., and Larry M. Bartels. *Democracy for Realists: Why Elections Do Not Produce Responsive Government*. Princeton, NJ: Princeton University Press, 2016.

Albertson, Bethany, and Shana Kushner Gadarian. *Anxious Politics: Democratic Citizenship in a Threatening World*. New York: Cambridge University Press, 2015.

Campbell, David. *Why We Vote: How Schools and Communities Shape Our Civic Life*. Princeton, NJ: Princeton University Press, 2006.

Cramer, Katherine J. *The Politics of Resentment: Rural Consciousness in Wisconsin and the Rise of Scott Walker*. Chicago: University of Chicago Press, 2016.

Davenport, Christian. *Media Bias, Perspective, and State Repression: The Black Panther Party*. New York: Cambridge University Press, 2010.

Green, Donald P., Bradley Palmquist, and Eric Schickler. *Partisan Hearts and Minds*. New Haven, CT: Yale University Press, 2002.

Hibbing, John R., and Elizabeth Theiss-Morse. *Congress as Public Enemy: Public Attitudes toward American Political Institutions*. New York: Cambridge University Press, 1995.

Iyengar, Shanto. *Media Politics: A Citizen's Guide*. 4th ed. New York: W. W. Norton, 2019.

Marcus, George E., John L. Sullivan, Elizabeth Theiss-Morse, and Sandra L. Wood. *With Malice toward Some: How People Make Civil Liberties Judgments*. New York: Cambridge University Press, 1995.

Mendelberg, Tali. *The Race Card: Campaign Strategy, Implicit Messages, and the Norm of Equality*. Princeton, NJ: Princeton University Press, 2001.

Peffley, Mark, and Jon Hurwitz. *Justice in America: The Separate Realities of Blacks and Whites*. New York: Cambridge University Press, 2010.

Prior, Markus. *Post-Broadcast Democracy: How Media Choice Increases Inequality in Political Involvement and Polarizes Elections*. New York: Cambridge University Press, 2007.

Schlozman, Kay Lehman, Sidney Verba, and Henry E. Brady. *The Unheavenly Chorus: Unequal Political Voice and the Broken Promise of American Democracy*. Princeton, NJ: Princeton University Press, 2013.

Zaller, John. *The Nature and Origins of Mass Opinion*. New York: Cambridge University Press, 1992.

Political Parties

How do political parties organize American politics?

> **"Our diversity is our strength, our unity is our power."[1]**
> *Speaker of the House Nancy Pelosi (D-CA)*

> **"I've got news for the Republican establishment. I've got news for the Democratic establishment. They can't stop us."**
> *Senator Bernie Sanders (I-VT)*

The power and limits of American political parties are best illustrated by the 2020 Democratic presidential nomination contest. Over a dozen candidates ran serious, well-funded campaigns, beginning over a year before the first caucus in Iowa. None of them, not even billionaire Mike Bloomberg, seriously considered running as an Independent. The rules of the contest were set by the Democratic National Committee, which even decided which candidates would appear in DNC-sponsored debates. There was extensive live coverage of the party's presidential nomination convention in August 2020, including the acceptance speech by the winner of the contest, former vice president Joe Biden. At the same time, many critics argued that the nomination process was drawn out and highlighted divisions between liberals and moderates in the party that will complicate Democratic policy initiatives over the next two years.

The 2020 Democratic nomination contest is an example of what political scientist Julia Azari calls "strong partisanship, weak parties."[2] On the one hand, decades of research have shown that most Americans have a long-term attachment to one of the major parties and that this attachment shapes their political behavior—even if they say they are voting for the better candidate rather than according to their party identification. Parties organize elections: although President Trump campaigned in 2016 as a political outsider, he won the presidency as the candidate of the Republican Party. And once candidates are elected to office, parties are also players in the legislative process. Congressional party leaders, such as Senate Majority Leader Mitch McConnell or House Minority Leader Nancy Pelosi during the 116th Congress, are important spokespeople and dealmakers. In these ways, parties unify and mobilize disparate groups, simplify the choices that voters face, and bring efficiency and coherence to government policy making.

During the 2020 Democratic primary, the field was initially crowded with several candidates from a variety of backgrounds. Ultimately, Joe Biden won the nomination and defeated incumbent president Donald Trump.

CHAPTER GOALS

Define *political parties* **and show how American political parties and party systems have evolved over time.** pages 220–224

Describe the main characteristics of American parties as organizations, in the government, and in the electorate. pages 224–232

Explain the important functions that parties perform in the political system. pages 232–242

At the same time, American political parties seem unable to carry through on their promises. While Joe Biden won the nomination, there were doubts about whether he would be able to reach policy compromises and gain the support of the more progressive side of the party that had been excited about the policy proposals championed by Bernie Sanders, including Medicare for All, a Green New Deal, and free higher education. (And as Sanders's quote indicates, he made no secret of his opposition to both party organizations.[3]) But Biden is not the first nominee to receive these criticisms. Many Democrats had doubts about Senator Hillary Clinton's electability in 2016. And even though Donald Trump ran that year on promises to fully repeal Obamacare, build a wall at the Mexican border, and reform federal welfare programs, he was largely unsuccessful— even with Republican control of the presidency and both houses of Congress after his election in 2016. Congressional Democrats were similarly unable to deliver on their pledge to remove President Trump from office through impeachment, despite winning majority control of the House of Representatives in the 2018 midterms. Given the diversity of House Democrats, party leaders face a daunting task in trying to build unity around controversial policy initiatives. Many Americans report that they dislike both major parties—even the one they identify with.

Our task in this chapter is to understand that American political parties can simultaneously be strong and weak, or influential yet disliked and irrelevant. Why is it impossible to describe American politics without talking about Republicans and Democrats? At the same time, why do the parties seem like bystanders as nominees are chosen and policies are debated?

DEFINE *POLITICAL PARTIES* **AND SHOW HOW AMERICAN POLITICAL PARTIES AND PARTY SYSTEMS HAVE EVOLVED OVER TIME**

What are political parties and where did today's parties come from?

Political parties are organizations that run candidates for political office and coordinate the actions of officials elected under the party banner. Looking around the world, we find many different kinds of parties. In numerous western European countries, the major political parties have millions of dues-paying members and party leaders control what their elected officials do. These countries typically have several major parties competing for office. In contrast, candidates in many new democracies run as representatives of a party, but party leaders have no control over what candidates say during the campaign or how they act in office.

America's two major political parties, the Republican Party and the Democratic Party, lie somewhere between these extremes. However, rather than being unified organizations with party leaders at the top, candidates and party workers in the middle, and citizen-members at the bottom, American political parties are decentralized, each one a loose network of organizations, groups, and individuals who share a party label but are under no obligation to work together.[4]

The **party organization** is the structure of national, state, and local parties, including party leaders and workers. The **party in government** is made up of the politicians who are elected as candidates of the party. And the **party in the electorate** includes all the citizens who identify with the party. For example, the Republican Party's national organization, the RNC, functions independently of Republican leaders in

party organization
A specific political party's leaders and workers at the national, state, and local levels.

party in government
The group of officeholders who belong to a specific political party and were elected as candidates of that party.

party in the electorate
The group of citizens who identify with a specific political party.

government like Senate Majority Leader Mitch McConnell during the 116th Congress; neither one is in charge of the other. Although McConnell is the leader of Republican senators, he cannot tell them what to do. While McConnell's colleagues may be somewhat sympathetic to his arguments, they are under no obligation to do what he asks. Moreover, while many Americans think of themselves as members of a political party, someone who identifies with the Republican Party is not obligated to work for or give money to the party or to vote for its candidates. As you will see, organization matters: the fact that American political parties are split into three parts has important implications for what they do and for their impact on the nation's politics.

The Republican and Democratic parties have existed for a long time—the Republicans since 1854 and the Democrats since the early 1800s. Over this time, the parties have been transformed in every respect except their names. These changes are the first important clue about the nature of American political parties: there is nothing inevitable about what the parties stand for, the types of candidates who run under each party's banner, and the groups that support each party. The sharply polarized parties in today's America did not exist a generation ago. American political parties may look very different in the future.

The Republican and Democratic parties have survived throughout most of American history even though they often have not been very popular, even among their supporters. Their survival is partly due to state and local laws that make it easier for candidates to get on the ballot if they run as a major-party candidate. Both parties also work to find good candidates and raise money for their campaigns. In addition, the fact that America elects officeholders from states or geographic districts makes it harder for new parties to form, keeping the two existing parties in place, a result known as Duverger's Law.[5]

Political scientists use the term **party system** to describe periods when the major parties' names, their groups of supporters, and the issues dividing them have all been constant (the beginning and end years that we use throughout this section are approximate). As Table 7.1 shows, there have been six party systems in America.[6] For each party system, the table gives the names of the two major parties, indicates which party dominated (that is, won the most presidential elections or controlled Congress), and describes the principal issues dividing the parties.

The evolution of American political parties

While most of the Founders held a dim view of political parties, many of them participated in the formation of such parties soon after the Founding of the United States. The Federalists and the Democratic-Republicans were primarily parties in government that consisted of like-minded legislators: Federalists wanted a strong central government and a national bank; Democratic-Republicans took the opposite positions. These political parties were quite different from their modern

American political parties have three largely separate components: the party organization, represented here by Tom Perez, chair of the DNC; the party in government, represented here by Speaker of the House Nancy Pelosi and Senate Minority Leader Chuck Schumer during the 116th Congress; and the party in the electorate, exemplified here by the crowd at a rally for Representative Alexandria Ocasio-Cortez (D-NY) and New York attorney general candidate Zephyr Teachout.

party system
Periods in which the names of the major political parties, their supporters, and the issues dividing them have remained relatively stable.

TABLE
7.1

American Party Systems

There have been six party systems in the United States since 1789.

Party System	Major Parties (dominant party in boldface)	Key Issues
First (1789–1828)	Federalists, Democratic-Republicans (neither party was dominant)	Location of the capital, financial issues (e.g., national bank)
Second (1829–1856)	**Democrats**, Whigs	Tariffs (farmers vs. merchants), slavery
Third (1857–1896)	Democrats, **Republicans**	Slavery (pre–Civil War), Reconstruction (post–Civil War), industrialization
Fourth (1897–1932)	Democrats, **Republicans**	Industrialization, immigration
Fifth (1933–1968)	**Democrats**, Republicans	Size and scope of the federal government
Sixth (1969–present)	Democrats, Republicans (neither party is dominant)	Size and scope of the federal government, civil rights, social issues, foreign policy

Source: Compiled by the authors.

counterparts. In particular, there were no national party organizations, few citizens thought of themselves as party members, and candidates for office did not campaign as representatives of a political party. Even so, the goals of those who developed these parties were similar to the goals of party leaders today: like-minded individuals banded together to help enact their preferred policies and defeat their opponents.

For two decades, the two parties were more or less evenly matched in Congress, although the Federalists did not win a presidential contest after 1800. However, in the 1814 elections Federalist legislators, who had opposed the War of 1812 and supported a politically unpopular pay raise for members of Congress, lost most of their congressional seats.[7] These defeats led to the Era of Good Feelings, when there was only one political party: the Democratic-Republican Party. Following the election of President Andrew Jackson in 1828, this party became known as the Democratic Party. At the same time, another new party, the Whig Party, was formed in opposition to Democratic policy priorities, beginning the second party system.

The new Democratic Party cultivated electoral support by building organizations to mobilize citizens and bind them to the party. The operations of the party reflected two new concepts: the **party principle**, the idea that a party is not just a group of elected officials but an organization that exists apart from its candidates, and the **spoils system**, whereby party workers were rewarded with benefits such as federal jobs.[8]

In the 1840s, the issue of slavery split the second party system, leading to a third party system. Most Democratic politicians either supported slavery outright or wanted to avoid debating the issue.[9] The Whig Party was split between abolitionists, who wanted to end slavery, and politicians who agreed with the Democrats. Ultimately, antislavery Whigs left the party and formed the Republican Party, which also attracted antislavery Democrats, leading to the demise of the Whig Party. This move divided the country into a largely Republican Northeast, a largely Democratic South, and politically split midwestern and border states.[10]

Even after the Civil War, the Republicans and Democrats remained the two prominent national parties. The parties were divided over whether the federal

party principle
The idea that a political party exists as an organization distinct from its elected officials or party leaders.

spoils system
The practice of rewarding party supporters with benefits like federal government positions.

government should help farmers and rural residents or inhabitants of rapidly expanding cities and whether it should regulate America's rapidly growing industrial base. Democrats built a coalition of rural and urban voters by proposing a larger, more active federal government and other policies that would help both groups. A similar shift occurred during the transition to the fourth party system, in which the parties were divided on the government's response to industrialization and restrictions on immigration. There were also significant moves during this time in expanding who was eligible to vote, although women did not gain this right until the early twentieth century, and minorities were generally barred by a combination of laws and practices until the 1960s.[11]

The fifth party system was born out of the Great Depression. Many Republicans argued that conditions would improve over time and that government intervention would do little good, while Democrats proposed new government programs that would help people in need and spur economic growth. The Democratic landslide in the 1932 elections led to the New Deal, a series of federal programs designed to stimulate the national economy, help needy people, and impose a variety of new regulations.

Debate over the New Deal brought together the New Deal coalition of African Americans, Catholics, Jews, union members, and White southerners, who became strong supporters of Democratic candidates over the next generation.[12] This transformation established the basic division between the parties that exists to the present day: Democrats generally favor a large federal government that takes an active role in managing the economy and regulating behavior, while Republicans generally believe that many such programs should be provided by state and local governments or not provided at all.

A sixth party system emerged as new political questions and debates divided the parties.[13] Beginning in the late 1940s, many Democratic candidates and party leaders, particularly outside the South, came out against the "separate but equal" system of racial discrimination in southern states and in favor of programs designed to ensure equal opportunity for minority citizens. Then, during the 1960s, many Democratic politicians argued for expanding the role of the federal government into health care, antipoverty programs, and education. Most Republicans opposed these initiatives, although a significant portion did not.

At the same time, these new issues also began to divide American citizens and organized groups, leading to a gradual but significant shift in the groups that identified with each party.[14] White southerners and some Catholics moved to the Republican Party, and minorities, particularly African Americans, started identifying more strongly as Democrats. Democrats also gained supporters in New England and West Coast states. By the late 1980s, all three elements of the Republican and Democratic parties (organization, government, and electorate) were much more like-minded than they had been a generation earlier, a trend that continues to the present day.

Broadly speaking, Democrats tend to favor a larger government that provides more benefits to citizens and regulates corporate and individual behavior, while Republicans advocate for a small government that does less. However, there are exceptions to these rules. On many social issues such as abortion and LGBTQ rights, most Democrats favor individual choice and equality, while most Republicans favor limits on abortion and oppose equality for same-sex couples on issues such as marriage and adoption.[15] Moreover, as the 2020 Democratic presidential nomination contest demonstrates, issues such as expanding government-provided health care divide candidates and their supporters within each party.

"THAT'S WHAT'S THE MATTER."

Boss Tweed. "As long as I count the Votes, what are you going to do about it? say?"

The Tammany Hall political machine, depicted here as a rotund version of one of its leaders, William "Boss" Tweed, controlled New York City politics for most of the nineteenth and early twentieth centuries. Its strategy was "honest graft," rewarding party workers, contributors, and voters for their efforts to keep the machine's candidates in office.

Debate over Roosevelt's New Deal programs established the basic divide between Democrats and Republicans that continues to this day: in the main, Democrats favor a larger federal government that takes an active role in managing the economy; Republicans prefer a smaller federal government and fewer programs and regulations.

realignment
A change in the size or composition of the party coalitions or in the nature of the issues that divide the parties. Realignments typically occur within an election cycle or two, but they can also occur gradually over the course of a decade or longer.

Realignments Each party system is separated from the next by a **realignment**—a change in one or more of the factors that define a party system. These factors include the issues that divide the parties, the nature and function of the party organizations, the composition of the party coalitions, and the specifics of government policy. Early work on realignments argued that realignments began with the emergence of a new question or issue debate that captured the attention of large numbers of ordinary citizens, activists, and politicians.[16] For example, as noted, the fifth party system (1933–1968) was born during the Great Depression, when the parties were primarily divided by their positions on the appropriate size of the federal government.

"Why Should I Care?"

Looking at American political parties today, you might think that Democratic and Republican parties have been around forever, that they are evenly split in party identifiers and officeholders, and that their main disagreement has always concerned the size and scope of government. None of these ideas is true. Moreover, the changes over time in the Republican and Democratic parties illustrate how these organizations adapt to shifts in public opinion. Thus, American political parties may look very different 10 years from now than they do today.

DESCRIBE THE MAIN CHARACTERISTICS OF AMERICAN PARTIES AS ORGANIZATIONS, IN THE GOVERNMENT, AND IN THE ELECTORATE

American political parties today

We've seen that, almost from the beginning, political parties have been a central feature of American politics. The next steps are to examine the different aspects (the party organization, the party in government, and the party in the electorate) of American political parties, describe the role they play in elections and in government, and understand how their organization and operations shape American democracy.

The party organization

national committee
An American political party's principal organization, comprising party representatives from each state.

The principal body in each party organization is the **national committee** (the Democratic National Committee or the Republican National Committee), which consists of representatives from state party organizations, usually one man and one woman per state. The state party organizations in turn are made up of professional staff plus thousands of party organizations at the county, city, and town levels. The job of these organizations is to run the party's day-to-day operations, recruit candidates and supporters, raise money for future campaigns, and work to build a consensus on major issues.

Both national party committees include a number of *constituency groups* (the Democrats' term) or *teams* (the Republicans' term). These organizations within the party work to attract the support of demographic groups considered likely to share the party's issue concerns—such as African Americans, Latinos, people with strong religious beliefs, senior citizens, women, and many others—and assist in fund-raising.

Each party organization also includes groups designed to build support for, or coordinate the efforts of, particular individuals or politicians. These groups include the Democratic and the Republican Governors' Associations, the Young Democrats, the Young Republicans, and more specialized groups such as the Republican Lawyers' Organization or the Democratic Leadership Council (DLC), an organization of moderate Democratic politicians.[17]

Other Allied Groups Many other groups, such as **political action committees (PACs)** or **527 organizations**, labor unions, and other interest groups and organizations, are loosely affiliated with one of the major parties. For example, the organization MoveOn.org typically supports Democratic candidates. Similar organizations on the Republican side include the Club for Growth, Americans for Prosperity, Crossroads GPS, and many evangelical groups. Though these groups often favor one party over the other, they are not part of the party organization and do not always agree with the party's positions or support its candidates—in fact, many have to operate independently of the parties and their candidates in order to preserve their tax-exempt status. (For more details on campaign finance, see Chapters 8 and 9.)

As this description suggests, the party organization has a fluid structure rather than a rigid hierarchy.[18] Individuals and groups work with a party's leaders and candidates when they share the same goals, but unless they are paid party employees, they are under no obligation to do so. (Even paid party workers can quit rather than work for a candidate or a cause they oppose. The strong support for President Trump from within the Republican party organization was partly due to departures—both voluntary and forced—of party workers and officials who opposed Trump's nomination and his policies.)

Party Brand Names The Republican and Democratic party organizations have well-established "brand names." Because the parties stand for different things, in terms of both their preferred government policies and their ideological leanings, the party names themselves become a shorthand way of providing information to voters about the parties' candidates.[19] Hearing the term "Democrat" or "Republican" calls to mind ideas about what kinds of positions the members of each party support, what kinds of candidates each party runs, and how these candidates will probably vote if they are elected to office. Citizens can use these brand names as a cue to decide whom to vote for in an election. (See Chapter 8 for more information about voting cues.)

Limits of the Party Organization One critical thing to understand about the Democratic and Republican party organizations is that they are not hierarchies. No one person or group in charge determines what either organization does—which often makes them look disorganized. Within the RNC and the DNC, the party organization's issue positions are set not by the committee chair but by RNC or DNC members from all 50 states. If the committee chair and the committee disagree, the chair cannot force the committee members to do what he or she wants.

The national party organization is also unable to force state and local parties to share its positions on issues or comply with other requests. State and local parties make their own decisions about state- and local-level candidates and issue positions. The national committee can ask nicely, cajole, or even threaten to withhold funds (although such threats are rare), but if a state party organization, an independent group, or even an individual candidate disagrees with the national committee, there's little the national committee can do to force compliance.

The party in government

The party in government consists of elected officials holding national, state, and local offices who have taken office as candidates of a particular party. They are the public face

political action committee (PAC)
An interest group or a division of an interest group that can raise money to contribute to campaigns or to spend on ads in support of candidates. The amount a PAC can receive from each of its donors and the amount it can spend on federal electioneering are strictly limited.

527 organization
A tax-exempt group formed primarily to influence elections through voter mobilization efforts and to issue ads that do not directly endorse or oppose a candidate. Unlike PACs, they are not subject to contribution limits and spending caps.

I am not a member of an organized political party. I am a Democrat.

—**Will Rogers,** American actor

of the party, somewhat like the players on a sports team. Although players are only one part of a sports franchise—along with owners, coaches, trainers, and support staff—the players' identities are what most people call to mind when they think of the team. Because the party in government is made up of officeholders, it has a direct impact on government policy. Members of the party organization can recruit candidates, write platforms, and pay for campaign ads, but only those who win elections—that is, the party in government—serve as members of Congress or as executive officials and actually propose, debate, vote on, and sign the legislation that determines what government does.

Caucuses and Conferences In the House and Senate, the Democratic and Republican parties are organized around working groups called a **caucus** (Democrats) and a **conference** (Republicans). The party caucus or conference serves as a forum for debate, compromise, and strategizing among a party's elected officials. Under **unified government** (in which the same party controls Congress and the presidency) these discussions focus on finding common ground within the party, as in the negotiations that led to the Republican tax cut legislation in 2016, which was enacted without Democratic support. Under **divided government** (in which one party controls at least one house of Congress and the other party controls the presidency, as in 2019–2020), the focus changes to finding opportunities to work with the other party or strategizing on how to block the other party's initiatives. Divided government was relatively rare before the 1960s, but has become increasingly common since then. Particularly when control is divided, partisan differences can yield policy gridlock, as neither side is willing to compromise and neither side has the votes to push its preferred package through. Measures such as the economic stimulus legislation enacted rapidly in response to the COVID-19 pandemic in March 2020 are very much the exception to the rule.

Each party's caucus or conference also meets to decide on legislative committee assignments, leadership positions on committees, and leadership positions within the caucus or conference.[20] Caucus or conference leaders serve as spokespeople for their respective parties, particularly when the president is from the other party. The party in government also contains groups that recruit and support candidates for political office: the Democratic Congressional Campaign Committee (DCCC), the Democratic Senatorial Campaign Committee (DSCC), the National Republican Congressional Committee (NRCC), and the National Republican Senatorial Committee (NRSC).

caucus (congressional)
The organization of Democrats within the House and Senate that meets to discuss and debate the party's positions on various issues in order to reach a consensus and to assign leadership positions.

conference
The organization of Republicans within the House and Senate that meets to discuss and debate the party's positions on various issues in order to reach a consensus and to assign leadership positions.

unified government
A situation in which one party holds a majority of seats in the House and Senate and the president is a member of that same party.

divided government
A situation in which the House, Senate, and presidency are not controlled by the same party—for example, when Democrats hold the majority of House and Senate seats and the president is a Republican.

Activist volunteers, such as these two canvassing in the crucial swing state of Ohio, undertake most of the one-on-one efforts to mobilize support for a party and its candidates.

Are the Parties More Polarized than Ever?

For the last 20 years, it seems as though all the news about political parties has been about conflict and stalemate. It seems like political campaigns are increasingly negative, compromise is rare, and Republicans and Democrats have divided into camps that never agree on anything. Is this trend new? What do the facts say?

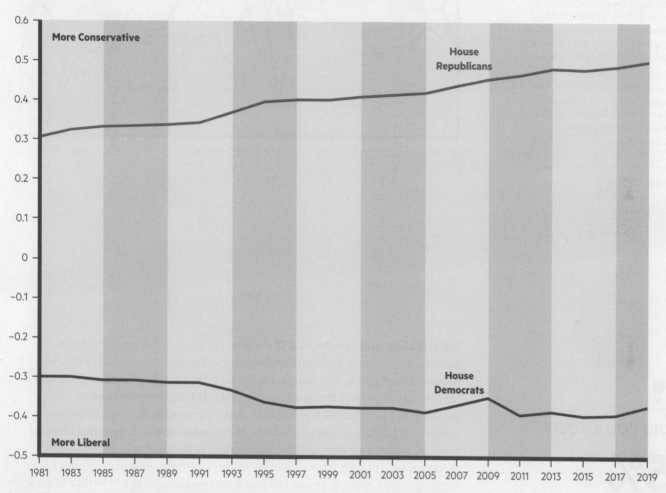

Source: Jeffrey B. Lewis et al., Voteview (congressional roll call votes database), https://voteview.com/ (accessed 3/19/20).

Think about it

- **This graph uses voting behavior to measure** the average ideology (liberal–conservative) of House Democrats and Republicans. Scores near 1 indicate a conservative ideology, while scores near –1 indicate a liberal ideology. Since the 1980s, have Republicans gotten more conservative, have Democrats become more liberal, or both? Has one party moved more than the other?

- **How might these changes make it harder** for members of the contemporary Congress to enact major changes in government policy? What is more likely: compromise or gridlock?

FIGURE 7.1

Party ID Trends among American Voters

In terms of party ID, the parties have moved from rough parity in the 1990s to a slight Democratic advantage in the early twenty-first century, although this change has eroded in recent years. What events might have caused these changes in party ID?

Sources: 1992–2003 data from Pew Research Center, "Party Identification Trends, 1992–2017," March 20, 2018, www.people-press.org (accessed 6/15/20); 2004–2020 data from Gallup, "Party Affiliation," May 2020, https://news.gallup.com/poll/15370/party-affiliation.aspx (accessed 5/30/20).

DID YOU KNOW?

5%

of Americans say they worked for a political candidate or issue campaign during the last presidential election.

Source: Pew Research Center

Polarization and Ideological Diversity The modern Congress is polarized: in both the House and the Senate, Republicans and Democrats hold different views on government policy. The graph in the What Do the Facts Say? feature tells us that over the last 60 years the magnitude of ideological differences between the parties in Congress has increased. Up until the 1980s there was some overlap between the positions of Democrats and Republicans, but this overlap has disappeared in recent years. However, if we expanded the figure to look at the ideologies of individual members, we'd find a mixture of ideologies, not a uniform consensus opinion. In the contemporary Congress, Democrats vary from the relatively liberal left end of the scale to the moderate (middle) and even somewhat conservative right end. The same is true for Republican members of Congress: while most are conservative, there are some moderates, as well as a range of conservative opinions.

The ideological diversity within each party in government can create situations in which a caucus or conference is divided on a policy question. Compromise within a party's working group is not inevitable—even though legislators share a party label, they may not be able to find common ground. In the last few years, congressional Republicans have been divided on issues such as immigration, health care, taxation and spending levels, and the federal budget deficit.[21] Differences between the parties are present on virtually all major issues—with the support for the bipartisan COVID-19 legislations being a rare exception.

The party in the electorate

The party in the electorate consists of citizens who identify with a particular political party. Most Americans say they are either Democrats or Republicans, although the percentage has declined slightly over the last two generations. **Party identification (party ID)** is a critical variable in understanding votes and other forms of political participation.

Party ID To say you identify with a party is a personal orientation or decision that does not commit you to anything, nor does it give you any control over a party's actions. Although the Republicans and the Democrats have websites where people can sign up to receive e-mail alerts and contribute online to party causes, joining a party does not give a citizen any direct influence over what the party does. Rather, the party leaders and the candidates themselves make the day-to-day decisions. These individuals often heed citizens' demands, but there is no requirement that they do so. Real participation in party operations is open to citizens who become activists by working for a party organization or one of its candidates. Activists' contributions vary widely and may include stuffing envelopes, helping out with a phone bank, being a delegate to a party convention, attending campaign rallies, or campaigning door-to-door.

Figure 7.1 gives data on party ID in America from 1992 to 2020, measured when respondents were given the option to say whether they were a Democrat, a Republican, or an Independent. Over this time period, the parties have been nearly evenly split. At various times in the past, one party has opened some advantage over the other (as the Democrats did in the early 2000s), but there is no consistent trend.

Looking more closely at vote decisions, we see that Figure 7.2 shows how Democrats, Republicans, and Independents voted in the 2020 presidential election

party identification (party ID)
A citizen's loyalty to a specific political party.

There's no evidence from decades of Pew Research surveys that public opinion, in the aggregate, is more extreme now than in the past. But what has changed—and pretty dramatically—is the growing tendency of people to sort themselves into political parties based on their ideological differences.

—Pew Research Center

FIGURE 7.2

The Impact of Party ID on Voting Decisions in the 2020 Presidential Election

Americans are much more likely to vote for candidates who share their party affiliation. What does this relationship tell us about the impact of campaign events (including speeches, debates, and gaffes) on voting decisions?

Source: Data compiled from CNN Exit Poll, www.cnn.com/election/2020/exit-polls/president/national-results (accessed 11/5/20).

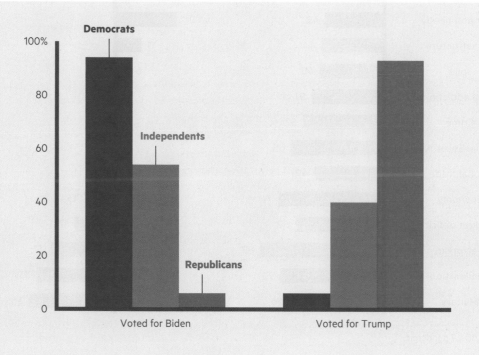

party coalitions
The groups that identify with a political party, usually described in demographic terms such as African-American Democrats or evangelical Republicans.

("closet partisan" Independents are grouped with the party they actually affiliate with). This figure shows that if you are trying to predict how someone will vote, the most important thing to know is his or her party ID.[22] Over 90 percent of Democrats voted for Joe Biden, the Democratic nominee, and about the same percentage of Republicans voted for Donald Trump.

Party Coalitions Data on party ID enable scholars to determine the **party coalitions**, or groups of citizens who identify with each party, as well as the nature of disagreements between the parties.

FIGURE 7.3

Democrats' and Republicans' Top Priorities

The Republican and Democratic party coalitions have different priorities on many issues, ranging from environmental protection to deficit reduction—and their differences are small on a few issues, such as fighting drug addiction and reducing the crime rate. Do these differences make sense in light of each party's "brand name"?

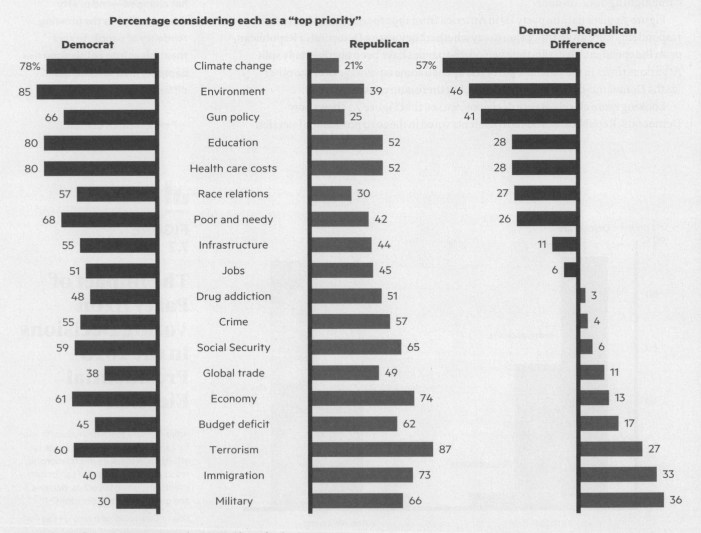

Percentage considering each as a "top priority"

Democrat	Issue	Republican	Democrat–Republican Difference
78%	Climate change	21%	57%
85	Environment	39	46
66	Gun policy	25	41
80	Education	52	28
80	Health care costs	52	28
57	Race relations	30	27
68	Poor and needy	42	26
55	Infrastructure	44	11
51	Jobs	45	6
48	Drug addiction	51	3
55	Crime	57	4
59	Social Security	65	6
38	Global trade	49	11
61	Economy	74	13
45	Budget deficit	62	17
60	Terrorism	87	27
40	Immigration	73	33
30	Military	66	36

Note: Chart reflects priorities prior to the COVID-19 pandemic.

Source: Pew Research Center, "As Economic Concerns Recede, Environmental Protection Rises on the Public's Policy Agenda," February 13, 2020, www.people-press.org (accessed 3/18/20).

The contemporary Republican and Democratic party coalitions differ systematically in terms of their policy preferences—what they want government to do—as shown in Figure 7.3. This data indicate the extent to which partisans disagree about the relative importance of issues such as providing health insurance to the uninsured, addressing global warming, and strengthening the military. These differences hammer home the idea that party labels are meaningful: if you know someone is a Republican (or a Democrat), this information tells you something about what that person probably wants government to do and how he or she will likely vote in the next election. These differences also create opportunities for **issue ownership**: candidates from a party tend to concentrate their campaigns on issues that are part of their party's brand names and ignore issues that belong to the other party.

These policy disagreements reflect sharp differences in the composition of the party coalitions, as shown in Figure 7.4. As you can see, some groups are disproportionately likely to identify as Democrats (African Americans), some are disproportionately likely

issue ownership
The theory that voters associate certain issues or issue positions with certain parties (like Democrats and support for government-provided health insurance).

The Party Coalitions

FIGURE 7.4

Many groups, such as African Americans and White evangelicals, are much more likely to affiliate with one party than the other. What are the implications of these differences for the positions taken by each party's candidates?

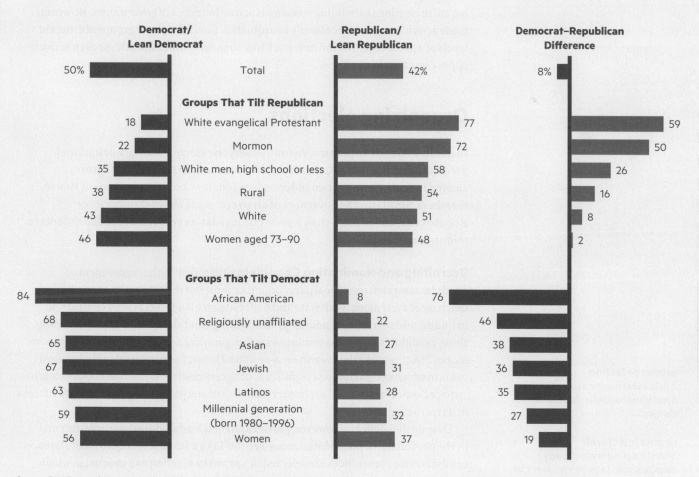

Source: Pew Research Center, "Wide Gender Gap, Growing Educational Divide in Voters' Party Identification," March 20, 2018, www.people-press.org (accessed 3/20/20).

to identify as Republicans (White evangelicals), and other groups have no clear favorite party (women born before 1945). Again, these coalitions have shifted over time. For example, the Republican advantage among White southerners and White evangelical Protestants has existed only since the 1980s.[23]

Knowing that someone is a Democrat or a Republican tells you a lot about the issues that person cares about, whether he or she will like or dislike different candidates, and whom he or she will vote for in an election. Taken together, information about the kinds of people who identify with each party tells you a lot about the kinds of candidates who will run under the party banner and the platforms they will campaign on.

EXPLAIN THE IMPORTANT FUNCTIONS THAT PARTIES PERFORM IN THE POLITICAL SYSTEM

The role of political parties in American politics

Political parties play an important dual role in American politics, from helping to organize elections to building consensus across branches of government. However, these activities are not necessarily coordinated. Candidates and groups at different levels of a party organization may work together, refuse to cooperate, or even actively oppose one another's efforts.

Organizing elections

In modern American politics, virtually everyone elected to a state or national political office is either a Republican or a Democrat. In the 117th Congress, elected in 2020, there are two Independent senators and no Independent House members. Similarly, the governors of all 50 states are either Democrats or Republicans, and of more than 7,300 state legislators very few are Independents or minor-party candidates.

Recruiting and Nominating Candidates Historically, the recruitment of candidates was left up to local party organizations. But the process has become much more systematic, with state and national party leaders playing a central role in finding and recruiting, endorsing, and funding candidates—and often promising those candidates help in assembling a staff, organizing a campaign, and raising more money.[24] Actions like these can have a profound impact on congressional elections; years in which one party gains significant congressional seats (such as Republicans in 2010 or Democrats in 2018) are in part the result of one party's disproportionate success in its recruiting efforts.

Despite these efforts, however, parties and their leaders do not control who runs in House, Senate, or presidential races (see the Take a Stand feature). In most states, candidates for these offices are selected in a **primary election** or a **caucus**, in which they compete for a particular party's spot on the ballot. Most states use primaries;

primary election
A ballot vote in which citizens select a party's nominee for the general election.

caucus (electoral)
A local meeting in which party members select a party's nominee for the general election.

Should Parties Choose Their Candidates?

One of the facts of life for the leaders of the Democratic and Republican parties is that they cannot determine who runs as their party's candidate for political office. They can encourage some candidates to run and attempt to discourage others by endorsing their favorites and funneling money, staff support, and other forms of assistance to the candidates they prefer. But in the end, congressional candidates get on the ballot by winning a primary or a vote at a state party convention; presidential candidates compete in a series of primaries and caucuses. Is this system a good one?

Let the party decide. Many scholars have argued that letting parties choose their candidates increases the chances of getting experienced, talented candidates on the ballot.[a] After all, party leaders probably know more than the average voter about who would make a good candidate or elected official. Plus, party leaders have a strong incentive to find good candidates and convince them to run: their party's influence over government policy increases with the number of people they can elect to political office. And finally, in states that have no party registration or day-of-election registration, giving the nomination power to party leaders would ensure that a group of outsiders could not hijack a party primary to nominate a candidate who disagreed with a party's platform or who was unqualified to serve in office.

While cases of outright hijacking of party nominations are fairly rare, political parties don't always get the nominees their leaders want and party leaders cannot force candidates out of a race. In the 2016 election cycle, for example, many Republican Party leaders believed that Donald Trump was not the party's strongest nominee. Trump gained the nomination over their objections by winning the party's caucus and primary contests. You can judge whether his performance in office refutes or justifies their concerns.

Let the people decide. One argument in favor of giving the nomination power to the people is that party leaders have not always shown good judgment in picking either electable or qualified candidates. Many of the same Republican leaders who opposed Trump had supported party nominees John McCain in 2008 and Mitt Romney in 2012, both of whom went on to lose their general-election contest. This track record suggests that party leaders are far from infallible. In 2020, most Democratic leaders believed that Joe Biden was more electable than the alternatives. While the COVID-19 pandemic complicates judgments about the 2020 election, the party leaders were probably right: Biden was best suited to win back White, less educated, midwestern voters who had defected to Trump in 2016.

The second argument for letting the people decide hinges on a judgment about whose wishes should prevail in nomination contests: the people who make up the party in the electorate or the people in the party organization. What right does the party organization have to select nominees, given that support for the party from the electorate (its contributions and votes in elections) is essential for electoral success? Moreover, shouldn't voters have a say in determining what their electoral choices look like? If party leaders choose, voters may not like any of the options put before them.

Why, then, do voters in America get to pick party nominees in primaries? Direct primaries were introduced in American politics during the late 1800s and early 1900s.[b] The goal was explicit: reform-minded party activists wanted to take the choice of nominees out of the hands of party leaders and give it to the electorate, with the assumption that voters should be able to influence the choice of candidates for the general election. Moreover, reformers believed that this goal outweighed the expertise held by party leaders.

Here is the trade-off: If party leaders select nominees, they will likely (but not inevitably) choose electable candidates who share the policy goals held by party leaders. If voters choose nominees, they can pick whomever they want, using whatever criteria they like—but there is no guarantee that these candidates will be skilled general-election campaigners or effective in office.

In the end, some groups must be given control over the selection of a party's nominees. Should this power be given to party leaders or to the people?

 Both political parties organize a series of candidate debates during their presidential contests, giving candidates a chance to present themselves before a national audience.

take a stand

1. One reform proposal would increase the importance of the parties as sources of campaign funds. Would this change have made much of a difference in the 2020 Democratic presidential contest?

2. What kind of nomination procedure would be favored by insurgent groups?

Types of Primaries and Caucuses

Primary Election	An election in which voters choose the major-party nominees for political office, who subsequently compete in a general election.
Closed primary	A primary election system in which only registered party members can vote in their party's primary.
Nonpartisan primary	A primary election system in which candidates from both parties are listed on the same primary ballot. Following a nonpartisan primary, the two candidates who receive the most votes in the primary compete in the general election, even if they are from the same party.
Open primary	A primary election system in which any registered voter can participate in either party's primary, regardless of the voter's party affiliation.
Semi-closed primary	A primary election system in which voters registered as party members must vote in their party's primary, but registered Independents can vote in either party's primary.
Caucus Election	A series of local meetings at which registered voters select a particular candidate's supporters as delegates who will vote for the candidate in a later, state-level convention. (In national elections, the state-convention delegates select delegates to the national convention.) Caucuses are used in some states to select delegates to the major parties' presidential nominating conventions. Some states' caucuses are open to members of any party, while others are closed.

Source: Compiled by the authors.

"Why Should I Care?" People often wonder if their vote really counts. Primaries give citizens the opportunity to select the candidates who will run in the upcoming election, but each format has its own advantages and disadvantages. Even the time of the year in which a primary occurs can matter. We saw this in play during the 2020 Democratic primary. Voters in states with primaries earlier in the year had many candidates on the ballot to choose from, while those whose primaries fell later in the year had far fewer options, as many of the original candidates had long since dropped out.

a few state parties use conventions to select candidates (see Nuts & Bolts 7.1). Most notably, Donald Trump won the 2016 Republican presidential nomination by virtue of his victories in the party's primaries and caucuses over the objections of many party leaders. Trump's victory demonstrates that party endorsements, while significant, are not the only factor in shaping nomination contests.

Running as a major party's nominee, as opposed to running as an Independent, is almost always the easiest way to get on the general-election ballot. Even Vermont senator Bernie Sanders, who won his Senate seat by running as an Independent, ran for the Democratic presidential nomination in 2016 and 2020. Some states give the Republican and Democratic nominees an automatic spot on the ballot. Even in states that don't automatically allocate ballot slots this way, the requirements for the major parties to get a candidate on the ballot are much less onerous than those for minor parties and Independents. In California, for example, a party and its candidates automatically qualify for a position on the ballot if any of the party's candidates for statewide office received more than 2 percent of the vote in the previous election. In contrast, Independent candidates need to file petitions with more than 150,000 signatures to get on the ballot without a major-party label—an expensive, time-consuming task.[25] These advantages help explain why virtually all prominent candidates for Congress and the presidency run as Democrats or Republicans. Even billionaires Mike Bloomberg and Tom Steyer, who could have easily self-financed Independent campaigns for the presidency, chose to run as Democrats in 2020.

National parties also manage the nomination process for presidential candidates. This process involves a series of primaries and caucuses held over a six-month period beginning in January of a presidential election year. The type of election (primary or caucus; about two-thirds of states use primaries) and its date are determined by state legislatures, although national party committees can limit the allowable dates, using their control over seating delegates at the party conventions to motivate compliance. Voters in these primaries and caucuses don't directly select the parties' nominees. Instead, citizens' votes are used to determine how many of each candidate's supporters become delegates to the party's national **nominating convention**, where delegates vote to choose the party's presidential and vice-presidential nominees. The national party organizations determine how many delegates each state sends to the convention based on factors such as state population, the number of votes the party's candidate received in each state in the last presidential election, and the number of House members and senators from the party that each state elected (see How It Works: Nominating Presidential Candidates).

Campaign Assistance One of the most visible ways that the political parties support candidates is by contributing to and spending money on campaign activities. By and large, federal law mandates that these funds be spent by the organization that raised them; the national party, for example, is limited in the amount of money it can directly contribute to congressional and presidential candidates or to state party organizations. As we discuss in Chapter 9, however, party organizations can use the campaign funds they raise to help candidates in other ways, for example, through independent expenditures—running their own ads in a candidate's district or state.

Figure 7.5 shows the amount of money raised by the top groups within the Republican and Democratic parties for the 2020 election (through November 3). The final figures show that the parties and their various committees raised over $2 billion.

nominating convention
A meeting held by each party every four years at which states' delegates select the party's presidential and vice-presidential nominees and approve the party platform.

FIGURE 7.5

Democratic and Republican Fund-Raising in the 2019–2020 Election Cycle

In the 2019–2020 election cycle, party and leadership committees raised more than $2 billion in campaign funds. Although most of this money was raised by the national committees, the state, local, and candidate committees also raised significant sums. To what extent might these funds allow the national committees to force candidates to run on the party platform?

Source: The Center for Responsive Politics, www.opensecrets.org (accessed 11/4/20).

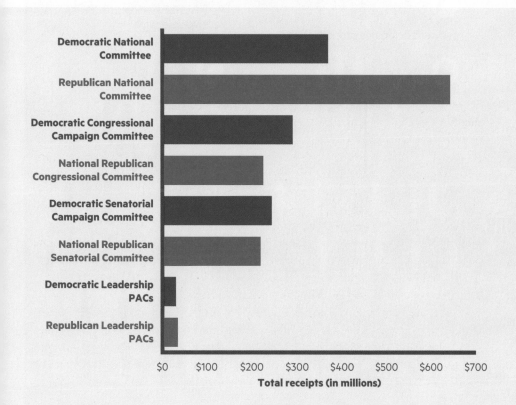

Nominating Presidential Candidates

Primaries and caucuses . . .

Closed Primaries
Only voters registered with party vote

Open Primaries
Open to voters from any political party and Independents

Caucus or Local Convention
Party members meet in groups to select delegates

are used to select delegates . . .

Republican Party
States can award all delegates to the winning candidate

or award delegates proportionally.

Democratic Party
The state's delegates are divided proportionally. A candidate must receive at least 15 percent of the vote either statewide or in a congressional district to receive delegates.

who attend national nominating conventions.

Delegates from all states attend the national convention, where they vote for the party's presidential and vice-presidential nominees based on the primary and caucus results. Superdelegates—important party leaders—also vote at the convention.

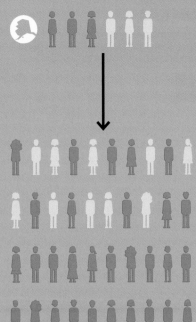

The Nomination of Joe Biden for President, 2020

While Joe Biden was the clear winner in the 2020 Democratic presidential nomination contest, his campaign benefited from the 15 percent threshold rule and the fact that many of the early contests were in states with high percentages of African-American voters, who were strong Biden supporters.

% Percentage of popular vote won
ı Delegates allocated
† Caucus

Note: For the contests in which allocated delegates do not add up to the number available or for which the popular vote percentages do not total 100 percent, other candidates omitted here also received delegates or votes. If a candidate drops out of the race before the national convention, any delegates he or she has earned may be reallocated.

Source: Table compiled by the authors from press accounts and U.S. Census data.

Critical Thinking

1. **What would have happened to Biden's candidacy** if more of the early states had lower percentages of African-American voters?

2. **One argument about caucuses is that they allow** lesser-known candidates to build support. Did this work for any candidates in 2020?

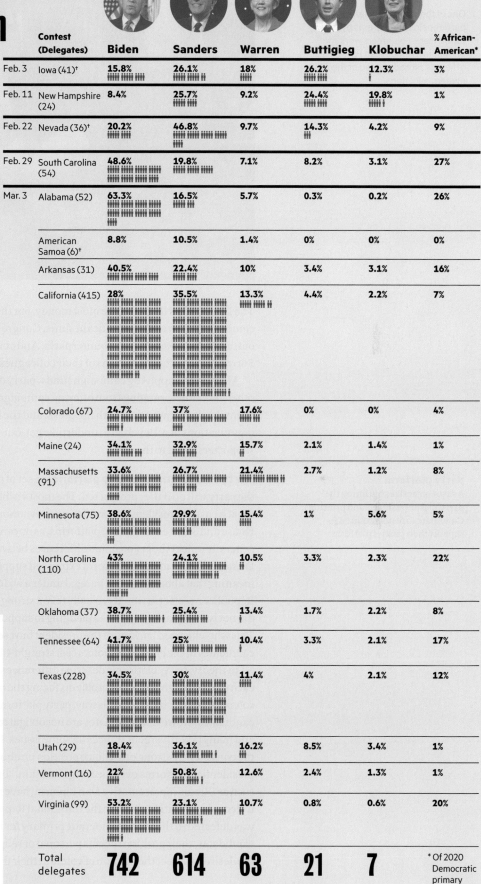

	Contest (Delegates)	Biden	Sanders	Warren	Buttigieg	Klobuchar	% African-American*
Feb. 3	Iowa (41)†	15.8%	26.1%	18%	26.2%	12.3%	3%
Feb. 11	New Hampshire (24)	8.4%	25.7%	9.2%	24.4%	19.8%	1%
Feb. 22	Nevada (36)†	20.2%	46.8%	9.7%	14.3%	4.2%	9%
Feb. 29	South Carolina (54)	48.6%	19.8%	7.1%	8.2%	3.1%	27%
Mar. 3	Alabama (52)	63.3%	16.5%	5.7%	0.3%	0.2%	26%
	American Samoa (6)†	8.8%	10.5%	1.4%	0%	0%	0%
	Arkansas (31)	40.5%	22.4%	10%	3.4%	3.1%	16%
	California (415)	28%	35.5%	13.3%	4.4%	2.2%	7%
	Colorado (67)	24.7%	37%	17.6%	0%	0%	4%
	Maine (24)	34.1%	32.9%	15.7%	2.1%	1.4%	1%
	Massachusetts (91)	33.6%	26.7%	21.4%	2.7%	1.2%	8%
	Minnesota (75)	38.6%	29.9%	15.4%	1%	5.6%	5%
	North Carolina (110)	43%	24.1%	10.5%	3.3%	2.3%	22%
	Oklahoma (37)	38.7%	25.4%	13.4%	1.7%	2.2%	8%
	Tennessee (64)	41.7%	25%	10.4%	3.3%	2.1%	17%
	Texas (228)	34.5%	30%	11.4%	4%	2.1%	12%
	Utah (29)	18.4%	36.1%	16.2%	8.5%	3.4%	1%
	Vermont (16)	22%	50.8%	12.6%	2.4%	1.3%	1%
	Virginia (99)	53.2%	23.1%	10.7%	0.8%	0.6%	20%
	Total delegates	**742**	**614**	**63**	**21**	**7**	* Of 2020 Democratic primary and caucus voters

One of the most important ways parties help candidates is by raising funds. Here, volunteers work the phones in a Republican Party field office in Colorado ahead of the 2018 midterm elections.

The DNC and RNC raised the most money, but the congressional campaign committees also raised significant sums. Congressional Democratic committees outraised their Republican counterparts. And congressional leaders raised over $60 million for the campaigns of their colleagues.[26]

Along with supplying campaign funds, party organizations give candidates other assistance, ranging from offering campaign advice (including which issues to emphasize, how to deal with the press, and the like) to conducting polls. Party organizations at all levels also undertake get-out-the-vote activities, encouraging supporters to get to the polls.

party platform
A set of objectives outlining the party's issue positions and priorities. Candidates are not required to support their party's platform.

Party Platforms The **party platform** is a set of promises about what candidates from the party will do if they are elected. The most visible party platform is the one approved at each party's presidential nominating convention, but the party organizations in the House and Senate also release platforms, as do other major-party groups. Party platforms generally reflect the brand name differences between the parties. For example, the 2020 Democratic presidential platform expressed support for a woman's right to choose, meaning that abortion would be legal under a wide range of conditions. While the Republican platform would typically take a strong anti-abortion stand, in 2020 that party did not issue a platform, instead pledging to support President Trump and his policies. This wholehearted backing of the president hurt some Republican congressional candidates in the election as voters cast straight-ticket votes against Republicans.

In theory, party platforms describe differences between the major parties, capture each party's diagnosis of the problems facing the country, and present the party's plan for solving those problems. In this way, party platforms give citizens an easy way to evaluate candidates. However, candidates are not obligated to support their party's platform and many take divergent stances on some issues. For example, notwithstanding the consistently strong pro-choice position on abortion in the Democratic Party's presidential platforms over the last generation, some Democratic members of Congress, such as Illinois representative Dan Lipinski, have promised to vote to restrict abortions if elected—a position closer to the traditional Republican platform.[27] (Lipinski, however, was defeated in the 2020 Democratic primary for his House seat.) For some of these candidates, their position reflects personal or religious beliefs; for others, it is driven by the desire to reflect the opinion of voters in their district or state.

Cooperation in government

Parties also play an important role in enabling like-minded politicians to cooperate on policy plans and strategies for enacting their proposals. Parties in government develop agendas, coordinate the actions of members across branches of government, and provide accountability to voters.

Agenda-Setting Throughout the year, the parties in government meet to devise strategies for legislative action—that is, to set agendas. What proposals should they offer, and in what order should these proposals be considered? Should the parties try to make a deal with the president or with legislators from the other party?

However, the party in government can act collectively this way only when its members can agree on what they want. Such agreement is not always possible or may require extensive negotiation and compromise. Even with unified Republican control of Congress in the 2017–2018 legislative term, legislators were unable to agree on immigration reform, Obamacare repeal, or infrastructure spending. Part of the problem was the narrow Republican majority in the Senate, yet the deeper issue was splits in Republican ranks that would have made compromise difficult even if Republicans had held a larger majority.

Coordination Political parties play an important role in coordinating the actions taken in different branches of government. Such coordination is extremely important for enacting new laws, because unless supporters in Congress can amass a two-thirds majority to override a veto, they need the president's support. Similarly, the president needs congressional support to enact the proposals he or she favors. To these ends, the president routinely meets with congressional leaders from his or her party and occasionally meets with the entire caucus or conference. Various members of the president's staff also meet with House and Senate members to present the president's proposals and hear what members of Congress from both parties want to enact.

During 2019 and 2020, President Trump held many meetings with Republican members of Congress to lobby them to support his policy proposals and to persuade them to oppose efforts to impeach him. Trump was successful on impeachment, in that virtually all Republicans voted against impeachment. But in other areas, including cuts to some federal programs and a plan to enact substantial reductions in legal immigration to the United States, Trump had little success. These two examples illustrate the limits of presidential persuasion: presidential victories have more to do with proposing something that members of Congress are inclined to support (in the case of impeachment, because most Republican voters approve of Trump) than with pressuring them to support a proposal they oppose.

Coordination can also occur between caucuses or conferences in the House and Senate. During the COVID-19 pandemic in 2020, for example, unified Democratic opposition to Republican-proposed economic stimulus legislation forced Senate Republicans to include many Democratic provisions in the final version. Similarly, the need for party unity partly explains Trump's September 2020 nomination of Amy Coney Barrett to the Supreme Court, as other short-listed candidates raised more opposition among Senate Republicans. Such coordination efforts require real compromise, as party leaders in Congress do not have authority over each other or the elected members of their party. Nor can the president order a House member or senator to do anything, even if the legislator is from the president's own party.

Accountability One of the most important functions political parties play in a democracy is to give citizens identifiable groups to reward or punish for government action or inaction. Using the ballot box, voters will reward and punish elected officials, often based on their party affiliation and on the behavior of that party's members in

Parties don't exert total control over their members. Republican Party leaders could not stop then–freshman senator Ted Cruz (R-TX) from filibustering for 23 hours in an attempt to stop a budget compromise.

office. In this way, the party system gives the electorate a mechanism that can be used to hold officials accountable for outcomes such as the state of the economy or America's relations with other nations. This mechanism is most clear during periods of unified government, when one party holds majorities in both the House and the Senate *and* controls the presidency, meaning that party has enough votes to enact policies in Congress and a good chance of having them signed into law by the president. During times of divided government, when one party controls Congress but not the presidency or when different parties control the House and Senate (such as during most of Obama's presidency as well as the second half of Trump's), it is not clear which party should be held accountable for the state of the nation.

Focusing on parties makes it easy for citizens to issue rewards and punishments. Is the economy doing well? Then citizens are likely to vote for the candidates from the party in power. But if the economy is doing poorly or if citizens feel that government is wasting tax money or enacting bad policies, voters can punish the party in power by supporting candidates from the party that is currently out of power. When citizens behave this way, they strengthen the incentive for elected officials from the party in power to work together to develop policies that address voters' concerns—on the premise that if they do, voters will reward them with another term in office. Consider the 2020 elections. Although Democrats lost about nine seats in the House and Senate, most Democratic incumbents were reelected. Why? Some were elected from states or districts dominated by Democratic identifiers. But many others were reelected because they campaigned on a platform of promoting Democratic party ideals or because of their efforts to help local constituents; in effect, these candidates said, "Instead of punishing me for my party affiliation, reward me for working on your behalf."

In the end, reelecting members of the party in power despite a poor economy or other troubles makes sense given how American political parties are organized and their lack of control over individual officeholders. Of course, insofar as incumbent members of the party in power present themselves as loyal party members and cast votes in accordance with the wishes of party leaders, they will increase the chances that their constituents will take account of their party label when casting their votes—which will help them get reelected in good times but will increase their chances of defeat when conditions turn against their party.

Democrats framed the 2020 election as a referendum on President Trump's performance in office, particularly his mismanagement of the COVID-19 pandemic. While this strategy did not lead to as many Senate pickups as the party had hoped, it did help some candidates, including former astronaut Mark Kelly, who defeated incumbent Martha McSally (R-AZ) by arguing that McSally had been an uncritical supporter of Trump's policies. Following Kyrsten Sinema's (D-AZ) election to the Senate in 2018, Arizona is now represented by two Democratic senators for the first time since 1952.

Minor parties

So far, this chapter has focused on the major American political parties—the Republicans and the Democrats—and paid less attention to other party organizations. The reason is that minor political parties in America are *so* minor that they are generally not significant players on the political stage. Many such parties exist, but few run candidates in more than a handful of races and very few minor-party candidates win political office. Few Americans identify with minor parties, and most exist for only a relatively short period.

Even so, you may think we are giving minor parties too little attention. Consider Howie Hawkins and Jo Jorgensen, who ran as the Green and Libertarian party candidates for president in 2020. If the votes they received had gone to Donald Trump instead, he might have prevailed in close states and thereby won reelection. In this sense, you might think of minor parties and their supporters as the kingmakers in modern American politics. However, the size of the minor party vote in 2020 doesn't so much highlight the importance of minor parties as it illustrates the closeness of elections in some states. If Hawkins and Jorgensen had not run, Trump might have received enough additional support to win. But given that Biden's margin of victory in several states was so small, any number of seemingly minor events (rain in some areas and sunshine in others, or some small number of additional pro-Trump ads) could have had the same effect.

Even in terms of lower offices, minor-party candidates typically attract only meager support. While the Libertarian Party claims to have over 200 officeholders, many of these officials hold unelected positions such as seats on county planning boards or ran unopposed for relatively minor offices.[28] In 2020, Justin Amash, who was elected as a Republican representative for the state of Michigan, changed his party affiliation to become a Libertarian and in doing so became the party's first member to serve in Congress, though he chose not to seek reelection.

Looking back in history, we see that some minor-party candidates for president have attracted a substantial percentage of citizens' votes. George Wallace (governor of Alabama at the time) ran as the candidate of the American Independent Party in 1968, receiving

Minor-party presidential candidates, such as Libertarian Jo Jorgensen in 2020, sometimes attract considerable press attention because of their distinctive policy preferences, but they rarely effect election outcomes.

about 13 percent of the popular vote nationwide. Texas millionaire Ross Perot, the Reform Party candidate for president in 1996, won 8.4 percent of the popular vote. Perot also ran as an Independent in 1992, winning 18.2 percent of the popular vote. And environmental and consumer activist Ralph Nader received about 5 percent of the popular vote in 2000.

Unique Issues Facing Minor Parties The differences between major and minor political parties in contemporary American politics grow even more substantial when considered in terms other than election outcomes. For most minor parties, the party in government does not exist, as few of their candidates win office.[29] Many minor parties have virtually no organization beyond a small party headquarters and a website. Some minor parties, such as the Green Party, the Libertarian Party, and the Reform Party, have local chapters that meet on a regular basis. But these modest efforts pale in comparison with the nationwide network of offices, thousands of workers, and hundreds of millions of dollars deployed by Republican and Democratic party organizations.

The issues and issue positions taken by minor parties and their candidates are almost always very different from those espoused by the major parties. The Constitution Party, for example, advocates ending government civil service regulations; banning compulsory school attendance laws; withdrawing from the UN and all international trade agreements; abolishing foreign aid, the income tax, the Internal Revenue Service (IRS), and all federal welfare programs; and repealing all campaign finance legislation, the Endangered Species Act, and federal firearms regulations. These positions are extreme, not in the sense of being silly or dangerous but in the sense that relatively few Americans agree with them.

"Why Should I Care?"

You may dislike political parties or party leaders in Congress, but the fact is, the parties are key players in congressional policy making and in negotiations between Congress and the president. If you are trying to decide whether a new program (or nominee) has a chance of being approved, one of the first things you need to consider is whether the party caucuses in the House and Senate (particularly the majority-party caucuses) are in favor or opposed.

Unpacking the Conflict

Considering all that we've discussed in this chapter, let's apply what we know about how political parties work to the examples of party dysfunction from the beginning of this chapter. Why is it impossible to describe American politics without talking about Republicans and Democrats? At the same time, why do the parties seem like bystanders as nominees are chosen and policies are debated?

The answer is that we have strong partisanship, but weak parties. Party identification organizes how we think about politics as well as our political behavior as much as or more than it ever has in the past. However, at the same time Americans generally dislike political parties, even the one they identify with. And the laws governing elections allow candidates to claim a party label without having to support or even talk about their party's platform.

As a result, while America's political system gives enormous opportunities to political parties, from organizing elections to working inside Congress to build coalitions behind policy proposals, the fact that these opportunities exist does not ensure that political parties will be able to follow through on them. As we have seen, American political parties are often beset by internal conflicts over who should run for office and what their campaign platforms should look like. The party organization has little control over the party in government (or vice versa). And neither group can order party members in the electorate to work for the party, support its candidates, or do anything they don't want to do.

As a result of these organizational features, there is no guarantee that officeholders and election winners of the same party affiliation will have the same policy priorities or be able to compromise over their differences. This has been true even in recent years, when differences between Republicans and Democrats have been as large as ever. It will be just as hard for Democrats to agree amongst themselves about policy priorities as it will be to gain support for these proposals from the Republican-controlled Senate. Republicans will face the same problem even if they gain unified control of government in the future. At the same time, while Americans may not approve of these outcomes, they show no signs of totally abandoning the Republicans or the Democrats in favor of new party organizations.

"What's Your Take?"

Are American political parties too dysfunctional to be useful?

Or do the benefits they provide outweigh their drawbacks?

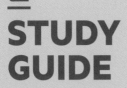

STUDY GUIDE

What are political parties and where did today's parties come from?

Define *political parties* and show how American political parties and party systems have evolved over time. (Pages 220–224)

Summary

Political parties are a central feature of American politics, although they look and act very differently today than they have in the past. Political scientists use the term "party system" to refer to a period of party stability; in all, there have been six different party systems in the country's history. Party systems have been separated by realignments, which occur when some of the defining factors of the party system are changed or specified and when rifts in the group develop because of these changes.

Key terms

party organization (p. 220)
party in government (p. 220)
party in the electorate (p. 220)
party system (p. 221)
party principle (p. 222)
spoils system (p. 222)
realignment (p. 224)

Practice Quiz Questions

1. **Which were the first well-known parties in the United States?**

   a   Federalists and Democratic-Republicans

   b   Democrats and Republicans

   c   Whigs and Federalists

   d   Democrats and Whigs

   e   Whigs and Republicans

2. **The idea that a party is not just a group but an organization that exists apart from its candidate is called the _____ .**

   a   party system

   b   spoils system

   c   conditional party government

   d   party ID

   e   party principle

American political parties today

Describe the main characteristics of American parties as organizations, in the government, and in the electorate. (Pages 224–232)

Summary

The modern party is composed of three parts. The party organization is a loosely defined group of individuals and organizations that are focused on supporting political candidates when they share the same policy goals. The party in the government consists of elected officials who are the members of a particular party. The party in the electorate consists of citizens who identify with a particular political party.

Key terms

national committee (p. 224)
political action committee (PAC) (p. 225)
527 organization (p. 225)
caucus (congressional) (p. 226)
conference (p. 226)
unified government (p. 226)
divided government (p.226)
party identification (party ID) (p. 229)
party coalitions (p. 230)
issue ownership (p. 231)

Practice Quiz Questions

3. **The Democratic and Republican party organizations _____ hierarchical; they are _____ to force state and local parties to share their positions on issues.**

   a   are not; able

   b   are not; unable

   c   are; able

   d   are; unable

   e   are; sometimes able

4. **A group of elected officials of the same party who come together to organize and strategize is called a _____ .**

   a   cabal

   b   conditional party government

   c   primary

   d   PAC

   e   caucus

5. **The modern Congress is _____ ; the distance between the parties has _____ over the past 60 years.**

   a   polarized; increased

   b   polarized; stayed the same

   c   not polarized; decreased

   d   not polarized; stayed the same

   e   not polarized; increased

The role of political parties in American politics

Explain the important functions that parties perform in the political system. (Pages 232–242)

Summary

Political parties serve two major roles in the political system. First, they compete in elections by recruiting and nominating candidates and supporting candidate campaigns. Second, they facilitate cooperation in government by providing a framework for agenda-setting, coordination, and accountability among members of the same party. There are many different minor political parties, and while they rarely make a significant impact on the political stage, they do occasionally influence election outcomes. The two big issues facing minor parties are that their platforms do not appeal to a large portion of Americans and that the electoral system makes it hard for minor parties to win elections.

Key terms

primary election (p. 232) **nominating convention** (p. 235)
caucus (electoral) (p. 232) **party platform** (p. 238)

Practice Quiz Questions

6. Which is *not* one of the ways political party organizations support candidates?

a   by controlling who runs in House and Senate races

b   by contributing money to campaign activities

c   by offering advice on how to deal with the press

d   by organizing get-out-the-vote activities

e   by offering advice on which issues to emphasize

7. Why do most candidates support their party platforms?

a   because candidates are required to support the platforms

b   because all candidates vote on the platforms that are written

c   because candidates get kicked out of the party for not doing so

d   because both major parties' platforms are essentially the same

e   because most candidates and their constituents generally agree with the platform

8. When the president, House, and Senate are controlled by the same party, this is called _____.

a   party in government

b   responsible party government

c   unified government

d   divided government

e   conditional party government

9. In American politics, minor parties _____.

a   are very prominent at the state and local levels

b   are prominent only in congressional elections

c   win few offices at any level of government

d   win a significant number of offices at all levels

e   are more influential today than in the past

10. The issue positions of minor parties are usually _____.

a   very different from those of the major parties and most Americans

b   very similar to those of the major parties and most Americans

c   developed with input from a national network

d   based on the preferences of the party's members in government

e   not the reason people vote for minor-party candidates

Suggested Reading

Aldrich, John. *Why Parties?*, 2nd ed. Chicago: University of Chicago Press, 2014.

Anderson, Sarah E., Daniel M. Butler, and Laurel Harbridge-Yong. *Rejecting Compromise: Legislators' Fear of Primary Voters*. New York: Cambridge University Press, 2020.

Bartels, Larry M. *Unequal Democracy: The Political Economy of the New Gilded Age*. New York: Russell Sage Foundation, 2008.

Binder, Sarah A. *Minority Rights, Majority Rule: Partisanship and the Development of Congress*. New York: Cambridge University Press, 1997.

Blum, Rachel M. *How the Tea Party Captured the GOP: Insurgent Factions in American Politics*. Chicago: University of Chicago Press, 2020.

Cohen, Marty, David Karol, Hans Noel, and John Zaller. *The Party Decides: Presidential Nominations before and after Reform*. Chicago: University of Chicago Press, 2008.

Klar, Samara, and Yanna Krupnikov. *Independent Politics: How American Disdain for Parties Leads to Political Inaction*. New York: Cambridge University Press, 2016.

Noel, Hans. *Political Ideologies and Political Parties in America*. New York: Cambridge University Press, 2014.

Norrander, Barbara. *The Imperfect Primary: Oddities, Biases, and Strengths of U.S. Presidential Nomination Politics*, 3rd ed. New York: Routledge, 2019.

Schattschneider, E. E. *Party Government*. New York: McGraw-Hill, 1942.

Sinclair, Betsy. *The Social Citizen: Peer Networks and Political Behavior*. Chicago: University of Chicago Press, 2012.

Elections

Who gets to represent the people?

 "I won the election, got 71,000,000 legal votes. Bad things happened which our observers were not allowed to see. Never happened before. Millions of mail-in ballots were sent to people who never asked for them!"[1]
President Donald Trump, November 7, 2020

 " I've worked extensively with the election officials in the city of Detroit, and they take it very seriously.... Are there errors that happen? Sure. But that's not fraud.... I never saw any sort of fraud.... It never happens. Because you can't get away with it. It's way easier to just try and win the election."[2]
Josh Venable, Michigan Republican political operative

Every two years, Americans elect 435 House members and 33 or so senators; every four years (as in 2020), we also elect a president. The outcomes of these elections are scrutinized because they provide insights into what voters are thinking, because they reveal the usefulness of different campaign strategies, or simply because of what's at stake.

One example in 2020 was the Senate election in Maine between Republican incumbent Susan Collins and her Democratic challenger, Speaker of the Maine House of Representatives Sara Gideon. One reason this election was important was that Democrats needed to flip only four Senate seats to gain control of the chamber, and Maine was one of the few states in 2020 where a Democratic challenger had a good chance of unseating an incumbent. Another was that Collins was one of the few remaining moderate Republicans in the Senate, as well as an occasional supporter of Democratic initiatives. But Collins had also supported many of President Trump's policy initiatives, although she did not vote for Trump's last-minute Supreme Court nominee, Amy Coney Barrett.

Ultimately, Collins won reelection, a surprise to observers who had predicted a Gideon win based on her popularity, her well-funded campaign, and discontent with Collins. Collins's victory illustrates an important truth: even though most Americans are thoroughly disgusted with politicians and politics, most congressional incumbents are reelected. Our task is to understand this outcome. Did Mainers support Collins because she was a Republican, or because of Donald Trump? What role did the campaign play, or the challenger's record? Did Maine's use of a ranked-choice voting system help or hurt Gideon? Answers to these questions help explain whether Collins's victory is a one-off, idiosyncratic win or an indication of how U.S. elections will play out in 2022 and beyond.

The 2020 senate race in Maine between Democrat Sara Gideon and Republican incumbent Susan Collins (shown here) captured the country's attention. Was Collins's surprise victory a result of smart campaigning, approval of her record as a senator, widespread dissatisfaction with Gideon or the Democratic Party, or something else?

CHAPTER GOALS

Present the major rules and procedures of American elections. pages 248–257

Describe the features, strategies, and funding of campaigns for federal office. pages 258–270

Explain the key factors that influence voters' choices. pages 270–274

Analyze the issues and outcomes in the 2018 and 2020 elections. pages 275–281

The 2020 Senate election in Maine is also a good example of the central themes of this text. Elections matter: no one watching the Maine race would think that Collins and Gideon would support the same policies if elected. Candidates competing for political office offer the people distinct, competing visions of what the federal government should do—from what the tax code should look like to what regulations the government should impose on individuals and corporations. In a very real sense, elections are how Americans resolve conflict over whose vision of government policy should prevail—at least until the next election.

American elections are structured by rules. Maine is somewhat unique in using ranked-choice voting, a system wherein voters rank all the candidates running for a given office instead of choosing just one. If no candidate wins a majority of first-place votes, the candidate with the lowest number of first-place votes is eliminated, and that candidate's votes are redistributed according to his or her supporters' second-place votes. In other states, an outcome where neither candidate wins an outright majority leads to a runoff between the two top finishers. These rules matter—runoff elections often produce surprising outcomes because they occur a month or more after Election Day, allowing candidates to refine their message, but also forcing them to motivate supporters to return to the polls a second time. And in 2020, party control of the Senate hinged on the results of two runoffs in Georgia.

The 2020 Senate contest in Maine highlights fundamental facts about American elections. Candidates run for different offices and represent different constituents. Locally set rules determine who runs, who votes, and how money is raised and spent. Even ballot layouts and how votes are cast and counted vary across states. Who wins is up to ordinary citizens. After his defeat, Donald Trump alleged that American elections were rigged, but there is no evidence to support his claims. Rather, as Republican operative Josh Venable asserts, the only way to win is to convince voters that you are the best person for the job. In this chapter, we show how elections are run, how they are decided, and how they affect policy making. Ultimately, how meaningful was Susan Collins's victory in Maine in 2020—or Democrats' failure to win a Senate majority? What do election results tell us about why some candidates win and others lose? Why do these outcomes matter in American politics?

★
PRESENT THE MAJOR RULES
AND PROCEDURES OF
AMERICAN ELECTIONS

How do American elections work?

The American political system is a representative democracy: Americans do not make policy choices themselves, but they vote for individuals who make these choices on their behalf. Thus, we begin by describing the rules and procedures that define American national elections. Our working assumption for explaining the rules and processes of elections as well as the behavior of candidates and voters is that they are tied directly to what elections do: select representatives, give citizens the ability to influence the direction of government policy, and provide citizens with the opportunity to reward and punish officeholders seeking reelection.

The most visible function of American elections is the selection of officeholders, including, at the national level, members of the House and Senate and the president and vice president. Candidates can be **incumbents**, running for reelection to their current office, or challengers, running for the office for the first time. Because America is a representative democracy, by voting in elections, Americans have an indirect effect

incumbent
A politician running for reelection to the office he or she currently holds.

on government policy. Although citizens do not make policy choices themselves, they determine which individuals get to make these choices. In this way, elections connect citizen preferences and government actions.

Although the fundamental choice in an election is between two or more candidates running for some political office, elections also involve a choice between candidates' policy platforms: the set of policies and programs they promise to carry out if elected. By investigating candidates' platforms, citizens learn about the range of options for government policy. Moreover, their voting decisions determine who gets to make choices about future government policy and thereby shape policy itself. For example, in the 2020 elections, Democrats wanted to ensure they kept their House majority, which would allow them to block Republican policy initiatives and investigate the Trump administration's actions if Trump was reelected. They also wanted to gain a Senate majority and win the presidency, which would allow them to formulate and enact new policies rather than responding to Republican initiatives.

The election process also creates a way to hold incumbents accountable. When citizens choose between voting for an incumbent or a challenger, they can consider the incumbent's performance over his or her previous terms in office and ask, "Has he [or she] done a good job on the issues I care about?"[3] Citizens who answer yes typically vote for the incumbent, and those who say no typically vote for the challenger. These evaluations are significant because they make incumbents responsive to their constituents' demands.[4] If an elected official anticipates that some constituents will consider his or her performance objectively when making their decision (rather than simply reflecting their partisanship), the official will try to take actions that these constituents will look back upon favorably when they're in the voting booth. Otherwise, voters can opt to remove the official from office because they disapprove of his or her performance and believe the country will fare better if a different candidate wins.

Two stages of elections

Candidates running for federal office (House, Senate, or president) face a two-step procedure. First, if prospective candidates want to run on behalf of a political party, they must win the party's nomination in a **primary** election. If the would-be candidates want to run as Independents, they need to gather signatures on a petition to secure a spot on the ballot. Different states hold either **open primaries**, **semi-closed primaries**, or **closed primaries**, and state law sets the timing of these elections. For House and Senate seats, a few states hold single primaries, in which there is one election involving candidates from both parties, with the top two finalists (regardless of party) receiving nominations to the general election.

The second step in the election process is the **general election**, which is held throughout the nation on the first Tuesday after the first Monday in November. Federal law designates this day as Election Day. General elections determine who wins elected positions in government. The offices at stake vary depending on the year. Presidential elections occur every four years (2012, 2016, 2020, …). In a presidential election year, Americans elect the entire House of Representatives, one-third of the Senate, and a president and vice president. During midterm elections (2014, 2018, 2022, …), there is no presidential contest, but the entire House and another one-third of the Senate are up for election.

One implication of this two-step process of primary and general elections is that sometimes the winner of a primary is not a party's best candidate for the general election. For example, in the 2020 presidential race, one of the principal arguments for

Though incumbents generally fared well in the 2020 congressional elections, some, such as Representative Dan Lipinski (D-IN), a former political science professor and eight-term member of Congress, lost in the primaries.

DID YOU KNOW?

There are a total of

510,000

federal, state, and local elected offices in the United States.
Source: Jennifer Lawless, *Becoming a Candidate*

primary
A ballot vote in which citizens select a party's nominee for the general election.

open primary
A primary election in which any registered voter can participate in the contest, regardless of party affiliation.

semi-closed primary
A primary in which anyone who is a registered member of the party or registered as an Independent can vote.

closed primary
A primary election in which only registered members of a particular political party can vote.

general election
The election in which voters cast ballots for House members, senators, and (every four years) a president and vice president.

choosing someone other than Joe Biden as the Democratic nominee (such as Senator Bernie Sanders, Senator Amy Klobuchar, or Senator Elizabeth Warren) was that this candidate would have had a better chance of winning the general election. While Biden had many enthusiastic supporters, a first-rate campaign organization, and considerable Washington experience as senator and vice president, he was also strongly disliked by a sizable fraction of the American electorate—because of his age, his moderately liberal policy stances, and his career in politics. In the end, Biden was a good fit for the unique circumstances of the 2020 election, as he attracted support from working-class White midwestern voters who had supported Donald Trump in 2016, while increasing turnout from minority voters in crucial swing states.

Mechanics of elections

The Constitution limits voting rights to American citizens who are at least 18 years old. There are also restrictions on voter eligibility that vary across states, including residency requirements (usually 30 days) and prohibitions for people convicted of a major crime. A recent development in American elections is an increase in the practice of automatic absentee voting, in which someone can request an absentee ballot without having to provide a reason, such as being out of town on election day. Most states also allow early voting in the weeks prior to Election Day and some allow voters to send in ballots by mail.[5]

The most fundamental feature of American elections is that officeholders are elected in single-member districts in which only the winner of the most votes takes office. (Although both of each state's senators represent the whole state, they are elected separately, usually in different years.) Senate candidates compete statewide; House candidates compete in congressional districts. In most states, the congressional district lines are drawn by state legislatures. In some states, nonpartisan commissions or committees of judges perform this function. (For details on redistricting, see Chapter 10.)

Because members of the House and Senate are elected from specific geographic areas, they often represent very different kinds of people. Their constituents differ in terms of age, race, income level, occupation, and political leaning, including party affiliation and ideology. Therefore, legislators from different areas of the country face highly diverse demands from their constituents—leading them to pursue very dissimilar kinds of policies.

For example, Democratic senator Charles Schumer represents the fairly liberal state of New York, where most people take some sort of pro-choice position on abortion rights, while Republican senator Richard Shelby represents the conservative state of Alabama, where most voters have long been opposed to abortions. Suppose the Senate votes on a proposal to ban all abortions after the twelfth week of pregnancy. Shelby knows that most of his constituents would probably want him to vote for the proposal, and Schumer knows that most of his constituents would probably want him to vote against it. This example illustrates that congressional conflicts over policy often reflect differences in constituents' demands. Schumer and Shelby themselves may hold different views on abortion rights, but even if they agreed, their constituents' distinct demands would make it likely that as legislators they would vote differently.

Most House and Senate contests involve **plurality voting**: the candidate who gets the most votes wins. However, some states use **majority voting**, meaning that a candidate needs more than 50 percent of the vote to win. In these states, if no candidate has a majority, a **runoff election** takes place between the top two finishers.

plurality voting
A voting system in which the candidate who receives the most votes within a geographic area wins the election, regardless of whether that candidate wins a majority (more than half) of the votes.

majority voting
A voting system in which a candidate must win more than 50 percent of votes to win the election. If no candidate wins enough votes to take office, a runoff election is held between the top two vote-getters.

runoff election
Under a majority voting system, a second election is held only if no candidate wins a majority of the votes in the first general election. Only the top two vote-getters in the first election compete in the runoff.

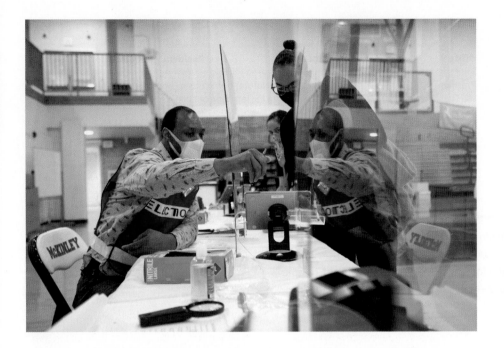

Ballots and Vote Counting Americans vote by using a variety of machines and ballot structures based on where they live. States either use electronic touch screen voting machines, usually with some sort of paper receipt to allow manual recounts, or have voters fill out paper ballots that are then scanned and recorded. When the polls close, workers transcribe vote totals from the various machines, then hand-carry the totals and individual ballots or receipts to county boards of election, where totals are aggregated and sent to state agencies, which certify the results. The process is largely run by volunteers, with both major parties having participants or observers at all stages.

Most states have laws that allow vote recounts if a race is sufficiently close (typically within 1 percent or less). Even when a recount occurs, it may be impossible to definitively determine who won a particular election, as the statutes that determine which ballots are valid are often open to interpretation.

What *is* clear is that election rules can affect results. Particularly in close races, small changes in the rules governing elections can easily change outcomes.

Presidential elections

Many of the rules governing elections, such as who is eligible to vote, are the same for both presidential and congressional elections. However, presidential contests have several unique rules regarding how nominees are determined and how votes are counted. Moreover, the constitutional requirements for presidential candidates are also somewhat stricter than those for congressional candidates (see Nuts & Bolts 8.1).

The Nomination: Primaries and Caucuses Presidential nominees from the Democratic and Republican parties are determined by the outcomes of state-level primaries and **caucuses** held over a five-month period beginning in January of an election year.[6] Primary and caucus voters select a candidate, but their votes do not count directly toward the election of that candidate; their votes instead count toward the selection of delegates who have pledged to support the candidate, who then go on to attend the party nominating conventions. There, the delegates cast votes that determine their party's presidential and vice-presidential nominees. The format of these elections, including their timing and the number of delegates selected per state,

caucus
A local meeting in which party members select a party's nominee for the general election.

Constitutional Requirements for Candidates

Source: U.S. Constitution.

Office	Minimum Age	Residency Requirement
President	35	Natural-born citizen (born in the United States or on U.S. territory, or child of citizen parent)
Senator	30	Resident of state; U.S. citizen for at least nine years
Representative	25	Resident of state; U.S. citizen for at least seven years

"Why Should I Care?" These age and citizenship requirements are the most fundamental limits on who can run for political office. They are one explanation for why there are no college-age people elected to Congress—they are prevented from running in the first place.

proportional allocation
During the presidential primaries, the practice of determining the number of convention delegates allotted to each candidate based on the percentage of the popular vote cast for each candidate. All Democratic primaries and caucuses use this system, as do some states' Republican primaries and caucuses.

winner-take-all
During the presidential primaries, the practice of assigning all of a given state's delegates to the candidate who receives the most popular votes. Some states' Republican primaries and caucuses use this system.

Campaigns don't end—they run out of money.

—**Richard Gephardt,** former Speaker of the House and presidential candidate

is determined on a state-by-state basis by the state and national party organizations.[7] A candidate's principal goal is to win as many delegates as possible.

The details of translating primary and caucus votes into convention delegates vary from state to state, but some general rules apply. All Democratic primaries and caucuses use **proportional allocation** to divide each state's delegate seats between the candidates; thus, if a candidate receives 40 percent of the votes in a state's primary the candidate gets roughly 40 percent of the convention delegates from that state. Some Republican contests use proportional allocation, but others use a **winner-take-all** system. In these states, the candidate who receives the most votes gets all the convention delegates. These rules can have a significant effect on candidates' campaign strategies and the outcome of the nomination process. (See How It Works: Nominating Presidential Candidates in Chapter 7.)

The order in which the primaries and caucuses in different states take place is another important factor, because many candidacies do not survive beyond the early contests.[8] Most presidential candidates pour everything they have into the first few contests. Candidates who do well early on attract financial contributions, campaign workers, endorsements, and additional media coverage, all of which enable them to move on to subsequent primaries or caucuses. But for candidates who do poorly in the first contests, contributions and coverage dry up, leaving these candidates with no alternative but to drop out of the race. For example, more than 20 candidates entered the race for the 2020 Democratic presidential nomination. Several withdrew before any convention delegates were selected. By mid-March, two months into the process and five months before the convention where the nominee would actually be selected, the race was down to only two serious candidates, Sanders and Biden.

For many years, Iowa and New Hampshire have held the first presidential nomination contests, with the Iowa Caucuses taking place a week before the New Hampshire primary. These states' position at the beginning of the process is largely a historical accident, but party officials from other states often complain about the disproportionate influence of these states.

The parties' national committees can issue rules and requirements about the timing of state presidential primaries, but state law sets the election dates, meaning that a national committee's directives may not be followed. As a result, the initial 2020 nomination process was roughly the same as in previous years (with the exception of California's move to March), with Iowa and New Hampshire holding the initial contests in early February 2020, followed by a primary in South Carolina and a caucus in Nevada later in the month and the remaining contests beginning in March and continuing through June, although some were delayed due to COVID-19.

The National Convention Presidential nominating conventions happen late in the summer of an election year. Their main task is to select the party's presidential nominee, although usually the vote at the convention is a formality; in most recent presidential contests, one candidate has emerged from the nomination process leading up to the convention with a clear majority of delegates and has been able to win the nomination on the first ballot. To get the nomination, a candidate needs the support of a majority of the delegates. If no candidate receives a majority after the first round of voting at the convention, the voting continues until someone does. When a sitting president runs for reelection, as Donald Trump did in 2020, he or she typically faces little opposition for the party's general-election nomination.

After the delegates nominate a presidential candidate, they nominate a vice-presidential candidate. The presidential nominee chooses this running mate (generally shortly before the convention), and the delegates almost always ratify this choice without much debate. Convention delegates also vote on the party platform, which describes what kinds of policies the party's candidates will supposedly seek to enact if they are elected.

The final purpose of a convention is to attract public attention to the party and its nominees. Public figures give speeches during the evening sessions when all major television networks have live coverage. At some recent conventions, both parties have drawn press attention by recruiting speakers who support their political goals despite being associated with the opposing party. At the 2020 Democratic convention, Republicans John Kasich (former governor of Ohio) and Colin Powell (secretary of state under George W. Bush) gave televised primetime speeches voicing their support for Joe Biden.

Once presidential candidates are nominated, the general-election campaign officially begins—although it often unofficially starts much earlier, as soon as the presumptive nominees are known. We will say more about presidential campaigns in a later section.

Counting Presidential Votes Let's assume for a moment that the campaigning is over and that Election Day has arrived. Even though in the voting booth people choose between the candidates by name, a choice that constitutes the **popular vote**, this vote is not directly for a presidential candidate. Rather, when you select your preferred candidate's name, you are choosing that person's slate of pledged supporters from your state to serve as electors, who will then vote to elect the president. The number of electors for each state equals the state's number of House members (which varies by state population) plus the number of senators (two per state). Altogether, the electors chosen by the citizens of each state constitute the **Electoral College**, the body that casts **electoral votes** to formally select the president.

In most states, the electoral votes are allocated on a winner-take-all basis: the candidate who receives the most votes from a given state's citizens gets all of that state's electoral votes. But two states, Maine and Nebraska, allocate most of their electoral votes at the congressional district level: in those states, the candidate who wins the most votes in each congressional district wins that district's single electoral vote. Then the remaining 2 electoral votes go to the candidate who gets the most votes statewide.[9] (See Nuts & Bolts 8.2 for state-by-state electoral vote totals.)

The winner-take-all method of allocating most states' electoral votes makes candidates focus their attention on two kinds of states: high-population states with lots of electoral votes and so-called swing states, where the contest is relatively close.

Senate campaign appearances almost always involve extensive print and electronic media coverage. Here, Shelley Moore Capito, a West Virginia Republican senator who ran for reelection in 2020, speaks to the media. They helped get out her message and policy agenda, and as a result, she won her contest.

popular vote
The votes cast by citizens in an election.

Electoral College
The body that votes to select America's president and vice president based on the popular vote in each state. Each candidate nominates a slate of electors who are selected to attend the meeting of the college if their candidate wins the most votes in a state or district.

electoral votes
Votes cast by members of the Electoral College; after a presidential candidate wins the popular vote in a given state, that candidate's slate of electors casts electoral votes for the candidate on behalf of that state.

NUTS & BOLTS
8.2

Electoral Votes and Swing States

Presidential campaigns focus their attention on states with high electoral votes and swing states where each candidate has a good chance of winning. In this box, we group states into categories based on their number of electoral votes and whether one party has consistently won the state in recent presidential elections.

Source: Compiled by the authors.

Number of Electoral Votes	Yes (Not a Swing State)	No (Swing State)
3–5	D.C., Delaware, Alaska, Montana, North Dakota, South Dakota, Vermont, Wyoming, Hawaii, Maine, Rhode Island, Idaho, Nebraska, West Virginia	New Hampshire, New Mexico
6–10	Arkansas, Kansas, Utah, Connecticut, Oregon, Oklahoma, Kentucky, Louisiana, Alabama, South Carolina, Maryland, Mississippi, Missouri, Minnesota	Iowa, Nevada, Colorado, Wisconsin
More than 10	Massachusetts, Indiana, Tennessee, Washington, New Jersey, Illinois, New York, Texas, California, Ohio, Virginia	Arizona, North Carolina, Florida, Michigan, Pennsylvania, Georgia

"Why Should I Care?" Data on a state's electoral votes and status as a swing state tell us why presidential candidates campaign in some states more than in others. For the most part, the crucial factor is whether both presidential candidates see a state as winnable—if they do, they will campaign there aggressively.

You win some, you lose some. And then there's that little-known third category.

—Al Gore, who lost the 2000 presidential vote in the Electoral College despite winning the most votes on Election Day

It's better for a candidate to spend a day campaigning in California (55 electoral votes) than in Montana (3 electoral votes). However, if one candidate is sure to win a particular state, both candidates will direct their efforts elsewhere. This is why, during the final weeks of the 2020 campaign, the Trump team was on defense, trying to hold Florida and key Rust Belt states (following the strategy described in the How It Works feature), while the Biden campaign was targeting former Republican strongholds Georgia, Texas, and Arizona.

While most Americans believe that the winner of the presidential election is decided on Election Day, this outcome is actually just the first step in a process that determines the winner. After citizens' votes are counted, each state's slate of electors meets in December in the state capitals. At their meetings, the electors almost always vote for the presidential candidate they have pledged to support. After the votes are certified by a joint session of Congress, the candidate who wins a majority of the nation's electoral votes (at least 270) is the new president. If no candidate receives a majority of the Electoral College votes, the members of the House of Representatives choose the winner. They follow a procedure in which the members from each state decide which candidate to support and then cast one collective vote per state, with the winner needing a majority of these state-level votes to win. This procedure has not been used since 1824, although it might be required if a third-party candidate wins a significant number of electoral votes or if a state's electors refuse to cast their votes.[10]

Popular Vote versus Electoral Vote Percentages, 2000–2020

FIGURE 8.1

Political scientists argue that the Electoral College system tends to magnify the winning candidate's margin of victory. Do the data presented here support this view?

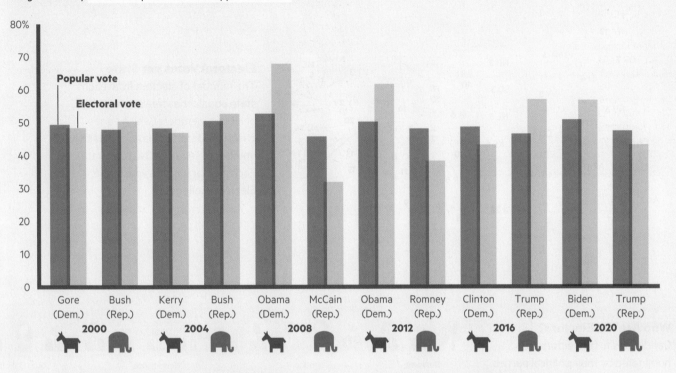

Source: 2000–2016 data from U.S. National Archives and Records Administration, www.archives.gov/federal-register/electoral-college/historical.html (accessed 5/11/18); 2020 data calculated by the authors from election results as of 11/12/20.

A presidential candidate can win the Electoral College vote, and thus the election, without receiving a majority of the votes cast by citizens (see Figure 8.1). In 2016, Democrat Hillary Clinton received several million more votes than Donald Trump because of large majorities in states such as California and New York, but Trump won a majority in the Electoral College because of narrow victories in states such as Wisconsin and Pennsylvania. A similar outcome occurred in 2000, leading to Republican George W. Bush's victory over Democrat Al Gore.

American elections incorporate a complex set of laws, rules, and procedures. And these rules matter—the candidates who win under current rules might lose given other reasonable ways to conduct elections. For example, in 2016, Democrat Hillary Clinton won the popular vote but lost the electoral vote (and the election) due to close losses in Florida, Michigan, Pennsylvania, and Wisconsin. Even small changes in voter registration, voter ID regulations, and other laws in these states might have given Clinton victories in these states—and the presidency.

"Why Should I Care?"

The Electoral College

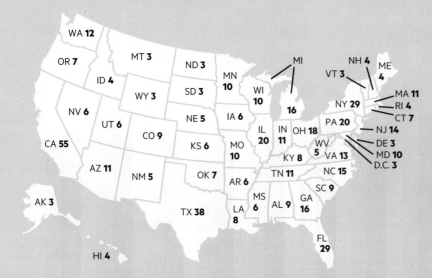

WA 12
OR 7
MT 3
ND 3
MN 10
ID 4
WY 3
SD 3
WI 10
MI
NV 6
UT 6
CO 9
NE 5
IA 6
IL 20
IN 11
OH 18
MI 16
CA 55
KS 6
MO 10
KY 8
WV 5
VA 13
NC 15
AZ 11
NM 5
OK 7
AR 6
TN 11
AK 3
TX 38
MS 6
LA 8
AL 9
GA 16
SC 9
HI 4
FL 29
VT 3
NH 4
ME 4
NY 29
MA 11
RI 4
CT 7
PA 20
NJ 14
DE 3
MD 10
D.C. 3

Electoral Votes per State

The number of electors from each state equals the state's number of House members (which varies based on state population) plus the number of senators (two per state). Each elector has one vote in the Electoral College.

Who Are the Electors?

Candidates to be electors are nominated by their political parties. They pledge to support a certain candidate if they are elected to the Electoral College. When you cast your vote for a presidential candidate, you are in fact voting for the slate of potential electors who support that candidate.

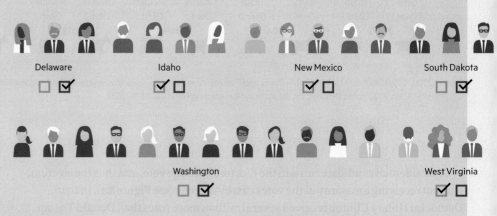

Delaware
Idaho
New Mexico
South Dakota

Washington
West Virginia

California Popular Vote

40%

60%

California Electoral Votes (55)

100%

Winning a State

Most states give all of their Electoral College votes to the candidate who wins the most votes in that state. So, even if a candidate only gets 51 percent of the vote in the state, his or her entire slate of electors is elected, and he or she gets all of the state's votes in the Electoral College.

100%
of electoral votes go to winner

Donald Trump's Electoral College Strategy, 2020

Trump's campaign started with the electoral map that produced its 2016 victory with 304 electoral votes. It focused on two groups of states—Rust Belt states where it won narrow victories in 2016 (Michigan, Pennsylvania, and Wisconsin) and states where increasing minority populations might swing the outcome toward Democrat Joe Biden (Arizona, Georgia, North Carolina, and Texas)—in an attempt to amass at least 270 electoral votes, the threshold required to win the election.

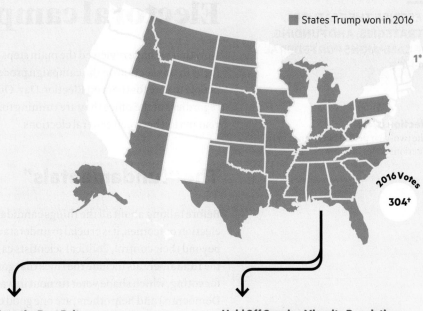

■ States Trump won in 2016

1*

2016 Votes
304†

Keep the Rust Belt:
Michigan, Pennsylvania, and Wisconsin
Trump won these states by small margins in 2016.

WI **10**
MI **16**   1
PA **20**

260+46
306

Hold Off Growing Minority Populations:
Arizona, Georgia, North Carolina, Texas
Growing minority populations in these states were a significant worry for the Trump campaign.

1
AZ **11**
NC **15**
GA **16**
TX **38**   226+80
306

1*
4§

Total Votes
232

2020 Results

This strategy did not succeed for Trump in 2020 like it did in 2016. While he did manage to hold on to Texas and North Carolina, **higher overall turnout and growing Democratic support among minority populations and in the suburbs** helped Biden secure victories across the Rust Belt and in Arizona and Georgia, which ultimately won Biden the election.

Trump's Final Electoral College Map

AL **9**	KS **6**	NE **4**	TN **11**
AK **3**	KY **8**	NC **15**	TX **38**
AR **6**	LA **8**	ND **3**	UT **6**
FL **29**	ME **1**	OH **18**	WV **5**
ID **4**	MS **6**	OK **7**	WY **3**
IN **11**	MO **10**	SC **9**	
IA **6**	MT **3**	SD **3**	

❓ Critical Thinking

1. **Why didn't the Trump campaign** focus on some delegate-rich states like California and New York?

2. **In what state do you think the Trump campaign** spent the most money? Where do you think Trump made the most personal appearances? Why?

---

* Maine splits its electoral votes: in 2016, Trump received 1, Clinton 3; in 2020, Trump received 1, Biden 3.

† Two electors in Texas did not cast their electoral votes for Trump in 2016.

§ Nebraska splits its electoral votes: in 2020, Trump received 4, Biden 1.

election cycle
The two-year period between general elections.

Electoral campaigns

Now that we have reviewed the main steps of how American elections work, we will focus in this section on the campaign process and what candidates do to convince people to vote for them on Election Day. Our emphasis is on things that candidates do regardless of the office they are running for, across the entire **election cycle**, the two-year period between general elections.

The "fundamentals"

Before talking about all the things candidates and their supporters do to shape election outcomes, it is crucial to understand that many important factors are beyond their control. Political scientists call these factors the *fundamentals*. In part, the fundamentals include the rules that govern elections. Photo ID requirements for voting, which shape voter turnout in ways that hurt some candidates (usually Democrats) and help others, are one good example of electoral rules that affect outcomes. Another fundamental is how many people in a candidate's district share his or her party ID. As we showed in Chapter 7, an individual's party ID is a strong influence on his or her voting decisions. Political scientists refer to states or districts that have roughly equal numbers of Democrats and Republicans as swing districts, meaning that candidates from both parties have a good chance of winning. Safe districts are those where one party has a significant majority, so candidates from that party are likely to win election and those from the other party are not. Over the last two generations, the number of safe districts and states has increased somewhat, with rural areas becoming more solidly Republican and urban areas trending Democratic.

Particularly in presidential elections, economic conditions also have a strong effect on who wins. As you can see in the What Do the Facts Say? feature on p. 259, a stronger economy benefits incumbent presidents running for reelection (for example, Obama in 2012), while a weak economy hurts incumbents (Jimmy Carter in 1980) and their successors (John McCain in 2008). Of course, fundamentals have to be taken in context. Big one-time shocks have unique effects. For example, the COVID-19 pandemic caused a drop in second-quarter GDP that was so big we can't even include it in the figure (that's why there's an asterisk next to the 2020 data point). As we discuss later, while most voters gave Trump low marks for his management of the pandemic and the economic downturn, his approval ratings did not change very much. That said, Trump's ratings were already low prior to the pandemic, and the social and economic turmoil limited his ability to attract the additional support he needed to get reelected.

Candidates might like to think that they can convince people to vote for them regardless of circumstances. But the fundamentals like party ID and economic conditions tell us which candidates face an uphill fight or an easy ride—either because voters are well aware of these factors before the campaign begins or because campaigns are mechanisms by which voters become informed about them.[11] It may not be fair to reward or blame candidates for the state of the economy, as even presidents have only limited control over economic growth or unemployment levels. For better or worse, however, a significant fraction of American voters behave this way.[12] Similarly, for some challengers, defeat is a foregone conclusion because they are running in a state or district that is safe for the other party—no matter what they do, most of the electorate is unlikely to support them.

It's important to remember, though, that the fundamentals are not the final word in an election. The backgrounds of the candidates, their qualifications for office, and the decisions they make about their campaigns sometimes have significant, even decisive, effects.

"The Fundamentals" and Presidential Elections

Vote Share for President's Party vs. Economic Growth

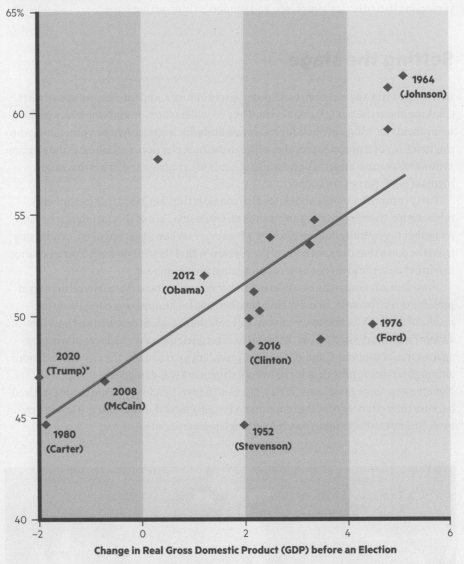

*In 2020 the change in real GDP was −31.4% due to the COVID-19 pandemic.

Source: Data calculated by the authors.

Think about it

- **Why do incumbent presidents do better** when the economy is strong than when it is weak?
- **Candidates who lose, such as Clinton in 2016 or Romney in 2012, are criticized** for running poor campaigns. Look at the data points that describe economic conditions in these elections and the percentage of the popular vote received by Obama in 2012 and Clinton in 2016. Given the state of the economy in these years, is there any evidence that Romney or Clinton did worse than you would expect?
- **What signs are there in the graph** that other factors besides "the fundamentals" might influence presidential election outcomes?

Political scientists argue that "the fundamentals" play a key role in American elections. For example, the state of the economy is thought to influence voter decisions in presidential elections—a strong economy benefits incumbent presidents or their successors. However, most candidates (and journalists) argue that the things candidates say and do during the campaign determine who wins and who loses. What do the facts say?

To answer this question, let's examine this figure, which shows the relationship between presidential election outcomes (vote share for the incumbent president or the candidate from the president's party) and economic conditions (the growth in real gross domestic product [GDP] in the year before the election). The blue line gives the predicted relationship between economic conditions and the popular vote, showing that on average, as economic conditions improve, the president or candidate from the president's party receives more votes.

For example, Democrat Conor Lamb won a 2018 special election in a strongly Republican Pennsylvania congressional district—although President Trump won there in 2016 by a 20-point margin. At least part of Lamb's victory was due to a decline in Trump's popularity and the resignation of the district's Republican incumbent due to scandal. But Lamb, who took moderate positions on issues such as gun control, was widely regarded as the stronger, more energetic candidate. Under these conditions, Republican voters appear to have seen Lamb as someone who would do a better job protecting their district's interests, and supported him on that basis.

Setting the stage

On the day after any election, candidates, party officials, and interest groups all start thinking about the next election cycle. They consider who won and who lost, which incumbents look like safe bets for reelection and which ones might be vulnerable, who might retire soon or run for another office in the next election, and whether the election returns reveal new information about the kinds of campaigns or issues that might increase voter turnout or support.

Party committees and candidates also consider the likelihood that incumbents might retire, thereby creating an **open seat**. Open seats are of special interest because incumbents generally hold an election advantage.[13] When a seat opens up, candidates from the party that does not control the seat know that they might have a better chance to win because they will not have to run against an incumbent.

Presidential campaigns also take incumbency into account. Virtually all first-term presidents run for reelection. Potential challengers in the opposing party study the results of the last election to see how many votes the president received and how this support was distributed across the states to determine their own chances of winning against the incumbent. Candidates in the president's party make the same calculations, although no sitting president in the twentieth century was denied renomination. Nonetheless, some presidents (Harry Truman in 1952, Lyndon Johnson in 1968) retired because their chances of being renominated were not good, while others (Gerald Ford in 1976, Jimmy Carter in 1980) barely won tough primary contests.[14]

open seat
An elected position for which there is no incumbent.

Each term, members of Congress decide whether to retire or run for another term. In December 2018, Senator Lamar Alexander (R-TN) announced his decision not to seek reelection in 2020, leaving his seat in the Senate open. Retirement decisions, which create open-seat races, are an opportunity for one party to gain seats from the other.

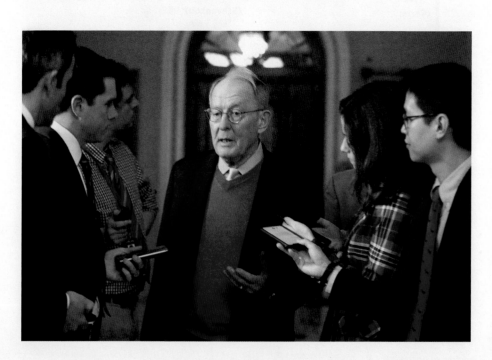

Before the campaign

While in Office Most sitting House members, senators, and presidents work throughout the election cycle to secure their reelection. Political scientists describe this activity as the permanent campaign.[15] To stay in office, incumbents have to do two things: keep the constituents happy and raise money for the campaign. As we will see in Chapter 10, congressional incumbents pursue the first goal by taking actions that reflect the demands of their constituents. This, in turn, boosts voters' retrospective evaluations of the incumbents at election time.[16] Incumbent presidents make the same calculations. For example, during the COVID-19 pandemic, Donald Trump faced the decision of when to relax social distancing advisories and allow the economy to reopen. Part of Trump's calculation was to balance safety (preventing the spread of the virus) with the goal of preventing a prolonged economic downturn. But Trump's calculations undoubtedly included the goal of ensuring that voters would remember his actions in a positive way when they returned to the polls in November 2020. Of course, many presidential actions are taken in response to events rather than initiated to gain voter support. Particularly in the case of wars and pandemic, it is far-fetched to say that presidents take hostile actions for political gain. Even so, presidents, just like other politicians, are keenly aware of the political consequences of their actions and the need to build a record they can run on in the next election.

Fund-Raising Candidates for all offices, incumbents and challengers alike, also devote considerable time before the campaign to raising campaign funds. Fund-raising helps an incumbent in two ways.[17] First, it ensures that if the incumbent faces a strong opponent, he or she will have enough money to run an aggressive campaign. Second, successful fund-raising deters opposition. Potential challengers are less likely to run against an incumbent if that individual is well funded with a sizable campaign war chest.[18] We'll discuss campaign fund-raising in more detail later in the chapter.

Promises and Party Positions Candidates also spend time before (and sometimes during) a campaign developing or refining their campaign platform, which includes stances on issues and promises about how the candidate will act in office.

Most officeholders are always campaigning—traveling around their states or districts, talking with constituents, and explaining their actions in office—all in the hope of winning and keeping support for the next election. Here, Representative Nanette Diaz Barragán (D-CA) meets with service members.

In writing their platforms, candidates may be constrained by positions they have taken in the past or by their party affiliation. For one thing, candidates whose positions vary from one election to another or between the primary and general elections often lose support from voters who see the changes as a sign of manipulation.[19] As we saw in Chapter 7, the parties have strong brand identities that lead many citizens to associate Democrats with liberal policies and Republicans with conservative ones. As a result, candidates often find it difficult to make campaign promises that contradict these perceptions. A candidate's positions are also influenced by demands from potential supporters. For example, in a state or district with many conservative or Republican voters, opposition to Obamacare or to amnesty for illegal immigrants might be a winning electoral strategy—just as support for these proposals would generally be helpful for candidates running in states or districts where most voters are moderate to liberal or Democrats.

The two-step electoral process in American elections also influences candidate positions. To win office, candidates have to campaign three times: first to build a staff and gain contributors and volunteers (the so-called silent primary or money primary), then in a primary to get on the ballot, and then in a general election. This process gives candidates an incentive to take relatively extreme policy positions—and encourages the entry of relatively extreme candidates—because party activists, contributors, and primary voters (the people whose support candidates need to attract in the first two steps) hold more extreme positions than voters in the general election. Thus, in the typical congressional district, Republican candidates win primaries by taking conservative positions, while Democratic candidates win primaries by upholding liberal views.

However, a position or promise that attracts votes in a primary election might not work so well in the general election, or vice versa. For example, during the 2020 Democratic presidential nomination campaign, challenger Bernie Sanders attracted support by promising to expand government health insurance programs. While this promise was popular among Democratic activists, contributors, and primary voters and helped Sanders compete in a close race against Joe Biden for the nomination, it would likely have cost Sanders (or any Democratic candidate) considerable support in the general election.

A candidate's issue positions as described in his or her platform help mobilize supporters and attract volunteers, activists, interest-group endorsements, and contributions. Issue positions also define what a government will seek to do differently depending on who gets elected. Even so, there is considerable evidence that many voters do not know much about candidates' issue positions, particularly in House and Senate races. As a result, when a candidate wins a race or a party wins seats across the country, it is risky to read the outcome as a sign that the winners had the most popular set of issue positions.

Campaign Staff Another thing candidates do before the campaign is build their campaign organization.[20] The success or failure of these efforts is another signal of a candidate's prospects. If experienced, well-respected people work for a candidate's campaign, observers conclude that the candidate's prospects for being elected are probably good. Indeed, skilled campaign consultants are highly desirable. They plan strategies, run public-opinion polls, assemble ads and buy television time, and talk with members of the media on the candidate's behalf, among other things. While only the most well-funded campaigns can afford top consultants, almost all campaigns have paid and volunteer staff, ranging from the dozen or so people who work for a typical House candidate to the thousands who run a major-party candidate's presidential campaign.

American presidential campaigns depend on thousands of paid and volunteer staff. Here Joe Biden makes phone calls to potential supporters before the Iowa Caucuses from a campaign office in Cedar Rapids in January 2020.

Candidates may gain media attention and (if they are not incumbents) name recognition by hosting campaign events. During the 2020 presidential race, this became challenging due to the need for social distancing. While Biden scheduled town halls online, Trump held in-person events throughout the summer, including this one in Tulsa, Oklahoma, which was ultimately poorly attended.

Primaries and the general election

Officially, the general-election campaigns begin in early September. By then, candidates have announced their intent to run and have built their campaign organizations, primary campaigns and elections have taken place, and both parties have chosen their presidential nominees and their congressional candidates. Interest groups, candidates, and party committees have raised most of the funds they will use or donate in the campaign. The race is on.

Name Recognition One fundamental campaign strategy, particularly in congressional campaigns, is to build name recognition. Since many citizens know fairly little about congressional candidates, efforts to increase a candidate's name recognition can deliver a few extra percentage points of support—enough to turn a close defeat into a victory. If the only thing a citizen knows is the name of one of the candidates, that citizen will almost surely vote for that candidate on Election Day. The importance of name recognition is one reason why campaigns invest in buttons, bumper stickers, and yard signs—all of which help ensure that voters know a candidate's name.

Getting Out the Vote A second basic strategy is mobilization. Turnout is not automatic: candidates have to make sure that their supporters actually go to the polls and vote (or make sure they have an absentee ballot). Campaign professionals refer to voter mobilization efforts as **GOTV ("get out the vote")** or the **ground game**.[21] Most campaigns for Congress or the presidency use extensive door-to-door canvassing in which volunteers knock on doors and present their candidate's message to voters one at a time. Campaigns also commonly use phone banks, e-mail campaigns, and social media to reach out to potential supporters. To determine how best to contact these people and convince them to vote, both Republican and Democratic campaigns use sophisticated databases, combining voter registration data with demographics.[22] Sometimes these contacts are made through social media, but many campaigns still use volunteers to knock on doors and present their candidate's messages to voters one at a time.

GOTV ("get out the vote") or the **ground game**
A campaign's efforts to "get out the vote" or make sure its supporters vote on Election Day.

Debates Candidates often contrast their own records or positions with those of opposing candidates or make claims designed to lower voters' opinions of their opponents. Sometimes these interactions occur during a formal debate. Most congressional campaigns involve debates in front of an audience of likely voters, a group of reporters, or the editorial board of a local newspaper. Typically candidates take questions from reporters or a debate moderator, although sometimes candidates question each other or answer questions from the audience.

Presidential campaigns involve multiple debates during the primary and caucus season. Throughout the months before the first primaries and caucuses, each party's candidates gather for many single-party debates using a variety of formats. During the general election, the Republican and Democratic nominees meet for several debates. The number and format are negotiated between the campaigns and the Commission on Presidential Debates, a nonpartisan organization that organizes the debates.[23] The 2020 presidential campaign featured two debates between the presidential nominees and one between the vice-presidential nominees. The debates offer valuable free exposure: given a relatively uninterested electorate, candidates must present themselves in a way that captures voters' attention and gains their support.

Campaign Advertising: Getting the Word Out

One of the realities of modern American electoral campaigns is that they are, for the most part, conducted indirectly—through social media, through news coverage of events, and (most important) through paid campaign advertising. Candidates, party committees, and interest groups spend more than several billion dollars during each election cycle for federal office. Most of that money is spent on 30-second television spots. Such advertising is critical because, as we discussed in Chapter 6, candidates cannot assume that citizens will take the time to learn from other sources about the candidates, their qualifications, and their issue positions.

Campaign advertising has evolved considerably over the last generation.[24] During the early years of television, many campaign ads consisted of speeches by candidates or endorsements from supporters and they ran several minutes in length. Today, in contrast, campaign ads are short, feature arresting images, and often use photomontages and bold text to engage a distracted citizenry. Content varies depending on who is running the ads. Yet despite all the money and effort poured into campaign advertising, these ads must deliver a message that all viewers can understand without too much interpretation.

One critical question about campaign advertising is whether the ads work— whether they shape what people know or influence their voting decisions or other forms of participation. Some observers have complained that campaign ads (particularly negative ads) depress voter turnout and reinforce citizens' negative perceptions of government, although political science research has uncovered no evidence for either effect.[25]

Insofar as ads matter and Americans pay attention to politics, studies of campaign advertising suggest that Americans are reasonably thoughtful when assessing campaign ads. Evidence suggests that campaign advertising has several beneficial effects. Researchers have found that people who are exposed to campaign ads tend to be more interested in the campaign and know more about the candidates.[26] Moreover, many campaign ads highlight real differences between the candidates and the parties.[27] Even so, average citizens know that they cannot believe everything they see on television, so campaign advertising, if it does anything at all, captures their attention without necessarily changing their minds.[28] (See the What Do the Facts Say? feature on p. 265 for more on evaluating facts in the media.)

In the 2020 presidential race, many of the ads aired by the Trump campaign and Republican groups criticized Joe Biden for his son Hunter's business dealings in Ukraine. As you can see in this ad, these groups questioned whether the Bidens asked for money in return for political favors—a quid pro quo arrangement.

Do Maps Offer "Just the Facts"?

When reading media coverage of politics, it's important to consider the source—the author of the story. In many cases, stories that ostensibly offer "just the facts" are cherry-picking data to support a particular point of view. When a story is written by an overtly partisan individual or publication, a closer look often reveals that the story's facts have been misreported or interpreted in an incorrect or limited way.

One example is the "try to impeach this" map that was featured on Fox News host Sean Hannity's Web page and other conservative, pro-Trump media outlets in fall 2019 during the House impeachment hearings.[a] Counties where Trump received a majority of votes in 2016 were shown in red, while counties Hillary Clinton won were shown in blue. As you see, most of the country is red, with some blue counties on the coasts—supporting Hannity's argument that the Democratic move to impeach Trump amounted to undoing Trump's 2016 electoral victory.

Should we take this map as a serious, fair depiction of political reality? One reason to be suspicious is that Hannity makes no secret of his conservative ideology or the fact that his audience consists mostly of conservative Republicans. This is not to say that Hannity intentionally lies or misrepresents the facts, but simply to point out that his website is hardly the place to look for dispassionate analysis. In fact, the Fox TV network, which broadcasts Hannity's show, classifies it as opinion rather than news.

It also turns out that the map is both incorrect and misleading.[b] For one thing, it mistakenly classifies some counties in the middle of the country as red that should be blue. The bigger problem is that the red/blue classification doesn't consider population density—most of Trump's wins were in low-population rural counties, while Clinton won many high-population urban centers. Even though Trump won more counties than Clinton, Clinton received over 3 million more votes.

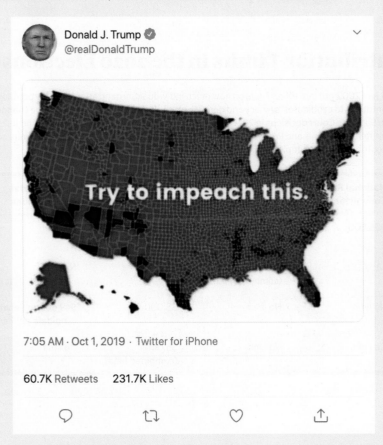

Donald J. Trump ✔
@realDonaldTrump

Try to impeach this.

7:05 AM · Oct 1, 2019 · Twitter for iPhone

60.7K Retweets   231.7K Likes

Campaign finance

"Campaign finance" refers to money collected for and spent on campaigns and elections by candidates, political parties, and other organizations and individuals. The **Federal Election Commission** is in charge of administering election laws, including the complex regulations pertaining to how campaigns can spend money. Changes in campaign finance rules, which were passed as the Bipartisan Campaign Reform Act (BCRA), took effect after the 2002 elections and have been modified by subsequent Supreme Court decisions—most notably *Citizens United v. Federal Election Commission* (2010) and *McCutcheon v. Federal Election Commission* (2014), which we describe later.

While campaign finance law is complex, most Americans believe the effects of campaign finance are simple: candidates cannot win without spending money, victory goes to the candidate with the larger budget, and, as a result, candidates listen to large donors and ignore average citizens. They also believe that elections cost too much. The reality is much more complex. Candidates need money to run effective campaigns (particularly to pay for campaign ads), but spending does not guarantee victory. And while candidates court large donors, they are even more obsessed with winning the support of ordinary citizens, because in the end, elections are about votes, not money.

Types of Contributions and Funding Organizations The limits on campaign contributions in the BCRA—also known as the McCain-Feingold Act—vary depending on whether contributions are made by an individual or a group and by the type of group, as Table 8.1 shows. These limits were modified in April 2014 by a 5-4 ruling in *McCutcheon v. Federal Election Commission*, in which the Supreme Court struck down limits on overall campaign contributions to candidates and PACs. A second Supreme

TABLE 8.1

Contribution Limits in the 2020 Elections

The BCRA of 2002 put into effect limits on how much individuals, organizations, and corporations could contribute to candidates' primary and general-election campaigns. The limits were changed based on Supreme Court decisions in 2010 and 2014. At present, although there are still limits on contributions that individuals and PACs can make to each individual candidate, there are no limits on total overall contributions to multiple candidates by individuals and PACs.

	Individual Candidates	National Party Committees	State, District, and Local Parties	PACs	Limit on Total Contributions
Individuals	$2,800	$35,500	$10,000 (combined limit)	$5,000	No limit
PACs	$5,000	$15,000	$5,000 (combined limit)	$5,000	No limit
National Party Committees	$5,000	No limit	No limit	$5,000	$49,600 to Senate candidate per campaign
State, District, and Local Party Committees	$5,000 (combined limit)	No limit	No limit	$5,000 (combined limit)	No limit

Source: Federal Election Commission, "Contribution Limits for 2019–2020," www.fec.gov/resources/cms-content/documents/contribution_limits_chart_2019-2020.pdf (accessed 3/1/20).

Court decision, *Citizens United v. Federal Election Commission*, also eliminated restrictions on campaign advertising by corporations, organizations, and labor unions within 30 days of a primary or 60 days of a general election, which had led to large increases in spending by these groups.

Current law distinguishes between independent expenditures, in which a party or group spends money to advocate for a candidate but the candidate or the campaign does not control, direct, or approve the activity, and coordinated expenditures, in which the candidate has some control. Independent expenditures are not limited, but coordinated expenditures are. For example, in Senate races, there is a cap on coordinated expenditures by political parties, ranging from several hundred thousand dollars in small states like Delaware to several million dollars in California.

A second distinction in campaign finance laws is between **hard money**, meaning contributions to a candidate, party organization, or other group that are intended to help elect or defeat a specific candidate, and **soft money**, meaning funds that are used for other activities and are not subject to the limits imposed on hard money. Groups defined by IRS regulations as 527 organizations, for example, can raise unlimited soft money from individuals or corporations for voter mobilization and for issue advocacy, but these expenditures must not be coordinated with a candidate or a party. Ads by 527s cannot advocate the election or defeat of a particular candidate or political party.[29] Another type of organization, again described using the IRS code, is the 501(c)(4), which often collects and spends soft money. The principal difference between 527s and 501(c)(4)s is that the latter type of organization does not have to disclose the names of its contributors.

A third type of organization, the political action committees (PAC), is a group that aims to elect or defeat particular candidates or a particular political party. A company or an organization can form a PAC and solicit contributions from employees or group members. As Table 8.1 shows, the amount PACs can give to each candidate in an election is limited, but these limits pertain only to hard money. PACs can also form 527s, which can then accept unlimited amounts of soft money. So-called Super PACs are PACs that do not donate to candidates but use soft money to make unlimited independent expenditures in campaigns.

As discussed in Chapter 7, political party committees are entities within the Republican and Democratic parties. Both major parties have a national committee and a campaign committee in each house of Congress. Party committees are limited in the amount of hard money they can give to any given candidate's campaign and in the amount they can spend on behalf of the candidate as a coordinated expenditure. However, a party committee (and, after *Citizens United*, organizations, corporations, and labor unions) can spend an unlimited amount in independent expenditures to elect a candidate or candidates.

Current law gives presidential candidates the ability to receive federal campaign funds for the primary and general-election campaign (in the primary, these are matching funds; in the general election, they are a block grant). These federal funds are generated, in part, by money that taxpayers voluntarily allocate out of their federal taxes by checking off a box on their tax return form. However, in order to accept federal funds, presidential candidates must abide by overall spending limits (and, during the nomination process, by state-by-state spending caps). During the last two presidential campaigns, all the major candidates decided against accepting these funds during the nomination and general-election campaign, which meant that they were not bound by the spending caps (although individual contributors were still limited to the amounts shown in Table 8.1).

These complex campaign finance regulations reflect two simple truths. First, any limits on campaign activities involve balancing the right to free speech about candidates and issues with the idea that rich people or well-funded

Political action committees spend millions on campaign advertising. Often, their ads are highly negative. This one attacks Donald Trump for being homophobic in his rhetoric.

TABLE
8.2

Candidate, Party, and Interest-Group Election Fund-Raising, 2018–2020

Candidates and political parties raise and spend a great deal of money in their campaigns. Do these numbers help explain the high reelection rates for members of Congress?

Source: Calculated by the authors from data at www.opensecrets.org (accessed 11/11/20).

	2018	2020
Presidential Candidates		
Republican	—	$595,630,157
Democrat	—	$937,673,077
Congressional Candidates		
House incumbents	$711,117,909	$1,007,981,450
House challengers	$438,927,947	$427,837,316
House open-seat candidates	$384,890,754	$274,002,516
Senate incumbents	$539,389,767	$627,228,374
Senate challengers	$350,187,926	$765,656,874
Senate open-seat candidates	$82,890,927	$80,371,448
Political Parties		
Republicans	$859,438,792	$2,303,011,274
Democrats	$802,172,215	$1,022,879,060
Independent Expenditures	$1,110,325,920	$2,973,234,720
Totals	$5,279,342,217	$11,015,506,266

organizations should not be allowed to dominate what voters hear during the campaign. Second, an enormous amount of money is spent on American elections (see Table 8.2).

The Effects of Money in Politics The raw data on campaign finance do not always tell the whole story. For example, while total spending is often quite high, it is important to remember that a large percentage of campaign expenditures are for advertising. A 30-second ad on a major network can cost tens or hundreds of thousands of dollars.[30] Given that even House campaigns may run hundreds of ads and presidential campaigns run tens of thousands, it is easy to see why campaign costs pile up so quickly.

The principal concern about all this campaign cash is that the amount of money spent on a candidate's campaign might matter more than the candidate's qualifications or issue positions. That is, candidates—in particular, wealthy ones who can self-fund their campaigns—could get elected regardless of how good a job they would do, simply because they have more money than competing candidates to pay for ads, polls, a large staff, and mobilization efforts. Another concern is that individuals and organizations or corporations that can afford to make large contributions (or fund their own electioneering efforts) might be able to dictate election outcomes or, by funding certain candidates' campaigns, garner disproportionate influence over the subsequent behavior of elected officials (see the Take a Stand feature).

However, there is little evidence that campaign contributions alter legislators' behavior or that contributors are rewarded with votes supporting their causes or favorable policies.[31] On the other hand, contributions may help with access, getting

Is There Too Much Money in Politics?

Campaign finance regulations place restrictions on what Americans can do to influence election outcomes—but should they? Suppose you are a wealthy individual who wants to help elected candidates who agree with your worldview. Under current law, you can make relatively small direct contributions to these candidates, but you can also form one of several types of organizations that can spend unlimited money to run campaign ads, or you can donate to an existing organization that will do the same thing. Clearly, having money gives you options for participation in American elections that are not open to the average citizen. (This is the chief criticism of the *Citizens United* decision that struck down limits on independent spending.) Is that a good thing?

It's a free country, and spending money on politics is part of that freedom. Limits on campaign spending conflict with fundamental tenets of American democracy. The Bill of Rights states that Congress cannot abridge "freedom of speech, or of the press; or the right of the people peaceably to assemble, and to petition the Government for a redress of grievances." One interpretation of the First Amendment that has shaped recent Supreme Court decisions on campaign finance is that people should be free to spend whatever they want on contesting elections—excluding bribes, threats, and other illegal actions, of course.

Another argument for eliminating limits on political activities is that with one exception—donations to 501(c)(4) organizations—donors and political activists are required to file quarterly reports on their campaign activities. Therefore, other activists and even ordinary citizens would quickly learn of any large-scale attempts to manipulate election outcomes and could decide to work for the other side or simply vote against a big donor's preferred candidates.

And ultimately, given that campaign spending is no guarantee of electoral success, it is not clear that eliminating spending limits would give big donors control over election outcomes.

Campaign contributions need to be constrained. Even if there's no evidence that money buys elections, there is also no guarantee that under the right circumstances a big donation or ad campaign would not make the difference for one or more candidates. Because money for ads is a necessary component of a political campaign, the possibility remains that a rich donor could change election outcomes by giving large sums to challengers in congressional elections. And in close races, giving a candidate extra funds to increase his or her GOTV efforts or to run additional campaign ads might be enough to change the outcome.

With this possibility in mind, it makes sense to place broad limits on campaign contributions and independent expenditures to level the playing field between ordinary citizens and political activists with deep pockets. The fact that someone is rich shouldn't give him or her additional ways to influence election outcomes.

 Does money equal speech or should campaign contributions be limited?

Moreover, while it is true that limiting campaign activities requires imposing limits on speech rights, limitations on civil liberties are nothing new. All the individual rights set out in the Bill of Rights are limited in one way or the other. Even freedom of speech is limited in areas such as hate speech and statements that pose a clear and present danger. Imposing limits on campaign activities could be justified on the grounds that maintaining free and fair elections is important enough to justify a modest limitation on what individuals and organizations can do to influence election outcomes.

Does the risk of allowing rich donors disproportionate power over elections outweigh the dangers associated with restricting their speech rights?

take a stand

1. Limits on individual campaign contributions guard against allowing wealthy people to dominate elections. What are some of the possible drawbacks of such regulations?

2. Under current law, corporations and unions (not just individuals) are allowed unlimited political expenditures as long as they are independent of a candidate's campaign organization. Why do you think independent expenditures are less regulated than direct contributions to campaigns?

the donor an appointment to present arguments to a politician or his or her staff.[32] But people and organizations who contribute are already friendly with the politicians they support, so the politicians would likely hear their arguments in any case.

It's also clear that having a lot of campaign cash doesn't make a candidate into a winner—and that winners don't always outspend their opponents. The poster-children for this argument are billionaires Tom Steyer and Mike Bloomberg, who both ran for the Democratic presidential nomination in 2020. Both candidates spent millions on their campaigns, running thousands of ads, opening field offices, and hiring large staffs. Even so, both failed to attract much support. And in the 2016 general election, Hillary Clinton's campaign outspent Trump's by nearly $200 million. The Democratic Party and allied outside groups also outspent the Republican Party and its groups by a similar amount. Even so, Trump won. Of course, Trump entered the campaign with high levels of name recognition and his campaign message resonated with Republican primary voters. But that is exactly the point: victories aren't bought with campaign cash. Candidates need a base level of funding to hire staff, travel, and run some campaign ads. Beyond that point, success is a function of what candidates say and do, not the dollar amount of contributions they receive or the number of ads run on their behalf.[33]

"Why Should I Care?"

When you follow the news about political campaigns, pay attention to the money candidates raise (and spend), where they campaign (and to whom they appeal), the tone and message of their campaigns, and larger fundamentals, such as the strength of the economy. These factors can provide strong clues about who is likely to win (or lose). Remember, though, that politicians don't win elections just by spending a lot of money. Sometimes candidates win despite lower budgets. The other factors listed here and examined in this chapter often have stronger effects on the outcome than money alone.

★

EXPLAIN THE KEY FACTORS THAT INFLUENCE VOTERS' CHOICES

How do voters decide?

All the electoral activities we have considered so far are directed at citizens: making sure they are registered to vote, influencing their voting decisions, and getting them to the polls. Now we examine how citizens respond to these influences. The first things to understand are that only a minority of citizens report high levels of interest in campaigns, many people know little about the candidates or the issues, and many people do not vote.[34]

Who votes, and why?

Politics is everywhere, but getting involved is your choice. Voting and other forms of political participation are optional. Even a strong preference between two candidates may not drive citizens to the polls. They may not be motivated to vote because each person's vote is just one of many.[35] And it's true that the only time a vote "counts," in the sense that it changes the outcome, is when the other votes are split evenly so that one vote breaks the tie. Moreover, voting involves costs. Even if citizens don't learn about the candidates but want to vote anyway, they still have to get to the polls on Election Day. Thus, the **paradox of voting** is this: Why does anyone vote, given that voting is costly and the chances of affecting the outcome are small?

paradox of voting
The question of why citizens vote even though their individual votes stand little chance of changing the election outcome.

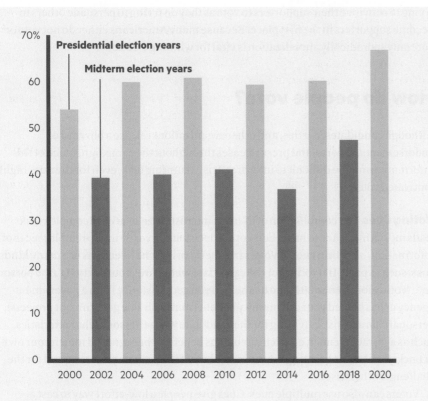

**FIGURE
8.2**

Turnout in Presidential and Midterm Elections, 2000–2020

The figure shows how turnout of registered voters varies both over time and between presidential and midterm elections. Why don't more people vote in midterm election years? Why don't more people vote in any given year?

Source: United States Election Project, www.electproject.org (accessed 11/9/20).

Figure 8.2 shows that among Americans the percentage of registered voters who actually voted in recent presidential elections has been around 60 percent, although actual turnout (votes as a percentage of the total adult population) has been closer to 50 percent.[36] As the figure shows, turnout is significantly higher in presidential elections than in midterm elections. Turnout is even lower in primaries and caucuses.

In the main, turnout is higher for Whites than for non-Whites (African Americans were an exception in 2008 and 2012, when Barack Obama was on the ballot), for older Americans than for younger Americans, and for college graduates than for people with a high school education or less. Men and women, however, say they vote at roughly the same rate. Many factors explain variation in turnout. Turnout is also affected by structural factors, such as state laws that prohibit convicted felons from voting, laws that require citizens to be registered to vote a set number of days before an election, variation in early-voting and voting-by-mail laws, laws requiring a photo ID to vote, and laws that make it easier or harder to obtain an absentee ballot.

However, turnout is far below 100 percent, even in areas of the country where all of these factors are set to make it easy for people to vote. Analysis shows that turnout is much higher among people who consider going to the polls an obligation of citizenship, feel guilty when they do not vote, or think that the election matters. Turnout is much lower among those who are angry with the government, think that government actions do not affect them, or think that voting will have no impact on government policy.[37]

These findings demonstrate the importance of mobilization in elections. As discussed earlier, many candidates for political office spend at least as much time

DID YOU KNOW?

Voter turnout was

66.5%

for African Americans in the 2020 presidential election.
Source: Calculated by the authors from exit polls and historical data

trying to convince their supporters to vote as they do trying to persuade others to become supporters in the first place. Because many Americans either do not vote or vote only sporadically, mobilization is vital for winning elections.

How do people vote?

Although candidates, parties, and other organizations release a blizzard of endorsements, reports, and press releases throughout the campaign, much of this information may be difficult to interpret. It is a daunting task, even for the rare, highly motivated voter.

Voting Cues The combination of a lack of interest and a relatively complex task leads most Americans to base their voting decisions on easily interpretable pieces of information, or **voting cues**.[38] Voters in American national elections use many kinds of cues, such as party ID (voting for the candidate who shares your party ID), the personal vote (voting for a candidate who has helped you get assistance from a government agency or has helped your community benefit from desirable government projects), personal characteristics (voting for the candidate whose personal characteristics such as age, race, gender, ethnicity, religious beliefs, or background match your own), or pocketbook voting (voting for the incumbent if the economy is strong and for the challenger otherwise).

Voters can also use multiple cues. Cues give people a low-effort way to cast a vote that, more likely than not, is consistent with the voter's true preference among candidates.[39] Studies have found that citizens who use cues and are politically well informed are more likely to cast a reasonable vote (one that's consistent with their underlying policy preferences relative to candidates' positions) than those who use cues but are otherwise relatively politically ignorant. In essence, knowing something about the candidates and the issues at stake in an election helps people select the right cue on which to base their vote.[40]

All the strategies identified here for making voting decisions are used to some extent in every election. In normal elections, when congressional reelection rates are high

voting cues
Pieces of information about a candidate that are readily available, easy to interpret, and lead a citizen to decide to vote for a particular candidate.

Are you better off than you were four years ago?

—**Ronald Reagan,** running for president against incumbent Jimmy Carter

After registering and informing themselves about the election, voters have to take the time to go to the polls and possibly wait in line. Voting is costly in terms of time and effort. In 2020, during the coronavirus pandemic, it became a calculated health risk too, as people struggled to socially distance while waiting.

and the seat shift between the parties is small, voters generally use cues that focus on the candidates themselves—such as incumbency, partisanship, a personal connection to a candidate, or the candidate's personal characteristics or past performance. This behavior is consistent with the saying that "all politics is local": many congressional elections are independent, local contests in which a candidate's chances of winning depend on what voters think of the candidate in particular—not the president, Congress, or national issues. It also explains why electoral **coattails** are typically very weak in American elections and why so many Americans cast **split tickets** rather than **straight tickets**. In the main, voting decisions in presidential and congressional elections are made independently of each other.

Voting in wave elections

"Wave" elections generally occur when a large number of voters vote against incumbents because of poor economic conditions, political scandal, or a costly, unpopular war. In 2010, many Americans were concerned about the state of the economy, the size of corporate bailouts, the apparent ineffectiveness of economic stimulus legislation, and the enactment of health care reform, and they blamed the party in power (Democrats) for all of these outcomes. As a result, a significant percentage of Americans voted against Democratic congressional candidates, either as a protest vote, because they disapproved of their performance, or as an effort to put different individuals in charge in the hope that new members would bring about improved conditions. In contrast, 2020 was not a wave election: while Democrats won the presidency, Republicans captured House seats and prevented Democrats from gaining majority control of the Senate.

coattails
The ability of a popular president to generate additional support for candidates affiliated with his or her party. Coattails are weak or nonexistent in most American elections.

split ticket
A ballot on which a voter selects candidates from more than one political party.

straight ticket
A ballot on which a voter selects candidates from only one political party.

During campaigns, candidates often seek to strengthen the perception that they share (or at least are sympathetic to) average Americans' beliefs and interests. Here, Senator Kamala Harris (D-CA, center), who became the vice presidential candidate on the Democratic ticket, meets with constituents at the Martin Luther King Jr. Kingdom Day Parade in Los Angeles.

FIGURE 8.3

Percentage of House Incumbents Reelected, 2000–2020

The figure shows that, despite public dissatisfaction with Congress, incumbents still tend to be reelected in their respective districts. According to the chart, which congressional elections were wave elections? Which were normal elections?

Source: Calculated by the authors from election results.

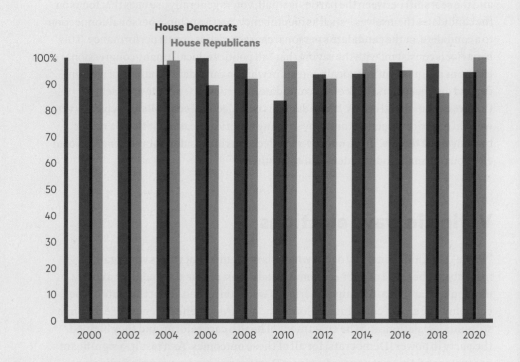

Even in wave elections, reelection rates for members of Congress (the percentage of incumbents who successfully run for reelection) are generally high, as Figure 8.3 shows for the House of Representatives over the last generation. During that period, neither party had a House reelection rate of less than 80 percent; even in 2006, when 100 percent of Democratic House incumbents running for reelection were reelected, the reelection rate for House Republican incumbents was almost 90 percent.

Reelection rates for members of Congress are so high because senators and representatives work to insulate themselves from electoral challenges through tactics we discuss in this chapter and will discuss further in Chapter 10. Even so, congressional incumbents are not necessarily safe from electoral defeat. Rather, their high reelection rates result from the actions they take every day, which are calculated to win favor with their constituents. In normal elections, these strategies are generally enough to ensure reelection. In nationalized elections, however, they are not enough to guarantee reelection for some legislators from the disadvantaged party, such as Democrats in 2010.

"Why Should I Care?"

After each election, people look at the results and try to figure out what the election was about—why some candidates won and others lost. Before each election, would-be candidates wonder whether this is "the year" to run for office (you may be one of these candidates someday). The most important thing to understand is that there are no easy explanations and no guarantees. The problem is not that voters are fickle or clueless or that the rules are too complex. Rather, elections boil down to voters and the many different ways they decide how to vote. Knowing what is likely to influence voters can help you make predictions about who will win elections and thus what policies and issues government will tackle.

Understanding the 2018 and 2020 elections

In recent years, every election has been described as "the most important election in American history." And in truth, elections always matter because they determine who exercises power in Washington—who sets government policy. During the 2016 campaign, for example, it seemed likely that America's next president would appoint several Supreme Court justices, leading to significant policy changes on issues like abortion and affirmative action. Republican control of the presidency would make it easier to change President Obama's health care and financial reforms, as well as his executive orders. As we discuss throughout this book, the election of Donald Trump in 2016 has brought many of these outcomes to pass.

At one level, the essential question in 2020 was whether voters would support the Trump-Republican policy agenda of tax cuts, reductions in domestic spending and increases in military spending, loosening of business and environmental regulations, reestablishment of tariffs, further restrictions on immigration, and selection of conservatives to the federal judiciary. All of these issues were overshadowed by the debate over how to address the ongoing COVID-19 pandemic and its damage to America's economy and society, and who to blame for missteps in federal policy.

In political terms, the 2020 elections were scrutinized to see if the patterns seen in the 2018 elections would prove lasting or transitory. Would Democrats retain gains in rural and suburban areas, and among Republicans disenchanted with President Trump? Would the gender gap widen or narrow? Would minority turnout, which dropped in 2016 and bounced back somewhat in 2018, increase to earlier levels or grow even more, buoyed by nationwide protests demanding systemic changes in government and policing after the killing of George Floyd? How would the pandemic that still threatened the country impact voter turnout rates, especially for those groups particularly at risk for COVID-19—including the elderly, who are typically one of the most reliable voting blocs? The answers would determine which party held majorities in the House and Senate, and thereby shape the trajectory of government policy over the next two years.

The path to 2020: the 2018 elections

The 2018 elections involved campaigns for all 435 seats in the House of Representatives, as well as 35 Senate elections. At first glance, electoral forces favored Republicans in 2018, with a strong economy and no major international conflicts. However, sustained partisan polarization meant that economic factors were relatively less important than in previous elections. For many Americans, vote decisions were driven by party identification and their approval or disapproval of President Trump's performance in office.

The most important structural feature of 2018 was the partisan division of Senate seats: of the 35 seats contested, Democrats controlled 26 and the Republicans only 9. Moreover, of the dozen or so seats that were truly in play, 10 were Democratic, many of them in strongly Republican states such as North Dakota. Because Democrats had to divide campaign resources among a much larger number of seats than Republicans did, the odds favored Republican rather than Democratic gains.

In contrast, Democrats had notable opportunities in House contests. Democrats needed 23 seats to regain majority control—a number smaller than the average number of seats (about 30) gained by the party out of power in midterm House elections. Moreover, an abnormally high number of Republican incumbents retired rather than pursue another term. Some left because the party's rules forced them to step down from committee chairs, some departed to pursue other offices, some retired because of scandals, and some left because they feared losing a primary or general election. These retirements raised Democratic hopes for gains in Republican-held suburban districts.

A final fundamental factor was a Democratic advantage in enthusiasm—national polls consistently showed higher levels of interest among Democrats compared to Republicans, as well as a Democratic advantage in polls asking which party respondents would like to control Congress.

The Campaign The early months of the election cycle set the tone for the entire campaign. In House campaigns, Democrats fielded many well-funded, politically experienced candidates, while Republicans struggled to find good replacements for retiring incumbents or as challengers against Democrats. And while Senate Republicans reinforced their structural advantage by nominating a slate of well-qualified candidates (including several House members and governors), Democratic incumbents such as Jon Tester (D-MT) and Joe Manchin (D-WV) ran effective campaigns that highlighted their attention to local concerns and willingness to vote with President Trump on issues vital to their states. Democrats also outraised their Republican opponents in many races. In the closing weeks of the campaign, most national-level predictions were close to expectations at the beginning of the election cycle: Democrats were likely to win a House majority, while Republicans would hold the Senate.

Within the parties, however, the campaign revealed important disagreements on policy. In several Democratic primaries, liberal challengers unseated long-time incumbent House members, including Joe Crowley (D-NY), who was chair of the Democratic Caucus. Many other Democratic challengers refused to commit to voting for Minority Leader Nancy Pelosi as Speaker if Democrats regained the majority. On the Republican side, several incumbents, including Senators Jeff Flake (R-AZ) and Bob Corker (R-TN), retired in the face of strong conservative opposition.

The Election During the final weeks of the campaign, polls revealed that many House and Senate seats were still in play, as President Trump also crisscrossed the country, holding rallies in strongly Republican areas. In the end, the 2018 election met expectations: Democrats gained a House majority by capturing Republican suburban districts and capitalizing on Republican open seats. In Senate elections, Democrats captured two seats (Nevada and Arizona) but lost other races, allowing Republicans to retain their Senate majority.

Exit polls that asked respondents about their vote in House elections showed that, for the most part, vote decisions reflected partisanship and opinions about President Trump. The 2018 results also showed a strong gender gap, with higher rates of Democratic voting among women, as well as a strong correlation of Democratic voting with race and with education. Moreover, voters in lower income brackets were much more likely to vote Democratic, while voters in higher income brackets showed similarly high rates of voting for Republicans (though interestingly, the gap between Democratic and Republican voters narrowed for those making over $100,000 per year).

The 2020 elections

The Nomination Process When Joe Biden entered the race for the Democratic presidential nomination in the summer of 2019, many people (and some political scientists) argued that he would have little chance of winning. Biden was a career politician who had held elected office for 47 years, running at a time when trust in government was near all-time lows. He had run two disorganized, unsuccessful presidential nomination campaigns. If elected, he would be 78 years old on Inauguration Day, making him the oldest person to begin a presidency by more than seven years.

In retrospect, however, Biden was a perfect fit for the political moment. His reputation as a centrist Democrat helped secure votes from moderate voters (especially White voters in the Midwest who were not college educated) who had defected to Trump in 2016. At the same time, his willingness to listen and respond to demands from liberal Democratic groups helped unify the party. Biden also had strong support from Black voters (a key Democratic constituency) in part because of his service as Barack Obama's vice president.

Biden faced strong opposition for the nomination from Senators Kamala Harris, Bernie Sanders, and Elizabeth Warren, as well as former mayor of South Bend, Indiana, Pete Buttigieg (the first openly gay candidate for a major-party presidential nomination), former New York City mayor (and billionaire) Michael Bloomberg, and a number of other candidates. While Biden did not do well in the early nomination contests, he scored a decisive win in the South Carolina primary in late February and won the most delegates in the Super Tuesday contests on March 3. By mid-March, as other candidates dropped out of the contest, Biden emerged as the clear favorite for the nomination. He spent the months until the Democratic National Convention in August 2020 building party unity. He further cemented his position by choosing Kamala Harris, a daughter of Indian and Jamaican immigrants, as his vice-presidential nominee.

The COVID-19 pandemic also worked against President Trump's reelection chances. A strong majority of Americans believed that Trump had mismanaged the pandemic, from failing to stockpile medical supplies or order early lockdowns, to discouraging mask wearing and frequently claiming that the end of the pandemic was almost in sight, only to be contradicted by increasing virus caseloads and fatalities.[41] These perceptions were reinforced after Trump, First Lady Melania Trump, and many senior aides caught the coronavirus after a public event in September 2020—an event at which most participants did not wear masks or socially distance. The shutdown of large parts of the economy as a result of the virus led to the loss of 22 million jobs from February through April; just over half of those jobs had been restored by Election Day, presenting an additional hurdle for Trump's reelection. While the pandemic and economic collapse did not cause a sharp decline in Trump's approval rating, they presented a strong, visible counterargument to his attempts to convince Americans that he deserved another term.

President Trump did not face significant opposition in the Republican nomination process. In fact, the entire process demonstrated his control over the party. He received a unanimous endorsement from the Republican National Committee in February 2020. Several states canceled their primaries and caucuses because Trump was the only candidate, and others used winner-take-all voting to ensure that only Trump would receive convention delegates. Finally, national committee members decided against producing a new party platform, instead endorsing the president and the platform adopted at the 2016 convention.

After promising to choose a woman as his running mate, Joe Biden selected California senator Kamala Harris as the Democratic vice-presidential nominee in the 2020 presidential election. With the success of the Biden-Harris ticket, Harris made history as the first woman, the first Black American, and the first South Asian American to serve as vice president of the United States.

The 2020 General Election Campaign The 2020 general election campaign played out in the middle of the COVID-19 pandemic. In addition to being a major campaign issue, the pandemic transformed the campaign itself. To minimize risks to campaign workers and voters, the Biden campaign did almost no door-to-door canvassing, although Democratic-affiliated groups and the Trump campaign had modest operations. Joe Biden campaigned largely from the basement of his home via Zoom, holding only small, socially distanced events. The Trump campaign relied on large rallies as in 2016. While the Trump campaign began the nomination campaign with a significant financial advantage, it spent much of this cushion on early ads and field offices, forcing it to curb advertising during the general election campaign. In contrast, the Biden campaign raised unprecedented amounts of funds, allowing it to dominate the airwaves during the last few months of the election.

The campaign revolved around two sets of issues. The first involved the candidates themselves. Trump claimed that Biden was a moderate in name only, or that he would defer to the more liberal Harris. On this point, Biden's extensive career in office gave him an effective counter, as it demonstrated his relatively moderate leanings. Trump also argued that Biden lacked the energy and the mental acuity to serve as president, calling him "Sleepy Joe." Here again, Biden's campaign performance, including two national debates, effectively countered these attacks. At the same time, Trump was himself an issue. After four years of outrageous tweets, threats, and blustering against political opponents, and his apparent lack of interest in the details of governing (as exemplified by his perceived mismanagement of the COVID-19 pandemic), Trump's approval ratings were stuck in the low 40s.

The second set of campaign issues reflected the enduring split between the parties. In essence, Trump promised to continue tax cuts, limits on immigration, nominations of conservative judges, and rollbacks of government regulations. The Biden-Harris campaign promised to expand the size and scope of government, including new health care programs, more efforts to combat climate change, fewer limits on immigration (and a path to citizenship for undocumented individuals), and new efforts to limit police brutality against minority citizens.

Because COVID-19 had reduced the amount of campaigning by both candidates and generated uncertainty about turnout, both sides focused on the potential for an "October surprise"—an event that would cause citizens to reconsider their judgments about the candidates. The Trump campaign held high hopes for the first televised debate, believing that Trump could demonstrate that Biden was not up to the job. However, Trump's constant interruptions, muttered asides, and abrupt attacks on Biden only reinforced existing impressions of both candidates. Trump moderated his behavior in the second (and final) debate but was unable to make a convincing attack on Biden or his record. Late in October, the *New York Post* ran a story about a laptop owned by Biden's son Hunter that allegedly contained compromising e-mails. This story collapsed after a few days when it became clear that Trump supporters (including Trump's personal lawyer, former New York mayor Rudy Giuliani) had been involved in bringing the story to the *Post* and that there was no evidence that the laptop actually belonged to Hunter Biden.

The General Election Throughout the general election campaign, polls showed Biden with a significant national lead and smaller but consistent advantages in swing states. Biden's lead widened in early October, after Trump's poor performance in the first debate and his hospitalization for the coronavirus, then contracted slightly as the election approached. There was also uncertainty about who would actually cast votes, as most states expanded early voting and allowed no-excuse absentee (mail-in) voting in order to reduce the risks of holding an election during the pandemic. These concerns were magnified after President Trump repeatedly claimed during the campaign that mail-in voting would encourage fraud and urged his supporters to vote in person.

On Election Day, many observers were surprised by the strength of Trump's support in early returns. He outperformed the polls in several swing states, including Florida and Iowa. Democrats were unsuccessful in capturing Texas, although Biden did much better than other recent Democratic nominees. However, it soon became apparent that Trump's support was overstated by early returns, as several key states had not yet counted the large number of mail-in ballots, which were expected to favor Biden.

In the days after the election, county election boards processed the remaining ballots, giving Biden victories in Wisconsin, Michigan, and Pennsylvania (the "blue wall" of Democratic midwestern support that Trump won in 2016) as well as victories in Nevada, Arizona, and Georgia. Turnout was almost 67 percent, the highest in 120 years.[42] Biden had strong support from young voters, women, and minorities. In all, Biden received 306 electoral votes (see Figure 8.4).

During the few days it took to determine a clear winner in Pennsylvania, Nevada, and Georgia, President Trump issued numerous tweets and campaign press releases claiming that the extended vote count was fraudulent and that local election officials were stealing the election from him. While Trump was right in claiming that a high percentage of mail-in ballots favored Joe Biden, there was no evidence of misconduct at any level.[43] Biden's strength in the mail-in vote reflected the fact that Trump had discouraged his supporters from voting in this way, and that many mail-in ballots came from urban counties where many voters supported Biden.

After the major networks declared Biden the winner, Trump refused to concede the election or call Biden to congratulate him, and his campaign pursued legal

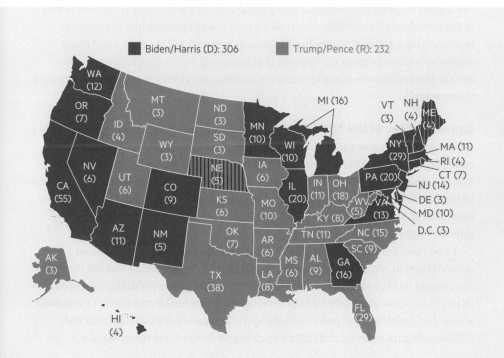

FIGURE 8.4

The 2020 Presidential Election: State by State

Note: 2020 Electoral map represents the authors' estimates as of 11/13/20. Two states split their electoral votes: in Maine, Trump received 1 vote and Biden 3; in Nebraska, Trump received 4 votes and Biden 1.

Source: Compiled by the authors.

The 2020 presidential race was called for Joe Biden by all the major media outlets on November 7, four days after Election Day. Biden and his running mate, Kamala Harris, addressed the nation that night from Biden's hometown of Wilmington, Delaware, vowing to serve all Americans and unite the country—strong promises given the ongoing conflicts in American politics.

challenges in some states. However, the courts did not sustain these claims, as the Trump campaign had no evidence to back them up. While some Republicans, including Senators Ted Cruz and Lindsey Graham, supported Trump's attacks, others, such as Senator Mitt Romney and former president George W. Bush, congratulated Biden and called for Trump to concede. What Trump faced was a reality we have noted throughout this chapter: American elections are decided by counting votes. There is no requirement that the loser concede, accept defeat, or literally do anything. Even for candidates who happen to be president, elections are out of their hands.

In congressional races, Democrats netted only one Senate seat, leaving them still short of majority control with two outstanding runoff elections in Georgia, and in the biggest surprise of the election, they lost about eight seats in the House. Here and in the presidential race, it is hard to read a strong policy mandate into the election results. Table 8.3 shows clear policy differences between Biden voters and Trump voters—but given Democrats' losses in the House and their failure to capture the Senate, it is unclear whether Biden can capitalize on his victory to pursue an aggressive policy agenda.

Consequences of the 2020 Election It is easy to imagine that Joe Biden's victory will lead to significant policy changes. Biden has reassembled the Democratic coalition that elected Barack Obama twice and regained control of the House of Representatives in 2018. Biden received millions more votes than Hillary Clinton did in 2016.[44] He leads a Democratic party that unified behind his candidacy, achieving record turnout despite the COVID-19 pandemic, including large numbers of new minority voters.

To be sure, Biden can accomplish a great deal using executive orders and personal action, such as rejoining the World Health Organization and the Paris Agreement on climate change, deprioritizing federal pursuit of undocumented individuals, increasing admissions of refugees, and rebuilding America's relations with other countries. But policies that require legislative action will occur only if Biden can gain votes from Senate Republicans. At the same time, Senate

TABLE 8.3

Exit Polls in the 2020 Elections

		Biden	Trump
Approval of President Trump	Approve (47%)	9%	90%
	Disapprove (51%)	96	3
Most important issue	Racial inequality (20%)	91	8
	Coronavirus pandemic (17%)	82	14
	Economy (35%)	17	82
	Health care (11%)	63	36
Gender	Male (47%)	48	49
	Female (53%)	56	43
Race	White (65%)	42	57
	Non-White (35%)	72	26
Education	College graduate (44%)	55	42
	Not college graduate (56%)	49	49
Partisanship	Democrats (37%)	94	6
	Republicans (35%)	6	93
	Independents (28%)	54	40

Source: 2020 CNN Exit Polls, www.cnn.com/election/2020/exit-polls/president/national-results (accessed 11/5/20).

Note: Data may not always add up to 100 percent due to rounding.

Republicans are unlikely to agree to institutional changes that would help Biden, such as eliminating the filibuster or increasing the size of the Supreme Court. There are also deep splits among Democratic officeholders over policy priorities, including hot-button issues of climate change and renewable energy, police reform, immigration, and health care.

Biden also inherits the COVID-19 pandemic, and much of his first few years in office will be focused on developing and deploying an effective vaccine and on returning the country to something approaching normal politics. Indeed, one of his first actions as president-elect was to appoint an informal task force to review current policies and make recommendations for new initiatives.

Finally, Biden leads a country that is as divided as ever. Biden's clear victory in the popular vote and the Electoral College is overshadowed by his razor-thin victories in Georgia, Michigan, Pennsylvania, and Wisconsin and the fact that over 70 million people voted for Donald Trump. Given that Trump vigorously contested the legitimacy of Biden's win, claiming without evidence that the election was stolen from him, many of his supporters are unlikely to ever accept Biden's presidency. Achieving policy victories under these conditions is certainly not guaranteed. What we know for sure is that politics matters, so the fight to win elections and shape government policy will continue unabated.

Unpacking the Conflict

Considering all that we've discussed in this chapter, let's apply what we know about how elections work to the example of Sara Gideon's loss in the 2020 Maine Senate election introduced at the beginning of this chapter. Ultimately, how meaningful was Susan Collins's victory in Maine in 2020—or Democrats' failure to win a Senate majority? What do election results tell us about why some candidates win and others lose? Why do these outcomes matter in American politics?

Candidates in American national elections compete for different offices using a variety of rules that determine who can run for office, who can vote, and how ballots are counted and winners determined. Election outcomes are shaped not only by who runs for office and how they campaign, who decides to vote, and how they decide whom to support, but also by the rules that govern electoral competition. By taking these factors into account for the 2020 election, we can explain why Susan Collins beat Sara Gideon, why Joe Biden defeated Donald Trump—and why Republicans maintained control of the Senate but failed to recapture the House.

It is easy to complain about American elections. Citizens are not experts on public policy. They often know little about the candidates running for office. Candidates sensationalize, attack, and dissemble rather than giving details about what they would do if elected. Even so, however candidates campaign and voters vote, elections matter: there are clear, systematic differences between Democratic and Republican candidates that translate into different government policies depending on who holds office. Government policy will be different as a result of Biden's victory in 2020, but complicated by division in Congress, with Republicans controlling the Senate and Democrats controlling the House.

Campaigns and election outcomes would surely be different if more Americans were well informed about candidates and campaign platforms, if turnout was higher, if campaigns always focused on important issues facing the country, and if attack ads never worked. Even so, despite all their limitations, elections are how we decide who gets to run the government. And as we have discussed, election outcomes are somewhat predictable—they are the product of national and local rules and regulations; the fundamentals of district factors and national forces; candidates' campaign strategies; and citizens' decisions about whether to vote and whom to vote for. The outcome of every election is the result of all these individual-level choices added together. In that sense, election outcomes reflect the preferences of the American people.

"What's Your Take?"

Do the campaigns that candidates run significantly affect election outcomes, or are the outcomes out of the candidates' control?

Are individual election outcomes representative of larger trends?

STUDY GUIDE

How do American elections work?

Present the major rules and procedures of American elections. (Pages 248–257)

Summary

Elections in America generally have two steps. Primary elections select candidates for each party, and general elections determine who wins the office. Some of the rules for presidential elections differ from those for other elections; notably, the Electoral College system determines the winner of the general election.

Key terms

incumbent (p. 248)

primary (p. 249)

open primary (p. 249)

semi-closed primary (p. 249)

closed primary (p. 249)

general election (p. 249)

plurality voting (p. 250)

majority voting (p. 250)

runoff election (p. 250)

caucus (p. 251)

proportional allocation (p. 252)

winner-take-all (p. 252)

popular vote (p. 253)

Electoral College (p. 253)

electoral votes (p. 253)

Practice Quiz Questions

1. **Runoff elections occur only in states that use _____.**

a   majority voting

b   primary elections

c   plurality voting

d   absentee ballots

e   proportional allocation

2. **The winner-take-all method of allocating most states' electoral votes results in candidates focusing on _____ states and _____ states.**

a   low-population; safe

b   high-population; safe

c   low-population; swing

d   high-population; swing

e   safe; swing

Electoral campaigns

Describe the features, strategies, and funding of campaigns for federal office. (Pages 258–270)

Summary

Party organizations and candidates begin preparing for the next election the day after the last election ends. They focus on fund-raising and determining which races are likely to be competitive. Incumbents work throughout the election cycle to maintain their good standing among the voters and secure their reelection bids. During a campaign, candidates work hard, particularly through the use of advertisements, to increase their name recognition and mobilize their supporters.

Key terms

election cycle (p. 258)

open seat (p. 260)

GOTV ("get out the vote") or the **ground game** (p. 263)

Federal Election Commission (p. 266)

hard money (p. 267)

soft money (p. 267)

Practice Quiz Questions

3. **An open-seat election is one in which _____.**

a   there is no challenger in the race

b   there is no incumbent in the race

c   an incumbent loses his or her seat due to redistricting

d   an incumbent faces a challenger in his or her own primary

e   an incumbent faces a challenger in the general election

4. **What effect does fund-raising have for incumbents?**

a   It ensures the potential for an aggressive campaign, but it has no effect on opposition.

b   It ensures the potential for an aggressive campaign, and it deters opposition.

c   It ensures the potential for an aggressive campaign, and it encourages opposition.

d   It has no effect on the potential for an aggressive campaign, but it does deter opposition.

e   It has no effect on the potential for an aggressive campaign, nor does it deter opposition.

5. **"GOTV" and "ground game" refer to a candidate's attempts to _____.**

a   boost name recognition

b   mobilize supporters

c   increase fund-raising

d   deter opposition

e   win endorsements

6. Research shows that modern campaign ads are likely to _____ .

a change voters' minds

b feature speeches by the candidate

c have beneficial effects, such as informing voters

d run several minutes in length

e increase turnout

7. What is soft money?

a money that can be given directly to a candidate

b money that is given by members of the opposing party

c money that can be spent to mobilize voters for a specific candidate

d money that candidates spend to boost the party's reputation

e money that is not tied to a specific candidate

How do voters decide?

Explain the key factors that influence voters' choices. (Pages 270–274)

Summary

Although politics is everywhere, ordinary voters don't pay much attention to politics. Turnout rates are modest, and people know relatively little about the candidates and their positions. While some voters are highly interested in politics and collect all the information they can about the candidates, most voters make their decision based on voting cues. Most elections are determined by local-level politics, but occasionally national issues come to the fore.

Key terms

paradox of voting (p. 270)   **split ticket** (p. 273)

voting cues (p. 272)   **straight ticket** (p. 273)

coattails (p. 273)

Practice Quiz Questions

8. What is the paradox of voting?

a Voting is costly, and the chances of affecting the election outcome are small.

b Voting is costly, and approval for government is high.

c Voting is easy, and the chances of affecting the election outcome are large.

d Voting is easy, but informing yourself about the candidates takes time.

e Approval for government is low, but voter turnout rates are high.

9. Voters who rely on voting cues to determine their voting choice are _____ .

a likely to cast a reasonable vote, regardless of their information level

b unlikely to cast a reasonable vote, regardless of their information level

c likely to cast a reasonable vote, and more so if they are informed

d unlikely to cast a reasonable vote, and less so if they are informed

e neither more nor less likely to cast a reasonable vote than voters who ignore cues

10. Weak coattails and split tickets serve as indicators that _____ .

a most voters don't know anything about the candidates

b most elections are determined by local issues

c most elections are determined by national issues

d most voters use political parties as their dominant voting cue

e most voters use incumbency as their dominant voting cue

Understanding the 2018 and 2020 elections

Analyze the issues and outcomes in the 2018 and 2020 elections. (Pages 275–281)

Summary

The 2020 campaign played out amidst the COVID-19 pandemic and revolved around two sets of issues: the first involved the candidates themselves and the second reflected the enduring split between the parties. Trump promised to continue tax cuts, limits on immigration, nomination of conservative judges, and rollbacks of government regulations. The Biden-Harris campaign promised new health care programs, more policies to combat climate change, fewer limits on immigration, and new efforts to reduce police brutality against minority citizens.

Practice Quiz Questions

11. How did the electoral map favor Republican Senate candidates in 2018?

a Democratic efforts at redistricting gave the Democrats a sharp advantage in Senate contests.

b Economic growth was uneven across the states, particularly in Senate seats controlled by the Democrats.

c Democrats had to defend a disproportionate number of Senate seats, and many of these seats were in states where Republicans outnumbered Democrats.

d Independent candidates drew votes away from Democratic candidates.

e Republican candidates were more likely to lose in states where a majority of voters supported Donald Trump.

12. What is one likely challenge that the Biden administration will face?

a   rejoining the Paris Agreement on climate change

b   garnering policy support from Senate Republicans

c   increasing admissions of refugees

d   garnering policy support from House Democrats

e   rebuilding foreign relations with other countries

13. Which of the following is an accurate conclusion about the 2020 elections?

a   The COVID-19 pandemic caused the lowest voter turnout in the last 50 years.

b   Democrats performed better than expected in Senate races.

c   Despite claims, there was no evidence of widespread voter fraud.

d   Republicans performed worse than expected in House races.

e   Donald Trump performed better with voters who chose to vote by mail.

Suggested Reading

Abramson, Paul, John Aldrich, and David Rohde. *Change and Continuity in the 2012 and 2014 Elections*. Washington, DC: CQ Press, 2015.

Bartels, Larry M., and Christopher H. Achen. *Democracy for Realists: Why Elections Do Not Produce Responsive Government*. Princeton, NJ: Princeton University Press, 2016.

Cramer, Richard Ben. *What It Takes: The Way to the White House*. New York: Vintage Books, 1993.

Fiorina, Morris P. *Retrospective Voting in American National Elections*. New Haven, CT: Yale University Press, 1981.

Grimmer, Justin, Sean J. Westwood, and Solomon Messing. *The Impression of Influence: Legislator Communication, Representation, and Democratic Accountability*. Princeton, NJ: Princeton University Press, 2015.

Halperin, Mark, and John Heilemann. *Double Down: Game Change 2012*. New York: Penguin Books, 2013.

Key, V. O. *The Responsible Electorate*. New York: Vintage Books, 1966.

Popkin, Samuel. *The Reasoning Voter*. Chicago: University of Chicago Press, 1991.

Sides, John, and Lynn Vavreck. *The Gamble: Choice and Chance in the 2012 Presidential Election*. Princeton, NJ: Princeton University Press, 2013.

9

Interest Groups

Do interest groups serve the needs of the many, or the privileged few?

» **"This provision isn't about coronavirus, working families or small businesses struggling to stay afloat. It is just more insider politics to get millions to those who have millions, especially real estate investors and hedge fund managers."[1]**
Representative Lloyd Doggett (D-TX)

« **"The attempt to paint this tax provision as a boon for real estate and hedge fund investors completely misses the mark.... This misleading talking point ignores the unimaginable economic losses that are painfully occurring across my state of Iowa and the rest of America."[2]**
Senator Chuck Grassley (R-IA)

When a staggering number of Americans lost their jobs in 2020 as the coronavirus pandemic crossed the United States, it was clear Congress needed to act. In quick succession, it passed four relief bills that pumped trillions of dollars into the economy. The largest of these, the Coronavirus Aid, Relief, and Economic Security (CARES) Act, provided $2.2 trillion for direct payments to individuals, forgivable loans to small businesses, and assistance to state and local governments and hospitals. There were huge logistical problems with quickly distributing that much money and there were some significant glitches: millions of people didn't receive their $1,200 checks for several months, and more than 200 large businesses engaged in the time-honored tradition of "feeding at the public trough" by taking billions of dollars that were intended for small businesses. Chastened by the public scrutiny and a stern warning from Treasury Secretary Steven Mnuchin that large companies would face "severe consequences" if they took money they weren't entitled to, dozens of businesses returned the taxpayers' money, including Potbelly, Shake Shack, Ruth's Chris Steak House, and the Los Angeles Lakers basketball team.[3]

While these problems made headlines, a much more significant misuse of taxpayers' funds initially slid through with little attention: a set of changes to the 2017 tax cuts,

Donald Trump signed the CARES Act into law on March 27, 2020. The historic $2.2 trillion bill was passed as a part of the emergency response to the 2020 COVID-19 pandemic.

CHAPTER GOALS

Define *interest groups* and describe the characteristics of different types of groups.
pages 288–296

Explore the ways interest groups try to influence government policies. pages 296–305

Evaluate interest group influence.
pages 305–309

which had been a key legislative success of the Trump administration and a fulfillment of a campaign promise to reduce the tax burden on businesses. These changes, when integrated into the coronavirus legislation, illustrate the power of interest groups in the political system. In the 2017 tax cut legislation, Congress placed income limits on some of the more generous tax cuts to reduce the loss of revenue, but in the CARES Act it repealed those limits, which could result in a staggering loss of $135 billion in tax revenue over the next 10 years. The details get a little complicated, which is probably why this didn't get as much attention. After all, it is easier for people to understand why the L.A. Lakers, one of the most highly valued teams in the world (at $3.7 billion), shouldn't get a $4.6 million loan that was intended for small businesses than it is to understand arcane details of tax policy.

We don't need to get into the details here to understand the broad issues at play.[4] These income limit rollbacks affect how business owners can use losses from their businesses to cancel out other nonbusiness income. Another provision rolls back the restrictions on how much debt some companies can deduct from their taxes. How did this happen? Well, large corporations had lobbied hard to change these restrictions since they were enacted in 2017, and in an example that illustrates the power of these corporations' lobbying efforts, Congress snuck the provisions into the massive bill.

Once these changes in the tax law came to light shortly after the CARES bill was signed, an analysis by the nonpartisan Joint Committee on Taxation revealed that 80 percent of the tax cuts included in the bill went to business owners making more than $1 million (because only couples with $500,000 of nonbusiness income benefited from the policy change). And 43,000 business owners received a tax cut of an average of $1.6 million each, which means they received more total dollars than the 47 *million* people earning less than $20,000, who got $1,200 each. The $135 billion for the tax credits is three times more than the CARES Act is spending on safety-net programs like food and housing aid ($42 billion) and is more than is being spent on hospitals and other public health services ($100 billion).[5] Perhaps the most outrageous part of the policy is that wealthy business owners can exploit losses unrelated to the pandemic because the law allows them to retroactively write off losses from 2018 and 2019, well before we even knew about the virus.

This chapter surveys the wide range of interest groups in American politics—from large, powerful groups such as the National Rifle Association (NRA) to small organizations that lobby on issues that concern only a few Americans. Our aim is to get to the bottom of examples in which the lobbyists lose and understand examples in which it seems like the lobbyists always win, as with the CARES Act tax cuts. Some people, such as Senator Chuck Grassley, argue that such policies are good for the overall economy and *are* in the public's interest. However, many others always root for lobbyists, with their perceived insider connections and undue influence, to lose their battles. Is it fair to characterize all interest groups as self-interested organizations that undermine the public good? Are interest groups really too-powerful manipulators of the American policy process?

DEFINE *INTEREST GROUPS* **AND DESCRIBE THE CHARACTERISTICS OF DIFFERENT TYPES OF GROUPS**

What are interest groups?

Interest groups are organizations that seek to influence government policy. Interest groups may represent very specific or more general interests and they use a variety of tactics, such as lobbying elected officials and bureaucrats, helping draft legislation, mobilizing members and the public to apply pressure on and work with legislators and government agencies, and helping to elect candidates who support the organizations' policy goals. **Lobbying** involves persuasion and monitoring policy development by using reports, protests, informal meetings, or other techniques to convince an elected official or bureaucrat to help enact a law, craft a regulation, or do something else that a group wants. In this way, interest groups serve as a **linkage institution** between the people and their elected representatives. The members of an interest group can be individual citizens, local governments, businesses, foundations or nonprofit organizations, churches, or virtually any other entity. An interest group's employees or members may lobby on the group's behalf, or a group may hire a lobbyist or lobbying firm to do the work for it. Nuts & Bolts 9.1 gives some examples of the types of interest groups found in contemporary American politics.

Single-issue groups, ideological groups, and protest movements form with the goal of influencing society and policy making. One such group is Public Citizen, which conducts research projects, lobbies legislators and bureaucrats, and tries to rally public opinion on a range of environmental, health, and energy issues. In other cases, lobbying is only one part of what an organization does. The NRA, for example, endorses candidates, contributes to campaigns, and lobbies elected officials, but it also runs gun safety classes, holds competitions, and sells gun accessories to its members. Interest group activity is almost hidden within other organizations. For example, most drivers

interest group
An organization of people who share common political interests and aim to influence public policy by electioneering and lobbying.

lobbying
Efforts to influence public policy through contact with public officials on behalf of an interest group.

linkage institutions
Institutions such as political parties, interest groups, the media, and elections that are channels through which individuals can communicate their preferences to policy makers.

NUTS & BOLTS 9.1

Types of Interest Groups

Scholars often divide interest groups into categories based on who their members are or the number or kinds of things they lobby for

- *Institutional interest groups* are formed by nonprofits such as universities, think tanks, or museums. For example, the Big Ten Academic Alliance is a group of universities that prepares research to help individual universities make the case for continued federal support.
- *Businesses* are for-profit enterprises that aim to influence policy in ways that will increase profits or satisfy other goals. Many corporations, such as Google, Exxon Mobil, Boeing, Facebook, Citibank, and Sallie Mae, have lobbying operations that petition government for contracts or favorable regulations of their firm or industry.
- *Trade or peak associations* are groups of businesses (often in the same industry) that band together to lobby for policies that benefit all of them. For example, the National Beer Wholesalers Association, a nationwide group of local businesses that buy beer from brewers and resell it to stores and restaurants, lobbies to require intermediaries between beer producers and the stores, bars, and restaurants that sell beer to consumers.

- *Professional associations* represent individuals who have a common interest in a profession; examples include the American Society of Civil Engineers, National Education Association, American Medical Association, and American Bar Association.
- *Labor organizations* lobby for regulations that make it easy for workers to form labor unions, as well as for a range of other policies. The largest of these is the American Federation of Labor and Congress of Industrial Organizations (AFL-CIO).
- *Citizen groups* range from those with mass membership (such as the Sierra Club) to those that have no members but claim to speak for particular segments of the population. One such group is the Family Research Council (FRC), which describes itself as "promoting the Judeo-Christian worldview as the basis for a just, free, and stable society." FRC Action (the lobbying arm of the organization) promotes a range of policies, from legislation that defines marriage as between a man and a woman to legislation that would eliminate estate taxes.

Source: Compiled by the authors.

"Why Should I Care?" Categorizing interest groups can help you see which groups are working for the collective interests and which groups are working for more particular or special interests. Which of the types above do you think would fall into each category?

know that AAA (formerly the American Automobile Association) provides emergency roadside service and maps, but many people are not aware that AAA is also an interest group that lobbies for policies such as limiting new drivers to daylight-only hours.

As these descriptions suggest, interest groups and lobbying are ubiquitous in American politics. You may think that you don't belong to a group that lobbies the federal government, but the odds are that you do.

Organizational structures

Interest groups differ in how they are organized—whether the group is one body or made up of many smaller, local groups. How a group is organized makes a difference for the kinds of lobbying tactics it can use, as well as how decisions are made about what to lobby for.

Centralized Groups or Confederations There are two main models of interest group structure. Most large, well-known organizations like the AARP and the NRA are **centralized groups**, which means the organization's leadership is concentrated in its headquarters. These national organizations typically have headquarters in Washington, D.C., field offices in large state capitals, and members nationwide. Their leaders determine the group's lobbying goals and tactics. The other structural model is a **confederation**, which comprises largely independent, local organizations. For example, the National Independent Automobile Dealers Association (NIADA) encompasses 50 state-level organizations that provide membership benefits to car dealers who join and that also raise much of the money that NIADA contributes to political candidates (several million dollars in recent elections).

Both organizational structures have advantages and disadvantages. A centralized organization controls all the group's resources and can deploy them efficiently, but it can be challenging for these groups to find out what their members want. In contrast, because confederations maintain independent chapters at the state and local levels, their national headquarters can easily learn what the members want simply by contacting the local groups. But this strength is related to a weakness: because state and local chapters mostly function independently of the national headquarters, confederated groups often experience conflict, as different local chapters disagree over what to lobby for and which candidates to support.

Mass Associations or Peak Associations Interest groups can be categorized in terms of the size of their membership and the members' role in the group's activities. **Mass associations**, with many dues-paying members, tend to be citizens' groups and labor organizations. One example is the Sierra Club, which has over 3 million members. Besides keeping its members informed about the implementation of environmental policy in Washington, D.C., the Sierra Club endorses judicial nominees and candidates for elected positions, files lawsuits to increase environmental protection on government projects, and works with members of Congress to develop legislative proposals. The group's members elect the organization's board of directors.

Yet not all mass associations give members a say in selecting their leaders or determining their mission. For example, the AARP claims to lobby for policies its members favor, but members actually have no control over which legislative causes the group chooses. Moreover, the AARP does not poll members to determine its issue positions, nor do members elect AARP leadership.

The members of **peak associations** are businesses or other organizations rather than individuals.[6] Individuals cannot join peak associations—they may work for

centralized groups
Interest groups that have a headquarters, usually in Washington, D.C., as well as members and field offices throughout the country. In general, these groups' lobbying decisions are made at headquarters by the group leaders.

confederations
Interest groups made up of several independent, local organizations that provide much of their funding and hold most of the power.

mass associations
Interest groups that have a large number of dues-paying individuals as members.

peak associations
Interest groups whose members are businesses or other organizations rather than individuals.

member companies or organizations, but they cannot become dues-paying members on their own. The Business–Industry Political Action Committee (BIPAC), an association of several hundred businesses and trade associations that aims to elect "pro-business individuals" to Congress, is a good example of a peak association.[7]

Membership: benefits and incentives

Attracting members is important for an interest group's success. Society is full of groups of like-minded people who do not organize to lobby or who choose to engage in **free riding** and thus enjoy the benefits of organizations without participating. Therefore, most organizations develop mechanisms to promote participation. These **selective incentives** fall into three categories: benefits from participation, coercion, and material goods.

Studies of political parties and interest groups find that some individuals volunteer out of a sense of duty or because they enjoy working together toward a common goal. These benefits of participation are called either **solidary benefits**, which come from working with like-minded people, or **purposive benefits**, which come from working to achieve a desired policy goal.[8] If most people were spurred to political action because of participation benefits, the free rider problem wouldn't exist.

A second mechanism is **coercion**, or required participation. Consider labor unions. They provide public goods to workers by negotiating with management on behalf of worker-members over pay issues and work requirements. In many cases, worker-members have to join the union: union shop laws require them to pay union dues as a condition of their employment.

Finally, **material benefits** (also called material incentives) are benefits given only to the members of a given interest group. Thus, for example, AAA members can call AAA at any time for emergency service when they have car trouble. AAA also provides its members with annotated maps and travel guides, discounts at hotels and restaurants, and other benefits. These services mask the interest group role of AAA. For example, its Foundation for Traffic Safety delivers research reports to legislators on topics ranging from lowering the blood alcohol level threshold that legally defines drunk driving to increasing the restrictions on driving by senior citizens.[9] It's unlikely that many AAA members—who join for the selective incentives—are aware of the organization's lobbying efforts. The incentives drive membership, which funds the organization's lobbying operation.

Resources and challenges

Interest groups use three key resources to support their lobbying efforts: people (the members), money, and expertise. The resources that a group has at its disposal significantly influence its available lobbying strategies. (We will examine some of these strategies in more detail in a later section.) Some large groups have sufficient funding and staff to pursue a wide range of strategies, whereas some smaller groups with fewer resources face more significant challenges when it comes to the lobbying options they have at their disposal.

A crucial resource for most interest groups is their membership. Group members can write to or meet with elected officials, travel to Washington for demonstrations, and even offer expertise or advice to the group's leaders. When the "members" of a group are corporations, as is the case with trade associations, CEOs and other corporate staff can help with the group's lobbying efforts.

free riding
Relying on others to contribute to a collective effort while failing to participate on one's own behalf, yet still benefiting from the group's successes.

selective incentives
Benefits that can motivate participation in a group effort because they are available only to those who participate, such as member services offered by interest groups.

solidary benefits
Satisfaction derived from the experience of working with like-minded people, even if the group's efforts do not achieve the desired impact.

purposive benefits
Satisfaction derived from the experience of working toward a desired policy goal, even if the goal is not achieved.

coercion
A method of eliminating nonparticipation or free riding by potential group members by requiring participation, as in many labor unions.

material benefits
Benefits that are provided to individuals for joining a group, such as a coffee mug or a T-shirt, that are distinct from the collective benefits provided by the group.

AAA (formerly the American Automobile Association) is a well-known provider of emergency road service, yet few people are aware of its role as an interest group that lobbies for a wide range of policy changes and builds awareness of key transportation issues.

Money is another important resource. Virtually everything interest groups do can be purchased as services: groups can spend money on hiring people to meet with elected officials and to fight for what they want in court. Money can also go toward campaign contributions or developing and running campaign ads. And, of course, money is necessary to fund interest groups' everyday operations. Well-funded interest groups and firms have a considerable advantage in the lobbying process. If they need an expert, a lobbyist, or a lawyer, they can hire one, or they can open a Washington office to increase contacts with legislators and bureaucrats. They can pay for campaign ads and make contributions to candidates and parties, while groups with less cash cannot use these strategies. Smaller firms might join a trade association to lobby for policies that help all of the association's members.

Expertise is a third type of group resource. It takes many forms. Groups can employ staff (or hire experts) to conduct research or develop policy proposals related to their interests. A firm's in-house lobbyists can provide information about how a change in government policy will affect the firm's profits and employment. Some lobbying firms (especially those that employ former members of Congress or congressional staff) may also have inside information on the kinds of policies that are likely to be enacted in the House or Senate. Interest groups with dues-paying members (such as the Sierra Club) can poll them to find out what they would like government to do. All of this information can be deployed to persuade elected officials or bureaucrats about the merits of a group's or a firm's demands (as well as the political consequences of inaction) and offer ready-made policy solutions to the problems the group has identified.

Staff

Interest group staff fall into two categories: experts on the group's main policy areas and people with useful government connections and knowledge of procedures. The first group includes scientists, engineers, and others with advanced degrees; the second primarily comprises people who have worked inside government as elected officials, bureaucrats, or legislative staff.[10] Sometimes these former members of government are also policy experts, but their unique contribution is their knowledge of how government works and their already-existing relationships with officeholders and other former coworkers in government.

The practice of moving from a government position to a job with an interest group or lobbying firm, or of transitioning from a lobbyist to an officeholder, is often called the **revolving door**.[11] For example, as of 2020, more than one half of the members of Congress who retired at the end of the 115th Congress and were employed had moved to lobbying jobs.[12] The percentages are similar for congressional staff and bureaucrats. Many observers view this dynamic as potentially sowing seeds of corruption; they fear that past government employees might capitalize on personal ties with their former colleagues to negotiate favorable deals for their interest groups—or that people working in government may give special treatment to a corporation or interest group that might hire them as a lobbyist in the future. These concerns have led to proposed restrictions on the revolving door, including banning former elected officials, staff, and bureaucrats from working as lobbyists for some time period after they have left government service, as well as banning former lobbyists in government positions from administering programs that they previously lobbied for.

revolving door
The movement of individuals from government positions to jobs with interest groups or lobbying firms, and vice versa.

The business of lobbying

Interest group lobbying is regulated. Lobbying firms must file quarterly reports identifying their clients, specifying how much each client paid, and the issues they lobbied on. Similarly, interest groups and corporations must file reports that list staff members who spent more than 20 percent of their time lobbying Congress and total expenditures to lobbying firms.[13] Data from these sources and others offer insight into the extent of lobbying in American politics.

Today lobbying involves billions of dollars a year. Figure 9.1 (top) presents annual lobbying expenditures for 2000 through 2019. As the figure shows, a total of $3.51 billion was spent on lobbying in 2019. The amount spent, as well as the number of groups lobbying government, increased significantly from 2000 to 2010 and has held steady since then.

Why are there so many interest groups and registered lobbyists, and why are their numbers increasing? Figure 9.1 (bottom) suggests that this proliferation is related to the large size and widespread influence of the federal government. Simply put, the federal government does so many things and spends so much money that many individuals, organizations, and corporations have strong incentives for lobbying: corporations may lobby for a government contract or for regulations that favor their business sector. Corporations may also lobby to prevent new regulations or reverse existing rules that hurt their profits: in the first two months of the Trump administration, Congress reversed 14 regulations that were passed at the end of Obama's presidency, and 100 environmental rules were overturned by 2020.[14] Energy companies lobbied hard on the Keystone XL pipeline, offshore drilling in the Atlantic and Arctic Oceans, and calculations of the social cost of carbon, and they won. The Environmental Protection Agency (EPA) also replaced the Obama-era emissions rules for power plants and vehicles, weakened protections for more than half the nation's wetlands, and eased restrictions on mercury emissions from power plants. While business dominates lobbying spending, individuals may lobby the government to place limits on what citizens can do or to relax restrictions on behavior—or to change corporate behavior. Trade unions and single-issue groups also spend millions of dollars on lobbying.

Expenditures on lobbying pay for many things. The largest expense is for salaries. For example, in 2018 the top 20 defense contractors hired 645 former senior government officials and legislative staff, top military leaders, and members of Congress; 90 percent of these former officials became registered lobbyists. Top-level officials don't come cheap.[15] Lobbyists also spend on publicity and outreach.

DID YOU KNOW?

446

former members of Congress had been registered lobbyists as of 2020 (and 356 were currently lobbyists).

Source: OpenSecrets.org

**FIGURE
9.1**

Growth in Spending on Lobbying and Total Federal Spending, 2000–2019

These data show that in recent years interest groups have spent several billion dollars lobbying the federal government. Does this amount seem surprisingly large or surprisingly small, given what lobbyists do and given the total federal outlays of money?

Total spending on lobbying (billions)

Total federal outlays (trillions)

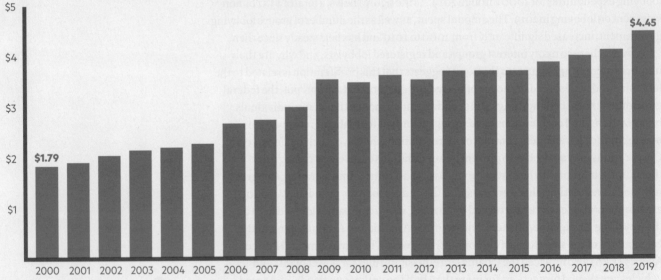

Sources: Lobbying data available at Center for Responsive Politics, "Lobbying Database," www.opensecrets.org/federal-lobbying; federal spending from Congressional Budget Office, Historical Budget Data, August 2019, www.cbo.gov/about/products/budget-economic-data#2 (both accessed 5/11/20).

For example, when Lockheed Martin Corporation lobbied Congress on contracts for the new F-35 fighter-attack plane for the military, Lockheed's lobbyists ran ads in newspapers in Washington, D.C., promoting its new warplane.[16] Lobbying firms also may also spend money to generate "grassroots" support by getting people to contact their members of Congress, as we discuss later in the chapter.

Figure 9.2 shows lobbying expenditures for several different firms and associations for two years (2018–2019). Three associations and one policy center were the highest spenders on lobbying during this time. It's not hard to imagine why each group devotes so much effort to lobbying: realtors, for example, might be concerned about maintaining government policies that make it almost essential to hire a realtor to help buy or sell a home. While the $121 million the National Association of Realtors spent on lobbying may sound like a lot, it really isn't that much.[17] After all, over a million people work in real estate, generating billions of dollars in profits every year. The surprise is that real estate brokers are willing to spend only a tiny fraction of their profits to keep their near monopoly in place. The same is true for the large firms listed in Figure 9.2. Apple, for example, is one of the largest firms in the United States, but it spends only about $7 million per year on lobbying ($14.1 million over two years). And only one of the influential interest groups in Figure 9.2 (the AARP) spends more than $10 million per year on lobbying. Clearly, the big spenders on lobbying are exceptions to the rule, and most interest groups and firms spend relatively little on lobbying.[18] For example, the group that sends a turkey to the White House for a ceremonial pardon every year at Thanksgiving, the National Turkey Federation, spends $140,000 a year to lobby the federal government on a relatively small range of issues. Many other groups spend even less, barely scraping together enough cash to send someone to plead their case in Washington. In fact, a few groups account for a substantial fraction of total lobbying expenditures.

DID YOU KNOW?

38%

of total lobbying expenditures are made by the top 100 interest groups.

Source: OpenSecrets.org

FIGURE 9.2

Variation in Lobbying Expenditures, 2018–2019

Lobbying expenditures vary widely. Some influential groups (such as the U.S. Chamber of Commerce) spend hundreds of millions of dollars a year, but many other influential groups (such as NARAL Pro-Choice America and the Family Research Council) spend relatively little. How can groups have influence over government policy despite spending almost nothing on lobbying?

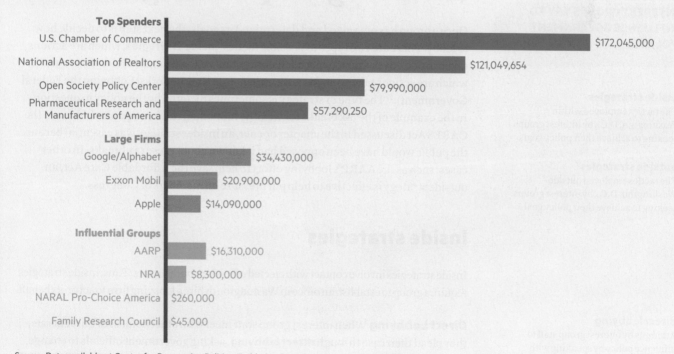

Source: Data available at Center for Responsive Politics, "Lobbying Data Summary," www.opensecrets.org/federal-lobbying (accessed 5/12/20).

That concentration of spending is evident in another way as well: a large proportion of lobbying is done by the business sector and relatively little by political or public interests. According to the Center for Responsive Politics, the top six sectors in 2018–2019 were all business interests (health, finance, miscellaneous business, communication, energy, and transportation), with 77 percent of the total spending on lobbying, while education, nonprofits, and public officials (categorized as "Other") and ideological/single-issue political groups came in seventh and eighth, spending 7.4 and 4.4 percent respectively.[19]

Although the amount of money spent on lobbying by interest groups may seem like a lot (and often leads to calls for restrictions on lobbying, as discussed in the Take a Stand feature), it is small compared with how much is at stake.[20] The federal government now spends more than $4 trillion every year (with spending more than double that in 2020 because of the extraordinary response to the COVID-19 pandemic and economic recession). In recent years, spending by interest groups and by the lobbying arms of organizations and corporations has amounted to $3.5 billion every year. That's a lot of money, but it's still less than one-tenth of 1 percent of total federal spending. This difference raises a critical question: If interest groups can control policy choices by spending money on lobbying, why aren't they spending more? We will address this question throughout the remainder of this chapter, focusing on how groups lobby and the limits of their influence over government policy.

"Why Should I Care?"

When you think of a lobbyist, don't imagine a person in an expensive suit carrying a briefcase of cash (or a campaign contribution). More often, people become lobbyists because they believe in the goals of the group they represent. And they generally don't wear expensive suits. Understanding who lobbyists really are, and the boundaries of what they can really do, is key to evaluating whether or not they have too much influence in American politics.

EXPLORE THE WAYS INTEREST GROUPS TRY TO INFLUENCE GOVERNMENT POLICIES

inside strategies
The tactics employed within Washington, D.C., by interest groups seeking to achieve their policy goals.

outside strategies
The tactics employed outside Washington, D.C., by interest groups seeking to achieve their policy goals.

direct lobbying
Attempts by interest group staff to influence policy by speaking with elected officials or bureaucrats.

Interest group strategies

Once a group has organized and determined its goals, the next step is to decide how to lobby. There are two types of possible tactics: **inside strategies**, which are actions taken inside government (whether federal, state, or local), and **outside strategies**, which are actions taken outside government (see How It Works: Lobbying the Federal Government).[21] The type of strategy is sometimes dictated by the policy in question. In the example of the tax breaks for wealthy individuals and companies hidden in the CARES Act discussed in the chapter opener, an insider strategy was essential because the public would have been opposed had it known about these tax breaks. In other cases, such as the AARP's lobbying effort to help save the Affordable Care Act, an outside strategy is effective to help put pressure on members of Congress.

Inside strategies

Inside strategies involve contact with elected officials or bureaucrats. Thus, inside strategies require a group to establish an office in Washington or hire a lobbying firm to act on its behalf.

Direct Lobbying When interest group staff meet with officeholders or bureaucrats, they plead their case through **direct lobbying**, asking government officials to change policy in line with the group's goals.[22] Direct lobbying is generally aimed at officials and

Restrictions on Interest Group Lobbying

Under current rules, members of Congress and their staffs are severely limited in the size of gifts they can receive from lobbyists. These restrictions were tightened in the mid-2000s after it was revealed that former-congressional-staffer-turned-lobbyist Jack Abramoff had used "golf junkets, free meals at the restaurant he owned, seats at sporting events, and, in some cases, old-fashioned cash" to lobby members of Congress.[a] The current restrictions limit members and their staffs to accepting gifts only if they are valued at less than $50—moreover, the total worth of the gifts that any lobbyist can give to a particular member of Congress or staffer is limited to $100 per year. In addition, "cooling off" rules, which prevent staffers and former members of Congress from lobbying for one year after leaving their government job, were instituted in an attempt to limit the revolving door between government and lobbying firms. President Trump vowed to "drain the swamp" of lobbyist influence in Washington, but lobbyists have gained even more access in his administration. Are current restrictions fair? Do they help or hurt the political process? Are even stronger limitations needed?

Keep the rules, and maybe tighten them. Supporting this option seems like a no-brainer. These regulations are based on a sensible intuition that laws are needed to prevent well-funded, unscrupulous lobbyists from offering inducements to members of Congress and their staffs in return for policy change. Simply put, groups that can send people to Washington to wine and dine members of Congress, congressional staff, and bureaucrats might gain a significant advantage over those who are unable to do so. Even if a fancy lunch doesn't buy a legislator's vote, it might help with access—that is, it might give the group a chance to make its arguments and perhaps change some minds. In this way, rules that allow even small gifts create an advantage for interest groups that have a Washington office or hire lobbyists and a disadvantage for those that do not. As a result, many reform proposals should go further, preventing lobbyists from giving anything to a member of Congress, legislative staffer, or bureaucrat—even a cup of coffee.

Relax the rules (a little). Some argue that worries about interest group influence seem a little overstated. Congressional staff and the legislators they work for are going to support a group's proposals only if they help the member's constituents or if they move policy in a way the member favors, not just because of an interest group's free lunch.

 When scandals surrounding Jack Abramoff came to light in 2005, many Americans considered him a typical lobbyist. Abramoff's actions were illegal, but the question remains: Are his tactics common in Washington, or was he a rare exception?

There are also downsides to tight controls on these gifts and perks. The current rules on lobbyists' gifts create a lot of paperwork for members and their staffs, who have to file reports on just about anything they receive from a lobbyist, even if that individual is a former colleague, neighbor, or friend. The rules are also extremely complicated—for example, legislators are allowed to eat the hors d'oeuvres provided at a reception, but they cannot sit down to a full meal without violating the gift restrictions. The disclosure requirements are also a burden to smaller interest groups and firms, which have to document everything they do on complex forms. As a result, members of Congress, their staff, interest groups, and lobbying firms spend considerable time and effort on documenting small gifts that are unlikely to have any effect on policy outcomes.

Do both. Another approach would be to relax some of the rules and strengthen others. For example, one suggestion is to get rid of the "cooling off" periods, but have better disclosure of who is lobbying so constituents will be able to hold their elected officials accountable. Many lobbyists skirt current disclosure rules by generously interpreting the 20 percent rule mentioned earlier in the chapter to exclude what most would consider lobbying activity. These "shadow lobbyists" would be exposed by stricter disclosure rules.[b]

take a stand

1. To what extent do you think current congressional rules limiting the size of gifts that members of Congress and their staffers can receive from lobbyists have curbed illegal behavior by interest groups?

2. Are these rules aimed at exceptional cases or average interest groups?

bureaucrats who are sympathetic to the group's goals.[23] Through these efforts, interest groups and their representatives help like-minded legislators secure policy changes that they both want.[24] Groups can assist in a number of ways, from sharing information about the proposed changes, to providing lists of legislators who might be persuaded to support the group's goals, to drafting legislative proposals or regulations.

Interest groups also contact "fence-sitters" who neither support or oppose them, with the goal of converting them to supporters. These efforts are less extensive than the lobbying of supporters, because opponents are unlikely to change their minds unless a group can provide new information that causes them to rethink their position.

As these descriptions indicate, interest groups place a high priority on maintaining access to their lobbying targets and being able to present their arguments, regardless of whether they expect to get what they want. Of course, interest groups want to achieve their policy goals, but access is the first step that makes persuasion possible. Therefore, many interest groups try to keep their efforts low-key, providing information to friends and opponents alike and avoiding threats or harsh words, in the hope that they will leave a favorable impression and be able to gain access the next time they want to lobby their opponents. After all, people who oppose a group's current priorities one day may agree with the group on some future issue.

In their efforts at direct lobbying, interest groups contact elected officials, members of the president's staff, and bureaucrats in the executive branch. They seek this wide range of contacts because different officials play distinct roles in the policy-making process and thus have various types of influence. Members of Congress shape legislation and budgets, members of the president's staff influence the formation of new policies and obtain presidential consent for new laws, and executive branch bureaucrats change the ways regulations are written and policies are implemented.

Drafting Legislation and Regulations Interest groups sometimes draft legislative proposals and regulations, which they deliver to legislators and bureaucrats as part of their lobbying efforts.[25] In recent years, the role of lobbyists in drafting legislation has become more prominent because Congress has less internal capacity to write the laws due to cuts in committee staff.[26]

Interest groups do not give proposals to just anyone: they seek out legislators who already support their cause and who have significant influence within Congress. For example, a lobbying effort aimed at cutting interest rates on student loans would target supporters of this change who are also members of the congressional committee with jurisdiction over student loan programs—preferably someone who chairs the committee or one of its subcommittees.[27] Interest groups also lobby bureaucrats to influence the details of new regulations.[28] If the types of regulations involved can go into effect without congressional approval, then lobbying the bureaucracy can result in groups' getting exactly what they want. If new regulations require approval by Congress or White House staff, then interest groups can increase their chances of success by getting involved in the initial drafting of policy.

Research Interest groups often prepare research reports on topics of interest to the group. For example, Public Citizen features on its website a series of research reports on topics such as protecting democracy, making government work, consumer and worker safety, globalization and trade, climate and energy, health care, and justice and the courts.[29] Such reports may sway public opinion or help persuade elected officials or bureaucrats. They also help interest group staff claim expertise on some aspect of public policy. Members of Congress are more likely to accept a group's legislative proposal if they think that the group's staff has solid research to back up its claims. Journalists are also more likely to respond to an interest group's requests for publicity if they think that the group's staff has supporting evidence.

Hearings Interest group staff often testify before congressional committees. In part, this activity seeks to inform members of Congress about issues that matter to the group. For example, the NRA's website shows that its staff has testified in state legislatures and in the U.S. congress in favor of right-to-carry laws as well as laws that would grant immunity to gun manufacturers for harm committed with weapons they produced, and against universal background checks and federal funding for research on gun violence.[30]

Litigation Another inside strategy involves taking the government to court. In bringing their case, interest groups can argue that the government's actions are not consistent with the Constitution or that the government has misinterpreted existing law.[31] Interest groups can also become involved in an existing case by filing amicus curiae ("friend of the court") briefs; these are documents that offer the group's rationale for how the judges should decide the case. The drawback of litigation is that it is costly and time-consuming; cases can take years to work through the federal courts system. In fact, most groups that use the litigation strategy combine it with direct lobbying or other strategies.

The American Civil Liberties Union is an interest group that often uses litigation strategies in its efforts to change government policy. Here, members of the ACLU chapter in Washington State announce their filing of an abortion rights lawsuit against several local hospitals.

Working Together To increase their chances for success, interest groups can work together in their lobbying efforts, formulating a common strategy and future plans. Legislators are more likely to respond, or at least provide access, when many groups with large or diverse memberships are all asking for the same thing.[32] In general, these collaborations are short-term efforts focused on achieving a specific outcome, like supporting or opposing the confirmation of judicial and cabinet nominees.[33] The tax giveaway discussed in the chapter opener had unlikely allies such as Coca-Cola, Hewlett Packard Enterprise, Morgan Stanley, and the National Association of Manufacturers (whose members include companies such as Exxon Mobil, Raytheon, and Caterpillar), which would all gain billions of dollars from the change in the tax law.[34]

The problem with working together is that groups may agree on general goals but disagree on specifics. If differences cannot be bridged, groups may undertake separate and possibly conflicting lobbying efforts or decide against lobbying entirely. For example, although there are many groups pressing for climate change legislation, they have not developed a unified lobbying effort. The problem? The groups disagree on which policies should be implemented, who should pay for them, and whether the government should aid companies that would be forced to purchase new antipollution equipment.[35] Here, again, we see how conflict and compromise infuse another aspect of the American political process.

Lobbying the Federal Government: Inside and Outside Strategies

Inside Strategies

Groups **lobby government officials directly** in Washington, D.C.

Examples:

meeting with lawmakers

drafting legislation

providing research and testimony

taking the government to court

Outside Strategies

Groups use **public pressure, elections, and the media** to influence government.

Examples:

grassroots e-mail, letter, or phone campaigns

contributing to election campaigns

getting media coverage of their cause

AIPAC and the Iran Nuclear Deal

Throughout negotiations between Iran and the United States and its allies over limiting Iran's nuclear research program, the American Israel Public Affairs Committee (AIPAC)—an influential pro-Israel interest group—strongly opposed the deal. AIPAC engaged in a diverse set of lobbying activities with the goal of persuading members of Congress to disapprove the deal before a crucial deadline passed and the deal was enacted.

● Inside strategies

● Outside strategies

Critical Thinking

1. **Despite its lobbying efforts, AIPAC's** side initially did not prevail in this situation. It wasn't until they had a more sympathetic ear in the White House that the policy was changed. If you were advising them, what strategy would you suggest they spend time on: inside or outside? Why?

2. **Suppose you are the head of AIPAC.** How could you use the Iran agreement to illustrate AIPAC's power and influence in Washington, despite the fact that the group's position did not prevail in Congress? Given the ultimate outcome, would you change how your group allocates its time and resources?

Do we have a deal?

July 14, 2015
The United States and its negotiation partners announce details of their **nuclear agreement with Iran**.

And they're off!

July 15, 2015
AIPAC announces its opposition to the Iran deal and **forms a new advocacy group to lobby** against the agreement.

Gathering forces.

July 2015
AIPAC organizes a series of **speeches and town hall meetings** in congressional districts and states of undecided legislators.

Making introductions.

July 28–29, 2015
AIPAC arranges a "Washington fly-in"— a series of **meetings between lawmakers and hundreds of constituents** who are opposed to the deal.

Running ads.

August 2015
AIPAC spends over **$20 million running television ads** opposing the deal in 23 states.

Funding trips.

August 2015
AIPAC organizes a **trip to Israel for 58 members of Congress** to meet with Israeli citizens and officials.

Going right to the source.

August 2015
AIPAC representatives **lobby undecided senators** to oppose the agreement.

No luck for AIPAC.

September 2, 2015
Deadline for Congress to disapprove the deal **passes without action**.

But there's a new sheriff in town!

May 8, 2018
Despite initially extending the deal, **President Trump withdraws from the agreement**, saying, "This was a horrible one-sided deal that should have never, ever been made."

While AIPAC's efforts were ultimately unsuccessful, they illustrate the many ways interest groups can work to influence the policy process.

Outside strategies

Outside strategies involve actions that interest groups undertake across the country rather than in Washington. Again, these activities can be orchestrated by the group or can be organized by a firm that the group hires.

Grassroots Lobbying Directly involving interest group members in lobbying efforts is called **grassroots lobbying**. Members may send letters, make telephone calls, participate in a protest, or express their demands in other ways. Mass protests, another form of grassroots lobbying, seek to capture the attention of government officials and also to draw media coverage, with the idea of publicizing the group's goals and perhaps gaining new members or financial support.

Grassroots strategies are useful because elected officials do not like to act against a large group of citizens who care enough about an issue to express their position.[36] Officials may not agree with the group's goals, but they will likely arrange a meeting with its staff so that they appear willing to learn about their constituents' demands.[37] However, these member-based strategies work only for interest groups with a large number of members, because legislators pay attention to a letter-writing campaign only when they receive several thousand pieces of mail.

In addition, the letters or other efforts have to come from a Congress member's own constituents. The effectiveness of grassroots lobbying also depends on perceptions of how much a group has done to motivate participation. Suppose a representative gets 10,000 e-mails demanding an increase in federal student aid, but virtually all the messages contain the same appeal because they were generated and sent from a group's website. Congressional staff refer to these efforts as **Astroturf lobbying**.[38] Given the letters' similarity, the representative may discount the effort, believing that it says more about the group's ability to make campaign participation accessible than it does about the number of district residents who strongly support an increase in federal student aid. Even so, politicians are sometimes reluctant to completely dismiss Astroturf efforts—the fact that so many people participated, even with facilitation by an interest group, means that their demands should at least be considered.

Mobilizing Public Opinion One strategy related to grassroots lobbying involves trying to change what the public thinks about an issue in the hope that elected officials will notice this change and respond by enacting (or opposing) new laws or regulations in order to keep their constituents happy.

Virtually all interest groups try to influence opinion. Most maintain a website that presents their message and write press releases to get media coverage. Most groups are also very active on social media, using Facebook, Twitter, and Instagram to keep in touch with members and let them know about issues that the group is working on. Any contact with citizens, whether to encourage them to join the group, contribute money, or engage in grassroots lobbying, also involves elements of persuasion—trying to transform citizens into supporters and supporters into true believers and even activists. In the case of gun control, for example, the NRA has an aggressive campaign to encourage members to contact their elected officials and to express their opinions.

A focused mobilization effort involves contacting large numbers of potential supporters (beyond just members) through e-mail, phone calls, direct mail, television advertising, print media, social media, and websites. In order to get legislators to respond, a group has to persuade large numbers of people to become involved.

Electioneering Interest groups get involved in elections by making contributions to candidates, urging people to help in a campaign, endorsing candidates, funding

The Black Lives Matter movement, formed in 2013 in support of issues of racial justice and police reform, utilizes protests for grassroots lobbying. In 2020, after the killing by police of George Floyd, an unarmed Black man in Minneapolis, Minnesota, mass protests across the country brought increased attention to and support for the group's goals, including ending police brutality and systemic racism.

campaign ads, or mobilizing a candidate's or party's supporters. All these efforts seek to influence who gets elected, with the expectation that changing who gets elected will affect what government does.

Federal laws limit groups' electioneering and lobbying efforts (see Nuts & Bolts 9.2). For example, most private organizations and associations in America are organized as 501(c)(3) organizations, a designation based on their IRS classification, which means that donations to the group are tax deductible. However, 501(c)(3) organizations must not advocate for or against political candidates, and lobbying must not constitute more than 20 percent of the group's total expenditures (certain public-education programs or voter-registration drives that are conducted in a nonpartisan manner do not count toward that 20 percent), although some groups are always looking for loopholes in these restrictions. Groups that want to engage in lobbying or electioneering without looking for exceptions can incorporate under other IRS designations and operate as a **political action committee (PAC)**, a **527 organization**, or a 501(c)(4) organization. Although contributions to these organizations are not tax deductible, such organizations have fewer restrictions on the size of the contributions or how their money is spent—for example, 527 organizations have no contribution or spending limits.

Two new options for electioneering by interest groups emerged in recent elections: Super PACs and 501(c)(4) organizations. The former was a consequence of the *Citizens United* Supreme Court decision that authorized unlimited independent spending by corporations and labor unions in federal elections.[39] Many groups set up new PACs to take advantage of these latest rules—the "Super" label reflects the fact that these groups take in and spend much more money than the typical PAC. All the major 2020 presidential candidates had an independent Super PAC running ad campaigns on their behalf.

In 2020, federally focused PACs and Super PACS spent more than $7 billion for electioneering and contributions to candidates and parties, of which ActBlue raised a staggering $3.45 billion and WinRed raised $1.35 billion.[40] However, these large numbers mask some important details. To begin with, some of the largest firms in America (Google, Walmart, and Exxon Mobil, for example) have PACs that spend only a million or so on contributions. Another large firm, Apple, has no PAC. The PAC for the Pharmaceutical Research and Manufacturers of America is also small, and the other influential interest groups mentioned earlier in Figure 9.2 (the AARP, NARAL Pro-Choice America, and the Family Research Council) spend even less or don't have a PAC or a 527. These numbers suggest that money doesn't buy elections or policy outcomes—if it did, these organizations would probably spend a lot more on campaign donations and television ads.

Spending totals can also be deceptive. The National Association of Realtors, for example, made about $3.5 million in contributions in 2020—but spread out the funds over 500 candidates, with slightly more going to Democrats than Republicans. The PAC for EMILY's List collected over $72 million but only $16.9 million went to contributions to candidates and parties, with the rest for fundraising and overhead. Another large spender, NextGen Climate Action, was funded largely by a single wealthy donor but did not make any contributions to federal candidates in the 2020 cycle—their spending was on issue ads. (The founder, billionaire entrepreneur Tom Steyer, ran as a candidate for president during the 2020 Democratic primary.) And some groups used most of their money against candidates they opposed: the conservative Super PAC America First Action spent almost all of its $134 million against Democratic contenders.

Finally, while the $7 billion that these groups raised together seems large, only about two-thirds was spent on behalf of or as contributions to candidates. Most PACs contributed to only a few candidates. And while more than a thousand Super PACs were active in the 2020 election, most were small, and the average group spent just over $500,000. These data highlight a sharp difference in electioneering strategies between the very few large,

political action committee (PAC)
An interest group or a division of an interest group that can raise money to contribute to campaigns or to spend on ads in support of candidates. The amount a PAC can receive from each of its donors and the amount it can spend on federal campaigning are strictly limited.

527 organization
A tax-exempt group formed primarily to influence elections through voter mobilization efforts and issue ads that do not directly endorse or oppose a candidate. Unlike PACs, 527s are not subject to contribution limits and spending caps.

well-funded interest groups and everyone else. A few 527s, Super PACs, 501(c)(4)s, and PACs have the money to deploy massive advertising and mobilization efforts for a candidate or issue they like or against those they don't like. There are also some very large associations that can persuade large numbers of members to work and vote for candidates that the group supports or against candidates that the group wants to defeat. And just a very few rich individuals can make outsized contributions to a candidate they favor.

But these strategies are not available to the vast majority of interest groups, which simply don't have the resources. They give modest help to a few candidates who are sympathetic to their goals in the hope that, once elected, the officeholder will remember their contribution when their group asks for a meeting. Some groups do no electioneering at all, possibly because they lack sufficient funds, because they want to avoid making enemies based on whom they do or do not support, or because other strategies are more promising given the resources that are available to them. Many groups opt for quiet lobbying efforts that use their expertise or undertake grassroots efforts to build public support for their policy goals. Massive electioneering operations by interest groups are relatively rare.

Cultivating Media Contacts Media coverage helps a group publicize its concerns without spending any money. Such attention may mobilize public opinion indirectly by getting people to join the group, contribute money, or demand that elected officials support the group's agenda. Favorable media coverage also helps a group's leaders assure members that they are actively working on members' concerns.

NUTS & BOLTS 9.2

Interest Groups and Electioneering: Types of Organizations

An interest group's ability to engage in electioneering depends on how it is organized—specifically, what section of the IRS code applies to the organization. The following table gives details on four common organizations: 501(c) organizations, 527 organizations, PACs, and so-called Super PACs. Many individuals choose to contribute money to nonprofits organized as 501(c)(4) groups, which can lobby and engage in electioneering as long as their "primary activity" (at least half of their overall activity) is not political.

Type of Organization	Advantages	Disadvantages
501(c)(3)	Contributions tax deductible	Cannot engage in political activities, and lobbying can be no more than 20 percent of spending (but voter education and mobilization are permitted)
527	Can spend unlimited amounts on issue advocacy and voter mobilization	Cannot make contributions to candidates or coordinate efforts with candidates or parties
501(c)(4)	Can spend unlimited amounts on electioneering; does not have to disclose contributors	At least half of its activities must be nonpolitical; cannot coordinate efforts with candidates or parties
PAC	Can contribute directly to candidates and parties	Strict limits on direct contributions
Super PACs	Can spend unlimited amounts on electioneering; can support or oppose specific candidates	Cannot make contributions to candidates or coordinate efforts with candidates or parties

Source: Compiled by the authors.

"Why Should I Care?" This may seem a little deep in the weeds, but understanding the different types of interest groups is important for understanding how they influence elections. Some types of groups have to disclose their donors and others don't. It is more difficult for voters to hold their leaders accountable if voters don't know who is supporting candidates' campaigns.

Conservative Super PACs, such as the Conservative Political Action Conference (CPAC), hold conventions that give candidates a venue to present themselves to conservative activists and donors.

Journalists listen when interest groups call if they feel that a group's story will catch their readers' attention or address their concerns. Smart interest group leaders make it easy for journalists to cover their cause, holding events that produce intriguing news stories. These stories may not change anyone's mind, but the media coverage provides free publicity for the groups' policy agendas.

How much power do interest groups have?

★
EVALUATE INTEREST GROUP INFLUENCE

Two 2020 presidential candidates, Democrats Bernie Sanders and Elizabeth Warren, focused much of their campaigns on the need to reduce the power of large corporations and special interests over policy making in Washington. While neither Sanders nor Warren gained the nomination, their campaigns spoke for the widely held belief about how Washington works: that interest groups have too much power and something drastic must be done to end their domination over policy making in Washington. Donald Trump capitalized on this same sentiment with his pledge to "drain the swamp" in 2016.

As we discuss in the What Do the Facts Say? feature, some studies of interest group influence support Sanders and Warren's claims—but others tell a very different story, one in which a group's chances of getting what it wants depend on whether there is organized opposition to its demand. In other words, as one analysis put it, "the solution to lobbying is more lobbying."[41]

I will Make Our Government Honest Again—believe me. But First, I'm going to have to #DrainTheSwamp in DC.

—President Donald Trump

Interest Group Power

Conventional wisdom says that business interest groups have too much power over policy outcomes in Washington. But what do the facts say?

To address this question, a group of political scientists tracked a series of issues through years of lobbying, congressional debate, legislative action, and implementation by the bureaucracy. Their goal was to determine whether business groups were successful in getting what they want from Congress, particularly when their efforts were opposed by citizen groups or government officials. This figure shows what they found.

Think about it

- **Many people believe that business groups** always succeed in their lobbying efforts. Does this figure confirm or deny these suspicions?
- **After looking at these data,** do you think business groups have too much power? How do these data help us understand the winners and losers in the tax benefits in the CARES Act discussed at the beginning of this chapter?

Which Interest Groups Win . . . and When?

After four years ...

■ Business Groups Win   ■ Other Side Wins   ■ Both/Neither Win

Business groups vs. citizen groups or unions

40%   40%   20%

Business groups vs. government (executive branch, members of Congress)

36%   36%   27%

Business groups unopposed

89%   11%

Source: Marie Hojnacki, Kathleen Marchetti, Frank Baumgartner, Jeffrey M. Berry, David C. Kimball, and Beth L. Leech, "Assessing Business Advantage in Washington Lobbying," *Interest Groups and Advocacy* 4 (2015): 206–24.

What determines when interest groups succeed?

Three factors shape interest group influence. The first is the group's goal: Does it want to change a policy (including enacting a new policy) or to prevent change? The second is the amount of public attention a group gets: How many Americans care about what a group is trying to do? The third is conflict: To what extent do other groups or the public oppose the policy change?

Change versus Preventing Change In general, groups are going to have an easier time preventing a change than working to implement one. As we discuss in Chapter 2, enacting a new policy requires the approval of both houses of Congress, the president's signature (or a veto override), and implementation from the appropriate bureaucratic agency. Each of these steps provides an opportunity for interest groups to lobby members of government to do nothing. So if the groups are successful, change will not occur. Studies show that groups are much more likely to be successful when their goals involve this kind of negative lobbying that seeks to block changes in policy.[42] Most of the NRA's legislative victories in recent years fit this description: the NRA has successfully lobbied against a new ban on assault weapons, against reforms to the system of national background checks for handgun purchases, and against new limits on ownership of guns by mentally ill people.

While the success of the NRA's negative lobbying attracts considerable attention, its failures in lobbying for policy change do not. Consider the NRA's advocacy of concealed carry laws. As noted earlier, there is little doubt that the NRA's leaders and most of its members favor the passage of such laws nationwide, but efforts to lobby Congress in favor of such laws are unlikely to be successful given public opposition and well-funded interest groups that are against concealed carry. These groups could respond with negative lobbying against any effort the NRA might make. As a result, while the NRA lobbies for concealed carry, it has failed to help enact national legislation, and the limits on its power over legislation do not get much publicity.

Amount of Public Attention Interest groups are more likely to succeed when their request attracts little public attention.[43] When the average voter does not know or care about a group's request, legislators and bureaucrats do not have to worry about the political consequences of giving the group what it wants. The only question is whether the officials themselves favor the request or can be convinced that the group's desired change is worthwhile. In contrast, when the issue attracts a lot of public attention, legislators' response to lobbying will hinge on their judgment of constituent opinion: Do voters favor what the group wants? After all, the average legislator has a strong interest in reelection and is unlikely to act against his or her constituents' wishes. As a result, lobbying may count for nothing in the face of public opposition or may be superfluous when the group's position already has public support.[44]

While the idea of interest group lobbying probably brings to mind titanic struggles on controversial issues, such as gun control, abortion rights, or judicial nominations, low-profile issues are surprisingly common. Many groups are indeed active for or against these high-profile issues and try to capture public attention as a way of pressuring the government. But not all interest group lobbying is so high-profile. Remember the National Turkey Federation—the people who give the president a turkey every Thanksgiving? In the winter of 2014, the federation successfully lobbied federal bureaucrats to increase propane supplies to Midwest states facing record cold temperatures, including areas where the federation's members use propane to heat their barns. The policy change resulting from the federation's lobbying efforts attracted no publicity, which is precisely the point. When few people know or care about a policy change, interest groups are able to dominate the policy-making process.

> **But this is the great danger America faces. That we will cease to be one nation and become instead a collection of interest groups: city against suburb, region against region, individual against individual. Each seeking to satisfy private wants.**
>
> —**Barbara Jordan,** civil rights leader and former member of Congress

If you have ever heard of the National Turkey Federation, it's probably because of its participation in the annual presidential "pardoning" of a turkey before Thanksgiving. The federation's relative anonymity has been beneficial: its effort to increase the amount of turkey served in federally funded school lunches was aided by most Americans' lack of awareness of the proposal.

While many observers credit lobbying by the pharmaceutical industry for policies such as the Medicare Prescription Drug Benefit (and its ban on importing medicines), favorable public opinion, the efforts of the AARP, and bureaucrats' independent judgments probably had greater influence on passing the Drug Benefit Act.

Level of Conflict Interest group influence is much less apparent on highly conflictual issues—those over which public opinion is split and groups are active on all sides of the issue. Consider gun control. The ongoing debate over gun control attracts many well-funded interest groups and coalitions, which support different versions of gun control or want no change to current policy. There is no consensus among members of Congress, interest groups, or the American public about which policy changes are needed. Under these conditions, access doesn't count for much; legislators have a keen sense of the political costs of accommodating a group's demands. As a result, stalemate is the likely result, which is exactly what has happened over the last few years: gun control laws have not been strengthened, but other than an increase in concealed carry laws, there have not been significant changes in either direction. After the 2017 mass shooting in Las Vegas, in which 58 people were killed and 546 injured, the NRA said it would favor additional regulation of "bump stocks," which allow 90 rounds to be fired in 10 seconds. President Trump started the process of banning bump stocks through an executive order in March 2018 (the final rule went into effect on March 26, 2019). If policy change occurs at all, it is likely to reflect a complex process of bargaining and compromise, with no groups getting exactly what they want—which is what generally happens with gun control.

The case of gun control also illustrates that the fact that a group is large or well funded does not mean government officials will always comply with its requests. Although many people worry that well-funded interest groups will use their financial resources to dominate the policy-making process, even if public opinion is against them, these fears are largely unfounded. The conditions that are ripe for well-funded interest groups to become involved in a policy debate typically ensure that there will be well-funded groups on all sides of a question. Under these conditions, no group is likely to get everything it wants and no group's lobbying efforts are likely to be decisive. Some groups may not get anything.

However, gun control is not a typical case. Most cases of interest group influence look a lot like the National Turkey Federation's request for more propane: a group asks for something, there is relatively little opposition, and Congress or the bureaucracy responds with appropriate policy changes. The situation might have been very different if another group had lobbied on the other side against the Turkey Federation. If so, satisfying one group would have required displeasing at least one other group. Faced with this no-win situation, bureaucrats or legislators would be less likely to give the group what it wanted. At a minimum, they would have had to measure the Turkey Federation's arguments against those made by the other groups.

Suppose you want to change some federal government policy—you want more funding for a program or an end to some regulation. Does having enough money guarantee a win? Generally speaking, the answer is no. What matters more is the importance of the policy or regulation you're trying to change and whether there is organized opposition on the other side. If your group is the only one lobbying, chances are good that you'll win. But if the issue is important to constituents or controversial and you have opposition, your prospects aren't good, regardless of the size of your bankroll.

Unpacking the Conflict

Considering all that we've discussed in this chapter, let's apply what we know about how interest groups work to the example of the tax credits discussed at the beginning of this chapter. Is it fair to characterize all interest groups as self-interested organizations that undermine the public good? Are interest groups really too-powerful manipulators of the American policy process?

Many Americans think that interest groups are powerful manipulators of the American policy process and that they are able to get what they want regardless of the impact on everyone else. Sometimes it seems like "Heads they win. Tails we lose." While the chapter opener's example of income limit repeals in the CARES Act would support this view, there are countless counterexamples of laws that have been passed over the objections of corporations, including environmental protections, worker safety laws, consumer product and food safety regulations, and minimum wages laws.

So the truth is much more complex. Interest groups represent many different Americans, many of whom are unaware that lobbying occurs on their behalf. Moreover, for many groups, the challenge is to get organized in the first place or scrape together enough resources to start lobbying. These efforts don't always succeed because of the collective action problem. Interest groups are more likely to get what they want when their demands attract little public attention and no opposition from other groups. When a group asks for a large or controversial policy change, it stands little chance of success, even if the group has many members, a large lobbying budget, or an influential leader directing its operation.

The CARES Act also reflects this complexity. While lobbyists were able to sneak in the tax provisions that benefited their clients to the tune of $135 billion over 10 years, the bill also did a lot of good for millions of Americans who were in desperate need. Small businesses, hospitals, state and local governments, and researchers rushing to make a vaccine all received necessary aid. Most Americans received a $1,200 check just in time to help them make their next rent payment, and millions of people who lost their jobs benefited from the extension of unemployment compensation. So the special interests had their big chunk of the pie, but the American people received more of what they needed to try to get back on their feet.

In sum, while individual lobbying efforts often reflect the efforts of small groups to achieve favored policy outcomes at the expense of the majority, when we look across the entire range of interest group activities, a different picture emerges: in the main, interest groups reflect the conflictual nature of American politics and the resulting drive of individuals, groups, and corporations to shape American public policy in line with their policy goals. The average citizen benefits as well as loses from lobbying activities.

"What's Your Take?"

Are interest groups really too-powerful manipulators of the American policy process?

Or do groups play an important role in helping all citizens' voices be heard?

STUDY GUIDE

What are interest groups?

Define *interest groups* and describe the characteristics of different types of groups. (Pages 288–296)

Summary

Interest groups are organizations that seek to influence government policy by helping elect candidates who support their policy goals and by lobbying elected officials and bureaucrats. Although they are generally viewed with disdain, interest groups are ubiquitous—most organizations have lobbyists working on their behalf.

Key terms

interest group (p. 289)
lobbying (p. 289)
linkage institutions (p. 289)
centralized groups (p. 290)
confederations (p. 290)
mass associations (p. 290)
peak associations (p. 290)

free riding (p. 291)
selective incentives (p. 291)
solidary benefits (p. 291)
purposive benefits (p. 291)
coercion (p. 291)
material benefits (p. 291)
revolving door (p. 293)

Practice Quiz Questions

1. In contrast to political parties, interest groups _____.

a   run candidates for office

b   coordinate the activities of elected officials

c   guarantee that certain candidates appear on electoral ballots

d   directly influence government activity

e   indirectly influence government activity

2. Why is the number of lobbyists increasing?

a   The federal government is growing in size and influence.

b   Lobbying is not closely regulated.

c   Citizens are now more supportive of special interests.

d   Politicians can concurrently serve their terms and work as lobbyists.

e   Interest groups have more money to spend.

3. One of the main advantages of a centralized interest group is that it _____.

a   maintains a number of independent chapters

b   often has local chapters competing over resources

c   deploys the group's resources more efficiently

d   is able to easily find out what its members want

e   has no weaknesses

4. The practice of moving from government positions to working for interest groups is called _____.

a   interest-group capture

b   the revolving door

c   an iron triangle

d   escalator politics

e   the spoils system

5. Purposive benefits come from _____, while solidary benefits come from _____.

a   working with like-minded people; working to achieve a desired policy goal

b   receiving material goods; working with like-minded people

c   receiving material goods; working to achieve a desired policy goal

d   working to achieve a desired policy goal; receiving material goods

e   working to achieve a desired policy goal; working with like-minded people

Interest group strategies

Explore the ways interest groups try to influence government policies. (Pages 296–305)

Summary

Interest groups have two types of tactics for lobbying elected officials. They can attempt to influence politics by taking action in Washington, or they can take action elsewhere. The decision to pursue an inside or outside strategy comes down to the interest group's resources and which strategy members think will be most effective.

Key terms

inside strategies (p. 296)
outside strategies (p. 296)
direct lobbying (p. 296)
grassroots lobbying (p. 302)

Astroturf lobbying (p. 302)
political action committee (PAC) (p. 303)
527 organization (p. 303)

Practice Quiz Questions

6. Asking government officials to change policy in line with the group's goals is _____.

a   revolving door lobbying

b   Astroturf lobbying

c   direct lobbying

d   indirect lobbying

e   outside lobbying

7. **Interest groups generally _____ draft legislation; they generally _____ provide testimony before committees.**

a do; do

b do not; do

c do; do not

d do not; do not

e are not allowed to; are not allowed to

8. **Directly involving interest group members in lobbying efforts is called _____ .**

a Astroturf lobbying

b grassroots lobbying

c democratic lobbying

d lobbying through referendum

e inside lobbying

9. **For grassroots lobbying to be effective, _____ .**

a only a few pieces of mail are necessary

b mail must come from all over the country

c all messages have to have exactly the same appeal

d letters have to come from constituents

e letters have to come from prominent officials

How much power do interest groups have?

Evaluate interest group influence. (Pages 305–309)

Summary

It is commonly argued that elected officials are letting interest groups define their agenda. However, the evidence on interest groups does not support these claims: there is no correlation between the amount of money spent on lobbying and a group's success, nor is there conclusive evidence that group lobbying influences policy. Groups are generally most influential when the issues attract little public attention and when an issue does not have organized opposition.

Practice Quiz Question

10. **Interest groups are more likely to succeed when their request has _____ importance and when it has _____ conflict.**

a low; little

b high; little

c low; high

d high; high

e high; zero

Suggested Reading

Ainsworth, Scott. *Analyzing Interest Groups: Group Influence on People and Policies*. New York: W. W. Norton, 2002.

Baumgartner, Frank, Jeffrey M. Berry, Marie Hojnacki, David C. Kimball, and Beth L. Leech. *Lobbying and Policy Change: Who Wins, Who Loses, and Why*. Chicago: University of Chicago Press, 2009.

Carpenter, Daniel. *The Forging of Bureaucratic Autonomy: Reputations, Networks, and Policy Innovation in Executive Agencies, 1862-1928*. Princeton, NJ: Princeton University Press, 2002.

Drutman, Lee. *The Business of America Is Lobbying: How Corporations Became Politicized and Politics Became More Corporate*. New York: Oxford University Press, 2015.

Gilens, Martin, and Benjamin Page. "Testing Theories of American Politics: Elites, Interest Groups, and Average Citizens." *Perspectives on Politics* 12:3 (September 2014): 564-81.

Kollman, Kenneth. *Outside Lobbying: Public Opinion and Interest Group Strategies*. Princeton, NJ: Princeton University Press, 1998.

Olson, Mancur. *The Logic of Collective Action*, 2nd ed. Cambridge, MA: Harvard University Press, 1971.

Schattschneider, E. E. *The Semisovereign People*. New York: Harper and Row, 1959.

Schlozman, Kay Lehman, and John Tierney. *Organized Interests and American Democracy*. New York: HarperCollins, 1986.

Schlozman, Kay Lehman, Sidney Verba, and Henry E. Brady. *The Unheavenly Chorus: Unequal Political Voice and the Broken Promise of American Democracy*. Princeton, NJ: Princeton University Press, 2012.

Stigerwalt, Amy. *The Battle over the Bench: Senators, Interest Groups, and Lower Court Confirmations*. Charlottesville: University of Virginia Press, 2010.

10

Congress

Who does Congress represent?

» **"As President of the United States, I am asking for a legal solution on DACA, not a political one, consistent with the rule of law. The Supreme Court is not willing to give us one, so now we have to start this process all over again."[1]**
President Donald Trump

» **"I do not believe we should be granting a path to citizenship to anybody here illegally."[2]**
Senator Ted Cruz (R-TX)

« **"We can't allow these young people to continue to live in fear, to be at risk."[3]**
Representative Joe Neguse (D-CO)

Representatives Nydia Velázquez (D-NY) and Adriano Espaillat (D-NY) announce the Dream and Promise Act, a bill designed to provide DACA recipients, known as "Dreamers," with a path to U.S. citizenship.

Late in the first year of his presidency, Donald Trump announced that he would end President Obama's Deferred Action for Childhood Arrivals (DACA) program on March 5, 2018. The program allowed residents who were brought illegally to the United States as children to remain in the country if they had graduated from high school, were currently in school, or had served in the military, and had not committed a felony. President Trump expressed strong support for the program, calling the 700,000 people enrolled "incredible kids." However, Trump believed that President Obama had overstepped his authority by creating the program through executive action, so Trump asked Congress to create a legislative solution.[4] In a meeting with congressional leaders early in 2018, President Trump said that he would sign whatever compromise on DACA that Congress could agree to. Polls showed that between 73 and 87 percent of Americans favored allowing the Dreamers, as program participants are called, to stay and have a path to citizenship.[5]

One would think that enacting a policy that is supported by more than three-fourths of Americans, the president, and both parties in Congress would be a no-brainer. But shortly before the March 5 deadline, the wheels came off. Democrats initially tried to attach the DACA bill to a must-pass budget bill, but this effort failed after a three-day government shutdown. Democrats agreed to a two-year budget bill three weeks later, but without a resolution to the DACA issue. In a reversal of

his earlier position that he would sign any DACA bill that Congress put forward, President Trump took a hard line against bills that did not include $25 billion in funding for the border wall with Mexico and that did not replace the lottery program for legal immigration and family-based immigration with a merit-based system. Critics on the far right, such as Senator Ted Cruz, called it amnesty for illegal immigrants, while those on the far left called for a "clean bill" that addressed only the Dreamers. After Democrats took control of the House in 2019, they passed a bill that would have provided a path to citizenship for 2.3 million undocumented immigrants, including the Dreamers, but the bill was not taken up in the Senate. (See What Do the Facts Say? on p. 316.)

Given Congress's inability to solve the problem, DACA supporters turned to the courts, which stopped the deportation of the Dreamers. Then, in June 2020 the Supreme Court ruled in a 5–4 decision that President Trump had not provided legal justification for ending the program, and as a result he could not disassemble it. The ruling granted a reprieve to the close to 650,000 people in the program who had been brought to the United States as children.

On a basic level, this appears to be an example of congressional incompetence and dysfunction. How could a policy with such broad support and positive consequences for the economy not be passed? But it is not unusual for congressional leaders to use a consensual policy such as DACA to help pass more controversial legislation such as building the wall with Mexico. Some would argue that it is an essential feature of the legislative process.

The essential nature of conflict and compromise in the legislative process is not very well understood by the general public. Americans often view the type of wheeling and dealing that is necessary to reach compromises as improper and wonder why there is so much conflict. A typical sentiment is "Why does there have to be so much partisan bickering? Can't they just implement the best solutions to our problems?"

In this chapter, we argue that Congress members' behavior is driven by their desire to respond to constituent interests (and the closely related goal of reelection) and constrained by the institutional structures within which they operate (such as the committee system, parties, and leadership). At the same time, members try to be responsible for broader national interests, which are often at odds with their constituents' interests and, consequently, the goal of reelection.

This tension between being responsible and responsive is a source of conflict and requires members of Congress to make tough decisions, often involving political trade-offs and compromises. Should a House member vote for dairy price supports for her local farmers even if it means higher milk prices for families around the nation? Should a senator vote to subsidize the production of tobacco, the biggest cash crop in his state, despite the tremendous health costs it imposes on millions of Americans? Should a member vote to close a military base, as requested by the Pentagon, even if it means the loss of thousands of jobs back home? These are difficult questions. On a complex issue, such as immigration, there is no obvious "responsible" solution and fair-minded people can disagree. These disagreements take on a partisan edge, as most Republicans favor building a stronger border with more limits on legal immigration while most Democrats do not, which obviously leads to conflict. Why is it so hard for Congress to compromise on issues that appear to be consensual, like protecting the Dreamers? How can members of Congress best serve the collective interests of the nation while also representing their local constituents?

Congress and the people

Congress and the Constitution

Congress was the "first branch" early in our nation's history. The Constitution specified for Congress a vast array of enumerated powers, including regulating commerce, coining money, raising and supporting armies, creating the courts, establishing post offices and roads, declaring war, and levying taxes (see Article I, Section 8, of the Constitution in the appendix). The president, in contrast, was given few explicit powers and played a much less prominent role early in our history. Furthermore, much of Congress's authority came from its implicit powers, which were rooted in the elastic clause of Article I of the Constitution, which gives Congress the power "to make all Laws which shall be necessary and proper for carrying into Execution the foregoing Powers."

The compromises that gave rise to Congress's initial structure reflected an attempt to reconcile the competing interests of the day (large versus small states, northern versus southern interests, and proponents of strong national power versus state power). These compromises included establishing a system of **bicameralism**, that is, a bicameral (two-chambered) institution made up of a popularly elected House reflecting the relative populations of the states and a Senate chosen by state legislatures, representing each state equally; allowing each enslaved person to count as three-fifths of a person for purposes of apportionment for the House; and setting longer terms for senators (six years) than for House members (two years).

But these compromises also laid the foundation for the split loyalties that members of Congress have: they must respond to both their local constituencies and the nation's interests. Although the Founders hoped that Congress would pass legislation emphasizing the national good over local interests, they also recognized the importance of local constituencies. Thus, the relatively short two-year House term was intended to tie legislators to public sentiment.

In general, the Founders viewed the Senate as the more likely institution to speak for the national interests; it was intended to check the more responsive and passionate House. Because senators were indirectly elected and served longer terms than House members, the Senate was more insulated from the people. A famous (although maybe fictional) story of an argument between George Washington and Thomas Jefferson points out the differences between the House and Senate. Jefferson did not think the Senate was necessary, while Washington supported having two chambers. During the argument, Jefferson poured some coffee he was drinking into his saucer. Washington asked him why he had done so. "To cool it," replied Jefferson. "Even so," said Washington, "we pour legislation into the senatorial saucer to cool it."

This idea of a more responsible Senate survived well into the twentieth century, even after the Seventeenth Amendment in 1913 allowed the direct, popular election of senators. Today the Senate is still more insulated than the House. Because of the six-year terms of senators, only one-third of the 100 Senate seats are contested in each election, while all 435 House members are elected every two years. However, differences between the House's and Senate's representational roles have become muted, as senators seem to campaign for reelection 365 days a year, every year, just like House members.[6] This "**permanent campaign**" means that senators are now less insulated from electoral forces than they were in the past.

The relationship between the president and Congress has also evolved significantly. In the nineteenth century, Congress's roots in geographic constituencies made it well suited for the politics of the time. Although several great presidents left their mark on

bicameralism
The system of having two chambers within one legislative body, like the House and Senate in the U.S. Congress.

A ROW IN CONGRESS.

The Founders viewed the House as more passionate than the Senate, or as the "hot coffee" that needed to be cooled in the "saucer" of the Senate. This perception probably did not include coming to blows over differences in policy as Congressmen Albert G. Brown and John A. Wilcox did in 1851 about whether Mississippi should secede from the Union.

permanent campaign
The continual quest for reelection that is rooted in high-cost professional campaigns that are increasingly reliant on consultants and expensive media campaigns.

Are the DACA Dreamers "Hardened Criminals"?

While Twitter became the preferred method for President Trump to communicate his thoughts on policy issues, the medium has raised some questions. How do we fact-check a tweet? What safeguards are in place to ensure accuracy? The day that the Supreme Court heard oral arguments in the DACA case, the president tweeted his thoughts, presenting an excellent example of this challenge: How do we assess the claim that some DACA recipients have become "hardened criminals"?

It is well known that President Trump often played fast-and-loose with the facts—the *Washington Post* documented 22,247 "false or misleading claims" the president uttered from his first day in office through August 27, 2020.[a] To figure out how to wrestle with this, think about the size of the claim.

Big claims need to be investigated with multiple sources and more extensive reading, but smaller claims can usually be settled by the various media fact-checkers. The claim made by the president is that some DACA recipients are "hardened criminals." This is a very specific claim that can be checked pretty easily with a credible source. For example, FactCheck.org, part of the Annenberg Public Policy Center, provides an excellent analysis. An article on the site points out that on its face, the claim doesn't make sense because "DACA applicants have to meet several eligibility criteria, including not having been convicted of a felony, significant misdemeanor or three or more other misdemeanors." That is, they can't be in the program if they are "hardened criminals."

However, there is something to the president's claim. First, 2,130 DACA recipients from fiscal years 2013–2017 had their status revoked because of criminal or gang activity (this is less than 0.5 percent), so they are no longer in the program. Second, in 2018 the U.S. Citizen and Immigration Services found that of the "770,628 approved DACA applications from 2012 to 2018, 53,792 had a prior arrest or apprehension, and 7,814 had a later arrest or apprehension, after approval and before renewal." This is a much larger number (about 7 percent) and these are people who were in the program. However, on closer inspection most of the arrests were for driving or immigration violations and there was no indication that any of the DACA recipients were convicted of any crimes (or they would not have been allowed in the program). Also, the article points out that the *Wall Street Journal* reports an average arrest rate of 30 percent for the U.S. adult population, so the DACA participants have an arrest rate that is less than one-fourth the rate of the general public.

Source: Lori Robertson, "The Data on DACA and Crime," FactCheck.org, November 13, 2019, www.factcheck.org/2019/11/the-data-on-daca-and-crime/ (accessed 6/10/20).

Donald J. Trump ✓
@realDonaldTrump

Many of the people in DACA, no longer very young, are far from "angels." Some are very tough, hardened criminals. President Obama said he had no legal right to sign order, but would anyway. If Supreme Court remedies with overturn, a deal will be made with Dems for them to stay!

6:45 AM · Nov 12, 2019 · Twitter for iPhone

30.5K Retweets   **77.3K** Likes

Think about it

- **When you read something** in a news story or in a tweet, do you have a favorite fact-checker you consult? This can be a very useful tool for being a good consumer of the news.

- **How do you decide** about the size of the claim that is being made? When would you need to consult more sources to get to the bottom of a story?

national politics early in U.S. history (George Washington and Abraham Lincoln, among others), Congress dominated much of the day-to-day politics, which revolved around issues such as the tariff (taxes on imported or exported goods), slavery, and internal improvements such as building roads and canals. Given the tendency to address these issues with patronage and the **pork barrel**—that is, jobs and policies targeted to benefit specific constituents—Congress was better suited for the daily task of governing than the president was.

Beginning around the turn of the twentieth century and accelerating with the New Deal of the 1930s (which established modern social welfare and regulatory policies), the scope of national policy expanded and politics became more centered in Washington. With this nationalization of politics and the increasing importance of national security issues, the president assumed a more central policy-making role. However, the tensions between representing local and national interests remain essential in understanding the legislative process and the relationship between members of Congress and their constituents.

Congress represents the people (or tries to)

Americans have a love–hate relationship with Congress; that is, we generally love our own member of Congress, but we hate Congress as a whole. Well, "hate" is a strong word, but as we show later in this section, individual members of Congress routinely have approval ratings 30 to 40 points higher than the institution's. One poll found that members of Congress landed third from the bottom in a ranking of 22 professions in terms of perceived honesty and ethical standards, narrowly ahead of car salespeople and lobbyists (nurses and military officers were at the top).[7] A more whimsical poll by Public Policy Polling asked respondents questions such as "What do you have a higher opinion of, Congress or root canals?" Root canals won handily, 56 percent to 32 percent. Congress was also less popular than head lice, traffic jams, and cockroaches, but narrowly beat out telemarketers and had a comfortable margin over North Korea, the Kardashians, and meth labs.[8] Why is Congress so unpopular? How do members of Congress try to represent their constituents? And how do elections influence this important dynamic?

Types of Representation The relationships between constituents and their member of Congress can be characterized in two basic ways: as both descriptive and substantive. **Descriptive representation** occurs when members of Congress "look like" their constituents in demographic or socioeconomic terms. For example, are members African American, Latino, or White; male or female; Catholic, Protestant, or some other religion; middle-class or upper-class? Many people believe that this kind of representation is a distinct value in itself. Having positive role models for various demographic groups helps create greater trust in the system. Moreover, constituents benefit from being represented by someone who shares something as basic as their skin color.

Descriptive representation is also related to the perceived responsiveness of a member of Congress. In general, constituents report higher levels of satisfaction with representatives who are of their same racial or ethnic background.[9] If you doubt that descriptive representation makes a difference, ask yourself whether it would be fair if all 435 House members and 100 senators were White male Protestants. Although the demographics of Congress are considerably more diverse than this, the legislature does not come close to "looking like us" on a nationwide scale (see the What Do the Facts Say? feature on p. 318).

More important than a member's race, gender, or religion, many people argue, is the *substance* of what that person does. **Substantive representation** involves *how* the

pork barrel
Legislative appropriations that benefit specific constituents, created with the aim of helping local representatives win reelection.

The American Republic will endure until the day Congress discovers that it can bribe the public with the public's money.

—**Alexis de Tocqueville,** French diplomat and author

DID YOU KNOW?

$1 million

was the average net worth of the 116th Congress (2019–2021). More than half of all members of Congress are millionaires.

Source: Center for Responsive Politics

descriptive representation
Representation in which a member of Congress shares the characteristics (such as gender, race, religion, or ethnicity) of his or her constituents.

substantive representation
Representation in which a member of Congress serves constituents' interests and shares their policy concerns.

Descriptive Representation in the 116th Congress

Compared with a generation ago, the number of women and racial and ethnic minorities in Congress has increased. But on these dimensions, how representative of the people is Congress? How close does Congress come to "looking like us"? What do the facts say?

Gender in Congress

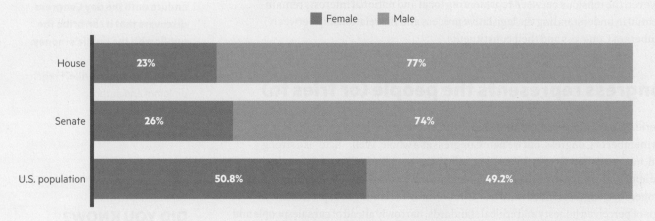

Female   Male

House	23%	77%
Senate	26%	74%
U.S. population	50.8%	49.2%

Racial and Ethnic Composition of Congress

White   Latino (any race)   African American
Asian American   Other

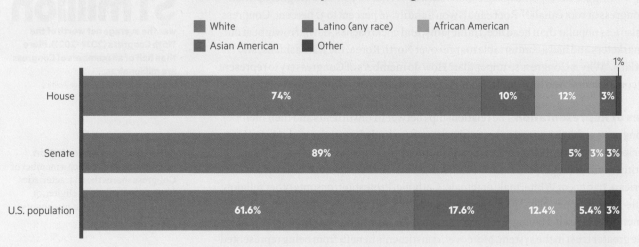

				1%
House	74%	10%	12%	3%
Senate	89%		5%	3% 3%
U.S. population	61.6%	17.6%	12.4%	5.4% 3%

Sources: Congressional data from Jennifer Manning, "Membership of the 116th Congress: A Profile," Congressional Research Service, June 1, 2020, https://fas.org/sgp/crs/misc/R45583.pdf ; population data from U.S. Census Bureau, "Quick Facts: United States," July 1, 2019, www.census.gov/quickfacts/fact/table/US/PST045219 (both accessed 6/11/20).

Think about it

- **Which comes closer to "looking like us,"** the House or the Senate?
- **How could having more women or racial and ethnic minorities** in Congress affect legislation and policy decisions?
- **Latinos now make up the largest ethnic minority** in the United States, yet they still lag behind African Americans in terms of representation in the House. Why do you think this is?

member serves his or her constituents' interests. Two long-standing models of this kind of representation are (1) the **trustee**, who represents the constituents' interests from a distance, weighing numerous national, collective, local, and moral concerns; and (2) the **delegate**, who carries out the direct desires of the voters. In a sense, trustees are more concerned with being responsible and delegates are more interested in being responsive.

Trustees, by definition, will do what they think is in the best long-term interests of their constituents and the nation, even though it may mean voting against their constituents' immediate wishes and risking defeat in the next election. Delegates, in contrast, do not have to worry about angering voters because they simply do what their constituents want. Truth be told, the trustee/delegate distinction is mostly important as a theoretical point of departure for talking about representation roles. Nearly all members of Congress act like trustees in some circumstances and like delegates in others. A third model of representation captures this reality: the **politico** is more likely to act as a delegate on issues that are especially important to his or her constituency (such as immigration reform or farm subsidies) but as a trustee on less salient or very complex issues (such as some foreign policies). Therefore, the crucial component of representation is the nature of the constituency and how the member of Congress attempts to balance and represent constituents' conflicting needs and desires.

The Role of the Constituency Most voters do not monitor their representatives' behavior closely. Can representation work if voters are not paying attention? Members of Congress behave as if voters were paying attention, even when constituents are inattentive. Incumbents know that at election time the challengers may raise issues that become important after the public thinks about them, so they try to deter challengers by anticipating what the constituents would want *if* they were fully informed.[10] For example, the public hadn't thought much about voting by mail, but it became an issue in the 2020 elections when the COVID-19 pandemic forced many states to cut down on in-person voting. President Trump claimed that voting by mail was an effort by Democrats to steal the election, while many states argued that it was a way to protect voters from being exposed to the virus. Savvy incumbents would have tried to stake out a position consistent with what the voters would want *before* a strong challenger raised the issue in a campaign.

trustee
A member of Congress who represents constituents' interests while also taking into account national, collective, and moral concerns that sometimes cause the member to vote against the preference of a majority of constituents.

delegate
A member of Congress who loyally represents constituents' direct interests.

politico
A member of Congress who acts as a delegate on issues that constituents care about (such as immigration reform) and as a trustee on more complex or less salient issues (such as some foreign policy or regulatory matters).

Members of Congress spend a good deal of time in their districts, developing relationships with constituents. Here Representative Elise Stefanik (R-NY) speaks with constituents at a community open house at the Fort Drum Youth Center in Fort Drum, New York.

Another way to examine the representative–constituency relationship is to look at differences across districts. How do districts vary? First, they differ in size: Senate "districts" (that is, states) vary in terms of both area and population. House districts all have about 760,000 people, but they vary tremendously in geographic size, from Alaska's 663,000 square miles to New York's 13th district with 10.25 square miles. Second, districts also differ in terms of who lives there and what they want from government.

Because districts are so multifaceted, the legislators they elect differ from one another as well. Regardless of the office, most voters want to elect someone whose policy positions are close to theirs. As a result, legislators tend to reflect the central tendencies of their districts. At one level, electing a legislature that "thinks like America" sounds good: if legislators act and think like their districts, then the legislature will contain a good mixture of the interests representing the country or state. But this often makes finding compromise difficult. We elect legislators to get things done, but they may be unable to agree on anything because their disagreements are too fundamental to bridge. For example, the country is sharply divided on abortion rights, as are the House, the Senate, and most state legislatures. The fact that legislators have not come to a decision on this issue is no surprise: just as citizens disagree, so do their elected representatives.

Despite the vast differences among congressional constituencies, voters nationwide want many of the same things: a healthy economy, a safe country (in terms of national defense and local crime), good schools, and effective and affordable health care. Figure 10.1 reports responses to a survey about how citizens feel that

FIGURE 10.1

What Do People Want from Congress?

Members of Congress are often criticized for being out of touch with their constituents. Based on a *USA Today* poll, Americans seem to want their congressional members to vote in line with their constituents' views, to work across party lines, and to spend more time in the district rather than Washington, D.C. But what happens if these goals conflict? What if the member represents a very partisan district where the majority does not want him or her to work with the other party? Also, is there no room for trustees who follow their conscience and stick to their principles?

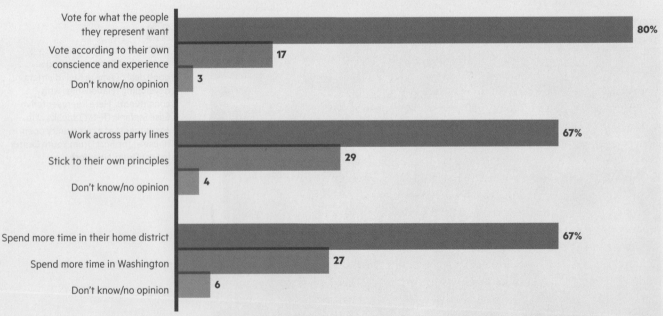

Vote for what the people they represent want — 80%
Vote according to their own conscience and experience — 17
Don't know/no opinion — 3

Work across party lines — 67%
Stick to their own principles — 29
Don't know/no opinion — 4

Spend more time in their home district — 67%
Spend more time in Washington — 27
Don't know/no opinion — 6

Source: Susan Page and Kendall Breitman, "Divided We Still Stand—and Getting Used to It," *USA Today*, March 23, 2014, www.usatoday.com/story/news/politics/2014/03/23/congress-divided-poll/6792585/ (accessed 6/10/20).

legislators should do their jobs. The survey shows tensions between being a delegate and a trustee. Respondents want their representatives to "vote for what the people they represent want" and "spend more time at home," and they show little interest in having their representatives "spend more time in Washington." Thus, responsibilities for national interests may be more difficult for members of Congress to explain to their constituents.

Members of Congress want to keep their jobs

Members' relationships to their constituents also must be understood within the context of their desire to be reelected. Political scientist David R. Mayhew argues that members of Congress are "single-minded seekers of reelection."[11] Members certainly hold multiple goals, including making good policy, but if they cannot maintain their seats, then they cannot attain other goals while in office.

After assuming that reelection is central, Mayhew asks this question: "Members of Congress may be electorally motivated, but are they in a position to do anything about it?"[12] Although individual members of Congress cannot do much to alter national economic or political forces that may affect voters' choices, they can control their own activities in the House or Senate. The importance of the **electoral connection** in explaining members' behavior seems especially clear for marginal incumbents who are constantly trying to shore up their electoral base, but even incumbents in "safe" districts realize that their job security is not guaranteed.

Mayhew outlines three ways that members of Congress promote their chances for reelection: advertising, credit claiming, and position taking. Each approach shapes the way members relate to their constituents. "Advertising" in this context refers to appeals or appearances without issue content that get the member's name in front of the public in a favorable way. Advertising includes "working the district," such as attending town meetings, appearing in a parade, or sending letters of congratulation for graduations, birthdays, or anniversaries. Members of Congress also spend a fair amount of time meeting with constituents in Washington, D.C., including seeing school groups, tourists, and interest groups from their districts.

In "credit claiming," the member of Congress takes credit for something of value to voters—most commonly, pork-barrel policies targeted to benefit specific constituents or the district as a whole. Another source of credit claiming is **casework** for individual constituents who request help with tasks such as tracking down a lost Social Security check or expediting the processing of a passport. This activity, like advertising, has both district-based and Washington-based components.

"Position taking" refers to any public statement—such as a roll call vote, speech, editorial, or position paper—about a topic of interest to constituents or interest groups. This may be the toughest aspect of a member's job, because on many issues the member is likely to alienate a certain segment of the population no matter what position he or she takes. Members try to appeal to specific audiences within their district. For example, while speaking to the Veterans of Foreign Wars members might emphasize their support for a particular new weapons program, but in meetings with college students they might highlight their opposition to the NSA's collection of millions of phone records.

Representatives' focus on reelection has some costs, two of which reflect widespread public opinion. First, the perception that Congress has granted itself too many special privileges aimed at securing reelection (such as funding for large staffs and the privilege of sending mail at no cost) leads to harsh criticism. Second, there is concern that members' time spent actively campaigning takes time away from

electoral connection
The idea that congressional behavior is centrally motivated by members' desire for reelection.

casework
Assistance provided by members of Congress to their constituents in solving problems with the federal bureaucracy or addressing other specific concerns.

incumbency advantage
The relative infrequency with which members of Congress are defeated in their attempts for reelection.

the responsibilities of enacting laws and overseeing their implementation. Another cost is the possibility of passing contradictory policies in an effort to satisfy diverse interest groups.

The desire to be reelected influences House members' and senators' behavior both in the district and in Congress. As we have mentioned, incumbents look for opportunities to shore up support for the next election, and their success at pleasing constituents produces large election rewards. As Figure 10.2 shows, few members are defeated in reelection races. This is known as the **incumbency advantage**. In the past two decades, incumbent reelection rates have been near record high levels, with 95–98 percent of House incumbents winning.[13] For example, in 2008, in an election that many called transformational, 94 percent of House incumbents were still reelected. Even in the "tsunami" election of 2010, in which Republicans made the largest gains in the House since 1948, picking up 63 seats, 86 percent of incumbents were reelected. In the 2018 midterm, in which Democrats picked up 41 seats and regained control of the House, 91 percent of incumbents were reelected. Why are incumbents so successful? Scholars have offered several reasons for this incumbency advantage.

In the District: Home Style One explanation for the increasing incumbency advantage is rooted in the diversity of congressional districts and states. Members of Congress typically respond to the diversity in their districts by developing an appropriate home style—a way of relating to the district.[14] A home style shapes the way members allocate resources, the way incumbents present themselves to their district, and the way they explain their policy positions.

Given the variation among districts, members' home styles vary as well. In some rural districts, it is important for representatives to have local roots and voters expect extensive contact with members. Urban districts expect a different kind of style. Because they have a more mobile population, voters there expect less direct contact and place more emphasis on how their elected members of Congress explain their policy positions.

Incumbency advantage may be explained in part by the skill with which members have cultivated their individual home styles in the last two decades. Members spend

House reelection rates have gone upwards of 90 percent for decades, but incumbents still campaign vigorously. Congressman Steve King (R-IA), a nine-term incumbent, lost his 2020 primary bid to Iowa state senator Randy Feenstra following widespread scrutiny over King's history of racist remarks.

House and Senate Reelection Rates, 1956–2020

FIGURE 10.2

The whole House is up for reelection every two years, so the line showing the reelection of House members in a given election year represents the percentage of the entire House. Since senators are up for reelection every six years, only one-third of the members are seeking reelection every two years. The line for the Senate represents the percentage of those who won who were up for reelection in that election year. Why do you think that House members have an easier time getting reelected than senators?

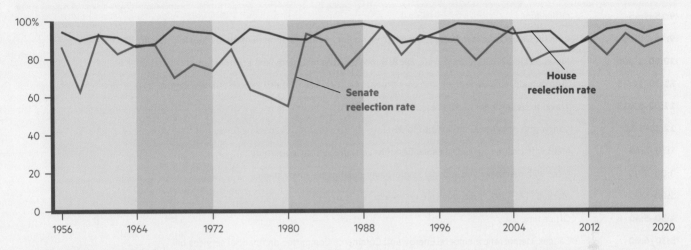

Sources: 1956–2012 percentages were compiled from Norman J. Ornstein, Thomas E. Mann, Michael J. Malbin, and Andrew Rugg, "Vital Statistics on Congress," www.brookings.edu/vitalstats, pp. 49–50 (accessed 7/30/20); 2014–2018 percentages were calculated from OpenSecrets.org (accessed 11/7/18) and 2020 percentages from CNN Politics, www.cnn.com/election/2020/results (accessed 11/8/20).

more time at home and less time in Washington than was true a generation ago. This familiarity with voters has helped them remain in office. Table 10.1 shows how one member, Senator Tammy Baldwin, spent her time in Washington and in her district as a House member before running for the Senate.

Campaign Fund-Raising Raising money is also key to staying in office. Incumbents need money to pay for campaign staff, travel, and advertising. It takes at least $1 million to make a credible challenge to an incumbent in most districts, and in many areas with expensive media markets the minimum price tag is $2 million or more. Few challengers can raise that much money. The gap between incumbent and challenger spending has grown dramatically in the past decade, with incumbents now spending about three times as much as challengers. Incumbents have far greater potential to raise vast sums of money, in part because PACs are unwilling to risk alienating an incumbent by donating to challengers. However, for the first time ever, Senate challengers outspent incumbents in 2020, but only three of them won. (For more on campaign finance, see Chapters 8 and 9.)

Money also functions as a deterrent to potential challengers. A sizable reelection fund signals that an incumbent knows how to raise money and will run a strong campaign. The aim is to convince would-be challengers that they have a slim chance of beating the incumbent—and to convince contributors and party organizations that there's no point in trying to support a challenger. This point is crucial in explaining incumbency advantage because it is nearly impossible for a weak challenger to beat an incumbent. Consider that only 10–15 percent of challengers in a typical election year have any previous elective experience; when such a high proportion of challengers are amateurs, it is not surprising that so many incumbents win.

DID YOU KNOW?

On average, House incumbents raised

$1,870,700

for their campaigns in 2020. The average Senate incumbent raised $17,083,000. This is compared with $626,411 and $18,497,000 for the average House and Senate challengers.

Source: OpenSecrets.org

TABLE
10.1

Typical Workdays for a Congressional Representative

Members of Congress are generally busy from morning until late at night, both in Washington, D.C., and in their districts, attending meetings and events. This is the actual schedule for Tammy Baldwin when she represented Wisconsin's 2nd congressional district in the House.

In Washington, D.C. (votes scheduled throughout the day)

9:15–9:45	Office time
9:45–10:00	Caucus, Democratic members, Subcommittee on Energy and Environment on markup legislation
10:00–12:00	Markup H.R. 3276, H.R. 3258, H.R. 2868, Subcommittee on Energy and Environment
11:30–11:45	Step outside markup to meet with constituents on specifics of health care reform legislation
12:00–12:15	Travel to Department of Justice
12:15–1:15	Lunch with Attorney General Eric Holder
1:30–1:45	Meet with health care CEO on specifics of health care reform legislation
2:00–3:00	Meet with members who support single-payer health care amendment
3:00–4:30	Markup H.R. 3792, Subcommittee on Health
4:30–5:30	Office time
5:30–6:00	Caucus, Democratic members, Energy and Commerce Committee on financial services bill
6:00–6:30	Meet with legislative staff
6:30–7:00	Meet with chief of staff
7:00–7:50	Office time
8:00–10:00	Dinner with chief of staff and political adviser

In the District

7:00 ET–8:00 CT	Fly from Washington, D.C., to Madison, WI
8:15–10:30	Free time at home
10:30–10:40	Phone interview with area radio station on constituent survey, health care reform, and upcoming listening session
12:15–12:25	Travel to office
12:25–1:00	Office time, edit/sign correspondence
1:00–1:20	Travel to Madison West High School
1:30–1:55	Remarks at school plaza dedication ceremony
2:00–2:30	Travel to Stoughton, WI
2:45–5:00	Listening session (originally scheduled for one hour but continued until all present could speak)
5:00–5:40	Travel home
5:15–5:20	Phone interview with University of Wisconsin student radio station
6:15–6:45	Travel to Middleton, WI
7:00–8:00	Attend and give brief remarks at NAACP annual banquet
8:05–8:25	Travel home

Note: The authors would like to thank then-representative Tammy Baldwin and her press secretary, Jerilyn Goodman, for sharing this information. Ms. Goodman emphasized that there really isn't a "typical day" for a member but said that these two days illustrate the workload. Baldwin was reelected to the U.S. Senate in 2018 (having won her first Senate term in 2012).

Constituency Service Another thing incumbents do to get reelected is "work their districts," taking every opportunity to meet with constituents, listen to their concerns, and perform casework (helping constituents interact with government programs or agencies). High levels of constituency service may help explain why some incumbents have become electorally secure.

Members of Congress love doing constituency service because it is an easy way to make voters happy. If a member can help a constituent solve a problem, that person will be more likely to support the member in the future.[15] Many voters might give the incumbent some credit simply for being willing to listen. Therefore, most members devote a significant portion of their staff to constituency service, publish newsletters that tout their good deeds on behalf of constituents, and solicit citizens' requests for help through their newsletters and websites.

This combination of factors gives incumbents substantial advantages over candidates who might run against them. By virtue of their position, they can help constituents who have problems with an agency or a program. They attract media attention because of their actions in office. And they use their official position as a platform for raising campaign cash. Finally, most incumbents represent states or districts whose partisan balance (the number of likely supporters of their party versus the number likely to prefer the other party) is skewed in their favor—if it weren't, they probably wouldn't have won the seat in the first place.

Redistricting connects representation and elections

The shape and makeup of congressional districts are critical to understanding representation in Congress and the electoral connection. District boundaries determine who is eligible to vote in any given congressional race, and these boundaries are re-drawn every 10 years, after each national census. **Redistricting** is usually the task of state legislatures. Its official purpose is to ensure that districts are roughly equal in population, which in turn ensures that every vote counts equally in determining the composition of the legislature. This decennial process placed additional significance on state elections in 2020, as control over redistricting was at stake. Final results were not available as this edition went to press, but it appears that Republicans picked up

redistricting
Re-drawing the geographic boundaries of legislative districts. This happens every 10 years to ensure that districts remain roughly equal in population.

Representative Lauren Underwood (D-IL, center) speaks to constituents at the 2019 Fox Valley Women's March in Geneva, Illinois. "Position taking," such as in this speech, is an important way representatives show they are responsive to their constituents' interests.

control of a net of two state legislative chambers and two governorships and now have unified control in 23 states. Democrats control 15 state governments and 12 states have split control.

District populations vary over time as people move from state to state or from one part of a state to another. At the national level, states gain or lose legislative seats after each census through a process called **apportionment**, which is the process of dividing the fixed number of House seats (435) among the states based on increases and decreases in state populations. Thus, states growing the fastest gain seats, and states that are not growing as fast lose seats (for example, after the 2010 census Texas gained four seats in Congress while Ohio lost two). After the 2020 census, Texas is projected to pick up three seats, Florida will gain two seats, and at least 15 more states will gain or lose a single seat.[16] The one legislature in America that is not redistricted is the U.S. Senate, which has two legislators elected per state. Voters in small states thus have proportionally more influence than those in large states when it comes to the Senate.

In theory, redistricting proceeds from a set of principles that define what districts should look like. One criterion is that districts should be roughly equal in population based on the principles of "one-person, one-vote" established by the Supreme Court with *Baker v. Carr* in the 1960s.[17] They should also reflect "communities of interest" by grouping like-minded voters in the same district. There are also technical criteria, including compactness (districts should not have extremely bizarre shapes) and contiguity (one part of a district cannot be completely separated from the rest of the district). Mapmakers also try to respect traditional natural boundaries, avoid splitting municipalities, preserve existing districts, and avoid diluting the voting power of racial minorities.

Partisan Redistricting Although the preceding principles are important, they are not the driving force in the redistricting process. Suppose a Democrat holds a House seat from an urban district populated mainly by citizens with strong Democratic Party ties. After a census, the Republican-dominated state legislature develops a new plan that extends the representative's district into the suburbs, claiming that the change counteracts population declines within the city by adding suburban voters. However, these suburban voters will likely be Republicans, thus increasing the chance that the Democrat will face strong opposition in future elections and lose his or her seat. Such changes have an important impact on voters as well. Voters who are "shifted" to a new district by a change in boundaries may be unable to vote for the incumbent they have supported for years and may instead get a representative who doesn't share their views.

In congressional redistricting, a reduction in the number of seats allocated to a state can lead to districting plans that put two incumbents in the same district, forcing them to run against each other. Incumbents from one party use these opportunities to defeat incumbents from the other party. Both parties use this technique and other tools of creative cartography to gain partisan advantage.

Attempts to use the redistricting process for political advantage are called **gerrymandering**. The term is named after Elbridge Gerry, an early Massachusetts House member and governor, vice president under James Madison, and author of the original partisan redistricting plan in 1812 (including a district with a thin, winding shape resembling a salamander). While partisan motivations have produced some funny-looking districts (see Nuts & Bolts 10.1 for examples of a partisan gerrymander and redistricting strategies), the courts have allowed the practice to continue until recently. More than 30 years ago, the Supreme Court ruled that partisan gerrymandering *may* be unconstitutional, but over the next three decades the Court struggled to find a standard that allowed it to distinguish between partisan bias so extreme that it violated the Constitution and normal partisan politics.[18]

apportionment
The process of assigning the 435 seats in the House to the states based on increases or decreases in state population.

gerrymandering
Attempting to use the process of re-drawing district boundaries to benefit a political party, protect incumbents, or change the proportion of minority voters in a district.

Types of Gerrymanders

We have learned that the redistricting process is a powerful tool politicians can use to help their party, or individual members, win and maintain seats in Congress. Let's look at two key types of gerrymandering.

Partisan gerrymanders

Elected officials from one party draw district lines that benefit candidates from their party and hurt candidates from other parties. This usually occurs when one party has majorities in both houses of the state legislature and occupies the governorship and can therefore enact redistricting legislation without input from the minority party.

Racial gerrymanders

Redistricting is used to help or hurt the chances of minority legislative candidates. The Voting Rights Act (VRA) of 1965 mandated that districting plans for many parts of the South be approved by the U.S. Department of Justice or a Washington, D.C., district court. Subsequent interpretations of the 1982 VRA amendments and Supreme Court decisions led to the creation of districts in which racial minorities are in the majority. The aim of these majority-minority districts was to raise the percentage of African-American and Latino elected officials.

Redistricting

■ The new 9th district

Previous Districts

■ 10th—Dennis Kucinich
■ 13th—Betty Sutton
■ 9th—Marcy Kaptur

Chicago

■ The new 4th congressional district

After the 2010 census, Ohio lost two seats in Congress (see our discussion of apportionment on p. 326). Republicans controlled the redistricting process and wanted the loss of seats to come from the Democrats. So the Republicans drew a new 9th congressional district that cut across the districts of three existing Democratic members of Congress. Obviously only one could win the Democratic primary—that happened to be Marcy Kaptur. Democrats Kucinich and Sutton had to leave Congress.

Illinois's 4th congressional district is a clear example of racial gerrymandering. The district has a very odd shape, but it incorporates two heavily Latino areas. (The northern part has a high Puerto Rican population and the southern part is largely Mexican; both areas are heavily Democratic.) This district was a stronghold of Democrat Luis Gutiérrez, who is of Puerto Rican descent, and is currently held by Chuy García, who is of Mexican descent. It is seen as a safe district for Democrats.

"Why Should I Care?" Many people question whether or not their vote "counts." While all votes count, actions like gerrymandering are attempts to manipulate the results to ensure particular geographic areas are overwhelmingly Republican or Democratic, thus diluting the influence of minority-party voters in those regions.

Then, from 2016 through 2018, a flood of litigation in federal and state courts showed judges' increasing willingness to rule that parties had gone too far in their redistricting plans. Sophisticated mapping programs and access to detailed political data allowed parties to slice and dice districts with increasing precision, yielding partisan maps that were no longer acceptable to the courts. In Wisconsin, North Carolina, Maryland, and Pennsylvania, federal and state courts struck down state legislative and congressional maps that they ruled to be unfairly partisan (see the Take a Stand feature for more on the debate on this topic). However, in June 2018 the Supreme Court took up cases from North Carolina and Maryland and concluded that "partisan gerrymandering claims present political questions beyond the reach of the federal courts" because they lacked a "limited and precise standard" for evaluating the extent of partisan bias. While recognizing that partisan gerrymandering may "reasonably seem unjust" and is "incompatible with democratic principles," the Court left it up to states to resolve this problem. Justice Kagan issued a scathing dissent, writing, "For the first time ever, this Court refuses to remedy a constitutional violation because it thinks the task beyond judicial capabilities. . . . Of all times to abandon the Court's duty to declare the law, this was not the one. The practices challenged in these cases imperil our system of government. Part of the Court's role in that system is to defend its foundations. None is more important than free and fair elections."[19]

Racial Redistricting Redistricting may yield boundaries that look highly unusual, especially when such efforts address population groups based on race. During the 1992 redistricting in North Carolina, the Justice Department told state legislators that they needed to create two districts with majority populations of minority voters (called majority-minority districts). Figure 10.3 shows the plan the legislature enacted, in which the district boundaries look like a pattern of spiderwebs and ink blots. Moreover, one of the districts had parts that ended up being only as wide as I-85, following the highway off an exit ramp, over a bridge, and down the entrance ramp on the other side. This move prevented the I-85 district from bisecting the district it was traveling through, which would have violated the state law requiring contiguous districts.

FIGURE 10.3

North Carolina Redistricting, 1992

This set of House districts was the subject of the landmark Supreme Court ruling *Shaw v. Reno* (1993), in which the Court said that "appearances matter" when drawing district lines. Do you agree? Should other factors such as race, party, and competitiveness play a greater role than district shape?

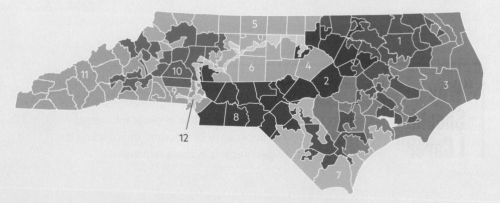

Source: North Carolina General Assembly, 1992 Congressional Base Plan No. 10, www.ncleg.gov/Files/GIS/ReferenceDocs/2011/NC%20Congressional%20Districts%20-%20Historical%20Plans%20-%201941-1992.pdf (accessed 7/30/20).

TAKE A STAND

Partisan Redistricting

Partisan redistricting is the re-drawing of legislative district lines in a way that gives one party an advantage. As we have noted, until recently the courts allowed the practice as a normal part of politics: of course, the majority party that controls the redistricting process has tried to stack the deck in its favor. When combined with the reluctance of the Supreme Court to address "political questions"—those that are better left to the elected branches—there was a powerful incentive to stay out of the "political thicket."[a] But as mapping software and "big data" political tools became readily available, the extent of partisan bias in redistricting became more pronounced. In Pennsylvania, a Republican gerrymander gave the party 13 of the state's 18 U.S. House seats, despite the Republicans' failure to win a majority of the statewide vote in the House races. In Maryland, a Democratic gerrymander turned a safe Republican House seat into a Democratic seat. Should this practice be reined in by the Court? Is it fair that some votes seem to count more than others?

Redistricting is always partisan. Those who say that the courts should stay out of redistricting argue that the practice is inherently partisan. The majority party will always try to solidify or expand its power when it has the opportunity. This has been true since the earliest years of our nation. Furthermore, those on this side of the argument say that courts are not well suited to draw legislative maps; this responsibility should remain with the state legislatures.

A second line of argument concedes that the process has gotten a little out of hand, but contends that the standard for redistricting should be partisan *neutrality* rather than partisan *fairness*. That is, rather than trying to make sure that the votes for candidates of one party have the same collective impact on the outcome of elections as the votes for the other party (fairness), the redistricting process should simply ignore partisanship (neutrality). Another perspective, adopted by the Supreme Court when it deemed partisan gerrymandering to be a political question, is that there are no objective standards to identify partisan fairness, so the problem cannot be resolved by the courts.

Partisan redistricting undermines democracy. The other side of the debate counters that just because we have always had partisan gerrymandering doesn't make it right. Indeed, democracy means that voters should be able to choose their representatives, not the other way around. Because politicians have a self-interest in maintaining their political power and will work to further this self-interest through redistricting, unfairly drawn districts undermine democratic accountability.

The strategy of emphasizing neutrality instead of fairness in redistricting is plausible, but does not convince those who support this side of the argument. While it is true that Republicans would continue to have some advantage in most states if districts were neutrally drawn, it is possible to draw maps that follow traditional districting principles but also promote partisan fairness.

take a stand

1. If you were a Supreme Court justice, how would you have ruled in the Pennsylvania and Maryland cases? Should partisan redistricting be limited?

2. Is the appropriate standard for evaluating a legislative map partisan neutrality or partisan fairness? Or should the courts stay out of redistricting entirely?

Maryland's 6th congressional district from 2011 map.

Pennsylvania's 7th congressional district from 2011 map.

The North Carolina example shows how convoluted redistricting plans can become. Part of the complexity is due to the availability of census databases that enable line drawers to divide voters as closely as they want, moving neighborhood by neighborhood, even house by house. Why bother with this level of detail? Because redistricting influences who gets elected. It is active politicking in its most fundamental form. The North Carolina plan was ultimately declared unconstitutional by the Supreme Court in *Shaw v. Reno*—a ruling that opened the door for dozens of lawsuits about racial redistricting. (See the discussion in Chapter 5 of the Voting Rights Act of 1965 and more recent Supreme Court rulings on racial redistricting, especially the 2013 case in which the Court struck down the part of the law that identified states that needed to have their redistricting plans preapproved by the Justice Department.[20]) The current legal standard is that race cannot be the *predominant* factor in drawing congressional district lines, but it can be one of the factors.

The responsibility–responsiveness dilemma

As mentioned earlier, polls show that despite generally approving of their own member of Congress, people hold Congress itself in very low esteem. This is rooted in the conflicts that arise from Congress's dual roles: responsibility for national policy making and responsiveness to local constituencies.[21] Part of the national frustration with Congress arises because we want our representatives to be both responsible *and* responsive; we want them to be great national leaders *and* to take care of our local and, at times, personal concerns.

Rather than understanding these issues as inherent in the legislative process, we often accuse members of **gridlock** and partisan bickering when our conflicting demands are not met. For example, public-opinion polls routinely show that the public wants lower taxes; more spending on education, the environment, and health care; and balanced budgets—but those three things cannot happen simultaneously. We often expect the impossible from Congress and then are frustrated when it doesn't happen.

The responsibility-responsiveness dilemma brings us back to the puzzle we posed at the beginning of this section: Why is there a persistent 30-40 percent gap between approval ratings for individual members and for the institution? The answer may simply be that members of Congress tend to respond more to their constituents' demands than to take on the responsibility of solving national problems. And when Congress becomes embroiled in debates about constituencies' conflicting demands, the institution may appear ineffectual. But as long as members keep the "folks back home" happy, their individual popularity will remain high.

gridlock
An inability to enact legislation because of partisan conflict within Congress or between Congress and the president.

"Why Should I Care?"

How would you like your member of Congress to represent you? Should members represent the interests of just their district or the broader nation? Should they be responsive or responsible? Constituents have an interest in holding their members accountable, yet most congressional elections are not very competitive. So if you don't like how your member is representing you, what can you do about it? Understanding the nature of representation and the incumbency advantage can help answer these important questions.

The structure of Congress

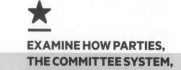

EXAMINE HOW PARTIES, THE COMMITTEE SYSTEM, AND STAFFERS ENABLE CONGRESS TO FUNCTION

As we have seen, the goal of getting reelected greatly influences the behavior of members of Congress. The reelection goal also has a strong influence on the way that Congress is structured, both formally (staff, the committee system, parties, and leadership roles) and informally (norms). Despite the importance of the electoral connection, the goal of being reelected cannot explain everything about members' behavior and the congressional structure. This section examines some other explanations that underlie the informal and formal structures of Congress: the policy motivations of members, the partisan basis for congressional institutions, and the importance of the committee system.

Informal structures

Various norms provide an informal structure for the way that Congress works. *Universalism* is the norm that when benefits are divided up, they should be awarded to as many districts and states as possible. Thus, for example, when it comes to handing out federal highway dollars or expenditures for the Pentagon's weapons programs, the benefits are broadly distributed across the entire country. (This means, however, that votes on such bills tend to be lopsided, as some areas of the country need the federal funds more urgently than others.)

Another norm, **logrolling**, reinforces universalism with the idea that "if you scratch my back, I'll scratch yours." This norm leads members of Congress to support bills that they otherwise might oppose in exchange for other members' votes on bills that are very important to them. For example, House members from a dairy state might vote for tobacco price supports even if their state has no tobacco farmers, and in return they would expect a member from the tobacco state to vote for the dairy price support bill. This norm can produce wasteful pork-barrel spending. In the 2011 budget, a $1.1 trillion omnibus appropriations bill contained more than 6,488 **earmarks** worth $8.3 billion, so nearly everyone gained something by passing it. The $1.4 trillion 2020 omnibus appropriations bill did not include any traditional earmarks (or "pork," as they are informally known), following the ban on formal earmarks in both the House and the Senate in 2011, but there were still billions of dollars in targeted spending as members of Congress found ways to secure funding for their district or state. Representative Jim Banks (R-IN) complained about the wasteful spending in the sprawling bill, saying, "Like 'mystery meat,' you don't want to know what's in it. Also like 'mystery meat'—you can bet at least one ingredient is a whole lot of pork."[22]

The norm of *specialization* is also important, both for the efficient operation of Congress and for members' reelection. By specializing and becoming an expert on a given issue, members provide valuable information to the institution as a whole and also create a basis for credit claiming. This norm is stronger in the House, where members often develop a few areas of expertise, whereas senators tend to be policy generalists.

The **seniority** norm also serves individual and institutional purposes. This norm holds that the member with the longest service on a given committee will chair that committee. Although there have been numerous violations of this norm, whereby the most senior member has been passed over for someone whom the party leaders favored, the norm benefits the institution by ensuring orderly succession in committee leadership.[23] The norm also benefits members by providing a tangible reason why voters should return them to Congress year after year.

logrolling
A form of reciprocity in which members of Congress support bills that they otherwise might not vote for in exchange for other members' votes on bills that are very important to them.

earmarks
Federally funded local projects attached to bills passed through Congress.

seniority
The informal congressional norm of choosing the member who has served the longest on a particular committee to be the committee chair.

Representative Bill Flores (R-TX) poses with Faye, a potbellied pig, after a news conference held by Citizens Against Government Waste at the Phoenix Park Hotel to release the "2017 Congressional Pig Book," which identifies pork-barrel spending in Congress.

Formal structures

Formal structures also shape members' behavior in Congress. Political parties, party leadership, the committee system, and staff provide the context within which members of Congress make policy and represent their constituents (see Nuts & Bolts 10.2).

Parties and Party Leaders Political parties are important for allocating power in Congress. Party leaders are always elected on straight party-line votes, and the majority party determines committee leadership, the division of seats on committees, and the allocation of committee resources. Without parties, the legislative process would be much more fractured because members would be autonomous agents in battle with one another. Parties provide a team framework that allows members to work together for broadly beneficial goals. Just think how difficult it would be for a member of Congress to get a bill passed if he or she had to build a coalition from scratch every time. Instead, parties provide a solid base from which coalition building may begin. As discussed in Chapter 7, political parties provide brand name recognition for members.

The top party leader in the House—and the only House leader mentioned in the Constitution—is the **Speaker of the House**. This individual is the head of the majority party, and he or she influences the legislative agenda, committee assignments, scheduling, and overall party strategy. The Speaker is aided by the **Majority Leader**, the Majority Whip, and the conference or caucus chair (in addition to many other lower-level party positions). The Majority Leader not only is a key national spokesperson for the party but also helps with the day-to-day operation of the legislative process.

The Majority Whip oversees the extensive **whip system**, which has three functions: information gathering, information dissemination, and coalition building. The whips meet regularly to discuss legislative strategy and scheduling. The whips then pass along this information to colleagues in their respective parties and indicate the party's position on a given bill. Whips also take a head count of party members in the House on specific votes and communicate this information to the party leaders. If a vote looks close, whips try to persuade members to support the party's position. ("Whip"

Speaker of the House
The elected leader of the House of Representatives.

Majority Leader
The elected head of the party holding the majority of seats in the House or Senate.

whip system
An organization of House leaders who work to disseminate information and promote party unity in voting on legislation.

Majority-Party Structure in the House of Representatives and the Senate

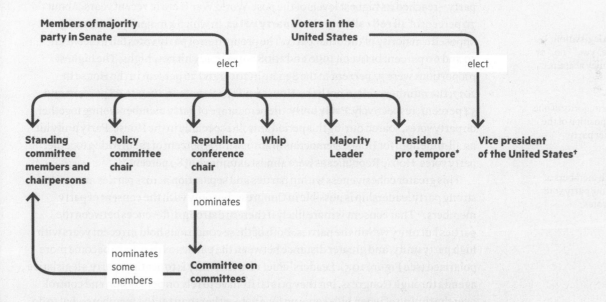

*Steering committee includes the Speaker, Majority Leader, and whip, and some members who are appointed by the Speaker and some who are elected by the conference.

*The president pro tempore is elected by the majority-party members, but by custom is the most senior member of the majority party.

†The vice president of the United States is the president of the Senate, but rarely presides over the floor. The vice president's most important role is to break tie votes.

Source: Compiled by the authors.

comes from English fox hunting, referring to the person who keeps the hounds from wandering too far from the pack—the "whipper-in.")

The conference chair for the Republicans (or caucus chair for the Democrats) runs the party meetings to elect floor leaders, make committee assignments, and set legislative agendas. The minority party in the House has a parallel structure: its leader is the **Minority Leader,** and the second in command is the Minority Whip.

The Senate leadership does not have as much power as the House leadership, mostly because individual senators have more power than individual House members due to the Senate's rule of unlimited debate, as we will discuss later. The Majority Leader and Minority Leader are the leaders of their respective parties; second in command are the Assistant Majority and Minority Leaders. The Senate also has a whip system, but it is not as extensive as the House system. Republicans have a separate position for the conference chair, while the Democratic leader also serves as the caucus chair. Officially, the country's vice president is also the president of the Senate, but he or she appears in the chamber only when needed to cast a tie-breaking vote. The Constitution also mentions the **president pro tempore** of the Senate, whose formal duties involve presiding over the Senate when the vice president is not present. This is typically the member of the majority party with the greatest seniority, although the position does not have any real power. In fact, the actual president pro tempore rarely presides over the Senate and the task is typically given to a more junior senator.

The Role of Parties Political parties in Congress reflect the individualism of the institution. In the U.S. Congress, the parties do not impose a party line or penalize members who vote against the party. Indeed, they have virtually no ability to impose electoral restrictions (such as denying the party's nomination) on renegade members.

Parties in Congress have greatly strengthened since the 1960s (see Figure 10.4). Partisanship—evident when party members stick together in opposition to the other party—reached its highest levels of the post–World War II era in recent years. About 70 percent of all **roll call votes** were **party votes,** in which a majority of one party opposed a majority of the other party. The proportion of party votes fell to between 50 and 60 percent between 1996 and 2008 but recently hit new highs. The highest proportions were 72 percent in the Senate in 2009 and 76 percent in the House in 2017; the numbers fell in both the House and the Senate in 2019 to 68 percent and 54 percent, respectively. **Party unity,** the percentage of party members voting together on party votes, soared during this period as well, especially in the House. Party unity hit an all-time high for House Democrats in 2019, with 95 percent of them voting together on party votes. House Republicans were almost as unified, at 89 percent.[24]

This greater cohesiveness within parties and separation across parties means that strong party leadership is possible in Congress, but only with the consent of party members.[25] That consent is more likely if there are strong differences between the parties but unity within the parties. Both of these conditions hold in recent years with high party unity, and greater distance between the parties as they have become more polarized (see Figure 10.5). Leaders' chief responsibility is to get their party's legislative agenda through Congress, but they primarily have to rely on persuasion and control over the timing of when bills come up for a vote rather than telling members what to do. Leaders' success largely depends on their personal skills, communicative abilities, and trustworthiness. Some of the most successful leaders, such as Lyndon Johnson (D-TX), Majority Leader of the Senate from 1955 to 1961, and Sam Rayburn (D-TX), Speaker of the House for more than 17 years, kept in touch with key members on a daily basis. Another important tool of the leadership is agenda control: both positive (getting bills to the floor that are favored by the party) and negative (preventing votes on bills that would divide the majority party).

Minority Leader
The elected head of the party holding the minority of seats in the House or Senate.

president pro tempore
A largely symbolic position usually held by the most senior member of the majority party in the Senate.

roll call vote
A recorded vote on legislation; members may vote "yes," "no," or "present," or they may abstain.

party vote
A vote in which the majority of one party opposes the position of the majority of the other party.

party unity
The extent to which members of Congress in the same party vote together on party votes.

FIGURE
10.4

Party Votes and Unity in Congress, 1962–2019

Party votes are said to occur when a majority of one party opposes a majority of the other party, and party unity refers to the percentage of the party members who vote together on party votes. These two graphs make two important points. First, partisanship has increased in the last two decades, in terms of both the proportion of party votes and the level of party unity. Second, despite these increased levels of partisanship, only about two-thirds of all votes in the House and Senate divide the two parties. Given these potentially conflicting observations, how would you assess the argument that partisanship in Congress is far too intense?

Party votes in Congress

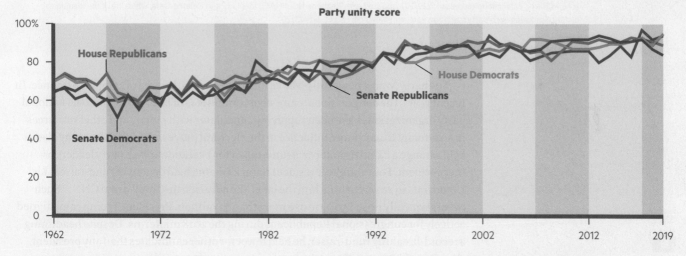

Party unity score

Source: Congressional Quarterly, "CQ Federal Congressional Bill Tracker," https://info.cq.com/legislative-tracking/cq-federal/ (accessed 8/1/20).

Leaders must also have the ability to bargain and compromise. One observer noted, "To Senator Johnson, public policy evidently was an inexhaustibly bargainable product."²⁶ Such leaders find solutions where none appear possible. Leaders also do favors for members (such as making campaign appearances, helping with fund-raising, contributing to campaigns, helping them get desired committee assignments, or guiding pet projects through the legislative process) to engender a feeling of personal obligation to the leadership when it needs a key vote.

If you want to get along, go along.

—**Sam Rayburn,** former Speaker of the House

FIGURE 10.5

Ideological Polarization in Congress, 1879–2019

Although party polarization in Congress has been high in the past, it lessened in the early twentieth century. Polarization has increased steadily in the last 70 years, and today's Congress is more polarized than ever. What do you think causes this extreme polarization?

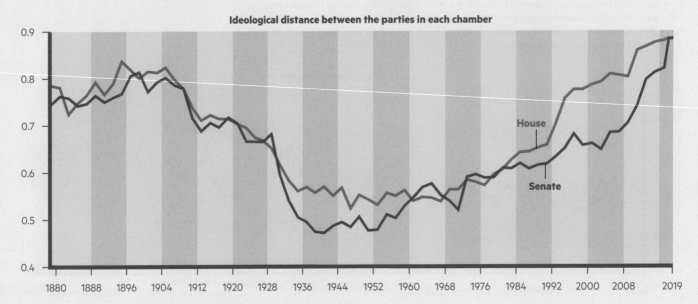

Ideological distance between the parties in each chamber

Source: Polarization in Congress, "Liberal-Conservative Partisan Polarization by Chamber," Jeff Lewis, March 11, 2018, https://voteview.com/articles/party_polarization (accessed 7/29/20); updated with Realtime NOMINATE Ideology and Related Data, which track the ideological distance between each party's average vote, voteview.com (accessed 6/3/20).

A sitting president can be a powerful ally in a campaign. Here, President Trump uses his Twitter account to endorse Representative Mo Brooks (R-AL), who was reelected to the House in 2020.

> **Donald J. Trump** ✓
> @realDonaldTrump
>
> .@MoInTheHouse Brooks is running for Congress in the Great State of Alabama. He is a huge supporter of the #MAGA Agenda. Mo fully supports Securing our Border w/the WALL, he Loves our Military & Vets, & is Strong on the #2A. Mo has my Complete Endorsement!

The party's most powerful positive incentives are in the area of campaign finance. In recent years, the congressional campaign committees of both parties and the national party organizations have been supplying candidates with money and other resources in an attempt to gain more influence in the electoral process. Party leaders may also help arrange a campaign stop or a fund-raiser for a candidate with party leaders or the president. For example, President Barack Obama held dozens of fund-raisers for Democrats in 2014, earning him the label "Fundraiser-in-Chief" from CNN.[27] Such events typically raise $500,000 to more than $1 million. President Trump campaigned actively for congressional Republicans during the 2018 midterms. Despite headlining a record-breaking fund-raiser, he held fewer for other candidates than any president since Ronald Reagan.[28]

Despite these positive reinforcements, members' desire for reelection always comes before party concerns, and leadership rarely tries to force a member to vote against his or her constituents' interests. For example, Democrats from rural areas, where most constituents support gun ownership and many are hunters, would not be expected to vote the party line favoring a gun control bill. But if a member of Congress did something much more extreme that crossed the party's leadership—for example, supporting the opposing party's candidate for Speaker or passing strategic information to the opposition—he or she could expect to be disciplined by the party's leaders. In such cases, disciplinary measures might involve stripping the member of all committee assignments or even expelling the member from his or her seat. Despite occasional strong-arm tactics, party leaders have moved toward a service-oriented leadership, recognizing that their power is only as strong as the leeway granted by the rank-and-file membership.

The Committee System The committee system in the House and Senate is another crucial part of the legislative structure. There are four types of committees: standing, select, joint, and conference. **Standing committees**, which have ongoing membership and jurisdictions, are where most of the work of Congress gets done. These committees draft legislation and oversee the implementation of the laws they pass. For example, the Agriculture Committees in the House and Senate have jurisdiction over farm programs such as commodity price supports, crop insurance, and soil conservation. But they also create and oversee policy for rural electrification and development, nutrition programs like the Supplemental Nutrition Assistance Program (SNAP), and the inspection of livestock, poultry, seafood, and meat products. Many committees share jurisdiction on policy: for example, the House Natural Resources Committee oversees the U.S. Forest Service and forests on federally owned lands, and the Agriculture Committee oversees policy for forests on privately owned lands. There are 21 standing committees in the House and 20 in the Senate.

Select committees typically address a specific topic for one or two terms, such as the House Select Committee on the Climate Crisis. These committees do not have the same legislative authority as standing committees; rather, they mostly collect information, provide policy options, and draw attention to a given issue.

There are four **joint committees** made up of members of the House and Senate, and they rarely have legislative authority. The Joint Committee on Taxation, for example, does not have authority to send legislation concerning tax policy to the floor of the House or Senate. Instead, it gathers information and provides estimates of the consequences of proposed tax legislation. Joint committees may also be temporary, such as the "Supercommittee" (officially, the Joint Select Committee on Deficit Reduction) that was formed in 2011 to try to reach bipartisan agreement on a deficit reduction plan. The committee failed to reach agreement and was disbanded in 2012.

Conference committees are formed as needed to resolve differences between the House and Senate versions of legislation that are passed in each chamber. These committees mostly comprise standing committee members from each chamber who worked on the bill in question.

The committee system creates a division of labor that helps members get reelected by facilitating specialization and credit claiming. For example, a chair of the Agriculture Committee or of a key agricultural subcommittee may reasonably take credit for passing an important bill for the farmers back home, such as the Cottonseed Payment Program that provides assistance to cottonseed farmers who have lost crops due to hurricanes.[29] The number of members who could make these credible claims expanded dramatically in the 1970s with the proliferation of subcommittees (there are 102 in the House and 67 in the Senate). Speaking about the House, one observer said, with some exaggeration, that if you ever forget a member's name, you can simply refer to him or her as "Mr. or Ms. Chairman" and you will be right about half the time.

This view of congressional committees is based on the *distributive theory*, which is rooted in the norm of reciprocity and representatives' incentives to provide benefits for their districts. The theory holds that members will seek committee assignments to best serve their district's interests, the leadership will accommodate those requests, and the floor will respect the views of the committees (that is, committee members will support one another's legislation). This means that members tend to have an interest in and to support the policies produced by the committees they serve on. For example, members from farm states would want to serve on the Agriculture Committee and members with a lot of military bases or defense contractors in their districts would want to be on the Armed Services Committee.

standing committees
Committees that are a permanent part of the House or Senate structure, holding more importance and authority than other committees.

select committees
Committees in the House or Senate created to address a specific issue for one or two terms.

joint committees
Committees that contain members of both the House and Senate but have limited authority.

conference committees
Temporary committees created to negotiate differences between the House and Senate versions of a piece of legislation that has passed through both chambers.

Nonetheless, the committee system does not exist simply to further members' electoral goals. It also provides collective benefits to the rest of the members through committee members' expertise on policy, which helps reduce uncertainty about policy outcomes.[30] By deferring to expert committees, members are able to achieve beneficial outcomes while using their own time more efficiently.

Committees also serve the policy needs of the majority party, largely because the party in power controls a majority of seats on every committee. The party ratios on each committee generally reflect the partisan distribution in the overall chamber, but the majority party gives itself somewhat larger majorities on the important committees such as Ways and Means (which controls tax policy), Appropriations, and Rules. The Rules Committee is important to the majority party because it structures the nature of debate in the House by setting the length of debate and the type and number of amendments to a bill that will be allowed. These decisions must be approved by a majority of the House members. The Rules Committee has become an arm of the majority-party leadership, and in many instances it provides rules that support the party's policy agenda or protect its members from having to take controversial positions. For example, the Rules Committee prevented amendments on the articles of impeachment brought against President Trump in December 2019, fearing that amendments could have divided the Democratic Party.[31] Majority members are expected to support their party on votes concerning rules, even if they end up voting against the related legislation.

Congressional Staff The final component of the formal structure of Congress is congressional staff. The size of personal and committee staff exploded in the 1970s and 1980s but has since leveled off. Today the total number of congressional staff is more than four times as large as it was 50 years ago. Part of the motivation for this growth was to reduce the gap between the policy-making capability of Congress and the president, especially with regard to fiscal policy. The larger committee staffs gave members of Congress independent sources of information and expertise with which to challenge the president. The other primary motivation was electoral. By increasing the size of their personal staff, members were able to open multiple district offices and expand opportunities for helping constituents.

"Why Should I Care?"

The Constitution says very little about the internal structure of Congress, so the institution is largely the creation of its members. The norms of the institution and its formal structure facilitate members' electoral and policy goals, so if they don't like the way something works, they can change it. While this may sound very self-serving, members of Congress also work to serve broader collective and policy goals—or else they would be booted out of office. Understanding this fundamental point provides great insight into why Congress is structured the way that it is.

★
TRACE THE STEPS IN THE LEGISLATIVE PROCESS

How a bill becomes a law

Every introductory textbook on American politics presents a diagram that describes how a bill becomes a law (see How It Works: Passing Legislation). This book is no exception. However, we provide an important truth-in-advertising disclosure: many important laws do not follow this orderly path.[32] After presenting the standard view, we describe the most important deviations from that path.

The conventional process

The details of the legislative process can be incredibly complex, but its basic aspects are fairly simple. The most important thing to understand about the process is that before a piece of legislation can become a law it must be passed *in identical form* by both the House and the Senate and signed by the president. If the president vetoes the bill, it can still be passed with a two-thirds vote in each chamber. Note, however, that all legislation that is signed by the president (or for which Congress overrides a veto) carries the weight of the law; legislation that is not signed by the president has only internal legislative or symbolic purposes. Here are the basic steps of the process to pass a bill:

1. A member of Congress introduces the bill.
2. A subcommittee and committee craft the bill.
3. Floor action on the bill takes place in the first chamber (House or Senate).
4. Committee and floor action takes place in the second chamber.
5. The conference committee works out any differences between the House and Senate versions of the bill. (If the two chambers pass the same version, steps 5 and 6 are not necessary.)
6. The floor of each chamber passes the final conference committee version.
7. The president either signs or vetoes the final version.
8. If the bill is vetoed, both chambers can attempt to override the veto with a two-thirds vote in both chambers.

Early Steps The first part of the process, unchanged from the earliest Congresses, is the introduction of the bill. Only members of Congress can introduce a bill, either by dropping it into the "hopper," a wooden box at the front of the chamber in the House, or by presenting it to one of the clerks at the presiding officer's desk in the Senate. Even the president would need to have a House member or senator introduce his or her bill. Each bill has one or more sponsors and often many co-sponsors. (See Nuts & Bolts 10.3 for a description of the different types of legislation.)

Types of Legislation

NUTS & BOLTS 10.3

- **Bill:** A legislative proposal that becomes law if it is passed by both the House and the Senate in identical form and approved by the president. Each is assigned a bill number, with "H.R." indicating bills that originated in the House and "S.R." denoting bills that originated in the Senate. Private bills are concerned with a specific individual or organization and often address immigration or naturalization issues. Public bills affect the general public if enacted into law.
- **Simple resolution:** Legislation used to express the sense of the House or Senate, designated by "H.Res." or "S.Res." Simple resolutions affect only the chamber passing the resolution, are not signed by the president, and cannot become public law. Resolutions are often used for symbolic legislation, such as congratulating sports teams or naming a post office after a famous person.
- **Concurrent resolution:** Legislation used to express the position of both chambers on a nonlegislative matter to set the annual budget or to fix adjournment dates, designated by "H.Con.Res" or "S.Con.Res." Concurrent resolutions are not signed by the president and therefore do not carry the weight of law.
- **Joint resolution:** Legislation that has few practical differences from a bill (passes both chambers in identical form, signed by the president) unless it proposes a constitutional amendment. In that case, a two-thirds majority of those present and voting in both the House and the Senate, and ratification by three-fourths of the states, are required for the amendment to be adopted and it does not require the president's signature.

How it works: in theory
Passing Legislation

Speaker of House Receives Bill

Committee*†

Subcommittee*†

Bill Reported Out by Full Committee

Rules Committee*†

House Floor*†

Amends or Approves Bill from Committee

House Bill

President of Senate Receives Bill

Committee*†

Subcommittee*†

Bill Reported Out by Full Committee

Majority Leader

Senate Floor*†

Amends or Approves Bill from Committee

Senate Bill

House Amends Senate Bill*†

House Floor†

Senate Amends House Bill*†

Senate Floor†

Conference Committee*†

House Modifies Senate Bill

Senate Modifies House Bill

Conference Report*†

House Approves Senate Bill†

Adoption by Both Houses†

Senate Approves House Bill†

White House†

Veto

Approve

House and Senate Floor†

Law

Veto Override

*Points at which a bill can be amended.
†Points at which a bill can die.

In the House...

The House Ways and Means Committee crafted H.R. 1, the House version of the Tax Bill. **All tax bills must originate in the House**.

In the Senate...

The Senate Finance Committee **crafted the initial Senate version**.

Passing the Tax Cuts and Jobs Act

The 2017 Tax Cuts and Jobs Act provides an example of how passing legislation often deviates from the conventional method.

House passes its version.

Not so fast.

Republicans **cannot pass the Finance Committee's version** without the 60 votes needed to break a filibuster.

So the Budget Committee saves the day.

The Senate Budget Committee packages the Finance Committee's bill with a bill on drilling for oil as a reconciliation bill (which only needs 51 votes, rather than a filibuster-proof 60, to be approved). **It keeps the title of the House bill, H.R. 1, on this new bill to preserve the fiction that it originated in the House** and then submits it in the Senate.

Vote-a-rama!

After 355 amendments to the reconciliation bill are proposed, key provisions ratifying McConnell's deals are approved and the **Democrats' efforts are defeated** in a marathon of overnight voting.

Meanwhile, on the Left...

10 Democratic senators **try to slow the bill down** by sending it to the Finance Committee.

Meanwhile, on the Right...

Several Republican senators say **they will vote against the bill if changes are not made**, so Majority Leader Mitch McConnell cuts some deals.

Conference committee **works out the differences** in the House version of H.R. 1 and the revamped Senate version of H.R. 1.

Senate passes its version.

Passed!

House passes the conference report.

Passed!

Passed!

House passes the Senate's amendments.

Senate passes the conference report—with amendments.

Signed into law.

President Trump signs the **bill into law**.

❓ Critical Thinking

1. **What are the most significant ways in which** the process to pass the 2017 Tax Cuts and Jobs Act deviated from the conventional method?

2. **Do you think the 2017 Tax Cuts and Jobs Act could have been** passed without this unconventional process? Why or why not?

The next step is to send the bill to the relevant committee. House and Senate rules specify committee jurisdictions (there are more than 200 categories), and the bill is matched with the committee that best fits its subject matter. In the House, major legislation may be sent to more than one committee in a practice known as multiple referral, but one of the committees is designated the primary committee and the bill is reviewed by other committees sequentially or in parts. The practice is less common in the Senate, partly because senators have more opportunities to amend legislation on the floor.

Once the bill goes to a committee, the chair refers it to the relevant subcommittee, where much of the legislative work occurs. One important point: 80–90 percent of bills die at this stage of the process; they never make it out of the subcommittee or committee. For bills that see some action, the subcommittee holds hearings, calls witnesses, and gathers the information necessary to rewrite, amend, and edit the bill. The final language of the bill is determined in a collaborative process known as the **markup**. During this meeting, members debate aspects of the issue and offer amendments to change the language or content of the bill. After all amendments have been considered, a final vote is taken on whether to send the bill to the full committee. The full committee then considers whether to pass it along to the floor. This committee also has the option of amending the bill, passing it as is, or tabling it (which kills the bill). Every bill sent to the floor by a committee is accompanied by a report and full documentation of all the hearings. These documents constitute the bill's legislative history, which the courts, executive departments, and the public use to determine the purpose and meaning of the law.

Debating the Bill

When the bill makes it to the floor, it is placed on one of the various legislative calendars. Bills are removed from the calendar to be considered by the floor under a broad range of possible rules. When the bill reaches the floor, the majority party and minority party each designate a bill manager, who is responsible for guiding the debate on the floor. Debate in the House proceeds according to tight time limits and rules governing the nature of amendments. Senate debate is much more open and unlimited in most circumstances (unless all the senators agree to a limit).

Unless restricted by a unanimous consent agreement, senators can speak as long as they want and offer any amendment to a bill, even if it isn't germane (that is, directly related to the underlying bill). Debate may be cut off only if a supermajority of 60 senators agree in a process known as invoking **cloture**. Therefore, one senator can stop any bill by threatening to talk the bill to death if 40 of his or her colleagues agree. This practice, which is known as a **filibuster**, strengthens the hand of the minority party in the Senate, giving it veto power over legislation unless the majority party has 60 senators who unanimously support a bill.

When debate is completed and all amendments have been considered, the presiding officer calls for a voice vote, with those in favor saying "aye" and those opposed "no." If it is unclear which side has won, any member may call for a "division vote," which requires members on each side to stand and be counted. At that point, any member may call for a recorded vote (there is no way of recording members' positions on voice votes and division votes). If at least 25 members agree that a recorded vote is desired, buzzers go off in the office buildings and committee rooms, calling members to the floor for the vote. Once they reach the floor, members vote by an electronic system in which they insert ATM-like cards into slots and each vote is recorded on a big board at the front of the chamber.

Resolving Discrepancies

If the bill passes the House and the Senate in different forms, the discrepancies have to be resolved. On many minor bills, one chamber

markup
One of the steps through which a bill becomes a law, in which the final wording of the bill is determined.

cloture
A procedure through which the Senate can limit the amount of time spent debating a bill (cutting off a filibuster) if a supermajority of 60 senators agree.

filibuster
A tactic used by senators to block a bill by continuing to hold the floor and speak—under the Senate rule of unlimited debate—until the bill's supporters back down.

may simply accept the other chamber's version to solve the problem. On other minor bills and some major bills, differences are resolved through a process known as amendments between the chambers. In this case, one chamber modifies a bill passed by the other chamber and sends it back. These modifications can go back and forth several times before both chambers agree on an identical bill. A complicated version of this approach was used to pass health care reform in 2010.

The most common way to resolve differences on major legislation is through a conference committee made up of key players in the House and the Senate. A majority of major bills go to a conference committee, but minor bills rarely do.[33] Sometimes the conferees split the difference between the House and Senate versions, but at other times the House and Senate approaches are so different that one must be chosen—an especially tricky prospect when different parties control the two chambers. Sometimes the conference committee cannot resolve differences and the bill dies. If the committee can agree on changes, each chamber must pass the final version—the conference report—by a majority vote and neither chamber is allowed to amend it.

Presidential Approval or Veto The bill is then sent to the president. If the president approves and signs the measure within 10 days (not counting Sundays), it becomes law. If the president objects to the bill, he or she may **veto** it within 10 days by sending it back to the chamber where it originated, along with a statement of objections. Unless both the House and the Senate vote to override the veto by a two-thirds majority, the bill dies. If the president does not act within 10 days and Congress is in session, the bill becomes law without the president's approval. If Congress is not in session, the measure dies through a **pocket veto**.

Appropriations Bills One final point on how a bill becomes a law is important: any bill that appropriates money must pass through the two-step process of authorization and appropriation. In the authorization process, members debate the merits of the bill, determine its language, and limit the amount that can be spent on the bill. The appropriations process involves the Budget Committees in both the House and the Senate, which set the overall guidelines for the national budget, and the Appropriations Committees in the two chambers, which determine the actual amounts of money that will be spent (see How It Works in Chapter 14). In recent years, Congress has been unable to pass appropriations bills in time for the start of the new fiscal year, so it ends up passing "continuing resolutions" that spend money at the previous year's levels in order to keep the government open. Congress passed eight continuing resolutions for the 2019 fiscal year (but only two for 2020). That may sound like a lot, but the record is 21 for the 2001 fiscal year.[34]

Deviations from the conventional process

There are many ways in which legislation may not follow the typical path. First, in some Congresses up to 20 percent of *major* bills bypass the committee system. This may be done by a discharge petition, in which a majority of the members force a bill out of its assigned committee, or by a special rule in the House. In some cases, a bill may go to the relevant committee, but then party leadership may impose its version of the bill later in the process. Consider the USA PATRIOT Act, which Congress passed in the wake of the terrorist attacks of September 11 to give the government stronger surveillance powers. It was unanimously reported by the Judiciary Committee after five days of hard bipartisan work; but a few days later, according to committee member Representative Jerrold Nadler (D-NY), "[t]hen the bill just

veto
The president's rejection of a bill that has been passed by Congress. A veto can be overridden by a two-thirds vote in both the House and Senate.

pocket veto
The automatic death of a bill passed by the House and Senate when the president fails to sign the bill in the last 10 days of a legislative session.

disappeared. And we had a new several hundred-page bill revealed from the Rules Committee" that had to be voted on the next day. Most members of Congress did not have a chance to read it.[35] The Affordable Care Act (ACA) also deviated from the standard path.

Second, about one-third of major bills are adjusted post-committee and before the legislation reaches the floor by supporters of the bills to increase the chances of passage. Sometimes the bill goes back to the committee after these changes, and sometimes it does not. One good example of this approach was the ACA, which was altered by House and Senate leadership after the committees deadlocked on different versions of the bill. The legislation also bypassed the conference committee; party leadership worked out the differences between the House and Senate versions directly. Thus, although most of the legislative work is accomplished in committees, a significant amount of legislation bypasses committee review.

Third, summit meetings between the president and congressional leaders may bypass or jump-start the normal legislative process. For example, rather than going through the Budget Committees to set budgetary targets, the president may meet with top leaders from both parties and hammer out a compromise that is presented to Congress as a done deal.

Fourth, **omnibus legislation**—massive bills that run hundreds of pages long and cover many different subjects and programs—often requires creative approaches by the leadership to guide the bill through the legislative maze. In addition, the massive legislation often carries riders—extraneous legislation attached to the "must pass" bill to secure approval for pet projects that would otherwise fail. This form of pork-barrel legislation is another mechanism used in the quest for reelection.

omnibus legislation
Large bills that often cover several topics and may contain extraneous, or pork-barrel, projects.

Key differences between House and Senate legislative processes

There are three central differences between the legislative processes of the House and the Senate: the continuity of the membership and the impact that has on the rules; the way in which bills get to the floor; and the structure of the floor process, including debate and amendments. Because the Senate is a continuing body, with two-thirds of its members returning every session without facing reelection, there has been greater stability in the rules of the Senate than in those of the House. However, Senate rules can be changed at the start of a session to meet the needs of new members.

The floor process itself is simpler and less structured in the Senate than in the House. This is partly due to the relative size of the two chambers: the House, with 435 members, needs more rules than the Senate, with 100 members. Moreover, the Senate is a more individualistic body, with unlimited debate and a very open amendment process. As mentioned earlier, unless restricted by a unanimous consent agreement, senators can speak as long as they want and offer any type of amendment to a bill. In contrast, the House is a more complex institution. The Rules Committee governs the nature of debate on a bill there: closed rules do not allow any amendments, open rules allow related amendments, and modified rules allow some amendments but not others. Floor managers control general debate under a five-minute rule, although that restriction is frequently circumvented through an elaborate process that allows more time.

Ironically, although the Senate is formally committed to unlimited debate, senators often voluntarily place limits on themselves, which makes the Senate operate more like the House. Similarly, although the House has strict rules concerning debate and amendments, there are ways of bending those rules to make that chamber operate more like the potentially freewheeling Senate.

Oversight

DESCRIBE HOW CONGRESS ENSURES THAT THE BUREAUCRACY IMPLEMENTS POLICIES CORRECTLY

Once a bill becomes a law, Congress plays another crucial role by overseeing the implementation of the law to make sure the bureaucracy interprets it as Congress intended. Other motivations driving the oversight process are the desire to gain publicity that may help in the reelection quest or to embarrass the president if he or she is of the opposite party. For example, in 2015 Republicans used their oversight powers to call attention to Hillary Clinton's use of private servers for her work-related e-mail as secretary of state and the way that she handled the attack on the U.S. embassy in Benghazi. Similarly, when Democrats investigated President Trump's withholding of funds to Ukraine until its president promised to investigate the Bidens (see Chapter 2), there were serious concerns about an abuse of executive power that undermined national security. While these hearings were, at least in part, politically motivated, the most important motivation for oversight is to ensure that laws are implemented properly.[36]

Congress may use several mechanisms to accomplish this goal (see Chapter 12). First, the bluntest instrument is the power of the purse. If members of Congress think an agency is not properly implementing their programs, they can simply cut off the funds. However, this approach is rarely used because budget cuts often eliminate good aspects of the agency along with the bad.

Second, Congress can hold hearings and investigations. By summoning administration officials and agency heads to a public hearing, Congress can use the media spotlight to focus attention on problems within the bureaucracy or on issues that have been overlooked. For example, the House Oversight Committee has investigated Russian interference in the 2016 election, violations of the emoluments clause by President Trump (with a focus on his hotel in Washington, D.C.), the process for providing security clearances, immigration policy, and voting rights.[37] This type of oversight is known as "fire alarm oversight"—that is, members wait until there is a crisis before they spring to action.[38] It is in contrast to "police patrol" oversight, which involves constant vigilance in overseeing the bureaucracy. For example, House Democrats were very concerned about the executive branch interfering with the Justice Department, dating back to President Trump's firing of FBI Director James Comey in 2017 and Attorney General William Barr's handling of the Mueller report, which documented Russian interference in the 2016 election and possible

The director of the National Institute of Allergy and Infectious Diseases, Dr. Anthony Fauci, testified via video before the Senate Health Committee in May 2020 in the midst of the COVID-19 outbreak. Hearings such as this are an important tool used in congressional oversight.

obstruction of justice by the White House. Tensions between Democrats in Congress and the Justice Department continued throughout Trump's impeachment trial into the summer of 2020, with congressional hearings on prosecutorial independence.[39] Of the two, fire alarm oversight is more common because Congress does not have the resources to constantly monitor the entire bureaucracy.

Last, the Senate exercises specific control over other executive functions through its constitutional responsibilities to provide "advice and consent" on presidential appointments and approval of treaties. The Senate typically defers to the president on these matters, but it may assert its power, especially when constituent interests are involved. Two current examples would be the Senate's increasing skepticism about free-trade agreements negotiated by the president's trade representatives and the Senate's holds on presidential nominations (however, those holds were less effective as Majority Leader Mitch McConnell [R-KY] was quite successful in getting President Trump's executive branch and court nominations approved).

The ultimate in congressional oversight is the process of removing the president, vice president, other civil officers, or federal judges through impeachment. The House and Senate share this power. The House issues articles of impeachment, which outline the charges against the official, and the Senate conducts the trial of the impeached officials. Three presidents have been impeached: Andrew Johnson in the controversy over Reconstruction after the Civil War, Bill Clinton over the scandal involving White House intern Monica Lewinsky, and Donald Trump for the abuse of power and obstruction of Congress concerning his interactions with Ukraine. However, none of them were convicted and removed by the Senate.

As should be clear from this summary, one important aspect of congressional oversight is to serve as a check on the executive branch. The boundaries of the system of checks and balances may be fundamentally altered, depending on the outcome of three cases concerning President Trump's claims of absolute executive immunity from congressional subpoenas. The first case concerns a House subpoena requiring White House Counsel Donald McGahn to testify in the impeachment inquiry. President Trump refused to allow McGahn to testify, so the House sued in federal court to enforce the subpoena. An appeals court ruled in Congress's favor, but it was unlikely that McGahn would testify before the elections.[40] The other two cases involve President Trump's financial records and tax returns, to which Congress is attempting to gain access.[41] Most presidents have claimed immunity against some congressional requests for information, but no previous president has claimed absolute immunity. In June 2020, the Supreme Court ruled 7–2 against the president in both cases. Chief Justice John Roberts wrote the majority opinions, concluding, "In our system, the public has a right to every man's evidence … since the founding of the Republic, every man has included the President of the United States."[42] However, as in the McGahn case, the White House was able to delay the release of any documents until after the election.

An even more far-reaching erosion of congressional oversight is playing out in the context of the COVID-19 relief bills. One of the key provisions of the laws was to provide oversight to make sure that the trillions of dollars were being properly spent. However, the president refused to allow executive branch officials to testify before the Democrat-controlled House, while those same officials were routinely appearing before Senate committees. The *Washington Post* reported, "Since the virus outbreak in early March, House Democrats have sent at least 203 letters to agencies, 173 directly related to the pandemic, and almost all have been rejected or have yet to receive a response. President Trump explained he didn't want his people to appear before Speaker Nancy Pelosi's committees because they are 'a bunch of Trump haters.'"[43] Congress can't do its job if executive branch officials refuse to testify.

Unpacking the Conflict

Considering all that we've learned in this chapter about how Congress works, let's return to our discussion of DACA. Why is it so hard for Congress to compromise on issues that appear to be consensual, like protecting the Dreamers? How can members of Congress best serve the collective interests of the nation while also representing their local constituents?

Although the details of the legislative process and the institutions of Congress can be complicated, the basic explanations for member behavior are straightforward when viewed in terms of the trade-off between responsiveness and responsibility. Members of Congress want to be reelected, so they are generally quite responsive to constituents' interests. They spend considerable time on casework—meeting with people in their district and delivering benefits for the district. At the same time, members are motivated to be responsible—to rise above local interests and attend to the nation's best interests. The conflict between these two impulses can create contradictory policies that contribute to Congress's image problem. The chapter opener discussed the difficulty of reaching a compromise on DACA. Both parties and the president appeared to want to help the Dreamers, but there was strong opposition from conservatives in the Republican Party who were opposed to providing any path to citizenship. Clearly the country as a whole benefits from the economic and social contributions of the Dreamers, but some members of Congress responded to their political base by opposing a compromise. The tension between responsible lawmaking and responsiveness to constituents is evident on many issues.

Considering members' motivations is crucial to understanding how Congress functions, but their behavior is also constrained by the institutions in which they operate. When moderate House Republicans were on the verge of forcing a vote on the Dreamers, the Senate Republican Leader stood firm in his opposition, saying he would not bring a bill to a vote in the Senate that did not have President Trump's approval. So ultimately, it did not matter that the House was able to find a compromise solution. In this instance, party leadership served as a constraint, but the committee system

can provide a positive vehicle for lawmaking as an important source of expertise and
information, and it provides a platform from which members can take positions and
claim credit. When they aren't obstructing legislation, parties in Congress can provide
coherence to the legislative agenda and help structure voting patterns on bills. Rules
and norms constrain the nature of debate and the legislative process. Although these
institutions shape members' behavior, members can also change those rules and
institutions. Therefore, Congress has the ability to evolve with changing national
conditions and demands from voters, groups, and the president.

In this context, much of what Congress does can be understood in terms of the
conflicts inherent in politics. As we have seen, even on consensual issues like DACA,
conflict and political strategy may doom the common ground that is within reach. The
extremes on the right and left did not want to compromise on DACA: the former viewed
any path to citizenship as amnesty and the latter wanted a "clean bill" with no money
for the wall or other changes to immigration policy. There was a huge majority in the
middle that could have passed a DACA bill with some money for border security and
the wall, but President Trump and Republicans wanted to leverage the consensual
issue of DACA to enact the broader immigration policies they favored. Their approach
did not work, and we got deadlock instead. Congress does not always live up to the
expectations of being the "first branch" of government, but it tries to do the best it can
to balance the conflicting pressures it faces.

"What's Your Take?"

Does Congress do
a reasonable job of
representing both national
and local interests?

If not, how should
Congress change?

STUDY GUIDE

Congress and the people

Explain how members of Congress represent their constituents and how elections hold members accountable. (Pages 315–330)

Summary

The Constitution gave Congress vast enumerated powers, making it the "first branch" of government. While Congress has long dominated day-to-day politics, the president has become considerably more powerful over time. Despite the low approval ratings for Congress itself, most voters like their members of Congress. Members of Congress work hard to strike a balance between responding to what constituents want and doing what is in the nation's best interest. In the balance, however, they prioritize district interests over national policy.

Key terms

bicameralism (p. 315)
permanent campaign (p. 315)
pork barrel (p. 317)
descriptive representation (p. 317)
substantive representation (p. 317)
trustee (p. 319)
delegate (p. 319)

politico (p. 319)
electoral connection (p. 321)
casework (p. 321)
incumbency advantage (p. 322)
redistricting (p. 325)
apportionment (p. 326)
gerrymandering (p. 326)
gridlock (p. 330)

Practice Quiz Questions

1. What did the Seventeenth Amendment do?

a   repeal Prohibition

b   grant women's suffrage

c   give senators six-year terms

d   allow for direct election of senators

e   lower the voting age to 18

2. Why do senators have longer terms than members of the House of Representatives?

a   to reduce the number of candidates in each election

b   to make sure senators are tied to public sentiment

c   to provide more opportunities for pork-barrel legislation

d   to make elections easier to administer

e   to make sure that senators are somewhat insulated from the people

3. What is the most common style of representation in Congress?

a   trustee

b   politico

c   delegate

d   consulate

e   adviser

4. Members of Congress generally hold multiple goals. Which goal comes first?

a   getting reelected

b   passing good policy

c   serving their political party

d   blocking the opposing party

e   serving special interests

5. What is apportionment?

a   determining presidential primary winners

b   determining whether the state legislature or courts will re-draw district lines

c   determining which states gain/lose seats in the Senate

d   determining which states gain/lose seats in the House

e   determining how many seats a party has in Congress

6. On average, incumbents spend _____ times as much as challengers on campaigning.

a   one and one-half

b   four

c   five

d   ten

e   twenty

The structure of Congress

Examine how parties, the committee system, and staffers enable Congress to function. (Pages 331–338)

Summary

Many aspects of Congress are set up to meet the needs of its members. The norms of universalism and reciprocity still dominate, meaning that members of Congress share resources more broadly than partisan politics would dictate.

Key terms

logrolling (p. 331)
earmarks (p. 331)
seniority (p. 331)
Speaker of the House (p. 332)
Majority Leader (p. 332)
whip system (p. 332)
Minority Leader (p. 334)
president pro tempore (p. 334)

roll call vote (p. 334)
party vote (p. 334)
party unity (p. 334)
standing committees (p. 337)
select committees (p. 337)
joint committees (p. 337)
conference committees (p. 337)

7. Under the norm of _____, federal highway dollars are likely to be divided up so that many districts benefit.

a reciprocity

b seniority

c party unity

d universalism

e specialization

8. Committee leadership, division of seats on committees, and allocation of committee resources are determined by _____.

a the majority party

b the size of the election margin

c unanimous consent

d seniority

e the president pro tempore

9. The Senate leadership is _____ the House leadership.

a more powerful than

b as powerful as

c less powerful than

d irrelevant to

e none of the above

10. Party leaders have the power to _____.

a force members of Congress to vote a particular way

b keep a member of Congress off the ballot in the next election

c force their members to share their campaign money

d exclude a member from a roll call vote

e help their members get favorable committee assignments

How a bill becomes a law

Trace the steps in the legislative process. (Pages 338–345)

Summary

Most bills become law in a conventional manner, but major legislation generally deviates considerably from this path. The legislative process differs for the House and Senate, sometimes making it difficult to reconcile differences between bills.

Key terms

markup (p. 342)
cloture (p. 342)
filibuster (p. 342)
veto (p. 343)
pocket veto (p. 343)
omnibus legislation (p. 344)

11. Compared with the Senate, the floor process in the House is very _____ and _____.

a unstructured; majoritarian

b structured; majoritarian

c unstructured; individualistic

d structured; individualistic

e individualistic; majoritarian

Oversight

Describe how Congress ensures that the bureaucracy implements policies correctly. (Pages 345–347)

Summary

After passing bills into law, Congress oversees the bureaucracy in its implementation of the law, making sure it fits Congress's intentions. Although controlling funding is the most powerful mechanism for this, Congress has a number of other mechanisms for achieving bureaucratic fidelity. Generally, Congress does not actively patrol the bureaucracy but waits until a crisis emerges to act.

Practice Quiz Question

12. Waiting for a crisis to emerge before taking action is called _____.

a police patrol oversight

b fire alarm oversight

c emergency room oversight

d reactionary oversight

e bureaucratic oversight

Suggested Reading

Adler, Scott E., Jeffery A. Jenkins, and Charles R. Shipan. *The United States Congress*, 2nd ed. New York: W. W. Norton, 2021.

Adler, Scott E., and John D. Wilkerson. *Congress and the Politics of Problem Solving*. New York: Cambridge University Press, 2013.

Bianco, William T. *Trust: Representatives and Constituents*. Ann Arbor: University of Michigan Press, 1994.

Canon, David T. *Race, Redistricting, and Representation: The Unintended Consequences of Black Majority Districts*. Chicago: University of Chicago Press, 1999.

Fenno, Richard F. *Congressmen in Committees*. Boston: Little, Brown, 1973.

Hall, Richard L. *Participation in Congress*. New Haven, CT: Yale University Press, 1996.

Jacobson, Gary C. *The Politics of Congressional Elections,* 8th ed. New York: Pearson, 2012.

Lapinski, John S. *The Substance of Representation: Congress, American Political Development, and Lawmaking*. Princeton, NJ: Princeton University Press, 2013.

Mayhew, David R. *Congress: The Electoral Connection*, 2nd ed. New Haven, CT: Yale University Press, 2004.

Theriault, Sean. *Party Polarization in Congress*. New York: Cambridge University Press, 2008.

11

The Presidency

Are there limits on presidential power?

» **"This is when somebody is the President of the United States, the authority is total and that's the way it's got to be. It's total, it's total—and that's the way it's got to be. And the governors know that."[1]**
President Donald Trump, in a COVID-19 briefing, April 13, 2020

« **"I will be speaking to all 50 governors very shortly and I will then be authorizing each individual governor of each individual state to implement a reopening and a very powerful reopening plan of their state at a time and in a manner as most appropriate."[2]**
President Donald Trump, in a COVID-19 briefing, April 14, 2020

Outlining the major achievements of Donald Trump's four years in office illustrates the immense power of the presidency. Trump commanded the most powerful military forces on earth—and pushed through budget increases that will make them even stronger. Working with Republicans in Congress, Trump enacted the largest tax cut in American history. His directives transformed federal policy in areas such as immigration, the environment, and federal regulations.[3] And he placed himself at the center of the government's response to COVID-19, personally fielding calls from state and local officials for allocations of federal medical supplies.

A look at the personal style that Trump brought to the office, too, seems to underline its power. Trump behaved very differently compared to his predecessors. He hired and fired people working at the highest levels of government, seemingly at whim. Anything he said—even an offhand comment or tweet—became the focus of public attention. He relied on social media to communicate directly with the American people; responded to criticism with strong, personal attacks; made abrupt, radical changes in America's domestic and foreign policy; routinely ignored many presidential traditions and norms; pushed the boundaries of formal and informal limits on presidential authority; and made personal loyalty a dominant criterion for his appointees.

Yet the two quotes at the beginning of this chapter illustrate that there are fundamental limits to presidential power. One day, Trump claimed the authority

President Trump placed himself at the center of the government's response to the coronavirus pandemic in 2020, often butting heads with his advisers, as well as state-level officials. The crisis raised many questions about the power of the presidency. Is the power of the president "total"? What powers does the Constitution grant the president? How do the other branches of the government "check" these powers?

to determine when states would ease COVID-19 lockdown and social-distancing regulations. The very next day, Trump said he would authorize governors to act as they thought best—a face-saving way to acknowledge the constitutional reality that this decision lies with the states. Other events during Trump's presidency illustrate limits on presidential power. While Trump frequently threatened to end the Justice Department's investigation into Russian collusion with the 2016 Trump campaign, he did not intervene. His attempts to force other nations to lower tariffs on American goods were largely unsuccessful. Although Trump campaigned on promises to repeal Obamacare and build a wall on the Mexican border, he did not succeed. He is one of only three presidents to be impeached by the House of Representatives, although he was later acquitted by the Senate. And the COVID-19 pandemic illustrates that the awesome power of the presidency does not always translate into the ability to prevent disaster.

Just like the other 44 individuals who have served as president—and like his successor, Joe Biden—Trump was often constrained by factors that were out of his control, from disagreements with other members of the federal government to the sometimes-fickle opinions of the American public. The fact is that the president is but one actor in a complex political system tasked with achieving often-impossible goals. This truth that has constrained all presidents, not just Trump.

Trump's at times unorthodox approach to the office of the presidency raised questions about where presidential power comes from and what limits there are on its exercise. Did Trump redefine what makes a successful president—or a failed one? What factors distinguish presidential successes from presidential failures?

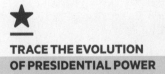

TRACE THE EVOLUTION OF PRESIDENTIAL POWER

The development of presidential power

As we consider the history of America's 46 presidents, four facts stand out: (1) Presidents matter. Their actions have had profound consequences for the nation, in both domestic and foreign policy. (2) Presidents get their power from a variety of sources, from provisions of the Constitution to their management of the actions taken by the executive branch of government. (3) Presidential power has increased over time, not because of changes in the Constitution but because of America's growth as a nation, its emergence as a dominant actor in international politics, the expansion of the federal government, and acts of legislation that have given new authority to the president. (4) There are sharp limits to presidential power. Presidents are often forced to compromise or abandon their plans in the face of public, congressional, or foreign opposition. It is also important to note that while all 46 presidents have been men, and almost all of them have been White, breaking this regularity is only a matter of time. In recent years, in addition to the election of Barack Obama in 2008 and 2012, the groundbreaking presidential campaign of Hillary Clinton in 2016, and the election of Kamala Harris as vice president in 2020, more women as well as minorities—including Senator Cory Booker (D-NJ), surgeon Ben Carson, and entrepreneur Andrew Yang—have been credible contenders for their party's presidential nominations.[4] In 2020, Pete Buttigieg, the mayor of South Bend, Indiana, became the first openly gay presidential candidate.

These lessons are particularly important as we consider the presidency of Donald Trump. Trump's background and behavior in office were often described as being radically different from those of past presidents. Even so, Trump had to contend with the same limits on presidential power faced by his predecessors, including voters' high expectations; unexpected events such as pandemics, natural disasters, or military actions by other countries; conflicts within his own party as well as between Republicans and Democrats in Congress; and differences between his goals and those held by federal bureaucrats who implement his decisions. Understanding how the accomplishments of past presidents were shaped by these constraints can help us begin to analyze and understand the Trump presidency.

Early years through World War I

Since the early years of the republic, presidents' actions have had profound consequences for the nation. Presidents George Washington, John Adams, and Thomas Jefferson forged compromises on domestic issues such as choosing a permanent location for the nation's capital, establishing the federal courts, and financing the government. Presidents Andrew Jackson and Martin Van Buren were instrumental in forming the Democratic Party and its local party organizations.[5]

In addition, early presidents made important foreign policy decisions. For example, the Monroe Doctrine, issued by President James Monroe in 1823, stated that America would remain neutral in wars involving European nations and that these nations must cease attempts to colonize or occupy areas in North and South America.[6] Presidents John Tyler and James Polk oversaw the admission of the huge territory of Texas into the Union following the Mexican-American War as well as the acquisition of land that later became Oregon, Washington, Idaho, and parts of Montana and Wyoming.[7]

Presidents also played key roles in the conflict over slavery. President Millard Fillmore's support helped enact the Compromise of 1850, which limited slavery in California, and Franklin Pierce supported the Kansas-Nebraska Act, which regulated slavery in those territories. And, of course, Abraham Lincoln, who helped form the Republican Party in the 1850s, played a transformative role during the Civil War. His orders raised the huge Union army, and as commander in chief he directed the conduct of the bloody war that ultimately ended slavery and brought the southern states back into the Union.[8]

During the late 1800s and early 1900s, presidents were instrumental in federal responses to the nation's rapid expansion and industrialization.[9] The country's growing size and economy generated conflict over which services the federal government should provide to citizens and the extent to which the government should regulate individual and corporate behavior.[10] Various acts of legislation created new federal agencies as well as new presidential powers and responsibilities. For example, Republican president Theodore Roosevelt used the Sherman Antitrust Act to break up the Northern Securities Company, a mammoth nationwide railroad trust. Roosevelt also expanded federal conservation programs and increased the power of the Interstate Commerce Commission to regulate businesses. At the same time, the foreign policy initiatives of President Woodrow Wilson illustrate the limits of presidential power. Although he campaigned in the 1916 election on a promise to keep America out of World War I, he ultimately ordered American troops to fight on the side of the Allies. After the war, Wilson offered a peace plan that proposed (1) reshaping the borders of European countries in order to prevent future conflicts; (2) creating an international organization, the League of Nations, to prevent future conflicts; and (3) taking other measures to encourage free trade and democracy.[11] However, America's allies rejected most of Wilson's proposals and the Senate refused to allow American participation in the League of Nations.

George Washington remains, for many Americans, the presidential ideal—a leader whose crucial domestic and foreign policy decisions shaped the growth of America's democracy.

The Great Depression through the present

Presidential actions defined the government's response to the Great Depression—the worldwide economic collapse in the late 1920s and 1930s marked by high unemployment, huge stock market declines, and many bank failures. After winning the 1932 presidential election, Democrat Franklin Roosevelt and his staff began reshaping American government in an effort to pull the country out of the Depression. Roosevelt's New Deal reforms created numerous federal agencies that helped individual Americans and imposed many new corporate regulations.[12] This expansion continued under Roosevelt's successors. Even Republican Dwight Eisenhower, whose party had initially opposed many New Deal reforms, presided over the creation of new agencies and the building of the interstate highway system.[13]

Presidents were instrumental in the civil rights reforms and expansion of the federal government in the 1960s. With congressional approval, President Lyndon Johnson's administration created a wide range of domestic programs, such as the Department of Housing and Urban Development, Medicare, Medicaid, and federal funding for schools. The job of enacting voting rights and civil rights legislation also took place during Johnson's presidency.

Both Johnson and his successor, Richard Nixon, directed America's involvement in the Vietnam War, with the goal of forcing the North Vietnamese to abandon their plans to unify North and South Vietnam. But presidential efforts in Vietnam did not meet with success. Despite enormous deployments of American forces and the deaths of more than 58,000 American soldiers, Nixon eventually signed an agreement that allowed American troops to leave but did not end the conflict, which concluded only after a North Vietnamese victory in 1975.

The two presidents immediately after Nixon, Republican Gerald Ford and Democrat Jimmy Carter, faced the worst economic conditions since the Great Depression, largely due to increased energy prices. Both presidents offered plans to reduce unemployment and inflation, restore economic growth, and enhance domestic energy sources. However, their efforts were largely unsuccessful, which became a critical factor in their failed reelection bids. The experiences of Ford and Carter highlight that presidents often face situations for which there are no good solutions. Given the realities of the American economy in the 1970s, it is hard to imagine policies that would have improved on Ford and Carter's performance.

The political and policy importance of presidential actions continued to increase during the presidency of Republican Ronald Reagan, despite the fact that he ran on a platform of tax cuts, fewer regulations, and smaller government. Reagan and his staff also negotiated important arms control agreements with the Soviet Union. Reagan's successor, George H. W. Bush, led American and international participation in the Persian Gulf War during 1990 and 1991, which succeeded in removing Iraqi forces from Kuwait with minimal American casualties.

Democrat Bill Clinton's presidency was marked by passage of the North American Free Trade Agreement, welfare reform, arms control agreements, and successful peacekeeping efforts by U.S. troops in Haiti and the Balkans. His presidency also was distinguished by having one of the longest periods of economic growth in U.S. history and the first balanced budgets since the 1960s. President George W. Bush won congressional approval of his tax cuts and education reforms, but he is best remembered for managing America's response to the September 11 attacks, including the wars in Iraq and Afghanistan.

President Obama secured several notable changes in foreign and domestic policy, including the enactment of health care reform, economic stimulus legislation, and new financial regulations and the appointment of two Supreme Court justices.

Presidents throughout the twentieth century expanded the power of the office in terms of both domestic and foreign policy making. President Franklin Delano Roosevelt called on the public to support his New Deal social programs through his signature "fireside chat" radio broadcasts.

However, Obama had to compromise in enacting many of these new policies, and in areas such as immigration reform and gun control he was largely unsuccessful. Obama's experience highlights a fundamental limit on presidential power: in many areas, presidents require congressional support in order to achieve their policy goals.

Despite the ways Donald Trump differed from past presidents (his personal wealth, life outside politics, and willingness to deviate from established norms), the Trump presidency still illustrates both the exercise of presidential power and the limits on presidential action. Trump had considerable success in forcing policy and regulatory changes though administrative actions. However, in many cases (and particularly after Democrats regained a House majority in 2019), his plans were blocked by lack of public support, the failure to build majorities in the House and Senate, his unwillingness to fully staff the executive branch because of concerns over disloyalty, and congressional investigations prompted by leaks and whistleblower reports. Thus, Trump sometimes looked decisive and influential—but at other times he appeared relatively constrained and weak.

After presidents leave office, their performance is often evaluated as though their powers and foresight during their term had been unlimited. The history of presidential successes and failures reminds us that, in fact, presidents are often constrained by circumstances. Many of the problems past presidents have faced were totally unanticipated or had no good solutions. Other times, attempts to address national needs failed because of congressional resistance. Thus, before we make judgments about presidential performance, we need to understand the president's job and the resources available to accomplish it.

"Why Should I Care?"

The president's job description

DESCRIBE THE CONSTITUTIONAL AND STATUTORY POWERS OF THE PRESIDENT TODAY

This section describes the president's **constitutional authority** (powers derived from the provisions of the Constitution) and **statutory authority** (powers that come from laws), as well as the additional capabilities that presidents derive from their position as the head of the executive branch of government. Constitutional and statutory powers are summarized in Nuts & Bolts 11.1. As the box indicates, some presidential powers arise from the Constitution, and others derive from a combination of constitutional and statutory authority. Questions about the sources and limits of presidential authority have bedeviled political scientists for several generations. In fact, one very influential book, Richard Neustadt's *Presidential Power*, argued that the main source was a president's power to persuade people to do what the president wanted.[14] Building on more recent research, our aim is to show how the provisions that define presidential authority operate in modern-day American politics: what kinds of opportunities and constraints they create for the current president and future holders of the office.

constitutional authority (presidential)
Powers derived from the provisions of the Constitution that outline the president's role in government.

statutory authority (presidential)
Powers derived from laws enacted by Congress that add to the powers given to the president in the Constitution.

Presidential Powers

Power	Source of Power
Head of government, head of state (vesting clause)	Constitutional authority
Implementation of laws ("faithful execution")	Constitutional and statutory authority
Executive orders and similar directives (rare)	Constitutional and statutory authority
Administration of executive branch	Constitutional authority
Nominations and appointments to executive branch and judiciary	Constitutional and statutory authority
Commander in chief of armed forces	Constitutional authority
Negotiation of treaties and executive agreements	Constitutional and statutory authority
Veto of congressional actions	Constitutional authority
Presidential pardons	Constitutional authority
Other ceremonial powers	Constitutional authority
Executive privilege	Other
Recommendation of spending levels and other legislative initiatives	Other

Source: Compiled by the authors.

"Why Should I Care?" The question of where a president's power comes from matters because it affects the extent of the power, and whether it can be taken away or blocked by other actors in American politics.

Head of the executive branch

vesting clause
Article II, Section 1, of the Constitution, which states: "The executive Power shall be vested in a President of the United States of America," making the president both the head of government and the head of state.

head of government
One role of the president, through which he or she has authority over the executive branch.

head of state
One role of the president, through which he or she represents the country symbolically and politically.

A president's responsibilities and the source of presidential power begin with the constitutional responsibilities of the office. The Constitution's **vesting clause**—"The executive Power shall be vested in a President of the United States of America"—makes the president the **head of government**, or the leader of the executive branch, as well as the **head of state**, or the symbolic and political representative of the country. The Constitution also places the president in charge of the implementation of laws, saying "he shall take Care that the Laws be faithfully executed." Sometimes the implementation of a law is nearly automatic and all the president needs to do is ensure that bureaucrats use proper, lawful procedures to accomplish the implementation, as was the case with the part of the 2020 COVID-19 stimulus package that provided $1,200 payments to most Americans. In this case, all the president needed to do to implement the directive was to ask Treasury bureaucrats to send the payments, either by direct deposit or mail.

More commonly, the president's authority to implement the law requires using judgment to translate legislative goals into programs, budgets, and regulations. For

Millions of Americans found themselves unemployed in the wake of the coronavirus pandemic, and small businesses especially suffered, scrambling to find loans and grants to stay in business throughout the crisis. As a temporary solution, the president approved a stimulus package that provided $1,200 payments to most Americans, and the secretary of the Treasury made grants and loans to firms to prevent additional layoffs and bankruptcies.

example, another part of the stimulus package directed the secretary of the Treasury to make grants and loans to firms in order to prevent layoffs and bankruptcies. However, the law did not specify which firms should get these funds or whether any conditions would be applied (repayment terms, guarantees about no layoffs, and so on). All of these provisions were left up to the Treasury bureaucrats, giving them and the president considerable discretion to set the terms of these bailouts.

Appointments

The president appoints ambassadors, senior bureaucrats, and members of the federal judiciary, including Supreme Court justices.[15] As head of the executive branch, the president can appoint individuals to about 8,000 positions, ranging from high-profile jobs such as secretary of state to routine administrative and secretarial positions. About 1,200 of these appointments—generally high-level positions such as cabinet secretaries—require Senate confirmation. These individuals "serve at the pleasure of the president," meaning that the president can remove them from their positions whenever he or she likes. Thus, when Donald Trump fired National Security Advisor John Bolton in November 2019, this action was a legitimate exercise of presidential authority, as was Trump's nomination of Robert O'Brien to succeed Bolton.

The president also nominates individuals to fill federal judgeships, including Supreme Court justices, although these nominations require Senate approval in order to take effect. Because these positions are lifetime appointments, they enable the president to put people into positions of power who will remain after the president leaves office. For example, President Trump nominated many young conservative justices to federal judgeships during his presidency, including Supreme Court associate justices Neil Gorsuch, Brett Kavanaugh, and Amy Coney Barrett. The full effects of these and future judicial appointments by Trump will not be completely apparent for years to come.

The need for Senate confirmation of the president's appointments is one of the fundamental limits on presidential power. Historically, the Senate has approved virtually all nominees without much debate or controversy, although in recent years senators (particularly Republicans during Obama's presidency) have blocked votes on judicial and agency nominees. Some of Trump's cabinet appointees, including Secretary of Education Betsy DeVos, were approved only because Vice President Mike Pence (who is the president of the Senate under the Constitution) voted to break a tie. In several cases, Trump has named individuals to serve as acting cabinet secretaries; these positions do not require Senate confirmation, but the officeholders can serve only for a limited time.

If the Senate is in recess (adjourned for more than three days), the president can make a **recess appointment**, whereby an appointee is temporarily given a position without a Senate vote and holds the office until the beginning of the next congressional session. All presidents make recess appointments, but typically for relatively minor offices and for noncontroversial nominees. For example, when the Republican-controlled Senate refused to vote on President Obama's 2016 Supreme Court nominee, Merrick Garland, it would have been highly unusual (and perhaps unconstitutional) for President Obama to appoint Garland to the Supreme Court via a recess appointment. In any case, the Senate can (and sometimes does) eliminate the possibility of recess appointments by holding brief working sessions as often as needed to ensure that no recess lasts more than three days.

Executive orders

Presidents have the power to issue **executive orders**—that is, proclamations that unilaterally change government policy without subsequent congressional consent[16]—as well as other kinds of orders that change policy, such as National Security Presidential Directives and Presidential Findings (see the How It Works feature in this chapter). For example, one of President Trump's orders in April 2020 put strict limits on immigration for 60 days. Another order used Trump's authority under the Defense Production Act to order companies to increase production of face masks during the coronavirus pandemic.

As the What Do the Facts Say? feature shows, all presidents issue many executive orders. Most are not consequential, like the annual order that gives federal employees an early dismissal on the last working day before Christmas. But some executive orders implement large changes in federal policy. Lincoln's Emancipation Proclamation was issued as an executive order. Similarly, President Trump issued a series of executive orders that have reduced the number of refugees admitted to the United States each year, from about 70,000 per year during the Obama administration to only about 18,000 in 2019.

Executive orders may appear to give the president authority to do whatever he or she wants, even when facing strong opposition from Congress. However, particularly during the Trump administration, executive orders have been used to signal intentions rather than directly change policy. For example, one of Trump's executive orders directed the Border Patrol to end its "catch and release" policy whereby people caught trying to enter the United States from Mexico illegally were simply escorted back to a border checkpoint and set free. However, the order did not command the Border Patrol to hold all illegal immigrants for trial; rather, it instructed the agency to determine what changes would be needed to implement this practice.

In the main, when the president issues an order that makes real policy changes and Congress does not respond, it means that congressional majorities agree with the president's actions or there is already a law giving the president the authority that he or she is exercising in the order. That said, presidents often turn to executive orders and other directives when they know they cannot secure congressional support for the policy changes they want to implement—as was likely the case for Trump's executive

---

recess appointment
Selection by the president of a person to be an ambassador or the head of a department while the Senate is not in session, thereby bypassing Senate approval. Unless approved by a subsequent Senate vote, recess appointees serve only to the end of the congressional term.

executive orders
Proclamations made by the president that change government policy without congressional approval.

President Trump's Executive Orders

Many critics (including then–presidential candidate Donald Trump) argued that President Obama issued an unprecedented number of executive orders in order to bypass a Republican Congress that was unsympathetic to his policy proposals. Was Obama an outlier? How has Trump behaved in office?

Executive Orders Issued by Recent Presidents

■ Divided government (president from one party and at least one branch of Congress from the other)

■ Unified government (president and both branches of Congress from the same party)

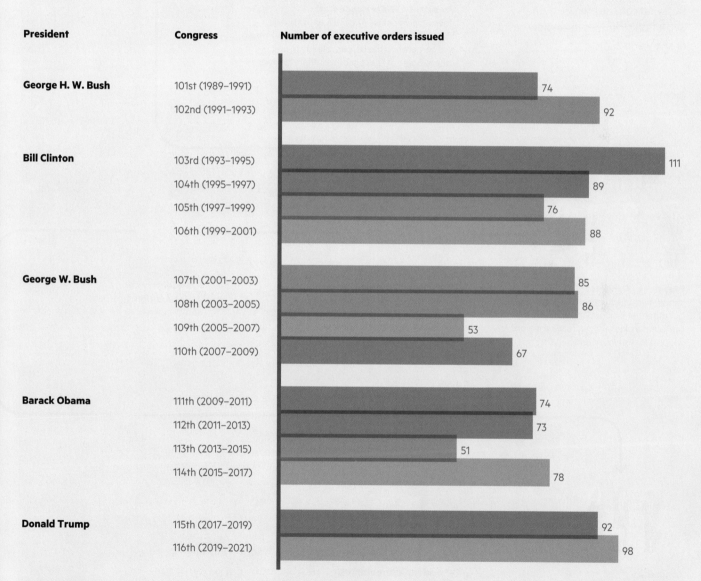

President	Congress	Number of executive orders issued
George H. W. Bush	101st (1989–1991)	74
	102nd (1991–1993)	92
Bill Clinton	103rd (1993–1995)	111
	104th (1995–1997)	89
	105th (1997–1999)	76
	106th (1999–2001)	88
George W. Bush	107th (2001–2003)	85
	108th (2003–2005)	86
	109th (2005–2007)	53
	110th (2007–2009)	67
Barack Obama	111th (2009–2011)	74
	112th (2011–2013)	73
	113th (2013–2015)	51
	114th (2015–2017)	78
Donald Trump	115th (2017–2019)	92
	116th (2019–2021)	98

Think about it

- **Is there any evidence** that Obama issued more executive orders than his predecessors?
- **How does Trump's behavior** compare to that of Obama and other presidents?

Note: Data current as of October 10, 2020.

Source: "Executive Orders Disposition Tables Index," *Federal Register*, www.federalregister. gov/presidential-documents/executive-orders (accessed 10/10/20).

How Presidents Make Policy Outside the Legislative Process

The Constitution describes the president's influence over new policy initiatives in terms of the power to sign or veto acts of Congress. But what can the president do when Congress fails to act how he or she wants?

President + White House staff develop proposals—they talk to the public, members of Congress, interest groups, union and corporation heads, party leaders, and others. Some of these groups initiate contact and submit their own ideas or even fully drafted plans.

President + Congress sometimes find compromise proposals—but other times negotiations reveal that the president's plans will not receive majority support in the House and Senate.

President + White House staff investigate whether some or all of the president's goals can be achieved through executive order or other means.

President issues appropriate orders and directives.

Congress decides whether to enact legislation reversing the president's actions. They need a two-thirds majority in both houses to override an expected presidential veto.

Presidential appointees, assuming congressional attempts to reverse the new policies are unsuccessful, administer implementation of the new policies.

Presidential Action and the Paris Agreement on Climate Change

The United States' involvement in the Paris Agreement on climate change illustrates how a president can bypass Congress and initiate meaningful policy change. Members of President Obama's executive branch participated in the initial talks to develop the accord, and Obama announced that the United States would comply with the agreement in late 2015. However, Donald Trump opposed the agreement during his 2016 campaign, and although he said he was open to keeping the United States in the accord if some of its provisions were renegotiated, the United States government ultimately submitted its formal notice to withdraw from the Paris Agreement on November 4, 2019.

Critical Thinking

1. **Why do you think President Obama decided to treat the accord as an executive agreement** rather than a treaty? Would the situation be different if Democrats were the majority party in the Senate?

2. **Candidate Trump campaigned against the Paris Agreement—** but President Trump did show some willingness to remain in a renegotiated accord. Why might he have reconsidered his initial position once he was in office?

President + staff + other nations

This is important.

During both of President Obama's campaigns for office, **he argued in favor** of new international agreements to fight climate change.

Let's talk.

Obama, White House staff, and others in the executive branch **discussed policy options** and negotiation strategies. **American diplomats were deeply involved** in negotiating the United Nations Framework Convention on Climate Change.

We have a deal.

Building on the Framework Convention, representatives from **196 nations developed the Paris Agreement on climate change**. U.S. Secretary of State John Kerry signed the accord in November 2015.

President + Congress

We want a say!

Many Republican senators who opposed the accord **demanded that President Obama submit the agreement** for ratification as a treaty.

You don't get one.

The Obama administration announced it would implement the accord as an executive agreement, so a **congressional vote was not required**.

This is a risk.

Although making the accord an executive agreement removed the risk that the Senate would reject the treaty, it also meant that **any future president** could end the United States' participation without further action by Congress.

A new president

We're out!

In August 2017, President Trump announced that the **United States intended to withdraw** from the agreement, though he did concede that he might be willing to remain if the terms of the agreement were renegotiated.

Not so fast.

Under the terms of the agreement, a country cannot submit a notice to withdraw **until the agreement has been in effect for four years, and it must then wait one year for the withdrawal to take effect**.

A formal withdrawal.

Renegotiation did not take place, and on November 4, 2019, **President Trump announced the United States' formal withdrawal from the Paris Agreement**, which would officially take place one year later, on November 4, 2020.

orders restricting immigration and Obama's executive orders limiting deportations of so-called Dreamers, who are undocumented individuals brought to the United States as children. While members of Congress can overrule the president, they may be too busy with other matters to do so, or simply not care enough about the change to take the steps needed to undo it.

Commander in chief

The Constitution makes the president the commander in chief of America's military forces but gives Congress the power to declare war. These provisions are potentially contradictory, and the Constitution leaves open the broader question of who controls the military.[17] In practice, however, the president controls day-to-day military operations through the Department of Defense and has the power to order troops into action without explicit congressional approval. For example, both the Trump and Obama administrations joined over a dozen other nations to aid rebel forces in the Syrian civil war. They provided arms and training to rebel fighters and conducted air strikes against ISIS and Syrian government forces. Even today, some American group forces remain in Syrian territory and limited air strikes continue. Similarly, the 2011 attack on Osama bin Laden's compound and the 2020 drone strike that killed Iranian general Qasem Soleimani were carried out without prior congressional approval. In fact, even though the United States has been involved in hundreds of military conflicts, there have been only five declarations of war: the War of 1812, the Mexican-American War (1846), the Spanish-American War (1898), World War I (1917), and World War II (1941).

As a way of restraining presidential war-making power, Congress enacted the War Powers Resolution of 1973 (Nuts & Bolts 11.2 lists the specific provisions of the resolution). However, a 2019 study found that the War Powers Resolution has been formally used by Congress to limit presidential authority only once, to limit the duration of a deployment of Marines in Lebanon on a peacekeeping mission.[18] Moreover, although it has been in effect for nearly 40 years, it has never faced

NUTS & BOLTS 11.2

The War Powers Resolution of 1973

1. The president is required to report to Congress any introduction of U.S. forces into hostilities or imminent hostilities.
2. The use of force must be terminated within 60 days unless Congress approves of the deployment. The time limit can be extended to 90 days if the president certifies that additional time is needed to safely withdraw American forces.
3. The president is required whenever possible to consult with Congress before introducing American forces into hostilities or imminent hostilities.
4. Any congressional resolution authorizing the continued deployment of American forces will be considered under expedited procedures.

Source: Richard F. Grimmett, "The War Powers Resolution: After Thirty Years," Congressional Research Service Report RL32267, March 11, 2004, www.hsdl.org/?view&did=446200 (accessed 6/23/20).

"Why Should I Care?"

While the War Powers Resolution is often described as a way for Congress to limit the president's control over America's armed forces, the reality is that the procedures do not address the vast majority of military operations.

Supreme Court review. Some scholars have even argued that the resolution actually expands presidential power because it gives the president essentially unlimited control for the first 90 days of a military operation—and in many cases, 90 days is more than enough time to complete military action without getting Congress involved.[19]

Even with its limitations, the War Powers Resolution has had some impact on presidential decisions regarding the use of force. Threats by members of Congress to invoke the War Powers Resolution were one factor in President Obama's 2011 decision to curtail American involvement in the NATO-led mission to end the Libyan civil war. The impact of the War Powers Resolution is also evident in the fact that presidents often consult with congressional leaders or try to gain congressional approval before committing troops to battle. It is important to remember, too, that the act is not the only tool available to members of Congress who disagree with a president's policy: they can curb a president's war-making powers through budget restrictions, legislative prohibitions, public appeals, and, ultimately, impeachment.[20]

Treaty making and foreign policy

Treaty-making power is shared between Congress and the president: presidents and their staff negotiate treaties, which are then sent to the Senate for approval. (Many need the support of a two-thirds majority of senators to be approved, but some need only a simple majority.) However, the president has a first-mover advantage in the treaty-making process. Congress considers treaties only after negotiations have ended; there is no way for members of Congress to force the president to negotiate a treaty or limit its scope. That said, the need for congressional approval often leads presidents to consider senators' preferences when negotiating treaties, which often results in significant compromise between the two branches.

Presidents have two strategies for avoiding a congressional treaty vote. One is to announce that the United States will voluntarily abide by a treaty without ratifying it. In the case of the 2015 Paris Agreement on climate change, one of the reasons why President Obama supported voluntary targets for reductions in greenhouse gases was that such an agreement did not require Senate approval. Of course, this strategy allowed Obama's successor, Donald Trump, to unilaterally withdraw from the agreement in 2017.

It is also possible to structure a deal as an **executive agreement** between the executive branch and a foreign government, which does not require Senate approval. This strategy was followed in the case of the deal between the United States, its allies, and the Iranian government to curtail Iran's nuclear weapons research program. In this case, Congress passed (and President Obama signed) a law giving members 30 days to review the deal and the opportunity to pass a resolution rejecting it. The deal ultimately went into effect, although Donald Trump ended United States participation in early 2018.

The president also serves as the principal representative of the United States in foreign affairs other than treaty negotiations. Presidential duties include communicating with foreign leaders, nongovernmental organizations, and even ordinary citizens to persuade them to act in ways that the president believes are in the best interest of the United States. For example, in February 2020 President Trump attended the World Economic Forum in Davos, Switzerland, where he met with leaders of the European Union as well as the prime minister and other officials from Iraq. While such meetings generally have no direct effect on policy, they signal presidential interest and highlight the importance of ongoing negotiations and joint efforts to address issues of mutual concern.

executive agreement
An agreement between the executive branch and a foreign government, which acts as a treaty but does not require Senate approval.

The president often meets with foreign leaders in both formal and informal settings. For example, in March 2016 President Barack Obama watched a baseball game in Havana, Cuba, with Cuban leader Raúl Castro, and in June 2018 President Trump met with Kim Jong-un, the supreme leader of North Korea, in Singapore. Such meetings provide a venue for the president not only to present American views and mediate disagreements but also to act as a visible symbol of America's position as a world superpower.

State of the Union
An annual speech in which the president addresses Congress to report on the condition of the country and to recommend policies.

The amount of time the administration devotes to foreign policy is subject to domestic and world events and therefore not entirely under presidential control. While President Trump promised to limit overseas military operations, he largely continued his predecessor's policies. In the case of North Korea, Trump's public pressure on the North Korean regime (including threats to respond with "fire and fury" if North Korea were to attack the United States) was a departure from the Obama administration in terms of tone, as was Trump's willingness to hold two meetings with North Korean leader Kim Jong-un. Even so, there were a few observable policy differences between Trump's and Obama's policies toward North Korea, as well as toward Syria, as Trump ultimately removed U.S. troops from the conflict there.

Legislative power

The Constitution establishes lawmaking as a shared power between the president and Congress, and compromise between the two branches is fundamental to passing laws that satisfy both.[21] The president recommends policies and legislative priorities to Congress, notably in the annual **State of the Union** address. Presidents and their legislative staff also work with Congress to develop legislative proposals: they spend considerable time lobbying members of Congress to support their proposals and negotiating with legislative leaders over policy details. Although the president cannot formally introduce legislation, it is typically easy to find a member of Congress willing to sponsor a presidential proposal.[22]

The president's legislative power also stems from the ability to veto legislation. Once both chambers of Congress have passed a bill by simple majority, the president must decide within two weeks whether to sign it or issue a veto. Signed bills become law, but vetoed bills return to the House and Senate for a vote to override the veto. If both chambers enact the bill again with at least two-thirds majorities, the bill becomes law; otherwise, it is defeated. If Congress adjourns before the president has made a decision, the president can *pocket veto* the proposal by not responding to it. Pocket vetoes cannot be overridden, but congressional leaders can avoid them by keeping Congress in session for two weeks after a bill is enacted.

Figure 11.1 shows the number of vetoes issued by recent presidents—and the number overridden by Congress. In general, vetoes are most likely to occur under divided government, when a president from one party faces a House and Senate controlled by the other party (in the case of Obama, the relatively small number of vetoes reflects a sharp reduction in the number of laws enacted by Congress).[23] Vetoes are much less likely under unified government, when one party controls both Congress and the

Presidential Vetoes from H. W. Bush to Trump

FIGURE
11.1

The figure shows the number of vetoes issued by recent presidents in each congressional term they held office, along with whether the term involved unified or divided government. Do the data support the argument that vetoes are less likely given unified government? Compared with other presidents, did Presidents Trump and Obama issue an inordinately high or low number of vetoes?

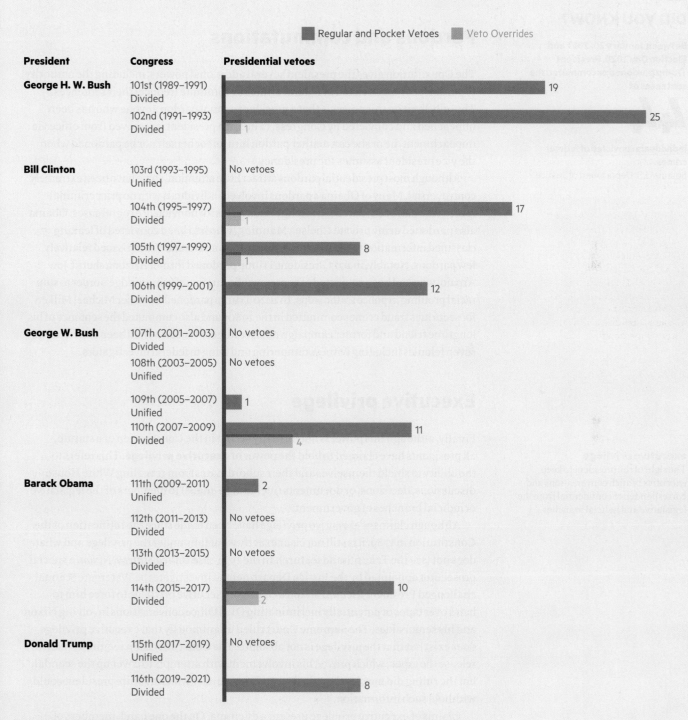

- ■ Regular and Pocket Vetoes
- ■ Veto Overrides

President	Congress	Presidential vetoes
George H. W. Bush	101st (1989–1991) Divided	19
	102nd (1991–1993) Divided	25 / 1
Bill Clinton	103rd (1993–1995) Unified	No vetoes
	104th (1995–1997) Divided	17 / 1
	105th (1997–1999) Divided	8 / 1
	106th (1999–2001) Divided	12
George W. Bush	107th (2001–2003) Divided	No vetoes
	108th (2003–2005) Unified	No vetoes
	109th (2005–2007) Unified	1
	110th (2007–2009) Divided	11 / 4
Barack Obama	111th (2009–2011) Unified	2
	112th (2011–2013) Divided	No vetoes
	113th (2013–2015) Divided	No vetoes
	114th (2015–2017) Divided	10 / 2
Donald Trump	115th (2017–2019) Unified	No vetoes
	116th (2019–2021) Divided	8

Note: Data current as of October 1, 2020.

Source: United States House of Representatives, History, Art, & Archives, "Presidential Vetoes," https://history.house.gov/Institution/Presidential-Vetoes/Presidential-Vetoes (accessed 10/1/20); data aggregated by the authors.

presidency, because the chances are much higher that the president and legislators from his or her party hold similar policy priorities. Thus, in the first two years of the Trump administration, when a Republican president faced a Republican Congress, the president did not veto any legislation. A president's veto threats also allow the president to specify what kinds of proposals he or she is willing or unwilling to accept from Congress. Legislators then know that they need to write a proposal that attracts two-thirds support in both houses or else accede to the president's demands.

Pardons and commutations

The Constitution gives the president several additional powers, including the authority to pardon people convicted of federal crimes or commute (reduce) their sentences. The only limit on this power is that a president cannot pardon anyone who has been impeached and convicted by Congress. (Thus, if a president is removed from office via impeachment, he or she can neither pardon himself or herself nor be pardoned when the vice president assumes the presidency.)

Although most presidential pardons attract little attention, some have been extremely controversial. Many of Obama's pardons involved individuals with no prior criminal record who had been sentenced to long prison terms for nonviolent drug offenses. Obama also pardoned army private Chelsea Manning, who had been convicted of leaking classified information to the WikiLeaks organization. Donald Trump issued relatively few pardons. Notably, in 2017 President Trump pardoned former Arizona sheriff Joe Arpaio, who had been convicted of contempt of court for refusing a judge's order to stop racial profiling in police traffic stops. In 2020 Trump pardoned financier Michael Milken for securities fraud crimes committed in the 1980s and also commuted the sentence of his longtime friend and former campaign adviser Roger Stone, who had been convicted of seven felonies including witness tampering and lying to federal investigators.

Executive privilege

Finally, although this power is not formally set out in the Constitution or a statute, all presidents have claimed to hold the power of **executive privilege**. This refers to the ability to shield themselves and their subordinates from revealing White House discussions, decisions, or documents (including e-mails) to members of the legislative or judicial branches of government.[24]

Although claims of executive privilege have been made since the ratification of the Constitution in 1789, it is still not clear exactly what falls under the privilege and what does not (see the Take a Stand feature). In the 1974 case *United States v. Nixon*, a special prosecutor appointed by the Justice Department to investigate the Watergate scandal challenged President Richard Nixon's claims of executive privilege to force him to hand over tapes of potentially incriminating Oval Office conversations involving Nixon and his senior aides. The Supreme Court ruled unanimously that executive privilege does exist but that the privilege is not absolute. The Court's decision required Nixon to release the tapes, which proved his involvement with attempts to cover up the scandal, but the ruling did not clearly state the conditions under which a future president could withhold such information.[25]

Claims of executive privilege present a dilemma. On the one hand, members of Congress need to know what is happening in the executive branch. In the case of President Nixon and the Watergate scandal, claims of executive privilege allowed the Watergate cover-up to continue for more than a year and would have kept this

DID YOU KNOW?

Between January 20, 2017 and Election Day 2020, President Trump pardoned or commuted the sentences of

44

individuals convicted of federal crimes.

Source: U.S. Department of Justice

executive privilege
The right of the president to keep executive branch conversations and correspondence confidential from the legislative and judicial branches.

The Limits of Executive Privilege

Deciding what information a president can be compelled to release to the public or to other branches of government and what information can be kept confidential requires confronting fundamentally political questions. There are no right answers, and the limits of executive privilege remain unclear. On the one hand, members of Congress need facts, predictions, and estimates from the executive branch to make good public policy. On the other hand, the president and his or her staff have a right to keep their deliberations confidential, as well as a practical need to keep some things secret.

Consider the controversy over the practice (begun during the Bush administration and continued under Presidents Obama and Trump) of targeting terrorists using attacks by unmanned drone aircraft. Compared with deployments of other military forces, drone attacks have the advantages of surprise (drones are small and fly high enough to be invisible), low cost (drones are cheaper than fighters or bombers), and lower risk (the drones can be controlled from anywhere, so there is no risk of American casualties in an attack). Nonetheless, drone attacks carry the risk of collateral damage—an attack may also hurt or kill innocent civilians. Moreover, because drone attacks are conducted in secret, there is little to no congressional oversight of who gets targeted by drone strikes or the potential for collateral damage. Should drone attacks fall under executive privilege?

Keep the attacks secret. Clearly, revealing the targets of drone strikes in advance of the actual attacks would destroy the secrecy that makes these strikes so effective—terrorists could stop using cell phones, stay indoors as much as possible, travel only at night, and take other actions to make themselves hard to spot from the air. But there would be danger even in forcing an administration to release information after an attack, as such documents would reveal the criteria used to decide which terrorists to target, the limits of the drone technology, and what factors made it easier to carry out a successful attack. All of this information would help terror targets evade future drone attacks and perhaps require a return to using Special Forces to attack terror targets, which would place American lives at risk.

Reveal the information. The problem with imposing a high level of secrecy on drone attacks is that it is an exception to the rule of keeping Congress informed about the use of military force. In the end, a drone is simply a different way of attacking terrorists or their organization. While the need for secrecy in advance of an attack makes sense, it is not obvious why it should continue after an attack has been carried out. In general, presidents are required to give Congress (in the case of secret operations, the chairs and ranking members of the Intelligence Committees) "prompt notification" of all secret operations. This rule was intended to govern reporting of all covert operations. Should drone attacks be given a higher level of secrecy, or should presidents be forced to keep members of Congress informed?

The president's role as commander in chief of America's armed forces gives him or her a tremendous amount of power—power that often can be exercised secretly. What should be the limits on presidential secrecy?

take a stand

1. One argument for using drones to attack terrorist targets highlights their greater effectiveness and lower costs than other options. But drone attacks also involve lower political risks to the president. Explain why this is so.

2. Under current law, the president has to inform only a few members of Congress about covert operations and can wait until an operation is in progress before releasing information. Why would members of Congress want expanded notification requirements, such as informing more members or requiring disclosure during the planning of an operation?

During the Congressional impeachment hearings, Trump claimed executive privilege in order to prevent his aides from testifying in the Ukraine investigation. Numerous expert witnesses, as seen being sworn in here, testified on constitutional issues raised by these proceedings, including executive privilege.

information secret permanently if the Supreme Court had ruled in Nixon's favor.[26] Exercising executive privilege can also weaken accountability to the public, as restricting information may leave the average voter unaware of what an administration is doing. On the other hand, the president and his or her staff need to be able to communicate freely and discuss alternative strategies, hypothetical situations, or national security secrets without fear that they will be forced to reveal conversations that could become politically embarrassing or costly.

"Why Should I Care?"

Criticisms of presidents often center on cases of inaction or failure, in which they do nothing to address a national problem or they try to change policy but are unsuccessful. The underlying expectation is that presidents are powerful and can do anything. The reality is that presidents are more powerful in some areas than in others. For example, they are more powerful when they negotiate with foreign leaders than when they propose changes in spending, which require congressional approval. Thus, when we judge presidents' performance, we must consider whether achieving their goals required the assistance of others to make their proposals a reality.

EXPLAIN HOW THE EXECUTIVE OFFICE OF THE PRESIDENT, THE VICE PRESIDENT, AND THE CABINET HELP THE PRESIDENT

The presidency as an institution

As head of the executive branch, the president runs a huge, complex organization with hundreds of thousands of employees. We speak of this organization as an "institution" to emphasize that both the *structure* of the executive branch (the division of responsibilities across different agencies and offices) and the *individuals* who serve in different positions (their experience, skills, and ideological leanings) can have a profound impact on government policies. This section describes the organizations and staff who help the president exercise these vast responsibilities, from managing disaster-response efforts to implementing policy changes.[27] Among these employees are appointees who hold senior positions in the government. These individuals serve as the president's eyes and ears in the bureaucracy, making sure that bureaucrats are following presidential directives.

The Executive Office of the President

The executive branch's organizational chart begins with the **Executive Office of the President (EOP)**, which has employed several thousand people in recent administrations, divided between policy-making positions and administrating personnel. About a third of these employees are concentrated in two offices, the Office of Management and Budget, which develops the president's budget proposals and monitors spending by government agencies, and the Office of the United States Trade Representative, which negotiates trade agreements with other nations. Nuts & Bolts 11.3 lists the organizations that make up the EOP.

One of the most important duties of EOP staff is helping presidents achieve their policy goals and get reelected. In the Trump White House, for example, Senior Adviser Stephen Miller focused on domestic policy (especially immigration policy) but also helped write Trump's speeches, including his State of the Union addresses. Trump's daughter Ivanka and her spouse, Jared Kushner, also played important advisory roles. These three individuals, as well as other influential EOP staff, occupied offices in the West Wing of the White House. The West Wing contains the president's office, known as the Oval Office,

Executive Office of the President (EOP)
The group of policy-related offices that serve as support staff to the president.

NUTS & BOLTS 11.3

The Executive Office of the President

Source: Compiled by the authors from whitehouse.gov.

Council of Economic Advisers	Office of National Drug Control Policy
Council on Environmental Quality	Office of Science and Technology Policy
Domestic Policy Council	Office of the First Lady
Homeland Security Council	Office of the United States Trade Representative
National Economic Council	President's Foreign Intelligence Advisory Board
National Security Council	Privacy and Civil Liberties Oversight Board
Office of Administration	USA Freedom Corps
Office of Faith-Based and Community Initiatives	White House Fellows Office
Office of Management and Budget	White House Military Office
Office of National AIDS Policy	White House Office

"Why Should I Care?" Organizations in the EOP play a major role in bringing information to the president and executing his or her directives. They are a reflection of presidential priorities and policy goals.

and space for the president's chief aide and personal secretary, as well as senior aides such as the vice president, the president's press secretary, and the chief of staff, who manages all aspects of White House operations—including, as former Reagan chief of staff James Baker put it, who gets to play tennis on the White House courts. Some recent chiefs of staff have been central in the development of policy proposals and negotiations with members of Congress. However, the chief of staff serves as the agent of the president—what matters is what the president wants, not a chief of staff's policy preferences.

Most EOP staff members are presidential appointees who retain their positions only as long as the president who appointed them remains in office, although some EOP offices—such as the Office of Management and Budget, the Office of the United States Trade Representative, and the National Security Council (NSC)—also have a significant number of permanent staff analysts and experts.[28] When the president appoints people to EOP positions, the primary expectation of them is loyalty rather than a concern for the general public or policy expertise.[29] The president needs staff who understand what he or she wants the government to do and who will dedicate themselves to implementing the president's vision.[30] However, the emphasis on loyalty in presidential appointments has obvious drawbacks: appointees may not know much about the jobs they are given and may not be very effective at managing the agencies they are supposed to control. For example, Trump's son-in-law, Jared Kushner, was given responsibility for American efforts to negotiate a peace deal between Israel and the Palestinian Authority, even though his prior experience was as a real estate developer and he had never served in government.

The vice president

As set out in the Constitution, the vice president's job is to preside over Senate proceedings. This largely ceremonial job is, in practice, usually delegated to the president pro tempore of the Senate, who in turn typically gives the duty to a more junior member. The vice president also has the power to cast tie-breaking votes in the Senate. Mike Pence, for example, cast several such votes in 2018 to break ties on presidential nominees. The vice president's other formal responsibility is to become president if the current president dies, becomes incapacitated, resigns, or is impeached, convicted, and ultimately removed from office. Of the 46 people who have become president, 9 were vice presidents who became president in midterm.

These rather limited official duties of the vice president pale in comparison with the influential role played by recent vice presidents. Vice President Dick Cheney,

While many people perceive the vice president's position to be ceremonial and relatively powerless, recently the vice president's role has expanded significantly. President Trump's vice president, Mike Pence, served as a trusted policy adviser and directed several initiatives such as the Coronavirus Task Force.

who served with President George W. Bush, exerted a significant influence over many policy decisions, including the rights of terror suspects, tax and spending policy, environmental decisions, and the writing of new government regulations.[31] Although Cheney's level of influence was unique, other recent vice presidents have also had real power, and it is likely that Kamala Harris will play a similar role, particularly given the possibility that President Biden will opt for a single term in office.

The president's Cabinet

The president's **Cabinet** is composed of the heads of the 15 executive departments in the federal government, along with other appointees given cabinet rank by the president. Nuts & Bolts 11.4 lists the Cabinet and cabinet-level positions. The cabinet members' principal job is to be the frontline implementers of the president's agenda in their executive departments. As we discuss in Chapter 12, these appointees monitor the actions of the lower-level bureaucrats who retain their jobs regardless of who is president and are not necessarily sympathetic to the president's priorities.

Cabinet
The group of 15 executive department heads who implement the president's agenda in their respective positions.

Cabinet and Cabinet-Level Positions

NUTS & BOLTS 11.4

The president's Cabinet is composed of the heads of the 15 executive departments along with other appointees given cabinet rank by the president.

Secretary of Agriculture	Secretary of Transportation
Secretary of Commerce	Secretary of the Treasury
Secretary of Defense	Secretary of Veterans Affairs
Secretary of Education	Vice President
Secretary of Energy	White House Chief of Staff
Secretary of Health and Human Services	Attorney General
Secretary of Homeland Security	Head of the Environmental Protection Agency
Secretary of Housing and Urban Development	Head of the Office of Management and Budget
Secretary of the Interior	Head of the Office of National Drug Control Policy
Secretary of Labor	United States Trade Representative
Secretary of State	

Source: Compiled by the authors from whitehouse.gov.

"Why Should I Care?" Cabinet secretaries are the president's eyes and ears in the executive branch, carrying out the president's wishes and serving as the public faces of the departments they lead.

Like other presidential appointees, cabinet members are chosen for a combination of loyalty to the president and expertise. Trump's second secretary of state, Mike Pompeo, served as a member of Congress from Kansas and as director of the Central Intelligence Agency. Trump's secretary of the Treasury, Steven Mnuchin, was a former hedge fund manager and investor who held a senior position in the 2016 Trump campaign.

"Why Should I Care?"

Having read the job description for America's president, you might reasonably ask, How does any one person handle all of these responsibilities? The answer is that presidents have help: trusted advisers and people chosen for policy knowledge, political skills, and loyalty. Put another way, if you want to know whether someone will make a good president, don't look at his or her experience or campaign promises—look at the people he or she picks to help run the government.

★

EXPLAIN HOW MODERN PRESIDENTS HAVE BECOME EVEN MORE POWERFUL

Presidential power today

As we have discussed, presidential authority comes from two sources, on paper: the limited powers granted by the Constitution, and laws that have expanded the president's power. Even so, assessing presidential power requires expanding our notions of where this power actually comes from. Saying that presidents have become more powerful over time because of the expansion of the United States or the increased size of the federal budget or bureaucracy tells only part of the story. What about these circumstances made presidents more powerful?

One important clue about where presidential power comes from is that, after more than two centuries, many of the limits to these powers are not well defined. It is unclear, for example, which executive actions require congressional approval and which ones can be reversed by Congress. The very ambiguity of the Constitution and most statutes also creates opportunities for the exercise of presidential power. As we have seen, the Constitution makes the president military commander in chief but gives Congress the power to declare war and to raise and support armies, without specifying which branch of government is in charge of the military. Thus, at least part of presidential authority must be derived or assumed from what the Constitution and statutes *do not say*—the ways in which they fail to define or delineate presidential power—and how presidents use this ambiguity to pursue their goals.

In addition to these ambiguities, presidents also gain real power from other, more informal aspects of their office. Recall our discussion of the president's ability to influence the legislative process. In the Constitution, the president's powers in this realm are limited to advising Congress on the state of the union and to vetoing legislation (subject to congressional override). But presidents often have very real influence at all points in the legislative process: they can offer a variety of small inducements, such as visits to the Oval Office and campaign assistance, and they can draw on the natural respect that most people (including members of Congress) feel for the presidency regardless of who holds the office, thereby securing compromises that achieve the president's policy goals.[32]

Donald Trump made no secret of his willingness to push the boundaries of presidential authority in areas such as executive privilege, to keep key executive branch positions open or rely on acting appointments, and to build relationships with the leaders of nondemocratic regimes such as Vladimir Putin of Russia, Xi Jinping of China, and Kim Jong-un of North Korea. He also removed individuals from high-level jobs in the executive branch because they advised against these actions or informed Congress about them (as they were obligated to do under law). Regardless of whether or not you support these moves, they are not clearly in violation of the Constitution or established law. In fact, what is notable about Trump's behavior in office is that despite his strong rhetoric, he backed off threats when challenged by the courts or Congress. For example, during negotiations over additional funding for small businesses during the 2020 COVID-19 pandemic, Trump administration officials originally said they would not approve any bill that gave funding to hospitals and an expanded testing effort, only to reverse course when it was clear that both provisions had support among congressional Republicans.[33] While Joe Biden is unlikely to follow these strategies, he will, like all other presidents, use his informal authority to pursue policy and political goals.

Presidents, unilateral action, and policy making

Constitutional and statutory ambiguities in some cases enable presidents to take **unilateral action**—that is, changing policy on their own without consulting Congress or anyone else.[34] The 2018 debate over U.S. attacks on suspected chemical weapons facilities in Syria provides a good example of how constitutional ambiguities create opportunities for unilateral action. The Trump administration argued that because the operation involved only air strikes, it did not trigger the provisions of the "hostilities or imminent hostilities" provisions of the War Powers Resolution. While some in Congress disagreed and wanted to vote on whether to authorize the operation, no such vote was ever taken.

This example is far from the first time that a president has argued that military operations were not subject to congressional review. For example, the arguments advanced by the Trump administration were very similar to those made by the Obama administration when it sent military aid and advisers to Syria in 2011. Even during the Iraq War, when some Democrats in Congress wanted to cut off war funding to force the withdrawal of American forces, supporters of the Bush administration maintained that the Constitution's description of the president as commander in chief meant that even if Congress refused to appropriate funds for the war, the president could (1) order American forces to stay in Iraq and (2) order the Treasury Department to spend any funds necessary to continue operations. Ultimately, members of Congress approved a funding resolution.

Even when a president takes a unilateral action, it may not lead to policy change. Presidents and their staffs still have to monitor subsequent actions by bureaucrats to make sure they are implementing the president's decision. Most presidents have tried to control the implementation of laws by issuing **signing statements** when signing bills into law. These documents, which explain the president's interpretation of a new law, are issued most often when the president wishes to approve a bill but disagrees with the way that supporters of the bill in Congress interpret the legislation. Presidents issue signing statements so that if the courts have to resolve uncertainties about the bill's intent, judges can take into account not only the views expressed during congressional debates about the bill but also the president's interpretation of it.[35]

Congressional responses to unilateral action

In theory, members of Congress can undo a president's unilateral action by enacting a law to overturn it, but this is harder than it may sound.[36] Some members of Congress may approve of what the president has done or be indifferent to it, or they may give a higher priority to enacting other laws, making it hard to assemble a majority of legislators who are motivated enough to pass a law overturning the president's action. For example, the Trump administration went far enough on its implementation of the Russia sanctions that only a minority of House members and senators were willing to invest the time to enact a new bill that went farther. Still, reversals do happen: Congress enacted a Russia sanctions bill in the first place in a reversal of the Trump administration's refusal to agree that Russians actually interfered in the 2016 election or that America should impose sanctions as a response. And the impeachment of Donald Trump can be seen as a response to claims that Trump had pressured the government of Ukraine to investigate his 2020 political rival, Democrat Joe Biden.

Members of Congress can also write laws in a way that limits the president's authority over their implementation.[37] However, this strategy has drawbacks. The problem is that members of Congress delegate authority to the president or the executive branch bureaucracy for good reasons—either because it is difficult for legislators to predict how a policy should be implemented or because they cannot agree among themselves on an implementation plan.[38] In the case of Russia sanctions, for example, members of Congress may have been unsure of whom to sanction or what appropriate punishments would look like. Members of Congress from the president's party may also want to grant authority to the president because they hold policy goals similar to the president's and would therefore benefit from the exercise of unilateral power.

In sum, ambiguities in the Constitution create opportunities for unilateral presidential action. These actions are subject to reversal through legislation, court decisions, and impeachment, but members of Congress face significant costs if they undertake any of these options. As long as the president is careful to limit the exercise of unilateral power

President Trump's closeness to Russian president Vladimir Putin led to speculation about the nature of their relationship. After President Trump refused to agree that Russians actually interfered in the 2016 election, Congress enacted a Russia sanctions bill. This is an example of members of Congress undoing a president's unilateral action by enacting a law to overturn it.

to actions that do not generate intense opposition in Congress, he or she can implement a wide range of policy goals without official congressional consent—provided that bureaucrats go along with the president's wishes (see Chapter 12). Thus, presidential power has important consequences for government policy—but it is not unlimited.

Presidents as politicians

Aside from situations in which the president has (or has been given) the authority to act unilaterally, the reality of presidential power is that much of what presidents do (or want to do) requires support from others, including legislators, bureaucrats, and citizens. As a result, the presidency is an inherently political office—something that all presidents learn is true, regardless of their expectations when they take office.[39] Presidents have to take into account the political consequences of their decisions: the effects on their political support, reelection prospects, and party. A president must also contend with the fact that achieving policy goals often requires bargaining and compromising with others, both inside and outside government. Many accounts of Trump's presidency have emphasized that Trump's experience as a CEO, the head of an organization in which his word was law, did not prepare him for being president, a role in which he faced members of Congress and bureaucrats who often had the power to reject presidential initiatives.

In part, presidents must keep their eye on the political implications of their actions in office because they want to be reelected to a second term. One important indicator of presidential performance is the **presidential approval rating**, the percentage of the public who think the president is doing a good job in office. Figure 11.2, which shows approval ratings for the last ten presidents who ran for reelection, reveals that first-term presidents with less than 50 percent approval are in real trouble. No recent president has been reelected with less than a 50 percent approval rating. Donald Trump's approval rating in reputable polls never moved higher than the mid-40s despite a strong economy. Criticism of his mismanagement of the COVID-19 pandemic did not reduce his popularity by much, but it likely prevented any increase in his rating—and his chances of reelection.

"

He'll sit here, and he'll say, "Do this! Do that!" And nothing will happen. Poor Ike—it won't be a bit like the Army. He'll find it very frustrating.

—President Harry Truman,
describing incoming president Dwight Eisenhower

presidential approval rating
The percentage of Americans who think that the president is doing a good job in office.

FIGURE 11.2

Presidential Popularity and Reelection

This figure shows the preelection-year average approval ratings for recent presidents who ran for reelection. It shows that a president's chances of winning reelection are related to his or her popularity. At what level of approval would you say that an incumbent president is likely to be reelected?

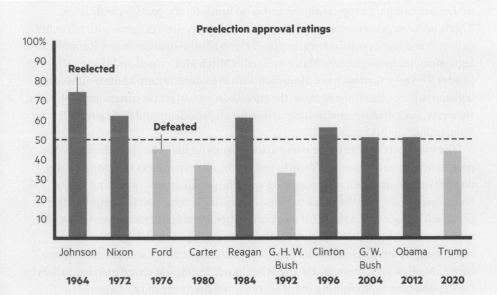

Preelection approval ratings

Johnson	Nixon	Ford	Carter	Reagan	G. H. W. Bush	Clinton	G. W. Bush	Obama	Trump
1964	1972	1976	1980	1984	1992	1996	2004	2012	2020

Reelected

Defeated

Source: Approval data from the Roper Center for Public Opinion Research, Cornell University, "Presidential Approval," https://presidential.roper.center (accessed 11/2/20).

Of course, it would be wrong to say that presidents are single-mindedly focused on keeping their approval rating as high as possible. For one thing, presidential approval is shaped by factors that they have only limited control over, such as the state of the economy. And all presidents have taken actions that were politically costly because they believed that the policies were worthwhile. For example, many of President Trump's decisions (such as the travel ban) and legislative initiatives (such as the tax cuts enacted in 2017) were opposed by a majority of Americans. Even so, presidents and their advisers are keenly aware of the political consequences of their actions, and there is no doubt that these consequences shape both their decisions and how they explain these actions to American citizens. This was probably one reason why Donald Trump appeared at daily press conferences during the COVID-19 pandemic.

The president as party leader

The president is the unofficial head of his or her political party and generally picks the party's day-to-day leaders (or at least has considerable influence over their selection). This process begins when a presidential candidate captures the party's nomination and continues through the president's time in office. For example, while many members of the Republican National Committee (RNC) opposed Donald Trump's nomination in 2016, the party organized to help Trump get elected and ran countless campaign ads on his behalf. After the election, Trump supporters, including the chair of the RNC at the time, Ronna McDaniel, moved into positions within the party organization.

The connection between the president and the party reflects their intertwined interests. The president needs support from members of his or her party in Congress to enact legislation, and the party and its candidates need the president to compile a record of policy achievements that reflect well on the organization and to help raise the funds needed for the next election. Therefore, party leaders generally defer to a presidential candidate's (or a president's) staffing requests, and most presidents and presidential candidates take time to meet with national party leaders and the congressional leadership from their party to plan legislative strategies, make joint campaign appearances, and raise funds for the party's candidates. This is not to say that members of the president's party always agree with his or her behavior and issue positions: during the Trump administration, many Republican legislators, including Senate Majority Leader Mitch McConnell and House Minority Leader Kevin McCarthy, have disagreed with President Trump's policy views and legislative proposals (for example, the travel ban and an end to sanctions on Russia). However, such disagreements have arisen for all presidents and their party; Trump is not unique in this regard.

The president's value to the party also depends on his or her popularity. When presidential approval ratings drop to low levels, most members of Congress see no political advantage in campaigning with the president or supporting White House proposals, and they may become increasingly reluctant to comply with the president's requests. In the 2020 elections, when President Trump was unpopular in many urban and suburban parts of the country, Republican legislators from these areas de-emphasized their connection to the president and did not request joint campaign appearances. On the other hand, Trump appeared at many rallies for Republicans campaigning in rural areas, and many candidates appeared with Vice President Mike Pence, whose popularity was significantly higher than Trump's.

Going Public and Public Opinion Presidents are in an excellent position to communicate with the American people because of their prominent role and the extensive media coverage devoted to anything the president says to the nation. Broadcast and cable networks even give the president prime-time slots for the State of the Union speech and other major addresses. The media attention that comes with the presidency provides the president with a unique strategy for shaping government policy: **going public**, or appealing directly to American citizens, in the hope of getting the electorate to pressure members of the House and Senate to do what the president wants.[40]

Going public sometimes works—but more often it is ineffectual or even counterproductive. A president's appeals may energize supporters, but they may also have a similar effect on opponents.[41] Thus, rather than facilitating compromise (or a wholesale presidential victory), publicizing an issue may deepen existing conflicts. More generally, studies suggest that most Americans ignore or reject a president's attempts to go public. As presidency scholar George C. Edwards III notes, people who disapprove of a president's time in office are not going to change their minds just because of a presidential speech.[42] Other times, presidential efforts to shape opinion fail spectacularly, such as President Trump's use of a Sharpie to alter a National Oceanographic and Atmospheric Administration (NOAA) hurricane prediction map to justify his tweeted assertion that the storm might hit Alabama.[43] While few Americans are political experts, most citizens are not gullible.

George C. Edwards's findings explain why most recent presidents have had little success with their efforts to go public. President George W. Bush gave many speeches to build support for his Iraq War policies and for his proposal to privatize Social Security. President Barack Obama did the same in an effort to enact gun control legislation.

going public
A president's use of speeches and other public communications to appeal directly to citizens about issues the president would like the House and Senate to act on.

DID YOU KNOW?

Since becoming president in 2017, President Trump held over

300

rallies (often televised) calling for enactment of his policy priorities.
Source: *New York Times*

After mistakenly tweeting that Alabama was under threat from Hurricane Dorian in September 2019, President Donald Trump appeared during a briefing by federal agencies with a map that seems to have been updated with a Sharpie marker to extend the range of at-risk areas into Alabama. The National Weather Service never included Alabama in its projected path for Dorian, leaving many Americans confused about whom to trust.

And while President Trump used a broader range of media outlets compared to his predecessors (most notably, Twitter and his campaign rallies), his efforts to shape public opinion on issues such as the travel ban, the border wall, or immigration reform have not significantly changed public opinion. Thus, while presidents have a unique platform from which to deliver their arguments directly to the American people, in practice they are often frustrated in their ability to shape public opinion.

Unpacking the Conflict

Considering all that we've discussed in this chapter, let's apply what we know about how the office of the president works to the questions we presented at the beginning of this chapter. Did Trump and the outcomes of his tenure in office redefine what makes a successful president—or a failed one? What factors distinguish presidential successes from presidential failures?

The president occupies an office whose power is derived from constitutional authority, statutory authority, and ambiguities that enable unilateral action. While Trump promised during the 2016 campaign to transform America, his presidency highlights the difficulties that any president would face in trying to deliver on this promise. Although presidents are given considerable powers, big policy changes generally require congressional consent. And as we have seen, even with unified government, Trump was no more successful than his predecessors at persuading members of Congress to accept his policy plans such as building a border wall. Trump also faced opposition from within the bureaucracy and from citizens pursuing their claims through the federal judicial system.

Even so, Trump had some notable successes, particularly in areas where he could act unilaterally using executive orders or directives, as well as in shaping American foreign policy. Trump's appointees to posts in cabinet departments and federal agencies made significant progress in implementing his agenda in the form of regulatory changes and new interpretations of existing laws. Considering these successes along with the failures that we've noted, we should not conclude that President Trump had some special powers that his predecessors lacked or that he was deficient in some crucial talent. While his day-to-day behavior in office was sometimes different from what we have come to expect from our presidents, Trump's overall performance was not surprising. Rather, it illustrates both the possibilities and the limitations of the presidency in contemporary American politics.

"What's Your Take?"

Did Trump's presidency represent a departure from the norm?

How do the results he achieved in office compare with those of previous presidents?

STUDY GUIDE

Summary

The president's formal powers arise from a combination of constitutional provisions and additional laws that give him or her increased responsibilities. The president has many duties, but the primary responsibilities of the office are to oversee the executive branch and implement laws passed by Congress. Although some presidents might prefer to focus on either domestic or foreign policy, most find that their priorities are determined by domestic and world events.

The development of presidential power

Trace the evolution of presidential power. (Pages 354–357)

Key terms

constitutional authority (presidential) (p. 357)	head of state (p. 358)
statutory authority (presidential) (p. 357)	recess appointment (p. 360)
	executive orders (p. 360)
vesting clause (p. 358)	executive agreement (p. 365)
head of government (p. 358)	State of the Union (p. 366)
	executive privilege (p. 368)

Summary

Presidents get their powers from a variety of sources: some powers are from the Constitution; others have more informal origins. Although the president's constitutional powers have not changed, presidential power has grown substantially over time. Nonetheless, even presidents' power is still limited in a number of contexts.

Practice Quiz Questions

1. **Which of the following is *not* a reason why presidential power has increased over time?**

   a changes in the Constitution

   b America's growth as a nation

   c America's emergence as a dominant actor in international politics

   d the expansion of the federal government

   e acts of legislation passed by Congress

2. **The government's response to the Great Depression was defined by _____.**

   a presidential actions

   b presidential inaction

   c congressional action

   d popular protest

   e international pressure

Practice Quiz Questions

3. **Presidents use recess appointments when they are trying to _____.**

   a fill a judicial vacancy outside the scheduled period

   b fill a vacant seat in Congress

   c temporarily dodge the need for Senate approval

   d temporarily dodge the need for House approval

   e fill vacancies with a permanent replacement

4. **A presidential proclamation that unilaterally changes government policy without congressional consent is called _____.**

   a an executive privilege

   b a fast-track authority

   c an executive agreement

   d an executive order

   e statutory authority

5. **Some scholars argue that the War Powers Resolution has effectively expanded the power of _____.**

   a the president

   b Congress

   c the Supreme Court

   d the Department of Defense

   e the State Department

The president's job description

Describe the constitutional and statutory powers of the president today. (Pages 357–370)

The presidency as an institution

Explain how the Executive Office of the President, the vice president, and the Cabinet help the president. (Pages 370–374)

Summary

The executive branch is a huge, complex organization that helps the president exercise vast responsibilities. Appointees to the branch serve as the president's eyes and ears on the bureaucracy. Almost all appointees are replaced when a new administration begins.

Key terms

Executive Office of the President (EOP) (p. 371)

Cabinet (p. 373)

Practice Quiz Questions

6. **In most appointments to EOP positions, presidents generally emphasize _____ .**

   a experience

   b expertise

   c effectiveness

   d public opinion

   e loyalty

7. **Recent vice presidents have had _____ official duties and _____ been influential in their role.**

   a no; have not

   b limited; have

   c limited; have not

   d extensive; have

   e extensive; have not

Presidential power today

Explain how modern presidents have become even more powerful. (Pages 374–380)

Summary

While presidents have gained power over time, the Constitution grants the president rather limited powers. The growth of presidential power is closely related to the fact that most limits on it are not well defined and presidents have succeeded in taking advantage of these ambiguities.

Key terms

unilateral action (presidential) (p. 375)

signing statement (p. 375)

presidential approval rating (p. 377)

going public (p. 379)

Practice Quiz Questions

8. **Most presidents use the _____ to control the interpretation and implementation of laws.**

   a line-item veto

   b recess appointment

   c executive order

   d signing statement

   e pocket veto

9. **Congressional challenges to presidential unilateral action are _____ used and are generally _____ at constraining presidential power.**

   a rarely; successful

   b rarely; unsuccessful

   c commonly; successful

   d commonly; unsuccessful

   e never; unsuccessful

10. **Presidential reelection is often tied to _____ .**

    a economic conditions

    b policy positions

    c presidential actions

    d presidential appointments

    e an absence of scandals

11. **For most presidents, the problem with going public is that _____ .**

    a the public is more focused on Congress

    b the president's speeches are not very persuasive

    c they energize their opponents

    d they generally address unimportant issues

    e they do not reach their target audience

Suggested Reading

Azari, Julia R. *Delivering the People's Message: The Changing Politics of the Presidential Mandate*. Ithaca, NY: Cornell University Press, 2014.

Campbell, Karlyn Kohrs, and Kathleen Hall Jamieson. *Presidents Creating the Presidency: Deeds Done in Words*. Chicago: University of Chicago Press, 2008.

Canes-Wrone, Brandice. *Who Leads Whom? Presidents, Policy, and the Public*. Chicago: University of Chicago Press, 2006.

Edwards, George C., III. *Predicting the Presidency: The Potential of Persuasive Leadership*. Princeton, NJ: Princeton University Press, 2015.

Graham, Mary. *Presidents' Secrets: The Use and Abuse of Hidden Power*. New Haven: Yale University Press, 2017.

Howell, William G. *Power without Persuasion: The Politics of Direct Presidential Action*. Princeton, NJ: Princeton University Press, 2003.

Katznelson, Ira. *Fear Itself: The New Deal and the Origins of Our Time*. New York: W. W. Norton, 2013.

Lewis, David E. *Presidents and the Politics of Agency Design: Political Insulation in the United States Government Bureaucracy, 1946-1997*. Palo Alto, CA: Stanford University Press, 2003.

Rudalevige, Andrew. *Managing the President's Program: Presidential Leadership and Legislative Policy Formation*. Princeton, NJ: Princeton University Press, 2002.

Skowronek, Stephen. *Presidential Leadership in Political Time: Reprise and Reappraisal*. Lawrence: University of Kansas Press, 2008.

12

The Bureaucracy
What's with all this red tape?

 "Government! Three fourths parasitic and the other fourth stupid fumbling."[1]
Robert A. Heinlein, American writer

 "Bureaucracy is not an obstacle to democracy but an inevitable complement to it."[2]
Joseph A. Schumpeter, American economist

Throughout the COVID-19 pandemic, one of the most important pieces of information was the number of people who died each day from the disease. Death statistics captured not only changes in how many people were suffering from the virus but also our success at treating these cases. At the same time, death statistics were politically significant, as they were a visible indicator of the government's effectiveness at dealing with the pandemic. Particularly in the earliest-affected states, sharp increases in the number of daily COVID-related deaths highlighted gaps in state and local government preparedness, including a lack of protective equipment and other medical supplies, a reluctance to impose lockdown measures, and an overall unwillingness to take the problem seriously.

The political significance of death statistics was one reason for an ongoing debate within the federal government over measuring COVID-related deaths. For example, if a patient with a compromised immune system caught the virus and died, was the death due to COVID-19 or the underlying condition that increased that person's vulnerability? Scientists at the federal Centers for Disease Control and Prevention wanted to ignore underlying conditions, while members of President Trump's staff favored excluding cases from the pandemic's mortality statistics if an underlying condition could be identified.

This example highlights three essential features of the federal bureaucracy. First, bureaucrats are often engaged in highly technical tasks that require expertise and judgment. Second, these tasks have political consequences—for President Trump, a reduction in death statistics would have helped him argue during the 2020 election campaign that his administration had responded effectively to the pandemic. Third, while Trump wields considerable power as president, he cannot simply order bureaucrats to do whatever he wants. Throughout his time as president, Trump described the bureaucracy as a more or less autonomous "deep state," raising the

In the midst of the coronavirus outbreak, the White House Coronavirus Task Force held daily television briefings to disseminate information to the public. Here, Dr. Anthony Fauci, director of the National Institute of Allergy and Infectious Diseases, can be seen placing his hand over his face in dismay as President Trump makes a comment about "deep state" conspiracies during a briefing, demonstrating the often-contentious relationship between President Trump and the federal bureaucracy.

CHAPTER GOALS

Define *bureaucracy* and explain its major functions. pages 386–393

Trace the expansion of the federal bureaucracy over time. pages 394–397

Describe the size and structure of the executive branch today. pages 397–402

Describe who bureaucrats are and the regulations that govern their employment. pages 402–405

Explain how Congress and the president oversee the executive branch. pages 405–410 question of whether bureaucratic actions reflect expertise or a political agenda (in this case, opposition to Trump's reelection).

Up to now, we've described the policy-making process in terms of three steps: (1) citizens elect representatives, (2) these representatives go to Washington and enact laws, and (3) bureaucrats are given these laws to implement. The reality in our system is that the responsibility for implementing laws conveys policy-making power. When bureaucrats write regulations, sign contracts with private corporations, deliver services to citizens, or make judgments about how to measure things like deaths due to COVID-19, they are translating often-vague statutes into concrete decisions. Moreover, because of their training and experience, bureaucrats are often better informed than elected officials about the details of government policy. Bureaucratic expertise creates a new problem for elected officials: if they ignore what bureaucrats tell them or force bureaucrats to implement laws and directives as written, the result may be policy failures. However, if elected officials acknowledge that bureaucrats are experts and allow them to make as well as implement government policy, elected officials in effect give up all their power to the bureaucracy—something that the Trump administration was unwilling to risk. Were bureaucrats really obstructing the Trump agenda, or were they just doing their jobs? How do elected officials control a bureaucracy of experts, in the midst of a pandemic or in more routine times?

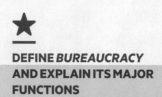

DEFINE *BUREAUCRACY* AND EXPLAIN ITS MAJOR FUNCTIONS

bureaucracy
The system of civil servants and political appointees who implement congressional or presidential decisions; also known as the *administrative state.*

civil servants
Employees of bureaucratic agencies within the government.

political appointees
People selected by an elected leader, such as the president, to hold a government position.

What is the federal bureaucracy?

The federal **bureaucracy** is the vast network of agencies that makes up the government's executive branch. It is composed of millions of **civil servants**, who work for the government in permanent positions, and thousands of **political appointees**, who hold short-term, usually senior positions and are appointed by an elected leader, such as the president. Another name for the bureaucracy is the *administrative state.*[3]

In general, the job of the federal bureaucracy includes a wide range of tasks, from regulating the behavior of individuals and corporations to buying everything from pencils to jet fighters. These activities are inherently political and often conflictual: ordinary citizens, elected officials, and bureaucrats themselves often disagree about aspects of these activities, and they work to influence bureaucratic actions to suit their policy goals.

What do bureaucrats do?

The task of the bureaucracy is to develop and implement policies established by congressional acts or presidential decisions. Sometimes the tasks are very specific. For example, in the appropriations bill for fiscal year 2020, Congress mandated that the navy purchase 98 F-35 attack jets from defense contractor Lockheed Martin. This provision required no discretion on the part of the bureaucrats who were tasked to implement it—all they needed to do was sign the contract, make sure that the jets were delivered, and pay Lockheed Martin.

More commonly, however, legislation provides only general guidelines for meeting governmental goals. Bureaucrats thus have considerable latitude to develop particular policies and programs. For example, the 1938 Federal Food, Drug, and Cosmetic Act gave the Food and Drug Administration (FDA) the job of determining which drugs are safe and effective (including drugs to treat COVID-19 symptoms and vaccines to prevent people from getting the disease), but it allowed FDA bureaucrats to develop their own procedures for making these determinations.[4]

Developing Regulations A **regulation** is a rule that allows the government to exercise control over individuals and corporations by allowing or prohibiting behavior, setting out the conditions under which certain behaviors can occur, or assessing costs or granting benefits based on behavior. Bureaucrats gain the authority to write regulations from acts passed by Congress, either through the statute that initially sets up their agency or through subsequent laws. For example, the Environmental Protection Agency (EPA) has many regulations that limit the amount of various pollutants that can be emitted from factories, automobiles, and electrical power plants. The EPA's authority to develop these regulations, as well as limits on other power plant emissions, comes from the Clean Air Act of 1970 as well as subsequent reauthorizations (newer versions) of this legislation (for more details, see How It Works: Bureaucracy and Legislation).

Regulations are developed according to the **notice-and-comment procedure**.[5] Before most proposed regulations can take effect, they are published in the *Federal Register*, an official journal that includes rules, proposed rules, and other types of government documents. Individuals and companies potentially affected by the regulation can then comment, or respond to the agency that proposed it, either supporting or opposing the regulation or offering different versions for consideration. They can also appeal to members of Congress or to the president's staff for help in lobbying bureaucrats to revise the proposal. The agency then issues a final regulation that incorporates changes based on the comments. This final regulation is also published in the *Federal Register* and then put into effect. The process is time-consuming. For example, an ongoing effort of the Federal Aviation Administration (FAA) to develop regulations on the use of drone aircraft began with a congressional mandate issued in 2012. Current regulations limit the size and weight of drones that can be flown without registering with the agency, but the FAA is still developing rules to govern larger package-delivery drones that must fly over populated areas. Many regulations can take even longer to craft from beginning to end.

regulation
A rule that allows the government to exercise control over individuals and corporations by restricting certain behaviors.

notice-and-comment procedure
A step in the rule-making process in which proposed rules are published in the *Federal Register* and made available for debate by the general public.

What is the federal bureaucracy? **387**

Bureaucracy and Legislation

After Congress passes legislation and the president signs it, the transition from legislation to regulation begins. Input from local government officials, interest groups, and others helps to refine the regulations as they are developed, and has a strong influence on how regulations will affect people "on the ground."

Congress passes legislation.

The president signs the bill into law.

Bureaucrats interpret the law and design appropriate regulations.

Courts respond to challenges to the law, and they can provide guidelines for implementation.

Other bureaucrats disseminate regulations to state and local governments, corporations, and individuals, and they monitor compliance.

Citizens and interest groups provide information and proposals to bureaucrats, and they lobby for their preferred implementation of the legislation.

Regulations can be revised in light of changing circumstances, different political climates, or unanticipated consequences.

Regulating Greenhouse Gas Emissions

In November 2017, the Trump administration announced a plan to repeal and replace the Environmental Protection Agency (EPA)'s Clean Power Plan regulations that limited CO_2 emissions from fossil fuel power plants, and in May 2019 announced further plans to issue new regulations dealing with CO_2 emissions. These actions were some of the latest steps in a 20-year process of court cases, presidential directives, and actions by EPA bureaucrats.

New Acts!

Congressional Action: Congress enacts two Clean Air Acts, in 1963 and 1970 respectively, with amendments in 1977 and 1990, authorizing the government to monitor and limit emissions of harmful chemicals into the atmosphere.

Although... maybe not?

Bureaucratic Action (2003): The EPA announces that the **Clean Air Act does not give it the authority to regulate CO_2** and other greenhouse gases.

Actually... yes.

Judicial Action (2007): In response to a case brought by 12 states, the Supreme Court rules that **greenhouse gases are covered by the Clean Air Act**.

Obama weighs in.

Presidential Directive (June 2013): President Obama **directs the EPA to develop additional regulations** for limiting CO_2 emissions from new and existing power plants.

Results?

September 2013: The EPA modifies its draft regulations to place **CO_2 standards** on new power plants and issues a revised proposal.

June 2014: The EPA proposes an additional rule that aims to **cut CO_2 emissions from existing power plants**.

Third try!

New Regulations Finalized (August 2015): After receiving over 6 million comments, the EPA **announces its Clean Power Plan**, which will regulate CO_2 emissions from both new and existing power plants.

Critical Thinking

1. **Critics of the regulatory process complain that unelected** bureaucrats make most of the decisions while elected officials sit on the sidelines. Is this complaint supported by the case of the Clean Power Plan?

2. **The Clean Power Plan illustrates how acts of legislation are often** reinterpreted years after their passage. Why don't members of Congress write legislation in ways that prevent this from happening?

Stand by.

February 2016: The Supreme Court **puts implementation of the Clean Power Plan for existing plants on hold**, pending litigation. Moreover, these regulations are subject to change by the Trump administration.

Up in the air?

November 2017: Under the Trump administration, **the EPA announces a plan to repeal and replace the Clean Power Plan**.

More to come.

May 2019: Following President Trump's directive, **the EPA announces plans to issue a new set of regulations** dealing with CO_2 emissions, beginning the entire process over again.

This process of devising or modifying regulations is often political. Members of Congress and the president usually have strong opinions about how new regulations should look—and even when they don't, they may still get involved on behalf of a constituent or an interest group. Bureaucrats take account of these pressures for two reasons: (1) the bureaucrats' policy-making power may derive from a statute that members of Congress could overturn; and (2) bureaucrats need congressional support to get larger budgets and to expand their agency's mission. Thus, despite bureaucrats' power to develop and implement policies, their agencies' budgets, appointed leaders, and overall missions are subject to elected officials' oversight.

Federal regulations affect most aspects of everyday life. They influence the gas mileage of cars sold in the United States, the materials used to build roads, and the price of gasoline. They determine the amounts that doctors can charge senior citizens for medical procedures; the hours that medical residents can work; the criteria used to determine who gets a heart, lung, or kidney transplant; and the allowable emissions from power plants. Regulations set the eligibility criteria for student loans, limit how the military can recruit on college campuses, determine who can get a home mortgage and what the interest rate will be, and describe what constitutes equal funding for men's and women's college sports teams. Regulations also shape contribution limits and spending decisions in political campaigns.

Regulations are often controversial because they involve trade-offs between incompatible goals as well as decisions made under uncertain circumstances. For example, the regulations that guide the FDA drug-approval process prioritize the goal of preventing harmful drugs from coming to market.[6] As a result, patients sometimes cannot get access to experimental treatments because FDA approval has not been granted, even when those treatments are the patients' only remaining option.[7] Advocates for patients have argued that people with dire prognoses should be allowed to use these treatments as a potentially lifesaving last resort.[8] However, current FDA regulations prevent patients from doing so except under very special circumstances.

Federal regulations influence many aspects of everyday life that would seem unlikely to be affected by government actions. The increase in the number of women's intercollegiate athletic teams is partly due to regulations that require equal funding for men's and women's teams. Pictured here is Baylor University's 2019 NCAA women's basketball championship team.

In the case of COVID-19, exceptions were made for the drugs hydroxychloroquine and remdesivir, both which had been tested for safety and approved for treatment of other diseases. However, follow-up studies found that hydroxychloroquine did not improve survival rates and also caused severe side effects for some patients, illustrating the risks associated with bypassing the FDA review process.

Bringing Expertise to Policy Making Bureaucrats are also an important source of new government policies. For example, Congress and the president give civilian and military personnel in the Department of Defense the job of revising military doctrines—broad directives on how our armed forces should go about accomplishing specific tasks such as protecting civilian freighters from attacks by Somali pirates, deploying troops to rescue American civilians in hostile territory, or running military training operations in Africa. While military doctrines reflect input from members of Congress, the State Department and the president's appointees, and groups outside government (including lobbyists, think tanks, and defense contractors), they also reflect the preferences of the bureaucrats assigned to the task. Thus, as in the case of regulations, when it comes to government policy, bureaucrats are not just implementers; they have a significant influence on what government does and does not do.

Delivering Services Some bureaucrats are the face of the federal government, interacting directly with citizens to provide services and other benefits. People working in the Department of Agriculture assist farmers by processing crop loans and providing advice on new technologies and techniques. Members of the Park Service operate the network of national parks and wilderness areas. And the Transportation Security Administration staffs the security checkpoints at American airports. These and other jobs are a reminder of how intertwined the federal government is with the lives of ordinary Americans. We may like to think of the federal government as something that exists only in Washington, D.C., but the reality is that bureaucrats are spread out across the country and are deeply involved with all elements of American society.

Bureaucratic expertise and its consequences

Bureaucrats are experts. Even compared with most members of Congress or presidential appointees, the average bureaucrat is a specialist in a certain policy area (often holding an advanced degree), with a good grasp of his or her agency's mission. For example, people who hold scientific or management positions in the FDA usually know more about the benefits and risks of new drugs than people outside the agency do. A bureaucracy of experts is an important part of **state capacity**—the knowledge, personnel, and institutions needed to effectively implement policies.[9] It is an important check on elected officials, helping to ensure that government policies are effective and efficient.

While having an expert bureaucracy seems like an obvious good idea, it creates a new problem for elected officials. Bureaucrats can bring expertise to their policy choices only if elected officials stop ordering bureaucrats around and instead allow them to act as they think best. But when elected officials allow such discretion, they risk losing control over the policy-making process and having to live with policy choices that serve bureaucratic interests without satisfying the elected officials or their constituents.

The Problem of Control: Principals and Agents The difficulty that elected officials and their staff face when trying to interpret or influence bureaucratic actions is the **problem of control**.[10] A classic illustration of this situation is the **principal–agent game**, which describes an interaction in which an individual or a group (an "agent")

state capacity
The knowledge, personnel, and institutions that the government requires to effectively implement policies.

problem of control
A difficulty faced by elected officials in ensuring that when bureaucrats implement policies they follow these officials' intentions but still have enough discretion to use their expertise.

principal–agent game
The interaction between a principal (such as the president or Congress), who needs something done, and an agent (such as a bureaucrat), who is responsible for carrying out the principal's orders.

Despite their policy expertise, bureaucrats still make mistakes. When the Medicare program implemented the Prescription Drug Benefit in 2006, information about the coverage was available on an easy-to-read website, but the agency soon learned that many seniors who needed the information did not own a computer or even know how to use a Web browser.

The nine most terrifying words in the English language are: I'm from the government, and I'm here to help.

—President Ronald Reagan

acts on behalf of another (the "principal"). In the federal government, the president and Congress are principals and bureaucrats are agents. An agent in the bureaucracy may prefer outcomes that the principal does not like. Moreover, because the agent is an expert at the task he or she has been given, the agent has additional knowledge and experiences that are inaccessible to the principal. The conundrum for the principal, then, is this: giving the agent very specific orders prevents the agent from acting based on his or her expertise, but if the principal gives the agent the freedom to make decisions based on expertise, the principal has less control over the agent's actions.

Suppose Congress and the president directed the FDA to shorten its drug-approval process to approve new drugs or vaccines to fight COVID-19. FDA officials might have mandated a lengthy process based on their expert assessment of the best way to screen out harmful drugs. By giving orders that superseded the FDA officials' screening process, elected officials would be sacrificing the valuable bureaucratic expertise behind the policy and risking the hasty approval of unsafe drugs. But if Congress and the president allowed FDA bureaucrats to devise their own procedures and regulations, there would be a chance that the FDA could use this freedom to pursue goals that have nothing to do with drug safety. For example, critics of the FDA's procedures have asserted that a drawn-out approval process favors large companies that already have drugs on the market over smaller companies trying to get approval for drugs that would compete with existing products.

The principal–agent game can also be framed in terms of citizens. Figure 12.1 shows that a majority of survey respondents agreed that the federal government is typically inefficient and wasteful—although the percentage agreeing with this assessment declined from its peak in 1994 until more recent years, when it again increased. Such opinions give citizens a strong motivation to demand that elected officials control the bureaucracy—to reduce the waste and inefficiency or, as the quote from Ronald Reagan suggests, to prevent bureaucrats from overly intruding into American society.

One important consequence of the problem of control is the complexity of bureaucratic organizations and procedures. Despite bureaucrats' policy expertise,

FIGURE 12.1

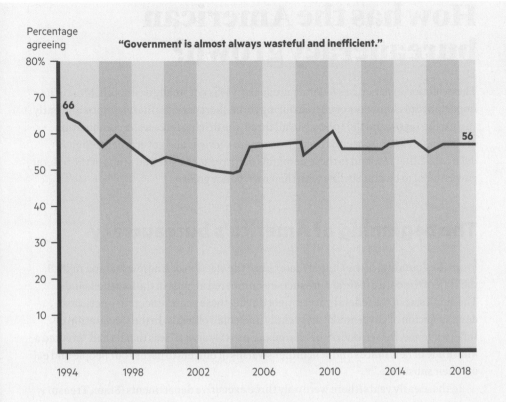

Percentage agreeing

"Government is almost always wasteful and inefficient."

66

56

1994 1998 2002 2006 2010 2014 2018

How Americans View the Federal Bureaucracy

Many Americans believe the bureaucracy is wasteful and inefficient. Note, however, that the magnitude of negative feelings varies over time. Consider the time frame represented in the graph. What happened during these years that might explain the changes in citizens' opinions about the government?

Source: Pew Research Center, "In a Politically Polarized Era, Sharp Divides in Both Partisan Coalitions," December 17, 2019, www.pewresearch.org/politics/2019/12/17/views-of-government-and-the-nation/ (accessed 5/20/20).

their decisions often appear to take too much time, rely on arbitrary judgments of what is important, and have unintended consequences—to the point that actions designed to solve one problem may create worse ones. Examples include **red tape**, which refers to excessive or unnecessarily complex regulations, and **standard operating procedures (SOPs)**, which are the rules that lower-level bureaucrats must follow, regardless of whether they actually apply, when implementing policies.

The problem of control has existed throughout the history of the federal government. It affects both the kinds of policies that bureaucrats implement and the structure of the federal bureaucracy, including the number of agencies and their missions, staff, and tasks. Moreover, elected officials use a variety of methods to solve the problem of control, including making it easier for people outside government to learn about agency actions before they take effect. However, all these tactics are at best partial solutions to the problem of control. The trade-off between expertise and control remains.

red tape
Excessive or unnecessarily complex regulations imposed by the bureaucracy.

standard operating procedures (SOPs)
Rules that lower-level bureaucrats must follow when implementing policies.

Bureaucrats aren't mindless paper pushers. Rather, they are experts who have considerable power to shape what government does. The way many elected officials talk, it's easy to think that once they pass a piece of legislation or issue an executive order, government policy automatically changes. In most cases, however, these directives are only the first step. To bring these changes to life, bureaucrats must step in to translate often-vague goals into concrete regulations, budgets, and actions. In other words, while you might not think much about bureaucrats, they can have a profound effect on your daily life.

"Why Should I Care?"

How has the American bureaucracy grown?

The evolution of America's federal bureaucracy was not steady or smooth. Most of its important developments occurred during three short periods: the late 1890s and early 1900s, the 1930s, and the 1960s.[11] In all three, the driving force was a combination of citizens' demands for enhanced government services and government officials' desires to either respond to these demands or increase the size and scope of the federal government to be more in line with their own policy goals.

The beginning of America's bureaucracy

From the Founding of the United States until the election of Andrew Jackson in 1828, the staff of the entire federal bureaucracy numbered at most in the low thousands. The small size of the federal government during these years reflected Americans' deep suspicion of government, especially unelected officials. In the Declaration of Independence, in fact, one of the charges against George III was that he had "erected a multitude of new offices and sent hither swarms of officers to harass our people and eat out their substance."[12]

In these early years, there were only three executive departments (State, Treasury, and War), along with a postmaster general,[13] and executive branch offices were formed only when absolutely necessary. This small bureaucracy performed a very narrow range of tasks. It collected taxes on imports and exports and delivered the mail. The national army consisted of a small Corps of Engineers and a few frontier patrols. The attorney general was a private attorney who had the federal government as one of his clients. Members of Congress outnumbered civil servants in Washington, and the president had very little staff at all.[14]

The election of Andrew Jackson in 1828 brought the first large-scale use of the spoils system: people who had worked for Jackson's campaign were rewarded with new positions in the federal government (usually as local postmasters).[15] The spoils system was extremely useful to party organizations, as it gave them a powerful incentive with which to convince people to work for the party—and it was a particularly important tool for Jackson. His campaign organization was at that time the largest ever organized.

The challenge facing the spoils system was ensuring that these government employees, who often lacked experience in their new fields, could actually carry out their jobs. The solution was to develop procedures that guided them on exactly what to do even if they had no experience or training.[16] These instructions became one of the earliest uses of standard operating procedures. They ensured that the government could function even if many employees had been hired in reward for political work rather than because of their qualifications.[17]

As America expanded, so did the federal government, which saw an almost eightfold increase in the bureaucracy between 1816 and the beginning of the Civil War in 1861. This growth did not reflect fundamental changes in what the government did; in fact, much of the increase came in areas such as the Post Office, which needed to serve a geographically larger nation—and, of course, to provide "spoils" for party workers in the form of government jobs.[18] Even by the end of the Civil War, the federal government still had very little involvement in the lives of ordinary Americans. State and local governments provided services such as education, public works, and

This cartoon of a monument depicting President Andrew Jackson riding a pig decries his involvement in the spoils system, which allowed politicians to dole out government service jobs in return for political support.

welfare benefits, if they were provided at all. The federal government's role in daily life was limited to mail delivery, the collection of import and export taxes, and a few other sectors.

Building a new American state: the Progressive Era

Political developments in the second half of the nineteenth century transformed America's bureaucracy.[19] While the transformation began after the Civil War, the most significant changes occurred during the Progressive Era, from 1890 to 1920. Many laws and executive actions increased the government's regulatory power during this period, including the Sherman Antitrust Act of 1890, the Pure Food and Drug Act of 1906, the Federal Meat Inspection Act of 1906, expansion of the Interstate Commerce Commission, and various conservation measures.[20] Now the federal government had an indirect impact on several aspects of everyday life: when Americans bought food or other products, went to work, or traveled, the choices available to them were shaped by the actions of federal bureaucrats.

These developments were matched by a fundamental change in the federal bureaucracy following passage of the 1883 Pendleton Civil Service Act. This measure created the **federal civil service**, in which the merit system (qualifications, not political connections) became the basis for hiring and promoting bureaucrats.[21] In other words, when new presidents took office they could not replace government workers with their own campaign workers. Initially, only about 13,000 federal jobs acquired civil service protections, but subsequently many additional positions were incorporated into the civil service. These reforms created a bureaucracy in which people could build a career in government without having to fear being fired when a new president or Congress took office.[22] In the modern era, virtually all full-time, permanent government employees have civil service protections—although many individuals lack these protections because they work for a company that contracts services to the government, or because they are senior political appointees.

federal civil service
A system created by the 1883 Pendleton Civil Service Act in which bureaucrats are hired on the basis of merit rather than political connections.

The New Deal, the Great Society, and the Reagan Revolution

Dramatic expansion of the federal bureaucracy occurred during the New Deal period in the 1930s and during the mid-1960s Great Society era. In both cases, the changes were driven by a combination of citizen demands and the preferences of elected officials who favored an increased role of government in society. These expansion trends were only marginally curtailed during the Reagan Revolution of the 1980s.

The New Deal The New Deal comprised government programs implemented during Franklin Roosevelt's first term as president in the 1930s. These programs were partly a response to the Great Depression and the inability of local governments and private charities to provide adequate support to Americans during this economic crisis. Many advocates of the New Deal also favored an expanded role for government in American society, regardless of the immediate need for intervention.[23] Roosevelt's programs included reforms to the financial industry as well as efforts to help people directly,

Franklin Roosevelt's New Deal programs greatly expanded the power of the federal government and the bureaucracy. As this cartoon shows, these changes were controversial, with some seeing them as moving too much power from Congress to the president and bureaucracy.

including the stimulation of employment and economic growth, and the formation of labor unions. The Social Security Act, the first federally funded pension program for all Americans, was also passed as part of the New Deal.[24]

These reforms resulted in a vast increase in the size and responsibilities of the bureaucracy, as well as a large transfer of power to bureaucrats and to the president.[25] Before the New Deal, the federal government influenced citizens' choices through activities such as regulating industries and workplace conditions. Afterward, it took on the role of directly delivering a wide range of benefits and services to its citizens, from jobs to electricity. It also increased regulations on many industries, including those in the banking and financial sectors.

Expansion of the federal government and the subsequent delegation of power to bureaucrats and to the president were controversial changes.[26] Many Republicans opposed New Deal reforms because they believed that the federal government could not deliver services efficiently and that an expanded federal bureaucracy would create a modern spoils system. Many southerners worried that the federal government's increased involvement in everyday life would endanger the system of racial segregation in southern states.[27] Even so, Democratic supporters of the New Deal, aided by public support, carried the day.

The Great Society The Great Society was a series of federal programs enacted during Lyndon Johnson's presidency (1963–1969) that further expanded the size, capacity, and activities of the bureaucracy. Johnson proposed and Congress passed programs that funded bilingual education, loans and grants for college students, special education, preschools, construction of elementary and secondary schools, mass-transit programs in many cities, health care for seniors and poor people, job training and urban renewal, enhanced voting rights and civil rights for minorities, environmental protection, funding for the arts and cultural activities, and space exploration.[28]

The Great Society programs had mixed success. Voting rights and civil rights reforms ended the "separate but equal" system of social order in southern states and dramatically increased political participation by African Americans.[29] At the same time, many antipoverty programs were dismal failures. During the 1960s and 1970s, poverty rates among most groups remained relatively constant, and other indicators, such as the rate of teen pregnancy, actually increased.[30] In retrospect, the people who designed and implemented these programs did not realize the complexities of the problems they were trying to address.[31] Despite these shortcomings, the expansion of the federal government during the New Deal and Great Society has remained in place well into the twenty-first century.

The Reagan Revolution and Afterward The election of Ronald Reagan to the presidency in 1980, along with a Republican takeover of the Senate and Republican gains in the House of Representatives, created an opportunity for conservatives to roll back the size and scope of the federal government. These efforts were largely unsuccessful. In the years since Reagan, members of Congress and presidents from both parties have fought for large expansions in government policy. For example, while Democrat Barack Obama's administration issued many new environmental regulations and profoundly changed the American health care system, these changes are not too different in magnitude from the reforms championed by Republican George W. Bush, including education policies that increased federal control over local school districts, new drug financing benefits for seniors, and changes to financial regulations that increased financial reporting requirements for corporations. After four years in office, the Trump administration had little success in cutting overall federal spending

Under President George W. Bush, the federal bureaucracy continued to expand. Programs like No Child Left Behind increased the role of government in society.

or in reducing the size of specific agencies. For example, the administration initially proposed a one-third cut in the budget of the State Department for fiscal year 2018, only to ultimately accept a congressional budget that kept spending levels constant.

Though sometimes their rhetoric seems to tell a different story, the difference between Republicans and Democrats is not over the size of the federal government but over what government should do. While Republicans often argue for making government smaller and Democrats respond by highlighting the consequences of even a small cut in services, the truth is that most people on both sides accept the fact that a large federal government is here to stay. Knowing how the federal bureaucracy has grown, as well as evaluating whether this growth has caused problems or created benefits, is central to building your own ideas about what government should do.

"Why Should I Care?"

DESCRIBE THE SIZE AND STRUCTURE OF THE EXECUTIVE BRANCH TODAY

The modern federal bureaucracy

The size and scope of the modern federal bureaucracy reflect the expansion of the federal government over the last half century and its increased role in citizens' lives. The bureaucracy's structure also reflects ongoing attempts by presidents, members of Congress, and others to control bureaucratic actions in line with their policy goals.

The structure of the federal government

Nuts & Bolts 12.1 shows the structure of the executive branch of the federal government. As discussed in Chapter 11, the Executive Office of the President (EOP) contains organizations that support the president and implement presidential policy initiatives. Individuals working in these organizations aim to ensure that bureaucrats (agents) act appropriately to implement the president's (principal's) priorities and preferences.[32] Among its many offices, the EOP contains the **Office of Management and Budget**, which prepares the president's annual budget proposal to Congress and monitors government spending as well as the development of new regulations. Below the EOP are the 15 executive departments, from the Department of Agriculture to the Department of Veterans Affairs. The heads of these 15 organizations (plus others added by presidential order) make up the president's Cabinet. One thing to remember: while the diagram places the EOP above the cabinet departments and all other government agencies, the president's authority to direct agency decisions is not absolute, as it is limited by statute, regulations, and the Constitution, as well as by the pressure of business and a lack of information. These limits are discussed later in this chapter as well as in Chapter 11. Each executive department contains many smaller, sometimes diverse organizations. For example, Nuts & Bolts 12.2 shows the organizational chart for the Department of Agriculture.

In addition to executive departments, the government contains a group of agencies, commissions, and government corporations that are called **independent agencies** to highlight that they are not part of an executive department. Most of these agencies carry out specialized functions, regulating a particular activity (these are called independent regulatory agencies) or carrying out policy in a narrow area.

Office of Management and Budget
An office within the EOP that is responsible for creating the president's annual budget proposal to Congress, reviewing proposed rules, and performing other budget-related tasks.

independent agencies
Government offices or organizations that provide government services and are not part of an executive department.

NUTS & BOLTS 12.1

The Executive Branch of the Federal Government

The executive branch includes the 15 cabinet offices, as well as several independent agencies, commissions, and government corporations.

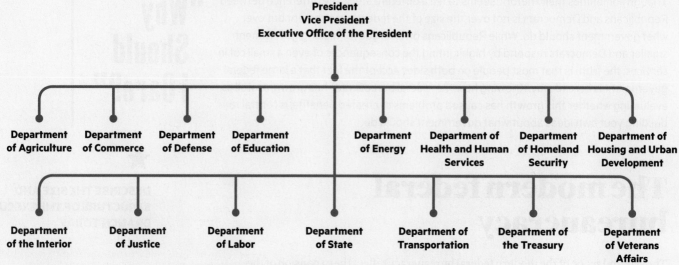

Selected Independent Establishments and Government Corporations

Central Intelligence Agency
Consumer Financial Protection Bureau
Consumer Product Safety Commission
Environmental Protection Agency
Equal Employment Opportunity Commission
Federal Communications Commission
Federal Deposit Insurance Corporation
Federal Election Commission

Federal Reserve System
Federal Trade Commission
General Services Administration
National Aeronautics and Space Administration
National Foundation on the Arts and the Humanities
National Labor Relations Board
National Railroad Passenger Corporation (Amtrak)
National Science Foundation

Occupational Safety and Health Review Commission
Peace Corps
Securities and Exchange Commission
Selective Service System
Small Business Administration
Social Security Administration
U.S. Agency for International Development
U.S. Postal Service

Source: United States General Services Administration, "Government Organizational Chart," www.usgovernmentmanual.gov/ReadLibraryItem.ashx?SFN=Myz95sTyO4rJRM/nhlRwSw==&SF=VHhnJrOeEAnGaa/rtk/JOg== (accessed 6/19/20).

 "Why Should I Care?" The list of cabinet departments and agencies illustrates the priorities of the federal government—the issues that are a high enough priority to be given an agency to address them.

The Federal Reserve System, for example, manages the money supply, banking system, and interest rates, while the National Aeronautics and Space Administration (NASA) directs aviation research and space exploration. Nuts & Bolts 12.1 includes only some noteworthy agencies; there are many more.

There are two important lessons to draw from these charts. First, the federal government handles an enormous range of functions. Second, the division of activities among executive departments and independent agencies does not always have an obvious logic. Why, for example, does the Department of Agriculture administer rural utilities programs and the Supplemental Nutritional Assistance Program (SNAP; formerly known as food stamps)? Similarly, it is not always clear why certain tasks are handled by

The Structure of the Department of Agriculture

The Department of Agriculture is headed by the secretary of agriculture and the deputy secretary of agriculture and includes various assistant secretaries and undersecretaries for specific areas, such as natural resources and the environment, farm services, rural development, and food safety.

Source: U.S. Department of Agriculture, "USDA Organization Chart," www.usda.gov/sites/default/files/documents/usda-organization-chart.pdf (accessed 7/30/20).

"Why Should I Care?" Organizational charts illustrate both governmental priorities and which agencies are subordinate to others. For example, if the Forest Service were in the Department of the Interior instead of Agriculture, America would likely have different policies concerning the management of forests and timber.

an independent agency while others fall within the scope of an executive department.[33] Why is the Food and Drug Administration (FDA) an independent agency rather than part of the Department of Commerce—and why is the Federal Aviation Administration (FAA) located within the Department of Transportation rather than being independent?

Part of the difference between independent agencies and the organizations contained within executive departments has to do with the president's ability to control these organizations' activities. Organizations that fall within an executive department, such as the FAA or the Federal Highway Administration (FHA) (both within the Department of Transportation) can be subject to presidential control (to some extent) through his or her appointees.[34] In contrast, independent agencies are

TABLE
12.1

Employment in Cabinet Departments

Source: Office of Management and Budget. "A Budget for America's Future: Analytical Perspectives, Fiscal Year 2021," 2020, www.whitehouse.gov/wp-content/uploads/2020/02/spec_fy21.pdf (accessed 5/22/20).

Organization	Total Employees
Defense (civilian only)	741,500
Veterans Affairs	375,800
Homeland Security	192,400
Justice	111,900
Treasury	88,000
Agriculture	81,400
Health and Human Services	73,000
Interior	70,000
Transportation	53,100
Commerce	45,000
State	27,100
Labor	14,800
Energy	14,000
Housing and Urban Development	7,400
Education	3,600

often designed to have more freedom from oversight and control by the president and Congress. For example, governors of the Federal Reserve, though nominated by the president and confirmed by the Senate, serve for 14 years—outlasting the administration that nominated them. Outside the nomination and confirmation process, the president and Congress have very little control over the Federal Reserve's policies; the organization is self-financing, and its governors can be removed from office only if Congress impeaches them. These kinds of details about the hiring and firing of bureaucrats and the location of agencies in the structure of the federal government matter because they determine the amount of political control that other parts of the government can exercise over an agency, as well as which individuals (the president or members of Congress) get to exercise this power.[35]

The size of the federal government

The federal government employs millions of people. Table 12.1 shows the number of employees in each executive department. Millions of additional people work for the government as members of the armed forces, as employees of the Postal Service, as employees of civilian companies that contract with the government, or as recipients of federal grant money.

The What Do the Facts Say? feature in this chapter shows the number of civilian federal employees from 1961 to 2020. Clearly, the federal workforce has steadily increased over time, although it has declined from its peak in the 1990s and remained

DID YOU KNOW?

In the first two years of the Trump presidency, 12 of 15 Cabinet Departments reduced their number of employees, some by almost

10%

Source: Office of Personnel Management

Is the Federal Bureaucracy Too Big?

One of the most intense conflicts in American political life is over the size of the federal government. Generally, Republicans say that the size of the federal bureaucracy should be reduced, while Democrats tend to favor increasing the size of government programs, including adding more employees if needed. Has the size of government increased over time?

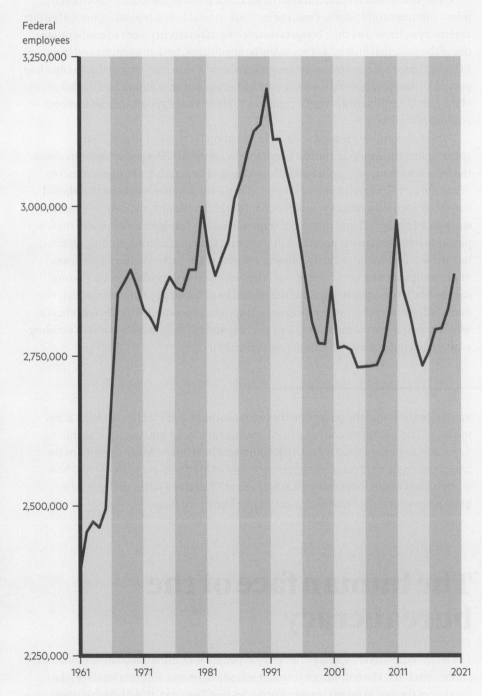

Source: Based on Federal Reserve Bank, St. Louis, "All Employees: Government: Federal," https://fred.stlouisfed.org/series/CES9091000001#0 (accessed 5/21/20).

WHAT DO THE FACTS SAY?

Think about it

- **During the 2016 presidential campaign,** candidate Donald Trump claimed that the size of the bureaucracy had significantly increased under President Obama. Do the data support this assertion?
- **The size of the federal bureaucracy** increased significantly during the 1960s and 1970s, then declined after about 1990. What political or historical events explain these changes?

budget maximizers
Bureaucrats who seek to increase funding for their agency whether or not that additional spending is worthwhile.

steady in recent years. Some observers argue that growth in employment was driven by the fact that bureaucrats are **budget maximizers** who never pass up a chance to increase the size of their organization regardless of whether the increase is worthwhile.[36] Of course, the fact that federal employment has remained steady in recent years suggests that something besides budget maximization is at work. The best explanation for the overall size of the federal government is the size of America itself—nearly 330 million people spread out over an area more than twice the size of the European Union—combined with America's position as the most powerful nation in the world with the largest military, and the increased costs associated with some government services, such as health care.

Those who blame bureaucrats for the increasing size of the federal government miss some important points. First, the increase in total federal spending masks the fact that many agencies see their budgets shrink.[37] Particularly in recent administrations, one of the principal missions of presidential appointees, both in agencies and in the EOP, has been to scrutinize budget requests with an eye to cutting spending as much as possible.[38] And in most years, some government agencies are eliminated (in fact, most of the executive department head counts in Table 12.1 have grown smaller in recent editions of this text).[39]

Public-opinion data also provide an explanation for the overall growth in government: the American public's demand for services.[40] Despite complaints about the federal bureaucracy, polls find little evidence of demands for less government. When the Pew Research Center asked people in 2019 to name programs that should have their spending cut as a way of reducing the budget deficit, the only program that was named by more than a quarter of respondents was foreign economic aid. Far fewer people favored cuts in the programs that account for most federal spending: defense, health care, and Social Security.[41] In other words, while in the abstract Americans might want a smaller government that is less involved in everyday life, they do not support the large-scale budget cuts that would be necessary to achieve this goal. The public's desire for more government services is often encouraged by elected officials, who create new government programs (and expand existing ones) as a way of building support and improving their chances of reelection.

"Why Should I Care?"

You might think that the government spends too much and that the bureaucracy is too large. The questions you have to ask yourself are: What am I willing to sacrifice to make government smaller? Am I OK with a smaller military, fewer regulations on banks and credit card companies, less oversight of food and drug safety? And how much money would these changes actually save? We have a large, costly federal government because, in the end, most people want it that way.

DESCRIBE WHO BUREAUCRATS ARE AND THE REGULATIONS THAT GOVERN THEIR EMPLOYMENT

The human face of the bureaucracy

The term "bureaucrat" applies to an array of people with different qualifications and job descriptions. The federal government includes so many different kinds of jobs because of the vast array of services it provides (see Figure 12.2). Although citizens and politicians often complain about federal bureaucrats' efficiency or motivations,

FIGURE 12.2

Types of Federal Workers

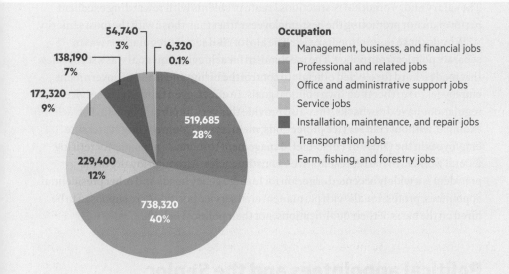

Occupation
- Management, business, and financial jobs
- Professional and related jobs
- Office and administrative support jobs
- Service jobs
- Installation, maintenance, and repair jobs
- Transportation jobs
- Farm, fishing, and forestry jobs

54,740 — 3%
6,320 — 0.1%
138,190 — 7%
172,320 — 9%
519,685 — 28%
229,400 — 12%
738,320 — 40%

Source: Bureau of Labor Statistics, "Occupational Employment Statistics," www.bls.gov/oes/current/naics4_999100.htm#00-0000 (accessed 5/22/20).

Note: Data may not total 100 percent due to rounding.

surveys show that many employees in these positions have a strong interest in public service or the implementation of good public policy. In fact, these motivations are often strong enough that scholars such as James L. Perry have argued against attempts to motivate federal workers with monetary incentives—bureaucrats who work hard because they feel it is the right thing to do may resent incentive schemes that presume they are lazy or only interested in money.[42]

Civil service regulations

Most jobs in the federal bureaucracy are subject to civil service regulations.[43] The current civil service system sets out job descriptions and pay ranges for all federal jobs.[44] The system also establishes tests that determine who is hired for low-level clerical and secretarial positions. People with less than a college degree are generally eligible for entry-level jobs, and as in the private sector, a college degree or an advanced degree and work experience qualify an individual for higher-level positions. Federal salaries are supposed to be comparable to what people earn in similar, private-sector positions, and salaries are somewhat higher for federal employees who work in areas with a high cost of living.

Civil service regulations provide job security. After three years of satisfactory performance, employees cannot be fired except "for cause," meaning that the firing agency must cite a reason. Civil service regulations set out a multistep procedure for firing someone, beginning with low performance evaluations, then warning letters given to the employee, followed by a lengthy appeals process before a firing takes place.[45] It is hard to get exact data, but most estimates are that about 10,000 federal employees are fired every year—out of a total workforce of over 2 million. A subpar performer may be assigned other duties, transferred to another office, or even given nothing to do in the hope that the person will leave voluntarily out of boredom or embarrassment.

Civil service regulations are extraordinarily cumbersome.[46] The hiring criteria remove a manager's discretion to hire someone who would do an excellent job but lacks the education or work experience that the regulations specify as necessary for the position. The firing requirements make it difficult to remove poor performers.

DID YOU KNOW?

28%

of federal bureaucrats have an advanced degree (post-bachelor). The corresponding percentage for large private businesses is about 11 percent.

Source: U.S. Census

The salary and promotion restrictions create problems with rewarding excellent performance or promoting the best employees rather than those with the most seniority.

Why do these requirements exist? The aim of civil service regulations was to separate politics from policy. The mechanism for achieving this goal was a set of rules that made it hard for elected officials to control the hiring and firing of government employees to further their own political goals. In effect, even though civil service regulations have drawbacks, they also provide this very important benefit. For example, without civil service protections, members of Congress might pressure employees in the Office of Personnel Management to increase pensions for retiring federal workers in the representatives' constituencies. Although loyalty to the president is a widely accepted criterion for hiring agency heads and other presidential appointees, professionals with permanent civil service positions are supposed to be hired on the basis of their qualifications, not their political beliefs.

Political appointees and the Senior Executive Service

Not every federal employee is a member of the civil service. About 3,000 senior positions in the executive branch—such as the leaders of executive departments and independent agencies like NASA, as well as members of the EOP—are not subject to civil service regulations. The president appoints individuals to these positions, and, in some cases, the Senate must confirm them.

The majority of a president's appointees act as his or her eyes, ears, and hands throughout the executive branch. They hold positions of power within government agencies, serving as secretaries of executive departments, agency heads, or senior deputies. Their jobs involve finding out what the president wants from their agency and ordering or persuading their subordinates to implement presidential directives.

In many agencies, people in the top positions are members of the Senior Executive Service (SES), who are also exempt from civil service restrictions.[47] As of 2020, there are about 8,000 SES members—mostly career government employees who held relatively high-level agency positions before moving to the SES. This change of employment status costs them their civil service protections but allows them to apply for senior leadership positions in the bureaucracy. Some political appointees are also given SES positions, although most do not have the experience or expertise held by career bureaucrats who typically move to the SES.

The president's ability to appoint bureaucrats in many different agencies helps him or her control the bureaucracy. By selecting people who are loyal or like-minded, the president can attempt to control the actions of lower-level bureaucrats and implement his or her policy agenda. The SES also provides civil servants an incentive to do their jobs well, as good performance in an agency position can help build a career that might allow them to transfer to the SES.

Federal employees must be careful that their comments to the media comply with Hatch Act restrictions. Kellyanne Conway, former counselor to President Trump, violated the Hatch Act when she advocated for and against candidates in the 2017 Senate special election in Alabama on CNN and Fox News programs.

Limits on political activity

Legislation places limits on the political activities that federal employees can undertake. The Hatch Act, enacted in 1939 and amended in 1940, prohibited federal employees from engaging in organized political activities: employees could vote and contribute to candidates but could not work for candidates or for political parties.[48] These restrictions were modified in the 1993 Federal Employees Political Activities Act, which allows federal employees to participate in a wider range of political activities, including fund-raising and serving as an officer of a political party. Senior members of the president's White House staff and political appointees are exempt from most of these restrictions, although they cannot use government resources for political activities.

The problem of control shapes the kinds of people who are hired as bureaucrats as well as their job protections. Political appointees and members of the SES are supposed to ride herd on the rest of the bureaucracy. Civil service protections exist to ensure that bureaucrats' decisions reflect expertise rather than political considerations.

"Why Should I Care?"

★

EXPLAIN HOW CONGRESS AND THE PRESIDENT OVERSEE THE EXECUTIVE BRANCH

Controlling the bureaucracy

As the expert implementers of legislation and presidential directives, bureaucrats hold significant power to influence government policy. This situation creates the problem of control illustrated by the principal–agent game, as we discussed earlier: elected officials must figure out how to reap the benefits of bureaucratic expertise without simply giving bureaucrats free rein to do whatever they want.

One strategy is to take away discretion and give bureaucrats simple, direct orders. For example, from 1996 to 2015 a law passed by Congress forbade the U.S. Centers for Disease Control and Prevention (CDC) from conducting research that would "advocate or promote gun control"—which was interpreted by the CDC as limiting all gun-related research by agency scientists or by outside researchers who received agency funds.[49] (The ban was repealed after a series of mass shootings in 2013, although to this day the CDC conducts very little gun-related research.)

The problem with eliminating bureaucrats' discretion in this way is that it limits the positive influence of their expertise. Particularly when new policies are being developed, taking away bureaucratic discretion is costly for legislators or presidential appointees because it forces them to work out the policy details themselves—and it may produce less effective policies than those constructed by bureaucrats with specialized knowledge.[50] Moreover, preventing bureaucrats from using their judgment makes it impossible for them to craft policies that take into account new developments or unforeseen circumstances.[51] For all these reasons, elected officials must find other ways to reduce or eliminate **bureaucratic drift**—that is, bureaucrats' pursuit of their own goals rather than their assignments from officeholders or appointees—while still reaping the benefits of bureaucratic expertise. This section describes two common strategies: changing the way agencies are organized and staffed and using standardized procedures for monitoring agency actions (see the Take a Stand feature).

bureaucratic drift
Bureaucrats' tendency to implement policies in a way that favors their own political objectives rather than following the original intentions of the legislation.

Agency organization

Political scientists have shown how agencies can be organized to minimize bureaucratic drift.[52] Specifically, when an agency is set up or given new responsibilities, the officials who initiated the change don't simply tell the new agency what to do. To ensure that the agency pursues the policies officials want, they also determine where the agency is located within the federal government structure and who runs it.

Is Political Control of the Bureaucracy Beneficial?

Civil service protections help ensure that agency scientists will continue to do cutting-edge research and report their findings, even if their conclusions conflict with the views of their political superiors.

When working with bureaucrats, elected officials (the president or members of Congress) face the problem of political control: Should they allow bureaucrats to exercise judgment when implementing policies or give them specific, narrow directives? Compounding this problem is the fact that most bureaucrats are civil service employees, meaning they cannot be fired except under very extreme circumstances. As a result, even when elected officials give very specific directives to an agency, they may find that bureaucrats essentially ignore the directives and that very little can be done to force compliance (after all, regardless of what bureaucrats do or don't do, they will still have a job). Civil service protections also mean that members of Congress or a new presidential administration cannot clean house in an agency, replacing untrustworthy bureaucrats with individuals who will do what they are told. Should civil service protections be abolished?

Get rid of civil service protections. The civil service system began in an era when few government jobs required specialized knowledge, expertise, or an advanced degree.

The modern federal bureaucracy is exactly the opposite: most jobs, particularly those that involve real policy-making power, require expertise to be done effectively. Under these conditions, civil service protections are to some extent unnecessary, as bureaucrats have considerable job security because of their expertise and experience. Getting rid of recalcitrant bureaucrats involves significant costs: by removing their knowledge of the policies being decided and the procedures by which decisions are made, it may become impossible for an agency to function at all. Moreover, a bureaucrat's reluctance to behave as ordered may be a sign that something is wrong—that the directive makes no sense or that there are easier ways of accomplishing the task.

Consider the U.S. Environmental Protection Agency. There is little doubt that most EPA scientists believe that climate change is real and that it is the result of human actions. Both of these views were in opposition to President Trump's stated positions. Were civil service protections the only thing preventing Trump from firing these scientists? Doing so would have decimated the EPA and made it impossible for the agency to carry out many of its functions, some of which (like cleaning up Superfund sites) were things Trump favored. Trump may not have liked having EPA scientists that disagree with him, but he would probably have liked the consequences of a mass firing even less. Moreover, the

replacements would have operated within existing resource, regulatory, and legal constraints, so their actions might not have looked different from those of their predecessors.

Civil service protections are still needed. The fact that firing bureaucrats costs the government the benefit of their experience and expertise does not mean that elected officials will never threaten to do so, or even carry out their threats. Removing civil service protections—making bureaucrats vulnerable to threats about their future employment—could easily lead to bad policy outcomes. Eliminating civil service protections would also change the kinds of people who undertake careers in government service. Civil service protections enable policy experts to work for the government without fearing that they will be fired for simply voicing their concerns or because a new administration places a high value on loyalty. Without the protections afforded by civil service regulations, these individuals might choose a different career, depriving the federal government (and the American people) of the benefits of their knowledge and training.

In the case of the EPA, civil service protections helped ensure that agency scientists continued to do cutting-edge research and report their findings—even if their conclusions conflicted with the views of their political superiors—and that these scientists work for the agency in the first place.

take a stand

1. In general, contemporary Democratic politicians tend to favor civil service protections, while Republicans want to weaken them. Does this preference make sense in light of what we know about the differences between the parties in their beliefs about the size and scope of government?

2. Not all jobs in the federal bureaucracy require specialized knowledge and expertise. Would it make sense to abandon civil service protections for low-level jobs such as clerical positions? Why or why not?

These efforts may occur solely within Congress, may involve both Congress and the president, or may be arranged by presidential actions.[53]

For example, one of the Obama administration's responses to the 2008 financial crisis was to form a new agency, the Consumer Financial Protection Bureau (CFPB), which would help enforce new bank regulations and investigate consumer complaints about financial firms. However, Republican senators opposed Obama's initial nominee to run the agency, Elizabeth Warren, believing she would encourage her subordinates to be excessively pro-consumer. Similarly, in 2017 President Trump appointed Michael Mulvaney (a former Republican congressman and the head of the Office of Management and Budget and chief of staff in the Trump administration) to run the agency, even though Mulvaney was a longtime opponent of the CFPB who as a member of Congress had sought to abolish the agency. Both Trump and Obama's appointments were intended to shape agency operations by appointing an individual who was expected to act in line with the then-president's preferences.

Monitoring

One of the most important ways elected officials prevent bureaucratic drift is by keeping an eye on what bureaucrats are doing or planning to do. Information gathering by members of Congress about bureaucratic actions is termed **oversight**. Congressional committees often hold hearings to question agency heads, secretaries of executive departments, or senior agency staff. Similarly, one responsibility of presidential appointees is to monitor how lower-level bureaucrats are responding to presidential directives. However, appointees may be unable to fulfill this role. Because they are chosen for their loyalty to the president, they may lack the experience needed to fully understand what bureaucrats in their agency are doing. Moreover, given that appointees typically hold their position for only a year or two, they have little time to learn the details of agency operations.

oversight
Congressional efforts to make sure that laws are implemented correctly by the bureaucracy after they have been passed.

Advance Warning Members of Congress, the president, and his or her staff gain advance knowledge of planned bureaucratic actions through the notice-and-comment procedure described earlier, which requires bureaucrats to disclose proposed regulations before they take effect.[54] This delay gives opponents the opportunity to register complaints with their congressional representatives, and it allows these legislators time either to pressure the agency to revise the regulation or to even enact another law undoing or modifying the agency action. Members of Congress also pressure bureaucrats to release memos, working drafts, and other documents as a way of keeping track of what bureaucrats are doing. For example, in 2020 members of Congress requested documents from the State Department in the wake of the removal of Inspector General Steve Linick—the concern was that Linick was fired because he was investigating complaints that Secretary of State Mike Pompeo had used State Department staff to run personal errands.[55]

Investigations: Police Patrols and Fire Alarms

Investigations: Police Patrols and Fire Alarms Congress, legislative staff, or presidential appointees may initiate investigations of government programs or offices to scrutinize the organizations, their expenditures, and their activities. There are two types of investigation: police patrol oversight and fire alarm oversight. Ideally, every agency would be investigated on a consistent basis, with agencies that have large budgets or carry out important functions being investigated more frequently. These investigations may involve fact-finding trips to local offices, interviews with senior personnel, audits of agency accounts, and calls to the agency to see how it responds to citizens' requests. This method of investigation is called **police patrol oversight.**[56] Think of a police officer walking his or her beat, rattling doors to see if they are locked, checking out broken windows, and looking down alleys for suspicious behavior.

The disadvantage of police patrol oversight is that it is costly in terms of money and staff time. Moreover, these investigations often find that agencies are doing what they should be doing. Because of these problems, Congress and the president often follow a different strategy. Rather than initiating investigations, they wait until they receive a complaint about bureaucratic actions and then focus investigative efforts on those cases, a practice labeled **fire alarm oversight.**[57]

The so-called fire alarm that sets off an investigation can take many different forms. Constituents may let their congressional representatives or their staff know of a problem with the bureaucracy. Similarly, lobbyists, corporate executives, and ordinary citizens often contact the president and his or her staff with complaints. Newspaper reporters and Internet bloggers also provide information about what bureaucrats are doing. In addition, some agencies have advisory committees that not only help make agency decisions but also keep Congress and the president informed about their agencies' actions.[58] Such fire alarm communications tell Congress and the president where to focus their efforts to monitor the bureaucracy, removing the need to try to oversee the entire government at once.

Correcting violations

When the president or members of Congress find a case of bureaucratic drift, they can choose from many tactics to bring a wayward agency into line. Legislation or an executive order can send a clear directive to an agency or remove its discretion, tasks and programs can be moved to an agency more closely aligned with elected officials' goals, political appointees at an agency can be replaced, and agencies can be reorganized.

A significant difficulty in dealing with bureaucratic drift is disagreement between members of Congress and the president about whether an agency is doing the right thing—regardless of whether it is following its original orders. Many strategies for influencing an agency's behavior require joint action by the president and congressional majorities. Without presidential support, members of Congress need a two-thirds majority to impose corrections. Without congressional support, the president can only threaten to cut an agency's proposed budget, change its home within the federal bureaucracy, or establish a new agency to do what the errant agency refuses to do; actually carrying out these threats requires congressional approval. As a result, disagreements between the president and Congress can give an agency significant freedom, as long as it retains the support of at least one branch of government.

An agency may also be able to fend off elected officials' attempts to take political control if it has a reputation for expertise. For example, one reason that attempts to pass legislation forcing the FDA to alter its drug-approval process have had little success is that the FDA's process is thought to have worked mostly as intended, approving new drugs that are safe and effective and keeping ineffective or unsafe drugs off the market.

---

police patrol oversight
A method of oversight in which members of Congress constantly monitor the bureaucracy to make sure that laws are implemented correctly.

fire alarm oversight
A method of oversight in which members of Congress respond to complaints about the bureaucracy or problems of implementation only as they arise rather than exercising constant vigilance.

During the coronavirus pandemic, government was divided on the best way to get the country back to work and reopen the economy after the shutdown. John Howard, MD, the director of the National Institute for Occupational Safety and Health, testified on how to protect workers from COVID-19 at a U.S. House Committee on Education and Labor Subcommittee on Workforce Protections hearing.

At the same time, the FDA has responded to pressure from Congress and the president to revise some rules on its own.[59]

Finally, agencies can sometimes combat attempts to control their behavior by appealing to groups that benefit from agency actions.[60] For example, since the 1980s the Occupational Safety and Health Administration (OSHA) has resisted attempts by Republican presidents and Republican members of Congress to eliminate the agency or limit its operations.[61] One element of its strategy has been to build strong ties to labor unions; as a result, OSHA is much more likely to receive complaints about workplace safety from companies with strong unions. The strategy has also involved building cooperative arrangements with large companies to prevent workplace accidents, an approach that not only protects workers but also can save companies a lot of money over the long term. Moreover, when OSHA levies fines against companies that violate safety regulations, the fines are generally much less than the maximum fines that would be allowed by law. As a result, when proposals to limit or eliminate OSHA are debated in Congress, members hear from unions as well as many large corporations in support of keeping the agency in place. Over time, this strategy has generated support for the agency from congressional Democrats and Republicans.

The consequences of control

Elected officials' competing desires to both control what bureaucrats do and tap their expertise explain many of the seemingly dysfunctional aspects of the bureaucracy. Part of the problem is the nature of the tasks given to bureaucrats: even when members of Congress and the president agree on which problems deserve attention, bureaucrats face the much harder task of translating these goals into concrete policies. Given the magnitude of this job, it is no surprise that even the best efforts of government agencies do not always succeed.

Most important, the use of standard operating procedures is rooted partly in the complexity of bureaucrats' tasks—but also in the desire of agency heads and elected officials to control the actions of lower-level staff. In some disaster relief efforts, government agencies have found that preset plans and procedures worked against the need to respond quickly to alleviate human suffering. And while the FDA's drug-approval process succeeds for the most part in preventing harmful drugs from coming to market, the delays imposed by the process do prevent some patients from receiving lifesaving treatments. However, in all these cases the decisions do not reflect incompetence or malice. Rules and procedures are needed in any organization to ensure that decisions are fair and reflect the goals of the organization. Yet it is impossible to find procedures that will work well in all cases, particularly for the kinds of policy decisions bureaucrats must make.

Cases of bureaucratic failure (poorly conceived policies or regulations, inaction, red tape) are often cited to "prove" that bureaucrats are incompetent, lazy, or dumb. The real story is that bureaucrats are often given nearly impossible tasks or political mandates that limit their authority. In this sense, complaints about bureaucrats have more to do with what we want them to do than with their unwillingness or inability to execute these missions.

Unpacking the Conflict

Considering all that we've discussed in this chapter, let's return to President Trump's often-contentious relationship with members of the federal bureaucracy. Were bureaucrats really obstructing the Trump agenda, or were they just doing their jobs? How do elected officials control a bureaucracy of experts, in the midst of a pandemic or in more routine times?

A deeper look shows that some of the time, conflicts between President Trump and bureaucratic officials reflected real disagreements. In the case of counting deaths from COVID-19, for example, it is not hard to see why Trump or the politically minded people around him preferred a definition that minimized casualties. However, the fact that many bureaucrats are policy experts suggests an alternative explanation of their preference for a different accounting scheme. Rather than trying to embarrass Trump or ensure his defeat, bureaucrats may have been acting from expertise, working to account for the pandemic in a way that facilitated an effective governmental response.

Bureaucratic expertise and the resulting problem of control also explain the cumbersome procedures for hiring, firing, and decision making that are a feature of operations in many government agencies. Sometimes bureaucrats simply make mistakes, choosing the wrong policy because they—and, in some cases, all the people involved—lack information about the tasks they were given. Bureaucrats may drag their feet when they oppose their tasks on policy grounds. But in many cases, cumbersome procedures are the result of a fundamental trade-off faced by elected officials between wanting to exercise control over the bureaucracy and wanting to ensure that changes in policy produce their intended effect. Put another way, conflict over public policy often translates into conflicting ideas about what bureaucrats should do, resulting in complex, often-contradictory mandates and directions imposed on bureaucrats. In this way, politics shapes virtually all aspects of the bureaucracy and of the choices bureaucrats make, even in places where it is hard to discern political motivations.

Should elected officials defer to bureaucratic expertise?

Or should the president's agenda override other concerns?

STUDY GUIDE

What is the federal bureaucracy?

Define *bureaucracy* and explain its major functions.
(Pages 386–393)

Summary

The bureaucracy is composed of both civil servants and political appointees and is in charge of interpreting and implementing a wide range of government policies. While bureaucrats are policy experts, most members of Congress are not. Nonetheless, Congress tries to control how the bureaucracy operates, which can result in inefficiencies.

Key terms

bureaucracy (p. 386)
civil servants (p. 386)
political appointees (p. 386)
regulation (p. 387)
notice-and-comment
   procedure (p. 387)

state capacity (p. 391)
problem of control (p. 391)
principal–agent game (p. 391)
red tape (p. 393)
standard operating
   procedures (SOPs) (p. 393)

Practice Quiz Questions

1. **A government rule that affects the choices that individuals or corporations make is called _____.**

a   an initiative
b   a referendum
c   a regulation
d   a procurement
e   an appropriation

2. **One of the reasons bureaucrats respond to pressure from elected officials is that _____.**

a   bureaucrats need congressional support to get larger budgets
b   elected officials are experts
c   bureaucrats are all appointed by members of Congress
d   bureaucrats' offices are housed in the Congress
e   bureaucrats are required by law to do so

3. **In the problem of control, the _____ is the principal and the _____ is the agent.**

a   bureaucracy; president
b   bureaucracy; Congress
c   president; Congress
d   president; bureaucracy
e   Congress; president

How has the American bureaucracy grown?

Trace the expansion of the federal bureaucracy over time.
(Pages 394–397)

Summary

The bureaucracy has grown substantially since the turn of the twentieth century, largely in response to citizens' demands that the government do more for the people. The federal government had a very limited role in daily life for much of the nineteenth century, but it expanded during the Progressive Era, when regulatory activity increased and the spoils system was replaced by the federal civil service. The bureaucracy expanded again with the New Deal and Great Society programs, which increased the number of services the government provided.

Key term

federal civil service (p. 395)

Practice Quiz Questions

4. **How did the bureaucracy change during the Progressive Era?**

a   It expanded the delivery of government services directly to individuals.
b   The spoils system was first established.
c   It created a number of antipoverty and educational programs.
d   It reduced the government's regulatory activity.
e   It increased the government's regulatory activity.

5. **The civil service reforms of the Progressive Era _____ the spoils system and _____ the power of party organizations.**

a   ended; increased
b   ended; decreased
c   instituted; increased
d   instituted; decreased
e   expanded; increased

6. **How has the bureaucracy changed since the Reagan Revolution?**

a   The government stopped passing regulatory policies.
b   The size of the federal government shrank.
c   The size of the federal government increased.
d   The civil service reforms were weakened.
e   The civil service reforms were strengthened.

The modern federal bureaucracy

Describe the size and structure of the executive branch today. (Pages 397–402)

Summary

The modern bureaucracy serves a wide range of functions, but the division of labor within the bureaucracy does not always have an obvious logic. Overlapping or confusing jurisdictions can be the result of elected officials' attempts to shape agency behavior by assigning a task to an executive department rather than an independent agency. The overall size of the bureaucracy reflects the demands of constituents but also fits the needs of elected officials to improve their chances of reelection.

Key terms

Office of Management and Budget (p. 397)

independent agencies (p. 397)

budget maximizers (p. 402)

Practice Quiz Questions

7. What is the job of the Office of Management and Budget?

a to prepare the president's annual budget proposal for Congress

b to prepare a response to the budget passed by Congress

c to prepare annual budget proposals for the states

d to monitor government spending for the Supreme Court

e to monitor government spending for Congress

8. Independent agencies have _____ freedom from oversight than executive departments do and _____ be controlled by the president through his or her appointees.

a more; cannot

b more; can

c less; cannot

d less; can

e in some situations more; can in some situations

9. The federal budget is growing in size because _____.

a bureaucrats are budget maximizers

b politicians do not scrutinize budget requests

c government agencies are never eliminated

d the public does not support large-scale budget cuts

e a growing percentage of Americans are going into civil service

The human face of the bureaucracy

Describe who bureaucrats are and the regulations that govern their employment. (Pages 402–405)

Summary

The regulations within the civil service system were established to separate politics from policy. Rather than getting and retaining a job for political reasons, individuals are hired based on merit and are quite difficult to fire. However, the president makes senior-level appointments that are not protected by civil service regulations and are more political in nature. These appointments are instrumental in helping the president control the bureaucracy.

Practice Quiz Questions

10. Compared with employees in private business, government employees are motivated _____ by salary and benefits than/as by the chance to make a difference.

a more

b just as much

c less

d increasingly since the 1980s

e none of the above; government employees are not paid

11. The civil service regulations _____ the flexibility that managers have in their hiring decisions and _____ the influence of elected officials.

a decrease; decrease

b increase; increase

c increase; decrease

d decrease; increase

e increase; have no effect on

Controlling the bureaucracy

Explain how Congress and the president oversee the executive branch. (Pages 405–410)

Summary

With their expertise, bureaucrats have the power to significantly influence government policy. This creates a dilemma for elected officials, who want to enjoy the benefits of the expertise while retaining control of the bureaucracy. Lawmakers can generally organize agencies and monitor their behavior to reduce, but not eliminate, bureaucratic drift.

Key terms

bureaucratic drift (p. 405)

oversight (p. 407)

police patrol oversight (p. 408)

fire alarm oversight (p. 408)

Practice Quiz Questions

12. When bureaucrats pursue their own goals rather than their assignments from officeholders, this is called _____.

a an iron triangle

b regulatory capture

c the problem of control

d turkey farming

e bureaucratic drift

13. Giving direct orders to bureaucrats _____ the influence of their policy expertise and _____ the potential to respond to unforeseen circumstances.

a   limits; reduces

b   increases; reduces

c   limits; increases

d   increases; increases

e   limits; has no effect on

14. While police patrol oversight has the advantage of being _____, it has the drawback of being _____.

a   affordable; unresponsive

b   responsive; costly

c   affordable; generally unnecessary

d   responsive; unpopular

e   affordable; ineffective

Suggested Reading

Brehm, John, and Scott Gates. *Teaching, Managing Tasks, and Brokering Trust: Functions of the Public Executive.* New York: Russell Sage Foundation, 2008.

Carpenter, Daniel P. *The Forging of Bureaucratic Autonomy: Reputations, Networks, and Policy Innovation in Executive Agencies, 1862–1928.* Princeton, NJ: Princeton University Press, 2001.

Herd, Pamela, and Daniel P. Moynihan. *Administrative Burden: Policymaking by Other Means.* New York: Russell Sage Foundation, 2019.

Lerman, Amy E. *Good Enough for Government Work: The Public Reputation Crisis in America (and What We Can Do to Fix It).* Chicago: University of Chicago Press, 2018.

Lewis, David E. *The Politics of Presidential Appointments: Political Control and Bureaucratic Performance.* Princeton, NJ: Princeton University Press, 2010.

Moffitt, Susan L. *Making Policy Public: Participatory Bureaucracy in American Democracy.* New York: Cambridge University Press, 2014.

Nelson, Michael. "A Short, Ironic History of American National Bureaucracy." *Journal of Politics* 44 (1982): 747–78.

Potter, Rachel Augustine. *Bending the Rules: Procedural Politicking in the Bureaucracy.* Chicago: University of Chicago Press, 2020.

Rivlin, Alice M. *Divided We Fall: Why Consensus Matters.* Washington, DC: Brookings Institution Press, 2021.

Skowronek, Stephen. *Building a New American State: The Expansion of National Administrative Capacities, 1877–1920.* New York: Cambridge University Press, 1982.

Workman, Samuel. *The Dynamics of Bureaucracy in the U.S. Government.* New York: Cambridge University Press, 2015.

13

The Courts

What is the role of courts in our political system?

 "He is a faker. He has no consistency about him. He says whatever comes into his head at the moment."
Justice Ruth Bader Ginsburg, commenting on Donald Trump

 "Justice Ginsburg of the U.S. Supreme Court has embarrassed all by making very dumb political statements about me. Her mind is shot—resign![1]
President Donald Trump

In the heat of the 2016 presidential campaign, the late Justice Ruth Bader Ginsburg cut loose with a series of comments about a possible Trump presidency. In addition to labeling Trump a "faker" in an interview conducted by CNN,[2] Ginsburg told the *New York Times*, "I can't imagine what this place would be—I can't imagine what the country would be—with Donald Trump as our president."[3]

These comments set off a firestorm, not just from Trump and his supporters but also from left-leaning editorial boards such as that of the *Washington Post*. It called her observations "inappropriate," noting that the Code of Conduct for United States Judges "flatly states" that a "judge should not . . . publicly endorse or oppose a candidate for public office."[4] Under the headline "Donald Trump Is Right about Justice Ruth Bader Ginsburg," the *New York Times* was even more critical, saying, "Justice Ruth Bader Ginsburg needs to drop the political punditry and the name-calling."[5] We have come to expect such personal attacks from politicians, but not from Supreme Court justices, which is why Ginsburg's words were so jarring.

Bowing to the public pressure, Justice Ginsburg backed off, saying, "On reflection, my recent remarks in response to press inquiries were ill-advised and I regret making them. Judges should avoid commenting on a candidate for public office. In the future I will be more circumspect."[6]

Chief Justice John G. Roberts Jr. also weighed in on the topic of judicial independence, rebuking the president for complaining about an "Obama judge" who ruled against him in a political asylum case. "We do not have Obama judges or Trump judges, Bush judges or Clinton judges," Roberts said. "What we have is an extraordinary group of dedicated judges doing their level best to do equal right to those appearing before them. That independent judiciary is something we should all be thankful for."[7]

Justice Ginsburg broke from the image of the blindfolded Lady Justice when she expressed her opinions on a Trump presidency. Here, Justice Ginsburg (left), along with other Supreme Court justices, looks on as President Trump makes a speech during the swearing-in ceremony for Justice Brett Kavanaugh.

CHAPTER GOALS

Explain how the power of judicial review was established. pages 416–420

Outline the structure of the court system. pages 420–429

Describe how cases reach the Supreme Court. pages 430–432

Describe the Supreme Court's procedures for hearing a case. pages 433–436

Analyze the factors that influence Supreme Court decisions. pages 436–441

Why all the fuss? Why should a sitting justice's political comments or a president's remark about something that is obviously true (judges do have political biases) be so controversial? The simple answer is that our political system is strongly committed to the image of the blindfolded Lady Justice, holding the scales, neutrally applying the law. As Chief Justice Roberts famously said, justices are like baseball umpires, just calling the balls and strikes within the constitutional system. After all, the guiding principles of the "rule of law" in the American political system—embodied in the words carved above the entrance to the Supreme Court ("Equal Justice under Law") and the image of Lady Justice—seem to contradict the view of a political Supreme Court. We normally think of the courts as objectively applying the law and interpreting the Constitution for each case. Indeed, there is often consensus among the justices on how to rule in a given case. In the 2019–2020 term, 36 percent of the cases decided were unanimous (22 of 61) and 6 more had only one dissenting vote.[8]

However, a massive body of political science research shows that the Supreme Court can be quite political. In the most recent term, 23 percent of cases were decided by a 5–4 vote, including controversial cases concerning the Deferred Action for Childhood Arrivals program, hospital admitting privileges for abortion providers, and the counting of absentee ballots in the Wisconsin primary. As justices interpret the Constitution, they also play one of two roles in our political system: either asserting their own policy-making authority or deferring to the decisions of others (Congress, the president, or the people). The Court's decision about which path to take in a given case is often political, involving conflict, trade-offs, and compromise, much like decision making in Congress.

For those who resist the view that the courts are a policy-making institution, the theme "political process matters" may not seem to apply in this chapter. However, the courts often *do* make policy, and the way they make decisions has an impact on outcomes. To see how political process matters for the courts, it is important to answer the following questions: What are the different roles of the courts and the structure of the judicial system? How do court decisions shape policy? In a nutshell, what is the nature of judicial decision making? With this context in mind, we can reexamine the controversy over Justice Ginsburg's comments. Did Justice Ginsburg overstep her boundaries with her remarks on Donald Trump, or was it appropriate for her to express her opinions? Was Justice Roberts overreacting to Trump's comments about political judges? What is the proper place of the courts within our political system? Should judges attempt to neutrally apply the law, or should their political views play a role?

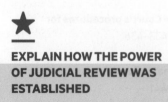

EXPLAIN HOW THE POWER OF JUDICIAL REVIEW WAS ESTABLISHED

The development of an independent and powerful federal judiciary

The Constitution did not definitively establish the role of the courts in American politics or the Supreme Court's authority as the ultimate interpreter of the Constitution. The powers of the Supreme Court evolved over time, and debates about its proper role continue to this day.

The Founders' views of the courts: the weakest branch?

The Federalists and Antifederalists did not see eye to eye on much, and the judiciary was no exception. Alexander Hamilton, writing in *Federalist 78*, said that the Supreme Court would be "beyond comparison the weakest of the three departments of power." In contrast, an author of the *Antifederalist Papers* wrote: "The supreme court under this constitution would be exalted above all other power in the government and subject to no control."[9] Hmmm, which is it: weakest or strongest? While the framers could not agree on how powerful the Court was likely to be relative to the other branches of government, there was surprisingly little debate at the Constitutional Convention about the judiciary. Article III of the Constitution, which concerns the judicial branch of government, created one Supreme Court and gave the courts independence by providing federal judges with lifetime terms (assuming "good behavior").

The main disagreements about the judiciary had to do with how independent the courts should be vis-à-vis the other branches of government and how much power to give the courts. Some of the framers feared a tyrannical Congress and wanted to create judicial and executive branches that could check this power. Others argued for making the executive and judicial branches more closely related so that they would be better able to balance Congress. A central debate was whether to give the judiciary some "revisionary power" over Congress, similar to the president's veto power. This idea of judicial review would have given the Supreme Court the power to strike down laws passed by Congress that violated the Constitution. The framers could not agree on judicial review, so the Constitution remained silent on the matter.

While the Constitution clearly specified the kinds of cases over which the Court would have **original jurisdiction** (see Nuts & Bolts 13.1), many details about the Supreme Court were left up to Congress, including its size, the time and place it would meet, and its internal organization. These details, as well as the system of lower federal courts, were outlined in the **Judiciary Act of 1789**. This law set the number of justices at six (one chief justice and five associates). The number of justices gradually increased to ten by the end of the Civil War and was then restricted to seven under Reconstruction policies. In 1869 the number was set at nine, where it has remained since.[10] The 1789 act also created a system of federal courts, which included 13 **district courts** and 3 circuit courts—the intermediate-level courts with **appellate jurisdiction**. Since the circuit courts hear cases on appeal from lower courts, they are now more commonly called appeals courts. The district courts each had one judge, while the circuit courts were each staffed by two Supreme Court justices and one district judge. Today separate judges are appointed to fill the appeals courts.

The Supreme Court had a rough start. Indeed, it seemed determined to prove Alexander Hamilton right, that it was the weakest branch. Of the six original justices appointed by George Washington, one declined to serve and another never showed up for a formal session. The Court's first sessions lasted only a few days because it did not have much business. In fact, the Court did not decide a single case in 1791 or 1792. When Justice Rutledge resigned in 1791 to take a state court position, two potential appointees turned down the job in order to keep their positions in their state legislatures! Such career decisions would be unimaginable today, when serving on the Supreme Court is considered the pinnacle of a legal career.[11]

original jurisdiction
The authority of a court to handle a case first, as in the Supreme Court's authority to initially hear disputes between two states. However, original jurisdiction for the Supreme Court is not exclusive; it may assign such a case to a lower court.

Judiciary Act of 1789
The law in which Congress laid out the organization of the federal judiciary. The law refined and clarified federal court jurisdiction and set the original number of justices at six. It also created the office of the attorney general and established the lower federal courts.

district courts
Lower-level trial courts of the federal judicial system that handle most U.S. federal cases.

appellate jurisdiction
The authority of a court to hear appeals from lower courts and change or uphold the decision.

Jurisdiction of the Federal Courts

Source: Lee Epstein and Thomas G. Walker,
*Constitutional Law for a Changing America:
Institutional Powers and Constraints*, 5th
ed. (Washington, DC: CQ Press, 2004), p. 65.

Jurisdiction of Lower Federal Courts

- Cases involving the U.S. Constitution, federal laws, and treaties.
- Controversies between two or more states. (Congress passed a law giving the Supreme Court exclusive jurisdiction over these cases.)
- Controversies between citizens of different states.
- Controversies between a state and citizens of another state. (The Eleventh Amendment removed federal jurisdiction in these cases.)
- Controversies between a state or its citizens and any foreign states, citizens, or subjects.
- Cases affecting ambassadors, public ministers, and consuls.
- Cases of admiralty and maritime jurisdictions.
- Controversies between citizens of the same state claiming lands under grants of different states.

Jurisdiction of the Supreme Court

Original Jurisdiction*

- Cases involving ambassadors, public ministers, and consuls.
- Cases that involve a state.

Appellate Jurisdiction

- Cases falling under the jurisdiction of the lower federal courts, "with such exceptions, and under such Regulations as the Congress shall make."

*This does not imply exclusive jurisdiction. For example, the Supreme Court may refer to a district court for a case involving an ambassador (the more likely outcome).

"Why Should I Care?" Understanding the type of cases that are heard by the federal courts is essential for recognizing their role in the system of checks and balances. Congress has some power to limit the jurisdiction of the federal courts.

Judicial review and *Marbury v. Madison*

The Court started to gain more power when John Marshall was appointed chief justice in 1801. Marshall single-handedly transformed the Court into an equal partner in the system of checks and balances. The most important step was the decision *Marbury v. Madison* (1803), which gave the Supreme Court the power of **judicial review**. As noted, the framers were split on the wisdom of giving the Court the power to strike down laws passed by Congress, and the Constitution does not explicitly address the issue. However, historians have established that a majority of the framers, including the most influential ones, favored judicial review. Given that the Constitution did not address the issue of judicial review, Marshall simply asserted that the Supreme Court had the power to determine when a law was unconstitutional.

Although the idea was not original to Marshall (the framers debated the issue and Hamilton endorsed it in some detail in *Federalist 78*), the Court had never before exercised its authority to rule on the constitutionality of a federal law. The facts of the *Marbury* case involved a partisan dispute over last-minute appointments to a lower court by the outgoing Adams administration. The new Jefferson administration did not honor those appointments, and one of the people who didn't get his position, Mr. Marbury, brought the case to the Supreme Court. Marshall said that Marbury was due his commission, but the Court could not give him his job because the part of the Judiciary

judicial review
The Supreme Court's power to strike down a law or an executive branch action that it finds unconstitutional.

Act of 1789 that gave it the power to do so was unconstitutional! The portion of the act in question was Section 13, which gave the Court the power to issue orders (writs of mandamus) to anyone holding federal office. Because this section expanded the original jurisdiction of the Supreme Court, Marshall ruled that Congress had overstepped its bounds in passing it. The original jurisdiction of the Court is clearly specified in the Constitution, so any attempt by Congress to change that jurisdiction through legislation would be unconstitutional; the only way to change original jurisdiction would be through a constitutional amendment.[12] Marshall wrote: "It is emphatically the province and duty of the judicial department to say what the law is.... If two laws conflict with each other, the courts must decide on the operation of each. So if a law be in opposition to the Constitution ... the courts must determine which of these conflicting rules governs the case. This is of the very essence of judicial duty."[13]

By asserting its power to review the constitutionality of laws passed by Congress, the Court became an equal partner in the institutional balance of power. Although more than 50 years would pass before the Court would use judicial review again to strike down a law passed by Congress (in the unfortunate 1857 *Dred Scott* case concerning slavery that effectively led to the Civil War), the reasoning behind *Marbury* has never been challenged by subsequent presidents or Congresses.[14]

Interpreting federal laws may seem a logical responsibility for the Supreme Court, but what about state laws? Should the Supreme Court have final say over them as well? The Constitution does not answer this question. However, the supremacy clause requires that the Constitution and national laws take precedence over state constitutions and state laws when they conflict. And the Judiciary Act of 1789 made it clear that the Supreme Court would rule on these matters.

Chief Justice John Marshall favored the idea of judicial review and claimed this power for the Court in the *Marbury v. Madison* decision.

Judicial review in practice

The contours of the relationship between the national government and the states have been largely defined by the Supreme Court's assertion of judicial review and its willingness to intervene in matters of state law. For much of the nineteenth century, the Court embraced dual federalism, in which the national government and the states operated on two separate levels (see Chapter 3). Later the Court involved itself more in state law as it moved toward an increasingly active role for the national government in regulating interstate commerce and using the Fourteenth Amendment to selectively incorporate the amendments that constitute the Bill of Rights (see Chapter 4).

All in all, the Court has struck down more than 205 acts of Congress (and about 1,400 state laws). This sounds like a lot, but Congress passed more than 60,000 laws in its first 230 years. Over time, the Court has ruled on state laws in many important areas, including civil liberties, desegregation and civil rights, abortion, privacy, redistricting, labor laws, employment and discrimination, and business and environmental regulation.

When the Supreme Court strikes down a congressional or state law, it engages in **constitutional interpretation**—that is, it determines that the law is unconstitutional. But the Supreme Court also engages in **statutory interpretation**—that is, it applies national and state laws to particular cases (statutes are laws that are passed by legislatures). Often the language of a statute may be unclear and the Court must interpret how to apply the law. For example, should the protection of endangered species prevent economic development that destroys the species' habitat? How does one determine whether an employer is responsible for punishing sexual harassment in the workplace? How should the voting rights of minorities be protected? In cases such as these, the Court must interpret the relevant statutes to determine what Congress or the state legislatures really meant.

constitutional interpretation
The process of determining whether a piece of legislation or governmental action is supported by the Constitution.

statutory interpretation
The various methods and tests used by the courts for determining the meaning of a law and applying it to specific situations. Congress may overturn the courts' interpretation by writing a new law; thus, it also engages in statutory interpretation.

Although politicians and other political actors accept judicial review as a central part of the political system, critics are concerned about its antidemocratic nature. Why, for example, do we give nine unelected justices such awesome power over our elected representatives? Debates about the proper role for the Court will continue as long as it is involved in controversial decisions. We will take up this question later in this chapter when we address the concepts of judicial activism and judicial restraint.

"Why Should I Care?"

Judicial review may seem like "inside baseball" that doesn't really matter for most Americans. However, the power to strike down laws and government actions means that the Court may act against political majorities to strike down unconstitutional actions such as segregating schools by race and discriminating against same-sex marriage. Judicial review may also be used, however, to frustrate popular majorities during times of political change, such as during the New Deal of the 1930s. Recently, the Court has done some of both—requiring the government to have a court order to search cell phone records but also deciding that states must collect sales taxes on Internet sales, despite public opposition to the practice. In either case, this is an awesome political power that puts the Supreme Court on an equal institutional footing with Congress and the president.

OUTLINE THE STRUCTURE OF THE COURT SYSTEM

The American legal and judicial system

Two sets of considerations shed light on the overall nature of our judicial system: the fundamentals of the legal system that apply to all courts in the United States, and the structure of the court system within our system of federalism.

Court fundamentals

plaintiff
The person or party who brings a case to court.

defendant
The person or party against whom a case is brought.

plea bargaining
Negotiating an agreement between a plaintiff and a defendant to settle a case before it goes to trial or the verdict is decided. In a civil case, this usually involves an admission of guilt and an agreement on monetary damages; in a criminal case, this often involves an admission of guilt in return for a reduced charge or sentence.

The general characteristics of the court system begin with the people who are in the courtroom. The **plaintiff** brings the case, and the **defendant** is the party who is being sued or charged with a crime. If the case is appealed, the petitioner is the person bringing the appeal and the respondent is on the other side of the case. In a civil case, the plaintiff sues to determine who is right or wrong and to gain something of value, such as monetary damages, the right to vote, or admission to a university. In a criminal case, the plaintiff is the government and the prosecutor attempts to prove the guilt of the defendant (the person accused of the crime).

Many, but not all, civil and criminal cases are heard before a jury that decides the outcome in the case, which is called the verdict. Often cases get settled before they go to trial (or even in the middle of the trial) in a process known as **plea bargaining**. In a civil case, this would mean that the plaintiff and the defendant agree on a monetary settlement and admission of guilt (or not; in some cases, the defendant may agree to pay a fine or damages but not to admit guilt). In a criminal case, the defendant may agree to plead guilty in exchange for being charged with a lesser crime or for receiving a shorter sentence than might be imposed in a jury trial. More than 95 percent of federal felony cases that result in a conviction are settled in this way.[15] Plea bargaining is an excellent example of how legal conflict between two parties can be resolved through compromise.

In 2019, several celebrities were accused of participating in a college admissions scandal that involved using their wealth and influence to improve the odds of their children being admitted to selective colleges; the scheme included falsifying SAT scores and academic records. Actress and producer Lori Loughlin, center, was accused of bribing an athletic coach to get her two daughters admitted to the University of Southern California. She ultimately accepted a plea bargain to reduce her prison sentence and fine.

One type of civil suit is the **class-action lawsuit**, a case brought by a group of individuals on behalf of themselves and others in similar circumstances. Their target may be a corporation that produced hazardous or defective products or that harmed a particular group through illegal behavior. For example, 1.5 million current and former female Walmart employees sued the retailing giant for sex discrimination in 2011, claiming that the store had paid women less than men for the same work and had promoted fewer women than men.[16] Class-action suits are often filed on behalf of shareholders of companies that have lost value because of fraud committed by corporate leaders. Cases like these are an important mechanism for providing accountability and justice in our economic system.

Common Law and Precedent Forty-nine of the 50 states and the federal courts operate under a system of **common law**, which means that legal decisions build from precedents established in previous cases and apply commonly throughout the jurisdiction of the court. The alternative, which is practiced only in Louisiana, is the civil law tradition that is based on a detailed codification of the law that is applied to each specific case.

The notion of **precedent** (or stare decisis: "let the decision stand") deserves special attention. Precedent is a previously decided case or set of cases that serves as a guide for future cases on the same topic. Lower courts are bound by Supreme Court decisions when there is a clear precedent that is relevant for a given case. In many cases, following precedent is not clear-cut because several precedents may seem relevant. The lower courts have considerable discretion in sorting out which precedents are the most important. The Supreme Court tries to follow its own precedents, but in the past 70 years justices have been willing to deviate from earlier decisions when they think that the precedent is flawed. The Court has developed four factors that it uses to decide if a case should be overturned: the quality of the past decision's reasoning, its consistency with related decisions, legal developments since the past decision, and reliance on the decision throughout the legal system and society. But in some cases, the Court overturns a precedent simply because the ideological composition of the Court has changed. For example, in a case concerning states' immunity from lawsuits in another state's courts, the Court overturned a 40-year precedent even though none of the four factors were met.[17] Precedent is not a rule the Court must follow but a norm that constrains its behavior.

class-action lawsuit
A case brought by a group of individuals on behalf of themselves and others in the general public who are in similar circumstances.

common law
Law based on the precedent of previous court rulings rather than on legislation. It is used in all federal courts and 49 of the 50 state courts.

precedent
A legal norm established in court cases that is then applied to future cases dealing with the same legal questions.

How it works: in theory
The Court System

If federal question →

State Supreme Courts or Courts of Last Resort

52 courts (Texas and Oklahoma each have two courts of last resort)

346 judges; about 75,000 cases per year

Final Appeals Courts

U.S. Supreme Court

Received 6,442 filings in the 2018–2019 term; 73 cases were argued; 69 were disposed of in 66 signed opinions.

Courts of Appeals

94 courts in 41 states

939 judges; about 257,000 cases per year

Intermediate Appeals Courts

U.S. Courts of Appeals

12 regional courts and the U.S. Court of Appeals for the Federal Circuit

48,486 filings in the 2018–2019 term

Trial Courts of Limited and Special Jurisdiction

16,920 judges; about 55 million cases per year

Examples: juvenile court, traffic court, small claims court, justice of the peace, family court

Trial Courts of General and Original Jurisdiction

10,650 judges; about 30 million cases per year

Examples: district courts, county courts, municipal courts

Trial Courts

Trial Courts of General and Original Jurisdiction

94 district courts

297,877 civil cases and 92,678 criminal cases filed in the 2018–2019 term

Trial Courts of Limited and Special Jurisdiction

Examples: federal claims court, tax court, Court of International Trade, Court of Veterans Appeals

State and Local Courts

Federal Courts

Sources: Data on federal courts are from U.S. Supreme Court, "2019 Year-End Report on the Federal Judiciary," www.supremecourt.gov/publicinfo/year-end/ 2019year-endreport.pdf (accessed 6/12/20). Data on state courts are from National Center for State Courts, www.ncsc.org; Ballotpedia.org, "Intermediate Appellate Courts," https://ballotpedia.org/Intermediate_appellate_courts; and Ron Malega and Thomas H. Cohen, "State Court Organization, 2011," U.S. Department of Justice, Bureau of Justice Statistics, www.bjs.gov/content/pub/pdf/sco11.pdf (all accessed 6/12/20).

Partisan Gerrymandering through the Court System

Partisan gerrymandering has been **addressed** in dozens of state and federal court cases in the past 30 years. A landmark case decided in June 2019 illustrates how cases make their way through the court system and how the Supreme Court may decide *not* to resolve a conflict.

We *still* don't like it!

North Carolina and Maryland stuck to their guns and **struck down their maps again**. Michigan and Ohio agreed.

Okay, let's resolve this—or not!

Supreme Court:
In a landmark ruling in June 2019, the Supreme Court got out of the partisan gerrymandering business, saying it is a "non-justiciable political question." The majority opinion **recognized it as a problem but said the Court does not have a measure to determine when a set of districts is unconstitutional**. The dissenters feared for the future of democracy.

We will just leave this sticky problem to the states.

The majority opinion noted that **states would still be free to address partisan gerrymandering**, but this path would not be open to states where politicians don't want to reform the process and voters don't have the initiative and referendum process to impose the change.

It's unconstitutional.

Federal courts:
In Ohio, North Carolina, Maryland, and Wisconsin, federal courts **struck down state legislative or congressional maps as unconstitutional**.

Hang on, don't get too excited...

In June 2018, the Court punted in cases from Wisconsin and Maryland, **sending the cases back to the lower courts**.

The states don't like it either!

State courts:
In Pennsylvania and Florida, state courts **struck down partisan gerrymanders, and voters in more than a dozen states took the control over redistricting out of the hands of politicians** and gave it to nonpartisan commissions.

Well, maybe, maybe not...

Over the next decade, state and federal courts struggled with various issues concerning redistricting, but **conflicting decisions left the issue unresolved**.

It's okay to do this, right?

State and Federal Trial Courts:
From 1986 to 2004, the Supreme Court **upheld partisan gerrymanders but left the door open for proving they were unconstitutional** if the right evidence was presented.

Critical Thinking

1. **What are the advantages and disadvantages** of having such a complex court system?

2. **When is it appropriate for the Supreme Court to decide** an issue is a "political question"? Do you think it was appropriate in this case? Can you think of an issue other than partisan gerrymandering for which this is likely to occur?

standing
Legitimate justification for bringing a civil case to court.

Standing Another characteristic common to all cases is that the person bringing the case must have **standing** to sue in a civil case, which means that there is a legitimate basis for bringing the case. This usually means that the individual has suffered some direct and personal harm from the action addressed in the court case. Standing is easy to establish for private parties—for example, if your neighbor destroys your fence, you have been harmed. However, determining who has standing gets more interesting when the government is the one being sued. For example, when an environmental group challenged the Interior Department's interpretation of the Endangered Species Act, the Supreme Court ruled that the group did not have standing to sue because it had not demonstrated that the government's policy would cause it "imminent" injury.[18] Later, in the section discussing how cases get to the Supreme Court, we will see that justices have some leeway in defining standing.

jurisdiction
The sphere of a court's legal authority to hear and decide cases.

Jurisdiction The final general characteristic of the legal system is the **jurisdiction** of the court. When bringing a case before the court, you must choose a court that actually has the power to hear your case. For example, if you wanted to contest a speeding ticket, you would not file your case in the state supreme court or in the federal district court; you would file it in your local traffic court. What if you believed you were the victim of discrimination in the workplace? Would you sue in state or federal court? You probably could do either, but the decision would be based on which set of laws would provide you with more protection from discrimination. This varies by state, so the proper jurisdiction for a given case is often a judgment call based on specific legal questions.

Structure of the court system and federalism

The structure of the court system is like that of the rest of the political system: it is divided within and across levels of government. Across the levels of government, the court system operates on two parallel tracks within the state and local courts and the federal courts. Within each level of government, both tracks include courts of original jurisdiction, appeals courts, and courts of special jurisdiction. As the How It Works graphic shows, the state courts are entirely separate from the federal courts, with the exception of the small proportion of cases that are appealed from a state supreme court to the U.S. Supreme Court. There is much variation between the states in terms of how they structure their court systems. However, they all follow the same general pattern of trial courts with limited and general original jurisdiction and appeals courts (either one or two levels, depending on the state).

District Courts Workhorses of the federal system, the district courts handle more than a quarter of a million filings a year. There are 89 districts in the 50 states, with at least one district court for each state. There are also district courts in Puerto Rico, the Virgin Islands, the District of Columbia, Guam, and the Northern Mariana Islands; this brings the total to 94 districts with 677 judges.[19] There are two limited-jurisdiction district courts: the Court of International Trade, which addresses cases involving international trade and customs issues, and the U.S. Court of Federal Claims, which handles most claims for money damages against the United States, disputes over federal contracts, unlawful "takings" of private property by the federal government, and other claims against the United States.

appeals courts
The intermediate level of federal courts that hear appeals from district courts. More generally, an appeals court is any court with appellate jurisdiction.

Appeals Courts The **appeals courts** (officially called circuit courts until 1948)[20] are the intermediate courts of appeals, but in practice they are the final court for most federal cases that are appealed from the district courts. The losing side in a federal case can appeal to the Supreme Court, but the highest court in the land hears so few cases that the appeals courts usually get the final word. Appeals courts did not always have this much power; in fact, through much of the nineteenth century they had very limited appellate jurisdiction and did not hear many significant cases.

The number of appeals courts in the nation slowly expanded as the workload of these courts grew. Currently, there are 12 regional courts and the Court of Appeals for the Federal Circuit, which handles specialized cases from all over the country.

The Supreme Court The Supreme Court sits at the top of the federal court system. The Supreme Court is the "court of last resort" for cases coming from both the state and the federal courts. One important function of the Court is to resolve conflicts between lower courts, or between state law and federal law, or between laws in different states, to ensure that the application and interpretation of the Constitution are consistent nationwide. A district court or appeals court ruling is applicable only within the specific region of that court, whereas Supreme Court rulings apply to the entire country.

Although the Supreme Court is the most important interpreter of the Constitution, the president and Congress also interpret the Constitution on a regular basis. This means that the Supreme Court does not always have the final say. For example, if the Court strikes down a federal law for being overly vague, Congress can rewrite the law to clarify the offending passage. When this happens, Congress may have the final word. For example, Congress overturned *Ledbetter v. Goodyear Tire & Rubber Co.* (2007) when it passed the Lilly Ledbetter Fair Pay Act in 2009. The law explicitly states that the Supreme Court had misinterpreted the 1964 Civil Rights Act when it ruled in 2007 that Ledbetter would have had to file her pay discrimination suit within 180 days of being hired.[21]

Even on matters of constitutional interpretation rather than statutory interpretation, Congress can fight back by passing a constitutional amendment. However, this is a difficult and time-consuming process (see Chapter 2). Nevertheless, that option is available as a way of overturning an unpopular Court decision.

How judges are selected

Although the Constitution provides detailed stipulations for serving in Congress and as president, it does not specify requirements for serving on the federal courts. Federal judges don't even have to have a law degree! (This is probably due to the limited number of law schools at the time of the Founding; when the Constitution was written, someone who wanted to be a lawyer generally would serve as an apprentice in a law office to learn the trade.) The president appoints federal judges with the "advice and consent" of the Senate, which in practice means that the Senate must approve the nominees with a majority vote.

Nomination battles for federal judges can be intense, because the stakes are high: the Supreme Court plays a central role in the policy process, and because justices have life tenure, a justice's impact can outlive the president and Senate who put him or her on the Court. Justices often serve for decades, much longer than the people who appoint them.

The Role of the President Given the Constitution's silence on the qualifications of federal judges, presidents have broad discretion over whom to nominate. Presidents have always tried to influence the direction of the federal courts, especially the Supreme Court, by picking people who share their views. Because the Senate often has different ideas about the proper direction for the Court, nomination disputes end up being a combination of debates over the merit of a nominee and partisan battles about the ideological composition of the Court.

Although presidents would *like* to influence the direction of the Court, it is not always possible to predict how judges will behave once they are on the bench (see the Take a Stand feature). However, the president can make a good guess about how a

DID YOU KNOW?

49

of the 115 people to serve on the Supreme Court have had law degrees. However, all since 1957 have had law degrees, and all but one of the current Court justices attended either Harvard or Yale law school (the newest justice, Amy Coney Barrett, attended Notre Dame).
Source: SupremeCourt.gov

President Trump, who nominated Judge Neil Gorsuch to the Supreme Court, watches as Supreme Court Justice Anthony Kennedy swears him in during a ceremony in the Rose Garden of the White House.

The Independence of the Courts

Many presidents have been frustrated by federal court decisions that they perceived to be unreasonable. Some have responded by lashing out at the courts—an action that never fails to stir controversy. Recently, both Presidents Obama and Trump have criticized high-profile Court decisions. In Obama's 2010 State of the Union address, he noted his disagreement with the Court's ruling in *Citizens United v. Federal Election Commission* (2010) and stated that he believed the decision had opened the floodgates for corporate spending—including by foreign corporations—in elections. Justice Alito was caught on camera mouthing the words "not true" in response. Washington was abuzz for days about whether the president's comment or Alito's response was out of line.[a] President Trump, for his part, was incensed with the Supreme Court's "horrible and politically charged decisions" on LGBTQ rights and the Dreamers, calling them "shotgun blasts into the face of people that are proud to call themselves Republicans or Conservatives."[b] Though it is not very common for presidents to openly criticize the federal courts, they routinely try to influence the courts through nominations to the federal bench. As we discussed earlier, all presidents try to pick justices who share their political views. Is this kind of influence different from that of presidents who directly express their opinions on Court decisions? Is either kind of influence acceptable?

Presidents should be able to influence the courts.

Some argue that whether it is President Obama criticizing the Court's ruling on campaign finance or President Trump expressing his views on its decisions on LGBTQ rights and DACA, presidents should be able to express their views on the important issues of the day. Furthermore, presidents are not obligated to nominate centrist judges. If a Republican president can nominate conservative judges, that is certainly his or her right. Trump exercised this right, to the dismay of some observers who believe that he picked extremely conservative judges to push his policy agenda.

Trump's appointees, like those of any other president, had to be confirmed by the Senate. If people don't like the ideological makeup of the judges the president selects, they can vote out the president and their senator in the next election. Besides, the president speaks for the people who elected him or her, while the courts are less democratic because they are not elected.

President Barack Obama was criticized during his 2010 State of the Union address for his comments on *Citizens United v. Federal Election Commission*, a federal court decision that he perceived to be unreasonable.

The independence of the courts is crucial: the president needs to back off.

Others argue that while it is fine for presidents to express their policy views on issues that come before the Court, they should refrain from direct criticism of specific cases or judges. Just as it was improper for Justice Ginsburg to criticize Trump during the campaign, presidents should not interject politics into the Court.

And though it is true that all presidents try to influence the Court through their nominations, moderation here would also serve the long-term interests of the country better than wild swings between ideological extremes.

The ballot box is the ultimate recourse for accountability, but even the mighty power of the vote is limited when it comes to holding judges responsible: many judges will serve on the bench for 25 years or more, much longer than the president or most senators.

take a stand

1. Where would you draw the line on presidents' criticizing the courts?

2. Does it bother you that courts are not accountable to the people and yet make important policy decisions? If so, how should presidents be able to influence the courts?

3. Should presidents be able to nominate whomever they want to the courts (subject to Senate approval, of course), or should the process be less partisan and less ideological?

justice is likely to vote based on the nominee's party affiliation and the nature of his or her legal writings and decisions (if the nominee has prior judicial experience). Not surprisingly, 105 of the 115 justices who have served on the Supreme Court have shared the nominating president's party (91 percent). Overall, more than 90 percent of the lower-court judges appointed by presidents in the twentieth and twenty-first centuries also belonged to the same party as the president.

The most partisan move to influence the Court was President Franklin Delano Roosevelt's infamous plan to pack the Court. FDR was frustrated because the Court had struck down several pieces of important New Deal legislation, so to get a more sympathetic Court, he proposed nominating a new justice for every justice who was more than 70 years old. Six justices were over 70, so this would have increased the size of the Court to 15 justices. The plan to pack the Court ran into opposition, but once the Court started ruling in favor of the New Deal legislation, the plan was dropped.

In addition to ideological considerations about whom to nominate, the president also considers the individual's reputation as a legal scholar and his or her personal relationship to the candidate. Further considerations are the candidate's ethical standards, religion, gender, and race (see Figure 13.1.) The religion of justices has undergone a complete transformation: for the nation's first 125 years, nearly all justices were Protestants. Now there are six Catholic justices, two Jewish justices, and one unknown (Gorsuch was raised Catholic but most recently attended an Episcopal church).[22] Over time, the federal courts have steadily become more diverse in terms of race and gender. However, Donald Trump

Race and Gender on Federal Circuit Courts

FIGURE 13.1

Since the 1980s, the proportion of women on the federal bench has gone up fivefold while the percentage of White men has plummeted by more than half. Do you think that descriptive representation in the judicial branch is important?

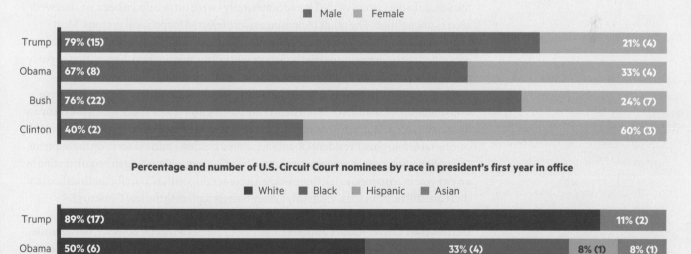

Percentage and number of U.S. Circuit Court nominees by gender in president's first year in office

■ Male   ■ Female

	Male	Female
Trump	79% (15)	21% (4)
Obama	67% (8)	33% (4)
Bush	76% (22)	24% (7)
Clinton	40% (2)	60% (3)

Percentage and number of U.S. Circuit Court nominees by race in president's first year in office

■ White   ■ Black   ■ Hispanic   ■ Asian

	White	Black	Hispanic	Asian
Trump	89% (17)	11% (2)		
Obama	50% (6)	33% (4)	8% (1)	8% (1)
Bush	86% (25)	10% (3)	3% (1)	
Clinton	80% (4)	20% (1)		

Source: Barry J. McMillion, "U.S. Circuit and District Court Nominations during President Trump's First Year in Office: Comparative Analysis with Recent Presidents," Congressional Research Service, May 2, 2018, http://fas.org/sgp/crs/misc/R45189.pdf (accessed 8/19/20). Data may not add up to 100 percent due to rounding.

President Obama nominated Judge Merrick Garland (right) to the Supreme Court. Here, the nominee meets with Senator Cory Booker (D-NJ). Judge Garland, however, was not confirmed prior to the end of Obama's term, and in 2017 President Trump nominated Judge Gorsuch to fill the vacancy left by Justice Scalia's death.

reversed this trend. Of his first 87 nominees to the federal courts, only one was African American and only one was Latino. Judges' demographic backgrounds also became an issue in the 2016 campaign when Trump said that federal district judge Gonzalo P. Curiel could not be objective in the lawsuit concerning Trump University because Curiel was a Mexican (the judge was born in Indiana and his parents are from Mexico).

The Role of the Senate The Senate is the other half of the equation to determine the composition of the federal courts. It has shifted from a very active role in providing "advice and consent" on court appointments to a passive role and then back to an active role. One constant is that the Senate rarely rejects nominees because of their qualifications; rather, it tends to reject them for political reasons. Of 28 Supreme Court nominees rejected by the Senate in the history of the United States, only 2 were turned down because they were seen as unqualified. The other 26 nominees were rejected for political reasons. Most commonly, when a president makes a nomination close to an election and the Senate is controlled by the opposing party, the Senate will kill the nomination, hoping that its party will win the presidency and nominate a justice more to its liking.

President Bill Clinton's two Supreme Court picks were judicial moderates who were overwhelmingly confirmed—Ruth Bader Ginsburg by a 96-3 vote and Stephen Breyer by an 87-9 vote. George W. Bush's nominees, John Roberts and Samuel Alito Jr., were confirmed by comfortable margins. President Obama appointed the first Latina to serve on the Supreme Court, Sonia Sotomayor, who was confirmed by a 68-31 vote. Elena Kagan's confirmation by a 63-37 vote in 2010 meant that three women were serving on the Court for the first time (and there are still three in 2021, with Amy Coney Barrett replacing the late Ginsburg).

Battles over Lower-Court Judges Contentious battles do occur, however, between the president and the Senate over nominees to the federal bench and the Supreme Court, and these have recently expanded to include nominees to the district and appeals courts. For much of the nation's history, the president did not play a very active role in the nomination process for district courts; instead, he deferred to the home-state senators of his own party to suggest candidates—a norm called **senatorial courtesy**. If neither senator from the state was from the president's party, he would consult House members from his party and other high-ranking party members from the state for district court nominees. The president typically has shown more interest in appeals court nominations. The Justice Department plays a key role in screening candidates, but the local senators of the president's party remain active.

senatorial courtesy
A norm in the nomination of district court judges in which the president consults with his or her party's senators from the relevant state in choosing the nominee.

FIGURE
13.2

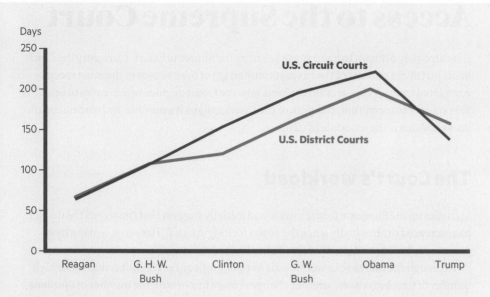

Days

U.S. Circuit Courts

U.S. District Courts

Reagan   G. H. W. Bush   Clinton   G. W. Bush   Obama   Trump

Average Confirmation Delay for Federal Court Nominations, 1981–2018

Since the 1980s, the length of time needed to confirm federal court nominations has increased dramatically. Why do you think this happened? Why does it matter?

Sources: Reagan–Obama: Barry J. McMillion, "Length of Time from Nomination to Confirmation for 'Uncontroversial' U.S. Circuit and District Court Nominees: Detailed Analysis," Congressional Research Service, September 18, 2012, http://fas.org (accessed 8/21/20); Trump: Rory Spill Solberg and Eric N. Waltenburg, "Are Trump's Judicial Nominees Being Confirmed at a Record Pace? The Answer is Complicated," *Washington Post*, June 14, 2018, www.washingtonpost.com/news/monkey-cage/wp/2018/06/14/are-trumps-judicial-nominees-really-being-confirmed-at-a-record-pace-the-answer-is-complicated (accessed 8/19/20).

Recently the process has become much more contentious. While the confirmation rate for federal judges has been relatively stable in the past 35 years (between 80 and 90 percent), the average time to confirm nominees has increased dramatically. The average length of delay from nomination to confirmation has also increased from a little over 50 days in the 1980s to over 200 days in recent years (see Figure 13.2), and the situation has intensified. Democrats blocked 39 of President George W. Bush's nominees between 2001 and 2009,[23] and Republicans returned the favor, blocking dozens of President Obama's nominees, which included employing a record number of filibusters of lower-court nominees. After the Senate blocked three nominees to the D.C. Court of Appeals, the second-most-important court in the nation, Democrats responded in November 2013 by eliminating the filibuster on lower-court and executive branch nominations but not Supreme Court nominations.[24] This move was originally labeled the "nuclear option" by Democrats who had threatened to shut down the Senate if the Republican leadership got rid of the filibuster during the George W. Bush presidency. In response to the detonation of the nuclear option, the confirmation process slowed to a trickle in President Obama's last year, which produced a near-record level of vacancies (more than 10 percent of all federal judgeships).

It is safe to assume that most Americans do not follow the details of battles over court nominations. However, these battles are every bit as important as the elections that *do* capture much attention. Unelected judges often serve for 20 or 30 years, much longer than the average member of Congress, and have the power to strike down laws that Congress passes. Confirmation battles also support our argument that politics is conflictual and that we should expect it to be that way. The Founders certainly did not expect that the process would be free of politics or that the Senate would be an essentially passive and subordinate player in a nominally joint enterprise. Even George Washington had two of his nominations turned down by the Senate for political reasons. Therefore, politics will continue to play an important role in deciding who serves on the federal bench.

"Why Should I Care?"

Access to the Supreme Court

It is extremely difficult to have a case heard by the Supreme Court. Currently the Court hears just over 1 percent of the cases submitted (73 of 6,442 cases in the most recent completed term).[25] This section explains how the Court decides which cases to hear. When a case is submitted, the clerk of the Court assigns it a number and places it on the docket, which is the schedule of cases.

The Court's workload

Statistics on the Supreme Court's workload initially suggest that the size of the docket has increased dramatically since the 1970s (see Figure 13.3). However, a majority of cases are frivolous and are dismissed after limited review.

Although the increase in workload is not as significant as it appears due to the high number of frivolous cases, another change is more important: the number of opinions issued by the Court has fallen by more than half in the past 35 years. The Court heard about 150 cases each year through the 1980s, but this number has fallen to only 65 to 95 in recent years (see again Figure 13.3).[26] There is no good explanation for why the Court issues half as many opinions as it used to, other than that the chief justices have decided that the Court shouldn't issue so many opinions.

FIGURE 13.3

The Court Sees More Opportunities ... but Hears Fewer Cases

The Supreme Court's workload appears to be headed in two directions: the Court is receiving more cases but hearing fewer of them. What are the implications of having the Supreme Court hear fewer cases? Should something be done to try to get the Court to hear more cases?

Source: Data compiled from John Roberts, "2019 Year-End Reports on the Federal Judiciary," U.S. Supreme Court, December 31, 2019, www.supremecourt.gov/publicinfo/year-end/2019year-endreport.pdf (accessed 3/21/20).

Cases available for review

Cases argued before the Court

Rules of access

With the smaller number of cases being heard, it is even more important to understand how the Court decides which ones to consider. There are four paths that a case may take to get to the Supreme Court.

First, Article III of the Constitution specifies that the Court has original jurisdiction in cases involving foreign ambassadors or foreign countries and cases in which a state is a party. As a practical matter, the Court shares jurisdiction with the lower courts on these issues. In recent years, the Court has invoked original jurisdiction only in cases involving disputes between two or more states over territorial or natural resource issues. For example, New Jersey and New York disagreed over which state should control about 24 acres of filled land that the federal government had added around Ellis Island, and Texas and New Mexico disagreed over which state should have access to water from the Rio Grande river (recent disputes often concern water rights).[27] One water dispute between Texas and New Mexico over the Pecos River Compact has been going on since 1960! In the history of our nation, only about 190 cases have made it to the Court through this path, and typically these cases do not have any broader significance beyond the interest of the parties involved.[28]

The other three routes to the Court are all on appeal: as a matter of right (usually called "on appeal"), through certification, or through a writ of *certiorari* (from the Latin "to be informed"). Cases on appeal are those that Congress has determined to be so important that the Supreme Court must hear them. Lately, Congress has given the Court much more discretion on these cases; the only ones that the Court is still compelled to take on appeal are some voting rights and redistricting cases.

The fourth path is the most common: at least 95 percent of the cases in most sessions arrive through a **writ of *certiorari***. In these cases, a litigant who lost in a lower court can file a petition to the Supreme Court explaining why it should hear the case. If four justices agree, the case will get a full hearing (this is called the Rule of Four). This process may sound simple, but sifting through the 6,500 or so cases that the Court receives every year and deciding which 70 to 75 of them will be heard is daunting. In fact, former justice William O. Douglas said that this winnowing process is "in many respects the most important and interesting of all our functions."[29]

writ of *certiorari*
The most common way for a case to reach the Supreme Court, in which at least four of the nine justices agree to hear a case that has reached them via an appeal from the losing party in a lower court's ruling.

The Court's criteria

How does the Court decide which cases to hear? Several factors come into play, including the specific characteristics of the case and the broader politics surrounding it. Although several criteria generally must be met before the Court will hear the case, justices still have leeway in defining the boundaries of these conditions.

Collusion, Standing, and Mootness First, there are the constitutional guidelines, which are sparse. The Constitution limits the Court to hearing actual "cases and controversies," which has been interpreted to mean that the Court cannot offer advisory opinions about hypothetical situations but must deal with actual cases. The term "actual controversy" also includes several other concepts that limit whether a case will be heard: collusion, standing, and mootness. *Collusion* simply means that the litigants in the case cannot want the same outcome and cannot be testing the law without an actual dispute occurring between the two parties.[30]

Standing, as noted earlier, means that the party bringing the case must have a personal stake in the outcome. The Court has discretion in defining standing: it may hear cases that the justices think are important even when the plaintiff may not have standing as traditionally understood, or it may duck cases that may be politically sensitive on the grounds that there is no standing. In an example of the former, the Court decided several important racial redistricting cases even when the White plaintiffs had not suffered any personal harm by being in the Black-majority districts.[31] In an example of the latter, the Court decided not to hear a politically sensitive case involving the Pledge of Allegiance and the First Amendment, saying that the father of the student who brought the case did not have standing because he did not have sufficient custody over his daughter (he was divorced and the mother had primary custody).[32] Clearly, the Court was more eager to voice its views on redistricting than on the Pledge of Allegiance, because it could have just as easily ducked the former case by saying that the plaintiffs did not have standing, and taken up the latter case despite the concern over custody (it was his daughter after all, which should have given him some stake!). This is an important point to consider: the Court often avoids hearing a controversial case based on a "threshold" issue such as standing and then does not have to decide on the merits of the case.

A controversy must still be relevant when the Court hears the case; **mootness** occurs when a case is irrelevant by the time it is brought before a federal court. Nonetheless, there are exceptions to this principle because some types of cases are necessarily moot by the time they get to the Supreme Court. For example, exceptions have been made for abortion cases because a pregnancy lasts only nine months, and it always takes longer than that for a case to get from district court to the appeals court to the Supreme Court.

Thousands of cases every year meet these basic criteria. One very simple guideline eliminates the largest number of cases: if a case does not involve a "substantial federal question," it will not be heard. This essentially means that the Court does not have to hear a case if the justices do not think it is important enough. Of course, the "federal" part of this standard is also important: if a case is governed by state law rather than by federal law, the Court will decline to hear the case unless there are constitutional implications.

Internal Politics Since the late 1970s, most justices have used a **cert pool**, whereby their law clerks take a first cut at the cases. Law clerks to the justices are top graduates of elite law schools who help the justices with background research at several stages of the process. Clerks write joint memos about groups of cases, providing their recommendations about which cases should be heard. The ultimate decisions are up to the justices, but clerks have significant power to help shape the agenda.

The chief justice has an important agenda-setting power: he or she decides the "discuss list" for a given day. Any justice can add a case to the list, but there is no systematic evidence on how often this happens. Only 20–30 percent of the cases are discussed in conference, which means that about three-quarters of the cases that are submitted to the Supreme Court are never even discussed by the justices. The decision not to discuss certain cases is often justified because of the high proportion of frivolous suits submitted to the Court.[33]

Many factors outside the legal requirements or internal processes of the Court influence access to the Court and which cases will be heard. Cases that have generated a lot of activity from interest groups or other governmental parties, such as the solicitor general, are more likely to be heard. The **solicitor general** is a presidential appointee who works in the Justice Department and supervises the litigation of the executive branch. In cases in which the federal government is a party, the solicitor general or someone else from that office will represent the government in court. The Court accepts about 70–80 percent of cases in which the U.S. government is a party, compared to about 1 percent overall.[34]

Even with these influences, the Court has a great deal of discretion on which cases it hears. Well-established practices such as standing and mootness may be ignored (or modified) if the Court wants to hear a specific case. However, one final point is important: although the justices may pick and choose their cases, they cannot completely set their own agenda. They can select only from the cases that come to them.

mootness
The irrelevance of a case by the time it is received by a federal court, causing the Supreme Court to decline to hear the case.

cert pool
A system initiated in the Supreme Court in the 1970s in which law clerks screen cases that come to the Supreme Court and recommend to the justices which cases should be heard.

solicitor general
A presidential appointee in the Justice Department who conducts all litigation on behalf of the federal government before the Supreme Court and supervises litigation in the federal appellate courts.

Hearing cases before the Supreme Court

A surprisingly small proportion of the Court's time—only about 37 days per term—is actually spent hearing cases. The Court's term extends from the first Monday in October through the end of June. It hears cases on Mondays through Wednesdays in alternating two-week cycles in which it is in session from 10 A.M. to 3 P.M., with a one-hour break for lunch. In the two weeks of the cycle when it is not in session, justices review briefs, write opinions, and sift through the next batch of petitions. On most Fridays during the Court's term, the justices meet in conference to discuss cases that have been argued and decide which cases they will hear. Opinions are released throughout the term, but the bulk of them come in May and June.[35]

The Court is in recess from July through September. The justices may take some vacation, but they mostly use the time for studying, reading, writing, and preparing for the next term. During the summer, the Court also considers emergency petitions (such as stays of execution) and occasionally hears exceptionally important cases—as it did in 2009, for example, when the Court heard a challenge to the Bipartisan Campaign Reform Act, more commonly known as the McCain–Feingold Act after its two principal sponsors. Congress urged the Court to give the law a speedy review given its importance for the upcoming 2010 elections. In the blockbuster case *Citizens United v. Federal Election Commission*, the Supreme Court decided that independent spending in campaigns by corporations and labor unions is protected by the First Amendment.

Briefs

During its regular sessions, the Court follows rigidly set routines. The justices prepare for a case by reading the briefs submitted by both parties. Because the Supreme Court hears only appeals, it does not call witnesses or gather new evidence. Instead, in structured briefs of no more than 50 pages the parties present their arguments about why they either support the lower-court decision or believe the case was improperly decided. Interest groups often submit **amicus curiae** ("friend of the court") briefs that convey their opinions to the Court; in fact, 85 percent of cases before the Supreme Court have at least one amicus brief.[36] The federal government also files amicus briefs on important issues such as school busing, school prayer, abortion, reapportionment of legislative districts, job discrimination against women and minorities, and affirmative action in higher education.

It is difficult to determine the impact of amicus briefs on the outcome of a case, but those that are filed early in the process increase the chances that the case will be heard.[37] Given the limited information that the justices have about any given case, interest group involvement can be a strong signal about the importance of a case. There is also some evidence that briefs from the solicitor general have an impact on the outcome of a case.[38]

amicus curiae
Latin for "friend of the court," referring to an interested group or person who shares relevant information about a case to help the Court reach a decision.

Oral argument

Once the briefs are filed and have been reviewed by the justices, cases are scheduled for **oral arguments**. Except in unusual circumstances, each case gets one hour, which is divided evenly between the two parties. In especially important cases, extra time may be granted (for example, the Obamacare case had six hours of oral argument, which was the most since a Voting Rights Act case in 1966).[39] Usually there is only one lawyer for each side who presents the case, but parties that have filed amicus briefs may

oral arguments
Spoken presentations made in person by the lawyers of each party to a judge or an appellate court outlining the legal reasons their side should prevail.

Cameras are not allowed in the Supreme Court, so artists' sketches are the only available images of oral arguments. Depicted here is the first round of oral arguments that Justice Kavanaugh participated in following his confirmation by the Senate.

DID YOU KNOW?

The late Justice Scalia was the funniest justice. According to one study, he holds the record, prompting

77

rounds of laughter in the 2004–2005 term, which made him 19 times funnier than his friend Justice Ginsburg.

Source: thedailybeast.com

participate if their arguments "would provide assistance to the Court not otherwise available." Given the tight time pressures, the Court generally does not extend the allotted time to allow "friends of the court" to testify.[40]

Some lawyers may not use all their time because their train of thought is interrupted by aggressive questioning. Transcripts reveal that justices jump in with questions almost immediately and some attorneys never regain their footing. The frequency and pointedness of the questions vary by justice, with Justices Breyer, Kagan, Roberts, and Sotomayor being the most aggressive on the current Court. Justice Thomas went more than 10 years without asking a single question but broke his streak in 2016, perhaps feeling the need to fill the void created by the death of Justice Scalia.[41] Cameras are not allowed in the courtroom, so most Americans have never seen the Court in action—although a small live audience is admitted every morning the Court is in session, and live audio was streamed online for the first time ever in 2020 as a result of the COVID-19 pandemic. If you are curious about oral arguments, audio recordings of every case since 1995 are available at www.oyez.org.

Conference

After oral arguments, the justices meet in conference to discuss and then vote on the cases. As with the initial conferences, these meetings are conducted in secret. We know, based on notes in the personal papers of retired justices, that the conferences are orderly and structured but can become quite heated. The justices take turns discussing the cases and outlining the reasons for their positions.

Opinion writing

After the justices indicate how they are likely to vote on a case, if the chief justice is in the majority (which is most of the time), the chief justice decides who will write the majority opinion. Otherwise, the most senior justice in the majority assigns the opinion. Several considerations determine how an opinion will be assigned. First, the chief justice will try to ensure the smooth operation of the Court, including considerations such as which justices may be able to take on the work of writing a given opinion. A second factor is the justices' individual areas of expertise. For example, Justice Sandra Day O'Connor developed expertise in racial redistricting cases and authored most of those decisions in the 1990s, while Justice Samuel Alito has specialized in criminal justice cases in recent years.[42]

Strategy on the Court Other factors in how opinions are assigned are more strategic, taking into account the Court's external relations, internal relations, and the personal policy goals of the opinion assigner. The Court must be sensitive to how others might respond to its decisions because it must rely on the other branches of government to enforce them. One famous example of this consideration in an opinion assignment came in a case from the 1940s that struck down a practice that had prevented African Americans from voting in Democratic primaries.[43] Originally, the opinion was assigned to Justice Felix Frankfurter, but Justice Robert Jackson wrote a memo suggesting that it might be unwise to have a liberal, politically independent Jew from the Northeast write an opinion that was sure to be controversial in the South. Chief Justice Harlan Fiske Stone agreed and reassigned the opinion to Justice Stanley Reed, a Protestant and Democrat from Kentucky.[44] It may not seem that the Court is sensitive to public opinion, but these kinds of considerations happen fairly frequently in important cases. Internal considerations occasionally cause justices to vote strategically—that is, differently from their sincere preferences—so they can put themselves in the majority. If they are the most senior justice in the majority, they then have the power to assign the opinion, and they often assign it to themselves.

After the opinions are assigned, the justices work on writing a draft opinion. Law clerks typically help with this process. The drafts are circulated to the other justices for comments and reactions. Some bargaining may occur, in which a justice says he or she will withdraw support unless a provision of the opinion is changed. Justices may join the majority opinion, may write a separate concurring opinion, or may dissent (see Nuts & Bolts 13.2 for details on the types of opinions).

Chief Justice John Roberts (left foreground) stands with Associate Justices Elena Kagan, Neil Gorsuch, and Brett Kavanaugh as they await the arrival of President Trump before his 2020 State of the Union address.

NUTS & BOLTS 13.2

Types of Supreme Court Decisions

- **Majority opinion:** The core decision of the Court that must be agreed upon by at least five justices. The majority opinion presents the legal reasoning for the Court's decision.
- **Concurring opinion:** Written by a justice who agrees with the outcome of the case but not with part of the legal reasoning. Concurring opinions may be joined by other justices. A justice may sign on to the majority opinion and write a separate concurring opinion.
- **Plurality opinion:** Occurs when a majority cannot agree on the legal reasoning in a case. The plurality opinion is the one that has the most agreement (usually three or four justices). Because of the fractured nature of these opinions, they typically are not viewed as having as much clout as majority opinions.

- **Dissent:** Submitted by a justice who disagrees with the outcome of the case. Other justices can sign on to a dissent or write their own, so there can be as many as four dissents. Justices can also sign on to part of a dissent but not the entire opinion.
- **Per curiam (Latin for "by the court") opinion:** An unsigned opinion of the Court or a decision written by the entire Court. However, this is not the same as a unanimous decision that is signed by the entire Court. Per curiam opinions are usually very short opinions on noncontroversial issues, but not always. For example, *Bush v. Gore*, which decided the outcome of the 2000 presidential election, was a per curiam opinion. Per curiam decisions may also have dissents.

Source: Compiled by the authors.

"Why Should I Care?" The type of decision influences how to interpret the impact of the decision. Majority opinions generally carry more weight than plurality opinions, concurring opinions are important for developing some of the nuances on the winning side, and dissent may lay the groundwork for future shifts in the opinions of the Court.

Dissents Two final points about the process of writing and issuing opinions are important. First, until 1940, a premium was placed on unanimous decisions. This changed dramatically in the 1940s, when most cases had at least one dissent.[45] Lately, about two-thirds of cases have had a dissent. However, in the 2013–2014 term two-thirds of the cases were unanimous, the highest proportion since at least 1946. That proportion fell to 36 percent in the 2019–2020 term.[46] Second, dissents serve an important purpose: not only do they allow the minority view to be expressed, but they also often provide the basis for subsequently reversing a poorly reasoned case. Moreover, when justices strongly oppose the majority decision, they may take the unusual step of reading a portion of their dissent from the bench.

"Why Should I Care?"

The process of hearing cases before the Court, including the written briefs, oral arguments, discussions in conference, and opinion assignment, is a very political one. As discussed in the chapter opener, it may be disturbing to think of the Court as a political institution that bargains and considers external forces like public opinion. Although justices do not have to answer to voters, they are still sensitive to a broad range of considerations in hearing cases.

★

ANALYZE THE FACTORS THAT INFLUENCE SUPREME COURT DECISIONS

Supreme Court decision making

Judicial decision making is influenced by many different factors, but the two main categories are *legal* and *political*. Legal factors include the precedents of earlier cases and the norm that justices must follow the language of the Constitution. Political influences include the justices' preferences or ideologies, their stances on whether the Court should take a restrained or activist role with respect to the elected branches, and external factors such as public opinion and interest group involvement.

Legal factors

The most basic legal factor is precedent, which we discussed earlier. Precedent does not determine the outcome of any given case, because every case has a range of precedents that can serve to justify a justice's decision. The "easy" cases, in which settled law makes the outcome obvious, are less likely to be heard by the Court because of the justices' desire to focus on the more controversial areas of unsettled law or cases in which there is conflict between lower courts' decisions. However, in some areas of the law—such as free speech, the death penalty, and search and seizure—precedent is an important explanation for how the justices decide a case.

The Constitution is the obvious starting point for any Supreme Court case that involves a constitutional right.[47] However, there are various perspectives on exactly how, and to what degree, the language of the Constitution can and should influence judicial decision making today.

People in one camp argue that the *language* used in the Constitution is the most important guiding factor. Their perspectives fall under the heading of **strict construction**. The most basic of these is the literalist view of the Constitution. Literalists argue that

strict construction
A way of interpreting the Constitution based on its language alone.

justices need to look no further than the actual words of the Constitution. However, critics of strict construction point out that the Constitution is silent on many important points (such as a right to privacy) and could not have anticipated the changes in technology in the twentieth and twenty-first centuries that have many legal implications, such as eavesdropping devices, cloning, and the Internet. Also, although the language of the First Amendment is relatively clear when it comes to political speech, other equally important words of the Constitution such as "necessary and proper," "executive power," "equal protection," and "due process" are open-ended and vague.

Those in the other camp are often described as supporting a **living Constitution** perspective on the document (see Chapter 2). They argue that strict construction can "make a nation the prisoner of its past, and reject any constitutional development save constitutional amendment."[48] If the justices are bound to follow the literal words of the Constitution, *with the meaning they had when the document was written*, we certainly could be legally frozen in time. Amending the Constitution is a long and difficult process, so that option is not always a viable way for the Constitution to reflect changing norms and values.

Political factors

The living Constitution perspective points to the second set of influences on Supreme Court decision making: political factors. Indeed, many people are uncomfortable thinking about the Court in political terms and prefer to think of the image of "blind justice," in which constitutional principles are fairly applied. However, political influences are clearly evident in the Court—maybe less than in Congress or the presidency, but they are certainly present. This means that the courts respond to and shape politics in ways that often involve compromise, both within the courts themselves and in the broader political system.

Political Ideology and Attitudes There is evidence that justices' ideology or attitudes about various issues influence their decisions. Those who argue that this is the most important factor in understanding Supreme Court decision making are said to take an attitudinalist approach. Liberal judges are strong defenders of individual

living Constitution
A way of interpreting the Constitution that takes into account evolving national attitudes and circumstances rather than the text alone.

The words of the Constitution ... are so unrestricted by their intrinsic meaning or by their history or by tradition or by prior decisions that they leave the individual Justice free, if indeed they do not compel him, to gather meaning not from reading the Constitution but from reading life.

—Felix Frankfurter,
former Supreme Court justice

In a survey taken about the judicial branch, most respondents were unable to name any Supreme Court justices. Just so you are not in danger of falling into that category, for much of 2020 the justices were (front row, left to right) Stephen Breyer, Clarence Thomas, John G. Roberts Jr. (chief justice), Ruth Bader Ginsburg, Samuel Alito Jr., (standing, left to right) Neil Gorsuch, Sonia Sotomayor, Elena Kagan, and Brett Kavanaugh. Justice Ginsburg died shortly before the 2020 elections, in September 2020, and was replaced by Amy Coney Barrett.

civil liberties (including defendants' rights), tend to be pro-choice on abortion, support regulatory policy to protect the environment and workers, support national intervention in the states, and favor race-conscious policies such as affirmative action. Conservative judges favor state regulation of private conduct (especially on moral issues), support prosecutors over defendants, tend to be pro-life on abortion, and support the free market and property rights over the environment and workers, states' rights over national intervention, and a color-blind policy on race. These are, of course, just general tendencies. However, they do provide a strong basis for explaining patterns of decisions, especially on some types of cases. See the What Do the Facts Say? feature for more on how the balance between liberal and conservative judges has shifted.

Other Justices' and Politicians' Preferences Another approach to understanding Supreme Court decision making, known as the strategic model, focuses on justices' calculations about the preferences of the other justices, the president, and Congress; the choices that other justices are likely to make; and the institutional context within which they operate. After all, justices do not operate alone: at a minimum, they need the votes of four of their colleagues if they want their position to prevail. Therefore, it makes sense to focus on the strategic interactions that take place to build coalitions.

The median voter on the Court—the one in the middle when the justices are arrayed from the most liberal to the most conservative—has an especially influential role in the strategic model. For many years, the median justice was Anthony M. Kennedy. The four conservatives to his right and the four liberals to his left all wanted to attract his vote. When Justice Sotomayor replaced Justice Souter, Justice Kagan replaced Justice Stevens, and Justice Gorsuch replaced Justice Scalia, Kennedy remained the median voter on the Court. When Kennedy retired and Brett Kavanaugh took his place, Roberts became the median and the center of the Court stayed in roughly the same place. With Justice Barrett replacing Ginsburg, Kavanaugh is the new median, with the center moving slightly to the right. Research shows that at least one justice switches his or her vote at some stage in the process (from the initial conference to oral arguments to the final vote) on at least half the cases, so strategic bargaining appears to be fairly common.[49] Our earlier discussion of opinion assignment and writing opinions to attract the support of a specific justice is more evidence in support of the strategic model.

Separation of Powers Another political influence on justices' decision making is their view of the place of the Court with respect to the democratically elected institutions (Congress and the president). Specifically, do they favor an activist or a restrained role for the Court? Advocates of **judicial restraint** argue that judges should defer to the elected branches and not strike down their laws or other actions. In contrast, advocates of **judicial activism** argue that the Court must play an active role in interpreting the Constitution to protect minority rights even if this means overturning the actions of the elected branches. Yet another approach says that these normative arguments about how restraint or activism ought to work don't really matter because the Court usually follows public opinion and rarely plays a lead role in promoting policy change.

Judicial Activism A central question concerning the role of the Court within our political system revolves around judicial review: Should the Court strike down laws passed by Congress and actions of the executive (activism) or defer to the elected branches (restraint)? Often the answer to this question varies when considered in light of specific lines of cases. A political conservative may favor "activist" decisions striking

judicial restraint
The idea that the Supreme Court should defer to the democratically elected executive and legislative branches of government rather than contradicting existing laws.

judicial activism
The idea that the Supreme Court should assert its interpretation of the law even if it overrules the elected executive and legislative branches of government.

The Shifting Ideological Balance of the Court

After Justice Antonin Scalia died in early 2016, the open seat on the Supreme Court became a major issue in the presidential election. Why? As this figure shows, when justices are replaced, the ideological shifts can be quite large (as when Thurgood Marshall, a very liberal justice, was replaced by a strong conservative, Clarence Thomas) or nonexistent (as when Sonia Sotomayor replaced David Souter—they both were moderate liberals). Many people said that replacing Scalia with Merrick Garland— Obama's nominee who was never confirmed—would have drastically altered the ideological makeup of the Court, given the 4–4 split on the Court between liberal and conservative justices. When Scalia was replaced by Neil Gorsuch instead of Garland, what happened to the ideological balance of the Court? Then, when Kennedy retired in 2018, he was replaced by conservative Brett Kavanaugh and the center of the Court was kept in about the same place. What do you think will happen now that Amy Coney Barrett has replaced Ruth Bader Ginsburg? What do the facts say?

WHAT DO THE FACTS SAY?

Think about it

- **Look at where Scalia is on the ideological scale.** If the Democratic candidate, Hillary Clinton, had been elected in 2016 and all but ensured Garland joining the Court, where would Scalia's dot have likely moved?
- **Did the median justice change** with the addition of Neil Gorsuch and Brett Kavanaugh to the Court?
- **What happened when John Roberts replaced Kennedy** as the median justice for the 2018 term?

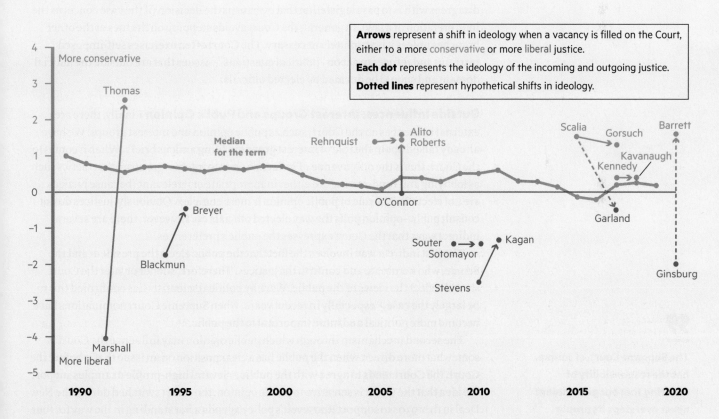

> **Arrows** represent a shift in ideology when a vacancy is filled on the Court, either to a more conservative or more liberal justice.
>
> **Each dot** represents the ideology of the incoming and outgoing justice.
>
> **Dotted lines** represent hypothetical shifts in ideology.

Sources: Alicia Parlapiano and Margot Sanger-Katz, "A Supreme Court with Merrick Garland Would Be the Most Liberal in Decades," *New York Times*, March 16, 2016, www.nytimes.com/interactive/2016/02/18/upshot/potential-for-the-most-liberal-supreme-court-in-decades.html; data for Scalia, Gorsuch, Kennedy, and Kavanaugh are from Martin Quinn Scores, "Measures," http://mqscores.lsa.umich.edu/measures.php; estimate for Garland is from Adam Bonica et al., "New Data Show How Liberal Merrick Garland Really Is," *Washington Post*, March 30, 2016, www.washingtonpost.com/news/monkey-cage/wp/2016/03/30/new-data-show-how-liberal-merrick-garland-really-is/ (all accessed 6/24/20); estimate for Barrett is from "The Supreme Court May Be About to Take a Hard Right Turn," *The Economist*, September 21, 2020, www.economist.com/graphic-detail/2020/09/21/the-supreme-court-may-be-about-to-take-a-hard-right-turn (accessed 11/10/20).

Students at a middle school in Alton, Illinois, gather around a flagpole for prayers before the start of the school day. Unless someone complains, it is difficult to enforce the ban on prayer in public schools.

The Supreme Court, of course, has the responsibility of ensuring that our government never oversteps its proper bounds or violates the rights of individuals. But the Court must also recognize the limits on itself and respect the choices made by the American people.

—Justice Elena Kagan

down environmental laws or workplace regulations but oppose activist decisions that defend flag burning or defendants' rights. Political liberals may do the opposite—calling for judicial restraint on the first set of cases but for judicial activism to protect civil liberties. The term "activist judges" often appears in the media. Sometimes the media mistakenly assert that liberal justices are more activist than conservative justices. In fact, however, that is not always the case. The current Court is quite conservative, but it is also activist.[50]

The separation of powers continues to play a role after the justices have issued their rulings. In some instances, the Court can force its view on the other branches; in other cases, it needs their support to enforce its decisions. The Court's lack of enforcement power is especially evident when a ruling applies broadly to millions of people who care deeply about the issues. Consider school prayer, which still exists in hundreds of public schools despite having been ruled unconstitutional nearly 60 years ago. It is impossible to enforce the ban unless someone in a school complains and brings a lawsuit.

The president and Congress often fight back when they think the Court is exerting too much influence, which can limit the Court's power as a policy-making institution. For example, the president can fail to enforce a decision vigorously and Congress can block appointments it disagrees with, limit the jurisdiction of the federal courts, change the size of the Court, or even impeach a judge. The latter three options are rarely used. The most common way for Congress to respond to a Court decision that it disagrees with is to pass legislation that overturns the decision (if the case concerns the interpretation of a law). In general, the Court avoids stepping on the toes of the other branches unless it is absolutely necessary. The Court often exercises self-imposed restraint and refuses to act on "political questions"—issues that are outside the judicial domain and should be decided by elected officials.

Outside Influences: Interest Groups and Public Opinion Finally, there are external influences on the Court, such as public opinion and interest groups. We have already talked about the role of interest groups in filing amicus briefs. When it comes to the Court, this is the only avenue of influence open to interest groups; other tactics such as lobbying and fund-raising are either inappropriate or irrelevant (because justices are not elected). The role of public opinion is more complex. Obviously, justices do not consult public-opinion polls the way elected officials do. However, there are several indirect ways that the Court expresses the public's preferences.

The first indirect way involves the fact that the public elects the president and the Senate, who nominate and confirm the justices. Therefore, sooner or later the Court should reflect the views of the public. Work by political scientists has confirmed this to be largely the case,[51] especially in recent years, when Supreme Court nominations have become more political and more important to the public.[52]

The second mechanism through which public opinion may influence the Court is somewhat more direct: when the public has a clear position on an issue that is before the Court, the Court tends to agree with the public.[53] Several high-profile examples support the idea that the Court is sensitive to public opinion: the Court switched during the New Deal in the 1930s to support Roosevelt's policy agenda after standing in the way for four years, gave in to wartime opinion to support the internment of Japanese Americans during World War II, limited an accused child molester's right to confront his or her accuser in a courtroom, and supported same-sex marriage. In each of these cases, the justices reflected the current public opinion of the nation rather than a strict reading of the Constitution or the Founders' intent. On the other hand, there are plenty of decisions in which the Court has stood up for unpopular views, such as banning prayer in schools, allowing flag burning, and protecting criminal defendants' rights.

The Court has been an important protector of minority rights, including in the civil rights era. This picture from 1953 shows people waiting in line at the Supreme Court to hear oral arguments in *Brown v. Board of Education*. But at other times, the Court has supported the will of the majority.

Another way that the Court may consider the public mood is to shift the timing of a decision. The best example here is the landmark school desegregation case *Brown v. Board of Education* (1954), which the Court sat on for more than two years—until after the 1952 presidential election—because it didn't think the public was ready for its bombshell ruling.[54] Others have argued that the Court rarely *changes* its views to reflect public opinion,[55] but at a minimum the evidence supports the notion that the Court is usually in step with the public.[56]

Shouldn't the Court be neutrally applying the words of the Constitution to the cases it hears? While a normatively appealing view, this textualist view ignores many of the realities of how the Court actually operates. Justices often let their own political views shape their decisions, but more neutral forces such as precedent and deferring to the elected branches also play important roles. A realistic perception of the various factors that go into a justice's decision can help you understand why the Court strikes down some laws and upholds others.

"Why Should I Care?"

Unpacking the Conflict

Considering all that we've discussed in this chapter, let's apply what we know about how the courts work to the events introduced at the beginning of this chapter: Justice Ginsburg's comments about Donald Trump during the 2016 presidential campaign and Chief Justice Roberts's defense of the independence of the courts in rebutting Trump's complaint about an "Obama judge." Did Justice Ginsburg overstep her boundaries with her remarks on Donald Trump, or was it appropriate for her to express her opinions? Was Justice Roberts overreacting to Trump's comments about political judges? What is the proper place of the courts within our political system? Should judges attempt to neutrally apply the law, or should their political views play a role?

The chapter-opening examples demonstrate that we often have a difficult time coming to grips with the political nature of the Supreme Court and prefer the comforting image of the neutral and fair Lady Justice: that is why there was such a strong reaction to Justice Ginsburg's comments about Trump. We *want* our courts to be politically neutral, but the reality is very different.

Politics is indeed everywhere, even in the courts, where you would least expect to see it. Politics affects everything from the selection of judges to the decisions they make. Some characteristics of the federal courts (most important of which is judges' lifetime tenure) insulate the system from politics. However, courts are subject to influence by judges' ideologies, interest groups, and the president and Senate, who try to shape the courts' composition through the nomination process.

While many recoil from a politicized Court, we also value its independence and don't want the president and Congress stepping on its toes. Thus, if the federal courts are allowed to play their proper role, they can serve as a referee between the other branches of government, and between the national and state governments, by defining the boundaries of permissible conduct.

The courts demonstrate that politics is conflictual. And many conflicts demonstrate that the courts are political. Although plenty of unanimous Supreme Court decisions do not involve much conflict among the justices, many landmark cases deeply divide the Court on constitutional interpretation and how to balance those competing interpretations against other values and interests. These conflicts in the Court often reveal deeper fault lines in the broader political system.

"What's Your Take?"

What should the proper place of the courts be in our political system?

How much influence should the executive and legislative branches have over the courts, and vice versa?

STUDY GUIDE

The development of an independent and powerful federal judiciary

Explain how the power of judicial review was established.
(Pages 416–420)

Summary

The Constitution offers few specifics on the organization of the judiciary, in contrast to other branches of government. In fact, most of the details on the arrangement of the judiciary do not come from the Constitution at all, but from congressional action. In addition, the Supreme Court's strongest power—judicial review—is not even mentioned in the Constitution but was established in the *Marbury v. Madison* decision.

Key terms

original jurisdiction (p. 417)
Judiciary Act of 1789 (p. 417)
district courts (p. 417)
appellate jurisdiction (p. 417)

judicial review (p. 418)
constitutional interpretation (p. 419)
statutory interpretation (p 419)

Practice Quiz Questions

1. **Most of the details about the Supreme Court were established in _____.**

   a   the Judiciary Act of 1789

   b   Article I of the Constitution

   c   Article II of the Constitution

   d   the *Federalist Papers*

   e   *Marbury v. Madison*

2. ***Marbury v. Madison* is significant because it _____.**

   a   established the Supreme Court

   b   introduced the process of selective incorporation

   c   changed the manner of judicial selection

   d   established judicial review

   e   gave Supreme Court justices lifetime appointments

3. **Judicial review enables the Supreme Court to _____.**

   a   submit legislation to Congress

   b   strike down laws passed by Congress

   c   revise laws passed by Congress

   d   oversee presidential appointments to the bureaucracy

   e   approve judicial appointments to lower courts

The American legal and judicial system

Outline the structure of the court system.
(Pages 420–429)

Summary

All courts within the United States have a similar set of fundamental attributes, such as the distinction between civil and criminal cases and the reliance on legal precedent. The judicial system is divided between state and federal courts, and within each level of government there are courts of original jurisdiction and appeals courts.

Key terms

plaintiff (p. 420)
defendant (p. 420)
plea bargaining (p. 420)
class-action lawsuit (p. 421)
common law (p. 421)

precedent (p. 421)
standing (p. 424)
jurisdiction (p. 424)
appeals courts (p. 424)
senatorial courtesy (p. 428)

Practice Quiz Questions

4. **A system of _____ relies on legal decisions that are built from precedent established in previous cases.**

   a   common law

   b   civil law

   c   statutory law

   d   stare decisis

   e   plea bargaining

5. **When one has suffered direct and personal harm from the action addressed in a case, it is called _____.**

   a   precedent

   b   appellant

   c   plea bargaining

   d   jurisdiction

   e   standing

6. **The president appoints federal judges with the "advice and consent" of the _____.**

   a   House of Representatives

   b   Senate

   c   Supreme Court

   d   attorney general

   e   vice president

Access to the Supreme Court

Describe how cases reach the Supreme Court.
(Pages 430–432)

Summary

The Supreme Court hears only about 1 percent of the cases that are brought to it. To help decide which cases to hear, the Court generally uses three factors: collusion, standing, and mootness. Ultimately, the justices have a great deal of discretion in deciding to hear a case, but they can hear only cases that come to them.

Key terms

writ of *certiorari* (p. 431)   cert pool (p. 432)

mootness (p. 432)   solicitor general (p. 432)

Practice Quiz Questions

7. When a litigant who lost in a lower court files a petition, the case reaches the Supreme Court _____ .

a   as a matter of right

b   through a writ of certification

c   through a writ of *certiorari*

d   as a matter of original jurisdiction

e   through senatorial courtesy

8. _____ means that the controversy is not relevant when the Court hears the case.

a   Mootness

b   Amicus

c   Collusion

d   Standing

e   Precedent

9. Most justices _____ in initially deciding which cases should be heard.

a   personally review all cases

b   personally review a random sample of cases

c   follow the recommendations of the chief justice

d   use a random selection process

e   use a cert pool

Hearing cases before the Supreme Court

Describe the Supreme Court's procedures for hearing a case. (Pages 433–436)

Summary

When hearing a case, the justices prepare by reading briefs before they hear the oral arguments. After oral arguments, the justices meet in conference to discuss and vote on the cases. The majority opinion

explains the rationale for how a decision is reached, although justices can also write dissenting and concurring opinions if they agree with the outcome of the case but not the legal reasoning.

Key terms

amicus curiae (p. 433)   oral arguments (p. 433)

Practice Quiz Questions

10. The most important impact of a large number of amicus curiae briefs on a case is that _____ .

a   the decision is more likely to be unanimous

b   the case is more likely to be heard

c   the decision is more likely to go against the government

d   the case is less likely to be heard

e   the decision is more likely to have a liberal outcome

11. Oral arguments generally last _____ , and justices _____ wait until the end of the arguments to ask questions.

a   one hour; will

b   one hour; do not

c   one day; will

d   one week; will

e   one week; do not

12. Generally, the chief justice or the _____ justice decides who writes the majority opinion; justices' individual areas of expertise _____ a factor in making this assignment.

a   most junior; are not

b   most junior; are

c   most senior; are not

d   most senior; are

e   dissenting; are not

Supreme Court decision making

Analyze the factors that influence Supreme Court decisions. (Pages 436–441)

Summary

The Court makes decisions based on legal factors such as precedent and informal norms, and political factors such as the justices' own ideologies and positions on the role that the Court plays in government. Although the Court does not consider public opinion the way elected officials do, most decisions generally stay in step with the views of the public.

Key terms

strict construction (p. 436)   judicial restraint (p. 438)

living Constitution (p. 437)   judicial activism (p. 438)

Practice Quiz Questions

13. Advocates of _____ argue that the Court must defer to the elected branches and not strike down their laws.

a   judicial restraint

b   judicial activism

c   judicial limitation

d   legal maximization

e   the strategic model

14. In general, the Court _____ challenges with the elected branches and often _____ to act on "political questions."

a   avoids; agrees

b   avoids; refuses

c   pursues; agrees

d   pursues; refuses

e   wins; tries

Suggested Reading

Baum, Lawrence. *Judges and Their Audiences: A Perspective on Judicial Behavior*. Princeton, NJ: Princeton University Press, 2006.

Black, Ryan C., and Ryan J. Owens. *The Solicitor General and the United States Supreme Court: Executive Influence and Judicial Decisions*. New York: Cambridge University Press, 2012.

Cornell University Law School's Legal Information Institute, Justia, and Chicago-Kent College of Law, Oyez: Supreme Court Multimedia, www.oyez.org.

Cornell University Law School, Supreme Court Collection, www.law.cornell.edu/supremecourt/text/home.

Hansford, Thomas G., and James F. Spriggs II. *The Politics of Precedent on the U.S. Supreme Court*. Princeton, NJ: Princeton University Press, 2006.

O'Brien, David M. *Storm Center: The Supreme Court in American Politics*, 12th ed. New York: W. W. Norton, 2020.

Posner, Richard A. *The Federal Judiciary: Strengths and Weaknesses*. Cambridge, MA: Harvard University Press, 2017.

Rosen, Jeffrey. *The Most Democratic Branch: How the Courts Serve America*. New York: Oxford University Press, 2006.

Sunstein, Cass R., David Schkade, Lisa M. Ellman, and Andres Sawicki. *Are Judges Political? An Empirical Analysis of the Federal Judiciary*. Washington, DC: Brookings Institution Press, 2006.

Tushnet, Mark. *A Court Divided: The Rehnquist Court and the Future of Constitutional Law*. New York: W. W. Norton, 2006.

U.S. Supreme Court website, www.supremecourt.gov.

14

Economic and Social Policy

What should the government do to promote a strong economy and provide a social safety net?

 "Forget about this $3 trillion left-wing wish list that even House Democrats are criticizing. It ain't gonna happen."[1]
Senate Majority Leader Mitch McConnell (R-KY)

 "Sen. McConnell's months-long refusal to engage in bipartisan talks on the next phase of federal relief legislation has created needless uncertainty and pain for millions of families who are still reeling from the public health and economic crises."[2]
Senate Minority Leader Chuck Schumer (D-NY)

Lawmakers continued working throughout the COVID-19 pandemic in an attempt to pass legislation that would help soften the blow of the deepening recession. Here, Senate Minority Leader Chuck Schumer can be seen in the halls of the Capitol wearing a mask.

As the COVID-19 pandemic swept the country early in 2020, most state governments responded by ordering all nonessential businesses to close and recommending or requiring that people stay at home to slow the spread of the virus. Schools and universities closed and went online (to the extent that was possible); airlines and the service industry, especially hotels and restaurants, were hard-hit; sports, entertainment, and the arts were completely shut down. As a result, the economy shed 20.5 million jobs in April, leaving nearly 24 million people out of work and increasing the unemployment rate to 14.7 percent—the highest since the Great Depression in the 1930s. By June 20, nearly 33 million people had claimed unemployment benefits.[3]

Congress responded with four bills, totaling nearly $3 trillion in spending, with the centerpiece the $2.2 trillion Coronavirus Aid, Relief, and Economic Security Act, or CARES Act, which passed with unanimous support in the Senate (96–0) and by a voice vote in the House. The bills provided $600 billion in payments to individuals ($1,200 each for people making less than $75,000), $600 billion to small businesses,

A major feature of the March 2020 CARES Act legislation was the $1,200 stimulus check paid out to Americans as a means to offset the negative effects of the COVID-19 recession.

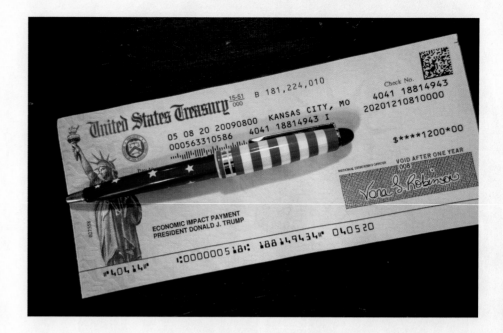

$500 billion to large corporations (such as airlines), $154 billion to health care, $340 billion to state and local governments, and $44 billion to education.[4]

The Federal Reserve also moved aggressively to ensure stability in the financial sector by pumping nearly $3 trillion into the economy. In addition to buying federal treasuries, state and municipal bonds, and (for the first time) corporate debt, the Fed dropped its target interest rate to 0.25 percent, eliminated the reserve requirement for banks, and relaxed regulations on capital requirements to encourage more lending, backstopped money market mutual funds, and supported loans to medium-sized businesses that were too big to qualify for congressionally funded aid.[5]

The bipartisan response was unprecedented in its scope and size, but by the middle of the summer it became clear that more action was needed. The House moved first, passing the $3 trillion Health and Economic Recovery Omnibus Emergency Solutions Act (yes, the HEROES Act!). However, as the chapter-opening quotes indicate, this bill was "dead on arrival" in the Senate because the Majority Leader dismissed it as a "left-wing wish list." Speaker Nancy Pelosi and Treasury Secretary Steven Mnuchin were close to a $1.8 trillion compromise bill shortly before the election, but the deal fell apart as McConnell continued to express skepticism. The bipartisan harmony that existed in the first part of the crisis gave way to the familiar partisan conflict in Washington.

Conflict over economic policy goes beyond emergency responses to the economic downturn caused by the COVID-19 pandemic. Many of America's political debates concern economic policy: Should we try to protect domestic industries from foreign competition or promote free trade? Should we have a largely unregulated free market—or regulations for things like pollution and health care? Should we spend more money to create "green jobs" and promote alternative energy, or subsidize offshore oil drilling and build more natural gas pipelines? Democrats tend to favor a more activist government that supports a broader range of redistributive programs and regulates the economy to ensure a range of public goods, such as rebuilding the infrastructure. Republicans tend to favor a more limited approach to government that promotes lower taxes and less regulation and allows the free market to determine more social and economic decisions, such as allowing greater development of domestic energy sources.

As our political leaders debate how best to support a growing economy, it becomes increasingly important to understand the economic policy–making process. How much should the government do to get us out of a recession? Which side is right about trade policy or environmental policy? More generally, what is the proper role of the government in a free market economy? How do political players deal with the conflict that is inherent in economic policy making?

Making public policy

Public policy is a course of action pursued by government to address a specific problem. For example, various social policies, such as Medicare and Social Security, are aimed at addressing the medical and economic needs of retired American citizens. In this section, we outline the policy-making process and discuss the key players in shaping economic and social policy.

The policy-making process

How are policies shaped and implemented? All policies go through similar stages in this process. The first stage involves defining a problem as an issue that requires the federal government's attention. Of the thousands of possible issues, Congress acts on a relatively small number. Consider food assistance programs: poor and hungry people have been part of American society since the arrival of the first settlers, but this was not seen as a problem requiring government intervention until the twentieth century. What causes a society to change its assumptions about whether and how government should address social problems?

Sometimes there is a triggering event: the assassination of President John F. Kennedy led to the passage of gun control legislation, the energy crisis of the early 1970s led to the first comprehensive discussions of energy policy, and Hurricane Katrina and the COVID-19 pandemic led to a reexamination of our readiness for emergencies and our social safety net. Sometimes redefining an issue can move the policy to the next step of the process. For example, the estate tax has been part of our tax system since 1917, but when Republican leaders in Congress redefined it as the "death tax" in the late 1990s, they transformed the politics of the debate and made it a problem that needed a solution. After all, who could support a tax on dead people? (Of course, dead people don't pay taxes—the estate's heirs do—but that nuance was lost in the redefinition of the problem.)

Recognizing and defining a problem is just the first step; it still needs to come to the attention of political leaders and get on the **policy agenda**. When conditions are right, with the appropriate national political mood and participation from key interest groups and government actors, an issue can reach the agenda.

Once the issue is on the active agenda, alternatives are proposed and debated and the final version of the policy is formulated in Congress (if it is a bill) or the executive branch (if it is an administrative action). Enactment involves either (1) a roll call vote in the House and the Senate and then a signature by the president, (2) a regulatory decision or administrative action by the bureaucracy, or (3) unilateral action by the president (such as an executive order or agreement).

Many factors determine whether the finalized policy is implemented successfully. First, the problem the policy is designed to fix has to be solvable. Second, the policy

TRACE THE STEPS THROUGH WHICH PROBLEMS ARE ADDRESSED BY GOVERNMENT POLICIES

public policy
A course of action pursued by government to address a specific problem.

policy agenda
The set of desired policies that political leaders view as their top priorities.

The disagreements over policy run deep. Conflicts over "Trumpcare," the proposed replacement to Obamacare, for example, led to the legislative failure of any repeal or replacement of the Affordable Care Act.

must be clear and consistent in its objectives. It wouldn't make sense for Congress to pass a law telling the Department of Health and Human Services to "make sure everyone has health care," because such a law would not indicate how to accomplish that broad goal. Third, the policy must be funded adequately and administered by competent bureaucrats who have the required expertise. Finally, external support from the public and relevant interest groups may be critical to the policy's success. For example, AARP's support is absolutely essential for the success of any social policy that affects older Americans. Its support helped pass the Prescription Drug Benefit that was added to Medicare in 2003 and comprehensive health care reform in 2010.[6]

Implementation of a policy is an ongoing process. To ensure that the desires of Congress and the president are being followed, policy evaluation is a critical stage of the policy-making process. (See Chapter 12 for a discussion of Congress's and the president's attempts to control the bureaucracy.) Evaluation has become more visible since passage of the Government Performance and Results Act of 1993, which requires agencies to publish strategic plans and performance measures. Though these efforts sound impressive, it is incredibly difficult to assess whether a government program is achieving its aims.

Political scientist James Q. Wilson explains the difference in measuring success in the private sector and the public sector—specifically, he compares McDonald's with the Department of Motor Vehicles (DMV).[7] It is relatively easy to know whether McDonald's is doing a good job: simply compare the profits being generated with those of the previous period. If profits are going up at a reasonable pace, the burger flippers and fry cooks are doing their jobs. The DMV's performance is much more difficult to assess because there is no simple measure, such as profit, to look at. Maybe you could review the number of people served per hour or the average time that people have to wait to get their driver's license. But that would ignore many other considerations, such as how well the DMV serves disadvantaged populations or people for whom English is a second language. In a DMV office where 50 percent of the applicants don't speak English, we wouldn't expect the workers to be as efficient as in one where all applicants speak English.

Evaluating a public agency such as the State Department is even more difficult. How do we know if diplomacy is being conducted in a manner consistent with congressional and presidential preferences? Would success be defined as staying out of war? Increasing economic activity or cultural exchanges between countries? Strengthening democratic institutions in emerging democracies? Getting cooperation in the war on terrorism? Measuring the achievement of objectives like these is very difficult even if those goals can be clearly defined.

Despite these limitations, extensive efforts to evaluate policy do provide decision makers with some basis for deciding whether to modify, expand, or terminate a policy. Programs are notoriously difficult to cut or eliminate.

The key players in economic and social policy making

Congress, the president, and the bureaucracy all play important roles in making economic and social policy. Congress, through the "power of the purse," has the constitutional authority to determine the nation's fiscal policy, but the president also can shape taxing and spending policy for the nation. The Federal Reserve and the Treasury implement the nation's monetary policy, while other bureaucratic agencies implement social policy. Additional significant players include the courts, state governments, and interest groups.

Congress The Constitution places Congress at the center of economic policy making by giving legislators the "power of the purse"—that is, power over the nation's fiscal policy of taxing and spending. In a way, everything Congress does has an impact on the economy, whether it is providing money for an interstate highway or a student loan, regulating the level of air pollutants, or funding the Social Security system. Some committees are more directly related to economic policy. Budget Committees, Appropriations Committees, and tax committees (Ways and Means in the House and Finance in the Senate; see Chapter 10) direct **fiscal policy**, while the banking committees have a hand in overseeing aspects of **monetary policy**. The Commerce Committees, especially in the House, also influence a range of economic policies. The budget process is the most important of Congress's economic policy–making responsibilities.

Budget making in Congress was decentralized through much of the nation's history, with no real way to coordinate activity among the various committees and subcommittees involved in the process. The Appropriations Committees had a difficult time keeping spending requests from other committees in line with overall budgetary expectations because of Congress's two-step process to approve spending: the authorizing committee writes the law that authorizes the spending, and then the Appropriations Committee approves the level of spending.[8] As a result, budgetary power shifted from Congress to the president, starting with the Budget and Accounting Act of 1921. Since then, presidents have played a central role in the budget process by submitting their budgets to Congress. The president's budget often serves as the starting point for the congressional budget (see How It Works: The Budget Process).

Today, as evidence that politics is conflictual, increased partisan polarization is occurring in Congress over budget making. Differences between Democrats' and Republicans' views of taxing and spending policy have made it difficult to pass a budget on time. Recently Congress has relied on "continuing resolutions," which keep spending at the level of the previous year's budget, when members cannot agree

fiscal policy
Government decisions about how to influence the economy by taxing and spending.

monetary policy
Government decisions about how to influence the economy using control of the money supply and interest rates.

budget making
The processes carried out in Congress to determine how government money will be spent and revenue will be raised.

How it works: in theory
The Budget Process

First Monday in February:
The president submits budget request to Congress.

February 15:
Congressional Budget Office (CBO) issues budget and economic outlook report.

Within six weeks of president's submission:
Other committees with budgetary responsibilities submit "views and estimates" to Budget Committees.

Early April:
House Budget Committee creates its budget resolution and the House votes on it.

Early April:
Senate Budget Committee creates its budget resolution and the Senate votes on it.

Early April:
Budget Conference Committee reconciles the House and Senate versions of the budget resolution.

By April 15:
House votes on conference version.
Senate votes on conference version.

Appropriations:
After both houses approve the budget resolution, Appropriations Committees draft legislation authorizing expenditures to the relevant agencies. Each appropriations bill must be passed by both houses and signed into law by the president. If this process is not completed by October 1 and no temporary measure (a "continuing resolution") is in place, the government will shut down.

October 1:
Start of the fiscal year.

The 2020 Budget Process

Although there is a "textbook" path that politicians try to follow when passing a budget, they almost always deviate wildly from it. In fact, it has been 24 years since Congress passed all 12 appropriations bills using the regular process. In 2020, the budget resolution was six months late, so Congress resorted to continuing resolutions, a government shutdown (complicated by negotiations over DACA and the Dreamers), and eventually an omnibus bill that combined the 12 appropriations bills.

Critical Thinking

1. **How might the type of "brinkmanship" budgeting** described here—that is, using the threat of a government shutdown to achieve policy goals—affect the economy?

2. **If you were a businessperson trying to decide** whether or not to expand, would the uncertainty created by a threatened shutdown affect your decision?

Cleaning up last year's mess.

January 25 and February 15, 2019: Congress passes two spending bills to end the longest government shutdown in U.S. history (35 days). **These bills should have been passed by October 1, 2018.**

Whatever...

Over the summer, the Budget Committees **fail to pass a budget resolution**. This should have been passed by April 15.

The sequester ax looms.

August 1: Facing deep spending cuts that would have been imposed through sequestration, **Congress raises the budget caps by $320 billion**.

Shutdown, anyone?

November 21: With a few hours to spare, the Senate passes another CR, passed by the House on November 19, **keeping the government open through December 20**.

Starting a little late.

March 11: President Trump submits his budget for the 2020 fiscal year—**35 days late**.

Wait, can they do that?

May–June: House and Senate Appropriations Committees **forge ahead without a budget resolution**. (Yes, they can do that, through a procedure called "deeming.")

Um, we have a deadline, guys...

September 26: Five days before the start of the new fiscal year, the Senate **passes a continuing resolution (CR)**, which was passed by the House a week earlier, extending government funding through November 21.

Better late than never!

December 17–20: Trump signs the $1.8 trillion budget bill. The process was wrapped up 80 days after the deadline, which was the quickest in 10 years and two months shorter than the average since 1998 of 140 days late.

CBO does its thing.

May 9: CBO submits its analysis of the president's budget—**83 days late**. (But who's counting? Oh, I guess we are.)

Making some progress, but...

June 25: The House **passes 10 of its 12 appropriation bills**, but things grind to a halt in the Senate.

Jump on the minibus?

October 31: The Senate **passes four appropriation bills in "minibus 2"** (get it? instead of a bigger omnibus bill), but minibus 1 fails due to disagreement over funding for the wall with Mexico.

COVID-19 blows a hole in the budget.

March–April 2020: Congress passes four spending bills totaling $2.4 trillion to fight the recession caused by the pandemic (and this doesn't include the $4 trillion spent by the Fed).

on a new budget. Even traditionally noncontroversial aspects of fiscal policy, such as increasing the debt ceiling to authorize government borrowing, have become opportunities for partisan politics. And even unified control of government for the first time since 2010 did not make the budget process work more smoothly in 2017.

Congress also plays a central role in shaping social policy. Many important social policies, such as Social Security, Medicare, Medicaid, and SNAP (formerly known as food stamps), started out as presidential initiatives. But Congress writes the laws and then reforms and expands them over the years.

The President Presidents know that the public expects them to promote a healthy economy. Indeed, the state of the economy influences the public's assessment of presidential performance and also influences election outcomes. President Obama focused on the economy in his first months in office, pushing through a massive stimulus bill; later, facing high levels of unemployment, Obama also signed legislation aimed at creating more jobs. The signature achievement of President Trump's first two years was enacting the $1.5 trillion tax cut, which gave a short-term boost to the economy.[9]

As we discussed in Chapter 11, the president cannot accomplish much single-handedly on the economic front: Congress, the Fed, and broader domestic and international economic forces all have an impact on the health of the economy. However, the executive branch has a large advising structure that helps the president formulate economic policy. The Office of Management and Budget (OMB), the Council of Economic Advisers (CEA), the Office of the **United States Trade Representative (USTR)**, and the **National Economic Council (NEC)** all provide important economic advice.

The OMB solicits spending requests from all federal agencies, suggests additional cuts, and then coordinates these requests with presidential priorities. It ultimately puts together the president's budget, which is then submitted to Congress. The OMB also oversees government reorganization plans and recommends improvements in departmental operations.

The CEA primarily provides the president with objective data on the state of the economy and expert advice on economic policy. The agency is responsible for creating the *Annual Economic Report of the President*, which has a wealth of data on the economy and an overview of the president's policies. Although presidents have varied in how closely they work with the CEA or other parts of their economic team, some prominent CEA members have significantly influenced the administration's tax policy and jobs program.

Understanding the interactions between Congress and the president is central to understanding economic and social policy. If the president's party controls Congress, then the president's budget becomes the starting point for congressional negotiations over the budget. If the opposing party controls Congress, then the president's budget is usually considered "dead on arrival" and Congress creates its own document. But even in 2018, Trump's budget was ignored by congressional leadership, although the president and the leadership belonged to the same party. Of course, the president can use the veto threat to try to move Congress closer to his or her position, but when the budget is contained in one large package that must be signed or vetoed in its entirety, it is difficult to carry out such threats.[10]

Similarly, in some instances the president may take the lead in formulating social policy, as Franklin Delano Roosevelt did with the New Deal and Lyndon Johnson with the Great Society. In other instances, Congress plays a central role, as with health care reform in 2009–2010. In all cases, the president and Congress must find some common ground.

United States Trade Representative (USTR)
An agency founded in 1962 to negotiate with foreign governments to create trade agreements, resolve disputes, and participate in global trade-policy organizations. Treaties negotiated by the USTR must be ratified by the Senate.

National Economic Council (NEC)
A group of economic advisers created in 1993 to work with the president to coordinate economic policy.

The Bureaucracy You might assume that the bureaucracy makes little difference in social policy and simply implements the policies determined by Congress and the president. That is somewhat true for some policies—such as Social Security, whose benefit levels are determined by law. Implementing this policy largely involves determining that the proper amount of money is going to the right people and making sure that they receive their payments. However, as discussed in Chapter 12, with many social policies the "on-the-ground" public employees have a great deal of discretion. One study found that welfare agencies that distributed **Aid to Families with Dependent Children (AFDC)** benefits had a more "hostile and punitive" attitude toward their clients than those that administered the disability program under Social Security.[11] Welfare offices in general tend not to be very welcoming places. People often have to wait for hours, and office workers are sometimes rude. Some potential welfare recipients are so alienated by the process that they give up. (This is not true of all welfare offices, but there are general differences in how recipients are treated in different types of social welfare programs.) Sometimes problems of bureaucratic implementation may be at the top, as when problems concerning Veterans Affairs (VA) hospitals came to light in 2014. Thousands of veterans had long waits for services that were covered up by VA hospital administrators. Veterans Affairs Secretary Eric Shinseki was forced to resign for his failure to address the problem.[12]

Bureaucratic discretion may also serve more positive ends. In fact, many bureaucratic agencies in the late nineteenth and early twentieth centuries developed political autonomy and strong reputations that enabled them to analyze and solve problems, create new programs, and plan and administer programs efficiently.[13] Many of the same insights apply to agencies that deliver social policies today, such as the Social Security Administration, which has a very strong base of popular and political support.

In terms of economic policy, two bureaucratic agencies are key in creating monetary policy: the **Federal Reserve System** (an independent agency, commonly known as "the Fed") and the **Treasury Department** (a cabinet-level department). The Treasury Department's mission "is to promote the conditions for prosperity and stability in the

Aid to Families with Dependent Children (AFDC)
The federal welfare program in place from 1935 until 1996, when it was replaced by TANF under President Clinton.

Federal Reserve System
An independent agency that serves as the central bank of the United States to bring stability to the nation's banking system.

Treasury Department
A cabinet-level agency that is responsible for managing the federal government's revenue. It prints currency, collects taxes, and sells government bonds.

Sometimes, problems in social service administration can stem from poor management. Veterans Affairs (VA) hospitals have been plagued by long wait times in recent years, forcing veterans to wait much longer for care than patients at non-VA hospitals.

United States and encourage prosperity and stability in the rest of the world." Some of these responsibilities overlap with the Fed's, especially supervising banks and managing the public debt. In most instances, the responsibilities are complementary rather than competing, such as the management of currency and coins: the Treasury produces currency and coins, and the Fed distributes them to member banks.[14] Financing federal debt is another matter. The Treasury generally prefers to lower interest rates to keep down the cost of financing the debt and to promote economic growth, whereas the Fed is concerned about keeping rates high enough to avoid inflation. Therefore, the Fed and the Treasury must coordinate their policies to avoid working at cross-purposes. One unanticipated consequence of the COVID-19 recession was an extreme shortage of coins and bills as people stopped circulating cash. The Fed was unable to meet the requests for coins and bills from retailers and banks through much of the summer of 2020.[15]

Other Important Players By providing a necessary legal foundation, *the courts* ensure fair application of economic and social policy laws and regulations. For example, contract law, patent law, banking and finance law, and property rights are all elements of a legal system that provides the foundation for economic development. Courts issue rulings on the regulation of telecommunications, banking, and energy industries and decisions on environmental law and eminent domain that affect property rights. All these policies have an impact on economic policy. Courts are also important in helping to shape economic and social policy by deciding when laws passed by Congress may be unconstitutional.

State governments have a central role in areas such as education and welfare. Welfare has always been administered at the state and local level, with varying degrees of national control. Medicaid is administered at the state level (with federal assistance), and education is almost completely controlled by local and state governments. One sticking point with health care reform in 2009–2010 was the extent to which policy would be centered in the states or have a stronger national component. The stronger national approach failed, but the new law signaled a definite shift to a more national role in health care.

Education policy, too, is seeing more involvement by the national government. But even with the national accountability mechanisms and testing requirements established by President George W. Bush's No Child Left Behind Act and the incentives provided by President Barack Obama's Race to the Top program, education policy remains largely a state and local affair. President Trump's education policy has been consistent with maintaining the central role for state and local government, calling for cuts in many federal programs but big increases in spending for public and private school choice programs.[16]

The importance of the states has been extremely clear in the response to the COVID-19 pandemic. The national government took a hands-off approach, leaving it to the states to determine the best way to respond. The White House's "Opening Up America Again" website listed ten "Core State Preparedness Responsibilities," including testing and contact tracing, hospital system capacity, and plans for protecting workers in critical industries; seven specific responsibilities for individuals (such as washing hands and not going to work when you feel sick); and five for employers, but there were no "core national responsibilities."[17] This state flexibility makes sense because what would be appropriate for New York City would not be useful in rural North Dakota. Also, it probably would not be constitutional for the president to either order everyone to stay home for six months or open up states' economies. These decisions ultimately reside with governors and state legislatures.[18] Some states responded with strict stay-at-home orders and very slowly opened up their economies, and others never implemented strict orders and opened up their economies while the virus was still spreading. As a result, by mid-July, infection rates in some states were 50 times higher than in others.[19]

In contrast, economic policy making is more of a national responsibility. States are severely constrained in making fiscal policy because they must have balanced budgets every year (unlike the national government, which may run deficits to stimulate the economy). Monetary policy is entirely the domain of the national government.

Interest groups constitute another important player in shaping policy, although those advocating for social policy are not as influential as groups focusing on business, labor, the environment, or gun ownership. A major exception is AARP, a highly powerful lobby that addresses policy issues affecting the elderly (see Chapter 9). AARP has had an especially strong voice on behalf of Social Security and Medicare.

Many other interest groups and think tanks work on behalf of the poor, the homeless, and other disadvantaged people, but Washington is generally less responsive to their concerns because these groups are not politically powerful. The poor tend not to vote or donate money to political campaigns. Many politicians in Washington care deeply about issues concerning poverty, homelessness, and other social-policy problems, but the interest groups and think tanks that try to focus politicians' attention on these issues face a particularly difficult task because of the relatively disadvantaged position of the people they represent.

Alternative perspectives on the policy-making process

The "stages model" of policy making described earlier is a pretty basic description of the process. Several elaborations and extensions provide a more nuanced understanding of the process.[20] For example, the first two steps, problem recognition and agenda setting, were conceptualized by John Kingdon as multiple streams of problems, politics, and policies. These three streams are independent and may or may not intersect. Objective conditions may or may not turn into problems. For example, the abuse of opioid painkillers has been evident for many years. But the death of the musician Prince called attention to this condition and turned it into a problem that policy makers felt more pressure to address. There are typically various policy options available to address any given problem, but whether or not policy makers act on them depends on either the presence of a policy entrepreneur who pushes for change or, more broadly, the occurrence of a political change that creates a "policy window"—an opportunity to implement the policy. Political change may occur thanks to a change in the national mood, interest group pressure, or an administrative or legislative change in control.[21] All this is to say that agenda setting and eventually passing a law are not as linear and static as implied by the basic stages model.

Frank R. Baumgartner and Bryan D. Jones provide additional insight into *how* policy change happens with their "punctuated equilibrium" model. They argue that the policy process features long periods of incremental change punctuated by brief periods of major policy change. Change comes about when an alternative "policy image" can expand an issue beyond the control of the policy specialists who resist change. For example, the Affordable Care Act (ACA) overcame decades of resistance to major change in health insurance by emphasizing a policy image that focused on the millions of Americans who did not have insurance.[22]

One final question about the policy-making process concerns policy diffusion: Why do some policies quickly spread across the country while others are adopted in only a few states? The idea that states are "laboratories of democracy" is an invitation to explore that variation. One comprehensive study took up the challenge and examined 130 policy innovations, explaining the relative rates of diffusion by the type of policy, the involvement of interest groups, and the level of government attention. For example, the Amber Alert child abduction notification system that was adopted in more than 30 states in less than six years is an example of a "policy outbreak" that quickly spread across the states (and now exists in all 50 states).[23] And an analysis of anti-smoking policy found that learning from early adopters, economic competition between proximate cities, imitation of larger cities, and coercion from state governments all explained whether or not a city adopted an anti-smoking policy.[24]

"Why Should I Care?"

Understanding the role of the "key players" is obviously important for understanding how social policy is made. However, it is also important for a reason more directly linked to this class: the policy section of the book allows you to pull together all the material that you learned earlier in the semester. Now that you understand the role of Congress, the president, the bureaucracy, parties, and interest groups, this discussion of how these key players influence the policy-making process should make sense to you.

EXPLAIN THE MAIN PURPOSES OF GOVERNMENT INVOLVEMENT IN THE ECONOMY AND HOW FISCAL, MONETARY, AND REGULATORY POLICIES INFLUENCE THE ECONOMY

Economic policy

Here we take a closer look at the goals and theories that influence specific economic policies passed by the government. We also examine the trade-offs among various goals.

Goals of economic policy

Policy makers have specific goals in mind when they try to influence the economy. Many seem obvious, such as full employment (it's better to have more people working than not working), but others may be less clear. Also, it is difficult to pursue all the goals simultaneously because there are trade-offs among some of them.

Full Employment Employment seems like a good starting point for a healthy economy. If people have jobs, they pay taxes and do not depend directly on the government for support. Despite this, **full employment** was not an explicit goal of economic policy until 1946, when Congress passed the Employment Act. Leaders were concerned that with millions of World War II veterans returning and the wartime economy gearing down, the nation might slide back into the **economic depression** that had created so much hardship in the 1930s. Although the act was largely symbolic (it did not create a guaranteed right to employment), it did create the **Council of Economic Advisers (CEA)**, which provides the president with economic information and advice. A more concrete effort to ensure that returning veterans could find jobs was the 1944 Servicemen's Readjustment Act (the GI Bill). By the time this law expired in 1956, it had provided higher education assistance and low-interest home mortgages for millions of veterans. Today the government seeks to support the creation of as many jobs as possible by maintaining a strong economy.

Stable Prices The importance of price stability is not as obvious as the need for jobs. Why are rising prices—**inflation**—a problem? (See Figure 14.1.) This is a common

full employment
The theoretical point at which all citizens who want to be employed have a job.

economic depression
A deep, widespread downturn in the economy, like the Great Depression of the 1930s.

Council of Economic Advisers (CEA)
A group of economic advisers, created by the Employment Act of 1946, that provides objective data on the state of the economy and makes economic policy recommendations to the president.

inflation
The increase in the price of consumer goods over time.

Inflation and Unemployment, 1960–2020

FIGURE 14.1

The Misery Index is the sum of the unemployment rate and the inflation rate. Which periods have had the highest misery rate since 1960? Were there any external explanations for the high misery rate? How did the government respond to the high levels of unemployment and inflation?

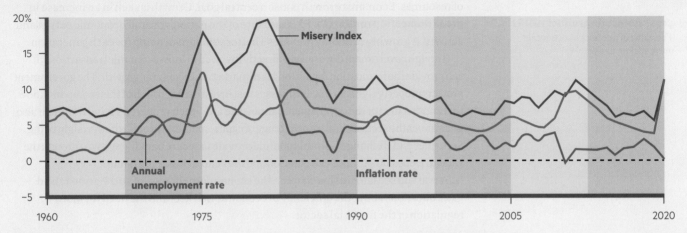

Source: Data from the U.S. Department of Labor, Bureau of Labor Statistics, www.bls.gov (accessed 7/13/20).

question during periods of low inflation. Especially for workers who have automatic raises (cost of living adjustments, or COLAs) as part of their basic pay package, moderate inflation isn't much of a problem. For example, if your rent goes up 4 percent, the price of groceries goes up 3 percent, and you get a 4 percent raise, you will probably be at least as well-off as you were in the previous year.

However, high inflation can have serious effects on the economy. First, some people will experience an erosion of their purchasing power. If your rent goes up by 10 percent and groceries go up by 15 percent, but your pay goes up by only 4 percent, you will be substantially worse off. Second, high inflation penalizes savers as inflation outstrips savings interest rates (so savings are worth *less* over time). On the other hand, inflation may benefit debtors, because people can repay their debts with dollars that are worth less in the future. Finally, long-term economic planning by businesses becomes more difficult when inflation is high: investors will demand high interest rates to compensate for the added risk of future inflation, and businesses will be reluctant to accept loans at these rates.

As counterintuitive as it may sound, *falling* prices, or **deflation**, may be equally as devastating for an economy as prices that are rising too quickly. During the Great Depression, prices fell by 10 percent each year from 1930 to 1933. This trend exacerbated the depression as businesses made less money, wages fell (for those who were still working), production fell, and real debt increased. American policy makers were concerned about possible deflation after the Great Recession of 2008–2009, but those fears subsided as inflation remained at a low level.[25]

Typically, unemployment and inflation are not high at the same time, so there can be a trade-off in focusing on one or the other in economic policy. There tend to be basic partisan differences on the goals of full employment and stable prices, with Democrats being more concerned about employment and Republicans more concerned about inflation. This is no surprise, given the Democratic Party's base of support within labor unions and blue-collar workers and the Republican Party's stronger support on Wall Street and with investors whose income is likely to be eroded by high inflation.

deflation
A decrease in the general prices of goods and services.

gross domestic product (GDP)
The value of a country's economic output taken as a whole.

Promoting the Free Market and Growth The American economy is a capitalist system, which means that most economic decisions are voluntarily made between individuals and firms for their mutual benefit. The government generally stays out of most economic activity, except to regulate the market when it produces too much of something that is not in the public's interest, such as pollution or unsafe products. Economists tout the advantage of the free market as promoting the most efficient use of resources. Economic growth is also a central goal. Growth is seen in an increase in **gross domestic product (GDP)**, a measure of the nation's overall economic output and activity. A growing economy provides a better standard of living for each generation.

Though government does not get directly involved in most economic transactions, it can provide the foundation for a strong free market and economic growth. The government protects property rights so that businesses that invest in the growth of their company know that another firm or the government cannot take away their property. The government also guarantees the security and transparency of capital markets through the oversight of the Securities and Exchange Commission and provides a secure banking system through the Federal Deposit Insurance Corporation and the Federal Reserve System.

As we will see later in this chapter, the economic meltdown of 2008–2009 raised basic questions about the efficiency of economic markets and the need for more regulation of the financial sector.

balanced budget
A spending plan in which the government's expenditures are equal to its revenue.

budget deficit
The amount by which a government's spending in a given fiscal year exceeds its revenue.

Balanced Budgets Maintaining a **balanced budget** has been a central economic goal since the 1980s, when **budget deficits** skyrocketed (see Nuts & Bolts 14.1). However, because of the need to address the deepest recessions since the 1930s, first the 2008–2009 recession and then the 2020 COVID-19 recession, this has been more of a theoretical goal than a practical one. Yet, in the long term, large deficits (the deficit for fiscal year 2020 was $3.1 trillion) are a concern for several reasons. First, the debt accumulated over years of running budget deficits takes a big bite out of current spending. About $390 billion, or 8.7 percent, of the 2019 fiscal year budget is for financing the federal debt.[26] These dollars

NUTS & BOLTS 14.1

Deficits and Debt

Budget deficits and the federal debt are related concepts that are easily confused.

- A *budget deficit* occurs when tax revenue is not sufficient to cover government spending in a given year. If tax revenue is higher than spending, then there is a budget surplus.
- The *federal debt* is the total accumulation of all outstanding borrowing by the government.
- The concepts of deficit and debt are related because when the government runs a deficit it must borrow money to cover the gap. This borrowing then builds up the federal debt.

Source: Compiled by the authors.

"Why Should I Care?" You can think of this in terms of your own spending habits. Any time you spend more money in a given month than you earn, you are running a deficit. You must borrow money to make up that deficit from a bank, from your parents, or by running up the balance on your credit card. The accumulated sum of your monthly deficits is the total debt that you owe. However, there is one obvious point that should be made: you cannot print your own money, unlike the government!

went to people and financial institutions that earn interest on the money that they loaned to the federal government; this money did not pay for a single uniform for a soldier, highway exit ramp, or student loan. Second, the total federal debt is a burden on future generations. Each man, woman, and child in the United States in effect carries more than $57,000 of federal debt (total debt has grown steadily; see What Do the Facts Say?).

However, as we discuss below in the section on fiscal policy, deficit spending is sometimes necessary to stimulate the economy during a recession. When there is slack in the economy, the negative effects of too much government borrowing will not be as significant, especially if the debt is funded by foreign investors or the Federal Reserve (Modern Monetary Theory suggests that the latter approach can be pursued with no negative consequences in an economic downturn).[27]

Tools and theories of economic policy

Now that we know the key players in economic policy and their goals, it is time to examine the tools those policy makers use to accomplish those goals. Policy makers cannot pull levers and push buttons to achieve desired outcomes, nor are they immune from external forces that can sink the economy despite their best efforts. However, leaders can do certain things to move the massive U.S. economy in the right direction.

Fiscal Policy Fiscal policy is the use of the government's taxing and spending power to influence the direction of the economy. Developed by economist John Maynard Keynes in the 1930s, **Keynesian economics** argues that policy makers can soften the effects of a recession by stimulating the economy when overall demand is low— during a recession, when people aren't spending much—through tax cuts or increased government spending. Tax cuts put more money in people's pockets, enabling them to spend more than they otherwise would. The government can also inject money into the economy by purchasing various goods, such as highways or military equipment, or by issuing direct payments to individuals, such as unemployment compensation. From this perspective, it is acceptable to run budget deficits to increase employment and national income, which in turn gives a short-term boost to the economy. Keynes also pointed out that if overall demand is too high, which might result in inflation, policy makers should cool off the economy by cutting spending or raising taxes.[28]

A competing theory of fiscal policy was the basis for Ronald Reagan's tax cuts in 1981 and has been the centerpiece of economic policy for many Republicans since then. **Supply-side economics** focuses on the effects of tax policy and regulations on the labor supply (how much people work) rather than their effects on overall demand (how much people spend). The idea is that if tax rates are too high, people will work less because a large percentage of their income goes to the government.

However, when the Reagan administration cut taxes in 1981, with the top marginal rate (the income tax rate paid on the top slice of earned income) going from 70 to 50 percent, revenue fell and budget deficits exploded. Supporters of the supply-side theory argued that the problem was on the spending side of the equation rather than on the tax revenue side. That is, deficits went up because the Democratic Congress spent too much, not because of Reagan's tax cuts. However, both tax revenue and government spending as a share of the overall economy fell during the Reagan presidency, which suggests that spending was not the source of the budget deficits in the 1980s.[29] A similar relationship between a cut in tax rates and a decline in revenue was observed after Bush's tax cuts in 2001 and Trump's tax cuts in 2017.[30] The latter are a good example of supply-side thinking because clearly the tax cut could not be justified on Keynesian grounds, given that the economy was moderately growing and at full employment at the time of the tax cuts.

Keynesian economics
The theory that governments should use economic policy, like taxing and spending, to maintain stability in the economy.

supply-side economics
The theory that lower tax rates will stimulate the economy by encouraging people to save, invest, and produce more goods and services.

No nation has ever taxed itself into prosperity.

—**Rush Limbaugh,** conservative radio host

Are Deficits and the National Debt out of Control?

Economic policy is difficult for most American to understand. Even something as basic as the implications of the size of the federal debt can be difficult to grasp, especially when dueling headlines say, "National Debt: Will It Destroy America's Economy?"[a] and "Debt? What Debt? At $22 Trillion, Here's the Argument the National Debt Doesn't Matter."[b]

Being a good consumer of media can help you sort out the dueling headlines. Is the claim too simple? Will national debt really destroy our economy? Does it really not matter at all? In both of those cases, the claims are too extreme and therefore too simple. If an explanation is too simple, it means that it is ignoring the complexity of the issue. Too much debt can create certain problems for the economy, but in some circumstances, such as a deep recession, taking on more debt may be necessary.

Often this type of over-the-top headline can be clickbait to get you to read the article. You should read such pieces with a healthy dose of skepticism. Another tip for being a good consumer of economic news is to seek out trusted government sources, such as the Congressional Budget Office, or bipartisan organizations, such as the Committee for a Responsible Federal Budget (see its recent article "Why Should We Worry about the National Debt?").[c] These sources are less likely to rely on simple arguments and will provide reliable facts to support an argument. For example, look at the two figures below. The first shows the budget deficit, which can look extreme out of context. The second figure shows the percentage of the GDP that that deficit represents. What do the facts say? Which headline is right?

Budget Deficits

Note: Deficits include the Social Security Trust Fund. 2020 data reflect pre-pandemic projections, not actual figures.

Source: Congressional Budget Office, Budget Projections, various documents from www.cbo.gov/topics/budget (accessed 6/1/20).

Think about it

- **Economists argue that debt** becomes a potentially serious problem when it is as big as the overall economy. Have we ever hit that level since 1940?
- **After examining these data,** do you think the United States' budget deficits are out of control? Why or why not?

How Much Can Fiscal Policy Really Affect the Economy? Economists continue to debate the extent to which fiscal policy can influence the economy. Two factors have limited the effectiveness of fiscal policy. First, fiscal policies often cannot be implemented quickly enough to have the intended impact on the **business cycle**—the normal expansion and contraction of the economy. This is especially true when one party controls Congress and the other controls the presidency, but it can also be the case even during unified government. The $787 billion American Recovery and Reinvestment Act of 2009, designed to stimulate the economy and create jobs after the 2008 economic crisis, encountered problems along these lines. Although the legislation had a limited immediate impact on the economy, it is impossible to spend that much money (or implement tax cuts) without some time lag. Republicans criticized Democrats, who controlled Congress and the presidency at the time, for spending too much money and not enacting policies that would have had a more immediate effect (such as payroll tax cuts). Critics on the left, meanwhile, argued that the stimulus wasn't big enough.

Second, on the other side of the Keynesian coin, tax increases or spending cuts during good economic times are much more difficult to implement than tax cuts or spending increases, which are more politically popular. After all, politicians do not like to raise taxes or cut spending. Furthermore, even if politicians *wanted* to cut spending to influence the economy or to reduce the federal deficit, it is becoming increasingly difficult to do so because a growing portion of the federal budget is devoted to **mandatory spending**—that is, entitlements such as Social Security, which must be spent by law, and interest on the federal debt, which must be paid (if the United States defaulted on its debt, there would be an international economic meltdown). In order for Congress to balance the budget and eliminate the deficit ($3.1 trillion in 2020), it would have to cut all **discretionary spending**—spending that can be cut from the budget without changing the underlying law. Discretionary spending, currently $1.3 trillion in non-defense spending and $700 billion in defense spending, accounts for everything other than entitlements and interest on the debt. But even if Congress eliminated 100 percent of this spending, it would still be $1.1 trillion short of balancing the budget.[31] (See Figure 14.2.)

business cycle
The normal pattern of expansion and contraction of the economy.

mandatory spending
Expenditures that are required by law, such as the funding for Social Security.

discretionary spending
Expenditures that can be cut from the budget without changing the underlying law, which is everything other than defense, entitlements, and interest on the debt.

**FIGURE
14.2**

Mandatory and Discretionary Spending, 1970–2030

The percentage of the budget allocated for discretionary spending has been shrinking since the 1970s. What implications does this have for members of Congress and the president as they try to reduce the federal deficits?

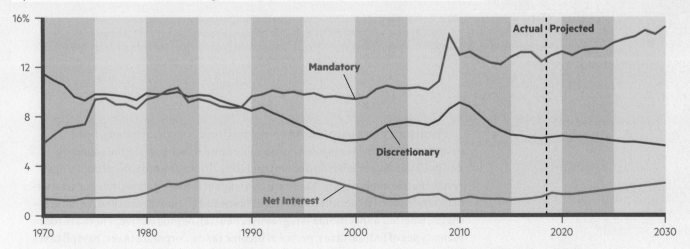

Source: Congressional Budget Office, *The Budget and Economic Outlook: 2020 to 2030*, January 2020, www.cbo.gov/publication/56073 (accessed 7/13/20).

FIGURE
14.3

Federal Revenues and Spending, 1962 and 2019

A much larger share of tax revenue comes from payroll taxes than was true in the 1960s. What implications does this have for the redistributive nature of federal taxes? What have been the biggest changes since the 1960s in the way the federal tax dollar is spent? Are these trends likely to reverse or continue in the next 30 years?

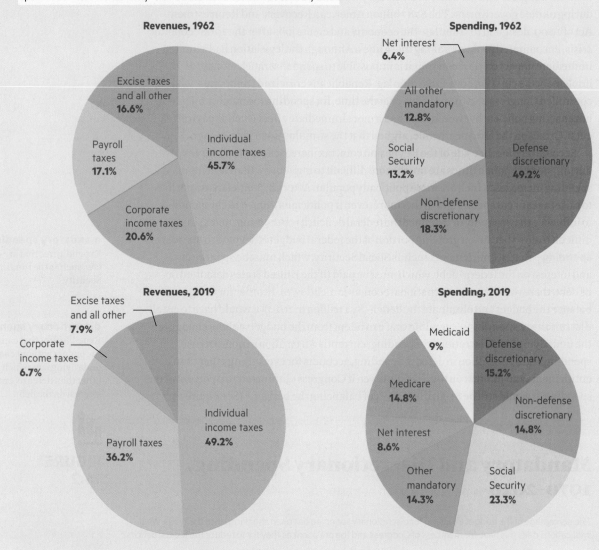

Revenues, 1962

- Excise taxes and all other **16.6%**
- Payroll taxes **17.1%**
- Corporate income taxes **20.6%**
- Individual income taxes **45.7%**

Spending, 1962

- Net interest **6.4%**
- All other mandatory **12.8%**
- Social Security **13.2%**
- Non-defense discretionary **18.3%**
- Defense discretionary **49.2%**

Revenues, 2019

- Excise taxes and all other **7.9%**
- Corporate income taxes **6.7%**
- Payroll taxes **36.2%**
- Individual income taxes **49.2%**

Spending, 2019

- Medicaid **9%**
- Medicare **14.8%**
- Net interest **8.6%**
- Other mandatory **14.3%**
- Defense discretionary **15.2%**
- Non-defense discretionary **14.8%**
- Social Security **23.3%**

Source: The Tax Foundation, "Federal Tax Revenue by Source, 1934–2018," Table 2, https://taxfoundation.org/federal-tax-revenue-source-1934-2018/#per; Mindy R. Levit, D. Andrew Austin, and Jeffrey M. Stupak, "Mandatory Spending Since 1962," Congressional Research Service, March 18, 2015, https://fas.org/sgp/crs/misc/RL33074.pdf; Congressional Budget Office, "The Federal Budget in 2019: An Infographic," April 15, 2020, www.cbo.gov/publication/56324 (all accessed 9/21/20).

Fiscal policy may have a relatively modest impact on the economy, but it determines how the tax burden is distributed and which parts of the economy and policy areas benefit from federal spending. In other words, fiscal policy has *redistributive* implications. There are two ways of thinking about the characteristics of federal taxes: (1) the different types of taxes and (2) their redistributive nature—that is, whether a specific tax is regressive, neutral, or progressive. There are four major types of federal taxes: personal income taxes, corporate taxes, payroll taxes (for Social Security and Medicare), and excise taxes (such as taxes on cigarettes, alcohol, gasoline, air travel, and telephone lines). Figure 14.3 shows how the distribution of tax revenue changed between 1962 and 2019. The proportion of personal income taxes held fairly steady, but excise taxes and corporate taxes fell and payroll taxes more than doubled.

The increasing share of revenue that comes from payroll taxes has important implications for the redistributive nature of taxes. Payroll taxes are **regressive** because everyone who works pays the same rate of 6.2 percent, up to a certain income level ($137,700 in 2020; also, all workers pay an additional 1.45 percent on all income to support Medicare). Thus, someone who earns $137,700 pays the same *amount* of Social Security tax ($8,537) as a wealthy individual such as Bill Gates does, but the tax represents a much larger share of the lesser-paid person's income than it does of Gates's. Income taxes, in contrast, are **progressive**: upper-income people pay a larger portion of their income in taxes than low-income people do.

One criticism of Donald Trump's tax cut was that a disproportionate share of the cuts went to the wealthiest people in the country, making taxes less progressive. This may make sense from one perspective, given that the bottom 45 percent of taxpayers do not pay any personal income tax because of the standard deduction (which was $24,800 for married couples and $12,400 for individuals in 2020) and the Earned Income Tax Credit. However, poor and lower-middle-income people do pay a large share of the total payroll tax. Thus, the top quintile of the income distribution earned 55 percent of the total income and paid 70 percent of all income taxes but only 40 percent of payroll taxes.[32] So income tax cuts will help wealthier people because they pay most of the income tax, whereas payroll tax cuts will help poor and middle-income people more. At the same time, the top marginal tax rate is close to the lowest it has been since the 1920s (see Figure 14.4). As a result, the overall personal income tax rate for the

regressive
Describes taxes that take a larger share of poor people's income than wealthy people's income, such as sales taxes and payroll taxes.

progressive
Describes taxes that require upper-income people to pay a higher tax rate than lower-income people, such as income taxes.

DID YOU KNOW?

45%
of Americans pay no income tax.
Source: Tax Policy Center

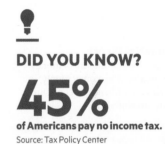

FIGURE 14.4

Top Marginal Tax Rates, 1915–2020

The top marginal tax rate, which is the tax rate paid by the richest Americans on their income above some threshold ($518,400 in 2020 for a single taxpayer), declined from 94 percent in 1945 to 35 percent in 2012, rose back up to 39.6 percent in 2013, and then fell back down to 37 percent in 2018, where it remained in 2019 and 2020. What are the arguments for and against increasing the top marginal tax rate?

Sources: Data from the Internal Revenue Service, "SOI Tax Stats–Historical Table 23," www.irs.gov/statistics/soi-tax-stats-historical-table-23 (accessed 9/17/20); 2008–2020 rates from www.irs.gov (accessed 7/13/20).

top 1 percent of the income distribution dropped from 40 percent in 1945 to 26 percent in 2015. This lower overall tax rate for the wealthy is also explained by the lower 15 percent rate for capital gains and dividends.[33]

Monetary Policy and the Federal Reserve System Monetary policy includes influencing interest rates and the money supply and regulating the lending activity of banks. The Federal Reserve Act of 1913 established the Federal Reserve System to bring stability and continuity to the nation's banking system. The chair, vice-chair, and five other governors serve on the Federal Reserve Board. The board is responsible for establishing monetary policy for the nation. There are 12 regional Federal Reserve Banks, more than 3,000 member banks, and about 17,000 other depository institutions (which include nonmember commercial banks, savings and loan associations, savings banks, and credit unions).[34] The Fed monitors levels of bank lending, the money supply, and interest rates. Bank lending is important for economic growth because businesses borrow money to expand, and as they grow they add jobs. If credit is tight and businesses cannot borrow money, economic growth will suffer, as became painfully evident in late 2008 and 2009.

The money supply is also central to economic growth and directly related to levels of lending activity. The Fed can influence the amount of money in the system by making it easier or harder for banks to lend money. According to the **monetarist theory**, the amount of money in circulation is the most important determinant of economic activity and inflation. If too much money is chasing too few goods, there could be inflationary pressure on the economy and prices might rise too quickly.[35] In contrast, if there isn't enough money available, a recession could occur.

Perhaps the most obvious targets of monetary policy are interest rates. Changing interest rates affects the economy by making borrowing money either less or more expensive. Businesses and consumers are more likely to borrow if the interest rate is 5 percent than if it is 10 percent. Consumer purchases of big-ticket items—things that are financed by borrowing rather than being purchased with cash—also increase when interest rates are low. These purchases dry up when interest rates are high. That is why so many appliance stores and car dealers advertise: "Zero dollars down, and zero percent interest until next January!" Entire sectors of the economy, such as housing, construction, consumer durables, and cars, are very sensitive to interest rates.

What can the Fed do to meet its targets on credit availability, the money supply, and interest rates? It uses three central tools of monetary policy. The first tool, the **reserve requirement**, is the most potentially powerful tool for affecting the availability of credit: banks are required to have a certain amount of money in reserve to ensure they have cash on hand to cover withdrawals. By simply changing the amount of money that banks are required to hold for every deposit, the Fed can significantly influence the amount of money that those institutions can lend. However, because changing the reserve requirement has such a powerful impact on the economy, the Fed has rarely used this tool.[36] But in March 2020, in response to the massive unemployment caused by the COVID-19 pandemic, the Fed dropped the reserve requirement to zero for the first time in the nation's history. The rate had been unchanged since 1992, when it was reduced from 12 percent to 10 percent. *Forbes* published an article headlined "The Fed Fires 'the Big One,'" along with a picture of a mushroom cloud, indicating the dramatic nature of the move.[37]

The second monetary-policy tool, interest rates, is more difficult to manage than the reserve requirement. With the reserve requirement, the Fed simply announces the change in the rate. With interest rates, there is only one rate—the **discount rate**—that the Fed directly sets. This is the rate the Fed charges to member banks for short-term

monetarist theory
The idea that the amount of money in circulation (the money supply) is the primary influence on economic activity and inflation.

It is well enough that people of the nation do not understand our banking and monetary system, for if they did, I believe there would be a revolution before tomorrow morning.

—**Henry Ford,** founder of Ford Motor Company

reserve requirement
The minimum amount of money that a bank is required to have on hand to back up its assets.

discount rate
The interest rate that a bank must pay on a short-term loan from the Federal Reserve Bank.

loans. However, it is far less important as a policy tool than the **federal funds rate (FFR)**, the rate that member banks charge one another on overnight loans, which are short-term loans that banks use to meet their reserve requirements. Beginning in 1995, the FFR has been the central interest rate target for the Fed.[38] The FFR is set by the demand for overnight loans that are necessary to settle accounts, but the Fed greatly affects those rates.

Despite the Fed's ability to influence short-term interest rates, it has only an indirect impact on long-term interest rates, including consumer rates such as those for mortgages, car loans, and student loans. Long-term rates are set by the market. If an investor thinks that inflation will increase from 3 percent to 6 percent over the next five years, he or she will demand a higher interest rate for lending money to the government or a corporation than if the investor thinks inflation will hold steady at about 3 percent.

The third tool the Fed uses to meet its monetary targets is **open market operations**—the buying and selling of securities. This is the Fed's most important tool because it influences the FFR and the level of bank reserves—and thus the money supply. If the Fed wants to increase the money supply and put downward pressure on the FFR, it will purchase securities such as government bonds from a bank. The bank gives the Fed its bonds, and the Fed deposits the appropriate amount of money into the bank's account at the Fed. The bank can use this money to support new loans. Open market operations may also serve to contract the money supply or raise interest rates; if this is the desired outcome, the Fed will sell government securities. The member bank will give the Fed money to cover the cost of the bond and therefore take money out of circulation.

One example of when new money was desperately needed in the economy was the "credit crunch" that emerged with the meltdown of the subprime mortgage market and related problems in the bond markets in 2008. Fed chair Ben Bernanke responded by "flooding the street with money," as the famous banker Benjamin Strong had advocated as the appropriate response to the Great Depression.[39] The Fed increased its assets from $927 billion on September 10, 2008, to what seemed like an eye-popping $2.26 trillion by November 11, 2008. Assets held by the Fed, mostly government securities and mortgage-backed securities, peaked at $4.5 trillion in October 2015

federal funds rate (FFR)
The interest rate that a bank must pay on an overnight loan from another bank.

open market operations
The process by which the Federal Reserve System buys and sells securities to influence the money supply.

U.S. Federal Reserve chair Jerome Powell testifies before a congressional panel in the midst of the COVID-19 pandemic in 2020, offering insight into how long it will take the U.S. economy to recover from the COVID-induced recession.

and then fell a bit until the record-breaking purchase of assets starting in March 2020. As of mid-July 2020, the Fed's balance sheet increased another *$3 trillion* to just over $7 trillion![40] These unprecedented interventions in the financial sector prevented more serious crises and deeper recessions, but critics argue that the Fed has become a too powerful, unaccountable player in economic policy making.

One crucial characteristic of the Fed is its political independence: its decisions are not subject to presidential or congressional review. A strong indication of the Fed's independence is that presidents typically reappoint chairs who were initially appointed by presidents of the other party.[41] For example, Ben Bernanke was nominated by Bush and renominated by Obama for one term. However, Trump broke that tradition by replacing Janet Yellen with Jerome Powell. But the Fed is not immune to political influence. In fact, one line of research argues that the Fed tries to help presidents during reelection years by encouraging a pro-growth economy.[42] Evidence on this point is mixed, but at a minimum presidents do have the ability to make it clear when they disagree with the Fed's policies. Presidents also have the opportunity to appoint the chair and vice-chair of the Fed, but presidents usually go for continuity over change because they do not want to upset the financial markets. Other research has shown that the Fed is at least somewhat sensitive to the preferences of the president and Congress, who may publicly criticize the Fed when they disagree with its policies.[43] For example, in the early days of the pandemic, President Trump threatened to demote Powell, saying he was "not happy with the Fed" because it was "following" and "we should be leading."[44] Shortly after these comments, the Fed took more aggressive action to address the economic downturn.

The Fed's ultimate accountability is to Congress, because if things really got out of hand—for example, if the Fed were to increase interest rates to 20 percent without good reason—Congress could amend the Federal Reserve Act and remove the Fed's responsibility or autonomy in specific areas. The Fed must report to Congress annually on its activities and to the Banking Committees of Congress twice a year on its plans for monetary policy. The Fed's annual report is subject to an outside audit. Fed officials also frequently testify before Congress on a range of issues.

Regulatory Policy Government regulation has a huge impact on the economy. For example, the federal government regulates the quality of food and water, the safety of workplaces and airspaces, and the integrity of the banking and finance system. In general, regulations address market failures such as monopolies and imperfect information. There are two main types of regulation: economic and social. Economic regulation sets prices or conditions for entry of firms into an industry, whereas social regulation addresses issues of quality and safety.[45] Both types influence the economy.

A common type of economic regulation involves price regulation of monopolies. A monopoly occurs when a single firm controls the entire market for a product and thus is not subject to competition. In this event, the firm with the monopoly could charge extremely high prices if the government did not regulate it. Concern about this type of behavior led to the Interstate Commerce Act (1887), which created the Interstate Commerce Commission to regulate railroad rates, and the Sherman Antitrust Act (1890), which served to break up Standard Oil in 1910, among other monopolies. More common than a true monopoly are firms that control most of a market rather than all of it and start acting like a monopoly. In such cases, the government will try to make sure that free market forces continue to operate and the monopoly-like companies cannot jack up prices. For example, Microsoft was sued by the Justice Department and 19 states in 1998 for trying to quash its competition in the rapidly growing area of Internet browsers. In a more recent similar case, the European Union fined Google three different times—first, $2.7 billion in 2017 for illegally steering users toward its comparative shopping site; then, $5 billion in 2018 for forcing Android phones to install the Google search app and the Chrome Web browser; and finally, $1.7 billion in 2019 for using its online advertising to limit its rivals from working with companies that had deals with Google.[46]

The most common market failures that lead to social regulation occur when the costs of a firm's behavior are not entirely borne by the firm and are passed on to other people. The classic example is pollution. In a free market, the owners of a coal-fired power plant do not bear the cost of the pollution spewing out of its smokestacks; instead, the people who live downwind from the plant bear the cost. Therefore, the power plant owners have little incentive to curb pollution unless a government agency, like the Environmental Protection Agency (EPA), regulates it. Other examples of agencies that set social regulations are those that promote safety, such as the National Highway Traffic Safety Administration, the Consumer Product Safety Commission, and the Occupational Safety and Health Administration. Carbon emissions are another good example of a product (carbon) that would be overproduced by the market if there were no regulations.

Regulatory policy also involves interbranch politics between Congress and the bureaucracy. Even when members of Congress agree on a general policy goal—for example, limiting air pollution—they often cannot agree on the precise mechanisms for achieving that goal, so they delegate authority to a regulatory agency. As discussed in Chapter 12, this produces a "principal–agent problem" in which Congress (the principal) cannot be sure that the bureaucracy (the agent) will implement policy according to its legislative goals. Another area in which regulatory policy has generated political heat concerns the debate about the trade-off between regulation and economic growth. Regulations impose costs on the free market, which may limit job growth. The Trump administration moved aggressively to limit regulations and allow the free market to make more decisions. Nonetheless, some environmentalists have learned that using market principles can work to their advantage, as the example of grazing rights in the West shows (see the Take a Stand feature).

Thus, while political debates over regulatory policy can still be intense, common ground may be found in pursuing market solutions to regulatory problems. In general, the public interest is often served by regulations that protect the environment, ensure the safety of the food supply, and regulate the dumping of hazardous chemicals, whether it is through traditional economic regulations or market approaches. In each instance, *politics* defines how the public interest is served through regulation.

Grazing Rights and Free Market Environmentalism

Grazing rights, environmental policy, and control of western lands have been controversial for decades. The issue received attention in the 2016 presidential campaign when Senator Marco Rubio said that "the federal government controls far too much land in the western parts of the United States," indicating that he favors transferring some federal lands to the states.[a] The federal government owns more than 600 million acres, including 47 percent of the land in western states, and there are intense disagreements between environmentalists and ranchers, loggers, and miners about how those lands should be used.

There are three basic positions on this issue: the pro-business and antiregulation stance (ranchers, loggers), the pro-environment regulatory approach (conservationists and recreational users), and a middle ground called free market environmentalism that attempts to find free market solutions to protect the environment.

The scenario that you have to consider here is an actual case publicized in a *New York Times* op-ed piece.[b] The case involves a fifth-generation rancher in southern Utah named Dell LeFevre. He is no friend of environmentalism, saying, "We've got easterners who don't know the land telling us what to do with it. I am a bitter old cowboy." His bitterness was deepened back in 1991 when he found two dozen of his cows shot to death. He thinks the deed was done by an environmentalist who was trying to get ranchers to leave a scenic part of the Escalante River canyon. So LeFevre seems to be an unlikely candidate to have sat down with an environmentalist named Bill Hedden to accomplish that very goal of ending ranching in the area. Hedden works for a group called the Grand Canyon Trust (GCT) that, as the *New York Times* article explained, "doesn't use lobbyists or lawsuits (or guns) to drive out ranchers. These environmentalists get land the old-fashioned way. They buy it." The GCT spent about $100,000 to buy and retire the grazing rights from LeFevre for this scenic canyon area. The environmentalists are happy because the vegetation is coming back, and LeFevre is happy because he doesn't have to battle the environmentalists anymore and was able to buy grazing rights in a different area that is better for his cattle. Supporters of "free market environmentalism" say this is a perfect example of allowing the market to determine the best use of the land.

The pro-business approach. If the story ended here, there would be no controversy. But local groups, such as the Canyon Country Rural Alliance, which opposed all limitations on ranchers' grazing rights, lobbied Congress and the Interior

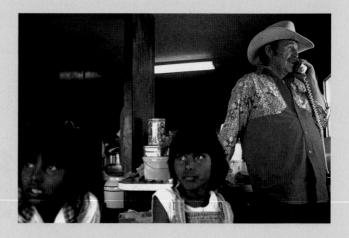

Rancher Dell LeFevre and two of his children.

Department to disallow arrangements that remove grazing rights from some public lands. Bowing to pressure, the Interior Department decided that "only Congress may permanently exclude lands from grazing use," so the GCT had no guarantee that the Bureau of Land Management would not change its mind and allow grazing. The process of resolving this conflict bounced around the Interior Department and the federal courts for nearly 10 years.

The free market environmental compromise. GCT members went to plan B: they decided to become ranchers. If the Interior Department wouldn't grant permanent conservation use permits on land designated for grazing, they would buy some cattle. The GCT is now one of the largest ranchers in the Colorado Plateau, with 1,000 acres of private land and grazing permits that cover 860,000 acres of federal and state lands, including a large part of the Kaibab National Forest adjacent to the North Rim of the Grand Canyon. It is managing the land in an eco-friendly manner with only 800 head of cattle. Though it may seem odd that an environmental group had to take up ranching to get the policy outcome it wanted, this compromise made all sides of the dispute relatively happy. As one opponent of the GCT put it, "We turned them from environmentalists into cowboys. I guess what they can do is get their cows and start losing money like the rest of us."[c]

take a stand

1. Do you favor the regulatory approach of permanently removing grazing rights from land that an environmental group would buy, the business approach of not having any permanent limits on grazing rights, or the free market environmental approach of allowing the environmental groups to buy land and grazing rights and become ranchers to protect the land?

2. Does the compromise position in which the GCT took up ranching strike you as a reasonable middle ground? Why or why not?

Putting it all together: the 2008–2009 economic crisis and the 2020 COVID-19 recession

The Economic Crisis The economic meltdown of 2008–2009 is an excellent example of how policy makers respond to a crisis and how they can influence the direction of the economy.

Problems in the subprime, or high-risk, mortgage market; the collapse of housing prices; and the tightening of credit markets had been putting pressure on the economy through the spring and summer of 2008. The first sign of serious trouble came in March, when the New York Federal Reserve loaned $30 billion to JPMorgan Chase to facilitate the buyout of Bear Stearns, an investment bank that was going bankrupt because of its exposure to mortgage-backed securities. Over the next six months, several of the nation's largest financial institutions, such as investment bank Merrill Lynch and the world's largest insurance company, American International Group (AIG), had to be bailed out by the federal government. When investment bank Lehman Brothers went bankrupt and Washington Mutual, the nation's sixth-largest bank, failed, the markets panicked.

This series of disasters and near disasters led to around-the-clock meetings of Fed and Treasury leaders, who produced a plan for the government to buy mortgage-related assets from banks and other financial institutions. A month before the election, after initially rejecting the plan in a stunning rebuke to party leaders and President Bush, Congress passed the $700 billion Troubled Asset Relief Program (TARP) to buy up to $700 billion in bad assets to help stabilize the banks. Despite this significant rescue plan, the crisis spiraled out of control in the following weeks. Stock markets plunged worldwide, with the U.S. stock market shedding 35 percent of its value in the two months after the crisis began. Credit markets remained frozen, and it became clear that an alternative approach was needed. European leaders swiftly agreed to an approach in which governments would directly invest in banks, providing them with desperately needed capital in return for equity stakes in the banks. The United States followed suit with an initial allocation of $250 billion to directly invest in banks, followed by an announcement that the Treasury would abandon its plan to buy toxic debt created by the subprime mortgage mess and to use all the funds to directly invest in banks. By mid-November, the economic panic had eased, but the situation remained fragile.

When President Obama took office in 2009, things were still very grim. Congress acted quickly to pass the Recovery Act, which allocated $831 billion over 10 years, roughly split among tax cuts, federal spending, and support for state and local governments.[47] Stocks finally bottomed in March 2009 (down 56 percent from their October 2007 high), shortly after Treasury Secretary Timothy Geithner announced the administration's Financial Stability Plan. The plan focused on four problems: frozen credit markets, weakened bank capital, a backlog of troubled mortgage assets on bank balance sheets, and falling home prices. Working with the Fed to stabilize the financial markets, the Treasury had largely resolved three of those four problems one year later. Credit markets were operating, and banks were in much better shape, having raised more than $140 billion in capital and $60 billion in unsecured debt. Banks used these funds to repay the Treasury. The Treasury expects to eventually recover all the TARP expenditures (with 96.2 percent recovered as of March 2020).[48] The housing market has also stabilized, with sales up and prices slowly rising in most markets. For several years after, troubled mortgage assets remained on the balance sheets of many banks, but with their stronger base of capital and the strengthened housing market, these securities were in much better shape.[49]

Despite the broad success of the financial rescue, it remained a political liability. The rescue was widely perceived as a bailout of Wall Street. Many citizens were outraged over corporate salaries and bonuses, the government bailouts, and the perception that not

During the financial crisis of 2008–2009, the government had to take unprecedented action to avoid an even deeper crisis. Here, then–Senate Majority Leader Harry Reid (D-NV, center) speaks to reporters. He is joined by other congressional leaders and Ben Bernanke (far right), who was Federal Reserve chairman at the time.

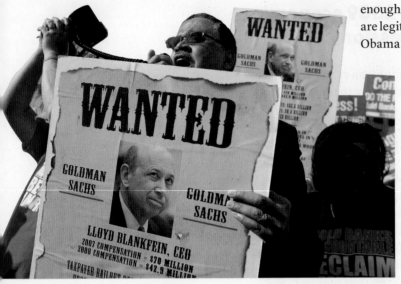

enough was being done to help average Americans. While these are legitimate concerns, the overall response of the Bush and Obama administrations was a textbook example of the use of fiscal policy (the 2008 TARP law and the 2009 Recovery Act) and monetary policy (the various actions by the Fed and Treasury to stabilize the banks) to address an economic crisis.

The COVID-19 Recession The CARES Act discussed in the chapter opener is another great example of fiscal stimulus: when businesses were shutting down, workers were laid off, and millions of people were having a hard time paying their bills, Congress pumped trillions of dollars into the economy. But as with the 2008–2009 recession, Congress needed help from the Treasury and Fed to provide the needed stimulus. For example, the Paycheck Protection Program provided forgivable loans to small businesses to maintain their payroll and hire back employees, and this was supported by a lending facility from the Fed.[50]

Despite this fiscal stimulus, financial markets were disrupted due to economic uncertainty. The Fed responded with aggressive action to buy Treasury securities, stabilizing financial markets, and support the flow of credit in the economy while keeping the federal funds rate close to zero.[51]

Despite all of these steps, early in October Fed chair Jerome Powell warned Congress that the economy could see "tragic" results without additional government support.[52] Joe Biden has promised action early in 2021, but he needs to get the Senate onboard.

Protesters at a rally against government bailouts for Wall Street called for the resignation of the chief executive of Goldman Sachs and cancellation of bonuses for all Goldman employees. Huge profits and bonuses on Wall Street in 2009–2010 were very controversial, as the national unemployment rate held at nearly 10 percent.

"Why Should I Care?"

Tax and spending policy, monetary policy, regulatory policy, and trade have more effect on your everyday life than anything else the government does. From the taxes you pay, to the interest rate on your student loan, to the quality of the air you breathe and the water you drink, to the cheap consumer goods that you are able to buy, decisions by policy makers, the president, Congress, and the Fed have a tremendous effect on your economic world.

★

EXPLAIN WHAT WE MEAN BY SOCIAL POLICY, DISCUSS HOW THE NATIONAL GOVERNMENT'S ROLE IN SOCIAL POLICY HAS EVOLVED, AND ANALYZE THE CURRENT MAJOR AREAS OF SOCIAL POLICY

Social policy

Social policy is generally defined in terms of the "social safety net," or **welfare**, which is financial or other assistance provided to individuals by the government, usually based on need. A broader conception of social policy includes government programs aimed at achieving a general social goal, such as programs that support public education, the income tax deduction for interest paid on home mortgages (to encourage home ownership), or policies designed to promote job creation and growth. This section addresses both types of social policies and also discusses how some traditional social welfare programs such as Social Security are not based on need.

History and context of social policy

First, we'll outline the evolution of social policy in the United States and describe the various types of social policy. It is also important to understand the need for social policy by examining the nature of poverty in the United States.

Historical Overview Early in our nation's history, the federal government took little responsibility for social welfare. Private charities, churches, and families largely took responsibility for the poor and disadvantaged. The first significant social policy appeared in the nineteenth century in the form of federal financial support for Civil War veterans and their families. Between 1880 and 1910, the national government spent more than a quarter of its budget on Civil War pensions and support for veterans' widows.[53] During the recession of the mid-1890s, populist and progressive reformers sought a national system of unemployment compensation, but the desire for such extensive policies was several decades ahead of its time.

Not until the 1930s and Franklin Delano Roosevelt's presidency did the government undertake broad-scale social policies. The stock market crash in 1929 and the ensuing Great Depression created a desperate economic situation for millions of Americans. An immediate concern was to alleviate the suffering caused by unemployment, but FDR also wanted to implement a broader "preventative social policy."[54] Thus, his **New Deal** included the following policies enacted between 1933 and 1935:

- The Agricultural Adjustment Administration provided farmers with much-needed assistance. Farmers were hit hard in the depression when plummeting commodity prices forced many family farms into bankruptcy.
- The National Recovery Administration and Public Works Administration reinvigorated the business sector.
- The Federal Emergency Relief Administration provided $500 million in emergency aid for the poor (about $7 billion in today's dollars).
- Jobs programs such as the Civil Works Administration and Civilian Conservation Corps put more than 2 million people to work. Later the Works Progress Administration, a broader program, employed at least one-third of the nation's unemployed.
- Social Security, including the familiar retirement policy, also supported the states with funds to spend on unemployment compensation, disability programs, and support for dependent children of single mothers. This New Deal–era program was the precursor of the central welfare program, Aid to Families with Dependent Children (AFDC), which existed until 1996.
- The National Labor Relations Act guaranteed the right to organize a union and set regulations for collective bargaining between management and labor.[55]

With these policies, the role of the federal government in social policy was forever changed. Although some aspects of the New Deal, such as the jobs programs, were never repeated on a similarly broad scale, most of its other programs became the cornerstone of social policy for subsequent generations.

The next major expansion of social policy occurred during the **Great Society**, the wide-ranging social agenda promoted by President Lyndon Johnson in the mid-1960s that aimed to improve Americans' quality of life through governmental social programs. In Chapter 5, we discussed one pillar of this social agenda: the civil rights movement, which culminated with the passage of the Civil Rights Act in 1964 and the Voting Rights Act in 1965. The other important aspect of Johnson's Great Society included the War on Poverty and programs concerning health, education, urban redevelopment, and housing. Perhaps most significant was the creation of Medicare,

social policy
An area of public policy related to maintaining or enhancing the well-being of individuals.

welfare
Financial or other assistance provided to individuals by the government, usually based on need.

The test of our progress is not whether we add more to the abundance of those who have much; it is whether we provide enough for those who have too little.

—President Franklin D. Roosevelt

New Deal
The set of policies proposed by President Franklin Roosevelt and enacted by Congress between 1933 and 1935 to promote economic recovery and social welfare during the Great Depression.

Before the New Deal programs in the 1930s, poverty relief was provided mainly by private charities. Here, future First Lady Eleanor Roosevelt serves meals to unemployed women and their children in a New York restaurant.

Great Society
The wide-ranging social agenda promoted by President Lyndon Johnson in the mid-1960s that aimed to improve Americans' quality of life through governmental social programs.

the national program that funds medical care for the elderly, and Medicaid, which funds health care for the poor.[56] By the late 1960s, the mounting costs of the Vietnam War had created a trade-off: it wasn't possible to continue funding both ambitious social programs and the war without causing inflation. In addition, conservative backlash against the "welfare state," especially during the Reagan years (1981–1989), led to cuts in spending on social programs.

President George W. Bush maintained most programs with some cuts and one major expansion—the addition of a prescription benefit to Medicare. As a "compassionate conservative," Bush attempted to place his stamp on American social policy with the idea of an **ownership society**, in which people take more responsibility for their own social welfare. He proposed privatizing part of Social Security and creating private savings accounts to cover more out-of-pocket medical expenses, in combination with more free market forces and a bigger role for private and religious charity. President Obama favored an approach that emphasized the market and community, while preserving an important role for government.

Poverty and Income Inequality Today The persistence of poverty remains the primary motivator for most social policy today. In 2020, the poverty line for a family of four was an annual income of $26,200; for a single person it was $12,760.[57] In 2019, official estimates determined that 34 million Americans were living in poverty— 10.5 percent of the population. Even the social programs that do not directly help the poor and disadvantaged, such as Social Security and Medicare, affect poverty. The percentage of the elderly population living in poverty plummeted from more than 35 percent in 1959 to 8.9 percent in 2019.[58]

Another source of concern is the growing income and wealth inequality in the United States. From 1993 to 2018, the top 1 percent of the income distribution had 48 percent of the net income gains. The real income of the top 1 percent rose 101 percent during this period compared to an 18.3 percent gain for the bottom 99 percent. These trends have produced a growing concentration of income at the top. In 2018, the top 10 percent of households—those earning more than $134,900 a year—earned more than half the nation's income, which was the highest proportion since 1917; and in 2020, the top 1 percent—those earning more than $538,000—earned 22 percent of the nation's income.[59] The wealth gap is even greater: the median (meaning that half are above this level and half are below) net worth of U.S. households in 2019 was $121,760, but the median wealth for the top 10 percent was nearly $2.6 million, and this group held 74 percent of the nation's wealth. Racial wealth inequality received extensive attention in 2020 with the renewed focus on racial justice: in 2019, the median wealth of a White family was $189,000, while the median wealth of a Black family was just 13 percent of that amount: $24,000.[60]

One important point to recognize when considering social policy as a tool to address income inequality is that government policies help middle-income people and even the wealthy, in addition to the poor. Consider, for example, that 73 percent of the tax savings from deducting mortgage interest goes to people in the top 20 percent.[61] Other government policies that help the wealthy include patent and copyright law, bankruptcy law, bailouts of the financial sector, immigration policy, enforcement of tax law, and monetary policy.[62] Government programs that help the wealthy also benefit corporations. These policies, often called corporate welfare, include programs such as crop subsidies to large corporate farmers and tax deductions for oil companies to encourage exploration and drilling, with annual expenditures of more than $100 billion.[63] Clearly, there is much more to welfare policies than programs for the poor.

Politicians' differing reactions to the types of statistics presented here remind us that politics is conflictual. Republicans, on the one hand, argue that the best way to address poverty is through supply-side tax cuts that promote the creation of capital, investment,

ownership society
The term used to describe the social-policy vision of President George W. Bush, in which citizens take responsibility for their own social welfare and the free market plays a greater role in social policy.

There's class warfare, all right, but it's my class, the rich class, that's making war, and we're winning.

—**Warren Buffett,** America's fourth-wealthiest person

and jobs, and thus ensure a healthy economy. Democrats, on the other hand, argue that making the wealthy pay a larger share of their income in taxes could fund programs to help the poor directly and would be more efficient than waiting for the trickle-down effect of tax cuts for the wealthy. From this perspective, a trade-off exists between income inequality and reducing poverty, and progressive taxes are needed to help the poor.

Social policy today

As of the 2019 fiscal year, Social Security, Medicare, and Medicaid constitute nearly half of all federal spending ($2.1 trillion out of $4.4 trillion; the 2020 ratio will be smaller because of COVID-related spending). With an aging population and health care costs that are rising as a percentage of the economy, these policies will take an even greater share of the budget in the future. Here we explain the nature of these important programs and discuss recent efforts to reform them.

Social Security Social Security is the most popular social program in the United States. Consequently, it has developed a reputation as the "third rail" of politics (like the dangerous, power-conducting rail on electrified train tracks) because a politician who dares to touch Social Security risks political death. Despite serious problems concerning its long-term solvency, Social Security has proven remarkably immune to any steps that could be taken to shore up its financial health, such as cutting benefits, raising taxes, or privatizing the program.

One reason that Social Security is so popular is its universal quality—that is, nearly every working American participates in the program, from Donald Trump to the teenager flipping burgers at McDonald's. Once people reach a certain age, they are all entitled to Social Security checks without regard to how much income they have from other sources, such as dividends, interest, or other pensions. Thus, Social Security does not pit citizens from different classes or ethnic groups against one another. The program is also popular because it works. Fewer than 10 percent of the nation's elderly are in poverty today. (See Nuts & Bolts 14.2.) Census data show that 38 percent of the elderly would be in poverty today without their Social Security payments.[64]

Despite its successes and overall popularity, Social Security faces long-term problems. Basic changes in the nation's demographic profile are driving the projected shortfall. The **baby-boom generation** (people born between 1946 and 1964) is starting to retire. Between 2000 and 2030 the number of Americans over age 65 will more than double, while the number of working-age Americans (20–64) will grow by only 19 percent.[65] This trend means that there will be fewer workers to support the increasing number of retirees. "Wait a minute," you may be saying. "Why does it matter how many workers there are for each retiree? I thought that Social Security was a pension program that you pay into while you're working and then get the benefits when you retire." Not exactly. Social Security is a "pay as you go" system under which today's workers support today's retirees through the payroll tax discussed earlier. Therefore, the huge increase in the number of retirees will strain the system because each worker will have to pay higher taxes to maintain the same level of Social Security benefits.

Before we examine the various proposals to change Social Security, it is important to understand how the program works. Social Security is funded by a payroll tax of 6.2 percent on income up to $137,700 (in 2020) with an equal 6.2 percent that is paid by employers. Faced with its first real crisis in the early 1980s, as benefits had increased faster than payroll taxes throughout the 1970s, several changes were made to Social Security in 1983 to strengthen its long-term finances. One significant change was a gradual increase in the retirement age from 65 to 67. People born in 1937 or earlier could

baby-boom generation
Americans born between 1946 and 1964, who are retiring in large numbers over the next 20 years.

Note: The maximum benefit for the couple is based on the spousal benefit; if both people worked at least 35 years at or above the contribution base, the couple's benefit would be simply twice the individual benefit.

Sources: Figures on the number of recipients are from the U.S. Social Security Administration Office of Policy, "Monthly Statistical Snapshot, June 2020," Table 2, www.ssa.gov/policy/docs/quickfacts/stat_snapshot/; figures on monthly benefits are from Social Security Administration, *2020 OASDI Trustees Report*, June 5, 2018, Table V.C7, p. 150, www.ssa.gov/OACT/TR/2018/tr2018.pdf (both accessed 7/14/20).

Social Security

Number of Recipients for Old-Age, Survivors, and Disability Insurance

Old-Age Insurance (the basic retirement program)	48,945,000
Survivors Insurance (retirement program for widows, widowers, and the children of deceased primary wage earners)	5,899,000
Disability Insurance (payments for people and their families who cannot work because of a disability and are not yet retired)	9,844,000

Monthly Retirement Benefits

Individual	Average: $1,514	Maximum: $3,110
Couple	Average: $2,300	Maximum: $4,666

"Why Should I Care?" Social Security is the main source of financial support for many retired people in the United States.

DID YOU KNOW?

15.9%

of women and 24 percent of men 65 and older are working full-time.

Source: Bureau of Labor Statistics

retire in 2002 at age 65 and receive full benefits. Between 2003 and 2027 the retirement age increases gradually to 67 for full benefits. Early retirement at 62 is an option, if the retiree is willing to accept a permanently reduced benefit level. Delaying retirement until age 70 permanently increases the retiree's Social Security benefits.

In addition to increasing the retirement age, the 1983 reforms increased payroll taxes to generate a surplus for a trust fund to take care of the additional burden of the boomers' retirement. The trust fund is a source of great confusion and controversy. The idea behind the trust fund was sound: build up a surplus while the boomers are working, and use that money to pay for their retirement. The problem is that this money wasn't really saved: the government spent it elsewhere, for example, to fund the war in Afghanistan, nutritional programs, school loans, and the FBI. In turn, the government gave the Social Security trust fund an IOU in the form of "special public-debt obligation." This means that the government will pay off these IOUs, but the only way it can do so is by increasing taxes, cutting spending in other areas, or borrowing even more. The trust fund is expected to run out in 2035, at which point the Social Security system will be able to fund only about 76 percent of its obligations (see Figure 14.5).[66]

So what is to be done? Dozens of plans have been suggested. There is a surprising amount of agreement that saving Social Security requires a mixture of benefit cuts and tax increases. The calculations get very complicated in terms of the projected fiscal impact of various reforms, but a mixture of these options would take care of the long-term fiscal problems of Social Security:[67]

- Raise payroll taxes by 1 percent and increase the income ceiling that is taxable.
- Lower benefits for nonworking spouses (that is, spouses who did not work during their earning years). Currently, nonworking spouses receive 50 percent of the benefits that their working partners do. Some proposals would cut that benefit to 33 percent.

**FIGURE
14.5**

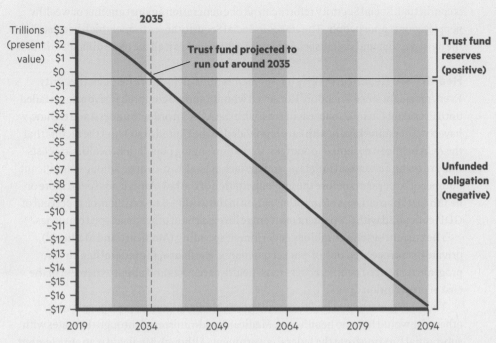

2035

Trillions (present value)

$3
$2
$1
$0
−$1
−$2
−$3
−$4
−$5
−$6
−$7
−$8
−$9
−$10
−$11
−$12
−$13
−$14
−$15
−$16
−$17

Trust fund projected to run out around 2035

Trust fund reserves (positive)

Unfunded obligation (negative)

2019   2034   2049   2064   2079   2094

Social Security Trust Fund

Since 2010, the cost of the Social Security program has exceeded Social Security payroll taxes, so taxes will need to be raised to cover the trust fund's obligations and the program's ongoing expenses. What do you think are the best solutions to address the long-term future of Social Security? What are the politically viable solutions?

Source: Social Security Administration, "The 2020 Annual Report of the Board of Trustees of the Federal Old-Age and Survivors Insurance and Federal Disability Insurance Trust Funds," April 22, 2020, Figure II.D5, www.ssa.gov/OACT/TR/2020/tr2020.pdf (accessed 7/15/20).

- Index current and future benefits to inflation instead of wages. Currently benefit increases are linked to national average wage increases. Because inflation does not increase as fast as wages, linking benefit increases to inflation would generate significant savings.
- Gradually raise the retirement age to 70 (by 2030). Changing the retirement age to 70 would save $620 billion by 2040.

More controversial proposals include these:

- Lower benefits for wealthier recipients. The strongest argument in favor of this approach is that wealthy people don't need the measly couple of thousand dollars they will receive each month from Social Security. The main argument against this proposal is that it would end the universal nature of Social Security and possibly turn it into another welfare program.
- Partial or full **privatization** of Social Security. This is the main issue that divides Democrats and Republicans: Democrats favor maintaining the basic structure of Social Security's public social insurance system, and Republicans favor moving part or all of the "pay as you go" system to private accounts. The central argument in favor of private accounts is that over the long term investing in the stock market has historically provided returns higher in value than Social Security. Advocates argue that if all workers were able to take their 6.2 percent payroll tax and put that in a retirement account, they would have a modest nest egg by the time they retired. Democrats point out the problems with this approach—most important, the transition costs. Because the current system is "pay as you go," if we stopped taking payroll taxes and allowed people to put the money into private accounts, there wouldn't be any money to pay for today's retirees and everyone else who has paid into the system for a substantial number of years. These transition costs are estimated to be $7 to $8 *trillion*! A second criticism of these plans is that investing in the stock market is fine as a supplement to Social Security, but it is too risky to be counted on as a sole source of retirement income.

privatization
The process of transferring the management of a government program (like Social Security) from the public sector to the private sector.

These issues are not likely to be resolved any time soon, which illustrates that politics is conflictual. Social Security reform can pit one generation against another or wealthy people against poor people. The stakes in Social Security are extremely high because it is the most popular and visible social program, which makes it all the more difficult to handle.

Health Care Health care policy has seemed as difficult to reform as Social Security. Every president since Theodore Roosevelt who attempted comprehensive reform failed until President Obama's success in 2010 with the ACA. In order to understand the law, we have to understand how health care is provided in the United States and the factors that the ACA has been designed to address: the nation's aging population, health care costs that are rising faster than inflation, and the lack of health insurance among a significant number of Americans before the implementation of the law. Americans spend more on health care than citizens of any other nation in the world—$3.64 trillion, or 17 percent of GDP, compared with 8.8 percent on average for citizens of other developed countries.[68]

The current system combines government spending (Medicare and Medicaid), private insurance, and out-of-pocket payments. Medicare, the federal health care program for retired people, covers most health care costs and about 75 percent of the cost of prescription drugs.

The other government health care program, Medicaid, serves poor people who otherwise would have no health care. Medicaid is administered through the states with substantial funding from the federal government. Although Medicaid is an entitlement, states have considerable discretion over the program. Each state (1) establishes its own eligibility standards; (2) determines the type, amount, duration, and scope of services; (3) sets the rate of payment for services; and (4) administers its own program.[69]

The variation in state Medicaid coverage means that some states cover virtually all poor people and others cover as few as one-third of those in need. Overall, 75 million Americans receive health care through Medicaid at a projected cost of $600 billion. The federal government reimburses the states for 62 percent of the costs ($370 billion in 2018), but this percentage varies by the relative total personal income in the states (that is, poorer states get more of their costs reimbursed than wealthier states).[70] Like Medicare, Medicaid faces growing budgetary pressures in the coming years.

Medicare
The federal health care plan created in 1965 that provides coverage for retired Americans for hospital care (Part A), medical care (Part B), and prescription drugs (Part D).

Medicaid
An entitlement program funded by the federal and state governments that provides health care coverage for low-income Americans who would otherwise be unable to afford health care.

entitlement
Any federal government program that provides benefits to Americans who meet requirements specified by law.

Proposed budgetary solutions to Medicare and Social Security's unfunded liabilities involve politically unpopular benefit cuts and tax increases. Similarly, public support for Medicare for All, a proposed program that would extend government-funded health care benefits to all Americans, has increased significantly in recent years, and gained further traction during the 2020 Democratic presidential primary, with candidates Elizabeth Warren, Kirsten Gillibrand, Kamala Harris, and Bernie Sanders voicing their support for the proposal.

An increasing share of Medicaid's costs is for long-term nursing home care for the indigent elderly, and the need for this service continues to grow as the population ages.

The long-term fiscal problems of Medicare and Medicaid are severe. In fact, they dwarf Social Security's problems. The *2020 Medicare Trustees Report* estimates that Social Security's unfunded liabilities through 2095, or the amount of additional money (beyond the current payroll tax) required to fund all the program's commitments, are $19.7 trillion, while Medicare has unfunded liabilities of $45.7 trillion.[71] Even though such projections depend on assumptions about future economic performance, demographic trends, and other uncertain variables, the *relative* difference between the two programs is significant. Medicare's troubles are more than twice as serious as Social Security's!

Another study estimates that by 2049 federal spending on health care, Social Security, and interest on the debt will reach 28.2 percent of GDP. That is, if the size of the federal government stays around its historic average of 20 percent of GDP, the two major social-policy programs will constitute nearly all of federal spending that is not interest on the debt by 2049. The choices are clear: either everything else must be cut from the budget (defense, education, transportation), health care costs and Social Security must be reined in, or the size of government must grow. Clearly, the current trends are not sustainable (see Figure 14.6 for a breakdown of spending on health care).

President Obama's primary focus when he took office in 2009 was to get the economy going; however, he also campaigned on reforming our health care

The Health Care Dollar: Where It Comes From and Where It Goes, 2018

FIGURE 14.6

Funding for our current health care system comes from a variety of sources and is spent on many types of care. In an effort to slow the increases in health care costs, which areas should receive the most attention?

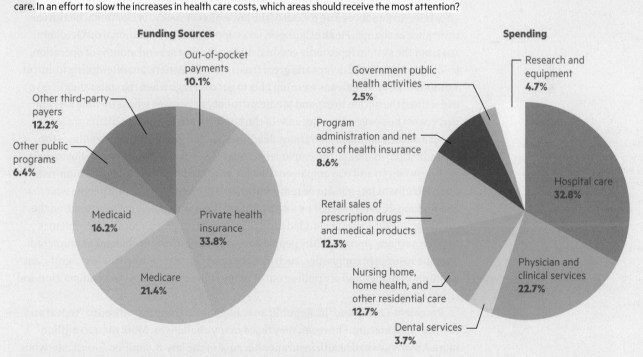

Funding Sources

- Out-of-pocket payments **10.1%**
- Other third-party payers **12.2%**
- Other public programs **6.4%**
- Medicaid **16.2%**
- Private health insurance **33.8%**
- Medicare **21.4%**

Spending

- Government public health activities **2.5%**
- Program administration and net cost of health insurance **8.6%**
- Retail sales of prescription drugs and medical products **12.3%**
- Nursing home, home health, and other residential care **12.7%**
- Dental services **3.7%**
- Research and equipment **4.7%**
- Hospital care **32.8%**
- Physician and clinical services **22.7%**

Note: Percentages shown may not add up to 100 percent due to rounding.

Source: Centers for Medicare and Medicaid Services, National Health Expenditures 1960–2018, spending data from Table 2, funding sources from Table 3, www.cms.gov/Research-Statistics-Data-and-Systems/Statistics-Trends-and-Reports/NationalHealthExpendData/NationalHealthAccountsHistorical (accessed 7/14/20).

system—controlling costs, providing as close to universal coverage as possible, and paying for the program without adding to the deficit. His goal of comprehensive coverage was essential. If insurance companies were forced to cover people with preexisting conditions without a mandate that everyone have insurance, people would wait until they were seriously ill to get coverage. Healthy people had to be pooled with sick people to spread the costs of expensive care. Comprehensive coverage was achieved by requiring businesses with more than 50 employees to provide coverage and by requiring all individuals without employer coverage to purchase insurance through new state-regulated private health insurance exchanges (which were implemented in 2014). Businesses and individuals that did not comply with the mandate would face fines. However, individuals who could not afford insurance would receive federal subsidies on a sliding scale (a formula that provides the biggest subsidies to the poorest people and some support to people with incomes all the way up to four times the federal poverty rate). The individual mandate was one of the most controversial parts of the bill, but it was repealed, effective in 2019. Other features of the law include incentives to computerize medical records, seen as a way to reduce medical mistakes, facilitate medical evaluations, and, as a result, improve the overall quality of care.

Another goal was that health care had to pay for itself. With a price tag of just under $1 trillion over the first 10 years, the bill was a challenge to finance. However, a combination of higher Medicare taxes, a new investment tax on the wealthy, an excise tax on insurers for expensive "Cadillac" health care plans, new fees for drug companies and health insurers, and cuts in Medicare reimbursement meant that the law would actually reduce the federal deficit by $143 billion over the first decade.[72] While some of those taxes were never fully implemented (such as the "Cadillac tax"), the law actually did a better job of cutting costs than initial estimates predicted. One study estimated that the Affordable Care Act saved $2.3 trillion in health care costs over 10 years.[73]

Yet the battle over health care reform was not over when Obama signed the bill into law. House Republicans repeatedly attempted to repeal the law. While these efforts were not successful, rollout of the law was very rocky. The national health care insurance exchange, HealthCare.gov, was supposed to be operational on October 1, 2013, but the system repeatedly crashed during the first several months of operation, leading to substantial delays and great frustration for Americans attempting to enroll. Millions of poor Americans were not able to get coverage when the states they lived in declined the option to expand Medicaid to cover everyone whose income was 138 percent of the poverty line. Because of the bumpy start, President Obama granted about a dozen extensions of various deadlines, including enrollment deadlines for the individual mandate, the employer mandate to cover all employees for businesses with between 50 and 100 employees (which was extended until 2016), the high-risk pool (which was intended to be temporary), and the requirement that people who had previously been covered by a substandard insurance policy get insurance on the exchange (this, too, was extended until the end of 2016).[74] An additional problem is that not as many young healthy people have signed up on the exchanges as predicted. So some insurance companies, such as Aetna and United Health, have lost significant amounts of money and are pulling out of many states. This means less competition and rising rates.

President Trump and the Republican leadership in Congress vowed to "repeal and replace" Obamacare. However, they faced many challenges. More than 20 million more Americans had health insurance because of the law: 8.3 million Americans who previously did not have health insurance successfully used the exchanges to sign up for insurance, and more than 6 million young adults were able to remain on their parents' health insurance until age 26.[75] Also, 12 million new enrollees were covered through the expansion of Medicaid.[76]

However, President Trump and congressional Republicans tried to keep the popular parts of Obamacare while getting rid of the unpopular parts (such as the individual mandate). The difficulty is that if insurance companies must provide coverage for people with preexisting conditions but people are not required to buy insurance, then people will wait until they have some serious condition before they sign up for insurance, while healthy people will opt out. This means that rates will go up for everyone, making it even more difficult to get coverage. This appears to have happened in some markets: premiums for health insurance on the state exchanges increased by double digits, while several million people dropped their coverage once they were no longer required to have it.[77] Although Republicans agreed on repealing Obamacare, no single Republican alternative had universal support within the party. Most Republicans argued for market-based reforms that would introduce more competition into the system to help keep costs down and for health savings accounts that would be tax deductible. But the basic problem of how to maintain coverage for the 20 million people who currently have insurance under Obamacare was not resolved.

Income Support and Welfare Welfare is usually thought of as cash support for people who cannot support themselves. However, **income support** can take many forms, including nutritional support benefits, unemployment insurance, and the Earned Income Tax Credit (EITC). Moreover, a significant reform of welfare occurred in 1996.

The Supplemental Nutrition Assistance Program (SNAP) provides nutritional support benefits, which today are government-issued debit cards that may be used as cash to buy groceries. Anyone whose income is less than 130 percent of the poverty level and whose resources do not exceed specific levels may qualify for SNAP. In 2020, the maximum monthly gross income for a family of four to qualify for SNAP was $2,838. As the effects of the recent economic crisis lingered through 2013, the number of people using SNAP peaked at a record of nearly 47.8 million in June 2013, with an average monthly benefit of $133 per person. With improvements in the economy, by February 2020 the numbers had dropped to 38.6 million and $121 per person, but those numbers jumped to 42.9 million and $125 per person in April 2020 because of the massive unemployment caused by the COVID-19 pandemic.[78]

The Federal-State Unemployment Compensation Program was established in 1935 as part of the Social Security Act. The U.S. Department of Labor oversees the program, but it is administered by the states. The program provides temporary and partial wage replacement for people who have been laid off and helps stabilize the economy during recessions. States set a broad range in benefit levels, minimum amount of income earned, and hours worked during the period leading up to unemployment. Also, laid-off workers have to make themselves "available for work." About 97 percent of all workers are covered by unemployment insurance, but only about half of the eligible unemployed make use of the benefit. The regular state programs provide up to 26 weeks of income support, and the Federal-State Extended Benefits Program temporarily provides up to 20 additional weeks in states with relatively high unemployment rates. The COVID-19 pandemic overwhelmed the unemployment compensation programs because 30 million people had claimed regular state unemployment insurance by mid-May 2020, up from an average of 2 million in a typical week.[79]

The EITC is one of the most successful programs for providing income support for the working poor. Established in 1975, the program aims to help poor people move from welfare to work: it provides tax credits to those who do not earn enough to pay income taxes and are relatively poor. It is intended to offset the burden of Social Security taxes, which all workers pay as part of payroll taxes. In 2020, you could qualify for an EITC as a couple if you had two children and earned less than $53,330, one child and earned less than $47,646, or no children and earned less than $21,710; the figures were about

income support
Government programs that provide support to low-income Americans, such as welfare, nutritional support benefits, unemployment compensation, and the EITC.

DID YOU KNOW?

Sixty percent of uninsured Americans can get health care coverage for

$100

or less per month, and 87 percent of those with a marketplace account get some assistance.

Source: ObamacareFacts.com

$5,800 lower if you were single.[80] The federal government provided $65 billion in EITCs in 2019 to more than 25 million recipients, with an average annual benefit of $2,476.[81]

Welfare is straight cash assistance for people who are not working and do not qualify for unemployment compensation. The primary welfare program for the latter half of the twentieth century was Aid to Families with Dependent Children (AFDC). This program became increasingly unpopular through the 1980s, and in 1992 Bill Clinton was the first Democratic presidential nominee to campaign against welfare, promising to "end welfare as we know it."[82] He began addressing welfare reform in 1993 by appointing a task force on the issue. When the Republicans took over Congress in 1994, the momentum for reform grew. Clinton and Congress haggled over the specifics for two years but then agreed on a major reform called **Temporary Assistance for Needy Families (TANF)**.

The new law set a five-year lifetime limit on welfare benefits, required single mothers with children above age five to find work after two years of receiving benefits, required unmarried mothers who were under age 18 to live with an adult and attend school to get full benefits, denied benefits to drug users who were convicted of a felony, and limited people who were not raising children and were between the ages of 18 and 50 to three months of food stamps in any three-year period in which they were not working. Perhaps most important, welfare lost its status as an entitlement and would be administered by the states with the assistance of federal block grants. In 2006, Congress reauthorized TANF and required that half the recipients in a state's caseload participate in work activities for at least 30 hours per week. Welfare reform significantly reduced the number of people on welfare, as Figure 14.7 shows, but it has been criticized for being too hard on the people who need government assistance the most. When the policy was enacted in 1996, two-thirds of all families in poverty received TANF assistance; in 2018 the fraction was less than one-quarter (22 percent). Critics also point out that TANF block grants have not been adjusted for inflation in most states since they were first created and were worth nearly 40 percent less in 2018 than in 1996.[83]

Education policy

Education policy is largely the domain of state and local governments. For the first century of our nation's history, the national government played virtually no role in education. One important exception was the Morrill Act in 1862, also known as the Land Grant College Act, which gave land to eligible states to establish colleges focusing on practical professions such as agriculture and mechanical arts. More than 75 colleges and universities today are land grant institutions. The next major forays by the federal government into education policy came with the GI Bill of Rights in 1944, which provided access to higher education for returning World War II veterans, and the Elementary and Secondary Education Act of 1965, which was part of President Johnson's War on Poverty. The Department of Education was created in 1980, signaling the government's interest in playing an important role in education policy.

A recent debate concerning the national government's role in education policy has focused on standards-based education reform: Should the national government establish standards and impose accountability as a way to improve public schools? The No Child Left Behind Act of 2001 required yearly statewide standardized testing in math and reading. If the test results showed that a school was not meeting annual academic benchmarks, it lost some federal funding and its students could transfer to another public school. Critics argue that standardized test results are a poor measurement of progress, because top-down standards incentivize schools to "teach to the test" and manipulate other aspects of the evaluation system. Responding to these concerns that one size does not fit all, Congress enacted the Every Student Succeeds

Temporary Assistance for Needy Families (TANF)
The welfare program that replaced AFDC in 1996, eliminating the entitlement status of welfare, shifting implementation of the policy to the states, and introducing several new restrictions on receiving aid. These changes led to a significant decrease in the number of welfare recipients.

Participation in Means-Tested Programs

FIGURE
14.7

The social-policy "safety net" is supposed to protect poor Americans during periods of economic recession. A deep recession happened in the early 1980s, and the other recession during the time frame depicted here was in the early 1990s. To what extent did the safety net accomplish the goal for which it was intended?

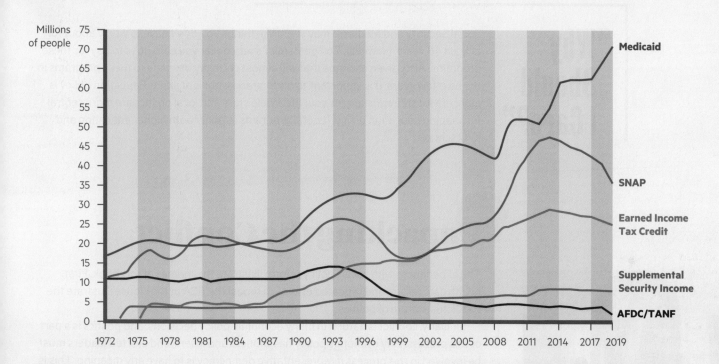

Sources: Data for 1972–2013 are from Congressional Research Service, based on data from the U.S. Department of Health and Human Services; and Congressional Budget Office, "Changes in Participation in Means-Tested Programs," February 2013, www.cbo.gov (both accessed 11/15/16). Data for 2014–2018 were collected by the author from various sources. Data for 2019 are from Medicaid.gov, "March 2020 Medicaid & CHIP Enrollment Data Highlights," www.medicaid.gov/medicaid/program-information/medicaid-and-chip-enrollment-data/report-highlights/index.html#:~:text=.Medicaid.gov.-,March%202020%20Medicaid%20%26%20CHIP%20Enrollment,individuals%20were%20enrolled%20in%20Medicaid; U.S. Department of Agriculture, Food and Nutrition Service, "SNAP Data Tables," www.fns.usda.gov/pd/supplemental-nutrition-assistance-program-snap; U.S. Department of Health and Human Services, Administration for Children and Families, "TANF Total Number of Recipients," www.acf.hhs.gov/sites/default/files/ofa/fy2019_tanf_caseload_trec.pdf; IRS, "EITC Fast Facts," www.eitc.irs.gov/partner-toolkit/basic-marketing-communication-materials/eitc-fast-facts/eitc-fast-facts; and Center on Budget and Policy Priorities, "Policy Basics: Supplemental Security Income," www.cbpp.org/research/social-security/policy-basics-supplemental-security-income#:~:text=SSI%20recipients%20are%20limited%20to,and%20%241%2C157%20for%20a%20couple (all accessed 7/16/20).

Act in 2015. The new law maintains annual testing but gives states more control over setting student performance targets and school ratings.

President Obama's Race to the Top grant program used a "carrot" rather than a "stick" approach to educational innovation, dedicating $4.35 billion to competitive grants from 2010 to 2013 to encourage schools to adopt more challenging standards and better tools of assessment, promote better leadership and methods for assessing and rewarding excellent teaching, create better data systems for tracking students' progress, and obtain stronger commitments for improving the worst-performing schools. These grants were aimed at strengthening the quality of public education while improving accountability.[84] The emphasis on accountability was criticized by both the left and the right. There was more bipartisan support behind Obama's effort to expand programs to improve access to higher education, such as increasing the number of Pell Grant recipients to 9.3 million and, in 2016, launching a new online "college scorecard" to provide objective information about college costs and quality.

Even with these efforts at imposing a national approach, there can be variations in state and local implementation of the national law. States and local school districts are also experimenting with policies aimed at introducing more competition for public schools, including public school choice and publicly funded vouchers for attending private schools.

Unpacking the Conflict

The experiences with social-policy reform illustrate the themes of this book. First, health care reform and repeated efforts to repeal the ACA in the House illustrate the conflictual nature of politics.

Similarly, conflict is natural in many economic policy decisions, and politics is a part of this process. Any economic policy has winners and losers, and elected leaders must be involved in this process if representative democracy is to have any meaning. This is especially true of the budget process because the redistributive implications of taxing and spending are so clear, but even monetary policy is not insulated from politics. This role for politics is guaranteed by our system of checks and balances: Congress, the president, and to some extent the courts all have a hand in shaping economic policy. What is the proper role of the government in a free market economy? How do political players deal with the conflict that is inherent in economic policy making?

It shouldn't be surprising when politics enters the economic policy debate. Elected leaders should be responsive to what their constituents think about the central questions concerning the direction of the economy. The struggles over economic and social policies—especially in Congress—demonstrate that political process matters. Politicians' decisions have a key impact on policy outcomes, and the timing and politics of the policy-making process drive the results. Finally, politics is everywhere: social and economic policies touch every American, and the struggles over reforming these policies are at the core of contemporary American politics.

STUDY GUIDE

Making public policy

Trace the steps through which problems are addressed by government policies. (Pages 449–458)

Summary

Once an issue is recognized and defined as a problem and when the conditions are right, the issue reaches the congressional agenda. Once a policy is in place, its effectiveness and implementation are evaluated in an ongoing process, although very few programs are ultimately terminated.

Key terms

public policy (p. 449)
policy agenda (p. 449)
fiscal policy (p. 451)
monetary policy (p. 451)
budget making (p. 451)
United States Trade
   Representative (USTR) (p. 454)
National Economic Council
   (NEC) (p. 454)
Aid to Families with
   Dependent Children
   (AFDC) (p. 455)
Federal Reserve System (p. 455)
Treasury Department (p. 455)

Practice Quiz Questions

1. What is the policy agenda?

a   the set of desired policies that political leaders view as priorities

b   the set of issues that political leaders view as priorities

c   the set of issues that issue groups view as priorities

d   the set of desired policies that issue groups view as priorities

e   the set of desired policies that issue groups and political leaders view as priorities

2. Relative to the private sector, public-sector programs are _____ to evaluate.

a   easier

b   equally easy

c   harder

d   equally as hard

e   not important

3. States influence policies on _____ , but not _____ .

a   Social Security; education

b   Social Security; Medicaid

c   education; Medicaid

d   Medicaid; education

e   Medicaid; Social Security

4. The difference between fiscal policy and monetary policy is that fiscal policy is concerned with _____ , while monetary policy is concerned with _____ .

a   controlling the money supply and spending; taxing and interest rates

b   taxing and controlling the money supply; spending and interest rates

c   taxing and spending; controlling the money supply and interest rates

d   controlling the money supply and interest rates; taxing and spending

e   taxing and interest rates; spending and controlling the money supply

5. The Treasury generally prefers _____ interest rates; the Federal Reserve Board generally prefers _____ interest rates.

a   higher; lower

b   higher; higher

c   lower; lower

d   lower; higher

e   stable; lower

Economic policy

Explain the main purposes of government involvement in the economy and how fiscal, monetary, and regulatory policies influence the economy. (Pages 458–472)

Summary

Policy makers' pursuit of economic goals—such as full employment, stable prices, or growth—is a complex process. Policy makers have a variety of tools at their disposal to help push the economy in their desired direction. The government utilizes fiscal policy, monetary policy, and regulation to influence the country's economic performance, but the pursuit of one goal often comes at the expense of other economic goals.

Key terms

full employment (p. 458)

economic depression (p. 458)

Council of Economic Advisers (CEA) (p. 458)

inflation (p. 458)

deflation (p. 459)

gross domestic product (GDP) (p. 460)

balanced budget (p. 460)

budget deficit (p. 460)

Keynesian economics (p. 461)

supply-side economics (p. 461)

business cycle (p. 463)

mandatory spending (p. 463)

discretionary spending (p. 463)

regressive (p. 465)

progressive (p. 465)

monetarist theory (p. 466)

reserve requirement (p. 466)

discount rate (p. 466)

federal funds rate (FFR) (p. 467)

open market operations (p. 467)

Practice Quiz Questions

6. The CEA was established _____ .

a by the Employment Act of 1946

b by the Balanced Budget Amendment

c in Article I of the Constitution

d in Article III of the Constitution

e by the Federal Reserve Board

7. Keynesian economics argues that the effects of an economic recession can be reduced by _____ .

a decreasing government spending

b increasing government spending

c increasing income taxes

d reducing the budget deficit

e discouraging consumer spending

8. Reducing the federal deficit by cutting spending is difficult because _____ .

a the interest rates are too high

b the majority of the budget is mandatory spending

c the majority of the budget is discretionary spending

d members of Congress put too much pork in budgetary bills

e large deficits benefit the economy in the long run

9. Regressive taxes, like the payroll tax, mean that compared with the wealthy, poor people spend _____ of their income on taxes.

a none

b much less

c slightly less

d an equal amount

e more

10. The "reserve requirement" refers to _____ .

a the interest rates the Fed charges to member banks

b the rate member banks charge one another on overnight loans

c the minimum activity level of the Fed's open market operations

d the lowest price for government bonds

e the minimum level of money banks must always have on hand

Social policy

Explain what we mean by social policy, discuss how the national government's role in social policy has evolved, and analyze the current major areas of social policy. (Pages 472–484)

Summary

"Social policy" is the catchall term for government programs that are designed to achieve a general social goal. While the early federal government took little responsibility for social welfare, the federal government currently plays a significant role in ensuring the welfare of its people. Today the most important social programs center on the issues of poverty, an aging population, and health care. Unfortunately, the political realities of the system make reforms difficult.

Key terms

social policy (p. 473)

welfare (p. 473)

New Deal (p. 473)

Great Society (p. 473)

ownership society (p. 474)

baby-boom generation (p. 475)

privatization (p. 477)

Medicare (p. 478)

Medicaid (p. 478)

entitlement (p. 478)

income support (p. 481)

Temporary Assistance for Needy Families (TANF) (p. 482)

Practice Quiz Questions

11. Social Security was established under the _____; Medicare was established under the _____ .

a New Deal; Great Society

b New Deal; New Deal

c Great Society; Great Society

d Great Society; New Deal

e New Deal; Opportunity Society

12. The principle of the "ownership society" is that _____ .

a the government has responsibility for the people's social welfare

b the government has responsibility for the poor's social welfare

c the government has responsibility for health care but not education

d the rich have responsibility for the poor's social welfare

e people have responsibility for their own welfare

13. The primary motivator for social policy is _____ .

a intergenerational equality

b poverty

c the deficit

d care for the elderly

e gender inequality

14. The primary reason Social Security will be financially strained in the coming years is that _____ .

a it is a pay-as-you-go program

b its stipends are indexed to inflation

c it is transitioning to privately held accounts

d compensation to nonworking spouses is equal to benefits for the working spouses

e most Americans don't approve of Social Security

15. In President Obama's health care plan, why was it essential to guarantee comprehensive coverage?

a to make sure enough people were paying into the system

b to pool risk between sick and healthy people

c to reduce the risks of fraud

d to prevent individuals from having only one price to pay

e to win broad political support

Suggested Reading

Altman, Nancy J. *The Battle for Social Security: From FDR's Vision to Bush's Gamble*. New York: Wiley, 2005.

Bartels, Larry M. *Unequal Democracy: The Political Economy of the New Gilded Age*, 2nd ed. Princeton, NJ: Princeton University Press, 2016.

Friedman, Milton. *Capitalism and Freedom*, 40th anniversary ed. Chicago: University of Chicago Press, 2002.

Friedman, Thomas L. *The World Is Flat: A Brief History of the Twenty-First Century*. New York: Farrar, Straus and Giroux, 2005.

Keynes, John Maynard. *The General Theory of Employment, Interest and Money*. 1936. Reprint, New York: Macmillan, 2007.

King, Ronald F. *Budgeting Entitlements: The Politics of Food Stamps*. Washington, DC: Georgetown University Press, 2000.

Lewis, Michael. *The Big Short: Inside the Doomsday Machine*. New York: W. W. Norton, 2010.

Oberlander, Jonathan. *The Political Life of Medicare*. Chicago: University of Chicago Press, 2003.

Phillips, Kevin. *Bad Money: Reckless Finance, Failed Politics, and the Global Crisis of American Capitalism*. New York: Viking, 2008.

Piketty, Thomas. *Capital in the Twenty-First Century*. Cambridge, MA: Belknap Press, 2014.

Skocpol, Theda. *Social Policy in the United States: Future Possibilities in Historical Perspective*. Princeton, NJ: Princeton University Press, 1995.

Soros, George. *The New Paradigm for Financial Markets: The Credit Crash of 2008 and What It Means*. New York: PublicAffairs Books, 2008.

Soss, Joe. *Unwanted Claims: The Politics of Participation in the U.S. Welfare System*. Ann Arbor: University of Michigan Press, 2000.

Stiglitz, Joseph E. *Globalization and Its Discontents Revisited: Anti-globalization in the Era of Trump*. New York: W. W. Norton, 2017.

Weaver, R. Kent. *Ending Welfare as We Know It*. Washington, DC: Brookings Institution Press, 2000.

15

Foreign Policy

What is America's role in the world?

 》 "Presidents from Roosevelt to Obama have sought to help allies protect themselves and to engage in collective defense against common dangers. We did this not in a spirit of charity but because we had learned the hard way that problems abroad, if unaddressed, could, before long, imperil us."[1]

Madeleine Albright, former secretary of state

 《 "Upon my inauguration, I announced that the United States would return to a simple principle: The first duty of our government is to serve its citizens, many of whom have been forgotten. But they are not forgotten any more. With every decision and every action, we are now putting America first."[2]

President Donald Trump

From the first day of his 2016 campaign, Donald Trump argued he was a dealmaker, someone who would use insight, brinksmanship, and grit to transform America's relations with the world. He claimed that other countries were taking advantage of America, tapping its open markets while keeping American firms shut out of their own. More than that, Trump argued that this problem could be fixed quickly and easily with tough talk and an unwillingness to accept the status quo.

The photo on the facing page is a good illustration of Trump's approach. It shows a tense moment at a 2018 meeting of the G7 (an informal group of the world's major industrialized democracies) with Trump facing off against the leaders of the other countries, including Germany's longtime prime minister, Angela Merkel. The meeting did not go well. Trump arrived late, left early, and refused to agree to a joint statement on fighting climate change, eliminating retaliatory tariffs, and criticizing Russia for its support of Syrian president Bashar al-Assad—all positions that previous American presidents had strongly supported. At one point, Trump even tossed two Starburst candies on the table in front of Prime Minister Merkel, saying, "Here, Angela. Don't say I never give you anything."[3]

Tough talk, including threats of an international trade war, characterized the Trump administration's foreign policy strategy in the first year of his presidency. For example, during the June 2018 G7 summit, President Trump's confrontational attitude toward American allies garnered praise from his supporters but left fellow world leaders on edge.

CHAPTER GOALS

Describe the major approaches to understanding foreign policy, and trace how America's role in the world has evolved. pages 491–498

Explain how the various branches of government shape foreign policy. pages 498–507

Examine the ways American foreign policy is implemented. pages 507–511

Analyze several major areas of foreign policy and why they are often controversial. pages 511–517

In his time in office, Trump combined strong rhetoric with concrete policy change. He imposed punitive tariffs on America's major trading partners, ordered the renegotiation of long-standing trade agreements, and made it clear that America expected to get more from these agreements than it had in the past. However, other nations did not respond as Trump had predicted. Rather, they put additional tariffs on American goods and stood firm against Trump's demands for renegotiation, raising the possibility of a global trade war that could reduce global economic growth.

The case of Donald Trump's attempt to reshape the global economy illustrates the importance of foreign policy in American politics, as well as some common misconceptions about how foreign policy gets made. Take America's economy. Over the last generation American politicians have approved a series of treaties that reduced tariffs on imports and exports, generating enormous profits for some American companies. However, trade liberalization has hurt companies that could not respond to increased foreign competition. Many of their workers have been laid off or have taken incentives to quit their jobs or retire early rather than face an uncertain future of layoffs and wage cuts. At the same time, Americans enjoy cheaper prices for many products that can now be sold in U.S. markets.

Many Americans expect foreign policy to be an area of consensus—believing that as Americans we hold similar ideas of what our country should be doing outside our borders. As a result, many Americans agree with late Senator Arthur Vandenberg, who is often credited for the saying "Politics stops at the water's edge." Americans tend to see disagreement over foreign policy as somehow unpatriotic. But as the trade example suggests, foreign policy choices create winners and losers, just as in the domestic arena. Lowering trade barriers made some Americans better off and some worse off. The same was true for Donald Trump's trade policies, and this would have been the case even if they worked as advertised.

Foreign policy is political even in the case of national security. Are diplomacy and economic sanctions the right response to North Korea's nuclear weapons program, or is a military attack warranted? And after two decades of combat operations in Afghanistan, is it time for America to withdraw its forces and leave the Afghan population on its own? These examples illustrate that we should expect disagreement over foreign policy, including between the political parties, inside the executive branch, and even between civilians and military personnel. Although these debates often have political consequences, with lawmakers sometimes taking positions for political gain, in the main they reflect sincere differences of opinion. In this way, foreign policy closely resembles domestic policy.

The COVID-19 pandemic is another example of how foreign and domestic events (and government policy) are linked. Our ability to understand and control the virus depends on the existence of business, cultural, and scientific linkages with other nations as well as policies that encourage or discourage international travel (including by students from other countries, who are an increasing presence on U.S. campuses). Yet many Americans disagree about whether such linkages and policies are good or bad, and the debate in Washington reflects these differences as well as broader ideas about the proper role of America in the modern world.

The reality of disagreement about foreign policy options raises the question of how these differences are resolved. Were President Trump's unilateral moves an exception or the rule? What choices will our new president, Joe Biden, make differently? What is the role of Congress, the courts, and the bureaucracy in the making of foreign policy? Where does public opinion enter into this process? Who gets to decide America's foreign policy? How is foreign policy made?

What is foreign policy?

Foreign policy encompasses government actions involving countries, corporations, groups, and individuals that lie outside America's borders. Foreign policy includes military operations, economic interactions, human rights policies, environmental agreements, foreign aid, helping build or sustain democratic systems, interventions in civil wars and other conflicts, and international efforts to limit weapons of mass destruction (WMDs), including nuclear weapons.

Foreign policy principles and perspectives

Foreign policy actions are often rooted in general principles or rules that guide people in their decision making. These principles and rules capture the decision to act, whether America acts alone or with other nations, and the motivations for actions. (See Nuts & Bolts 15.1 for a summary of these guiding principles.)

Should We Act Alone? There are three important distinctions in foreign policy. The first is between unilateral action and multilateral action. Unilateral action occurs when one country does something on its own, without coordinating with other countries. For example, some U.S. antiterrorism operations under recent presidents have been undertaken without any consultation with U.S. allies, such as the 2020 attack on Iranian general Qasem Soleimani in the Baghdad airport, which was carried out by U.S. forces without even informing the Iraqi government. American foreign policy more commonly involves multilateral action by the United States alongside other countries or international organizations such as the UN. For example, in 2018, after the Syrian government used chemical weapons against civilians, the United States, Great Britain, and France launched a coordinated missile attack to destroy several Syrian chemical weapons manufacture and storage facilities.

foreign policy
Government actions that affect countries, corporations, groups, or individuals outside America's borders.

unilateral action (national)
Independent acts of foreign policy undertaken by a nation without the assistance or coordination of other nations.

multilateral action
Foreign policy carried out by a nation in coordination with other nations or international organizations.

When the United States acts multilaterally in foreign policy, it often works through organizations such as the UN. Here, Donald Trump addresses a session of the UN General Assembly, where he promoted nationalist policies and spoke skeptically about globalization.

isolationism
The idea that a country should refrain from involvement in international affairs.

internationalism
The idea that a country should be involved in the affairs of other nations, out of both self-interest and moral obligation.

realism
The idea that a country's foreign policy decisions are motivated by self-interest and the goal of gaining more power.

idealism
The idea that foreign policy decisions reflect normative goals such as justice, equality, and human rights.

nation building
The use of a country's resources, including the military, to help nondemocratic nations transform themselves into democracies.

Should We Intervene? A second important distinction in foreign policy is between **isolationism** and **internationalism**. Isolationists believe that the United States should avoid making alliances and agreements with other nations, concentrate on defending America's borders, and let the people in other countries work out their problems for themselves. In the case of the humanitarian crisis in Syria, an isolationist might argue that U.S. intervention would be futile or potentially counterproductive, too costly, or simply inappropriate—that it is not America's problem to solve.[4]

An internationalist, however, would likely argue that the United States should establish many agreements with other nations and intervene in international crises whenever it may be able to help, both because of possible economic and security gains and because intervening in civil wars and helping solve humanitarian crises are morally right. In the case of terrorist organizations such as ISIS (the Islamic State in Iraq and Syria), internationalists would at a minimum support efforts to help and protect the local population, either in concert with other nations or alone if other nations are unwilling to intervene.[5]

Are We Only Out for Ourselves? The third major distinction in foreign policy making is between **realism** and **idealism** (also known as liberalism, although the term has a very different meaning than the liberal ideology in domestic politics).[6] Realists believe that countries pursue their own interests, seeking to increase their economic and military power and their international influence. In approaching a policy decision, a realist would choose the policy that maximizes U.S. military and economic power relative to that of other states. Idealists, in contrast, believe that states' concerns extend beyond increasing their power, including the promotion of principles such as freedom, liberty, or democracy. For an idealist, upholding these principles should be a primary goal of U.S. foreign policy—for example, idealists generally believe in helping nondemocratic nations transform themselves into democracies with strong court systems (also called **nation building**).

Realism and idealism are used often in foreign policy debates because they offer convenient ways to summarize the motivations behind policy decisions. That is how we use the terms in this chapter, but in reality neither of them provides a fully accurate

NUTS
& BOLTS
15.1

Theories of Foreign Policy

Realism	Foreign policy is driven by a state's national interest, as defined by its leaders.
Idealism	Foreign policy reflects the ideals held by a state's leaders, such as protection of human rights.
Internationalism	States should, whenever possible, pursue their foreign policy goals by working together with other nations.
Isolationism	States should, whenever possible, work alone to define and implement their foreign policy, working with other nations only when absolutely necessary.

Source: Compiled by the authors.

"Why Should I Care?" Foreign policy theories can help us understand why a president or Congress decides to take action or refrain from taking action.

definition of what motivates nations or individuals. As the quote from President Barack Obama illustrates, no one is a realist or an idealist all the time. For example, Obama's support for intervention in the Libyan civil war was squarely idealist in its motivation—done with the hope that dissident elements in Libya could unite to build a stable democracy. Conversely, Obama's reluctance to undertake a large-scale operation in Syria is a classic example of realism: while the situation was a human rights catastrophe, it put no fundamental American interests at stake.

History of American foreign policy

In this section, we review the evolution of American foreign policy. Our aim is to illustrate the types of choices American politicians face, how these policy options have changed over time, and the lack of agreement among American politicians about how to resolve foreign policy issues.

The Founding to World War I Until America's entry into World War I in 1917, American foreign policy was largely isolationist. Isolationism made sense during this period for several reasons: America's distance from Europe reduced the potential for international economic interactions, lowered the level of military threat, and gave early America room to expand without conflicting with European nations.[7] The **Monroe Doctrine**, established by President James Monroe in 1823, stated that America would remain neutral in wars involving European nations and that the United States expected these nations to stop trying to colonize or occupy areas in North and South America.[8]

America's foreign policy was never completely isolationist, however, even in the early years. The American navy was deployed on many occasions to protect U.S. ships and citizens, and America had several colonies far beyond its borders. Even in the early years, the United States expanded by purchasing land from other countries or from Native Americans—adding much of the Midwest through the Louisiana Purchase— and by annexing land after military conflicts, such as the large section of the Southwest acquired from Mexico following the Mexican-American War. Later, America built the Panama Canal, leasing land from Panama in the process, and sent troops into conflicts in Nicaragua and other Central American countries. America also maintained significant trading relationships with nations in Europe and elsewhere.

Still, America's involvement in World War I (1914–1918) marked a sharp departure in foreign policy, in terms of both the country's participation in an international alliance and the president's willingness to continue alliance membership after the conflict.[9] With the war almost over, President Woodrow Wilson offered a peace plan, the Fourteen Points, which proposed reshaping the borders of European countries to mitigate future conflict, creating measures to encourage free trade and democracy, and establishing an international organization that would prevent wars.[10] American diplomats participated in the negotiations that culminated in the Treaty of Versailles, which officially ended the war.[11] The treaty created the League of Nations, an organization similar to the modern UN, but the U.S. Senate rejected the treaty, which meant that the United States never joined the League of Nations.[12]

The Rise of Internationalism World War II (1939–1945) marked a great transition in American foreign policy. The United States became directly involved in the conflict on December 8, 1941, declaring war on Japan the day after the country carried out air attacks on Pearl Harbor in Hawaii and American bases in the Philippines. Germany subsequently declared war on the United States on December 11. However, even before the United States officially became involved, the U.S. military had been supplying

You take victories where you can. You make things a little bit better rather than a little bit worse. And that's in no way a concession to this idea that America is withdrawing or there's not much we can do. It's just a realistic assessment of how the world works.

—President Barack Obama

Monroe Doctrine
The American policy, initiated under President James Monroe in 1823, stating that the United States would remain neutral in conflicts between European nations and that these nations should stop colonizing or occupying areas of North and South America.

Great Britain and its allies with arms, ships, and other supplies in return for payments and long-term leases on British military bases throughout the world—actions that only narrowly escaped a congressional vote to reverse. During the war, the Allied Powers—the United States, Great Britain, the Soviet Union, and other countries—fought as a formal alliance, making joint plans and sharing military hardware and intelligence.

After World War II, American politicians and scholars felt that the United States should be a central actor in world affairs. This new policy was justified by realist arguments, such as the need to deter future conflicts and the desire for economic benefits from trading with other nations.[13] Idealists argued for the same policies on the grounds that America had a moral obligation to preserve world peace.[14] However, this shift toward internationalism only increased the amount of conflict in American foreign policy, as actors disagreed on where the United States should get involved; what its goals should be; whether intervention should involve military force, foreign aid, diplomacy, or some other policy tool; and whether the country should act alone or in concert with other nations.

The Cold War Soon after World War II ended, the **Cold War** (1945–1991) began, as the victorious Allies disagreed—with the United States and Great Britain on one side and the Soviet Union on the other—over the reconstruction of Germany and the reformation of Eastern European countries that Germany had occupied during the war. In a 1946 speech, former British prime minister Winston Churchill referred to an "iron curtain" that had split Eastern and Western Europe, leaving the East under Soviet domination with few political freedoms.[15] American diplomat George F. Kennan argued that America should use diplomatic, economic, and military means to prevent the Soviet Union from expanding the set of countries that it controlled or was allied with—a strategy that he deemed "**containment**."[16] This idea served as a guiding principle for American foreign policy over the next generation.[17]

During this period, the United States implemented several measures to build and strengthen alliances against the Soviet threat. The first was the Marshall Plan, a series of aid and development programs enacted in the late 1940s to restore the economies of Western European countries that had been devastated during World War II.[18]

Cold War
The period of tension and arms competition between the United States and the Soviet Union that lasted from 1945 until 1991.

containment
An important feature of American Cold War policy in which the United States used diplomatic, economic, and military strategies in an effort to prevent the Soviet Union from expanding its influence.

The Marshall Plan, which helped European nations rebuild their economies after World War II, was part of America's strategy to build alliances against the Soviet Union.

In addition, the United States was instrumental in the formation of the World Bank and the International Monetary Fund (IMF), as well as other international trade agreements.

The United States also formed alliances with other countries, including the North Atlantic Treaty Organization (NATO) in 1949. The goal of these alliances and organizations was collective security, based on the principle that "an attack against one is an attack against all."[19] The aim was to deter Soviet attacks throughout the world by formalizing America's commitment to defend its allies. Of course, the Soviets formed their own alliances, most notably the Warsaw Pact with nations in Eastern Europe.[20]

On another front the United States was behind the 1945 creation of the UN, an international organization with the goal of preventing wars by facilitating negotiations between combatants and, if necessary, sending military forces from member states to stop conflicts. Other aspects of the UN's role have included administering relief efforts for refugees, undertaking development efforts, codifying international law, and publicizing and condemning human rights violations.

Clearly, the goal of containment influenced every aspect of American foreign policy after World War II.[21] America maintained large military forces, beginning its first peacetime draft in the 1950s and building up a large store of nuclear weapons. These weapons were intended to deter war with the Soviet Union through the threat of **mutually assured destruction**—the idea that even if the Soviet Union unleashed an all-out nuclear assault on the United States, enough American weapons would remain intact to deliver a similarly devastating counterattack. As part of this effort, throughout much of the mid-twentieth century the United States stationed hundreds of thousands of troops in Western Europe and elsewhere to deter the Soviet threat. Yet in 1962, war nearly broke out during the Cuban missile crisis, when the Soviets tried to place nuclear missiles in Cuba—within striking range of the United States. However, the issue was defused by a Soviet withdrawal in the face of an American naval blockade of Cuba and a secret American promise to withdraw similar missiles from Turkey in return.

In the early 1960s, America also became involved in the conflict in Vietnam, believing that North Vietnam's drive to take over South Vietnam was part of the Soviet Union's plan for world domination.[22] A popular theory at the time held that if the United States did not prevent the fall of South Vietnam, the next step would be a Soviet-backed conflict in the Philippines, in Australia, or in the territory of some other American ally. However, the conflict between North and South Vietnam was a civil war rather than an international event.[23] Although the North Vietnamese accepted Soviet support, they did not take orders from the Soviets.

Beginning in the early 1970s, President Richard Nixon began a process of **détente** with the Soviet Union. This involved a series of negotiations and cultural exchanges designed to reduce tensions and promote cooperation.[24] These efforts culminated in the 1972 Strategic Arms Limitation Treaty (SALT I), which limited the growth of U.S. and Soviet missile forces.[25] At the same time, the Arab nations' embargo prohibiting oil shipments to Western nations after the 1973 Arab-Israeli war was a reminder that containment of the Soviet Union could not be America's only foreign policy priority. Tensions over oil increased again when the Organization of the Petroleum Exporting Countries (OPEC) raised prices in 1979. Both events contributed to a recession in America and the electoral defeats of two incumbent presidents: Gerald Ford in 1976 and Jimmy Carter in 1980.

After the Cold War: Human Rights, Trade, and Terrorism
In 1991, the Soviet Union splintered into 15 countries, effectively ending the Cold War. The end of this conflict, along with the growing number of democracies worldwide and the development of democratic peace theories (which argue that democracies will not fight other democracies), suggested to some observers that military conflicts would become much rarer, so that other concerns would more strongly influence America's

mutually assured destruction
The idea that two nations that possess large stores of nuclear weapons—like the United States and the Soviet Union during the Cold War—would both be annihilated in any nuclear exchange, thus making it unlikely that either country would launch a first attack.

détente
An approach to foreign policy in which cultural exchanges and negotiations are used to reduce tensions between rival nations, such as between the United States and the Soviet Union during the 1970s.

foreign policy.[26] Events early in the post–Cold War era seemed to support this thesis. For example, human rights became a more important foreign policy topic[27] and the United States became involved in humanitarian relief and nation-building efforts in Somalia, Bosnia, and Kosovo. Moreover, a series of agreements, including the North American Free Trade Agreement (NAFTA) in 1994 and the formation of the World Trade Organization (WTO) in 1995, lowered tariffs throughout the world. Technological advances in transportation also lowered the cost of shipping goods worldwide, and the industrialization of many developing countries made them low-cost suppliers of manufactured goods to the United States, causing many domestic factories to close. The world's nations also began to negotiate over voluntary limits on carbon emissions in order to address climate change. These developments are consistent with the idea of "soft power": that is, America's exertion of influence over other nations through increased economic interactions and cultural ties rather than the use of military force.[28]

Near the end of the twentieth century, new security threats emerged in the form of terrorist groups, most notably Al Qaeda, led by Osama bin Laden, who organized the September 11, 2001, attacks on the World Trade Center in New York and the Pentagon in Washington, D.C. Some analysts and politicians, including President George W. Bush, described these attacks as part of a worldwide "clash of civilizations" resulting in a global war on terrorism, pitting the secular, open West against radical Islam.[29] After the attacks, President George W. Bush announced a new U.S. policy, the **Bush Doctrine**, or the doctrine of preemption, whereby the United States would not wait until after an attack to respond but, instead, would use military force to eliminate potential threats before they could be put in motion. This policy change was intended to prevent another September 11 attack, as the quote from Bush's National Security Advisor and Secretary of State Condoleezza Rice illustrates.

President Obama emphasized improving foreign perceptions of America and Americans, ending the ground war in Iraq, and avoiding unilateral action in favor of multilateral coalitions. However, many of Obama's policies in regard to the War on Terror, such as his emphasis on drone attacks (see the Take a Stand feature in this chapter) and America's limited involvement in the Syrian civil war, were quite similar to those established by the Bush administration.

We don't want the smoking gun to be a mushroom cloud.

—**Condoleezza Rice,** secretary of state under George W. Bush

Bush Doctrine
The foreign policy of President George W. Bush, under which the United States would use military force preemptively against threats to its national security.

The Al Qaeda terrorist organization headed by Osama bin Laden was the driving force behind many terrorist attacks on Americans, including the 2001 attacks on the World Trade Center and the Pentagon. In 2011, American forces killed bin Laden, but the group, along with newer organizations such as ISIS, remains a significant threat.

Should America Carry Out Drone Attacks against Terrorists?

One of the elements of America's strategy to fight terrorist groups is the increased use of drones—small, pilotless aircraft that fly into foreign airspace, monitor the activities of terror suspects on the ground, and launch missiles against these targets. Over the last 15 years, drone attacks in countries such as Syria, Afghanistan, Yemen, and Pakistan have decimated the leadership and infrastructure of terrorist groups and inflicted significant casualties on lower-level fighters. Drones also played a key role in identifying the safe house in Pakistan where Al Qaeda leader Osama bin Laden was located, making possible the attack that resulted in bin Laden's death in 2011. However, the use of drones by American forces continues to be highly controversial inside the United States and throughout the world.

Drones are an effective tool. Drone attacks allow the United States to combat terrorists throughout the world without putting American troops at risk. Drone attacks are also less expensive than conventional forces. For example, rather than sending a special operations unit across the world to attack a target in the Middle East, American crews working at a base in Nevada can remotely control drones launched from a secure base in the Middle East or a ship in the Persian Gulf. Because drones have no crew, they can be small and quiet and stay in the air for long periods of time, making a surprise attack more feasible. Even if an attack is not being planned, drones allow the United States to monitor suspected terrorists and collect intelligence.

Describing drones as a tool also highlights their similarity to other examples of military force. How different is it if a terrorist camp is attacked by a drone rather than U.S. ground troops? Any argument against drones (the danger of civilian casualties or that terrorists can publicize the attack as a way of galvanizing public opposition to the U.S. strategy) can be applied just as well to other ways the United States might attack terrorists.

Drones bring risks and negatively affect decision making. Some people foresee that the very advantages ascribed to drones—that they are relatively inexpensive and require no human pilots—could likely lead decision makers to use drones more quickly than they might use conventional weapons. In a similar vein, there are those who believe that

The use of drones is controversial. Here, a protester in Yemen holds a sign denouncing the practice.

drones remove the personal element from warfare, making it easier to disregard the moral implications of an attack.

Moreover, at least up to now, drone strikes have occurred with little congressional oversight or approval. As we discussed in Chapter 11, Congress has the power to limit military operations—but doing so in the case of drones would be difficult because most of these operations are carried out in secret. How could members stop an operation they didn't know about until after it occurred?

While mistakes are possible in any military operation, drone attacks involve special risks. Because drone operators view their targets through long-range cameras mounted on the drones, the chances of civilian casualties or other collateral damage are probably higher than with Special Forces units who carry out their attacks at short range.

The problem for decision makers is this: prohibiting drone attacks on suspected terrorists does not mean that these individuals and organizations will go scot-free; most of these operations will instead be carried out by American armed forces, with the risk that some of these troops will be wounded, killed, or taken hostage. Should decision makers use drones or send in the troops?

take a stand

1. If you were writing a letter to your member of Congress about the use of drones, what position would you take? What arguments would you use to support your position?

2. If you favor the use of drones, are there situations in which we shouldn't use them? If you oppose them, are there situations in which drones have advantages over traditional troops?

On one level, Donald Trump's foreign policy, with its emphasis on "putting America first," was a sharp departure from that of his predecessors, particularly the imposition of trade tariffs on other countries such as China and the withdrawal from trade agreements with other nations; threats to use military force against countries such as North Korea; efforts to reduce admissions of refugees to the United States; and the emphasis on enhanced border security (including efforts to build a wall between the United States and Mexico). On another level, while all these changes were significant, major portions of America's foreign policy remained unchanged. For example, while Trump's rhetoric emphasized attacking ISIS forces in Syria rather than helping rebel forces fighting the Syrian government, America and its allies continued to give military aid and technical support to rebel forces. And Trump was not the first president to pressure China to alter its trade policies or regulations on intellectual property.

"Why Should I Care?"

Maybe you don't care about foreign policy—although as we discuss throughout this chapter, you probably should. In the modern era, no nation can separate itself from the rest of the world. The same is true for individual citizens, even you. Your job, cost of living, and even your personal safety are affected by America's foreign policy. Making sense of foreign policy (or deciding where you stand on foreign policy questions) requires you to know some history and some basic terminology. History helps you understand America's place in the world and how different issues came about. Knowing the basic terminology used in foreign affairs helps you understand what politicians and pundits are talking about when they discuss foreign policy issues.

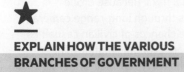

★

EXPLAIN HOW THE VARIOUS BRANCHES OF GOVERNMENT SHAPE FOREIGN POLICY

Foreign policy makers

We begin with the president and the executive branch, and then we consider Congress, the courts, and, finally, other groups and individuals outside the government. Nuts & Bolts 15.2 summarizes the foreign policy powers of the two most important actors, the president and Congress.

The president and the executive branch

The president is the dominant actor in American foreign policy.[30] Working with staff, the president can negotiate treaties or executive agreements with other nations, change policy through executive orders or findings, mobilize public opinion to prompt action by Congress, and shape foreign policy by appointing people to agencies and departments that administer these policies (see Chapter 11). The president also serves as commander in chief of America's armed forces. Furthermore, the president is the first point of contact between America and other world leaders—in fact, the 2019–2020 impeachment proceedings against President Trump began because of comments Trump made to the president of Ukraine in a routine phone conversation about Russian aid to rebel groups in Eastern Ukraine.

Within the Executive Office of the President (EOP), the principal foreign policy agency is the **National Security Council (NSC)**, which develops foreign policy options and presents them to the president. The EOP also includes the Office of the

National Security Council (NSC)
An agency within the EOP that advises the president on matters of foreign policy.

Foreign Policy Powers of the President and Congress

President	Congress
Commander in chief of armed forces	Can declare war
Nominates and appoints senior officials in Department of Defense	Senate must approve Defense nominees
Negotiates treaties and executive agreements with other nations	Treaties take effect only if approved by Senate
Changes policy with executive orders and findings	Can overturn orders and findings with legislation
Attempts to mobilize public opinion behind foreign policy goals	Makes policy using "power of the purse" (annual budget)

Source: Compiled by the authors.

"Why Should I Care?" Foreign policy powers determine who can act, what they can do, and what process is necessary before they can move forward. Knowing about these powers helps us understand when and why the United States engages abroad.

United States Trade Representative, which focuses on tariffs and trade disputes; the president's Foreign Intelligence Advisory Board, a group of academics, politicians, and former government officials who advise the president; and the Office of Management and Budget, which prepares the president's annual budget proposals for federal agencies and departments, including those with foreign policy responsibilities.

The Department of State The principal foreign policy department in the executive branch is the Department of State. Its head, the secretary of state, acts as the official spokesperson for the United States in foreign relations and is an important adviser to the president. Aside from senior staff such as the secretary of state, who is nominated by the president and confirmed by the Senate, State Department personnel are generally career civil servants who remain in their positions even after a new president takes office.

State Department officials operate U.S. embassies abroad and interact extensively with the leaders of other countries; they also offer expertise on the politics, economics, and cultures of other nations. There are many different offices and working groups in the State Department, from people who deal with treaties to coordinators of international aid, arms control, or assistance for refugees.

The Department of Defense The Department of Defense carries out military actions as ordered by civilian authorities, ranging from large military operations such as those in Afghanistan to smaller operations such as the ongoing drone attacks against Al Qaeda and ISIS forces throughout the Middle East or the deployment of troops, ships, and aircraft for training, humanitarian relief, and other purposes. For example, crewed and uncrewed navy ships and submarines routinely transit the South China Sea to contest China's sovereignty claims and to gather information on Chinese ships and military installations.

DID YOU KNOW?

In 2019, American military personnel acted as advisers or trainers in

152

countries.
Source: State Department report

The military's role in foreign policy is not limited to uses of force. Military personnel also deliver humanitarian aid or help American citizens evacuate from areas of conflict. For example, U.S. ships and helicopters deliver medical supplies and assist relief operations after natural disasters. In addition, some military planes were used to return citizens to the United States during the COVID-19 pandemic. The American military advises and trains armed forces in other countries, including hot spots such as Syria, Somalia, and Yemen. And military personnel may also play a role in foreign policymaking, with senior military officials serving as consultants during policy debates and midlevel officers serving in the NSC and on the staff of some congressional committees. For example, former general H. R. McMaster served as one of President Trump's National Security Advisors, and former general James Mattis was Trump's first secretary of defense.

The overriding principle of America's military is the concept of **civilian control**—the idea that military personnel do not formulate policy but, rather, implement directives from their civilian leaders in the executive branch (the president and senior leaders in the Defense Department) and Congress. In general, the norm is that disagreements between the civilians and the military are accepted as long as (1) they are kept private and (2) military leaders carry out without hesitation the orders they are ultimately given.

The Department of Homeland Security The Department of Homeland Security was formed after the September 11 attacks by combining the Coast Guard, the Transportation Security Administration, the Border Patrol, and several other agencies. The department's responsibilities are to secure America's borders, prevent future terrorist attacks, and coordinate intelligence gathering. On the one hand, Homeland Security's record is exemplary: there has not been a major terrorist attack on American soil since September 11, 2001. On the other hand, there is concern that many Homeland Security policies (such as requiring extensive screening for all airline passengers) impose large societal costs while having a marginal impact on safety.[31]

Intelligence Agencies Agencies such as the Central Intelligence Agency (CIA) and National Security Agency (NSA) are primarily responsible for government intelligence gathering. Most of their work consists of gathering information from public or semipublic sources, such as data on industrial outputs. However, these agencies also undertake covert operations to acquire intelligence, use satellites and other

civilian control
The idea that military leaders do not formulate military policy but rather implement directives from civilian leaders.

Unilateral presidential powers in the foreign policy arena allow presidents to make foreign policy decisions as they see fit. Despite Democratic opposition in Congress and opposition among the American people, President Trump elected to remove the United States from the Paris Agreement on climate change.

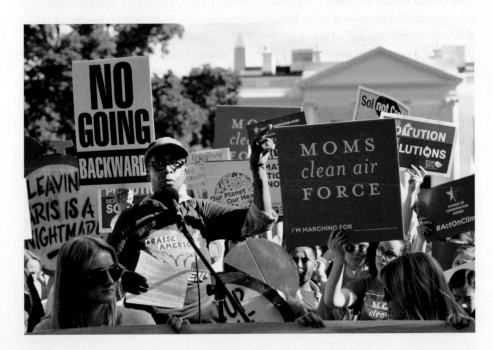

technology to monitor communications, or even attack individuals, other nations, or organizations. The Director of National Intelligence in the EOP leads and coordinates the activities of the various intelligence agencies.

Congress

Congress holds three types of influence over foreign policy. The first is the power of the purse. Since members of Congress write annual budgets for every government department and agency, one way for members to shape foreign policy is to forbid expenditures on activities that members want to prevent.

Second, the Senate has the power to approve treaties and confirm the appointments of senior members of the president's foreign policy team, including the secretaries of state and defense, the Director of National Intelligence, and America's ambassador to the UN. Although it is rare for senators to reject a treaty or nominee, sometimes they issue preemptive warnings about what kinds of treaties they will accept (in response, presidents often avoid asking for a vote on treaties they know will be rejected).

Third, the Constitution grants Congress the power to declare war on other nations. However, the Constitution does not say that this declaration must occur before hostilities can begin or whether the declaration is necessary at all. In an attempt to codify war-making powers, in 1973 Congress adopted the War Powers Resolution, although the question of which branch of the government ultimately controls America's armed forces remains controversial. (See the How It Works graphic for more details.)

Although the president dominates foreign policy, several groups within Congress participate in making foreign policy and Congress can reverse or thwart any presidential initiatives. The Committee on Foreign Affairs in the House and the Foreign Relations Committee in the Senate are responsible for writing legislation that deals with foreign policy, including setting the annual budget for agencies that carry out those policies. These committees also hold hearings in which they pose questions to foreign policy experts from inside and outside the government.

There is an Intelligence Committee in both the House and the Senate; these committees oversee covert operations and the actions of the CIA, the NSA, and similar agencies. Current law requires the president to give Congress "timely notification" of covert intelligence operations (although there is some dispute over what "timely" means).[32] These arrangements help ensure that someone outside the executive branch knows about secret operations and can organize congressional opposition if these actions are deemed illegal, immoral, or unwise.

Of course, members of Congress always have the power to block a president's foreign policy initiatives, but doing so requires enacting a law with enough votes to override a presidential veto (often an impossible task). For example, after Congress passed a resolution in 2019 disapproving of a sale of U.S. military equipment to the United Arab Emirates, President Trump vetoed the measure and the Senate failed to override, meaning the sale went through. In other cases, such as during the debate over U.S. participation in the NATO operations in Libya or interventions in Syria, resolutions were offered to cut off funding but were not passed by either house of Congress.

The federal courts

The federal courts, including the Supreme Court, weigh in on foreign policy questions through judicial review, determining whether laws, regulations, and presidential actions are consistent with the Constitution. For example, a series of lower-court and

War Powers: Who Controls the Armed Forces?

The President

Has the power to deploy troops as commander in chief

Under the War Powers Resolution, has to notify Congress, and the use of force must be terminated within 60 days if Congress does not approve. However, Congress has never voted to terminate military action, and most presidents have argued that the act is unconstitutional.

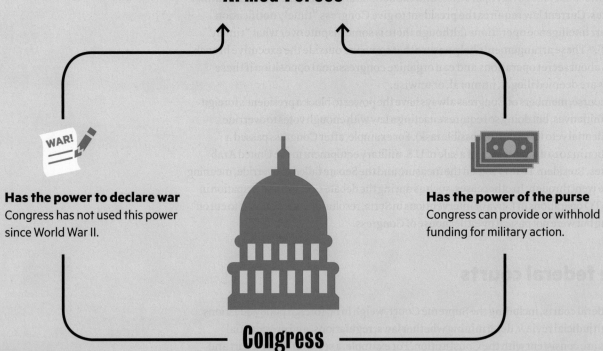

Armed Forces

Has the power to declare war
Congress has not used this power since World War II.

Has the power of the purse
Congress can provide or withhold funding for military action.

Congress

America's Role in Syria's Civil War

America's ongoing intervention in the Syrian civil war illustrates how the constitutional allocation of war powers plays out in practice. Although presidents Obama and Trump had the authority to order U.S. forces into combat, their actions were taken after consultation with other nations and debate within the United Nations, and were subject to congressional review and limitations.

Civil war!

March 2011: A civil war begins between the Syrian government and opposition forces.

Taking sides.

Soon after the conflict begins, the United States and its allies **send assistance to opposition** forces, while Russia helps the Syrian government.

Uh oh...

January 2012: ISIS forces move from Iraq to Syria, **capturing territory** from both government and opposition forces.

It gets worse.

2012–2014: Reports surface of **Syrian government attacks on civilians** (some using chemical weapons). Civilians fleeing the conflict flood into refugee camps in neighboring countries.

Nope.

September 2013: Attempts by Senate Democrats to authorize intervention in the Syrian civil war are **defeated**.

International agreement.

September 2013: Under pressure from the international community and the United Nations, the Syrian government **agrees to destroy** all of its chemical weapons.

?

Critical Thinking

1. **As you see in this example,** though the president is commander in chief, military action generally follows an extended process of consultation and negotiation with members of Congress and representatives from other nations. What are the benefits and costs of this deliberative process?

2. **At the beginning of this chapter,** we noted that some Americans believe that "politics stops at the water's edge." Does the United States' intervention in the Syrian civil war support or disprove this statement?

Giving the go-ahead.

September 2014: President Obama requests that Congress appropriate funds to aid Syrian rebels and **orders airstrikes against ISIS forces**. Congress approves both actions, and airstrikes soon begin.

Change, or the same?

Incoming president Trump promises a **more aggressive** U.S. policy in Syria.

We're out (mostly).

October 2019: President Trump announces **withdrawal of U.S. forces from Syria**, although some troops remain to continue the fight against ISIS.

Supreme Court decisions forced the Bush administration to revise its policy of holding terror suspects indefinitely without charges; the rulings required that the suspects be charged with crimes and tried on those charges. Although this example shows how the courts can reverse presidential actions, three points are key. First, the decisions were not a complete defeat for President Bush. While his policy was overturned, the courts acknowledged that similar policies would be constitutional. Second, court proceedings require time: adjudicating the terror suspect cases required several years, during which the administration's policy remained in place and the defendants were imprisoned without trial or any way to contest their imprisonment.[33] And third, in many cases, such as President Trump's travel ban, the courts have ultimately supported presidential orders.

Groups outside the federal government

A variety of individuals, groups, and forces outside government influence foreign policy. These include interest groups, the media, and public opinion, as well as intergovernmental, nongovernmental, and international organizations.

Interest Groups Interest groups are organizations that work to convince elected officials and bureaucrats to implement policy changes in line with the group's goals. Diverse groups and organizations lobby government over foreign policy.[34] For example, during the congressional debate in the summer of 2015 over the agreement with Iran regarding its nuclear weapons program and President Trump's subsequent decision in 2018 to withdraw from the deal, the American-Israel Public Affairs Committee (AIPAC), one of the most powerful interest groups in Washington, led the opposition to the deal. A coalition of smaller groups (including J Street, another pro-Israel lobbying organization that often opposes AIPAC on issues relating to Israel, as well as groups of scientists and the left-leaning organization Move On) lobbied in favor of approval.

Lobbying efforts can even involve foreign governments. In these cases, lobbying efforts center on economic and military aid, trade deals, and more general efforts to

DID YOU KNOW?

Since 2016, foreign governments have spent more than

$2 billion

to lobby the U.S. federal government.

Source: OpenSecrets.org

U.S. politicians and government officials regularly speak at AIPAC events. Vice President Mike Pence is shown here addressing AIPAC's annual convention. However, it would be a mistake to conclude that the attention paid to this or other interest groups automatically translates into U.S. government support for the groups' policy proposals.

improve a country's image among members of Congress and the bureaucracy. In the case of the Iran deal, Israel's ambassador to the United States called many members of Congress to try to persuade them to oppose the deal when it was negotiated and, later, to support President Trump's withdrawal.

Sometimes interest group lobbying pits business interests against other concerns such as national security. For example, during both the Obama and Trump presidencies, the Chinese government and two of its major telecommunications technology firms, Huawei and ZTE, complained that the U.S. government had prevented these firms from expanding into U.S. markets. The United States had also discouraged its allies from purchasing equipment from these companies. U.S. technology firms argued that Huawei and ZTE should be kept out of the United States because their equipment could be used for spying or cyberattacks. Although the U.S. technology firms' claims might have been true (the evidence was classified), it was also the case that the U.S. firms had lost market share to Chinese firms in recent years. Raising national security concerns may have just been a way for the U.S. firms to force the federal government to keep Huawei and ZTE out of the lucrative American market.

Finally, some groups focus on publicizing international events in the hope of prompting citizens to demand government action. For example, in recent years religious groups met with elected officials and worked to gain press coverage of the plight of refugees fleeing the civil war in Syria. At the same time, major American media outlets published photos of squalid refugee camps and refugee children who drowned after the boat they were traveling on sank in the Mediterranean.

As mentioned in Chapter 9, the impact of lobbying efforts like these is hard to determine. At the same time that groups were lobbying in favor of Syrian refugees, the Obama administration was granting asylum to thousands of refugees each year. However, it is likely that the individuals making these asylum decisions (including, at the top, President Obama) were sympathetic to the refugees and would have admitted them in any case. And in fact, despite the ongoing problems in Syria and other countries, overall refugee admissions to the United States have plunged to near zero under President Trump, highlighting the limits of lobbying efforts.

The Media Television, radio, print media, and the Internet all inform the public about events in America and elsewhere. As discussed in Chapter 6, although media coverage is a prime source of information about domestic and foreign policy for most Americans, one cannot say that evaluations of America's foreign policy are driven solely by the news media's decisions about what to cover and how to report it. The press informs individuals about events and may to some extent frame the criteria people use to judge America's foreign policy and consider alternatives, but as we have seen elsewhere, most of the time, media attention to a foreign policy question or problem has a limited impact on opinions and policy choices.

Public Opinion Foreign policy decisions are also sensitive to public opinion. As with many domestic issues, elected officials are well aware of their constituents' views and are reluctant to support policies that conflict with opinions held by a majority of their constituents. On issues such as lowering tariffs with other countries, congressional voting is highly correlated with constituents' support of or opposition to these measures. However, public opinion is not a decisive influence on foreign policy. For example, in the case of Syrian refugees, American public opinion has consistently been opposed to allowing them to live in the United States. (This finding is not exceptional—in many other cases, Americans have opposed admission of refugees from political crises.[35])

When citizens are relatively less interested in foreign policy and uninformed about it, elected officials can place a low priority on responding to public opinion and can instead pursue their own foreign policy goals. For example, President Obama ordered American forces to intervene in the Syrian civil war with air strikes, arms shipments, and military assistance, although a strong majority of the American public favored different policies (some Americans wanted a more aggressive effort, while others favored disengagement).

Intergovernmental Organizations, Nongovernmental Organizations, and International Organizations America's relationship with the rest of the world is not just about government action; it also reflects actions on the part of several types of organizations. For example, members of **intergovernmental organizations (IGOs)** and **nongovernmental organizations (NGOs)** provide information and humanitarian assistance and carry out other activities that the U.S. government is unable or unwilling to undertake. IGOs are associations of sovereign states, while NGOs are private organizations. Thousands of IGOs and NGOs operate throughout the world.[36]

A primary goal of NGOs and IGOs is to promote global economic development and growth. Thus, one of the largest IGOs, the **World Bank**, funds economic development projects worldwide. Another IGO, the **International Monetary Fund (IMF)**, helps countries manage budget deficits and control the value of their currencies. Many NGOs, such as the Asia Foundation, focus on development in a particular region or on certain activities.

A second goal of NGOs is to provide humanitarian relief. In the wake of a disaster such as an earthquake or a flood, or during a famine or a war, organizations such as Oxfam International supply populations in crisis with basic necessities. Other groups such as Doctors without Borders provide medical care to populations threatened by violence, epidemics, or natural disasters. These groups played a key role in the response to COVID-19 outbreaks in Africa and elsewhere. Some NGOs also promote human rights. For example, Amnesty International spotlights international cases of people jailed for their political beliefs or held without trial, and the use of cruel punishments such as stoning. Amnesty's campaigns, as well as those of other NGOs, are not always supportive of U.S. policy. In recent years, for example, Amnesty has criticized the rendition of terror suspects by the United States.[37]

Finally, NGOs help build democracies. The Open Society Foundations fund efforts to increase mass political participation, strengthen political organizations, and verify the fairness of elections in new democracies throughout the world. The National Democratic Institute and the International Republican Institute conduct similar activities. Both organizations, for example, are working with groups in countries such as Myanmar, Ukraine, and Pakistan to increase the transparency of electoral institutions, recruit candidates, and help citizens build political organizations.

The United States is also a member of many international organizations. Best known is the **United Nations (UN)**, an assembly of ambassadors representing almost all of the world's nations that addresses issues of worldwide concern. The UN is involved in economic development, environmental protection, humanitarian relief, and peacekeeping efforts. Inside the UN, the Security Council—a group of 15 nations (permanent members Britain, China, France, Russia, and the United States, plus 10 rotating nations)—makes the most important decisions, particularly those involving UN military missions. The UN General Assembly, in which each nation has one vote, debates and votes on other concerns.

intergovernmental organizations (IGOs)
Organizations that seek to coordinate policy across member nations.

nongovernmental organizations (NGOs)
Groups operated by private institutions (rather than governments) to promote growth, economic development, and other agendas throughout the world.

World Bank
An intergovernmental organization established in 1944 that provides financial support for economic development projects in developing nations.

International Monetary Fund (IMF)
An intergovernmental organization established in 1944 to help stabilize the international monetary system, improve economic growth, and aid developing nations.

United Nations (UN)
An international organization made up of representatives from nearly every nation, with a mission to promote peace and cooperation, uphold international law, and provide humanitarian aid.

It may look to you like foreign policy is all about what the president wants. However, for the most part, the same kinds of people (in many cases, the same people) who influence domestic policy choices also shape America's foreign policy—including elected officials, interest groups, and the public at large. The president is a key player in making foreign policy choices, but he or she is far from being the only voice that matters.

"Why Should I Care?"

★

EXAMINE THE WAYS AMERICAN FOREIGN POLICY IS IMPLEMENTED

The tools of foreign policy

Now that we know the key players in foreign policy making, what are the tools and methods these players use to implement policy?

Diplomacy

The process of diplomacy involves using personal contact and negotiations with national leaders and representatives to work out international agreements or persuade other nations to change their behavior. Sometimes these efforts involve the threat of military action or economic sanctions, or incentives such as economic assistance or other forms of aid. The United States may participate directly in such efforts or mediate between parties in a dispute. Diplomacy has often been a limited but useful foreign policy tool. For example, the efforts of American and Russian diplomats were instrumental in establishing a brief cease-fire in Syria in 2016 and in getting both sides to allow convoys carrying relief supplies to enter besieged areas of the country—although this agreement had little impact on the larger conflict.

Diplomacy often involves protracted negotiations and many participants. The Singapore Summit between North Korea and the United States, which yielded a promise for peaceful relations and denuclearization of the Korean Peninsula, required months of preparation and the cooperation of the Singaporean government.

FIGURE 15.1

U.S. Imports and Exports as a Percentage of GDP

This figure illustrates the importance of trade to the U.S. economy. In recent years imports and exports have accounted for almost 30 percent of U.S. economic activity. Based on these data, what arguments would you make for lowering or increasing barriers to trade?

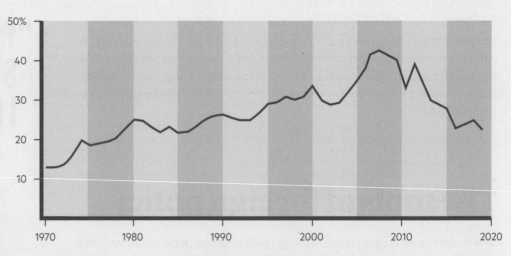

Source: Office of the United States Trade Representative, *2020 Trade Policy Agenda and 2019 Annual Report*, February 2020, https://ustr.gov/sites/default/files/2020_Trade_Policy_Agenda_and_2019_Annual_Report.pdf (accessed 6/12/20).

Trade and economic policies

Trade and economic policies can be crucial instruments of foreign policy: they can sustain economic growth in the United States and elsewhere, as well as create foreign markets for the goods produced by America's domestic industries. Figure 15.1 shows total American trade (imports and exports) with other countries over the last 50 years, expressed as a percentage of U.S. gross domestic product (GDP), which measures the size of the U.S. economy. In recent years, imports and exports together have constituted almost 30 percent of GDP.

The main tools of trade policy are tariffs and trade agreements. A **tariff** is a tax on the import or export of certain commodities, and a trade agreement sets tariff levels or limits the quantities of particular items that can be imported or exported. The United States International Trade Commission maintains a list of all tariffs in effect.[38] By adjusting tariff rates, the government can help or hurt domestic industries: high tariffs on imports help American producers charge lower prices than foreign competitors can, and low tariffs on exports help American producers sell to overseas markets.

Over the last two generations, the United States and most other nations have lowered tariffs and established free-trade zones, which reflect agreements to eliminate tariffs on all imports and exports among specific nations. Examples include a long-standing free trade agreement with Canada and Mexico and the Central America Free Trade Agreement (CAFTA) among the United States, five Central American nations, and the Dominican Republic. Other organizations, such as the **World Trade Organization (WTO)**, facilitate negotiations over tariffs and provide a mechanism for adjudicating cases in which one nation believes that another is using tariffs unfairly. Finally, the United States has granted many other countries **most-favored-nation status**: tariffs on imports to the United States from these nations are set at the lowest rate placed on any other nation.

Trade deals are inherently controversial because they almost always involve winners and losers. Even if a deal increases overall economic growth in the United States, some people will be made worse off. For example, if a deal makes it possible for an entrepreneur in a developing nation to sell a product in the United States at a lower price than domestic suppliers of the same product are charging, Americans who buy the imported goods are

tariff
A tax levied on imported or exported goods.

World Trade Organization (WTO)
An international organization created in 1995 to oversee trade agreements between nations by facilitating negotiations and handling disputes.

most-favored-nation status
A standing awarded to countries with which a nation has good trade relations, providing the lowest possible tariff rate. WTO members must give one another this preferred status.

better off (they pay less for the same product). However, the people who work for the U.S. suppliers are in trouble (their employers may go out of business if they cannot find another market for their products). One reason for Donald Trump's victory in 2016 was strong support from rural communities (particularly in the Midwest Rust Belt) that have lost manufacturing jobs because companies responded to lower tariffs by moving factories overseas and because companies face competition from foreign suppliers.

Trade is an important part of foreign policy. The United States can use free-trade agreements and tariffs to bargain with countries for concessions in noneconomic policy areas or to cement international alliances. One of the reasons why America played a central role in crafting trade agreements with Asian nations was that the government wanted to strengthen its political and economic ties with these nations, as a counter to the increased regional economic and military power of China. Withdrawing from these agreements, as Trump has decided to do, means that these foreign policy issues will need to be addressed using other means.

Economic policies are also used to threaten or sanction countries as a way of inducing them to change their behavior. For example, the UN Security Council authorized **economic sanctions** in the early 2000s against Iran aimed at forcing the nation to stop enriching uranium, a first step in the production of nuclear weapons. These sanctions banned arms sales to the country and made it all but impossible for Iranian citizens and corporations to do business outside their nation's borders. The damage caused by sanctions was one important reason why Iran agreed to negotiate a deal with the United States and the EU, resulting in the 2016 deal in which Iran agreed to curb its nuclear research programs and Western nations agreed to remove economic sanctions. This outcome also explains why President Trump's decision to withdraw from the deal is unlikely to change Iranian behavior: none of the sanctions formerly imposed by EU nations have been reinstated.

Foreign aid

Foreign aid comprises money, products, or services given to other countries or the citizens of these countries. Sometimes foreign aid reflects the desire to provide basic assistance to satisfy fundamental human needs. For example, American military ships and aircraft are often used to deliver food and medical supplies to the victims of earthquakes and other natural disasters. Foreign aid also serves to stimulate economic growth in other nations and to facilitate international agreements. For example, the peace treaty between Egypt and Israel in 1979 was facilitated by America's agreement to provide substantial military and economic assistance to both countries.[39]

Figure 15.2 shows the level of American nonmilitary foreign aid in 2019 measured as a percentage of gross national income (GNI, which includes GDP as well as investment income from other countries) and total volume in U.S. dollars, compared with that of the six other countries that are members of the G7 group of major industrialized nations. Compared to these countries, America gives a relatively low percentage of GNI in foreign aid, although part of the explanation lies in the size of the U.S. economy: America's foreign aid contributions are the largest of any country when measured in total dollars, but it also has the largest GNI of any country.

Alliances and treaties

A treaty is an agreement between nations to work together on economic or security issues. An alliance is an agreement that commits nations to security guarantees, which are assurances that one country will help another if it is attacked. America is a member of many international alliances, most notably NATO. This alliance was formed by

One of the most conflictual issues of the Trump administration's foreign policy strategy was tariffs. Touted initially as a defense of the United States' national security, President Trump's steel tariff had unintended consequences, including the increase of steel prices domestically and the escalation of a trade war abroad.

economic sanctions
Penalties applied by one country or group of countries on another, usually in the form of tariffs or other trade barriers.

DID YOU KNOW?

The United States spends

<1%

of its annual budget on foreign aid. According to one poll, Americans on average think the country spends 28 percent.

Source: Kaiser Family Foundation Poll

U.S. Foreign Aid in Comparative Perspective

This figure shows foreign aid contributions expressed both in total volume and as a percentage of gross national income (GNI). Do these data imply that America is less generous with aid than other nations are? What other explanations are there for the differences across countries?

Note: Bars represent aid in volume and dots represent aid as percent GNI. Data are from 2019.

Source: Organization for Economic Cooperation and Development, *Development Co-operation Report 2019*, December 18, 2019, www.oecd.org/dac/development-co-operation-report-20747721.htm (accessed 6/12/20).

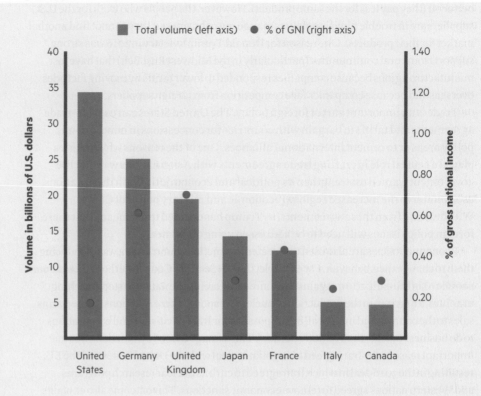

the North Atlantic Treaty after World War II to provide collective security against the Soviet Union and Warsaw Pact countries. The organization's mission shifted after the Cold War to focus on coordinating military force toward common goals, with the organization's 2011 intervention in the Libyan civil war the first instance of operations outside Europe. Historically, the United States has paid a disproportionate share of the cost of NATO operations and devoted a larger share of GNI to defense spending. In recent years, the United States has successfully pressured its NATO allies to increase their spending on defense. Such demands continued under President Trump, who made doing so one of the central themes of his presidential campaign.

The United States is a party to treaties with many countries.[40] Treaties and alliances enable the United States to commit itself to a course of action or signal its intentions to other nations.[41] By helping form NATO and stationing troops in Europe, the United States guaranteed that if Warsaw Pact troops invaded the West, U.S. forces would be directly involved in the defense of Western Europe. More recently, after Russia's invasion of Crimea (a region of Ukraine) in 2014, America and its NATO partners sent aircraft, troops, and ships to countries adjacent to Ukraine and other countries that were part of the former Soviet Union to signal their opposition to Russia's plans and their support for these governments.

Military force

Military force is a fundamental tool of foreign policy. America's military forces serve throughout the world as a deterrent to conflict, and military exercises by U.S. troops, aircraft, and ships serve to remind potential adversaries of America's military power.

For example, as mentioned earlier, in 2016, in response to Chinese claims of sovereignty over the South China Sea, U.S. military aircraft and ships began to regularly transit the region to underscore the U.S. position that the sea is international waters and to demonstrate that America is ready to keep the sea open by using force if necessary.

The United States has also fought wars and lesser conflicts to further its foreign policy goals. Some were all-out military operations, such as the invasions of Iraq and Afghanistan. More commonly, these deployments were short-lived operations, such as the evacuation of American civilians from areas of unrest, the delivery of humanitarian assistance, or the use of ship-launched cruise missiles to attack terrorist camps and similar targets.[42] In the case of fighting ISIS, America has sent military advisers and training personnel to several nations, carried out numerous attacks by Special Forces and drones, and, in the case of Syria and Iraq, conducted many air strikes against ISIS forces and infrastructure as well as Syrian ground forces.

The size and power of America's military provide numerous options for policy makers. For example, after the September 11 attacks, in an attempt to prevent future terror attacks by Al Qaeda, U.S. forces invaded Afghanistan, which had been used as a base of operations for the organization.[43] It is highly unlikely that any other country could carry out such a large-scale operation so far from home.

Nonetheless, military force is not all-powerful. For example, despite over a decade of combat operations in Afghanistan and large amounts of economic and military aid to the Afghan government, the Taliban (a religious–political organization) still controls a significant percentage of the Afghan countryside, and the Afghan government's ability to defeat the Taliban without American help is highly questionable. Similarly, while air strikes in Iraq and Syria have reduced ISIS's military might, the organization remains able to plan future terror attacks throughout the world. Moreover, it is not clear whether any level of military force can remove this threat.

The politics of foreign policy today

ANALYZE SEVERAL MAJOR AREAS OF FOREIGN POLICY AND WHY THEY ARE OFTEN CONTROVERSIAL

The making of foreign policy, like everything else in the federal government, is a political act—a contest involving elected officials, bureaucrats, interest groups, and other actors, all with their own goals. In this sense, there are always conflicts over what America's foreign policy should look like and compromise is fundamental to the making of it. This section discusses three of the major foreign policy issues facing America in the contemporary era: trade, terrorism, and nuclear proliferation—and how all of these issues raise human rights concerns. These issues demonstrate the complexity of America's foreign policy choices and how these decisions are shaped both by conflicts and by political processes.

Managing international trade: China

For the United States, trade is a necessity. America imports a wide range of resources and manufactured goods from other countries. Increased trade or outsourcing of manufacturing and service delivery can also enhance economic growth and thereby create new jobs for Americans.

These practices are examples of **globalization**, reflecting the trend toward increasing interaction and connections among individuals, corporations, and nations. New technologies have leveled the global playing field, allowing suppliers of goods and services to sell their products throughout the world. At the same time, there have been many new international agreements to reduce or eliminate tariffs among nations and adjudicate disputes.[44]

America's relations with China are a prime example of these developments. Many American companies have factories in China to serve American markets. China is a major producer of rare earth metals that are used to build computer chips. American corporations are also opening stores in China—the coffee chain Starbucks, for example, opens more than one store per day there.[45] In recent years, China has been one of America's largest trading partners, with over $500 billion in imports and exports during 2019.[46]

Although these moves generate significant benefits, the changes do not make everyone better off. American jobs have been lost as factories that could not compete with cheaper foreign suppliers have closed.[47] Support from individuals hurt by these changes was one reason for Donald Trump's victory in 2016. Moreover, there have been numerous complaints that Chinese companies have stolen trade secrets from American corporations or violated American copyright laws—in some cases, with the apparent support of the Chinese government.

President Trump departed from previous administrations in his aggressive use of punitive tariffs to force China and other countries to change their trade

globalization
The increase over the last generation in trade, travel, and the flow of ideas and beliefs between nations.

What I'm saying is this: I'm saying that we do it, but if they [China] don't start treating us fairly and stop devaluing and let their currency rise so that our companies can compete and we don't lose all of these millions of jobs that we're losing I would certainly start taxing goods that come in from China. Who the hell has to lose $505 billion a year?

—President Donald Trump

Globalization has transformed economics and society in the United States and abroad. Brands such as Starbucks have spread around the world. Revenue growth for the company in China and Southeast Asia has been substantially higher than in the United States.

practices. The problem is, in a global economy in which America is only one potential market, such threats may simply lead foreign companies to sell their goods elsewhere, raising the prices paid by American consumers. Trump's tariffs also triggered increased tariffs on American goods, which reduced American exports and hurt employees of affected companies. Most important, however, even if trade barriers disappear and global markets become completely open, some American communities will still suffer because of increased foreign imports. It is often extremely difficult to retrain people to compete for new jobs that will provide pay and benefits comparable to what they received in their former positions. In addition, there are no systematic American efforts to help citizens of other countries who are hurt by globalization.

Finally, globalization raises new human rights questions. For example, do U.S. companies such as Apple, which has outsourced the production of iPhones to factories in China, have a responsibility to monitor conditions in these factories and ensure that workers are paid a fair wage? More generally, should the United States increase its trade with a country such as China that restricts the freedoms of its citizens in ways that most Americans would find objectionable? Or should it increase trade, on the grounds that exposure to American commerce and culture will encourage the other country's citizens to press their government for reforms?

One way to respond to these complications is to take a stand along the lines of Donald Trump's punitive tariffs—that the United States should renegotiate trade agreements to protect American workers and increase American exports, with the threat that America will impose high import tariffs on countries that refuse to comply with these demands. This attitude illustrates a central truth: decisions to encourage trade and globalization are real choices, choices that are sure to generate high levels of conflict in American politics. While U.S. policy can encourage or discourage trade, outsourcing, and other interactions that cross national borders, all these choices will make some people better off and some worse off. As in so many other areas of American politics, because of the wide range of interests that Americans bring to the table, there is no one trade policy that is clearly better than all the others.

One of the effects of globalization is outsourcing—moving jobs to different countries, usually to take advantage of lower wages and looser restrictions on manufacturing practices. Here, workers in China assemble electronic products for a foreign company.

Fighting terrorism: ISIS

There have been no major terrorist attacks on the United States since September 11, 2001, and Al Qaeda and ISIS have been decimated by U.S. counterattacks. Nevertheless, the potential for terrorism remains, and groups such as ISIS have continued to carry out smaller operations, such as attacks in various European cities. ISIS has also encouraged individuals to plan and execute their own attacks, such as the attacks by an American citizen in a Miami nightclub in June 2016 and by a New York City resident who drove a truck through a crowd of pedestrians in October 2017.

The fight against global terror is different from a conventional war. In a conventional war, there are clear victory criteria: the losing nation's government capitulates. In contrast, terrorism involves multiple organizations with fluid memberships. Eliminating one individual or group may not reduce the danger of future attacks, because these victories do not address the factors that drive terrorism, including poverty and a deep-set anger that some individuals have against Western interests. For example, while the United States and its allies have recaptured land in Syria and Iraq that was controlled by ISIS and have killed or captured many ISIS fighters, offshoots of the organization still exist throughout the world, as do anti-American, anti-West sentiments among some groups.

The same is true for Al Qaeda. Over the last 20 years, the United States has invaded Afghanistan and removed the Afghan Taliban government that supported Al Qaeda, destroyed many camps and other centers in Afghanistan and elsewhere, and captured or killed many operatives and leaders of the organization. However, while Al Qaeda is far weaker than it was in 2001, the possibility of an attack on Americans in the United States or abroad by the remnants of Al Qaeda remains very real (although, as we discuss in the What Do the Facts Say? feature, many Americans overestimate the threat of terrorist attacks). Moreover, even after over a decade of military action and efforts to build a stable democracy and a growing economy, Afghanistan remains a dangerous, unstable place. Should the United States be responsible for creating a stable, prosperous Afghan nation? What will happen if America withdraws its support? Would the Taliban and Al Qaeda return, or would another equally bad group emerge?

Human rights concerns also shape antiterrorism efforts. American attacks against terror groups have the potential to cause civilian casualties—especially in places such as Afghanistan, where these groups have tried to hide among civilians to discourage such attacks. In addition, investigating terror groups may involve increased surveillance of Americans and their communications. American decision makers must also decide whether they will overlook problems in other countries to pursue terror suspects. For example, the government of Pakistan is routinely cited for human rights abuses, but Pakistani officials have aided in the capture of Taliban fighters in Afghanistan and have allowed the United States to use Pakistani airspace to send drones into Iraq and Iran.

In sum, regardless of what happens in Syria, Afghanistan, and other areas where ISIS and other terrorist organizations operate, the fight against global terrorism will continue for the foreseeable future. It is easy to work backward from this conclusion to a critique of past policies—to conclude, for example, that things would be better if the United States had sent more troops or economic aid to Afghanistan, had not invaded Iraq, or had refused to intervene in the Syrian civil war. However, because terror attacks can come from many sources, because the fight against these organizations

One of the United States' strategies to increase stability in Afghanistan is to train the Afghan National Army and police in order to provide the Afghan government with a greater level of control over the region.

touches on human rights concerns, and because it is not clear how to eliminate the threat, there is no clearly best strategy in the War on Terror. As a result, the threat from terrorism, and the debate over how to respond, will persist.

Preventing the spread of WMDs: North Korea

The term "**weapons of mass destruction (WMDs)**" refers to nuclear bombs, chemical weapons such as nerve gas, and biological weapons such as anthrax. Given the potential for these weapons to inflict mass casualties, the United States has placed a high priority on (1) limiting the number of nations that have these weapons and (2) preventing terrorist organizations from obtaining or developing them.

The enduring problem for the United States is to determine how to respond to North Korea's nuclear capabilities. Military operations are problematic, as North Korea's weapons and the factories that manufacture them are buried deep underground and may not be destroyed even by a massive attack. An unsuccessful attack might goad the North Korean government to launch its remaining weapons against U.S., South Korean, or Japanese targets. Moreover, how should America respond to a nuclear attack against its citizens or its allies, particularly if it is unclear which nation or group is responsible?

Historically, America's policy toward North Korea as well as other near-nuclear powers has emphasized incentives as well as threats. Economic and military sanctions serve to pressure nations that continue to develop weapons, while offers of economic aid and even civilian nuclear reactors serve to persuade nations to give up their weapons programs.[48] Of course, because these agreements are voluntary, nations giving up their nuclear weapons programs get something in return. In the case of the deal with Iran, the United States and its allies made crucial concessions—the lifting of economic sanctions and the return of Iranian assets held after the Iranian Revolution of 1979. These concessions were hugely valuable to the Iranian regime because of their importance in the Iranian economy. While President Trump moved beyond previous administrations by making threats about the magnitude of the U.S. response to a North Korean attack, as well as by meeting with North Korea's leader, Kim Jong-un, in 2018, in concrete terms his policies were not significantly different from those of his predecessors.

weapons of mass destruction (WMDs)
Weapons that have the potential to cause large-scale loss of life, such as nuclear bombs and chemical or biological weapons.

North Korea has one of the world's least predictable and most isolated political regimes. Its nuclear capabilities and large military make North Korea a threat to the stability of the region. However, because of the poor state of the country's economy, economic sanctions are unlikely to foster movement toward democracy and openness.

The Threat of Terrorism

As the Gallup poll here indicates, a substantial percentage of Americans worry that they or members of their family will be the victims of a terrorist attack—in fact, these concerns even predate the September 11 attacks. Are these fears justified? How great is the risk? What do the facts say?

How Worried Are You That You or Someone in Your Family Will Become a Victim of Terrorism?

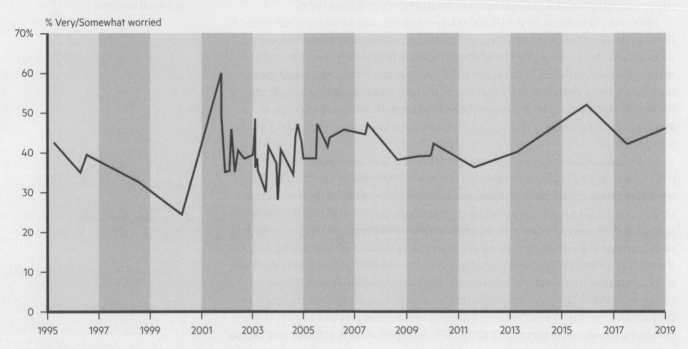

% Very/Somewhat worried

Think about it

- **Is the public's concern over the dangers of terrorist attacks** justified by the fatality data?
- **Suppose you are a bureaucrat from the Department of Homeland Security** who is testifying before Congress on the need to increase funding for antiterrorism programs. One of the members of Congress at the hearing argues that such funding is unnecessary because the likelihood of dying from a terrorist incident is so low. How would you respond?

Hazard	Annual Fatality Risk
Traffic accidents	1 in 8,200
Homicide	1 in 22,000
Industrial accidents	1 in 53,000
Natural disasters	1 in 480,000
Drowning in bathtub	1 in 950,000
Home appliances	1 in 1,500,000
Deer accidents	1 in 2,000,000
Commercial aviation	1 in 2,300,000
Peanut allergies	1 in 6,000,000
Lightning	1 in 7,000,000
Terrorist attack	1 in 110,000,000

Sources: Gallup Poll, "Terrorism in the United States," https://news.gallup.com/poll/4909/terrorism-united-states.aspx (accessed 6/12/20); John Mueller and Mark G. Stewart, *Chasing Ghosts: The Policing of Terrorism* (New York: Oxford University Press, 2015).

The problem with America's carrots and sticks is that the North Korean economy is already in shambles and the country has relatively little trade with other nations. As a result, economic sanctions are not very threatening. The North Korean government has essentially isolated its citizens from the outside world and carried out a widespread program of indoctrination to reinforce beliefs that building nuclear weapons is an appropriate response to threats from the rest of the world. The government also imprisons dissidents and withholds basic resources from the North Korean people, focusing instead on building a strong military. Under these conditions, the offer to reopen commercial and cultural ties is not very attractive to the North Korean leadership.

The difficulty of the problem does not eliminate conflict in American politics over what policy to follow. The disagreement is in part over the potential for success of different tactics. Some believe that North Korea's weapons could be destroyed by a bombing attack, for example. Despite ongoing missile tests, it is also uncertain whether North Korea has the means to reliably launch nuclear weapons against American targets. Others see a wider range of motivations, agreeing that North Korea's nuclear capability must be eliminated but also arguing that it is America's responsibility to free the North Korean people from an oppressive dictatorship.

Unpacking the Conflict

Foreign policy matters. National security is a top priority for many Americans. The state of the American economy, from home prices to the unemployment rate, is affected by economic conditions elsewhere. Trade agreements with other nations determine how much American companies are allowed to export and what taxes and fees they must pay to import raw materials and other goods. It is hard to find a domestic issue that does not have a foreign policy component. And the COVID-19 pandemic highlights that in an interconnected world, problems that start within one nation's borders can expand to threaten countries across the entire globe. Who gets to decide America's foreign policy? How is foreign policy made?

As with many other issues in politics, the importance of foreign policy is not matched by the ability of elected officials to manage events and achieve desired outcomes. President Trump and his supporters believed that a combination of punitive tariffs and demands for renegotiation of existing agreements would increase U.S. exports and improve the American economy, only to find that foreign leaders responded with their own punishments and demands, leading to an outcome in which everyone was worse off. The problem is not that Trump's desire to reward his supporters by protecting American manufacturers and exporters was bad per se. But in a world where all countries want to maximize exports and protect domestic industries, the United States cannot have it both ways—it cannot demand that other countries open their economies but accept U.S. restrictions.

One significant difference between foreign and domestic policies is the preeminent role played by the president in determining America's relations with other nations and its role in the world. Even so, other actors, especially Congress, can block presidential initiatives or set policy on their own. In fact, many presidential foreign policy powers, such as the ability to change tariffs, have been delegated to the executive branch by Congress.

The most important thing to remember about foreign policy making is that it is conflictual. It is tempting to think that because foreign policy involves dealing with other countries, Americans should hold similar preferences and stand united. The reality is that disagreements among elected officials over what to do about terrorist groups, trade agreements, worldwide pandemics, or any other question of foreign policy are not just attempts to attract political support or get media attention. These differences of opinion reflect real dilemmas over what government should do and how it should do it.

In all these respects, the issues discussed in this chapter, including the fight against global terrorism, the Middle East, conflicts with China over trade policy, and persuading Iran and North Korea to curb their nuclear ambitions, are not exceptions to the rule; rather, they epitomize just how close to home foreign policy is. Ordinary Americans are finding their lives increasingly affected by actions taken outside U.S. borders—a trend that is likely to continue over the next generation. And the political process will determine how these pressing foreign policy questions will be resolved.

"What's Your Take?"

What should be America's foreign policy objectives? Should foreign policy makers focus on providing foreign aid to stimulate growth in other countries, as well as intervening to support foreign governments?

Or should the goal be to return to isolationism, focusing on domestic rather than international issues, as Trump proposed in his inauguration speech?

STUDY GUIDE

What is foreign policy?

Describe the major approaches to understanding foreign policy, and trace how America's role in the world has evolved. (Pages 491–498)

Summary

Foreign policy is any government action toward a group outside America's borders. Foreign policy goals are complex, and debates on what America's goals should be are traditionally framed in terms of general principles. The goals of American foreign policy have changed over time and have become increasingly internationalist.

Key terms

foreign policy (p. 491)
unilateral action (national) (p. 491)
multilateral action (p. 491)
isolationism (p. 492)
internationalism (p. 492)
realism (p. 492)
idealism (p. 492)

nation building (p. 492)
Monroe Doctrine (p. 493)
Cold War (p. 494)
containment (p. 494)
mutually assured destruction (p. 495)
détente (p. 495)
Bush Doctrine (p. 496)

Practice Quiz Questions

1. When one country does something on its own without coordinating with other countries, it is _____.

a   isolationist
b   internationalist
c   acting unilaterally
d   acting multilaterally
e   nation building

2. _____ believe that countries pursue their own interests.

a   Realists
b   Idealists
c   Constructivists
d   Internationalists
e   Comparativists

3. The Monroe Doctrine stated that in European wars America would _____.

a   support Britain
b   support the attacking country
c   support the attacked country
d   provide arms but not troops
e   remain neutral

4. American foreign policy became increasingly internationalist following _____.

a   the Civil War
b   World War I
c   World War II
d   the Vietnam War
e   the Cold War

5. The goal of containment influenced the _____ and _____.

a   war in Iraq; the war in Afghanistan
b   Korean War; the war in Iraq
c   Vietnam War; the war in Iraq
d   Vietnam War; the Cuban missile crisis
e   Vietnam War; World War II

Foreign policy makers

Explain how the various branches of government shape foreign policy. (Pages 498–507)

Summary

The major actors in foreign policy are the president and Congress, although the Supreme Court, interest groups, and public opinion all influence foreign policy decisions to a degree. The president's advantage over Congress lies in the ambiguity in the Constitution and the unilateral presidential power.

Key terms

National Security Council (NSC) (p. 498)
civilian control (p. 500)
intergovernmental organizations (IGOs) (p. 506)
nongovernmental organizations (NGOs) (p. 506)

World Bank (p. 506)
International Monetary Fund (IMF) (p. 506)
United Nations (UN) (p. 506)

6. The principal foreign policy department in the executive branch is _____ .

a   the Department of Defense

b   the Council on Foreign Relations

c   the Department of International Relations

d   the Department of State

e   the Foreign Intelligence Advisory Board

7. The idea that military personnel do not formulate policy but rather implement directives from civilians is _____ .

a   military deference

b   civilian control

c   the Geneva system

d   civilian–military alliance

e   the Bush Doctrine

8. Congress holds the _____ and the _____ , which both influence foreign policy.

a   power to deploy troops; power of the purse

b   power to approve treaties; power to deploy troops

c   power to declare war; power of the purse

d   power to deploy troops; power to declare war

e   power to approve appointments; power to deploy troops

9. The War Powers Resolution was designed to _____ .

a   limit the president's war-making powers

b   limit Congress's war-making powers

c   limit the Department of Defense's war-making powers

d   limit the Pentagon's war-making powers

e   limit the State Department's war-making powers

The tools of foreign policy

Examine the ways American foreign policy is implemented. (Pages 507–511)

Summary

American foreign policy is implemented using a variety of tools—beyond the use of military force, other tools include the provision of foreign aid or changes to trade policy. Though all tools can be used in pursuit of desired policy outcomes, the specific tool is selected based on careful consideration of context.

Key terms

tariff (p. 508)

World Trade Organization (WTO) (p. 508)

most-favored-nation status (p. 508)

economic sanctions (p. 509)

10. The process of _____ involves using personal contact and negotiations with leaders to work out international agreements.

a   nation building

b   diplomacy

c   unilateralism

d   the Bush Doctrine

e   the use of force

11. When a country is given most-favored-nation status, it means that the United States _____ any other nation.

a   gives the country higher levels of foreign aid than

b   gives the country higher levels of military aid than

c   sets tariffs on imports to the United States to the lowest rate given to

d   sets tariffs on exports from the United States to the lowest rate given to

e   sends that country more troops than

The politics of foreign policy today

Analyze several major areas of foreign policy and why they are often controversial. (Pages 511–517)

Summary

Focusing on three contemporary foreign policy issues—trade, terrorism, and WMDs—reveals a variety of conflicts among citizens and elected officials alike over how America's foreign policy should look. Notwithstanding this conflict, it is clear that America's policy choices on these issues will have enormous consequences both for American citizens and for people throughout the world.

Key terms

globalization (p. 512)

weapons of mass destruction (WMDs) (p. 515)

12. What factor limits the American response to potential terrorist threats?

a   American public opinion opposes attacks on terrorist organizations.

b   The War Powers Resolution limits military actions to those approved by Congress.

c   Other nations would impose economic sanctions on American corporations.

d   It is difficult to identify terrorists or determine their plans.

e   Addressing terrorism requires a multilateral effort, which is difficult to coordinate.

13. The American government hesitates to pressure Pakistan on human rights violations most likely because _____.

a doing so would threaten economic ties with Pakistan

b attempts to protect human rights may make it harder for the United States to achieve goals in Afghanistan

c evidence of human rights violations in Pakistan is unreliable

d there is little international condemnation for the Pakistani violations of human rights

e Pakistan enforces a Bill of Rights

14. Efforts to eliminate the threat of North Korean WMDs are limited by all of these factors *except* _____.

a Russian support for the North Korean regime

b the limited impact of economic sanctions

c the possibility that North Korea would respond militarily to an attack

d the isolation of North Korea's population

e the fact that North Korean WMDs are stored in well-protected facilities

Suggested Reading

Bueno de Mesquita, Bruce. *Principles of International Politics.* Washington, DC: CQ Press, 2005.

Finnemore, Martha. *The Purpose of Intervention: Changing Beliefs about the Use of Force.* Ithaca, NY: Cornell University Press, 2003.

Fortna, V. Page. *Does Peacekeeping Work? Shaping Belligerents' Choices after Civil War.* Princeton, NJ: Princeton University Press, 2008.

Huntington, Samuel P. *The Clash of Civilizations and the Remaking of World Order.* New York: Free Press, 2002.

Mearsheimer, John J. *The Tragedy of Great Power Politics.* New York: W. W. Norton, 2001.

Milner, Helen V., and Dustin Tingley. *Sailing the Water's Edge: The Domestic Politics of American Foreign Policy.* Princeton, NJ: Princeton University Press, 2015.

Mueller, John, and Mark G. Stewart. *Chasing Ghosts: The Policing of Terrorism.* New York: Oxford University Press, 2015.

Nye, Joseph. *Soft Power: The Means to Success in World Politics.* New York: PublicAffairs, 2009.

Peters, Margaret E. *Trading Barriers: Immigration and the Remaking of Globalization.* Princeton, NJ: Princeton University Press, 2017.

Rubenstein, Jennifer C. *Between Samaritans and States: The Political Ethics of Humanitarian INGOs.* New York: Oxford University Press, 2015.

Sen, Amartya. *Identity and Violence: The Illusion of Destiny.* New York: W. W. Norton, 2007.

Simmons, Beth A. *Mobilizing for Human Rights: International Law in Domestic Politics.* New York: Cambridge University Press, 2009.

APPENDIX

The Declaration of Independence

In Congress, July 4, 1776

The unanimous Declaration of the thirteen united States of America,

When in the Course of human events, it becomes necessary for one people to dissolve the political bands which have connected them with another, and to assume among the powers of the earth, the separate and equal station to which the Laws of Nature and of Nature's God entitle them, a decent respect to the opinions of mankind requires that they should declare the causes which impel them to the separation.

We hold these truths to be self-evident, that all men are created equal, that they are endowed by their Creator with certain unalienable Rights, that among these are Life, Liberty and the pursuit of Happiness.—That to secure these rights, Governments are instituted among Men, deriving their just powers from the consent of the governed.—That whenever any Form of Government becomes destructive of these ends, it is the Right of the People to alter or to abolish it, and to institute new Government, laying its foundation on such principles and organizing its powers in such form, as to them shall seem most likely to effect their Safety and Happiness. Prudence, indeed, will dictate that Governments long established should not be changed for light and transient causes; and accordingly all experience hath shewn, that mankind are more disposed to suffer, while evils are sufferable, than to right themselves by abolishing the forms to which they are accustomed. But when a long train of abuses and usurpations, pursuing invariably the same Object evinces a design to reduce them under absolute Despotism, it is their right, it is their duty, to throw off such Government, and to provide new Guards for their future security.—Such has been the patient sufferance of these Colonies; and such is now the necessity which constrains them to alter their former Systems of Government. The history of the present King of Great Britain is a history of repeated injuries and usurpations, all having in direct object the establishment of an absolute Tyranny over these States. To prove this, let Facts be submitted to a candid world.

He has refused his Assent to Laws, the most wholesome and necessary for the public good.

He has forbidden his Governors to pass Laws of immediate and pressing importance, unless suspended in their operation till his Assent should be obtained; and when so suspended, he has utterly neglected to attend to them.

He has refused to pass other Laws for the accommodation of large districts of people, unless those people would relinquish the right of Representation in the Legislature, a right inestimable to them and formidable to tyrants only.

He has called together legislative bodies at places unusual, uncomfortable, and distant from the depository of their public Records, for the sole purpose of fatiguing them into compliance with his measures.

He has dissolved Representative Houses repeatedly, for opposing with manly firmness his invasions on the rights of the people.

He has refused for a long time, after such dissolutions, to cause others to be elected; whereby the Legislative powers, incapable of Annihilation, have returned to the People at large for their exercise; the State remaining in the mean time exposed to all the dangers of invasion from without, and convulsions within.

He has endeavoured to prevent the population of these States; for that purpose obstructing the Laws for Naturalization of Foreigners; refusing to pass others to encourage their migrations hither, and raising the conditions of new Appropriations of Lands.

He has obstructed the Administration of Justice, by refusing his Assent to Laws for establishing Judiciary powers.

He has made Judges dependent on his Will alone, for the tenure of their offices, and the amount and payment of their salaries.

He has erected a multitude of New Offices, and sent hither swarms of Officers to harrass our people, and eat out their substance.

He has kept among us, in times of peace, Standing Armies without the Consent of our legislatures.

He has affected to render the Military independent of and superior to the Civil power.

He has combined with others to subject us to a jurisdiction foreign to our constitution, and unacknowledged by our laws; giving his Assent to their Acts of pretended Legislation:

For Quartering large bodies of armed troops among us:

For protecting them, by a mock Trial, from punishment for any Murders which they should commit on the Inhabitants of these States:

For cutting off our Trade with all parts of the world:

For imposing Taxes on us without our Consent:

For depriving us in many cases, of the benefits of Trial by Jury:

For transporting us beyond Seas to be tried for pretended offences:

For abolishing the free System of English Laws in a neighboring Province, establishing therein an Arbitrary government, and enlarging its Boundaries so as to render it at once an example and fit instrument for introducing the same absolute rule into these Colonies:

For taking away our Charters, abolishing our most valuable Laws, and altering fundamentally the Forms of our Governments:

For suspending our own Legislatures, and declaring themselves invested with power to legislate for us in all cases whatsoever.

He has abdicated Government here, by declaring us out of his Protection and waging War against us.

He has plundered our seas, ravaged our Coasts, burnt our towns, and destroyed the lives of our people.

He is at this time transporting large Armies of foreign Mercenaries to compleat the works of death, desolation and tyranny, already begun with circumstances of Cruelty & perfidy scarcely paralleled in the most barbarous ages, and totally unworthy the Head of a civilized nation.

He has constrained our fellow Citizens taken Captive on the high Seas to bear Arms against their Country, to become the executioners of their friends and Brethren, or to fall themselves by their Hands.

He has excited domestic insurrections amongst us, and has endeavoured to bring on the inhabitants of our frontiers, the merciless Indian Savages, whose known rule of warfare, is an undistinguished destruction of all ages, sexes and conditions.

In every stage of these Oppressions We have Petitioned for Redress in the most humble terms: Our repeated Petitions have been answered only by repeated injury. A Prince whose character is thus marked by every act which may define a Tyrant, is unfit to be the ruler of a free people.

Nor have We been wanting in attentions to our Brittish brethren. We have warned them from time to time of attempts by their legislature to extend an unwarrantable jurisdiction over us. We have reminded them of the circumstances of our emigration and settlement here. We have appealed to their native justice and magnanimity, and we have conjured them by the ties of our common kindred to disavow these usurpations, which, would inevitably interrupt our connections and correspondence. They too have been deaf to the voice of justice and of consanguinity. We must, therefore, acquiesce in the necessity, which denounces our Separation, and hold them, as we hold the rest of mankind, Enemies in War, in Peace Friends.

We, Therefore, the Representatives of the United States of America, in General Congress, Assembled, appealing to the Supreme Judge of the world for the rectitude of our intentions, do, in the Name, and by Authority of the good People of these Colonies, solemnly publish and declare, That these United Colonies are, and of Right ought to be Free and Independent States; that they are Absolved from all Allegiance to the British Crown, and that all political connection between them and the State of Great Britain, is and ought to be totally dissolved; and that as Free and Independent States, they have full Power to levy War, conclude Peace, contract Alliances, establish Commerce, and to do all other Acts and Things which Independent States may of right do. And for the support of this Declaration, with a firm reliance on the protection of divine Providence, we mutually pledge to each other our Lives, our Fortunes and our sacred Honor.

The foregoing Declaration was, by order of Congress, engrossed, and signed by the following members:

John Hancock

New Hampshire
Josiah Bartlett
William Whipple
Matthew Thornton

Massachusetts Bay
Samuel Adams
John Adams
Robert Treat Paine
Elbridge Gerry

Rhode Island
Stephen Hopkins
William Ellery

Connecticut
Roger Sherman
Samuel Huntington
William Williams
Oliver Wolcott

New York
William Floyd
Philip Livingston
Francis Lewis
Lewis Morris

New Jersey
Richard Stockton
John Witherspoon
Francis Hopkinson
John Hart
Abraham Clark

Pennsylvania
Robert Morris
Benjamin Rush
Benjamin Franklin
John Morton
George Clymer
James Smith
George Taylor
James Wilson
George Ross

Delaware
Caesar Rodney
George Read
Thomas M'Kean

Maryland
Samuel Chase
William Paca
Thomas Stone
Charles Carroll, of Carrollton

Virginia
George Wythe
Richard Henry Lee
Thomas Jefferson
Benjamin Harrison
Thomas Nelson, Jr.
Francis Lightfoot Lee
Carter Braxton

North Carolina
William Hooper
Joseph Hewes
John Penn

South Carolina
Edward Rutledge
Thomas Heyward, Jr.
Thomas Lynch, Jr.
Arthur Middleton

Georgia
Button Gwinnett
Lyman Hall
George Walton

Resolved, That copies of the Declaration be sent to the several assemblies, conventions, and committees, or councils of safety, and to the several commanding officers of the continental troops; that it be proclaimed in each of the United States, at the head of the army.

The Articles of Confederation

Agreed to by Congress November 15, 1777;
ratified and in force March 1, 1781

To all whom these Presents shall come, we the undersigned Delegates of the States affixed to our Names, send greeting. Whereas the Delegates of the United States of America, in Congress assembled, did, on the fifteenth day of November, in the Year of Our Lord One thousand Seven Hundred and Seventy seven, and in the Second Year of the Independence of America, agree to certain articles of Confederation and perpetual Union between the States of Newhampshire, Massachusetts-bay, Rhodeisland and Providence Plantations, Connecticut, New-York, New-Jersey, Pennsylvania, Delaware, Maryland, Virginia, North-Carolina, South-Carolina and Georgia in the words following, viz. "Articles of Confederation and perpetual Union between the states of Newhampshire, Massachusettsbay, Rhodeisland and Providence Plantations, Connecticut, New-York, New-Jersey, Pennsylvania, Delaware, Maryland, Virginia, North-Carolina, South-Carolina and Georgia.

Art. I. The Stile of this confederacy shall be "The United States of America."

Art. II. Each state retains its sovereignty, freedom and independence, and every Power, Jurisdiction and right, which is not by this confederation expressly delegated to the United States, in Congress assembled.

Art. III. The said states hereby severally enter into a firm league of friendship with each other, for their common defence, the security of their Liberties, and their mutual and general welfare, binding themselves to assist each other, against all force offered to, or attacks made upon them, or any of them, on account of religion, sovereignty, trade, or any other pretence whatever.

Art. IV. The better to secure and perpetuate mutual friendship and intercourse among the people of the different states in this union, the free inhabitants of each of these states, paupers, vagabonds and fugitives from Justice excepted, shall be entitled to all privileges and immunities of free citizens in the several states; and the people of each state shall have free ingress and regress to and from any other state, and shall enjoy therein all the privileges of trade and commerce, subject to the same duties, impositions and restrictions as the inhabitants thereof respectively, provided that such restriction shall not extend so far as to prevent the removal of property imported into any state, to any other state, of which the Owner is an inhabitant; provided also that no imposition, duties or restriction shall be laid by any state, on the property of the united states, or either of them.

If any Person guilty of, or charged with treason, felony, or other high misdemeanor in any state, shall flee from Justice, and be found in any of the united states, he shall, upon demand of the Governor or executive power, of the state from which he fled, be delivered up and removed to the state having jurisdiction of his offence.

Full faith and credit shall be given in each of these states to the records, acts and judicial proceedings of the courts and magistrates of every other state.

Art. V. For the more convenient management of the general interests of the united states, delegates shall be annually appointed in such manner as the legislature of each state shall direct, to meet in Congress on the first Monday in November, in every year, with a power reserved to each state, to recall its delegates, or any of them, at any time within the year, and to send others in their stead, for the remainder of the Year.

No state shall be represented in Congress by less than two, nor by more than seven Members; and no person shall be capable of being a delegate for more than three years in any term of six years; nor shall any person, being a delegate, be capable of holding any office under the united states, for which he, or another for his benefit receives any salary, fees or emolument of any kind.

Each state shall maintain its own delegates in a meeting of the states, and while they act as members of the committee of the states.

In determining questions in the united states, in Congress assembled, each state shall have one vote.

Freedom of speech and debate in Congress shall not be impeached or questioned in any Court, or place out of Congress, and the members of congress shall be protected in their persons from arrests and imprisonments, during the time of their going to and from, and attendance on congress, except for treason, felony, or breach of the peace.

Art. VI. No state without the Consent of the united states in congress assembled, shall send any embassy to, or receive any embassy from, or enter into any conference, agreement, or alliance or treaty with any King, prince or state; nor shall any person holding any office or profit or trust under the united states, or any of them, accept of any present, emolument, office or title of any kind whatever from any king, prince or foreign state; nor shall the united states in congress assembled, or any of them, grant any title of nobility.

No two or more states shall enter into any treaty, confederation or alliance whatever between them, without the consent of the united states in congress assembled, specifying accurately the purposes for which the same is to be entered into, and how long it shall continue.

No state shall lay any imposts or duties, which may interfere with any stipulations in treaties, entered into by the united states in congress assembled, with any king, prince or state, in pursuance of any treaties already proposed by congress, to the courts of France and Spain.

No vessels of war shall be kept up in time of peace by any state, except such number only, as shall be deemed necessary by the united states in congress assembled, for the defence of such state, or its trade; nor shall any body of forces be kept up by any state, in time of peace, except such number only, as in the judgment of the united states, in congress assembled, shall be deemed requisite to garrison the forts necessary for the defence of such state; but every state shall always keep up a well regulated and disciplined militia, sufficiently armed and accoutred, and shall provide and constantly have ready for use, in public stores, a due number of field pieces and tents, and a proper quantity of arms, ammunition and camp equipage.

No state shall engage in any war without the consent of the united states in congress assembled, unless such state be actually invaded by enemies, or shall have received certain advice of a resolution being formed by some nation of Indians to invade such state, and the danger is so imminent as not to admit of a delay, till the united states in congress asssembled can be consulted; nor shall any state grant commissions to any ships or vessels of war, nor letters of marque or reprisal, except it be after a declaration of war by the united states in congress assembled, and then only against the kingdom or state and the subjects thereof, against which war has been so declared, and under such regulations as shall be established by the united states in congress assembled, unless such state be infested by pirates; in which case vessels of war may be fitted out for that occasion, and kept so long as the danger shall continue, or until the united states in congress assembled shall determine otherwise.

Art. VII. When land-forces are raised by any state for the common defence, all officers of or under the rank of colonel, shall be appointed by the legislature of each state respectively, by whom such forces shall be raised, or in such manner as such state shall direct, and all vacancies shall be filled up by the state which first made the appointment.

Art. VIII. All charges of war, and all other expences that shall be incurred for the common defence or general welfare, and allowed by the united states in congress assembled, shall be defrayed out of a common treasury, which shall be supplied by the several states in proportion to the value of all land within each state, granted to or surveyed for any Person, as such land and the buildings and improvements thereon shall be estimated according to such mode as the united states in congress assembled, shall from time to time direct and appoint.

The taxes for paying that proportion shall be laid and levied by the authority and direction of the legislatures of the several states within the time agreed upon by the united states in congress assembled.

Art. IX. The united states in congress assembled, shall have the sole and exclusive right and power of determining on peace and war, except in the cases mentioned in the sixth article—of sending and receiving ambassadors—entering into treaties and alliances, provided that no treaty of commerce shall be made whereby the legislative power of the respective states shall be restrained from imposing such imposts and duties on foreigners, as their own people are subjected to, or from prohibiting the exportation of any species of goods or commodities whatsoever—of establishing rules for deciding in all cases, what captures on land or water shall be legal, and in what manner prizes taken by land or naval forces in the service of the united states shall be divided or appropriated—of granting letters of marque and reprisal in times of peace—appointing courts for the trial of piracies and felonies committed on the high seas and establishing courts for receiving and determining finally appeals in all cases of captures, provided that no member of congress shall be appointed a judge of any of the said courts.

The united states in congress assembled shall also be the last resort on appeal in all disputes and differences now subsisting or that hereafter may arise between two or more states concerning boundary, jurisdiction or any other cause whatever; which authority shall always be exercised in the manner following. Whenever the legislative or executive authority or lawful agent of any state in controversy with another shall present a petition to congress stating the matter in question and praying for a hearing, notice thereof shall be given by order of congress to the legislative or executive authority of the other state in controversy, and a day assigned for the appearance of the parties by their lawful agents, who shall then be directed to appoint by joint consent, commissioners or judges to constitute a court for hearing and determining the matter in question: but if they cannot agree, congress shall name three persons out of each of the united states, and from the list of such persons each party shall alternately strike out one, the petitioners beginning, until the number shall be reduced to thirteen; and from that number not less than seven, nor more than nine names as congress shall direct, shall in the presence of congress be drawn out by lot, and the persons whose names shall be so drawn or any five of them, shall be commissioners or judges, to hear and finally determine the controversy, so always as a major part of the judges who shall hear the cause shall agree in the determination: and if either party shall neglect to attend at the day appointed, without shewing reasons, which congress shall judge sufficient, or being present shall refuse to strike, the congress shall proceed to nominate three persons out of each state, and the secretary of congress shall strike in behalf of such party absent or refusing; and the judgment and sentence of the court to be appointed, in the manner before prescribed, shall be final and conclusive; and if any of the parties shall refuse to submit to the authority of such court, or to appear to defend their claim or cause, the court shall nevertheless proceed to pronounce sentence, or judgment, which shall in like manner be final and decisive, the judgment or sentence and other proceedings being in either case transmitted to congress, and lodged among the acts of congress for the security of the parties concerned: provided that every commissioner, before he sits in judgment, shall take an oath to be administered by one of the judges of the supreme or superior court of the state, where the cause shall be tried, "well and truly to hear and determine the matter in question, according to the best of his judgment, without favour, affection or hope of reward:" provided also, that no state shall be deprived of territory for the benefit of the united states.

All controversies concerning the private right of soil claimed under different grants of two or more states, whose jurisdictions as they may respect such lands, and the states which passed such grants are adjusted, the said grants or either of them being at the same time claimed to have originated antecedent to such settlement of jurisdiction, shall on the petition of either party to the congress of the united states, be finally determined as near as may be in the same manner as is before prescribed for deciding disputes respecting territorial jurisdiction between different states.

The united states in congress assembled shall also have the sole and exclusive right and power of regulating the alloy and value of coin struck by their own authority, or by that of the respective states—fixing the standard of weights and measures throughout the united states—regulating the trade and managing all affairs with the Indians, not members of any of the states, provided that the legislative right of any state within its own limits be not infringed or violated—establishing and regulating post-offices from one state to another, throughout all the united states, and exacting such postage on the papers passing thro' the same as may be requisite to defray the expences of the said office—appointing all officers of the land forces, in the service of the united states, excepting regimental officers—appointing all the officers of the naval forces, and commissioning all officers whatever in the service of the united states—making rules for the government and regulation of the said land and naval forces, and directing their operations.

The united states in congress assembled shall have authority to appoint a committee, to sit in the recess of congress, to be denominated "A Committee of the States," and to consist of one delegate from each state; and to appoint such other committees and civil officers as may be necessary for managing the general affairs of the united states under their direction—to appoint one of their number to preside, provided that no person be allowed to serve in the office of president more than one year in any term of three years; to ascertain the necessary sums of Money to be raised for the service of the united states, and to appropriate and apply the same for defraying the public expenses—to borrow money, or emit bills on the credit of the united states, transmitting every half year to the respective states an account of the sums of money so borrowed or emitted,—to build and equip a navy—to agree upon the number of land forces, and to make requisitions from each state for its quota, in proportion to the number of white inhabitants in such state; which requisition shall be binding, and thereupon the legislature of each state shall appoint the regimental officers, raise the men and cloath, arm and equip them in a soldier like manner, at the expense of the united states; and the officers and men so cloathed, armed and equipped shall march to the place appointed, and within the time agreed on by the united states in congress assembled: But if the united states in congress assembled shall, on consideration of circumstances judge proper that any state should not raise men, or should raise a smaller number than its quota, and that any other state should raise a greater number of men than the quota thereof, such extra number shall be raised, officered, cloathed, armed and equipped in the same manner as the quota of such state, unless the legislature of such state shall judge that such extra number cannot be safely spared out of the same, in which case they shall raise officer, cloath, arm and equip as many of such extra number as they judge can be safely spared. And the officers and men so cloathed, armed and equipped, shall march to the place appointed, and within the time agreed on by the united states in congress assembled.

The united states in congress assembled shall never engage in a war, nor grant letters of marque and reprisal in time of peace, nor enter into any treaties or alliances, nor coin money, nor regulate the value thereof, nor ascertain the sums and expenses necessary for the defence and welfare of the united states, or any of them, nor emit bills, nor borrow money on the credit of the united states, nor appropriate money, nor agree upon the number of vessels of war, to be built or purchased, or the number of land or sea forces to be raised, nor appoint a commander in chief of the army or navy, unless nine states assent to the same: nor shall a question on any other point, except for adjourning from day to day be determined, unless by the votes of a majority of the united states in congress assembled.

The congress of the united states shall have power to adjourn to any time within the year, and to any place within the united states, so that no period of adjournment be for a longer duration than the space of six Months, and shall publish the Journal of their proceedings monthly, except such parts thereof relating to treaties, alliances or military operations, as in their judgment require secrecy; and the yeas and nays of the delegates of each state on any question shall be entered on the Journal, when it is desired by any delegate; and the delegates of a state, or any of them, at his or their request shall be furnished with a transcript of the said Journal, except such parts as are above excepted, to lay before the legislatures of the several states.

Art. X. The committee of the states, or any nine of them, shall be authorised to execute, in the recess of congress, such of the powers of congress as the united states in congress assembled, by the consent of nine states, shall from time to time think expedient to vest them with; provided that no power be delegated to the said committee, for the exercise of which, by the articles of confederation, the voice of nine states in the congress of the united states assembled is requisite.

Art. XI. Canada acceding to this confederation, and joining in the measures of the united states, shall be admitted into, and entitled to all the advantages of this union: but no other colony shall be admitted into the same, unless such admission be agreed to by nine states.

Art. XII. All bills of credit emitted, monies borrowed and debts contracted by, or under the authority of congress, before the assembling of the united states, in pursuance of the present confederation, shall be deemed and considered as a charge against the united states, for payment and satisfaction whereof the said united states and the public faith are hereby solemnly pledged.

Art. XIII. Every state shall abide by the determinations of the united states in congress assembled, on all questions which by this confederation are submitted to them. And the Articles of this confederation shall be inviolably observed by every state, and the union shall be perpetual; nor shall any alteration at any time hereafter be made in any of them; unless such alteration be agreed to in a congress of the united states, and be afterwards confirmed by the legislatures of every state.

And Whereas it hath pleased the Great Governor of the World to incline the hearts of the legislatures we respectively represent in congress, to approve of, and to authorize us to ratify the said articles of confederation and perpetual union. Know Ye that we the undersigned delegates, by virtue of the power and authority to us given for that purpose, do by these presents, in the name and in behalf of our respective constituents, fully and entirely ratify and confirm each and every of the said articles of confederation and perpetual union, and all and singular the matters and things therein contained: And we do further solemnly plight and engage the faith of our respective constituents, that they shall abide by the determinations of the united states in congress assembled, on all questions, which by the said confederation are submitted to them. And that the articles thereof shall be inviolably observed by the states we respectively represent, and that the union shall be perpetual. In Witness whereof we have hereunto set our hands in Congress. Done at Philadelphia in the state of Pennsylvania the ninth day of July, in the Year of our Lord one Thousand seven Hundred and Seventy-eight, and in the third year of the independence of America.

The Constitution of the United States of America

[PREAMBLE]

We the People of the United States, in Order to form a more perfect Union, establish Justice, insure domestic Tranquility, provide for the common defence, promote the general Welfare, and secure the Blessings of Liberty to ourselves and our Posterity, do ordain and establish this Constitution for the United States of America.

Article I

SECTION 1

[LEGISLATIVE POWERS]

All legislative Powers herein granted shall be vested in a Congress of the United States, which shall consist of a Senate and House of Representatives.

SECTION 2

[HOUSE OF REPRESENTATIVES, HOW CONSTITUTED, POWER OF IMPEACHMENT]

The House of Representatives shall be composed of Members chosen every second Year by the People of the several States, and the Electors in each State shall have the Qualifications requisite for Electors of the most numerous Branch of the State Legislature.

No Person shall be a Representative who shall not have attained to the Age of twenty five Years, and been seven Years a Citizen of the United States, and who shall not, when elected, be an Inhabitant of that State in which he shall be chosen.

Representatives and *direct Taxes*[1] shall be apportioned among the several States which may be included within this Union, according to their respective Numbers, *which shall be determined by adding to the whole Number of free Persons, including those bound to Service for a Term of Years, and excluding Indians not taxed, three fifths of all other Persons.*[2] The actual Enumeration shall be made within three Years after the first Meeting of the Congress of the United States, and within every subsequent Term of ten Years, in such Manner as they shall by Law direct. The Number of Representatives shall not exceed one for every thirty Thousand, but each State shall have at Least one Representative; *and until such enumeration shall be made, the State of New Hampshire shall be entitled to chuse three, Massachusetts eight, Rhode-Island and Providence Plantations one, Connecticut five, New-York six, New Jersey four, Pennsylvania eight, Delaware one, Maryland six, Virginia ten, North Carolina five, South Carolina five, and Georgia three.*[3]

When vacancies happen in the Representation from any State, the Executive Authority thereof shall issue Writs of Election to fill such Vacancies.

The House of Representatives shall chuse their Speaker and other Officers; and shall have the sole Power of Impeachment.

SECTION 3

[THE SENATE, HOW CONSTITUTED, IMPEACHMENT TRIALS]

The Senate of the United States shall be composed of two Senators from each State, *chosen by the Legislature thereof,*[4] for six Years; and each Senator shall have one Vote.

Immediately after they shall be assembled in Consequence of the first Election, they shall be divided as equally as may be into three Classes. The Seats of the Senators of the first Class shall be vacated at the Expiration of the second Year, of the second Class at the Expiration of the fourth Year, and of the third Class at the Expiration of the sixth Year, so that one third may be chosen every second Year; *and if Vacancies happen by Resignation, or otherwise, during the Recess of the Legislature of any State, the Executive thereof may make temporary Appointments until the next Meeting of the Legislature, which shall then fill such Vacancies.*[5]

No Person shall be a Senator who shall not have attained to the Age of thirty Years, and been nine Years a Citizen of the United States, and who shall not, when elected, be an Inhabitant of that State for which he shall be chosen.

The Vice President of the United States shall be President of the Senate, but shall have no Vote, unless they be equally divided.

The Senate shall chuse their other Officers, and also a President pro tempore, in the Absence of the Vice President, or when he shall exercise the Office of President of the United States.

The Senate shall have the sole Power to try all Impeachments. When sitting for that Purpose, they shall be on Oath or Affirmation. When the President of the United States is tried, the Chief Justice shall preside: And no Person shall be convicted without the Concurrence of two thirds of the Members present.

Judgment in Cases of Impeachment shall not extend further than to removal from Office, and disqualification to hold and enjoy any Office of honor, Trust or Profit under the United States: but the Party convicted shall nevertheless be liable and subject to Indictment, Trial, Judgment and Punishment, according to Law.

SECTION 4

[ELECTION OF SENATORS AND REPRESENTATIVES]

The Times, Places and Manner of holding Elections for Senators and Representatives, shall be prescribed in each State by the Legislature thereof; but the Congress may at any time by Law make or alter such Regulations, except as to the Places of chusing Senators.

The Congress shall assemble at least once in every Year, and such Meeting shall be on the first Monday in December, unless they shall by Law appoint a different Day.[6]

SECTION 5

[QUORUM, JOURNALS, MEETINGS, ADJOURNMENTS]

Each House shall be the Judge of the Elections, Returns and Qualifications of its own Members, and a Majority of each shall constitute a Quorum to do Business; but a smaller Number may adjourn from day to day, and may be authorized to compel the

---

[1] Modified by Sixteenth Amendment.
[2] Modified by Fourteenth Amendment.
[3] Temporary provision.
[4] Modified by Seventeenth Amendment.
[5] Modified by Seventeenth Amendment.
[6] Modified by Twentieth Amendment.

Attendance of absent Members, in such Manner, and under such Penalties as each House may provide.

Each House may determine the Rules of its Proceedings, punish its Members for disorderly Behaviour, and, with the Concurrence of two thirds, expel a Member.

Each House shall keep a Journal of its Proceedings, and from time to time publish the same, excepting such Parts as may in their Judgment require Secrecy; and the Yeas and Nays of the Members of either House on any questions shall, at the Desire of one fifth of those Present, be entered on the Journal.

Neither House, during the Session of Congress, shall, without the Consent of the other, adjourn for more than three days, nor to any other Place than that in which the two Houses shall be sitting.

SECTION 6
[COMPENSATION, PRIVILEGES, DISABILITIES]

The Senators and Representatives shall receive a Compensation for their Services, to be ascertained by Law, and paid out of the Treasury of the United States. They shall in all Cases, except Treason, Felony and Breach of the Peace, be privileged from Arrest during their Attendance at the Session of their respective Houses, and in going to and returning from the same; and for any Speech or Debate in either House, they shall not be questioned in any other Place.

No Senator or Representative shall, during the Time for which he was elected, be appointed to any civil Office under the Authority of the United States, which shall have been created, or the Emoluments whereof shall have been encreased during such time; and no Person holding any Office under the United States, shall be a Member of either House during his Continuance in Office.

SECTION 7
[PROCEDURE IN PASSING BILLS AND RESOLUTIONS]

All Bills for raising Revenue shall originate in the House of Representatives; but the Senate may propose or concur with Amendments as on other Bills.

Every Bill which shall have passed the House of Representatives and the Senate, shall, before it become a Law, be presented to the President of the United States: If he approve he shall sign it, but if not he shall return it, with his Objections to that House in which it shall have originated, who shall enter the Objections at large on their Journal, and proceed to reconsider it. If after such Reconsideration two thirds of that House shall agree to pass the Bill, it shall be sent, together with the Objections, to the other House, by which it shall likewise be reconsidered, and if approved by two thirds of that House, it shall become a Law. But in all such Cases the Votes of both Houses shall be determined by yeas and Nays, and the Names of the Persons voting for and against the Bill shall be entered on the Journal of each House respectively. If any Bill shall not be returned by the President within ten Days (Sundays excepted) after it shall have been presented to him, the Same shall be a Law, in like Manner as if he had signed it, unless the Congress by their Adjournment prevent its Return, in which Case it shall not be a Law.

Every Order, Resolution, or Vote to which the Concurrence of the Senate and House of Representatives may be necessary (except on a question of Adjournment) shall be presented to the President of the United States; and before the Same shall take Effect, shall be approved by him, or being disapproved by him, shall be repassed by two thirds of the Senate and House of Representatives, according to the Rules and Limitations prescribed in the Case of a Bill.

SECTION 8
[POWERS OF CONGRESS]

The Congress shall have Power

To lay and collect Taxes, Duties, Imposts and Excises, to pay the Debts and provide for the common Defence and general Welfare of the United States; but all Duties, Imposts and Excises shall be uniform throughout the United States;

To borrow Money on the credit of the United States;

To regulate Commerce with foreign Nations, and among the several States, and with the Indian Tribes;

To establish an uniform Rule of Naturalization, and uniform Laws on the subject of Bankruptcies throughout the United States;

To coin Money, regulate the Value thereof, and of foreign Coin, and fix the Standard of Weights and Measures;

To provide for the Punishment of counterfeiting the Securities and current Coin of the United States;

To establish Post Offices and post Roads;

To promote the Progress of Science and useful Arts, by securing for limited Times to Authors and Inventors the exclusive Right to their respective Writings and Discoveries;

To constitute Tribunals inferior to the supreme Court;

To define and punish Piracies and Felonies committed on the high Seas, and Offences against the Law of Nations;

To declare War, grant Letters of Marque and Reprisal, and make Rules concerning Captures on Land and Water;

To raise and support Armies, but no Appropriation of Money to that Use shall be for a longer Term than two Years;

To provide and maintain a Navy;

To make Rules for the Government and Regulation of the land and naval Forces;

To provide for calling forth the Militia to execute the Laws of the Union, suppress Insurrections and repel Invasions;

To provide for organizing, arming, and disciplining, the Militia, and for governing such Part of them as may be employed in the Service of the United States, reserving to the States respectively, the Appointment of the Officers, and the Authority of training the Militia according to the discipline prescribed by Congress;

To exercise exclusive Legislation in all Cases whatsoever, over such District (not exceeding ten Miles square) as may, by Cession of particular States, and the Acceptance of Congress, become the Seat of the Government of the United States, and to exercise like Authority over all Places purchased by the Consent of the Legislature of the State in which the Same shall be, for the Erection of Forts, Magazines, Arsenals, dock-Yards, and other needful Buildings;—And

To make all Laws which shall be necessary and proper for carrying into Execution the foregoing Powers, and all other Powers vested by this Constitution in the Government of the United States, or in any Department or Officer thereof.

SECTION 9
[SOME RESTRICTIONS ON FEDERAL POWER]

The Migration or Importation of such Persons as any of the States now existing shall think proper to admit, shall not be prohibited by the Congress prior to the Year one thousand eight hundred and eight, but a Tax or duty may be imposed on such Importation, not exceeding ten dollars for each Person.[7]

---

[7] Temporary provision.

The Privilege of the Writ of Habeas Corpus shall not be suspended, unless when in Cases of Rebellion or Invasion the public Safety may require it.

No Bill of Attainder or ex post facto Law shall be passed.

No Capitation, or other direct, Tax shall be laid, unless in Proportion to the Census or Enumeration herein before directed to be taken.[8]

No Tax or Duty shall be laid on Articles exported from any State.

No Preference shall be given by any Regulation of Commerce or Revenue to the Ports of one State over those of another; nor shall Vessels bound to, or from, one State, be obliged to enter, clear, or pay Duties in another.

No Money shall be drawn from the Treasury, but in Consequence of Appropriations made by Law; and a regular Statement and Account of the Receipts and Expenditures of all public Money shall be published from time to time.

No Title of Nobility shall be granted by the United States: And no Person holding any Office of Profit or Trust under them, shall, without the Consent of the Congress, accept of any present, Emolument, Office, or Title, of any kind whatever, from any King, Prince, or foreign State.

SECTION 10
[RESTRICTIONS UPON POWERS OF STATES]

No State shall enter into any Treaty, Alliance, or Confederation; grant Letters of Marque and Reprisal; coin Money; emit Bills of Credit; make any Thing but gold and silver Coin a Tender in Payment of Debts; pass any Bill of Attainder, ex post facto Law, or Law impairing the Obligation of Contracts, or grant any Title of Nobility.

No State shall, without the Consent of the Congress, lay any Imposts or Duties on Imports or Exports, except what may be absolutely necessary for executing its inspection Laws: and the net Produce of all Duties and Imposts, laid by any State on Imports or Exports, shall be for the Use of the Treasury of the United States; and all such Laws shall be subject to the Revision and Control of the Congress.

No State shall, without the Consent of Congress, lay any Duty of Tonnage, keep Troops, or Ships of War in time of Peace, enter into any Agreement or Compact with another State, or with a foreign Power, or engage in War, unless actually invaded, or in such imminent Danger as will not admit of delay.

Article II

SECTION 1
[EXECUTIVE POWER, ELECTION, QUALIFICATIONS OF THE PRESIDENT]

The executive Power shall be vested in a President of the United States of America. *He shall hold his Office during the Term of four Years, and, together with the Vice President, chosen for the same Term, be elected, as follows*[9]

Each State shall appoint, in such Manner as the Legislature thereof may direct, a Number of Electors, equal to the whole Number of Senators and Representatives to which the State may be entitled in the Congress: but no Senator or Representative, or Person holding an Office of Trust or Profit under the United States, shall be appointed an Elector.

The electors shall meet in their respective States, and vote by ballot for two Persons, of whom one at least shall not be an Inhabitant of the same State with themselves. And they shall make a List of all the Persons voted for, and of the Number of Votes for each; which List they shall sign and certify, and transmit sealed to the Seat of the Government of the United States, directed to the President of the Senate. The President of the Senate shall, in the Presence of the Senate and House of Representatives, open all the Certificates, and the Votes shall then be counted. The Person having the greatest Number of Votes shall be the President, if such Number be a Majority of the whole Number of Electors appointed; and if there be more than one who have such Majority, and have an equal Number of Votes, then the House of Representatives shall immediately chuse by Ballot one of them for President; and if no Person have a Majority, then from the five highest on the List the said House shall in like Manner chuse the President. But in chusing the President, the Votes shall be taken by States, the Representation from each State having one Vote; A quorum for this Purpose shall consist of a Member or Members from two thirds of the States, and a Majority of all the States shall be necessary to a Choice. In every Case, after the Choice of the President, the person having the greatest Number of Votes of the Electors shall be the Vice President. But if there should remain two or more who have equal Votes, the Senate shall chuse from them by Ballot the Vice President.[10]

The Congress may determine the Time of chusing the Electors, and the Day on which they shall give their Votes; which Day shall be the same throughout the United States.

No Person except a natural born Citizen, or a Citizen of the United States, at the time of the Adoption of this Constitution, shall be eligible to the Office of President; neither shall any Person be eligible to that Office who shall not have attained to the Age of thirty five Years, and been fourteen Years a Resident within the United States.

In Case of the Removal of the President from Office, or his Death, Resignation, or Inability to discharge the Powers and Duties of the said Office, the Same shall devolve on the Vice President, and the Congress may by Law provide for the Case of Removal, Death, Resignation or Inability, both of the President and Vice President, declaring what Officer shall then act as President, and such Officer shall act accordingly, until the Disability be removed, or a President shall be elected.

The President shall, at stated Times, receive for his Services, a Compensation, which shall neither be increased nor diminished during the Period for which he shall have been elected, and he shall not receive within that Period any other Emolument from the United States, or any of them.

Before he enter on the Execution of his Office, he shall take the following Oath or Affirmation:—"I do solemnly swear (or affirm) that I will faithfully execute the Office of President of the United States, and will to the best of my Ability, preserve, protect and defend the Constitution of the United States."

SECTION 2
[POWERS OF THE PRESIDENT]

The President shall be Commander in Chief of the Army and Navy of the United States, and of the Militia of the several States, when called into the actual Service of the United States; he may require the Opinion, in writing, of the principal Officer in each of the executive Departments, upon any Subject relating to the Duties of their respective Offices, and he shall have Power to grant Reprieves and Pardons for Offences against the United States, except in Cases of Impeachment.

He shall have Power, by and with the Advice and Consent of the Senate, to make Treaties, provided two thirds of the Senators present concur; and he shall nominate, and by and with the Advice

---

[8] Modified by Sixteenth Amendment.
[9] Number of terms limited to two by Twenty-second Amendment.
[10] Modified by the Twelfth and Twentieth Amendments.

and Consent of the Senate, shall appoint Ambassadors, other public Ministers and Consuls, Judges of the supreme Court, and all other Officers of the United States, whose Appointments are not herein otherwise provided for, and which shall be established by Law: but the Congress may by Law vest the Appointment of such inferior Officers, as they think proper, in the President alone, in the Courts of Law, or in the Heads of Departments.

The President shall have Power to fill up all Vacancies that may happen during the Recess of the Senate, by granting Commissions which shall expire at the End of their next Session.

SECTION 3
[POWERS AND DUTIES OF THE PRESIDENT]

He shall from time to time give to the Congress Information of the State of the Union, and recommend to their Consideration such Measures as he shall judge necessary and expedient; he may, on extraordinary Occasions, convene both Houses, or either of them, and in Case of Disagreement between them, with Respect to the Time of Adjournment, he may adjourn them to such Time as he shall think proper; he shall receive Ambassadors and other public Ministers; he shall take Care that the Laws be faithfully executed, and shall Commission all the Officers of the United States.

SECTION 4
[IMPEACHMENT]

The President, Vice President and all civil Officers of the United States, shall be removed from Office on Impeachment for, and Conviction of, Treason, Bribery, or other high Crimes and Misdemeanors.

Article III

SECTION 1
[JUDICIAL POWER, TENURE OF OFFICE]

The judicial Power of the United States, shall be vested in one supreme Court, and in such inferior Courts as the Congress may from time to time ordain and establish. The Judges, both of the supreme and inferior Courts, shall hold their Offices during good Behaviour, and shall, at stated Times, receive for their Services, a Compensation, which shall not be diminished during their Continuance in Office.

SECTION 2
[JURISDICTION]

The judicial Power shall extend to all Cases, in Law and Equity, arising under this Constitution, the Laws of the United States, and Treaties made, or which shall be made, under their Authority;—to all Cases affecting Ambassadors, other public Ministers and Consuls;—to all Cases of admiralty and maritime Jurisdiction;—to Controversies to which the United States shall be a Party;—to Controversies between two or more States;—*between a State and Citizens of another State;*—between Citizens of different States,—between Citizens of the same State claiming Lands under Grants of different States, *and between a State,* or the Citizens thereof, *and foreign States, Citizens or Subjects.*[11]

In all Cases affecting Ambassadors, other public Ministers and Consuls, and those in which a State shall be Party, the supreme Court shall have original Jurisdiction. In all the other Cases before mentioned, the supreme Court shall have appellate Jurisdiction, both as to Law and Fact, with such Exceptions, and under such Regulations as the Congress shall make.

The Trial of all Crimes, except in Cases of Impeachment, shall be by Jury; and such Trial shall be held in the State where the said Crimes shall have been committed; but when not committed within any State, the Trial shall be at such Place or Places as the Congress may by Law have directed.

SECTION 3
[TREASON, PROOF, AND PUNISHMENT]

Treason against the United States, shall consist only in levying War against them, or in adhering to their Enemies, giving them Aid and Comfort. No Person shall be convicted of Treason unless on the Testimony of two Witnesses to the same overt Act, or on Confession in open Court.

The Congress shall have Power to declare the Punishment of Treason, but no Attainder of Treason shall work Corruption of Blood, or Forfeiture except during the Life of the Person attainted.

Article IV

SECTION 1
[FAITH AND CREDIT AMONG STATES]

Full Faith and Credit shall be given in each State to the public Acts, Records, and judicial Proceedings of every other State. And the Congress may by general Laws prescribe the Manner in which such Acts, Records and Proceedings shall be proved, and the Effect thereof.

SECTION 2
[PRIVILEGES AND IMMUNITIES, FUGITIVES]

The Citizens of each State shall be entitled to all Privileges and Immunities of Citizens in the several States.

A Person charged in any State with Treason, Felony or other Crime, who shall flee from Justice, and be found in another State, shall on Demand of the executive Authority of the State from which he fled, be delivered up, to be removed to the State having Jurisdiction of the Crime.

No person held to Service or Labour in one State, under the Laws thereof, escaping into another, shall, in Consequence of any Law or Regulation therein, be discharged from such Service or Labour, but shall be delivered up on Claim of the Party to whom such Service or Labour may be due.[12]

SECTION 3
[ADMISSION OF NEW STATES]

New States may be admitted by the Congress into this Union; but no new State shall be formed or erected within the Jurisdiction of any other State; nor any State be formed by the Junction of two or more States, or Parts of States, without the Consent of the Legislatures of the States concerned as well as of the Congress.

The Congress shall have Power to dispose of and make all needful Rules and Regulations respecting the Territory or other Property belonging to the United States; and nothing in this Constitution shall be so construed as to Prejudice any Claims of the United States, or of any particular State.

---

[11] Modified by the Eleventh Amendment.

[12] Repealed by the Thirteenth Amendment.

SECTION 4
[GUARANTEE OF REPUBLICAN GOVERNMENT]

The United States shall guarantee to every State in this Union a Republican Form of Government, and shall protect each of them against Invasion; and on Application of the Legislature, or of the Executive (when the Legislature cannot be convened), against domestic Violence.

Article V
[AMENDMENT OF THE CONSTITUTION]

The Congress, whenever two thirds of both Houses shall deem it necessary, shall propose Amendments to this Constitution, or, on the Application of the Legislatures of two thirds of the several States, shall call a Convention for proposing Amendments, which, in either Case, shall be valid to all Intents and Purposes, as Part of this Constitution, when ratified by the Legislatures of three fourths of the several States, or by Conventions in three fourths thereof, as the one or the other Mode of Ratification may be proposed by the Congress; *Provided that no Amendment which may be made prior to the Year One thousand eight hundred and eight shall in any Manner affect the first and fourth Clauses in the Ninth Section of the first Article;* and that no State, without its Consent, shall be deprived of its equal Suffrage in the Senate.

Article VI
[DEBTS, SUPREMACY, OATH]

All Debts contracted and Engagements entered into, before the Adoption of this Constitution, shall be as valid against the United States under this Constitution, as under the Confederation.

This Constitution, and the Laws of the United States which shall be made in Pursuance thereof; and all Treaties made, or which shall be made, under the Authority of the United States, shall be the supreme Law of the Land; and the Judges in every State shall be bound thereby, any Thing in the Constitution or Laws of any State to the Contrary notwithstanding.

The Senators and Representatives before mentioned, and the Members of the several State Legislatures, and all executive and judicial Officers, both of the United States and of the several States, shall be bound by Oath or Affirmation, to support this Constitution; but no religious Test shall be required as a Qualification to any Office or public Trust under the United States.

Article VII
[RATIFICATION AND ESTABLISHMENT]

The Ratification of the Conventions of nine States, shall be sufficient for the Establishment of this Constitution between the States so ratifying the Same.

Done in Convention by the Unanimous Consent of the States present the Seventeenth Day of September in the Year of our Lord one thousand seven hundred and Eighty seven and of the Independence of the United States of America the Twelfth. *In Witness* whereof We have hereunto subscribed our Names,

G:° WASHINGTON—
Presidt. and deputy from Virginia

New Hampshire
John Langdon
Nicholas Gilman

Massachusetts
Nathaniel Gorham
Rufus King

Connecticut
Wm. Saml. Johnson
Roger Sherman

New York
Alexander Hamilton

New Jersey
Wil: Livingston
David Brearley
Wm. Paterson
Jona: Dayton

Pennsylvania
B Franklin
Thomas Mifflin
Robt. Morris
Geo. Clymer
Thos. FitzSimons
Jared Ingersoll
James Wilson
Gouv Morris

Delaware
Geo: Read
Gunning Bedford jun
John Dickinson
Richard Bassett
Jaco: Broom

Maryland
James McHenry
Dan of St Thos. Jenifer
Danl. Carroll

Virginia
John Blair—
James Madison Jr.

North Carolina
Wm. Blount
Richd. Dobbs Spaight
Hu Williamson

South Carolina
J. Rutledge
Charles Cotesworth Pinckney
Charles Pinckney
Pierce Butler

Georgia
William Few
Abr Baldwin

Amendments to the Constitution

Proposed by Congress and Ratified by the Legislatures of the Several States, Pursuant to Article V of the Original Constitution.

Amendments I–X, known as the Bill of Rights, were proposed by Congress on September 25, 1789, and ratified on December 15, 1791.

Amendment I
[FREEDOM OF RELIGION, OF SPEECH, AND OF THE PRESS]

Congress shall make no law respecting an establishment of religion, or prohibiting the free exercise thereof; or abridging the freedom of speech, or of the press; or the right of the people peaceably to assemble, and to petition the Government for a redress of grievances.

Amendment II
[RIGHT TO KEEP AND BEAR ARMS]

A well regulated Militia, being necessary to the security of a free State, the right of the people to keep and bear Arms, shall not be infringed.

Amendment III
[QUARTERING OF SOLDIERS]

No Soldier shall, in time of peace be quartered in any house, without the consent of the Owner, nor in time of war, but in a manner to be prescribed by law.

Amendment IV
[SECURITY FROM UNWARRANTABLE SEARCH AND SEIZURE]

The right of the people to be secure in their persons, houses, papers, and effects, against unreasonable searches and seizures, shall not be violated, and no Warrants shall issue, but upon probable cause, supported by Oath or affirmation, and particularly describing the place to be searched, and the persons or things to be seized.

Amendment V
[RIGHTS OF ACCUSED PERSONS IN CRIMINAL PROCEEDINGS]

No person shall be held to answer for a capital, or otherwise infamous crime, unless on a presentment or indictment of a Grand Jury, except in cases arising in the land or naval forces, or in the Militia, when in actual service in time of War or in public danger; nor shall any person be subject for the same offence to be twice put in jeopardy of life or limb; nor shall be compelled in any criminal case to be a witness against himself, nor be deprived of life, liberty, or property, without due process of law; nor shall private property be taken for public use, without just compensation.

Amendment VI
[RIGHT TO SPEEDY TRIAL, WITNESSES, ETC.]

In all criminal prosecutions, the accused shall enjoy the right to a speedy and public trial, by an impartial jury of the State and district wherein the crime shall have been committed, which district shall have been previously ascertained by law, and to be informed of the nature and cause of the accusation; to be confronted with the witnesses against him; to have compulsory process for obtaining witnesses in his favor, and to have the Assistance of Counsel for his defence.

Amendment VII
[TRIAL BY JURY IN CIVIL CASES]

In suits at common law, where the value in controversy shall exceed twenty dollars, the right of trial by jury shall be preserved, and no fact tried by a jury, shall be otherwise reexamined in any Court of the United States, than according to the rules of the common law.

Amendment VIII
[BAILS, FINES, PUNISHMENTS]

Excessive bail shall not be required, nor excessive fines imposed, nor cruel and unusual punishments inflicted.

Amendment IX
[RESERVATION OF RIGHTS OF PEOPLE]

The enumeration in the Constitution, of certain rights, shall not be construed to deny or disparage others retained by the people.

Amendment X
[POWERS RESERVED TO STATES OR PEOPLE]

The powers not delegated to the United States by the Constitution, nor prohibited by it to the States, are reserved to the States respectively, or to the people.

Amendment XI
[*Proposed by Congress on March 4, 1794; declared ratified on January 8, 1798.*]
[RESTRICTION OF JUDICIAL POWER]

The Judicial power of the United States shall not be construed to extend to any suit in law or equity, commenced or prosecuted against one of the United States by Citizens of another State, or by Citizens or Subjects of any Foreign State.

Amendment XII
[*Proposed by Congress on December 9, 1803; declared ratified on September 25, 1804.*]
[ELECTION OF PRESIDENT AND VICE PRESIDENT]

The Electors shall meet in their respective states and vote by ballot for President and Vice-President, one of whom, at least, shall not be an inhabitant of the same state with themselves; they shall name in their ballots the person voted for as President, and in distinct ballots the person voted for as Vice-President, and they shall make distinct lists of all persons voted for as President, and of all persons voted for as Vice-President, and of the number of votes for each, which lists they shall sign and certify, and transmit sealed to the seat of the government of the United States, directed to the President of the Senate;—the President of the Senate shall, in presence of the Senate and House of Representatives, open all the certificates and the votes shall then be counted;—The person having the greatest number of votes for President, shall be the President, if such number be a majority of the whole number of Electors appointed; and if no person have such majority, then from the persons having the highest numbers not exceeding three on the list of those voted for as President, the House of Representatives shall choose immediately, by ballot, the President. But in choosing the President, the votes shall be taken by states, the representation from each state having one vote; a quorum for this purpose shall consist of a member or members from two-thirds of the states, and a majority of all the states shall be necessary to a choice. And if the House of Representatives shall not choose a President whenever the right of choice shall devolve upon them, before the fourth day of March next following, then the Vice-President shall act as President, as in the case of the death or other constitutional disability of the President.—The person having the greatest number of votes as Vice-President, shall be the Vice-President, if such number be a majority of the whole number of Electors appointed, and if no person have a majority, then from the two highest numbers on the list, the Senate shall choose the Vice-President; a quorum for the purpose shall consist of two-thirds of the whole number of Senators, and a majority of the whole number shall be necessary to a choice. But no person constitutionally ineligible to the office of President shall be eligible to that of Vice-President of the United States.

Amendment XIII

[*Proposed by Congress on January 31, 1865; declared ratified on December 18, 1865.*]

SECTION 1
[ABOLITION OF SLAVERY]

Neither slavery nor involuntary servitude, except as a punishment for crime whereof the party shall have been duly convicted, shall exist within the United States, or any place subject to their jurisdiction.

SECTION 2
[POWER TO ENFORCE THIS ARTICLE]

Congress shall have power to enforce this article by appropriate legislation.

Amendment XIV

[*Proposed by Congress on June 13, 1866; declared ratified on July 28, 1868.*]

SECTION 1
[CITIZENSHIP RIGHTS NOT TO BE ABRIDGED BY STATES]

All persons born or naturalized in the United States, and subject to the jurisdiction thereof, are citizens of the United States and of the State wherein they reside. No State shall make or enforce any law which shall abridge the privileges or immunities of citizens of the United States; nor shall any State deprive any person of life, liberty, or property, without due process of law; nor deny to any person within its jurisdiction the equal protection of the laws.

SECTION 2
[APPORTIONMENT OF REPRESENTATIVES IN CONGRESS]

Representatives shall be apportioned among the several States according to their respective numbers, counting the whole number of persons in each State, excluding Indians not taxed. But when the right to vote at any election for the choice of electors for President and Vice-President of the United States, Representatives in Congress, the Executive and Judicial officers of a State, or the members of the Legislature thereof, is denied to any of the male inhabitants of such State, being twenty-one years of age, and citizens of the United States, or in any way abridged, except for participation in rebellion, or other crime, the basis of representation therein shall be reduced in the proportion which the number of such male citizens shall bear to the whole number of male citizens twenty-one years of age in such State.

SECTION 3
[PERSONS DISQUALIFIED FROM HOLDING OFFICE]

No person shall be a Senator or Representative in Congress, or elector of President and Vice-President, or hold any office, civil or military, under the United States, or under any State, who, having previously taken an oath, as a member of Congress, or as an officer of the United States, or as a member of any State legislature, or as an executive or judicial officer of any State, to support the Constitution of the United States, shall have engaged in insurrection or rebellion against the same, or given aid or comfort to the enemies thereof. But Congress may by a vote of two-thirds of each House, remove such disability.

SECTION 4
[WHAT PUBLIC DEBTS ARE VALID]

The validity of the public debt of the United States, authorized by law, including debts incurred for payment of pensions and bounties for services in suppressing insurrection or rebellion, shall not be questioned. But neither the United States nor any State shall assume or pay any debt or obligation incurred in aid of insurrection or rebellion against the United States, or any claim for the loss or emancipation of any slave; but all such debts, obligations and claims shall be held illegal and void.

SECTION 5
[POWER TO ENFORCE THIS ARTICLE]

The Congress shall have power to enforce, by appropriate legislation, the provisions of this article.

Amendment XV

[*Proposed by Congress on February 26, 1869; declared ratified on March 30, 1870.*]

SECTION 1
[BLACK SUFFRAGE]

The right of citizens of the United States to vote shall not be denied or abridged by the United States or by any State on account of race, color, or previous condition of servitude.

SECTION 2
[POWER TO ENFORCE THIS ARTICLE]

The Congress shall have power to enforce this article by appropriate legislation.

Amendment XVI

[*Proposed by Congress on July 2, 1909;
declared ratified on February 25, 1913.*]
[AUTHORIZING INCOME TAXES]

The Congress shall have power to lay and collect taxes on incomes, from whatever source derived, without apportionment among the several States, and without regard to any census or enumeration.

Amendment XVII

[*Proposed by Congress on May 13, 1912;
declared ratified on May 31, 1913.*]
[POPULAR ELECTION OF SENATORS]

The Senate of the United States shall be composed of two Senators from each State, elected by the people thereof, for six years; and each Senator shall have one vote. The electors in each State shall have the qualifications requisite for electors of the most numerous branch of the State legislatures.

When vacancies happen in the representation of any State in the Senate, the executive authority of such State shall issue writs of election to fill such vacancies: *Provided,* That the legislature of any State may empower the executive thereof to make temporary appointments until the people fill the vacancies by election as the legislature may direct.

This amendment shall not be so construed as to affect the election or term of any Senator chosen before it becomes valid as part of the Constitution.

Amendment XVIII

[*Proposed by Congress December 18, 1917; declared ratified on January 29, 1919.*]

SECTION 1
[NATIONAL LIQUOR PROHIBITION]

After one year from the ratification of this article the manufacture, sale, or transportation of intoxicating liquors within, the importation thereof into, or the exportation thereof from the United States and all territory subject to the jurisdiction thereof for beverage purposes is hereby prohibited.

SECTION 2
[POWER TO ENFORCE THIS ARTICLE]

The Congress and the several States shall have concurrent power to enforce this article by appropriate legislation.

SECTION 3
[RATIFICATION WITHIN SEVEN YEARS]

This article shall be inoperative unless it shall have been ratified as an amendment to the Constitution by the legislatures of the several States, as provided in the Constitution, within seven years from the date of the submission hereof to the States by the Congress.[1]

Amendment XIX

[*Proposed by Congress on June 4, 1919;
declared ratified on August 26, 1920.*]

---

[1] Repealed by the Twenty-first Amendment.

[WOMAN SUFFRAGE]

The right of citizens of the United States to vote shall not be denied or abridged by the United States or by any State on account of sex.

Congress shall have power to enforce this article by appropriate legislation.

Amendment XX

[*Proposed by Congress on March 2, 1932; declared ratified on February 6, 1933.*]

SECTION 1
[TERMS OF OFFICE]

The terms of the President and Vice President shall end at noon on the 20th day of January, and the terms of Senators and Representatives at noon on the 3d day of January, of the years in which such terms would have ended if this article had not been ratified; and the terms of their successors shall then begin.

SECTION 2
[TIME OF CONVENING CONGRESS]

The Congress shall assemble at least once in every year, and such meeting shall begin at noon on the 3d day of January, unless they shall by law appoint a different day.

SECTION 3
[DEATH OF PRESIDENT-ELECT]

If, at the time fixed for the beginning of the term of the President, the President elect shall have died, the Vice President elect shall become President. If a President shall not have been chosen before the time fixed for the beginning of his term, or if the President elect shall have failed to qualify, then the Vice President elect shall act as President until a President shall have qualified; and the Congress may by law provide for the case wherein neither a President elect nor a Vice President elect shall have qualified, declaring who shall then act as President, or the manner in which one who is to act shall be selected, and such person shall act accordingly until a President or Vice President shall have qualified.

SECTION 4
[ELECTION OF THE PRESIDENT]

The Congress may by law provide for the case of the death of any of the persons from whom the House of Representatives may choose a President whenever the right of choice shall have devolved upon them, and for the case of the death of any of the persons from whom the Senate may choose a Vice President whenever the right of choice shall have devolved upon them.

SECTION 5
[AMENDMENT TAKES EFFECT]

Sections 1 and 2 shall take effect on the 15th day of October following the ratification of this article.

SECTION 6
[RATIFICATION WITHIN SEVEN YEARS]

This article shall be inoperative unless it shall have been ratified as an amendment to the Constitution by the legislatures of three-fourths of the several States within seven years from the date of its submission.

Amendment XXI

[*Proposed by Congress on February 20, 1933; declared ratified on December 5, 1933.*]

SECTION 1
[NATIONAL LIQUOR PROHIBITION REPEALED]

The eighteenth article of amendment to the Constitution of the United States is hereby repealed.

SECTION 2
[TRANSPORTATION OF LIQUOR INTO "DRY" STATES]

The transportation or importation into any State, Territory, or Possession of the United States for delivery or use therein of intoxicating liquors, in violation of the laws thereof, is hereby prohibited.

SECTION 3
[RATIFICATION WITHIN SEVEN YEARS]

This article shall be inoperative unless it shall have been ratified as an amendment to the Constitution by conventions in the several States, as provided in the Constitution, within seven years from the date of the submission hereof to the States by the Congress.

Amendment XXII

[*Proposed by Congress on March 21, 1947; declared ratified on February 27, 1951.*]

SECTION 1
[TENURE OF PRESIDENT LIMITED]

No person shall be elected to the office of President more than twice, and no person who has held the office of President or acted as President, for more than two years of a term to which some other person was elected President shall be elected to the office of the President more than once. But this Article shall not apply to any person holding the office of President when this Article was proposed by the Congress, and shall not prevent any person who may be holding the office of President, or acting as President, during the term within which this Article becomes operative from holding the office of President or acting as President during the remainder of such term.

SECTION 2
[RATIFICATION WITHIN SEVEN YEARS]

This article shall be inoperative unless it shall have been ratified as an amendment to the Constitution by the legislatures of three-fourths of the several States within seven years from the date of its submission to the States by the Congress.

Amendment XXIII

[*Proposed by Congress on June 16, 1960; declared ratified on March 29, 1961.*]

SECTION 1
[ELECTORAL COLLEGE VOTES FOR THE DISTRICT OF COLUMBIA]

The District constituting the seat of Government of the United States shall appoint in such manner as the Congress may direct:

A number of electors of President and Vice President equal to the whole number of Senators and Representatives in Congress to which the District would be entitled if it were a State, but in no event more than the least populous State; they shall be in addition to those appointed by the States, but they shall be considered, for the purposes of the election of President and Vice President, to be electors appointed by a State; and they shall meet in the District and perform such duties as provided by the twelfth article of amendment.

SECTION 2
[POWER TO ENFORCE THIS ARTICLE]

The Congress shall have power to enforce this article by appropriate legislation.

Amendment XXIV

[*Proposed by Congress on August 27, 1962; declared ratified on January 23, 1964.*]

SECTION 1
[ANTI-POLL TAX]

The right of citizens of the United States to vote in any primary or other election for President or Vice President, for electors for President or Vice President, or for Senator or Representative of Congress, shall not be denied or abridged by the United States or any State by reason of failure to pay any poll tax or other tax.

SECTION 2
[POWER TO ENFORCE THIS ARTICLE]

The Congress shall have power to enforce this article by appropriate legislation.

Amendment XXV

[*Proposed by Congress on July 6, 1965; declared ratified on February 10, 1967.*]

SECTION 1
[VICE PRESIDENT TO BECOME PRESIDENT]

In case of the removal of the President from office or his death or resignation, the Vice President shall become President.

SECTION 2
[CHOICE OF A NEW VICE PRESIDENT]

Whenever there is a vacancy in the office of the Vice President, the President shall nominate a Vice President who shall take the office upon confirmation by a majority vote of both houses of Congress.

SECTION 3
[PRESIDENT MAY DECLARE OWN DISABILITY]

Whenever the President transmits to the President pro tempore of the Senate and the Speaker of the House of Representatives his written declaration that he is unable to discharge the powers and duties of his office, and until he transmits to them a written declaration to the contrary, such powers and duties shall be discharged by the Vice President as Acting President.

SECTION 4
[ALTERNATE PROCEDURES TO DECLARE AND TO END PRESIDENTIAL DISABILITY]

Whenever the Vice President and a majority of either the principal officers of the executive departments, or of such other body as Congress may by law provide, transmit to the President pro tempore of the Senate and the Speaker of the House of Representatives their written declaration that the President is unable to discharge the powers and duties of his office, the Vice President shall immediately assume the powers and duties of the office as Acting President.

Thereafter, when the President transmits to the President pro tempore of the Senate and the Speaker of the House of Representatives his written declaration that no inability exists, he shall resume the powers and duties of his office unless the Vice President and a majority of either the principal officers of the executive department, or of such other body as Congress may by law provide, transmit within four days to the President pro tempore of the Senate and the Speaker of the House of Representatives their written declaration that the President is unable to discharge the powers and duties of his office. Thereupon Congress shall decide the issue, assembling within forty eight hours for that purpose if not in session. If the Congress, within twenty one days after receipt of the latter written declaration, or, if Congress is not in session, within twenty one days after Congress is required to assemble, determines by two-thirds vote of both Houses that the President is unable to discharge the powers and duties of his office, the Vice President shall continue to discharge the same as Acting President; otherwise, the President shall resume the powers and duties of his office.

Amendment XXVI

[*Proposed by Congress on March 23, 1971; declared ratified on July 1, 1971.*]

SECTION 1
[EIGHTEEN-YEAR-OLD VOTE]

The right of citizens of the United States, who are eighteen years of age or older, to vote shall not be denied or abridged by the United States or by any State on account of age.

SECTION 2
[POWER TO ENFORCE THIS ARTICLE]

The Congress shall have power to enforce this article by appropriate legislation.

Amendment XXVII

[*Proposed by Congress on September 25, 1789; declared ratified on May 8, 1992.*]
[CONGRESS CANNOT RAISE ITS OWN PAY]

No law varying the compensation for the services of the Senators and Representatives, shall take effect, until an election of representatives shall have intervened.

The Federalist Papers

No. 10: Madison

The Same Subject Continued: The Utility of the Union as a Safeguard against Domestic Faction and Insurrection

Among the numerous advantages promised by a well constructed Union, none deserves to be more accurately developed than its tendency to break and control the violence of faction. The friend of popular governments never finds himself so much alarmed for their character and fate, as when he contemplates their propensity to this dangerous vice. He will not fail therefore to set a due value on any plan which, without violating the principles to which he is attached, provides a proper cure for it. The instability, injustice, and confusion introduced into the public councils have, in truth, been the mortal diseases under which popular governments have everywhere perished, as they continue to be the favorite and fruitful topics from which the adversaries to liberty derive their most specious declamations. The valuable improvements made by the American constitutions on the popular models, both ancient and modern, cannot certainly be too much admired; but it would be an unwarrantable partiality to contend that they have as effectually obviated the danger on this side, as was wished and expected. Complaints are everywhere heard from our most considerate and virtuous citizens, equally the friends of public and private faith and of public and personal liberty, that our governments are too unstable, that the public good is disregarded in the conflicts of rival parties, and that measures are too often decided, not according to the rules of justice and the rights of the minor party, but by the superior force of an interested and overbearing majority. However anxiously we may wish that these complaints had no foundation, the evidence of known facts will not permit us to deny that they are in some degree true. It will be found, indeed, on a candid review of our situation, that some of the distresses under which we labor have been erroneously charged on the operation of our governments; but it will be found, at the same time, that other causes will not alone account for many of our heaviest misfortunes; and, particularly, for that prevailing and increasing distrust of public engagements and alarm for private rights which are echoed from one end of the continent to the other. These must be chiefly, if not wholly, effects of the unsteadiness and injustice with which a factious spirit has tainted our public administration.

By a faction I understand a number of citizens, whether amounting to a majority or minority of the whole, who are united and actuated by some common impulse of passion, or of interest, adverse to the rights of other citizens, or to the permanent and aggregate interests of the community.

There are two methods of curing the mischiefs of faction: the one, by removing its causes; the other, by controlling its effects.

There are again two methods of removing the causes of faction: the one, by destroying the liberty which is essential to its existence; the other, by giving to every citizen the same opinions, the same passions, and the same interests.

It could never be more truly said than of the first remedy, that it is worse than the disease. Liberty is to faction what air is to fire, an aliment without which it instantly expires. But it could not be a less folly to abolish liberty, which is essential to political life, because it nourishes faction, than it would be to wish the annihilation of air, which is essential to animal life, because it imparts to fire its destructive agency.

The second expedient is as impracticable, as the first would be unwise. As long as the reason of man continues fallible, and he is at liberty to exercise it, different opinions will be formed. As long as the connection subsists between his reason and his self-love, his opinions and his passions will have a reciprocal influence on each other; and the former will be objects to which the latter will attach themselves. The diversity in the faculties of men, from which the rights of property originate, is not less an insuperable obstacle to a uniformity of interests. The protection of these faculties is the first object of Government. From the protection of different and unequal faculties of acquiring property, the possession of different degrees and kinds of property immediately results; and from the influence of these on the sentiments and views of the respective proprietors, ensues a division of the society into different interests and parties.

The latent causes of faction are thus sown in the nature of man; and we see them everywhere brought into different degrees of activity, according to the different circumstances of civil society. A zeal for different opinions concerning religion, concerning Government, and many other points, as well of speculation as of practice; an attachment to different leaders ambitiously contending for pre-eminence and power; or to persons of other descriptions whose fortunes have been interesting to the human passions, have in turn divided mankind into parties, inflamed them with mutual animosity, and rendered them much more disposed to vex and oppress each other, than to co-operate for their common good. So strong is this propensity of mankind to fall into mutual animosities, that where no substantial occasion presents itself, the most frivolous and fanciful distinctions have been sufficient to kindle their unfriendly passions, and excite their most violent conflicts. But the most common and durable source of factions has been the various and unequal distribution of property. Those who hold and those who are without property have ever formed distinct interests in society. Those who are creditors, and those who are debtors, fall under a like discrimination. A landed interest, a manufacturing interest, a mercantile interest, a moneyed interest, with many lesser interests, grow up of necessity in civilized nations, and divide them into different classes, actuated by different sentiments and views. The regulation of these various and interfering interests forms the principal task of modern Legislation, and involves the spirit of party and faction in the necessary and ordinary operations of Government.

No man is allowed to be judge in his own cause, because his interest would certainly bias his judgment and, not improbably, corrupt his integrity. With equal, nay with greater reason, a body of men are unfit to be both judges and parties at the same time; yet what are many of the most important acts of legislation but so many judicial determinations, not indeed concerning the rights of single persons, but concerning the rights of large bodies of citizens; and what are the different classes of legislators but advocates and parties to the causes which they determine? Is a law proposed concerning private debts? It is a question to which the creditors are parties on one side and the debtors on the other. Justice ought to hold the balance between them. Yet the parties are, and must be, themselves the judges; and the most numerous party, or in other words, the most powerful faction must be expected to prevail. Shall domestic manufacturers be encouraged, and in what degree, by restrictions on foreign manufacturers? are questions which would be differently decided by the landed and the manufacturing classes, and probably by neither with a sole regard to justice and the public good. The apportionment of taxes on the various descriptions of property is an act which seems to require the most exact impartiality; yet there is, perhaps, no legislative act in which greater opportunity and temptation are given to a predominant party to trample on the rules of justice. Every shilling with which they overburden the inferior number is a shilling saved to their own pockets.

It is in vain to say that enlightened statesmen will be able to adjust these clashing interests and render them all subservient to the public good. Enlightened statesmen will not always be at the helm. Nor, in many cases, can such an adjustment be made at all without taking into view indirect and remote considerations, which will rarely prevail over the immediate interest which one party may find in disregarding the rights of another or the good of the whole.

The inference to which we are brought is that the *causes* of faction cannot be removed and that relief is only to be sought in the means of controlling its *effects*.

If a faction consists of less than a majority, relief is supplied by the republican principle, which enables the majority to defeat its sinister views by regular vote. It may clog the administration, it may convulse the society; but it will be unable to execute and mask its violence under the forms of the Constitution. When a majority is included in a faction, the form of popular government, on the other hand, enables it to sacrifice to its ruling passion or interest both the public good and the rights of other citizens. To secure the public good and private rights against the danger of such a faction, and at the same time to preserve the spirit and the form of popular government, is then the great object to which our enquiries are directed. Let me add that it is the great desideratum by which alone this form of government can be rescued from the opprobrium under which it has so long labored and be recommended to the esteem and adoption of mankind.

By what means is this object attainable? Evidently by one of two only. Either the existence of the same passion or interest in a majority at the same time must be prevented, or the majority, having such co-existent passion or interest, must be rendered, by their number and local situation, unable to concert and carry into effect schemes of oppression. If the impulse and the opportunity be suffered to coincide, we well know that neither moral nor religious motives can be relied on as an adequate control. They are not found to be such on the injustice and violence of individuals, and lose their efficacy in proportion to the number combined together, that is, in proportion as their efficacy becomes needful.

From this view of the subject it may be concluded that a pure Democracy, by which I mean a Society consisting of a small number of citizens, who assemble and administer the Government in person, can admit of no cure for the mischiefs of faction. A common passion or interest will, in almost every case, be felt by a majority of the whole; a communication and concert results from the form of Government itself; and there is nothing to check the inducements to sacrifice the weaker party or an obnoxious individual. Hence it is that such Democracies have ever been spectacles of turbulence and contention; have ever been found incompatible with personal security or the rights of property; and have in general been as short in their lives as they have been violent in their deaths. Theoretic politicians, who have patronized this species of Government, have erroneously supposed that by reducing mankind to a perfect equality in their political rights, they would at the same time be perfectly equalized and assimilated in their possessions, their opinions, and their passions.

A Republic, by which I mean a Government in which the scheme of representation takes place, opens a different prospect and promises the cure for which we are seeking. Let us examine the points in which it varies from pure Democracy, and we shall comprehend both the nature of the cure and the efficacy which it must derive from the Union.

The two great points of difference between a Democracy and a Republic are: first, the delegation of the Government, in the latter, to a small number of citizens elected by the rest; secondly, the greater number of citizens and greater sphere of country over which the latter may be extended.

The effect of the first difference is, on the one hand, to refine and enlarge the public views by passing them through the medium of a chosen body of citizens, whose wisdom may best discern the true interest of their country and whose patriotism and love of justice will be least likely to sacrifice it to temporary or partial considerations. Under such a regulation it may well happen that the public voice, pronounced by the representatives of the people, will be more consonant to the public good than if pronounced by the people themselves, convened for the purpose. On the other hand, the effect may be inverted. Men of factious tempers, of local prejudices, or of sinister designs, may, by intrigue, by corruption, or by other means, first obtain the suffrages, and then betray the interests of the people. The question resulting is, whether small or extensive Republics are most favorable to the election of proper guardians of the public weal; and it is clearly decided in favor of the latter by two obvious considerations.

In the first place it is to be remarked that however small the Republic may be, the Representatives must be raised to a certain number in order to guard against the cabals of a few; and that however large it may be they must be limited to a certain number in order to guard against the confusion of a multitude. Hence, the number of Representatives in the two cases not being in proportion to that of the Constituents, and being proportionally greatest in the small Republic, it follows that if the proportion of fit characters be not less in the large than in the small Republic, the former will present a greater option, and consequently a greater probability of a fit choice.

In the next place, as each Representative will be chosen by a greater number of citizens in the large than in the small Republic, it will be more difficult for unworthy candidates to practise with success the vicious arts by which elections are too often carried; and the suffrages of the people being more free, will be more likely to centre on men who possess the most attractive merit and the most diffusive and established characters.

It must be confessed that in this, as in most other cases, there is a mean, on both sides of which inconveniencies will be found to lie. By enlarging too much the number of electors, you render the representative too little acquainted with all their local circumstances and lesser interests; as by reducing it too much, you render him unduly attached to these, and too little fit to comprehend and pursue great and national objects. The Federal Constitution forms a happy combination in this respect; the great and aggregate interests being referred to the national, the local and particular to the State legislatures.

The other point of difference is the greater number of citizens and extent of territory which may be brought within the compass of Republican than of Democratic Government; and it is this circumstance principally which renders factious combinations less to be dreaded in the former than in the latter. The smaller the society, the fewer probably will be the distinct parties and interests composing it; the fewer the distinct parties and interests, the more frequently will a majority be found of the same party; and the smaller the number of individuals composing a majority, and the smaller the compass within which they are placed, the more easily will they concert and execute their plans of oppression. Extend the sphere and you take in a greater variety of parties and interests; you make it less probable that a majority of the whole will have a common motive to invade the rights of other citizens; or if such a common motive exists, it will be more difficult for all who feel it to discover their own strength and to act in unison with each other.

Besides other impediments, it may be remarked, that where there is a consciousness of unjust or dishonorable purposes, communication is always checked by distrust in proportion to the number whose concurrence is necessary.

Hence, it clearly appears that the same advantage which a Republic has over a Democracy in controlling the effects of faction is enjoyed by a large over a small republic—is enjoyed by the Union over the States composing it. Does this advantage consist in the substitution of representatives whose enlightened views and virtuous sentiments render them superior to local prejudices and to schemes of injustice? It will not be denied that the representation of the Union will be most likely to possess these requisite endowments. Does it consist in the greater security afforded by a greater variety of parties, against the event of any one party being able to outnumber and oppress the rest? In an equal degree does the increased variety of parties comprised within the Union increase this security? Does it, in fine, consist in the greater obstacles opposed to the concert and accomplishment of the secret wishes of an unjust and interested majority? Here again the extent of the Union gives it the most palpable advantage.

The influence of factious leaders may kindle a flame within their particular States but will be unable to spread a general conflagration through the other States: a religious sect may degenerate into a political faction in a part of the Confederacy; but the variety of sects dispersed over the entire face of it must secure the national Councils against any danger from that source: a rage for paper money, for an abolition of debts, for an equal division of property, or for any other improper or wicked project, will be less apt to pervade the whole body of the Union than a particular member of it; in the same proportion as such a malady is more likely to taint a particular county or district than an entire State.

In the extent and proper structure of the Union, therefore, we behold a republican remedy for the diseases most incident to Republican Government. And according to the degree of pleasure and pride we feel in being republicans ought to be our zeal in cherishing the spirit and supporting the character of Federalists.

PUBLIUS

No. 51: Madison

The Structure of the Government Must Furnish the Proper Checks and Balances between the Different Departments

To the People of the State of New York:

To what expedient, then, shall we finally resort, for maintaining in practice the necessary partition of power among the several departments as laid down in the constitution? The only answer that can be given is that as all these exterior provisions are found to be inadequate the defect must be supplied, by so contriving the interior structure of the government as that its several constituent parts may, by their mutual relations, be the means of keeping each other in their proper places. Without presuming to undertake a full development of this important idea I will hazard a few general observations which may perhaps place it in a clearer light, and enable us to form a more correct judgment of the principles and structure of the government planned by the convention.

In order to lay a due foundation for that separate and distinct exercise of the different powers of government, which to a certain extent is admitted on all hands to be essential to the preservation of liberty, it is evident that each department should have a will of its own; and consequently should be so constituted that the members of each should have as little agency as possible in the appointment of the members of the others. Were this principle rigorously adhered to, it would require that all the appointments for the supreme executive, legislative, and judiciary magistracies should be drawn from the same fountain of authority, the people, through channels having no communication whatever with one another. Perhaps such a plan of constructing the several departments would be less difficult in practice than it may in contemplation appear. Some difficulties, however, and some additional expense would attend the execution of it. Some deviations, therefore, from the principle must be admitted. In the constitution of the judiciary department in particular, it might be inexpedient to insist rigorously on the principle: first, because peculiar qualifications being essential in the members, the primary consideration ought to be to select that mode of choice which best secures these qualifications; second, because the permanent tenure by which the appointments are held in that department must soon destroy all sense of dependence on the authority conferring them.

It is equally evident that the members of each department should be as little dependent as possible on those of the others for the emoluments annexed to their offices. Were the executive magistrate, or the judges, not independent of the legislature in this particular, their independence in every other would be merely nominal.

But the great security against a gradual concentration of the several powers in the same department consists in giving to those who administer each department the necessary constitutional means and personal motives to resist encroachments of the others. The provision for defence must in this, as in all other cases, be made commensurate to the danger of attack. Ambition must be made to counteract ambition. The interest of the man must be connected with the constitutional rights of the place. It may be a reflection on human nature that such devices should be necessary to control the abuses of government. But what is government itself but the greatest of all reflections on human nature? If men were angels, no government would be necessary. If angels were to govern men, neither external nor internal controls on government would be necessary. In framing a government which is to be administered by men over men, the great difficulty lies in this: You must first enable the government to control the governed; and in the next place oblige it to control itself. A dependence on the people is, no doubt, the primary control on the government; but experience has taught mankind the necessity of auxiliary precautions.

This policy of supplying, by opposite and rival interests, the defect of better motives, might be traced through the whole system of human affairs, private as well as public. We see it particularly displayed in all the subordinate distributions of power, where the constant aim is to divide and arrange the several offices in such a manner as that each may be a check on the other; that the private interest of every individual may be a sentinel over the public rights. These inventions of prudence cannot be less requisite in the distribution of the supreme powers of the State.

But it is not possible to give to each department an equal power of self-defense. In republican government, the legislative authority necessarily predominates. The remedy for this inconveniency is to divide the legislature into different branches; and to render them, by different modes of election and different principles of action, as little connected with each other as the nature of their common functions and their common dependence on the society will admit. It may even be necessary to guard against dangerous encroachments by still further precautions. As the weight of the legislative authority requires that it should be thus divided, the weakness of the executive may require, on the other hand, that it should be fortified. An absolute negative on the legislature appears, at first view, to be the natural defense with which the executive magistrate should be armed. But perhaps it would be neither altogether safe nor alone sufficient. On ordinary occasions it might not be exerted with the requisite firmness, and on extraordinary occasions it might be perfidiously abused. May not this defect of an absolute negative be supplied by some qualified connection between this weaker branch of the stronger department, by which the latter may be led to support the constitutional rights of the former, without being too much detached from the rights of its own department?

If the principles on which these observations are founded be just, as I persuade myself they are, and they be applied as a criterion to the several State constitutions, and to the federal Constitution, it will be found that if the latter does not perfectly correspond with them, the former are infinitely less able to bear such a test.

There are, moreover, two considerations particularly applicable to the federal system of America, which place that system in a very interesting point of view.

First. In a single republic, all the power surrendered by the people is submitted to the administration of a single government; and usurpations are guarded against by a division of the government into distinct and separate departments. In the compound republic of America, the power surrendered by the people is first divided between two distinct governments, and then the portion allotted to each subdivided among distinct and separate departments. Hence a double security arises to the rights of the people. The different governments will control each other, at the same time that each will be controlled by itself.

Second. It is of great importance in a republic not only to guard the society against the oppression of its rulers, but to guard one part of the society against the injustice of the other part. Different interests necessarily exist in different classes of citizens. If a majority be united by a common interest, the rights of the minority will be insecure.

There are but two methods of providing against this evil: The one by creating a will in the community independent of the majority—that is, of the society itself; the other, by comprehending in the society so many separate descriptions of citizens as will render an unjust combination of a majority of the whole very improbable, if not impracticable. The first method prevails in all governments possessing an hereditary or self-appointed authority. This, at best, is but a precarious security; because a power independent of the society may as well espouse the unjust views of the major as the rightful interests of the minor party, and may possibly be turned against both parties. The second method will be exemplified in the federal republic of the United States. Whilst all authority in it will be derived from and dependent on the society, the society itself will be broken into so many parts, interests and classes of citizens, that the rights of individuals, or of the minority, will be in little danger from interested combinations of the majority.

In a free government the security for civil rights must be the same as that for religious rights. It consists in the one case in the multiplicity of interests, and in the other in the multiplicity of sects. The degree of security in both cases will depend on the number of interests and sects; and this may be presumed to depend on the extent of country and number of people comprehended under the same government. This view of the subject must particularly recommend a proper federal system to all the sincere and considerate friends of republican government: Since it shows that in exact proportion as the territory of the Union may be formed into more circumscribed Confederacies, or States, oppressive combinations of a majority will be facilitated; the best security, under the republican form, for the rights of every class of citizens, will be diminished; and consequently the stability and independence of some member of the government, the only other security, must be proportionally increased. Justice is the end of government. It is the end of civil society. It ever has been and ever will be pursued until it be obtained, or until liberty be lost in the pursuit. In a society under the forms of which the stronger faction can readily unite and oppress the weaker, anarchy may as truly be said to reign as in a state of nature, where the weaker individual is

not secured against the violence of the stronger: And as, in the latter state, even the stronger individuals are prompted, by the uncertainty of their condition, to submit to a government which may protect the weak as well as themselves: So, in the former state, will the more powerful factions or parties be gradually induced, by a like motive, to wish for a government which will protect all parties, the weaker as well as the more powerful.

It can be little doubted that if the State of Rhode Island was separated from the Confederacy and left to itself, the insecurity of rights under the popular form of government within such narrow limits would be displayed by such reiterated oppressions of factious majorities that some power altogether independent of the people would soon be called for by the voice of the very factions whose misrule had proved the necessity of it. In the extended republic of the United States, and among the great variety of interests, parties, and sects which it embraces, a coalition of a majority of the whole society could seldom take place on any other principles than those of justice and the general good; and there being thus less danger to a minor from the will of the major party, there must be less pretext, also, to provide for the security of the former, by introducing into the government a will not dependent on the latter, or, in other words, a will independent of the society itself. It is no less certain than it is important, notwithstanding the contrary opinions which have been entertained, that the larger the society, provided it lie within a practicable sphere, the more duly capable it will be of self-government. And happily for the *republican cause,* practicable sphere may be carried to a very great extent by a judicious modification and mixture of the *federal principle.*

PUBLIUS

No. 78: Hamilton

To the People of the State of New York:

We proceed now to an examination of the judiciary department of the proposed government.

In unfolding the defects of the existing Confederation, the utility and necessity of a federal judicature have been clearly pointed out. It is the less necessary to recapitulate the considerations there urged, as the propriety of the institution in the abstract is not disputed; the only questions which have been raised being relative to the manner of constituting it, and to its extent. To these points, therefore, our observations shall be confined.

The manner of constituting it seems to embrace these several objects: 1st. The mode of appointing the judges. 2d. The tenure by which they are to hold their places. 3d. The partition of the judiciary authority between different courts, and their relations to each other.

First. As to the mode of appointing the judges; this is the same with that of appointing the officers of the Union in general, and has been so fully discussed in the two last numbers, that nothing can be said here which would not be useless repetition.

Second. As to the tenure by which the judges are to hold their places; this chiefly concerns their duration in office; the provisions for their support; the precautions for their responsibility.

According to the plan of the convention, all judges who may be appointed by the United States are to hold their offices DURING GOOD BEHAVIOR; which is conformable to the most approved of the State constitutions and among the rest, to that of this State. Its propriety having been drawn into question by the adversaries of that plan, is no light symptom of the rage for objection, which disorders their imaginations and judgments. The standard of good behavior for the continuance in office of the judicial magistracy, is certainly one of the most valuable of the modern improvements in the practice of government. In a monarchy it is an excellent barrier to the despotism of the prince; in a republic it is a no less excellent barrier to the encroachments and oppressions of the representative body. And it is the best expedient which can be devised in any government, to secure a steady, upright, and impartial administration of the laws.

Whoever attentively considers the different departments of power must perceive, that, in a government in which they are separated from each other, the judiciary, from the nature of its functions, will always be the least dangerous to the political rights of the Constitution; because it will be least in a capacity to annoy or injure them. The Executive not only dispenses the honors, but holds the sword of the community. The legislature not only commands the purse, but prescribes the rules by which the duties and rights of every citizen are to be regulated. The judiciary, on the contrary, has no influence over either the sword or the purse; no direction either of the strength or of the wealth of the society; and can take no active resolution whatever. It may truly be said to have neither FORCE nor WILL, but merely judgment; and must ultimately depend upon the aid of the executive arm even for the efficacy of its judgments.

This simple view of the matter suggests several important consequences. It proves incontestably, that the judiciary is beyond comparison the weakest of the three departments of power; that it can never attack with success either of the other two; and that all possible care is requisite to enable it to defend itself against their attacks. It equally proves, that though individual oppression may now and then proceed from the courts of justice, the general liberty of the people can never be endangered from that quarter; I mean so long as the judiciary remains truly distinct from both the legislature and the Executive. For I agree, that "there is no liberty, if the power of judging be not separated from the legislative and executive powers." And it proves, in the last place, that as liberty can have nothing to fear from the judiciary alone, but would have every thing to fear from its union with either of the other departments; that as all the effects of such a union must ensue from a dependence of the former on the latter, notwithstanding a nominal and apparent separation; that as, from the natural feebleness of the judiciary, it is in continual jeopardy of being overpowered, awed, or influenced by its co-ordinate branches; and that as nothing can contribute so much to its firmness and independence as permanency in office, this quality may therefore be justly regarded as an indispensable ingredient in its constitution, and, in a great measure, as the citadel of the public justice and the public security.

The complete independence of the courts of justice is peculiarly essential in a limited Constitution. By a limited Constitution, I understand one which contains certain specified exceptions to the legislative authority; such, for instance, as that it shall pass no bills of attainder, no ex-post-facto laws, and the like. Limitations of this kind can be preserved in practice no other way than through the medium of courts of justice, whose duty it must be to declare all acts contrary to the manifest tenor of the Constitution void. Without this, all the reservations of particular rights or privileges would amount to nothing.

Some perplexity respecting the rights of the courts to pronounce legislative acts void, because contrary to the Constitution, has arisen from an imagination that the doctrine would imply a superiority of the judiciary to the legislative power. It is urged that the authority which can declare the acts of another void, must necessarily be superior to the one whose acts may be declared void. As this doctrine is of great importance in all the American constitutions, a brief discussion of the ground on which it rests cannot be unacceptable.

There is no position which depends on clearer principles, than that every act of a delegated authority, contrary to the tenor of the commission under which it is exercised, is void. No legislative act, therefore, contrary to the Constitution, can be valid. To deny this, would be to affirm, that the deputy is greater than his principal; that the servant is above his master; that the representatives of the people are superior to the people themselves; that men acting by virtue of

powers, may do not only what their powers do not authorize, but what they forbid.

If it be said that the legislative body are themselves the constitutional judges of their own powers, and that the construction they put upon them is conclusive upon the other departments, it may be answered, that this cannot be the natural presumption, where it is not to be collected from any particular provisions in the Constitution. It is not otherwise to be supposed, that the Constitution could intend to enable the representatives of the people to substitute their will to that of their constituents. It is far more rational to suppose, that the courts were designed to be an intermediate body between the people and the legislature, in order, among other things, to keep the latter within the limits assigned to their authority. The interpretation of the laws is the proper and peculiar province of the courts. A constitution is, in fact, and must be regarded by the judges, as a fundamental law. It therefore belongs to them to ascertain its meaning, as well as the meaning of any particular act proceeding from the legislative body. If there should happen to be an irreconcilable variance between the two, that which has the superior obligation and validity ought, of course, to be preferred; or, in other words, the Constitution ought to be preferred to the statute, the intention of the people to the intention of their agents.

Nor does this conclusion by any means suppose a superiority of the judicial to the legislative power. It only supposes that the power of the people is superior to both; and that where the will of the legislature, declared in its statutes, stands in opposition to that of the people, declared in the Constitution, the judges ought to be governed by the latter rather than the former. They ought to regulate their decisions by the fundamental laws, rather than by those which are not fundamental.

This exercise of judicial discretion, in determining between two contradictory laws, is exemplified in a familiar instance. It not uncommonly happens, that there are two statutes existing at one time, clashing in whole or in part with each other, and neither of them containing any repealing clause or expression. In such a case, it is the province of the courts to liquidate and fix their meaning and operation. So far as they can, by any fair construction, be reconciled to each other, reason and law conspire to dictate that this should be done; where this is impracticable, it becomes a matter of necessity to give effect to one, in exclusion of the other. The rule which has obtained in the courts for determining their relative validity is, that the last in order of time shall be preferred to the first. But this is a mere rule of construction, not derived from any positive law, but from the nature and reason of the thing. It is a rule not enjoined upon the courts by legislative provision, but adopted by themselves, as consonant to truth and propriety, for the direction of their conduct as interpreters of the law. They thought it reasonable, that between the interfering acts of an equal authority, that which was the last indication of its will should have the preference.

But in regard to the interfering acts of a superior and subordinate authority, of an original and derivative power, the nature and reason of the thing indicate the converse of that rule as proper to be followed. They teach us that the prior act of a superior ought to be preferred to the subsequent act of an inferior and subordinate authority; and that accordingly, whenever a particular statute contravenes the Constitution, it will be the duty of the judicial tribunals to adhere to the latter and disregard the former.

It can be of no weight to say that the courts, on the pretense of a repugnancy, may substitute their own pleasure to the constitutional intentions of the legislature. This might as well happen in the case of two contradictory statutes; or it might as well happen in every adjudication upon any single statute. The courts must declare the sense of the law; and if they should be disposed to exercise WILL instead of judgment, the consequence would equally be the substitution of their pleasure to that of the legislative body. The observation, if it prove any thing, would prove that there ought to be no judges distinct from that body.

If, then, the courts of justice are to be considered as the bulwarks of a limited Constitution against legislative encroachments, this consideration will afford a strong argument for the permanent tenure of judicial offices, since nothing will contribute so much as this to that independent spirit in the judges which must be essential to the faithful performance of so arduous a duty.

This independence of the judges is equally requisite to guard the Constitution and the rights of individuals from the effects of those ill humors, which the arts of designing men, or the influence of particular conjunctures, sometimes disseminate among the people themselves, and which, though they speedily give place to better information, and more deliberate reflection, have a tendency, in the meantime, to occasion dangerous innovations in the government, and serious oppressions of the minor party in the community. Though I trust the friends of the proposed Constitution will never concur with its enemies, in questioning that fundamental principle of republican government, which admits the right of the people to alter or abolish the established Constitution, whenever they find it inconsistent with their happiness, yet it is not to be inferred from this principle, that the representatives of the people, whenever a momentary inclination happens to lay hold of a majority of their constituents, incompatible with the provisions in the existing Constitution, would, on that account, be justifiable in a violation of those provisions; or that the courts would be under a greater obligation to connive at infractions in this shape, than when they had proceeded wholly from the cabals of the representative body. Until the people have, by some solemn and authoritative act, annulled or changed the established form, it is binding upon themselves collectively, as well as individually; and no presumption, or even knowledge, of their sentiments, can warrant their representatives in a departure from it, prior to such an act. But it is easy to see, that it would require an uncommon portion of fortitude in the judges to do their duty as faithful guardians of the Constitution, where legislative invasions of it had been instigated by the major voice of the community.

But it is not with a view to infractions of the Constitution only, that the independence of the judges may be an essential safeguard against the effects of occasional ill humors in the society. These sometimes extend no farther than to the injury of the private rights of particular classes of citizens, by unjust and partial laws. Here also the firmness of the judicial magistracy is of vast importance in mitigating the severity and confining the operation of such laws. It not only serves to moderate the immediate mischiefs of those which may have been passed, but it operates as a check upon the legislative body in passing them; who, perceiving that obstacles to the success of iniquitous intention are to be expected from the scruples of the courts, are in a manner compelled, by the very motives of the injustice they meditate, to qualify their attempts. This is a circumstance calculated to have more influence upon the character of our governments, than but few may be aware of. The benefits of the integrity and moderation of the judiciary have already been felt in more States than one; and though they may have displeased those whose sinister expectations they may have disappointed, they must have commanded the esteem and applause of all the virtuous and disinterested. Considerate men, of every description, ought to prize whatever will tend to beget or fortify that temper in the courts: as no man can be sure that he may not be to-morrow the victim of a spirit of injustice, by which he may be a gainer to-day. And every man must now feel, that the inevitable tendency of such a spirit is to sap the foundations of public and private confidence, and to introduce in its stead universal distrust and distress.

That inflexible and uniform adherence to the rights of the Constitution, and of individuals, which we perceive to be indispensable in the courts of justice, can certainly not be expected from judges who hold their offices by a temporary commission. Periodical appointments, however regulated, or by whomsoever made, would, in some way or other, be fatal to their necessary independence. If the power of making them was committed either to the Executive or legislature, there would be danger of an improper complaisance to the branch which possessed it; if to both, there would be an unwillingness to hazard the displeasure of either; if to the people, or to persons chosen by them for the special purpose, there would be too great a disposition to consult popularity, to justify a reliance that nothing would be consulted but the Constitution and the laws.

There is yet a further and a weightier reason for the permanency of the judicial offices, which is deducible from the nature of the qualifications they require. It has been frequently remarked, with great propriety, that a voluminous code of laws is one of the inconveniences necessarily connected with the advantages of a free government. To avoid an arbitrary discretion in the courts, it is indispensable that they should be bound down by strict rules and precedents, which serve to define and point out their duty in every particular case that comes before them; and it will readily be conceived from the variety of controversies which grow out of the folly and wickedness of mankind, that the records of those precedents must unavoidably swell to a very considerable bulk, and must demand long and laborious study to acquire a competent knowledge of them. Hence it is, that there can be but few men in the society who will have sufficient skill in the laws to qualify them for the stations of judges. And making the proper deductions for the ordinary depravity of human nature, the number must be still smaller of those who unite the requisite integrity with the requisite knowledge. These considerations apprise us, that the government can have no great option between fit character; and that a temporary duration in office, which would naturally discourage such characters from quitting a lucrative line of practice to accept a seat on the bench, would have a tendency to throw the administration of justice into hands less able, and less well qualified, to conduct it with utility and dignity. In the present circumstances of this country, and in those in which it is likely to be for a long time to come, the disadvantages on this score would be greater than they may at first sight appear; but it must be confessed, that they are far inferior to those which present themselves under the other aspects of the subject.

Upon the whole, there can be no room to doubt that the convention acted wisely in copying from the models of those constitutions which have established good behavior as the tenure of their judicial offices, in point of duration; and that so far from being blamable on this account, their plan would have been inexcusably defective, if it had wanted this important feature of good government. The experience of Great Britain affords an illustrious comment on the excellence of the institution.

PUBLIUS

Endnotes

Chapter 1

1. John Wagner, "'Very Much Our Friend': Romney Speaks Out Against Trump Calling the Media 'the Enemy of the People,'" *Washington Post*, November 1, 2018, www.washingtonpost.com/politics/very-much-our-friend-romney-speaks-out-against-trump-calling-the-media-the-enemy-of-the-people/2018/11/01/d28b0000-ddf7-11e8-85df-7a6b4d25cfbb_story.html (accessed 2/18/20).

2. "'Spies and Treason': Read a Transcript of Trump's Remarks Related to the Whistle-Blower," *New York Times*, September 26, 2019, www.nytimes.com/2019/09/26/us/politics/trump-treason-spies-whistle-blower.html (accessed 2/18/20).

3. Ben Gilbert, "The 10 Most-Viewed Fake-News Stories on Facebook in 2019 Were Just Revealed in a New Report," *Business Insider*, November 6, 2019, www.businessinsider.com/most-viewed-fake-news-stories-shared-on-facebook-2019-2019-11 (accessed 12/20/19); Mihir Zaveri, Allie Conti, and Sandra E. Garcia, "Fireworks Conspiracy Theories: Why You Should Be Skeptical," *New York Times*, September 1, 2020, www.nytimes.com/2020/06/25/nyregion/fireworks-nyc-conspiracy.html (accessed 9/30/20)..

4. Thomas Hobbes, *Leviathan* (1651; repr., Indianapolis, IN: Bobbs, Merrill, 1958).

5. Alexander Hamilton, James Madison, and John Jay, *The Federalist Papers*, ed. Roy P. Fairfield, 2nd ed. (1788; repr., Baltimore, MD: Johns Hopkins University Press, 1981), p. 160.

6. Hamilton, Madison, and Jay, *The Federalist Papers*, p. 18.

7. E. E. Schattschneider, *The Semisovereign People: A Realist's View of Democracy in America* (New York: Holt, Rinehart, and Winston, 1960).

8. Irving L. Janis, *Victims of Groupthink: A Psychological Study of Foreign-Policy Decisions and Fiascoes* (Boston: Houghton Mifflin, 1972).

9. Larry M. Bartels, *Unequal Democracy: The Political Economy of the New Gilded Age,* 2nd ed. (Princeton, NJ: Princeton University Press, 2016); Lawrence Baum, *Ideology in the Supreme Court* (Princeton, NJ: Princeton University Press, 2017).

10. Robert S. Erikson and Kent L. Tedin, *American Public Opinion*, 9th ed. (New York: Routledge, 2015).

11. John R. Hibbing and Elizabeth Theiss-Morse, *Stealth Democracy: Americans' Beliefs about How Government Should Work* (New York: Cambridge University Press, 2002), p. 147. See Diana E. Hess, *Controversy in the Classroom: The Democratic Power of Discussion* (New York: Routledge, 2009), for evidence that diverse viewpoints in the classroom have important effects on discussion.

12. For various surveys on abortion, see www.pollingreport.com/abortion.htm (accessed 1/16/18).

13. Donald Green, Bradley Palmquist, and Eric Schickler, *Partisan Hearts and Minds* (New Haven, CT: Yale University Press, 2004); Christopher Achen, "Parental Socialization and Rational Party Identification," *Political Behavior* 24:2 (2002): 151-70.

14. Robert S. Erikson, Michael B. MacKuen, and James A. Stimson, *The Macro Polity* (New York: Cambridge University Press, 2002); Christopher H. Achen and Larry M. Bartels, *Democracy for Realists: Why Elections Do Not Produce Responsive Government* (Princeton, NJ: Princeton University Press, 2016).

15. Office of Personnel Management, September 2019, www.fedscope.opm.gov/; Congressional Budget Office, November 2019, www.cbo.gov/topics/budget; Code of Federal Regulations, www.govinfo.gov/help/cfr#about (all accessed 12/20/19).

16. Andrew Heywood, *Political Theory: An Introduction*, 4th ed. (New York: Macmillan, 2015).

17. Morris P. Fiorina, with Samuel J. Abrams and Jeremy C. Pope, *Culture War: The Myth of a Polarized America*, 3rd ed. (New York: Pearson, Longman, 2010), pp. 46-7.

18. For more on political culture, see Pippa Norris, *Democratic Deficit: Critical Citizens Revisited* (New York: Cambridge University Press, 2011).

19. Frank M. Bryan, *Real Democracy: The New England Town Meeting and How It Works* (Chicago: University of Chicago Press, 2004).

Chapter 2

1. Donald Trump, Twitter, November 10, 2019, 2:43 P.M., https://twitter.com/realDonaldTrump/status/1193615188311912449 (accessed 2/20/20).

2. Nancy Pelosi, Twitter, October 29, 2019, 9:59 A.M., https://twitter.com/speakerpelosi/status/1189179898960715776 (accessed 4/16/20).

3. Alexander Hamilton, John Jay, and James Madison, *The Federalist Papers*, ed. Roy P. Fairfield, 2nd ed. (1788; repr., Baltimore, MD: Johns Hopkins University Press, 1981).

4. For a good overview of the political thought of the American Revolution, see Gordon S. Wood, *The Radicalism of the American Revolution* (New York: Vintage Books, 1993). For an excellent summary of the history, see Wood's *The American Revolution: A History* (New York: Modern Library, 2003).

5. J. W. Peltason, *Corwin and Peltason's Understanding the Constitution*, 7th ed. (Hinsdale, IL: Dryden Press, 1976), p. 12.

6. The pamphlet sold 120,000 copies within a few months of publication, a figure that would leave the Harry Potter books in the dust in terms of the proportion of the literate public that purchased the book.

7. John Locke, *Second Treatise of Government* (1690; repr., Indianapolis, IN: Bobbs, Merrill, 1952), Section 160.

8. Many delegates probably assumed that the electors would reflect the wishes of the voters in their states, but there is no clear indication of this in Madison's notes. (Hamilton makes this argument in the *Federalist Papers*.) Until the 1820s, many electors were directly chosen by state legislatures rather than by the people. In the first presidential election, George Washington won the unanimous support of the electors, but in only five states were the electors chosen by the people.

9. Beeman, Richard, *Plain Honest Men: The Making of the American Constitution* (New York: Random House, 2009), pp. 66-67.

10. The actual language of the section avoids the term "slavery." Instead, it says: "The Migration or Importation of such Persons as any of the States now existing shall think proper to admit, shall not be prohibited by Congress prior to the Year one thousand eight hundred and eight." The ban on the importation of enslaved people was implemented on the earliest possible date, January 1, 1808.

11. Brutus 1, October 18, 1787, The Constitution Society, www.constitution.org/afp/brutus01.htm (accessed 6/28/18).

12. Sharon LaFraniere, "Court Throws Out Emoluments Case Brought against Trump by Democrats," *New York Times*, February 7, 2020, www.nytimes.com/2020/02/07/us/emoluments-trump-democrats.html (accessed 2/12/20); Byron Tau, "Supreme Court Won't Review Democrats' Emoluments Case Against Trump," *Wall Street Journal*, October 13, 2020, www.wsj.com/articles/supreme-court-wont-review-democrats-emoluments-case-against-trump-11602616606 (accessed 11/5/20).

13. Charlie Savage, "Can Trump Pardon Himself? Explaining Presidential Clemency Powers," *New York Times*, July 21, 2017, www.nytimes.com/2017/07/21/us/politics/trump-pardon-himself-presidential-clemency.html (accessed 8/17/17).

14. Thomas B. Edsall, "The Savage Injustice of Trump's Military Pardons," *New York Times*, December 4, 2019, www.nytimes.com/2019/12/04/opinion/trump-military-pardons.html (accessed 12/6/19).

15. Associated Press, "House Overwhelmingly Votes Bipartisan Condemnation of Trump Withdrawal of U.S. Troops from Syria," October 16, 2019, www.nbcnews.com/politics/congress/house-overwhelmingly-votes-bipartisan-condemnation-trump-withdrawal-u-s-troops-n1067586 (accessed 12/6/19).

16. Cass R. Sunstein, "Making Amends," *New Republic*, March 3, 1997, p. 42.

17. *Furman v. Georgia*, 408 U.S. 238 (1972).

18. The case concerning minors was *Roper v. Simmons*, 543 U.S. 551 (2005), and the case concerning the mentally impaired was *Atkins v. Virginia*, 536 U.S. 304 (2002).

19. Valerie Strauss, "In the Age of Trump, a New Surge of Interest in the Constitution," *Washington Post*, August 17, 2017, www.washingtonpost.com/news/answer-sheet/wp/2017/08/17/in-the-age-of-trump-a-new-surge-of-interest-in-the-u-s-constitution/?utm_term=.e3abb53b9976 (accessed 8/18/2017).

20. Walter F. Murphy, "The Nature of the American Constitution," The Edmund Janes James lecture, December 6, 1987 (Department of Political Science, University of Illinois at Urbana-Champaign, 1989), p. 8, http://babel.hathitrust.org/cgi/pt?id=mdp.39015078286518;view=1up;seq=12 (accessed 1/22/20).

Take a Stand

a. Kristen Bialik, "Growing Share of Americans Say Supreme Court Should Base Its Rulings on What Constitution Means Today," Pew Research Center, May 11, 2018, www.pewresearch.org/fact-tank/2018/05/11/growing-share-of-americans-say-supreme-court-should-base-its-rulings-on-what-constitution-means-today/ (accessed 12/6/19).

b. Clarence Thomas, "How to Read the Constitution," *Wall Street Journal*, October 20, 2008.

c. *State of Missouri v. Holland*, 252 U.S. 416 (1920), 252.

d. William Rehnquist, "The Notion of a Living Constitution," *Harvard Journal of Law and Public Policy* 29 (2006): 402.

e. Rehnquist, "The Notion," p. 405.

f. Thurgood Marshall at the Annual Seminar of the San Francisco Patent and Trademark Law Association, Maui, Hawaii, May 6, 1987, www.thurgoodmarshall.com/speeches/constitutional_speech.htm (accessed 12/20/13).

Chapter 3

1. Paul A Einstein, "Trump Axes California's Right to Set Own Auto Emissions Standards," NBC News, September 18, 2019, www.nbcnews.com/business/autos/trump-about-strip-california-its-right-overrule-emissions-regulations-n1055811 (accessed 2/27/20).

2. United States Environmental Protection Agency, "Administrator Wheeler Addresses National Automobile Dealers Association," September 17, 2019, www.epa.gov/newsreleases/administrator-wheeler-addresses-national-automobile-dealers-association (accessed 2/27/20).

3. Slaughterhouse Cases, 83 U.S. 36 (1873). See Ronald M. Labbe and Jonathan Lurie, *The Slaughterhouse Cases: Regulation, Reconstruction, and the Fourteenth Amendment* (Lawrence: University Press of Kansas, 2003).

4. Civil Rights Cases, 109 U.S. 3 (1883).

5. *Hammer v. Dagenhart*, 247 U.S. 251 (1918).

6. Four key cases are *West Coast Hotel Company v. Parrish* (1937); *Wright v. Vinton Branch* (1937); *Virginia Railway Company v. System Federation* (1937); and *National Labor Relations Board v. Jones and Laughlin Steel Corporation* (1937).

7. Martin Grodzins, *The American System* (New York: Rand McNally, 1966).

8. *Brown v. Board of Education*, 347 U.S. 483 (1954); *Swann v. Charlotte-Mecklenburg Board of Education*, 402 U.S. 1 (1971).

9. *Miranda v. Arizona*, 384 U.S. 436 (1966); *Mapp v. Ohio*, 367 U.S. 643 (1961).

10. Barry Rabe, "Environmental Policy and the Bush Era: The Collision between the Administrative Presidency and State Experimentation," *Publius* 37:3 (May 2007): 413–31.

11. Lois Beckett, "Nullification: How States Are Making It a Felony to Enforce Federal Gun Laws," *ProPublica*, May 2, 2013, www.propublica.org/article/nullification-how-states-are-making-it-a-felony-to-enforce-federal-gun-laws (accessed 11/15/13).

12. From a review of Michael S. Greve, *Real Federalism: Why It Matters, How It Could Happen* (Washington, DC: American Enterprise Institute Press, 1999), www.federalismproject.org/publications/books (accessed 10/10/07).

13. *City of Boerne v. Flores*, 521 U.S. 507 (1997), 520.

14. *Kimel et al. v. Florida Board of Regents*, 528 U.S. 62 (2000).

15. *United States v. Lopez*, 514 U.S. 549 (1995).

16. *United States v. Morrison*, 529 U.S. 598 (2000); Nia-Malika Henderson, "Obama Signs a Strengthened Violence Against Women Act," *Washington Post*, March 7, 2013, www.washingtonpost.com/politics/obama-signs-a-strengthened-violence-against-women-act/2013/03/07/e50d585e-8740-11e2-98a3-b3db6b9ac586_story.html (accessed 3/21/14).

17. *Romer v. Evans*, 517 U.S. 620 (1996).

18. *National Federation of Independent Business v. Sebelius*, 132 S. Ct. 2566 (2012).

19. *National Federation of Independent Business v. Sebelius*, 132 S. Ct. 2566 (2012), p. 51.

20. Martha Derthick, *Keeping the Compound Republic: Essays on American Federalism* (Washington, DC: Brookings Institution, 2001), pp. 9–32.

What Do the Facts Say?

a. One example is Umair Irfan, "The EPA Refuted Its Own Bizarre Justification for Rolling Back Fuel Efficiency Standards," Vox, August 16, 2018, www.vox.com/2018/4/2/17181476/epa-fuel-economy-standards-tesla (accessed 11/18/19).

Chapter 4

1. Donald J. Trump, "Remarks by President Trump at Signing of Executive Order, 'Improving Free Inquiry, Transparency, and Accountability at Colleges and Universities,'" The White House, March 21, 2019, www.whitehouse.gov/briefings-statements/remarks-president-trump-signing-executive-order-improving-free-inquiry-transparency-accountability-colleges-universities/ (accessed 1/29/20).

2. Katherine Timpf, "Biden Is Right and Kasich Is Wrong on Campus Free Speech," *National Review*, October 18, 2017, www.nationalreview.com/2017/10/john-kasich-joe-biden-campus-free-speech-debate/ (accessed 1/29/20).

3. Patrick Strudwick, "Milo Yiannopoulos Calls Abuse Victims 'Whinging, Selfish Brats' In A Newly Emerged Video," BuzzFeed, March 11, 2017, www.buzzfeed.com/patrickstrudwick/milo-yiannopoulos-described-sexual-abuse-victims-as-whinging?utm_term=.sgZNwrBGy#.kmGkJoeZd; Graeme Wood, "His Kampf: Richard Spencer Is a Troll and an Icon for White Supremacists," *The Atlantic*, June 2017, www.theatlantic.com/magazine/archive/2017/06/his-kampf/524505 (both accessed 4/11/18).

4. A partial list of campuses that have protested conservative speakers includes Middlebury College; University of California, Berkeley; University of Florida; DePaul; Harvard; Auburn; Emory; Georgetown; and the University of Washington. For an insightful discussion of the broader debate, see Lee C. Bollinger, "Free Speech on Campus Is Doing Just Fine, Thank You," *The Atlantic*, June 12, 2019, www.theatlantic.com/ideas/archive/2019/06/free-speech-crisis-campus-isnt-real/591394/ (accessed 1/29/20).

5. Michael S. Roth, "Free Speech Wars Miss the Point of College," CNN, September 10, 2019, www.cnn.com/2019/09/10/opinions/free-speech-on-campus-roth/index.html (accessed 1/29/20).

6. Meghan Keneally and Julia Jacobo, "Police: Suspect Shouted 'Heil Hitler' before Shooting Incident after Spencer Event," ABC News, October 20, 2017, http://abcnews.go.com/US/security-ramped-white-nationalist-richard-spencers-florida-event/story?id=50585570 (accessed 10/24/17).

7. Trump, "Remarks by President Trump." President Trump also explained that the federal government would require private institutions that receive federal grants to follow "their own policies on free speech."

8. Yanan Wang, "Obama to Campus Protesters: Don't 'Shut Up' Opposing Viewpoints," *Washington Post*, December 22, 2015, www.washingtonpost.com/news/morning-mix/wp/2015/12/22/obama-to-campus-protesters-dont-shut-up-opposing-viewpoints (accessed 12/30/15).

9. "Speech on Campus," American Civil Liberties Union, www.aclu.org/other/speech-campus (accessed 1/16/20).

10. Bollinger, "Free Speech on Campus."

11. Foundation for Individual Rights in Education (FIRE), Disinvitation Database, www.thefire.org/research/disinvitation-database/#home/?view_2_sort=field_6|desc&view_2_page=7 (accessed 1/29/20).

12. *Arar v. Ashcroft et al.*, WL 346439 (E.D. N.Y. 2006). The case was dismissed because Arar, a Canadian citizen, did not have standing to sue the U.S. government. Supporters of this decision (and the practice more generally) say that it is an essential part of the War on Terror and that the enemy combatants who are arrested have no legal rights. Opponents say that the practice violates international law and our own standards of decency; furthermore, torture almost never produces useful information because people will say anything to get the torture to stop.

13. Max Farrand, ed., *The Records of the Federal Convention of 1787*, rev. ed. (New Haven, CT: Yale University Press, 1937), pp. 587–88, 617–18.

14. The two that were not ratified by the states were a complicated amendment on congressional apportionment and a pay raise amendment.

15. There is an intense scholarly debate on whether the authors of the Fourteenth Amendment intended for it to apply the Bill of Rights to the states. The strongest argument against this position is Raoul Berger, *The Fourteenth Amendment and the Bill of Rights* (Norman: University of Oklahoma Press, 1989), and a good book in support is Akhil Reed Amar, *The Bill of Rights* (New Haven, CT: Yale University Press, 1998).

16. *Slaughterhouse Cases*, 83 U.S. 36 (1873).

17. *Gitlow v. New York*, 268 U.S. 652 (1925).

18. James Hutson, "A Wall of Separation," *Library of Congress Information Bulletin* 57: 6 (June 1998), www.loc.gov/loc/lcib/9806/danbury.html (accessed 3/3/08).

19. *Engel v. Vitale*, 370 U.S. 421 (1962).

20. *Wallace v. Jaffree*, 482 U.S. 38 (1985).

21. *Lee v. Weisman*, 505 U.S. 577 (1992); *Santa Fe Independent School District v. Doe*, 530 U.S. 290 (2000).

22. *Marsh v. Chambers*, 463 U.S. 783 (1983); *Jones v. Clear Creek Independent School*, 61 LW 3819 (1993).

23. *Town of Greece, New York v. Galloway*, 572 U.S. 565 (2014).

24. *Lemon v. Kurtzman*, 403 U.S. 602 (1971).

25. *Lynch v. Donnelly*, 465 U.S. 668 (1984), 672–73.

26. Jeffrey Rosen, "Big Ten," *The New Republic*, March 14, 2004, p. 11.

27. *American Legion v. American Humanist Association*, 588 U.S.——(2019).

28. *Arizona Christian School Tuition Organization v. Winn*, U.S. Supreme Court slip. op. 09-987 and 09-991 (2011).

29. *Mitchell v. Helms*, 530 U.S. 793 (2000).

30. *Zobrest v. Catalina Foothills School District*, 509 U.S. 1 (1993). A similar decision in 1997 allowed a public school teacher to teach in a special program in a parochial school, *Agostini v. Felton*, 521 U.S. 203 (1997).

31. *Espinoza v. Montana Department of Revenue*, 591 U.S.——(2020).

32. We will not cite all of the cases here. See Henry J. Abraham and Barbara A. Perry, *Freedom and the Court: Civil Rights and Liberties in the United States*, 8th ed. (Lawrence: University Press of Kansas, 2003), Chapter 6, for a summary of cases on this topic, especially Tables 6.1 and 6.2.

33. *Employment Division, Department of Human Resources of Oregon v. Smith*, 494 U.S. 872 (1990), 878–80. This case is often erroneously reported as having banned the religious use of peyote. In fact, the Court said: "Although it is constitutionally permissible to exempt sacramental peyote use from the operation of drug laws, it is not constitutionally required."

34. *City of Boerne v. Flores*, 521 U.S. 527 (1997); *Cutter v. Wilkinson*, No. 03-9877 (2005); *Gonzales v. O Centro Espirita Beneficente Uniao do Vegetal (UDV) et al.*, 546 U.S. 418 (2006). The Sherbert test requires that whenever the government limits religious expression it must prove a compelling interest that is narrowly tailored to achieve that interest if a person is substantially burdened by the law (*Sherbert v. Verner*, 374 U.S. 398 [1963]).

35. *Burwell v. Hobby Lobby*, 573 U.S. 682 (2014).

36. In *Little Sisters of the Poor Saints Peter and Paul Home v. Pennsylvania*, 591 U.S. ___ (2020), the Supreme Court upheld an administrative rule that overturned an Obama-era rule that had provided a workaround by having insurance pay directly for contraception for employees of private employers who objected to paying for it on religious grounds. The playground case, *Trinity Lutheran Church of Columbia, Inc. v. Comer*, 582 U.S. ___ (2017), would appear to be an establishment clause case (can the state provide direct funds to a church?), but it was decided on free exercise grounds. This opens the door to a broader range of protections for religious activity. See Garrett Epps, "A Major Church-State Ruling That Shouldn't Have Happened," *The Atlantic*, June 27, 2017, www.theatlantic.com/politics/archive/2017/06/a-major-church-state-case-that-shouldnt-have-happened/531789 (accessed 10/18/17).

37. *Masterpiece Cakeshop v. Colorado Civil Rights Commission*, 584 U.S. ___ (2018).

38. *Police Department of Chicago v. Mosley*, 408 U.S. 92 (1972).

39. *United States v. O'Brien*, 391 U.S. 367 (1968); *Ladue v. Gilleo*, 512 U.S. 43 (1994).

40. *Schenck v. United States*, 249 U.S. 47 (1919), 52.

41. Alan Dershowitz, *Shouting Fire: Civil Liberties in a Turbulent Age* (New York: Little, Brown, 2002).

42. *Brandenburg v. Ohio*, 395 U.S. 444 (1969).

43. *Snyder v. Phelps*, 131 S.Ct. 1207 (2011).

44. *Smith v. Goguen*, 415 U.S. 566 (1974).

45. *Tinker v. Des Moines School District*, 393 U.S. 503 (1969).

46. *Spence v. Washington*, 418 U.S. 405 (1974).

47. *Texas v. Johnson*, 491 U.S. 397 (1989).

48. *United States v. Eichman*, 496 U.S. 310 (1990).

49. David Wright, "Trump: Burn the Flag, Go to Jail," CNN, November 29, 2016, www.cnn.com/2016/11/29/politics/donald-trump-flag-burning-penalty-proposal/index.html (accessed 10/18/17).

50. *Buckley v. Valeo*, 424 U.S. 1 (1976).

51. *Davis v. Federal Election Commission*, 554 U.S. 724 (2008).

52. *Citizens United v. Federal Election Commission*, 558 U.S. 310 (2010).

53. *McCutcheon v. Federal Election Commission*, 572 U.S. (2014).

54. *McConnell v. Federal Election Commission*, 540 U.S. 93 (2003).

55. One example was a speech code adopted at the University of Michigan that prohibited "any behavior, verbal or physical, that stigmatizes or victimizes an individual on the basis of race, ethnicity, religion, sex, sexual orientation, creed, national origin, ancestry, age, marital status, handicap, or Vietnam veteran status" and "creates an intimidating, hostile, or demeaning environment for educational pursuits, employment or participation in University-sponsored extra-curricular activities." Kermit L. Hall, "Free Speech on Public College Campuses: Overview," www.firstamendmentcenter.org/speech/pubcollege/overview.aspx (accessed 2/10/08).

56. Liam Stack, "Yale's Halloween Advice Stokes a Racially Charged Debate," *New York Times*, November 8, 2015, www.nytimes.com/2015/11/09/nyregion/yale-culturally-insensitive-halloween-costumes-free-speech.html?_r=0 (accessed 12/30/15).

57. Michael D. Regan, "Yale Lecturer Resigns over Halloween Costume Email Controversy," *Christian Science Monitor*, December 8, 2015, www.csmonitor.com/USA/Education/2015/1208/Yale-lecturer-resigns-over-Halloween-costume-email-controversy (accessed 12/30/15).

58. One of the authors of this book took Introduction to American Politics in that lecture hall, and the other has taught many classes

59. *City of St. Paul v. RAV*, 505 U.S. 377 (1992).

60. *Virginia v. Black*, 538 U.S. 343 (2003).

61. The Editorial Board, "Hate Speech on Facebook," *New York Times*, May 30, 2013, www.nytimes.com/2013/05/31/opinion/misogynist-speech-on-facebook.html (accessed 1/28/14).

62. Facebook "community standards" on hate speech, www.facebook.com/communitystandards (accessed 1/28/14).

63. Jeff Rosen, "Who Decides? Civility v. Hate Speech on the Internet," *Insights on Law and Society* 13:2 (Winter 2013): 32–36.

64. Mike Isaac, "Why Everyone Is Angry at Facebook over Its Political Ads Policy," *New York Times*, November 22, 2019, www.nytimes.com/2019/11/22/technology/campaigns-pressure-facebook-political-ads.html (accessed 1/29/20).

65. *Packingham v. North Carolina*, 582 U.S. ___ (2017).

66. *De Jonge v. State of Oregon*, 299 U.S. 353 (1937); *Edwards v. South Carolina*, 372 U.S. 229 (1963).

67. The Supreme Court declined to review the case in *Smith v. Collin*, 439 U.S. 916 (1978), which meant that the lower-court rulings stood: 447 F. Supp. 676 (1978), 578 F 2d 1197 (1978). See Donald A. Downs, *Nazis in Skokie: Freedom, Community and the First Amendment* (Notre Dame, IN: University of Notre Dame Press, 1985), for an excellent analysis of this important case.

68. *Frisby et al. v. Schultz et al.*, 487 U.S. 474 (1988).

69. See https://freespeech.ufl.edu/ for a discussion of all the related issues (accessed 3/7/18).

70. *McCullen v. Coakley*, 573 U.S. 464 (2014).

71. *New York Times Co. v. United States*, 403 U.S. 713 (1971).

72. *Chaplinsky v. State of New Hampshire*, 315 U.S. 568 (1942).

73. *Chaplinsky v. State of New Hampshire*, 315 U.S. 568 (1942).

74. *New York Times v. Sullivan*, 376 U.S. 254 (1964), cited in Abraham and Perry, *Freedom and the Court*, p. 193

75. *Hustler v. Falwell*, 485 U.S. 46 (1988).

76. *Virginia State Board of Pharmacy v. Virginia Citizens Consumer Council, Inc.*, 425 U.S. 748 (1976); *City of Cincinnati v. Discovery Network, Inc., et al.*, 507 U.S. 410 (1993).

77. *Central Hudson Gas & Electric Corp. v. Public Service Commission*, 447 U.S. 557 (1980).

78. *Matal v. Tam*, 582 U.S. ___ (2017).

79. In 1996, Congress passed the Child Pornography Prevention Act. This law makes the possession, production, or distribution of child pornography a criminal offense punishable with up to 15 years in jail and a fine. However, two parts of the law were struck down by the Court for being "overbroad and unconstitutional." *Ashcroft v. Free Speech Coalition*, 353 U.S. 234 (2002).

80. *Jacobellis v. Ohio*, 378 U.S. 184, 197 (1964).

81. *Miller v. California*, 413 U.S. 15 (1973).

82. David French, "Of Course the Second Amendment Protects an Individual Right to Keep and Bear Arms," *National Review*, April 13, 2016, www.nationalreview.com/2016/04/second-amendment-protects-individual-right-keep-bear-arms (accessed 3/29/18).

83. Dorothy Samuels, "The Second Amendment Was Never Meant to Protect an Individual's Right to a Gun," *The Nation*, September 23, 2015, www.thenation.com/article/how-the-roberts-court-undermined-sensible-gun-control/; John Paul Stevens, "Repeal

in the room. For a description of the controversy, see Dwight Adams and Holly V. Hays, "IU: Room with Mural of KKK Rally Will No Longer Be a Classroom," *Indianapolis Star*, September 29, 2017, www.indystar.com/story/news/2017/09/29/indiana-university-no-longer-use-room-mural-showing-kkk-rally-classroom/717308001 (accessed 10/18/17).

the Second Amendment," *New York Times*, March 27, 2018, www. nytimes.com/2018/03/27/opinion/john-paul-stevens-repeal-second-amendment.html (accessed 3/29/18).

84. Gun Violence Archive, www.gunviolencearchive.org (accessed 9/23/20).

85. The FBI defines an active shooter as "an individual actively engaged in killing or attempting to kill people in a confined and populated area." For data on active shooters, see Federal Bureau of Investigation, Office of Partner Engagement, "Quick Look: 277 Active Shooter Incidents in the United States from 2000 to 2018," www.fbi.gov/about/partnerships/office-of-partner-engagement/active-shooter-incidents-graphics (accessed 1/30/20).

86. Giffords Law Center, "Gun Law Trend Watch, 2017 Year-End Review," http://lawcenter.giffords.org/wp-content/uploads/2017/12/Trendwatch-2017-Year-End-12.19.17-pages.pdf; Giffords Law Center, "Concealed Carry," http://lawcenter.giffords.org/gun-laws/policy-areas/guns-in-public/concealed-carry (both accessed 4/9/18).

87. *District of Columbia v. Heller,* 554 U.S. 290 (2008).

88. *McDonald v. Chicago,* 561 U.S. 742 (2010)

89. The second-place country to the United States is actually the Falkland Islands (at 62.1), but there are only 3,000 people in that nation. All data are from the Switzerland-based Small Arms Survey; see especially Aaron Karp, "Estimating Global Civilian-Held Firearms Numbers," June 2018, www.smallarmssurvey.org/fileadmin/docs/T-Briefing-Papers/SAS-BP-Civilian-Firearms-Numbers.pdf; for a complete list of nations, see www.smallarmssurvey.org/fileadmin/docs/Weapons_and_Markets/Tools/Firearms_holdings/SAS-BP-Civilian-held-firearms-annexe.pdf (both accessed 1/31/20).

90. Juliet Eilperin and David Nakamura, "An Emotional Obama Flexes His Executive Muscle on Gun Control," *Washington Post*, January 5, 2016, www.washingtonpost.com/politics/obama-moves-on-guns-with-executive-actions-that-circumvent-congress/2016/01/05/97f23336-b3bc-11e5-a76a-0b5145e8679a_story.html?hpid=hp_hp-top-table-main_obamaguns-1215pm%3Ahomepage%2Fstory (accessed 1/5/16).

91. See Abraham and Perry, *Freedom and the Court*, Chapter 4, for a discussion of these cases.

92. *Florence v. Board of Chosen Freeholders,* 566 U.S. 318 (2012).

93. *Maryland v. King,* 133 S.Ct. 1958 (2013).

94. *Riley v. California,* 573 U.S. 373 (2014)

95. *United States v. Jones,* 565 U.S. 400 (2012).

96. *Carpenter v. United States,* 585 U.S. ____ (2018).

97. *Mapp v. Ohio,* 367 U.S. 643 (1961).

98. *Herring v. United States,* 555 U.S. 135 (2009).

99. *Vernonia School District v. Acton,* 515 U.S. 646 (1995); *Board of Education of Pottawatomie County v. Earls,* 536 U.S. 822 (2002).

100. *Chandler v. Miller,* 520 U.S. 305 (1997).

101. National Public Radio, "Political Comebacks: The Art of the Putdown," *Morning Edition*, May 12, 2008, www.npr.org/templates/story/story.php?storyId=90337494 (accessed 5/7/20).

102. Leslie Cauley, "NSA Has Massive Database of Americans' Phone Calls," *USA Today*, May 11, 2006, p. 1.

103. Andrew Crocker and David Ruiz, "How Congress's Extension of Section 702 May Expand the NSA's Warrantless Surveillance Authority," Electronic Frontier Foundation, February 1, 2018, www.eff.org/deeplinks/2018/02/how-congresss-extension-section-702-may-expand-nsas-warrantless-surveillance (accessed 6/14/18).

104. Lorraine Woellert and Dawn Kopecki, "The Snooping Goes beyond Phone Calls," *Business Week*, May 29, 2006, p. 38; "Data Mining: Federal Efforts Cover a Wide Range of Uses," GAO Report 04-548, May 2004, www.gao.gov/assets/250/242241.pdf (accessed 5/13/14).

105. *Miranda v. Arizona,* 384 U.S. 436 (1966).

106. *Dickerson v. United States,* 530 U.S. 428 (2000).

107. *Benton v. Maryland,* 395 U.S. 784 (1969).

108. This "separate sovereigns" exception was established in *Abbate v. United States,* 359 U.S. 187 (1959) and recently confirmed in *Gamble v. United States,* 587 U.S. ____ (2019).

109. *Kelo v. City of New London,* 505 U.S. 469 (2005).

110. National Conference of State Legislatures, "Eminent Domain Overview," www.ncsl.org/research/environment-and-natural-resources/eminent-doman-overview.aspx (accessed 1/31/14).

111. The 2017 case, *Murr v. Wisconsin,* 582 U.S. ____ (2017), involved a property owner who tried to sell a lot that was contiguous to another lot that he owned; he did not have to be compensated for the value of that lot when it was rendered worthless by a state regulation. The recent cases that ruled in favor of property owners were *Arkansas Game and Fish Commission v. United States,* 568 U.S. 23 (2012); *Koontz v. St. Johns River Water Management District,* 568 U.S. 936 (2013); and *Horne v. United States Department of Agriculture,* 569 U.S. 513 (2013).

112. *Knick v. Township of Scott, Pennsylvania,* 588 U.S. ____ (2019). The overruled precedent was *Williamson County Regional Planning Commission v. Hamilton Bank of Johnson City,* 473 U.S. 172 (1985).

113. *Powell v. Alabama,* 287 U.S. 45 (1932).

114. *Gideon v. Wainwright,* 372 U.S. 335 (1963).

115. *Evitts v. Lucy,* 469 U.S. 387 (1985); *Wiggins v. Smith,* 539 U.S. 510 (2003). See Elizabeth Gable and Tyler Green, "*Wiggins v. Smith*: The Ineffective Assistance of Counsel Standard Applied Twenty Years after *Strickland*," *Georgetown Journal of Legal Ethics* (Summer 2004): 755–71, for a discussion of many of these issues.

116. *Klopfer v. North Carolina,* 386 U.S. 213 (1967).

117. The law is 18 U.S.C. § 3161(c)(1), and the ruling is *Zedner v. United States,* 47 U.S. 489 (2006).

118. The case concerning African Americans is *Batson v. Kentucky,* 106 S.Ct. 1712 (1986); the case about Latinos is *Hernandez v. New York,* 500 U.S. 352 (1991); and the gender case is *J.E.B. v. Alabama ex rel. T.B.,* 511 U.S. 127 (1994). Three more-recent cases affirming that peremptory challenges cannot be used in a racially discriminatory fashion are *Miller-El v. Dretke,* 545 U.S. 231 (2005); *Snyder v. Louisiana,* 552 U.S. 472 (2008); and *Flowers v. Mississippi,* 588 U.S. ____ (2019).

119. Death Penalty Information Center, "Number of Executions since 1976," www.deathpenaltyinfo.org/executions-year (accessed 3/25/20); *Hall v. Florida,* 572 U.S. 701 (2014).

120. Erik Eckholm, "One Execution Botched, Oklahoma Delays the Next," *New York Times*, April 29, 2014, www.nytimes.com/2014/04/30/us/oklahoma-executions.html (accessed 5/13/14).

121. *Furman v. Georgia,* 408 U.S. 238 (1972); *Gregg v. Georgia,* 428 U.S. 513 (1976).

122. See Abraham and Perry, *Freedom and the Court*, pp. 72–73, for a discussion of the earlier cases, and Charles Lane, "5–4 Supreme Court Abolishes Juvenile Executions," *Washington Post*, March 2, 2005, p. A1, for a discussion of the 2002 and 2005 cases. The 2008 case was *Kennedy v. Louisiana,* 554 U.S. 407 (2008).

123. *Griswold v. Connecticut,* 381 U.S. 479 (1965), 482–86.

124. *Griswold v. Connecticut,* 381 U.S. 479 (1965), 512–13.

125. *Roe v. Wade,* 410 U.S. 113 (1973), 129.

126. *Planned Parenthood of Southeastern Pennsylvania v. Casey*, 505 U.S. 833 (1992).

127. Katharine Q. Seelye, "Mississippi Voters Reject Anti-abortion Measure," *New York Times*, November 8, 2011, www.nytimes.com/2011/11/09/us/politics/votes-across-the-nation-could-serve-as-a-political-barometer.html (accessed 12/5/11).

128. Erik Eckholm, "Access to Abortion Falling as States Pass Restrictions," *New York Times*, January 3, 2014, www.nytimes.com/2014/01/04/us/women-losing-access-to-abortion-as-opponents-gain-ground-in-state-legislatures.html (accessed 1/31/14).

129. *Whole Woman's Health v. Hellerstedt*, 579 U.S. ____ (2016).

130. *Lawrence v. Texas*, 539 U.S. 558 (2003).

Take a Stand

a. *Florida v. Jardines*, 569 U.S. 1 (2013), 6–7.

b. Oral arguments in *U.S. v. Jones* (2012), November 8, 2011, www.supremecourt.gov/oral_arguments/argument_transcripts/2011/10-1259.pdf, p. 44 (accessed 4/9/18).

Chapter 5

1. Joseph Goldstein, "Judge Rejects New York's Stop-and-Frisk Policy, *New York Times*, August 12, 2013, www.nytimes.com/2013/08/13/nyregion/stop-and-frisk-practice-violated-rights-judge-rules.html (accessed 11/7/17).

2. Rocco Parascandola and Thomas Tracy, "NYPD Stop-and-Frisk Numbers Jumped by 22% in 2019 from Prior Year: Report," *New York Daily News*, February 10, 2020, www.nydailynews.com/new-york/nyc-crime/ny-stop-question-and-frisk-numbers-jump-20200210-vamjtzdfcvdorot57ajtrhnghu-story.html (accessed 3/4/20).

3. *Face the Nation*, CBS News, June 19, 2016, transcript, www.cbsnews.com/news/face-the-nation-transcripts-june-19-2016-trump-lynch-lapierre-feinstein/ (accessed 11/7/17).

4. *Meet the Press*, NBC News, May 9, 2010, transcript, www.nbcnews.com/id/37024384/ns/meet_the_press/t/meet-press-transcript-may/#.WgIRPXZryiM (accessed 11/7/17).

5. Howard Dodson, "How Slavery Helped Build a World Economy," February 3, 2003, in Schomburg Center for Research in Black Culture of the New York City Public Library, *Jubilee: The Emergence of African-American Culture* (Washington, DC: National Geographic Press, 2003).

6. Other provisions of the Compromise of 1850, which was a package of five bills, included creating the current boundaries for Texas as it dropped its claim to land in parts of five current states in exchange for the federal government's assumption of $10 million in debt from the old Texas Republic. Also, the trading of enslaved people, but not slavery itself, was abolished in the District of Columbia. See "The Compromise of 1850," Primary Documents in American History, Library of Congress, www.loc.gov/rr/program/bib/ourdocs/Compromise1850.html (accessed 10/26/17).

7. John W. Wright, ed., *New York Times 2000 Almanac* (New York: Penguin Reference, 1999), p. 165. Estimates from various online sources are quite a bit higher, averaging about 620,000 deaths.

8. Chandler Davidson, "The Voting Rights Act: A Brief History," in *Controversies in Minority Voting: The Voting Rights Act in Perspective*, ed. Bernard Grofman and Chandler Davidson (Washington, DC: Brookings Institution, 1992), p. 21.

9. Equal Justice Initiative, *Lynching in America: Confronting the Legacy of Racial Terror*, 3rd ed. (2017), https://lynchinginamerica.eji.org/report/ (accessed 3/6/20).

10. "Indian Removal: 1814–1848," Public Broadcasting System, www.pbs.org/wgbh/aia/part4/4p2959.html (accessed 1/26/12).

11. Donald L. Fixico, "When Native Americans Were Slaughtered in the Name of 'Civilization,'" August 16, 2019, www.history.com/news/native-americans-genocide-united-states (accessed 3/12/20).

12. Bruce E. Johansen, *The Native Peoples of North America* (New Brunswick, NJ: Rutgers University Press, 2006); Russell Thornton, *American Indian Holocaust and Survival: A Population History since 1492* (Norman: University of Oklahoma Press, 1990), pp. 26–32; Henry F. Dobyns, *Their Number Become Thinned: Native American Population Dynamics in Eastern North America* (Knoxville: University of Tennessee Press, 1983).

13. *Cherokee Nation v. Georgia*, 30 U.S. 1 (1831).

14. Andrea Smith, "Soul Wound: The Legacy of Native American Schools," *Amnesty International Magazine*, posted on News around Indian Country, Lara Trace Hentz, October 9, 2015, https://laratracehentz.wordpress.com/2015/10/09/soul-wound-the-legacy-of-native-american-schools/ (accessed 3/12/20).

15. *United States v. Wong Kim Ark*, 169 U.S. 649 (1898).

16. Bilal Qureshi, "From Wrong to Right: A U.S. Apology for Japanese Internment," National Public Radio, August 9, 2013, www.npr.org/sections/codeswitch/2013/08/09/210138278/japanese-internment-redress (accessed 1/29/16).

17. *Trump v. Hawaii*, 585 U.S. ____ (2018).

18. This Day in History, "Abigail Adams Urges Husband to 'Remember the Ladies,'" Abigail Adams to John Adams, March 31, 1776, www.history.com/this-day-in-history/abigail-adams-urges-husband-to-remember-the-ladies (accessed 4/13/18).

19. Lucian K. Truscott IV, "The Real Mob at Stonewall," *New York Times*, June 25, 2009, p. A19.

20. "LGBT" (various surveys), www.pollingreport.com/lgbt.htm; Justin McCarthy, "Gallup First Polled on Gay Issues in '77. What Has Changed?," June 6, 2019, https://news.gallup.com/poll/258065/gallup-first-polled-gay-issues-changed.aspx; Justin McCarthy, "U.S. Support for Gay Marriage Stable, at 63%," May 22, 2019, https://news.gallup.com/poll/257705/support-gay-marriage-stable.aspx (all accessed 3/13/20).

21. *Obergefell v. Hodges*, 576 U.S. ____ (2015).

22. Sean Cahill, "Trump Administration Amasses Striking Anti-LGBT Record in First Year," *The Hill*, January 19, 2018, http://thehill.com/opinion/campaign/369790-trump-administration-amasses-striking-anti-lgbt-record-in-first-year (accessed 4/13/18).

23. Davidson, "The Voting Rights Act," p. 22. See U.S. Department of Justice, Civil Rights Division, "About Section 5 of the Voting Rights Act," www.justice.gov/crt/about-section-5-voting-rights-act (accessed 4/13/18), for a complete list of cases in which the Justice Department has denied "preclearance" of a change in an electoral practice under Section 5 of the Voting Rights Act. Note that in racially homogeneous single-member districts, minority candidates usually win. But in at-large elections, in which representatives are elected citywide or countywide (and which thus may contain a mix of minority and White voters from the districts making up the city or county), the majority-White voters can outvote the minority voters and elect an all-White city council or school board.

24. "Voting Laws Roundup 2020," Brennan Center for Justice, February 4, 2020, www.brennancenter.org/our-work/research-reports/voting-laws-roundup-2020 (accessed 3/21/20).

25. *Husted v. A. Philip Randolph Institute*, 584 U.S. ___ (2018).

26. Office of the Assistant Secretary for Planning and Evaluation, "HHS Poverty Guidelines for 2020," U.S. Department of Health and Human Services, January 8, 2020, https://aspe.hhs.gov/poverty-guidelines (accessed 10/2/20).

27. Jessica Semega, Melissa Kollar, Emily A. Shrider, and John F. Creamer, "Income and Poverty in the United States: 2019," U.S. Census Bureau, September 15, 2020, Figure 1, www.census.gov/library/publications/2020/demo/p60-270.html (accessed 9/23/20).

28. Federal Reserve Board, "Survey of Consumer Finances (SCF), 2019," September 28, 2020, www.federalreserve.gov/econres/scf/dataviz/scf/chart/ (accessed 10/21/20).

29. Life expectancy information is from Elizabeth Arias, Jiaquan Xu, and Kenneth D. Kochanek, "United States Life Tables, 2016," *National Vital Statistics Reports*, Centers for Disease Control and Prevention, May 7, 2019, Table A, p. 3, www.cdc.gov/nchs/data/nvsr/nvsr68/nvsr68_04-508.pdf. Infant mortality numbers are from "Infant Mortality," Centers for Disease Control and Prevention, www.cdc.gov/reproductivehealth/maternalinfanthealth/infantmortality.htm. Maternal mortality rates are from "Pregnancy Mortality Surveillance System," November 9, 2017, Centers for Disease Control and Prevention, www.cdc.gov/reproductivehealth/maternalinfanthealth/pmss.html (all accessed 3/31/20).

30. See the National Resources Defense Council's program on environmental justice, www.nrdc.org/about/environmental-justice, and the Environmental Justice and Health Alliance for Chemical Policy reform's report "Who's in Danger? Race, Poverty, and Chemical Disasters," May 2014, www.comingcleaninc.org/assets/media/images/Reports/Who's%20in%20Danger%20Report%20and%20Table%20FINAL.pdf (both accessed 4/13/18).

31. Steve Carmody, "5 Years after Flint's Crisis Began, Is The Water Safe?," National Public Radio, April 25, 2019 www.npr.org/2019/04/25/717104335/5-years-after-flints-crisis-began-is-the-water-safe (accessed 3/22/20).

32. Ariane de Vogue and Devan Cole, "Supreme Court Won't Block Lawsuit Brought by Flint Water Crisis Victims," CNN, January 21, 2020, www.cnn.com/2020/01/21/politics/supreme-court-flint-michigan-lawsuit-water-crisis/index.html (accessed 3/22/20).

33. "Fatal Force," *Washington Post*, March 16, 2020, www.washingtonpost.com/graphics/2019/national/police-shootings-2019/ (accessed 3/22/20).

34. "Herstory," Black Lives Matter, https://blacklivesmatter.com/about/herstory/ (accessed 4/17/18).

35. Holly Yan, Khushbu Shah, and Emanuella Grinberg, "Ex-officer Michael Slager Pleads Guilty in Shooting Death of Walter Scott," CNN, May 2, 2017, www.cnn.com/2017/05/02/us/michael-slager-federal-plea/ (accessed 2/23/18).

36. Janell Ross, "Police Officers Convicted for Fatal Shootings Are the Exception, Not the Rule," NBC News, March 13, 2019, www.nbcnews.com/news/nbcblk/police-officers-convicted-fatal-shootings-are-exception-not-rule-n982741 (accessed 3/22/20).

37. Lynne Peeples, "What the Data Say about Police Shootings: How Do Racial Biases Play into Deadly Encounters with the Police?," *Scientific American*, September 5, 2019, www.scientificamerican.com/article/what-the-data-say-about-police-shootings/ (accessed 3/22/20).

38. Hundreds of studies have examined these patterns, and, not surprisingly, there are divergent findings. However, most have found differences in sentencing based on race. A 2015 Bureau of Justice Statistics study found that "black men received roughly 5% to 10% longer prison sentences than white men for similar crimes, after accounting for the facts surrounding the case." See "Federal Sentencing Disparity: 2005–2012," Bureau of Justice Statistics, October 2015, www.bjs.gov/content/pub/pdf/fsd0512_sum.pdf. Government statistics on crime may be found on the FBI site at www.fbi.gov. (Both sources accessed 11/2/17.)

39. "2018 Hate Crime Statistics," U.S. Department of Justice, https://ucr.fbi.gov/hate-crime/2018/topic-pages/tables/table-1.xls (accessed 3/22/20).

40. Clayborne Carson et al., eds., *The Eyes on the Prize Civil Rights Reader* (New York: Penguin Books, 1997).

41. Matt Broomfield, "Women's March against Donald Trump Is the Largest Day of Protests in US History, Say Political Scientists," *Independent*, January 23, 2017, www.independent.co.uk/news/world/americas/womens-march-anti-donald-trump-womens-rights-largest-protest-demonstration-us-history-political-a7541081.html (accessed 10/26/17). Jeremy Pressman of the University of Connecticut and Erica Chenoweth of the University of Denver collected data on the Women's March, https://docs.google.com/spreadsheets/d/1xa0iLqYKz8x9Yc_rfhtmSOJQ2EGgeUVjvV4A8LsIaxY/edit#gid=0 (accessed 10/26/17). The low end of their estimate is 3,267,134, the high end is 5,246,670, and their "best guess" is 4,157,894.

42. See https://blacklivesmatter.com/ for more information about the movement, including the "Black Lives Matter 4-Year Anniversary Report" and news about recent events (accessed 10/26/17).

43. By the end of the 2019 regular season, only three teams featured at least one player regularly sitting or kneeling on the sidelines for the anthem. See Mark Maske, "NFL Owners Approve New National Anthem Policy with Hope of Ending Protests, *Washington Post*, May 23, 2018, www.washingtonpost.com/news/sports/wp/2018/05/23/nfl-owners-leaning-towards-requiring-players-to-stand-for-national-anthem-or-remain-in-locker-room/?utm_term=.71eed9fa2d60; and Associated Press, "NFL Stops Anthem Policy after Dolphins Criticized for Considering Suspensions for Players Who Protest," NBC News, July 19, 2018, www.nbcnews.com/news/sports/nfl-halts-anthem-policy-after-dolphins-criticized-considering-suspensions-players-n893021 (both accessed 3/22/20).

44. *Shelley v. Kraemer*, 334 U.S. 1 (1948).

45. *Brown v. Board of Education*, 347 U.S. 483 (1954).

46. *Brown v. Board of Education II*, 349 U.S. 294 (1955).

47. Paul Brest and Sanford Levinson, *Process of Constitutional Decision Making: Cases and Material* (Boston: Little, Brown, 1982), pp. 471–80.

48. *Swann v. Charlotte-Mecklenburg Board of Education*, 402 U.S. 1 (1971).

49. *Milliken v. Bradley*, 418 U.S. 717 (1974).

50. *Parents Involved in Community Schools Inc. v. Seattle School District*, 05-98 (2007); *Meredith v. Jefferson County (Ky.) Board of Education*, 551 U.S. 701 (2007).

51. *Griggs v. Duke Power*, 401 U.S. 424 (1971).

52. *Easley v. Cromartie*, 532 U.S. 234 (2001), rehearing denied, 532 U.S. 1076 (2001).

53. *Easley v. Cromartie*, 532 U.S. 1076 (2001).

54. *Bethune-Hill v. Virginia State Board of Elections*, 580 U.S. ___ (2017); *Cooper v. Harris*, 581 U.S. ___ (2017). In *Alabama Legislative Black Caucus v. Alabama* 575 U.S. ___ (2015), the Court also struck down state legislative districts in Alabama as unconstitutional "packing." In January 2017, a three-judge panel also struck down the state's next attempt to draw the districts, and finally, in October 2017, the third attempt was upheld.

55. Richard L. Hasen, "The Gerrymandering Decision Drags the Supreme Court Further into the Mud: Ignoring the Racial Redistricting Problem Won't Make It Go Away," *New York Times*, June 27, 2019, www.nytimes.com/2019/06/27/opinion/gerrymandering-rucho-supreme-court.html (accessed 3/22/20). The case is *Rucho v. Common Cause*, 588 U.S. ____ (2019).

56. *Shelby County v. Holder*, 570 U.S. 529 (2013).

57. *Reed v. Reed*, 404 U.S. 71 (1971). As a young women's rights attorney, Ruth Bader Ginsburg wrote the plaintiff's brief in this case. She argued more than three hundred gender discrimination cases, including six before the Supreme Court, before becoming a federal judge.

58. *Frontiero v. Richardson*, 411 U.S. 677 (1973).

59. *Craig v. Boren*, 429 U.S. 190 (1976).

60. *United States v. Virginia*, 518 U.S. 515 (1996).

61. *Johnson v. Transportation Agency of Santa Clara*, 480 U.S. 616 (1987).

62. *Harris v. Forklift Systems*, 510 U.S. 17 (1993).

63. Jan Ransom, "Harvey Weinstein's Stunning Downfall: 23 Years in Prison," *New York Times*, March 11, 2020, www.nytimes.com/2020/03/11/nyregion/harvey-weinstein-sentencing.html (accessed 3/22/20).

64. Stephanie Zacharek, Eliana Dockterman, and Haley Sweetland Edwards, "Person of the Year 2017: The Silence Breakers," *Time*, http://time.com/time-person-of-the-year-2017-silence-breakers (accessed 4/18/18).

65. *Ledbetter v. Goodyear Tire & Rubber Co.*, 550 U.S. 618 (2007).

66. Julie Hirschfeld Davis, "Obama Moves to Expand Rules Aimed at Closing Gender Pay Gap," *New York Times*, January 29, 2016, www.nytimes.com/2016/01/29/us/politics/obama-moves-to-expand-rules-aimed-at-closing-gender-pay-gap.html (accessed 1/30/16).

67. "Presidential Executive Order on the Revocation of Federal Contracting Executive Orders," The White House, March 27, 2017, www.whitehouse.gov/presidential-actions/presidential-executive-order-revocation-federal-contracting-executive-orders/ (accessed 3/22/20).

68. *Bowers v. Hardwick*, 478 U.S. 186 (1986), rehearing denied, 478 U.S. 1039 (1986).

69. *Romer v. Evans*, 517 U.S. 620 (1996).

70. *Lawrence v. Texas*, 539 U.S. 558 (2003). Because the basis for the decision was the due process clause of the Fourteenth Amendment and not the equal protection clause, this ruling upheld a civil liberty rather than a civil right. As such, it applied to all laws regarding sodomy, not just those that applied to gays. However, the decision has been widely regarded as a landmark civil rights case because it provided equal rights for gays.

71. The three cases are *Hollingsworth v. Perry*, 570 U.S. 693 (2013), *United States v. Windsor*, 570 U.S. 744 (2013), and *Obergefell v. Hodges*, 576 U.S. ____ (2015).

72. *Bostock v. Clayton County*, 590 U.S. ____ (2020).

73. *Altitude Express Inc. v. Zarda*, 590 U.S. ____ (2020); *R.G. & G.R. Harris Funeral Homes Inc. v. Equal Employment Opportunity Commission*, 590 U.S. ____ (2020).

74. Drew S. Days III, "Section 5 Enforcement and the Justice Department," in *Controversies in Minority Voting: The Voting Rights Act in Perspective*, ed. Bernard Grofman and Chandler Davidson (Washington, DC: Brookings Institution Press, 1992), p. 52; Frank R. Parker, *Black Votes Count* (Chapel Hill: University of North Carolina Press, 1990), p. 1.

75. "Fair Housing: It's Your Right," U.S. Department of Housing and Urban Development, www.hud.gov/program_offices/fair_housing_equal_opp/online-complaint (accessed 4/18/18).

76. Alexandra DeSanctis, "Would the Equal Rights Amendment Enshrine Abortion Rights in the Constitution?," *National Review*, February 17, 2020, www.nationalreview.com/2020/02/would-the-equal-rights-amendment-enshrine-abortion-rights-in-the-constitution/ (accessed 3/22/20).

77. *United States v. Morrison*, 529 U.S. 598 (2000).

78. *Board of Trustees of the University of Alabama v. Garrett*, 531 U.S. 356 (2001). Also, in *State of Tennessee v. George Lane and Beverly Jones*, 541 U.S. 509 (2004), the Court ruled that disabled people must have access to courthouses.

79. The White House, "Remarks by the President at Reception Commemorating the Enactment of the Matthew Shepard and James Byrd Jr. Hate Crimes Prevention Act," October 28, 2009, https://obamawhitehouse.archives.gov/the-press-office/remarks-president-reception-commemorating-enactment-matthew-shepard-and-james-byrd- (accessed 4/18/18).

80. Tim Mak, "Post-'Don't Ask,' Gay Navy Lt. Marries," Politico, September 20, 2011, www.politico.com/news/stories/0911/63909.html (accessed 1/12/12).

81. Justin Jouvenal, "Federal Judge in D.C. Blocks Part of Trump's Transgender Military Ban," *Washington Post*, October 30, 2017, www.washingtonpost.com/local/public-safety/federal-judge-in-dc-blocks-part-of-trumps-transgender-military-ban/2017/10/30/41d41526-bd94-11e7-959c-fe2b598d8c00_story.html?utm_term=.fe88c4776b62 (accessed 11/6/17).

82. Rebecca Kheel, "Navy Officer Sues Pentagon over Transgender Military Ban," *The Hill*, March 18, 2020, https://thehill.com/policy/defense/488240-navy-officer-sues-pentagon-over-transgender-military-ban (accessed 3/22/20).

83. The first poll is from the Pew Research Center, October 4, 2017, www.people-press.org/2017/10/05/4-race-immigration-and-discrimination/4_7-6/, and the second from Gallup, July 8, 2016, news.gallup.com/poll/193508/oppose-colleges-considering-race-admissions.aspx (both accessed 4/18/18).

84. A training program case was *United Steel Workers of America v. Weber*, 443 U.S. 193 (1979); a labor union case was *Sheet Metal Workers v. EEOC*, 478 U.S. 421 (1986); and a case involving Alabama state police was *U.S. v. Paradise*, 480 U.S. 149 (1987).

85. *Ricci v. DeStefano*, 557 U.S. 557 (2009).

86. *Regents of the University of California v. Bakke*, 438 U.S. 265 (1978).

87. *Grutter v. Bollinger*, 539 U.S. 306 (2003), was the law school case, and *Gratz v. Bollinger*, 539 U.S. 244 (2003), was the undergraduate admissions case.

88. In *Bakke*, Justice Lewis Powell was the only member of the Court who held this position, even though it became the basis for all affirmative action programs over the next 25 years. Four justices in the *Bakke* decision wanted to get rid of race as a factor in admissions, and another four thought that the "strict scrutiny" standard should not even be applied in this instance.

89. *Schuette v. Coalition to Defend Affirmative Action*, 572 U.S. 291 (2014).

90. *Fisher v. University of Texas, Austin*, 579 U.S. ____ (2016).

91. Adam Harris, "In Trump Era, the Use of Race in Admissions Comes under New Scrutiny," *Chronicle of Higher Education*, August 2, 2017, www.chronicle.com/article/In-Trump-Era-the-Use-of-Race/240821?cid=rclink (accessed 11/6/17).

92. *Trump v. Hawaii*, 535 U.S. ____ (2018).

93. *Arizona v. United States*, 567 U.S. 387 (2012).

94. Fernanda Santos, "Arizona Immigration Law Survives Ruling," *New York Times*, September 6, 2012, www.nytimes.com/2012/09/07/us/key-element-of-arizona-immigration-law-survives-ruling.html?_r=0 (accessed 10/5/12).

95. Andrew Daniller, "Americans' Immigration Policy Priorities: Divisions between—and within—the Two Parties," Pew Research Center, November 12, 2019, www.pewresearch.org/fact-tank/2019/11/12/americans-immigration-policy-priorities-divisions-between-and-within-the-two-parties/ (accessed 3/22/20).

96. Emily Kassie, "Detained: How the US Built the World's Largest Immigrant Detention System," *Guardian*, September 24, 2019, www.theguardian.com/us-news/2019/sep/24/detained-us-largest-immigrant-detention-trump (accessed 3/22/20).

97. "An Act Providing for the Collection of Data Relative to Traffic Stops," Massachusetts state law, Chapter 228 of the Acts of 2000, www.mass.gov/legis/laws/seslaw00/sl000228.htm (accessed 7/22/08).

Take a Stand

a. *Fisher v. University of Texas, Austin*, 579 U.S. ____ (2016).

b. *Schuette v. Coalition to Defend Affirmative Action*, 572 U.S. 291 (2014).

Chapter 6

1. Shirley Chisholm, "Vote Chisholm 1972: Unbought and Unbossed," January 25, 1972, 4President.org, www.4president.org/speeches/shirleychisholm1972announcement.htm (accessed 10/27/20).

2. Quoted in Mark Dawidziak, "Jon Stewart Blurs the Lines between Jester and Journalist," *Cleveland Plain Dealer*, March 28, 2019.

3. V. O. Key, *The Responsible Electorate* (Cambridge, MA: Harvard University Press, 1966).

4. Josh Clinton and Carrie Roush, "Poll: Persistent Partisan Divide over 'Birther' Question," NBC News, August 10, 2016, www.nbcnews.com/politics/2016-election/poll-persistent-partisan-divide-over-birther-question-n627446 (accessed 1/28/20).

5. Berinsky, Adam. "Telling the Truth about Believing the Lies? Evidence for the Limited Prevalence of Expressive Survey Responding," *Journal of Politics* 80:1 (2018): 211-24.

6. Joanna Piacenza, "Can You Locate Iran? Few Voters Can," Morning Consult, January 8, 2020, https://morningconsult.com/2020/01/08/can-you-locate-iran-few-voters-can/ (accessed 1/28/20).

7. For a review, see Arthur Lupia and Mathew D. McCubbins, *The Democratic Dilemma* (New York: Cambridge University Press, 1998).

8. Robert S. Erikson, Michael B. MacKuen, and James A. Stimson, *The Macro Polity* (New York: Cambridge University Press, 2002).

9. John Zaller, "Coming to Grips with V. O. Key's Concept of Latent Opinion" (unpublished paper, University of California, Los Angeles, 1998).

10. Morris Fiorina, *Retrospective Voting in American National Elections* (Cambridge, MA: Harvard University Press, 1981).

11. Virginia Sapiro, "Not Your Parents' Political Socialization: Introduction for a New Generation," *Annual Review of Political Science* 7 (2004): 1-23.

12. Robert Putnam, *Bowling Alone: The Collapse and Revival of American Community* (New York: Simon and Schuster, 2000).

13. Richard G. Niemi and Mary Hepburn, "The Rebirth of Political Socialization," *Perspectives on Politics* 24 (1995): 7-16.

14. David Campbell, *Why We Vote: How Schools and Communities Shape Our Civic Life* (Princeton, NJ: Princeton University Press, 2006).

15. Sidney Verba, Kay Schlozman, and Henry Brady, *Voice and Equality: Civic Volunteerism in American Politics* (Cambridge, MA: Harvard University Press, 1995).

16. Paul Allen Beck and M. Kent Jennings, "Pathways to Participation," *American Political Science Review* 76 (1982): 94-108.

17. Pew Research Center, "In Gay Marriage Debate, Both Supporters and Opponents See Legal Recognition as 'Inevitable,'" June 6, 2013, www.people-press.org/2013/06/06/in-gay-marriage-debate-both-supporters-and-opponents-see-legal-recognition-as-inevitable (accessed 10/30/15).

18. Richard Nadwau et al., "Class, Party and South-Nonsouth Differences," *American Politics Research* 32 (2004): 52-67.

19. Donald P. Green, Bradley Palmquist, and Eric Schickler, *Partisan Hearts and Minds* (New Haven, CT: Yale University Press, 2002).

20. Pew Research Center, "Young Voters Supported Obama Less, but May Have Mattered More," November 26, 2012, www.people-press.org/2012/11/26/young-voters-supported-obama-less-but-may-have-mattered-more (accessed 3/17/14).

21. Lupia and McCubbins, *The Democratic Dilemma*.

22. Lawrence R. Jacobs and Robert Y. Shapiro, *Politicians Don't Pander: Political Manipulation and the Loss of Democratic Responsiveness* (Chicago: University of Chicago Press, 2000).

23. John Zaller, *The Nature and Origins of Mass Opinion* (New York: Cambridge University Press, 1992).

24. R. Michael Alvarez and John Brehm, *Hard Choices, Easy Answers* (Princeton, NJ: Princeton University Press, 2002).

25. John Zaller and Stanley Feldman, "A Theory of the Survey Response: Revealing Preferences versus Answering Questions," *American Journal of Political Science* 36 (1992): 579-616.

26. Janet M. Box-Steffensmeier and Susan DeBoef, "Macropartisanship and Macroideology in the Sophisticated Electorate," *Journal of Politics* 63:1 (2001): 232-48.

27. Shanto Iyengar, Gaurav Sood, and Yphtach Lelkes, "Affect, Not Ideology: A Social Identity Perspective on Polarization," *Public Opinion Quarterly* 76:3 (2012): 405-31.

28. R. Michael Alvarez and John Brehm, "American Ambivalence towards Abortion Policy: Development of a Heteroskedastic Probit Model of Competing Values," *American Journal of Political Science* 39:4 (1995): 1055-82.

29. Christopher Wlezien and Robert S. Erikson, "The Horse Race: What Polls Reveal as the Election Campaign Unfolds," *International Journal of Public Opinion Research* 19:1 (2007): 74-88.

30. Anton J. Nederhof, "Methods of Coping with Social Desirability Bias: A Review," *European Journal of Social Psychology* 15:3 (2006): 263-80.

31. Sarah Kliff, "Obamacare Is 5 Years Old, and Americans Are Still Worried about Death Panels," Vox, May 23, 2015, www.vox.com/2015/3/23/8273007/obamacare-poll-death-panels (accessed 11/2/15).

32. Michael X. Delli Carpini and Scott Keeter, *What Americans Know about Politics and Why It Matters* (New Haven, CT: Yale University Press, 1997).

33. Delli Carpini and Keeter, *What Americans Know about Politics*.

34. Lilliana Mason, "'I Disrespectfully Agree': The Differential Effects of Partisan Sorting on Social and Issue Polarization, *American Journal of Political Science* 59:1 (2015): 128–45.

35. Shanto Iyengar and Sean J. Westwood, "Fear and Loathing across Party Lines: New Evidence on Group Polarization," *American Journal of Political Science* 59:3 (2015): 690–707.

36. For a review of the literature on trust in government, see Karen Cook, Russell Hardin, and Margaret Levi, *Cooperation without Trust* (New York: Russell Sage Foundation, 2005); and Marc J. Hetherington, *Why Trust Matters: Declining Political Trust and the Demise of American Liberalism* (Princeton, NJ: Princeton University Press, 2004).

37. William T. Bianco, *Trust: Representatives and Constituents* (Ann Arbor: University of Michigan Press, 1994).

38. Sean M. Theriault, *The Power of the People: Congressional Competition, Public Attention, and Voter Retribution* (Columbus: Ohio State University Press, 2005).

39. Thomas Rudolph and Jillian Evans, "Political Trust, Ideology, and Public Support for Government Spending," *American Journal of Political Science* 49 (2005): 660–71.

40. Patricia Moy and Michael Pfau, *With Malice toward All? The Media and Public Confidence in Democratic Institutions* (Boulder, CO: Praeger, 2000).

41. Erikson, MacKuen, and Stimson, *The Macro Polity*.

42. James A. Stimson, *Public Opinion in America: Moods, Swings, and Cycles* (Boulder, CO: Westview Press, 1999).

43. Robert S. Erikson, Michael B. MacKuen, and James A. Stimson, "American Politics: The Model" (unpublished manuscript, Columbia University, 2000).

44. Pew Research Center, "As Economic Concerns Recede, Environmental Protection Rises on the Public's Policy Agenda," Feb. 13, 2020, www.people-press.org/2020/02/13/as-economic-concerns-recede-environmental-protection-rises-on-the-publics-policy-agenda/ (accessed 4/7/20).

45. Pew Research Center, "Public's Policy Priorities for 2019," January 24, 2019, www.people-press.org/2019/01/24/publics-2019-priorities-economy-health-care-education-and-security-all-near-top-of-list/pp_2019-01-24_political-priorities_0-02/ (accessed 5/3/20).

46. Larry Bartels, "Constituency Opinion and Congressional Policy Making: The Reagan Defense Buildup," *American Political Science Review* 85 (June 1991): 457–74; Jonathan Kastellec, Jeffrey R. Lax, and Justin H. Phillips, "Public Opinion and Senate Confirmation of Supreme Court Nominees," *Journal of Politics* 72 (2010): 767–84.

47. Jacobs and Shapiro, *Politicians Don't Pander: Political Manipulation and the Loss of Democratic Responsiveness*.

48. See www.themonkeycage.org (accessed 1/25/18) and www.vox.com/mischiefs-of-faction (accessed 2/23/18).

49. To see the difference between facts and opinions, take this Pew Research quiz: www.pewresearch.org/quiz/news-statements-quiz/ (accessed 3/7/20).

50. The Project for Excellence in Journalism, "State of the News Media," www.pewresearch.org/topics/state-of-the-news-media (accessed 5/3/18).

51. The *Columbia Journalism Review* maintains a list of holdings for major media companies at Who Owns What, www.cjr.org/resources (accessed 3/7/20).

52. For a discussion of these concepts, see Paul M. Sniderman and Sean M. Theriault, "The Structure of Political Argument and the Logic of Issue Framing," in *Studies in Public Opinion*, ed. William E. Saris and Paul M. Sniderman (Princeton, NJ: Princeton University Press, 2004); and Shanto Iyengar and Donald Kinder, *News That Matters* (Chicago: University of Chicago Press, 1987). See also Maxwell McCombs and Donald L. Shaw, "The Agenda-Setting Functions of Mass Media," *Public Opinion Quarterly* 36 (1972): 176–87; and Amos Tversky and Daniel Kahnemann, "The Framing of Decisions and the Psychology of Choice," *Science* 211 (1981): 453–58.

53. Markus Prior, "Media and Political Polarization," *Annual Review of Political Science* 16 (2013): 101–27.

54. Kevin Arceneaux et al., "The Influence of News Media on Political Elites: Investigating Strategic Responsiveness in Congress," *American Journal of Political Science* 60:1 (2016): 5–29.

55. Matthew S. Levendusky, "Why Do Partisan Media Polarize Viewers?," *American Journal of Political Science* 57:3 (2013): 611–23.

56. Kevin Arceneaux, Martin Johnson, and Chad Murphy, "Polarized Political Communication, Oppositional Media Hostility, and Selective Exposure," *Journal of Politics* 74:01 (2012): 174–86.

What Do the Facts Say?

a. Gianno Caldwell, "Violence in Chicago Proves Black Lives Don't Matter to Liberal Politicians," *New York Post*, November 9, 2019, https://nypost.com/2019/11/09/chicagos-crime-proves-black-lives-dont-matter-to-democrats/ (accessed 4/14/20).

b. The data are available at www.chicagotribune.com/news/breaking/ct-chicago-homicides-data-tracker-htmlstory.html (accessed 1/29/20).

c. "Daily Chart: Murder Rates in 50 American Cities," *The Economist*, February 7, 2017, www.economist.com/blogs/graphicdetail/2017/02/daily-chart-3 (accessed 2/3/18).

Chapter 7

1. Nancy Pelosi, "Transcript of Pelosi Weekly Press Conference Today," May 23, 2019, www.speaker.gov/newsroom/52319 (accessed 10/30/20).

2. Julia Azari, "Weak Parties and Strong Partisanship Are a Bad Combination," Vox, November 3, 2016, www.vox.com/mischiefs-of-faction/2016/11/3/13512362/weak-parties-strong-partisanship-bad-combination (accessed 4/13/20).

3. Bernie Sanders, Twitter, February 25, 2020, 8:02 P.M., https://twitter.com/BernieSanders/status/1231021453270769664 (accessed 4/2/20).

4. Joseph Schlesinger, *Political Parties and the Winning of Office* (Ann Arbor: University of Michigan Press, 1994).

5. Kenneth Benoit, "Duverger's Law and the Study of Electoral Systems," *French Politics* 4:1 (2006): 69–83.

6. William Nesbit Chambers and Walter Dean Burnham, *The American Party Systems: Stages of Political Development* (Oxford, UK: Oxford University Press, 1966).

7. Donald H. Hickey, "Federalist Party Unity and the War of 1812," *Journal of American Studies* 12 (April 1978): 23–39; William T. Bianco, David B. Spence, and John D. Wilkerson, "The Electoral Connection in the Early Congress: The Case of the Compensation Act of 1816," *American Journal of Political Science* 40 (February 1996): 145–71.

8. John Aldrich, *Why Parties?* (Chicago: University of Chicago Press, 2005).

9. James MacPherson, *Battle Cry of Freedom: The Civil War Era* (New York: Oxford University Press, 1988).

10. Michael F. Holt, *The Rise and Fall of the Whig Party: Jacksonian Politics and the Onset of the Civil War* (New York: Oxford University Press, 1999).

11. David A. Bateman, *Disenfranchising Democracy: Constructing the Electorate in the United States, the United Kingdom, and France* (New York: Cambridge University Press, 2018).

12. Harold W. Stanley, William T. Bianco, and Richard G. Niemi, "Partisanship and Group Support over Time: A Multivariate Analysis," *American Political Science Review* 80 (1986): 969–76.

13. Eric Schickler, *Racial Realignment: The Transformation of American Liberalism, 1932–1965* (Princeton, NJ: Princeton University Press, 2016).

14. Hans Noel, *Political Ideologies and Political Parties in America* (New York: Cambridge University Press, 2014).

15. Ben Protess, Danielle Ivory, and Steve Eder, "Where Trump's Hands-Off Approach to Governing Does Not Apply," *New York Times*, September 10, 2017, www.nytimes.com/2017/09/10/business/trump-regulations-religious-conservatives.html, (accessed 3/20/20).

16. James L. Sundquist, *Dynamics of the Party System*, rev. ed. (Washington, DC: Brookings Institution, 1983).

17. Jon F. Hale, "The Making of the New Democrats," *Political Science Quarterly* 110:2 (1995): 207–32.

18. James Monroe, *The Political Party Matrix* (Albany: SUNY Press, 2001).

19. Gary Cox and Mathew McCubbins, *Legislative Leviathan* (Berkeley: University of California Press, 1993); James M. Snyder and Michael M. Ting, "An Informational Rationale for Political Parties," *American Journal of Political Science* 46 (2002): 90–110.

20. Jason Roberts and Steven Smith, "Procedural Contexts, Party Strategy, and Conditional Party Government," *American Journal of Political Science* 47:2 (2003): 305–17.

21. Catherine Rampell, "Tax Pledge May Scuttle a Deal on Deficit," *New York Times*, November 18, 2011, p. B1.

22. Larry M. Bartels, "Partisanship and Voting Behavior, 1952–1996," *American Journal of Political Science* 44:1 (2000): 35–50.

23. Daniel Schlotzman, *When Movements Anchor Parties: Electoral Alignments in American History* (Princeton, NJ: Princeton University Press, 2015).

24. Jill Lawrence, "Party Recruiters Lead Charge for '06 Vote; Choice of Candidates to Run in Fall May Decide Who Controls the House," *USA Today*, May 25, 2006, p. A5.

25. Compiled from information available at www.ballot-access.org (accessed 2/18/18).

26. The Center for Responsive Politics, opensecrets.org (accessed 11/4/20).

27. Heather Caygle, "Anti-abortion Democrat Snubbed by Party for Reelection," Politico, February 26, 2018, www.politico.com/story/2018/02/25/lipinski-democrats-abortion-chicago-illinois-423431 (accessed 5/9/18).

28. Libertarian National Committee, "Elected Officials," www.lp.org/elected-officials (accessed 7/14/20).

29. Lee Drutman, *Breaking the Two-Party Doom Loop* (New York: Oxford University Press, 2019).

Take a Stand

a. Nelson Polsby, *Consequences of Party Reform* (New York: Oxford University Press, 1983).

b. Daniel A. Smith and Caroline J. Tolbert, *Educated by Initiative: The Effects of Direct Democracy on Citizens and Political Organizations in the American States* (Ann Arbor: University of Michigan Press, 2004).

Chapter 8

1. Donald Trump, Twitter, November 7, 2020, 4:53 P.M., https://twitter.com/realdonaldtrump/status/1325194709443080192 (accessed 11/17/20).

2. Quoted in Tim Alberta, "The Election That Broke the Republican Party," Politico, November 6, 2020, www.politico.com/news/magazine/2020/11/06/the-election-that-broke-the-republican-party-434797 (accessed 11/17/20).

3. Morris P. Fiorina, *Retrospective Voting in American National Elections* (New Haven, CT: Yale University Press, 1981); V. O. Key, *The Responsible Electorate* (New York: Vintage Books, 1966).

4. David Mayhew, *Congress: The Electoral Connection* (New Haven, CT: Yale University Press, 1973).

5. For details on early voting, see the Early Voting Information Center site at http://earlyvoting.net/resources (accessed 5/9/18).

6. Minor-party candidates are typically selected during party conventions.

7. Barbara Norrander, "Presidential Nomination Politics in the Post-reform Era," *Political Research Quarterly* 49 (1996): 875–90.

8. Larry Bartels, *Presidential Primaries and the Dynamics of Public Choice* (Princeton, NJ: Princeton University Press, 1988).

9. FairVote, "Maine and Nebraska," www.fairvote.org/maine_nebraska (accessed 5/9/18).

10. James Q. Wilson, "Is the Electoral College Worth Saving?," *Slate*, November 3, 2000, www.slate.com/id/92663 (accessed 10/19/12).

11. Robert Erikson and Christopher Wlezien, *The Timeline of Presidential Elections* (Chicago: University of Chicago Press, 2013).

12. Larry M. Bartels and Christopher H. Achen, *Democracy for Realists: Why Elections Do Not Produce Responsive Government* (Princeton, NJ: Princeton University Press, 2016).

13. Steven Ansolabehere and Alan Gerber, "Incumbency Advantage and the Persistence of Legislative Majorities," *Legislative Studies Quarterly* 22 (1997): 161–80.

14. For a discussion of Johnson's decision, see Robert A. Caro, *The Path to Power* (New York: Knopf, 1983).

15. Thomas Mann and Norman Ornstein, *The Permanent Campaign and Its Future* (Washington, DC: American Enterprise Institute, 2000).

16. Mayhew, *Congress: The Electoral Connection*.

17. Jonathan Krasno and Donald P. Green, "The Dynamics of Campaign Fundraising in House Elections," *Journal of Politics* 56 (1991): 459–74.

18. Michael J. Goff, *The Money Primary: The New Politics of the Early Presidential Nomination Process* (New York: Rowman & Littlefield, 2007).

19. Michael Babaro, "Candidates Stick to Script, If Not the Truth, in the 2016 Race," *New York Times*, November 7, 2015, p. A1.

20. Chris Cillizza, "Consulting Firms Face Conflict in 2008," *Roll Call*, June 20, 2005, p. 1.

21. Matt Bai, "Turnout Wins Elections," *New York Times Magazine*, December 14, 2003, p. 100.

22. Christopher Drew, "New Telemarketing Ploy Steers Voters on Republican Path," *New York Times*, November 6, 2006.

23. For a history of presidential debates, see the Commission on Presidential Debates site at www.debates.org (accessed 10/19/12).

24. For a video library of presidential campaign ads, see Museum of the Moving Image, "The Living Room Candidate: Presidential Campaign Commercials 1952–2012," http://livingroomcandidate.org (accessed 10/19/12).

25. Steven E. Finkel and John G. Geer, "A Spot Check: Casting Doubt on the Demobilizing Effect of Attack Advertising," *American Journal of Political Science* 42:2 (1998): 573–95; Richard R. Lau, Lee Sigelman, and Ivy Brown Rovner, "The Effects of Negative Political Campaigns: A Meta-analytic Reassessment," *Journal of Politics* 69:4 (2007): 1176–1209; Yanna Krupnikov, "When Does Negativity Demobilize? Tracing the Conditional Effect of Negative Campaigning on Voter Turnout," *American Journal of Political Science* 55:4 (2011): 797–813.

26. Paul Freeman, Michael Franz, and Kenneth Goldstein, "Campaign Advertising and Democratic Citizenship," *American Journal of Political Science* 48 (2004): 723–41.

27. Constantine J. Spilotes and Lynn Vavreck, "Campaign Advertising: Partisan Convergence or Divergence?," *Journal of Politics* 64 (2002): 249–61.

28. Kathleen Hall Jameson, *Packaging the Presidency: A History and Criticism of Presidential Campaign Advertising* (New York: Oxford University Press, 1996).

29. Jonathan Krasno and Frank J. Sorauf, "For the Defense," *Political Science and Politics* 37 (2004): 777–80.

30. Brian Stelter, "The Price of 30 Seconds," *New York Times*, October 1, 2007, http://mediadecoder.blogs.nytimes.com/2007/10/01/the-price-of-30-seconds (accessed 10/19/12).

31. For a review of this literature, see Michael Malbin, *The Election after Reform: Money, Politics, and the Bipartisan Campaign Reform Act* (Washington, DC: Rowman & Littlefield, 2006).

32. Lynda Powell, *The Influence of Campaign Contributions in State Legislatures* (Ann Arbor: University of Michigan Press, 2012).

33. David Karol, "If You Think Super PACs Have Changed Everything about Presidential Primaries, Think Again," September 21, 2015, www.washingtonpost.com/blogs/monkey-cage/wp/2015/09/21/if-you-think-super-pacs-have-changed-everything-about-the-presidential-primary-think-again (accessed 9/21/15).

34. For a discussion, see Thomas Patterson, *The Vanishing Voter* (New York: Knopf, 2002), especially Chapter 1, "The Incredible Shrinking Electorate," pp. 3–22.

35. William H. Riker and Peter Ordeshook, "A Theory of the Calculus of Voting," *American Political Science Review* 62 (1968): 25–39.

36. Michael McDonald, The United States Elections Project, www.electproject.org (accessed 5/11/18).

37. Pew Research Center, "Regular Voters, Intermittent Voters, and Those Who Don't," October 18, 2006, www.pewresearch.org/wp-content/uploads/sites/4/legacy-pdf/292.pdf (accessed 5/1/20).

38. Richard P. Lau and David P. Redlawsk, *How Voters Decide: Information Processing during Electoral Campaigns* (New York: Cambridge University Press, 2006).

39. Samuel Popkin, *The Reasoning Voter* (Chicago: University of Chicago Press, 1991).

40. Richard R. Lau and David P. Redlawsk, "Advantages and Disadvantages of Cognitive Heuristics in Political Decision Making," *American Journal of Political Science* 45 (2001): 951–71.

41. Mark Jurkowitz, "Majority of Americans Disapprove of Trump's COVID-19 Messaging, though Large Partisan Gaps Persist," Pew Research Center, September 15, 2020, www.pewresearch.org/fact-tank/2020/09/15/majority-of-americans-disapprove-of-trumps-covid-19-messaging-though-large-partisan-gaps-persist/ (accessed 11/17/20).

42. Kevin Schaul, Kate Rabinowitz, and Ted Mellnik, "2020 Turnout Is the Highest in Over a Century," *Washington Post*, November 5, 2020, www.washingtonpost.com/graphics/2020/elections/voter-turnout/ (accessed 11/17/20).

43. Nick Corasaniti, Reid J. Epstein, and Jim Rutenberg, "The Times Called Officials in Every State: No Evidence of Voter Fraud," *New York Times*, November 10, 2020, www.nytimes.com/2020/11/10/us/politics/voting-fraud.html (accessed 11/17/20).

44. Nicholas Riccardi, "Democrats Keep Winning the Popular Vote. That Worries Them," AP News, November 14, 2020, https://apnews.com/article/democrats-popular-vote-win-d6331f7e8b51d52582bb2d60e2a007ec (accessed 11/17/20).

What Do the Facts Say?

a. See "Trump's Challenge: The President Dares Congress to 'Impeach This,'" Sean Hannity, October 1, 2019, https://hannity.com/media-room/trumps-challenge-the-president-dares-congress-to-impeach-this/ (accessed 4/14/20).

b. Philip Bump, "The Four Simple Reasons Trump's 'Impeach This' Map Doesn't Make Any Sense," *Washington Post*, October 1, 2019, www.washingtonpost.com/politics/2019/10/01/four-simple-reasons-that-trumps-impeach-this-map-doesnt-make-any-sense/ (accessed 4/14/20).

Chapter 9

1. Quoted in Naomi Jagoda, "Democrats Offer Bill to Undo Business Tax Provisions in Coronavirus Law," *The Hill*, https://thehill.com/policy/finance/494647-democrats-offer-bill-to-undo-business-tax-provisions-in-coronavirus-law (accessed 5/18/20).

2. Chuck Grassley, "Coronavirus-Damaged Businesses Deserve Financial Relief," www.grassley.senate.gov/news/news-releases/grassley-op-ed-coronavirus-damaged-businesses-deserve-financial-relief (accessed 5/18/20).

3. Jim Zarroli, "Even the Los Angeles Lakers Got a PPP Small Business Loan," National Public Radio, April 27, 2020, www.npr.org/sections/coronavirus-live-updates/2020/04/27/846024717/even-the-la-lakers-got-a-ppp-small-business-loan (accessed 5/16/20).

4. For an excellent summary of the details, see Steven M. Rosenthal and Aravind Boddupalli, "Heads I Win, Tails I Win Too: Winners from the Tax Relief for Losses in the CARES Act," Tax Policy Center, April 20, 2020, www.taxpolicycenter.org/taxvox/heads-i-win-tails-i-win-too-winners-tax-relief-losses-cares-act (accessed 5/16/20).

5. Joint Committee on Taxation, "Estimated Revenue Effects of the Revenue Provisions Contained in an Amendment in the Nature of a Substitute to H.R. 748, the 'Coronavirus

Aid, Relief, And Economic Security ("CARES")' Act," JCX-11R-20, April 23, 2020, www.jct.gov/publications. html?func=startdown&id=5255 (accessed 5/16/20).

6. Robert H. Salisbury et al., "Who Works with Whom? Interest Group Alliances and Opposition," *American Political Science Review* 81 (1987): 1217-34.

7. Business-Industry Political Action Committee, "About BIPAC," www.bipac.org/about-us (accessed 6/5/18).

8. James Q. Wilson, *Political Organizations* (New York: Basic Books, 1974).

9. AAA, Foundation for Traffic Safety, www.aaafoundation.org/ home (accessed 7/29/16).

10. Scott Ainsworth, *Analyzing Interest Groups: Group Influence on People and Policies* (New York: W. W. Norton, 2002).

11. Timothy LaPira and Hershel F. Thomas III, "Revolving Door Lobbyists and Interest Representation," *Interest Groups and Advocacy* 3 (2013): 4-29.

12. One hundred and six members retired in January 2019; 58 of those were employed by mid-2020, and 31 of those were employed in lobbying jobs. Data available at www.opensecrets. org/revolving/departing.php (accessed 5/13/20).

13. Lobbying regulations are often changed; the discussion here is just a general guide. For a summary of federal law, see "Lobbying Disclosure Act Guidance," Office of the Clerk, U.S. House of Representatives, January 31, 2017, https:// lobbyingdisclosure.house.gov/amended_lda_guide.htmll; for state law, see Lobbying Regulation, National Conference of State Legislatures, www.ncsl.org/research/ethics/lobbyist-regulation.aspx (both accessed May 11, 2020).

14. Nadja Popovich, Livia Albeck-Ripka, and Kendra Pierre-Louis, "The Trump Administration Is Reversing 100 Environmental Rules. Here's the Full List," *New York Times*, July 15, 2020, www.nytimes.com/interactive/2020/climate/trump-environment-rollbacks.html (accessed 8/20/20).

15. Project on Government Oversight, "Brass Parachutes: Defense Contractors' Capture of Pentagon Officials through the Revolving Door," November 5, 2018, https://s3.amazonaws.com/ docs.pogo.org/report/2018/POGO_Brass_Parachutes_DoD_ Revolving_Door_Report_2018-11-05.pdf (accessed 5/12/20).

16. Roxana Tiron, "Lockheed Martin Leads Expanded Lobbying by US Defense Industry," *Washington Post*, January 26, 2012, www .washingtonpost.com/business/economy/lockheed-martin-leads-expanded-lobbying-by-us-defense-industry/2012/01/26/ gIQAlgQtaQ_story.html (accessed 2/4/14).

17. However, the sector of "finance, insurance, and real estate" spent $502,107,659 on lobbying in 2019, which is a lot!

18. Tim LaPira, Lee Drutman, and Matthew Grossmann, "The Interest Group Top Tier: More Groups, Concentrated Clout," paper presented at the 2014 American Political Science Association Annual Meeting.

19. 2018 Ranked Sectors, Center for Responsive Politics, www. opensecrets.org/federal-lobbying/ranked-sectors?cycle=2018; 2019 Ranked Sectors, Center for Responsive Politics, www. opensecrets.org/federal-lobbying/ranked-sectors?cycle=2019 (both accessed 5/12/20).

20. For more on this argument, see Tim Harford, "There's Not Enough Money in Politics," *Slate*, April 1, 2006, www. slate.com/id/2138874 (accessed 7/29/16); and Stephen Ansolabehere, John M. de Figueiredo, and James M. Snyder, "Why Is There So Little Money in American Politics?," *Journal of Economic Perspectives* 17 (2003): 105-30.

21. Kenneth Kollman, *Outside Lobbying: Public Opinion and Interest Group Strategies* (Princeton, NJ: Princeton University Press, 1998).

22. Jack Walker, *Mobilizing Interest Groups in America* (Ann Arbor: University of Michigan Press, 1991); Frank R. Baumgartner et al., *Lobbying and Policy Change: Who Wins, Who Loses, and Why* (Chicago: University of Chicago Press, 2009).

23. John P. Heinz, Edward O. Laumann, and Robert Salisbury, *The Hollow Core: Private Interests in National Policymaking* (Cambridge, MA: Harvard University Press, 1993).

24. Richard L. Hall and Alan V. Deardorff, "Lobbying as Legislative Subsidy," *American Political Science Review* 100 (2006): 69-84.

25. Key Lehman Schlozman and John T. Tierney, *Organized Interests and American Democracy* (New York: HarperCollins, 1986).

26. Anthony Madonna and Ian Ostrander, "If Congress Keeps Cutting Its Staff, Who Is Writing Your Laws? You Won't Like the Answer," *Washington Post*, August 20, 2015, www. washingtonpost.com/news/monkey-cage/wp/2015/08/20/ if-congress-keeps-cutting-its-staff-who-is-writing-your-laws-you-wont-like-the-answer/?utm_term=.d4773b24c7cf (accessed 12/20/17).

27. Christine A. DeGregorio, *Networks of Champions: Leadership, Access, and Advocacy in the U.S. House of Representatives* (Ann Arbor: University of Michigan Press, 1992).

28. Daniel Carpenter, *The Forging of Bureaucratic Autonomy: Reputations, Networks, and Policy Innovation in Executive Agencies, 1862-1928* (Princeton, NJ: Princeton University Press, 2002).

29. Public Citizen," Our Work," www.citizen.org (accessed 5/15/20).

30. Derived from a search of the NRA Institute for Legislative Action site, www.nraila.org (accessed 5/15/20).

31. Kim Scheppele and Jack L. Walker, "The Litigation Strategies of Interest Groups," in *Mobilizing Interest Groups in America*, ed. Jack Walker (Ann Arbor: University of Michigan Press, 1991).

32. Kevin W. Hula, *Lobbying Together: Interest Group Coalitions in Legislative Politics* (Washington, DC: Georgetown University Press, 1999).

33. Lauren Cohen Bell, *Warring Factions: Interest Groups, Money, and the New Politics of Senate Confirmation* (Columbus: Ohio State University Press, 2002).

34. Jesse Drucker, "The Tax-Break Bonanza Inside the Economic Rescue Package," *New York Times*, April 24, 2020 www. nytimes.com/2020/04/24/business/tax-breaks-wealthy-virus.html (accessed 5/15/20).

35. Jeanne Cummings, "Word Games Could Threaten Climate Bill," Politico, June 9, 2009, www.politico.com/news/ stories/0609/24059.html (accessed 9/19/12).

36. Richard Fenno, *Home Style: U.S. House Members in Their Districts* (Boston: Little, Brown, 1978). See also Brandice Caines-Wrone, David W. Brady, and John F. Cogan, "Out of Step, Out of Office: Electoral Accountability and House Members' Voting," *American Political Science Review* 96 (2002): 127-40.

37. Emily Yoffe, "Am I the Next Jack Abramoff?," *Slate*, April 1, 2006, www.slate.com/id/2137886 (accessed 8/28/09).

38. Kollman, *Outside Lobbying*.

39. *Citizens United v. Federal Election Commission*, 558 U.S. 310 (2010).

40. Data from www.opensecrets.org and www.fec.gov (accessed 11/8/20).

41. Lee Drutman, "The Solution to Lobbying Is More Lobbying," *Washington Post*, April 29, 2015, www.washingtonpost. com/blogs/monkey-cage/wp/2015/04/29/the-solution-to-lobbying-is-more-lobbying (accessed 2/16/16).

42. Amy McKay, "Negative Lobbying and Policy Outcomes," *American Politics Review* 40 (2011): 116-46.

43. Jeffrey M. Berry, *The Interest Group Society* (New York: HarperCollins, 1997); Raymond A. Bauer, Ithiel de Sola Pool, and Lewis Dexter, *American Business and Public Policy* (New York: Atherton Press, 1963).

44. Kollman, *Outside Lobbying*.

Take a Stand

a. Jacob Weisberg, "Three Cities, Three Scandals: What Jack Abramoff, Anthony Pellicano, and Jared Paul Stern Have in Common," *Slate*, April 9, 2006, www.slate.com/id/2140238 (accessed 10/25/12).

b. Herschel F. Thomas and Timothy M. LaPira, "How Many Lobbyists Are in Washington? Shadow Lobbying and the Gray Market for Policy Advocacy," *Interest Groups and Advocacy* 6:3 (2017): 199–214.

Chapter 10

1. Donald J. Trump, Twitter, June 18, 2020, 1:20 P.M., https://twitter.com/realDonaldTrump/status/1273666793362673665 (accessed 6/29/20).

2. Quoted in Morgan Gstalter, "Cruz: No Path to Citizenship for Dreamers," *The Hill*, January 25, 2018, https://thehill.com/latino/370771-cruz-no-path-to-citizenship-for-dreamers (accessed 6/11/20).

3. Quoted in Felicia Sonmez, "House Passes Immigration Bill to Protect 'Dreamers,' Offer a Path to Citizenship," *Washington Post*, June 4, 2019, www.washingtonpost.com/powerpost/house-poised-to-pass-immigration-bill-that-would-protect-dreamers/2019/06/04/bac5cf98-86d7-11e9-a491-25df61c78dc4_story.html (accessed 6/11/20).

4. Katie Reilly, "Here's What President Trump Has Said about DACA in the Past," *Time*, September 5, 2017, http://time.com/4927100/donald-trump-daca-past-statements/ (accessed 2/15/18).

5. Most of the poll questions specified the conditions of the DACA program for becoming a citizen: "To qualify, immigrants had to be under the age of 30 as of 2012, have no criminal record, and be a student, in the military, or have earned a high school diploma." A few only mentioned not having a criminal record. See www.pollingreport.com/immigration.htm for a record of the polls taken early in 2018 (accessed 2/9/18).

6. See Wendy J. Schiller and Charles Stewart III, *Electing the Senate: Indirect Democracy before the Seventeenth Amendment* (Princeton, NJ: Princeton University Press, 2015), for an analysis of Senate elections before the popular vote. See Paul Gronke, *The Electorate, the Campaign, and the Office: A Unified Approach to Senate and House Elections* (Ann Arbor: University of Michigan Press, 2000), for research showing that the House and Senate elections share many similar characteristics. See Richard F. Fenno, *Senators on the Campaign Trail: The Politics of Representation* (Norman: University of Oklahoma Press, 1996), for a good general discussion of Senate elections.

7. The poll data on Congress's general approval is from PollingReport.com; see www.pollingreport.com/CongJob.htm (accessed 5/3/20). The occupations poll was conducted by Gallup in December 2017; see http://news.gallup.com/poll/1654/honesty-ethics-professions.aspx (accessed 2/15/18). There has not been recent polling on DACA, but for a summary of public sentiment on the issue, see Giovanni Russonello, "The Supreme Court May Let Trump End DACA. Here's What the Public Thinks about It," *New York Times*, November 15, 2019, www.nytimes.com/2019/11/15/us/politics/daca-supreme-court-polls.html (accessed 5/23/20).

8. "Congress Less Popular than Cockroaches, Traffic Jams," Public Policy Polling, January 8, 2013, www.publicpolicypolling.com/pdf/2011/PPP_Release_Natl_010813_.pdf (accessed 4/11/14).

9. Claudine Gay, "Spirals of Trust? The Effect of Descriptive Representation on the Relationship between Citizens and Their Government," *American Journal of Political Science* 46:4 (October 2002): 717–32.

10. R. Douglas Arnold, *The Logic of Congressional Action* (New Haven, CT: Yale University Press, 1990), pp. 60–71.

11. David R. Mayhew, *Congress: The Electoral Connection* (New Haven, CT: Yale University Press, 1974).

12. Mayhew, *Congress*, p. 17.

13. Gary C. Jacobson, *The Politics of Congressional Elections*, 5th ed. (New York: Longman, 2001), pp. 24–30.

14. Richard F. Fenno, *Home Style: House Members in Their Districts* (Boston: Little, Brown, 1978).

15. Morris Fiorina, *Congress: Keystone of the Washington Establishment*, rev. ed. (New Haven, CT: Yale University Press, 1989).

16. Ed Kilgore, "Final Pre-census Estimates Show Which States Will Become More Powerful After 2020," *New York*, December 30, 2019, https://nymag.com/intelligencer/2019/12/pre-census-estimates-show-reapportionment-winners-losers.html (accessed 11/9/20).

17. The language used by the Court in 1960 was "one-man, one-vote." The Court ruled in *Baker v. Carr*, 369 U.S. 186 (1962), that state legislative districts that were unequal in population violated the equal protection clause of the Fourteenth Amendment. *Wesberry v. Sanders*, 376 U.S. 1 (1964), applied the same principle to U.S. House districts.

18. *Davis v. Bandemer*, 478 U.S. 109 (1986); *Vieth v. Jubelirer*, 541 U.S. 267 (2004); *League of United Latin American Citizens v. Perry*, 548 U.S. 399 (2006).

19. The North Carolina case is *Rucho v. Common Cause* 558 U.S. _____ (2019); this case was consolidated with the Maryland case, *Lamone v. Benisek* (No. 18-726) and was issued as a single opinion for both cases.

20. *Shelby County v. Holder*, 570 U.S. 529 (2013). The full citation for the North Carolina case is *Shaw v. Reno*, 509 U.S. 630 (1993).

21. See Kenneth R. Mayer and David T. Canon, *The Dysfunctional Congress: The Individual Roots of an Institutional Dilemma* (New York: Routledge, 2019), for an extended discussion of this argument.

22. Caitlin Emma, "House Swiftly Advances Behemoth $1.4T Spending Deal," Politico, December 17, 2019, www.politico.com/news/2019/12/17/house-passes-massive-deal-to-fund-government-and-avoid-shutdown-086514 (accessed 6/2/20).

23. An important qualification to the norm was imposed by Republicans in 1995 when they set a six-year term limit for committee and subcommittee chairs.

24. Congressional Quarterly, "CQ Federal Congressional Bill Tracker," https://info.cq.com/legislative-tracking/cq-federal/ (accessed 8/1/20).

25. David Rohde and John Aldrich, "The Transition to Republican Rule in the House: Implications for Theories of Congressional Politics," *Political Science Quarterly* 112:4 (Winter 1997–1998): 541–67.

26. Nelson W. Polsby, *Congress and the Presidency*, 4th ed. (Englewood Cliffs, NJ: Prentice Hall, 1986), p. 111.

27. Paul Steinhauser, "Obama 2014 Campaign Role: Fundraiser-in-Chief," CNN Politics, March 20, 2014, http://politicalticker.blogs.cnn.com/2014/03/20/obama-2014-campaign-role-fundraiser-in-chief (accessed 4/16/14).

28. Kathryn Watson, "Trump Addresses Record-Setting GOP Fundraiser," CBS News, March 20, 2018, www.cbsnews.com/

news/trump-addresses-one-of-the-biggest-gop-fundraisers-of-the-year (accessed 6/7/18).

29. However, recent research shows that members of Congress do not confine their credit claiming to legislative activity that is rooted in committee work. See Justin Grimmer, Sean J. Westwood, and Solomon Messing, *The Impression of Influence: Legislator Communication, Representation, and Democratic Accountability* (Princeton, NJ: Princeton University Press, 2014).

30. Keith Krehbiel, *Information and Legislative Organization* (Ann Arbor: University of Michigan Press, 1992).

31. Grace Segers, Stefan Becket, and Melissa Quinn, "House Committee Approves Rules for Impeachment Vote," CBS News, December 18, 2019, www.cbsnews.com/live-updates/trump-impeachment-house-rules-committee-debate-live-updates-live-stream-2019-12-17/ (accessed 6/3/20).

32. Barbara Sinclair, *Unorthodox Lawmaking* (Washington, DC: CQ Press, 2000), p. xiv.

33. Edward Epstein, "Dusting Off Deliberation," *CQ Weekly*, June 14, 2010, pp. 1434–42.

34. See Congressional Research Service, Appropriations Status Table, https://crsreports.congress.gov/AppropriationsStatusTable/Index/AppropriationsStatusTable?id=2019 (accessed 6/3/20).

35. USA Patriot Act, Hearing before the Subcommittee on the Constitution, Civil Rights and Civil Liberties, Committee on the Judiciary, House of Representatives, September 22, 2009, www.gpo.gov/fdsys/pkg/CHRG-111hhrg52409/html/CHRG-111hhrg52409.htm (accessed 6/7/18).

36. Philip Rucker and Robert Costa, "McCarthy's Comments on Benghazi Probe May Be a Political Gift to Clinton," *Washington Post*, October 1, 2015, www.washingtonpost.com/politics/mccarthys-comments-on-benghazi-probe-may-be-a-political-gift-to-clinton/2015/10/01/6ceb6e88-6857-11e5-9223-70cb36460919_story.html. For an account of the Ukraine investigation, see Jerrold Nadler, "Impeachment of Donald J. Trump, President of the United States," Report of the Committee on the Judiciary, House of Representatives, December 2019, https://docs.house.gov/billsthisweek/20191216/CRPT-116hrpt346.pdf (both accessed 6/3/20).

37. House Committee on Oversight and Reform, "Oversight of Trump Administration," https://oversight.house.gov/oversight-of-trump-administration (accessed 6/3/20).

38. Mathew McCubbins and Thomas Schwartz, "Congressional Oversight Overlooked: Police Patrol versus Fire Alarm," *American Journal of Political Science* 28:1 (February 1984): 165-77.

39. House Committee on the Judiciary, Hearing on "Oversight of the Department of Justice: Political Interference and Threats to Prosecutorial Independence," June 24, 2020, https://judiciary.house.gov/calendar/eventsingle.aspx?EventID=3034; House Committee on the Judiciary, Hearing on "Oversight of the Department of Justice," July 28, 2020, https://judiciary.house.gov/calendar/eventsingle.aspx?EventID=3140 (both accessed 8/6/20).

40. Hailey Fuchs, "House Can Sue to Force Testimony From McGahn, Appeals Court Rules," *New York Times*, August 7, 2020, www.nytimes.com/2020/08/07/us/politics/donald-mcgahn-congress-lawsuit.html (accessed 8/10/20).

41. The cases concerning financial records and tax returns are discussed in John Kruzel, "Supreme Court Divided over Fight for Trump's Financial Records," *The Hill*, May 12, 2020, https://thehill.com/regulation/497385-supreme-court-divided-over-fight-for-trumps-financial-records. The McGahn case is discussed in Jennifer Rubin, "What the McGahn Case Means and Does Not Mean," *Washington Post*, March 2, 2020 www.washingtonpost.com/opinions/2020/03/02/what-mcgahn-case-means-does-not-mean/ (both accessed 6/4/20).

42. Nina Totenberg, "Supreme Court Says Trump Not 'Immune' From Records Release, But Hedges On House Case," National Public Radio, July 9, 2020, www.npr.org/2020/07/09/884447882/supreme-court-says-trump-not-immune-from-records-release-pushes-back-on-congress (accessed 8/10/20).

43. Paul Kane, " Democrats Warn Republicans They Will Regret Backing Trump's Defiance of Congressional Oversight," *Washington Post*, May 20, 2020, www.washingtonpost.com/powerpost/democrats-warn-republicans-they-will-regret-backing-trumps-defiance-of-congressional-oversight/2020/05/20/3084f0ac-9ab8-11ea-ac72-3841fcc9b35f_story.html (accessed 6/3/20).

What Do the Facts Say?

a. Glenn Kessler, Meg Kelly, Salvador Rizzo, and Michelle Ye Hee Lee, "In 1,316 days, President Trump Has Made 22,247 False or Misleading Claims," *Washington Post*, August 27, 2020, www.washingtonpost.com/graphics/politics/trump-claims-database/ (accessed 11/8/20).

Take a Stand

a. The warning against entering the "political thicket" comes from *Colegrove v. Green*, 328 U.S. 549 (1946).

Chapter 11

1. Quoted in Meagan Flynn and Allyson Chiu, "Trump Says His 'Authority Is Total.' Constitutional Experts Have 'No Idea' Where He Got That," *Washington Post*, April 14, 2020, www.washingtonpost.com/nation/2020/04/14/trump-power-constitution-coronavirus/ (accessed 4/26/20).

2. Quoted in Morgan Chalfant and Brett Samuels, "Trump Eases Back on Asserting Power over Governors on Reopening," *The Hill*, April 14, 2020, https://thehill.com/homenews/administration/492837-trump-eases-back-on-asserting-power-over-governors-on-reopening (accessed 4/26/20).

3. Philip Bump, "What Trump Has Undone," *Washington Post*, August 24, 2017, www.washingtonpost.com/news/politics/wp/2017/08/24/what-trump-has-undone/ (accessed 4/24/20).

4. Lori Cox Han and Caroline Heldman, *Madam President? Gender and Politics on the Road to the White House* (Boulder, CO: Lynne Rienner, 2020).

5. John Aldrich, *Why Parties? A Second Look* (Chicago: University of Chicago Press, 1995).

6. Ernest R. May, *The Making of the Monroe Doctrine* (Cambridge, MA: Harvard University Press, 1975).

7. Arthur M. Schlesinger Jr., *The Age of Jackson* (Boston: Little, Brown, 1945).

8. David Greenberg, "Lincoln's Crackdown," *Slate*, November 30, 2001, www.slate.com/id/2059132 (accessed 8/8/16).

9. Stephen Skowronek, *Building a New American State: The Expansion of National Administrative Capacities* (New York: Cambridge University Press, 1982).

10. Theda Skocpol, *Protecting Soldiers and Mothers: The Political Origins of Social Policy in the United States* (Cambridge, MA: Harvard University Press, 1995).

11. Thomas J. Knock, *To End All Wars: Woodrow Wilson and the Quest for a New World Order* (New York: Oxford University Press, 1992).

12. William E. Leuchtenburg, *FDR Years: On Roosevelt and His Legacy* (New York: Columbia University Press, 1995).

13. Chester Pach and Elmo Richardson, *The Presidency of Dwight D. Eisenhower* (Lawrence: University Press of Kansas, 1991).

14. Richard E. Neustadt, *Presidential Power and the Modern Presidents* (1960; repr., New York: Free Press, 1991).

15. Thomas J. Weko, *The Politicizing Presidency: The White House Personnel Office, 1948-1994* (Lawrence: University Press of Kansas, 1995).

16. Kenneth Mayer, *With the Stroke of a Pen: Executive Orders and Presidential Power* (Princeton, NJ: Princeton University Press, 2001).

17. Brian Hallett, *Declaring War: Congress, the President, and What the Constitution Does Not Say* (New York: Cambridge University Press, 2012).

18. Frederick S. Tipson, "The War Powers Resolution: A Continuing Constitutional Struggle," in *Making Government Work: From White House to Congress*, ed. Robert E. Hunter (New York: Routledge, 2019), pp. 115-51.

19. Lewis Fisher and David G. Adler, "The War Powers Resolution: Time to Say Goodbye," *Political Science Quarterly* 113:1 (1998): 1-20.

20. William G. Howell and Jon C. Pevehouse, *While Dangers Gather: Congressional Checks on Presidential War Powers* (Princeton, NJ: Princeton University Press, 2007).

21. Mark A. Peterson, *Legislating Together: The White House and Capitol Hill from Eisenhower to Reagan* (Cambridge, MA: Harvard University Press, 1990).

22. Andrew Rudalevige, *Managing the President's Program: Presidential Leadership and Legislative Policy Formation* (Princeton, NJ: Princeton University Press, 2002).

23. Charles Cameron and Nolan M. McCarty, "Models of Vetoes and Veto Bargaining," *Annual Review of Political Science* 7 (2004): 409-35.

24. Mark J. Rozell, "The Law: Executive Privilege: Definition and Standards of Application," *Presidential Studies Quarterly* 29:4 (1999): 918-30.

25. For a summary of the case, see Oyez, *United States v. Nixon*, 418 U.S. 683 (1974), www.oyez.org/cases/1973/73-1766 (accessed 6/21/18).

26. Mark J. Rozell, *Executive Privilege: The Dilemma of Secrecy and Democratic Accountability* (Baltimore, MD: Johns Hopkins University Press, 1994).

27. John Hart, *The Presidential Branch: From Washington to Clinton* (Chatham, NY: Chatham House, 1987).

28. David E. Lewis, "Staffing Alone: Unilateral Action and the Politicization of the Executive Office of the President, 1988-2004," *Presidential Studies Quarterly* 35 (2005): 496-514.

29. Charles E. Walcott and Karen M. Hult, "White House Staff Size: Explanations and Implications," *Presidential Studies Quarterly* 29 (1999): 638-56.

30. Karen M. Hult and Charles E. Walcott, *Empowering the White House: Governance under Nixon, Ford, and Carter* (Lawrence: University Press of Kansas, 2004).

31. For a series of articles detailing Cheney's role, see "Angler: The Cheney Vice Presidency," *Washington Post*, June 24-27, 2007, http://voices.washingtonpost.com/cheney/ (accessed 5/8/20).

32. Richard E. Neustart, *Presidential Power and the Modern Presidents* (New York: Simon and Schuster, 1991).

33. Erika Werner and Seung Min Kim, "Senate Passes $484 Billion Bill That Would Expand Small-Business Aid, Boost Money for Hospitals and Testing," *Washington Post*, April 21, 2020, www.washingtonpost.com/us-policy/2020/04/21/congress-coronavirus-small-business/ (accessed 5/8/20).

34. Terry M. Moe and William G. Howell, "The Presidential Power of Unilateral Action," *Journal of Law, Economics, and Organization* 15 (1999): 132-46.

35. Louis Fisher, *Presidential War Power*, 2nd ed. (Lawrence: University Press of Kansas, 2004); James M. Lindsay, "Deference and Defiance: The Shifting Rhythms of Executive-Legislative Relations in Foreign Policy," *Presidential Studies Quarterly* 33:3 (2003): 530-46; Lawrence Margolis, *Executive Agreements and Presidential Power in Foreign Policy* (New York: Praeger, 1985), 209-32.

36. Christopher Deering and Forrest Maltzman, "The Politics of Executive Orders: Legislative Constraints on Presidential Power," *Political Research Quarterly* 52:4 (1999): 767-83.

37. David E. Lewis, *Presidents and the Politics of Agency Design: Political Insulation in the United States Government Bureaucracy, 1946-1997* (Palo Alto, CA: Stanford University Press, 2003).

38. David Epstein and Sharyn O'Halloran, *Delegating Powers* (Cambridge, UK: Cambridge University Press, 1999).

39. William G. Howell, *Thinking about the Presidency: The Primacy of Power* (Princeton, NJ: Princeton University Press, 2015).

40. George C. Edwards III, *The Public Presidency* (New York: St. Martin's Press, 1983); George C. Edwards III, *On Deaf Ears: The Limits of the Bully Pulpit* (New Haven, CT: Yale University Press, 2003).

41. For evidence, see Edwards, *On Deaf Ears*.

42. George C. Edwards III, *Predicting the Presidency: The Potential of Persuasive Leadership* (Princeton, NJ: Princeton University Press, 2015).

43. Eric Berger, "Email Release Reveals Chaos Sowed by President Trump's Hurricane Tweets," Ars Technica, February 1, 2020, https://arstechnica.com/science/2020/02/email-release-reveals-choas-sowed-by-president-trumps-hurricane-tweets/ (accessed 4/24/20).

Chapter 12

1. Robert Heinlein, *Stranger in a Strange Land* (1961; repr., New York: Berkley, 1983), p. 95.

2. Joseph A. Schumpeter, *Capitalism, Socialism and Democracy* (1943; repr., London: Routledge, 2013), p. 206.

3. Dwight Waldo, *The Administrative State: A Study of the Political Theory of American Public Administration* (1948; repr. Piscataway, NJ: Transaction, 2006).

4. For a history of the FDA, see John P. Swann, FDA History Office, "History of the FDA," www.fda.gov/AboutFDA/History/FOrgsHistory/EvolvingPowers/ucm124403.htm (accessed 7/6/18).

5. For details, see Cornelius Kerwin, *Rulemaking: How Government Agencies Write Law and Make Policy* (Washington, DC: CQ Press, 1999).

6. Andrew Pollack, "New Sense of Caution at FDA," *New York Times*, September 29, 2006, www.nytimes.com/2006/09/29/business/29caution.html?_r=0 (accessed 8/29/16).

7. There are two exceptions. A patient can enroll in a clinical trial for a new drug during the approval process, but there is a good chance that the patient will get a placebo or a previously approved treatment rather than the drug being tested. The FDA does allow companies to provide some experimental drugs to patients who cannot participate in a trial, but only those drugs that have passed early screening trials.

8. Susan Okie, "Access before Approval—a Right to Take Experimental Drugs?," *New England Journal of Medicine* 355 (2004): 437-40.

9. Stephen Skowronek, *Building a New American State: The Expansion of National Administrative Capacities, 1877-1920* (New York: Cambridge University Press, 1982).

10. Terry Moe, "An Assessment of the Positive Theory of Congressional Dominance," *Legislative Studies Quarterly* 4 (1987): 475-98.

11. Karen Orren and Steven Skowronek, "Regimes and Regime Building in American Government: A Review of the Literature on the 1940s," *Political Science Quarterly* 113 (1998): 689-702.

12. Michael Nelson, "A Short, Ironic History of American National Bureaucracy," *Journal of Politics* 44 (1982): 747-78.

13. Nelson, "A Short, Ironic History of American National Bureaucracy."

14. Nelson, "A Short, Ironic History of American National Bureaucracy."

15. John Aldrich, *Why Parties?* (Chicago: University of Chicago Press, 1995).

16. Nelson, "A Short, Ironic History of American National Bureaucracy."

17. Matthew A. Crenson, *The Federal Machine: Beginnings of Bureaucracy in Jacksonian America* (Baltimore, MD: Johns Hopkins University Press, 1975).

18. James Q. Wilson, "The Rise of the Bureaucratic State," in *The American Commonwealth*, ed. Nathan Glazer and Irving Kristol (New York: Basic Books, 1976).

19. Skowronek, *Building a New American State*.

20. Robert Harrison, *Congress, Progressive Reform, and the New American State* (New York: Cambridge University Press, 2004).

21. The National Archives and Records Administration has an excellent summary of the Pendleton Act at www.ourdocuments.gov/doc.php?flash=false&doc=48 (accessed 7/6/18).

22. Lawrence C. Dodd and Richard L. Schott, *Congress and the Administrative State* (New York: Wiley, 1979).

23. Ira Katznelson and Bruce Pietrykowski, "Rebuilding the American State: Evidence from the 1940s," *Studies in American Political Development* 5:2 (1991): 301-39.

24. David Plotke, *Building a Democratic Political Order: Reshaping American Liberalism in the 1930s and 1940s* (New York: Cambridge University Press, 1996).

25. Theda Skocpol and Kenneth Finegold, "State Capacity and Economic Intervention in the Early New Deal," *Political Science Quarterly* 97 (1999): 255-70.

26. Michael Brown, "State Capacity and Political Choice: Interpreting the Failure of the Third New Deal," *Studies in American Political Development* 9 (1995): 187-212.

27. Ira Katznelson, Kim Geiger, and Daniel Kryder, "Limiting Liberalism: The Southern Veto in Congress, 1933-1950," *Political Science Quarterly* 108 (1993): 283-306.

28. Joseph Califano, "What Was Really Great about the Great Society," *Washington Monthly*, October 1999, www. washingtonmonthly.com/1999/10/01/what-was-really-great-about-the-great-society/ (accessed 7/16/08).

29. David T. Canon, *Race, Redistricting, and Representation: The Unintended Consequences of Black Majority Districts* (Chicago: University of Chicago Press, 1999).

30. Charles Murray, *Losing Ground: American Social Policy, 1950-1980* (New York: Basic Books, 1984).

31. Henry J. Aaron, *Politics and the Professors: The Great Society in Perspective* (Washington, DC: Brookings Institution Press, 1978).

32. Richard P. Nathan, *The Administrative Presidency* (New York: Wiley, 1983).

33. Andrew Rudalevige, "The Structure of Leadership: Presidents, Hierarchies, and Information Flow," *Presidential Studies Quarterly* 35 (2005): 333-60.

34. David E. Lewis, *Presidents and the Policy of Agency Design* (Palo Alto, CA: Stanford University Press, 2003).

35. Terry M. Moe, "An Assessment of the Positive Theory of Congressional Dominance," *Legislative Studies Quarterly* 4 (1987): 475-98.

36. William A. Niskanen, *Bureaucracy and Public Economics* (Washington, DC: Edward Elgar, 1976); Robert Whaples and Heckelman, "Public Choice Economics: Where Is There Consensus?," *American Economist* 49 (2005): 66-78.

37. Alan Schick and Felix LoStracco, *The Federal Budget: Politics, Process, Policy* (Washington, DC: Brookings Institution Press, 2000).

38. Joel D. Aberbach, "The Political Significance of the George W. Bush Administration," *Social Policy and Administration* 39:2 (2005): 130-49.

39. David E. Lewis, "The Politics of Agency Termination: Confronting the Myth of Agency Immortality," *Journal of Politics* 64 (2002): 89-107.

40. Ronald A. Wirtz, "Put It on My ... Er, His Tab: Opinion Polls Show a Big Gap between the Public's Desire for Services and Its Willingness to Pay for These Services," *Fedgazette*, January 2004, www.minneapolisfed.org/publications/fedgazette/put-it-on-my-er-his-tab (accessed 6/25/18).

41. Pew Research Center, "Little Public Support for Reductions in Federal Spending," April 11, 2019, www.people-press. org/2019/04/11/little-public-support-for-reductions-in-federal-spending/ (accessed 5/22/20).

42. James L. Perry and Annie Hondeghem, *Motivation in Public Management: The Call of Public Service* (Oxford, UK: Oxford University Press, 2008).

43. Paul Light, *A Government Well-Executed: Public Service and Public Performance* (Washington, DC: Brookings Institution Press, 2003).

44. This discussion of the details of the civil service system is based on U.S. Office of Personnel Management General Schedule, www.opm.gov/policy-data-oversight/pay-leave/salaries-wages/2017/general-schedule/ (accessed 7/6/18).

45. Dennis Cauchon, "Some Federal Workers More Likely to Die Than Lose Jobs," *USA Today*, July 19, 2011, p. A1.

46. Ronald N. Johnson and Gary D. Liebcap, *The Federal Civil Service System and the Problem of Bureaucracy* (Chicago: University of Chicago Press, 1993).

47. For details on the SES, see www.opm.gov/policy-data-oversight/senior-executive-service/ (accessed 5/7/18).

48. For the details of the Hatch Act, see Daniel Engber, "Can Karl Rove Plot Campaign Strategy on the Government's Dime?," *Slate*, April 21, 2006, www.slate.com/id/2140418 (accessed 8/29/16).

49. Todd Frankel, "Why the CDC Still Isn't Researching Gun Violence, despite the Ban Being Lifted Two Years Ago," *Washington Post*, January 14, 2015, www.washingtonpost. com/news/storyline/wp/2015/01/14/why-the-cdc-still-isnt-researching-gun-violence-despite-the-ban-being-lifted-two-years-ago/ (accessed 6/5/20).

50. John D. Huber and Charles R. Shipan, *Deliberate Discretion? The Institutional Foundations of Bureaucratic Autonomy* (New York: Cambridge University Press, 2002).

51. David Epstein and Sharyn O'Halloran, *Delegating Powers: A Transaction Cost Politics Approach to Policy Making under Separate Powers* (New York: Cambridge University Press, 1999).

52. Barry R. Weingast, "Caught in the Middle: The President, Congress, and the Political–Bureaucratic System," in *Institutions of American Democracy: The Executive Branch*, ed. Joel D. Aberbach and Mark A. Peterson (New York: Oxford University Press, 2006).

53. Keith Whittington and Daniel P. Carpenter, "Executive Power in American Institutional Development," *Perspectives on Politics* 1 (2003): 495–513.

54. Roger Noll, Mathew McCubbins, and Barry Weingast, "Administrative Procedures as Instruments of Political Control," *Journal of Law, Economics, and Organization* 3 (1987): 243–77.

55. Hannah Knowles, "Top Democrats Launch Investigation into Late-Night Firing of State Department Inspector General," *Washington Post*, March 16, 2020, www.washingtonpost.com/politics/2020/05/16/state-department-inspector-general-fired-democrats-decry-dangerous-pattern-retaliation/ (accessed 6/5/20).

56. Mathew McCubbins and Thomas Schwartz, "Congressional Oversight Overlooked: Fire Alarms vs. Police Patrols," *American Journal of Political Science* 28 (1984): 165–79.

57. McCubbins and Schwartz, "Congressional Oversight Overlooked."

58. Steven J. Balla and John R. Wright, "Interest Groups, Advisory Committees, and Congressional Control of the Bureaucracy," *American Journal of Political Science* 45 (2001): 799–812.

59. Daniel P. Carpenter, "The Gatekeeper: Organizational Reputation and Pharmaceutical Regulation at the FDA" (unpublished paper, Harvard University, 2006).

60. Terry M. Moe, "Political Control and the Power of the Agent," *Journal of Law, Economics, and Organization* 22 (2006): 1–29.

61. See David Weil, "OSHA: Beyond the Politics," *Frontline*, January 9, 2003, www.pbs.org/wgbh/pages/frontline/shows/workplace/osha/weil.html (accessed 8/29/16).

Chapter 13

1. Donald J. Trump, Twitter, July 13, 2016, 12:54 A.M., https://twitter.com/realDonaldTrump/status/753090242203283457 (accessed 7/10/20).

2. Joan Biskupic, "Justice Ruth Bader Ginsburg Calls Trump a 'Faker,' He Says She Should Resign," July 13, 2016, CNN Politics, www.cnn.com/2016/07/12/politics/justice-ruth-bader-ginsburg-donald-trump-faker/index.html (accessed 3/13/18).

3. Adam Liptak, "Ruth Bader Ginsburg, No Fan of Donald Trump, Critiques Latest Term," *New York Times*, July 11, 2016, www.nytimes.com/2016/07/11/us/politics/ruth-bader-ginsburg-no-fan-of-donald-trump-critiques-latest-term.html (accessed 7/10/20).

4. Editorial Board, "Justice Ginsburg's Inappropriate Comments on Donald Trump," *Washington Post*, July 12, 2016, www.washingtonpost.com/opinions/justice-ginsburgs-inappropriate-comments-on-donald-trump/2016/07/12/981df404-4862-11e6-bdb9-701687974517_story.html?utm_term=.fed5635b0e1a (accessed 3/13/18).

5. Editorial Board, "Donald Trump Is Right about Justice Ruth Bader Ginsburg," *New York Times*, July 13, 2016, www.nytimes.com/2016/07/13/opinion/donald-trump-is-right-about-justice-ruth-bader-ginsburg.html (accessed 3/13/18).

6. Eliza Collins, "Ginsburg on Trump Comments: 'I Regret Making Them,'" *USA Today*, July 14, 2016, www.usatoday.com/story/news/politics/onpolitics/2016/07/14/ginsburg-apologizes-trump-comments/87074576/ (accessed 3/12/18).

7. Debra Cassens Weiss, "Chief Justice Roberts Defends Judicial Independence after Trump's 'Obama Judge' Criticism," *ABA Journal*, November 21, 2018, www.abajournal.com/news/article/chief_justice_roberts_criticizes_trumps_reference_to_obama_judge_in_asylum (accessed 6/15/20).

8. SCOTUSblog, Final Stat Pack for October Term 2019, July 20, 2020, www.scotusblog.com/wp-content/uploads/2020/07/Final-Statpack-7.20.2020.pdf (accessed 11/9/20).

9. Ralph Ketcham, *The Anti-Federalist Papers and the Constitutional Convention Debates* (New York: Penguin Putnam, 2003), p. 304.

10. Lester S. Jayson, ed., *The Constitution of the United States of America: Analysis and Interpretation* (Washington, DC: U.S. Government Printing Office, 1973), p. 585.

11. David D. Savage, *Guide to the U.S. Supreme Court*, 4th ed. (Washington, DC: CQ Press, 2004), pp. 5–7.

12. Winfield H. Rose, "*Marbury v. Madison*: How John Marshall Changed History by Misquoting the Constitution," *Political Science and Politics* 36:2 (April 2003): 209–14. Rose argues that in a key quotation in the case Marshall intentionally left out a clause of the Constitution that suggests that Congress did have the power to expand the original jurisdiction of the Court. Other constitutional scholars reject this argument.

13. *Marbury v. Madison*, 5 U.S. 1 Cranch 137 (1803).

14. Revisionist historians, legal scholars, and political scientists have challenged the landmark status of *Marbury v. Madison*. For example, Michael Stokes Paulsen's *Michigan Law Review* article points out that *Marbury* was not cited in subsequent Supreme Court cases as a precedent for judicial review until the late nineteenth century. Legal scholars in the early twentieth century were the first to promote the idea that *Marbury* was a landmark decision. Paulsen also notes that when the opinion was delivered in 1803 it was not controversial. Even the Jeffersonian Democrats, who were at odds with Marshall's Federalists, thought that it was a reasonable decision and not the institutional power grab that modern accounts describe. Finally, Marshall made a very narrow case for judicial review, arguing that the Supreme Court could declare legislation that was contrary to the Court's interpretation of the Constitution null and void only if it concerned judicial powers. Revisionists argue that what appear to be broad claims of judicial power in *Marbury* (e.g., the Court has the power "to say what the law is") are taken out of the context of a much more narrow claim of power. Michael Stokes Paulsen, "Judging Judicial Review: *Marbury* in the Modern Era: The Irrepressible Myth of *Marbury*," *Michigan Law Review* 101 (August 2003): 2706–43.

15. Bureau of Justice Statistics, "Criminal Cases," www.bjs.gov/index.cfm?ty=tp&tid=23 (accessed 3/20/20).

16. *Wal-Mart v. Dukes*, 564 U.S. (2011). However, in 2011 the Court struck down any class-action claim unless there was "convincing proof of a companywide discriminatory pay and promotion policy"—statistical evidence of pay disparities would not suffice. David Savage, "Supreme Court Blocks Huge Class-Action Suit against Wal-Mart," *Los Angeles Times*, June 21, 2011, http://articles.latimes.com/2011/jun/21/nation/la-na-court-walmart-20110621 (accessed 3/20/20).

17. *Franchise Tax Board of California v. Hyatt*, 587 U.S. ____ (2019). For a discussion of the implications of this case, see Henry Gass, "Overruled: Is Precedent in Danger at the Supreme Court?," *Christian Science Monitor*, June 25, 2019, www.csmonitor.com/USA/Justice/2019/0625/Overruled-Is-precedent-in-danger-at-the-Supreme-Court (accessed 6/15/20).

18. *Lujan v. Defenders of Wildlife*, 504 U.S. 555 (1992).

19. United States Courts, "Authorized Judgeships," www.uscourts. gov/judges-judgeships/authorized-judgeships (accessed 3/20/20).

20. The official name for each appeals court is the "United States Court of Appeals for the Circuit."

21. *Ledbetter v. Goodyear Tire & Rubber Co.*, 550 U.S. 618 (2007).

22. Allyson Escobar, "Why Do Catholics Make Up a Majority of the Supreme Court?," *America Magazine*, October 27, 2020, www. americamagazine.org/politics-society/2018/07/18/why-do-catholics-make-majority-supreme-court (accessed 11/10/20).

23. "President Bush Discusses Judicial Accomplishments and Philosophy," Cincinnati, Ohio, October 6, 2008, https://georgewbush-whitehouse.archives.gov/news/releases/2008/10/20081006-5.html (accessed 3/20/20).

24. Paul Kane, "Reid, Democrats Trigger 'Nuclear' Option; Eliminate Most Filibusters on Nominees," *Washington Post*, November 21, 2013, www.washingtonpost.com/politics/senate-poised-to-limit-filibusters-in-party-line-vote-that-would-alter-centuries-of-precedent/2013/11/21/d065cfe8-52b6-11e3-9fe0-fd2ca728e67c_story.html (accessed 5/2/14).

25. John Roberts, "2019 Year-End Report on the Federal Judiciary," U.S. Supreme Court, December 31, 2019, www.supremecourt. gov/publicinfo/year-end/2019year-endreport.pdf (accessed 6/16/20).

26. Roberts, "2019 Year-End Report on the Federal Judiciary."

27. *New Jersey v. New York*, No. 120 Orig., 118 S.Ct. 1726 (1998), and *Texas v. New Mexico*, 138 S.Ct. 954 (2018).

28. Henry J. Abraham, *The Judiciary: The Supreme Court in the Governmental Process*, 7th ed. (Boston: Allyn and Bacon, 1987), p. 25, says that original jurisdiction has been invoked "about 150 times." A Lexis search revealed an additional 27 original-jurisdiction cases between 1987 and December 2004. A search of the U.S. Supreme Court's website, www.supremecourt.gov, found 14 more original jurisdiction cases from 2005 to 2020.

29. Savage, *Guide to the U.S. Supreme Court*, p. 848.

30. See Thomas G. Walker and Lee Epstein, *The Supreme Court of the United States: An Introduction* (New York: St. Martin's Press, 1993), pp. 80–85, for a more detailed discussion of these concepts and citations to the relevant court cases.

31. *Shaw v. Reno*, 509 U.S. 630 (1993).

32. *Elk Grove Unified School District v. Newdow*, 542 U.S. 1 (2004).

33. Gregory A. Caldeira and John R. Wright, "The Discuss List: Agenda Building in the Supreme Court," *Law and Society Review* 24 (1990): 813; Benjamin Johnson, "The Supreme Court's Political Docket: How Ideology and the Chief Justice Control the Court's Agenda and Shape Law," *Connecticut Law Review* 50:3 (August 2018): 581–639.

34. Walker and Epstein, *Supreme Court*, p. 89; Ryan C. Black and Ryan J. Owens, *The Solicitor General and the United States Supreme Court: Executive Branch Influence and Judicial Decisions* (New York: Cambridge University Press, 2012).

35. U.S. Supreme Court, "The Court and Its Procedures," www. supremecourt.gov/about/procedures.aspx (accessed 3/21/20).

36. Lee Epstein et al., *The Supreme Court Compendium: Data, Decisions, and Developments*, 6th ed. (Washington, DC: CQ Press, 2015), Table 7-22.

37. Gregory A. Caldeira and John R. Wright, "*Amicus Curiae* before the Supreme Court: Who Participates, When, and How Much?," *Journal of Politics* 52 (August 1990): 803.

38. Richard L. Pacelle Jr., John M. Scheb II, Hemant K. Sharma, and David H. Scott, "The Influence of the Solicitor General as Amicus Curiae on the Roberts Court, 2005-2014: A Research Note," *Justice System Journal* 38:2 (2017): 202–8.

39. Andrew Christy, "'Obamacare' Will Rank among the Longest Supreme Court Arguments Ever," National Public Radio, November 15, 2011, www.npr.org/blogs/itsallpolitics/2011/11/15/142363047/obamacare-will-rank-among-the-longest-supreme-court-arguments-ever (accessed 3/21/20).

40. U.S. Supreme Court, *Rules of the Supreme Court of the United States*, adopted April 8, 2019, effective July 1, 2019, www. supremecourt.gov/ctrules/2019RulesoftheCourt.pdf (accessed 3/21/20).

41. Garrett Epps, "Clarence Thomas Breaks His Silence," *The Atlantic*, February 29, 2016, www.theatlantic.com/politics/archive/2016/02/clarence-thomas-supreme-court/471582/ (accessed 5/27/16).

42. Michael A. McCall and Madhavi M. McCall, "Quantifying the Contours of Power: Chief Justice Roberts & Justice Kennedy in Criminal Justice Cases," *Pace Law Review* 37:1 (2016): 115–74.

43. *Smith v. Allwright*, 321 U.S. 649 (1944).

44. Walker and Epstein, *Supreme Court*, p. 110.

45. Lee Epstein, William M. Landes, and Richard A. Posner, "Are Even Unanimous Decisions in the United States Supreme Court Ideological?," *Northwestern University Law Review* 106:2 (2012): 702.

46. SCOTUSblog, Final Stat Pack for October Term 2019.

47. In cases involving statutory interpretation, the language of the law passed by Congress would be the starting point. The logic of these various perspectives on constitutional interpretation generally applies to statutory interpretation as well.

48. Lee Epstein and Thomas G. Walker, *Constitutional Law for a Changing America: Institutional Powers and Constraints*, 5th ed. (Washington, DC: CQ Press, 2004), p. 31.

49. Forrest Maltzman and Paul J. Wahlbeck, "Strategic Policy Considerations and Vote Fluidity on the Burger Court," *American Journal of Political Science* 90 (1996): 581–92; Maltzman, Spriggs, and Wahlbeck, *Crafting Law on the Supreme Court: The Collegial Game* (New York: Cambridge University Press, 2000), p. 33.

50. Thomas M. Keck, *The Most Activist Supreme Court in History: The Road to Modern Judicial Conservatism* (Chicago: University of Chicago Press, 2004).

51. Robert Dahl, "Decision-Making in a Democracy: The Supreme Court as a National Policy-Maker," *Journal of Public Law* 6 (1957): 279–95, is the classic work on this topic. More recent work has challenged Dahl's methods but largely supports the idea that the Court follows the will of the majority.

52. Jeffrey A. Segal, Richard J. Timpone, and Robert M. Howard, "Buyer Beware? Presidential Success through Supreme Court Appointments," *Political Research Quarterly* 53:3 (September 2000): 557–73; Gregory A. Caldeira and Charles E. Smith Jr., "Campaigning for the Supreme Court: The Dynamics of Public Opinion on the Thomas Nomination," *Political Research Quarterly* 58:3 (August 1996): 655–81.

53. William Mishler and Reginald S. Sheehan, "The Supreme Court as a Countermajoritarian Institution? The Impact of Public Opinion on Supreme Court Decisions," *American Political Science Review* 87:1 (March 1993): 87–101.

54. David O'Brien, *Storm Center: The Supreme Court in American Politics*, 4th ed. (New York: W. W. Norton, 1996), p. 276.

55. Helmut Norpoth and Jeffrey A. Segal, "Popular Influence in Supreme Court Decisions," *American Political Science Review* 88 (1994): 711–16.

56. While it is clear that the Supreme Court is at least somewhat sensitive to public opinion, the reverse does not appear to be true. A survey experiment had half the respondents read Chief Justice Roberts's admonition to President Trump about how there were not "Obama judges and Trump judges" and the other half did not see that statement. Both were shown a story about a federal court's decision on a political asylum case that President Trump was unhappy about to see if the respondents who read Roberts's statement would respond any differently than those who did not. There were absolutely no differences. However, another study by the same authors found that those who saw a speech by Justice Sotomayor were more likely than those who did not see the speech to think that law rather than ideology determined court decisions. See David Fontana and Christopher Krewson, "Can the Supreme Court Learn to Speak Up for Itself?," *Washington Post*, February 26, 2020, washingtonpost.com/magazine/2020/02/26/can-supreme-court-learn-speak-up-itself/?arc404=true (accessed 6/17/20).

Take a Stand

a. Martin Kady II, "Justice Alito Mouths 'Not True,'" Politico, January 27, 2010, www.politico.com/blogs/politico-now/2010/01/justice-alito-mouths-not-true-0246088 (accessed 8/24/18).

b. Donald J. Trump, Twitter, June 28, 2020, 10:08 A.M., https://twitter.com/realDonaldTrump/status/1273633632742191106 (accessed 6/17/20).

Chapter 14

1. Mitch McConnell, Twitter, May 15, 2020, 3:04 P.M., https://twitter.com/senatemajldr/status/1261371804133646337 (accessed 7/14/20).

2. Quoted in Erica Werner, Jeff Stein, and Rachael Blade, "McConnell Calls for Five-Year Lawsuit Shield for Businesses as Part of Next Coronavirus Bill," *Washington Post*, July 6, 2020, www.washingtonpost.com/us-policy/2020/07/06/congress-departed-two-week-recess-without-addressing-coronavirus-spikes-economic-strains/ (accessed 7/14/20).

3. Department of Labor, "Unemployment Insurance Weekly Claims," July 9, 2020, www.dol.gov/ui/data.pdf (accessed 7/10/20).

4. Kelsey Snell, "What's Inside the Senate's $2 Trillion Coronavirus Aid Package," National Public Radio, March 26, 2020, www.npr.org/2020/03/26/821457551/whats-inside-the-senate-s-2-trillion-coronavirus-aid-package (accessed 7/10/20).

5. Jeffrey Cheng, Dave Skidmore, and David Wessel, "What's the Fed Doing in Response to the COVID-19 Crisis? What More Could It Do?," Brookings Institution, June 12, 2020, www.brookings.edu/research/fed-response-to-covid19/ (accessed 7/10/20).

6. See William T. Bianco, *Trust: Representatives and Constituents* (Ann Arbor: University of Michigan Press, 1994), Chapter 6, for a discussion of the repeal of the Catastrophic Coverage Act.

7. James Q. Wilson, *Bureaucracy: What Government Agencies Do and Why They Do It* (New York: Basic Books, 1989).

8. The classic work on the appropriations process in the pre-reform era is Richard F. Fenno's *The Power of the Purse: Appropriations Politics in Congress* (Boston: Little, Brown, 1966). D. Roderick Kiewiet and Mathew D. McCubbins reexamined the appropriations process in the post-reform era and found that the Appropriations Committees have maintained much of their power; see *The Logic of Delegation: Congressional Parties and the Appropriations Process* (Chicago: University of Chicago Press, 1991).

9. The size of the tax cut was initially estimated at $1.5 trillion over 10 years by the nonpartisan Joint Committee on Taxation. A few months later, the Office of Management and Budget estimated the tax cut at $2.3 trillion, and then in April, the Congressional Budget Office estimated the 10-year cost at $1.9 trillion (www.cbo.gov/publication/53787). For a discussion of the tax cuts' short-term economic impact, see Indradip Ghosh and Shrutee Sarkar, "Tax Cuts to Boost U.S. Economy, but Benefits to Be Short-Lived: Reuters Poll," Reuters Business News, January 22, 2018, www.reuters.com/article/us-economy-usa-poll/tax-cuts-to-boost-u-s-economy-but-benefits-to-be-short-lived-reuters-poll-idUSKBN1FC0FX (both accessed 8/3/20).

10. See Charles M. Cameron, *Veto Bargaining: Presidents and the Politics of Negative Power* (New York: Cambridge University Press, 2000), for a general discussion of the strategic elements of issuing veto threats.

11. Joe Soss, *Unwanted Claims: The Politics of Participation in the U.S. Welfare System* (Ann Arbor: University of Michigan Press, 2000).

12. Greg Jaffe and Ed O'Keefe, "Obama Accepts Resignation of VA Secretary Shinseki," *Washington Post*, May 30, 2014, www.washingtonpost.com/politics/shinseki-apologizes-for-va-health-care-scandal/2014/05/30/e605885a-e7f0-11e3-8f90-73e071f3d637_story.html (accessed 8/3/20).

13. Daniel P. Carpenter, *The Forging of Bureaucratic Autonomy: Reputations, Networks, and Policy Innovation in Executive Agencies, 1862-1928* (Princeton, NJ: Princeton University Press, 2001).

14. U.S. Department of the Treasury, Resource Center, www.treasury.gov/resource-center/faqs/Currency/Pages/edu_faq_currency_production.aspx; United States Mint, *2019 Annual Report*, January 2020, www.usmint.gov/wordpress/wp-content/uploads/2020/01/2019-Annual-Report.pdf (both accessed 7/8/20).

15. Matthew Gualt and Kevin Truong, "COVID-19 Is Causing a National Coin Shortage," Vice, July 7, 2020, www.vice.com/en_us/article/8895e4/covid-19-is-causing-a-national-coin-shortage (accessed 7/8/20).

16. Michael Stratford, "Budget Fleshes Out Trump Higher Ed Agenda," Politico, February 13, 2018, www.politico.com/newsletters/morning-education/2018/02/13/budget-fleshes-out-trump-higher-ed-agenda-103874 (accessed 8/3/20).

17. Opening Up America Again, www.whitehouse.gov/openingamerica/ (accessed 7/13/20).

18. Jennifer Selin, "Trump versus the States: What Federalism Means for the Coronavirus Response," The Conversation, April 17, 2020, https://theconversation.com/trump-versus-the-states-what-federalism-means-for-the-coronavirus-response-136361 (accessed 7/13/20).

19. For differences in state responses, see National Conference on State Legislatures, "State Action on Coronavirus (COVID-19)," July 13, 2020, www.ncsl.org/research/health/state-action-on-coronavirus-covid-19.aspx. For data on infection rates and death rates across the states, see Joe Fox et al., "At Least 132,000 People Have Died from Coronavirus in the U.S.," *Washington Post*, July 13, 2020, www.washingtonpost.com/graphics/2020/national/coronavirus-us-cases-deaths/?itid=hp_hp-top-table-main_gfx-virus-tracker%3Ahomepage%2Fstory-ans (both accessed 7/13/20).

20. The stages model was first presented in James E. Anderson, *Public Policy Making* (New York: Praeger, 1974). Also see Thomas R. Dye, *Understanding Public Policy*, 15th ed. (New York: Pearson, 2017).

21. John Kingdon, *Agendas, Alternatives, and Public Policy* (Boston: Little, Brown, 1984).

22. Frank R. Baumgartner and Bryan D. Jones, *Agendas and Instability in American Politics*, 2nd ed. (Chicago: University of Chicago Press, 2009); Nikolaos Zahariadis, "The Shield of Heracles: Multiple Streams and the Emotional Endowment Effect," *European Journal of Political Research* 54:3 (August 2015): 466–81.

23. Graeme Boushey, *Policy Diffusion Dynamics in America* (New York: Cambridge University Press, 2010). See U.S. Department of Justice, "AMBER Alert: America's Missing: Broadcast Emergency Response," https://amberalert.ojp. gov/#:~:text=Today%2C%20the%20AMBER%20Alert%20 system,through%20the%20AMBER%20Alert%20system (accessed 7/1/20).

24. Charles R. Shipan and Craig Volden, "The Mechanisms of Policy Diffusion," *American Journal of Political Science* 52:4 (October 2008): 840–57.

25. The classic article on deflation is Irving Fisher, "The Debt-Deflation Theory of Great Depressions," *Econometrica*, 1933, https://fraser.stlouisfed.org/docs/meltzer/fisdeb33.pdf (accessed 8/3/20). For articles on recent policies concerning deflation, see www.nytimes.com/topic/subject/deflation-economics (accessed 8/3/20).

26. Congressional Budget Office, *The Budget and Economic Outlook: 2018 to 2028*, April 2018, Table, 4-1, p. 81, www.cbo. gov/system/files/2019-04/53651-outlook-2.pdf (accessed 8/3/20).

27. Dylan Matthews, "Modern Monetary Theory, Explained: A Very Detailed Walkthrough of the Big New Left Economic Idea," Vox, April 16, 2019, www.vox.com/future-perfect/2019/4/16/18251646/modern-monetary-theory-new-moment-explained (accessed 7/10/20).

28. John Maynard Keynes, *The General Theory of Employment, Interest and Money* (1936; repr., New York: Macmillan, 2007).

29. These figures come from the Congressional Budget Office, "Historical Budget Data," www.cbo.gov (accessed 8/3/20). Tax revenue fell from 19.6 percent of GDP in 1981, the last year before the tax cuts went into effect, to 18.1 percent of GDP in 1988, the last year of the Reagan presidency. Individual income tax revenue fell from 9.3 percent to 8 percent of GDP over the same period, so most of the decrease in revenue was due to lower individual income taxes. While overall government spending did increase during the 1982–1983 recession, spending from the beginning of Reagan's term to the end dropped slightly, from 22.2 percent to 21.2 percent of GDP.

30. William G. Gale, "Did the 2017 tax cut—the Tax Cuts and Jobs Act—pay for itself?," Policy 2020 Brookings, February 14, 2020, www.brookings.edu/policy2020/votervital/did-the-2017-tax-cut-the-tax-cuts-and-jobs-act-pay-for-itself/ (accessed 7/8/20).

31. Congressional Budget Office, "Monthly Budget Review for June 2020," July 8, 2020, www.cbo.gov/publication/56458; Congressional Budget Office, "Discretionary Spending in 2019: An Infographic" April 15, 2020, www.cbo.gov/ publication/56326 (both accessed 7/9/20).

32. The payroll tax figure comes from Congressional Budget Office, "The Distribution of Household Income and Federal Taxes, 2010," December 2013, Table 3, p. 13, http://cbo.gov/sites/ default/files/cbofiles/attachments/44604-AverageTaxRates. pdf, and the income tax figure comes from Congressional Budget Office, "Projected Changes in the Distribution of Household Income, 2016 to 2021," December 2019, Table B-3, p. 33, www.cbo.gov/system/files/2019-12/55941-CBO-Household-Income.pdf (both accessed 7/9/20).

33. Robert McClelland and Nikhita Airi, "Effective Income Tax Rates Have Fallen for the Top One Percent Since World War II," Tax Policy Center, January 6, 2020, www.taxpolicycenter. org/taxvox/effective-income-tax-rates-have-fallen-top-one-percent-world-war-ii (accessed 7/9/20).

34. Federal Reserve, "The Structure and Functions of the Federal Reserve System," Federal Reserve Education.org, www. federalreserveeducation.org/about-the-fed/structure-and-functions (accessed 7/9/20).

35. Milton Friedman, "The Quantity Theory of Money: A Restatement," in *The Optimum Quantity of Money and Other Essays* (Chicago: Aldine, 1969), p. 52.

36. In reality, until the recent move to set the reserve requirement at zero, the Fed always had at least two different reserve requirements depending on the size of the bank, ranging from 3 percent to 26 percent at various points in our history. See Board of Governors of the Federal Reserve System, "Reserve Requirement," www.federalreserve.gov/monetarypolicy/ reservereq.htm; and Joshua N. Feinman, "Reserve Requirements: History, Current Practice, and Potential Reform," *Federal Reserve Bulletin* (June, 1993): 569–89, www. federalreserve.gov/monetarypolicy/0693lead.pdf (both accessed 7/9/20).

37. Bob Haber, "The Fed Fires 'the Big One,'" *Forbes*, March 16, 2020, www.forbes.com/sites/bobhaber/2020/03/16/the-fed-fires-the-big-one/#328525836aa8 (accessed 7/9/20).

38. In December 2002, the discount rate was effectively discontinued as an active policy tool and was pegged to 1 percent above the targeted FFR (which means that the "discount rate" is oddly named—it really should be called the premium rate). In the economic crisis of 2008–2009, the Fed temporarily dropped the difference between the FFR and the discount rate to 0.25 percent and then to 0.50 percent, where it remains today; see *Federal Reserve Bulletin*, December 2002, pp. 482–83. See also Federal Reserve, "Frequently Asked Questions—Discount Window Lending Programs," www.frbdiscountwindow.org/Archive/Frequently-Asked-Questions-Discount-Window-Lending-Programs (accessed 8/3/20).

39. William Greider, *Secrets of the Temple: How the Federal Reserve Runs the Country* (New York: Simon and Schuster, 1987), pp. 295–98.

40. Board of Governors of the Federal Reserve System, "Credit and Liquidity Programs and Balance Sheets," "Recent Balance Sheet Trends," www.federalreserve.gov/monetarypolicy/ bst_recenttrends.htm (accessed 7/9/20).

41. William McChesney Martin, who was appointed by Harry Truman, served through the presidencies of Eisenhower, Kennedy, and Johnson and part of Nixon's first term. Paul Volcker served under Carter and Reagan, while Alan Greenspan's tenure spanned the presidencies of Reagan, Bush, and Clinton and the second Bush. For a list of all Federal Reserve Board members, see Federal Reserve Board, "Board of Governors Members, 1914-Present," www.federalreserve.gov/ aboutthefed/bios/board/boardmembership.htm (accessed 8/3/20).

42. Edward R. Tufte, *Political Control of the Economy* (Princeton, NJ: Princeton University Press, 1978); Douglas Hibbs, "The Partisan Model of Macroeconomic Cycles: More Theory and Evidence for the United States," *Economics and Politics* 6 (1994): 1–23.

43. Jim Granato, "The Effect of Policy-Maker Reputation and Credibility on Public Expectations," *Journal of Theoretical Politics* 8 (1996): 449–70; Peter Conti-Brown, *The Power and Independence of the Federal Reserve* (Princeton, NJ: Princeton University Press, 2016).

44. Jeanna Smialek, "Trump Says He Could Demote Fed Chair Powell, Risking More Market Turmoil," *New York Times*, March 14, 2020, www.nytimes.com/2020/03/14/business/economy/trump-powell-fed-chair.html (accessed 7/9/20).

45. John B. Taylor, *Economics*, 4th ed. (New York: Houghton Mifflin, 2003), Chapter 10. Some economics textbooks also define regulation of externalities, such as pollution, as economic regulation.

46. Bill Chappell, "EU Fines Google $1.7 Billion over 'Abusive' Online Ad Strategies," National Public Radio," March 20, 2019, www.npr.org/2019/03/20/705106450/eu-fines-google-1-7-billion-over-abusive-online-ad-strategies#:~:text=The%20European%20Commission%20is%20hitting,working%20with%20companies%20that%20had (accessed 7/9/20).

47. American Recovery and Reinvestment Act of 2009 (Public Law 111–5), February 17, 2009, www.govinfo.gov/content/pkg/PLAW-111publ5/pdf/PLAW-111publ5.pdf (accessed 7/1/20).

48. U.S. Department of the Treasury, "TARP Tracker from November 2008 to March 2020," www.treasury.gov/initiatives/financial-stability/reports/Pages/TARP-Tracker.aspx#All (accessed 7/10/20).

49. The one area of loans that has not turned a profit yet is loans to the auto industry. See U.S. Department of the Treasury, "TARP Tracker from November 2008 to March 2020."

50. U.S. Department of the Treasury, "The CARES Act Works for All Americans," https://home.treasury.gov/policy-issues/cares (accessed 11/12/20).

51. Jane Ihrig, Gretchen Weinbach, and Scott Wolla, "How the Fed Has Responded to the COVID-19 Pandemic," Federal Reserve Bank of St. Louis, August 12, 2020, www.stlouisfed.org/open-vault/2020/august/fed-response-covid19-pandemic (accessed 11/12/20).

52. Jeanna Smialek, Emily Cochrane, and Jim Tankersley, "Trump Abruptly Ends Stimulus Talks After Fed Chair Urges Economic Support," *New York Times*, October 6, 2020, www.nytimes.com/2020/10/06/business/economy/jerome-powell-economic-recovery-coronavirus.html (accessed 11/12/20).

53. Theda Skocpol, *Social Policy in the United States: Future Possibilities in Historical Perspective* (Princeton, NJ: Princeton University Press, 1995), p. 37.

54. Skocpol, *Social Policy in the United States*, pp. 145–60.

55. David M. Kennedy, *Freedom from Fear: The American People in Depression and War, 1929-1945* (New York: Oxford University Press, 2001); Byron W. Daynes, William Pederson, and Michael P. Riccards, eds., *The New Deal and Public Policy* (New York: St. Martin's Press, 1998).

56. Robert Dallek, *Flawed Giant: Lyndon Johnson and His Times, 1961-1973* (New York: Oxford University Press, 1998); Irving Bernstein, *Guns or Butter: The Presidency of Lyndon Johnson* (New York: Oxford University Press, 1996).

57. U.S. Department of Health and Human Services, "HHS Poverty Guidelines for 2020," January 8, 2020, https://aspe.hhs.gov/poverty-guidelines (accessed 9/23/20).

58. Jessica Semega, Melissa Kollar, Emily A. Shrider, and John F. Creamer, "Income and Poverty in the United States: 2019," U.S. Census Bureau, September 15, 2020, Figure 8, p. 13, www.census.gov/library/publications/2020/demo/p60-270.html (accessed 11/12/20).

59. These figures include income from capital gains. Thomas Piketty and Emmanuel Saez, "Income Inequality in the United States, 1913–1998," *Quarterly Journal of Economics* 118:1 (2003): 1–39, with tables and figures updated to 2018, February 2020, https://eml.berkeley.edu/~saez/ (accessed 7/12/20); Samuel Stebbins and Evan Comen, "How Much Do You Need to Make to Be in the Top 1% in Every State? Here's the List," *USA Today*, July 1, 2020, www.usatoday.com/story/money/2020/07/01/how-much-you-need-to-make-to-be-in-the-1-in-every-state/112002276/ (accessed 10/9/20).

60. Federal Reserve Board, "Survey of Consumer Finances (SCF), 2019," September 28, 2020, www.federalreserve.gov/econres/scf/dataviz/scf/chart/ (accessed 10/9/20).

61. The housing expenditure figures are from U.S. Department of Housing and Urban Development, "Fiscal Year 2020, Budget in Brief," March 7, 2020, p. 8, www.hud.gov/sites/dfiles/CFO/documents/HUD2020BudgetinBrief03072019Final.pdf. The top 20 percent figure is from Ilya Somin, "Mortgage Interest Deduction Mostly Benefits the Rich—End It," *The Hill*, November 6, 2017, http://thehill.com/opinion/finance/358922-mortgage-interest-deduction-mostly-benefits-the-rich-end-it. Data on tax expenditures are from Joint Committee on Taxation, "Estimates of Federal Tax Expenditures for Fiscal Years 2018–2022," October 4, 2018, www.jct.gov/publications.html?id=5148&func=startdown (all accessed 7/12/20). Note that tax expenditures for housing are much lower as a result of recent changes in the tax law, because fewer people are itemizing due to the increase in the standard deduction and the cap on deducting state income taxes and local property taxes.

62. Dean Baker, *The Conservative Nanny State: How the Wealthy Use the Government to Stay Rich and Get Richer*, Center for Economic and Policy Research, May 2006, https://deanbaker.net/images/stories/documents/cnswebbook.pdf (accessed 8/3/20).

63. Doug Bandow, "Corporate Welfare Lives On and On," Cato Institute, August 29, 2018, www.cato.org/publications/commentary/corporate-welfare-lives (accessed 7/13/20).

64. Kathleen Romig, "Social Security Lifts More Americans above Poverty Than Any Other Program," Center on Budget and Policy Priorities, February 20, 2020, www.cbpp.org/research/social-security/social-security-lifts-more-americans-above-poverty-than-any-other-program (accessed 7/14/20).

65. Social Security Administration, *2020 OASDI Trustees Report*, April 22, 2020, Table V.A3, p. 95, www.ssa.gov/OACT/TR/2020/X2_trLOF.html (accessed 7/14/20).

66. Social Security Administration, *2020 OASDI Trustees Report*, Table II.B1, p. 7, and Summary, p.5.

67. For a detailed account of the fiscal impact of the various proposals, see Charles Pineles-Mark "Options for Social Security," Congressional Budget Office, March 8, 2017, www.cbo.gov/publication/52471 (accessed 8/3/20).

68. Organization for Economic Cooperation and Development, "OECD Health Statistics 2020," July 1, 2020, www.oecd.org/health/health-data.htm, (accessed 7/14/20).

69. Department of Health and Human Services, Centers for Medicare and Medicaid Services, "Brief Summaries of Medicare and Medicaid," www.cms.gov/Research-Statistics-Data-and-Systems/Statistics-Trends-and-Reports/MedicareProgramRatesStats/Downloads/MedicareMedicaidSummaries2017.pdf (accessed 8/3/20).

70. Department of Health and Human Services, *2018 Actuarial Report on the Financial Outlook for Medicaid*, April 9, 2020, Table 3, p. 14, www.cms.gov/files/document/2018-report.pdf (accessed 7/14/20).

71. *2020 Medicare Trustees Report*, April 22, 2020, Table V.F2, p. 202, www.cms.gov/files/document/2020-medicare-trustees-report.pdf (accessed 7/14/20).

72. Congressional Budget Office, "Cost Estimates for H.R. 4872, Reconciliation Act of 2010 (Final Health Care Legislation)," March 20, 2010, www.cbo.gov/doc.cfm?index=11355 (accessed 8/3/20).

73. Ezekiel J. Emanuel, "Name the Much-Criticized Federal Program That Has Saved the U.S. $2.3 Trillion. Hint: It Starts with Affordable," Stat, March 22, 2019, www.statnews.com/2019/03/22/affordable-care-act-controls-costs/ (accessed 7/20/20).

74. David Nather and Susan Levine, "A Brief History of Obamacare Delays," Politico, March 25, 2014, www.politico.com/story/2014/03/obamacare-affordable-care-act-105036.html#ixzz33QRP8biR (accessed 8/3/20).

75. Centers for Medicare and Medicaid Services, "2020 Federal Health Insurance Exchange Enrollment Period Final Weekly Enrollment Snapshot," January 8, 2020, www.cms.gov/newsroom/fact-sheets/2020-federal-health-insurance-exchange-enrollment-period-final-weekly-enrollment-snapshot (accessed 7/14/20).

76. Medicaid.gov, "Medicaid Enrollment Data Collected through MBES, April–June 2019 Medicaid MBES Enrollment Report," June 2020, https://data.medicaid.gov/Enrollment/2019-3Q-Medicaid-MBES-Enrollment/avy5-4pxa/data (accessed 7/31/20).

77. Joseph R. Antos and James C. Capretta, "The ACA: Trillions? Yes. A Revolution? No," Health Affairs Blog, April 10, 2020, www.healthaffairs.org/do/10.1377/hblog20200406.93812/full/ (accessed 7/14/20).

78. Eligibility information for SNAP may be found at U.S. Department of Agriculture Food and Nutrition Services, "SNAP Eligibility," August 14, 2019, www.fns.usda.gov/snap/recipient/eligibility (accessed 8/3/20).

79. U.S. Department of Labor, "Unemployment Insurance Data Summary, 1st Quarter 2018," http://workforcesecurity.doleta.gov/unemploy/content/data_stats/datasum18/DataSum_2018_1.pdf; Chad Stone, "CARES Act Measures Strengthening Unemployment Insurance Should Continue While Need Remains," Center on Budget and Policy Priorities, June 9, 2020, www.cbpp.org/research/federal-budget/cares-act-measures-strengthening-unemployment-insurance-should-continue (both accessed 7/14/20).

80. Internal Revenue Service, "Earned Income Tax Credit Income Limits and Maximum Credit Amounts," April 2, 2020, www.irs.gov/credits-deductions/individuals/earned-income-tax-credit/earned-income-tax-credit-income-limits-and-maximum-credit-amounts#:~:text=Investment%20income%20must%20be%20%243%2C650%20or%20less%20for%20the%20year.&text=The%20maximum%20amount%20of%20credit,%245%2C920%20with%20two%20qualifying%20children (accessed 7/14/20).

81. Internal Revenue Service, "EITC Fast Facts," January 16, 2020, www.eitc.irs.gov/partner-toolkit/basic-marketing-communication-materials/eitc-fast-facts/eitc-fast-facts (accessed 7/14/20).

82. R. Kent Weaver, Ending Welfare as We Know It (Washington, DC: Brookings Institution Press, 2000).

83. Ife Floyd, "Cash Assistance Should Reach Millions More Families," Center on Budget and Policy Priorities, March 4, 2020, www.cbpp.org/research/family-income-support/cash-assistance-should-reach-millions-more-families (accessed 7/14/20).

84. U.S. Department of Education, "Race to the Top Fund," www2.ed.gov/programs/racetothetop/index.html (accessed 8/3/20).

What Do the Facts Say?

a. Terry Jones, "National Debt: Will It Destroy America's Economy?," Investor's Business Daily, December 28, 2018, www.investors.com/politics/national-debt-economy-taxes/ (accessed 7/9/19).

b. Z. Byron Wolf, "Debt? What Debt? At $22 Trillion, Here's the Argument the National Debt Doesn't Matter," CNN, January 13, 2019, www.cnn.com/2019/01/13/politics/debt-spending-mmt/index.html (accessed 7/9/19).

c. Committee for a Responsible Federal Budget, "Why Should We Worry about the National Debt?," April 16, 2019, www.crfb.org/papers/why-should-we-worry-about-national-debt (accessed 7/9/19).

Take a Stand

a. The comment was in response to the takeover of a federal wildlife refuge in Oregon. Rubio called for the occupiers to lay down their arms but showed sympathy for their central demand that the federal government cede control over much of the Bureau of Land Management land. "Marco Rubio on Oregon Federal Land Business," Des Moines Register editorial board interview, January 6, 2016, www.desmoinesregister.com/videos/news/elections/presidential/caucus/2016/01/06/78384514/ (accessed 8/3/20).

b. John Tierney, "The Sagebrush Solution," New York Times, July 26, 2005, p. A19. Additional information was drawn from www.hcn.org (accessed 8/3/20).

c. A very detailed account of this saga may be found in Raymond B. Wrabley Jr., "Managing the Monument: Cows and Conservation in the Grand-Staircase-Escalante National Monument," Journal of Land, Resources and Environmental Law 29:2 (2009): 253–80.

Chapter 15

1. Madeleine Albright, Fascism: A Warning (New York: HarperCollins, 2018).

2. Donald J. Trump, "Remarks by President Trump on the Administration's National Security Strategy," December 18, 2017, www.whitehouse.gov/briefings-statements/remarks-president-trump-administrations-national-security-strategy/ (accessed 6/19/20).

3. Aris Folley, "Ian Bremmer: Trump Tossed Candy to Merkel at G-7, Said 'Don't Say I Never Give You Anything,'" June 20, 2018, https://thehill.com/blogs/blog-briefing-room/news/393311-ian-bremmer-trump-tossed-candy-to-merkel-during-g-7-said-dont (accessed 6/8/20).

4. For an example of the isolationist approach, see Patrick J. Buchanan, A Republic, Not an Empire, updated ed. (Washington, DC: Regnery, 2002).

5. Robert O. Keohane, After Hegemony: Cooperation and Discord in the International System (1984; repr., Princeton, NJ: Princeton University Press, 2005).

6. The distinction was first made in E. H. Carr, The Twenty Years' Crisis, 1919–1939: An Introduction to the Study of International Relations (London: Macmillan, 1939). Realism was elaborated as a general theory in Hans Morgenthau, Politics among Nations: The Struggle for Power and Peace (New York: Knopf, 1948). For a general overview, see Jonathan Haslam, No Virtue like Necessity: Realist Thought in International Relations since Machiavelli (New Haven, CT: Yale University Press, 2002).

7. A synoptic account of the United States as a world power, which takes the story up to the 2003 invasion of Iraq, is Niall Ferguson, Colossus: The Price of America's Empire (New York: Penguin Press, 2004).

8. Samuel Flagg Bemis, John Quincy Adams and the Foundations of American Foreign Policy (New York: Knopf, 1949); Ernest

R. May, *The Making of the Monroe Doctrine* (Cambridge, MA: Harvard University Press, 1975). The latter stresses domestic political considerations and argues that the Monroe Doctrine was "actually the by-product of an election campaign."

9. Daniel M. Smith, *The Great Departure: The United States and World War I, 1914–1920* (New York: Wiley, 1965).

10. Thomas J. Knock, *To End All Wars: Woodrow Wilson and the Quest for a New World Order* (New York: Oxford University Press, 1992).

11. Margaret MacMillan, *Paris 1919: Six Months That Changed the World* (New York: Random House, 2001).

12. John M. Cooper, *Breaking the Heart of the World: Woodrow Wilson and the Fight for the League of Nations* (New York: Cambridge University Press, 2001).

13. John Lewis Gaddis, *Strategies of Containment* (New York: Oxford University Press, 2005).

14. Tony Smith, "Making the World Safe for Democracy in the American Century," *Diplomatic History* 23:2 (1999): 173–88.

15. Winston Churchill, "Sinews of Peace (Iron Curtain)," Westminster College, Fulton, Missouri, March 5, 1946, International Churchill Society, https://winstonchurchill.org/resources/speeches/1946-1963-elder-statesman/the-sinews-of-peace/ (accessed 8/2/18). See also Klaus Larres, *Churchill's Cold War: The Politics of Personal Diplomacy* (New Haven, CT: Yale University Press, 2002).

16. George F. Kennan, "The Sources of Soviet Conduct," *Foreign Affairs* 25:4 (July 1947): 566–82.

17. Robert L. Beisner, *Dean Acheson: A Life in the Cold War* (New York: Oxford University Press, 2006); Dean Acheson, *Present at the Creation* (New York: W. W. Norton, 1969).

18. Michael J. Hogan, *The Marshall Plan: America, Britain, and the Reconstruction of Western Europe* (New York: Cambridge University Press, 1987). See also Martin Schain, ed., *The Marshall Plan: Fifty Years Later* (New York: Palgrave, 2001).

19. Marc Trachtenberg, *A Constructed Peace: The Making of the European Settlement, 1945–1963* (Princeton, NJ: Princeton University Press, 1999).

20. The balance of military power between NATO and the Warsaw Pact throughout the Cold War is traced in David Miller, *The Cold War: A Military History* (New York: St. Martin's Press, 1998).

21. Robert A. Packenham, *Liberal America and the Third World* (Princeton, NJ: Princeton University Press, 1973). For an overview, see David P. Forsythe, "Human Rights in U.S. Foreign Policy: Retrospect and Prospect," *Political Science Quarterly* 105:3 (Autumn 1990): 435–54.

22. Lawrence Freedman, *Kennedy's Wars: Berlin, Cuba, Laos, and Vietnam* (Oxford, UK: Oxford University Press, 2002).

23. William J. Duiker, *Sacred War: Nationalism and Revolution in a Divided Vietnam* (New York: McGraw-Hill, 1995).

24. Henry Kissinger, *Years of Upheaval* (Boston: Little, Brown, 1982); Jussi Hanhimäki, *The Flawed Architect: Henry Kissinger and American Foreign Policy* (New York: Oxford University Press, 2004).

25. Raymond Garthoff, *Détente and Confrontation: American–Soviet Relations from Nixon to Reagan* (Washington, DC: Brookings Institution Press, 1994).

26. Francis Fukuyama, *The End of History and the Last Man*, updated ed. (New York: Free Press, 2006).

27. For a summary of American human rights policy, see John W. Dietrich, "U.S. Human Rights Policy in the Post–Cold War Era," *Political Science Quarterly* 121:2 (Summer 2006): 269–94.

28. Joseph Nye, *Soft Power: The Means to Success in World Politics.* (New York: Hachette Book Group, 2009).

29. Samuel P. Huntington, *The Clash of Civilizations and the Remaking of World Order* (New York: Free Press, 2002).

30. Louis Fisher, *Presidential War Power* (Lawrence: University Press of Kansas, 2004).

31. John Mueller and Mark G. Stewart, *Chasing Ghosts: The Policing of Terrorism* (New York: Oxford University Press, 2015).

32. David Hoffman and David B. Ottaway, "Panel Drops Covert-Acts Notification; in Compromise, Bush Pledges to Inform Hill in All but Rare Cases," *Washington Post*, October 27, 1989, p. A1.

33. Dahlia Lithwick, "The Enemy Within," *Slate*, June 12, 2008, www.slate.com/id/2193468 (accessed 10/3/16).

34. Somini Sengupta, "As Musharraf's Woes Grow, Enter an Old Rival, Again," *New York Times*, April 6, 2007, p. A3; Leslie Wayne, "Airbus Seeks a Welcome in Alabama," *New York Times*, June 19, 2007, p. C1.

35. Pew Research Center, "U.S. Public Seldom Has Welcomed Refugees into Country," November 19, 2015, www.pewresearch.org/fact-tank/2015/11/19/u-s-public-seldom-has-welcomed-refugees-into-country/ (accessed 5/13/16).

36. A directory of NGOs can be found at the United Nations website, https://research.un.org/en/ngo (accessed 6/12/20).

37. See Amnesty International, "The Secretive and Illegal U.S. Programme of Rendition," April 5, 2006, www.amnesty.org/en/documents/amr51/056/2006/en/ (accessed 8/3/18).

38. United States International Trade Commission, Official Harmonized Tariff Schedule 2020, www.usitc.gov/tata/hts/index.htm (accessed 7/6/20).

39. William B. Quandt, *Camp David: Peacemaking and Politics* (Washington, DC: Brookings Institution Press, 1986).

40. U.S. Department of State, *Treaties in Force*, January 1, 2019, www.state.gov/treaties-in-force/ (accessed 7/6/20).

41. Lisa L. Martin, "The President and International Commitments: Treaties as Signaling Devices," *Presidential Studies Quarterly* 35:3 (2005): 440–65.

42. Johanna Neuman and Megan K. Stack, "Americans' Beirut Exodus Underway; Hundreds Are Evacuated by Ship and Helicopter," *Los Angeles Times*, July 20, 2006, p. A10. The Clinton administration resorted to cruise missile attacks five times: three against Iraq (1993, 1996, 1998), one in 1995 against Bosnian Serb forces in the former Yugoslavia, and one against targets in Afghanistan and Sudan in 1998. James Mann, "Foreign Policy of the Cruise Missile," *Los Angeles Times*, December 23, 1998, p. 5.

43. A comprehensive account of the Afghanistan invasion and its aftermath is in Barnett R. Rubin, "Saving Afghanistan," *Foreign Affairs* 86:1 (January/February 2007): 57–78.

44. For an optimistic review, see Joseph E. Stiglitz, *Making Globalization Work* (New York: W. W. Norton, 2007).

45. Angelica LaVito, "Starbucks Is Opening a Store in China Every 15 Hours," CNBC, December 5, 2017, www.cnbc.com/2017/12/05/starbucks-is-opening-a-store-in-china-every-15-hours.html (accessed 7/6/20).

46. U.S. Census Bureau, "Trade in Goods with China," www.census.gov/foreign-trade/balance/c5700.html (accessed 7/6/20).

47. Benjamin Applebaum, "Perils of Globalization When Factories Close and Towns Struggle," *New York Times*, May 17, 2015, p. A1.

48. Fred Kaplan, "North Korea's Nuclear Test Isn't as Dangerous as Kim Jong-un Wants Us to Believe," *Slate*, January 6, 2016, www.slate.com/articles/news_and_politics/politics/2016/01/north_korea_s_nuclear_test_isn_t_as_dangerous_as_kim_jong_un_wants_us_to.html (accessed 6/20/16).

Study Guide Answer Key

Chapter 1

1. C
2. B
3. C
4. D
5. D
6. C
7. A
8. E
9. A
10. E
11. C
12. B

Chapter 2

1. B
2. E
3. C
4. C
5. B
6. D
7. B
8. D
9. B
10. D
11. A
12. A
13. A
14. C
15. B

Chapter 3

1. C
2. B
3. B
4. C
5. C
6. B
7. B
8. B
9. A
10. D
11. B
12. D

Chapter 4

1. D
2. B
3. C
4. A
5. B
6. A
7. D
8. C
9. B
10. C
11. C
12. B
13. C

Chapter 5

1. A
2. C
3. B
4. E
5. E
6. B
7. C
8. E
9. A
10. B
11. C
12. C
13. D

Chapter 6

1. D
2. B
3. A
4. C
5. E
6. D
7. C
8. D
9. A
10. B
11. E
12. B
13. A

Chapter 7

1. A
2. E
3. B
4. E
5. A
6. A
7. E
8. C
9. C
10. A

Chapter 8

1. A
2. D
3. B
4. B
5. B
6. C
7. E
8. A
9. C
10. B
11. C
12. B
13. C

Chapter 9

1. E
2. A
3. C
4. B
5. E
6. C
7. A
8. B
9. D
10. A

Chapter 10

1. D
2. E
3. B
4. A
5. D
6. B
7. D
8. A
9. C
10. E
11. B
12. B

Study Guide Answer Key

Chapter 11

1. A
2. A
3. C
4. D
5. A
6. E
7. B
8. D
9. B
10. A
11. C

Chapter 12

1. C
2. A
3. D
4. E
5. B
6. C
7. A
8. A
9. D
10. C
11. A
12. E
13. A
14. B

Chapter 13

1. A
2. D
3. B
4. A
5. E
6. B
7. C
8. A
9. E
10. B
11. B
12. D
13. A
14. B

Chapter 14

1. A
2. C
3. E
4. C
5. D
6. A
7. B
8. B
9. E
10. E
11. A
12. E
13. B
14. A
15. B

Chapter 15

1. C
2. A
3. E
4. C
5. D
6. D
7. B
8. C
9. A
10. B
11. C
12. D
13. B
14. A

Credits

Line Art

Chapter 1, What Do the Facts Say? (p. 17): Map: "2020 Presidential Election, Purple America," by Robert J. Vanderbei, Princeton University, https://vanderbei.princeton.edu/JAVA/election2020/. Reprinted by permission of the author.

Figure 5.5 (p. 164): Map: Lifetime Wage Gap for Women Compared with Men, from National Women's Law Center, "The Lifetime Wage Gap, State by State," April 4, 2018. Reprinted by permission.

Figure 6.2 (p. 191): Graph from "The Iraq War continues to divide the U.S. public, 15 years after it began," Pew Research Center Fact Tank, Washington, D.C. (March 2018), https://www.pewresearch.org/fact-tank/2018/03/19/iraq-war-continues-to-divide-u-s-public-15-years-after-it-began/. Reprinted by permission.

Figure 6.5 (p. 204): Graph from "Economic Issues Decline Among Public's Policy Priorities," Pew Research Center, Washington, D.C. (January 2018), http://www.people-press.org/2018/01/25/economic-issues-decline-among-publics-policy-priorities/. Reprinted with permission.

Figure 7.4 (p. 231): Figure from "A Deep Dive Into Party Affiliation," Pew Research Center, Washington, D.C. (April 2015), http://www.people-press.org/2015/04/07/a-deep-dive-into-party-affiliation/. Reprinted with permission.

Figure 10.5 (p. 336): Graph: Liberal-conservative partisan polarization by chamber, from "Polarization in Congress," Jeffrey Lewis, Keith T. Poole, and Howard Rosenthal, March 11, 2018, voteview.com. Reprinted by permission.

Photographs

Front Matter

ii–iii: Morry Gash/AP/Shutterstock; **vi (top):** Paul B.; **vi (bottom):** Kolin Goldschmidt, University of Wisconsin-Madison; **ix (top):** Robert Alexander/Getty Images; **ix (bottom):** AP Photo/Evan Vucci; **x:** AP Photo/Andrew Harnik; **xi (top):** Noah Berger/REUTERS/Newscom; **xi (bottom):** Marilyn Humphries/Alamy Stock Photo; **xii (top):** David McNew/Getty Images; **xii (bottom):** SOPA Images Limited/Alamy Stock Photo; **xiii (top):** Jennifer Booher/Alamy Stock Photo; **xiii (bottom):** Storms Media Group/Alamy Stock Photo; **xiv (top):** UPI/Alamy Stock Photo; **xiv (bottom):** Hum Images/Alamy Stock Photo; **xv:** Jabin Botsford/The Washington Post via Getty Images; **xvi (top):** Brendan Smialowski/AFP via Getty Images; **xvi (bottom):** Michael Reynolds/EPA-EFE/Shutterstock; **xvii:** Jesco Denzel/German Federal Government via AP

Chapter 1

3: Robert Alexander/Getty Images; **5:** Mark Wilson/Getty Images; **8 (left):** US Army Photo/Alamy Stock Photo; **8 (right):** Melvyn Longhurst/Alamy Stock Photo; **10:** Allison Shelley/The Washington Post via Getty Images; **12:** Olivier Douliery/SIPA/Newscom; **13 (right):** Eva Marie Uzcategui T./Anadolu Agency/Getty Images; **15 (left):** Patrick Gorski/NurPhoto/Sipa USA/Newscom; **15 (center):** Williams Paul/Icon Sportswire via Getty Images; **15 (right):** Fox/Photofest; **18 (top):** AP Photo/Odessa American, Courtney Sacco;

18 (bottom): © Flip Schulke/CORBIS/Corbis via Getty Images; **20:** Chip Somodevilla/Getty Images; **23:** Xinhua/Alamy Stock Photo; **28:** Robert Alexander/Getty Images

Chapter 2

33: AP Photo/Evan Vucci; **35:** North Wind Picture Archives/Alamy Stock Photo; **39:** © North Wind Picture Archives—All rights reserved; **42:** Bettmann/Getty Images; **45:** Library of Virginia; **48:** Library of Congress/Corbis/VCG via Getty Images; **49:** Francis G. Mayer/Corbis/VCG via Getty Images; **51:** Mandel Ngan/AFP via Getty Images; **53 (top left):** Draper, Eric, 1964–, Photographer/National Archives; **53 (top center):** Spx Chrome/Getty Images; **53 (top right):** ZUMA Press, Inc./Alamy Stock Photo; **53 (center left):** Spx Chrome/Getty Images; **53 (center):** ZUMA Press, Inc./Alamy Stock Photo; **53 (center right):** Dpa Picture Alliance/Alamy Stock Photo; **53 (bottom left):** Stone/Shutterstock; **53 (bottom right):** Spx Chrome/Getty Images; **55:** ZUMA Press, Inc./Alamy Stock Photo; **58:** Porter Gifford/Corbis via Getty Images; **60:** Norma Jean Gargasz/Alamy Stock Photo; **61 (left):** Everett Collection Inc/Alamy Stock Photo; **61 (right):** Everett Collection Inc/Alamy Stock Photo; **62:** AP Photo/Evan Vucci

Chapter 3

67: AP Photo/Andrew Harnik; **69:** American Photo Archive/Alamy Stock Photo; **73:** AP Photo/Eric Gay; **76:** The Metropolitan Museum of Art, New York. The Edward W. C. Arnold Collection of New York Prints, Maps, and Pictures. Bequest of Edward W. C. Arnold, 1954 (54.90.491); **77:** MPI/Getty Images; **78:** Bettmann/Getty Images; **79:** GRANGER; **83 (top left):** J Main/Shutterstock; **83 (top center):** Ivana Star/Getty Images; **83 (top right):** Space Images/Getty Images; **83 (center left):** Food Collection/Getty Images; **83 (center):** Sam Edwards/Getty Images; **83 (center right):** Stone/Shutterstock; **83 (bottom left, top):** Ivana Star/Getty Images; **83 (bottom left, bottom):** Food Collection/Getty Images; **83 (bottom center, left):** Gado Images/Alamy Stock Photo; **83 (bottom center, right):** Sam Edwards/Getty Images; **83 (bottom right):** Michael Betts/Getty Images; **85:** DOE Photo/Alamy Stock Photo; **86:** AP Photo/Andrew Harnik; **89:** Joe Raedle/Getty Images; **91:** Justin Sullivan/Getty Images; **93:** Bill Pugliano/Getty Images; **94:** AP Photo/Andrew Harnik;

Chapter 4

99: Noah Berger/REUTERS/Newscom; **103 (top left):** Thinkstock Images/Getty Images; **103 (top center):** Spx Chrome/Getty Images; **103 (top right):** John Parra/Getty Images; **103 (center left):** Spx Chrome/Getty Images; **103 (center):** ZUMA Press, Inc./Alamy Stock Photo; **103 (center right):** Image Navi/Getty Images; **103 (bottom):** Stockbyte/Getty Images; **108 (left):** Rick Barbero/The Register-Herald via AP; **108 (right):** William Thomas Cain/Getty Images; **109:** Lawrence Hurley/REUTERS/Newscom; **110:** Matthew Staver/The New York Times/Redux; **114:** J. Lawler Duggan/For the Washington Post via Getty Images; **115:** Indiana University Campus Art Collection, THB X, Thomas Hart Benton, "Indiana Murals: Parks, the Circus, the Klan, the Press." Photograph by: Michael Cavanagh and Kevin Montague, Eskenazi Museum of Art at Indiana

University; **116:** Michael Nigro/Pacific Press/LightRocket via Getty Images; **117:** Shawn Thew/EPA-EFE/Shutterstock; **119:** Anthony Pidgeon/Redferns/Getty Images; **121 (left):** John Wingfield/Alamy Stock Photo; **121 (right):** Erin Schaff/The New York Times/Redux; **123:** Erin Schaff/The New York Times/Redux; **124:** AP Photo; **126:** Bettmann/Getty Images; **128:** Reuters/Newscom; **130:** AP Photo/Michael Stravato; **132:** Noah Berger/REUTERS/Newscom

Chapter 5

137: Marilyn Humphries/Alamy Stock Photo; **139 (left):** Library of Congress; **139 (right):** HB Lindsey/Underwood Archives/Getty Images; **142:** Alpha Stock/Alamy Stock Photo; **143:** Robyn Beck/AFP via Getty Images; **145:** AP Photo/Julia Weeks; **147:** AP Photo/Hillery Smith Shay; **151 (top left):** Feidin Santana via AP Images; **151 (top right):** Richard Ellis/Getty Images; **151 (bottom):** Curtis Compton/Atlanta Journal-Constitution via AP; **153:** Don Cravens/The LIFE Images Collection/Getty Images; **156 (right):** AP Photo/John Minchillo; **156 (left):** AFP/Getty Images; **157:** AP Photo; **158:** AP Photo/Bill Hudson; **163 (left):** David Schaffer/Getty Images; **163 (right):** Tetra Images/Getty Images; **167:** Kyodo via AP Images; **169:** ZUMA Press, Inc./Alamy Stock Photo; **171:** Liu Jie Xinhua News Agency/Newscom; **173:** Jose Luis Magana/Reuters/Newscom; **174:** ZUMA Press, Inc./Alamy Stock Photo; **175:** Marilyn Humphries/Alamy Stock Photo

Chapter 6

181: David McNew/Getty Images; **183:** AP Photo/Rogelio V. Solis; **187:** Alex Wong/Getty Images; **193 (top left):** Tetra Images/Getty Images; **193 (top center):** Evirgen/Getty Images; **193 (top right):** Daniel Grill/Getty Images; **193 (bottom left):** John Lamb/Getty Images; **193 (bottom center):** Hero Images/Getty Images; **193 (bottom right):** Image Navi/Getty Images; **197 (left):** Lucy Nicholson/REUTERS/Newscom; **197 (right):** AP Photo/David J. Phillip; **204:** CALVIN AND HOBBES © 1994 Watterson. Reprinted with permission of ANDREWS MCMEEL SYNDICATION. All rights reserved.; **213:** David McNew/Getty Images

Chapter 7

219: SOPA Images Limited/Alamy Stock Photo; **221 (left):** AP Photo/Patrick Semansky; **221 (center):** UPI/Alamy Stock Photo; **221 (right):** Pacific Press/Alamy Stock Photo; **223 (top):** © CORBIS/Corbis via Getty Images; **223 (bottom):** Sarin Images/GRANGER; **226:** Chris Hondros/Getty Images; **233:** AP Photo/John Locher; **237 (far left):** White House Photo/Alamy Stock Photo; **237 (left):** Matt Baron/Shutterstock; **237 (center):** Matt Baron/Shutterstock; **237 (right):** Matt Baron/Shutterstock; **237 (far right):** Michael Brochstein/Alamy Stock Photo; **238:** Denver Post via Getty Images; **239:** AP Photo/Charles Dharapak; **240:** Zuma Press, Inc./Alamy Stock Photo; **241:** SOPA Images Limited/Alamy Stock Photo; **242:** SOPA Images Limited/Alamy Stock Photo

Chapter 8

247: Jennifer Booher/Alamy Stock Photo; **249:** Bill Clark/CQ Roll Call/Newscom; **251:** UPI/Alamy Stock Photo; **253:** UPI/Alamy Stock Photo; **260:** AP Photo/Steve Helber; **261:** AB Forces News Collection/Alamy Stock Photo; **262:** ZUMA Press, Inc./Alamy Stock Photo; **263:** UPI/Alamy Stock Photo; **269:** Drew Angerer/Getty Images; **272:** John Spink/Atlanta Journal-Constitution via AP; **273:** ZUMA Press, Inc./Alamy Stock Photo; **277:** Shiiko Alexander/Alamy Stock Photo; **280:** Tasos Katopodis/POOL/EPAEFE/Shutterstock; **282:** Jennifer Booher/Alamy Stock Photo

Chapter 9

287: Storms Media Group/Alamy Stock Photo; **292:** JeffG/Alamy Stock Photo; **297:** Tom Williams/Roll Call/Newscom; **299:** AP Photo/Elaine Thompson; **301 (top left):** Pressmaster/Shutterstock; **301 (top right):** Yuri Arcurs/Getty Images; **301 (center left):** Image Source/Getty Images; **301 (center):** Tetra Images/Getty Images; **301 (center right):** Greg Bajor/Getty Images; **301 (bottom left):** Dpa Picture Alliance/Alamy Stock Photo; **301 (bottom right):** JStone/Shutterstock; **302:** Janine Wiedel Photolibrary/Alamy Stock Photo; **305:** Pacific Press Agency/Alamy Stock Photo; **307:** Xinhua/Alamy Stock Photo; **308 (left):** Jim West/Alamy Stock Photo; **308 (right):** Jim West/Alamy Stock Photo; **309:** Storms Media Group/Alamy Stock Photo

Chapter 10

313: UPI/Alamy Stock Photo; **315:** Sarin Images/GRANGER; **319:** Heather Ainsworth/AP Images for Boys and Girls Clubs of America; **322:** ZUMA Press, Inc./Alamy Stock Photo; **325:** Brian Hill/Daily Herald via AP; **329 (left):** United States Department of the Interior; **329 (right):** United States Department of the Interior; **332:** Tom Williams/CQ Roll Call via AP Images; **341 (row 1, left):** Xinhua/Alamy Stock Photo; **341 (row 1, right):** Dpa Picture Alliance/Alamy Stock Photo; **341 (row 2, left):** Xinhua/Alamy Stock Photo; **341 (row 2, center):** Beneda Miroslav/Shutterstock; **341 (row 2, right):** Dpa Picture Alliance/Alamy Stock Photo; **341 (row 3, left):** SOPA Images Limited/Alamy Stock Photo; **341 (row 3, center):** Photomaster/Shutterstock; **341 (row 3, right):** Beneda Miroslav/Shutterstock; **341 (row 4, left):** Xinhua/Alamy Stock Photo; **341 (row 4, right):** Dpa Picture Alliance/Alamy Stock Photo; **341 (row 5):** Xinhua/Alamy Stock Photo; **341 (row 6):** JStone/Shutterstock; **346:** Toni L. Sandys/The Washington Post via AP, Pool; **347:** UPI/Alamy Stock Photo

Chapter 11

353: Hum Images/Alamy Stock Photo; **355:** Painting/Alamy Stock Photo; **356:** Bettmann/Getty Images; **359:** ZUMA Press, Inc./Alamy Stock Photo; **363 (top left):** ZUMA Press, Inc./Alamy Stock Photo; **363 (top center):** Official White House Photo by Pete Souza/National Archives; **363 (top right):** A Katz/Shutterstock; **363 (center left):** Dpa Picture Alliance/Alamy Stock Photo; **363 (center):** Dpa Picture Alliance/Alamy Stock Photo; **363 (center right):** Nazlisart/Shutterstock; **363 (bottom left):** JStone/Shutterstock; **363 (bottom right):** JStone/Shutterstock; **366 (left):** AP Photo/Pablo Martinez Monsivais; **366 (right):** Doug Mills/The New York Times/Redux; **369:** Al-Mayadeen via AP video; **370:** Sipa USA/Alamy Stock Photo; **372 (left):** Al Drago/The New York Times/Redux; **372 (right):** Backgrid/Alamy Stock Photo; **376:** Mikhail Klimentyev, Sputnik, Kremlin Pool Photo via AP; **379:** UPI/Alamy Stock Photo; **380:** Hum Images/Alamy Stock Photo

Chapter 12

385: Jabin Botsford/The Washington Post via Getty Images; **387:** American Photo Archive/Alamy Stock Photo; **389 (top left):** J Main/Shutterstock; **389 (top center):** United States Environmental Protection Agency; **289 (top right):** Spx Chrome/Getty Images; **389 (center left):** ZUMA Press, Inc./Alamy Stock Photo; **389 (center):** United States Environmental Protection Agency; **389 (center right):** United States Environmental Protection Agency; **389 (bottom left):** JStone/Shutterstock; **389 (bottom right):** Corine van Kapel/Alamy Stock Photo; **390:** UPI/Alamy Stock Photo; **392:** CARLSON © 2005 Milwaukee Journal Sentinel. Reprinted with permission of ANDREWS MCMEEL

Glossary/Index

Annapolis Convention (1786), 36
Annenberg Public Policy Center, 316
Annual Economic Report of the President, 454
Anthony, Susan B., 152
Anti-Defamation League, 116
Antifederalist Papers, 417

Antifederalists, 40 Those at the Constitutional Convention who favored strong state governments and feared that a strong national government would be a threat to individual rights.
    on civil liberties, 101–4
    concerns about proposed Constitution, 44, 45, 49, 101–4
    on judiciary, 417
    and pluralism principle, 37
    on presidential powers, 56
    and Second Amendment, 120

anti-smoking policies, 458

appeals courts, 422, 423, 424–25 The intermediate level of federal courts that hear appeals from district courts. More generally, an appeals court is any court with appellate jurisdiction.

appellate jurisdiction, 417, *418* The authority of a court to hear appeals from lower courts and change or uphold the decision.

Apple, 295, *295*, 303, 469, 513
appointments:
    to federal bureaucracy, 386, 404
    to Federal Reserve Board, 468
    presidential power in, 54, 56, 60, 359–60, 372, 404, 468

apportionment, 326 The process of assigning the 435 seats in the House to the states based on increases or decreases in state population.

Appropriations Committee, 338, 343, 451
Arab Americans, 172
Arab-Israeli war (1973), 495
Argersinger v. Hamlin, 106
aristocracy, 9
Aristotle, 9
Arizona, 91, 109, 172–74, 240, 254, 257, 279
Arkansas, 130, 168
Armed Services Committee, 337
arms, right to bear, 120–22
Arpaio, Joe, 368

Articles of Confederation, 34, 35–37, 40 Sent to the states for ratification in 1777, these were the first attempt at a new American government. It was later decided that the Articles restricted national government too much, and they were replaced by the Constitution.
    compared to Constitution, *38*, 72

compromises in revision of, 40–47
confederal form of government in, 72
tax policies in, *38*, 47

Ashcroft, Gregory v., 88
Asia Foundation, 506
Asian Americans, *19*
    and affirmative action, 170, *171*, 173
    civil rights of, 138, 143–44, 175
    in Congress, 318
    diversity of, 144
    as federal court judges, *427*
    in internment camps, 144
    party identification of, 18
    voting by, *146*
assembly, freedom of, 102, 116–17, 120
assimilation of immigrants, 18, 172

Astroturf lobbying, 302 Any lobbying method initiated by an interest group that is designed to look like the spontaneous, independent participation of many individuals.

AT&T, 125
athletes, *see* sports
attitudinalist approach, 437
authoritarian governments, 22
authorization process for legislation, 343
Azari, Julia, 218

baby-boom generation, 475 Americans born between 1946 and 1964, who are retiring in large numbers over the next 20 years.

Baker, James, 372
Bakke, Allan, 171

balanced budget, 460–62 A spending plan in which the government's expenditures are equal to its revenue

Baldwin, Tammy, 323, 324
ballots, 251, 416
Baltimore, Barron v., 75, 105
Baltimore, Md., 150
banks:
    and Federal Deposit Insurance Commission, 460
    and Federal Reserve System, 456
    and financial crisis (2008), 471–72
    and monetary policy, 466–67
    reserve requirement on, 466
    Supreme Court on, 75
Banks, Jim, 331
bargaining in political conflicts, 12
Barr, William, 91, 345
Barrett, Amy Coney, 130, 239, 359, *437*, 439
Barron v. Baltimore, 75, 105
Batali, Mario, 161
Baumgartner, Frank, 457
Baylor University, *390*
Bear Stearns, 471
BellSouth, 125
Benton v. Maryland, 106
Bernanke, Ben, 467, 468, 471

Bezos, Jeff, *469*
bias:
    in media coverage, 210
    in public opinion polls, 193, 196
    social desirability bias, 196

bicameralism, 315 The system of having two chambers within one legislative body, like the House and Senate in the U.S. Congress.

Biden, Hunter, 278
Biden, Joe, 5, *13*, 32, 195, 252, 262, 282, 375
    centrist reputation of, 277
    and COVID-19 pandemic, 281, 472
    electoral votes for, 279, 281
    media coverage of, 211–12
    as oldest person elected president, 277
    popular votes for, 281
    in presidential election (2020), 34, 218–20, *219*, 230, 233, 237, 241, 250, 277–81, *277*, *280*
bilingual education, 172

Bill of Rights, 45, 50, 59, 79, *104*, 419 The first 10 amendments to the Constitution; they protect individual rights and liberties.
    on free speech, 269
    on liberty, 22
    origins of, 101–5
    selective incorporation of, 105, *106*
    see also specific amendments

bills, and legislative process, 338–43
bin Laden, Osama, 364, 496, *496*, 497
Bipartisan Campaign Reform Act (2002), 114, 266, *266*, 433
Birmingham, Alabama, 153, 154, *158*
birth control, 111, 129
bisexual people, *see* LGBTQ people
Bismarck, Otto von, 345
Black Lives Matter movement, 149, 154–55, *156*
Bladensburg, Md., 109
Bladensburg Cross, 109, *109*
Blake, Jacob, 155

block grants, 81, 87 Federal aid provided to a state government to be spent within a certain policy area, but the state can decide how to spend the money within that area.

blogs, political, 208
Bloomberg, Michael, 136, 218, 235, 270, 277
"blue states," 16, 17
Board of Education, Brown v., 141, 152, 156–57, 441, *441*
Board of Education II, Brown v., 141, 157
Board of Education of Ewing Township, Everson v., 106
Bollinger, Gratz v., 163
Bollinger, Grutter v., 163
Bolton, John, 359
Bond, United States v., 88
Booker, Cory, 354, 428
Border Patrol, 360, 500
Boren, Craig v., 163
Bosnia, 496

and presidential power, 355
Reconstruction period after, 78, 141
and slavery, 47, 48, 78, 140
states' rights issue in, 78

Civil War amendments, 105, 140 The Thirteenth, Fourteenth, and Fifteenth Amendments to the Constitution, which abolished slavery and granted civil liberties and voting rights to newly freed people after the Civil War.

Civil Works Administration, 473

class-action lawsuit, 421 A case brought by a group of individuals on behalf of themselves and others in the general public who are in similar circumstances.

Clean Air Acts, 66, 81, 83, 94, 387, 389
Clean Power Plan of EPA, 389
Clean Water Act (1972), 81, 83

clear and present danger test, 112–13 Established in *Schenck v. United States*, this test allowed the government to restrict certain types of speech deemed dangerous.

climate change, 4, 66–68, 67, 72, 86, 93, 281, 406, 500
    interest groups concerned about, 299
    Paris Agreement on, 13, 86, 280, 363, 365
    public opinion on, 185, 204, 205
Clinton, Bill:
    appointments and nominations of, 169, 427, 428, 429
    approval rating of, 377
    electoral votes for, 255
    executive orders of, 361
    and gays in military, 168
    impeachment of, 346
    presidential power of, 356
    social policies of, 482
    vetoes from, 367
Clinton, Hillary, 5, 26, 220, 241, 259, 270, 280, 354
    e-mail practices of, 212, 345
    media coverage of, 211–12
    presidential campaign of (2016), *see* presidential campaign and election of 2016
    public opinion on, 196

closed primary, 234, 236, 249 A primary election in which only registered members of a particular political party can vote.

cloture, 342 A procedure through which the Senate can limit the amount of time spent debating a bill (cutting off a filibuster) if a supermajority of 60 senators agree.
Club for Growth, 225
CNN, 196
coalitions in political parties, 230–32, 231
Coastal Zone Management Act, 83
Coast Guard, 500

coattails, 273 The ability of a popular president to generate additional support for candidates affiliated with his or her party. Coattails are weak or nonexistent in most American elections.

Coca-Cola, 299
Code of Federal Regulations, 15

coercion, 291 A method of eliminating nonparticipation or free riding by potential group members by requiring participation, as in many labor unions.

coercive federalism, 81, 82, 83, 84, 85 A form of federalism in which the federal government pressures the states to change their policies by using regulations, mandates, or conditions (often involving threats to withdraw federal funding).

Cold War, 494–95 The period of tension and arms competition between the United States and the Soviet Union that lasted from 1945 until 1991.

Cole, James, 91
Cole Memo, 91

collective action problems, 8, 15 Situations in which the members of a group would benefit by working together to produce some outcome, but each individual is better off refusing to cooperate and reaping benefits from those who do the work.

college:
    affirmative action in admission to, 138, 170–72, 173, 176
    controversial speech in, 98–100, 132
    land grant institutions, 482
    student loans for, 15, 298, 302
Collins, Susan, 246–48, 247, 282
collusion, 431
Colorado, 91, 111, 165, 237, 257
Colorado, Wolf v., 106
Colorado Civil Rights Commission, 111
color-blind jurisprudence, 156, 158–60, 171, 438
Comey, James, 60, 345
commander in chief, presidential power as, 54, 364–65, 374, 498
commerce clause, 79, 89–90
Commerce Department, 398, 399, 400

commercial speech, 119, 119 Public expression with the aim of making a profit. It has received greater protection under the First Amendment in recent years but remains less protected than political speech.

Commission on Civil Rights, 147
Commission on Presidential Debates, 264
committee system in Congress, 337–43
    in budget process, 343, 451, 452
    economic policy role of, 451

foreign policy role of, 501

common law, 421 Law based on the precedent of previous court rulings rather than on legislation. It is used in all federal courts and 49 of the 50 state courts.

Common Sense (Paine), 38
community, political socialization in, 185
commutations, presidential power in, 368

competitive federalism, 87, 92, 93 A form of federalism in which states compete to attract businesses and jobs through the policies they adopt.

compromise in political conflicts, 12
    at Constitutional Convention, 40–47, 41, 49–50
Compromise of 1850, 140, 355

concurrent powers, 70, 70 Responsibilities for particular policy areas, such as transportation, that are shared by federal, state, and local governments.

concurrent resolution, 339
concurring opinions, 435
Confederacy, 116, 140

confederal government, 9, 72 A form of government in which states hold power over a limited national government.

confederations, 290 Interest groups made up of several independent, local organizations that provide much of their funding and hold most of the power.

conference, 226, 239, 332 The organization of Republicans within the House and Senate that meets to discuss and debate the party's positions on various issues in order to reach a consensus and to assign leadership positions.

conference, of Supreme Court justices, 434

conference committees, 337, 343 Temporary committees created to negotiate differences between the House and Senate versions of a piece of legislation that has passed through both chambers.

confessions, Miranda rights in, 126
confidentiality, executive privilege for, 368–70
conflicts, political, 4, 5, 9, 10–13, 10, 11, 16, 41, 84
    compromise in, 12, 40–47, 49–50
    and Constitution, 34, 61–62
    critical analysis of political information in, 24–26, 27, 71, 209
    on economic policy, 20, 484
    on foreign policy, 511, 517–18
    gridlock in, 330

conflicts, political (*Continued*)
    on health care, 12–13, *450*
    as human nature, 39
    interest group influence in, 308
    resolution of, 21–24
    sources of, 16–21
Congress, 5, 312–27
    accountability in, 239–40, 319–21
    advice and consent role of, 55, 60, 346,
        425, 428, 429
    Articles of Confederation on, 35–36, *38*
    budget process in, 451–54
    campaigns and elections for, *see*
        congressional campaigns and
        elections
    casework of, 321, 347
    caucuses and conferences in, 226, 332–34
    checks and balances with other
        branches, 7, 52, 55–56, 62
    civil rights legislation of, 165–68
    committee system in, 337–43, 451, 452,
        501
    constituency of, 319–21, *320*, *325*
    Constitutional Convention compromise
        on, 42
    Constitution on, *38, 41*, 72, 315–17, 338,
        451, 501
    credit claiming in, 321, 331
    economic policy role of, 273, 451–54, 484
    enumerated powers of, 51, 315
    exclusive powers of, 51
    foreign policy role of, 498, *499*, 501
    formal structures in, 332–38
    gridlock in, 330
    home styles in, 322–23
    ideological polarization in, 228, 334, *336*
    impeachment power of, 55, 346, 376
    informal structures in, 331
    interest groups lobbying, 286–311
    legislative process in, 338–43, 366–68
    logrolling in, 331
    net worth of members in, 317
    oversight role of, 345–47, 407–10, 497
    in policy-making process, 449–54
    political parties in, 226, 239–40, 332–38
    pork-barrel spending of, 317
    power of the purse, 51, 55, 345, 451, 501,
        502
    public opinion on, 317, 319–21, *320*, 330
    racial and ethnic composition of, 158,
        317, 318
    relationship with president, 239, 315–17,
        365, 375–77
    representation in, 317–21
    and revolving door with interest groups,
        293, 297
    roll call votes in, 334
    seniority in, 331
    shared powers of, 54–55
    social policy role of, 454, 482
    specialization in, 331
    staff in, 338
    testimony at hearings of, 299, 345
    typical workday in, 324
    and unilateral presidential actions,
        375–77

    universalism in, 331
    war powers of, 54, 501, 502
    women in, 20, 318, 323, 324, *325*
    see also House of Representatives; Senate
Congressional Budget Office (CBO), 452,
    453
congressional campaigns and elections,
    246–51, *252*, 317–30
    in 1814, 222
    in 1994, 482
    in 2006, 274
    in 2008, 322
    in 2010, 232, 273, 322
    in 2014, 303, 336
    in 2017, 153, *404*
    in 2020, 246–48
    campaign finances in, *266, 268, 276*, 323,
        325, 336
    economic issues in, 273
    in, 2018–2020, 268
    plurality and majority in, 21
    recruiting and nominating candidates
        in, 232–35
    reelection of incumbents in, 240, 321–25,
        322, 336
    voter turnout in, 271, *271*, 276
congressional campaigns and elections of
    2018:
    campaign financing in, *235*, 238, *268, 276*
    outcome of, 232, 276, 280
    party affiliation in, 273
    in Pennsylvania, 260, *260*
    policy issues in, 276
    Trump involvement in, 276, 336
    voter turnout in, 276
congressional campaigns and elections of
    2020:
    accountability in, 240
    campaign financing in, *235, 266, 368*
    media coverage in, *253*
    outcome of, 240, 246, *246*, 248, 249, 273, 282
    party affiliation in, 232, 240, 249
    policy issues in, *203*, 249
    Trump involvement in, *336*
Connecticut, 42–43, *43*, 46, 120, 127, 129
Connecticut, Cantwell v., 106
Connecticut, Griswold v., 106, 129
Connecticut Compromise, 42, *43*
consent of the governed, 22, 38, 39
    see also popular sovereignty

conservative, 20, 90 The side of the
ideological spectrum defined by support
for lower taxes, a free market, and a more
limited government; generally associated
with Republicans.
    and ideological polarization, 199, *200*
    and media effects, 210–12
    as stable opinion, 183, *183*
    of Supreme Court justices, 426, 438, 439

Conservative Political Action Committee, *305*
considerations in public opinion, 188–91
constituency:
    of Congress, 319–21, *320*, *325*
    of political parties, 224

Constitution:
    on Congress, 501
    on presidential power, 353, 354
constitution, state, 47
Constitution, U.S., 32–65
    ambiguity of, 60
    amendments to, *see* amendments to
        Constitution
    Article I of, 59, 73, 315
    Article II of, 73, 358
    Article III of, 417, *418*, 431
    Article IV of, 74
    Article V of, 57, 59, 73
    Article VI of, 73
    Article VII of, 48
    Bill of Rights of, *see* Bill of Rights
    checks and balances in, 50–56
    commerce clause in, 79, 89–90
    compared to Articles of Confederation,
        38, 72
    on Congress, *38, 41*, 72, 315–17, 338, 451
    and Constitutional Convention, 35, 37–48
    enumerated powers in, 51
    exclusive powers in, 51–54
    executive powers in, 54, 60
    full faith and credit clause in, 74
    on goals of government, 7
    historical context of, 34–40, *36–37*
    implied powers in, 60, 70
    on judicial branch, *38*, 416, 417, *418*, 419,
        425, 431
    as living document, 57–61, 437
    national supremacy clause in, 45, 73, 75
    necessary and proper clause in, 51, 73
    originalist view of, 58
    preamble of, 7, 72
    on presidential authority, 357, *358*, 364,
        374, 380
    privileges and immunities clause in, 74
    on promotion of general welfare, 8
    public knowledge of, 62
    ratification of, *38*, 48–50, 101–4
    shared powers in, 54–55
    strict construction in interpretation of,
        436–37
    Supreme Court interpretation of, 58,
        60–61, 69, 416, 419, 425, 436
    and Trump, 34, 61, 62
    vesting clause in, 358

**constitutional authority, presidential, 357,
358, 364, 374, 380** Powers derived from the
provisions of the Constitution that outline
the president's role in government.

Constitutional Convention, 34, *35*, 37–48
    civil liberties motion in, 101
    compromises in, 40–47, *41*, 49–50
    economic interests in, *39*, 40, 42
    judiciary issues in, 417
    large and small state interests in, *41*,
        42–43, *43*
    political theories of Founders in, 37–39

**constitutional interpretation, 58, 60–61,
416, 419, 425, 436–37** The process of

determining whether a piece of legislation or governmental action is supported by the Constitution.

containment, 494–95 An important feature of American Cold War policy in which the United States used diplomatic, economic, and military strategies in an effort to prevent the Soviet Union from expanding its influence.

cooperative federalism, 79–80, 84, 92 A form of federalism in which national and state governments work together to provide services efficiently. This form emerged in the late 1930s, representing a profound shift toward less concrete boundaries of responsibility in national–state relations.

Council of Economic Advisers (CEA), 454, 458 A group of economic advisers, created by the Employment Act of 1946, that provides objective data on the state of the economy and makes economic policy recommendations to the president.

culture wars, 16 Political conflict in the United States between "red-state" Americans, who tend to have strong religious beliefs, and "blue-state" Americans, who tend to be more secular.

de facto, 157 Relating to actions or circumstances that occur outside the law or "by fact," such as the segregation of schools that resulted from housing patterns and other factors rather than from laws.

defendant, 420 The person or party against whom a case is brought.

deflation, 458–59 A decrease in the general prices of goods and services.

De Jonge v. Oregon, 106

de jure, 157 Relating to actions or circumstances that occur "by law," such as the legally enforced segregation of schools in the American South before the 1960s.

Delaware, *43, 46,* 254, 267, *280*

delegate, 319 A member of Congress who loyally represents constituents' direct interests.

democracy, 9, 21–22, 23 Government by the people. In most contexts, this means representative democracy in which the people elect leaders to enact policies. Democracies must have fair elections with at least two options.
  and nation building, 492, 496
  political parties in, 239–40
  public opinion in, 213–14
  representative, 21–22, 41
  republican, 37
  stealth, 12

Democratic Congressional Campaign Committee, 226, *235*
Democratic Governors' Association, 224
Democratic Leadership Council, 225, *235*
Democratic National Committee, 218, 221, 224, 225*n,* 235, 238
Democratic National Convention (2020), 218, 277
Democratic Party, 220, 242
  in "blue states," 16, 17
  as brand name, 225
  in budget-making process, 451
  in campaign financing, 235–38, *235, 268,* 270
  coalitions in, 231–32, *231*
  congressional caucuses of, 226, 332–34
  in congressional elections, 246–48, 249, 273–74, 325–26
  on Constitution as living document, 58
  economic policies of, 16, 448, 451, 463, 475
  in election process, 232–38
  and federal bureaucracy, 396, 397, *401*
  on federal government, 222–23, *223,* 448
  on health insurance, 480–82
  history of, 221–24, *222*
  identification with, 186, *228,* 229–30, *229*
  and ideological polarization, 199, *200,* 334, *336*
  Latinos in, 18, 143
  liberal ideology in, 20, 24
  and media effects, 212
  New Deal supported by, 396
  organization of, 223, 224–25
  party unity in, 334, *335*
  party votes in, 334, *335*
  platform of, 238
  policy priorities in, 228, *230,* 231–32, 238
  in presidential election (2020), 17, 218–20, *219,* 275
  public opinion in, 190
  racial, gender, and ethnic identity in, 18, *18*
  in Reconstruction era, 141
  recruiting and nominating candidates from, 232–38, 251–53
  in redistricting, 325–26, 327, 329
  reelection of incumbents in, 273–74, *274,* 322
  on slavery, 222
  social policies of, 475
  on Social Security, 477

Democratic-Republicans, 221–23, *222*
Democratic Senatorial Campaign Committee, 226, *235*
deregulation of media, 210
Dershowitz, Alan, 34
Derthick, Martha, 94

descriptive representation, 317 Representation in which a member of Congress shares the characteristics (such as gender, race, religion, or ethnicity) of his or her constituents.

desegregation:
  of hotels and restaurants, 158
  of public schools, 85, 141, 152–53, 157, 441
Des Moines School District, Tinker v., 113

détente, 495 An approach to foreign policy in which cultural exchanges and negotiations are used to reduce tensions between rival nations, such as between the United States and the Soviet Union during the 1970s.

DeVos, Betsy, *85,* 360
Diaz Barragán, Nanette, *261*
Dingell, John, 14
diplomacy, as foreign policy tool, 507, *507*

direct incitement test, 113 Established in *Brandenburg v. Ohio,* this test protects threatening speech under the First Amendment unless that speech aims to and is likely to cause imminent "lawless action."

direct lobbying, 296–98, 300 Attempts by interest group staff to influence policy by speaking with elected officials or bureaucrats.

Director of National Intelligence, 501
disabled people, 86, 93, 167, 455
disaster response, *69,* 85, 500

discount rate, 466–67 The interest rate that a bank must pay on a short-term loan from the Federal Reserve Bank.

discretionary spending, 463, *463* Expenditures that can be cut from the budget without changing the underlying law, which is everything other than defense, entitlements, and interest on the debt.

discrimination:
  against African Americans, *78,* 85, 87–88, 93, 136–38, 139–41, 156–60, 165–66, 175, 223
  age, 88, 93
  against Asian Americans, 138, 143–44, 173, 175
  civil rights in protection from, 136–38
  current issues in, 170–72
  against disabled people, 86, 93, 167
  in employment, 88, 158, 164, *164,* 167

  in housing, 156, 166, 175
  intermediate scrutiny test in, 160, 162–63
  against Latinos, 143
  in law enforcement, 136–38, 149–51
  against LGBTQ people, 93, 130, 138, 144–45, 164–65, 167–68, 175
  liberal policies against, 90
  against Muslims, 56
  political conflicts in, 19
  in protectionism, 144, 160
  rational basis test in, 160, 161, 162–63
  remedial legislation in, 88
  in restaurants, 79, 153
  reverse, 138, 170–72, 173
  separate but equal doctrine in, 141, 153, 156, 223, 396
  state laws on, 93
  strict scrutiny test in, 161, 162–63
  suspect classification in, 161, 162
  in voting access, 146–47, 158–60, 166
  against women, 138, 144, 160–64, 166–67, 425
dissenting opinions of Supreme Court, *435, 436*
distributive theory, 337

district courts, 417, 423, 424 Lower-level trial courts of the federal judicial system that handle most U.S. federal cases.

diversity, 19

divided government, 226, 240, 366 A situation in which the House, Senate, and presidency are not controlled by the same party—for example, when Democrats hold the majority of House and Senate seats and the president is a Republican.
  and policy gridlock, 226

DNA evidence, 124, 128
Doctors without Borders, 506
Dodd-Frank, 12
Doggett, Lloyd, 286
dogs, drug-sniffing, 123
DOMA (Defense of Marriage Act), 165, 168
Dominican Republic, 508
Don't Ask, Don't Tell Repeal Act, 168

double jeopardy, 126–27 Being tried twice for the same crime. This is prevented by the Fifth Amendment.

Douglas, William O., 113, 431
Dream and Promise Act and Dreamers, 312–14, *313,* 316, 347, 364
Dred Scott v. Sandford, 75, 76–77, *77,* 105, 140, 419
drinking age, 160–61, 163
drone aircraft, 369, 387, 496, 497
  antiterrorism use of, 369, 497, 499, 511
drugs:
  dogs detecting, 123
  FDA approval of, 387, 390–91, 392, 408–10, *409*
  marijuana, 16, 91

executive powers clause, 54, 60

executive privilege, 368–70, 370, 375 The right of the president to keep executive branch conversations and correspondence confidential from the legislative and judicial branches.

ex post facto laws, 101
Exxon Mobile, *295, 303*

F-35 fighter-attack plane, *294, 386*
Facebook, 115–16, 206, 210, 302, *469*
FactCheck.org, 316

factions, 7, 39, 42 Groups of like-minded people who try to influence the government. American government is set up to avoid domination by any one of these groups.

Fair Housing Act (1968), 165, 166
fairness doctrine of FCC, 208
fake news, 2–4, 28
Fallon, Jimmy, 207
Falwell, Jerry, 119
family, political socialization in, 184–85, *186*, 188
Family Research Council, *295, 303*
family values, 18
Fauci, Anthony, *346, 385*
Federal Aviation Administration (FAA), 387, 399
Federal Bureau of Investigation (FBI), 7, 212, 476

federal civil service, 395 A system created by the 1883 Pendleton Civil Service Act in which bureaucrats are hired on the basis of merit rather than political connections.

Federal Communications Commission (FCC), 208 A government agency created in 1934 to regulate American radio stations and later expanded to regulate television, wireless communications technologies, and other broadcast media.

federal debt, *460, 461, 462*
Federal Deposit Insurance Corporation, 460

Federal Election Commission, 114, 266 The government agency that enforces and regulates election laws; made up of six presidential appointees, of whom no more than three can be members of the same party.

Federal Election Commission, Citizens United v., 266, 267, 269, 303, 426, 433
Federal Election Commission, McCutcheon v., 266
Federal Emergency Management Agency (FEMA), *69*
Federal Emergency Relief Administration, 473

Federal Employees Political Activities Act (1993), 404
Federal Food, Drug, and Cosmetic Act (1938), 386–87

federal funds rate (FFR), 467 The interest rate that a bank must pay on an overnight loan from another bank.

federal government:
   Antifederalist concerns about, 49
   autonomy of, 69–70
   balance of power with state and local governments, 7, 9, 40, 45, 72–74
   budget of, 460–61; *see also* budget of federal government
   bureaucracy in, 384–413
   checks and balances in, 7, 42; *see also* checks and balances
   in cooperative federalism, 79–80
   in daily life, 14–15, *14, 15*
   economic policy of, 446–72
   education role of, 85, *85,* 456, 482–84
   employees in, 400, *400, 401,* 402–5, *402*
   environmental policies of, 83
   evolving concept of, 74–80
   in federalism, 7, 9, 40, 45, 68, 69–70, *70,* 73–74
   financial aid to states, 81–84
   forms of, 9
   goals of, 5–8
   historical growth of, 355–57
   lobbying of, 286–311
   party views on role of, 222–23, *223*
   policy priorities in, 201–5
   public opinion on, 187, 198–201, *202*
   responsibilities of, 69–70, *70*
   separation of powers in, 7, 9, 39, 42, 51, 56, 62, 68
   size of, 15, 400–402
   social policy of, 472–84
   spoils system in, 222
   Supreme Court rulings on, 74–80, *75*
   unfunded mandates of, 81
Federal Highway Administration, 399

federalism, 7, 50, 66–97 The division of power across the local, state, and national levels of government.
   advantages and disadvantages of, 90–93
   and Antifederalists, 40, 49
   assessment of, 90–93
   balance of power in, 9, 45, *70,* 72–74
   coercive, 81, 82, 83, *84,* 85
   competitive, 87, 92, 93
   concurrent powers in, *70, 70*
   cooperative, 79–80, 81, *84,* 92
   definition of, 68
   dual, 75, 76–79, 80, *84,* 85, 419
   and environmental policies, 83
   evolving concept of, 74–80, 82, *84*
   fiscal, 81–84, *84*
   levels of government and autonomy in, 70
   "marble cake" and "layer cake" models of, 80, 82, *84*

picket fence, 80, 82, 83, *84*
policy implications of, 90
and recreational marijuana, 91
states' rights in, 78, 87–90
Supreme Court rulings on, 74–80, *75, 88*

Federalist Papers, 34, 39, 49, 50, 417

Federalists, 40, 42, 75, 221–22, 221, 222 Those at the Constitutional Convention who favored a strong national government and a system of separated powers.
   on judiciary, 417
   on presidential powers, 56
   on proposed Constitution, 50

Federal Meat Inspection Act (1906), 395

federal preemption, 81 Imposition of national priorities on the states through national legislation that is based on the Constitution's supremacy clause.

Federal Register, 387
Federal Reserve, 448, 451
Federal Reserve Act (1913), 466, 468
Federal Reserve Board, 466
   appointment to, 468

Federal Reserve System, 8, 398, 400, 439–41, 455–56, 460 An independent agency that serves as the central bank of the United States to bring stability to the nation's banking system.
   in COVID-19 recession, 472
   and interest rates, 456, 466–68
   monetary policies of, 466
   open market operations of, 467
   political independence of, 468

Federal Speedy Trial Act (1974), 128
Federal-State Extended Benefits Program, 481
Federal-State Unemployment Compensation Program, 481
Feenstra, Randy, *322*
feminism, 19
fence-sitters, 298
Ferguson, Mo., *114,* 149, 150
Ferguson, Plessy v., 141
feudalism, 40
Fifteenth Amendment, 59, 78, 105, 140
Fifth Amendment, 76, *104,* 105, *106,* 126–27, 129, 165

fighting words, 118 Forms of expression that "by their very utterance" can incite violence. These can be regulated by the government but are often difficult to define.

filibuster, 342, 429 A tactic used by senators to block a bill by continuing to hold the floor and speak—under the Senate rule of unlimited debate—until the bill's supporters back down.

Fillmore, Millard, 355

filtering, 212 The influence on public opinion that results from journalists' and editors' decisions about which of many potential news stories to report.

Finance Committee, 451
financial crisis (2008), *12*, 85, 459, 467, 471–72, *471*
Financial Stability Plan, 471
Fiorina, Carly, 354

fire alarm oversight, 345–46, 408 A method of oversight in which members of Congress respond to complaints about the bureaucracy or problems of implementation only as they arise rather than exercising constant vigilance.

First Amendment, 28, 60, 100, 102–3, *104*, 107–20
    and campaign financing, 269
    establishment clause in, 102, 103, 107–9
    on freedom of religion, 102–3, 107–11
    on freedom of speech, assembly, and press, 111–20, 132
    on freedom of the press, 28
    free exercise clause in, 102, 103, 107, 109–11
    limits to freedoms in, 100
    and privacy rights, 129
    selective incorporation of, *106*
    Supreme Court on, 60, 437

fiscal federalism, 81–84 A form of federalism in which federal funds are allocated to the lower levels of government through transfer payments or grants.

fiscal policy, 451, 457, 461–66 Government decisions about how to influence the economy by taxing and spending.

Fisher, Abigail, 172, 173
Fisher v. Univ. of Texas, 163, 173
501(c)(3) organizations, 303, *304*
501(c)(4) organizations, 267, 269, 303, 304, *304*

527 organizations, 225, 267, 303, 304, *304* A tax-exempt group formed primarily to influence elections through voter mobilization efforts and to issue ads that do not directly endorse or oppose a candidate. Unlike PACs, 527 organizations are not subject to contribution limits and spending caps.

FiveThirtyEight, 26, 195, 206, 210, *211*
flag, of U.S., and symbolic speech, 113, *114*
Flag Protection Act (1989), 113
Flake, Jeff, 276
Flint, Mich., 149
Flores, Bill, *332*
Flores, City of Boerne v., 88
Florida, 326
    drug-sniffing dogs in, 123
    gun laws in, *89*

Latinos in, 143
presidential election in (2016), 257
presidential election in (2020), *13*, 254, 279
shooting incidents in, *89*, 120, 121, *121*
voting districts in, 159
women on juries in, 144
Florida, Seminole Tribe v., 88
Floyd, George, police killing of, 136, 150, 155, 275
Food and Drug Administration (FDA), 8, 390–91
    drug approval process of, 387, 390, 391, 392, 408–10, *409*
    as independent agency, 399
food stamps, 476, 481
Forbes, 466
Ford, Gerald, 260, 356, *377*, 495
Ford, Henry, 466
Foreign Affairs Committee, 501
foreign aid, 509, *510*
Foreign Intelligence Advisory Board, 499
Foreign Intelligence Surveillance Court, 125
Foreign Miners Tax, 144

foreign policy, 355, 365–66, *366*, 375, 488–521 Government actions that affect countries, corporations, groups, or individuals outside America's borders.
    alliances and treaties in, 365–66, 501, 509–10
    antiterrorism efforts in, 490, 492, 495, *496*, 497, 504, 511, 513–15
    congressional role in, 498, *498*, 501
    and COVID-19 pandemic, 490
    definition of, 491
    diplomacy in, 507
    economic sanctions in, 509, *515*, 517
    financial aid in, 509
    history of, 493–98
    interest group influence on, 504–5
    judicial branch in, 501–4
    media influence on, 505
    military in, 491–98, 499–500, 510–11
    of Obama, 365–66, *366*, 493, 496, 503, 505, 506
    political conflicts on, 511, 517–18
    presidential power in, 355, 365–66, 498–99, *499*, *500*, 517
    principles and perspectives in, 491–93
    and public opinion, 504
    public opinion on, 505–6
    soft power in, 496
    trade in, 495, 498, 508–9, 512–13, 517
    of Trump, 365–66, 488–90, 498, *500*, 503, 504, 505, 509, 510, 517
    weapons of mass destruction as factor in, 515–17

Foreign Relations Committee, 501
Foundation for Traffic Safety, 291
Founders:
    Articles of Confederation of, 35–36
    on Congress, 315, *315*
    at Constitutional Convention, 33–43, *35*
    on equality, 22
    on goals of government, 7
    on human nature, 7, 39

on impeachment, 34
on judiciary, 417
on liberty, 22
on political parties, 221
on republicanism, 37–38
on separation of church and state, 107
on strong national government, 72
Fourteen Point Plan, 493
Fourteenth Amendment, 59, 78, 79, 87–88, 90, 105–7
    on due process, 78, 88, 105, 165
    equal protection clause in, *see* equal protection clause
    and gay rights, 90, 130, 165
    and remedial legislation, 88
    and slavery, 140
    Supreme Court on, 105, 419
    and women's rights, 160, 161
Fourth Amendment, *104*, *106*, 122–26, 129
Fox News, 265

framing, 212 The influence on public opinion caused by the way a story is presented or covered, including the details, explanations, and context offered in the report.

France, 9, 72
    foreign aid from, *510*
    multilateral actions of, 491
    Paris terrorist attacks in (2016), 172
    as UN Security Council member, 506
Franken, Al, 161
Frankfurter, Felix, 435, 437
Franklin, Benjamin, 47
Freedmen's Bureau, 141
freedom:
    of assembly, 102, 116–17, 120
    of press, 2, 28, 100, 101, 102, 117–18, 120
    of religion, 102–3, 107–11
    of speech, *see* speech, freedom of

free exercise clause, 102, 103, 107, 109–11 Part of the First Amendment that states that Congress cannot prohibit or interfere with the practice of religion unless there are important secular reasons for doing so.

free market, 16, 460 An economic system based on competition among businesses without government interference.
    and grazing rights, 470

free rider problem, 8, 15 The incentive to benefit from others' work without making a contribution, which leads individuals in a collective action situation to refuse to work together.

free riding, 291 Relying on others to contribute to a collective effort while failing to participate on one's own behalf, yet still benefiting from the group's successes

French and Indian War (1754–1763), 34
Fugitive Slave Act (1850), 140
Fugitive Slave Clause, 47

gun laws (*Continued*)
  interest groups concerned with, 289,
    299, 302, 307, 308
  and mass shootings, 120
  party votes on, 336
  public opinion on, 184, 190–91, 205,
    308
  research limitations on, 405
  and Second Amendment, 120
  state differences in, 74, 87, 120
Gutiérrez, Luis, 327

habeas corpus rights, 101
Hague v. CIO, 106
Halloween costumes, 114
Hamdan v. Rumsfeld, 53
Hamilton, Alexander, 34, 36, 39, 49, 75, 417,
  418
Hamilton (musical), 44
*Hamilton v. Regents of the University of
  California*, 106
Hamlin, Argersinger v., 106
Hannity, Sean, 210, 265

hard money, 267 Donations that are used
to help elect or defeat a specific candidate.

Hardwick, Bowers v., 165
Harris, Kamala, 26, 273, 478
  in presidential campaign and election
    (2020), 26, 277, 277, 280
Harvard University, 171
  affirmative action policy of, 173
Hasen, Richard, 160
Hatch Act (1939), 404, 404
hate crimes, 151, 168

hate speech, 98, 114–15 Expression that is
offensive or abusive, particularly in terms
of race, gender, or sexual orientation.
It is currently protected under the First
Amendment.

Hawaii, 493
Hawaiians, Native, 19
Hawkins, Howie, 241

head of government, 358 One role of the
president, through which he or she has
authority over the executive branch.

head of state, 358 One role of the president, through which he or she represents the
country symbolically and politically.

Health and Economic Recovery Omnibus
  Emergency Solutions (HEROES) Act, 448
Health and Human Services Department,
  398, 400, 450
health care, 220, 223, 275, 281
  Affordable Care Act on, *see* Affordable
    Care Act
  annual spending on, 478, 479, 479
  computerized medical records in, 480
  congressional and presidential role in
    reform of, 454

as congressional election issue (2018), 276
  Great Society programs in, 473–74
  political conflicts on, 12–13, 450
  for preexisting conditions, 480, 481
  as presidential election issue (2020),
    262, 278
  public opinion on, 184, 187, 187, 198, 205
  as public policy priority, 203, 204, 204
  racial disparities in, 149
  social policy on, 456, 473–74, 478–81
  state role in, 81, 86, 90, 92, 456, 478, 480
  Trump on, 12–13, 480
  for veterans, 455
Health Committee, 346
hearings, congressional, 299
Hedden, Bill, 470
Heinlein, Robert A., 384
Hewlett Packard Enterprise, 299
Hibbing, John R., 12
*Hibbs, Nevada Department of Human
  Resources v.*, 88
Hispanics, 19, 427, 428
  see also Latinos
Hobbes, Thomas, 6
Hobby Lobby stores, 110–11
Hodges, Obergefell v., 10, 73, 165
Hogan, Malloy v., 106
Holder, Eric, 136, 138, 170
Holder, Shelby County v., 88
Hollings, Ernest, 125
Holmes, Oliver Wendell, 58
Homeland Security Department, 7, 398,
  400, 500
homelessness, 457
homosexuals, *see* LGBTQ people

hostile media effect, 211 The tendency of
people to see neutral media coverage of an
event as biased against their point of view.

House of Representatives:
  Affordable Care Act in, 480
  in budget process, 451, 452, 453
  committee system in, 337–38
  compared to Senate, 315, 320
  constituency of, 320
  Constitutional Convention compromise
    on, 42
  constitutional requirements to serve
    in, 252
  descriptive representation in, 317, 318
  districts represented in, 320
  economic policy role of, 451
  election to, *see* congressional campaigns
    and elections
  foreign policy role of, 501
  ideological polarization in, 336
  legislative process in, 338–43
  party structure in, 332, 333
  party unity in, 334, 335
  party votes in, 249, 334, 335
  redistricting of, 325–30; *see also*
    redistricting
  term in, 315, 323
  Three-Fifths Compromise on, 46, 47
  Trump impeached by, 5, 32–34, 33, 265, 354

typical workday in, 324
  whip system in, 332
  women in, 20, 323
housing:
  discrimination in, 156, 166, 175
  mortgages on, *see* mortgages
  price of, in financial crisis (2008),
    471–72
  restrictive covenants on, 156
  tax deductions related to, 473
Housing and Urban Development Department, 356, 398, 400
Huawei technology firm, 505
Hulu, 210, 211
human nature, view of Founders on, 7, 39
human rights issues, 495–96, 506
  in antiterrorism efforts, 514, 515
  in globalization of trade, 513
hunting, and right to bear arms, 121
Hurricane Dorian, 379, 379
Hurricane Katrina, 449
Hustler, 119
hydroxychloroquine, 391

Idaho, 160

idealism, 492, 492 The idea that foreign
policy decisions reflect normative
goals such as justice, equality, and human
rights.

ideological polarization, 199, 200 Sharp
differences in Americans' overall ideas of
the size and scope of the government.
  of Congress, 227, 228, 334, 336
  of political parties, 199, 200, 227,
    228, 334
  Trump affecting, 170

ideology, 20–21 A cohesive set of ideas and
beliefs used to organize and evaluate the
political world.
  conservative, *see* conservative ideology
  liberal, *see* liberal ideology
  libertarian, 20
  and public opinion, 183, 183, 184, 199,
    200
  of Supreme Court justices, 426, 435,
    437–38, 439, 442

iHeartMedia, 210
Illinois, 116, 327
  marijuana in, 91
immigration policies, 172–75, 281
  on Chinese, 143–44
  as congressional election issue (2018), 276
  and DACA program, 312, 347–48, 453
  of Obama, 174
  political conflicts on, 5, 18–19, 22
  public opinion on, 196, 197, 205
  of Trump, 4, 5, 62, 170, 172, 174–75, 196,
    239, 275, 278, 312–14, 347–48, 354,
    360, 504

impeachment, 7, 55, 346, 368, 376 A
negative or checking power over the other

branches that allows Congress to remove the president, the vice president, or other "officers of the United States" (including federal judges) for abuses of power.
    Founders on, 34
    of Trump, 5, 32–34, *33*, 220, 239, 265, 338, 354, *370*, *376*, 498

implied powers, 60, 70 Powers supported by the Constitution that are not expressly stated in it.

income inequality, 16, 23, 40, 148
    and group identity, *186*
    growth in, 474–75
    and race, 474
    in slavery, 140
    in southern states, 40, 140
    for women, 19, 164, *164*, 425

income support, 481–82 Government programs that provide support to low-income Americans, such as welfare, food assistance, unemployment compensation, and the EITC.

income taxes, 464–65, *464*
    marginal tax rate in, 465, *465*

incumbency advantage, 321–25 The relative infrequency with which members of Congress are defeated in their attempts for reelection.

incumbents, 248–49, 260 A politician running for reelection to the office he or she currently holds.
    accountability of, 249
    advantage of, 321–25
    constituency service of, 302
    credit claiming by, 321
    position taking by, 321
    redistricting affecting, 326
    reelection of, 240, 273–74, *274*, 319–25, 336
    retirement of, 260, 276
    seniority of, 331
    and wave elections, 273–74

independent agencies, 397–400, 455 Government offices or organizations that provide government services and are not part of an executive department.
    Federal Reserve System as, 468

Independents, 232, 234, 242
    identification with, *228*, *229*, 230
Indiana, Timbs v., 106
Indiana University, 115, *115*
Indian Removal Act (1830), 142
individualism, economic, 16
inequality, *see* equality

inflation, 458–59 The increase in the price of consumer goods over time.
    and interest rates, 458, 467

Misery Index on, *459*
    and monetary policies, 467
    and unemployment rate, *459*, *459*

information, political, *see* political information
infrastructure repairs, 93
In re Oliver 333 U.S. 257 (1948), *106*

inside strategies, 296–99 The tactics employed within Washington, D.C., by interest groups seeking to achieve their policy goals.

Instagram, 210, 302
institutional interest groups, *289*
intelligence agencies, 500–501
Intelligence Committees, 501

interest groups, 225, 286–311 An organization of people who share common political interests and aim to influence public policy by electioneering and lobbying.
    in campaign financing, 292, 302–4
    centralized, 290
    confederation model, 290
    congressional testimony of, 299
    definition of, 288–90
    direct lobbying by, 296–98, 300
    expertise in, 292
    foreign policy role of, 504–5
    gifts to Congress from, 297
    grassroots lobbying by, 302
    implementing or preventing change, 307
    incentives for participation in, 291
    inside strategies of, 296–99
    legislation and regulations drafted by, 298
    litigation strategies of, 299, *299*
    media coverage on, 304–5
    membership in, 291
    organizational structure of, 290–91
    outside strategies of, 296, 300–301, 302–5
    policy-making role of, 457
    political action committees, *see* political action committees
    power and influence of, *306*, 307–8
    research of, 298
    resources of, 291–92
    restrictions on, 297
    revolving door with Congress, 293, 297
    social policy issues of, 457
    spending by, 291–96, 304
    staff of, 292–93, 298
    and Supreme Court decisions, 440–41
    types of, *289*

interest rates:
    discount rate, 466–67
    federal funds rate, 467
    and Federal Reserve System, 456, 466
    on home loans, 458, 473
    and inflation rate, 459, 467
    monetary policies on, 466
    and Treasury Department, 456

intergovernmental organizations, 506 Organizations that seek to coordinate policy across member nations.

Interior Department, 80, 83, *398*, 400, 424
    and grazing rights, 470
Intermediate-Range Nuclear Forces (INF) Treaty, 54

intermediate scrutiny, 112, 160, 162–63 The middle level of scrutiny the courts can use when determining whether a law is constitutional. To meet this standard, the law or policy must be "content neutral," must further an important government interest in a way that is "substantially related" to that interest, and must use means that are a close fit to the government's goal and not substantially broader than is necessary to accomplish that goal.

Internal Revenue Service, 8, 242, 267, 303

internationalism, 492, *492* The idea that a country should be involved in the affairs of other nations, out of both self-interest and moral obligation.
    history of, 493–94

International Monetary Fund (IMF), 495, 506 An intergovernmental organization established in 1944 to help stabilize the international monetary system, improve economic growth, and aid developing nations.

International Republican Institute, 506
Internet:
    mass surveys and polls on, 195
    news and political information from, 193–94, 206, 210
    political ads on, 116
    speech on, 115–16
    surveillance of activity on, 125
internment camps, Japanese Americans in, 144
interrogation, Miranda rights in, 126
Interstate Commerce Act (1887), 468
Interstate Commerce Commission, 355, 395, 468
Iowa, 237, 252, 257, 279
iPhones, 513
Iran, 22, 213, 491, 504
    economic sanctions on, 509, 515
    lobbying on policy in, 504–5
    nuclear program of, 301, 365, 509
Iran nuclear agreement, and Trump, 54
Iraq, 190, 203–4, 375, 496, 511
Iraq war, public opinion on, *191*
iron curtain, 494
ISIS (Islamic State of Iraq and the Syria), 204, 492, 513–15
    air strikes against, 503, 511
    drone attacks against, 499
    in Syria, 364, 496, 498, 503, 511, 514
    threat of, *496*
Islam, 496

Islamic State of Iraq and Syria, *see* ISIS

isolationism, 492, 492, 493 The idea that a country should refrain from involvement in international affairs.

Israel, 72, 372, 504, 509

issue ownership, 231 The theory that voters associate certain issues or issue positions with certain parties (like Democrats and support for government-provided health insurance).

issue scale, 195
Italy, 72, *510*

Jackson, Andrew, 222, 355, 394, *394*
Jackson, Robert, 435
Japan, 9, 72, 468, *510*
Japanese Americans in internment camps, 144
Jardines, Joelis, 123
Jay, John, 39
Jefferson, Thomas, 22, 38, 44, 75
    on Congress, 315
    presidential election, 112, 418
    presidential power of, 355
    on separation of church and state, 107

Jim Crow laws, 78, 79, 141 State and local laws that mandated racial segregation in all public facilities in the South, many border states, and some northern communities between 1876 and 1964.

Johnson, Andrew, 346
Johnson, Lyndon, 85, 165–66, 168, *259*, 260, 335, 336
    on affirmative action, 168, 170
    approval rating of, *377*
    Great Society programs of, 85–86, *203*, 396, 473
    presidential power of, 356
    social policies of, 454
    War on Poverty of, 473, 482
Joint Committee on Taxation, 288

joint committees, 337 Committees that contain members of both the House and Senate but have limited authority.

joint resolution, 339
Jolie, Angelina, 161
Jones, Antoine, 124
Jones, Bryan D., 457
Jones and Laughlin Steel Corporation, National Labor Relations Board v., 80
Jordan, Barbara, 307
Jorgensen, Jo, *241*, 241
JP Morgan Chase, 471
J Street, 504
Judd, Ashley, 161

judicial activism, 160, 438–40 The idea that the Supreme Court should assert its interpretation of the law even if it overrules

the elected executive and legislative branches of government.

judicial branch, 414–45
    Articles of Confederation on, 35, *38*
    checks and balances with other branches, 7, 52, 56, 60, 62, 418–19, 440, 442
    Constitution on, *38*, 396, 416, 417, *418*, 419, 431
    exclusive powers of, 54
    foreign policy role of, 501–4
    historical development of, 416–20
    and political processes, 13
    selection of judges in, 425–29
    structure of, 424–25
    see also courts

judicial restraint, 438–40 The idea that the Supreme Court should defer to the democratically elected executive and legislative branches of government rather than contradicting existing laws.

judicial review, 56, 418–19, 438–40 The Supreme Court's power to strike down a law or executive branch action that it finds unconstitutional.
    activism and restraint in, 160, 438–40
    definition of, 56

Judiciary Act (1789), 417, 418–19 The law in which Congress laid out the organization of the federal judiciary. The law refined and clarified federal court jurisdiction and set the original number of justices at six. It also created the office of the attorney general and established the lower federal courts.

jurisdiction, 422, 424, 431 The sphere of a court's legal authority to hear and decide cases.

jury trials, 49, 127–28, 144
Justice Department, 5, *398*
    and affirmative action, 172
    and executive privilege, 368
    and Microsoft, 468
    and police discrimination, 149
    and recreational marijuana, 91
    and redistricting, 160, 327, 328
    and Russia investigation, 345, 354
    in screening of lower-court judges, 428–29
    size of, *400*
    solicitor general in, 432
    and Trump, 54, 354
    and Watergate investigation, 368

Kagan, Elena, 170, 328, 428, 434, *435*, *437*, 438, 440
Kaibab National Forest, 470
Kansas, 87
Kansas-Nebraska Act (1854), 140, 355
Kaptur, Marcy, 327
Kasich, John, 98, 253
Kavanaugh, Brett, *55*, 246, 360, *415*, 434, *435*, *437*, 438, 439

Keillor, Garrison, 161
Kelly, Mark, *240*
Kennan, George F., 494
Kennedy, Anthony M., 173, *425*, 438, 439
Kennedy, John F., 168, 449
Kentucky, 46, 157
Kerry, John, *255*, 363
Key, V. O., 180, 213
Keynes, John Maynard, 461

Keynesian economics, 461 The theory that governments should use economic policy, like taxing and spending, to maintain stability in the economy.

Keystone XL pipeline, 293
Kim Jong-un, 366, *366*, 375, 515
King, Martin Luther, Jr., 153, 154
King, Steve, 322
Kingdon, John, 457
Klobuchar, Amy, 26, 237
Kosovo, 496
Kraninger, Kathy, *407*
Kucinich, Dennis, 327
Kuebel, Schilb v., 106
Ku Klux Klan, 112, 115, *115*, 117
Kurtzman, Lemon v., 108
Kushner, Jared, 371, 372

Labor Department, *398*, *400*, 481
labor unions, 289, 291, 409, 473
laissez-faire capitalism, 79
Lamb, Conor, 260
Land Grant College Act (1862), 482
Las Vegas, Nev., 120

latent opinion, 183 An opinion formed on the spot, when it is needed (as distinct from a deeply held opinion that is stable over time).

Latinos:
    civil rights of, 143
    composition of U.S. population, *19*, 318
    in Congress, 158, 318
    discrimination against, 143, 171
    diversity of, 143
    as federal court judges, 427, 428
    party identification of, 18, 143
    police shooting of, 150
    presidential appointments of, 169
    socioeconomic indicators on, 148
    voting by, *146*, *147*
Lauer, Matt, 161
Laughlin, Lori, *421*
law enforcement:
    as government function, 6–7, 8, *8*
    Miranda rights in, 126
    and police brutality against minority citizens, 278
    and police shootings of African Americans, 136, 149–51, *151*, 155, 275
    racial profiling in, 136–38, 151, 172, 174, 175
    search and seizure in, 58, 100, 122–26
Lawrence, John Geddes, *130*, 154
Lawrence v. Texas, 130
laws, *see* legislation

lawsuits and litigation strategies of interest groups, 299, *299*

lawyers, right to counsel from, 127–28

"layer cake" and "marble cake" models of federalism, 80, 82, *84*

Leadership Conference on Civil and Human Rights, 116

lead in water supply, 149

League of Nations, 355, 493

leaking of information, 118

Lebanon, 364

Ledbetter, Lilly, 164, 425

Ledbetter v. Goodyear Tire & Rubber, 425

LeFevre, Dell, 470

legal counsel, right to, 127–28

legislation, 338–43
    and bureaucracy, 388
    on civil rights, 165–68
    enforcement of, *see* law enforcement
    interest groups drafting, 298
    judicial review of, 56, 417, 418–19, 438–40
    omnibus, 344, 453
    party influence on, 239–40
    pork barrel, 317, 321, 331, *332*, 344
    on presidential authority, 358–59, *358*
    presidential interpretation and implementation of, 375
    presidential veto of, 7, 56, 343, 366–68, 374, 454, 501
    signing statements on, 375
    types of, 339
    see also specific laws

legislative branch, 43–44
    Articles of Confederation on, 35–36
    checks and balances with other branches, 7, 52, 55–56, 62
    Constitutional Convention compromise on, 42
    Constitution on, *41*, 73, 315–17, 338, 451
    in parliamentary system, 44
    and separation of powers, 7
    shared powers of, 54–55
    see also Congress

legislative process, 338–43
    for Affordable Care Act, 344
    amendments in, 342–43, 344
    authorization and appropriation in, 343
    on budget, 452, 453
    committee system in, 337–43
    conventional, 339–43
    diagrams of, 340, 341
    discharge petition in, 343
    earmarks in, 331
    filibusters in, 342
    logrolling in, 331
    markup in, 342
    president in, 56, 343, 358–59, 366–68, 374
    reconciliation in, 341
    vetoes in, 7, 56, 343, 366–68, 374, 454, 501
    voting in, 334, 342

Lehman Brothers, 471

Lemon test, 108 The Supreme Court uses this test, established in *Lemon v. Kurtzman,* to determine whether a practice violates the First Amendment's establishment clause.

Lemon v. Kurtzman, 108–9

Leno, Jay, 62

lesbian people, *see* LGBTQ people

"Letter from Birmingham Jail" (King), 153

Levine, James, 161

Lewinsky, Monica, 346

LGBTQ people, 130, 139, 144–45
    civil rights of, 130, 138, 144–45, 164–65, 167–68, 175
    discrimination against, 93, 130, 138, 144–45, 164–65, 167–68, 175
    equal protection of, 90
    hate crimes against, 168
    and interest groups, 303
    liberal policies on, 90
    in military, 168, *169*, 175
    as presidential election issue (2016), *267*
    privacy rights of, 130
    and same-sex marriage, *see* same-sex marriage
    and social movements, 152
    and sodomy laws, 130, 164–65
    and Stonewall uprising, 145, *145*

LGBTQ rights, 223

libel, 118 Written false statements that damage a person's reputation. They can be regulated by the government but are often difficult to distinguish from permissible speech.

liberal, 20, 90 The side of the ideological spectrum defined by support for stronger government programs and more market regulation; generally associated with Democrats.
    in domestic policies, 492
    and ideological polarization, 199, *200*
    and media effects, 210–12
    as stable opinion, 183
    of Supreme Court justices, 426, 435, 437–38, 439

liberalism, 494 The idea that foreign policy decisions reflect normative goals such as justice, equality, and human rights.

libertarians, 20, 20, 241, 241, 242 Those who prefer very limited government and therefore tend to be conservative on issues such as social welfare policy, environmental policy, and government funding for education but liberal on issues involving personal liberty such as free speech, abortion, and the legalization of drugs.

liberty, 22–23, 38 Political freedom, such as the freedom of speech, press, assembly, and religion. These and other legal and due process rights protecting individuals from government control are outlined in the Bill of Rights of the U.S. Constitution.
    Antifederalist concerns about, 49
    and civil liberties, 98–135
    and conflict resolution, 22–23

Libya, 365, 493, 501, 510

life expectancy, 149

Lilly Ledbetter Fair Pay Act, 164, 425

limited government, 35 A political system in which the powers of the government are restricted to prevent tyranny by protecting property and individual rights.

Limbaugh, Rush, 461

Lincoln, Abraham, 140, 183, 317, 355, 360

Linick, Steve, 407

linkage institutions, 289

linking institution, 20

Lipinski, Dan, 238, 249

literacy tests for voting, 141

litigation strategies of interest groups, 299, *299*

living Constitution, 57–61, 437 A way of interpreting the Constitution that takes into account evolving national attitudes and circumstances rather than the text alone.

loans:
    interest rates on, 456, 459, 466, 473
    mortgage, *see* mortgages

lobbying, 15, 286–311 Efforts to influence public policy through contact with public officials on behalf of an interest group.
    Astroturf, 302
    definition of, 289
    direct, 296–98, 300
    on foreign policy, 504–5
    gifts to Congress members in, 297
    grassroots, 302
    on grazing rights, 470
    influence of, 307–8
    inside strategies in, 296–99
    outside strategies in, 296, 300–301, 302–5
    resources used in, 291–92
    restrictions on, 297
    and revolving door, 293, 297
    spending on, 291–96, *294*, 304

local government:
    balance of power with national government, 45, 72–74
    citizen participation in, 92, *93*
    in cooperative federalism, 80
    in daily life, 15
    education role of, 482
    environmental policies of, 83
    federal financial aid to, 81–84
    in federalism, 7, 9, 45, 68, 70, 74
    in health care, 456
    responsibilities of, 70

Locke, John, 44

Lockett, Clayton, 128

Lockheed Martin Corporation, 294, 386

logrolling, 331 A form of reciprocity in which members of Congress support bills that they otherwise might not vote for in exchange for other members' votes on bills that are very important to them.

Lopez, Alfonso, 89
Lopez, United States v., 88, 89, *89*
Los Angeles Lakers, 286–88
Louisiana, 130, 140, 159, 421
Louisiana, Duncan v., 106
Louisiana, Ramos v., 106
Louisiana Purchase, 493

Madison, James, 12, 34, 42, 57, 104
    at Annapolis Convention, 36
    on Bill of Rights, 104
    on common good, 7
    at Constitutional Convention, 42, 44
    on dual federalism, 75
    on factions, 7, 39, 42
    Gerry as vice president under, 326
    on human nature, 7, 39
    on liberty and conflict, 22
    and *Marbury* case, 56, 418–19, *419*
    on republicanism, 37
    on role of government, 7, 39
    on separation of church and state, 107
Madison, Marbury v., 56, 418–19, *419*
Maine, 91, 237, 253, 282
    Senate election in (2020), 246–48, *247*

Majority Leader, 332 The elected head of the party holding the majority of seats in the House or Senate.

majority opinions, *435*
majority rule, 41–42

majority voting, 21, 250 A voting system in which a candidate must win more than 50 percent of votes to win the election. If no candidate wins enough votes to take office, a runoff election is held between the top two vote-getters.

Malloy v. Hogan, 106
Manchin, Joe, 276

mandatory spending, 463, *463* Expenditures that are required by law, such as the funding for Social Security.

Manning, Chelsea, *117*, 368
Mapp, Dollree, 124, *124*
Mapp v. Ohio, 106
"marble cake" and "layer cake" models of federalism, 80, 82, *84*
Marbury, William, 418
Marbury v. Madison, 56, 418–19, *419*
March for Our Lives, 121, *121*
marginal tax rate, 465, *465*
margin of error, 192, 193, 194
marijuana, 16, 91
Marjory Stoneman Douglas High School, *89*, 121

markup, 342 One of the steps through which a bill becomes a law, in which the final wording of the bill is determined.

marriage, interracial, 21, 141, 158
marriage, same-sex, *see* same-sex marriage

Marshall, John, 56, 58, 59, 75–77, 418, *419*
Marshall, Thurgood, 58, 439
Marshall Plan, 494, *494*
Martin, Trayvon, 149
Maryland, 43, 46, 75, 157, 328, 329
    partisan gerrymandering in, 328
Maryland, Benton v., 106
Maryland, McCulloch v., 58, 75, *75*
Mason, George, 34, 49, 101
Massachusetts:
    abortion protests in, 117
    at Constitutional Convention, 43, *43*
    marijuana in, 91
    presidential campaign in (2020), 237
    ratification of Constitution, 50
    Shays's Rebellion in, 37
    slavery in, *46*

mass associations, 290–91 Interest groups that have a large number of dues-paying individuals as members.

mass media, 206 Sources that provide information to the average citizen, such as newspapers, television networks, radio stations, podcasts, and websites.
    see also media

mass protests, grassroots lobbying in, 302, *302*
mass shootings, 120, 405

mass surveys, 194–98, 213 A way to measure public opinion by interviewing a relatively small sample of a large population.
    on abortion, 12
    accuracy of, 196–98, 213
    reliability of, 192, 193, 196
    sample in, 192, 193, 194, 195
    on terrorism concern, 516
    on voting in congressional election (2018), 276
    wording of questions in, 192, 195, *196*, 214

material benefits, 291 Benefits that are provided to individuals for joining a group, such as a coffee mug or a T-shirt, that are distinct from the collective benefits provided by the group.

Matthew Shepard and James Byrd Jr. Hate Crimes Prevention Act (2009), 168
Mattis, James, 500
Mayhew, David R., 321
McCain, John, 233, *255, 258, 259*
McCain-Feingold Act, 266, 433
McCarthy, Kevin, 378
McConnell, Mitch, 218, 220–21, 341, 346, 378, 446
McCulloch v. Maryland, 58, 75, *75*
McCutcheon v. Federal Election Commission, 266
McDaniel, Ronna, 378

McDonald v. Chicago*, 106, 121, *121 The Supreme Court ruled in 2010 that the

Second Amendment's right to keep and bear arms for self-defense in one's home is applicable to the states through the Fourteenth Amendment.

McGahn, Donald, 346–47
McGowan, Rose, 161
McHenry, James, 49
McMaster, H. R., 500
McSally, Martha, *240*
means-tested programs, *483*
media, 9–10, 28, 206–12
    advertising in, *see* advertising
    and anonymous sources, 25
    bias in, 210–12
    broadcast, 208
    critical analysis of, 24–26, 27, 71, 209
    equal time provision on, 208
    fact and opinion increasingly blurred in, 208
    and fake news, 2–4, 28
    filtering of news in, 212
    foreign policy role of, 505
    framing of news in, 212
    and free press, 2, 102, 117–18, 120
    influence on audience, 210–12
    interest group coverage in, 304–5
    Internet sources of political information in, 206, 210
    leaks of information in, 118
    regulation and deregulation of, 208–10
    social, *see* social media
Media Checklist for Assessing Reporting on Politics, 25, 27

media conglomerates, 210, *211* Companies that control a large number of media sources across several types of media outlets.

media effects, 210–12 The influence of media coverage on average citizens' opinions and actions.

Medicaid, 356, 478, 480 An entitlement program funded by the federal and state governments that provides health care coverage for low-income Americans who would otherwise be unable to afford health care.
    and Affordable Care Act, 86, 90, 480
    categorical grants in, 81
    creation of, 474
    federal funds in, 81, 86, 90
    and fiscal federalism, 81
    long-term challenges for, 478–79
    participation in, *483*
    spending on, 475
    state role in, 81, 86, 90, 456, 478, 480

medical records, computerized, 480

Medicare, 356, 449, 472–74, 478–81 The federal health care plan created in 1965 that provides coverage for retired Americans for hospital care (Part A), medical care (Part B), and prescription drugs (Part D).

National Federation of Independent Business v. Sebelius, 88

National Football League, 155, 170

National Forest Service, 337

National Guard, 7, 120, 168

National Highway Traffic Safety Administration, 469

National Independent Automobile Dealers Association, 290

National Instant Criminal Background Check System, 121

National Institute of Allergy and Infectious Diseases, 346, 384

National Labor Relations Act, 473

National Labor Relations Board v. Jones and Laughlin Steel Corporation, 80

National Oceanographic and Atmospheric Administration (NOAA), 379

National Organization for Women, 116, 166

National Park Service, 391

National Recovery Administration, 473

National Republican Congressional Committee, 226, 235

National Republican Senatorial Committee, 226

National Rifle Association (NRA), 120, 288, 289, 295, 299, 307, 308
    as centralized group, 290
    in opposition to policy change, 307
    public opinion mobilization efforts of, 302

national security, 7, 72, 100, 490, 517

National Security Agency (NSA), 125, 132, 321, 500–501

National Security Council, 498, 500 An agency within the EOP that advises the president on matters of foreign policy.

national supremacy clause, 45, 73, 75 Part of Article VI, Section 2, of the Constitution stating that the Constitution and the laws and treaties of the United States are the "supreme Law of the Land," meaning national laws take precedence over state laws if the two conflict.

National Turkey Federation, 295, 307, 307, 308

National Weather Service, 379

nation building, 492, 496 The use of a country's resources, including the military, to help nondemocratic nations transform themselves into democracies.

Nation of Islam, 19

Native Americans, 19, 139, 493
    affirmative action policies for, 170
    civil rights of, 142–43, 142, 143
    forced assimilation of, 142, 142
    and smallpox, 142
    voting rights of, 142

Nativity displays, 107, 108–9

NATO (North Atlantic Treaty Organization), 495, 501, 509–10

Natural Resources Department, 80

natural rights, 39 Also known as "unalienable rights," these rights are defined in the Declaration of Independence as "Life, Liberty, and the pursuit of Happiness." The Founders believed that upholding these rights should be the government's central purpose.

Nazi marchers, 116–17, 132

NCAA women's basketball, 390

Near v. Minnesota, 106

Nebraska, 128, 253

necessary and proper clause, 51, 73 Part of Article I, Section 8, of the Constitution that grants Congress the power to pass all laws related to its expressed powers; also known as the elastic clause.

negative partisanship, 199

Neguse, Joe, 312

Neustadt, Richard, 357

Nevada:
    congressional midterm election (2018), 276
    marijuana in, 91
    mass shooting in, 120
    presidential campaign and election in (2016), 253, 257
    presidential campaign and election in (2020), 237, 279

Nevada Department of Human Resources v. Hibbs, 88

New Deal, 473 The set of policies proposed by President Franklin Roosevelt and enacted by Congress between 1933 and 1935 to promote economic recovery and social welfare during the Great Depression.
    and bureaucracy growth, 395–96, 395
    and federal government power, 79, 85, 317
    and party system, 223, 223
    and presidential power, 356, 356
    and social policy, 454, 473, 473
    and Supreme Court, 420, 427, 440

New Hampshire, 43, 46, 50, 237, 252

New Jersey, 43, 46, 431

New Jersey Plan, 42, 43, 57 A plan that was suggested in response to the Virginia Plan; smaller states at the Constitutional Convention proposed that each state should receive equal representation in the national legislature, regardless of size.

New Mexico, 140, 431

news, political information in, *see* political information

newspapers, 206
    circulation trends, 208
    media conglomerates in, 210
    recent changes in, 208

Newtown, Conn., Sandy Hook Elementary School in, 121

New York, 320
    Antifederalists in, 49

    at Constitutional Convention, 43, 49
    COVID-19 in, 69
    Ellis Island dispute with New Jersey, 431
    interstate commerce in, 76, 76
    presidential election in (2016), 255
    public prayer in, 108
    ratification of Constitution, 50
    slavery in, 46
    Stonewall uprising in, 145, 145
    "stop-and-frisk" policy in, 136, 137

New York, Gitlow v., 105, 106

New York, N.Y., 69
    "stop-and-frisk" in, 136, 137

New York Federal Reserve, 471

New York Post, 209, 278

New York Times, 470

***New York Times Co. v. United States,* 118** The Supreme Court ruled in 1971 that the government could not prevent the publication of the Pentagon Papers, which revealed lies about the progress of the war in Vietnam.

NextGen Climate Action, 303

Nicaragua, 493

Nineteenth Amendment, 19, 59, 61, 144, 152

Ninth Amendment, 104, 106

Nixon, Richard:
    affirmative action program of, 168, 170
    approval rating of, 377
    executive privilege of, 368
    foreign policy of, 495
    presidential power of, 356

Nixon, United States v., 368

NOAA, 379

No Child Left Behind Act (2001), 396, 456, 482

nominating conventions, 235, 236, 253 A meeting held by each party every four years at which states' delegates select the party's presidential and vice-presidential nominees and approve the party platform.

nongovernmental organizations, 506 Groups operated by private institutions (rather than governments) to promote growth, economic development, and other agendas throughout the world.

nonpartisan primary, 234

nonviolent protests, 153

norms, 21 Unwritten rules and informal agreements among citizens and elected officials about how government and society should operate.
    changes influencing constitutional interpretation, 60–61

North American Free Trade Agreement (NAFTA), 496

North Atlantic Treaty Organization (NATO), 495, 501, 509–10

North Carolina:
    civil rights movement in, 153
    at Constitutional Convention, 43

partisan gerrymandering in, 328
presidential campaign in (2020), 237
presidential election in (2016), 254, 257
ratification of Constitution, 50
slavery in, *46*
social media restrictions for sex offenders in, 116
voting districts in, 159–60, 328–30, *328*
North Dakota, 130, 275
Northern Securities Company, 355
North Korea, 366, *507*
economic sanctions on, *515*, 517
nuclear technology of, 490, 515
and Trump, 366, *366*, 498, 515
North Vietnam, 495

notice-and-comment procedure, 387, 407 A step in the rule-making process in which proposed rules are published in the *Federal Register* and made available for debate by the general public.

NSA, 125, 132, 321, 500–501
nuclear technology:
of Iran, 301, 365, 509
and mutually assured destruction, 495
of North Korea, 490, 515

Obama, Barack, 5, *12*, 275, 277, 280, 354
Affordable Care Act of, *see* Affordable Care Act
appointments and nominations of, 54, 169–70, 360, *427*, 428, 429, 468
bureaucracy under, 396, 407
citizenship of, *181*, 182, 213
as commander in chief, 364, 365
and congressional elections, 336
DACA program of, 312
and divided government, 240
and drone attacks, 369
economic policies of, 258, 454
economy under, 258, *259*, 471–72
education policies of, 456, 483
electoral votes for, *255*
environmental policies of, 363, 365–66, 389
executive orders of, 60, 164, 275, 361
and Federal Reserve System, 468
and Flint water crisis, 149
foreign policy of, 365–66, *366*, 493, 496, 503, 505, 506
on freedom of speech, 100
and gay rights, 145, *145*, 168, *169*
on gender pay disparities, 164
going public, 379
and Guantánamo Bay detention center, 53
and gun laws, 121
on hate crimes, 168
immigration policies of, 174
and marijuana laws, 91
pardons by, 368
presidential power of, 356–57
public opinion on, *181*, 182, 188, *189*, 190, *202*, *203*, 377
on same-sex marriage, 145
social policies of, 456, 474, 479–80
on Supreme Court decisions, 426

and Syria, 55
trade policies of, 505
unfunded mandates of, 86
unilateral actions of, 375
vetoes from, *366*, *367*
Obamacare, *see* Affordable Care Act
Obergefell, Jim, *73*
Obergefell v. Hodges, 10, *73*, 165
O'Brien, Robert, 359
obscenity, 119–20
obstruction of justice, 60
Ocasio-Cortez, Alexandria, 4, *221*
Occupational Safety and Health Administration (OSHA), 409, 469
O'Connor, Sandra Day, 87, 130, 435, 438

Office of Management and Budget, 71, 397, 454, 499 An office within the EOP that is responsible for creating the president's annual budget proposal to Congress, reviewing proposed rules, and performing other budget-related tasks.

Ogden, Gibbons v., *75*, 76
Ohio, 257, 326, 327
Ohio, Brandenburg v., 112
Ohio, Mapp v., 106
oil, *142*, 495
Oklahoma, 128, 142, 163, 237
Oliver, John, 207

omnibus legislation, 344, 453 Large bills that often cover several topics and may contain extraneous, or pork-barrel, projects.

"one-person, one-vote," 326
OPEC, 495

open market operations, 467 The process by which the Federal Reserve System buys and sells securities to influence the money supply.

open primary, 234, 236, 249 A primary election in which any registered voter can participate in the contest, regardless of party affiliation.

open seat, 260 An elected position for which there is no incumbent.

Open Society Foundations, 506
Open Society Policy Center, *295*
opinions, factors affecting formation of, 188–91
opinion writing by Supreme Court justices, 434–36, *435*
opioid overdose and addiction, 457
opportunity, equality of, 23, 159, 171

oral arguments, 433–34 Spoken presentations made in person by the lawyers of each party to a judge or an appellate court outlining the legal reasons their side should prevail.

order, provision of, 6–7

Oregon, 91, 110
Oregon, De Jonge v., *106*
O'Reilly, Bill, 161
Organization of the Petroleum Exporting Countries (OPEC), 495
originalism, 58

original jurisdiction, 417 The authority of a court to handle a case first, as in the Supreme Court's authority to initially hear disputes between two states. However, original jurisdiction for the Supreme Court is not exclusive; it may assign such a case to a lower court.

Orlando, Fla., 120, 121
Orwell, George, 25
OSHA, 409, 469
Ostrom, Elinor, 85

outside strategies, 296, 300–301, 302–5 The tactics employed outside Washington, D.C., by interest groups seeking to achieve their policy goals.

outsourcing, 513, *513*
Oval Office, 371, 373

oversight, 345–47, 407–10, 497 Congressional efforts to make sure that laws are implemented correctly by the bureaucracy after they have been passed.

ownership society, 474 The term used to describe the social policy vision of President George W. Bush, in which citizens take responsibility for their own social welfare and the free market plays a greater role in social policy.

Oxfam International, 506

Paine, Thomas, 37–38
Pakistan, 497, 506, 514
Palestinians, 372
Paltrow, Gwyneth, 161
Panama, 493

paradox of voting, 270 The question of why citizens vote even though their individual votes stand little chance of changing the election outcome.

pardons, 54, 62, 368
Paris Agreement on climate change, 13, 86, *86*, 280, 363, 365, *500*
and Trump, 54
Paris terrorist attacks (2016), 172
Paris Treaty (1783), 36
Parkland, Fla., *89*, 120, 121, *121*
Parks, Rosa, 152–53

parliamentary system, 9, 44 A system of government in which legislative and executive power are closely joined. The legislature (parliament) selects the chief executive (prime minister), who forms the cabinet from members of the parliament.

parochial schools, 108, 109
partisan gerrymandering, 328, 423
partisan redistricting, 326–28, 329
partisanship, negative, 199
party activists, 229

party coalitions, 230–32, *231* The groups that identify with a political party, usually described in demographic terms such as African-American Democrats or evangelical Republicans.

party identification, 183, 220–21, 229–30, 242 A citizen's loyalty to a specific political party.
    of African Americans, 18, *18*, 223, 231–32
    and group identity, 18–20, 186
    and opinion formation, 188–90
    and party in the electorate, 220, 229–32
    and political polarization, *200*, 227, 228
    and public opinion, 188, 190
    voter trends in, *228*, 229, *229*
    as voting cue, 258, 272
    of women, 18

party in government, 220, *221*, 259–28 The group of officeholders who belong to a specific political party and were elected as candidates of that party.

party in the electorate, 220, *221*, 229–32 The group of citizens who identify with a specific political party.

party leader, president as, 378–80

party organization, 220–21, *221*, 223, 224–25, 243 A specific political party's leaders and workers at the national, state, and local levels.

party platform, 238, 242, 249, 253, 261–62 A set of objectives outlining the party's issue positions and priorities. Candidates are not required to support their party's platform.

party principle, 222 The idea that a political party exists as an organization distinct from its elected officials or party leaders.

party system, 221, 223 Periods in which the names of the major political parties, their supporters, and the issues dividing them have remained relatively stable.

party unity, 334, *335* The extent to which members of Congress in the same party vote together on party votes

party vote, 334, *335* A vote in which the majority of one party opposes the position of the majority of the other party.

Patriot Act (2001), 122, 343
Paul, Rand, *20*
Paycheck Protection Program, 472
pay gap for women, 19, 164, *164*, 425

payroll taxes, 464–65, *464*
    for Social Security, 464, 475, 476, 477

peak associations, *289*, 290–91 Interest groups whose members are businesses or other organizations rather than individuals.

Pearl Harbor bombing, 493
Pell Grants, 483
Pelosi, Nancy, 4, 32, 218, 221, 276, 347
Pence, Mike, 360, 372, *372*, 378, *504*
Pendleton Civil Service Act (1883), 395
Pennsylvania, 37, *142*
    at Constitutional Convention, *43*
    presidential election in (2016), 255, 257
    presidential election in (2020), 279, 281
    redistricting in, 328, 329
    slavery in, *46*
    special election in (2018), 260
Pentagon, terrorist attack on, *496*
Pentagon Papers, 118
per curiam opinions, *435*
Perez, Tom, *221*
performance-enhancing drugs, 125
Pericles, 15

permanent campaign, 315 The continual quest for reelection that is rooted in high-cost professional campaigns that are increasingly reliant on consultants and expensive media campaigns.

Perot, Ross, 242
Perry, James L., 403
Perry, Rick, 87
Persian Gulf War, 356
Pew Research Center, 193, 229, 402
peyote in religious ceremonies, 110
pharmaceutical industry, 295, *308*
Pharmaceutical Research and Manufacturers of America, 295, 303, *308*
Philippines, 493
Phillips, Jack, *110*
phone use:
    privacy and security in, 124
    surveillance of, 125

picket fence federalism, 80, 82, 83, 84 A more refined and realistic form of cooperative federalism in which policy makers within a particular policy area work together across the levels of government.

Pierce, Franklin, 355
Pinckney, Charles, 101

plaintiff, 420 The person or party who brings a case to court.

Planned Parenthood, 129

plea bargaining, 420, *421* Negotiating an agreement between a plaintiff and a defendant to settle a case before it goes to trial or the verdict is decided. In a civil case, this usually involves an admission of guilt and

an agreement on monetary damages; in a criminal case, this often involves an admission of guilt in return for a reduced charge or sentence.

Pledge of Allegiance, 432
Plessy v. Ferguson, 141

pluralism, 42 The idea that having a variety of parties and interests within a government will strengthen the system, ensuring that no group possesses total control.

plurality opinions, *435*

plurality voting, 21, 250 A voting system in which the candidate who receives the most votes within a geographic area wins the election, regardless of whether that candidate wins a majority (more than half) of the votes.

pocket veto, 343, 366 The automatic death of a bill passed by the House and Senate when the president fails to sign the bill in the last 10 days of a legislative session.

Pointer v. Texas, 106
polarization, ideological, *see* ideological polarization
police, 7, *8*, 85
    brutality against minorities by, 278
    interrogations by, 126
    racial profiling by, 136–38, 151
    reform of, 281
    shooting African Americans, 136, 149–51, *151*, 155, 275

police patrol oversight, 345, 408 A method of oversight in which members of Congress constantly monitor the bureaucracy to make sure that laws are implemented correctly.

police powers, 70 The power to enforce laws and provide for public safety

policy agenda, 449 The set of desired policies that political leaders view as their top priorities.

policy-making process, 449–58
    bureaucracy in, 450, 455–56
    Congress in, 449–54
    president in, 450, 454
    punctuated equilibrium model on, 457
    stages model of, 457

policy mood, 201–5, *203*, *204* The level of public support for expanding the government's role in society; whether the public wants government action on a specific issue.

political action committees (PACs), 225, 303–4 An interest group or a division of an interest group that can raise money to contribute to campaigns or to spend on ads in support of candidates. The amount a PAC can receive from each of its donors and the amount it can spend on federal electioneering are strictly limited.

in campaign financing, 225, *235*, *266*, *267*, *267*, *303*, *304*, 323
definition of, 225, 303
party affiliation of, 225
and Super PACs, 303, *304*, *305*

political appointees, 386 People selected by an elected leader, such as the president, to hold a government position.

political equality, 23, 40
political influences on Supreme Court, 437–41
political information, 206–12
critical analysis of, 24–26, 27, 71, 209
fake news in, 2–4, 28
filtering of, 212
framing of, 212
Internet as source of, 206–10
leaking of, 118
sources used for, 206–10
and voting decisions, 272
political parties, 218–45
accountability function of, 239–40
brand identity of, 225, 262, 332
in campaign financing, 235–38, *235*, *238*, *266*, *267*, *268*, 270
coalitions in, 230–32, *231*
in Congress, 226, 239–40, 332–38
and cooperation in government, 239–40
in divided government, 226
economic policies of, 448, 474–75
in election process, 232–38, 239–40, 243, 246–48, 249, 261–62
on health insurance, 480–81
history of, 221–24, *222*
identification with, *see* party identification
and ideological polarization, 199, *200*, *227*, *228*, 334
ideology in, 20–21, 24
legislative influence of, 239–40
minor, 241–42, 255
organization of, 220–21, *221*, 223, 224–25, 243
party in government, 220, *221*, 225–28
party in the electorate, 220, *221*, 229–32
platform of, 238, 242, 249, 253, 261–62
policy priorities in, 228, *230*, 231–32, 238, 242
president as leader of, 378–80
public opinion on, 220, *221*
racial, gender, and ethnic identity in, 18–19
realignments of, 224
in recruiting and nominating candidates, 232–38
in redistricting, 326–28, 329
role of, 232–42
social policies of, 474–75
on Social Security, 477
in split ticket and straight ticket voting, 273
and spoils system, 222
in unified government, 226
in wave elections, 273–74
see also specific parties

political process, 9–10, 13–14
citizen involvement in, 92, *93*
in elections, 10, *13*
political socialization, 184–85 The process by which an individual's political opinions are shaped by other people and the surrounding culture.

political speech, freedom of, 112–13
politicians:
accountability of, 239–40, 249, 319–21
influence on public opinion, 187, *187*
presidents as, 377–78
public opinion polls influencing, 197, 205

politico, 319 A member of Congress who acts as a delegate on issues that constituents care about (such as immigration reform) and as a trustee on more complex or less salient issues (such as some foreign policy or regulatory matters).

Politico (Internet site), 206

politics, 9 The process that determines what government does.
conflicts in, *see* conflicts, political
in daily life, 10, 11, 14–15, *14*, *15*, 28
process in, 9–10, 13–14, 92
public opinion on, 198–206

polity, 9
Polk, James, 355
polling places, 147, 160, *251*, 272
polls, 26, 191–98, 213, 516
pollution, environmental regulations on, 66–68, *67*, 469, *469*
Pompeo, Mike, 374, 407

popular sovereignty, 39 The idea that government gains its legitimacy through regular elections in which the people living under that government participate to elect their leaders.

popular vote, 253, 255 The votes cast by citizens in an election.
in presidential election (2016), 195, 255, *259*
in presidential election (2020), 17, 229–30, *229*, *255*

population, 191 The group of people whom a researcher or pollster wants to study, such as evangelicals, senior citizens, or Americans.

pork barrel, 317, 332 Legislative appropriations that benefit specific constituents, created with the aim of helping local representatives win reelection.
earmarks in, 331
logrolling in, 331
omnibus legislation on, 344

pornography, 119, 124, *124*
position taking, by congressional incumbents, 321
Postal Service, 8, 15, 394, 400

Potbelly, 286
poverty, 147–49, *148*, 473, 474–75
Great Society programs in, 396, 473–74
social policies in, 457, 473–74
Powell, Colin, 253
Powell, Jerome, *467*, 468, 472
Powell v. Alabama, 106

power of the purse, *51*, 51, 55, 345, 451, 502 The constitutional power of Congress to raise and spend money. Congress can use this as a negative or checking power over the other branches by freezing or cutting their funding.

prayer in public schools, 103, 107–8, 440, *440*
preamble of Constitution, 7, 8, 72

precedent, 421, 436, 441 A legal norm established in court cases that is then applied to future cases dealing with the same legal questions.

president, 352–83
Cabinet of, 169–70, 373–74, *373*
constitutional requirements to serve as, 252
election of, *see* presidential campaigns and elections
Executive Office of, 371–72, *371*, 397, 402, 498
foreign policy power of, 499, 517
going public, 379–80
impeachment of, 5, 55, 346
as party leader, 378–80
as politicians, 377–78
power of, *see* presidential power
public opinion on, 26, 188–91, *189*, *191*, 202, 213, 354, 377–78
relationship with Congress, 239, 315–17, 365, 375–77

presidential approval ratings, 188–91, *189*, *202*, *213*, 258, 377–78 The percentage of Americans who think that the president is doing a good job in office.

presidential campaign and election of 2016, 275
campaign ads in, *267*
campaign financing in, 270
debates in, 264
economic issues in, 509
electoral votes in, 254, 257
fake news in, 3
Ginsburg comments on, 414, 416, 426, 441
grazing rights as issue in, 470
media coverage in, 211–12
minor parties in, 241–42
outcome prediction in, 195, 196–97
party organization in, 378
popular vote in, 5, 255, *259*
public opinion in, 196
recruitment and nomination of candidates in, 233, 234, 237

presidential campaign and election of 2016
(*Continued*)

president pro tempore, 334, 335 A largely symbolic position usually held by the most senior member of the majority party in the Senate.

principal-agent game, 391–93, 405, 469 The interaction between a principal (such as the president or Congress), who needs something done, and an agent (such as a bureaucrat), who is responsible for carrying out the principal's orders.

prior restraint, 117–18 A limit on freedom of the press that allows the government to prohibit the media from publishing certain materials.

privacy rights, 129–30 Liberties protected by several amendments in the Bill of Rights that shield certain personal aspects of citizens' lives from governmental interference, such as the Fourth Amendment's protection against unreasonable searches and seizures

privatization of Social Security, 474, 477 The process of transferring the management of a government program (like Social Security) from the public sector to the private sector.

privileges and immunities clause, 74 The part of Article IV of the Constitution requiring that states must treat nonstate residents within their borders as they would treat their own residents. This was meant to promote commerce and travel between states.

problem of control, 391–93, 404, 405 A difficulty faced by elected officials in ensuring that when bureaucrats implement policies they follow these officials' intentions but still have enough discretion to use their expertise.

progressive taxes, 464, 475 Describes taxes that require upper-income people to pay a higher tax rate than lower-income people, such as income taxes.

redistricting, 147, 158–59, 250, 325–30
Re-drawing the geographic boundaries of
legislative districts. This happens every 10
years to ensure that districts remain roughly
equal in population.
  gerrymandering in, 326, 327
  partisan, 326–28, 329
  racial, 327, 328–29, 432
  Supreme Court on, 326, 327, 328, *328*,
    329, 432

"red states," 16, 17

red tape, 393 Excessive or unnecessarily
complex regulations imposed by the
bureaucracy.

Reed, Stanley, 435
reelection of incumbents, 240, 273–74, *274*,
  319–25, 336
Reform Party, 242
refugees, 280, 505
Regents of the University of California,
  Hamilton v., 106
Regents of the University of California v.
  Bakke, 171

regressive taxes, 464–65 Describes taxes
that take a larger share of poor people's
income than wealthy people's income, such
as sales taxes and payroll taxes.

regulations, 387–91, 468–69 Rules that
allow the government to exercise control
over individuals and corporations by
restricting certain behaviors.
  economic, 468–69
  environmental, 83, 387, 389, 468, 469, *469*
  in everyday life, 15
  on interest group lobbying, 293, 297
  on media, 208–10
  in New Deal era, 396
  notice-and-comment procedure on, 387
  politics of, 469
  in Progressive Era, 395
  social, 468, 469

Rehnquist, William, 58
Reid, Harry, *471*
religion:
  and aid to religious organizations, 108, 111
  civil liberties in, 100
  and cultural values, 16
  and displays on government property, *109*
  and factions, 7
  freedom of, 102–3, 107–11
  and public safety, 107, *108*
  in public schools, 103, 107–8
  and same-sex marriage, 103, *110*, 111
  and separation of church and state, 103,
    107
  and theocracy, 22
Religious Freedom Restoration Act (1993), 110

remedial legislation, 88 National laws
that address discriminatory state laws.

Authority for such legislation comes from
Section 5 of the Fourteenth Amendment.

rendition of terror suspects, 506
Reno, Shaw v., 158, 328
representation in Congress, 317–21
  descriptive, 317–19
  substantive, 319
  trustee and delegate views of, 319
representative democracy, 21–22, 42
Republican Governors' Association, 224

republicanism, 37–38 As understood
by James Madison and the framers, the
belief that a form of government in which
the interests of the people are represented
through elected leaders is the best form of
government. Our form of government is
known as a republican democracy.

Republican Lawyers' Organization, 225
Republican National Committee, 220, 224,
  225, 235, 238, 277, 378
Republican National Convention (2020), 277
Republican Party, 218–20, 242
  as brand name, 225
  in budget-making process, 451
  in campaign financing, 235–38, *235*, *238*,
    268, 270
  in Civil War era, 140, 141
  coalitions in, 231–32, *231*
  congressional conferences of, 226, 332–34
  in congressional elections, 240, 246–48,
    273–74, 276, 325–26
  conservative ideology in, 20, 24
  on DACA, 347–48
  in divided government, 226
  economic policies of, 16, 448, 449, 451,
    461, 474–75
  in election process, 232–38
  and federal bureaucracy, 396, 397, *401*
  on federal government, 222–23, *223*, 449
  on health insurance, 480–81
  history of, 221–24, *222*
  identification with, 186, 220–21, *228*,
    229–30, *229*
  and ideological polarization, 199, *200*,
    334, *336*
  Latinos in, 143
  and media effects, 212
  on New Deal programs, 396
  organization of, 223, 224–25
  on original meaning of Constitution, 58
  party unity in, 334, *335*
  party votes in, 334, *335*
  platform of, 238, 262
  policy priorities in, 228, 230, 231–32, 238, 239
  in presidential election (2016), 233, 234, 237
  in presidential election (2020), 17, 235–38,
    281
  public opinion in, 190
  racial, gender, and ethnic identity in, 18
  recruiting and nominating election
    candidates from, 232–38, 251–53
  in redistricting, 325–26, 327, 329
  in "red states," 16, 17

reelection of incumbents in, 273–74, *274*,
  322
  on slavery, 222
  social policies of, 474–75
  on Social Security, 477
  on unfunded mandates, 81
republics, 9
research by interest groups, 298

**reserved powers, 45, 73–74, 76–78, 87,
104** As defined in the Tenth Amendment,
powers that are not given to the national
government by the Constitution, or not
prohibited to the states, are reserved by the
states or the people.

reserve requirement, 466 The minimum
amount of money that a bank is required to
have on hand to back up its assets.

residency requirement for citizenship, 161
resolutions, 339, 343
resources, distribution of, 93
restraint, judicial, 438–40
retirement:
  age at time of, 475–76, 477
  of baby-boom generation, 475
  from Congress, lobbying work after,
    293–94, 297
  of incumbents, 260, 276
reverse discrimination, 138, 171, 173
Revolutionary War, 35–36

revolving door, 293, 297 The movement of
individuals from government positions to
jobs with interest groups or lobbying firms,
and vice versa.

R.G. & G.R. Harris Funeral Homes Inc.
  v. Equal Employment Opportunity
  Commission, 165
Rhode Island, 42, *43*, 46, 50
Rice, Condoleezza, 496
rights:
  Antifederalist concerns about, 49
  to bear arms, 120–22
  Bill of Rights on, *see* Bill of Rights
  civil, *see* civil rights
  of defendants, 122–29
  of minority in majority rule, 42
  natural, 39
  in republicanism, 37
  of states, 76–78, 80, 87–90
  voting, *see* voting rights
"rights revolution," 85–86
Roberts, John G., Jr., 130, 347, 414, 416, 428,
  434, *435*, 437, *438*, 439, 441
Robinson, Jackie, 141
Robinson v. California, 106

Roe v. Wade, 129–30, 131, 167 This 1973
Supreme Court case extended the right
of privacy to a woman's decision to have
an abortion while recognizing legitimate
state interests in potential life and maternal
health. The Court noted that the "relative

September 11, 2001, terrorist attacks, 53, 122, 203, 356, 496, *496*, 500
   domestic surveillance after, 81, 125–26, 343
   foreign policy after, 511, 513
   immigration policies after, 172
   public opinions on, 182, 190, 214
Servicemen's Readjustment Act (1944), 458, 482
Sessions, Jeff, 91
Seventeenth Amendment, 59, 315
Seventh Amendment, *104*, *106*
sexual harassment, 161–64
sexual orientation, 144–45, 164–65
   see also LGBTQ people
Shake Shack, 286
shared powers, 54–55
Shaw v. Reno, 158, *328*
Shays, Daniel, 37

Shays's Rebellion, 37 An uprising of about 1500 men in Massachusetts in 1786 and 1787 to protest oppressive laws and gain payment of war debts. The unrest prompted calls for a new constitution.

Shelby, Richard, 250
Shelby County v. Holder, 88
Shepard, Matthew, 168
Sherman, Roger, 49
Sherman Antitrust Act (1890), 355, 395, 468
Shinseki, Eric, 455
Sierra Club, 290, 292

signing statements, 375 A document issued by the president when signing a bill into law explaining his or her interpretation of the law, which often differs from the interpretation of Congress, in an attempt to influence how the law will be implemented.

"Silence Breakers," 161
Silver, Nate, 195
simple resolution, 339
Simpsons, The, 15
Sinema, Kyrsten, *240*
Singapore Summit, *507*
single-member districts, 250
Sixteenth Amendment, 59
Sixth Amendment, 58, *104*, *106*, 127–28
"size principle", Madison on, 42
Slager, Michael, 149, *151*

slander, 118 Spoken false statements that damage a person's reputation. They can be regulated by the government but are often difficult to distinguish from permissible speech.

Slants (rock band), 119, *119*
slavery, 23, 139–40, 146
   and Civil War, 47, *48*, *78*, 140
   and Civil War amendments, 105, 140
   as Constitutional Convention issue, *41*, 45–48, *45*
   and *Dred Scott* decision, *75*, 76–77, *77*, 105, 140, 419

   as "original sin," *45*, *46*
   political party views on, 222
   and presidential power, 355
   state differences in, *41*, 45–48, 76
   Three-Fifths Compromise on, *46*, *47*
smallpox, Native Americans decimated by, 142
smoking, diffusion of policies on, 458
snake handling in religious practice, 107, *108*
SNAP, 337, 398, 481, *483*
SNCC, 153
Snowden, Edward, 125
socialization, political, 184–85
social media:
   interest group use of, 302
   and mass protest, 154
   political information on, 4, 194, 206
   speech restrictions on, 115–16
social movements on civil rights, 152–56
social networks in political socialization, 185

social policy, 472–84 An area of public policy related to maintaining or enhancing the well-being of individuals.
   bureaucracy role in, 455–56, *455*
   congressional role in, 454, 482
   definition of, 473
   diffusion of, 458
   on education, 456, 472, 474, 482–84
   evaluation of, 450
   in Great Society, 454, 473–74
   on health care, 456, 473–74, 478–81
   historical development of, 473–75
   on income support and welfare, 481–82
   interest group influence on, 457
   judicial influence on, 456
   in New Deal, 454, 473, *473*
   and ownership society, 474
   policy-making process for, 449–58
   in poverty and income inequality, 474–75
   presidential role in, 454
   regulatory, 468, 469
   Social Security in, 475–78
   state role in, 456–57

Social Security, 8, 449, 476
   bureaucracy in, 455
   disability program in, 455
   enactment of, 396, 473
   interest group support of, 457
   long-term challenges for, 475–78, 484
   mandatory spending on, 463
   and Medicare, 479
   number of recipients, 475, 476
   privatization of, 474, 477
   public opinion on, 475
   reform proposals, 476–78
   retirement age in, 475–76, 477
   tax revenue for, 464, 475, 476, 477
   trust fund for, 476, 477
Social Security Administration, 455
socioeconomic indicators of inequality, 147–49
   and affirmative action programs, 171
   and political equality, 40
sodomy laws, 130, 164–65

soft money, 114, 267 Contributions that can be used for voter mobilization or to promote a policy proposal or point of view as long as these efforts are not tied to supporting or opposing a particular candidate.

soft power in foreign policy, 496
Soleimani, Qasem, 364, 491

solicitor general, 432 A presidential appointee in the Justice Department who conducts all litigation on behalf of the federal government before the Supreme Court and supervises litigation in the federal appellate courts.

solidary benefits, 291 Satisfaction derived from the experience of working with like-minded people, even if the group's efforts do not achieve the desired impact.

Somalia, 496, 500
Sotomayor, Sonia, 170, 428, 434, *437*, 438, 439
Souter, David, 438, 439
South Carolina, 43, *43*
   active shooter incidents in, 120
   hate crimes in, 151, *151*
   police shooting of unarmed Blacks in, 149–51, *151*
   presidential primary elections in, 237, 253, 277
   slavery in, *46*, 140
South China Sea, 499, 511
Southeast Asia, *512*
southern states:
   civil rights in, 93, 152–53
   Jim Crow laws in, *78*, 79, 141
   in New Deal era, 396
   party identification in, 222, 223, 232
   school desegregation in, 157
   slavery in, 45–48, 139–40
   voting rights of African Americans in, 140, 166
   see also specific states
South Vietnam, 495

sovereign power, 68 The supreme power of an independent state to regulate its internal affairs without foreign interference.

Soviet Union, 494, 510
Spacey, Kevin, 161
Spanish-American War, 364

Speaker of the House, 332 The elected leader of the House of Representatives.

specializing, 337
speech, freedom of, 60, 98–100, 102, 105, 111–20
   in campaigns, 113–14, 269
   clear and present danger test in, 112–13
   in commercial speech, 119, *119*
   in controversial speech on college campuses, 98–100, 132
   direct incitement test in, 113

and fighting words, 118
in free press, 117–18
generally protected expression in, 111–18
in hate speech, 98, 114–15
intermediate scrutiny in, 112
on Internet, 115–16
limits to, 100
in money as speech, 113–14
and obscenity, 119–20
in political speech, 112–13
public opinion on, *186*
and slander or libel, 118–19
standards for protection in, 112
strict scrutiny in, 112
in symbolic speech, 113
speedy trial, right to, 127–28
Spencer, Richard, 98, 117, 132
spending:
on campaigns, 267, 269, 270, 300
compared to revenues, *464*
congressional authority over, 51–54, 55
discretionary, 463, *463*
fiscal policy on, 461–66
on health care, 478, 479
in Keynesian economics, 461
in lobbying, 291–96, 304
mandatory, 463, *463*
pork barrel, *see* pork barrel
public opinion on, 183, *183*, 198, 201, *203*
on Social Security, 463, 475
state and local, *92*

split tickets, 273 A ballot on which a voter selects candidates from more than one political party.

spoils system, 222, 394–95, 394 The practice of rewarding party supporters with benefits like federal government positions.

sports:
African-American athletes in, 141
kneeling during national anthem in, 155, 170
performance-enhancing drugs in, 125
women athletes in, 166, *390*
Stamp Act (1765), 34
standardized testing in schools, 482–83

standard operating procedures (SOPs), 383, 394, 409 Rules that lower-level bureaucrats must follow when implementing policies.

standing, 424, 431–32 Legitimate justification for bringing a civil case to court.

standing committees, 337 Committees that are a permanent part of the House or Senate structure, holding more importance and authority than other committees.
Standing Rock Sioux tribe, *142*
"stand your ground" laws, 120
Stanton, Elizabeth Cady, 152
Starbucks, 512, *512*

state capacity, 391 The knowledge, personnel, and institutions that the government requires to effectively implement policies.

State Department, 391, 394, 407
evaluation of, 451
in executive branch, *398*
foreign policy role of, 499
number of employees in, *404*
spending on, 397
state government:
Articles of Confederation on, 35–37
autonomy of, 70, 74
balance of power with national government, 9, 40, 45, 72–74
Constitution on, 74
and COVID-19 pandemic, 456–57
in daily life, 15
economic policy role of, 456–57
education role of, 68, 87, 456, 482
environmental policies of, 83, 86, *86*, 92
federal grants to, 81–84
in federalism, 7, 9, 80–84; *see also* federalism
forms of, 9
in health care, 81, 87, 90, 92, 456, 478, 480
judicial review on laws of, 419
marijuana policies of, 91
in policy-making process, 456–57
political parties in, 232
reserved powers of, 45, 65, 76–78, 87, *104*
responsibilities of, 70, *70*
social policy role of, 81, 456–57
spending trends for, *92*
strong role of, 90–93
Supreme Court rulings on, 74–80, *75*
Tenth Amendment on, 45, 76, 87
unfunded mandates for, 81, 86
and Welfare reform, 92
Staten Island, N.Y., 150

State of the Union, 366, 379 An annual speech in which the president addresses Congress to report on the condition of the country and to recommend policies.
media coverage of, 207, 379
of Obama, 426, *426*
of Trump, 371, *435*

states:
abortion rights in, 130, 131
at Constitutional Convention, *41*, 42–43, *43*, 45–48
economic interests of, 40
selective incorporation of civil liberties in, 105, *106*

states' rights, 78, 80, 87–90 The idea that states are entitled to a certain amount of self-government, free of federal government intervention. This became a central issue in the period leading up to the Civil War.

statutory authority, presidential, 357, *358*, 380 Powers derived from laws enacted by Congress that add to the powers given to the president in the Constitution.

statutory interpretation, 419 The various methods and tests used by the courts for determining the meaning of a law and applying it to specific situations. Congress may overturn the courts' interpretation by writing a new law; thus, it also engages in statutory interpretation.

stealth democracy, 12
steel industry, *509*
Stefanik, Elise, *319*
Stevens, John Paul, 438
Stevenson, Adlai, *259*
Stewart, Jon, 180, 182, 213
Stewart, Potter, 119
Steyer, Tom, 235, 270, 303
Stone, Harlan Fiske, 435
Stone, Roger, 368
Stonewall uprising, 145, *145*
"stop-and-frisk" policy, 136, *137*

straight ticket, 273 A ballot on which a voter selects candidates from only one political party.

Strategic Arms Limitation Treaty I (SALT I), 495
strategic model on Supreme Court, 438

strict construction, 436–37 A way of interpreting the Constitution based on its language alone.

strict scrutiny, 112, 161, 162–63 The highest level of scrutiny the courts can use when determining whether a law is constitutional. To meet this standard, the law or policy must be shown to serve a "compelling state interest" or goal, it must be narrowly tailored to achieve that goal, and it must be the least restrictive means of achieving that goal.

strip searches, 124
Strong, Benjamin, 467
student loans, 15, 298, 302
Student Nonviolent Coordinating Committee (SNCC), 153
subcommittees in Congress, 337, 342

substantive representation, 317–18 Representation in which a member of Congress serves constituents' interests and shares their policy concerns.

Superior Court, Michael M. v., 163
Super PACs, 267, 303, *304*, 305
Supplemental Nutrition Assistance Program (SNAP), 337, 398, 481, *483*
Supplemental Security Income (SSI), *483*

Third Amendment, *104*, *106*, 129
Thirteenth Amendment, 59, 78, 105, *139*, 140
Thomas, Clarence, 58, 434, *437*, 439

Three-Fifths Compromise, 46, 47 The states' decision during the Constitutional Convention to count each enslaved person as three-fifths of a person in a state's population for the purposes of determining the number of House members and the distribution of taxes.

Timbs v. Indiana, 106
Time, 161

Tinker v. Des Moines School District,
113 In 1969, the Supreme Court ruled that students may wear armbands to protest the Vietnam War. The Court noted that the students "were not disruptive and did not impinge upon the rights of others" and therefore their conduct was protected by the First and Fourteenth Amendments.

Title IX on sex discrimination in education, 166
Tocqueville, Alexis de, 317
Tories, 35
trade associations, *289*
trade policies:
 and Articles of Confederation, 36
 China in, 505, 512–13
 commerce clause on, 79, 89–90
 Constitutional Convention compromises on, *41*
 economic interests in, 40
 in federalism, 73, 76, *76*
 and foreign policy, 495–98, 508–9, 512–13, 517
 G7 Summit on (2018), 488–90, *489*
 and gross domestic product, 508, *508*
 human rights issues in, 513
 in intrastate and interstate commerce, 79
 most-favored-nation status in, 508
 of Obama, 505
 as presidential election issue (2016), 482
 Senate role in, 346
 Supreme Court on, *76*, *76*, 79
 tariffs in, *see* tariffs
 of Trump, 5, 211–12, 275, 354, 488–90, 505, *509*, *509*, 512–13
 U.S. trade representative in, 454, 499
Trail of Tears, 142
transgender people, 168, *169*
 see also LGBTQ people
Trans-Pacific Partnership, and Trump, 54
Transportation Department, *398*, 399, *400*
Transportation Security Administration, 391, 500
travel ban of Trump, 56, 60, 172, *174*, 378, 426

Treasury Department, 375, 394, 398, 400, 451, 455–56, 471–72 A cabinet-level agency that is responsible for managing the federal government's revenue. It prints currency, collects taxes, and sells government bonds.
treaties, 73, 365–66, 501, 509–10
Treaty of Paris (1783), 36
Treaty of Versailles, 493

trials, 122
 and double jeopardy, 126
 evidence in, 85, 124, 126–27
 fair and speedy, 127–28, *128*
 for illegal immigrants, 360
 by jury, 49, 127–28, 144
 plea bargaining in, 420
 Seventh Amendment on, *104*, *106*
 Sixth Amendment on, *104*, *106*, 127–28
 for suspected terrorists, *128*
Troubled Asset Relief Program (TARP), 471, 472
Truman, Harry, 141, 168, 206, 260, 377
Trump, Donald, *12*, 253, 270, 275, 276, 282, *287*, 305, *491*
 absolute immunity claim of, 347
 appointments and nominations of, 359, 407, 429, 468
 approval rating of, 26, 258, 276–78, 377
 and athletes kneeling during national anthem, 155
 baseless voter fraud allegations of, 279, 281
 and border wall with Mexico, *51*, 56, 220, 314, 380, 498
 budget process under, 453, 454
 and California's fuel economy waiver, 94
 campaign events of, *263*
 campaigning for congressional candidates, 246, 276, *336*
 CARES Act signed into law by, *287*
 on civil rights issues, 170
 as commander in chief, 364
 and Constitution, 34, 61, 62
 COVID-19 contracted by, 277, 278
 and COVID-19 pandemic, *240*, 261, 258, 277, 278, 352–54, *353*, 375, 377, 378, 384, *385*, 410
 on DACA program, 312, 314, 347–48
 and divided government, 240
 drone attacks deployed by, 369
 economic policies of, 4, 212, 275, 286–88, 453, 454, 461, 465, 468, 469
 education policies of, *85*, 456
 Electoral College strategy of, 257
 and emoluments clause, *51*, 345
 environmental policies of, 62, 66, 83, 94, 275, 363, 365, 389, 406, 469
 Executive Office staff of, 371–72
 executive orders of, 98, 360–64
 and fake news, 2, *2*
 and federal bureaucracy, 384–86, 396–97, 410
 federal court nominations of, 427–28, *427*
 and Federal Reserve System, 468
 on flag protection, 113
 foreign policy of, 365–66, 488–90, 498, 500, 503, 504, 505, *509*, 510, 517
 and gender politics, 20
 Ginsburg comments on, 414, 416, 426, 441
 going public, 379
 and Guantánamo Bay detention center, 57
 and gun laws, 122
 on health insurance, 12–13, 480–81
 and Hurricane Dorian, 379, *379*
 and ideological polarization, 170

 immigration policies of, 4, 5, 62, 170, 172, 174–75, *196*, 239, 275, 278, 312–14, 347–48, 353, 360, 504
 impeachment of, 5, 32–34, *33*, 220, 239, 265, 338, 346, 354, *370*, 376, 498
 and INF Treaty, 54
 and Iran nuclear agreement, 54, 301
 and Justice Department, 54, 353
 Latino support of, 143
 legislative priorities of, 239
 on LGBTQ rights, 145, 168, *169*
 lobbying policies of, 297
 and marijuana laws, 91
 media coverage on, 4, 28, 211–12
 misleading claims of, 316
 and North Korea, 366, *366*, 498, 515
 pardons granted by, 54, 368
 as party leader, 378
 political party of, 218, 233, 234
 in presidential campaign and election of (2016), *see* presidential campaign and election of 2016
 in presidential campaign and election (2020), *see* presidential campaign and election of 2020
 presidential power of, 34, 56, 352–54, *353*, 357, 375, 380, 384
 on profiling, 136, 138
 public opinion on, 26, 187, 188–90, *189*, 194, *196*, 213, 275, 276
 and refusal to concede 2020 presidential election, 279–80
 regulations repealed by, 164, 278, 469
 Republican opposition to, 233, 234, 275, 378
 and Russia, 54, 56, 60, *376*, *376*
 social policies of, 456
 on Supreme Court decisions, 426
 Supreme Court nominations of, 24, *55*, 359–60, *415*, *425*, 426
 and Syria, 55
 tax policies of, 275, 278, 286–88, 352, 378, 454, 465
 tax returns of, 346–47
 trade policies of, 5, 211–12, 275, 354, 488–90, 498, 505, 509, *509*, 512–13
 and Trans-Pacific Partnership, 54
 travel ban of, 53, 56, 60, 172, *174*, *196*, 378, 426
 Twitter use of, 2, 3, *5*, *207*, 278, *316*, 380
 and Ukraine, 345
 unfunded mandates of, 86
 unified government of, 13, 56, 380, 454
 unilateral actions of, 375, *376*, 380
 vetoes from, *367*, 368
 and voting by mail, 319
 and Women's March, 154
 and Zelensky, 32
Trump, Ivanka, 371
Trump, Melania, 277
Trump University, 428

trustee, 319 A member of Congress who represents constituents' interests while also taking into account national, collective, and moral concerns that sometimes cause the member to vote against the preference of a majority of constituents.

unfunded mandates, 81, 86 Federal laws that require the states to do certain things but do not provide state governments with funding to implement these policies.

unified government, 56, 226, 240, 249, 361, 366, 380 A situation in which one party holds a majority of seats in the House and Senate and the president is a member of that same party.

unilateral actions, national, 491 Independent acts of foreign policy undertaken by a nation without the assistance or coordination of other nations.

unilateral actions, presidential, 375, 380, 380 Any policy decision made and acted upon by the president and presidential staff without the explicit approval or consent of Congress.

unitary government, 9, 72 A system in which the national, centralized government holds ultimate authority. It is the most common form of government in the world.

United Nations (UN), 491, 491, 495, 501, 503, 506 An international organization made up of representatives from nearly every nation, with a mission to promote peace and cooperation, uphold international law, and provide humanitarian aid.

United States Trade Representative, 454, 499 An agency founded in 1962 to negotiate with foreign governments to create trade agreements, resolve disputes, and participate in global trade-policy organizations. Treaties negotiated by the USTR must be ratified by the Senate.

vesting clause, 358 Article II, Section 1, of the Constitution, which states: "The executive Power shall be vested in a President of the United States of America," making the president both the head of government and the head of state.

veto, 7, 44, 56, 343, 366–68, 374 The president's rejection of a bill that has been passed by Congress. A veto can be overridden by a two-thirds vote in both the House and Senate.

Virginia Plan, 42, 43, 57 A plan proposed by the larger states during the Constitutional Convention that based representation in the national legislature on population. The plan also included a variety of other proposals to strengthen the national government.

agree to hear a case that has reached them via an appeal from the losing party in a lower court's ruling.

Voter Registration Information

State	Registration Deadline before Election	Early Voting Permitted?	Identification Required to Vote?*	More Information
Alabama	15 days	No	Photo ID required	alabamavotes.gov
Alaska	30 days	Yes	ID requested; photo not required	elections.alaska.gov
Arizona	20 days**	Yes	ID required; photo not required	azsos.gov/elections
Arkansas	30 days	Yes	Photo ID required	sos.arkansas.gov
California	15 days; Election-Day registration permitted	Yes	No	sos.ca.gov
Colorado	8 days by mail or online; no in-person deadline	Yes (all voting by mail)	ID requested; photo not required	sos.state.co.us
Connecticut	7 days by mail or online; no in-person deadline	No	ID required; photo not required	portal.ct.gov/sots
Delaware	Fourth Saturday prior to election	No	ID requested; photo not required	elections.delaware.gov
District of Columbia	21 days by mail or online; no in-person deadline	Yes	No	dcboee.org
Florida	28 days**	Yes	Photo ID requested	dos.myflorida.com/elections
Georgia	28 days	Yes	Photo ID required	sos.ga.gov
Hawaii	30 days; no in-person deadline	Yes (all voting by mail)	Photo ID requested	hawaii.gov/elections
Idaho	25 days; Election-Day registration permitted	Yes	Photo ID requested	idahovotes.gov
Illinois	28 days by mail; 16 days online; no in-person deadline	Yes	No	elections.il.gov
Indiana	29 days	Yes	Photo ID required	in.gov/sos/elections
Iowa	10 days; Election-Day registration permitted	Yes	Photo ID required	sos.iowa.gov
Kansas	21 days	Yes	Photo ID required	kssos.org
Kentucky	29 days	Yes	Photo ID required	elect.ky.gov
Louisiana	30 days; 20 days online	Yes	Photo ID required	sos.la.gov
Maine	15 days by mail**; no in-person deadline	Yes	No	maine.gov/sos
Maryland	21 days	Yes	No	elections.state.md.us
Massachusetts	10 days**	No	Photo ID requested	sec.state.ma.us
Michigan	15 days online or by mail; no in-person deadline	No	Photo ID required	michigan.gov/sos
Minnesota	21 days; Election-Day registration permitted	Yes	No	mnvotes.org
Mississippi	30 days	No	Photo ID required	sos.ms.gov
Missouri	Fourth Wednesday prior to election	No	ID requested; photo not required	sos.mo.gov
Montana	37 days by mail**; no in-person deadline	Yes	ID requested; photo not required	sos.mt.gov
Nebraska	Third Friday prior to election by mail; second Friday prior to election in person; 10 days online	Yes	No	sos.nebraska.gov